P9-BBV-969

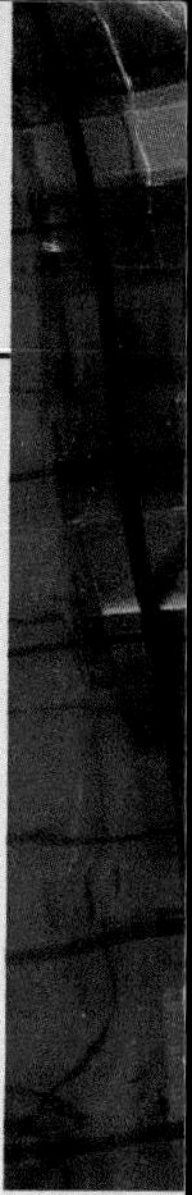

# A History of Western Society

Eighth Edition

Advanced Placement* Edition

# A History of Western Society

## Since 1300

John P. McKay
University of Illinois at Urbana-Champaign

Bennett D. Hill
Georgetown University

John Buckler
University of Illinois at Urbana-Champaign

HOUGHTON MIFFLIN COMPANY
Boston New York

**Publisher:** Charles Hartford
**Senior Sponsoring Editor:** Nancy Blaine
**Senior Development Editor:** Julie Swasey
**Editorial Associate:** Annette Fantasia
**Senior Project Editor:** Christina Horn
**Editorial Assistant:** Michelle O'Berg
**Senior Art and Design Coordinator:** Jill Haber
**Senior Photo Editor:** Jennifer Meyer Dare
**Senior Composition Buyer:** Sarah Ambrose
**Manufacturing Coordinator:** Chuck Dutton
**Senior Marketing Manager:** Sandra McGuire
**Marketing Assistant:** Molly Parke

**Text credits:**
**Page 558:** Poem by Joost van den Vondel, quoted in *Europe in the Seventeenth Century,* by David Ogg. Copyright © 1967 by A & C Black, Ltd. **Page 876:** Parody by Henry Labouchère, quoted in *The Social History of the Machine Gun,* by John Ellis. Reprinted by permission of Pantheon Books, a division of Random House, Inc.

**AP Edition cover image:** Natalia Goncharova (1881–1962), *Self-Portrait with Yellow Lillies,* © ARS, NY. Tretyakov Gallery, Moscow, Russia/Scala/Art Resource, NY.

*AP and Advanced Placement Program are registered trademarks of the College Entrance Examination Board, which was not involved in the production of, and does not endorse, this product.

Copyright © 2006 by Houghton Mifflin Company. All rights reserved.

No part of this work may be reproduced or transmitted in any form or by any means, electronic or mechanical, including photocopying and recording, or by any information storage or retrieval system without the prior written permission of Houghton Mifflin Company unless such copying is expressly permitted by federal copyright law. Address inquiries to College Permissions, Houghton Mifflin Company, 222 Berkeley Street, Boston, MA 02116-3764.

Printed in the U.S.A.

Library of Congress Control Number: 2004116683
ISBN: 0-618-52273-5
ISBN: 978-0-618-52273-6
4 5 6 7 8 9-VH-12 11 10 09 08 07

# About the Authors

**John P. McKay** Born in St. Louis, Missouri, John P. McKay received his B.A. from Wesleyan University (1961), his M.A. from the Fletcher School of Law and Diplomacy (1962), and his Ph.D. from the University of California, Berkeley (1968). He began teaching history at the University of Illinois in 1966 and became a professor there in 1976. John won the Herbert Baxter Adams Prize for his book *Pioneers for Profit: Foreign Entrepreneurship and Russian Industrialization, 1885–1913* (1970). He has also written *Tramways and Trolleys: The Rise of Urban Mass Transport in Europe* (1976) and has translated Jules Michelet's *The People* (1973). His research has been supported by fellowships from the Ford Foundation, the Guggenheim Foundation, the National Endowment for the Humanities, and IREX. He has written well over a hundred articles, book chapters, and reviews, which have appeared in numerous publications, including *The American Historical Review, Business History Review, The Journal of Economic History,* and *Slavic Review.* He contributed extensively to C. Stewart and P. Fritzsche, eds., *Imagining the Twentieth Century* (1997).

**Bennett D. Hill** A native of Philadelphia, Bennett D. Hill earned an A.B. from Princeton (1956) and advanced degrees from Harvard (A.M., 1958) and Princeton (Ph.D., 1963). He taught history at the University of Illinois at Urbana, where he was department chairman from 1978 to 1981. He has published *English Cistercian Monasteries and Their Patrons in the Twelfth Century* (1968), *Church and State in the Middle Ages* (1970), and articles in *Analecta Cisterciensia, The New Catholic Encyclopaedia, The American Benedictine Review,* and *The Dictionary of the Middle Ages.* His reviews have appeared in *The American Historical Review, Speculum, The Historian,* the *Journal of World History,* and *Library Journal.* He is one of the contributing editors to *The Encyclopedia of World History* (2001). He has been a Fellow of the American Council of Learned Societies and served on the editorial board of *The American Benedictine Review,* on committees of the National Endowment for the Humanities, and as Vice President of the American Catholic Historical Association (1995–1996). A Benedictine monk of St. Anselm's Abbey in Washington, D.C., he is also a Visiting Professor at Georgetown University.

**John Buckler** Born in Louisville, Kentucky, John Buckler received his B.A. (summa cum laude) from the University of Louisville in 1967. Harvard University awarded him the Ph.D. in 1973. From 1984 to 1986 he was an Alexander von Humboldt Fellow at the Institut für Alte Geschichte, University of Munich. He has lectured at the Fondation Hardt at the University of Geneva and at the University of Freiburg. He is currently a professor of Greek history at the University of Illinois. In 1980 Harvard University Press published his *Theban Hegemony, 371–362 B.C.* He has also published *Philip II and the Sacred War* (Leiden 1989) and co-edited *BOIOTIKA: Vorträge vom 5. Internationalen Böotien-Kolloquium* (Munich 1989). In 2003 he published *Aegean Greece in the Fourth Century B.C.* In the following year appeared his editions of W. M. Leake, *Travels in the Morea* (three volumes), and Leake's *Peloponnesiaca.* He has also published numerous articles in various international journals.

# Brief Contents

# Contents

## Chapter 14

### Reform and Renewal in the Christian Church 453



## Chapter 15

### The Age of Religious Wars and Overseas Expansion 489



## Chapter 16

### Absolutism and Constitutionalism in Western Europe (ca 1589–1715) 531

## Chapter 20



## Chapter 21

## Chapter 30



## Chapter 31

# Maps

# Listening to the Past

# Preface

**A History of Western Society** grew out of the authors' desire to infuse new life into the study of Western civilization. We knew that historians were using imaginative questions and innovative research to open up vast new areas of historical interest and knowledge. We also recognized that these advances had dramatically affected the subject of European economic, intellectual, and, especially, social history, while new research and fresh interpretations were also revitalizing the study of the traditional mainstream of political, diplomatic, and religious development. Despite history's vitality as a discipline, however, it seemed to us that both the broad public and the intelligentsia were generally losing interest in the past. That, fortunately for us all, has not proven the case.

It was our conviction, based on considerable experience introducing large numbers of students to the broad sweep of Western civilization, that a book reflecting current trends could excite readers and inspire a renewed interest in history and our Western heritage. Our strategy was twofold. First, we made social history a core element of our work. We not only incorporated recent research by social historians but also sought to recreate the life of ordinary people in appealing human terms. At the same time we were determined to give great economic, political, cultural, and intellectual developments the attention they unquestionably deserve. We wanted to give individual readers and instructors a balanced, integrated perspective so that they could pursue—on their own or in the classroom—those themes and questions that they found particularly exciting and significant. In an effort to realize fully the potential of our fresh yet balanced approach, we made many changes, large and small, in the editions that followed.

## Changes in the Eighth Edition

In preparing the Eighth Edition we have worked hard to keep our book up-to-date by including as much valuable and relevant scholarship as possible. We have also strengthened our distinctive yet balanced approach to a wide range of topics. Several main lines of revision have guided our many changes.

### "Images in Society" Feature

A photo essay, "Images in Society," represents a distinctive feature of this Eighth Edition. The complete text now contains seven essays (three new to this edition), each consisting of a short narrative with questions, accompanied by several pictures. The goal of the feature is to encourage students to think critically: to view and compare visual illustrations and draw conclusions about the societies and cultures that produced those objects. Thus, in Chapter 1 appears the discovery of the "Iceman," the frozen remains of an unknown herdsman. "The Roman Villa at Chedworth" in Britain mirrors Roman provincial culture (Chapter 6). The essay "From Romanesque to Gothic" treats the architectural shift in medieval church building, and aims to show how the Gothic cathedral reflected the ideals and values of medieval society (Chapter 11). Chapter 14 presents "From Reformation to Baroque," which examines both the Protestant and Catholic views of religious art. Moving to modern times, the focus in Chapter 19 changes to "London: The Remaking of a Great City," which depicts how Londoners rebuilt their city after a great catastrophe. "Class and Gender Boundaries in Women's Fashion, 1850–1914" studies women's clothing in relationship to women's evolving position in society and gender relations (Chapter 24). "Pablo Picasso and Modern Art" looks at some of Picasso's greatest paintings to gain insight into his principles and the modernist revolution in art (Chapter 28).

### "Individuals in Society" Feature

Included in each chapter is the feature "Individuals in Society," which offers a brief study of a woman, man, or group, informing us about the societies in which they lived. Each study or biographical sketch has been carefully integrated into the body of the text. The "Individuals in Society" feature grew out of our long-standing focus on people's lives and the varieties of historical experience, and we believe that readers will empathize with these human beings as they themselves seek to define their own identities. The spotlighting of individuals, both famous and obscure, perpetuates the greater attention to cultural and intellectual developments that we used to invigorate our social history in earlier editions, and it reflects changing interests within the historical profession as well as the development of "micro-history."

The range of men and women we consider is broad. For this edition, and sometimes at readers' suggestion, we have dropped some individuals and replaced them with others who add their own contributions to history. They include such fascinating people as Quintus Sertorius, who tried to create a Roman-style state in Spain (Chapter 5); Ebo of Reims, the son of a serf whom Charlemagne liberated, who rose to become archbishop under Louis the Pious (Chapter 8); Vera Brittain, an English writer and nurse during World War I who contributed a famous autobiographical work entitled *Testament of Youth* (1933) (Chapter 27); Primo Levi, an Italian Jew who wrote of his experiences in a Nazi concentration camp (Chapter 29); and Kofi Annan, the present secretary-general of the United Nations (Chapter 31).

## "Document-Based Questions" Feature

See DBQ 1

The Appendix of this edition includes a new feature of *A History of Western Society*—Document-Based Questions (DBQs) designed to help students hone their skills in writing essays for the Advanced Placement* European History Exam. Written by Ane Lintvedt (McDonogh School, Md.), Louise Forsyth (Poly Prep Country Day School, N.Y.), and David Gould (Durham Academy, N.C.) these questions are closely tied to the book's narrative structure. Fourteen total DBQs are connected with the various chapters of this book and are intended to help students think critically about major themes in those chapters. Students will find the DBQ icon (see above) beside the section in the textbook that first gets to the heart of answering the corresponding DBQ, as indicated by the number on the icon.

The beginning DBQs are accompanied by three to six primary source documents; the last three DBQs are designed like those on the AP* Exam. This will allow students to first gain confidence in working with a relatively small number of documents in the earlier exercises before advancing to those that offer the same number of documents as an actual AP* European History Exam.

*AP and Advanced Placement Program are registered trademarks of the College Entrance Examination Board, which was not involved in the production of, and does not endorse, this product.

## Expanded Ethnic and Geographic Scope

In the Eighth Edition we have added significantly more discussion of groups and regions that are frequently shortchanged in the general histories of Europe and Western civilization. This expanded scope reflects the renewed awareness within the profession of Europe's enormous historical diversity, as well as the efforts of contemporary Europeans to understand the ambivalent and contested meanings of their national, regional, ethnic, and pan-European identities. Examples of this enlarged scope include a new discussion of the Sea Peoples (Chapter 3); slavery in eastern Europe (Chapter 10); expanded coverage of the peasant revolts to include revolts in Flanders (Chapter 12); the Reformation in eastern Europe (Chapter 14); the Columbian Exchange (Chapter 15); an examination of the contribution of slaves to the Atlantic economy (Chapter 19); railroad construction in Africa, Asia, and Latin America and a discussion of British women and their role in imperial India (Chapter 26); and the Armenian genocide (Chapter 27). We have devoted special attention in the Eighth Edition to increasing the treatment of the Islamic world. Examples include an updated discussion of the basic tenets of Islam (Chapter 7); the slave trade between Europe and the Muslim world (Chapter 8); Moorish Spain (Chapter 9); the Arab influence in Sicily (Chapter 11); revised material on the Ottoman Empire (Chapter 17); the French conquest of Algeria (Chapter 23); the Ottomans and the war in Asia and Africa and peace treaties affecting Arab nations and the creation of Israel (Chapter 27); and the debate over Islamic headscarves in France, Islamic fundamentalists, and the wars in Afghanistan and Iraq (Chapter 31).

## Incorporation of Recent Scholarship

This edition includes the best of previous scholarship, while blending in the most important recent findings. Learning is fortunately never static. We have also strived to include new material on women and gender relations. The process has led to some organization changes, as can be seen below. In Chapter 1 the whole concept of "What Is History and Why" now explores the very concept of what we mean by the "West." Without Eurocentricism, the discussion simply points to the many contributions of

Western societies to the full realm of human progress. This new edition, as previous ones, highlights human contacts. Thus, in Chapter 2 updated material on the siege of Jerusalem includes both Jewish and Assyrian accounts of the episode. In so doing, readers understand how historians understand their sources. Chapter 3 gives expanded discussion of life in the countryside and revises material on Spartan and Athenian women. Cultural aspects include recent findings on religion, especially on local and domestic cults. Chapter 4 contains a new "Listening to the Past" that confronts the controversial notion that Alexander the Great wanted to create a "Brotherhood of Man" and includes new material on Antiochus II and his treatment of the Jews. Chapter 5 includes expanded discussion of clientage, of Roman women and child rearing, and of those client kingdoms that subsequently form part of the Roman Empire. Chapter 6 features a new discussion of the Lost Gospels, early Christian writings that were not included in the New Testament. There is also a fully updated section on the movement from the classical world to late antiquity.

In Chapter 7 readers can find an updated discussion of Islam and its tenets, including reference to the "Five Pillars of Islam." Chapter 8 continues the theme of contacts between the European and Islam worlds by including a new section on the slave trade between Europe and the Muslim world. Chapter 9 furthers the link between Europe and its Eastern neighbors, covering the Crusades and the role of women in them and adding a section on Moorish Spain. An important feature of Chapter 10 is the treatment of slavery in eastern Europe and new material on medieval rural economy. Chapter 11 incorporates a new discussion of the Arab influence in Sicily and offers a thoughtful appreciation of the rising commercial class. Chapter 14 inspects the somewhat neglected topic of the Reformation in eastern Europe, linking it to the changes occurring in western Europe. Chapter 15 examines not only the religious views of the period but also the debates among religious writers about the role of women in society, as well as scholarly debates over witch-hunts. A new section on the Columbian Exchange has also been added to this chapter. Chapter 16 is particularly important because it explores the evolution of the state and defines its relations with religious elements of society. Much of this chapter has been revised and new material on the Edict of Nantes added.

Chapters 17–20 present such topics as recent material on the Ottoman Empire, a discussion of slaves and the Atlantic economy, and treatment of abandoned children and the creation of foundling homes. Chapter 19 also contains a new "Images in Society" feature on "London: The Remaking of a Great City." Chapter 22 contributes attention to the consequences of industrialization for the working class of England. There is a new discussion of the French conquest of Algeria after 1830 in Chapter 23. Chapter 26 examines recent studies on railroad construction in Africa, Asia, and Latin America, as well as on British women and their role in imperial India. This chapter also includes a new "Listening to the Past" feature on British women in India. Chapter 27 has been fully revised to incorporate more material on the Middle East. There is expanded coverage of the breakup of the Ottoman Empire, the creation of Israel, and the effects of the peace treaties on Arab nations, as well as a new discussion of the Armenian genocide of 1915.

Chapter 30 includes a rewritten section on decolonization that stresses the agency of former colonies and new material on the development of the German Green political movement. Chapter 31 addresses such current topics as the challenges of globalization, the uncertainty of the effects of Russian president Putin's administration, and the entry of former communist states into the European Union. Also pertinent are the new sections on the al-Qaeda attack of September 11, 2001, and the wars in Afghanistan and Iraq and their effects on European-American relations.

### Revised Full-Color Art and Map Programs

Finally, the illustrative component of our work has been carefully revised. We have added many new illustrations to our extensive art program, which includes more than four hundred color reproductions, letting great art and important events come alive. As in earlier editions, all illustrations have been carefully selected to complement the text, and all carry informative captions, based on thorough research, that enhance their value. Artwork remains an integral part of our book; the past can speak in pictures as well as in words. The use of full color serves to clarify the maps and graphs and to enrich the textual material. The maps and map captions have been updated to correlate directly to the text, and new maps have been added in Chapters 8, 10, and 27.

## Distinctive Features

In addition to the "Images in Society" and "Individuals in Society" essays, distinctive features from earlier editions guide the reader in the process of historical understanding. Many of these features also show how historians sift through and evaluate evidence. Our goal is to suggest how historians actually work and think. We want the reader to think critically and to realize that history is neither a list of cut-and-dried facts nor a senseless jumble of conflicting opinions. To help students and instructors realize this goal, we have significantly expanded the discussion of "what is history" in Chapter 1 of this edition.

## Primary Sources

A two-page feature, entitled "Listening to the Past," extends and illuminates a major historical issue considered in each of the text's chapters. In the new edition we have reviewed our selections and made judicious substitutions. For example, in Chapter 4 comes a discussion of the much-debated topic of "Alexander and the Brotherhood of Man." Chapter 10 introduces the reader to the fascinating "Pilgrim's Guide to Santiago de Compostela." Chapter 11 provides a selection dealing with early Islamic views on trade, again based on recent scholarship. Chapter 26 treats the privileges and tribulations of British women in India. The feature in Chapter 29, "Stalin Justifies the Five-Year Plan," explores the controversies surrounding Stalin's attempt to turn the Soviet Union into one unified and modern government. Chapter 31 takes a contemporary examination of "The West in World Affairs" by including two contrasting documents on American foreign policy.

Each primary source opens with a problem-setting introduction and closes with "Questions for Analysis" that invite students to evaluate the evidence as historians would. Drawn from a range of writings addressing a variety of social, cultural, political, and intellectual issues, these sources promote active involvement and critical interpretation. Selected for their interest and importance and carefully fitted into their historical context, these sources do indeed allow the student to "listen to the past" and to observe how history has been shaped by individual men and women, some of them great aristocrats, others ordinary folk.

## Problems of Historical Interpretation

We believe that including examples of problems of historical interpretations in our text helps our readers develop the critical-thinking skills that are among the most precious benefits of studying history. Examples of this more open-ended, interpretative approach include the debate over the concept of history itself and our notion of "the West" (Chapter 1), an examination of the transition from antiquity to the early Middle Ages and a discussion of the importance of the Lost Gospels (Chapter 6), the question of European racism in the Middle Ages (Chapter 12), the issue of gender in the Italian cities of the Renaissance (Chapter 13), the renewed debate on personal and collective responsibility for the Holocaust (Chapter 29), the dynamics of the great purges in the Soviet Union (Chapter 29), the process of reconstruction in eastern Europe, the debate over globalization, and the issue of American unilateralism in the world today (Chapter 31).

## Improved Chapter Features

Other distinctive features from earlier editions have been reviewed and improved in this Eighth Edition. To help guide the reader toward historical understanding, we pose specific historical questions at the beginning of each chapter. These questions are then answered in the course of each chapter, and each chapter concludes with a concise summary of its findings. All of the questions and summaries have been re-examined and frequently revised in order to maximize the usefulness of this popular feature.

Comparative timelines begin each chapter and organize historical events into three categories: political/military, social/economic, and intellectual/religious. In addition, topic-specific timelines appear at key points throughout the book. Once again we provide a unified timeline at the end of the text. Comprehensive and easy to locate, this useful timeline allows students to compare simultaneous political, economic, social, cultural, intellectual, and scientific developments over the centuries.

A list of Key Terms concludes each chapter. These terms are highlighted in boldface in the text. The student may use these terms to test his or her understanding of the chapter's material.

In addition to posing chapter-opening questions and presenting more problems in historical interpretation, we have quoted extensively from a wide variety of primary sources in the narrative, demonstrating in our use of these quotations how historians evaluate evidence. Thus primary sources are examined as an integral part of the narrative as well as presented in extended form in the "Listening to the Past" chapter feature. We believe that such an extensive program of both integrated and separate primary source excerpts will help readers learn to interpret and think critically.

Each chapter concludes with carefully selected suggestions for further reading. These suggestions are briefly described to help readers know where to turn to continue thinking and learning about the Western world. Also, chapter bibliographies have been thoroughly revised and updated to keep them current with the vast amount of new work being done in many fields.

## Ancillaries

Learning and teaching ancillaries also contribute to the usefulness of the text. The new *Houghton Mifflin History Companion* is a collection of resources designed to complement the use of this edition. It is organized according to the chapters in the text and has three parts—the *Instructor Companion,* the *Student Research Companion,* and the *Student Study Companion.* First, the *Instructor Companion* is a free, searchable CD-ROM featuring hundreds of historical images and maps in PowerPoint format. Each image is accompanied by notes that place it in its proper historical context. The maps and images are correlated to the text's table of contents and are also searchable by other criteria. They are formatted for easy presentation in the classroom. The CD-ROM also includes the *HM Testing* program, a computerized version of the *Test Items* to enable instructors to alter, replace, or add questions, as well as resources from the *Instructor's Resource Manual.*

Second, the *Student Research Companion* is a free web-based tool with one hundred interactive maps and hundreds of primary sources. The primary sources include headnotes that provide pertinent background information and questions that students can answer and e-mail to their instructors. This website also provides students and teachers with additional information for the documents that are featured in the text. It has lengthy, searchable bibliographies that permit students to launch research assignments or pursue personal interests while giving teachers an outstanding opportunity to get directed guidance to the best historical literature in fields outside their own areas of expertise.

Third, the *Student Study Companion* is a free online study guide to accompany our text. It incorporates aspects of the last edition's print study guide and student website, as well as a variety of new interactive resources created by Laura Trauth of the Community College of Baltimore Country, Essex, and Carol Bresnahan Menning of the University of Toledo. The *Student Study Companion* contains a wealth of tutorial resources, including self-tests (ACE questions) with feedback, chronological ordering exercises, review questions, web activities, and interactive exercises on the "Individuals in Society" and "Images in Society" features. There are also a variety of review materials on the site, such as learning objectives, chapter summaries, outlines, a glossary of key terms, a searchable bibliography, links to web resources, and even general material on good study techniques. Finally, visitors to the site can also access some of the older "Individuals in Society" features that did not make it into the Eighth Edition.

An AP* Lesson Planning and Pacing Guide is available for high school teachers. This helpful resource extends the teaching support found in the *Instructor's Resource Manual* by providing specific guidelines and teaching notes for the AP* course in European History. Among its features are suggestions on how to cluster and pace the textbook lessons to ensure that all the key material for the AP* course is covered, and to most effectively prepare students to succeed on the AP* examination.

The print *Instructor's Resource Manual and Test Items,* thoroughly revised by John Reisbord of Vassar College, includes instructional objectives, annotated chapter outlines, suggestions for lectures and discussion, term paper and class activity topics, further information on the "Images in Society" features, primary source exercises, map activities, and lists of Internet and audiovisual resources. The test items section offers identification, multiple-choice, map, and essay questions for a total of approximately two thousand test items.

A correlation from the text to the Advanced Placement* course description ("acorn book") for European History is available from your McDougal Littell representative.

For institutions using either the Blackboard™ or WebCT™ platforms, we have designed course cartridges that include *HM Testing,* learning objectives, chapter summaries, study outlines, quizzes, and other study resources.

Finally, a set of full-color Map Transparencies of all the maps in the text is available on adoption.

## New for Adopters of Previous Editions

A separate **Document-Based Questions Practice Workbook** offers students and teachers the same DBQs found at the end of the Eighth Edition. A special "Tips and Analysis" section at the end of the workbook walks students through the process of approaching and answering each question, giving them a deeper understanding of the process of historical analysis. If you would like to see a copy of this newly available resource, please contact your McDougal Littell representative.

## Acknowledgments

It is a pleasure to thank the many instructors who read and critiqued the manuscript through its development:

Janice Amos
*Florida Community College–Jacksonville*

Jay Bergman
*Central Connecticut State University*

Margaret M. Bostwick
*John Jay College of Criminal Justice*

Allan Christelow
*Idaho State University*

James B. Collins
*Georgetown University*

Melissa Barden Dowling
*Southern Methodist University*

Joanne M. Ferraro
*San Diego State University*

Dennis Frey, Jr.
*Mercer County Community College*

Alison Futrell
*University of Arizona*

Elizabeth Heineman
*University of Iowa*

Blair T. Hinson
*Tri-County Technical College*

Thomas Kuehn
*Clemson University*

Lawrence Langer
*University of Connecticut*

Paul Douglas Lockhart
*Wright State University*

Elizabeth Makowski
*Texas State University at San Marcos*

Brent Maner
*Kansas State University*

Sarah Miller
*Lourdes College*

Jo Ann H. Moran Cruz
*Georgetown University*

Joe Perry
*Georgia State University*

Laura L. Phillips
*Eastern Washington University*

Anna Marie Roos
*University of Minnesota-Duluth*

Gavriel Rosenfeld
*Fairfield University*

Paul Teverow
*Missouri Southern State University–Joplin*

Leslie Tuttle
*University of Kansas*

It is also a pleasure to thank our many editors at Houghton Mifflin for their efforts over many years. To Christina Horn, who guided production in the ever-more intensive electronic age, and to Julie Swasey, our development editor, we express our special appreciation. And we thank Carole Frohlich for her contributions in photo research and selection.

Many of our colleagues at the University of Illinois and at Georgetown University continued to provide information and stimulation, often without even knowing it. We thank them for it. Bennett Hill wishes to express his appreciation to Donald Franklin for his support and encouragement in the preparation of this Eighth Edition. John Buckler thanks Professor Jack Cargill for his advice on topics in Chapter 2. And he wishes to thank Professor Nicholas Yalouris, former General Inspector of Antiquities, for his kind permission to publish the mosaic from Elis, Greece, in Chapter 3. He also wishes to thank Dr. Amy C. Smith, Curator of the Ure Museum of Archaeology of the University of Reading for her kind permission to publish the vase on page 63. John McKay expresses his deep appreciation to Jo Ann McKay for her sharp-eyed editorial support and unfailing encouragement.

Each of us has benefited from the criticism of his coauthors, although each of us assumes responsibility for what he has written. John Buckler has written the first six chapters; Bennett Hill has continued the narrative through Chapter 16; and John McKay has written Chapters 17 through 31. Finally, we continue to welcome the many comments and suggestions that have come from our readers, for they have helped us greatly in this ongoing endeavor.

**J. P. M.  B. D. H.  J. B.**

*Procession of the Magi.* Having bankrolled the entire Council of Florence (1439), including the presence of the Byzantine emperor John VIII Paleologus, who came seeking Western support against the Ottoman Turks, Cosimo de' Medici immortalized the event in the Medici chapel with Benozzo Gozzoli's frescoes. *(Scala/Art Resource, NY)*

chapter

# 12 The Crisis of the Later Middle Ages

**chapter outline**



During the later Middle Ages, the last book of the New Testament, the Book of Revelation, inspired thousands of sermons and hundreds of religious tracts. The Book of Revelation deals with visions of the end of the world, with disease, war, famine, and death. It is no wonder this part of the Bible was so popular. Between 1300 and 1450, Europeans experienced a frightful series of shocks: economic dislocation, plague, war, social upheaval, and increased crime and violence. Death and preoccupation with death make the fourteenth century one of the most wrenching periods of Western civilization. Yet, in spite of the pessimism and crises, important institutions and ideas, such as representative assemblies and national literatures, emerged.

The miseries and disasters of the later Middle Ages bring to mind a number of questions.

- What economic difficulties did Europe experience?
- What were the social and psychological effects of repeated attacks of plague and disease?
- Some scholars maintain that war is often the catalyst for political, economic, and social change. Does this theory have validity for the fourteenth century?
- What provoked schism in the church, and what impact did it have on the lives of ordinary people?
- How did new national literatures reflect political and social developments?
- How and why did the laws of settlers in frontier regions reveal a strong racial or ethnic discrimination?

This chapter will focus on these questions.

## Prelude to Disaster

In the first decade of the fourteenth century, the countries of northern Europe experienced a considerable price inflation. The cost of grain, livestock, and dairy products rose sharply. Severe weather, which historical geographers label the "Little Ice Age," made a serious situation frightful. An unusual number of storms brought torrential rains, ruining the wheat, oat, and hay crops on which people and animals almost everywhere depended. Since long-distance transportation of food was expensive and difficult, most urban areas depended for bread and meat on areas no more than a day's journey away. Poor harvests—and one in four was likely to be poor—led to scarcity and starvation. Almost all of northern Europe suffered a **"Great Famine"** in the years 1315–1322, which contemporaries interpreted as a recurrence of the biblical "seven lean years" (Genesis 42).

Reduced caloric intake meant increased susceptibility to disease, especially for infants, children, and the elderly. Workingmen and workingwomen on a reduced diet had less energy, which in turn meant lower productivity, lower output, and higher grain prices. The great famine proved a demographic disaster in France; in Burgundy perhaps one-third of the population died. The many religious houses of Flanders experienced a high loss of monks, nuns, and priests.

Hardly had western Europe begun to recover from this disaster when another struck. An epidemic of typhoid fever carried away thousands. In 1316, 10 percent of the population of the city of Ypres may have died between May and October alone. Then in 1318 disease hit cattle and sheep, drastically reducing the herds and flocks. Another bad harvest in 1321 brought famine and death.

The province of Languedoc in France presents a classic example of agrarian crisis. For over 150 years, Languedoc had enjoyed continual land reclamation, steady agricultural expansion, and enormous population growth. Then the fourteenth century opened with four years of bad harvests. Torrential rains in 1310 ruined the harvest and brought on terrible famine. Harvests failed again in 1322 and 1329. In 1332 desperate peasants survived the winter on raw herbs. In the half century from 1302 to 1348, poor harvests occurred twenty times. The undernourished population was ripe for the Grim Reaper, who appeared in 1348 in the form of the Black Death.

These catastrophes had grave social consequences. Poor harvests and famine led to the abandonment of homesteads. In parts of the Low Countries and in the Scottish-English borderlands, entire villages were abandoned. This meant a great increase in the number of vagabonds, what we call "homeless people." In Flanders and East Anglia (eastern England), where aspects of the famine have been carefully analyzed, some rustics were forced to mortgage, sublease, or sell their holdings to get money to buy food. Rich farmers bought out their poorer neighbors. When conditions improved, debtors tried to get their lands back, leading to a very volatile land market. To reduce the labor supply and the mouths to feed in the countryside, young males sought work in the towns.[1] Poor harvests probably meant that marriage had to be postponed. Later marriages and the deaths caused by famine and disease meant a reduction in population. Meanwhile, the international character of trade and commerce meant that a disaster in one country had serious implications elsewhere. For example, the infection that attacked English sheep in 1318 caused a sharp decline in wool exports in the following years. Without wool, Flemish weavers could not work, and thousands were laid off. Without woolen cloth, the businesses of Flemish, Hanseatic, and Italian merchants suffered. Unemployment encouraged people to turn to crime.

To none of these problems did governments have effective solutions. The three sons of Philip the Fair who sat on the French throne between 1314 and 1328 condemned speculators, who held stocks of grain back until conditions were desperate and prices high, forbade the sale of grain abroad, and published legislation prohibiting fishing with traps that took large catches. These measures had few positive results. As the subsistence crisis deepened, popular discontent and paranoia increased. Starving people focused their anger on the rich, speculators, and the Jews, who were targeted as creditors fleecing the poor through pawnbroking. (Expelled from France in 1306, Jews were readmitted in 1315 and granted the privilege of lending at high interest rates.) Rumors spread of a plot by Jews and their agents, the lepers, to kill Christians by poisoning the wells. With "evidence" collected by torture, many lepers and Jews were killed, beaten, or hit with heavy fines.

In England Edward I's incompetent son, Edward II (r. 1307–1327), used Parliament to set price controls, first on the sale of livestock after disease and poor lambing had driven prices up, and then on ale, which was made from barley (the severe rains of 1315 had contributed to molds and mildews, sharply reducing the crop). Baronial conflicts and wars with the Scots dominated Edward II's reign. Fearing food riots and violence, Edward condemned speculators, which proved easier than enforcing price controls. He did try to buy grain abroad, but yields in the Baltic were low; the French crown, as we have seen, forbade exports; and the grain shipped from Castile in northern Spain was grabbed by Scottish, English, and rogue Hanseatic pirates on the high seas. Such grain as reached southern English ports was stolen by looters and sold on the black market. The Crown's efforts at famine relief failed.

In Scandinavia and the Baltic countries, low cereal harvests, declines in meat and dairy production, economic

1300 | 1340 | 1380 | 1420 | 1460

**POLITICAL/MILITARY**

- 1250–1450 Beginnings of representative assemblies in England, Spain, the German Empire
- ca 1337–1453 Hundred Years' War
- 1346 English victory over the French at Crécy
- 1415 English smash the French at Agincourt
- 1429 French victory at Orléans; Charles VII crowned king
- 1431 Joan of Arc declared a heretic and burned at the stake

**SOCIAL/ECONOMIC**

- 1315–1322 Famine in northern Europe
- 1348 Black Death arrives in mainland Europe
- 1358 Jacquerie peasant uprising in France
- 1381 Peasants' Revolt in England

**INTELLECTUAL/RELIGIOUS**

- 1309–1376 Babylonian Captivity; papacy in Avignon
- 1310–1320 Dante, *Divine Comedy*
- 1324 Marsiglio, *Defensor Pacis*
- 1378–1417 Great Schism
- 1387–1400 Chaucer, *Canterbury Tales*

recessions, and the lack of salt, used for preserving herring, resulted in terrible food shortages. One scholar describes conditions there as "catastrophic."[2] Economic and social problems were aggravated by the appearance of a frightful disease.

## The Black Death

In 1291 Genoese sailors had opened the Strait of Gibraltar to Italian shipping by defeating the Moroccans. Then, shortly after 1300, important advances were made in the design of Italian merchant ships. A square rig was added to the mainmast, and ships began to carry three masts instead of just one. Additional sails better utilized wind power to propel the ship. The improved design permitted year-round shipping for the first time, and Venetian and Genoese merchant ships could sail the dangerous Atlantic coast even in the winter months. With ships continually at sea, shipboard rats were constantly on the move, and thus any rat-transmitted disease could spread rapidly.

Scholars dispute the origins of the bubonic plague, often known as the **Black Death.** One legend holds that the plague broke out in the Tartar (or Tatar) army under Khan Djani-Beg that was besieging the city of Caffa (modern Feodosiya) in the Crimea, in southern Russia. The Khan ordered the heads of Tartar victims hurled into Caffa to infect the defenders.[3] Some scholars hold that the plague broke out in China or Central Asia around 1331, and during the next fifteen years merchants and soldiers carried it over the caravan routes until in 1346 it reached the Crimea. Other scholars believe the plague was endemic in southern Russia. In either case, from the Crimea the plague had easy access to Mediterranean lands and western Europe.

In October 1347, Genoese ships brought the plague to Messina, from which it spread across Sicily. Venice and

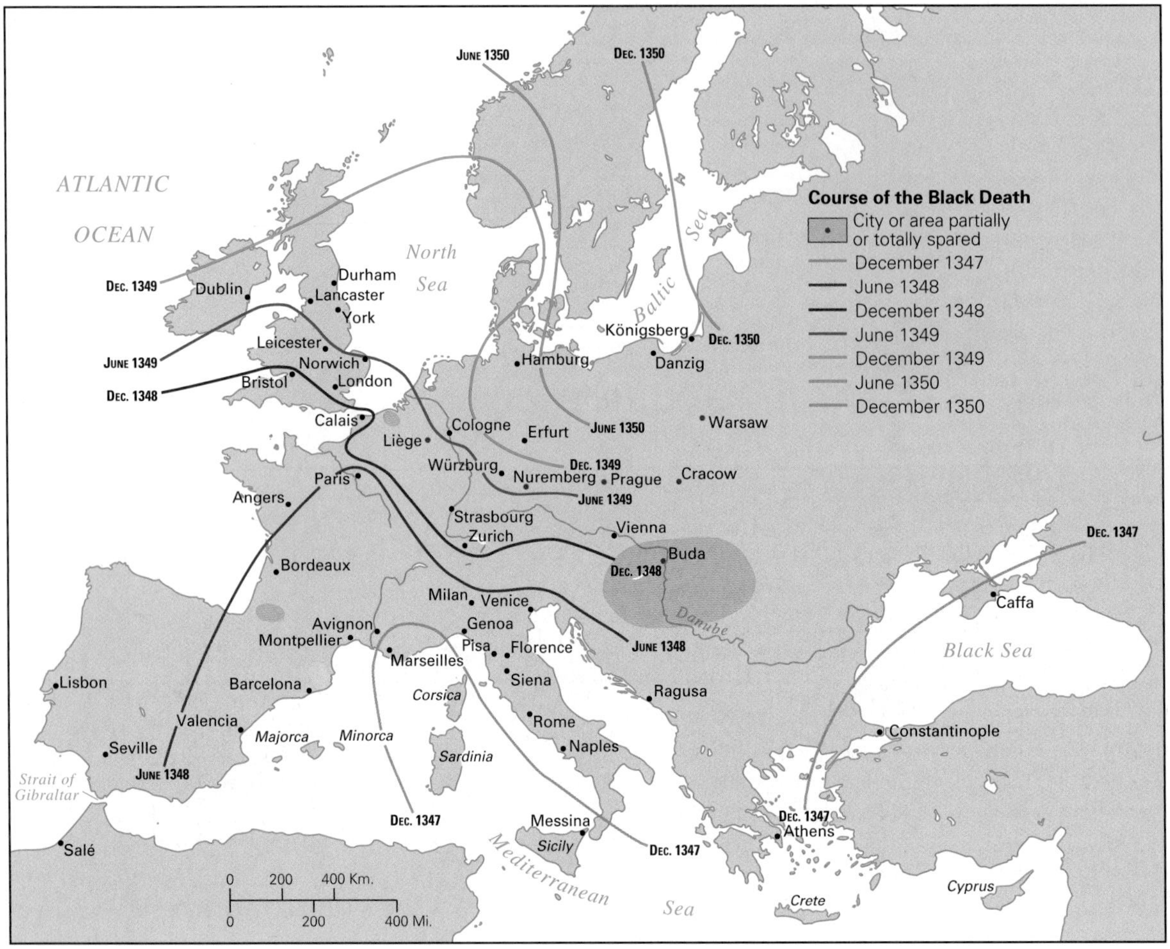


**MAP 12.1 The Course of the Black Death in Fourteenth-Century Europe** Note the routes that the bubonic plague took across Europe. How do you account for the fact that several regions were spared the "dreadful death"?

Genoa were hit in January 1348, and from the port of Pisa the disease spread south to Rome and east to Florence and all of Tuscany. By late spring, southern Germany was attacked. Frightened French authorities chased a galley bearing the disease from the port of Marseilles, but not before plague had infected the city, from which it spread to Languedoc and Spain. In June 1348, two ships entered the Bristol Channel and introduced it into England. All Europe felt the scourge of this horrible disease (see Map 12.1).

## Pathology and Care

Modern understanding of the bubonic plague rests on the research of two bacteriologists, one French and one Japanese, who in 1894 independently identified the bacillus that causes the plague, *Pasteurella pestis* (so labeled after the French scientist's teacher, Louis Pasteur). The bacillus liked to live in the bloodstream of an animal or, ideally, in the stomach of a flea. The flea in turn resided in the hair of a rodent, sometimes a squirrel but preferably the hardy, nimble, and vagabond black rat. Why the host black rat moved so much, scientists still do not know, but it often traveled by ship. There the black rat could feast for months on a cargo of grain or live snugly among bales of cloth. Fleas bearing the bacillus also had no trouble nesting in saddlebags.[4] Comfortable, well-fed, and having greatly multiplied, the black rats ended their ocean voyage and descended on the great cities of Europe.

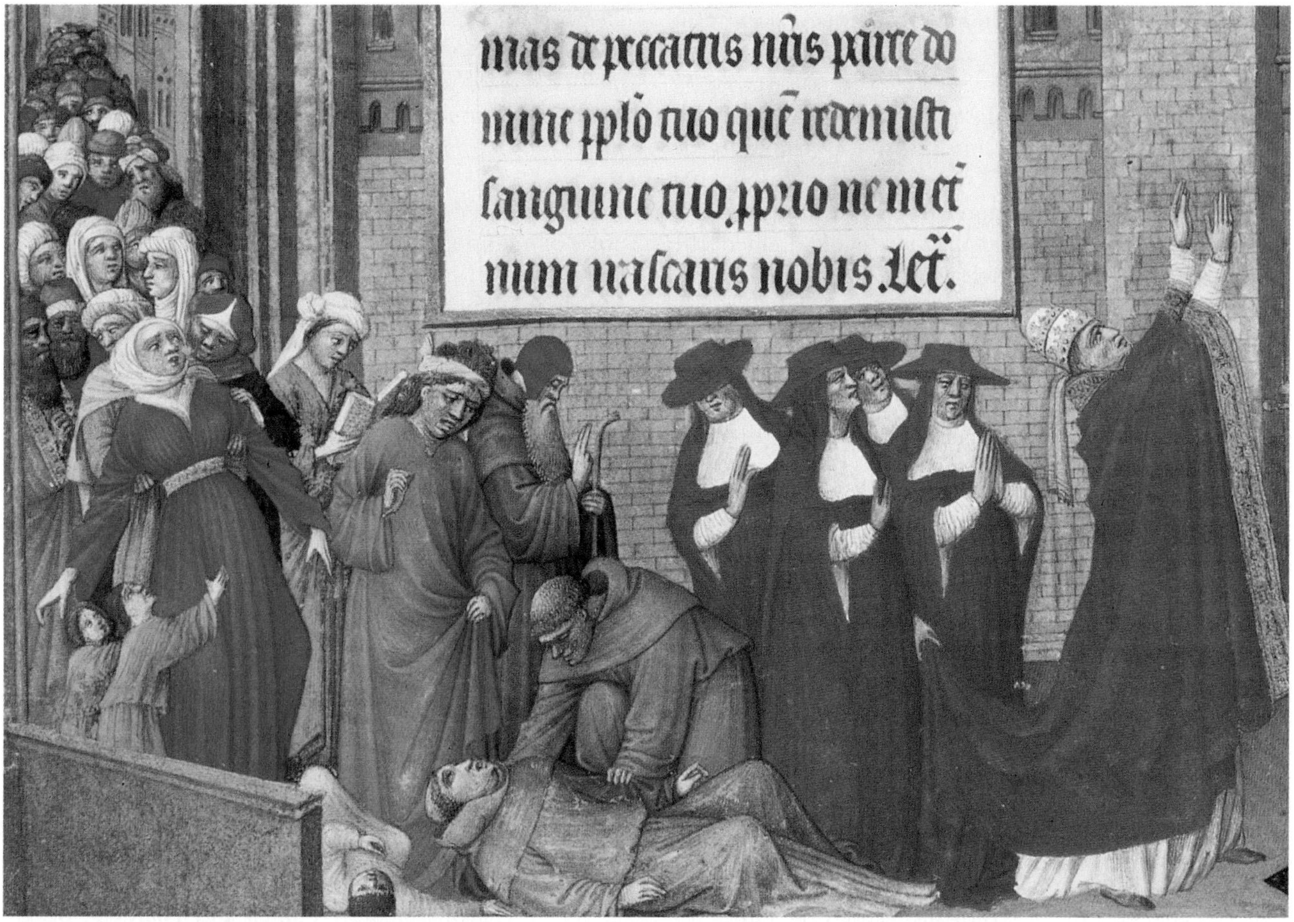

**Procession of Saint Gregory** According to the *Golden Legend,* a thirteenth-century collection of saints' lives, the bubonic plague ravaged Rome when Gregory I was elected pope (590–604). He immediately ordered special prayers and processions around the city. Here, as people circle the walls, new victims fall (*center*). The architecture, the cardinals, and the friars all indicate that this painting dates from the fourteenth, not the sixth, century. *(Musée Condé, Chantilly/Art Resource, NY)*

The plague took two forms—bubonic and pneumonic. In the bubonic form, the flea was the vector, or transmitter, of the disease. In the pneumonic form, the plague was communicated directly from one person to another.

Although by the fourteenth century urban authorities from London to Paris to Rome had begun to try to achieve a primitive level of sanitation, urban conditions remained ideal for the spread of disease. Narrow streets filled with refuse and human excrement were as much cesspools as thoroughfares. Dead animals and sore-covered beggars greeted the traveler. Houses whose upper stories projected over the lower ones blocked light and air. And extreme overcrowding was commonplace. When all members of an aristocratic family lived and slept in one room, it should not be surprising that six or eight persons in a middle-class or poor household slept in one bed—if they had one. Closeness, after all, provided warmth. Houses were beginning to be constructed of brick, but many remained of wood, clay, and mud. A determined rat had little trouble entering such a house.

Standards of personal hygiene remained frightfully low. True, most large cities had public bathhouses, but we have no way of knowing how frequently ordinary people used them. Lack of personal cleanliness, combined with any number of temporary ailments such as diarrhea and the common cold, weakened the body's resistance to serious disease. Fleas and body lice were universal afflictions: everyone from peasants to archbishops had them. One more bite did not cause much alarm. But if that nibble came from a bacillus-bearing flea, an entire household or area was doomed.

The classic symptom of the bubonic plague was a growth the size of a nut or an apple in the armpit, in the groin, or on the neck. This was the boil, or **buba,** that gave the disease its name and caused agonizing pain. If the buba was lanced and the pus thoroughly drained, the victim had a chance of recovery. The next stage was the appearance of black spots or blotches caused by bleeding under the skin. (This syndrome did not give the disease its common name; contemporaries did not call the plague the Black Death. Sometime in the fifteenth century, the Latin phrase *atra mors,* meaning "dreadful death," was translated "black death," and the phrase stuck.) Finally, the victim began to cough violently and spit blood. This stage, indicating the presence of millions of bacilli in the bloodstream, signaled the end, and death followed in two or three days. Rather than evoking compassion for the victim, a French scientist has written, everything about the bubonic plague provoked horror and disgust: "All the matter which exuded from their bodies let off an unbearable stench; sweat, excrement, spittle, breath, so fetid as to be overpowering; urine turbid, thick, black or red."[5]

Fourteenth-century medical literature indicates that physicians could sometimes ease the pain, but they had no cure. Most people—lay, scholarly, and medical—believed that the Black Death was caused by some "vicious property in the air" that carried the disease from place to place. When ignorance was joined to fear and ancient bigotry, savage cruelty sometimes resulted. Many people believed that the Jews had poisoned the wells of Christian communities and thereby infected the drinking water. This charge led to the murder of thousands of Jews across Europe. According to one chronicler, sixteen thousand were killed at the imperial city of Strasbourg alone in 1349. Though sixteen thousand is probably a typical medieval numerical exaggeration, the horror of the massacre is not lessened. Scholars have yet to explain the economic impact that the loss of such a productive people had on Strasbourg and other cities.

The Italian writer Giovanni Boccaccio (1313–1375), describing the course of the disease in Florence in the preface to his book of tales *The Decameron,* pinpointed the cause of the spread:

*Moreover, the virulence of the pest was the greater by reason that intercourse was apt to convey it from the sick to the whole, just as fire devours things dry or greasy when they are brought close to it. Nay, the evil went yet further, for not merely by speech or association with the sick was the malady communicated to the healthy with consequent peril of common death, but any that touched the clothes of the sick or aught else that had been touched or used by them, seemed thereby to contract the disease.*[6]

The highly infectious nature of the plague, especially in areas of high population density, was recognized by a few sophisticated Muslims. When the disease struck the town of Salé in Morocco, Ibu Abu Madyan shut in his household with sufficient food and water and allowed no one to enter or leave until the plague had passed. Abu Madyan was entirely successful. The rat that carried the disease-bearing flea avoided travel outside the cities. Thus the countryside was relatively safe. City dwellers who could afford to move fled to the country.

If medical science had no effective treatment, could victims' suffering be eased? Perhaps in hospitals. What was the geographical distribution of hospitals, and, although our estimates of medieval populations remain rough, what was the hospital-to-population ratio? How many patients could a hospital serve? Whereas earlier the feudal lord had made philanthropic foundations, beginning in the thirteenth century individual merchants—out of compassion, generosity, and the custom of giving to parish collections, and in the belief that the sick would be prayerful intercessors with God for the donors' sins—endowed hospitals. Business people established hospitals in the towns of northern France and Flanders; Milan, Genoa, and Venice were well served, and the 30 hospitals in Florence provided 1,000 beds in 1339. Sixty hospitals served Paris in 1328—but probably not enough for its population of 200,000. The many hospitals in the Iberian Peninsula continued the Muslim tradition of care for the poor and ill. Merchants in the larger towns of the German Empire, in Poland, and in Hungary also founded hospitals in the fourteenth century, generally later than those in western Europe. Sailors, long viewed as potential carriers of disease, benefited from hospitals reserved for them; in 1300 the Venetian government paid a surgeon to care for sick sailors. At the time the plague erupted, therefore, most towns and cities had hospital facilities.

When trying to determine the number of people a hospital could accommodate, the modern researcher considers the number of beds, the size of the staff, and the building's physical layout. Since each medieval hospital bed might serve two or more patients, we cannot calculate the number of patients on the basis of the beds alone. We do know that rural hospices usually had twelve to fifteen beds, and city hospitals, as at Lisbon, Narbonne,

**Patients in a Hospital Ward, Fifteenth Century** In many cities hospitals could not cope with the large numbers of plague victims. The practice of putting two or more adults in the same bed, as shown here, contributed to the spread of the disease. At the Hôtel-Dieu in Paris, nurses complained of being forced to put eight to ten children in a single bed in which a patient had recently died. *(Giraudon/The Bridgeman Art Library)*

and Genoa, had on average twenty-five to thirty beds, but these figures do not tell us how many patients were accommodated. Only the very rare document listing the number of wrapping sheets and coffins for the dead purchased in a given period provides the modern scholar with information on the number of patients a hospital had. Hospitals could offer only shelter, compassion, and care for the dying.[7]

Mortality rates cannot be specified, because population figures for the period before the arrival of the plague do not exist for most countries and cities. The largest amount of material survives for England, but it is difficult to use; after enormous scholarly controversy, only educated guesses can be made. Of a total English population of perhaps 4.2 million, probably 1.4 million died of the Black Death in its several visits.[8] Densely populated Italian cities endured incredible losses. Florence lost between one-half and two-thirds of its 1347 population of 85,000 when the plague visited in 1348.

Nor did central and eastern Europe escape the ravages of the disease. Moving northward from the Balkans, eastward from France, and southward from the Baltic, the plague swept through the German Empire. In the Rhineland in 1349, Cologne and Mainz endured heavy losses. In 1348 it swept through Bavaria, entered the Moselle Valley, and pushed into northern Germany. One chronicler records that in the summer and autumn of 1349, between five hundred and six hundred died every day in Vienna. Styria, in what today is central Austria, was very hard hit, with cattle straying unattended in the fields.

As the Black Death took its toll on the German Empire, waves of emigrants fled to Poland, Bohemia, and Hungary. The situation there was better, though not completely absent of disease. The plague seems to have entered Poland through the Baltic seaports and spread from there. Still, population losses were lower than elsewhere in Europe. The plague spread from Poland to Russia, reaching Pskov, Novgorod, and Moscow, where it felled Grand Duke Simeon.[9] No estimates have been made of population losses there or in the Balkans. In Serbia, though, the plague left vast tracts of land unattended, which prompted an increase in Albanian immigration to meet the labor shortage.

Across Europe the Black Death recurred intermittently from the 1360s to 1400. It reappeared many times with reduced virulence, making its last appearance in the French port city of Marseilles in 1721. Survivors became more prudent. Because periods of famine had caused malnutrition, making people vulnerable to disease, Europeans controlled population growth so that population did not outstrip food supply. Western Europeans improved navigation techniques and increased long-distance trade, which permitted the importation of grain from sparsely populated Baltic regions (see page 381). They strictly enforced quarantine measures.[10] They worked on the development of vaccines. But it was only in 1947, six centuries after the arrival of the plague in the West, that the American microbiologist Selman Waksman discovered an effective vaccine, streptomycin.

## Social, Economic, and Cultural Consequences

It is noteworthy that, in an age of mounting criticism of clerical wealth (see page 394), the behavior of the clergy during the plague was often exemplary. Priests, monks, and nuns cared for the sick and buried the dead. In places like Venice, from which even physicians fled, priests remained to give what ministrations they could. Consequently, their mortality rate was phenomenally high. The German clergy especially suffered a severe decline in personnel in the years after 1350. With the ablest killed off, the wealth of the German church fell into the hands of the incompetent and weak. The situation was ripe for reform (see Chapter 14).

In taking their pastoral responsibilities seriously, some clergy did things that the church in a later age would vigorously condemn. The institutional church has traditionally opposed laymen, and especially laywomen, administering the sacraments. But the shortage of priests was so great that in 1349 Ralph, bishop of Bath and Wells in England (1329–1363), advised his people that "if they are on the point of death and cannot secure the services of a priest, then they should make confession to each other, as is permitted in the teaching of the Apostles, whether to a layman or, if no man is present, even to a woman."[11]

Economic historians and demographers sharply dispute the impact of the plague on the economy in the late fourteenth century. The traditional view that the plague had a disastrous effect has been greatly modified. The clearest evidence comes from England, where the agrarian economy showed remarkable resilience. While the severity of the disease varied from region to region, it appears that by about 1375 most landlords enjoyed revenues near those of the pre-plague years. By the early fifteenth century, seigneurial prosperity reached a medieval peak. Why? The answer appears to lie in the fact that England and many parts of Europe suffered from overpopulation in the early fourteenth century. Population losses caused by the Black Death "led to increased productivity by restoring a more efficient balance between labour, land, and capital."[12]

What impact did visits of the plague have on urban populations? The rich evidence from a census of the city of Florence and its surrounding territory taken between 1427 and 1430 is fascinating. The region had suffered repeated epidemics since 1347. In a total population of 260,000 persons, 15 percent were age sixty or over (a very high proportion), suggesting that the plague took the young rather than the mature. Children and youths up to age nineteen constituted 44 percent of the people. Adults between the ages of twenty and fifty-nine, the most economically productive group, represented 41 percent of Florentine society.

The high mortality rate of craftsmen led Florentine guilds to recruit many new members. For example, between 1328 and 1347 the silk merchants guild accepted 730 members, and between 1408 and 1427 it admitted 784. It appears that economic organizations tried to keep their numbers constant, even though the size of the population and its pool of potential guild members was shrinking. Moreover, in contrast to the pre-1348 period, many new members of the guilds were not related to existing members. Thus the post-plague years represent an age of "new men."[13]

The Black Death brought on a general European inflation. High mortality produced a fall in production, shortages of goods, and a general rise in prices. The shortage of labor and workers' demands for higher wages put guild masters on the defensive. They retaliated with measures such as the Statute of Laborers (1351), an attempt by the English Parliament to freeze the wages of English workers at pre-1347 levels. Such statutes could not be enforced and thus were unsuccessful. The price of wheat in most of Europe increased, as did the costs of meat, sausage, and cheese. This inflation continued to the end of the fourteenth century. But wages in the towns rose faster, and the broad mass of people enjoyed a higher standard of living. "A more efficient balance between labour, land, and capital" brought increased productivity.[14] Population decline meant a sharp increase in per capita wealth. The greater demand for labor meant greater mobility for peasants in rural areas and for industrial workers in the towns and cities.

Labor shortages caused by the Black Death throughout the Mediterranean region, from Constantinople to Spain, presented aggressive businessmen with a golden opportunity. The price of slaves rose sharply. Venetian slavers from their colony at Tana on the Sea of Azov in the Crimea took advantage of the boom in demand as prices soared between 1350 and 1410. "By about 1408, no less than 78 per cent of Tana's export earnings came from slaves. Out of their misery, and out of the profits born of the Black Death, one palace after another was raised along the (Venetian) Rialto."[15]

Even more significant than the social effects were the psychological consequences. The knowledge that the disease meant almost certain death provoked the most profound pessimism. Imagine an entire society in the grip of the belief that it was at the mercy of a frightful affliction about which nothing could be done, a disgusting disease from which family and friends would flee, leaving one to die alone and in agony. It is not surprising that some sought release in orgies and gross sensuality, while others turned to the severest forms of asceticism and frenzied religious fervor. Some extremists joined groups of **flagellants,** who whipped and scourged themselves as penance for their and society's sins, in the belief that the Black Death was God's punishment for humanity's wickedness.

Plague ripped apart the social fabric. In the thirteenth century, funerals, traditionally occasions for the mutual consolation of the living as much as memorial services for the dead, grew increasingly elaborate, with large corteges and many mourners. In the fourteenth century, public horror at the suffering of the afflicted and at the dead reduced the size of mourning processions and eventually resulted in failure even to perform the customary death rites. Fear of infection led to the dead being buried hastily, sometimes in mass graves.

People often used pilgrimages to holy places as justification for their flight from cities. Suspected of being carriers of plague, travelers, pilgrims, and the homeless aroused deep hostility. All European port cities followed the example of Ragusa (modern Dubrovnik in southwestern Croatia on the Dalmatian coast) and quarantined arriving ships, crews, passengers, and cargoes to determine whether they brought the plague. Deriving from a Venetian word, the English term *quarantine* originally meant forty days' isolation.

Popular endowments of educational institutions multiplied. The years of the Black Death witnessed the foundation of new colleges at old universities, such as Corpus Christi and Clare Colleges at Cambridge and New College at Oxford, and of entirely new universities. The beginnings of Charles University in Prague (1348) and the Universities of Florence (1350), Vienna (1364), Cracow (1364), and Heidelberg (1385) were all associated with the plague: their foundation charters specifically mention the shortage of priests and the decay of learning. Whereas universities such as those at Bologna and Paris had an international student body, new institutions established in the wake of the Black Death had more national or local constituencies. Thus the international character of medieval culture weakened. The decline of cultural cohesion paved the way for schism in the Catholic church even before the Reformation.[16]

The literature and art of the fourteenth century reveal a terribly morbid concern with death. One highly popular artistic motif, the Dance of Death, depicted a dancing skeleton leading away a living person. A long international war added further misery to the frightful disasters of the plague.

## The Hundred Years' War (ca 1337–1453)

In January 1327, Queen Isabella of England, her lover Mortimer, and a group of barons, having deposed and murdered Isabella's incompetent husband, King Edward II, proclaimed his fifteen-year-old son king as Edward III. Isabella and Mortimer, however, held real power until 1330, when Edward seized the reins of government. In 1328 Charles IV of France, the last surviving son of Philip the Fair, died childless. With him ended the Capetian dynasty. An assembly of French barons, meaning to exclude Isabella—who was Charles's sister and the daughter of Philip the Fair—and her son Edward III from the French throne, proclaimed that "no woman nor her son could succeed to the [French] monarchy." French lawyers defended this position—that no woman or her descendant could rule France—with the claim that the Salic Law, a long-obsolete sixth-century Germanic law code (see page 210), was part of the fundamental law of France. The barons passed the crown to Philip VI of Valois (r. 1328–1350), a nephew of Philip the Fair. In these actions lie the origins of another phase of the centuries-old struggle between the English and French monarchies, one that was fought intermittently from 1337 to 1453.

## Causes

The Hundred Years' War had both distant and immediate causes. In 1259 France and England signed the Treaty of Paris, in which the English king agreed to become—for himself and his successors—vassal of the French crown for the duchy of Aquitaine. The English claimed Aquitaine as an ancient inheritance. French policy, however, was strongly expansionist, and the French kings resolved to absorb the duchy into the kingdom of France. In 1329 Edward III paid homage to Philip VI for Aquitaine. In 1337 Philip, eager to exercise full French jurisdiction in Aquitaine, confiscated the duchy. Edward III interpreted this action as a gross violation of the treaty of 1259 and as a cause for war. Moreover, Edward argued, as the eldest directly surviving male descendant of Philip the Fair, he must assume the title of king of France in order to wield his rightful authority in Aquitaine.[17] In short, Edward rejected the decision of the French barons excluding him from the throne. Edward III's dynastic argument upset the feudal order in France: to increase their independent power, French vassals of Philip VI used the excuse that they had to transfer their loyalty to a more legitimate overlord, Edward III. One reason the war lasted so long was that it became a French civil war, with some French barons supporting English monarchs in order to thwart the centralizing goals of the French crown.

Economic factors involving the wool trade and the control of Flemish towns had served as justifications for war between France and England for centuries. The wool trade between England and Flanders served as the cornerstone of both countries' economies; they were closely interdependent. Flanders was a fief of the French crown, and the Flemish aristocracy was highly sympathetic to the monarchy in Paris. But the wealth of Flemish merchants and cloth manufacturers depended on English wool, and Flemish burghers strongly supported the claims of Edward III. The disruption of commerce with England threatened their prosperity.

## The Popular Response

The governments of both England and France manipulated public opinion to support the war. Whatever significance modern scholars ascribe to the economic factor, public opinion in fourteenth-century England held that the war was waged for one reason: to secure for King Edward the French crown he had been unjustly denied.[18]

**Flanders and the English Merchant Staplers** Flanders was officially on the French side during the Hundred Years' War, but Flemish cities depended heavily on English wool for their textile manufacturing. Hence the Merchant Staplers, the English trading company with a monopoly on trade in wool, sought concessions. In this 1387 illustration, the master of the staple and his fellow merchants plead their case to the count of Flanders. *(British Library)*

Edward III issued letters to the sheriffs describing in graphic terms the evil deeds of the French and listing royal needs. Kings in both countries instructed the clergy to deliver sermons filled with patriotic sentiment. The royal courts sensationalized the wickedness of the other side and stressed the great fortunes to be made from the war. Philip VI sent agents to warn communities about the dangers of invasion and to stress the French crown's revenue needs to meet the attack.

The royal campaign to rally public opinion was highly successful, at least in the early stage of the war. Edward III gained widespread support in the 1340s and 1350s. The English developed a deep hatred of the French and feared that King Philip intended "to have seized and slaughtered the entire realm of England." When England was successful in the field, pride in the country's military proficiency increased.

Most important of all, the Hundred Years' War was popular because it presented unusual opportunities for wealth and advancement. Poor knights and knights who were unemployed were promised regular wages. Criminals who enlisted were granted pardons. The great nobles expected to be rewarded with estates. Royal exhortations to the troops before battles repeatedly stressed that, if victorious, the men might keep whatever they seized. The French chronicler Jean Froissart wrote that, at the time of Edward III's expedition of 1359, men of all ranks flocked to the English king's banner. Some came to acquire honor, but many came "to loot and pillage the fair and plenteous land of France."[19]

## The Course of the War to 1419

The war was fought almost entirely in France and the Low Countries (see Map 12.2). It consisted mainly of a series of random sieges and cavalry raids. In 1335 the French began supporting Scottish incursions into northern England, ravaging the countryside in Aquitaine, and

**Siege of the Castle of Mortagne Near Bordeaux (1377)** Medieval warfare usually consisted of small skirmishes and attacks on castles. This miniature shows the French besieging an English-held castle. Most of the soldiers use longbows, although at the left two men shoot primitive muskets above a pair of cannon. The castle held out for six months. Painted in the late fifteenth century, the scene reflects contemporary developments rather than fourteenth-century events. *(British Library)*

sacking and burning English coastal towns, such as Southampton. Such tactics lent weight to Edward III's propaganda campaign. In fact, royal propaganda on both sides fostered a kind of early nationalism.

During the war's early stages, England was highly successful. At **Crécy** in northern France in 1346, English longbowmen scored a great victory over French knights and crossbowmen. Although the aim of the longbow was not very accurate, it allowed for rapid reloading, and English archers could send off three arrows to the French crossbowmen's one. The result was a blinding shower of arrows that unhorsed the French knights and caused mass confusion. The firing of cannon—probably the first use of artillery in the West—created further panic. Thereupon the English horsemen charged and butchered the French.

This was not war according to the chivalric rules that Edward III would have preferred. Nevertheless, his son Edward the Black Prince used the same tactics ten years later to smash the French at Poitiers, where he captured the French king and held him for ransom. Again, at **Agincourt** near Arras in 1415, the chivalric English soldier-king Henry V (r. 1413–1422) gained the field over vastly superior numbers. Henry followed up his triumph at Agincourt with the reconquest of Normandy. By 1419 the English had advanced to the walls of Paris (see Map 12.2). But the French cause was not lost. Though England had scored the initial victories, France won the war.

## Joan of Arc and France's Victory

The ultimate French success rests heavily on the actions of an obscure French peasant girl, **Joan of Arc,** whose vision and work revived French fortunes and led to victory. A great deal of pious and popular legend surrounds Joan the Maid, because of her peculiar appearance on the scene, her astonishing success, her martyrdom, and her canonization by the Catholic church. The historical fact is that she saved the French monarchy, which was the embodiment of France.

Born in 1412 to well-to-do peasants in the village of Domrémy in Champagne, Joan of Arc grew up in a religious household. During adolescence she began to hear voices, which she later said belonged to Saint Michael, Saint Catherine, and Saint Margaret. In 1428 these voices spoke to her with great urgency, telling her that the dauphin (the uncrowned King Charles VII) had to be crowned and the English expelled from France. Joan went to the French court, persuaded the king to reject the rumor that he was illegitimate, and secured his support for her relief of the besieged city of Orléans.

The astonishing thing is not that Joan the Maid overcame serious obstacles to see the dauphin, not even that Charles and his advisers listened to her. What is amazing is the swiftness with which they were convinced. French fortunes had been so low for so long that the court believed only a miracle could save the country. Because Joan cut her hair short and dressed like a man, she scandalized the court. But hoping she would provide the miracle, Charles allowed her to accompany the army that was preparing to raise the English siege of Orléans.

In the meantime Joan, herself illiterate, dictated this letter calling on the English to withdraw:

> *King of England . . . , do right in the King of Heaven's sight. Surrender to* The Maid *sent hither by God the King of Heaven, the keys of all the good towns you have taken and laid waste in France. She comes in God's name to establish the Blood Royal, ready to make peace if you agree to abandon France and repay what you have taken. And you, archers, comrades in arms, gentles and others, who are before the town of Orléans, retire in God's name to your own country.*[20]

Joan arrived before Orléans on April 28, 1429. Seventeen years old, she knew little of warfare and believed that if she could keep the French troops from swearing and frequenting brothels, victory would be theirs. On May 8 the English, weakened by disease and lack of supplies, withdrew from Orléans. Ten days later, Charles VII was crowned king at Reims. These two events marked the turning point in the war.

Joan's presence at Orléans, her strong belief in her mission, and the fact that she was wounded enhanced her reputation and strengthened the morale of the army. In 1430 England's allies, the Burgundians, captured Joan and sold her to the English. When the English handed her over to the ecclesiastical authorities for trial, the French court did not intervene. While the English wanted Joan eliminated for obvious political reasons, sorcery (witchcraft) was the ostensible charge at her trial. Witch persecution was increasing in the fifteenth century, and Joan's wearing of men's clothes appeared not only aberrant but indicative of contact with the Devil. In 1431 the court condemned her as a heretic—her claim of direct inspiration from God, thereby denying the authority of church officials, constituted heresy—and burned her at the stake in the marketplace at Rouen. A new trial in 1456 rehabilitated her name. In 1920 she was canonized and declared a holy maiden, and today she is revered as the second patron saint of France. The nineteenth-

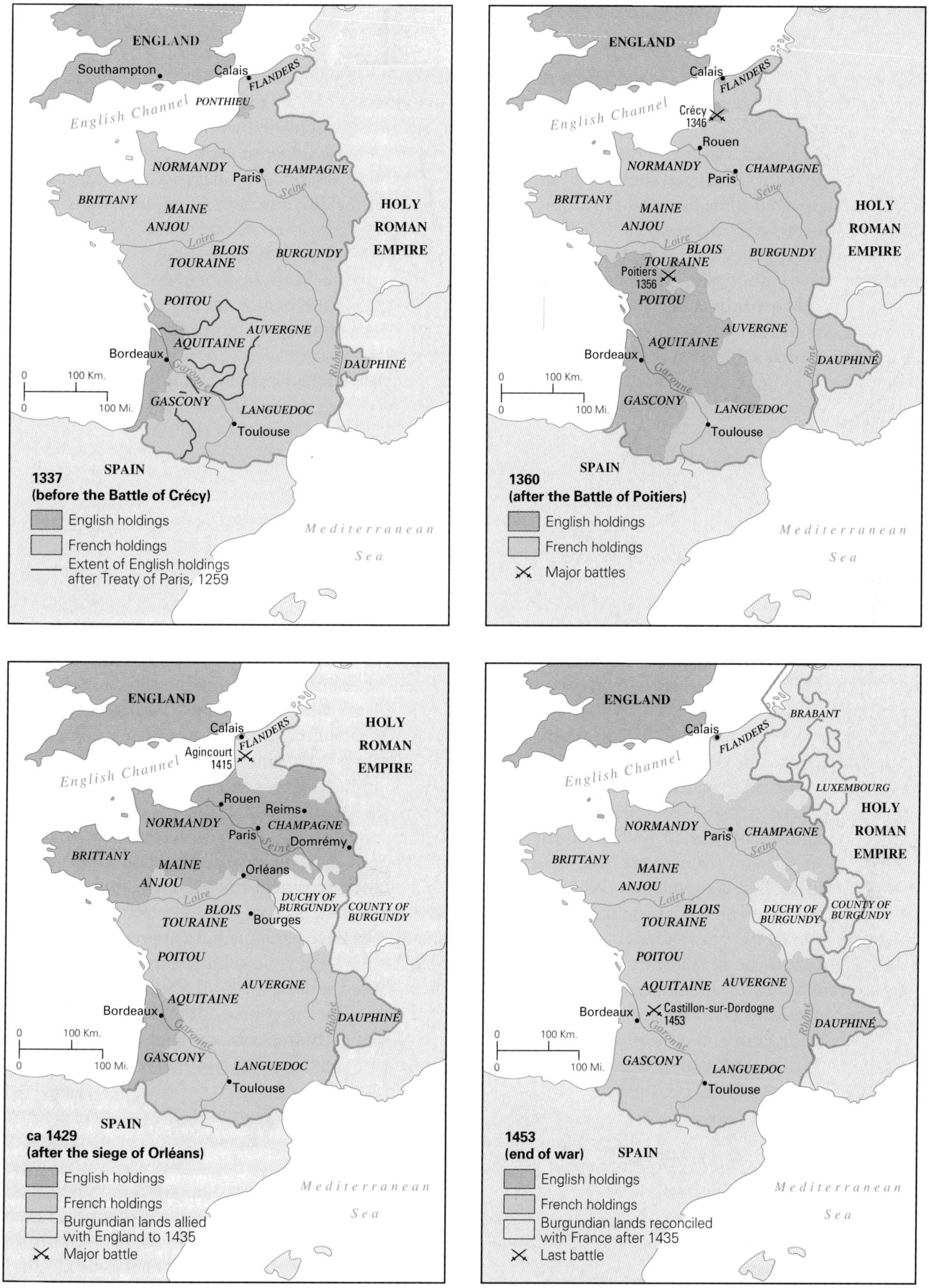


**MAP 12.2 English Holdings in France During the Hundred Years' War** The year 1429 marked the greatest extent of English holdings in France. Why is it unlikely that England could have held these territories permanently?

century French historian Jules Michelet extolled Joan of Arc as a symbol of the vitality and strength of the French peasant classes.

The relief of Orléans stimulated French pride and rallied French resources. As the war dragged on, loss of life mounted, and money appeared to be flowing into a bottomless pit, demands for an end increased in England. The clergy and intellectuals pressed for peace. Parliamentary opposition to additional war grants stiffened. Slowly the French reconquered Normandy and, finally, ejected the English from Aquitaine. At the war's end in 1453, only the town of Calais remained in English hands.

## Costs and Consequences

In France the English had slaughtered thousands of soldiers and civilians. In the years after the sweep of the Black Death, this additional killing meant a grave loss of population. The English had laid waste to hundreds of thousands of acres of rich farmland, leaving the rural economy of many parts of France a shambles. The war had disrupted trade and the great fairs, resulting in the drastic reduction of French participation in international commerce. Defeat in battle and heavy taxation contributed to widespread dissatisfaction and aggravated peasant grievances.

In England only the southern coastal ports experienced much destruction, and the demographic effects of the Black Death actually worked to restore the land-labor balance (see page 386). The costs of the war, however, were tremendous. England spent over £5 million on the war effort, a huge sum at the time. Manpower losses had greater social consequences. The knights who ordinarily handled the work of local government as sheriffs, coroners, jurymen, and justices of the peace were abroad, and their absence contributed to the breakdown of order at the local level. The English government attempted to finance the war effort by raising taxes on the wool crop. Because of steadily increasing costs, the Flemish and Italian buyers could not afford English wool. Consequently, raw wool exports slumped drastically between 1350 and 1450.

Many men of all social classes had volunteered for service in France in the hope of acquiring booty and becoming rich. The chronicler Walsingham, describing the period of Crécy, wrote: "For the woman was of no account who did not possess something from the spoils of . . . cities overseas in clothing, furs, quilts, and utensils . . . tablecloths and jewels, bowls of murra [semiprecious stone] and silver, linen and linen cloths."[21] Walsingham is referring to 1348, in the first generation of war. As time went on, most fortunes seem to have been squandered as fast as they were made.

If English troops returned with cash, they did not invest it in land. In the fifteenth century, returning soldiers were commonly described as beggars and vagabonds, roaming about making mischief. Even the large sums of money received from the ransom of the great—such as the £250,000 paid to Edward III for the freedom of King John of France—and the money paid as indemnities by captured towns and castles did not begin to equal the more than £5 million spent. England suffered a serious net loss.[22]

The long war also had a profound impact on the political and cultural lives of the two countries. Most notably, it stimulated the development of the English Parliament. Between 1250 and 1450, **representative assemblies** flourished in many European countries. In the English Parliament, German diets, and Spanish cortes, deliberative practices developed that laid the foundations for the representative institutions of modern liberal-democratic nations. While representative assemblies declined in most countries after the fifteenth century, the English Parliament endured. Edward III's constant need for money to pay for the war compelled him to summon not only the great barons and bishops, but knights of the shires and burgesses from the towns as well. Parliament met in thirty-seven of the fifty years of Edward's reign.[23]

The frequency of the meetings is significant. Representative assemblies were becoming a habit. Knights and burgesses—or the "Commons," as they came to be called—recognized their mutual interests and began to meet apart from the great lords. The Commons gradually realized that they held the country's purse strings, and a parliamentary statute of 1341 required that all nonfeudal levies have parliamentary approval. When Edward III signed the law, he acknowledged that the king of England could not tax without Parliament's consent. Increasingly, during the course of the war, money grants were tied to royal redress of grievances: if the government was to raise money, it had to correct the wrongs its subjects protested.

In England theoretical consent to taxation and legislation was given in one assembly for the entire country. France had no such single assembly; instead, there were many regional or provincial assemblies. Why did a national representative assembly fail to develop in France? The initiative for convening assemblies rested with the king, who needed revenue almost as much as the English ruler. But the French monarchy found the idea of representative assemblies thoroughly distasteful. Large gatherings of the nobility potentially or actually threatened the king's power. The advice of a counselor to King Charles VI (r. 1380–1422), "above all things be sure that no great assemblies of nobles or of *communes* take place in your kingdom," was accepted.[24] Charles VII (r. 1422–1461) even threatened to punish those proposing a national assembly.

No one in France wanted a national assembly. Linguistic, geographical, economic, legal, and political differences were very strong. People tended to think of themselves as Breton, Norman, Burgundian, or whatever, rather than French. Through much of the fourteenth and early fifteenth centuries, weak monarchs lacked the power to call a national assembly. Provincial assemblies, highly jealous of their independence, did not want a national assembly. The costs of sending delegates to it would be high, and the result was likely to be increased taxation.

In both countries, however, the war did promote the growth of **nationalism**—the feeling of unity and identity that binds together a people. After victories, each country experienced a surge of pride in its military strength. Just as English patriotism ran strong after Crécy and Poitiers, so French national confidence rose after Orléans. French national feeling demanded the expulsion of the enemy not merely from Normandy and Aquitaine but from French soil. Perhaps no one expressed this national consciousness better than Joan of Arc, when she exulted that the enemy had been "driven out of *France*."

## The Decline of the Church's Prestige

See DBQ 1

In times of crisis or disaster, people of all faiths have sought the consolation of religion. In the fourteenth century, however, the official Christian church offered little solace. In fact, the leaders of the church added to the sorrow and misery of the times.

### The Babylonian Captivity

From 1309 to 1376, the popes lived in Avignon in southeastern France. In order to control the church and its policies, Philip the Fair of France pressured Pope Clement V to settle in Avignon (see Map 11.5 on page 358). Clement, critically ill with cancer, lacked the will to resist Philip. This period in church history is often called the **Babylonian Captivity** (referring to the seventy years the ancient Hebrews were held captive in Mesopotamian Babylon).

The Babylonian Captivity badly damaged papal prestige. The Avignon papacy reformed its financial administration and centralized its government. But the seven popes at Avignon concentrated on bureaucratic matters to the exclusion of spiritual objectives. Though some of the popes led austere lives, the general atmosphere was one of luxury and extravagance. The leadership of the church was cut off from its historic roots and the source of its ancient authority, the city of Rome. In the absence of the papacy, the Papal States in Italy lacked stability and good government. The economy of Rome had been based on the presence of the papal court and the rich tourist trade the papacy attracted. The Babylonian Captivity left Rome poverty-stricken.

In 1377 Pope Gregory XI brought the papal court back to Rome. Unfortunately, he died shortly after the return. At Gregory's death, Roman citizens demanded an Italian pope who would remain in Rome. Between the time of Gregory's death and the opening of the conclave, great pressure was put on the cardinals to elect an Italian. At the time, none of them protested this pressure.

Sixteen cardinals—eleven Frenchmen, four Italians, and one Spaniard—entered the conclave on April 7, 1378. After two ballots, they unanimously chose a distinguished administrator, the archbishop of Bari, Bartolomeo Prignano, who took the name Urban VI. Each of the cardinals swore that Urban had been elected "sincerely, freely, genuinely, and canonically."

Urban VI (1378–1389) had excellent intentions for church reform. He wanted to abolish simony, *pluralism* (holding several church offices at the same time), absenteeism, and clerical extravagance. These were the very abuses being increasingly criticized by Christian people across Europe. Unfortunately, Pope Urban went about the work of reform in a tactless and bullheaded manner. The day after his coronation, he delivered a blistering attack on cardinals who lived in Rome while drawing their income from benefices elsewhere. His criticism was well-founded but ill-timed and provoked opposition before Urban had consolidated his authority.

In the weeks that followed, Urban stepped up attacks on clerical luxury, denouncing individual cardinals by name. He threatened to strike the cardinal archbishop of Amiens. Urban even threatened to excommunicate certain cardinals, and when he was advised that such excommunications would not be lawful unless the guilty had been warned three times, he shouted, "I can do anything, if it be my will and judgment."[25] Urban's quick temper and irrational behavior have led scholars to question his sanity. Whether he was medically insane or just drunk with power is a moot point. In any case, Urban's actions brought on disaster.

In groups of two and three, the cardinals slipped away from Rome and met at Anagni. They declared Urban's election invalid because it had come about under threats from the Roman mob, and they asserted that Urban himself was excommunicated. The cardinals then proceeded to the city of Fondi between Rome and Naples and elected Cardinal Robert of Geneva, the cousin of King Charles V of France, as pope. Cardinal Robert took the name Clement VII. There were thus two popes—Urban at Rome and the antipope Clement VII (1378–1394), who set himself up at Avignon in opposition to the legally elected Urban. So began the Great Schism, which divided Western Christendom until 1417.

## The Great Schism

The powers of Europe aligned themselves with Urban or Clement along strictly political lines. France naturally recognized the French antipope, Clement. England, France's historic enemy, recognized Pope Urban. Scotland, whose attacks on England were subsidized by France, followed the French and supported Clement. Aragon, Castile, and Portugal hesitated before deciding for Clement at Avignon. The emperor, who bore ancient hostility to France, recognized Urban VI. At first the Italian city-states recognized Urban; when he alienated them, they opted for Clement.

John of Spoleto, a professor at the law school at Bologna, eloquently summed up intellectual opinion of the **schism,** or division: "The longer this schism lasts, the more it appears to be costing, and the more harm it does; scandal, massacres, ruination, agitations, troubles and disturbances."[26] The common people, wracked by inflation, wars, and plague, were thoroughly confused about which pope was legitimate. The schism weakened the religious faith of many Christians and gave rise to instability and religious excesses. It brought the church leadership into serious disrepute. The schism also brought to the fore conciliar ideas about church government.

## The Conciliar Movement

Theories about the nature of the Christian church and its government originated in the very early church, but the years of the Great Schism witnessed their maturity. **Conciliarists** believed that reform of the church could best be achieved through periodic assemblies, or general councils, representing all the Christian people. While acknowledging that the pope was head of the church, conciliarists, such as the French theologian Pierre d'Ailly and the German Conrad of Gelnhausen, held that the pope derived his authority from the entire Christian community, whose well-being he existed to promote. Conciliarists favored a balanced or constitutional form of church government, with papal authority shared with a general council, in contrast to the monarchical one that prevailed.

A half century before the Great Schism, in 1324, Marsiglio of Padua, then rector of the University of Paris, had published *Defensor Pacis* (The Defender of the Peace). Marsiglio argued that the state was the great unifying power in society and that the church was subordinate to the state. He put forth the revolutionary ideas that the church had no inherent jurisdiction and should own no property. Authority in the Christian church, according to Marsiglio, should rest in a general council, made up of laymen as well as priests and superior to the pope. These ideas directly contradicted the medieval notion of a society governed by the church and the state, with the church supreme. *Defensor Pacis* was condemned by the pope, and Marsiglio was excommunicated.

Even more earthshaking than the theories of Marsiglio of Padua were the ideas of the English scholar and theologian John Wyclif (ca 1330–1384). Wyclif wrote that papal claims of temporal power had no foundation in the Scriptures and that the Scriptures alone should be the standard of Christian belief and practice. He urged the abolition of such practices as the veneration of saints, pilgrimages, pluralism, and absenteeism. Sincere Christians, according to Wyclif, should read the Bible for themselves. In response to that idea, the first English translation of the Bible was produced and circulated. Wyclif's views had broad social and economic significance. He urged that the church be stripped of its property. His idea that every Christian free of mortal sin possessed lordship was seized on by peasants in England during a revolt in 1381 and used to justify their goals.

In advancing these views, Wyclif struck at the roots of medieval church structure. Consequently, he has been hailed as the precursor of the Reformation of the sixteenth century. Although Wyclif's ideas were vigorously condemned by ecclesiastical authorities, they were widely disseminated by humble clerics and enjoyed great popularity in the early fifteenth century. Wyclif's followers were called "Lollards." The term, which means "mumblers of prayers and psalms," refers to what they criticized. Lollard teaching allowed women to preach. Women, some well educated, played a significant role in the movement. After Anne, sister of Wenceslaus, king of Germany and Bohemia, married Richard II of England, members of her household carried Lollard books back to Bohemia.

In response to continued calls throughout Europe for a council, the two colleges of cardinals—one at Rome, the other at Avignon—summoned a council at Pisa in 1409.

**Spoon with Fox Preaching to Geese (southern Netherlands, ca 1430)** Taking as his text a contemporary proverb, "When the fox preaches, beware your geese," the artist shows, in the bowl of a spoon, a fox dressed as a monk or friar, preaching with three dead geese in his hood, while another fox grabs one of the congregation. The preaching fox reads from a scroll bearing the word *pax* (peace), implying the perceived hypocrisy of the clergy. The object suggests the widespread criticism of churchmen in the later Middle Ages. *(Painted enamel and gilding on silver; 17.6 cm [6⅞ in]. Museum of Fine Arts, Boston, Helen and Alice Coburn Fund, 51.2472)*

That gathering of prelates and theologians deposed both popes and selected another. Neither the Avignon pope nor the Roman pope would resign, however, and the appalling result was the creation of a threefold schism.

Finally, because of the pressure of the German emperor Sigismund, a great council met at the imperial city of Constance (1414–1418). It had three objectives: to end the schism, to reform the church "in head and members" (from top to bottom), and to wipe out heresy. The council condemned the Czech reformer Jan Hus (see the feature "Individuals in Society: Jan Hus"), and he was burned at the stake. The council eventually deposed both the Roman pope and the successor of the pope chosen at Pisa, and it isolated the Avignon antipope. A conclave elected a new leader, the Roman cardinal Colonna, who took the name Martin V (1417–1431).

Martin proceeded to dissolve the council. Nothing was done about reform. The schism was over, and though councils subsequently met at Basel and at Ferrara-Florence, in 1450 the papacy held a jubilee, celebrating its triumph over the conciliar movement. In the later fifteenth century, the papacy concentrated on Italian problems to the exclusion of universal Christian interests. But the schism and the conciliar movement had exposed the crying need for ecclesiastical reform, thus laying the foundations for the great reform efforts of the sixteenth century.

## The Life of the People

In the fourteenth century, economic and political difficulties, disease, and war profoundly affected the lives of European peoples. Decades of slaughter and destruction, punctuated by the decimating visits of the Black Death, made a grave economic situation virtually disastrous. In many parts of France and the Low Countries, fields lay in ruin or untilled for lack of labor power. In England, as taxes increased, criticisms of government policy and mismanagement multiplied. Crime, aggravated economic troubles, and throughout Europe the frustrations of the common people erupted into widespread revolts. But for most people, marriage and the local parish church continued to be the center of their lives.

### Marriage

Marriage and the family provided such peace and satisfaction as most people attained. Scholars long believed that because peasants were illiterate and left very few statements about their marriages, generalizations could not be made about them. Recent research in English manorial, ecclesiastical, and coroners' records, however, has uncovered fascinating material. Evidence abounds of teenage flirtations, and many young people had sexual contacts—some leading to conception. Premarital pregnancy may have been deliberate: because children were economically important, the couple wanted to be sure of fertility before entering marriage.

"Whether rich or poor, male or female, the most important rite de passage for peasant youth was marriage."[27] Did they select their own spouses or accept parents' choices? Church law stressed that for a marriage to be valid, both partners must freely consent to it. The evidence overwhelmingly shows, above all where land or property accompanied the union, that parents took the lead in arranging their children's marriages; if the parents were dead, the responsibility fell to the inheriting son. Marriage determined not only the life partner and the economic circumstances in which the couple would live, but also the son-in-law who might take over the family land or the daughter-in-law who might care for her elderly in-laws. These kinds of interests required careful planning.

Most marriages were between men and women of the same village; where the name and residence of a husband is known, perhaps 41 percent were outsiders. Once the prospective bride or groom had been decided on, parents paid the **merchet** (fine to the lord for a woman's marriage—since he stood to lose a worker). Parents saw that the parish priest published on three successive Sundays the **banns,** public announcements that the couple planned to marry, to allow for objections to the union. And parents made the financial settlement. The couple then proceeded to the church door, where they made the vows, rings were blessed and exchanged, and the ceremony concluded with some kind of festivity.[28]

Although most peasants were illiterate, the gentry could write. The letters exchanged between Margaret and John Paston, who lived in Norfolk, England, in the fifteenth century, provide evidence for the experience of one couple. John and Margaret Paston were married about 1439, after an arrangement concluded entirely by their parents. John spent most of his time in London fighting through the law courts to increase his family properties and business interests; Margaret remained in Norfolk to supervise the family lands. Her enormous responsibilities involved managing the Paston estates, hiring workers, collecting rents, ordering supplies for the large household, hearing complaints and settling disputes among tenants, and marketing her crops. In these duties, she proved herself a remarkably shrewd businessperson. Moreover, when an army of over a thousand men led by the aristocratic thug Lord Moleyns attacked her house, she successfully withstood the siege. When the Black Death entered her area, Margaret moved her family to safety.

Margaret Paston did all this on top of raising eight children (there were probably other children who did not survive childhood). Her husband died before she was forty-three, and she later conducted the negotiations for the children's marriages. Her children's futures, like her estate management, were planned with an eye toward economic and social advancement. When one daughter secretly married the estate bailiff, an alliance considered beneath her, the girl was cut off from the family as if she were dead.[29]

The many letters surviving between Margaret and John reveal slight tenderness toward their children. They seem to have reserved their love for each other, and during many of his frequent absences they wrote to express mutual affection and devotion. How typical the Paston relationship was modern historians cannot say, but the marriage of John and Margaret, although completely arranged by their parents, was based on respect, responsibility, and love.[30]

At what age did people usually marry? The largest amount of evidence on age at first marriage survives from Italy. For girls, population surveys at Prato place the age at 16.3 years in 1372 and 21.1 in 1470. Chaucer's Wife of Bath (in England) says that she married first in her twelfth year. Among the German nobility, research has indicated that in the Hohenzollern family in the late Middle Ages, "five brides were between 12 and 13; five about 14, and five about 15." Generally in northern Europe, however, the evidence suggests that rural and urban women married in their twenties.

Men were older when they married. An Italian chronicler writing about 1354 says that men did not marry before the age of 30. At Prato in 1371, the average age of men at first marriage was 24 years, very young for Italian men, but these data may signal an attempt to regain population losses due to the recent attack of the plague. In England Chaucer's Wife of Bath describes her first three husbands as "goode men, and rich, and old." Among seventeen males in the noble Hohenzollern family, eleven were over 20 years when married, five between 18 and 19, one 16. The general pattern in late medieval Europe was marriage between men in their middle or late twenties and women under 20.[31] Poor peasants and wage laborers did not marry until their mid- or late twenties.

With marriage for men postponed, was there any socially accepted sexual outlet? Research on the southern French province of Languedoc in the fourteenth and fifteenth centuries has revealed the establishment of legal houses of prostitution. Prostitution involves "a socially definable group of women [who] earn their living primarily or exclusively from the [sexual] commerce of their bodies."[32] Municipal authorities in Toulouse, Montpellier, Albi, and other towns set up houses or red-light

# Individuals in Society

## Jan Hus

In May 1990, the Czech Republic's parliament declared July 6, the date of Jan Hus's execution in 1415, a Czech national holiday. The son of free farmers, Hus (ca 1369–1415) was born in Husinec in southern Bohemia, an area of heavy German settlement, and grew up conscious of the ethnic differences between Czechs and Germans. Most of his professors at Charles University in Prague were Germans. In 1396 he received a master's degree, and just before his ordination as a priest in 1400, he wrote that he would not be a "clerical careerist," implying that ambition for church offices motivated many of his peers.

The young priest lectured at the university and preached at the private Bethlehem Chapel. During his twelve years there, Hus preached only in Czech. He denounced superstition, the sale of indulgences, and other abuses, but his remarks were thoroughly orthodox. He attracted attention among artisans, the small Czech middle class, but not Germans. His austere life and lack of ambition enhanced his reputation.

Around 1400, Czech students returning from study at Oxford introduced into Bohemia the reforming ideas of the English theologian John Wyclif. When German professors condemned Wyclif's ideas as heretical, Hus and the Czechs argued "academic freedom," the right to read and teach Wyclif's works regardless of their particular merits. When popular demonstrations against ecclesiastical abuses and German influence at the university erupted, King Vaclav IV (1378–1419) placed control of the university in Czech hands. Hus was elected rector, the top administrative official.

The people of Prague, with perhaps the largest urban population in central Europe, 40 percent of it living below the poverty line and entirely dependent on casual labor, found Hus's denunciations of an overendowed church appealing. Hus considered the issues theological; his listeners saw them as socioeconomic.

Hus went into exile, where he wrote *On the Church*. He disputed papal authority, denounced abuses, and approved *utraquism,* the reception of the Eucharist under both species, bread and wine. Hus also defended transubstantiation (see page 460); insisted that church authority rested on Scripture, conscience, and tradition (in contrast to sixteenth-century Protestant reformers, who placed authority in Scripture alone); and made it clear that he had no intention of leaving the church or inciting a popular movement.

*The execution of Jan Hus.* (University Library, Prague)

In 1413 the emperor Sigismund urged the calling of a general council to end the schism. Hus was invited, and, given the emperor's safe conduct (protection from attack or arrest), agreed to go. What he found was an atmosphere of inquisition. The safe conduct was disregarded, and Hus was arrested. Under questioning about his acceptance of Wyclif's ideas, Hus repeatedly replied, "I have not held; I do not hold." Council members were more interested in proving Hus a Wyclifite than in his responses. They took away his priesthood, banned his teachings, burned his books, and burned Hus himself at the stake. He then belonged to the ages.

The ages have made good use of him. His death aggravated the divisions between the bishops at Constance and the Czech clerics and people. In September 1415, 452 nobles from all parts of Bohemia signed a letter saying that Hus had been unjustly executed and rejecting council rulings. This event marks the first time that an ecclesiastical decision was publicly defied. Revolution swept through Bohemia, with Hussites—Czech nobles and people—insisting on clerical poverty and Communion under both species, and German citizens remaining loyal to the Roman church. In the sixteenth century, reformers hailed Hus as the forerunner of Protestantism. In the eighteenth century, Enlightenment philosophes evoked Hus as a defender of freedom of expression. In the nineteenth century, central European nationalists used Hus's name to defend national sentiment against Habsburg rule. And in the twentieth century, Hus's name was used against German fascist and Russian communist tyranny.

### Questions for Analysis

1. Since Jan Hus lived and died insisting that his religious teaching was thoroughly orthodox, why has he been hailed as a reformer?
2. What political and cultural interests did the martyred Hus serve?

*The* **history companion** *features additional information and activities related to this topic.*
**history.college.hmco.com/students**

**Prostitute Invites a Traveling Merchant** Poverty and male violence drove women into prostitution, which, though denounced by moralists, was accepted as a normal part of the medieval social fabric. In the cities and larger towns where prostitution flourished, public officials passed laws requiring prostitutes to wear a special mark on their clothing, regulated hours of business, forbade women to drag men into their houses, and denied business to women with the "burning sickness," gonorrhea. *(Bodleian Library, MS. Bodl. 264, fol. 245V)*

districts either outside the city walls or away from respectable neighborhoods. For example, authorities in Montpellier set aside Hot Street for prostitution, required public women to live there, and forbade anyone to molest them. Prostitution thus passed from being a private concern to a social matter requiring public supervision.[33] Publicly owned brothels were more easily policed and supervised than privately run ones. Prostitution was an urban phenomenon, because only populous towns had large numbers of unmarried young men, communities of transient merchants, and a culture accustomed to a cash exchange. Although the risk of disease limited the number of years a woman could practice this profession, many women prospered. Some acquired sizable incomes. In 1361 Françoise of Florence, a prostitute working in a brothel in Marseilles, made a will in which she made legacies to various charities and left a large sum as a dowry for a poor girl to marry. Archives in several cities show expensive properties bought by women who named their occupation as prostitution.

The towns of Languedoc were not unique. Public authorities in Amiens, Dijon, Paris, Venice, Genoa, London, Florence, Rome, most of the larger German towns, and the English port of Sandwich set up brothels. Legalized prostitution suggests that public officials believed the prostitute could make a positive contribution to society; it does not mean the prostitute was respected. Rather, she was scorned and distrusted. Legalized brothels also reflect a greater tolerance for male than for female sexuality.[34]

In the later Middle Ages, as earlier—indeed, until the late nineteenth century—economic factors, rather than romantic love or physical attraction, determined whom and when a person married. The young agricultural laborer on the manor had to wait until he had sufficient land. Thus most men had to wait until their fathers died or yielded the holding. Late marriage affected the number of children a couple had. The journeyman craftsman in the urban guild faced the same material difficulties. Once a couple married, the union ended only with the death of one partner.

Deep emotional bonds knit members of medieval families. Most parents delighted in their children, and the church encouraged a cult of paternal care. The church stressed its right to govern and sanctify marriage, and it emphasized monogamy. Tighter moral and emotional unity within marriages resulted.

Divorce did not exist in the Middle Ages. The church held that a marriage validly entered into could not be dissolved. A valid marriage consisted of the mutual oral consent or promise of two parties. Church theologians of the day urged that the couple's union be celebrated and witnessed in a church ceremony and blessed by a priest.

Many couples did not observe the church's regulations. Some treated marriage as a private act—they made the promise and spoke the words of marriage to each other without witnesses and then proceeded to enjoy the sexual pleasures of marriage. This practice led to a great number of disputes, because one of the two parties could later deny having made a marriage agreement. The records of the ecclesiastical courts reveal many cases arising from privately made contracts. Evidence survives of marriages contracted in a garden, in a blacksmith's shop, at a tavern, and, predictably, in a bed. The records of church courts that relate to marriage reveal that, rather than suing for divorce, the great majority of petitions asked the court to enforce the marriage contract that one of the parties believed she or he had validly made. Annulments were granted in extraordinary circumstances, such as male impotence, on the grounds that a lawful marriage had never existed.[35]

## Life in the Parish

In the later Middle Ages, the land and the parish remained the focus of life for the European peasantry. Work on the land continued to be performed collectively. Both men and women cooperated in the annual tasks of planting and harvesting. The close association of the cycle of agriculture and the liturgy of the Christian calendar endured. The parish priest blessed the fields before the annual planting, offering prayers on behalf of the people for a good crop. If the harvest was rich, the priest led the processions and celebrations of thanksgiving.

How did the common people feel about their work? Since the vast majority were illiterate, it is difficult to say. Certainly the peasants hated the ancient services and obligations on the lords' lands and tried to get them commuted for money rents. When lords attempted to reimpose service duties, the peasants revolted.

In the thirteenth century, the craft guilds provided the small minority of men and women living in towns and cities with the psychological satisfaction of involvement in the manufacture of a superior product. The guild member also had economic security. The craft guilds set high standards for their merchandise. The guilds looked after the sick, the poor, the widowed, and the orphaned. Masters and employees worked side by side.

In the fourteenth century, those conditions began to change. The fundamental objective of the craft guild was to maintain a monopoly on its product, and to do so recruitment and promotion were carefully restricted. Some guilds required a high entrance fee for apprentices; others admitted only relatives of members. Apprenticeship increasingly lasted a long time, seven years. Even after a young man had satisfied all the tests for full membership in the guild and had attained the rank of master, other hurdles had to be passed, such as finding the funds to open his own business or special connections just to get into a guild. Restrictions limited the number of apprentices and journeymen to match the anticipated openings for masters.

Women experienced the same exclusion. A careful study of the records of forty-two craft guilds in Cologne shows that in the fifteenth century all but six had become male preserves, either greatly restricting women's participation or allowing so few female members that they cannot be considered mixed guilds.[36] Popular and educated culture, supporting a patriarchal system that held women to be biologically and intellectually inferior, consigned them to low-status and low-paying jobs.

The larger a particular business was, the greater was the likelihood that the master did not know his employees. The separation of master and journeyman and the decreasing number of openings for master craftsmen created serious frustrations. Strikes and riots occurred in the Flemish towns, in France, and in England.

The recreation of all classes reflected the fact that late medieval society was organized for war and that violence was common. The aristocracy engaged in tournaments or jousts; archery and wrestling had great popularity among ordinary people. Everyone enjoyed the cruel sports of bullbaiting and bearbaiting. The hangings and mutilations of criminals were exciting and well-attended events, with all the festivity of a university town before a Saturday football game. Chroniclers exulted in describing executions, murders, and massacres. Here a monk gleefully describes the gory execution of William Wallace (ca 1270–1305), the Scottish hero who led a revolt against Edward I of England and retains importance as a symbol of resistance to English rule and of Scottish nationalism:

*Wilielmus Waleis, a robber given to sacrilege, arson and homicide . . . was condemned to most cruel but justly deserved death. He was drawn through the streets of London at the tails of horses, until he reached a gallows of unusual height, there he was suspended by a halter; but taken down while yet alive, he was mutilated, his bowels torn out and burned in a fire, his head then cut off, his body divided into four, and his quarters transmitted to four principal parts of Scotland.*[37]

Violence was as English as roast beef and plum pudding, as French as bread, cheese, and *potage.*

If violent entertainment was not enough to dispel life's cares, alcohol was also available. Beer or ale commonly provided solace to the poor, and the frequency of drunkenness reflects their terrible frustrations.

**Spanish Bullfight** The Romans may have introduced bullfighting in Spain but the Muslims popularized it. The sport takes place in a large outdoor arena, the object being for the bullfighter or matador (*torero*) to kill a wild bull (*toro*) with a sword. Here unsporting spectators goad the bull with whips. *(From the* Cantigas *of Alfonso X, ca 1283. El Escorial/Laurie Platt Winfrey, Inc.)*

During the fourteenth and fifteenth centuries, the laity began to exercise increasing control over parish affairs. The constant quarrels of the mendicant orders (the Franciscans and Dominicans), the mercenary and grasping attitude of the parish clergy, the scandal of the Great Schism and a divided Christendom—all these did much to weaken the spiritual mystique of the clergy in the popular mind. The laity steadily took responsibility for the management of parish lands. Laypeople organized associations to vote on and purchase furnishings for the church. And ordinary laypeople secured jurisdiction over the structure of the church building and its vestments, books, and furnishings. These new responsibilities of the laity reflect the increased dignity of parishioners in the late Middle Ages.[38]

## Fur-Collar Crime

The Hundred Years' War had provided employment and opportunity for thousands of idle and fortune-seeking knights. But during periods of truce and after the war finally ended, many nobles once again had little to do. Inflation hurt them. Although many were living on fixed incomes, their chivalric code demanded lavish generosity and an aristocratic lifestyle. Many nobles turned to crime as a way of raising money. The fourteenth and fifteenth centuries witnessed a great deal of "fur-collar crime," so called for the miniver fur the nobility alone were allowed to wear on their collars.

Fur-collar crime rarely involved such felonies as homicide, robbery, rape, and arson. Instead, nobles used their superior social status to rob and extort from the weak and then to corrupt the judicial process. Groups of noble brigands roamed the English countryside stealing from both rich and poor. Sir John de Colseby and Sir William Bussy led a gang of thirty-eight knights who stole goods worth £3,000 in various robberies. Operating like modern urban racketeers, knightly gangs demanded that peasants pay "protection money" or else have their hovels burned and their fields destroyed.

Attacks on the rich often took the form of kidnapping and extortion. Wealthy travelers were seized on the highways and held for ransom. In northern England a gang of gentry led by Sir Gilbert de Middleton abducted Sir Henry Beaumont; his brother, the bishop-elect of Durham; and two Roman cardinals in England on a peacemaking visit. Only after a ransom was paid were the victims released.[39]

Fur-collar criminals were terrorists, but like some modern-day white-collar criminals who commit nonviolent crimes, medieval aristocratic criminals got away with their outrages. When accused of wrongdoing, fur-collar criminals intimidated witnesses. They threatened jurors. They used "pull" or cash to bribe judges. As a fourteenth-century English judge wrote to a young nobleman, "For the love of your father I have hindered charges being brought against you and have prevented execution of indictment actually made."[40]

The ballads of Robin Hood, a collection of folk legends from late medieval England, describe the adventures of the outlaw hero and his band of followers, who lived in Sherwood Forest and attacked and punished those who violated the social system and the law. Most of the villains in these simple tales are fur-collar criminals—grasping landlords, wicked sheriffs such as the famous sheriff of Nottingham, and mercenary churchmen. Robin and his merry men performed a sort of retributive justice. Robin Hood was a popular figure because he symbolized the deep resentment of aristocratic corruption and abuse; he represented the struggle against tyranny and oppression.

Criminal activity by nobles continued decade after decade because governments were too weak to stop it. Persecution by lords, on top of war, disease, and natural disaster, eventually drove long-suffering and oppressed peasants all across Europe to revolt.

## Peasant Revolts

Nobles, clergy, and city dwellers lived on the produce of peasant labor. Early in the thirteenth century, the French preacher Jacques de Vitry asked rhetorically, "How many serfs have killed their lords or burnt their castles?"[41] And in the fourteenth and fifteenth centuries, social and economic conditions caused a great increase in peasant uprisings (see Map 12.3). They were very common and provide most of the evidence of peasants' long-suffering and exploitation.

We will never be able fully to answer Jacques de Vitry's questions, for rustics were not literate and, apart from their explosive uprisings, left no record of their aspirations. The clerical writers who mentioned the rebellions viewed the peasants with aristocratic disdain and hostility. Recent research provides some insight into **peasant revolts** in Flanders in the 1320s. Although the vast majority of people engaged in agriculture, Flanders was the most highly urbanized region in northern Europe. The commercial cities of Ghent, Bruges, and Ypres were huge textile centers and the hearts of networks of smaller towns such as Arras, Lille, and Douai. Uprisings in Flanders were the first mass movements of the fourteenth century, perhaps unequaled anywhere in Europe before the German Peasants' Revolt of 1525 (see page 461). The English Peasants' Revolt of 1381 lasted five weeks, but the Flemish uprising extended over five years.[42]

Long-existing conflicts along the Flemish-French border came to a head at Courtrai in July 1302 when Flemish infantry smashed a French army, killing many knights and nobles (their golden spurs retrieved from the battlefield gave the battle its name, the Battle of the Spurs). The Flemish victory failed to resolve disputes over the French crown's claim to fiscal rights over the county of Flanders. Moreover, the peace agreements imposed heavy indemnities on Flemish peasants, who in 1323 began to revolt in protest of officials' demands for taxes and the misappropriation of the money collected. Also, monasteries pressed peasants for fees higher than the customary tithes. In retaliation, peasants subjected castles and aristocratic country houses to arson and pillage. At the same time, in Bruges and other Flemish cities, low- and middle-class workers deeply resented the widening social gap separating them from mercantile elites and the aristocracy. Eventually, rural and urban movements coalesced: peasants wanted "a world without corruption," and urban workers sought "a world without privilege." This amounted to revolutionary class warfare. A French army intervened and on August 23, 1328, near the town of Cassel in southwestern Flanders, crushed peasant forces. Savage repression and the confiscation of rustic property followed in the 1330s. In the towns, however, leaders of cloth guilds gained access to seats in town governments and used their influence to improve guild members' economic and political positions.[43]

In 1358, when French taxation for the Hundred Years' War fell heavily on the poor, the frustrations of the French peasantry exploded in a massive uprising called the **Jacquerie,** after a mythical agricultural laborer, Jacques Bonhomme (Good Fellow). Two years earlier, the English had captured the French king John and many nobles and held them for ransom. The peasants resented paying for their lords' release. Recently hit by plague, experiencing famine in some areas, and harassed by fur-collar criminals, peasants in Picardy, Champagne, and the Île-de-France erupted in anger and frustration. Crowds swept through the countryside slashing the throats of nobles, burning their castles, raping their wives and daughters, killing or maiming their horses and cattle. Peasants blamed the nobility for oppressive taxes, for the criminal brigandage of the countryside, for defeat in war, and for the general

**MAP 12.3 Fourteenth-Century Peasant Revolts** In the later Middle Ages and early modern times, peasant and urban uprisings were endemic, as common as factory strikes in the industrial world. The threat of insurrection served to check unlimited exploitation.

misery. Artisans, small merchants, and parish priests joined the peasants. Urban and rural groups committed terrible destruction, and for several weeks the nobles were on the defensive. Then the upper class united to repress the revolt with merciless ferocity. Thousands of the "Jacques," innocent as well as guilty, were cut down.

That forcible suppression of social rebellion, without some effort to alleviate its underlying causes, served to drive protest underground. Between 1363 and 1484, serious peasant revolts swept the Auvergne; in 1380 uprisings occurred in the Midi; and in 1420 they erupted in the Lyonnais region of France.

The Peasants' Revolt in England in 1381 involved thousands of people (see Map 12.3). Its causes were complex and varied from place to place. In general, though, the thirteenth century had witnessed the steady commutation of labor services for cash rents, and the Black Death had drastically cut the labor supply. As a result, peasants demanded higher wages and fewer manorial obligations. The parliamentary Statute of Laborers of 1351 (see page 386) had declared:

*Whereas to curb the malice of servants who after the pestilence were idle and unwilling to serve without securing excessive wages, it was recently ordained . . . that such servants, both men and women, shall be bound to serve in return for salaries and wages that were customary . . . five or six years earlier.*[44]

But this attempt to freeze wages and social mobility could not be enforced. Some scholars believe that the peasantry in most places was better off in the period 1350 to 1450 than it had been for centuries before or was to be for four centuries after.

Why then was the outburst in England in 1381 so serious? It was provoked by a crisis of rising expectations. The relative prosperity of the laboring classes led to demands that the upper classes were unwilling to grant. Unable to climb higher, the peasants sought release for their economic frustrations in revolt. But economic grievances combined with other factors. The south of England, where the revolt broke out, had been subjected to destructive French raids. The English government did little to protect the south, and villagers grew increasingly scared and insecure. Moreover, decades of aristocratic violence against the weak peasantry had bred hostility and bitterness. Social and religious agitation by the popular preacher John Ball fanned the embers of discontent. Ball's famous couplet "When Adam delved and Eve span; Who was then the gentleman?" reflected real revolutionary sentiment.

The straw that broke the camel's back in England was the reimposition of a head tax on all adult males. Despite widespread opposition to the tax in 1380, the royal council ordered the sheriffs to collect it again in 1381 on penalty of a huge fine. Beginning with assaults on the tax collectors, the uprising in England followed a course similar to that of the Jacquerie in France. Castles and manors were sacked. Manorial records were destroyed. Many nobles, including the archbishop of Canterbury, who had ordered the collection of the tax, were murdered.

The center of the revolt lay in the highly populated and economically advanced south and east, but sections of the north and the Midlands also witnessed rebellions. Violence took different forms in different places. Urban discontent merged with rural violence. In English towns where skilled Flemish craftsmen were employed, fear of competition led to their being attacked and murdered. Apprentices and journeymen, frustrated because the highest positions in the guilds were closed to them, rioted.

The boy-king Richard II (r. 1377–1399) met the leaders of the revolt, agreed to charters ensuring peasants' freedom, tricked them with false promises, and then crushed the uprising with terrible ferocity. The nobility tried to restore ancient duties of serfdom, but nearly a century of freedom had elapsed and the commutation of manorial services continued. Rural serfdom disappeared in England by 1550.

Conditions in Flanders, England, and France were not unique. In Florence in 1378, the *ciompi,* the poor propertyless workers, revolted. Serious social trouble occurred in Lübeck, Brunswick, and other German cities. In Spain in 1391, aristocratic attempts to impose new forms of serfdom, combined with demands for tax relief, led to massive working-class and peasant uprisings in Seville and Barcelona. These took the form of vicious attacks on Jewish communities. Rebellions and uprisings everywhere reveal deep peasant and working-class frustration and the general socioeconomic crisis of the time.

## Race and Ethnicity on the Frontiers

Large numbers of people in the twelfth and thirteenth centuries migrated from one part of Europe to another: the English into Scotland and Ireland; Germans, French, and Flemings into Poland, Bohemia, and Hungary; the French into Spain. In the fourteenth century, many Germans moved into eastern Europe, fleeing the Black Death. The colonization of frontier regions meant that peoples of different ethnic or racial backgrounds lived side by side. Race relations became a basic factor in the lives of peoples living in those frontier areas.

Racial categories rest on socially constructed beliefs and customs, not on any biological or anthropological classification. When late medieval chroniclers used the language of race—words such as *gens* (race or clan) and *natio* (species, stock, or kind)—they meant cultural differences. Medieval scholars held that peoples differed according to descent, language, customs, and laws. Descent or blood, basic to the color racism of the United States, played an insignificant part in eleventh- and twelfth-century ideas about race and ethnicity. Rather, the chief marks of an ethnic group were language (which could be learned), customs (for example, dietary practices, dance, marriage and death rituals, clothing, and hairstyles, all of which could be adopted), and laws (which could be changed or modified). How did the law reflect attitudes and race relations in the Middle Ages?

In the early periods of conquest and colonization, and in all frontier regions, a legal dualism existed: native peoples remained subject to their traditional laws; newcomers brought and were subject to the laws of the countries from which they came. On the Prussian and Polish frontier, for example, the law was that "men who come there . . . should be judged on account of any crime or contract engaged in there according to Polish custom if they are Poles and according to German custom if they are Germans."[45] Likewise, in Spain Mudéjars, Muslim subjects of Christian kings, received guarantees of separate but equal judicial rights. King Alfonso I of Aragon's charter to the Muslims of Toledo states, "They shall be in lawsuits and pleas under their (Muslim) qadi (judges) . . . as it was in the times of the Moors."[46] Thus conquered peoples, whether Muslims in Spain, or minority immigrant groups, such as Germans in eastern Europe, had legal protection and lived in their own juridical enclaves. Subject peoples experienced some disabilities, but the broad trend was toward a legal pluralism.

The great exception to this broad pattern was Ireland. From the start, the English practiced an extreme form of racial discrimination toward the native Irish. The English distinguished between the free and the unfree, and the entire Irish population, simply by the fact of Irish birth, was unfree. In 1210 King John declared that "English law and custom be established there (in Ireland)." Accordingly, a legal structure modeled on that of England, with county courts, itinerant justices, and the common law (see pages 342–344), was set up. But the Irish had no access to the common-law courts. In civil (property) disputes, an English defendant need not respond to his Irish plaintiff; no Irish person could make a will. In criminal procedures, the murder of an Irishman was not considered a felony. In 1317–1318, Irish princes sent a Remonstrance to the pope complaining that "any non-Irishman is allowed to bring legal action against an Irishman, but an Irishman . . . except any prelate (bishop or abbot) is barred from every action by that fact alone." An English defendant in the criminal matter would claim "that he is not held to answer . . . since he [the plaintiff] is Irish and not of free blood."[47] This emphasis on blood descent naturally provoked bitterness.

The later Middle Ages witnessed a movement away from legal pluralism or dualism and toward a legal homogeneity and an emphasis on blood descent. Competition for ecclesiastical offices and the cultural divisions between town and country people became arenas for ethnic tension and racial conflict. Since bishoprics and abbacies carried religious authority, spiritual charisma, and often rights of appointment to subordinate positions, they were natural objects of ambition. When prelates of a language or "nationality" different from those of the local people gained church positions, the latter felt a loss of influence. Bishops were supposed to be pastors. Their pastoral work involved preaching, teaching, and comforting, duties that could be performed effectively only when the bishop (or priest) could communicate with the people. Ideally in a pluralistic society, he should be bilingual; often he was not.

In the late thirteenth century, as waves of Germans migrated into Danzig on the Baltic, into Silesia, and into the Polish countryside and towns, they encountered Jakub Swinka, archbishop of Gniezno (1283–1314), whose jurisdiction included these areas of settlement. The bishop hated Germans and referred to them as "dog heads." His German contemporary, Bishop John of Cracow, detested the Poles, wanted to expel all Polish people, and refused to appoint Poles to any church office. In Ireland, English colonists and the native Irish competed for ecclesiastical offices until 1217, when the English government in London decreed:

*Since the election of Irishmen in our land of Ireland has often disturbed the peace of that land, we command you . . . that henceforth you allow no Irishman to be elected . . . or preferred in any cathedral . . . (and) you should seek by all means to procure election and promotion to vacant bishoprics of . . . honest Englishmen.*[48]

Although criticized by the pope and not totally enforceable, this law remained in effect in many dioceses for centuries.

Likewise, the arrival of Cistercians and mendicants (Franciscans and Dominicans) from France and Germany in Baltic and Slavic lands provoked racial and "national" hostilities. In the fourteenth and fifteenth centuries, in contrast to earlier centuries, racial or ethnic prejudices became conspicuous. Slavic prelates and princes saw the German mendicants as "instruments of cultural colonization," and Slavs were strongly discouraged from becoming friars. In 1333, when John of Drazic, bishop of Prague, founded a friary at Roudnice (Raudnitz), he specified that "we shall admit no one to this convent or monastery of any nation except a Bohemian [Czech], born of two Czech-speaking parents."[49]

Everywhere in Europe, towns recruited people from the countryside (see pages 346–347). In frontier regions, townspeople were usually long-distance immigrants and, in eastern Europe, Ireland, and Scotland, ethnically different from the surrounding rural population. In eastern Europe, German was the language of the towns; in Ireland, French, the tongue of Norman or English settlers, predominated. In fourteenth-century Prague, between 63 percent and 80 percent of new burgesses bore identifiable German names, as did almost all city council members. Towns in eastern Europe "had the character of German islands in Slav, Baltic, Estonian, or Magyar seas."[50] Although native peoples commonly held humbler positions, both immigrant and native townspeople prospered during the expanding economy of the thirteenth century. When economic recession hit during the fourteenth century, ethnic tensions multiplied.

On the frontiers of Latin Europe discrimination, ghettoization, and **racism**—now based on blood descent—characterized the attitudes of colonists toward native peoples. But the latter also could express racial savagery. In the ***Dalimil Chronicle,*** a survey of Bohemian history pervaded with Czech hostility toward Germans, one anti-German prince offered 100 marks of silver "to anyone who brought him one hundred noses cut off from the Germans."[51] Regulations drawn up by various guilds were explicitly racist, with protectionist bars for some groups and exclusionist laws for others. The Deutschtum paragraph of the *Chronicle,* applicable to parts of eastern Europe, required that applicants for guild membership be of German descent. Cobblers in fourteenth-century Beeskow, a town close to the large Slavic population of Lausitz in Silesia, required that "an apprentice who comes to learn his craft should be brought before the master and guild members. . . . We forbid the sons of barbers, linen workers, shepherds, Slavs." The bakers of the same town decreed:

*Whoever wishes to be a member must bring proof to the councillors and guildsmen that he is born of legitimate, upright, German folk. . . . No one of Wendish (Slavic) race may be in the guild. In Limerick and Dublin in Ireland, guild masters agreed to accept "noo apprentice but that he be of English berthe."*[52]

Intermarriage was forbidden in many places, such as Riga on the Baltic (now the capital of Latvia), where legislation for the bakers guild stipulated that "whoever wishes to have the privilege of membership in our company shall not take as a wife any woman who is ill-famed . . . or non-German; if he does marry such a woman, he must leave the company and office." Not only the guilds but eligibility for public office depended on racial purity, as at the German burgher settlement of Pest in Hungary, where a town judge had to have four German grandparents. The most extensive attempt to prevent intermarriage and protect racial purity is embodied in Ireland's **Statute of Kilkenny** (1366), which states that "there were to be no marriages between those of immigrant and native stock; that the English inhabitants of Ireland must employ the English language and bear English names; that they must ride in the English way (i.e., with saddles) and have English apparel; that no Irishmen were to be granted ecclesiastical benefices or admitted to monasteries in the English parts of Ireland. . . ."[53] Rulers of the Christian kingdoms of Spain drew up comparable legislation discriminating against the Mudéjars.

All these laws had an economic basis: to protect the financial interests of the privileged German, English, or Spanish colonial minorities. The laws also reflect a racism that not only pervaded the lives of frontier peoples at the end of the Middle Ages but also sowed the seeds of difficulties still unresolved today.

## Vernacular Literature

Across Europe people spoke the language and dialect of their particular locality and class. In England, for example, the common people spoke regional English dialects, while the upper classes conversed in French. Official documents and works of literature were written in Latin or French. Beginning in the fourteenth century, however, national languages—the vernacular—came into widespread use not only in verbal communication but in literature as well. Three masterpieces of European culture, Dante's *Divine Comedy* (1310–1320), Chaucer's *Canterbury Tales* (1387–1400), and Villon's *Grand Testament* (1461), brilliantly manifest this new national pride.

Dante Alighieri (1265–1321) descended from a landowning family in Florence, where he held several positions in the city government. Dante called his work a "comedy" because he wrote it in Italian and in a different style from the "tragic" Latin; a later generation added the adjective *divine,* referring both to its sacred subject and to Dante's artistry. The *Divine Comedy* is an allegorical trilogy of one hundred cantos (verses) whose three equal parts (1 + 33 + 33 + 33) each describe one of the realms of the next world: Hell, Purgatory, and Paradise. The Roman poet Virgil, representing reason, leads Dante through Hell, where he observes the torments of the damned and denounces the disorders of his own time, especially ecclesiastical ambition and corruption. Passing up into Purgatory, Virgil shows the poet how souls are purified of their disordered inclinations. From Purgatory, Beatrice, a woman Dante once loved and the symbol of divine revelation in the poem, leads him to Paradise. In Paradise, home of the angels and saints, Saint Bernard—representing mystic contemplation—leads Dante to the Virgin Mary. Through her intercession, he at last attains a vision of God.

The *Divine Comedy* portrays contemporary and historical figures, comments on secular and ecclesiastical affairs, and draws on Scholastic philosophy. Within the framework of a symbolic pilgrimage to the City of God, the *Divine Comedy* embodies the psychological tensions of the age. A profoundly Christian poem, it also contains bitter criticism of some church authorities. In its symmetrical structure and use of figures from the ancient world, such as Virgil, the poem perpetuates the classical tradition, but as the first major work of literature in the Italian vernacular, it is distinctly modern.

Geoffrey Chaucer (1342–1400), the son of a London wine merchant, was an official in the administrations of the English kings Edward III and Richard II and wrote poetry as an avocation. Chaucer's *Canterbury Tales* is a collection of stories in lengthy, rhymed narrative. On a pilgrimage to the shrine of Saint Thomas Becket at Canterbury (see page 343), thirty people of various social backgrounds each tell a tale. The Prologue sets the scene and describes the pilgrims, whose characters are further revealed in the story each one tells. For example, the gross Miller tells a vulgar story about a deceived husband; the earthy Wife of Bath, who has buried five husbands, sketches a fable about the selection of a spouse; and the elegant Prioress, who violates her vows by wearing jewelry, delivers a homily on the Virgin. In depicting the interests and behavior of all types of people, Chaucer

**Schoolmaster and His Wife Teaching** Ambrosius Holbein, elder brother of the more famous Hans Holbein, produced this signboard for the Swiss educator Myconius; it is an excellent example of what we would call commercial art—art used to advertise, in this case Myconius's profession. The German script above promised that all who enrolled would learn to read and write. By modern standards the classroom seems bleak: the windows have glass panes but they don't admit much light, and the schoolmaster is prepared to use the sticks if the boy makes a mistake. *(Kunstmuseum Basel/Martin Bühler, photographer)*

presents a rich panorama of English social life in the fourteenth century. Like the *Divine Comedy, Canterbury Tales* reflects the cultural tensions of the times. Ostensibly Christian, many of the pilgrims are also materialistic, sensual, and worldly, suggesting the ambivalence of the broader society's concern for the next world and frank enjoyment of this one.

Our knowledge of François Villon (1431–1463), probably the greatest poet of late medieval France, derives from Paris police records and his own poetry. Born to poor parents in the year of Joan of Arc's execution, Villon was sent by his guardian to the University of Paris, where he earned the master of arts degree. A rowdy and free-spirited student, he disliked the stuffiness of academic life. In 1455 Villon killed a man in a street brawl; banished from Paris, he joined one of the bands of wandering thieves that harassed the countryside after the Hundred Years' War. For his fellow bandits, he composed ballads in thieves' jargon.

Villon's *Lais* (1456) is a series of farcical bequests to friends and enemies. The word *lais* refers to short rhymed tales but is also a pun on the French word *legs,* meaning "legacy." Villon's greatest and most self-revealing work, the *Grand Testament,* contains another string of bequests, including a legacy to a prostitute, and describes his unshakable faith in the beauty of life on earth. The *Grand Testament* possesses elements of social rebellion, bawdy humor, and rare emotional depth. While the themes of Dante's and Chaucer's poetry are distinctly medieval, Villon's celebration of the human condition brands him as definitely modern. Although he used medieval forms of versification, Villon's language was the despised vernacular of the poor and the criminal.

Perhaps the most versatile and prolific French writer of the later Middle Ages was Christine de Pisan (1363?–1434?). The daughter of a professor of astrology at Bologna and then a prominent member of the French court, Christine had a broad knowledge of Greek, Latin, French, and Italian literature. The deaths of her father and husband left her with three small children and her mother to support; she had to earn her living with her pen. In addition to poems and books on love, religion, and morality, Christine produced the *Livre de la mutacion de fortune,* a major historical work; a biography of King Charles V; the *Ditié,* celebrating Joan of Arc's victory; and many letters. *The City of Ladies* lists the great women of history and their contributions to society, and *The Book of Three Virtues* provides practical advice on household management for women of all social classes. Christine de Pisan's wisdom and wit are illustrated in her autobiographical *Avison-Christine*. She records that a man told her an educated woman is unattractive, since there are so few, to which she responded that an ignorant man was even less attractive, since there are so many. (See the feature "Listening to the Past: Christine de Pisan" on pages 410–411.)

Beginning in the fourteenth century, a variety of evidence attests to the increasing literacy of laypeople. Wills and inventories reveal that many people, not just nobles, possessed books, mainly devotional, but also romances, manuals on manners and etiquette, histories, and sometimes legal and philosophical texts. In England the number of schools in the diocese of York quadrupled between 1350 and 1500. Information from Flemish and German towns is similar: children were sent to schools and received the fundamentals of reading, writing, and arithmetic. Laymen increasingly served as managers or stewards of estates and as clerks to guilds and town governments; such positions obviously required that they be able to keep administrative and financial records.

The penetration of laymen into the higher positions of governmental administration, long the preserve of clerics, also illustrates rising lay literacy. For example, in 1400 beneficed clerics held most of the posts in the English Exchequer; by 1430 clerics were the exception. With growing frequency, the upper classes sent their daughters to convent schools, where, in addition to instruction in singing, religion, needlework, deportment, and household management, girls gained the rudiments of reading and sometimes writing. Reading and writing represent two kinds of literacy. Scholars estimate that many more people, especially women, possessed the first literacy, but not the second. The spread of literacy represents a response to the needs of an increasingly complex society. Trade, commerce, and expanding governmental bureaucracies required more and more literate people. Late medieval culture remained an oral culture in which most people received information by word of mouth. But by the mid-fifteenth century, even before the printing press was turning out large quantities of reading materials, the evolution toward a literary culture was already perceptible.[54]

## Summary

The crises of the fourteenth and fifteenth centuries were acids that burned deeply into the fabric of traditional medieval society. Bad weather brought poor harvests, which contributed to the international economic depression. Disease, over which people also had little control, fostered widespread depression. Population losses caused by the Black Death and the Hundred Years' War encouraged the working classes to try to profit from the labor shortage by selling their services higher: they wanted to move up the economic ladder. The theological ideas of thinkers like John Wyclif, John Hus, and John Ball fanned the flames of social discontent. When peasant frustrations exploded in uprisings, the frightened nobility and upper middle class joined to crush the revolts and condemn heretical preachers as agitators of social rebellion.

The Hundred Years' War served as a catalyst for the development of representative government in England. In France, on the other hand, the war stiffened opposition to national assemblies.

The war also stimulated technological experimentation, especially with artillery. Cannon revolutionized warfare, because the stone castle was no longer impregnable. Because only central governments, and not private nobles, could afford cannon, they strengthened the military power of national states.

The migration of peoples from the European heartland to the frontier regions of Ireland, the Baltic, eastern Europe, and Spain led to ethnic frictions between native peoples and new settlers. Economic difficulties heightened ethnic consciousness and spawned a vicious racism.

Religion held society together. European culture was a Christian culture. But the Great Schism weakened the prestige of the church and people's faith in papal authority. The conciliar movement, by denying the church's universal sovereignty, strengthened the claims of secular government to jurisdiction over all their peoples. The later Middle Ages witnessed a steady shift of basic loyalty from the church to the emerging national states.

The increasing number of schools leading to the growth of lay literacy represents another positive achievement of the later Middle Ages. So also does the development of national literatures. The first signs of a literary culture appeared.

# Key Terms

Great Famine
Black Death
buba
flagellants
Crécy
Agincourt
Joan of Arc
representative assemblies
nationalism
Babylonian Captivity
schism
conciliarists
merchet
banns
peasant revolts
Jacquerie
racism
*Dalimil Chronicle*
Statute of Kilkenny

# Notes

1. W. C. Jordan, *The Great Famine: Northern Europe in the Early Fourteenth Century* (Princeton, N.J.: Princeton University Press, 1996), pp. 97–102.
2. Ibid., pp. 167–179.
3. N. Ascherson, *Black Sea* (New York: Hill & Wang, 1996), pp. 95–96.
4. W. H. McNeill, *Plagues and Peoples* (New York: Doubleday, 1976), pp. 151–168.
5. Quoted in P. Ziegler, *The Black Death* (Harmondsworth, England: Pelican Books, 1969), p. 20.
6. J. M. Rigg, trans., *The Decameron of Giovanni Boccaccio* (London: J. M. Dent & Sons, 1903), p. 6.
7. M. Mollatt, *The Poor in the Middle Ages: An Essay in Social History,* trans. A. Goldhammer (New Haven, Conn.: Yale University Press, 1986), pp. 146–153, 193–197.
8. Ziegler, *The Black Death,* pp. 232–239.
9. Ibid., p. 84.
10. G. Huppert, *After the Black Death: A Social History of Early Modern Europe* (Bloomington, Ind.: Indiana University Press, 1986), p. ix.
11. Quoted in D. Herlihy, *The Black Death and the Transformation of the West* (Cambridge, Mass.: Harvard University Press, 1997), p. 42.
12. J. Hatcher, *Plague, Population, and the English Economy, 1348–1530* (London: Macmillan Education, 1986), p. 33.
13. See Herlihy, *The Black Death,* pp. 43–45.
14. Ibid., pp. 46–47; Hatcher, *Plague,* p. 33. The quotation is from Hatcher.
15. Ascherson, *Black Sea,* p. 96.
16. See Herlihy, *The Black Death,* pp. 59–81.
17. See P. Cuttino, "Historical Revision: The Causes of the Hundred Years' War," *Speculum* 31 (July 1956): 463–472.
18. J. Barnie, *War in Medieval English Society: Social Values and the Hundred Years' War* (Ithaca, N.Y.: Cornell University Press, 1974), p. 6.
19. Quoted ibid., p. 34.
20. W. P. Barrett, trans., *The Trial of Jeanne d'Arc* (London: George Routledge, 1931), pp. 165–166.
21. Quoted in Barnie, *War in Medieval English Society,* pp. 36–37.
22. M. M. Postan, "The Costs of the Hundred Years' War," *Past and Present* 27 (April 1964): 34–53.
23. See G. O. Sayles, *The King's Parliament of England* (New York: W. W. Norton, 1974), app., pp. 137–141.
24. Quoted in P. S. Lewis, "The Failure of the Medieval French Estates," *Past and Present* 23 (November 1962): 6.
25. Quoted in J. H. Smith, *The Great Schism, 1378: The Disintegration of the Medieval Papacy* (New York: Weybright & Talley, 1970), p. 141.
26. Ibid., p. 15.
27. B. A. Hanawalt, *The Ties That Bound: Peasant Families in Medieval England* (New York: Oxford University Press, 1986), p. 197. This section leans heavily on Hanawalt's work.
28. Ibid., pp. 194–204.
29. A. S. Haskell, "The Paston Women on Marriage in Fifteenth Century England," *Viator* 4 (1973): 459–469.
30. Ibid., p. 471.
31. See D. Herlihy, *Medieval Households* (Cambridge, Mass.: Harvard University Press, 1985), pp. 103–111.
32. L. L. Otis, *Prostitution in Medieval Society: The History of an Urban Institution in Languedoc* (Chicago: University of Chicago Press, 1987), p. 2.
33. Ibid., pp. 25–27, 64–66, 100–106.
34. Ibid., pp. 118–130.
35. See R. H. Helmholz, *Marriage Litigation in Medieval England* (Cambridge: Cambridge University Press, 1974), pp. 28–29, et passim.
36. See M. C. Howell, *Women, Production, and Patriarchy in Late Medieval Cities* (Chicago: University of Chicago Press, 1986), pp. 134–135.
37. A. F. Scott, ed., *Everyone a Witness: The Plantagenet Age* (New York: Thomas Y. Crowell, 1976), p. 263.
38. See E. Mason, "The Role of the English Parishioner, 1000–1500," *Journal of Ecclesiastical History* 27 (January 1976): 17–29.
39. B. A. Hanawalt, "Fur Collar Crime: The Pattern of Crime Among the Fourteenth-Century English Nobility," *Journal of Social History* 8 (Spring 1975): 1–14.
40. Quoted ibid., p. 7.
41. Quoted in M. Bloch, *French Rural History,* trans. J. Sondeimer (Berkeley: University of California Press, 1966), p. 169.
42. W. H. TeBrake, *A Plague of Insurrection: Popular Politics and Peasant Revolt in Flanders, 1323–1328* (Philadelphia: University of Pennsylvania Press, 1993), pp. 1–9.
43. Ibid., pp. 15–99.
44. C. Stephenson and G. Marcham, eds., *Sources of English Constitutional History,* rev. ed. (New York: Harper & Row, 1972), p. 225.
45. Quoted in R. Bartlett, *The Making of Europe: Conquest, Colonization and Cultural Change, 950–1350* (Princeton, N.J.: Princeton University Press, 1993), p. 205. For an alternative, if abstract, discussion of medieval racism, see I. Hannaford, *Race: The History of an Idea in the West* (Baltimore: Johns Hopkins University Press, 1995), pp. 87–146.
46. Quoted in Bartlett, *The Making of Europe,* p. 208.
47. Quoted ibid., p. 215.
48. Quoted ibid., p. 224.
49. Quoted ibid., p. 228.
50. Quoted ibid., p. 233.
51. Quoted ibid., p. 236.
52. Quoted ibid., p. 238.
53. Quoted ibid., p. 239.
54. See M. Keen, *English Society in the Later Middle Ages, 1348–1500* (New York: Penguin Books, 1990), pp. 219–239.

## Suggested Reading

The best starting point for study of the great epidemic that swept the European continent is D. Herlihy, *The Black Death and the Transformation of the West* (1997), a fine treatment of the causes and cultural consequences of the disease. P. Binski, *Medieval Death: Ritual and Representation* (1995), discusses the impact of the Black Death on medieval art and literature. For the social implications of the Black Death, see L. Poos, *A Rural Society After the Black Death: Essex, 1350–1525* (1991), and G. Huppert, *After the Black Death: A Social History of Early Modern Europe* (1986). For the economic effects of the plague, see J. Hatcher, *Plague, Population, and the English Economy, ca. 1300–1450* (1977). The older study of P. Ziegler, *The Black Death* (1969), remains important.

For the background and early part of the long military conflicts of the fourteenth and fifteenth centuries, see the provocative M. M. Vale, *The Origins of the Hundred Years War: The Angevin Legacy, 1250–1340* (1996). See also C. Allmand, *The Hundred Years War: England and France at War, ca 1300–1450* (1988). The broad survey of J. Keegan, *A History of Warfare* (1993), contains a useful summary of significant changes in military technology during the war. The main ruler of the age has found his biographer in W. M. Ormrod, *The Reign of Edward III: Crown and Political Society in England, 1327–1377* (1990). J. Keegan, *The Face of Battle* (1977), chap. 2, "Agincourt," describes what war meant to the ordinary soldier. For strategy, tactics, armaments, and costumes of war, see H. W. Koch, *Medieval Warfare* (1978), a beautifully illustrated book. R. Barber, *The Knight and Chivalry* (1982), and M. Keen, *Chivalry* (1984), give interpretations of the cultural importance of chivalry.

For political and social conditions in the fourteenth and fifteenth centuries, see the works by Lewis, Sayles, Bloch, TeBrake, and especially Hanawalt and Helmholz cited in the Notes. C. Dyer, *Standards of Living in the Later Middle Ages* (1989), contains much valuable social history. The papers in R. H. Hilton and T. H. Aston, eds., *The English Rising of 1381* (1984), stress the importance of urban, as well as rural, participation in the movement, but see also R. Hilton, *Bond Men Made Free: Medieval Peasant Movements and the English Rising of 1381* (1973), a comparative study. T. F. Glick, *From Muslim Fortress to Christian Castle: Social and Cultural Change in Medieval Spain* (1995), is based in part on rare archaeological information and explores the reorganization of Spanish society after the reconquest. J. S. Gerber, *The Jews of Spain: A History of the Sephardic Experience* (1992), treats growing anti-Jewish sentiment in the wake of the Black Death. P. C. Maddern, *Violence and Social Order: East Anglia, 1422–1442* (1991), deals with social disorder in eastern England. I. M. W. Harvey, *Jack Cade's Rebellion of 1450* (1991), is an important work in local history. J. C. Holt, *Robin Hood* (1982), is a soundly researched and highly readable study of the famous outlaw. For the Pastons, see R. Barber, ed., *The Pastons: Letters of a Family in the Wars of the Roses* (1984). The starting point for study of the widespread starvation of the early fourteenth century is the prizewinning work by Jordan cited in the Notes. For social attacks on various ethnic and religious minorities, see D. Nirenberg, *Communities of Violence: Persecution of Minorities in the Middle Ages* (1996).

D. Herlihy, *Women, Family and Society in Medieval Europe: Historical Essays, 1978–1991* (1995), contains valuable articles dealing with the later Middle Ages, while the exciting study by B. Gottlieb, *The Family in the Western World from the Black Death to the Industrial Age* (1993), explores the family's political, emotional, and cultural roles. For prostitution, see, in addition to the title by Otis cited in the Notes, J. Rossiaud, *Medieval Prostitution* (1995), a very good treatment of prostitution's social and cultural significance.

For women's economic status in the late medieval period, see the titles by Howell and Hanawalt cited in the Notes. J. S. Bennett, *Ale, Beer, and Brewsters in England: Women's Work in a Changing World, 1300–1600* (1996), stresses the persistence of patriarchal attitudes. P. J. P. Goldberg, *Women, Work, and Life Cycle in a Medieval Economy: Women in York and Yorkshire, c 1300–1520* (1992), explores the relationship between economic opportunity and marriage.

The poetry of Dante, Chaucer, and Villon may be read in the following editions: D. Sayers, trans., *Dante: The Divine Comedy,* 3 vols. (1963); N. Coghill, trans., *Chaucer's Canterbury Tales* (1977); P. Dale, trans., *The Poems of Villon* (1973). The social setting of *Canterbury Tales* is brilliantly evoked in D. W. Robertson, Jr., *Chaucer's London* (1968). Students interested in further study of Christine de Pisan should consult A. J. Kennedy, *Christine de Pisan: A Bibliographical Guide* (1984), and C. C. Willard, *Christine de Pisan: Her Life and Works* (1984).

For religion and lay piety, A. D. Brown, *Popular Piety in Late Medieval England: The Diocese of Salisbury, 1250–1550* (1995), is a good case study showing the importance of guilds, charity, and heresy and how they affected parish life. F. Oakley, *The Western Church in the Later Middle Ages* (1979), is an excellent broad survey, while R. N. Swanson, *Church and Society in Late Medieval England* (1989), provides a good synthesis of English conditions. The important achievement of A. Vauchez, *The Laity in the Middle Ages: Religious Beliefs and Devotional Practices,* ed. D. E. Bornstein and trans. M. J. Schneider (1993), explores many aspects of popular piety and contains considerable material on women.

# Listening to the Past

## Christine de Pisan

*The passage below is taken from* The Book of the City of Ladies, *one of the many writings of Christine de Pisan (1363?–1434?). Christine was a highly educated woman who wrote prolifically in French, her native tongue. Her patron was the queen of France. Christine wrote amid the chaos of the Hundred Years' War about a wide range of topics. The excerpt below is not reflective of all French women. Rather, it focuses on the behavior of courtly women only. And it expresses Christine's and her patron's views about women's role in the creation and stabilization of an elite court culture during a time of political and social upheaval.*

Just as the good shepherd takes care that his lambs are maintained in health, and if any of them becomes mangy, separates it from the flock for fear that it may infect the others, so the princess will take upon herself the responsibility for the care of her women servants and companions, who she will ensure are all good and chaste, for she will not want to have any other sort of person around her. Since it is the established custom that knights and squires and all men (especially certain men) who associate with women have a habit of pleading for love tokens from them and trying to seduce them, the wise princess will so enforce her regulations that there will be no visitor to her court so foolhardy as to dare to whisper privately with any of her women or give the appearance of seduction. If he does it or if he is noticed giving any sign of it, immediately she should take such an attitude towards him that he will not dare to importune them any more. The lady who is chaste will want all her women to be so too, on pain of being banished from her company.

She will want them to amuse themselves with decent games, such that men cannot mock, as they do the games of some women, though at the time the men laugh and join in. The women should restrain themselves with seemly conduct among knights and squires and all men. They should speak demurely and sweetly and, whether in dances or other amusements, divert and enjoy themselves decorously and without wantonness. They must not be frolicsome, forward, or boisterous in speech, expression, bearing or laughter. They must not go about with their heads raised like wild deer. This kind of behaviour would be very unseemly and greatly derisory in a woman of the court, in whom there should be more modesty, good manners and courteous behaviour than in any others, for where there is most honour there ought to be the most perfect manners and behaviour. Women of the court in any country would be deceiving themselves very much if they imagined that it was more appropriate for them to be frolicsome and saucy than for other women. For this reason we hope that in time to come our doctrine in this book may be carried into many kingdoms, so that it may be valuable in all places where there might be any shortcoming.

We say generally to all women of all countries that it is the duty of every lady and maiden of the court, whether she be young or old, to be more prudent, more decorous, and better schooled in all things than other women. The ladies of the court ought to be models of all good things and all honour to other women, and if they do otherwise they will do no honour to their mistress nor to themselves. In addition, so that everything may be consistent in modesty, the wise princess will wish that the clothing and the ornaments of her women, though they be appropriately beautiful and rich, be of a modest fashion, well fitting and seemly, neat and properly cared for. There should be no deviation from this modesty

Christine de Pisan, shown here producing her *Collected Works,* was devoted to scholarship. *(British Library)*

nor any immodesty in the matter of plunging necklines or other excesses.

In all things the wise princess will keep her women in order just as the good and prudent abbess does her convent, so that bad reports about it may not circulate in the town, in distant regions or anywhere else. This princess will be so feared and respected because of the wise management that she will be seen to practise that no man or woman will be so foolhardy as to disobey her commands in any respect or to question her will, for there is no doubt that a lady is more feared and respected and held in greater reverence when she is seen to be wise and chaste and of firm behaviour. But there is nothing wrong or inconsistent in her being kind and gentle, for the mere look of the wise lady and her subdued reception is enough of a sign to correct those men and women who err and to inspire them with fear.

## Questions for Analysis

1. How did Christine think courtly women should behave around men?
2. How did women fit into the larger picture of court culture? What was their role at court?

*Source:* Christine de Pisan, "The Book of the City of Ladies," in *Treasures of the City of Ladies,* translated with an introduction by Sarah Lawson. Translation copyright © 1985 by Sarah Lawson. Reprinted by permission of Penguin Group UK.

Michelangelo painted the entire Sistine Chapel ceiling by himself, in 1508–1512. *(Vatican Museum)*

chapter

# 13 European Society in the Age of the Renaissance

## chapter outline



While the Four Horsemen of the Apocalypse seemed to be carrying war, plague, famine, and death across northern Europe, a new culture was emerging in southern Europe. The fourteenth century witnessed the beginnings of remarkable changes in many aspects of Italian society. In the fifteenth century, these phenomena spread beyond Italy and gradually influenced society in northern Europe. These cultural changes have been collectively labeled the "Renaissance."

- What does the term *Renaissance* mean?
- How was the Renaissance manifested in politics, government, and social organization?
- What were the intellectual and artistic hallmarks of the Renaissance?
- Did the Renaissance involve shifts in religious attitudes?
- What developments occurred in the evolution of the nation-state?

This chapter will concentrate on these questions.

## The Evolution of the Italian Renaissance

Economic growth laid the material basis for the Italian Renaissance. The period extending roughly from 1050 to 1300 witnessed phenomenal commercial and financial development, the growing political power of self-governing cities, and great population expansion. Then the period from the late thirteenth to the late sixteenth century was characterized by an incredible efflorescence of artistic energies.[1] Scholars commonly use the term **Renaissance** to describe the cultural achievements of the fourteenth through sixteenth centuries; those achievements rest on the economic and political developments of earlier centuries.

In the great commercial revival of the eleventh century, northern Italian cities led the way. By the middle of the twelfth century, Venice, supported by a huge merchant marine, had grown enormously rich through overseas trade. It profited tremendously from the diversion of the Fourth Crusade to Constantinople (see page 353). Genoa and Milan also enjoyed the benefits of a

**A Bank Scene, Florence** Originally a "bank" was just a counter; if covered with a carpet like this Ottoman geometric rug with a kufic border, it became a bank of distinction. Money-changers who sat behind the counter became "bankers," exchanging different currencies and holding deposits for merchants and business people. *(Prato, San Francesco/Scala/Art Resource, NY)*

large volume of trade with the Middle East and northern Europe. These cities fully exploited their geographical positions as natural crossroads for mercantile exchange between the East and West. Furthermore, in the early fourteenth century, Genoa and Venice made important strides in shipbuilding that allowed their ships for the first time to sail all year long. Advances in ship construction greatly increased the volume of goods that could be transported; improvements in the mechanics of sailing accelerated speed. Most goods were purchased directly from the producers and sold a good distance away. For example, Italian merchants bought fine English wool directly from the Cistercian abbeys of Yorkshire in northern England. The wool was transported to the bazaars of North Africa either overland or by ship through the Strait of Gibraltar. The risks in such an operation were great, but the profits were enormous. These profits were continually reinvested to earn more. The Florentine wool industry was the major factor in that city's financial expansion and population increase.

Scholars tend to agree that the first artistic and literary manifestations of the Italian Renaissance appeared in Florence, which possessed enormous wealth despite geographical constraints: it was an inland city without easy access to sea transportation. But toward the end of the thirteenth century, Florentine merchants and bankers acquired control of papal banking. From their position as tax collectors for the papacy, Florentine mercantile families began to dominate European banking on both sides of the Alps. These families had offices in Paris, London, Bruges, Barcelona, Marseilles, Tunis and other North African ports, and, of course, Naples and Rome. The profits from loans, investments, and money exchanges that poured back to Florence were pumped into urban industries. Such profits contributed to the city's economic vitality. Banking families, such as the Medici in Florence, controlled the politics and culture of their cities.

By the first quarter of the fourteenth century, the economic foundations of Florence were so strong that even severe crises could not destroy the city. In 1344 King Edward III of England repudiated his huge debts to Florentine bankers and forced some of them into bankruptcy. Florence suffered frightfully from the Black Death, losing at least half of its population. Serious labor unrest, such as the *ciompi* revolts of 1378 (see page 403), shook the political establishment. Nevertheless, the basic Florentine economic structure remained stable. Driving enterprise, technical know-how, and competitive spirit saw Florence through the difficult economic period of the late fourteenth century.

| 1420 | 1445 | 1470 | 1495 | 1520 | 1545 |
|---|---|---|---|---|---|

**POLITICAL/MILITARY**

- 1422–1461 Charles VII revives France and monarchy
- 1434–1494 Medici family in power in Florence
- 1469 Marriage of Isabella of Castile and Ferdinand of Aragon
- 1494 Invasion of Italy by Charles VIII of France
- 1521 Start of Habsburg-Valois Wars

**SOCIAL/ECONOMIC**

- 1420–1485 Flow of Balkan slaves to the eastern Mediterranean; flow of African slaves to the western Mediterranean

**INTELLECTUAL/RELIGIOUS**

- 1454 Invention of movable type
- 1456 Gutenberg's Bible
- 1500–1527 High Renaissance (Leonardo, Raphael, Michelangelo)
- 1506 Pope Julius II begins work on Saint Peter's Basilica
- 1508–1512 Michelangelo paints ceiling of Sistine Chapel
- 1513 Machiavelli, *The Prince*
- 1516 More, *Utopia*
- 1516 Erasmus publishes Greek New Testament
- 1528 Castiglione, *The Courtier*

## Communes and Republics

The northern Italian cities were **communes,** sworn associations of free men seeking complete political and economic independence from local nobles. The merchant guilds that formed the communes built and maintained the city walls, regulated trade, raised taxes, and kept civil order. In the course of the twelfth century, communes at Milan, Florence, Genoa, Siena, and Pisa fought for and won their independence from surrounding feudal nobles. The nobles, attracted by the opportunities of long-distance and maritime trade, the rising value of urban real estate, the new public offices available in the expanding communes, and the chances for advantageous marriages into rich commercial families, frequently settled within the cities. Marriage vows often sealed business contracts between the rural nobility and the mercantile aristocracy. This merger of the northern Italian feudal nobility and the commercial aristocracy constituted the formation of a new social class, an urban nobility. Within this nobility, groups tied by blood, economic interests, and social connections formed tightly knit alliances to defend and expand their rights.

This new class made citizenship in the communes dependent on a property qualification, years of residence within the city, and social connections. Only a tiny percentage of the male population possessed these qualifications and thus could hold office in the commune's political councils. A new force, called the **popolo,** disenfranchised and heavily taxed, bitterly resented their exclusion from power. The popolo wanted places in the communal government and equality of taxation. Throughout most of the thirteenth century, in city after city, the popolo used armed force and violence to take over the city governments. Republican governments—in which political power theoretically resides in the people and is exercised by their chosen representatives—were established in Bologna, Siena, Parma, Florence, Genoa, and other cities. The victory of the popolo, however, proved temporary. Because they practiced the same sort of political exclusivity as had the noble communes—denying influence to the classes below them, whether the poor, the unskilled, or new immigrants—the popolo never won the support of other groups. Moreover, the popolo could not establish civil order within their cities. Consequently, these movements for republican government failed. By 1300 **signori** (despots, or one-man rulers) or **oligarchies** (the rule of merchant aristocracies) had triumphed everywhere in Italy.[2]

For the next two centuries, the Italian city-states were ruled by signori or by constitutional oligarchies. In signorial governments, despots pretended to observe the law while actually manipulating it to conceal their basic illegality. Oligarchic regimes possessed constitutions, but through a variety of schemes a small, restricted class of wealthy merchants exercised the judicial, executive, and legislative functions of government. Thus in 1422 Venice had a population of eighty-four thousand, but two hundred men held all the power; Florence had about forty thousand people, but six hundred men ruled. Oligarchic regimes maintained only a façade of republican government. The Renaissance nostalgia for the Roman form of government, combined with calculating shrewdness, prompted the leaders of Venice, Milan, and Florence to use the old forms.

In the fifteenth century, political power and elite culture centered on the **princely courts** of despots and oligarchs. "A court was the space and personnel around a prince as he made laws, received ambassadors, made appointments, took his meals, and proceeded through the streets."[3] The princely court afforded the despot or oligarch the opportunity to display and assert his wealth and power. He flaunted his patronage of learning and the arts by munificent gifts to writers, philosophers, and artists. He used ceremonies connected with family births, baptisms, marriages, funerals, or triumphant entrances into the city as occasions for magnificent pageantry and elaborate ritual.

## The Balance of Power Among the Italian City-States

Renaissance Italians had a passionate attachment to their individual city-states: political loyalty and feeling centered on the local city. This intensity of local feeling perpetuated the dozens of small states and hindered the development of one unified state.

In the fifteenth century, five powers dominated the Italian peninsula: Venice, Milan, Florence, the Papal States, and the kingdom of Naples (see Map 13.1). The rulers of the city-states—whether despots in Milan, patrician elitists in Florence, or oligarchs in Venice—governed as monarchs. They crushed urban revolts, levied taxes, killed their enemies, and used massive building programs to employ, and the arts to overawe, the masses.

Venice, with its enormous trade and vast colonial empire, ranked as an international power. Though Venice had a sophisticated constitution and was a **republic** in name, an oligarchy of merchant aristocrats actually ran the city. Milan was also called a republic, but despots of the Sforza family ruled harshly and dominated the smaller cities of the north. Likewise in Florence the form of government was republican, with authority vested in several councils of state. In reality, between 1434 and 1494, power in Florence was held by the great Medici banking family. Though not public officers, Cosimo (1434–1464) and Lorenzo (1469–1492) ruled from behind the scenes.

Central Italy consisted mainly of the Papal States, which during the Babylonian Captivity had come under the sway of important Roman families. Pope Alexander VI (1492–1503), aided militarily and politically by his son Cesare Borgia, reasserted papal authority in the papal lands. Cesare Borgia became the hero of Machiavelli's *The Prince* (see page 429) because he began the work of uniting the peninsula by ruthlessly conquering and exacting total obedience from the principalities making up the Papal States.

South of the Papal States was the kingdom of Naples, consisting of virtually all of southern Italy and, at times, Sicily. The kingdom of Naples had long been disputed by the Aragonese and by the French. In 1435 it passed to Aragon.

The major Italian city-states controlled the smaller ones, such as Siena, Mantua, Ferrara, and Modena, and competed furiously among themselves for territory. The large cities used diplomacy, spies, paid informers, and any other available means to get information that could be used to advance their ambitions. While the states of northern Europe were moving toward centralization and consolidation, the world of Italian politics resembled a jungle where the powerful dominated the weak.

In one significant respect, however, the Italian city-states anticipated future relations among competing European states after 1500. Whenever one Italian state appeared to gain a predominant position within the peninsula, other states combined to establish a *balance of power* against the major threat. In 1450, for example, Venice went to war against Milan in protest against Francesco Sforza's acquisition of the title of duke of Milan. Cosimo de' Medici of Florence, a long-time sup-

**MAP 13.1 The Italian City-States, ca 1494** In the fifteenth century, the Italian city-states represented great wealth and cultural sophistication. The political divisions of the peninsula invited foreign intervention.

porter of a Florentine-Venetian alliance, switched his position and aided Milan. Florence and Naples combined with Milan against powerful Venice and the papacy. In the peace treaty signed at Lodi in 1454, Venice received territories in return for recognizing Sforza's right to the duchy. This pattern of shifting alliances continued until 1494. In the formation of these alliances, Renaissance Italians invented the machinery of modern diplomacy: permanent embassies with resident ambassadors in capitals where political relations and commercial ties needed continual monitoring. The resident ambassador was one of the great achievements of the Italian Renaissance.

**Uccello: Battle of San Romano** Fascinated by perspective—the representation of spatial depth or distance on a flat surface—the Florentine artist Paolo Uccello (1397–1475) celebrated the Florentine victory over Siena (1432) in a painting with three scenes. Though a minor battle, it started Florence on the road to domination over smaller nearby states. The painting hung in Lorenzo de' Medici's bedroom. *(National Gallery, London/Erich Lessing/Art Resource, NY)*

At the end of the fifteenth century, Venice, Florence, Milan, and the papacy possessed great wealth and represented high cultural achievement. However, their imperialistic ambitions at one another's expense and their resulting inability to form a common alliance against potential foreign enemies made Italy an inviting target for invasion. When Florence and Naples entered into an agreement to acquire Milanese territories, Milan called on France for support.

At Florence the French invasion had been predicted by Dominican friar Girolamo Savonarola (1452–1498). In a number of fiery sermons between 1491 and 1494, Savonarola attacked what he called the paganism and moral vice of the city, the undemocratic government of Lorenzo de' Medici, and the corruption of Pope Alexander VI. For a time, Savonarola enjoyed popular support among the ordinary people; he became the religious leader of Florence and as such contributed to the fall of the Medici dynasty. Eventually, however, people tired of his moral denunciations, and he was excommunicated by the pope and executed. Savonarola stands as proof that the common people did not share the worldly outlook of the commercial and intellectual elite. His career also illustrates the internal instability of Italian cities such as Florence, an instability that invited foreign invasion.

The invasion of Italy in 1494 by the French king Charles VIII (r. 1483–1498) inaugurated a new period in Italian and European power politics. Italy became the focus of international ambitions and the battleground of foreign armies. Charles swept down the peninsula with little opposition, and Florence, Rome, and Naples soon bowed before him. When Piero de' Medici, Lorenzo's son, went to the French camp seeking peace, the Florentines exiled the Medici and restored republican government.

Charles's success simply whetted French appetites. In 1508 his cousin and heir, Louis XII, formed the League of Cambrai with the pope and the German emperor Maximilian for the purpose of stripping rich Venice of its mainland possessions. Pope Leo X (1513–1521) soon found France a dangerous friend and in a new alliance called on the Spanish and Germans to expel the French from Italy. This anti-French combination was temporarily successful. In 1519 Charles V succeeded his grandfather Maximilian (1493–1519) as Holy Roman emperor. When the French returned to Italy in 1521, a series of conflicts called the Habsburg-Valois Wars (named for the German and French dynasties) began. The battlefield was often Italy.

In the sixteenth century, the political and social life of Italy was upset by the relentless competition for dominance between France and the empire. The Italian cities suffered severely from continual warfare, especially in the frightful sack of Rome in 1527 by imperial forces under Charles V. Thus the failure of the city-states to form some federal system, consolidate, or at least establish a common foreign policy led to the continuation of the centuries-old subjection of the peninsula by outside invaders. Italy was not to achieve unification until 1870.

## Intellectual Hallmarks of the Renaissance

See DBQ 1

The Renaissance was characterized by self-conscious awareness among fourteenth- and fifteenth-century Italians that they were living in a new era. The realization that something new and unique was happening first came to men of letters in the fourteenth century, especially to the poet and humanist Francesco Petrarch (1304–1374). Petrarch thought that he was living at the start of a new age, a period of light following a long night of Gothic gloom. He considered the first two centuries of the Roman Empire to represent the peak in the development of human civilization. Medieval people had believed that they were continuing the glories that had been ancient Rome and had recognized no cultural division between the world of the emperors and their own times. But for Petrarch, the Germanic migrations had caused a sharp cultural break with the glories of Rome and inaugurated what he called the "Dark Ages." He believed, with many of his contemporaries, that the thousand-year period between the fourth and the fourteenth centuries constituted a barbarian, Gothic, or "middle" age. The sculptors, painters, and writers of the Renaissance spoke contemptuously of their medieval predecessors and identified themselves with the thinkers and artists of Greco-Roman civilization. Petrarch believed that he was witnessing a new golden age of intellectual achievement—a rebirth or, to use the French word that came into English, a renaissance. The division of historical time into periods is often arbitrary and done for the convenience of historians. In terms of the way most people lived and thought, no sharp division exists between the Middle Ages and the Renaissance. Some important poets, writers, and artists, however, believed they were living in a new golden age.

The Renaissance also manifested itself in a new attitude toward men, women, and the world—an attitude that may be described as individualism. A humanism characterized by a deep interest in the Latin classics and a deliberate attempt to revive antique lifestyles emerged, as did a bold new secular spirit.

### Individualism

Though the Middle Ages had seen the appearance of remarkable individuals, recognition of such persons was limited. The examples of Saint Augustine in the fifth century and Peter Abelard and Guibert of Nogent in the twelfth—men who perceived themselves as unique and produced autobiographical statements—stand out for that very reason: Christian humility discouraged self-absorption. In the fourteenth and fifteenth centuries, moreover, such characteristically medieval and corporate attachments as the guild and the parish continued to provide strong support for the individual and to exercise great social influence. Yet in the Renaissance, intellectuals, unlike their counterparts in the Middle Ages, developed a new sense of historical distance from earlier periods. A large literature specifically concerned with the nature of individuality emerged. This literature represented the flowering of a distinctly Renaissance individualism.

The Renaissance witnessed the emergence of many distinctive personalities who gloried in their uniqueness. Italians of unusual abilities were self-consciously aware of their singularity and unafraid to be unlike their neighbors; they had enormous confidence in their ability to achieve great things. Leon Battista Alberti (1404–1474), a writer, architect, and mathematician, remarked, "Men can do all things if they will."[4] Florentine goldsmith and sculptor Benvenuto Cellini (1500–1574) prefaced his *Autobiography* with a declaration:

*My cruel fate hath warr'd with me in vain:*
*Life, glory, worth, and all unmeasur'd skill,*
*Beauty and grace, themselves in me fulfill*
*That many I surpass, and to the best attain.*[5]

Cellini, certain of his genius, wrote so that the whole world might appreciate it.

**Benvenuto Cellini: Saltcellar of Francis I (ca 1539–1543)** In gold and enamel, Cellini depicts the Roman sea god, Neptune (with trident, or three-pronged spear), sitting beside a small boat-shaped container holding salt from the sea. Opposite him, a female figure personifying Earth guards pepper, which derives from a plant. Portrayed on the base are the four seasons and the times of day, symbolizing seasonal festivities and daily meal schedules. The grace, poise, and elegance of the figures reflect Mannerism, an artistic style popular during the Italian High Renaissance (1520–1600). *(Kunsthistorisches Museum, Vienna/The Bridgeman Art Library)*

**Individualism** stressed personality, uniqueness, genius, and full development of one's capabilities and talents. Artist, athlete, painter, scholar, sculptor, whatever—a person's abilities should be stretched until fully realized. Thirst for fame, a driving ambition, and a burning desire for success drove such people to the complete achievement of their potential. The quest for glory was a central component of Renaissance individualism.

## Humanism

In the cities of Italy, especially Rome, civic leaders and the wealthy populace showed phenomenal archaeological zeal for the recovery of manuscripts, statues, and monuments. Pope Nicholas V (1447–1455), a distinguished scholar, planned the Vatican Library for the nine thousand manuscripts he had collected. Pope Sixtus IV (1471–1484) built that library, which remains one of the richest repositories of ancient and medieval documents.

The revival of antiquity also took the form of profound interest in and study of the Latin classics. This feature of the Renaissance became known as the "new learning," or simply **humanism,** the term of Florentine rhetorician and historian Leonardo Bruni (1370–1444). The words *humanism* and *humanist* derive ultimately from the Latin *humanitas,* which Cicero used to mean the literary culture needed by anyone who would be considered educated and civilized. Humanists studied the Latin classics to learn what they reveal about human nature. Humanism emphasized human beings, their achievements, interests, and capabilities. Although churchmen supported the new learning, by the later fifteenth century Italian humanism was increasingly a lay phenomenon.

Appreciation for the literary culture of the Romans had never died in the West. Bede and John of Salisbury, for example, had studied and imitated the writings of the ancients. Medieval writers, however, had studied the ancients in order to come to know God. Medieval scholars had interpreted the classics in a Christian sense and had invested the ancients' poems and histories with Christian meaning.

Renaissance humanists, although deeply Christian, approached the classics differently. Whereas medieval writers accepted pagan and classical authors uncritically, Renaissance humanists were skeptical of their authority, conscious of the historical distance separating themselves from the ancients, and fully aware that classical writers often disagreed among themselves. Whereas medieval writers looked to the classics to reveal God, Renaissance humanists studied the classics to understand human nature, and while they fully grasped the moral thought of pagan antiquity, Renaissance humanists viewed humanity from a strongly Christian perspective: men and women were made in the image and likeness of God. For example, in a remarkable essay, *On the Dignity of Man,* the Florentine writer Pico della Mirandola stressed that man possesses great dignity because he was made as Adam in the image of God before the Fall and as Christ after the Resurrection. According to Pico, man's place in the universe is somewhere between the beasts and the angels, but because of the divine image planted in him, there are no limits to what he can accomplish. Humanists rejected classical ideas that were opposed to Christianity. Or they sought through reinterpretation an underlying harmony between the pagan and secular and the Christian faith. The fundamental difference between Renaissance humanists and medieval ones is that the former were more self-conscious about what they were doing, and they stressed the realization of human potential.[6]

The fourteenth- and fifteenth-century humanists loved the language of the classics and considered it superior to the corrupt Latin of the medieval schoolmen. They eventually became concerned more about form than about content, more about the way an idea was expressed than about the significance and validity of the idea. Literary humanists of the fourteenth century wrote each other highly stylized letters imitating ancient authors, and they held witty philosophical dialogues in conscious imitation of the Platonic Academy of the fourth century B.C. Renaissance humanists heaped scorn on the "barbaric" Latin style of the medievalists. The leading humanists of the early Renaissance were rhetoricians, seeking effective and eloquent communication, both oral and written.

## Secular Spirit

**Secularism** involves a basic concern with the material world instead of with the eternal world of spirit. A secular way of thinking tends to find the ultimate explanation of everything and the final end of human beings within the limits of what the senses can discover. Even though medieval business people ruthlessly pursued profits and medieval monks fought fiercely over property, the dominant ideals focused on the otherworldly, on life after death. Renaissance people often held strong and deep spiritual interests, but in their increasingly secular society, attention was concentrated on the here and now, often on the acquisition of material things. Church doctrine, relying on Scripture (Leviticus 25:36–37, Psalms 37:26, Luke 11:15), frowned on usury (lending money at interest), but the law had always been difficult to enforce. In the twelfth century, Cistercian monks had been severely criticized for practicing usury. During the Renaissance, the practice became widespread, even acceptable. Considerable wealth derived from interest on loans. The fourteenth and fifteenth centuries witnessed the slow but steady growth of such secularism in Italy.

The economic changes and rising prosperity of the Italian cities in the thirteenth century worked a fundamental change in social and intellectual attitudes and values. Worries about shifting rates of interest, shipping routes, personnel costs, and employee relations did not leave much time for thoughts about penance and purgatory. The busy bankers and merchants of the Italian cities calculated ways of making and increasing their money. Such wealth allowed greater material pleasures, a more comfortable life, the leisure time to appreciate and patronize the arts. Money could buy many sensual gratifications, and the rich, social-climbing patricians of Venice, Florence, Genoa, and Rome came to see life more as an opportunity to be enjoyed than as a painful pilgrimage to the City of God.

In *On Pleasure,* humanist Lorenzo Valla (1406–1457) defends the pleasures of the senses as the highest good. Scholars praise Valla as a father of modern historical criticism. His study *On the False Donation of Constantine* (1444) demonstrates by careful textual examination that an anonymous eighth-century document supposedly giving the papacy jurisdiction over vast territories in western Europe was a forgery. Medieval people had accepted the Donation of Constantine as a reality, and the proof that it was an invention weakened the foundations of papal claims to temporal authority. Lorenzo Valla's work exemplifies the application of critical scholarship to old and almost-sacred writings as well as the new secular spirit of the Renaissance.

The tales in *The Decameron* by the Florentine Giovanni Boccaccio (1313–1375), which describe ambitious merchants, lecherous friars, and cuckolded husbands, portray a frankly acquisitive, sensual, and worldly society. Although Boccaccio's figures were stock literary characters, *The Decameron* contains none of the "contempt of the world" theme so pervasive in medieval literature. Renaissance writers justified the accumulation and enjoyment of wealth with references to ancient authors.

Nor did church leaders do much to combat the new secular spirit. In the fifteenth and early sixteenth centuries, the papal court and the households of the cardinals were just as worldly as those of great urban patricians. Of course, most of the popes and higher church officials had come from the bourgeois aristocracy. Renaissance popes beautified the city of Rome, patronized artists and men of letters, and expended enormous enthusiasm and huge sums of money. A new papal chancellery, begun in 1483 and finished in 1511, stands as one of the architectural masterpieces of the High Renaissance. Pope Julius II (1503–1513) tore down the old Saint Peter's Basilica and began work on the present structure in 1506. Michelangelo's dome for Saint Peter's is still considered his greatest work. Papal interests, which were far removed from spiritual concerns, fostered, rather than discouraged, the new worldly attitude.

The broad mass of the people and the intellectuals and leaders of society remained faithful to the Christian church. Few people questioned the basic tenets of the Christian religion. Italian humanists and their aristocratic patrons were anti-ascetic, anti-Scholastic, and ambivalent, but they were not agnostics or skeptics. The thousands of pious paintings, sculptures, processions, and pilgrimages of the Renaissance period prove that strong religious feeling persisted.

## Art and the Artist

No feature of the Renaissance evokes greater admiration than its artistic masterpieces. The 1400s (*quattrocento*) and 1500s (*cinquecento*) bore witness to a dazzling creativity in painting, architecture, and sculpture. In all the arts, the city of Florence led the way. According to Renaissance art historian Giorgio Vasari (1511–1574), the painter Perugino once asked why it was in Florence and not elsewhere that men achieved perfection in the arts. The first answer he received was, "There were so many good critics there, for the air of the city makes men quick and perceptive and impatient of mediocrity."[7] But Florence was not the only artistic center. In the period art historians describe as the "High Renaissance" (1500–1527), Rome took the lead. The main characteristics of High Renaissance art—classical balance, harmony, and restraint—are revealed in the masterpieces of Leonardo da Vinci (1452–1519), Raphael (1483–1520), and Michelangelo (1475–1564), all of whom worked in Rome.

### Art and Power

In early Renaissance Italy, art manifested corporate power. Powerful urban groups such as guilds or religious confraternities commissioned works of art. The Florentine cloth merchants, for example, delegated Filippo Brunelleschi to build the magnificent dome on the cathedral of Florence and selected Lorenzo Ghiberti to design the bronze doors of the Baptistry. These works represented the merchants' dominant influence in the community. Corporate patronage was also reflected in the Florentine government's decision to hire Michelangelo to create the sculpture of David, the great Hebrew hero and king. The subject matter of art through the early fifteenth century, as in the Middle Ages, remained overwhelmingly religious. Religious themes appeared in all media—woodcarvings, painted frescoes, stone sculptures, paintings. As in the Middle Ages, art served an educational purpose. A religious picture or statue was intended to spread a particular doctrine, act as a profession of faith, or recall sinners to a moral way of living.

Increasingly in the later fifteenth century, individuals and oligarchs, rather than corporate groups, sponsored works of art. Patrician merchants and bankers, popes and princes, supported the arts as a means of glorifying themselves and their families. Vast sums were spent on family chapels, frescoes, religious panels, and tombs. Writing about 1470, Florentine oligarch Lorenzo de' Medici declared that over the previous thirty-five years his family had spent the astronomical sum of 663,755 gold florins for artistic and architectural commissions. Yet "I think it casts a brilliant light on our estate [public reputation] and it seems to me that the monies were well spent and I am very pleased with this." Powerful men wanted to exalt themselves, their families, and their offices. A magnificent style of living, enriched by works of art, served to prove the greatness and the power of the despot or oligarch.[8]

In addition to power, art reveals changing patterns of consumption in Renaissance Italy. "Consumer habits introduced into economic life a creative and dynamic process for growth and change that was fundamental to the development of the West."[9] If modern consumerism has its roots in the eighteenth century, the latter period's consumer practices can be traced to the Italian Renaissance.

In the rural world of the Middle Ages, society had been organized for war. Men of wealth spent their money on military gear—swords, armor, horses, crenelated castles, towers, family compounds—all of which represent offensive or defensive warfare. As Italian nobles settled in towns (see page 415), they adjusted to an urban culture. Rather than employing knights for warfare, cities hired mercenaries. Expenditure on military hardware declined. For the rich merchant or the noble recently arrived from the countryside, the urban palace represented the greatest outlay of cash. It was his chief luxury, and although a private dwelling, the palace implied grandeur.[10] Within the palace, the merchant-prince's chamber, or bedroom, where he slept and received his intimate guests, was the most important room. In the fourteenth and fifteenth centuries, a large, intricately carved wooden bed, a chest, and perhaps a bench served as its sole decorations. The chest held the master's most precious goods—silver, tapestries, jewelry, clothing. Other rooms, even in palaces of fifteen to twenty rooms, were very sparsely furnished. As the fifteenth century advanced and wealth increased, other rooms were gradually furnished with carved chests, tables, benches, chairs, tapestries for the walls, paintings (an innovation), and sculptural decorations, and a private chapel was added. By the late sixteenth century, the Strozzi banking family of Florence spent more on household goods than on anything else except food; the value of those furnishings was three times that of their silver and jewelry.[11]

After the palace itself, the private chapel within the palace symbolized the largest expenditure. Equipped with

**Botticelli: Primavera, or Spring (ca 1482)** Framed by a grove of orange trees, Venus, goddess of love, is flanked on her left by Flora, goddess of flowers and fertility, and on her right by the Three Graces, goddesses of banquets, dance, and social occasions. Above, Venus's son Cupid, the god of love, shoots darts of desire, while at the far right the wind-god Zephyrus chases the nymph Chloris. The entire scene rests on classical mythology, though some art historians claim that Venus is an allegory for the Virgin Mary. *(Digital image © The Museum of Modern Art/Licensed by Scala/Art Resource, NY)*

the ecclesiastical furniture—tabernacles, chalices, thuribles, and other liturgical utensils—and decorated with religious scenes, the chapel served as the center of the household's religious life and its cult of remembrance of the dead. In fifteenth-century Florence, only the Medici had a private chapel, but by the late sixteenth century, most wealthy Florentine families had private chapels. Since the merchant banker or prince appointed the chaplain, usually a younger son of the family, religious power passed into private hands.[12]

As the fifteenth century advanced, the subject matter of art became steadily more secular. The study of classical texts brought deeper understanding of ancient ideas. Classical themes and motifs, such as the lives and loves of pagan gods and goddesses, figured increasingly in painting and sculpture. Religious topics, such as the Annunciation of the Virgin and the Nativity, remained popular among both patrons and artists, but frequently the patron had himself and his family portrayed. People were conscious of their physical uniqueness and wanted their individuality immortalized. Paintings were also means of displaying wealth.

The content and style of Renaissance art were decidedly different from those of the Middle Ages. The individual portrait emerged as a distinct artistic genre. In the fifteenth century, members of the newly rich middle

**Andrea Mantegna: Adoration of the Magi (ca 1495–1505)** Applying his study of ancient Roman relief sculpture, and elaborating on a famous scriptural text (Matthew 2:1), Mantegna painted for the private devotion of the Gonzaga family of Mantua this scene of the Three Kings coming to recognize the divinity of Christ. The Three Kings represent the entire world—that is, the three continents known to medieval Europeans: Europe, Asia, and Africa. They also symbolize the three stages of life: youth, maturity, and old age. Here Melchior, the oldest, his large cranium symbolizing wisdom, personifies Europe. He offers gold in a Chinese porcelain cup from the Ming Dynasty. Balthazar, with an olive complexion and dark beard, stands for Asia and maturity. He presents frankincense in a stunning vessel of Turkish tombac ware. Caspar, representing Africa and youth, gives myrrh in an urn of striped marble. The child responds with a blessing. The black background brings out the rich colors. *(© The J. Paul Getty Museum, Los Angeles. Mantegna, Andrea,* Adoration of the Magi, *ca 1495–1505, distemper on linen, 54.6 × 70.7 cm [85.PA.417])*

class often had themselves painted in a scene of romantic chivalry or courtly society. Rather than reflecting a spiritual ideal, as medieval painting and sculpture tended to do, Renaissance portraits mirrored reality. The Florentine painter Giotto (1276–1337) led the way in the use of realism; his treatment of the human body and face replaced the formal stiffness and artificiality that had for so long characterized representation of the human body. The sculptor Donatello (1386–1466) probably exerted the greatest influence of any Florentine artist before Michelangelo. His many statues express an appreciation of the incredible variety of human nature. Whereas medieval artists had depicted the nude human body only in a spiritualized and moralizing context, Donatello revived the classical figure, with its balance and self-awareness. The short-lived Florentine Masaccio (1401–1428), sometimes called the father of modern painting, inspired a new style characterized by great realism, narrative power, and remarkably effective use of light and dark. As important as realism was the new "international style," so called be-

**Renaissance Wedding Chest (Tuscany, late fifteenth century)** A wedding chest was a gift from the groom's family to the bride. Appreciated more for their decorative value than for practical storage purposes, these chests were prominently displayed in people's homes. This 37" × 47" × 28" chest is carved with scenes from classical mythology. *(Marriage chest with Ceres, Goddess of Agriculture searching for her abducted daughter, Prosperpina. Philadelphia Museum of Art. Purchased with the Joseph E. Temple Fund)*

cause of the wandering careers of influential artists, the close communications and rivalry of princely courts, and the increased trade in works of art. Rich color, decorative detail, curvilinear rhythms, and swaying forms characterized the international style. As the term *international* implies, this style was European, not merely Italian.

Narrative artists depicted the body in a more scientific and natural manner. The female figure is voluptuous and sensual. The male body, as in Michelangelo's *David* and *The Last Judgment,* is strong and heroic. Renaissance glorification of the human body revealed the secular spirit of the age. Filippo Brunelleschi (1377–1446) and Piero della Francesca (1420–1492) seem to have pioneered *perspective* in painting, the linear representation of distance and space on a flat surface. *The Last Supper* by Leonardo da Vinci, with its stress on the tension between Christ and the disciples, is an incredibly subtle psychological interpretation.

## The Status of the Artist

In the Renaissance, the social status of the artist improved. Whereas the lower-middle-class medieval master mason had been viewed in the same light as a mechanic, the Renaissance artist was considered a free intellectual worker. Artists did not produce unsolicited pictures or statues for the general public; that could mean loss of status. They usually worked on commission from a powerful prince. The artist's reputation depended on the support of powerful patrons, and through them some artists and architects achieved not only economic security but also very great wealth.

Lorenzo Ghiberti's salary of 200 florins a year compared very favorably with that of the head of the city government, who earned 500 florins. Moreover, at a time when a person could live in a princely fashion on 300 ducats a year, Leonardo da Vinci was making 2,000 annually.[13]

Renaissance society respected and rewarded the distinguished artist. In 1537 the prolific letter writer, humanist, and satirizer of princes Pietro Aretino (1492–1556) wrote to Michelangelo while he was painting *The Last Judgment* behind the altar in the Sistine Chapel:

*To the Divine Michelangelo:*
*Sir, just as it is disgraceful and sinful to be unmindful of God so it is reprehensible and dishonourable for any man of discerning judgment not to honour you as a brilliant and venerable artist whom the very stars use as a target at which to shoot the rival arrows of their favour. . . . It is surely my duty to honour you with this salutation, since the world has many kings but only one Michelangelo.*[14]

**Gentile and Giovanni Bellini: Saint Mark Preaching in Alexandria (1504–1507)** Reliable evidence does not support the tradition that Saint Mark preached and died in Alexandria, nor did either of the Bellinis ever visit there. Rather, they confected this painting from Gentile's stay in Constantinople, general information derived from Venice's long commercial contacts with Egypt, and their imagination. With a group of Venetians behind him, Saint Mark on a platform preaches to a group of heavily veiled Muslim women, behind whom stand Asian figures mingling with Europeans. A domed basilica reminiscent of Saint Mark's in Venice and of Sancta Sophia with minarets in Constantinople forms the background. The painting glorifies cosmopolitan Venice's patron saint, but the artists also wanted to acknowledge that Islamic society possessed not only commodities but scientific knowledge and business techniques more sophisticated than those in the West. *(Scala/Art Resource, NY)*

When Holy Roman Emperor Charles V (r. 1519–1556) visited the workshop of the great Titian (1477–1576) and stooped to pick up the artist's dropped paintbrush, the emperor was demonstrating that the patron himself was honored in the act of honoring the artist.

Renaissance artists were not only aware of their creative power; they also boasted about it. Describing his victory over five others, including Brunelleschi, in the competition to design the bronze doors of Florence's Baptistry, Ghiberti exulted, "The palm of victory was conceded to me by all the experts and by all my fellow-competitors. By universal consent and without a single exception the glory was conceded to me."[15] Some medieval painters and sculptors had signed their works; Renaissance artists almost universally did so, and many of them incorporated self-portraits, usually as bystanders, in their paintings.

The Renaissance, in fact, witnessed the birth of the concept of the artist as genius. In the Middle Ages, people believed that only God created, albeit through individuals; the medieval conception recognized no particular value in artistic originality. Renaissance artists and humanists came to think that a work of art was the deliberate creation of a unique personality who transcended traditions, rules, and theories. A genius had a peculiar gift, which ordinary laws should not inhibit. Cosimo de' Medici described a painter, because of his genius, as "divine," implying that the artist shared in the powers of God. The word *divine* was widely applied to Michelangelo. (See the feature "Individuals in Society: Leonardo da Vinci.")

But students must guard against interpreting Italian Renaissance culture in twenty-first-century democratic terms. The culture of the Renaissance was that of a small mercantile elite, a business patriciate with aristocratic pretensions. Renaissance culture did not directly affect the broad middle classes, let alone the vast urban proletariat. A small, highly educated minority of literary humanists and artists created the culture of and for an exclusive elite. The Renaissance maintained a gulf between

# Individuals in Society

## Leonardo da Vinci

What makes a genius? An infinite capacity for taking pains? A deep curiosity about an extensive variety of subjects? A divine spark as manifested by talents that far exceed the norm? Or is it just "one percent inspiration and ninety-nine percent perspiration," as Thomas Edison said? By whatever criteria, Leonardo da Vinci was one of the greatest geniuses in the history of the Western world.

He was born in Vinci, near Florence, the illegitimate son of Caterina, a local peasant girl, and Ser Piero da Vinci, a notary public. Caterina later married another native of Vinci. When Ser Piero's marriage to Donna Albrussia produced no children, they took in Leonardo, who remained with them until Ser Piero secured Leonardo's apprenticeship with the painter and sculptor Andrea del Verrocchio. In 1472, when Leonardo was just twenty years old, he was listed as a master in Florence's "Company of Artists."

Leonardo contributed to the modern concept of the artist as an original thinker and as a special kind of human being: an isolated figure with exceptional creative powers. Leonardo's portrait *Ginevra de' Benci* anticipates his most famous portrait, *Mona Lisa,* with the enigmatic smile that Giorgio Vasari described as "so pleasing that it seemed divine rather than human." Leonardo's experimental method of fresco painting of *The Last Supper* caused the picture to deteriorate rapidly, but it has been called "the most revered painting in the world." To the annoyance of his patrons, none of these paintings was ever completed to Leonardo's satisfaction. For example, *The Last Supper* was left unfinished because he could not find a model for the face of Christ that would evoke the spiritual depth he felt it deserved.

Leonardo once said that "a painter is not admirable unless he is universal." He left notes and plans on drawing, painting, sculpture, music, architecture, town planning, optics, astronomy, biology, zoology, mathematics, and various branches of engineering, such as a model for a submarine, designs for tank warfare, and cranes for dredging. These drafts suggest the astonishing versatility of his mind. One authority has said that Leonardo "saw art from the scientific point of view and science from the artist's point of view."

Vasari described Leonardo as a handsome man with a large body and physical grace, a "sparkling conversationalist" talented at singing while accompanying himself on the lyre. According to Vasari, "his genius was so wonderfully inspired by God, his powers of expression so powerfully fed by a willing memory and intellect . . . that his arguments confounded the most formidable critics."

In a famous essay, the Viennese psychiatrist Sigmund Freud argued that Leonardo was a homosexual who sublimated, pouring his sexual energy into his art. Freud wrote that it is doubtful that Leonardo ever touched a woman or even had an intimate spiritual relationship with one. Although as a master artist he surrounded himself with handsome young men and even had a long emotional relationship with one, Francesco Melzi, the evidence suggests that his male relationships never resulted in sexual activity. On a page of his *Codex Atlanticus,* which includes his sketch of the Florentine navigator Amerigo Vespucci, Leonardo wrote, "Intellectual passion drives out sensuality." For Freud, Leonardo transferred his psychic energy into artistic and scientific study. This thesis has attracted much attention, but no one has refuted it.

*Leonardo da Vinci,* Lady with an Ermine. *The whiteness of the ermine's fur symbolizes purity.* (Czartoryski Museum, Krakow/ The Bridgeman Art Library)

Leonardo worked in Milan for the despot Ludovico Sforza, planning a gigantic equestrian statue in honor of Ludovico's father, Duke Francesco Sforza. The clay model collapsed, and only notes survived. Leonardo also worked as a military engineer for Cesare Borgia (see page 416). In 1516 he accepted King Francis I's invitation to France. At the French court and in the presence of his faithful companion Francesco Melzi, Leonardo died in the arms of the king.

### Questions for Analysis

1. How would you explain Leonardo's genius?
2. Consider sublimation as a source of artistic and scientific creativity.

*Sources:* Giorgio Vasari, *Lives of the Artists,* vol. 1, trans. G. Bull (London: Penguin Books, 1965); S. B. Nuland, *Leonardo da Vinci* (New York: Lipper/Viking, 2000); Sigmund Freud, *Leonardo da Vinci: A Study in Psychosexuality* (New York: Random House, 1947).

*The* **history companion** *features additional information and activities related to this topic.*
**history.college.hmco.com/students**

the learned minority and the uneducated multitude that has survived for many centuries.

## Social Change

Renaissance ideals permeated educational theory and practice and political thought. The era's most stunning technological invention, printing, affected many forms of social life. Renaissance culture witnessed a shift in the status and experience of women. Slaves also played a role in Renaissance society.

### Education and Political Thought

One of the central preoccupations of the humanists was education and moral behavior. Humanists poured out treatises, often in the form of letters, on the structure and goals of education and the training of rulers. In one of the earliest systematic programs for the young, Peter Paul Vergerio (1370–1444) wrote Ubertinus, the ruler of Carrara:

*For the education of children is a matter of more than private interest; it concerns the State, which indeed regards the right training of the young as, in certain aspects, within its proper sphere. . . . Tutors and comrades alike should be chosen from amongst those likely to bring out the best qualities, to attract by good example, and to repress the first signs of evil. . . . Above all, respect for Divine ordinances is of the deepest importance; it should be inculcated from the earliest years. Reverence towards elders and parents is an obligation closely akin.*

*We call those studies liberal which are worthy of a free man; those studies by which we attain and practice virtue and wisdom.*[16]

Part of Vergerio's treatise specifies subjects for the instruction of young men in public life: history teaches virtue by examples from the past, ethics focuses on virtue itself, and rhetoric or public speaking trains for eloquence.

No book on education had broader influence than Baldassare Castiglione's *The Courtier* (1528). This treatise sought to train, discipline, and fashion the young man into the courtly ideal, the gentleman. According to Castiglione, the educated man of the upper class should have a broad background in many academic subjects, and his spiritual and physical as well as intellectual capabilities should be trained. The courtier should have easy familiarity with dance, music, and the arts. Castiglione envisioned a man who could compose a sonnet, wrestle, sing a song and accompany himself on an instrument, ride expertly, solve difficult mathematical problems, and, above all, speak and write eloquently.

In the sixteenth and seventeenth centuries, *The Courtier* was widely read. It influenced the social mores and patterns of conduct of elite groups in Renaissance and early modern Europe. The courtier became the model of the European gentleman.

In the cities of Renaissance Italy, well-to-do girls received an education similar to boys'. Young ladies learned their letters and studied the classics. Many read Greek as well as Latin, knew the poetry of Ovid and Virgil, and could speak one or two "modern" languages, such as French or Spanish. In this respect, Renaissance humanism represented a real educational advance for women. Some women, though a small minority among humanists, acquired great learning and fame. (See the feature "Listening to the Past: Christine de Pisan" on pages 410–411.) In the later sixteenth century, at least twenty-five women published books in Italy, Sofonisba Anguissola (1530–1625) and Artemisia Gentileschi (1593–1653) achieved international renown for their paintings, and Isabella Andreini (1562–1604) enjoyed a reputation as the greatest actress of her day.

Humanist Laura Cereta (1469–1499) illustrates the successes and failures of educated Renaissance women. Educated by her father, who was a member of the governing elite of Brescia in Lombardy, she learned languages, philosophy, theology, and mathematics. She also gained self-confidence and a healthy respect for her own potential. By the age of fifteen, when she married, her literary career was already launched, as her letters to several cardinals attest. For Laura Cereta, however, as for all educated women of the period, the question of marriage forced the issue: she could choose a husband, family, and full participation in social life or study and withdrawal from the world. Marriage brought domestic responsibilities and usually prevented women from fulfilling their scholarly potential. Although Cereta chose marriage, she was widowed at eighteen, and she spent the remaining twelve years of her life in study. But she had to bear the envy of other women and the hostility of men who felt threatened. In response, Cereta condemned "empty women, who strive for no good but exist to adorn themselves. . . . These women of majestic pride, fantastic coiffures, outlandish ornament, and necks bound with gold or pearls bear the glittering symbols of their captivity to men." For Laura Cereta, women's inferiority was derived not from the divine order of things but from women themselves: "For knowledge is not given as a gift, but through study. . . . The free mind, not afraid of labor, presses on to attain the good."[17] Despite Cereta's faith in women's potential, men frequently believed that in becoming learned, a woman violated nature and thus ceased to be a woman.

Laura Cereta was a prodigy. Ordinary girls of the urban upper middle class, in addition to a classical education, received some training in painting, music, and dance. What were they to do with this training? They were to be gracious, affable, charming—in short, decorative. So although Renaissance women were better educated than their medieval counterparts, their education prepared them for the social functions of the home. An educated woman was supposed to know how to attract artists and literati to her husband's court and how to grace her husband's household, whereas an educated man was supposed to know how to rule and participate in public affairs.

No Renaissance book on any topic, however, has been more widely read and studied in all the centuries since its publication (1513) than the short political treatise ***The Prince,*** by Niccolò Machiavelli (1469–1527). The subject of *The Prince* is political power: how the ruler should gain, maintain, and increase it. Machiavelli implicitly addresses the question of the citizen's relationship to the state. As a good humanist, he explores the problems of human nature and concludes that human beings are selfish and out to advance their own interests. This pessimistic view of humanity led him to maintain that the prince may have to manipulate the people in any way he finds necessary:

*For a man who, in all respects, will carry out only his professions of good, will be apt to be ruined amongst so many who are evil. A prince therefore who desires to maintain himself must learn to be not always good, but to be so or not as necessity may require.*[18]

The prince should combine the cunning of a fox with the ferocity of a lion to achieve his goals. Asking rhetorically whether it is better for a ruler to be loved or feared, Machiavelli writes: "It will naturally be answered that it would be desirable to be both the one and the other; but as it is difficult to be both at the same time, it is much more safe to be feared than to be loved, when you have to choose between the two."[19]

Medieval political theory had derived ultimately from Saint Augustine's view that the state arose as a consequence of Adam's fall and people's propensity to sin. The test of good government was whether it provided justice, law, and order. Political theorists and theologians from Alcuin to Marsiglio of Padua had stressed the way government *ought* to be; they had set high moral and Christian standards for the ruler's conduct.

Machiavelli maintained that the ruler should be concerned not with the way things ought to be but with the way things actually are. The sole test of a "good" government is whether it is effective, whether the ruler increases his power. Machiavelli did not advocate amoral behavior, but he believed that political action cannot be restricted by moral considerations. While amoral action might be the most effective approach in a given situation, he did not argue for generally amoral, rather than moral, behavior. Nevertheless, on the basis of a crude interpretation of *The Prince,* the word *Machiavellian* entered the language as a synonym for the politically devious, corrupt, and crafty, indicating actions in which the end justifies the means. The ultimate significance of Machiavelli rests on two ideas: first, that one permanent social order reflecting God's will cannot be established, and second, that politics has its own laws and ought to be a science.[20]

## The Printed Word

Sometime in the thirteenth century, paper money and playing cards from China reached the West. They were *block-printed*—that is, Chinese characters or pictures were carved into a wooden block, the block was inked, and the words or illustrations were transferred to paper. Since each word, phrase, or picture was on a separate block, this method of reproduction was extraordinarily expensive and time-consuming.

Around 1454, probably through the combined efforts of three men—Johann Gutenberg, Johann Fust, and Peter Schöffer, all experimenting at Mainz—movable type came into being. The mirror image of each letter (rather than entire words or phrases) was carved in relief on a small block. Individual letters, easily movable, were put together to form words; words separated by blank spaces formed lines of type; and lines of type were brought together to make up a page. Since letters could be arranged into any format, an infinite variety of texts could be printed by reusing and rearranging pieces of type.

By the middle of the fifteenth century, acquiring paper was no problem. The knowledge of paper manufacture had originated in China, and the Arabs introduced it to the West in the twelfth century (see page 286). Europeans quickly learned that durable paper was far less expensive than the vellum (calfskin) and parchment (sheepskin) on which medieval scribes had relied for centuries.

The effects of the invention of movable-type printing were not felt overnight. Nevertheless, within a half century of the publication of Gutenberg's Bible of 1456,

**The Print Shop** Sixteenth-century printing involved a division of labor. Two persons (*left*) at separate benches set the pieces of type. Another (*center, rear*) inks the chase (or locked plate containing the set type). Yet another (*right*) operates the press, which prints the sheets. The boy removes the printed pages and sets them to dry. Meanwhile, a man carries in fresh paper on his head. *(Giraudon/Art Resource, NY)*

movable type had brought about radical changes. Printing transformed both the private and the public lives of Europeans (see Map 13.2). Governments that "had employed the cumbersome methods of manuscripts to communicate with their subjects switched quickly to print to announce declarations of war, publish battle accounts, promulgate treaties or argue disputed points in pamphlet form. Theirs was an effort 'to win the psychological war.'" Printing made propaganda possible, emphasizing differences between opposing groups, such as Crown and nobility, church and state. These differences laid the basis for the formation of distinct political parties. Printed materials reached an invisible public, allowing silent individuals to join causes and groups of individuals widely separated by geography to form a common identity; this new group consciousness could compete with older, localized loyalties.[21]

Printing also stimulated the literacy of laypeople and eventually came to have a deep effect on their private lives. Although most of the earliest books and pamphlets dealt with religious subjects, students, housewives, businessmen, and upper- and middle-class people sought books on all subjects. Printers responded with moralizing, medical, practical, and travel manuals. Pornography as well as piety assumed new forms. For example, satirist Pietro Aretino (1492–1556) used the shock of sex in pornography as a vehicle to criticize: his *Sonnetti Lussuriosi* (1527) and *Ragionamenti* (1534–1536), sonnets accompanying sixteen engravings of as many sexual positions, attacked princely court life, humanist education, and false clerical piety.[22] Broadsides and flysheets allowed great public festivals, religious ceremonies, and political events to be experienced vicariously by the stay-at-home. Since books and other printed materials were read aloud to illiterate listeners, print bridged the gap between written and oral cultures.

## Clocks

The English word *quantification* was first used in 1840, but five centuries earlier, before the invention of movable type, Europeans learned how to quantify, or measure, time with the mechanical clock. Who invented the clock remains a subject of scientific debate. Between A.D. 700 and 1000, Arabs relied on the sundial, using their knowledge of astronomy to correct for the varying motion of the sun during the course of the year. The Arabs knew that the length of daylight, caused by the changing distance between the earth and the sun as the earth moves in elliptical orbit, varies with the seasons. Chinese knowledge of mechanical clocks may have allowed Gerbert, later Pope Sylvester II (999–1003), to build the first mechanical clock in the West.

The English word *clock* resembles the French *cloche* and the German *Glocke,* all meaning "bells." In monastic

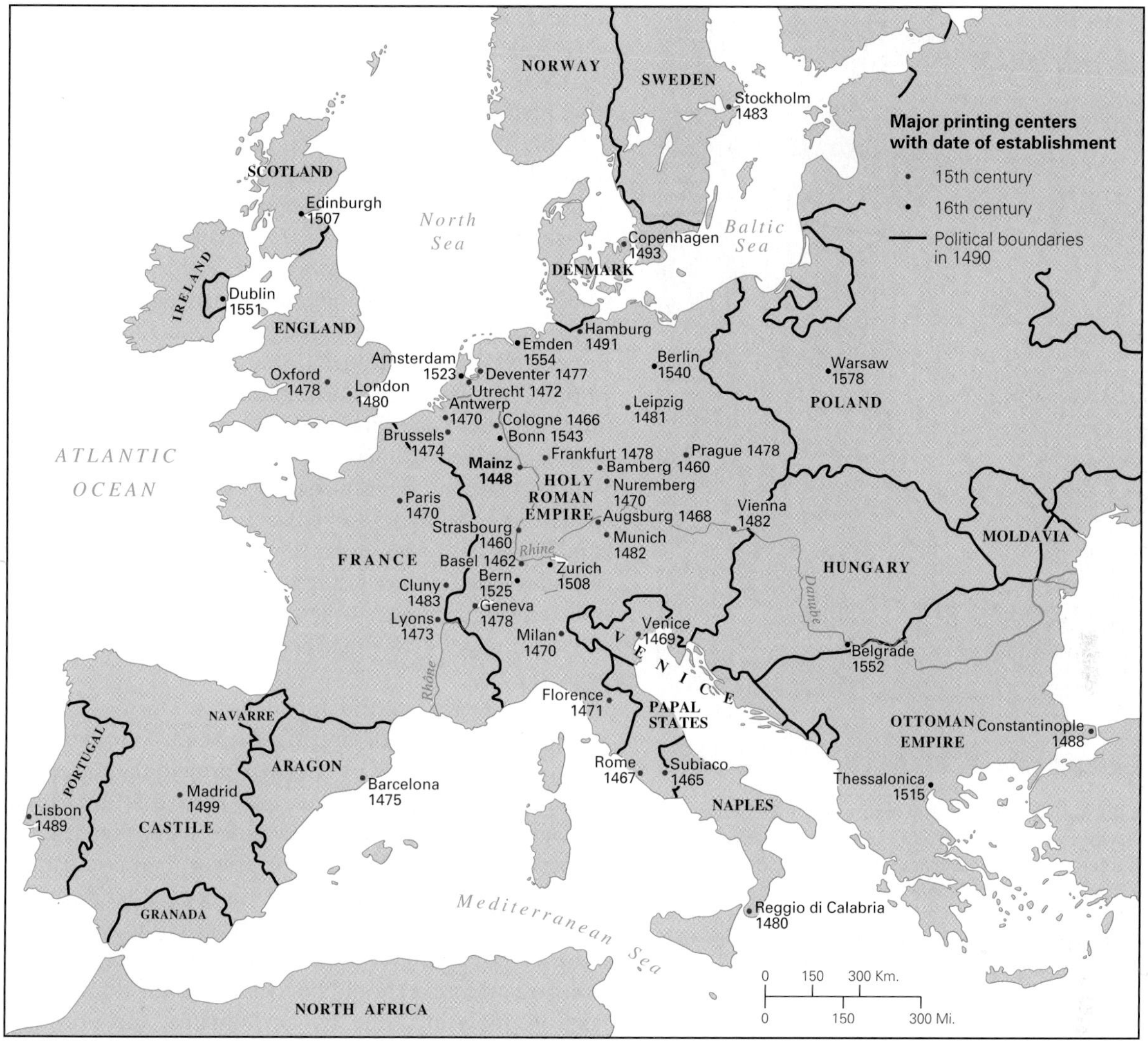


**MAP 13.2 The Growth of Printing in Europe** Although many commercial and academic centers developed printing technology, the press at Venice, employing between four hundred and five hundred people and producing one-eighth of all printed books, was by far the largest in Europe.

houses, bells determined the times for the recitation of the Hours, the Work of God. Bells also paced the life of the rural world nearby, but country people needed only approximate times—dawn, noon, sunset—for their work. The measurement of time played a much more urgent role for *city* people.

Buying and selling goods had initiated city people into the practice of quantification: they needed precise measurement of the day's hours. City people's time was what the American polymath Benjamin Franklin later called it: money. In the Italian cities, clocks must have been widespread, since the poet Dante, writing about 1320, took them for granted. Mechanical clocks, usually installed on the cathedral or town church, were in general use in Germany by the 1330s, in England by the 1370s, and in France by the 1380s.[23]

Clocks contributed to the development of a mentality that conceived of the universe in visual and quantitative terms. Measuring the world brought not only understanding of it but the urge to control it. The mechanical clock enabled Europeans to divide time into equal hours, allowing the working day to be fixed in both winter and

**Mechanical Clock** Slowly falling weights provide the force that pushes the figures' arms to strike the bells on the quarter-hour in this sixteenth-century German clock. The sound of a machine now marked time. *(Biblíothèque royale Albert 1er, Brussels)*

summer. The Maya in Central America and the Chinese had theoretical knowledge of time, but Europeans put that knowledge to practical use. Along with cannon and printing, clocks gave Europeans technological advantages over other peoples.[24]

## Women and Work

Early modern cultural values identified women with marriage and the domestic activities of the home. Revisionist scholarship today stresses that women's economic roles must include reproduction—defined not only as child-bearing but as everything connected with the care and nurturing of family members. In preindustrial societies, the production of goods often took place in the home in the intervals when women were not engaged in specific domestic chores; all family members benefited from that work. Women also worked outside the household. In whatever economic activity they engaged in, women were considered as "married or to be married." Their work was valued less than men's, and they earned half of what men did even for the same work.[25]

In the Venetian Arsenal, the state-controlled dock and shipbuilding area (the largest single industrial plant in Europe and the builder of the biggest fleet) women made the ships' sails. Women were heavily involved in the Florentine textile industry, weaving cloth and reeling and winding silk. In the 1560s, a woman named Suzanne Erkur managed the imperial silver mint at Kutná Hora in Bohemia. Women conducted the ferry service across the Rhône River at Lyons. Throughout Europe rural women assisted fathers and husbands in the many agricultural tasks, and urban women helped in shops and businesses. Widows often ran their husbands' establishments. Tens of thousands of women worked as midwives, maids, cooks, laundresses, and household servants. From the port city of Dubrovnik (formerly Ragusa) on the Dalmatian coast came tens of thousands of female slaves to enter domestic service in upper-class households throughout Italy[26] (see page 436).

What of women of the upper classes? During the Renaissance, the status of upper-class women declined. In terms of the kind of work they performed, their access to property and political power, and their role in shaping the outlook of their society, women in the Renaissance ruling classes generally had less power than comparable women in the feudal age. As mentioned earlier (see page 429), well-to-do girls generally received an education, but even so, men everywhere held the conviction that a woman's attention should be focused on the domestic affairs of family life. The Italian humanist and polymath Leon Battista Alberti (1404–1472), discussing morality in his *On the Family,* stressed that a wife's role should be restricted to the orderliness of the household, food and the serving of meals, the education of children, and the supervision of servants. The Spanish humanist Juan Luis Vives (1492–1540), in his *Instruction of the Christian Woman,* held that a woman's sphere should be the home, not the public arena, where she might compete with men. The English statesman Sir Thomas Smith (1513–1577) wrote in *The English Commonwealth* that women were "those whom nature hath made to keepe home and to nourish the familie and children, and not to meddle with affairs abroad."[27] Wealthy women might support charitable organizations, but men denied them any sort of political or legal activity.

Excluded from the public arena, the noblewoman or spouse of a rich merchant managed the household where

**Working Women** Women did virtually every kind of work in Renaissance Europe. They often sold food, cloth, handmade jewelry, trinkets, and other merchandise in the town marketplace, just as many women in developing countries do today. *(Scala/Art Resource, NY)*

the husband displayed his wealth and power (the larger the number of servants and retainers, the greater his prestige). Households depended on domestic servants, and the lady of the house had to have the shrewdness and managerial prudence to employ capable cooks, maids, tailors and seamstresses, laundresses, gardeners, coachmen, stable hands, nurses, and handymen. If a prosperous Florentine or Venetian merchant's household had fifteen to twenty servants, a great lord or a Medici banker could easily employ four times that number. The lady of the house had to make sure that all these people were adequately fed and clothed; to maintain harmony among them; to tend anyone who fell ill, meaning that she must have at least a rudimentary knowledge of medications; and to look after the girl who "accidentally" became pregnant and then her child. Custom also laid on the lady the responsibility for providing the servants with religious instruction. Then there was the education of her own children and possibly the care of aged or infirm in-laws. Her husband expected her to entertain (which, depending on his position, could be an elaborate and complicated undertaking) and preside over each occasion with grace and, if possible, charm. All of these burdens, in addition to her own pregnancies, added up to an enormous responsibility.

## Culture and Sexuality

With respect to love and sex, the Renaissance witnessed a downward shift in women's status. In contrast to the medieval tradition of relative sexual equality, Renaissance humanists laid the foundations for the bourgeois double standard. Castiglione, the foremost spokesman of Renaissance love and manners, completely separated love from sexuality. For women, sex was restricted entirely to marriage. Women were bound to chastity and then to the roles of wife and mother in a politically arranged marriage. Men, however, could pursue sensual indulgence outside marriage.[28]

Official attitudes toward rape provide an index of the status of women in the Renaissance. According to a study of the legal evidence from Venice in the years 1338 to 1358, rape was not considered a particularly serious crime against either the victim or society. Noble youths

**Artemesia Gentileschi: Judith Slaying Holofernes** The Old Testament Book of Judith tells the tale of the beautiful widow Judith, who first charms and then decapitates the Assyrian general Holofernes, thus saving Israel. The message is that trust in God will bring deliverance. The talented Roman artist Artemesia Gentileschi (1593–1652/3), elected to the Florentine Academy of Design at age twenty-three, rendered the story in this dramatic and gruesome painting, whose light and gushing blood give it great power. Some scholars hold that the painting is Gentileschi's pictorial revenge for her alleged rape by the decorative artist Agostino Tassi. *(Uffizi, Florence/Alinari/Art Resource, NY)*

committed a higher percentage of rapes than their small numbers in Venetian society would imply. The rape of a young girl of marriageable age or a child under twelve was considered a graver crime than the rape of a married woman. Nevertheless, the punishment for rape of a noble, marriageable girl was only a fine or about six months' imprisonment. In an age when theft and robbery were punished by mutilation, and forgery and sodomy by burning, this penalty was very mild indeed. When a youth of the upper class was convicted of the rape of a non-noble girl, his punishment was even lighter. By contrast, the sexual assault of a noblewoman by a working-class man, which was extraordinarily rare, resulted in severe penalization because the crime had social and political overtones.[29]

A new study of country women based on fifteenth-century Florentine court records raises interesting questions but provides inconclusive evidence about women's condition. These records read like twenty-first-century tabloids, with virtually every sensational criminal activity: incest, wife beatings, sexual assaults on children and nuns, murders provoked by adulterous relationships. For instance, one priest had a long love affair with a married woman and hired a "hit man" to kill the husband. Indicted for homicide and adultery, the priest was decapitated. In another case, while his wife was out shopping, middle-aged Muccino raped his eleven-year-old niece. The court ordered Muccino whipped with branches to the place of justice, where his penis was mutilated. The courts saw sexual crimes as "originating in bodily parts that had to be punished or removed."[30] But sexual crimes, however broadly defined, never constituted more than 5 percent of the courts' annual caseload. Fewer women appear in these fifteenth-century records than had appeared in similar records a century earlier. Why? We do not know.[31]

The term *homosexuality* was coined only in 1892, but erotic activity with a person of the same sex goes back very far in human history (see pages 79, 200–202). Medieval and Renaissance people used two terms concerning such activity: *sodomy,* meaning all sexual acts between persons of the same sex, whether male with male or female with female, and *sexual acts against nature,* meaning any act that did not lead to conception.[32] When early modern Italians used the term *sodomite,* they usually had males in mind, partly because those acts were most conspicuous, partly because theological and "scientific" teaching held that women could not have erotic pleasure without a man. While we tend to classify people according to the gender of their sexual partners, Renaissance people did not frame their understanding and representation of sexuality on this basis.

In the cities of Renaissance Italy, the sermons of the Franciscan Bernardino of Siena (1380–1444) and the Dominican Savonarola (1452–1498) severely condemned sodomitical activities, and civil authorities seem to have been preoccupied with it: Siena passed legislation against it in 1425, Venice in 1496, Florence in 1415, 1418, 1432, 1494, and 1542.[33] When a law is repeatedly put on the statute books, it is not observed or cannot be enforced. How prevalent was homosexuality? Florence provides a provocative case study.

On April 17, 1432, the Florentine government set up a special magistracy, the Office of the Night, to "root out . . . the abominable vice of sodomy." This board of professional men at least forty-five years of age and married was elected annually and charged with pursuing and punishing sodomitical activity between males.[34] The name of the magistracy derived from the nocturnal activities of most male encounters, especially in the spring and summer months, and on feast days and Sundays. Between 1432 and the abolition of the magistracy in 1502, about seventeen thousand men came to its attention, which, even over a seventy-year period, represents a great number in a population of about forty thousand. Sodomy was not a marginal practice.

**Thirteenth-Century Moral Code** This illustration, from a French book of morals, interprets female and male homosexuality as the work of devils; modern science offers other explanations. *(Österreichische Nationalbibliothek)*

Moreover, careful and statistical analysis of judicial records shows that all classes of society engaged in it—those in the textile trade, in commerce, in education, and in the food industry, especially butchers, as well as construction workers, tavern keepers, and innkeepers. Evidence also reveals that adult males rarely had sex together, or if they did, it did not come to the Office of the Night's attention. Rather, boys were the objects of desire. These roles carried cultural values. Florentines believed in a generational model in which different roles were appropriate to different stages in life. In a socially and sexually hierarchical world, the boy in the passive role was identified as subordinate, dependent, and mercenary, words usually applied to women. Florentines, however, never described the dominant partner in feminine terms, for he had not compromised his masculine identity or violated a gender ideal. Only if an adult male assumed the passive role was his masculinity jeopardized. Such cases were extremely rare.[35]

Why was this kind of sexual activity so common? The evidence offers a variety of explanations. First among these is the general seclusion of "respectable" women and the late marriages of men. Perhaps 30 percent of the adult male population never married because many men were clerics, and three-fourths of the men who eventually wed postponed marriage, largely for economic reasons, until about age thirty-two. An occasional sexual experience with a boy did not preclude sex with women. Other explanations include the construction of male identity and of forms of male sociability.

In 1476 an informer denounced the carpenter Piero di Bartolomeo for sexual relations with Bartolomeo di Jacopo, son of a grocer. When interrogated, fifteen-year-old Bartolomeo di Jacopo confessed that Piero "did [this] out of great love and good brotherhood, because they are in a confraternity together, and he did as good neighbors do." Bartolomeo di Jacopo understood their relationship as being based on the traditional emotional bonds between members of their confraternity and neighborhood associations.[36]

Other explanations for youthful homoerotic activity include the desire for gifts, money, or some material reward from the adult partner; parental complicity in urging attractive teenage sons to accept the attentions of wealthy suitors; the need for companionship and same-age cohorts—that is, peer pressure; gang rapes; and soldiers' demands that youthful servants satisfy their sexual needs. Sex among males—kinsmen, neighbors, coworkers, and groups of friends—fashioned the collective male experience. Homoerotic relationships played important roles in defining stages of life, expressing distinctions of status, and shaping masculine gender identity.[37]

## Slavery and Ethnicity

The French historian Marc Bloch once observed that "Western and Central Europe, taken as a whole, were never free of slaves during the High Middle Ages."[38] In central and eastern Europe, where political conditions were very unstable and permitted the enslavement of pagans, slavery allowed strong lords to satisfy cheaply the needs of their estates; slaves also offered merchants a commodity for profitable exchange with foreigners. Thus, in the period of eastward expansion (see Chapter 12), German lords seized Polish and Bohemian peoples; used them as agricultural laborers, domestics, and concubines; and sold the rest. In the thirteenth century, Prague was a large slave market. The word *slave* always carried a definite ethnic connotation: it meant an unfree person of Slavic background.[39]

In the fourteenth century, Genoa and Venice dominated the Mediterranean slave trade. The labor shortage caused by the Black Death led to the flow of Russians, Tartars, and Circassian slaves from Azov in the Crimea and of Serbs, Albanians, Greeks, and Hungarians from the Balkans. Venetian control of the northern regions of the Dalmatian coast enabled Venetian slavers to import large numbers of female slaves from the port city of Dubrovnik.[40] All of these people, Slavic but of different ethnic backgrounds, gradually intermingled with the native Italian population.

Ever since the time of the Roman republic, a few black people had lived in western Europe. They had come, along with white slaves, as the spoils of war. Even after the collapse of the Roman Empire, Muslim and Christian merchants continued to import them. The evidence of medieval art attests to the presence of Africans in Europe and to Europeans' awareness of them.

As in Slavic regions, unstable political conditions in many parts of Africa enabled enterprising merchants to seize people and sell them into slavery. Local authorities afforded them no protection. Long tradition, moreover, sanctioned the practice of slavery. Beginning in the fifteenth century, sizable numbers of black slaves entered Europe. Portuguese explorers imported perhaps a thousand a year and sold them at the markets of Seville, Barcelona, Marseilles, and Genoa. By the mid-sixteenth century, blacks, slave and free, constituted about 10 percent of the populations of the Portuguese cities of Lisbon and Évora; other cities had smaller percentages. In all, blacks made up roughly 3 percent of the Portuguese population. The Venetians specialized in the importation of white slaves, but blacks were so greatly in demand at the Renaissance courts of northern Italy that the Venetians defied papal threats of excommunication to secure them. Although blacks were concentrated in the Iberian Peninsula, there must have been some Africans in northern Europe as well. In the 1580s, for example, Queen Elizabeth I of England complained that there were too many "blackamoores" competing with needy English people for places as domestic servants.[41]

What roles did blacks play in Renaissance society? Although few written records survive, obviously black slaves in Europe hated the loss of their freedom, separation from their societal roots, and forced labor without compensation. No doubt, too, they disliked the alien culture, the cold climate, and the strange foods. But so far as we know, few who managed to secure their freedom through manumission or escape chose to return to Africa. The lack of black slave revolts in Europe, so common in South and North America and in Africa under colonial rule, attests to the small numbers and wide dispersion of blacks and to a relatively benign pattern of slavery. Moreover, the legal definition of *slave* never took on the rigid character in Europe that it did in the United States.

**Carpaccio: Black Laborers on the Venetian Docks (detail)** Enslaved and free blacks, besides working as gondoliers on the Venetian canals, served on the docks: here seven black men careen—clean, caulk, and repair—a ship. Carpaccio's reputation as one of Venice's outstanding painters rests on his eye for details of everyday life. *(Gallerie dell'Accademia, Venice/Scala/Art Resource, NY)*

Within Africa, the economic goals of rulers and merchants took priority over any cultural, ethnic, or racial hostilities they may have felt toward Europeans. For example, in 1492 the king of the Congo learned of the arrival of Portuguese ships off the Congo estuary. He needed support in a local war and new resources; his biggest asset was a large concentration of slaves near his capital. So he accepted Christian baptism and began to exchange slaves for weapons and other Portuguese goods. His son Alfonso Mbemba Nzinga adopted a European lifestyle: he renamed his capital São Salvador; took on Portuguese dress, etiquette, and literacy; and assigned Portuguese titles to his officials and courtiers. Meanwhile, the flow of slaves from the region accelerated. Between 1500 and 1525, about seventeen hundred slaves a year were traded to the Portuguese. By 1530 between four thousand and five thousand were being sold to the Portuguese each year.[42] What does this tell us about Africans' attitudes toward white Europeans? First, obviously, the interests of African rulers and those of their peoples diverged considerably. Second, African rulers' and merchants' desire for revenue and goods was the driving force in the sale of black people to white Europeans.

Westerners tend to lump all sub-Saharan Africans into one category: black. However, Africans, like Europeans and Asians, belonged to and identified themselves by ethnic groups. In Africa, the world's second-largest continent, there were (and are) more than six hundred distinct ethnic groups. In addition, African slaves in the Iberian Peninsula (and elsewhere in Europe), like Slavic ones in Italy, intermingled with the people they lived among, and their offspring were, in fact, biracial.

However Africans may have been defined in Europe, black servants were much sought after, as the medieval interest in curiosities, the exotic, and the marvelous continued into the Renaissance. In the late fifteenth century, Isabella, the wife of Gian Galazzo Sforza, took pride in the fact that she owned ten blacks, seven of them females. A black lady's maid was both a curiosity and a symbol of wealth. In 1491 Isabella of Este, duchess of Mantua, instructed her agent to secure a black girl between four and eight years old, "shapely and as black as possible." The duchess saw the child as a source of entertainment: "We shall make her very happy and shall have great fun with her." She hoped the girl would become "the best buffoon in the world,"[43] as the cruel ancient practice of a noble household retaining a professional "fool" for the family's amusement persisted through the Renaissance—and down to the twentieth century.

Adult black slaves served as maids, valets, and domestic servants. Italian aristocrats such as Marchesa Elena Grimaldi had their portraits painted with their black pageboys to indicate their wealth. The Venetians employed blacks—slave and free—as gondoliers and stevedores on the docks. In Portugal kings, nobles, laborers, monasteries and convents, and prostitutes owned slaves. They supplemented the labor force in virtually all occupations—as agricultural laborers, craftsmen, and seamen on ships going to Lisbon and Africa.[44] Tradition, stretching back at least as far as the thirteenth century, connected blacks with music and dance. In Renaissance Spain and Italy, blacks performed as dancers, as actors and actresses in courtly dramas, and as musicians, sometimes making up full orchestras.[45] Slavery during the Renaissance foreshadowed the American, especially the later Brazilian, pattern.

Before the sixteenth-century "discoveries" of the non-European world, Europeans had little concrete knowledge of Africans and their cultures. What Europeans did know was based on biblical accounts. The European attitude toward Africans was ambivalent. On the one hand, Europeans perceived Africa as a remote place, the home of strange people isolated by heresy and Islam from superior European civilization. Africans' contact, even as slaves, with Christian Europeans could only "improve" the blacks. Most Europeans' knowledge of the black as a racial type was based entirely on theological speculation. Theologians taught that God was light. Blackness, the opposite of light, therefore represented the hostile forces of the underworld: evil, sin, and the Devil. Thus the Devil was commonly represented as a black man in medieval and early Renaissance art (see the illustration on page 435). On the other hand, blackness possessed certain positive qualities. It symbolized the emptiness of worldly goods, the humility of the monastic way of life. Black clothes permitted a conservative and discreet display of wealth. Black vestments and funeral trappings indicated grief, and Christ had said that those who mourn are blessed. Until the exploration and observation of the sixteenth, seventeenth, and nineteenth centuries allowed, ever so slowly, for the development of more scientific knowledge, the Western conception of black people remained bound up with religious notions.[46] As for the sterile and meaningless concept of race, recent scholarship stresses that it emerged only in the late seventeenth century.[47] In Renaissance society, blacks, like women, were signs of wealth; both were used for display.

## The Renaissance in the North

See DBQ 1

In the last quarter of the fifteenth century, students from the Low Countries, France, Germany, and England flocked to Italy, imbibed the "new learning," and carried it back to their countries. Northern humanists interpreted Italian ideas about and attitudes toward classical antiquity, individualism, and humanism in terms of their own traditions. The cultural traditions of northern Europe tended to remain more distinctly Christian, or at least pietistic, than those of Italy. But in Italy, secular and pagan themes and Greco-Roman motifs received more humanistic attention. North of the Alps, the Renaissance had a distinctly religious character, and humanists stressed biblical and early Christian themes. What fundamentally distinguished Italian humanists from northern ones is that the latter had a program for broad social reform based on Christian ideals.

Christian humanists were interested in the development of an ethical way of life. To achieve it, they believed that the best elements of classical and Christian cultures should be combined. For example, the classical ideals of calmness, stoical patience, and broad-mindedness should be joined in human conduct with the Christian virtues of love, faith, and hope. Northern humanists also stressed the use of reason, rather than acceptance of dogma, as the foundation for an ethical way of life. Like the Italians, they were impatient with Scholastic philosophy. Christian humanists had a profound faith in the power of human intellect to bring about moral and institutional reform. They believed that, although human nature had been corrupted by sin, it was fundamentally good and capable of improvement through education.

The Englishman Thomas More (1478–1535) towered above other figures in sixteenth-century English social and intellectual history. Trained as a lawyer, More lived as a student in the London Charterhouse, a Carthusian monastery.

He subsequently married and practiced law but became deeply interested in the classics; his household served as a model of warm Christian family life and as a mecca for foreign and English humanists. In the career pattern of such Italian humanists as Petrarch, More entered government service under Henry VIII and was sent as ambassador to Flanders. There More found the time to write *Utopia* (1516), which presents a revolutionary view of society.

*Utopia,* which means "nowhere," describes an ideal socialistic community on an island somewhere off the mainland of the New World. All children receive a good education, primarily in the Greco-Roman classics, and learning does not cease with maturity, for the goal of all education is to develop rational faculties. Adults divide their days between manual labor or business pursuits and intellectual activities.

Because profits from business and property are held in common, there is absolute social equality. The Utopians use gold and silver to make chamber pots and to prevent wars by buying off their enemies. By this casual use of precious metals, More meant to suggest that the basic problems in society are caused by greed. Citizens of Utopia lead an ideal, nearly perfect existence because they live by reason; their institutions are perfect. More punned on the word *utopia,* which he termed "a good place. A good place which is no place."

More's ideas were profoundly original in the sixteenth century. Contrary to the long-prevailing view that vice and violence existed because women and men were basically corrupt, More maintained that acquisitiveness and private property promoted all sorts of vices and civil disorders. Since society protected private property, society's flawed institutions were responsible for corruption and war. According to More, the key to improvement and reform of the individual was reform of the social institutions that molded the individual. Today this view is so much taken for granted that it is difficult to appreciate how radical More's approach was in the sixteenth century.

Better known by contemporaries than Thomas More was the Dutch humanist Desiderius Erasmus (1466?–1536) of Rotterdam. Orphaned as a small boy, Erasmus was forced to enter a monastery. Although he hated the monastic life, he developed there an excellent knowledge of the Latin language and a deep appreciation for the Latin classics. During a visit to England in 1499, Erasmus met the scholar John Colet, who decisively influenced his life's work: the application of the best humanistic learning to the study and explanation of the Bible. As a mature scholar with an international reputation stretching from Cracow to London, a fame that rested largely on his exceptional knowledge of Greek, Erasmus could boast with truth, "I brought it about that humanism, which among the Italians . . . savored of nothing but pure paganism, began nobly to celebrate Christ."[48]

Erasmus's long list of publications includes *The Education of a Christian Prince* (1504), a book combining idealistic and practical suggestions for the formation of a ruler's character through the careful study of Plutarch, Aristotle, Cicero, and Plato; *The Praise of Folly* (1509), a satire of worldly wisdom and a plea for the simple and spontaneous Christian faith of children; and, most important, a critical edition of the Greek New Testament (1516). In the preface to the New Testament, Erasmus explained the purpose of his great work:

*For I utterly dissent from those who are unwilling that the sacred Scriptures should be read by the unlearned translated into their vulgar tongue, as though Christ had taught such subtleties that they can scarcely be understood even by a few theologians. . . . Christ wished his mysteries to be published as openly as possible. I wish that even the weakest woman should read the Gospel—should read the epistles of Paul. And I wish these were translated into all languages, so that they might be read and understood, not only by Scots and Irishmen, but also by Turks and Saracens.*[49]

Two fundamental themes run through all of Erasmus's work. First, education is the means to reform, the key to moral and intellectual improvement. The core of education ought to be study of the Bible and the classics. (See the feature "Listening to the Past: An Age of Gold" on pages 450–451.) Second, the essence of Erasmus's thought is, in his own phrase, "the philosophy of Christ." By this Erasmus meant that Christianity is an inner attitude of the heart or spirit. Christianity is not formalism, special ceremonies, or law; Christianity is Christ—his life and what he said and did, not what theologians have written. The Sermon on the Mount, for Erasmus, expresses the heart of the Christian message.

Whereas the writings of Erasmus and More have strong Christian themes and have drawn the attention primarily of scholars, the stories of French humanist François Rabelais (1490?–1553) possess a distinctly secular flavor and have attracted broad readership among the literate public. Rabelais's *Gargantua* and *Pantagruel* (serialized between 1532 and 1552) belong among the great comic masterpieces of world literature. These stories' gross and robust humor introduced the adjective *Rabelaisian* into the language.

*Gargantua* and *Pantagruel* can be read on several levels: as a comic romance about the adventures of the giant

**Rogier van der Weyden: Deposition** Taking as his subject the suffering and death of Jesus, a popular theme of Netherlandish piety, van der Weyden describes (in an inverted **T**) Christ's descent from the cross, surrounded by nine sorrowing figures. An appreciation of the human anatomy, the rich fabrics of the clothes, and the pierced and bloody hands of Jesus were all intended to touch the viewers' emotions. *(Museo del Prado/Scala/Art Resource, NY)*

Gargantua and his son, Pantagruel; as a spoof on contemporary French society; as a program for educational reform; or as an illustration of Rabelais's prodigious learning. The reader enters a world of Renaissance vitality, ribald joviality, and intellectual curiosity. In his travels, Gargantua meets various absurd characters, and within their hilarious exchanges occur serious discussions of religion, politics, philosophy, and education. Like More and Erasmus, Rabelais did not denounce institutions directly. Like Erasmus, Rabelais satirized hypocritical monks, pedantic academics, and pompous lawyers. But whereas Erasmus employed intellectual cleverness and sophisticated wit, Rabelais applied wild and gross humor. Like Thomas More, Rabelais believed that institutions molded individuals and that education was the key to a moral and healthy life. Whereas the middle-class inhabitants of More's Utopia lived lives of restrained moderation, the aristocratic residents of Rabelais's Thélèma lived for the gratification of their physical instincts and rational curiosity.

The distinctly religious orientation of the literary works of the Renaissance in the north also characterized northern art and architecture. Some Flemish painters, notably Rogier van der Weyden (1399/1400–1464) and Jan van

Eyck (1366–1441), were considered the artistic equals of Italian painters, were much admired in Italy, and worked a generation before Leonardo and Michelangelo. Van Eyck, one of the earliest artists to use oil-based paints successfully, shows the Flemish love for detail in paintings such as *Ghent Altarpiece* and the portrait *Giovanni Arnolfini and His Bride;* the effect is great realism and remarkable attention to human personality.

A quasi-spiritual aura infuses architectural monuments in the north. The city halls of wealthy Flemish towns such as Bruges, Brussels, Louvain, and Ghent strike the viewer more as shrines to house the bones of saints than as settings for the mundane decisions of politicians and business people. Northern architecture was little influenced by the classical revival so obvious in Renaissance Rome and Florence.

## Politics and the State in the Renaissance (ca 1450–1521)

The High Middle Ages had witnessed the origins of many of the basic institutions of the modern state. Sheriffs, inquests, juries, circuit judges, professional bureaucracies, and representative assemblies all trace their origins to the twelfth and thirteenth centuries (see pages 342–344). The linchpin for the development of states, however, was strong monarchy, and during the period of the Hundred Years' War, no ruler in western Europe was able to provide effective leadership. The resurgent power of feudal nobilities weakened the centralizing work begun earlier.

Beginning in the fifteenth century, rulers utilized the aggressive methods implied by Renaissance political ideas to rebuild their governments. First in Italy, then in France, England, and Spain, rulers began the work of reducing violence, curbing unruly nobles, and establishing domestic order. Divided into scores of independent principalities, Germany could not deal with the Roman church as an equal.

The dictators and oligarchs of the Italian city-states, together with Louis XI of France, Henry VII of England, and Ferdinand of Aragon, were tough, cynical, calculating rulers. In their ruthless push for power and strong governments, they subordinated morality to hard results. They preferred to be secure, if feared, rather than loved. They could not have read Machiavelli's *The Prince,* but they acted as though they understood its ideas.

Some historians have called Louis XI, Henry VII, and Ferdinand and Isabella in Spain "new monarchs." The term is only partly appropriate. These monarchs were new in that they invested kingship with a strong sense of royal authority and national purpose. They stressed that monarchy was the one institution that linked all classes and peoples within definite territorial boundaries. These rulers emphasized royal majesty and royal sovereignty and insisted on the respect and loyalty of all subjects. These monarchs ruthlessly suppressed opposition and rebellion, especially from the nobility. They loved the business of kingship and worked hard at it.

In other respects, however, the methods of these rulers, which varied from country to country, were not so new. They reasserted long-standing ideas and practices of strong monarchs in the Middle Ages. They seized on the maxim of the Justinian *Code,* "What pleases the prince has the force of law," to advance their authority. Some medieval rulers, such as Henry I of England, had depended heavily on middle-class officials. Renaissance rulers, too, tended to rely on middle-class civil servants. With tax revenues, medieval rulers had built armies to crush feudal anarchy. Renaissance townspeople with commercial and business interests naturally wanted a reduction of violence, and usually they were willing to pay taxes in order to achieve it.

### France

The Hundred Years' War left France drastically depopulated, commercially ruined, and agriculturally weak. Nonetheless, the ruler whom Joan of Arc had seen crowned at Reims, Charles VII (r. 1422–1461), revived the monarchy and France. He seemed an unlikely person to do so. Frail, indecisive, and burdened with questions about his paternity (his father had been deranged; his mother, notoriously promiscuous), Charles VII nevertheless began France's long recovery.

Charles reconciled the Burgundians and Armagnacs, who had been waging civil war for thirty years. By 1453 French armies had expelled the English from French soil except in Calais. Charles reorganized the royal council, giving increased influence to middle-class men, and strengthened royal finances through such taxes as the **gabelle** (on salt) and the *taille* (land tax). These taxes remained the Crown's chief sources of income until the Revolution of 1789.

By establishing regular companies of cavalry and archers—recruited, paid, and inspected by the state—Charles created the first permanent royal army. In 1438 Charles published the **Pragmatic Sanction of Bourges,** asserting the superiority of a general council over the papacy, giving the French crown major control over the appointment of bishops, and depriving the pope of

French ecclesiastical revenues. The Pragmatic Sanction established Gallican (or French) liberties because it affirmed the special rights of the French crown over the French church. Greater control over the church and the army helped to consolidate the authority of the French crown.

Charles's son Louis XI (r. 1461–1483), called the "Spider King" because of his treacherous character, was very much a Renaissance prince. Facing the perpetual French problem of reduction of feudal disorder, he saw money as the answer. Louis promoted new industries, such as silk weaving at Lyons and Tours. He welcomed foreign craftsmen and entered into commercial treaties with England, Portugal, and the towns of the Hanseatic League (see page 355). He used the revenues raised through these economic activities and severe taxation to improve the army. With the army, Louis stopped aristocratic brigandage and slowly cut into urban independence.

Luck favored his goal of expanding royal authority and unifying the kingdom. On the timely death of Charles the Bold, duke of Burgundy, in 1477, Louis invaded Burgundy and gained some territories. Three years later, the extinction of the house of Anjou brought Louis the counties of Anjou, Bar, Maine, and Provence.

Two further developments strengthened the French monarchy. The marriage of Louis XII (r. 1498–1515) and Anne of Brittany added the large western duchy of Brittany to the state. Then the French king Francis I and Pope Leo X reached a mutually satisfactory agreement in 1516. The new treaty, the Concordat of Bologna, rescinded the Pragmatic Sanction's assertion of the superiority of a general council over the papacy and approved the pope's right to receive the first year's income of new bishops and abbots. In return, Leo X recognized the French ruler's right to select French bishops and abbots. French kings thereafter effectively controlled the appointment and thus the policies of church officials within the kingdom.

## England

English society suffered severely from the disorders of the fifteenth century. The aristocracy dominated the government of Henry IV (r. 1399–1413) and indulged in mischievous violence at the local level. Population, decimated by the Black Death, continued to decline. Between 1455 and 1471, adherents of the ducal houses of York and Lancaster waged civil war, commonly called the Wars of the Roses because the symbol of the Yorkists was a white rose and that of the Lancastrians a red one. The chronic disorder hurt trade, agriculture, and domestic industry. Under the pious but mentally disturbed Henry VI, the authority of the monarchy sank lower than it had been in centuries.

The Yorkist Edward IV (r. 1461–1483) began establishing domestic tranquillity. He succeeded in defeating the Lancastrian forces and after 1471 began to reconstruct the monarchy. Edward, his brother Richard III (r. 1483–1485), and Henry VII (r. 1485–1509) of the Welsh house of Tudor worked to restore royal prestige, to crush the power of the nobility, and to establish order and law at the local level. All three rulers used methods that Machiavelli himself would have praised—ruthlessness, efficiency, and secrecy.

The Hundred Years' War had been financed by Parliament. Dominated by baronial factions, Parliament had been the arena where the nobility exerted its power. As long as the monarchy was dependent on the Lords and the Commons for revenue, the king had to call Parliament. Edward IV and subsequently the Tudors, excepting Henry VIII, conducted foreign policy on the basis of diplomacy, avoiding expensive wars. Thus the English monarchy did not depend on Parliament for money, and the Crown undercut that source of aristocratic influence.

Henry VII did summon several meetings of Parliament in the early years of his reign primarily to confirm laws, but the center of royal authority was the **royal council,** which governed at the national level. There Henry VII revealed his distrust of the nobility: though not completely excluded, very few great lords were among the king's closest advisers. Regular representatives on the council numbered between twelve and fifteen men, and while many gained high ecclesiastical rank (the means, as it happened, by which the Crown paid them), their origins were in the lesser landowning class, and their education was in law. They were, in a sense, middle-class.

The royal council handled any business the king put before it—executive, legislative, and judicial. For example, the council conducted negotiations with foreign governments and secured international recognition of the Tudor dynasty through the marriage in 1501 of Henry VII's eldest son, Arthur, to Catherine of Aragon, the daughter of Ferdinand and Isabella of Spain. The council dealt with real or potential aristocratic threats through a judicial offshoot, the **court of Star Chamber,** so called because of the stars painted on the ceiling of the room. The court applied principles of Roman law, and its methods were sometimes terrifying: accused persons were not entitled to see evidence against them, sessions were secret, torture could be applied to extract confessions, and juries were not called. These procedures ran directly counter to English common-law precedents, but they effectively reduced aristocratic troublemaking.

Unlike the continental countries of Spain and France, England had no standing army or professional civil service bureaucracy. The Tudors relied on the support of unpaid local officials, the **justices of the peace.** These influential landowners in the shires handled all the work of local government. They apprehended and punished criminals, enforced parliamentary statutes, fixed wages and prices, maintained proper standards of weights and measures, and even checked up on moral behavior.

The Tudors won the support of the influential upper middle class because the Crown linked government policy with the interests of that class. A commercial or agricultural upper class fears and dislikes few things more than disorder and violence. The Tudors promoted peace and social order, and the gentry did not object to arbitrary methods, like those of the court of Star Chamber, because the government had halted the long period of anarchy.

Secretive, cautious, and thrifty, Henry VII rebuilt the monarchy. He encouraged the cloth industry and built up the English merchant marine. English exports of wool and the royal export tax on that wool steadily increased. Henry crushed an invasion from Ireland and secured peace with Scotland through the marriage of his daughter Margaret to the Scottish king. When Henry VII died in 1509, he left a country at peace both domestically and internationally, a substantially augmented treasury, and the dignity and role of the royal majesty much enhanced.

## Spain

While England and France laid the foundations of unified nation-states during the Renaissance, Spain remained a conglomerate of independent kingdoms. Castile and León formed a single political organization, but Aragon consisted of the principalities of Aragon, Valencia, Majorca, Sicily, Cardeña, and Naples, each tied to the crown of Aragon in a different way. On the one hand, the legacy of Hispanic, Roman, Visigothic, Jewish, and Muslim peoples made for rich cultural diversity; on the other hand, the Iberian Peninsula lacked a common cultural tradition.

The centuries-long reconquista—the wars of the northern Christian kingdoms to control the entire peninsula (see pages 287–288)—had military and religious objectives: conversion or expulsion of the Muslims and Jews and political control of the south. By the middle of the fifteenth century, the kingdoms of Castile and Aragon dominated the weaker Navarre, Portugal, and Granada, and the Iberian Peninsula, with the exception of Granada, had been won for Christianity. But even the wedding in 1469 of the dynamic and aggressive Isabella of Castile and the crafty and persistent Ferdinand of Aragon did not bring about administrative unity. Rather, their marriage constituted a dynastic union of two royal houses, not the political union of two peoples. Although Ferdinand and Isabella (r. 1474–1516) pursued a common foreign policy, Spain existed until about 1700 as a loose confederation of separate kingdoms (see Map 13.3), each maintaining its own *cortes* (parliament), laws, courts, and systems of coinage and taxation.

To curb the rebellious and warring aristocracy, Ferdinand and Isabella revived an old medieval institution: the **hermandades,** or "brotherhoods," which were popular groups in the towns given authority to act as local police forces and as judicial tribunals. The hermandades repressed violence with such savage punishments that by 1498 they could be disbanded.

The decisive step Ferdinand and Isabella took to curb aristocratic power was the restructuring of the royal council. Aristocrats and great territorial magnates were rigorously excluded; thus the influence of the nobility on state policy was greatly reduced. Ferdinand and Isabella intended the council to be the cornerstone of their government system, with full executive, judicial, and legislative powers under the monarchy. The council was also to be responsible for the supervision of local authorities. The king and queen therefore appointed to the council only people of middle-class background. The council and various government boards recruited men trained in Roman law, which exalted the power of the Crown as the embodiment of the state.

In the extension of royal authority and the consolidation of the territories of Spain, the church was the linchpin. If the Spanish crown could select the higher clergy, then the monarchy could influence ecclesiastical policy, wealth, and military resources. Through a diplomatic alliance with the Spanish pope Alexander VI, the Spanish monarchs secured the right to appoint bishops in Spain and in the Hispanic territories in America. This power enabled the "Catholic Kings of Spain," a title granted Ferdinand and Isabella by the papacy, to establish, in effect, a national church.[50]

Revenues from ecclesiastical estates provided the means to raise an army to continue the reconquista. The victorious entry of Ferdinand and Isabella into Granada on January 6, 1492, signaled the culmination of eight centuries of Spanish struggle against the Arabs in southern Spain and the conclusion of the reconquista (see Map 9.3 on page 286). Granada in the south was incorporated into the Spanish kingdom, and in 1512 Ferdinand conquered Navarre in the north.

**MAP 13.3 Spain in 1492** The marriage of Ferdinand of Aragon and Isabella of Castile in 1469 represented a dynastic union of two houses, not a political union of two peoples. Some principalities, such as León (part of Castile) and Catalonia (part of Aragon), had their own cultures, languages, and legal systems. Barcelona, the port city of Catalonia, controlled a commercial empire throughout the Mediterranean. The culture of Granada was heavily Muslim.

There still remained a sizable and, in the view of the majority of the Spanish people, potentially dangerous minority, the Jews. During the long centuries of the reconquista, Christian kings had renewed Jewish rights and privileges; in fact, Jewish industry, intelligence, and money had supported royal power. While Christians of all classes borrowed from Jewish moneylenders, and while all who could afford them sought Jewish physicians, a strong undercurrent of resentment of Jewish influence and wealth festered. When the kings of France and England had expelled the Jews from their kingdoms (see pages 345–346), many had sought refuge in Spain. In the fourteenth century, Jews formed an integral and indispensable part of Spanish life. With vast numbers of Muslims, Jews, and Moorish Christians, medieval Spain represented the most diverse and cosmopolitan country in Europe. Diversity and cosmopolitanism, however, were not medieval social ideals.

Since ancient times, governments had seldom tolerated religious pluralism; religious faiths that differed from the official state religion were considered politically dangerous. But in the fourteenth century, anti-Semitism in Spain rose more from popular sentiment than from royal policies. Aggravated by fiery anti-Jewish preaching, by economic dislocation, and by the search for a scapegoat during the Black Death, the fourteenth century witnessed rising anti-Semitic feeling. In 1331 a mob attacked the Jewish community of Gerona in Catalonia. In 1355 royal troops massacred Jews in Toledo. On June 4, 1391, inflamed by "religious" preaching, mobs sacked and burned the Jewish community in Seville and compelled such Jews as survived to accept baptism. From Seville anti-Semitic pogroms swept the towns of Valencia, Barcelona, Burgos, Madrid, and Segovia. One scholar estimates that 40 percent of the Jewish population of Spain was killed or forced to convert.[51] Those converted were called *conversos, Marranos,* or **New Christians,** the three terms here used interchangeably.

King Ferdinand was not a religious fanatic. He was a Renaissance prince who wanted to *appear* as a moral and devout Christian, respectful of public opinion. He feared urban rioting and disorder, but he knew that the vast majority of the Spanish people hated the conversos. If the Crown protected them, it would lose popular support. Ferdinand resolved the dilemma by seeking papal permission to set up the Inquisition in Spain; if the actions of the Inquisition provoked public criticism, the papacy could be blamed. Pope Sixtus IV's bull authorizing the Inquisition reached Spain in November 1478, and on September 28, 1480, Ferdinand and Isabella ordered the establishment of tribunals to "search out and punish converts from Judaism who had transgressed against Christianity by secretly adhering to Jewish beliefs and performing rites of the Jews."[52]

What do we know of these New Christians? Why did they inspire such hostility? How did they view their

**Felipe Bigarny: Ferdinand the Catholic and Isabella the Catholic** All governments try to cultivate a popular image. For Ferdinand and Isabella, it was the appearance of piety. Contemporaries, such as the Burgundian sculptor Bigarny, portrayed them as paragons of Christian piety, as shown in these polychrome wooden statues. If Isabella's piety was perhaps more genuine, she used it—together with rich ceremony, elaborate dress, and a fierce determination—to assert royal authority. *(Capilla Real, Granada/Laurie Platt Winfrey, Inc.)*

religious position? In the administration of Castile, New Christians held the royal secretaryship, controlled the royal treasury, and composed a third of the royal council. In the church, they held high positions as archbishops, bishops, and abbots. In the administration of the towns, conversos often held the highest public offices; in Toledo they controlled the collection of royal revenues. They included some of the leading merchants and business people. They also served great magnates, and by intermarrying with the nobility, they gained political leverage. In the professions of medicine and law, New Christians held the most prominent positions. Numbering perhaps 200,000 in a total Spanish population of about 7.5 million, New Christians and Jews exercised influence disproportionate to their numbers. Aristocratic grandees resented their financial dependence, the poor hated the converso tax collectors, and churchmen doubted the sincerity of their conversions.

Recent scholarship has carefully analyzed documents written by New Christians for their reactions to the rising anti-Semitism. They identified themselves as Christians. In the 1480s, they unanimously insisted that they were happy to be Christians and failed to see why they should be labeled New Christians: many came from families that had received baptism generations before. They argued that just as Christ had never abandoned the ancient (Hebrew) Law, so they had not abandoned it; in fact, they had a better understanding of the Christian faith. For the New Christians, the issue was not that they had relinquished the faith of the Jews (and secretly reconverted); rather, in accepting Christianity, they had become real Jews and, in following Jesus, real Christians.[53]

This argument satisfied neither the Jews nor the conversos' enemies. The Jewish reaction to persecution of the conversos was, bluntly put, "Well, we told you so; it's just what you get."[54] Searching for a viable principle to use against both New Christians and Jews, their detractors hit not on what conversos believed, not on what they did, but on what they *were* as human beings. Hence arose the following racial theory: "Since race, they maintained, formed man's qualities and indeed his entire mental constitution, the Marranos, who were all offspring of Jews, retained the racial makeup of their forebears. . . . [E]thnically they were what they (or their ancestors) had been before their conversion to Christianity; in other words, they were Jews."[55] This absurd racist theory, which violated scriptural teaching, maintained that all conversos were malicious, immoral, and criminally inclined by their nature, and thus they could not be truly converted to Christianity.

Fifteenth-century Spanish anti-Semitism emerged at the very time a Spanish national feeling was emerging, a national sentiment that looked to the building of a single nation. Whereas earlier anti-Semitism, such as that during the time of the Black Death, alleged Jewish schemes to kill off entire Christian populations—by poisoning the wells, for example, from which Jews derived no profit—fifteenth-century theories held that Jews or New Christians planned to take over all public offices in Spain. Jews, therefore, represented a grave threat to national unity.[56]

Although the Inquisition was a religious institution established to ensure the Catholic faith, it was controlled by the Crown and served primarily as a politically unifying tool. Because the Spanish Inquisition commonly applied torture to extract confessions, first from lapsed conversos, then from Muslims, and later from Protestants, it gained a notorious reputation. Thus the word *inquisition,* meaning "any judicial inquiry conducted with ruthless severity," came into the English language. The methods of the Spanish Inquisition were cruel, though not as cruel as the investigative methods of some twentieth-century governments. Shortly after the reduction of the Moorish stronghold at Granada in 1492, Isabella and Ferdinand issued an edict expelling all practicing Jews from Spain. Of the community of perhaps 200,000 Jews, 150,000 fled. (Efforts were made, through last-minute conversions, to retain good Jewish physicians.) Absolute religious orthodoxy and purity of blood (untainted by Jews or Muslims) served as the theoretical foundation of the Spanish national state.

The diplomacy of the Catholic rulers of Spain achieved a success they never anticipated. Partly out of hatred for the French and partly out of a desire to gain international recognition for their new dynasty, Ferdinand and Isabella in 1496 married their second daughter, Joanna, heiress to Castile, to the archduke Philip, heir through his mother to the Burgundian Netherlands and through his father to the Holy Roman Empire. Philip and Joanna's son, Charles V (r. 1519–1556), thus succeeded to a vast patrimony. When Charles's son Philip II joined Portugal to the Spanish crown in 1580, the Iberian Peninsula was at last politically united. The various kingdoms, however, were administered separately.

## Summary

The Italian Renaissance rested on the phenomenal economic growth of the High Middle Ages. In the period from about 1050 to 1300, a new economy emerged based on Venetian and Genoese shipping and long-distance trade and on Florentine banking and cloth manufacture. These commercial activities, combined with the struggle of urban communes for political independence from surrounding feudal lords, led to the appearance of a new aristocratic class. The centuries extending roughly from 1300 to 1600 witnessed a remarkable intellectual flowering. Based on a strong interest in the ancient world, the Renaissance had a classicizing influence on many facets of culture: law, literature, government, education, religion, and art. In the city-states of fifteenth- and sixteenth-century Italy, oligarchic or despotic powers governed; Renaissance culture was manipulated to enhance the power of those rulers.

Expanding outside Italy, the intellectual features of this movement affected the culture of all Europe. The intellectual characteristics of the Renaissance were a secular attitude toward life, a belief in individual potential, and a serious interest in the Latin classics. The printing press revolutionized communication. Meanwhile, the status of women in society declined, and black people entered Europe in sizable numbers for the first time since the collapse of the Roman Empire. Male culture in Italian cities had a strongly homoerotic character, reflecting a significant contrast between Renaissance attitudes toward male sexuality and attitudes today. In northern Europe, city merchants and rural gentry allied with rising monarchies. With taxes provided by business people, kings established greater peace and order, both essential for trade. Northern humanism had a more pietistic strain than did the Italian. In Spain, France, and England, rulers also emphasized royal dignity and authority, and they utilized Machiavellian ideas to ensure the preservation and continuation of their governments. Feudal monarchies gradually evolved in the direction of nation-states.

## Key Terms

Renaissance
communes
popolo
signori
oligarchies
princely courts
republic
individualism
humanism
secularism
*The Prince*
gabelle
Pragmatic Sanction of Bourges
royal council
court of Star Chamber
justices of the peace
hermandades
New Christians

## Notes

1. See L. Martines, *Power and Imagination: City-States in Renaissance Italy* (New York: Vintage Books, 1980), esp. pp. 332–333.
2. Ibid., pp. 22–61.
3. Ibid., p. 221.
4. Quoted in J. Burckhardt, *The Civilization of the Renaissance in Italy* (London: Phaidon Books, 1951), p. 89.
5. *Memoirs of Benvenuto Cellini; A Florentine Artist; Written by Himself* (London: J. M. Dent & Sons, 1927), p. 2.
6. See C. Trinkaus, *In Our Image and Likeness: Humanity and Divinity in Italian Humanist Thought,* vol. 2 (London: Constable, 1970), pp. 505–529.
7. B. Burroughs, ed., *Vasari's Lives of the Artists* (New York: Simon & Schuster, 1946), pp. 164–165.
8. See Martines, *Power and Imagination,* chap. 13, esp. pp. 241, 243.
9. R. A. Goldthwaite, *Wealth and the Demand for Art in Italy, 1300–1600* (Baltimore: Johns Hopkins University Press, 1993), p. 5.
10. Ibid., p. 213.
11. Ibid., pp. 224–229.
12. Ibid., pp. 121–129.
13. See A. Hauser, *The Social History of Art,* vol. 2 (New York: Vintage Books, 1959), chap. 3, esp. pp. 60, 68.
14. G. Bull, trans., *Aretino: Selected Letters* (Baltimore: Penguin Books, 1976), p. 109.
15. Quoted in P. and L. Murray, *A Dictionary of Art and Artists* (Baltimore: Penguin Books, 1963), p. 125.
16. Quoted in W. H. Woodward, *Vittorino da Feltre and Other Humanist Educators* (Cambridge: Cambridge University Press, 1897), pp. 96–97.
17. M. L. King, "Book-Lined Cells: Women and Humanism in the Early Italian Renaissance," in *Beyond Their Sex: Learned Women of the European Past,* ed. P. H. Labalme (New York: New York University Press, 1980), pp. 66–81, esp. p. 73.
18. C. E. Detmold, trans., *The Historical, Political and Diplomatic Writings of Niccolò Machiavelli* (Boston: J. R. Osgood, 1882), pp. 51–52.
19. Ibid., pp. 54–55.
20. See F. Gilbert, *Machiavelli and Guicciardini: Politics and History in Sixteenth Century Florence* (New York: W. W. Norton, 1984), pp. 197–200.
21. E. L. Eisenstein, *The Printing Press as an Agent of Change: Communications and Cultural Transformations in Early Modern Europe,* vol. 1 (New York: Cambridge University Press, 1979), p. 135. For an overall discussion, see pp. 126–159.
22. See L. Hunt, *The Invention of Pornography: Obscenity and the Origins of Modernity, 1500–1800* (New York: Zone Books, 1993), pp. 10, 93–95.
23. See A. W. Crosby, *The Measure of Reality: Quantification and Western Society* (New York: Cambridge University Press, 1997), pp. 76–78.
24. Ibid., pp. 49–74.
25. See M. E. Wiesner, *Women and Gender in Early Modern Europe* (New York: Cambridge University Press, 1994), pp. 85–86 passim.
26. See Susan Mosher Stuard, "Ancillary Evidence for the Decline of Medieval Slavery," *Past and Present* 149 (November 1995): 3–28.
27. Quoted in J. Hale, *The Civilization of Europe in the Renaissance* (New York: Atheneum, 1994), p. 270.
28. This account rests on J. Kelly-Gadol, "Did Women Have a Renaissance?" in *Becoming Visible: Women in European History,* ed. R. Bridenthal and C. Koonz (Boston: Houghton Mifflin, 1977), pp. 137–161, esp. p. 161.
29. G. Ruggerio, "Sexual Criminality in Early Renaissance Venice, 1338–1358," *Journal of Social History* 8 (Spring 1975): 18–31.
30. For these and a variety of other remarkable court cases, see S. K. Cohn, Jr., *Women in the Streets: Essays on Sex and Power in*

*Renaissance Italy* (Baltimore: Johns Hopkins University Press, 1996), pp. 103–121.
31. Ibid., pp. 30–35, 105–115.
32. M. Rocke, *Forbidden Friendships: Homosexuality and Male Culture in Renaissance Florence* (New York: Oxford University Press, 1996), pp. 10–11.
33. Ibid.
34. Ibid., p. 45.
35. See ibid., chap. 3, "Age and Gender in the Social Organization of Sodomy," and chap. 4, "Social Profiles."
36. Ibid., p. 148.
37. Ibid., pp. 190–191.
38. Marc Bloch, *Slavery and Serfdom in the Middle Ages,* trans. William R. Beer (Berkeley: University of California Press, 1975), p. 30.
39. Ibid., p. 28.
40. See Stuard, "Ancillary Evidence for the Decline of Medieval Slavery."
41. Hale, *The Civilization of Europe,* p. 44.
42. J. Iliffe, *Africans: The History of a Continent* (Cambridge: Cambridge University Press, 1995), p. 130; H. Thomas, *The Slave Trade: The Story of the Atlantic Slave Trade, 1440–1870* (New York: Simon & Schuster, 1997), pp. 109–110.
43. Quoted in J. Devisse and M. Mollat, *The Image of the Black in Western Art,* vol. 2, trans. W. G. Ryan (New York: William Morrow, 1979), pt. 2, pp. 187–188.
44. See A. C. de C. M. Saunders, *A Social History of Black Slaves and Freedmen in Portugal, 1441–1555* (New York: Cambridge University Press, 1982), pp. 59, 62–88, 176–179.
45. Ibid., pp. 190–194.
46. Ibid., pp. 255–258.
47. See I. Hannaford, *Race: The History of an Idea in the West* (Washington, D.C.: Woodrow Wilson Center Press, 1996), pp. 3–182 passim, 182–187.
48. Quoted in E. H. Harbison, *The Christian Scholar and His Calling in the Age of the Reformation* (New York: Charles Scribner's Sons, 1956), p. 109.
49. Quoted in F. Seebohm, *The Oxford Reformers* (London: J. M. Dent & Sons, 1867), p. 256.
50. See J. H. Elliott, *Imperial Spain, 1469–1716* (New York: Mentor Books, 1963), esp. pp. 75, 97–108.
51. See B. F. Reilly, *The Medieval Spains* (New York: Cambridge University Press, 1993), pp. 198–203.
52. B. Netanyahu, *The Origins of the Inquisition in Fifteenth Century Spain* (New York: Random House, 1995), p. 921.
53. Ibid., pp. 934–935.
54. Ibid., p. 930.
55. Ibid., p. 982.
56. Ibid., pp. 996–1005.

## Suggested Reading

A comprehensive treatment of the period is J. Hale, *The Civilization of Europe in the Renaissance* (1994), a magisterial achievement, while G. Holmes, ed., *The Oxford History of Italy* (1997), contains valuable articles on politics, society, and culture. P. Burke, *The Historical Anthropology of Early Modern Italy* (1987), contains useful essays on Italian cultural history in a European framework. G. Holmes, ed., *Art and Politics in Renaissance Italy* (1993), treats the art of Florence and Rome against a political background. For an explanation of why Italy lagged in developing a national state, see G. Chittolini, "Cities, 'City-States,' and Regional States in North-Central Italy," in *Cities and the Rise of States in Europe, A.D. 1000 to 1800,* ed. C. Tilly and W. P. Blockmans (1994). For the Renaissance court, see the splendid work of G. Lubkin, *A Renaissance Court: Milan Under Galeazzo Maria Sforza* (1994), as well as the title by Martines cited in the Notes.

For Renaissance humanism and education, see D. R. Kelley, *Renaissance Humanism* (1991), a good survey of humanism as a cultural movement; A. Grafton and L. Jardine, *From Humanism to the Humanities: Education and the Liberal Arts in Fifteenth and Sixteenth Century Europe* (1986), a sophisticated study; P. F. Grendler, *Schooling in Renaissance Italy: Literacy and Learning, 1300–1600* (1989); and J. F. D'Amico, *Renaissance Humanism in Papal Rome: Humanists and Churchmen on the Eve of the Reformation* (1983), another work of outstanding scholarship.

J. R. Hale, *Machiavelli and Renaissance Italy* (1966), is a sound short biography, but advanced students may want to consult the intellectual biography S. de Grazia, *Machiavelli in Hell* (1989), which is based on Machiavelli's literary as well as political writing. C. Singleton, trans., *The Courtier* (1959), presents an excellent picture of Renaissance court life.

The best introduction to the Renaissance in northern Europe and a book that has greatly influenced modern scholarship is J. Huizinga, *The Waning of the Middle Ages: A Study of the Forms of Life, Thought, and Art in France and the Netherlands in the Dawn of the Renaissance* (1954): it challenges the whole idea of the Renaissance. R. J. Knecht, *Renaissance Warrior and Patron: The Reign of Francis I* (1994), is the standard study of that important French ruler. The leading northern humanist is sensitively treated in J. McConica, *Erasmus* (1991). Advanced students interested in his program for the reform of Christian society should see J. D. Tracy, *Erasmus of the Low Countries* (1996). R. Marius, *Thomas More: A Biography* (1984), is a useful study of the English humanist and statesman, while the works of Rabelais, the French humanist and wit, are available in J. Leclercq, trans., *The Complete Works of Rabelais* (1963).

For the experiences of women as wives, mothers, slaves, servants, and workers in the crafts, see B. Hanawalt, ed., *Women and Work in Pre-industrial Europe* (1986), and M. L. King, *Women of the Renaissance* (1991). For the status of women, see C. Klapisch-Zuper, ed., *A History of Women,* vol. 3 (1994); R. Chartier, ed., *A History of Private Life,* vol. 3: *Passions of the Renaissance* (1990); and I. Maclean, *The Renaissance Notion of Women* (1980). J. C. Brown, *The Life of a Lesbian Nun in Renaissance Italy* (1985), and J. M. Saslow, *Ganymede in the Renaissance* (1986), both treat sexual issues, as do the titles by Rocke and Cohn cited in the Notes.

Renaissance art has understandably inspired vast research. In addition to Burroughs's edited version of Vasari's volume of biographical sketches on the masters referred to in the Notes, see, for Vasari's aims and methods of interpretation, P. L. Rubin, *Giorgio Vasari: Art and History* (1995). For Venice, see the highly readable and beautifully illustrated G. Wills, *Venice, Lion City: The Religion of Empire* (2001), which tells the story of the republic through an appreciation of its art and architecture; P. F. Brown, *Venice and Antiquity: The Venetian Sense of the Past* (1997), which treats the ways Venice invented its past to celebrate the city and its people; P. F. Brown, *Venetian Narrative Painting in the Age of Carpaccio* (1989); P. Humfrey, *Painting in Renaissance Venice* (1995), a useful survey for the beginning student; and P. Humfrey, *Lorenzo Lotto* (1997), a fine study of a distinctive Venetian painter. For artist families, see P. Burke, *The Italian Renaissance: Culture and Society in Italy* (1986). For the city of Milan, see E. S. Welch, *Art and Authority in Milan* (1996); and for Rome, see C. Hibbert, *Rome: The Biography of a City* (1985), an elegantly illustrated work, and P. Partner, *Renaissance Rome, 1500–1559: A Portrait of a Society* (1979). For Florence, see R. W. B. Lewis, *The City of Florence: Historical Vistas and Personal Sightings* (1995), an evocative appreciation of the city with a good study of the Medici achievement; and D. C. Ahl, *Benozzo Gozzoli* (1996), which places Gozzoli's art in its social context. M. Baxandall, *Painting and Experience in Fifteenth Century Italy* (1988), has important material on Florentine art. The magisterial achievement of J. Pope-Hennessy, *Cellini* (1985), is a superb evocation of that artist's life and work, while R. Jones and N. Penny, *Raphael* (1983), celebrates the work of that master. Leonardo's scientific and naturalistic ideas and drawings are available in I. A. Richter, ed., *The Notebooks of Leonardo da Vinci* (1985). The best introduction to the art of northern Europe is C. Harbison, *The Mirror of the Artist: Northern Renaissance Art in Its Historical Context* (1995).

The following studies should be helpful to students interested in issues relating to the political and religious history of Spain: N. Rubin, *Isabella of Castile: The First Renaissance Queen* (1991); P. Lis, *Isabel the Queen: Life and Times* (1992); J. S. Gerber, *The Jews of Spain: A History of the Sephardic Experience* (1992); H. Kamen, *Inquisition and Society in Spain in the Sixteenth and Seventeenth Centuries* (1985); P. F. Albaladejo, "Cities and the State in Spain," in *Cities and the Rise of States in Europe, A.D. 1000 to 1800,* eds. C. Tilly and W. M. Blockmans (1994); and B. Netanyahu, *The Origins of the Inquisition in Fifteenth Century Spain* (1995).

# Listening to the Past

## An Age of Gold

*As the foremost scholar of the early sixteenth century and a writer with international contacts, Desiderius Erasmus (1466?–1536) maintained a vast correspondence. In the letters here, he explains his belief that Europe was entering a golden age. The letters also reflect the spiritual ideals of northern European humanists. Wolfgang Capito (1478?–1541), a German scholar, was professor of theology at the University of Basel. Pope Leo X (1513–1521), second son of Lorenzo de' Medici, extended the hospitality of the papal court to men of letters, sought to rebuild Rome as a Renaissance capital, and pushed the building of the new Saint Peter's Basilica by licensing the sale of indulgences (see pages 457–458).*

### To Capito

It is no part of my nature, most learned Wolfgang, to be excessively fond of life; whether it is that I have, to my own mind, lived nearly long enough, having entered my fifty-first year, or that I see nothing in this life so splendid or delightful that it should be desired by one who is convinced by the Christian faith that a happier life awaits those who in this world earnestly attach themselves to piety. But at the present moment I could almost wish to be young again, for no other reason but this, that I anticipate the near approach of a golden age, so clearly do we see the minds of princes, as if changed by inspiration, devoting all their energies to the pursuit of peace. The chief movers in this matter are Pope Leo and Francis, King of France.

There is nothing this king does not do or does not suffer in his desire to avert war and consolidate peace . . . and exhibiting in this, as in everything else, a magnanimous and truly royal character. Therefore, when I see that the highest sovereigns of Europe—Francis of France, Charles the King Catholic, Henry of England, and the Emperor Maximilian—have set all their warlike preparations aside and established peace upon solid and, as I trust, adamantine foundations, I am led to a confident hope that not only morality and Christian piety, but also a genuine and purer literature, may come to renewed life or greater splendour; especially as this object is pursued with equal zeal in various regions of the world—at Rome by Pope Leo, in Spain by the Cardinal of Toledo,* in England by Henry, eighth of the name, himself not unskilled in letters, and among ourselves by our young King Charles.† In France, King Francis, who seems as it were born for this object, invites and entices from all countries men that excel in merit or in learning. Among the Germans the same object is pursued by many of their excellent princes and bishops, and especially by Maximilian Caesar,‡ whose old age, weary of so many wars, has determined to seek rest in the employments of peace, a resolution more becoming to his own years, while it is fortunate for the Christian world. To the piety of these princes it is due, that we see everywhere, as if upon a given signal, men of genius are arising and conspiring together to restore the best literature.

Polite letters, which were almost extinct, are now cultivated and embraced by Scots, by Danes, and by Irishmen. Medicine has a host of champions. . . . The Imperial Law is restored at Paris by William Budé, in Germany by Udalric Zasy; and mathematics at Basel by Henry of Glaris. In the theological sphere there was no little to be done,

*Francisco Jiménez de Cisneros (1436–1517), Spanish statesman and adviser to Queen Isabella who gained renown for his reform of the monasteries and the Spanish church.

†After 1516 king of Spain and much of the Netherlands; after 1519 Holy Roman emperor.

‡Holy Roman emperor (1493–1519), he was succeeded by his grandson Charles (above).

because this science has been hitherto mainly professed by those who are most pertinacious in their abhorrence of the better literature,§ and are the more successful in defending their own ignorance as they do it under pretext of piety, the unlearned vulgar being induced to believe that violence is offered to religion if anyone begins an assault upon their barbarism. . . . But even here I am confident of success if the knowledge of the three languages continues to be received in schools, as it has now begun. . . .

The humblest part of the work has naturally fallen to my lot. Whether my contribution has been worth anything I cannot say; . . . although the work was not undertaken by me with any confidence that I could myself teach anything magnificent, but I wanted to construct a road for other persons of higher aims, so that they might be less impeded by pools and stumbling blocks in carrying home those fair and glorious treasures.

Why should I say more? Everything promises me the happiest success. But one doubt still possesses my mind. I am afraid that, under cover of a revival of ancient literature, paganism may attempt to rear its head—as there are some among Christians that acknowledge Christ in name but breathe inwardly a heathen spirit—or, on the other hand, that the restoration of Hebrew learning may give occasion to a revival of Judaism. This would be a plague as much opposed to the doctrine of Christ as anything that could happen. . . . Some books have lately come out with a strong flavour of Judaism. I see how Paul exerted himself to defend Christ against Judaism, and I am aware that some persons are secretly sliding in that direction. . . . So much the more do I wish you to undertake this province; I know that your sincere piety will have regard to nothing but Christ, to whom all your studies are devoted. . . .

### To Pope Leo X

While on the one hand, as a private matter, I acknowledge my own felicity in obtaining the approbation not only of the Supreme Pontiff but of Leo, by his own endowments supreme among the supreme, so on the other hand, as a matter of public concern, I congratulate this our age—which bids fair to be an age of gold, if ever such there was—wherein I see, under your happy auspices and by your holy counsels, three of the chief blessings of humanity are about to be restored to her. I mean, first, that truly Christian piety, which has in many ways fallen into decay; secondly, learning of the best sort, hitherto partly neglected and partly corrupted; and thirdly, the public and lasting concord of Christendom, the source and parent of piety and erudition. These will be the undying trophies of the tenth Leo, which, consecrated to eternal memory by the writings of learned men, will forever render your pontificate and your family‖ illustrious. I pray God that he may be pleased to confirm this purpose in you, and so protract your life, that after the affairs of mankind have been ordered according to your designs, Leo may make a long-delayed return to the skies.

§Latin, Greek, and Hebrew.

Hans Holbein the Younger, *Erasmus* (ca 1521). Holbein persuaded his close friend Erasmus to sit for this portrait and portrayed him at his characteristic work, writing. *(Louvre/Scala/Art Resource, NY)*

## Questions for Analysis

1. What does Erasmus mean by a "golden age"? What are its characteristics?
2. Do education and learning ensure improvement in the human condition?
3. What would you say are the essential differences between Erasmus's educational goals and those of modern society?

‖The Florentine House of Medici, whose interests Leo X, himself a Medici, was known always to support.

*Source:* Epistles 522 and 530, from *The Epistles of Erasmus*, trans. F. M. Nichols (London: Longmans, Green & Co. 1901).

Josse Lieferinxe, *Pilgrims in a Sanctuary.* Christians, especially those who were ill or handicapped, flocked to the shrines of saints in hopes of a cure. *(Scala/Art Resource, NY)*

chapter

# 14 Reform and Renewal in the Christian Church

## chapter outline

- The Condition of the Church (ca 1400–1517)
- Martin Luther and the Birth of Protestantism
- Germany and the Protestant Reformation
- The Growth of the Protestant Reformation
- The Catholic Reformation and the Counter-Reformation

The idea of reform is as old as Christianity itself. In his letter to the Christians at Rome, Saint Paul exhorted, "Do not model yourselves on the behavior of the world around you, but let your behavior change, reformed by your new mind. That is the only way to discover the will of God." In the early fifth century, Saint Augustine of Hippo, describing the final stage of world history, wrote, "In the sixth age of the world our reformation becomes manifest, in newness of mind, according to the image of Him who created us." In the middle of the twelfth century, Saint Bernard of Clairvaux complained about the church of his day: "There is as much difference between us and the men of the primitive Church as there is between muck and gold." The Christian humanists of the late fifteenth and early sixteenth centuries—More, Erasmus, and Colet—urged reform of the church on the pattern of the early church, primarily through educational and social change.

Men and women of every period believed the early Christian church represented a golden age, and critics in every period called for reform. Thus sixteenth-century cries for reformation were hardly new. What was new, however, were the criticisms of educated laypeople whose religious needs were not being met. Many scholars interpret the sixteenth-century Reformation against the background of reforming trends begun in the fourteenth century. Unlike any other period, the sixteenth century experienced religious changes that had profound social, political, and cultural consequences.

- What late medieval religious developments paved the way for the adoption and spread of Protestant thought?
- Why did the strictly theological ideas of Martin Luther trigger political, social, and economic reactions?
- What were the consequences of religious schism?
- Do the various reform movements represent revolution or continuity? How?

These are some of the questions that this chapter will explore.

## The Condition of the Church (ca 1400–1517)

The papal conflict with the German emperor Frederick II in the thirteenth century, followed by the Babylonian Captivity and then the Great Schism, badly damaged the prestige of church leaders. In the fourteenth and fifteenth centuries, leaders of the conciliar movement reflected educated public opinion when they called for the reform of the church "in head and members." Humanists denounced corruption in the church. As Machiavelli put it, "We Italians are irreligious and corrupt above others, because the Church and her representatives set us the worst example."[1] In *The Praise of Folly,* Erasmus condemned the superstitions of the parish clergy and the excessive rituals of the monks. The records of episcopal visitations of parishes, civil court records, and even such literary masterpieces as Chaucer's *Canterbury Tales* and Boccaccio's *Decameron* tended to confirm the sarcasm of the humanists.

### Signs of Disorder

The religious life of most people in early-sixteenth-century Europe took place at the village or local level. At this parish level, priests were peasants, and they were poor. All too frequently, the spiritual quality of their lives was not much better than that of the people to whom they ministered.

In the early sixteenth century, critics of the church concentrated their attacks on three disorders: clerical immorality, clerical ignorance, and clerical pluralism, with the related problem of absenteeism. There was little pressure for doctrinal change; the emphasis was on moral and administrative reform.

Since the fourth century, church law had required that candidates for the priesthood accept absolute celibacy. That requirement had always been difficult to enforce. Many priests, especially those ministering to country people, had concubines, and reports of neglect of the rule of celibacy were common. Immorality, of course, included more than sexual transgressions. Clerical drunkenness, gambling, and indulgence in fancy dress were frequent charges. Because such conduct was so much at odds with the church's rules and moral standards, it scandalized the educated faithful.

The bishops only casually enforced regulations regarding the education of priests. As a result, standards for ordination were shockingly low. When Saint Antonio, archbishop of Florence, conducted a visitation of his metropolitan see in the late fifteenth century, he found churches and service books in a deplorable state and many priests barely able to read and write. The evidence points consistently to the low quality of the Italian clergy, although in northern Europe—in England, for example—recent research shows an improvement in clerical educational standards in the early sixteenth century. Nevertheless, parish priests throughout Europe were not as educated as the educated laity. Predictably, Christian humanists, with their concern for learning, condemned the ignorance or low educational level of the clergy. Many priests could barely read and write, and critics laughed at the illiterate priest mumbling Latin words of the Mass that he could not understand.

In regard to absenteeism and **pluralism,** many clerics, especially higher ecclesiastics, held several *benefices* (or offices) simultaneously but seldom visited their benefices, let alone performed the spiritual responsibilities those offices entailed. Instead, they collected revenues from all of them and hired a poor priest, paying him just a fraction of the income to fulfill the spiritual duties of a particular local church. King Henry VIII's chancellor Thomas Wolsey was archbishop of York for fifteen years before he set foot in his diocese. The French king Louis XII's famous diplomat Antoine du Prat was perhaps the most notorious example of absenteeism: as archbishop of Sens, he entered his cathedral for the first time in his own funeral procession.

Many Italian officials in the papal curia held benefices in England, Spain, and Germany. Revenues from those countries paid the Italian priests' salaries, provoking not only charges of absenteeism but also nationalistic resentment. Critics condemned pluralism, absenteeism, and the way money seemed to change hands when a bishop entered into his office.

Although royal governments strengthened their positions and consolidated their territories in the fifteenth and sixteenth centuries, rulers lacked sufficient revenues to pay and reward able civil servants. The Christian church, with its dioceses and abbeys, possessed a large proportion of the wealth of the countries of Europe. What better way to reward government officials, who were usually clerics, than with high church offices? After all, the practice was sanctioned by centuries of tradition. Thus all over Europe—because church officials served their monarchs, those officials were allowed to govern the church. Churchmen served as royal councilors, diplomats, treasury officials, chancellors, viceroys, and judges. These positions had nothing whatsoever to do with spiritual matters. Bishops worked for their respective states as

1470 | 1500 | 1530 | 1560 | 1590

**POLITICAL/MILITARY**

- 1477 Union of Burgundy and Habsburg dynasties
- 1521–1555 Charles V's wars against Valois kings
- 1526 Turkish victory at Mohács leads to spread of Protestantism in Hungary
- 1553–1558 Reign of Mary Tudor and temporary restoration of Catholicism in England
- 1555 Peace of Augsburg
- 1558–1603 Reign of Elizabeth and the "Elizabethan Settlement" in England

**SOCIAL/ECONOMIC**

- 1525 Peasants' Revolt in Germany

**INTELLECTUAL/RELIGIOUS**

- 1517 Martin Luther, "Ninety-five Theses on the Power of Indulgences"
- 1521 Diet of Worms
- 1527 Henry VIII asks Pope Clement VII to annul his marriage to Catherine of Aragon
- 1541 John Calvin, *Genevan Catechism*
- 1542 Sacred Congregation of the Holy Office and Roman Inquisition
- 1545–1563 Council of Trent
- 1555 Peace of Augsburg officially recognizes Lutheranism

well as for the church, and they were paid by the church for their services to the state. It is astonishing that so many conscientiously tried to carry out their religious duties on top of their public burdens.

In most countries except England, members of the nobility occupied the highest church positions. The spectacle of proud, aristocratic prelates living in magnificent splendor contrasted very unfavorably with the simple fishermen who had been Christ's disciples.

## Signs of Vitality

Calls for reform testify to the spiritual vitality of the church as well as to its numerous problems. In the late fifteenth and early sixteenth centuries, both individuals and groups within the church were working actively for reform. In Spain, for example, Cardinal Francisco Jiménez de Cisneros (1436–1517) visited religious houses, encouraged the monks and friars to uphold their rules and constitutions, and set high standards for the training of the diocesan clergy.

In Holland beginning in the late fourteenth century, a group of pious laypeople called the "Brethren of the Common Life" lived in stark simplicity while daily carrying out the Gospel teaching of feeding the hungry, clothing the naked, and visiting the sick. The Brethren also taught in local schools with the goal of preparing devout candidates for the priesthood. The Brethren sought to make religion a personal, inner experience. The spirituality of the Brethren of the Common Life found its

**Arm Reliquary of Saint Babylas** Silver, glass paste, stones, rock crystals, and an amethyst were attached to an oak base to create this arm reliquary for a third-century martyred bishop of Antioch. Containers for relics were designed in forms related to the objects they held; here the bishop's hand is raised in blessing. Shrines possessing saints' relics drew pilgrims, who represented a demand for food, shelter, and souvenirs. *(Germany, Brunswick, 1467. Philadelphia Museum of Art, purchased with Museum funds. 1951-12-1)*

finest expression in the classic ***The Imitation of Christ*** by Thomas à Kempis, which gained wide appeal among laypeople. It urges Christians to take Christ as their model and seek perfection in a simple way of life. Like the later Protestants, the Brethren stressed the centrality of the Scriptures in spiritual life.[2] In the mid-fifteenth century, the movement had founded houses in the Netherlands, in central Germany, and in the Rhineland; it was a true religious revival.

If external religious observances are a measure of depth of heartfelt conviction, Europeans in the early sixteenth century remained deeply pious and loyal to the Roman Catholic church. Villagers participated in processions honoring the local saints. Middle-class people made pilgrimages to the great shrines, such as Saint Peter's in Rome. The upper classes continued to remember the church in their wills. In England, for example, between 1480 and 1490 almost 30,000 pounds, a prodigious sum in those days, was bequeathed to religious foundations. People of all social classes devoted an enormous amount of their time and income to religious causes and foundations.

The papacy also expressed concern for reform. Pope Julius II summoned an **ecumenical council,** which met in Rome from 1512 to 1517. Since most of the bishops were Italian and did not represent a broad cross section of international opinion, the term *ecumenical* (universal) is not really appropriate to describe their meetings. Nevertheless, the bishops and theologians present strove earnestly to reform the church. The council recommended higher standards for education of the clergy and instruction of the common people. The bishops placed the responsibility for eliminating bureaucratic corruption squarely on the papacy and suggested significant doctrinal reforms. But many obstacles stood in the way of ecclesiastical change. Meantime, difficulties were brewing in Germany.

## Martin Luther and the Birth of Protestantism

See DBQ 2

As the result of a personal religious struggle, a German Augustinian friar, Martin Luther (1483–1546), launched the Protestant Reformation of the sixteenth century. Luther was not a typical person of his time; miners' sons who become professors of theology are never typical. But Luther was representative of his time in the sense that he articulated the widespread desire for reform of the Christian church and a deep yearning for salvation. In the sense that concern for salvation was an important motivating force for Luther and other reformers, the sixteenth-century Reformation was in part a continuation of the medieval religious search.

### Luther's Early Years

Martin Luther was born at Eisleben in Saxony, the second son of a copper miner and, later, mine owner. At considerable sacrifice, his father sent him to school and then to the University of Erfurt, where he earned a master's degree with distinction at the young age of twenty-one. Hans Luther intended his son to proceed to the study of law and a legal career, which for centuries had been the steppingstone to public office and material success. Badly frightened during a thunderstorm, however, Martin Luther vowed to become a friar. Without consulting his father, he entered the monastery of the Augustinian friars at Erfurt in 1505. Luther was ordained a priest in 1507 and after additional study earned a doctorate of theology. From 1512 until his death in 1546, he served as professor of the Scriptures at the new University of Wittenberg. Luther was deadly serious when he said, years later, "I would not take all the world's goods for my doctorate." His doctorate led to his professorship, and his professorship conferred on him the *authority* to teach: throughout his life, he frequently cited his professorship as justification for his reforming work.

Martin Luther was a very conscientious friar. His scrupulous observance of the religious routine, frequent confessions, and fasting, however, gave him only temporary relief from anxieties about sin and his ability to meet God's demands. These apprehensions in turn led him to doubt the value of the monastic life itself. Since the medieval church had long held that the monastic life was a sure and certain road to salvation, Luther's confusion and anxieties increased.

Luther's wise and kindly confessor, John Staupitz, directed him to the study of Saint Paul's letters. Gradually, Luther arrived at a new understanding of the Pauline letters and of all Christian doctrine. He came to believe that salvation comes not through external observances and penance but through a simple faith in Christ. Faith is the means by which God sends humanity his grace, and faith is a free gift that cannot be earned. Thus Martin Luther discovered himself, God's work for him, and the centrality of faith in the Christian life.

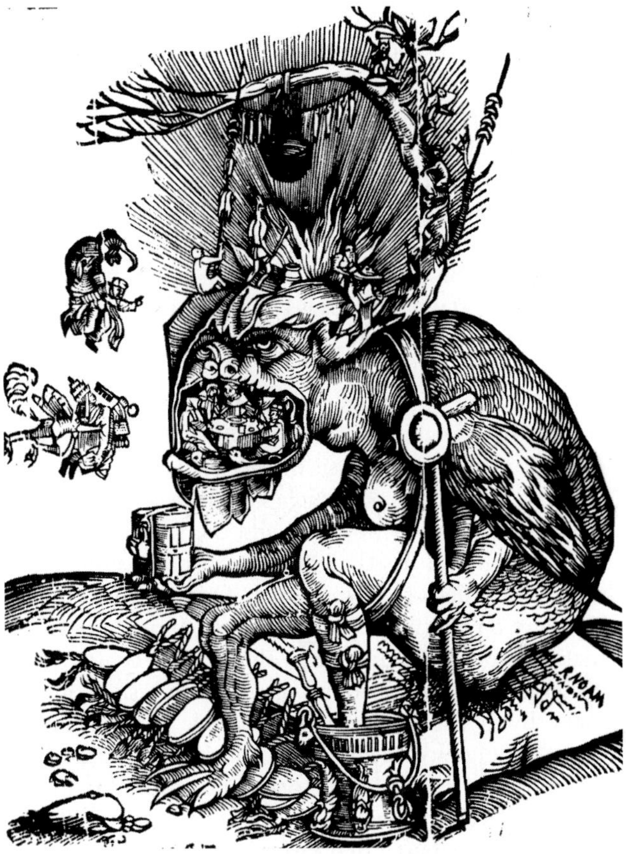

**The Folly of Indulgences** In this woodcut the church's sale of indulgences is viciously satirized. With one claw in the holy water symbolizing the rite of purification (Psalm 50), and the other claw resting on the coins paid for indulgences, the church, in the form of a rapacious eagle with its right hand stretched out for offerings, writes out an indulgence with excrement—which represents its worth. Fools, in a false security, sit in the animal's gaping mouth, representing Hell, to which a devil delivers the pope in a three-tiered crown and holding the keys to Heaven originally given to Saint Peter. *(Kunstsammlungen der Veste Coburg)*

## The Ninety-five Theses

An incident illustrative of the condition of the church in the early sixteenth century propelled Martin Luther onto the stage of history and brought about the Reformation. The University of Wittenberg lay within the ecclesiastical jurisdiction of the archdiocese of Magdeburg. The twenty-seven-year-old archbishop of Magdeburg, Albert, was also administrator of the see of Halberstadt and had been appointed archbishop of Mainz. To hold all three offices simultaneously—blatant pluralism—required papal dispensation. At that moment, Pope Leo X was eager to continue the construction of Saint Peter's Basilica but was hard-pressed for funds. Archbishop Albert borrowed money from the Fuggers, a wealthy banking family of Augsburg, to pay for the papal dispensation allowing him to hold the several episcopal benefices. Only a few powerful financiers and churchmen knew the details of the arrangement, but Leo X authorized Archbishop Albert to sell indulgences in Germany to repay the Fuggers.

Wittenberg was in the political jurisdiction of Frederick of Saxony, one of the seven electors of the Holy Roman Empire. When Frederick forbade the preaching and sale of indulgences within his duchy, the people of Wittenberg, including some of Professor Luther's students, streamed across the border from Saxony into Jütenborg in Thuringia to buy indulgences.

What exactly was an **indulgence?** According to Catholic theology, individuals who sin alienate themselves from God and his love. In order to be reconciled to God, the sinner must confess his or her sins to a priest and do the penance assigned. For example, a person who steals must first return the stolen goods and then perform the penance given by the priest, usually certain prayers or good works. This is known as the temporal (or earthly) penance since no one knows what penance God will ultimately require.

The doctrine of indulgence rested on three principles. First, God is merciful, but he is also just. Second, Christ and the saints, through their infinite virtue, established a "treasury of merits" on which the church, through its special relationship with Christ and the saints, can draw. Third, the church has the authority to grant sinners the spiritual benefits of those merits. Originally an indulgence was a remission of the temporal (priest-imposed) penalties for sin. Beginning in the twelfth century, the papacy and bishops had given Crusaders such indulgences. By the later Middle Ages, people widely believed that an indulgence secured total remission of penalties for sin—on earth or in purgatory—and ensured swift entry into Heaven.

Archbishop Albert hired Dominican friar John Tetzel to sell the indulgences. Tetzel mounted an advertising blitz. One of his slogans—"As soon as coin in coffer rings, the soul from purgatory springs"—brought phenomenal success. Men and women could buy indulgences not only for themselves but also for deceased parents, relatives, or friends. Tetzel even drew up a chart with specific prices for the forgiveness of particular sins.

Luther was severely troubled that ignorant people believed they had no further need for repentance once they had purchased an indulgence. He wrote a letter to Archbishop Albert on the subject and enclosed in Latin "Ninety-five Theses on the Power of Indulgences." His argument was that indulgences undermined the seriousness of the sacrament of penance, competed with the preaching of the Gospel, and downplayed the importance of charity in Christian life. After Luther's death, his disciple Philipp Melanchthon reported that the theses were also posted on the door of the church at Wittenberg Castle on October 31, 1517. Some modern scholars believe that event never happened, meaning all the subsequent dramatic and artistic renderings of it rest on myth.

In any case, Luther intended the theses for academic debate. By December 1517, they had been translated into German and were read throughout the empire.

Luther firmly rejected the notion that salvation could be achieved by good works, such as indulgences. Some of his theses challenged the pope's power to grant indulgences, and others criticized papal wealth. When questioned, Luther rested his fundamental argument on the principle that there was no biblical basis for indulgences. But, replied Luther's opponents, to deny the legality of indulgences was to deny the authority of the pope who had authorized them. The issue was drawn: where did authority lie in the Christian church?

Through 1518 and 1519, Luther studied the history of the papacy. In 1519 in a large public disputation with Catholic debater John Eck at Leipzig, Luther denied both the authority of the pope and the infallibility of a general council. The Council of Constance, he said, had erred when it had condemned Jan Hus (see page 397).

The papacy responded with a letter condemning some of Luther's propositions, ordering that his books be burned, and giving him two months to recant or be excommunicated. Luther retaliated by publicly burning the letter. By January 3, 1521, when the excommunication was supposed to become final, the controversy involved more than theological issues. The papal legate wrote, "All Germany is in revolution. Nine-tenths shout 'Luther' as their war cry; and the other tenth cares nothing about Luther, and cries 'Death to the court of Rome.'"[3]

In this highly charged atmosphere, the twenty-one-year-old emperor Charles V held his first diet (assembly of the Estates of the empire). Charles summoned Luther to appear before the **Diet of Worms.** When ordered to recant, Luther replied in language that rang all over Europe:

*Unless I am convinced by the evidence of Scripture or by plain reason—for I do not accept the authority of the Pope or the councils alone, since it is established that they have often erred and contradicted themselves—I am bound by the Scriptures I have cited and my conscience is captive to the Word of God. I cannot and will not recant anything, for it is neither safe nor right to go against conscience. God help me. Amen.*[4]

When Charles V declared Luther an outlaw, meaning he was denied legal protection, Duke Frederick of Saxony protected him.

Meanwhile, the Swiss humanist and admirer of Erasmus, Ulrich Zwingli (1484–1531), introduced the reformation in Switzerland. Elected People's Priest at the New Minster in Zurich, Zwingli first mounted the pulpit on January 1, 1519, and announced that he would preach not from the church's prescribed readings but, relying on Erasmus's New Testament, go right through the

**Jörg Ratgeb: The Last Supper** A painter in Heilbronn (modern Baden-Württemberg), Ratgeb (ca 1480–1526) moved his wife and children to that town but could not gain citizenship for them because they were serfs of the duke of Württemberg, who would not free them. This early work shows Ratgeb's innovative style: the disciples are grouped in pairs, wear lavish shimmering costumes, and seem engaged in private conversation as Jesus distributes the Eucharist. A roasted pascal lamb rests in the middle of the table, but a knife is the only eating utensil. *(Loan: The Netherlands Institute of Cultural Heritage. Museum Boijmans Van Beuningen, Rotterdam)*

New Testament "from A to Z," that is, from Matthew to Revelation. Zwingli was convinced that Christian life rested on the Scriptures, which were the pure words of God and the sole basis of religious truth. He went on to attack indulgences, the Mass, the institution of monasticism, and clerical celibacy. In his gradual reform of the church in Zurich, where he remained the rest of his life, he had the strong support of the town's civil authorities. He disagreed, however, with Luther on various theological issues, notably the nature of the Eucharist. The Colloquy of Marburg, summoned in 1529 to unite Protestant opinion, failed to resolve those differences.

## Protestant Thought

Between 1520 and 1530, Luther worked out the basic theological tenets that became the articles of faith for his new church and subsequently for all Protestant groups. The word **Protestant** derives from the protest drawn up by a small group of reforming German princes at the Diet of Speyer in 1529. The princes "protested" the decisions of the Catholic majority. At first Protestant meant "Lutheran," but with the appearance of many protesting sects, it became a general term applied to all non-Catholic Christians. Lutheran Protestant thought was officially formulated in the Confession of Augsburg in 1530.

Ernst Troeltsch, a German student of the sociology of religion, has defined Protestantism as a "modification of Catholicism, in which the Catholic formulation of questions was retained, while a different answer was given to them." Luther provided new answers to four old, basic theological issues.

First, how is a person to be saved? Traditional Catholic teaching held that salvation is achieved by both faith and good works. Luther held that salvation comes by faith alone. Women and men are saved, said Luther, by the arbitrary decision of God, irrespective of good works or the sacraments. God, not people, initiates salvation.

**Lucas Cranach the Elder: The Ten Commandments (early sixteenth century)** Protestants condemned images of all kinds but recognized their value for instructional purposes. Here Cranach, an early adherent of Luther's Reformation, illustrates the Ten Commandments. Can you name the commandments? Is it unfair to say that the painting has a misogynistic tinge, given the female devil in number 5 and the wife in number 9? The semicircular rainbow running through the ten scenes symbolizes the covenant between God and humankind. *(Lutherhalle, Wittenberg/The Bridgeman Art Library)*

Second, where does religious authority reside? Christian doctrine had long maintained that authority rests both in the Bible and in the traditional teaching of the church. Luther maintained that authority rests in the Word of God as revealed in the Bible alone and as interpreted by an individual's conscience. He used the Latin phrase ***sola scriptura,*** "scripture alone," to mean that authority in the church rested only on the Scriptures: for a doctrine or issue to be valid, it had to have a scriptural basis. (Luther, of course, did not have the advantage of modern biblical research, which has demonstrated that tradition *preceded* the writing of the New Testament—that is, the New Testament is not exactly contemporaneous with Jesus but is based on the traditional understanding of his life and teachings current in first-century Christian communities.) He urged that each person read and reflect on the Scriptures.

Third, what is the church? Luther re-emphasized the Catholic teaching that the church consists of the entire community of Christian believers. Medieval churchmen, in contrast, had tended to identify the church with the clergy.

Fourth, what is the highest form of Christian life? The medieval church had stressed the superiority of the monastic and religious life over the secular. Luther argued that all vocations have equal merit, whether ecclesiastical or secular, and that every person should serve God in his or her individual calling.[5]

As Protestant thought developed, it differed from Roman Catholic teaching on several other fundamental issues. Luther's idea of the church as a spiritual *priesthood of all believers,* an invisible fellowship not fixed in any place or person, differed markedly from the Roman Catholic practice of a clerical, hierarchical institution headed by the pope in Rome. Because faith required no institutional structure, Luther stressed the invisibility of the church. Whereas Catholic doctrine holds that there are seven sacraments, Luther believed that the Scriptures support only three sacraments—baptism, penance, and the Eucharist, or Lord's Supper. Protestant sects, as they emerged, developed a theology of the Eucharist. Catholics hold the dogma of **transubstantiation:** by the consecrating words of the priest during the Mass, the bread and wine become the actual body and blood of Christ, who is then fully present in the bread and wine. In opposition, Luther defined **consubstantiation,** the belief that after consecration the bread and wine undergo a spiritual change whereby Christ is really present (the Real Presence) but the bread and wine are not transformed. Swiss reformer Ulrich Zwingli affirmed that the **Lord's Supper** is a *memorial* of the Last Supper and that no change whatever occurs in the elements. John Calvin believed that the body and blood of Christ are spiritually but not physically present in the bread and wine and are consumed spiritually. Catholics and Protestants agreed that the sacrament must be received worthily and that it is a source of grace.

## The Social Impact of Luther's Beliefs

Every encounter Luther had with ecclesiastical or political authorities attracted attention. Pulpits and printing presses spread his message all over Germany. By the time of his death, people of all social classes had become Lutheran. What was the immense appeal of Luther's religious ideas?

Historical research on the German towns has shown that two significant late medieval developments prepared the way for Luther's ideas. First, since the fifteenth century, city governments had expressed resentment of clerical privileges and immunities. Priests, monks, and nuns paid no taxes and were exempt from civic responsibilities, such as defending the city. Yet religious orders frequently held large amounts of urban property. At Zurich in 1467, for example, religious orders held one-third of the city's taxable property. City governments were determined to integrate the clergy into civic life by reducing their privileges and giving them public responsibilities. Accordingly, the Zurich magistracy subjected the religious to taxes, inspected wills so that legacies to the church and legacies left by churchmen could be controlled, and placed priests under the jurisdiction of the civil courts.

Second, critics of the late medieval church, especially educated townspeople, condemned the irregularity and poor quality of sermons. As a result, prosperous burghers in many towns established **preacherships.** Preachers were men of superior education who were required to deliver about a hundred sermons a year, each lasting about forty-five minutes. Endowed preacherships had important consequences after 1517. Luther's ideas attracted many preachers, and in such towns as Stuttgart, Reutlingen, Eisenach, and Jena, preachers became Protestant leaders. Preacherships also encouraged the Protestant form of worship, in which the sermon, not the Eucharist, was the central part of the service.[6]

In the countryside, the attraction of German peasants to Lutheran beliefs was predictable. Luther himself came from a peasant background, and he admired the peasants' ceaseless toil. They thrilled to the words of Luther used in his treatise *On Christian Liberty* (1520)—"A Christian man is the most free lord of all and subject to none"—choosing to ignore the second clause of Luther's statement: "A Christian man is the most dutiful servant of all, and subject to everyone." (See the feature "Listening to the Past: Martin Luther, *On Christian Liberty*" on pages 486–487.) Taken by itself, the first clause contributed to social unrest.

Fifteenth-century Germany had witnessed several **peasant revolts**. In the early sixteenth century, the economic condition of the peasantry varied from place to place but was generally worse than it had been in the fifteenth century and was deteriorating. Crop failures in 1523 and 1524 aggravated an explosive situation. In 1525 representatives of the Swabian peasants met at the city of Memmingen and drew up the Twelve Articles, which expressed their grievances. The Twelve Articles condemned lay and ecclesiastical lords and summarized the agrarian crisis of the early sixteenth century. The articles complained that nobles had seized village common lands, which traditionally had been used by all; that they had imposed new rents on manorial properties and new services on the peasants working those properties; and that they had forced the poor to pay unjust death duties in the form of the peasants' best horses or cows. Wealthy, socially mobile peasants especially resented these burdens, which they emphasized as new.[7] The peasants believed their demands conformed to the Scriptures and cited Luther as a theologian who could prove that they did.

Luther wanted to prevent rebellion. Initially he sided with the peasants, and in his tract *An Admonition to Peace* (1525) he blasted the lords:

> *We have no one on earth to thank for this mischievous rebellion, except you lords and princes, especially you blind bishops and mad priests and monks. . . . In your government you do nothing but flay and rob your subjects in order that you may lead a life of splendor and pride, until the poor common folk can bear it no longer.*[8]

But, he warned, nothing justified the use of armed force: "The fact that rulers are unjust and wicked does not excuse tumult and rebellion; to punish wickedness does not belong to everybody, but to the worldly rulers who bear the sword." As for biblical support for the peasants' demands, he maintained that Scripture had nothing to do with earthly justice or material gain.[9]

Massive revolts first broke out near the Swiss frontier and then swept through Swabia, Thuringia, the Rhineland,

**German Burgher Domestic Scene** With what Jesus called the greatest commandment ("You shall love the Lord your God with all your heart and all your soul and your neighbor as yourself" [Deut. 6, Matt. 22]) inscribed on tablets over the room, a German family begins a meal. The father listens as his son says grace, the mother passes bread, the older daughters seem to have begun eating, and a small child biting a chicken drumstick seems dangerously close to the fire. The little dog begs for food; the cat laps milk. *(Mary Evans Picture Library)*

and Saxony. The crowds' slogans came directly from Luther's writings. "God's righteousness" and the "Word of God" were invoked in an effort to secure social and economic justice. The peasants who expected Luther's support were soon disillusioned. Freedom for Luther meant independence from the authority of the Roman church; it did *not* mean opposition to legally established secular powers. Firmly convinced that rebellion would hasten the end of civilized society, he wrote the tract *Against the Murderous, Thieving Hordes of the Peasants:* "Let everyone who can smite, slay, and stab [the peasants], secretly and openly, remembering that nothing can be more poisonous, hurtful or devilish than a rebel."[10] The nobility ferociously crushed the revolt. Historians estimate that over seventy-five thousand peasants were killed in 1525.

Luther took literally these words of Saint Paul's Letter to the Romans: "Let every soul be subject to the higher powers. For there is no power but of God: the powers that be are established by God. Whosoever resists the power, resists the ordinance of God: and they that resist shall receive to themselves damnation."[11] As Lutheran theology developed, it exalted the state, subordinated the church to the state, and everywhere championed "the powers that be." The German Peasants' Revolt of 1525 greatly strengthened the authority of lay rulers. Peasant economic conditions, however, moderately improved. For example, in many parts of Germany, enclosed fields, meadows, and forests were returned to common use.

Scholars in many disciplines have attributed Luther's fame and success to the invention of the printing press, which rapidly reproduced and made known his ideas. (See the feature "Images in Society: From Reformation to Baroque" on pages 464–465.) Equally important was Luther's incredible skill with language. Some thinkers have lavished praise on the Wittenberg reformer; others have bitterly condemned him. But in the words of psychologist Erik Erikson:

*The one matter on which professor and priest, psychiatrist and sociologist, agree is Luther's immense gift for language: his receptivity for the written word; his memory for the significant phrase; and his range of verbal expression (lyrical, biblical, satirical, and vulgar) which in English is paralleled only by Shakespeare.*[12]

Language proved to be the weapon with which this peasant's son changed the European world.

Like the peasants, educated people and humanists were much attracted by Luther's words. He advocated a simpler, personal religion based on faith, a return to the spirit of the early church, the centrality of the Scriptures in the liturgy and in Christian life, and the abolition of elaborate ceremonies—precisely the reforms the northern humanists had been calling for.

Luther's linguistic skill, together with his translation of the New Testament into German in 1523, led to the acceptance of his dialect of German as the standard version of German. His insistence that everyone should read and reflect on the Scriptures attracted the literate and thoughtful middle classes partly because Luther appealed to their intelligence. Moreover, the business classes envied the church's wealth, disapproved of the luxurious lifestyle of some churchmen, and resented tithes and ecclesiastical taxation. Luther's doctrines of salvation by faith and the priesthood of all believers not only raised the religious status of the commercial classes but also protected their pocketbooks.

Hymns, psalms, and Luther's two catechisms (1529), compendiums of basic religious knowledge, also show the power of language in spreading the ideals of the Reformation. The reformers knew "that rhyme, meter, and melodies could forcefully impress minds and affect sensibilities." Such hymns as the famous "A Mighty Fortress Is Our God" expressed deep human feelings, were easily remembered, and imprinted on the mind central points of doctrine. Luther's *Larger Catechism* contained brief sermons on the main articles of faith, whereas the *Shorter Catechism* gave concise explanations of doctrine in question-and-answer form. Both catechisms stressed the importance of the Ten Commandments, the Lord's Prayer, the Apostle's Creed, and the sacraments for the believing Christian. Although originally intended for the instruction of pastors, these catechisms became powerful techniques for the indoctrination of men and women of all ages, especially the young.[13]

What appeal did Luther's message have for women? Luther's argument that all vocations have equal merit in the sight of God gave dignity to those who performed ordinary, routine, domestic tasks. The abolition of monasticism in Protestant territories led to the exaltation of the home, which Luther and other reformers stressed as the special domain of the wife. The Christian home, in contrast to the place of business, became the place for the exercise of the gentler virtues—love, tenderness, reconciliation, the carrying of one another's burdens. The Protestant abolition of private confession to a priest freed women from possibly embarrassing explorations of their sexual lives. Protestants established schools where girls as well as boys became literate in the catechism and the

**Martin Luther and Katharina von Bora** The couple married on June 13, 1525, when Katharina was twenty-six and Luther forty-two. His parents were present for the ceremony. She brewed beer; managed the house, garden, and accounts; and produced six children. She also gave her husband her complete devotion, but having a no-nonsense character, she scolded him for what she perceived as his excessive generosity. For Luther, it was an exceptionally happy union. *(Uffizi, Florence/Scala/Art Resource, NY)*

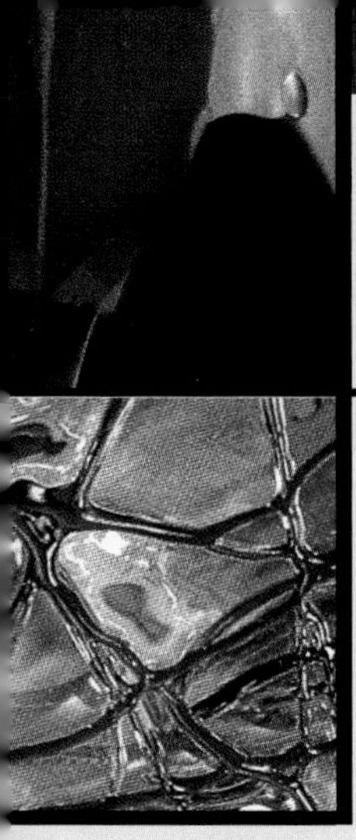

# Images in Society

## From Reformation to Baroque

In the Reformation era, controversy raged over the purpose and function of art. Protestants and Catholics disagreed, and Protestant sects disagreed with one another. The Latin phrase *sola scriptura* ("scripture alone") summarizes the fundamentalist Protestant position. The Bible specifically prohibits the making of images of anything

·Protestant leaders stressed the idea that anything Holy should not be represented in art.
·Martin Luther disagreed saying it will better educate the illiterate
·Calvin accepted biblical scenes, as long as they did not include God or Jesus as it would "bring God down to human level"

... aters ... omy ... the ... l in ... ed, ... eved ... the ... are ... by ... ruc- ... utter ... pt to ... or- ... d ... vin ... ving ... n tolerated narrative biblical scenes, as long as they did not include pictures of God or Jesus Christ, his son.

Many of the formerly Catholic churches in the Netherlands were redesigned with a stark, bare simplicity that mirrored the ideal of Protestant architecture. Notice the interior of the church of Saint Bavo in Haarlem (Image 1). The medieval Gothic structure was stripped of all statues, images, and decoration.

Lucas Cranach the Elder (1472–1553), a close friend of Luther's, is the finest representative of Protestant Reformation artists. He and Luther collaborated on the production of woodcuts and paintings, such as *The Ten Commandments* (see page 460), that spread the new evangelical theology. Protestants condemned images of all kinds but recognized their value for instructional purposes. Each square in the elder Cranach's painting represents one of the Ten Commandments. How many of the commandments can you name? Notice the female devil figure in number 5 and the portrayal of the wife in number 9. What conclusions can you draw from these representations of women? The semicircular rainbow running through the ten scenes symbolizes the covenant between God and humankind.

Lucas Cranach the Younger (1515–1586) continued his father's work. His wood engraving *The True and False Churches* (Image 2) shows the "true church" listening as Luther (gesturing from the pulpit) preaches the word of God from an open Bible. The engraving reveals a sacramental piety through Christ's presence on the altar as shown in the lamb of God and crucified Savior distributed to all in both bread and wine (left). An open mouth (right) symbolizing the jaws of Hell engulfs the pope, cardinals, and friars—the "false church."

The Catholic church officially addressed the subject of art at the Council of Trent in December 1563. The church declared that honor and veneration should be given to likenesses of Christ, the Virgin Mary, and the saints; that images would remind people of the saints' virtues, which should be imitated; and that pictorial art would promote piety and the love of God. Examine the

**Image 1** Church of Saint Bavo, Haarlem *(Pieter Jansz. Saenredam,* S. Bavo in Haarlem. *John G. Johnson Collection, Philadelphia Museum of Art)*

Image 2 Lucas Cranach the Younger: The True and False Churches (Staatliche Kunstsammlungen Dresden)

**Image 3** Jesuit Priest Distributing Holy Pictures *(From Pierre Chenu,* The Reformation *[New York: St. Martin's Press, 1986])*

**Image 4** Ceiling of the Gésu *(Scala/Art Resource, NY)*

painting *Jesuit Priest Distributing Holy Pictures* (Image 3). Such pictures and images of saints were often given to children to help educate them on matters of doctrine. How do these pictures serve the same function as the Protestant *Ten Commandments*?

Both Protestants and Catholics used religious art for propaganda purposes, to oppose religious heterodoxy, and to arouse piety in laypeople. Catholic Reformation art came into full flowering with the style later known as baroque (see page 582). Baroque art originated in Rome and reflected the dynamic and proselytizing spirit of the Counter-Reformation. The church encouraged artists to appeal to the senses, to touch the souls and kindle the faith of ordinary people while proclaiming the power and confidence of the reformed Catholic church.

In addition to this underlying religious emotionalism, the baroque drew from the Catholic Reformation its sense of drama, motion, and ceaseless striving. The interior of the Jesuit church of Jesus—the Gésu—combined all these characteristics in its lavish, shimmering, wildly active decorations and frescoes (Image 4). This triumphant, elaborate, and flamboyant church celebrates both the Catholic baroque and Rome as the artistic capital of Europe. What is the purpose of the ornate gilded ceiling and three-dimensional painting? How would you compare the Gésu with the Saint Bavo church (Image 1)?

*The* **history companion** *features additional information and activities related to this topic.*
**history.college.hmco.com/students**

Bible. Finally, the reformers stressed marriage as the cure for clerical concupiscence. Protestantism thus proved attractive to the many women who had been priests' concubines and mistresses: now they became legal and honorable wives.[14]

For his time, Luther held enlightened views on matters of sexuality and marriage. He wrote a letter to a young man, "Dear lad, be not ashamed that you desire a girl, nor you my maid, the boy. Just let it lead you into matrimony and not into promiscuity, and it is no more cause for shame than eating and drinking."[15] Luther was confident that God took delight in the sexual act and denied that original sin affected the goodness of creation. He believed, however, that marriage was a woman's career. A student recorded Luther as saying early in his public ministry, "Let them bear children until they are dead of it; that is what they are for." A happy marriage to ex-nun Katharina von Bora mellowed him, and another student later quoted him as saying, "Next to God's Word there is no more precious treasure than holy matrimony. God's highest gift on earth is a pious, cheerful, God-fearing, home-keeping wife, with whom you may live peacefully, to whom you may entrust your goods, and body and life."[16] With many relatives and constant visitors, Luther's home was a large and happy household, a model for Protestants but an abomination for Catholics. The wives of other reformers, though they exercised no leadership role in the reform, shared their husbands' work and concerns.

## Germany and the Protestant Reformation

Unlike Spain, France, and England, the German Empire lacked a strong central power. The Golden Bull of 1356 legalized what had long existed—government by an aristocratic federation. Each of seven electors—the archbishops of Mainz, Trier, and Cologne, the margrave of Brandenburg, the duke of Saxony, the count palatine of the Rhine, and the king of Bohemia—gained virtual sovereignty in his own territory. The agreement ended disputed elections in the empire; it also reduced the central authority of the emperor. Germany was characterized by weak borders, localism, and chronic disorder. The nobility strengthened its hold on its territories, while imperial power declined.

Against this background of decentralization and strong local power, Martin Luther had launched a movement to reform the church. Two years after Luther published the Ninety-five Theses, the electors chose as emperor a nineteen-year-old Habsburg prince who ruled as Charles V. Luther's interests and motives were primarily religious, but many people responded to his teachings for political, social, or economic reasons.

### The Rise of the Habsburg Dynasty

The marriage in 1477 of Maximilian I of the house of Habsburg and Mary of Burgundy was a decisive event in early modern European history. Burgundy consisted of two parts: the French duchy, with its capital at Dijon, and the Burgundian Netherlands, with its capital at Brussels. Through this union with the rich and powerful duchy of Burgundy, the Austrian house of Habsburg, already the strongest ruling family in the empire, became an international power.

In the fifteenth and sixteenth centuries, as in the Middle Ages, relations among states continued to be greatly affected by the connections of royal families. Marriage often determined the diplomatic status of states. The Habsburg-Burgundian marriage angered the French, who considered Burgundy French territory and had lusted after the Burgundian Netherlands (Flanders) for centuries. Louis XI of France repeatedly ravaged parts of the Burgundian Netherlands until he was able to force Maximilian to accept French terms: the Treaty of Arras (1482) declared French Burgundy a part of the kingdom of France. The Habsburgs, however, never really renounced their claim to Burgundy, and intermittent warfare over it continued between France and Maximilian. But Louis could not conquer it. It remained outside French control. Within the empire, German principalities that resented Austria's preeminence began to see that they shared interests with France. The marriage of Maximilian and Mary inaugurated centuries of conflict between the Austrian house of Habsburg and the kings of France. And Germany was to be the chief arena of the struggle.

"Other nations wage war; you, Austria, marry." Historians dispute the origins of this adage, but no one questions its accuracy. The heir of Mary and Maximilian, Philip of Burgundy, married Joanna of Castile, daughter of Ferdinand and Isabella of Spain. Philip and Joanna's son Charles V (1500–1558) fell heir to a vast conglomeration of territories. Through a series of accidents and unexpected deaths, Charles inherited Spain from his mother, her New World possessions, and the Spanish dominions in Italy, Sicily, and Sardinia. From his father he inherited the Habsburg lands in Austria, southern Germany, the Low Countries, and Franche-Comté in east-central France.

## The Heritage of Charles V

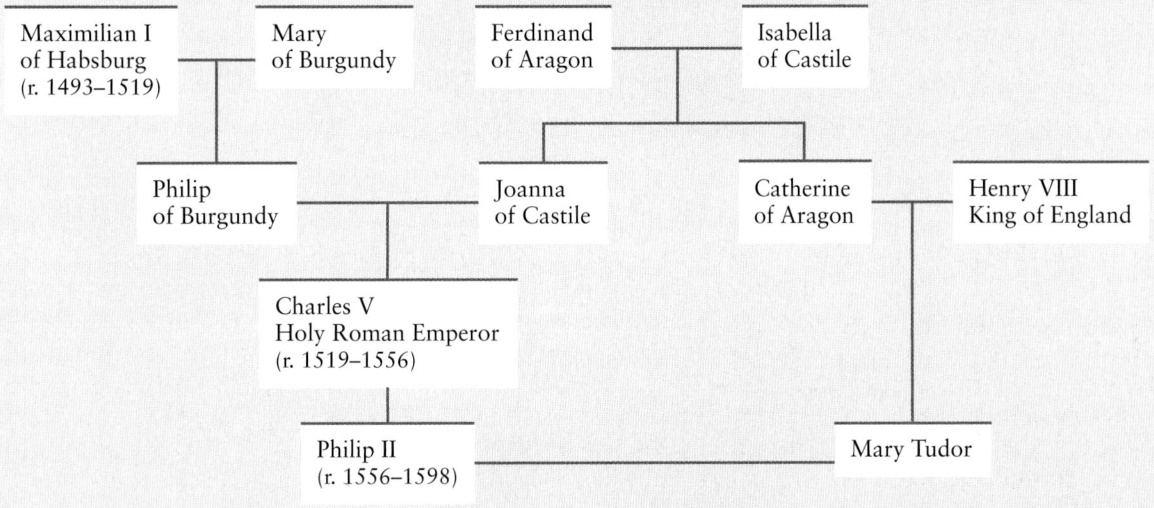


From his Habsburg grandparents, Charles V inherited claims to the imperial title, Austria, and Burgundy; through his mother, Charles acquired Spain, the Spanish territories in Italy, and the vast uncharted Spanish possessions in the New World.

Charles's inheritance was an incredibly diverse collection of states and peoples, each governed in a different manner and held together only by the person of the emperor (see Map 14.1). Charles's Italian adviser, the grand chancellor Gattinara, told the young ruler, "God has set you on the path toward world monarchy." Charles not only believed this, but also was convinced that it was his duty to maintain the political and religious unity of Western Christendom. In this respect, Charles V was the last medieval emperor.

Charles needed and in 1519 secured the imperial title. Forward-thinking Germans proposed placing the administration in the hands of an imperial council whose president, the emperor's appointee, would have ultimate executive power. Reforms of the imperial finances, the army, and the judiciary were also recommended. Such ideas did not interest the young emperor at all. When he finally arrived in Germany from Spain and opened his first diet at Worms in January 1521, he naively announced that "the empire from of old has had not many masters, but one, and it is our intention to be that one." In view of the long history of aristocratic power, Charles's notions were pure fantasy. He continued the Burgundian policy of his grandfather Maximilian. That is, German revenues and German troops were subordinated to the needs of other parts of the empire, first Burgundy and then Spain. Habsburg international interests came before the need for reform in Germany.

### The Political Impact of Luther's Beliefs

In the sixteenth century, the practice of religion remained a public matter. Everyone participated in the religious life of the community, just as almost everyone shared in the local agricultural work. Whatever spiritual convictions individuals held in the privacy of their consciences, the emperor, king, prince, magistrate, or other civil authority determined the official form of religious practice within his jurisdiction. Almost everyone believed that the presence of a faith different from that of the majority represented a political threat to the security of the state. Only a tiny minority, and certainly none of the princes, believed in religious liberty.

Against this background, the religious storm launched by Martin Luther swept across Germany. Elements in his religious reformation stirred patriotic feelings. Anti-Roman sentiment ran high. Humanists lent eloquent intellectual support. And Luther's translation of the New Testament evoked national pride.

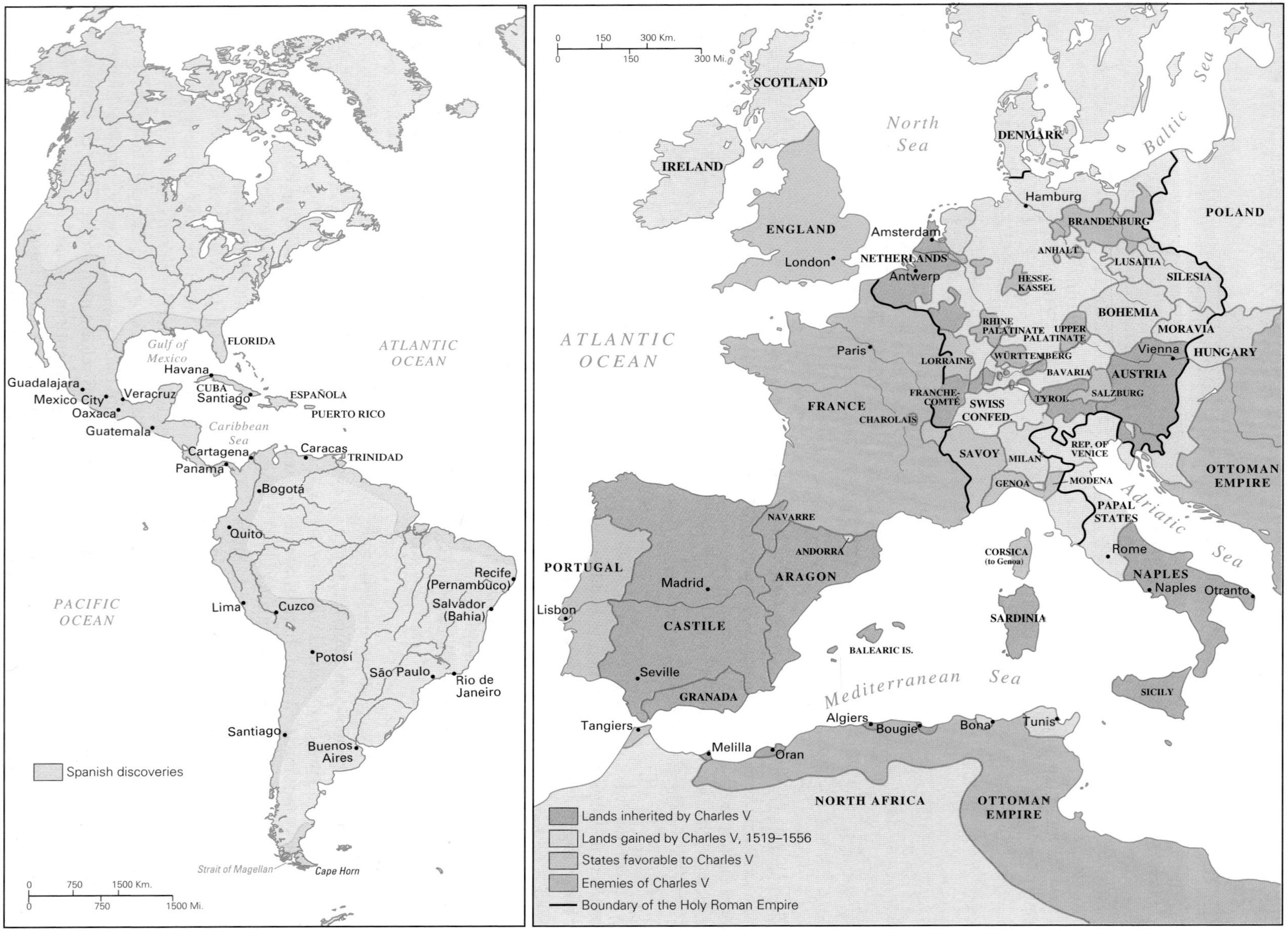


**MAP 14.1 The Global Empire of Charles V** Charles V exercised theoretical jurisdiction over more European territory than anyone since Charlemagne. He also claimed authority over large parts of North and South America.

For decades devout laypeople and churchmen had called on the German princes to reform the church. In 1520 Luther took up the cry in his *Appeal to the Christian Nobility of the German Nation*. Unless the princes destroyed papal power in Germany, Luther argued, reform was impossible. He urged the princes to confiscate ecclesiastical wealth and to abolish indulgences, dispensations, pardons, and clerical celibacy. He told them that it was their public duty to bring about the moral reform of the church. Luther based his argument in part on the papacy's financial exploitation of Germany:

*How comes it that we Germans must put up with such robbery and such extortion of our property at the hands of the pope? If the Kingdom of France has prevented it, why do we Germans let them make such fools and apes of us? It would all be more bearable if in this way they only stole our property; but they lay waste the churches and rob Christ's sheep of their pious shepherds, and destroy the worship and the Word of God. As it is they do nothing for the good of Christendom; they only wrangle about the incomes of bishoprics and prelacies, and that any robber could do.*[17]

These words fell on welcome ears and itchy fingers. Luther's appeal to German patriotism gained him strong support, and national feeling influenced many princes otherwise confused by or indifferent to the complexities of the religious issues.

The rejection of Roman Catholicism and adoption of Protestantism would mean the legal confiscation of lush farmlands, rich monasteries, and wealthy shrines. Some German princes, such as the prince-archbishop of Cologne, Hermann von Wied, were sincerely attracted to Lutheranism, but material considerations swayed many others to embrace the new faith. A steady stream of duchies, margraviates, free cities, and bishoprics secularized church property, accepted Lutheran theological doctrines, and adopted simpler services conducted in German. The decision reached at Worms in 1521 to condemn Luther and his teaching was not enforced because the German princes did not want to enforce it.

Charles V was a vigorous defender of Catholicism, and contemporary social and political theory denied the possibility of two religions coexisting peacefully in one territory. Thus many princes used the religious issue to extend their financial and political independence. When doctrinal differences became linked to political ambitions and financial receipts, the results were unfortunate for the improvement of German government. The Protestant movement ultimately proved a political disaster for Germany.

Charles V must share blame with the German princes for the disintegration of imperial authority in the empire. He neither understood nor took an interest in the constitutional problems of Germany, and he lacked the material resources to oppose Protestantism effectively there. Throughout his reign, he was preoccupied with his Flemish, Spanish, Italian, and American territories. Moreover, the Turkish threat prevented him from acting effectively against the Protestants; Charles's brother, Ferdinand, needed Protestant support against the Turks who besieged Vienna in 1529.

**Fresco of Pope Clement VII and the Emperor Charles V by Giorgio Vasari** Since Vasari's *Lives of the Most Eminent Italian Painters, Sculptors, and Architects* (rev. ed. 1568), still the basic historical source for Renaissance art and culture, held that "art is the imitation of nature," we may assume that these are faithful likenesses of the Medici pope and the Holy Roman emperor. *(Palazzo Vecchio, Florence/Scala/Art Resource, NY)*

Five times between 1521 and 1555, Charles V went to war with the Valois kings of France. The issue each time was the Habsburg lands acquired by the marriage of Maximilian and Mary of Burgundy. Much of the fighting occurred in Germany. The cornerstone of French foreign policy in the sixteenth and seventeenth centuries was the desire to keep the German states divided. Thus Europe witnessed the paradox of the Catholic king of France supporting the Lutheran princes in their challenge to his fellow Catholic, Charles V. French foreign policy contributed to the continuing division of Germany. The long dynastic struggle commonly called the Habsburg-Valois Wars advanced the cause of Protestantism and promoted the political fragmentation of the German Empire.

Finally, in 1555 Charles agreed to the Peace of Augsburg, which, in accepting the status quo, officially recognized Lutheranism. Each prince was permitted to determine his territory's religion. Most of northern and central Germany became Lutheran, while the south remained Roman Catholic. There was no freedom of religion, however. Princes or town councils established state churches to which all subjects of the area had to belong. Dissidents, whether Lutheran or Catholic, had to convert or leave. The political difficulties Germany inherited from the Middle Ages had been compounded by the religious crisis of the sixteenth century.

## The Growth of the Protestant Reformation

See DBQ 2

By 1555 much of northern Europe had broken with the Roman Catholic church. All of Scandinavia, England (except under Mary Tudor), Scotland, and such self-governing cities as Geneva and Zurich in Switzerland and Strasbourg in Germany had rejected the religious authority of Rome and adopted new faiths. Because a common religious faith had been the one element uniting all of Europe for almost a thousand years, the fragmentation of belief led to profound changes in European life and society. The most significant new form of Protestantism was Calvinism, of which the Peace of Augsburg had made no mention at all.

### Calvinism

In 1509 while Luther was studying for a doctorate at Wittenberg, John Calvin (1509–1564) was born in Noyon in northwestern France. Luther inadvertently launched the Protestant Reformation. Calvin, however, had the greater impact on future generations. His theological writings profoundly influenced the social thought and attitudes of Europeans and English-speaking peoples all over the world, especially in Canada and the United States. Although he had originally intended to have an ecclesiastical career, Calvin studied law, which had a decisive impact on his mind and later thought. In 1533 he experienced a religious crisis, as a result of which he converted to Protestantism.

Convinced that God selects certain people to do his work, Calvin believed that God had specifically called him to reform the church. Accordingly, he accepted an invitation to assist in the reformation of the city of Geneva. There, beginning in 1541, Calvin worked assiduously to establish a Christian society ruled by God through civil magistrates and reformed ministers. Geneva, "a city that was a Church," became the model of a Christian community for sixteenth-century Protestant reformers.

To understand Calvin's Geneva, it is necessary to understand Calvin's ideas. These he embodied in ***The Institutes of the Christian Religion,*** first published in 1536 and definitively issued in 1559. The cornerstone of Calvin's theology was his belief in the absolute sovereignty and omnipotence of God and the total weakness of humanity. Before the infinite power of God, he asserted, men and women are as insignificant as grains of sand.

Calvin did not ascribe free will to human beings because that would detract from the sovereignty of God. Men and women cannot actively work to achieve salvation; rather, God in his infinite wisdom decided at the beginning of time who would be saved and who damned. This viewpoint constitutes the theological principle called **predestination:**

> *Predestination we call the eternal decree of God, by which he has determined in himself, what he would have become of every individual. . . . For they are not all created with a similar destiny; but eternal life is foreordained for some, and eternal damnation for others. . . . In conformity, therefore, to the clear doctrine of the Scripture, we assert, that by an eternal and immutable counsel, God has once for all determined, both whom he would admit to salvation, and whom he would condemn to destruction. . . . To those whom he devotes to condemnation, the gate of life is closed by a just and irreprehensible, but incomprehensible, judgment. How exceedingly presumptuous it is only to inquire into the causes of the Divine will; which is in fact, and is justly entitled to be, the cause of everything that exists. . . . For the will of God is the highest justice; so that what he wills must be considered just, for this very reason, because he wills it.*[18]

Many people have found the doctrine of predestination, which dates back to Saint Augustine and Saint Paul, a pessimistic view of the nature of God, who, they feel, revealed himself in the Old and New Testaments as merciful as well as just. But "this terrible decree," as even Calvin called it, did not lead to pessimism or fatalism. Rather, the Calvinist believed in the redemptive work of Christ and was confident that God had elected (saved) him or her. Predestination served as an energizing dynamic, forcing a person to undergo hardships in the constant struggle against evil.

Calvin aroused Genevans to a high standard of morality. He had two remarkable assets: complete mastery of the Scriptures and exceptional eloquence. Through his sermons and a program of religious education, God's laws and man's were enforced in Geneva. Calvin's powerful sermons delivered the Word of God and thereby monopolized the strongest contemporary means of communication: preaching. Through his *Genevan Catechism,* published in 1541, children and adults memorized set questions and answers and acquired a summary of their faith and a guide for daily living. Calvin's sermons and his *Catechism* gave a whole generation of Genevans thorough instruction in the reformed religion.[19]

In the reformation of the city, the Genevan Consistory also exercised a powerful role. This body consisted of twelve laymen plus the Company of Pastors, of which Calvin was the permanent moderator (presider). The duties of the Consistory were "to keep watch over every man's life [and] to admonish amiably those whom they see leading a disorderly life." Even though Calvin emphasized that the Consistory's activities should be thorough and "its eyes may be everywhere," corrections were considered only "medicine to turn sinners to the Lord."[20]

Although all municipal governments in early modern Europe regulated citizens' conduct, none did so with the severity of Geneva's Consistory under Calvin's leadership. Nor did it make any distinction between what we would consider crimes against society and simple un-Christian conduct. Absence from sermons, criticism of ministers, dancing, card playing, family quarrels, and heavy drinking were all investigated and punished by the Consistory. Serious crimes and heresy were handled by the civil authorities, which, with the Consistory's approval, sometimes used torture to extract confessions. Between 1542 and 1546 alone, seventy-six persons were banished from Geneva and fifty-eight executed for heresy, adultery, blasphemy, and witchcraft.

Calvin reserved his harshest condemnation for religious dissenters, declaring them "dogs and swine":

*God makes plain that the false prophet is to be stoned without mercy. We are to crush beneath our heel all affections of nature when His honor is concerned. The father should not spare his child, . . . nor husband his own wife or the friend who is dearer to him than life. No human relationship is more than animal unless it be grounded in God.*[21]

**Young John Calvin** Even in youth, Calvin's face showed the strength and determination that was later to characterize his religious zeal. *(Geneva, CIG, coll. Bibliotèque publique et universitaire)*

In the 1550s, Spanish humanist Michael Servetus had gained international notoriety for his publications denying the Christian dogma of the Trinity. Servetus had been arrested by the Inquisition but escaped to Geneva, where he was promptly rearrested. At his trial, he not only held to his belief that there is no scriptural basis for the Trinity but also rejected child baptism and insisted that a person under twenty cannot commit a mortal sin. The city fathers considered this last idea dangerous to public morality, "especially in these days when the young are so corrupted." Though Servetus begged that he be punished by banishment, Calvin and the town council maintained that the denial of child baptism and the Trinity amounted to a threat to all society. Servetus was burned at the stake.

To many sixteenth-century Europeans, Calvin's Geneva seemed "the most perfect school of Christ since the days of the Apostles." Religious refugees from France, England, Spain, Scotland, and Italy visited the city. Subsequently, the Reformed church of Calvin served as the model for the Presbyterian church in Scotland, the Huguenot church in France, and the Puritan churches in England and New England. For women, the Calvinist provision for congregational participation and vernacular liturgy helped satisfy their desire to belong to and participate in a meaningful church organization.

On women the views of reformers such as Calvin did not differ much from those of medieval Scholastic theologians. Protestants exalted marriage, stressing the husband's authority over his family and the wife's duty of obedience to her husband. Marriage provided the outlet for women's sexual urges, which reformers believed were stronger than men's. Calvin and other reformers did not distinguish between noblewomen and commoners, but they recognized that noblewomen had influence and power. Thus Calvin maintained a large correspondence with them and worked hard to persuade Marguerite d'Angoulême and her daughter Jeanne of Navarre to support the Calvinist cause. Most women expressed their religious feelings in a domestic setting—praying, reciting the catechism, and reading the Bible with their children and servants. As public welfare, long the responsibility of local Catholic institutions, became secularized, well-to-do Protestant women aided the poor on a case-by-case basis; some wealthy women founded and endowed schools, orphanages, and dowries for girls and provided funds for poor widows. Women's charitable interests focused specifically on other women.[22]

Calvinism became the compelling force in international Protestantism. The Calvinist ethic of the "calling" dignified all work with a religious aspect. Hard work, well done, was pleasing to God. This doctrine encouraged an aggressive, vigorous activism. These factors, together with the social and economic applications of Calvin's theology, made Calvinism the most dynamic force in sixteenth- and seventeenth-century Protestantism.

## The Anabaptists

The name *Anabaptist* derives from a Greek word meaning "to baptize again." The **Anabaptists** believed that only adults could make a free choice about religious faith, baptism, and entry into the Christian community. Thus they considered the practice of baptizing infants and children preposterous and claimed there was no scriptural basis for it. They wanted to rebaptize believers who had been baptized as children. Anabaptists took the Gospel and, at first, Luther's teachings absolutely literally and favored a return to the kind of church that they thought had existed among the earliest Christians—a voluntary association of believers who had experienced an inner light.

Anabaptists maintained that only a few people would receive the inner light. This position meant that the Christian community and the Christian state were not identical. In other words, Anabaptists believed in religious toleration. They almost never tried to force their values on others. In an age that believed in the necessity of state-established churches, Anabaptist views on religious liberty were thought to undermine that concept. Each Anabaptist community or church was entirely independent; it selected its own ministers and ran its own affairs.

Anabaptists admitted women to the ministry. They shared goods as the early Christians had done, refused all public offices, and would not serve in the armed forces. In fact, they laid great stress on pacifism. A favorite Anabaptist scriptural quotation was "By their fruits you shall know them," suggesting that if Christianity was a religion of peace, then the Christian should not fight. Good deeds were the sign of Christian faith, and to be a Christian meant to imitate the meekness and mercy of Christ. With such beliefs Anabaptists were inevitably a minority. Anabaptism later attracted the poor, the unemployed, and the uneducated. Geographically, Anabaptists drew their members from depressed urban areas—from among the followers of Zwingli in Zurich and from Basel, Augsburg, and Nuremberg.

Ideas such as absolute pacifism and the distinction between the Christian community and the state brought down on these unfortunate people fanatical hatred and bitter persecution. Zwingli, Luther, Calvin, and Catholics all saw—quite correctly—the separation of church and state as leading ultimately to the complete secularization of society. The powerful rulers of Swiss and German society immediately saw the connection between religious heresy and economic dislocation. Civil authorities feared that the combination of religious differences and economic grievances would lead to civil disturbances. In Saxony, in Strasbourg, and in the Swiss cities, Anabaptists were either banished or cruelly executed by burning, beating, or drowning. Their community spirit and the edifying example of their lives, however, contributed to the survival of Anabaptist ideas. Later, the Quakers, with their gentle pacifism; the Baptists, with their emphasis on an inner spiritual light; the Congregationalists, with their democratic church organization; and, in 1787, the authors of the U.S. Constitution, with their opposition to the "establishment of religion" (state churches), would all trace their origins, in part, to the Anabaptists of the sixteenth century.

## The English Reformation

As on the continent, the Reformation in England had economic causes as well as religious ones. When the personal matter of the divorce of King Henry VIII (r. 1509–1547) became enmeshed with political issues, a complete break with Rome resulted.

Demands for ecclesiastical reform dated back at least to the fourteenth century. The Lollards (see page 394) had been driven underground in the fifteenth century but survived in parts of southern England and the Midlands. Working-class people, especially cloth workers, were attracted to their ideas. The Lollards stressed the individual's reading and interpretation of the Bible, which they considered the only standard of Christian faith and holiness. Consequently, they put no stock in the value of the sacraments and were vigorously anticlerical. Lollards opposed ecclesiastical wealth, the veneration of the saints, prayers for the dead, and all war. Although they had no notion of justification by faith, like Luther they insisted on the individual soul's direct responsibility to God.

Recent scholarship indicates that the English church was in a very healthy condition in the early sixteenth century. Traditional Catholicism exerted an enormously strong and vigorous hold over the imagination and loyalty of the people. The teachings of Christianity were graphically represented in the liturgy, reiterated in sermons, enacted in plays, carved and printed on walls, screens, and the windows of churches. A zealous clergy, increasingly better educated, engaged in a "massive catechetical enterprise." No substantial gulf existed between the religion of the clergy and educated elite and the broad mass of the English people.[23] The Reformation in England was an act of state initiated by the king's emotional life.

In 1527, having fallen in love with Anne Boleyn, Henry wanted his marriage to Catherine of Aragon annulled. When Henry had married Catherine, he had secured a dispensation from Pope Julius II eliminating all legal technicalities about Catherine's previous union with Henry's late brother, Arthur. Henry claimed that a disputed succession and the anarchy of the Wars of the Roses would be repeated if a woman, the princess Mary, sole surviving child of his marriage to Catherine, inherited the throne. Accordingly, Henry petitioned Pope Clement VII for an annulment, stating that a valid marriage to Catherine had never existed. The pope was an indecisive man whose attention at the time was focused on the Lutheran revolt in Germany and the Habsburg-Valois struggle for control of Italy. But there is a stronger reason Clement could not grant Henry's petition. Henry argued that Pope Julius's dispensation had contradicted the law of God—that a man may not marry his brother's widow. The English king's request reached Rome at the very time that Luther was publishing tracts condemning the papacy as the core of wickedness. Had Clement granted Henry's annulment and thereby admitted that his recent predecessor, Julius II, had erred, Clement would have given support to the Lutheran assertion that popes substituted their own evil judgments for the law of God. This Clement could not do, so he delayed acting on Henry's request.[24] The capture and sack of Rome in 1527 by the emperor Charles V (see the chart on page 467), Queen Catherine's nephew, thoroughly tied the pope's hands.

Since Rome appeared to be thwarting Henry's matrimonial plans, he decided to remove the English church from papal jurisdiction. Henry used Parliament to legalize the Reformation in England. The Act in Restraint of Appeals (1533) declared the king to be the supreme sovereign in England and forbade judicial appeals to the papacy, thus establishing the Crown as the highest legal authority in the land. The Supremacy Act (1534) declared the king the supreme head of the Church of England. Both the Act in Restraint of Appeals and the Supremacy Act led to heated debate in the House of Commons. An authority on the Reformation Parliament has written that probably only a small number of those who voted for the Restraint of Appeals actually knew they were voting for a permanent break with Rome.[25] Some opposed the king. John Fisher, the bishop of Rochester, a distinguished scholar and a humanist, lashed the clergy with scorn for its cowardice in abjectly bending to the king's will. Another humanist, Thomas More, resigned the chancellorship: he could not take the oath required by the Supremacy Act because it rejected papal authority and made the king head of the English church. Fisher, More, and other dissenters were beheaded.

When Anne Boleyn failed twice to produce a male child, Henry VIII charged her with adulterous incest and in 1536 had her beheaded. Parliament promptly proclaimed Anne's daughter, the princess Elizabeth, illegitimate and, with the royal succession thoroughly confused, left the throne to whomever Henry chose. His third wife, Jane Seymour, gave Henry the desired son, Edward, but died in childbirth. Henry went on to three more wives. Before he passed to his reward in 1547, he got Parliament to reverse the decision of 1536, relegitimating Mary and Elizabeth and fixing the succession first in his son and then in his daughters.

Between 1535 and 1539, under the influence of his chief minister, Thomas Cromwell, Henry decided to dissolve the English monasteries because he wanted their wealth. The king ended nine hundred years of English monastic life, dispersed the monks and nuns, and confiscated their lands. Hundreds of properties were sold to the middle and upper classes and the proceeds spent on war. The dissolution of the monasteries did not achieve a more equitable distribution of land and wealth. Rather, the "bare ruined choirs where late the sweet birds sang"—as Shakespeare described in Sonnet 73 the desolate religious houses—testified to the loss of a valuable cultural force in English life. The redistribution of land strengthened the upper classes and tied them to the Tudor dynasty.

Did the religious changes accompanying this political upheaval have broad popular support? The surviving evidence does not allow us to gauge the degree of opposition to (or support for) Henry's break with Rome. Certainly, many laypeople wrote to the king begging him to spare the monasteries. "Most laypeople acquiesced in the Reformation because they hardly knew what was going on, were understandably reluctant to jeopardise life or limb, a career or the family's good name."[26] But all did not quietly acquiesce. In 1536 popular opposition in the north to the religious changes led to the Pilgrimage of Grace, a massive multiclass rebellion that proved the largest in English history. The "pilgrims" accepted a truce, and their leaders were arrested, tried, and executed. In 1546 serious rebellions in East Anglia and in the west, despite possessing economic and Protestant components, reflected considerable public opposition to the state-ordered religious changes.[27]

Henry's motives combined personal, political, social, and economic elements. Theologically he retained such traditional Catholic practices and doctrines as auricular confession, clerical celibacy, and transubstantiation. Meanwhile, Protestant literature circulated, and Henry approved the selection of men of Protestant sympathies as tutors for his son.

The nationalization of the church and the dissolution of the monasteries led to important changes in government administration. Vast tracts of formerly monastic land came temporarily under the Crown's jurisdiction, and new bureaucratic machinery had to be developed to manage those properties. Cromwell reformed and centralized the king's household, the council, the secretariats, and the Exchequer. New departments of state were set up. Surplus funds from all of the departments went into a liquid fund to be applied to areas where there were deficits. This balancing resulted in greater efficiency and economy. Henry VIII's reign saw the growth of the modern centralized bureaucratic state.

In the short reign of Henry's sickly son, Edward VI (r. 1547–1553), strongly Protestant ideas exerted a significant influence on the religious life of the country. Archbishop Thomas Cranmer simplified the liturgy, invited Protestant theologians to England, and prepared the first ***Book of Common Prayer*** (1549). In stately and dignified English, the *Book of Common Prayer* included, together with the Psalter, the order for all services of the Church of England.

The equally brief reign of Mary Tudor (r. 1553–1558) witnessed a sharp move back to Catholicism. The devoutly Catholic daughter of Catherine of Aragon, Mary rescinded the Reformation legislation of her father's reign and restored Roman Catholicism. Mary's marriage to her cousin Philip of Spain, son of the emperor Charles V, proved highly unpopular in England, and her execution of several hundred Protestants further alienated her subjects. During her reign, many Protestants fled to the continent. Mary's death raised to the throne her sister, Elizabeth (r. 1558–1603), and inaugurated the beginnings of religious stability.

Elizabeth had been raised a Protestant, but at the start of her reign sharp differences existed in England. On the one hand, Catholics wanted a Roman Catholic ruler. On the other hand, a vocal number of returning exiles wanted all Catholic elements in the Church of England eliminated. The latter, because they wanted to "purify" the church, were called "Puritans." Probably one of the shrewdest politicians in English history, Elizabeth chose a middle course between Catholic and Puritan extremes. She insisted on dignity in church services and political order in the land. She did not care what people believed as long as they kept quiet about it. Avoiding precise doctrinal definitions, Elizabeth had herself styled "Supreme Governor of the Church of England, Etc.," and left it to her subjects to decide what the "Etc." meant.

The parliamentary legislation of the early years of Elizabeth's reign—laws sometimes labeled the **Elizabethan Settlement**—required outward conformity to the Church of England and uniformity in all ceremonies. Everyone had to attend Church of England services; those who refused were fined. In 1563 a convocation of bishops approved the Thirty-nine Articles, a summary in thirty-nine

**Allegory of the Tudor Dynasty** The unknown creator of this work intended to glorify the virtues of the Protestant succession; the painting has no historical reality. Enthroned Henry VIII (r. 1509–1547) hands the sword of justice to his Protestant son Edward VI (r. 1547–1553). The Catholic Queen Mary (r. 1553–1558) and her husband Philip of Spain are followed by Mars, god of war, signifying violence and civil disorder. At right the figures of Peace and Plenty accompany the Protestant Elizabeth I (r. 1558–1603), symbolizing England's happy fate under her rule. *(Yale Center for British Art, Paul Mellon Collection/The Bridgeman Art Library)*

short statements of the basic tenets of the Church of England. During Elizabeth's reign, the Anglican church (from the Latin *Ecclesia Anglicana*), as the Church of England was called, moved in a moderately Protestant direction. Services were conducted in English, monasteries were not re-established, and clergymen were allowed to marry. But the episcopate was not abolished and the bishops remained as church officials; apart from language, the services were quite traditional.

## The Establishment of the Church of Scotland

In Scotland as elsewhere, political authority was the decisive influence in reform. The monarchy was weak, and factions of virtually independent nobles competed for power. King James V and his daughter, Mary, Queen of Scots (r. 1560–1567), staunch Catholics and close allies of Catholic France, opposed reform. The Scottish nobles supported it. One man, John Knox (1505?–1572), dominated the movement for reform in Scotland.

In 1559 Knox, a dour, single-minded, and fearless man with a reputation as a passionate preacher, set to work reforming the church. He had studied and worked with Calvin in Geneva and was determined to structure the Scottish church after the model of Calvin's Geneva. In 1560 Knox persuaded the Scottish parliament, which was dominated by reform-minded barons, to enact legislation ending papal authority. The Mass was abolished. Knox then established the Presbyterian Church of Scotland, so named because *presbyters,* or ministers, not bishops, governed it. The Church of Scotland was strictly Calvinist in doctrine, adopted a simple and dignified service of worship, and laid great emphasis on preaching. Knox's *Book of Common Order* (1564) became the liturgical directory for the church. The Presbyterian Church of Scotland was a national, or state, church, and many of its members maintained close relations with English Puritans.

## Protestantism in Ireland

To the ancient Irish hatred of English political and commercial exploitation, the Reformation added the bitter antagonism of religion. Henry VIII wanted to "reduce that realm to the knowledge of God and obedience to us." English rulers in the sixteenth century regarded the Irish as barbarians, and a policy of complete extermination was rejected only because "to enterprise [attempt] the whole extirpation and total destruction of all the Irishmen in the land would be a marvelous sumptious charge and great difficulty."[28] In other words, it would have cost too much.

In 1536 on orders from London, the Irish parliament, which represented only the English landlords and the people of the Pale (the area around Dublin), approved the English laws severing the church from Rome and making the English king sovereign over ecclesiastical organization and practice. The Church of Ireland was established on the English pattern, and the (English) ruling class adopted the new reformed faith. Most of the Irish, probably for political reasons, defiantly remained Roman Catholic. Monasteries were secularized. Catholic property was confiscated and sold and the profits were shipped to England. With the Roman church driven underground, Catholic churchmen acted as national as well as religious leaders.

## Lutheranism in Sweden, Norway, and Denmark

In Sweden, Norway, and Denmark, the monarchy took the initiative in the religious Reformation. The resulting institutions were Lutheran state churches. Since the late fourteenth century, the Danish kings had ruled Sweden and Norway as well as Denmark. In 1520 Swedish nobleman Gustavus Vasa (r. 1523–1560) led a successful revolt against Denmark, and Sweden became independent. As king, Gustavus Vasa seized church lands and required the bishops' loyalty to the Swedish crown. Wittenberg-educated Swedish reformer Olaus Petri (1493–1552) translated the New Testament into Swedish and, with the full support of Gustavus Vasa, organized the church along strict Lutheran lines. This consolidation of the Swedish monarchy in the sixteenth century was to profoundly affect the development of Germany in the seventeenth century.

Christian III (r. 1503–1559) king of Denmark and of Norway (r. 1534–1559), secularized church property and set up a Lutheran church. Norway, which was governed by Denmark until 1814, adopted Lutheranism as its state religion under Danish influence.

## The Reformation in Eastern Europe

While political and economic issues determined the course of the Reformation in western and northern Europe, ethnic factors often proved decisive in eastern Europe. In the later Middle Ages, the migration of diverse peoples into Bohemia, Poland, and Hungary meant that in the sixteenth century those countries had heterogeneous populations. Ethnic background tended to resolve religious matters.

In Bohemia in the fifteenth century, the ethnic grievances of the Czech majority against German economic and ecclesiastical domination (see page 404) fused with Czech resentment at the corruption of the Roman church. By 1500, most Czechs had adopted Jan Hus's utraquist position (communion in both bread and wine). Germans adhered to the Roman Catholic tenet. Martin Luther's approval of utraquism led to the rapid spread of Lutheranism among Germans in Bohemia in the 1520s and 1530s; many Germans lived near the border of Luther's Saxony. Though a practicing Catholic and brother of the Habsburg emperor Charles V, King Ferdinand I of Bohemia had to acquiesce in the establishment of utraquism to become king, thereby aiding the spread of Lutheranism. Moreover, the nobility's identification of Lutheranism with opposition to the Habsburgs contributed, as in Germany, to the growth of Protestantism. Ferdinand's successors Maximilian II and Rudolf II had more tolerant religious policies, but the forces of Counter-Reformation spearheaded by the Council of Trent (see pages 479–480) promoted a Catholic spiritual revival in Bohemia. The contest between the ruler and the nobility would be resolved only in the Thirty Years' War (see pages 497–501).

By 1500 Poland and the Grand Duchy of Lithuania were united in a dynastic union. A king, senate, and diet (parliament) governed, but the two territories retained separate officials, judicial systems, armies, and forms of citizenship. In the fifteenth century, rulers had granted the Polish *szlachta* (nobility) extensive rights; though hereditary, the monarchy was weak and had to cooperate with the szlachta. The combined realms covered about 440,150 square miles, making Poland-Lithuania the largest European polity. A population of only about 7.5 million people was very thinly scattered over that land.

In comparison with western Europe, Poland-Lithuania was overwhelmingly rural, its largest cities Gdansk (30,000) and Cracow (15,000) very small in population by Italian or French standards. Yet with Germans, Italians, Tartars, and Jews, Poland-Lithuania represented great diversity. Such peoples had come as merchants, invited by medieval rulers because of their wealth or to make agricultural improvements. Each group spoke its native language, though all educated people spoke Latin. In the late fifteenth century, Italian Renaissance humanism influenced Polish art, architecture, literature, and historical writing.

Luther's ideas spread first to the German-speaking Baltic towns, then to the University of Cracow, where his works were translated. His ideas met two major obstacles: King Sigismund I (r. 1506–1548) banned Luther's teachings in Poland, and strong anti-German feeling among Poles meant that Lutheranism would have limited success outside Germanized towns.

The Reformed tradition of John Calvin, with its stress on the power of church elders, appealed to the Polish szlachta, however. The fact that Calvinism originated in France, not in Germany, also made it more attractive than Lutheranism. Several Polish magnates, including Jan Laski (1499–1560), converted to Calvinism, and Calvinist nobles dominated the important diet of 1555. But doctrinal differences among Calvinists, Lutherans, and other sects prevented united opposition to Catholicism.

Under Stanislaus Hosius (1505–1579), who attended the Council of Trent, a systematic Counter-Reformation gained momentum. Hosius pressed for reform within the Catholic church, held provincial synods, and published a comprehensive and clear statement of Roman Catholic faith and morals. The Jesuits (see page 483) complemented his work by establishing schools for the sons of the szlachta. By 1650, the identification of Poland and Roman Catholicism was well established.

Merchants from Poland carried the first news about Martin Luther to Hungary in 1521. Hungarian students flocked to Wittenberg; they became the major agents for the spread of Lutheranism in Hungary, and sympathy for it developed at the royal court at Buda. But concern about "the German heresy" in the Catholic hierarchy and among the magnates found expression in a decree of the Hungarian diet in 1523 that "all Lutherans and those favoring them . . . should have their property confiscated and themselves punished with death as heretics."[29]

A military event on August 26, 1526, had profound consequences for both the Hungarian state and the Protestant Reformation there. On the plain of Mohács in southern Hungary, the Ottoman sultan Suleiman the Magnificent (see page 570) inflicted a crushing defeat on the Hungarians, killing King Louis II, many of the magnates, and over sixteen thousand ordinary soldiers. Rival factions elected different kings, and the Hungarian kingdom was divided into three parts: the Ottoman Turks absorbed the great plains, including the capital, Buda; the Habsburgs ruled the north and west; Ottoman-supported Janos Zapolya held eastern Hungary and Transylvania. The Turks were indifferent to the religious conflicts of the infidels.

Mohács led to a great advance of Protestantism. Many Magyar (Hungarian) magnates accepted Lutheranism; Lutheran schools and parishes headed by men educated at Wittenberg multiplied; peasants welcomed the new faith. In spite of the foundation of Jesuit colleges, in 1585 the papal nuncio noted that 85 percent of the population was Protestant, 10 percent remained Greek Orthodox, and just 5 percent (concentrated in Croatia) stayed Catholic. Hungary seemed lost to Catholicism. Then in the late seventeenth century, Hungarian nobles' recognition of Habsburg (Catholic) rule, and Ottoman Turkish withdrawal in 1699, led to Catholic restoration.

## The Catholic Reformation and the Counter-Reformation

Between 1517 and 1547, the reformed versions of Christianity known as Protestantism made remarkable advances. Nevertheless, the Roman Catholic church made a significant comeback. After about 1540, no new large areas of Europe, except for the Netherlands, accepted Protestant beliefs (see Map 14.2).

Historians distinguish between two types of reform within the Catholic church in the sixteenth and seventeenth centuries. The Catholic Reformation began before 1517 and sought renewal basically through the stimulation of a new spiritual fervor. The Counter-Reformation started in the 1540s as a reaction to the rise and spread of Protestantism. The Counter-Reformation involved Catholic efforts to convince or coerce dissidents or heretics to return to the church lest they corrupt the entire community of Catholic believers. Fear of the "infection" of all Christian society by the religious dissident was a standard sixteenth-century attitude. If the heretic could not be persuaded to reconvert, counter-reformers believed it necessary to call on temporal authorities to defend Christian society by expelling or eliminating the dissident. The Catholic Reformation and the Counter-Reformation were not mutually exclusive; in fact, after about 1540 they progressed simultaneously.

### The Slowness of Institutional Reform

The Renaissance princes who sat on the throne of Saint Peter were not blind to the evils that existed. Modest reform efforts had begun with the Lateran Council called in 1512 by Pope Julius II. The Dutch pope Adrian VI

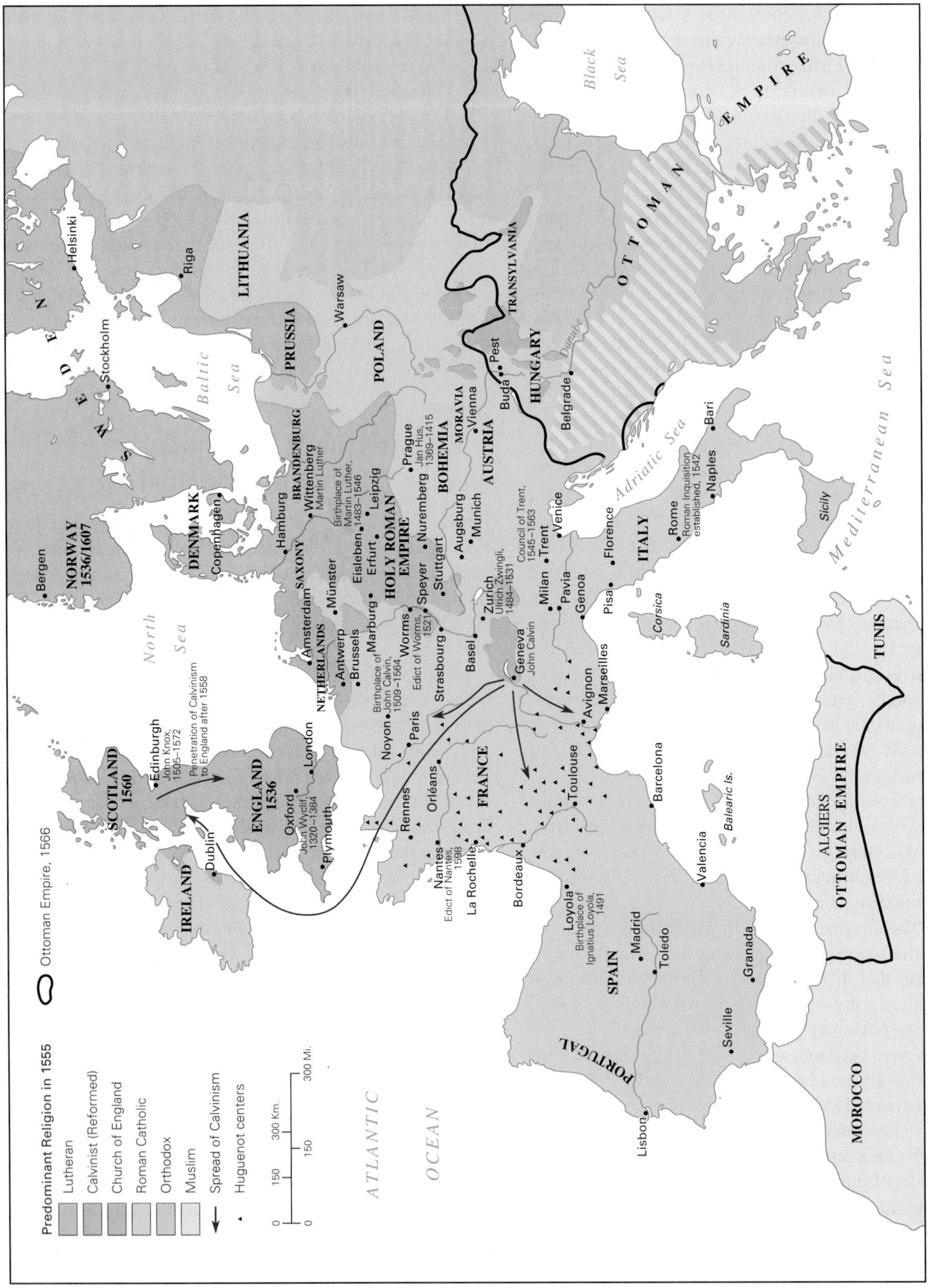


**MAP 14.2 The Protestant and the Catholic Reformations** The Reformations shattered the religious unity of Western Christendom. What common cultural traits predominated in regions where a particular branch of the Christian faith was maintained or took root?

(1522–1523) instructed his legate in Germany to "say that we frankly confess that God permits this [Lutheran] persecution of his church on account of the sins of men, especially those of the priests and prelates. . . . We know that in this Holy See now for some years there have been many abominations."[30] Adrian VI tried desperately to reform the church and to check the spread of Protestantism. His reign lasted only thirteen months, however, and the austerity of his life and his Dutch nationality provoked the hostility of pleasure-loving Italian curial bureaucrats.

Overall, why did the popes, spiritual leaders of the Western church, move so slowly? The answers lie in the personalities of the popes themselves, their preoccupation with political affairs in Italy, and the awesome difficulty of reforming so complicated a bureaucracy as the Roman curia.

Clement VII (r. 1523–1534), a true Medici, was far more interested in elegant tapestries and Michelangelo's painting of the Last Judgment than in theological disputes in barbaric Germany. Indecisive and vacillating, Pope Clement must bear much of the responsibility for the great spread of Protestantism. While Emperor Charles V and the French king Francis I competed for the domination of divided Italy, the papacy worried about the security of the Papal States. Clement tried to follow a middle course, backing first the emperor and then the French ruler. At the Battle of Pavia in 1525, Francis I suffered a severe defeat and was captured. In a reshuffling of diplomatic alliances, the pope switched from Charles and the Spanish to Francis I. In retaliation for Clement's diplomatic shift, and to pay his near mutinous soldiers, Charles allowed his German and Spanish troops to sack Rome (May 1527) and to capture the pope. With the city destroyed, its art treasures stolen, and its population decimated, a contemporary reported that "hell itself must have been a prettier sight." The event marked the end of the High Renaissance in Rome.

The idea of reform was closely linked to the idea of a general council representing the entire church. A strong contingent of countries beyond the Alps—Spain, Germany, and France—wanted to reform the vast bureaucracy of Latin officials, reducing offices, men, and revenues. Popes from Julius II to Clement VII, remembering fifteenth-century conciliar attempts to limit papal authority, resisted calls for a council. The papal bureaucrats who were the popes' intimates warned the popes against a council, fearing loss of power, revenue, and prestige.

## The Council of Trent

In the papal conclave that followed the death of Clement VII, Cardinal Alexander Farnese promised two German cardinals that if he was elected pope, he would summon a council. He won the election and ruled as Pope Paul III (1534–1549). This Roman aristocrat, humanist, and astrologer, who immediately made his teenage grandsons cardinals, seemed an unlikely person to undertake serious reform. Yet Paul III appointed as cardinals several reform-minded men, such as Gian Pietro Caraffa (later Pope Paul IV); established the Inquisition in the Papal States; and—true to his word—called a council, which finally met at Trent, an imperial city close to Italy.

The Council of Trent met intermittently from 1545 to 1563. It was called not only to reform the church but also to secure reconciliation with the Protestants. Lutherans and Calvinists were invited to participate, but their insistence that the Scriptures be the sole basis for discussion made reconciliation impossible. International politics repeatedly cast a shadow over the theological debates. Charles V opposed discussions on any matter that might further alienate his Lutheran subjects, fearing the loss of additional imperial territory to Lutheran princes. Meanwhile, the French kings worked against the reconciliation of Roman Catholicism and Lutheranism. As long as religious issues divided the German states, the empire would be weakened, and a weak and divided empire meant a stronger France. Portugal, Poland, Hungary, and Ireland sent representatives, but very few German bishops attended.

Another problem was the persistence of the conciliar theory of church government (see page 394). Some bishops wanted a concrete statement asserting the supremacy of a church council over the papacy, but the centralizing tenet was established that all acts of the council required papal approval.

In spite of the obstacles, the achievements of the Council of Trent were impressive. It dealt with both doctrinal and disciplinary matters. The council gave equal validity to the Scriptures and to tradition as sources of religious truth and authority. It reaffirmed the seven sacraments and the traditional Catholic teaching on transubstantiation. Thus it rejected Lutheran and Calvinist positions.

The council tackled the problems arising from ancient abuses by strengthening ecclesiastical discipline. Tridentine (from *Tridentum,* the Latin word for Trent) decrees required bishops to reside in their own dioceses, suppressed pluralism and simony, and forbade the sale of indulgences. Clerics who kept concubines were to give them up. The jurisdiction of bishops over all the clergy of their dioceses was made almost absolute, and bishops were ordered to visit every religious house within the diocese at least once every two years. In a highly original canon, the council required every diocese to establish a seminary for the education and training of the clergy; the council even

**School of Titian: The Council of Trent** Since the early sessions were sparsely attended, this well-attended meeting seems to be a later session. Few bishops from northern Europe, however, ever attended. The Swiss guards (*forefront*) of the Vatican were founded by Pope Julius II in 1505 to defend the papacy. *(Louvre/Réunion des Musées Nationaux/Art Resource, NY)*

prescribed the curriculum and insisted that preference for admission be given to sons of the poor. Seminary professors were to determine if candidates for ordination had *vocations,* genuine callings as determined by purity of life, detachment from the broader secular culture, and a steady inclination toward the priesthood. This was a novel idea since from the time of the early church, parents had determined their sons' (and daughters') religious careers (see page 205). Finally, great emphasis was laid on preaching and instructing the laity, especially the uneducated.

One decision had especially important social consequences for laypeople. Since the time of the Roman Empire, many couples had treated marriage as a completely personal matter, exchanged vows privately without witnesses, and thus formed what were called clandestine (secret) unions. This widespread practice frequently led later to denials by one party, conflicts over property, and disputes in the ecclesiastical courts that had jurisdiction over marriage once it became a sacrament (which occurred in the twelfth century). The Tridentine decree Tametsi (November 1563) stipulated that for a marriage to be valid, consent (the essence of marriage) as given in the vows had to be made publicly before witnesses, one of whom had to be the parish priest. Trent thereby ended secret marriages in Catholic countries. (They remained a problem for civil and church courts in England until the Hardwicke Act of 1753 abolished them.)

The Council of Trent did not meet everyone's expectations. Reconciliation with Protestantism was not achieved, nor was reform brought about immediately. Nevertheless, the Tridentine decrees laid a solid basis for the spiritual renewal of the church and for the enforcement of correction. For four centuries, the doctrinal and disciplinary legislation of Trent served as the basis for Roman Catholic faith, organization, and practice.

## New Religious Orders

The establishment of new religious orders within the church reveals a central feature of the Catholic Reformation. Most of these new orders developed in response to one crying need: to raise the moral and intellectual level

# Individuals in Society

## Teresa of Ávila

Her family derived from Toledo, center of the Moorish, Jewish, and Christian cultures in medieval Spain. Her grandfather, Juan Sanchez, made a fortune in the cloth trade. A "New Christian" (see pages 445–446), he was accused of secretly practicing Judaism. Although he endured the humiliation of a public repentance, he moved his family south to Ávila. Beginning again, he recouped his wealth and, aspiring to the prestige of an "Old Christian," bought noble status. Juan's son Alzonzo Sanchez de Cepeda married a woman of thoroughly Christian background, giving his family an aura of impeccable orthodoxy. The third of their nine children, Teresa, became a saint and the first woman declared a Doctor of the Church—a theologian of outstanding merit and saintliness (1970).

At age twenty, inspired more by the fear of Hell than the love of God, Teresa (1515–1582) entered the Carmelite Convent of the Incarnation in Ávila. The 140 nuns there were supported by rents from their lands; they did not practice poverty. Nor did they observe enclosure, as guests were frequently entertained. The nuns, privileged daughters of Ávila's leading citizens, were obsessed with status and social prestige.

For twenty years Teresa remained in this worldly atmosphere that contradicted the convent's religious ideals. Francesco de Osuna's book *The Third Spiritual Alphabet* introduced Teresa to a more meaningful spiritual life, and she began to devour devotional literature. In her late thirties, she had profound mystical experiences—visions and voices in which Christ chastised her for her frivolous life and friends. She described one such experience in 1560:

> *It pleased the Lord that I should see an angel. . . . Short, and very beautiful, his face was so aflame that he appeared to be one of the highest types of angels. . . . In his hands I saw a long golden spear and at the end of an iron tip I seemed to see a point of fire. With this he seemed to pierce my heart several times so that it penetrated to my entrails. When he drew it out . . . he left me completely afire with the great love of God.**

Teresa responded with a new sense of purpose: although she encountered stiff opposition, she resolved to found a reformed house. Four basic principles were to guide the new convent. First, poverty was to be fully observed, symbolized by the nuns being barefoot, hence *discalced*. Ending a long-established monastic practice, Teresa rejected rents: charity and the nuns' own work must support the community. Second, the convent must keep strict enclosure; the visits of powerful benefactors with material demands were forbidden. Third, Teresa intended an egalitarian atmosphere where class distinctions were forbidden. She had always rejected the emphasis on "purity of blood," a distinctive and racist feature of Spanish society especially out of place in the cloister. All sisters, including those of aristocratic background, must share the manual chores. Finally, like Ignatius Loyola and the Jesuits, Teresa placed great emphasis on obedience, especially to one's confessor.

*Seventeenth-century cloisonné enamelwork illustrating Teresa of Ávila's famous vision.* (By gracious permission of Catherine Hamilton Kappauf)

Between 1562 and Teresa's death in 1582, she founded or reformed fourteen other houses of nuns, no small feat for a woman in a very sexist society. She was the first spiritual author to provide a scientific description of the life of prayer from simple meditation to mystical union with God. Her books, along with her five hundred extant letters, show her as capable of great discernment of individual character. But for all her mystical experiences, Teresa was a motherly, practical, and down-to-earth woman with a strong sense of humor. From her brother who had obtained wealth in the Spanish colonies, Teresa learned about conditions in Peru and instructed her nuns "to pray unceasingly for the missionaries working among the heathens." In this way, they shared in evangelization.

Teresa of Ávila responded to change not with doubt, but with deeper belief.

### Questions for Analysis

1. How did sixteenth-century convent life reflect the values of Spanish society?
2. How does Teresa of Ávila represent the spirit of the Catholic Reformation?

**The Autobiography of St. Teresa of Ávila,* trans. and ed. E. A. Peers (New York: Doubleday, 1960), pp. 273–274.

*The* **history companion** *features additional information and activities related to this topic.*
**history.college.hmco.com/students**

**Juan de Valdes Leal: Pope Paul III Approves the Jesuit Constitutions** Although Paul III devoted considerable energy to advancing the interests of his (Farnese) family, he also tried to meet the challenge of Protestantism—through the Council of Trent and new religious orders. When the Jesuit constitutions were read to him, Paul III supposedly murmured, "There is the finger of God." The portrait of Ignatius Loyola is a reasonable likeness, that of the pope an idealization: in 1540 he was a very old man. *(Institut Amatller d'Art Hispanic)*

of the clergy and people. (See the feature "Individuals in Society: Teresa of Ávila.") Education was a major goal of the two most famous orders.

The Ursuline order of nuns, founded by Angela Merici (1474–1540), attained enormous prestige for the education of women. The daughter of a country gentleman, Angela Merici worked for many years among the poor, sick, and uneducated around her native Brescia in northern Italy. In 1535 she established the Ursuline order to combat heresy through Christian education. The first women's religious order concentrating exclusively on teaching young girls, the Ursulines sought to re-Christianize society by training future wives and mothers. Because the Council of Trent placed great stress on the *claustration* (strict enclosure) of religious women and called for the end of all active ministries for women, Angela had great difficulty gaining papal approval. Official recognition finally came in 1565, and the Ursulines rapidly spread to France and the New World. Their schools in North America, stretching from Quebec to New Orleans, provided superior education for young women and inculcated the spiritual ideals of the Catholic Reformation.

The Society of Jesus, founded by Ignatius Loyola (1491–1556), a former Spanish soldier, played a powerful international role in resisting the spread of Protestantism, converting Asians and Latin American Indians to Catholicism, and spreading Christian education all over Europe. While recuperating from a severe battle wound in his legs, Loyola studied a life of Christ and other religious books and decided to give up his military career and become a soldier of Christ. During a year spent in seclusion, prayer, and personal mortification, he gained insights that went into his great classic, *Spiritual Exercises* (1548). This work, intended for study during a four-week period of retreat, directed the individual imagination and will to the reform of life and a new spiritual piety.

Loyola was a man of considerable personal magnetism. After study at universities in Salamanca and Paris, he gathered a group of six companions and in 1540 secured papal approval of the new Society of Jesus, whose members were called **Jesuits.** The first Jesuits, recruited primarily from the wealthy merchant and professional classes, saw the Reformation as a pastoral problem, its causes and cures related not to doctrinal issues but to people's spiritual condition. Reform of the church, as Luther and Calvin understood that term, played no role in the future the Jesuits planned for themselves. Their goal was "to help souls." Loyola also possessed a gift for leadership that consisted in spotting talent and in seeing "how at a given juncture change is more consistent with one's scope than staying the course."[31]

The Society of Jesus developed into a highly centralized, tightly knit organization. Candidates underwent a two-year novitiate, in contrast to the usual one-year probation. In addition to the traditional vows of poverty, chastity, and obedience, professed members vowed "special obedience to the sovereign pontiff regarding missions."[32] Thus as stability—the promise to live his life in the monastery—was what made a monk, so mobility—the commitment to go anywhere for the help of souls—was the defining characteristic of a Jesuit. Flexibility and the willingness to respond to the needs of time and circumstance formed the Jesuit tradition. In this respect, Jesuits were very modern, and they attracted many recruits.

They achieved phenomenal success for the papacy and the reformed Catholic church. Jesuit schools adopted the modern humanist curricula and methods, and though they first concentrated on the children of the poor, they were soon educating the sons of the nobility. As confessors and spiritual directors to kings, Jesuits exerted great political influence. Operating on the principle that the end sometimes justifies the means, they were not above spying. Indifferent to physical comfort and personal safety, they carried Christianity to India and Japan before 1550, to Brazil, North America, and the Congo in the seventeenth century. Within Europe the Jesuits brought southern Germany and much of eastern Europe back to Catholicism.

### The Congregation of the Holy Office

In 1542 Pope Paul III established the Sacred Congregation of the **Holy Office,** with jurisdiction over the Roman Inquisition, a powerful instrument of the Counter-Reformation. The Inquisition was a committee of six cardinals with judicial authority over all Catholics and the power to arrest, imprison, and execute. Under the fanatical Cardinal Caraffa, it vigorously attacked heresy.

The Roman Inquisition operated under the principles of Roman law. It accepted hearsay evidence, was not obliged to inform the accused of charges against them, and sometimes applied torture. Echoing one of Calvin's remarks about heresy, Cardinal Caraffa wrote, "No man is to lower himself by showing toleration towards any sort of heretic, least of all a Calvinist."[33] The Holy Office published the *Index of Prohibited Books,* a catalogue of forbidden reading.

Within the Papal States, the Inquisition effectively destroyed heresy (and some heretics). Outside the papal territories, however, its influence was slight. In Venice, a major publishing center, the *Index* had no influence on scholarly research in nonreligious areas such as law, classical literature, and mathematics. As a result of the Inquisition, Venetians and Italians were *not* cut off from the main currents of European learning.

### The Reformations: Revolution or Continuity?

The introduction to this chapter casts reformation in general in terms of the individual Christian's and the institutional church's continual need and search for reform. Indeed, the first critical moment came with one man, Martin Luther, whose inner questioning about his own salvation led to his criticism of the Roman papacy. Historians ask a central question: do the sixteenth-century religious movements represent continuity—a constant feature of the institutional faith—or do those movements demonstrate revolution and radical discontinuity? Recent scholarly research argues that the Reformations constituted both.

Revolution, by definition, rejects the status quo. Protestantism rejected the authority of the Roman papacy. The appearance and growth of new churches—such as Lutheran, Calvinist, Anabaptist, and Anglican in the sixteenth century and Baptist, Quaker, and Methodist, among others, in the seventeenth and eighteenth centuries—represent revolution and a radical discontinuity from the religious situation in Europe over the previous thousand years. Whereas previously there had been one Christian church to which all Christians at least nominally belonged, after 1555 there were many. Protestantism meant fragmentation.

Moreover, some historians, mainly Protestant ones, have identified Protestantism with "modernity," by which they mean not only rejection of the Middle Ages and that period's main symbol, the Roman church, but also the embrace of light and genius. By contrast, students of the Catholic church have seen the Reformations in terms of continuity. While acknowledging that there were grave abuses in the institutional church, these scholars stress that serious movements for reform began in the fifteenth century. The Brethren of the Common Life in the Low Countries, the reforming efforts of Francisco Jiménez de Cisneros in Spain, the preaching programs of the friars, and the Lateran Council of 1512 all antedate Martin Luther. Within the Roman church, there was a great deal of spiritual vitality and many serious attempts to spread the Gospel message (see pages 455–456). After about 1550, the focus shifted from an emphasis on the church as an institution—its powers and prerogatives—to what both the Council of Trent and the Jesuits called "what's good for souls." The Catholic church became a pastoral and a missionary church.[34]

## Summary

Martin Luther's strictly religious call for reform, rapidly spread by preaching, hymns, and the printing press, soon became enmeshed in social, economic, and political issues. The German peasants interpreted Luther's ideas in an economic sense: Christian liberty for them meant the end of harsh manorial burdens. Princes used the cloak of the new religious ideas to acquire the material wealth of the church and to thwart the centralizing goals of the emperor. In England the political issue of the royal succession triggered that country's break with Rome, and in

Switzerland and France the political and social ethos of Calvinism attracted many people. The Protestant doctrine that all callings have equal merit in God's sight and its stress on the home as the special domain of women drew women to Protestantism. The reformulation of Roman Catholic doctrine at the Council of Trent and the new religious orders such as the Jesuits and the Ursulines represented the Catholic response to the demands for reform.

Religious belief remained tremendously strong. In fact, the strength of religious convictions caused political fragmentation. In the later sixteenth century and through most of the seventeenth, religion and religious issues continued to play a major role in the lives of individuals and in the policies and actions of governments. Religion, whether Protestant or Catholic, decisively influenced the growth of national states.

Although most of the church reformers rejected the idea of religious toleration, they helped pave the way for it. They also paved the way for the eighteenth-century revolt against the Christian God, one of the strongest supports of life in Western culture. In this respect, the Reformation marked the beginning of the modern world, with its secularism and rootlessness. At the same time, it can equally be argued that the sixteenth century represented the culmination of the Middle Ages. Martin Luther's anxieties about salvation showed him to be very much a medieval man. His concerns had deeply troubled serious individuals since the time of Saint Augustine. In modern times, such concerns have tended to take different forms.

## Key Terms

pluralism
*The Imitation of Christ*
ecumenical council
indulgence
Diet of Worms
Protestant
*sola scriptura*
transubstantiation
consubstantiation
Lord's Supper
preacherships
peasant revolts
*The Institutes of the Christian Religion*
predestination
Anabaptists
*Book of Common Prayer*
Elizabethan Settlement
Jesuits
Holy Office

## Notes

1. Quoted in J. Burckhardt, *The Civilization of the Renaissance in Italy* (London: Phaidon Books, 1951), p. 262.
2. See R. R. Post, *The Modern Devotion: Confrontation with Reformation and Humanism* (Leiden: E. J. Brill, 1968), esp. pp. 237–238, 255, 323–348.
3. Quoted in O. Chadwick, *The Reformation* (Baltimore: Penguin Books, 1976), p. 55.
4. Quoted in E. H. Harbison, *The Age of Reformation* (Ithaca, N.Y.: Cornell University Press, 1963), p. 52.
5. This passage leans on ibid., pp. 52–55.
6. See S. E. Ozment, *The Reformation in the Cities: The Appeal of Protestantism to Sixteenth-Century Germany and Switzerland* (New Haven, Conn.: Yale University Press, 1975), pp. 32–45.
7. See S. E. Ozment, *The Age of Reform, 1250–1550: An Intellectual and Religious History of Late Medieval and Reformation Europe* (New Haven, Conn.: Yale University Press, 1980), pp. 273–279.
8. Quoted ibid., p. 280.
9. Ibid., p. 281.
10. Quoted ibid., p. 284.
11. Romans 13:1–2.
12. E. Erikson, *Young Man Luther: A Study in Psychoanalysis and History* (New York: W. W. Norton, 1962), p. 47.
13. G. Strauss, *Luther's House of Learning: Indoctrination of the Young in the German Reformation* (Baltimore: Johns Hopkins University Press, 1978), esp. pp. 159–162, 231–233.
14. See R. H. Bainton, *Women of the Reformation in Germany and Italy* (Minneapolis: Augsburg, 1971), pp. 9–10; and Ozment, *The Reformation in the Cities,* pp. 53–54, 171–172.
15. Quoted in H. G. Haile, *Luther: An Experiment in Biography* (Garden City, N.Y.: Doubleday, 1980), p. 272.
16. Quoted in J. Atkinson, *Martin Luther and the Birth of Protestantism* (Baltimore: Penguin Books, 1968), pp. 247–248.
17. *Martin Luther: Three Treatises* (Philadelphia: Muhlenberg Press, 1947), pp. 28–31.
18. J. Allen, trans., *John Calvin: The Institutes of the Christian Religion* (Philadelphia: Westminster Press, 1930), bk. 3, chap. 21, paras. 5, 7.
19. E. W. Monter, *Calvin's Geneva* (New York: John Wiley & Sons, 1967), pp. 98–108.
20. Ibid., p. 137.
21. Quoted in Bainton, *Women of the Reformation,* pp. 69–70.
22. See M. E. Wiesner-Hanks, "Women," in *The Oxford Encyclopedia of the Reformation,* ed. H. J. Hillerbrand, vol. 4 (New York: Oxford University Press, 1996), pp. 290–298.
23. E. Duffy, *The Stripping of the Altars: Traditional Religion in England, 1400–1580* (New Haven, Conn.: Yale University Press, 1992), pp. 2–6.
24. See R. Marius, *Thomas More: A Biography* (New York: Alfred A. Knopf, 1984), pp. 215–216.
25. See S. E. Lehmberg, *The Reformation Parliament, 1529–1536* (Cambridge: Cambridge University Press, 1970), pp. 174–176, 204–205.
26. J. J. Scarisbrick, *The Reformation and the English People* (Oxford: Basil Blackwell, 1984), p. 81.
27. Ibid.
28. Quoted in P. Smith, *The Age of the Reformation,* rev. ed. (New York: Henry Holt, 1951), p. 346.
29. Quoted in D. P. Daniel, "Hungary," in *The Oxford Encyclopedia of the Reformation,* vol. 2, ed. H. J. Hillerbrand (New York: Oxford University Press, 1996), p. 273.
30. Quoted in Smith, *Age of the Reformation,* p. 84.
31. See J. W. O'Malley, *The First Jesuits* (Cambridge, Mass.: Harvard University Press, 1993), p. 376.
32. Ibid., p. 298.
33. Quoted in Chadwick, *The Reformation,* p. 270.
34. See J. W. O'Malley, *Trent and All That: Renaming Catholicism in the Early Modern Era* (Cambridge, Mass.: Harvard University Press, 2000), chap. 2, et passim.

## Suggested Reading

A. Levi, *Renaissance and Reformation: The Intellectual Genesis* (2002), surveys the ideas of major Reformation figures against the background of important political issues. The best reference work is H. J. Hillerbrand, ed., *The Oxford Encyclopedia of the Reformation,* 4 vols. (New York: Oxford University Press, 1996). E. Cameron, *The European Reformation* (1991), provides a comprehensive survey based on recent research; A. Pettegree, ed., *The Early Reformation in Europe* (1992), compares developments in different parts of Europe; and the books by Chadwick and Harbison listed in the Notes are good general introductions. L. W. Spitz, *The Protestant Reformation, 1517–1559* (1985), provides a comprehensive survey that incorporates sound scholarly research. For the trend in scholarship interpreting the Reformation against the background of fifteenth-century reforming developments, see the excellent study of J. F. D'Amico, *Renaissance Humanism in Papal Rome: Humanists and Churchmen on the Eve of the Reformation* (1983); and J. H. Overfield, *Humanism and Scholasticism in Late Medieval Germany* (1984), which portrays the intellectual life of the German universities, the milieu from which the Protestant Reformation emerged.

For the central figure of the early Reformation, Martin Luther, students should see the works by Atkinson, Erikson, and Haile mentioned in the Notes; and G. Brendler, *Martin Luther: Theology and Revolution* (1991), a response to the Marxist interpretation of Luther as a tool of the aristocracy who sold out the peasantry. Beginning as well as advanced students will find a vividly written interpretation of Luther's writings in the recent work by R. Marius, *Martin Luther: The Christian Between God and Death* (1999), which also contains a considerable amount of new information.

The scope of P. Benedict, *Christ's Churches Purely Reformed: A Social History of Calvinism* (2002), is indicated by its title; this is a most important work. The best study of John Calvin is W. J. Bouwsma, *John Calvin: A Sixteenth-Century Portrait* (1988), an authoritative study that situates Calvin within Renaissance culture. D. C. Steinmetz, *Calvin in Context* (1995), treats Calvin as an interpreter of the Bible. W. E. Monter, *Calvin's Geneva* (1967), shows the effect of Calvin's reforms on the social life of that Swiss city. R. T. Kendall, *Calvinism and English Calvinism to 1649* (1981), presents English conditions. Students interested in the left wing of the Reformation should see the profound, though difficult, work of G. H. Williams, *The Radical Reformers* (1962).

For various aspects of the social history of the period, see S. Ozment, *Magdalena and Balthasar* (1987), which reveals many features of social life through the letters of a Nuremberg couple. For women, see M. E. Wiesner, *Women and Gender in Early Modern Europe* (1993); L. Roper, *The Holy Household: Women and Morals in Reformation Augsburg* (1991), an important study in local religious history as well as the history of gender; and M. Wiesner, *Women in the Sixteenth Century: A Bibliography* (1983), a useful reference tool. The best recent treatment of marriage and the family is S. Ozment, *When Fathers Ruled: Family Life in Reformation Europe* (1983). Ozment's edition of *Reformation Europe: A Guide to Research* (1982), contains helpful references.

For England, in addition to the fundamental work by Duffy cited in the Notes, K. Thomas, *Religion and the Decline of Magic* (1971), provides a useful treatment of pre-Reformation popular religion. S. J. Gunn and P. G. Lindley, eds., *Cardinal Wolsey: Church, State and Art* (1991), is a useful study of that important prelate. The marital trials of Henry VIII are treated in both the sympathetic study by G. Mattingly, *Catherine of Aragon* (1949), and A. Fraser, *The Wives of Henry VIII* (1992). The legal implications of Henry VIII's divorces have been thoroughly analyzed in J. J. Scarisbrick, *Henry VIII* (1968), an almost definitive biography. On the dissolution of the English monasteries, see D. Knowles, *The Religious Orders in England,* vol. 3 (1959), one of the finest examples of historical prose in English written in the twentieth century. G. R. Elton, *The Tudor Revolution in Government* (1959), discusses the modernization of English government under Thomas Cromwell, whereas the same author's *Reform and Reformation: England, 1509–1558* (1977), combines political and social history in a broad study.

The definitive study of the Council of Trent was written by H. Jedin, *A History of the Council of Trent,* 3 vols. (1957–1961). For the Jesuits, see W. W. Meissner, *Ignatius of Loyola: The Psychology of a Saint* (1993), and J. W. O'Malley, *The First Jesuits* (1993). These books are basic not only for the beginnings of the Society of Jesus but also for the refutation of many myths. Perhaps the best recent work on the Spanish Inquisition is W. Monter, *Frontiers of Heresy: The Spanish Inquisition from the Basque Lands to Sicily* (1990). For the impact of the Counter-Reformation on ordinary Spanish people, see H. Kamen, *The Phoenix and the Flame: Catalonia and the Counter Reformation* (1993). In exceptionally lucid prose, J. W. O'Malley, *Trent and All That: Renaming Catholicism in the Early Modern Era* (2000), provides an excellent historiographical review of the literature and explains why and how early modern Catholicism influenced early modern European history.

# *Listening to the Past*

## Martin Luther, *On Christian Liberty*

*The idea of liberty has played a powerful role in the history of Western society and culture; that idea is unique to the European world. But the meaning and understanding of liberty has undergone continual change and interpretation. In the Roman world, where slavery was a basic institution, liberty meant the condition of being a free person, independent of obligations to a master. In the Middle Ages, possessing liberty meant having special privileges or rights that other persons or institutions did not have. A lord or a monastery, for example, might speak of his or its liberties. Likewise, the first chapter of Magna Carta (1215), often called the "Charter of Liberties," states: "Holy Church shall be free and have its rights entire and its* liberties *inviolate," meaning that the English church was independent of the authority of the king.*

*The idea of liberty also has a religious dimension, and the reformer Martin Luther formulated a classic interpretation of liberty in his treatise* On Christian Liberty, *arguably his finest piece. It contains the main themes of Luther's theology: the importance of faith, the relationship of Christian faith and good works, the dual nature of human beings, and the fundamental importance of Scripture in Christian life.*

Christian faith has appeared to many an easy thing; nay, not a few even reckon it among the social virtues, as it were; and this they do because they have not made proof of it experimentally, and have never tasted of what efficacy it is. For it is not possible for any man to write well about it, or to understand well what is rightly written, who has not at some time tasted of its spirit, under the pressure of tribulation; while he who has tasted of it, even to a very small extent, can never write, speak, think, or hear about it sufficiently. . . .

I hope that . . . I have attained some little drop of faith, and that I can speak of this matter, if not with more elegance, certainly with more solidity. . . .

A Christian man is the most free lord of all, and subject to none; a Christian man is the most dutiful servant of all, and subject to everyone.

Although these statements appear contradictory, yet, when they are found to agree together, they will do excellently for my purpose. They are both the statements of Paul himself, who says, "Though I be free from all men, yet have I made myself a servant unto all" (I Cor. 9:19), and "Owe no man anything but to love one another" (Rom. 13:8). Now love is by its own nature dutiful and obedient to the beloved object. Thus even Christ, though Lord of all things, was yet made of a woman; made under the law; at once free and a servant; at once in the form of God and in the form of a servant.

Let us examine the subject on a deeper and less simple principle. Man is composed of a twofold nature, a spiritual and a bodily. As regards the spiritual nature, which they name the soul, he is called the spiritual, inward, new man; as regards the bodily nature, which they name the flesh, he is called the fleshly, outward, old man. The Apostle speaks of this: "Though our outward man perish, yet the inward man is renewed day by day" (II Cor. 4:16). The result of this diversity is that in the Scriptures opposing statements are made concerning the same man, the fact being that in the same man these two men are opposed to one another; the flesh lusting against the spirit, and the spirit against the flesh (Gal. 5:17).

We first approach the subject of the inward man, that we may see by what means a man becomes justified, free, and a true Christian; that is, a spiritual, new, and inward man. It is certain that absolutely none among outward things, under whatever name they may be reckoned, has any influence in producing Christian righteousness or liberty, nor, on the other hand, unrighteousness or slavery. This can be shown by an easy argument.

What can it profit to the soul that the body should be in good condition, free, and full of life, that it should eat, drink, and act according to its pleasure, when even the most impious slaves of every kind of vice are prosperous in these matters? Again, what harm can ill health, bondage, hunger, thirst, or any other outward evil, do to the soul, when even the most pious of men, and the freest in the purity of their conscience, are harassed by these things? Neither of these states of things has to do with the liberty or the slavery of the soul.

And so it will profit nothing that the body should be adorned with sacred vestment, or dwell in holy places, or be occupied in sacred offices, or pray, fast, and abstain from certain meats, or do whatever works can be done through the body and in the body. Something widely different will be necessary for the justification and liberty of the soul, since the things I have spoken of can be done by an impious person, and only hypocrites are produced by devotion to these things. On the other hand, it will not at all injure the soul that the body should be clothed in profane raiment, should dwell in profane places, should eat and drink in the ordinary fashion, should not pray aloud, and should leave undone all the things above mentioned, which may be done by hypocrites.

. . . One thing, and one alone, is necessary for life, justification, and Christian liberty; and that is the most Holy Word of God, the Gospel of Christ, as He says, "I am the resurrection and the life; he that believeth in me shall not die eternally" (John 9:25), and also, "If the Son shall make you free, ye shall be free indeed" (John 8:36), and "Man shall not live by bread alone, but by every word that proceedeth out of the mouth of God" (Matt. 4:4).

Let us therefore hold it for certain and firmly established that the soul can do without everything except the Word of God, without which none at all of its wants is provided for. But, having the Word, it is rich and wants for nothing, since that is the Word of life, of truth, of light, of peace, of justification, of salvation, of joy, of liberty, of wisdom, of virtue, of grace, of glory, and of every good thing. . . .

But you will ask, "What is this Word, and by what means is it to be used, since there are so many words of God?" I answer, "The Apostle Paul (Rom. 1) explains what it is, namely the Gospel of God, concerning His Son, incarnate, suffering, risen, and glorified through the Spirit, the Sanctifier." To preach Christ is to feed the soul, to justify it, to set it free, and to save it, if it believes the preaching. For faith alone, and the efficacious use of the Word of God, bring salvation. "If thou shalt confess with thy mouth the Lord Jesus, and shalt believe in thine heart that God hath raised Him from the dead, thou

On effective preaching, especially to the uneducated, Luther urged the minister "to keep it simple for the simple." *(Church of St. Marien, Wittenberg/The Bridgeman Art Library)*

shalt be saved" (Rom. 9:9); . . . and "The just shall live by faith" (Rom. 1:17). . . .

But this faith cannot consist of all with works; that is, if you imagine that you can be justified by those works, whatever they are, along with it. . . . Therefore, when you begin to believe, you learn at the same time that all that is in you is utterly guilty, sinful, and damnable, according to that saying, "All have sinned, and come short of the glory of God" (Rom. 3:23). . . . When you have learned this, you will know that Christ is necessary for you, since He has suffered and risen again for you, that, believing on Him, you might by this faith become another man, all your sins being remitted, and you being justified by the merits of another, namely Christ alone.

. . . [A]nd since it [faith] alone justifies, it is evident that by no outward work or labour can the inward man be at all justified, made free, and saved; and that no works whatever have any relation to him. . . . Therefore the first care of every Christian ought to be to lay aside all reliance on works, and strengthen his faith alone more and more, and by it grow in knowledge, not of works, but of Christ Jesus, who has suffered and risen again for him, as Peter teaches (I Peter 5).

## Questions for Analysis

1. What did Luther mean by liberty?
2. Why, for Luther, was Scripture basic to Christian life?

*Source: Luther's Primary Works,* ed. H. Wace and C. A. Buchheim (London: Holder and Stoughton, 1896). Reprinted in *The Portable Renaissance Reader,* ed. James Bruce Ross and Mary Martin McLaughlin (New York: Penguin Books, 1981), pp. 721–726.

A detail from an early-seventeenth-century Flemish painting depicting maps, illustrated travel books, a globe, a compass, and an astrolabe. *(Reproduced by courtesy of the Trustees, The National Gallery, London)*

chapter

# 15 The Age of Religious Wars and Overseas Expansion

**chapter outline**

- Politics, Religion, and War
- Discovery, Reconnaissance, and Expansion
- Later Explorers
- Changing Attitudes
- Literature and Art

Between 1560 and 1648, two developments dramatically altered the world in which Europeans lived: the Reformations of the Christian churches and overseas expansion. The Renaissance and the Reformations drastically changed cultural, political, religious, and social life in Europe and inspired magnificent literary, artistic, and musical achievements. Overseas expansion broadened the geographical horizons of Europeans and brought them into confrontation with ancient civilizations in Africa, Asia, and the Americas. These confrontations led first to conquest, then to exploitation, and finally to profound social changes in both Europe and the conquered territories. War and religious issues dominated politics and were intertwined: religion was commonly used to rationalize wars, which were often fought for power and territorial expansion. Meanwhile, Europeans carried their political, religious, and social attitudes to their newly acquired territories.

- What were the causes and consequences of the religious wars in France, the Netherlands, and Germany?
- How and why, in the sixteenth and seventeenth centuries, did a relatively small group living on the edge of the Eurasian landmass gain control of the major sea-lanes of the world and establish political and economic influence on distant continents?
- What immediate effect did overseas expansion have on Europe and on the conquered societies?
- How and why did slave labor become the dominant form of labor organization in the New World?
- How did the religious crises of this period affect religious faith, literary and artistic developments, and the status of women?

This chapter will address these questions.

## Politics, Religion, and War

See DBQ 3

In 1559 France and Spain signed the **Treaty of Cateau-Cambrésis,** which ended the long conflict known as the Habsburg-Valois Wars. Spain was the victor. France, exhausted by the struggle, had to acknowledge Spanish dominance in Italy, where much of the wars had been fought. Spanish governors ruled in Sicily, Naples, and Milan, and Spanish influence was strong in the Papal States and Tuscany. The Treaty of Cateau-Cambrésis ended an era of dynastic wars and initiated a period of conflicts in which politics and religion played the dominant roles. Governments used religious faiths to persuade people to acquiesce to heavier taxation. Religious differences served as the motivating force for ordinary people to participate in wars. Religious passions conditioned the mindsets of all elements of European society.

Wars of the late sixteenth century differed considerably from earlier wars. Sixteenth- and seventeenth-century armies were bigger than medieval ones; some forces numbered as many as fifty thousand men. Because large armies were expensive, governments had to reorganize their administrations to finance these armies. The high cost of maintaining fortresses, such as those Philip II erected in Italy—at Milan, Sicily, Naples, and Sardinia—contributed heavily to state indebtedness.[1] The use of gunpowder altered the nature of war and popular attitudes toward it. Guns and cannon killed and wounded from a distance, indiscriminately. Writers scorned gunpowder as a coward's weapon that allowed a common soldier to kill a gentleman. Gunpowder weakened the notion, common during the Hundred Years' War, that warfare was an ennobling experience. At the same time, governments utilized propaganda, pulpits, and the printing press to arouse public opinion to support war.[2]

Late-sixteenth-century conflicts fundamentally tested the medieval ideal of a unified Christian society governed by one political ruler, the emperor, and one church to which all people belonged. The Protestant Reformation had killed this ideal, but few people recognized it as dead. Catholics continued to believe that Calvinists and Lutherans could be reconverted; Protestants persisted in thinking that the Roman church should be destroyed. Most people believed that a state could survive only if its members shared the same faith. Catholics and Protestants alike feared people of the other faith living in their midst. The settlement finally achieved in 1648, known as the Peace of Westphalia, signaled the end of the medieval ideal.

### The Origins of Difficulties in France (1515–1559)

In the first half of the sixteenth century, France continued the recovery begun under Louis XI (see page 442). The population losses caused by the plague and the disorders accompanying the Hundred Years' War had created such a labor shortage that serfdom almost disappeared. Cash rents replaced feudal rents and servile obligations. This development clearly benefited the peasantry. Meanwhile, the declining buying power of money hurt the nobility. The increase in France's population in the late fifteenth and sixteenth centuries brought new lands under cultivation, but the division of property among sons meant that most peasant holdings were very small. Domestic and foreign trade picked up, mercantile centers such as Rouen and Lyons expanded, and in 1517 a new port city was founded at Le Havre.

The charming and cultivated Francis I (r. 1515–1547) and his athletic, emotional son Henry II (r. 1547–1559) governed through a small, efficient council. Great nobles held titular authority in the provinces as governors, but Paris-appointed baillis and seneschals continued to exercise actual fiscal and judicial responsibility (see page 336). In 1539 Francis issued an ordinance that placed the whole of France under the jurisdiction of the royal law courts and made French the language of those courts. This act had a powerful centralizing impact. The taille, a tax on land, provided what strength the monarchy had and supported a strong standing army. Unfortunately, the tax base was too narrow for Francis's extravagant promotion of the arts and ambitious foreign policy.

The Habsburg-Valois Wars, waged intermittently through the first half of the sixteenth century, also cost more than the government could afford. Financing the wars posed problems. In addition to the time-honored practices of increasing taxes and engaging in heavy borrowing, Francis I tried two new devices to raise revenue: the sale of public offices and a treaty with the papacy. The former proved to be only a temporary source of money. The offices sold tended to become hereditary within a family, and once a man bought an office, he and his heirs were tax-exempt.

The treaty with the papacy was the Concordat of Bologna (see page 442), in which Francis agreed to recognize the supremacy of the papacy over a universal council. In return, the French crown gained the right to appoint all French bishops and abbots. This understanding gave the monarchy a rich supplement of money and offices and a power over the church that lasted until the Revolution of 1789. The Concordat of Bologna helps

1500 | 1540 | 1580 | 1620 | 1660

**POLITICAL/MILITARY**

- 1519–1522 Spanish under Cortés conquer Mexico
- 1531–1536 Spanish under Pizarro conquer Peru
- 1559 Treaty of Cateau-Cambrésis
- 1568–1578 Civil war in the Netherlands
- 1618–1648 Thirty Years' War
- 1587 Mary, Queen of Scots, is beheaded for plot to assassinate Elizabeth
- 1588 Spanish Armada defeated

**SOCIAL/ECONOMIC**

- 1510–1650 Biosocial exchange between Europe and the Americas includes the migration of peoples, fauna, flora, and disease
- 1560–1660 Height of the European witch-hunt
- 1560–1600 Much of Europe hit by price inflation
- 1602 Dutch East India Company founded

**INTELLECTUAL/RELIGIOUS**

- 1564–1616 Life of William Shakespeare
- 1598 Edict of Nantes
- 1572 Saint Bartholomew's Day massacre
- 1611 Publication of King James Bible

explain why France did not later become Protestant: in effect, it established Catholicism as the state religion. Because French rulers possessed control over appointments and had a vested financial interest in Catholicism, they had no need to revolt against Rome.

However, the Concordat of Bologna perpetuated disorders within the French church. Ecclesiastical offices were used primarily to pay and reward civil servants. Churchmen in France, as elsewhere, were promoted to the hierarchy not because they possessed any special spiritual qualifications but because they had rendered services to the state. Such bishops were unlikely to work to elevate the intellectual and moral standards of the parish clergy. Few priests devoted scrupulous attention to the needs of their parishioners. Thus the teachings of Luther and Calvin, as the presses disseminated them, found a receptive audience.

Luther's tracts first appeared in France in 1518, and his ideas attracted some attention. After the publication of Calvin's *Institutes* in 1536, sizable numbers of French people were attracted to the "reformed religion," as Calvinism was called. Because Calvin wrote in French rather than Latin, his ideas gained wide circulation. Initially, Calvinism drew converts from among reform-minded members of the Catholic clergy, the industrious middle classes, and artisan groups. Most Calvinists lived in major cities, such as Paris, Lyons, and Rouen.

In spite of condemnation by the universities, government bans, and massive burnings at the stake, the numbers of Protestants grew steadily. When Henry II died in

1559, there were 40 well-organized Calvinist churches and 2,150 mission stations in France. Perhaps one-tenth of the population had become Calvinist.

## Religious Riots and Civil War in France (1559–1598)

The feebleness of the French monarchy was the seed from which the weeds of civil violence sprang. The three weak sons of Henry II who occupied the throne could not provide the necessary leadership. Francis II (r. 1559–1560) died after seventeen months. Charles IX (r. 1560–1574) succeeded at the age of ten and was dominated by his mother, Catherine de' Medici. The intelligent, cultivated, and erratic Henry III (r. 1574–1589) followed his brother Charles on the French throne; Henry divided much of his attention between debaucheries with his male favorites and frantic acts of repentance. From 1560 to her death in 1589, Catherine genuinely wanted civil and religious peace—so long as her sons controlled the government; her actions were guided by political motives.

The French nobility took advantage of this monarchical weakness. In the second half of the sixteenth century, between two-fifths and one-half of the nobility at one time or another became Calvinist. Just as German princes in the Holy Roman Empire had adopted Lutheranism as a means of opposition to Emperor Charles V, so French nobles frequently adopted the reformed religion as a religious cloak for their independence. No one believed that peoples of different faiths could coexist peacefully within the same territory. The Reformation thus led to a resurgence of feudal disorder. Armed clashes between Catholic royalist lords and Calvinist antimonarchical lords occurred in many parts of France. Both Calvinists and Catholics believed that the others' books, services, and ministers polluted the community. Preachers incited violence, and ceremonies such as baptisms, marriages, and funerals triggered it.

A savage Catholic attack on Calvinists in Paris on August 24, 1572 (Saint Bartholomew's Day), followed the usual pattern. The occasion was a religious ceremony, the marriage of the king's sister Margaret of Valois to the Protestant Henry of Navarre, which was intended to help reconcile Catholics and **Huguenots,** as French Calvinists were called. Among the many Calvinists present for the wedding festivities was Admiral Gaspard de Coligny, head of one of the great noble families of France and leader of the Huguenot party. When, the night before the wedding, the leader of the Catholic aristocracy, Henry of Guise, had Coligny attacked, rioting and slaughter followed. The Huguenot gentry in Paris was massacred, and religious violence spread to the provinces. Between August 25 and October 3, perhaps twelve thousand Huguenots perished at Meaux, Lyons, Orléans, and Paris. The contradictory orders of Charles IX worsened the situation.

The **Saint Bartholomew's Day massacre** led to fighting called the War of the Three Henrys, a civil conflict among factions led by the Catholic Henry of Guise, the Protestant Henry of Navarre, and King Henry III, who succeeded the tubercular Charles IX. Though King Henry remained Catholic, he realized that the Catholic Guise group represented his greatest danger. The Guises wanted, through an alliance of Catholic nobles called the "Holy League," not only to destroy Calvinism but also to replace Henry III with a member of the Guise family. France suffered fifteen more years of religious rioting and domestic anarchy. Agriculture in many areas was destroyed, commercial life declined severely, and starvation and death haunted the land.

What ultimately saved France was a small group of moderates of both faiths called **politiques,** who believed that only the restoration of strong monarchy could reverse the trend toward collapse. No religious creed was worth the incessant disorder and destruction. Therefore, the politiques favored accepting the Huguenots as an officially recognized and organized pressure group. (But religious toleration, the full acceptance of peoples of different religious persuasions within a pluralistic society, with minorities having the same civil liberties as the majority, developed only in the eighteenth century.) The death of Catherine de' Medici, followed by the assassinations of Henry of Guise and King Henry III, paved the way for the accession of Henry of Navarre, a politique who became Henry IV (r. 1589–1610).

This glamorous prince, "who knew how to fight, to make love, and to drink," as a contemporary remarked, wanted above all a strong and united France. He knew, too, that the majority of the French were Roman Catholics. Allegedly saying "Paris is worth a Mass," Henry knelt before the archbishop of Bourges and was received into the Roman Catholic church. Henry's willingness to sacrifice religious principles to political necessity saved France. The **Edict of Nantes,** which Henry published in 1598, granted to Huguenots liberty of conscience and liberty of public worship in 150 fortified towns, such as La Rochelle. The reign of Henry IV and the Edict of Nantes prepared the way for French absolutism in the seventeenth century by helping restore internal peace in France.

**Giorgio Vasari: Massacre of Coligny and the Huguenots (1573)** Commissioned by Pope Gregory XIII to decorate a hall in the Vatican with frescoes asserting the church's struggle against "unbelief," Vasari here depicts the Saint Bartholomew's Day massacre in Paris: the Huguenot Admiral Coligny is hurled from a window while his followers are slaughtered. In another fresco Vasari glorified the Catholic victory over the Ottoman Turkish fleet at Lepanto. *(Vatican Palace/Scala/Art Resource, NY)*

## The Netherlands Under Charles V

In the last quarter of the sixteenth century, the political stability of England, the international prestige of Spain, and the moral influence of the Roman papacy all became mixed up with the religious crisis in the Low Countries. The Netherlands was the pivot around which European money, diplomacy, and war revolved. What began as a movement for the reformation of the church developed into a struggle for Dutch independence.

Emperor Charles V (r. 1519–1556) had inherited the seventeen provinces that compose present-day Belgium and Holland (see page 466). Since the time of the great medieval fairs, cities of the Low Countries (so called because much of the land lies below sea level) had been important sites for the exchange of products from the Baltic and Italy. Antwerp, ideally situated on the Scheldt River at the intersection of many trading routes, steadily expanded as the chief intermediary for international commerce and finance. English woolens; Baltic wheat, fur, and timber; Portuguese spices; German iron and copper; Spanish fruit; French wines and dyestuffs; Italian silks, marble, and mirrors; and vast amounts of cash—all were exchanged at Antwerp. The city's harbor could dock twenty-five hundred vessels at once, and five thousand merchants from many nations gathered daily in the **bourse** (or exchange). Other great towns—Bruges, Ghent, Brussels, Arras, and Amsterdam—made their living by trade and industry as well. The French-speaking southern towns produced fine linens and woolens, while the wealth of the Dutch-speaking northern cities rested on fishing, shipping, and international banking. In these cities, trade and commerce had produced a vibrant atmosphere, as personified in the urbane Erasmus of Rotterdam (see page 439).

Each of the seventeen provinces of the Netherlands possessed historical liberties: each was self-governing and enjoyed the right to make its own laws and collect its own taxes. In addition to important economic connections, only the recognition of a common ruler in the person of Emperor Charles V united the provinces. Delegates from the various provinces met together in the States General, but important decisions had to be referred back to each province for approval. In the middle of the sixteenth century, the provinces of the Netherlands had a limited sense of federation.

In the Low Countries as elsewhere, corruption in the Roman church and the critical spirit of the Renaissance provoked pressure for reform. Lutheran tracts and Dutch translations of the Bible flooded the seventeen provinces in the 1520s and 1530s, attracting many people to Protestantism. Charles V's government responded with condemnation and mild repression. This policy was not effective, however, because ideas circulated freely in the

## The Spanish and Habsburg Successions, 1493–1637

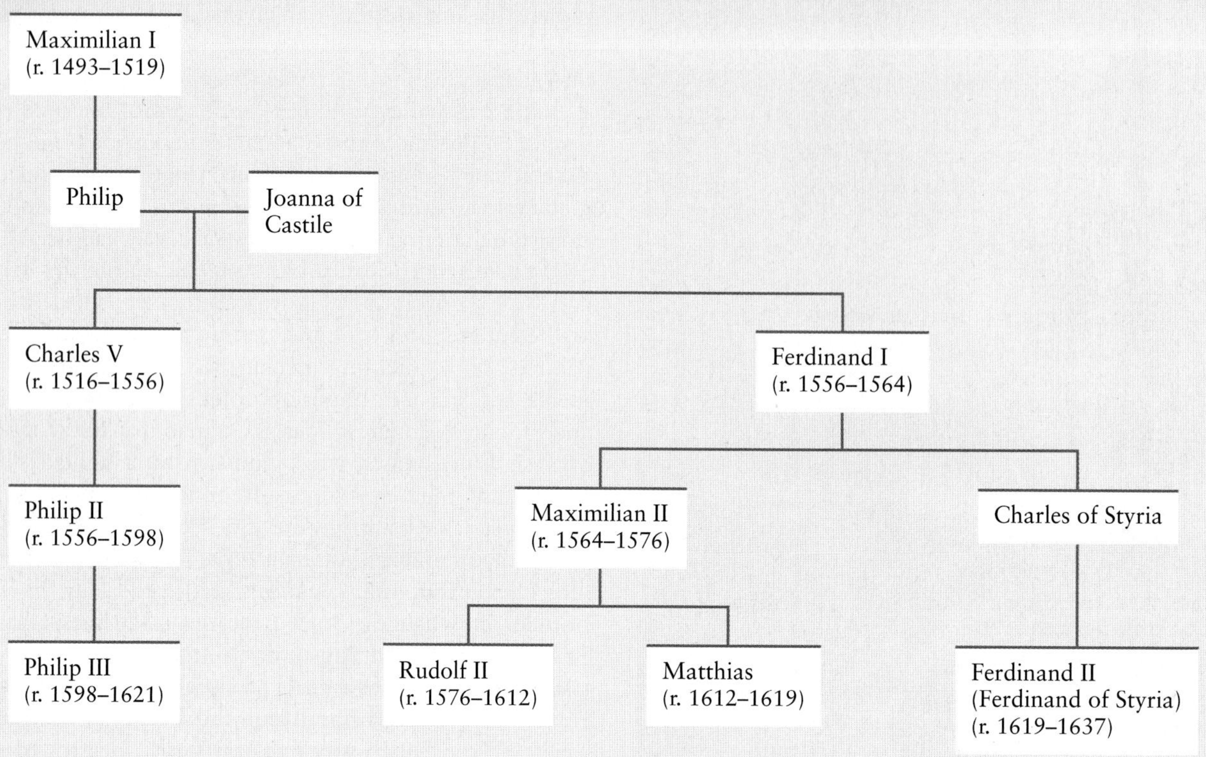


cosmopolitan atmosphere of the commercial centers. But Charles's loyalty to the Flemings checked the spread of Lutheranism. Charles had been born in Ghent and raised in the Netherlands; he was Flemish in language and culture. He identified with the Flemish and they with him.

In 1556, however, Charles V abdicated, dividing his territories between his brother Ferdinand, who received Austria and the Holy Roman Empire, and his son Philip, who inherited Spain, the Low Countries, Milan and the kingdom of Sicily, and the Spanish possessions in the Americas. Charles delivered his abdication speech before the States General at Brussels. The emperor was then fifty-five years old, white-haired, and so crippled in the legs that he had to lean for support on the young Prince William of Orange. According to one contemporary account of the emperor's appearance, "His under lip . . . was heavy and hanging, the lower jaw protruding so far beyond the upper that it was impossible for him to . . . speak a whole sentence in an intelligible voice."[3] Charles spoke in Flemish. Philip responded in Spanish; he could speak neither French nor Flemish. Netherlanders had always felt that Charles was one of their own. They were never to forget that Philip was Spanish.

### The Revolt of the Netherlands (1566–1587)

Lutheranism had posed no serious threat to Spanish rule; it was the spread of Calvinism that upset the apple cart. By the 1560s, there was a strong, militant minority of Calvinists in most of the cities of the Netherlands. The seventeen provinces possessed a large middle-class population, and the reformed religion, as a contemporary remarked, had a powerful appeal "to those who had grown rich by trade and were therefore ready for revolution."[4] Calvinism appealed to the middle classes because of its intellectual seriousness, moral gravity, and emphasis on any form of labor well done. It took deep root among the merchants and financiers in Amsterdam and the northern provinces. Working-class people were also converted, partly because their employers would hire only other Calvinists. Well organized and backed by rich merchants, Calvinists quickly gained a wide following. Whereas Lutherans taught respect for the powers that be, Calvinist reformed religion in the 1570s tended to encourage opposition to "illegal" civil authorities.

In August 1566, a year of very high grain prices, fanatical Calvinists, primarily of the poorest classes, embarked on a rampage of frightful destruction. As in France, Calvinist destruction in the Low Countries was incited by popular preaching, and attacks were aimed at religious images as symbols of false doctrines, not at people. The cathedral of Notre Dame at Antwerp was the first target.

Begun in 1124 and finished only in 1518, this church stood as a monument to the commercial prosperity of Flanders, the piety of the business classes, and the artistic genius of centuries. On six successive summer evenings, crowds embarked on a rampage of destruction. Before the havoc was over, thirty more churches had been sacked and irreplaceable libraries burned. From Antwerp the destruction spread to Brussels and Ghent and north to the provinces of Holland and Zeeland.

From Madrid Philip II sent twenty thousand Spanish troops under the duke of Alva to pacify the Low Countries. Alva interpreted "pacification" to mean the ruthless extermination of religious and political dissidents. On top of the Inquisition, he opened his own tribunal, soon called the "Council of Blood." On March 3, 1568, fifteen hundred men were executed.

For ten years, between 1568 and 1578, civil war raged in the Netherlands between Catholics and Protestants and between the seventeen provinces and Spain. Spanish generals could not halt the fighting. In 1576 the seventeen provinces united under the leadership of Prince William of Orange, called "the Silent" because of his remarkable discretion. In 1578 Philip II sent his nephew Alexander Farnese, duke of Parma, to crush the revolt once and for all. Farnese arrived with an army of German mercenaries. Avoiding pitched battles, he fought by patient sieges. One by one, the cities of the south fell—Maastricht, Tournai, Bruges, Ghent, and, finally, the financial capital of northern Europe, Antwerp (see Map 15.1). Calvinism was forbidden in these territories, and Protestants were compelled to convert or leave. The collapse of Antwerp marked the farthest extent of Spanish jurisdiction and ultimately the religious division of the Netherlands.

The ten southern provinces, the Spanish Netherlands (the future Belgium), remained under the control of the Spanish Habsburgs. The seven northern provinces, led by Holland, formed the **Union of Utrecht** and in 1581 declared their independence from Spain. The Dutch struggle for independence continued because it became inextricably tied up with English affairs.

Geography and sociopolitical structure differentiated the two countries. The northern provinces were ribboned with sluices and canals and therefore were highly defensible. Several times the Dutch had broken the dikes and flooded the countryside to halt the advancing Farnese. In the southern provinces, the Ardennes mountains interrupted the otherwise flat terrain. In the north, the commercial aristocracy possessed the predominant power; in the south, the landed nobility had the greater influence. The north was Protestant; the south remained Catholic. Philip II and Alexander Farnese did not accept this geographical division, and the struggle continued after 1581. The United Provinces repeatedly asked the Protestant queen of England, Elizabeth, for assistance.

**To Purify the Church** The destruction of pictures and statues representing biblical events, Christian doctrine, or sacred figures was a central feature of the Protestant Reformation. Here Dutch Protestant soldiers destroy what they consider idols in the belief that they are purifying the church. *(The Fotomas Index, U.K.)*

Three developments forced Elizabeth's hand. First, the wars in the Low Countries—the chief market for English

**MAP 15.1 The Netherlands, 1559–1609** Some provinces were overwhelmingly agricultural, some involved in manufacturing, others heavily commercial. Each of the seventeen was tied to the Spanish crown in a different way.

woolens—badly hurt the English economy. When wool was not exported, the Crown lost valuable customs revenues. Second, the murder of William the Silent in July 1584 eliminated not only a great Protestant leader but also the chief military check on the Farnese advance. Third, the collapse of Antwerp appeared to signal a Catholic sweep through the Netherlands. The next step, the English feared, would be a Spanish invasion of their island. For these reasons, Elizabeth pumped 250,000 pounds and two thousand troops into the Protestant cause in the Low Countries between 1585 and 1587.

## Philip II and the Spanish Armada

Philip pondered the Dutch and English developments at the **Escorial,** northwest of Madrid. The monastery of Saint Lawrence of the Escorial served as a residence for Jeromite monks, a tomb for the king's Habsburg ancestors, and a royal palace for Philip and his family. The vast buildings resemble a gridiron, the instrument on which Saint Lawrence (d. 258) had supposedly been roasted alive. The royal apartments were in the center of the Italian Renaissance building complex. King Philip's tiny bedchamber possessed a concealed sliding window that opened directly onto the high altar of the monastery church so that he could watch the services and pray along with the monks. In this somber atmosphere, surrounded by a community of monks and close to the bones of his ancestors, the Catholic ruler of Spain and much of the globe passed his days.

In 1587 Philip turned sixty, by the standards of his day an old man. Traditional scholarship, shaped largely by his Protestant enemies, has depicted Philip as morose and melancholic, a religious bigot determined to reimpose Roman Catholicism on northern Europe. Recent research portrays him as a more complicated, even paradoxical, figure. In his youth, "he had visited northern Italy, the Alps, southern Germany, the Rhineland, the Netherlands, parts of France, and southern England." He had walked the streets of Antwerp, Augsburg, Brussels, Cologne, London, and Trent. With the exception of his father, Charles V, no other European ruler of the time had traveled or seen so much, or accumulated so much political experience in international relations. Philip impressed ambassadors as formal, tight-lipped, and forbidding; he spoke only his native Castilian and Latin. He was deeply pious: he attended daily Mass, and every year he retired to a monastery during Holy Week. On the other hand, in his younger days, he was much given to pleasure, and a critical contemporary wrote, "He is dissipated with women, likes to go in disguise at night, and enjoys all types of gaming (gambling)." He also liked jokes and had a good sense of humor.[5]

After Philip buried his fourth wife (enough to make any man "melancholic"), Anna of Austria, to whom he had been deeply devoted, contemporaries noticed a more marked devotion to religion. He relied more and more on God for political help. On the issues of the Inquisition and religious toleration, Philip was completely inflexible. He identified toleration with the growth of heresy, civil disorder, violence, and bloodshed: "Had there been no inquisition (in Spain) there would have been more heretics, and the country would be in a lamentable state like others (the Netherlands) where there is no inquisition as we have in Spain."[6] In this respect, Philip II differed little from the Protestant reformers Luther and Calvin, who initially called for individual liberty of conscience and then insisted on the right of church and civil powers to extirpate heresy within their jurisdictions.

Philip was a man of his times, and the times did not favor religious toleration. And just as the Protestant princes of northern Europe governed religious life within their states, so Philip II controlled ecclesiastical appointments and revenues in Spain.

With his determination to crush heresy in the Low Countries, and with the enormous wealth of American silver enabling him to hire the mercenary armies he needed, why did Philip II have such trouble achieving his goal? Philip ruled the first global empire in history. He was preoccupied with other parts of that empire, especially the advance of the Ottoman Turks into the western Mediterranean. This issue, combined with the death of his son and heir, Don Carlos; the death of his third wife, Elizabeth of Valois; and then a revolt of the Moriscos (Muslims) in Granada, made it impossible to concentrate on the Netherlands. At one point in 1566 he complained, "I have so much on my mind that I rarely know what I am doing or saying." Only after Philip learned that Suleiman the Magnificent had led a Turkish army into Hungary, ordered his fleet from the Mediterranean to the Adriatic, and died, did Philip feel able to focus on the Netherlands.[7]

But the Netherlands could not be separated in Philip's mind from what he perceived as the "British problem." In 1586, Mary, Queen of Scots, cousin and heir of Elizabeth of England, became implicated in a plot to assassinate Elizabeth. Philip, hoping to reunite England with Catholic Europe through Mary, gave the conspiracy his full backing. Mary was discovered and beheaded on February 18, 1587. News of her execution reached Philip in mid-April. When Pope Sixtus V (1585–1590) learned of Mary's death on March 24 (the dates suggest the slowness of communication in the late sixteenth century), the pope promised to pay Philip 1 million gold ducats the moment Spanish troops landed in England. Alexander Farnese had repeatedly warned that to subdue the Dutch, he would have to conquer England and cut off the source of Dutch support. Two plans for an expedition were considered. Philip's naval adviser recommended that a fleet of 150 ships sail from Lisbon, attack the English navy in the Channel, and invade England. Another proposal was to assemble a collection of barges and troops in Flanders to stage a cross-Channel assault. With the expected support of English Catholics, Spain would achieve a great victory. Farnese opposed this plan as militarily unsound.

As plans for an armada proceeded in 1587, two serious difficulties burdened the king. First, he was so badly crippled by gout that he could not sign documents and could walk, painfully, only with a cane. Second, official reports indicated that the Ottoman Turks might seize the moment of preoccupation with the Netherlands and England to attack Spain from the Mediterranean. Philip prepared a vast fleet to sail from Lisbon to Flanders, fight off Elizabeth's navy if it attacked, rendezvous with Farnese, and escort his barges across the English Channel. The expedition's purpose was to transport the Flemish army.

On May 9, 1588, *la felícissima armada*—"the most fortunate fleet," as it was ironically called in official documents—sailed from Lisbon harbor. The **Spanish Armada** of 130 vessels met an English fleet of about 150 ships in the Channel. The English fleet was composed of smaller, faster, more maneuverable ships, many of which had greater firing power than their Spanish counterparts. A combination of storms and squalls, spoiled food and rank water, inadequate Spanish ammunition, and, to a lesser extent, English fire ships that caused the Spanish to scatter gave England the victory. Many Spanish ships went down on the journey home around Ireland; perhaps 65 managed to reach home ports.

The battle in the Channel has frequently been described as one of the decisive battles in the history of the world. In fact, it had mixed consequences. Spain soon rebuilt its navy, and after 1588 the quality of the Spanish fleet improved. The destruction of the Spanish Armada did not halt the flow of silver from the New World. More silver reached Spain between 1588 and 1603 than in any other fifteen-year period. The war between England and Spain dragged on for years.

The defeat of the Spanish Armada was decisive, however, in the sense that it prevented Philip II from reimposing religious unity on western Europe by force. He did not conquer England, and Elizabeth continued her financial and military support of the Dutch. In the Netherlands, neither side gained significant territory. The borders of 1581 tended to become permanent. In 1609 Philip III of Spain (r. 1598–1621) agreed to a truce, in effect recognizing the independence of the United Provinces. In seventeenth-century Spain, memory of the loss of the Spanish Armada contributed to a spirit of defeatism. In England the victory contributed to a David and Goliath legend that enhanced English national sentiment.

## The Thirty Years' War (1618–1648)

While Philip II dreamed of building a second armada and Henry IV began the reconstruction of France, the political-religious situation in central Europe deteriorated. An uneasy truce had prevailed in the Holy Roman Empire since the Peace of Augsburg of 1555 (see page 470). According to the Augsburg settlement, the faith of the prince determined the religion of his subjects. Later in the century, however, Catholics grew alarmed because Lutherans, in violation of the Peace of Augsburg, were steadily acquiring German bishoprics. The spread of Calvinism further confused the issue. The Augsburg settlement had pertained only to Lutheranism and Catholicism, so Calvinists ignored it and converted several princes. Lutherans feared that the Augsburg principles would be totally undermined by Catholic and Calvinist gains. Also, the militantly active Jesuits had reconverted several Lutheran princes to Catholicism. In an increasingly tense situation, Lutheran princes formed the **Protestant Union** (1608), and Catholics retaliated with the Catholic League (1609). Each alliance was determined that the other should make no religious (that is, territorial) advance. The empire was composed of two armed camps.

Dynastic interests were also involved in the German situation. The Spanish Habsburgs strongly supported the goals of their Austrian relatives: the unity of the empire and the preservation of Catholicism within it.

Violence erupted first in Bohemia (see Map 15.2), where in 1617 Ferdinand of Styria, the new Catholic king of Bohemia, closed some Protestant churches. On May 23, 1618, Protestants hurled two of Ferdinand's officials from a castle window in Prague. They fell seventy feet but survived: Catholics claimed that angels had caught them; Protestants said that the officials had fallen on a heap of soft horse manure. Called the "defenestration of Prague," this event marked the beginning of the Thirty Years' War (1618–1648).

Historians traditionally divide the war into four phases. The first, or Bohemian, phase (1618–1625) was characterized by civil war in Bohemia between the Catholic League, led by Ferdinand, and the Protestant Union, headed by Frederick, the elector of the Palatinate. The Bohemians fought for religious liberty and independence from Habsburg rule. In 1620 Frederick was defeated by Catholic forces at the Battle of the White Mountain. Ferdinand, recently elected Holy Roman emperor as Ferdinand II, followed up his victories by wiping out Protestantism in Bohemia through forcible conversions and the activities of militant Jesuit missionaries. Within ten years, Bohemia was completely Catholic.

The second, or Danish, phase of the war (1625–1629)—so called because of the participation of King Christian IV of Denmark (r. 1588–1648), the ineffective leader of the Protestant cause—witnessed additional Catholic victories. The Catholic imperial army led by Albert of Wallenstein scored smashing victories. It swept through Silesia, north through Schleswig and Jutland to the Baltic, and east into Pomerania. Wallenstein, who had made himself indispensable to the emperor Ferdinand, was an unscrupulous opportunist who used his vast riches to build an army loyal only to himself. The general seemed interested more in carving out an empire for himself than in aiding the Catholic cause. He quarreled with the Catholic League, and soon the Catholic forces were divided. Religion was eclipsed as a basic issue of the war.

The year 1629 marked the peak of Habsburg power. The Jesuits persuaded the emperor to issue the Edict of Restitution, whereby all Catholic properties lost to Protestantism since 1552 were to be restored and only Catholics and Lutherans (not Calvinists, Hussites, or other sects) were to be allowed to practice their faiths. When Wallenstein began ruthless enforcement of the edict, Protestants throughout Europe feared collapse of the balance of power in north-central Europe.

The third, or Swedish, phase of the war (1630–1635) began with the arrival in Germany of the Swedish king Gustavus Adolphus (r. 1594–1632). The ablest administrator of his day and a devout Lutheran, Gustavus Adolphus intervened to support the oppressed Protestants within the empire. Cardinal Richelieu, the chief minister of King Louis XIII of France (r. 1610–1643), subsidized the Swedes, hoping to weaken Habsburg power in Europe. In 1631, with a small but well-disciplined army equipped with superior muskets, Gustavus Adolphus won a brilliant victory at Breitenfeld. Again in 1632 he was victorious at Lützen, though he was fatally wounded in the battle.

The participation of the Swedes in the Thirty Years' War proved decisive for the future of Protestantism and later German history. When Gustavus Adolphus landed on German soil, he headed a Baltic empire under Swedish influence. The Swedish victories ended the Habsburg ambition of uniting all the German states under imperial authority.

The death of Gustavus Adolphus (r. 1611–1632) in 1632, followed by the defeat of the Swedes at the Battle of Nördlingen in 1634, prompted the French to enter the war on the side of the Protestants. Thus began the French, or international, phase of the Thirty Years' War (1635–1648). For almost a century, French foreign policy had been based on opposition to the Habsburgs because a weak empire divided into scores of independent principalities enhanced France's international stature. In 1635 Cardinal Richelieu declared war on Spain and again sent financial and military assistance to the Swedes and the German Protestant princes. The war dragged on. French, Dutch, and Swedes, supported by Scots, Finns, and German mer-

**Soldiers Pillage a Farmhouse** Billeting troops among civilian populations caused untold hardships. In this late-seventeenth-century Dutch illustration, brawling soldiers take over a peasant's home, eat his food, steal his possessions, and insult his family. Peasant retaliation sometimes proved swift and bloody. *(Rijksmuseum-Stichting Amsterdam)*

cenaries, burned, looted, and destroyed German agriculture and commerce. The Thirty Years' War lasted so long because neither side had the resources to win a quick, decisive victory. Finally, in October 1648, peace was achieved.

The treaties signed at Münster and Osnabrück, commonly called the **Peace of Westphalia,** marked a turning point in European political, religious, and social history. Conflicts fought over religious faiths ended. The treaties recognized the sovereign, independent authority of more than three hundred German princes; each would govern his territory and make war and peace. Since the time of Frederick II Hohenstaufen (see pages 340–341), Germany had followed a pattern of state building different from that of France and England: the imperial power (the emperor) had shared authority with the princes. After the Peace of Westphalia, the Habsburg emperors' power was severely limited, but the Holy Roman Empire continued to function as a federation.

The independence of the United Provinces of the Netherlands was acknowledged. Political divisions within the empire, Germany's weak frontiers, and the acquisition of the province of Alsace increased France's size and prestige. Sweden received a large cash indemnity and jurisdiction over German territories along the Baltic Sea. The powerful Swedish presence in northeastern Germany subsequently posed a major threat to the future kingdom of Brandenburg-Prussia. The treaties also denied the papacy the right to participate in German religious affairs—a restriction symbolizing the reduced role of the church in European politics.

In religion, the Westphalian treaties stipulated that the Augsburg agreement of 1555 should stand permanently.

**MAP 15.2 Europe in 1648** Which country emerged from the Thirty Years' War as the strongest European power? What dynastic house was that country's major rival in the early modern period?

**Dehumanization of the Enemy** During the Thirty Years' War, Protestants viewed Gustavus Adolphus as the savior of Protestantism, the leader of a "godly army." The Catholic Habsburgs saw him differently. To them, he was the Antichrist, and his soldiers were grotesque monsters. In this broadsheet, Lapps, Livonians (riding reindeer), and Scots in the Protestant Swedish army are portrayed as superhuman, brutal, and barbaric. *(Anon, Picture of the supernatural people to be found in the Swedish army, ca 1630)*

The sole modification was that Calvinism, along with Catholicism and Lutheranism, would become a legally permissible creed. The north German states remained Protestant; the south German states, Catholic.

## Germany After the Thirty Years' War

The Thirty Years' War was a disaster for the German economy and society, probably the most destructive event in German history before the twentieth century. Perhaps one-third of the urban residents and two-fifths of the inhabitants of rural areas died. Entire areas of Germany were depopulated, partly by military actions, partly by disease—typhus, dysentery, bubonic plague, and syphilis accompanied the movements of armies—and partly by the thousands of refugees who fled to safer areas.

In the late sixteenth and early seventeenth centuries, all Europe experienced an economic crisis primarily caused by the influx of silver from South America. Because the Thirty Years' War was fought on German soil, these economic difficulties were badly aggravated in the empire. Scholars still cannot estimate the value of losses in agricultural land and livestock, in trade and commerce. The trade of southern cities such as Augsburg, already hard hit by the shift in transportation routes from the Mediterranean to the Atlantic, was virtually destroyed by the fighting in the south. Meanwhile, towns such as Lübeck, Hamburg, and Bremen in the north and Essen in the Ruhr area actually prospered because of the many refugees they attracted. The destruction of land and foodstuffs, compounded by the flood of Spanish silver, brought on a severe price rise. During and after the war, inflation was worse in Germany than anywhere else in Europe.

Agricultural areas suffered catastrophically. The population decline caused a rise in the value of labor, and owners of great estates had to pay more for agricultural workers.

Farmers who needed only small amounts of capital to restore their lands started over again. Many small farmers, however, lacked the revenue to rework their holdings and had to become day laborers. Nobles and landlords bought up many small holdings and acquired great estates. In parts of Germany, especially in areas east of the Elbe River such as Mecklenburg and Pomerania, peasants' loss of land led to the rise of a new serfdom.[8] Thus the Thirty Years' War contributed to the legal and economic decline of the largest segment of German society.

## Discovery, Reconnaissance, and Expansion

Historians have variously called the period from 1450 to 1650 the "Age of Discovery," the "Age of Reconnaissance," and the "Age of Expansion." All three labels are appropriate. The Age of Discovery refers to the era's phenomenal advances in geographical knowledge and technology. In 1350 it took as long to sail from the eastern end of the Mediterranean to the western end as it had taken a thousand years earlier. Even in the fifteenth century, Europeans knew little more about the earth's surface than the Romans had. By 1650, however, Europeans had made an extensive reconnaissance—or preliminary exploration—and had sketched fairly accurately the physical outline of the whole earth. Much of the geographical information they had gathered was tentative and not fully understood—hence the appropriateness of the term the Age of Reconnaissance.

The designation of the era as the Age of Expansion refers to the migration of Europeans to other parts of the world. This colonization resulted in political control of much of South and North America; coastal regions of Africa, India, China, and Japan; and many Pacific islands. This political hegemony was accompanied by economic exploitation, religious domination, and the introduction of European patterns of social and intellectual life. Indeed, the sixteenth-century expansion of European society launched a new age in world history.

### Overseas Exploration and Conquest

The outward expansion of Europe began with the Viking voyages across the Atlantic in the ninth and tenth centuries. Under Eric the Red and Leif Ericson, the Vikings discovered Greenland and the eastern coast of North America. The Vikings also made permanent settlements in, and a legal imprint on, Iceland, Ireland, England, Normandy, and Sicily (see pages 256–257). The Crusades of the eleventh through thirteenth centuries were another phase in Europe's attempt to explore and exploit peoples on the periphery of the continent. But the lack of a strong territorial base, superior Muslim military strength, and sheer misrule combined to make the Crusader kingdoms short-lived. In the mid-fifteenth century, Europe seemed ill-prepared for further international ventures, and by 1450 a grave new threat had appeared in the East—the Ottoman Turks.

Combining excellent military strategy with efficient administration of their conquered territories, the Turks had subdued most of Asia Minor and begun to settle on the western side of the Bosporus. The Muslim Ottoman Turks under Sultan Mohammed II (r. 1451–1481) captured Constantinople in 1453, pressed northwest into the Balkans, and by the early sixteenth century controlled the eastern Mediterranean. The Turkish menace badly frightened Europeans. In France in the fifteenth and sixteenth centuries, twice as many books were printed about the Turkish threat as about the American discoveries. Yet these centuries witnessed a fantastic continuation, on a global scale, of European expansion.

Political centralization in Spain, France, and England helps explain those countries' outward push. In the fifteenth century, Isabella and Ferdinand had consolidated their several kingdoms to achieve a more united Spain and revamped the Spanish bureaucracy. The Spanish monarchy was stronger than before and in a position to support foreign ventures; it could bear the costs and dangers of exploration. But Portugal, situated on the extreme southwestern edge of the European continent, got a head start on the rest of Europe. Still insignificant as a European land power despite its recently secured frontiers, Portugal sought greatness in the unknown world overseas.

Portugal's taking of Ceuta, an Arab city in northern Morocco, in 1415 marked the beginning of European exploration and control of overseas territory. The objectives of Portuguese policy included the historic Iberian crusade to Christianize Muslims and to find gold, an overseas route to the spice markets of India, and the mythical Christian ruler of Ethiopia, Prester John.

In the early phases of Portuguese exploration, Prince Henry (1394–1460), called "the Navigator" because of the school he established for the study of geography and navigation and for the annual expeditions he sent down the western coast of Africa, played the leading role. In the fifteenth century, most of the gold that reached Europe came from the Sudan in West Africa and from the Akan peoples living near the area of present-day Ghana. Muslim caravans brought the gold from the African cities

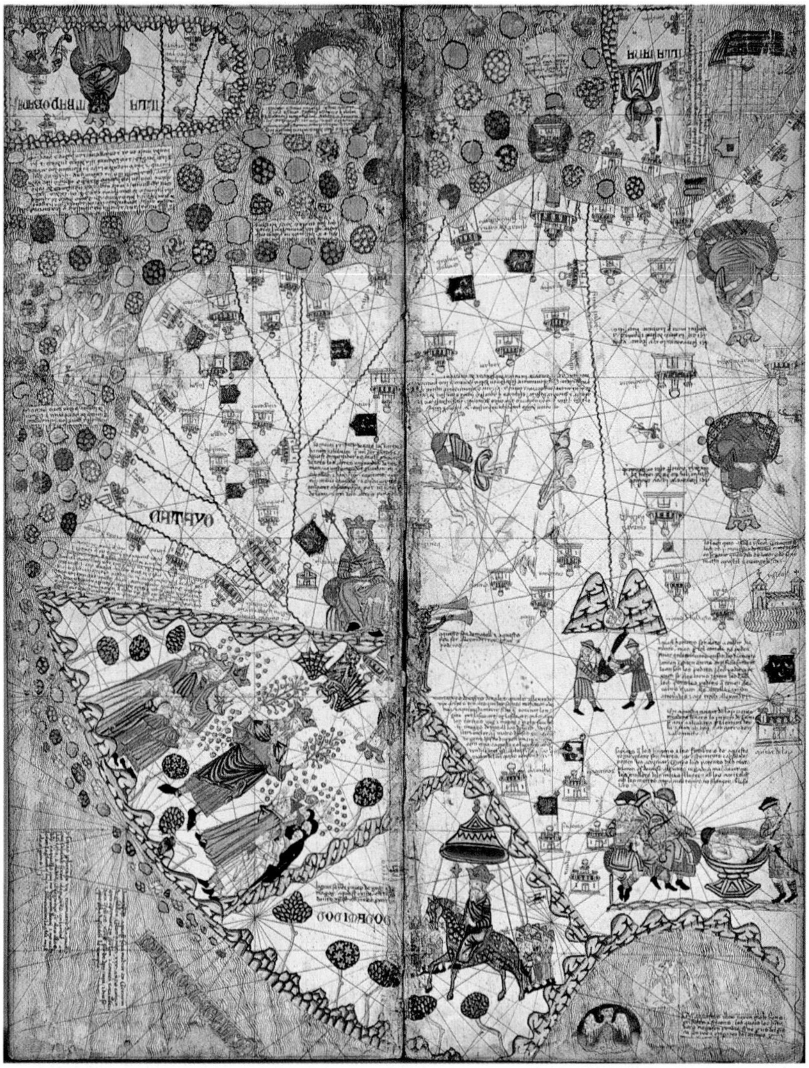

**Catalan Atlas, 1375** Abraham Cresques and his son Yehuda, Jews living in Palma on the island of Majorca (at the time, almost all the best mapmakers were Jewish), produced this atlas for Peter IV of Aragon. Consulting Marco Polo's manuscripts and interviewing Arabic seamen and European travelers, the Cresques aimed to produce a world map showing the various peoples inhabiting it. The atlas consists of twelve leaves mounted on boards to be folded like a screen. Primitive by modern standards, the atlas was at the time a masterpiece of empirical evidence. *(Bibliothèque nationale de France)*

of Niani and Timbuktu and carried it north across the Sahara to Mediterranean ports. Then the Portuguese muscled in on this commerce in gold. Prince Henry's carefully planned expeditions succeeded in reaching Guinea, and under King John II (r. 1481–1495) the Portuguese established trading posts and forts on the Guinea coast and penetrated into the continent all the way to Timbuktu (see Map 15.3). Portuguese ships transported gold to Lisbon, and by 1500 Portugal controlled the flow of gold to Europe. The golden century of Portuguese prosperity had begun.

Still the Portuguese pushed farther south down the west coast of Africa. In 1487 Bartholomew Diaz rounded the Cape of Good Hope at the southern tip, but storms and a threatened mutiny forced him to turn back. On a later expedition (1497–1499), the Portuguese mariner Vasco da Gama reached India and returned to Lisbon loaded with spices and samples of Indian cloth. King Manuel (r. 1495–1521) promptly dispatched thirteen ships under the command of Pedro Alvares Cabral, assisted by Diaz, to set up trading posts in India. On April 22, 1500, the coast of Brazil in South America was sighted and claimed for the Crown of Portugal. Cabral then proceeded south and east around the Cape of Good Hope and reached India. Half the fleet was lost on the return voyage, but the six spice-laden vessels that dropped anchor in Lisbon harbor in July 1501 more than paid for the entire expedition. Thereafter, convoys were sent out every March. Lisbon became the entrance port for Asian goods into Europe—but this was not accomplished without a fight.

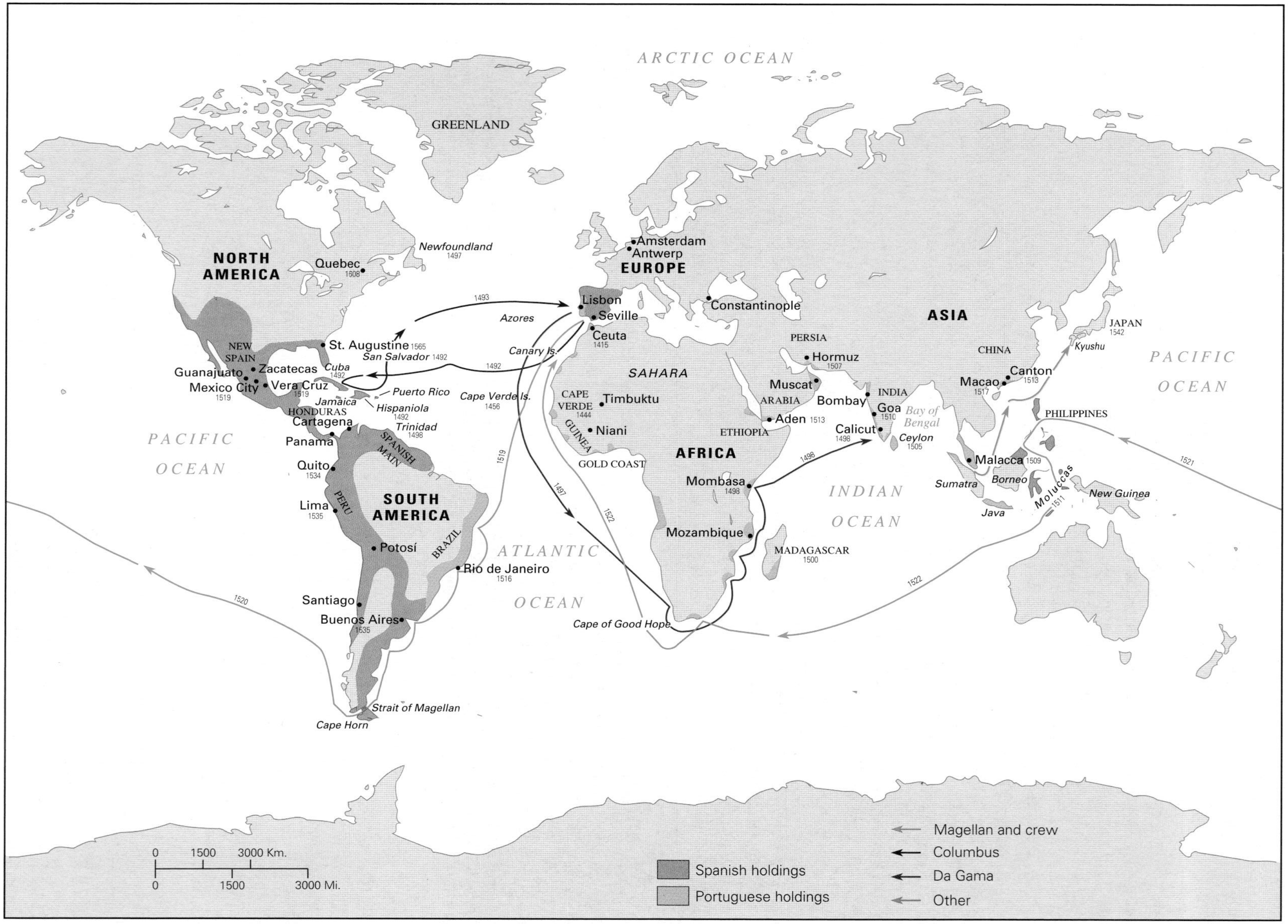


**MAP 15.3 Overseas Exploration and Conquest, Fifteenth and Sixteenth Centuries** The voyages of discovery marked another phase in the centuries-old migrations of European peoples. Consider the major contemporary significance of each of the three voyages depicted on the map.

For centuries the Muslims had controlled the rich spice trade of the Indian Ocean, and they did not surrender it willingly. Portuguese commercial activities were accompanied by the destruction or seizure of strategic Muslim coastal forts, which later served Portugal as both trading posts and military bases. Alfonso de Albuquerque, whom the Portuguese crown appointed as governor of India (1509–1515), decided that these bases, not inland territories, should control the Indian Ocean. Accordingly, his cannon blasted open the ports of Calicut, Ormuz, Goa, and Malacca, the vital centers of Arab domination of South Asian trade. This bombardment laid the foundation for Portuguese imperialism in the sixteenth and seventeenth centuries: a strange way to bring Christianity to "those who were in darkness." As one scholar wrote about the opening of China to the West, "while Buddha came to China on white elephants, Christ was borne on cannon balls."[9]

In March 1493, between the voyages of Diaz and da Gama, Spanish ships under a triumphant Genoese mariner named Christopher Columbus (1451–1506), in the service of the Spanish crown, entered Lisbon harbor. Spain also had begun the quest for an empire.

## Technological Stimuli to Exploration

Technological developments were the key to Europe's remarkable outreach. By 1350 *cannon*—iron or bronze guns that fired iron or stone balls—had been fully developed in western Europe. These pieces of artillery emitted frightening noises and great flashes of fire and could batter down fortresses and even city walls. Sultan Mohammed II's siege of Constantinople in 1453 provides a classic illustration of the effectiveness of cannon fire.

Constantinople had very strong walled fortifications. The sultan secured the services of a Western technician, who built fifty-six small cannon and a gigantic gun that could hurl stone balls weighing about eight hundred pounds. The gun could be moved only by several hundred oxen and loaded and fired only by about a hundred men working together. This awkward but powerful weapon breached the walls of Constantinople, which cracked on the second day of the bombardment. Lesser cannon finished the job.

Early cannon posed serious technical difficulties. Iron cannon were cheaper than bronze to construct, but they were difficult to cast effectively and were liable to crack and injure artillerymen. Bronze guns, made of copper and tin, were less subject than iron to corrosion, but they were very expensive. All cannon were extraordinarily difficult to move, required considerable time for reloading, and were highly inaccurate. They thus proved inefficient for land warfare. However, they could be used at sea.

The mounting of cannon on ships and improved techniques of shipbuilding gave impetus to European expansion. Since ancient times, most seagoing vessels had been narrow, open boats called *galleys,* propelled largely by manpower. Slaves or convicts who had been sentenced to the galleys manned the oars of the ships that sailed the Mediterranean, and both cargo ships and warships carried soldiers for defense. Though well suited to the placid and thoroughly explored waters of the Mediterranean, galleys could not withstand the rough winds and uncharted shoals of the Atlantic. The need for sturdier craft, as well as population losses caused by the Black Death, forced the development of a new style of ship that would not require soldiers for defense or much manpower to sail.

In the course of the fifteenth century, the Portuguese developed the *caravel,* a small, light, three-masted sailing ship. Though somewhat slower than the galley, the caravel held more cargo and was highly maneuverable. When fitted with cannon, it could dominate larger vessels, such as the round ships commonly used as merchantmen. The substitution of wind power for manpower and artillery fire for soldiers signaled a great technological advance and gave Europeans navigational and fighting ascendancy over the rest of the world.[10]

Other fifteenth-century developments in navigation helped make possible the conquest of the Atlantic. The

**Nocturnal** An instrument for determining the hour of night at sea by finding the progress of certain stars around the polestar (center aperture). *(National Maritime Museum, London)*

**magnetic compass** enabled sailors to determine their direction and position at sea. The **astrolabe,** an instrument developed by Muslim navigators in the twelfth century and used to determine the altitude of the sun and other celestial bodies, permitted mariners to plot their *latitude,* or position north or south of the equator. Steadily improved maps and sea charts gave information about distance, sea depths, and general geography.

## The Explorers' Motives

The expansion of Europe was not motivated by demographic pressures. The Black Death had caused serious population losses from which Europe had not recovered in 1500. Few Europeans immigrated to North or South America in the sixteenth century. Half of those who did sail to America died en route; half of those who reached the New World eventually returned to their homeland. Why, then, did explorers brave the Atlantic and Pacific Oceans, risking their lives to discover new continents and spread European culture?

The reasons are varied and complex. People of the sixteenth century were still basically medieval in the sense that their attitudes and values were shaped by religion and expressed in religious terms. In the late fifteenth century, crusading fervor remained a basic part of the Portuguese and Spanish national ideal. Queen Isabella of Spain, for example, showed a fanatical zeal for converting the Muslims to Christianity, and she concentrated her efforts on the Muslims in Granada. After the abortive crusading attempts of the thirteenth century, rulers realized full well that they lacked the material resources to mount the full-scale assault on Islam necessary for victory. Crusading impulses thus shifted from the Muslims to the pagan peoples of Africa and the Americas.

Moreover, after the reconquista, enterprising young men of the Spanish upper classes found their economic and political opportunities severely limited. As a study of the Castilian city of Ciudad Real shows, the ancient aristocracy controlled the best agricultural land and monopolized urban administrative posts. Great merchants and a few nobles (surprisingly, since Spanish law forbade participation by nobles in commercial ventures) dominated the textile and leather-glove manufacturing industries. Consequently, many ambitious men immigrated to the Americas to seek their fortunes.[11]

Government sponsorship and encouragement of exploration also accounted for the results of the various voyages. Mariners and explorers could not as private individuals afford the massive sums needed to explore mysterious oceans and control remote continents. The strong financial support of Prince Henry the Navigator led to Portugal's phenomenal success in the spice trade. Even the grudging and modest assistance of Isabella and Ferdinand eventually brought untold riches—and complicated problems—to Spain. The Dutch in the seventeenth century, through such government-sponsored trading companies as the Dutch East India Company, reaped enormous wealth, and although the Netherlands was a small country in size, it dominated the European economy in 1650.

Scholars have frequently described the European discoveries as a manifestation of Renaissance curiosity about the physical universe—the desire to know more about the geography and peoples of the world. Cosmography, natural history, and geography aroused enormous interest among educated people in the fifteenth and sixteenth centuries. Just as science fiction and speculation about life on other planets excite readers today, quasi-scientific literature about Africa, Asia, and the Americas captured the imaginations of literate Europeans. Fernández de Oviedo's ***General History of the Indies*** (1547), a detailed eyewitness account of plants, animals, and peoples, was widely read.

Spices were another important incentive for voyages of discovery. Introduced into western Europe by the Crusaders in the twelfth century, nutmeg, mace, ginger, cinnamon, and pepper added flavor and variety to the monotonous diet of Europeans. Spices were also used in the preparation of medicinal drugs and incense for religious ceremonies. In the late thirteenth century, Venetian Marco Polo (1254?–1324?), the greatest of medieval travelers, had visited the court of the Chinese emperor. The widely publicized account of his experiences in *Travels* (ca 1298) stimulated the trade in spices between Asia and Italy. The Venetians came to hold a monopoly of that trade in western Europe.

Spices were grown in India and China, shipped across the Indian Ocean to ports on the Persian Gulf, and then transported by Arabs across the Arabian Desert to Mediterranean ports. But the rise of the Ming Dynasty in China in the late fourteenth century resulted in the expulsion of foreigners. And the steady penetration of the Ottoman Turks into the eastern Mediterranean forced Europeans to seek a new route to the Asian spice markets.

The basic reason for European exploration and expansion, however, was the quest for material profit. Mariners and explorers frankly admitted this. As Bartholomew Diaz put the matter, his motives were "to serve God and His Majesty, to give light to those who were in darkness and to grow rich as all men desire to do." When Vasco da

**Pepper Harvest** To break the monotony of a bland diet, Europeans had a passion for pepper, which—along with cinnamon, cloves, nutmeg, and ginger—was the main object of the Asian trade. Since one kilo of pepper cost 2 grams of silver at the place of production in the East Indies, 10 to 14 grams of silver in Alexandria, Egypt, 14 to 18 grams in Venice, and 20 to 30 grams at the markets of northern Europe, we can appreciate the fifteenth-century expression "as dear as pepper." Here natives fill vats, while the dealer tastes a peppercorn for pungency. *(Bibliothèque nationale de France)*

Gama reached the port of Calicut, India, in 1498, a native asked what the Portuguese wanted. Da Gama replied, "Christians and spices."[12] The bluntest of the Spanish conquistadors, Hernando Cortés announced as he prepared to conquer Mexico, "I have come to win gold, not to plow the fields like a peasant."[13] A sixteenth-century diplomat, Ogier Gheselin de Busbecq, summed up this paradoxical attitude well: in expeditions to the Indies and the Antipodes, he said, "religion supplies the pretext and gold the motive."[14]

Spanish and Portuguese explorers carried the fervent Catholicism and missionary zeal of the Iberian Peninsula to the New World, and once in America they urged home governments to send clerics. At bottom, however, wealth was the driving motivation.

## The Problem of Christopher Columbus

The year 1992, which marked the quincentenary of Columbus's first voyages to the Americas, spawned an enormous amount of discussion about the significance of his voyages. Journalists, scholars, amateurs, and polemicists debated Columbus's accomplishments and failures. Until the 1980s, however, most writers would have generally agreed with Harvard historian Samuel Eliot Morison in his 1942 biography of the explorer:

*The whole history of the Americas stems from the Four Voyages of Columbus; today a score of independent nations and dominions unite in homage to Columbus, the stout-hearted son of Genoa, who carried Christian civilization across the Ocean Sea.*[15]

In 1942, the Western Powers believed they were engaged in a life-and-death struggle to defend "Christian civilization" against the evil of fascism.

In contrast to this lavish praise, Columbus has recently undergone severe criticism. He enslaved and sometimes killed the Indians he encountered. He was a cruel and ineffective governor of Spain's Caribbean colony. Moreover, he did not discover the continents: others—Africans and Europeans—had been there before him. And not only did he not discover the continents; he also misunderstood what he had found. In short, he was a fool who did not know what was going on around him. Some have criticized him because he abandoned the mother of his illegitimate son. Other writers have faulted Columbus as an opportunistic adventurer who loved the trappings of grand titles. Some claim he was the originator of European exploitation of the non-European world; he destroyed the paradise that had been the New World.[16] Because these judgments rest on social and ethical standards that did not exist in Columbus's world, responsible scholars consider them ahistorical.

Using the evidence of his journal (sea log) and letters, let us ask three basic questions. First, what kind of man was Columbus, and what forces or influences shaped him? Second, in sailing westward from Europe, what were his goals? Third, did he achieve his goals, and what did he make of his discoveries?

The central feature in the character of Christopher Columbus is that he was a deeply religious man. He began the *Journal* of his voyage to the Americas in the form of a letter to Ferdinand and Isabella of Spain:

*On 2 January in the year 1492, when your Highnesses had concluded their war with the Moors who reigned in Europe, I saw your Highnesses banners victoriously raised on the towers of the Alhambra, the citadel of the city, and the Moorish king come out of the city gates and kiss the hands of your Highnesses and the prince, My Lord. And later in that same month, on the grounds of information I had given your Highnesses concerning the lands of India . . . your Highnesses decided to send me, Christopher Columbus, to see these parts of India and the princes and peoples of those lands and consider the best means for their conversion.*[17]

Thus he had witnessed the Spanish reconquest of Granada and shared fully in the religious and nationalistic fervor surrounding that event. Just seven months separated Isabella and Ferdinand's entry into Granada on January 2 and Columbus's departure westward on August 3, 1492. In his mind, the two events were clearly linked. Long after Europeans knew something of Columbus's discoveries in the Caribbean, they nevertheless considered the restoration of Muslim Granada to Christian hands as Ferdinand and Isabella's greatest achievement; for the reconquest the Spanish pope Alexander VI rewarded them in 1494 with the title "Most Catholic Kings." Like the Spanish rulers and most Europeans of his age, Columbus understood Christianity as a missionary religion that should be carried to places and peoples where it did not exist. Although Columbus certainly had material and secular goals, first and foremost, as he wrote in 1498, he believed he was a divine agent: "God made me the messenger of the new heaven and the new earth of which he spoke in the Apocalypse of St. John . . . and he showed me the post where to find it."[18]

Columbus was also very knowledgeable about the sea. He was familiar with such fifteenth-century Portuguese navigational developments as *portolans*—written descriptions of the courses along which ships sailed, showing bays, coves, capes, ports, and the distances between these places—and the use of the magnetic needle as a nautical instrument. And, as he implied in his *Journal,* he had acquired not only theoretical but also practical experience: "I have spent twenty-three years at sea and have not left it for any length of time worth mentioning, and I have seen everything from east to west [meaning he had been to England] and I have been to Guinea [north and west Africa]."[19] Although some of Columbus's geographical theories, such as his measurement of the distance from Portugal to Japan at 2,760 miles, when it is actually 12,000, proved inaccurate, his successful thirty-three-day voyage to the Caribbean owed a great deal to his seamanship and his knowledge of the accurate use of instruments.

What was the object of this first voyage? He gave the answer in the very title of the expedition, "The Enterprise of the Indies." He wanted to find a direct ocean route to Asia that would provide the opportunity for a greatly expanded trade in which Spain would participate. Two recent scholars have written, "If Columbus had not sailed westward in search of Asia, someone else would have done so. The time was right for such a bold undertaking." Someone else might have done so, but the fact remains that Columbus, displaying a characteristic Renaissance curiosity and restless drive, actually did it.

How did Columbus interpret what he had found, and in his mind did he achieve what he had set out to do? His mind had been formed by the Bible and the geographical writings of classical authors, as had the minds of most educated people of his times. Thus as people have often done in every age, Columbus ignored the evidence of his eyes and described what he wanted to see in the Caribbean as an idyllic paradise, a peaceful garden of

Eden. (See the feature "Listening to the Past: Columbus Describes His First Voyage" on pages 526–527.) When accounts of his travels were published, Europeans' immediate fascination with this image of the New World meant that Columbus's propaganda created an instant myth. But having sensed that he had not found the spice markets and bazaars of Asia, Columbus shifted his goal from establishing trade with the (East) Indians and Chinese to establishing the kind of trade the Portuguese then conducted with Africa and with the Atlantic islands. That meant setting up some form of government in the islands, and Columbus had little interest in or capacity for governing. In 1496 he had forcibly subjugated the island of Hispaniola, enslaved the Indians, and laid the basis for a system of land grants tied to the Indians' labor service. Borrowing practices and institutions from reconquest Spain and the Canary Islands, Columbus laid the foundation for Spanish imperial administration. In all of this, Columbus was very much a man of his times. He never understood, however, that the scale of his discoveries created problems of trade, settlers, governmental bureaucracy, and, from a twenty-first-century perspective, the rights of native peoples.[20]

## Later Explorers

News of Columbus's first voyage rapidly spread across Europe. On April 1, 1493, a printer in Barcelona published in Spanish Columbus's letter describing what he believed he had found. By the end of that month, the letter had been translated into Latin and published in Rome as *De Insulis Inventis* (On the Discoveries of the Islands). Within a year, printers in Paris, Basel, Antwerp, and Venice had brought out six more Latin editions, which were soon followed by translations in German and Tuscan, the dialect of the Florentines. In a 1503 letter, Florentine navigator Amerigo Vespucci (1454–1512), in whose honor America was named, wrote, "Those new regions which we found and explored with the fleet . . . we may rightly call a New World." This letter, titled *Mundus Novus* (The New World), was the first document to describe America as a continent separate from Asia. Some scholars today try to avoid the terms *discovery* and *New World,* lest they be considered Eurocentric, but the use of those words rests on a tradition begun by the early explorers themselves.

The search for precious metals determined the direction of Spanish exploration and expansion into South America. When it became apparent that placer mining (in which ore is separated from soil by panning) in the Caribbean islands was slow and the rewards were slim, new routes to the East and new sources of gold and silver were sought.

In 1519 Spanish ruler Charles V commissioned Ferdinand Magellan (1480–1521) to find a direct route to the spices of the Moluccas off the southeast coast of Asia. Magellan sailed southwest across the Atlantic to Brazil and proceeded south around Cape Horn into the Pacific Ocean (see Map 15.3). He crossed the Pacific, sailing west, to the Malay Archipelago, which he called the "Western Isles." (Some of these islands were conquered in the 1560s and named the "Philippines" for Philip II of Spain.)

Though Magellan was killed, the expedition continued, returning to Spain in 1522 from the east by way of the Indian Ocean, the Cape of Good Hope, and the Atlantic. Terrible storms, mutiny, starvation, and disease haunted this voyage. Nevertheless, it verified the theory that the earth was round and brought information about the vastness of the Pacific. Magellan also proved that the earth was much larger than Columbus had estimated.

**Ecclesiastical Wealth (Yanhuitian Codex)** Through their control of tithes—taxes on agricultural production and livestock—the rulers of Spain and Portugal supported the colonial church and promoted the conversion of Amerindians. By 1600, the church was the largest property owner in the Americas and had vast agricultural, commercial, and mining interests. Here noble and commoner deliver payments to the bishop. *(Courtesy, M. E. Grenander Department of Special Collections and Archives, University of Albany, SUNY)*

In the West Indies, the slow recovery of gold, the shortage of a healthy labor force, and sheer restlessness speeded up Spain's search for wealth. In 1519, the year Magellan departed on his worldwide expedition, a brash and determined Spanish adventurer named Hernando Cortés (1485–1547) crossed from Hispaniola to mainland Mexico with six hundred men, seventeen horses, and ten cannon. Within three years, Cortés had taken captive the Aztec emperor Montezuma, conquered the fabulously rich Aztec Empire, and founded Mexico City as the capital of New Spain. The subjugation of northern Mexico took longer, but between 1531 and 1550 the Spanish gained control of Zacatecas and Guanajuato, where rich silver veins were soon tapped.

Another Spanish conquistador, Francisco Pizarro (1470–1541), repeated Cortés's feat in Peru. Between 1531 and 1536, with even fewer resources, Pizarro crushed the Inca Empire in western South America and established the Spanish viceroyalty of Peru, with its center at Lima. In 1545 the Spanish opened at Potosí in the Peruvian highlands what became the richest silver mines in the New World.

Between 1525 and 1575, the riches of the Americas poured into the Spanish port of Seville and the Portuguese capital of Lisbon. For all their new wealth, however, Lisbon and Seville did not become important trading centers. It was the Flemish city of Antwerp, controlled by the Spanish Habsburgs, that developed into the great entrepôt for overseas bullion and Portuguese spices and served as the commercial and financial capital of the entire European world (see page 493).

By the end of the sixteenth century, Amsterdam had overtaken Antwerp as the financial capital of Europe. The Dutch had also embarked on foreign exploration and conquest. The Dutch East India Company, founded in 1602, became the major organ of Dutch imperialism and within a few decades expelled the Portuguese from Ceylon and other East Indian islands. By 1650 the Dutch West India Company had successfully intruded on the Spanish possessions in the Americas, in the process gaining control of much of the African and American trade.

English and French explorations lacked the immediate, sensational results of those of the Spanish and Portuguese. In 1497 John Cabot, a Genoese merchant living in London, sailed for Brazil but discovered Newfoundland. The next year he returned and explored the New England coast and perhaps as far south as Delaware. Since these expeditions found no spices or gold, King Henry VII lost interest in exploration. Between 1534 and 1541, Frenchman Jacques Cartier made several voyages and explored the St. Lawrence region of Canada, but the first permanent French settlement, at Quebec, was not founded until 1608.

## The Economic Effects of Spain's Discoveries in the New World

The sixteenth century has been called the **Golden Century of Spain.** The influence of Spanish armies, Spanish Catholicism, and Spanish wealth was felt all over Europe. This greatness rested largely on the influx of precious metals from the New World. The mines at Zacatecas and Guanajuato in Mexico and Potosí in Peru poured out huge quantities of precious metals. To protect this treasure from French and English pirates, armed convoys transported it each year to Spain. Between 1503 and 1650, 16 million kilograms of silver and 185,000 kilograms of gold entered the port of Seville.

Meanwhile, Spain was experiencing a steady population increase, creating a sharp rise in the demand for food and goods. Spanish colonies in the Americas also represented a demand for products. Because Spain had expelled some of its best farmers and business people, the Jews in 1492 and the Muslims in the sixteenth and seventeenth centuries, the Spanish economy suffered and could not meet the new demands. Prices rose and with them the costs of manufacturing cloth and other goods. As a result, Spanish products could not compete in the international market with cheaper products made elsewhere. The textile industry was badly hurt. Prices spiraled upward faster than the government could levy taxes to dampen the economy. (Higher taxes would have cut the public's buying power; with fewer goods sold, prices would have come down.)

Did the flood of American silver bullion cause the inflation? Scholars have long debated this question. Prices rose most steeply before 1565, but bullion imports reached their peak between 1580 and 1620. Thus there is no direct correlation between silver imports and the inflation rate. Did the substantial population growth accelerate the inflation rate? Perhaps: when the population pressure declined after 1600, prices gradually stabilized. One fact is certain: the **price revolution** severely strained government budgets. Several times between 1557 and 1647, Philip II and his successors were forced to repudiate the state debt, which in turn undermined confidence in the government. By the seventeenth century, the economy was a shambles, and Spanish predominance was over.

As Philip II paid his armies and foreign debts with silver bullion, the Spanish inflation was transmitted to the rest of Europe. Between 1560 and 1600, much of Europe experienced large price increases. Prices doubled and in some cases quadrupled, and wages did not keep pace with prices. Spain suffered most severely, but all European countries were affected. People who lived on fixed incomes, such as the continental nobles, were badly hurt because their money bought less. Those who owed fixed sums of money, such as the middle class, prospered: in a time of rising prices, debts had less value each year. Food costs rose most sharply, and the poor fared worst of all.

## The Columbian Exchange

Besides the consequences of American silver and gold, what impact did contacts with the Americas have on Europeans? Europeans had had commercial relations with Asia and sub-Saharan Africa since Roman times. In the Carolingian era the slave trade had linked northern Europe and the Islamic Middle East. The High Middle Ages had witnessed a great expansion of trade between Europe and Africa and Asia (see pages 352, 356, and 437). But with the American discoveries, commercial and other relations for the first time became worldwide, involving all the continents except Australia. European involvement in the Americas led to the acceleration of global contacts. In time, these contacts had a profound influence on Europeans.

An important historical study asserts that the most significant changes brought about by the Columbian voyages were biosocial. The Age of Discovery led to the migration of peoples, which in turn led to an exchange of fauna and flora, of animals, plants, and disease. Spanish and Portuguese immigrants to the Americas wanted the foods with which they were familiar—wheat for bread, grapes for wine, olive oil for culinary and sacramental purposes. By 1535, Mexico was exporting wheat to Spain, and shortly after, wine and olive oil went to Spain from Chile and Peru. The Spanish and Portuguese also took back to Europe maize (corn) from Mexico (the main American cereal), white potatoes from Peru, and many varieties of beans, squash, pumpkins, and tomatoes (Europeans distrusted tomatoes, fearing they were sexually stimulating). Although they were initially contemptuous of white potatoes, once Europeans discovered their nutritional value, cultivation spread from Ireland and England in the seventeenth century to Germany, Poland, and Russia in the eighteenth. But maize—which grows in climates too dry for rice and too wet for wheat, has a short growing season, and gives a high yield per unit of land—proved to be the great Amerindian gift to Europe and the rest of the world.

Because Native Americans had only wild game for food and no large beasts of burden, on his second voyage to America Columbus brought horses, cattle, sheep, pigs, and chickens. The rapid multiplication of these animals allowed the Spaniards to take herds of swine on exploring expeditions; horses enabled them to move faster and farther. Columbus also introduced sugar cane into the Caribbean, Cortés took it to Mexico, and the European demand for sugar began to be satisfied.[21]

Europeans also brought something that had a devastating effect on the Amerindian population: disease.

**Physician Scraping Sores** In five years, syphilis spread across Europe, reaching Russia in 1499. The running sores, boils, and aches in the joints caused agonizing pain. European physicians first followed the treatment described by Arab doctors, scraping sores from the skin and rubbing the skin with mercury (shown here). Later, Europeans adopted a remedy common in Espaniola (Haiti, where syphilis was thought to have originated)—brewing a concoction made from shavings of the guaiacum tree and water, which the patient drank for thirty days. This treatment proved amazingly effective. The Fugger banking family of Augsburg gained a monopoly on the import of guaiacum, but because of its high cost only the rich could afford the remedy from the New World. *(Anon, from B. Steber,* A Mala Franzos Morbo Gallorum, Praeservatio ac Cura *[Venice, 1498])*

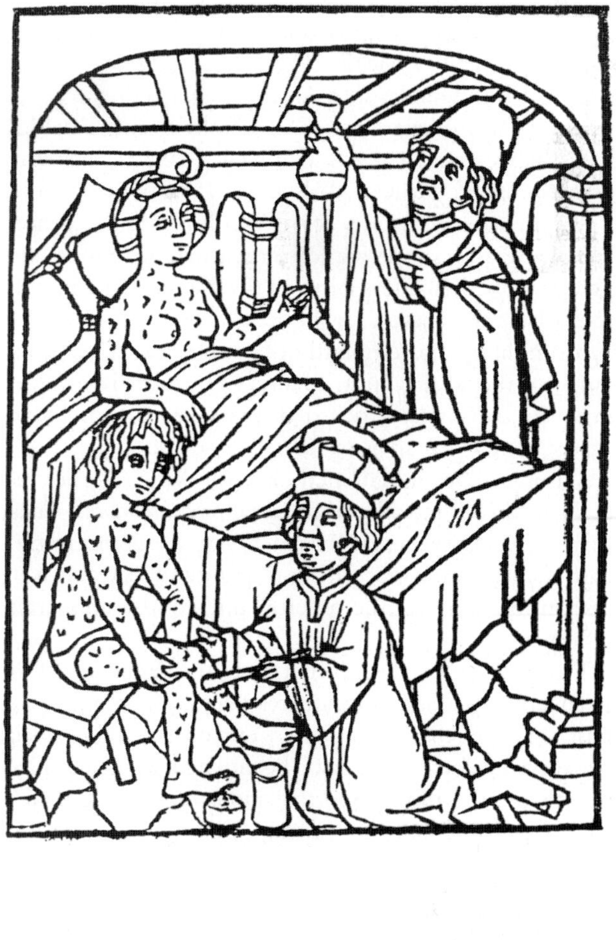

Long isolated from other peoples, Amerindians had no resistance to European diseases, especially smallpox. Students of the history of medicine estimate that the population of central Mexico fell from 25.3 million people in 1519 to 1 million in 1605 and the Andean population of Peru went from 1.3 million in 1570 to 600,000 in 1620. Some demographers dispute these figures, but all agree the decline of the native peoples was catastrophic.

In return, Amerindians gave the Spaniards the venereal disease syphilis. Sailors and settlers carried it back to Europe in 1493. Transmitted by sailors and armies to Europe after 1493, syphilis raced across the continent in the sixteenth century. Its precise origin is disputed, but no evidence for the disease in Europe exists before 1493.[22]

### Colonial Administration

Columbus, Cortés, and Pizarro claimed the lands they had "discovered" for the Crown of Spain. How were these lands to be governed? According to the Spanish theory of absolutism, the Crown was entitled to exercise full authority over all imperial lands. In the sixteenth century, the Crown divided its New World territories into four **viceroyalties,** or administrative divisions: New Spain, which consisted of Mexico, Central America, and present-day California, Arizona, New Mexico, and Texas, with the capital at Mexico City; Peru, originally all the lands in continental South America, later reduced to the territory of modern Peru, Chile, Bolivia, and Ecuador, with the viceregal seat at Lima; New Granada, including present-day Venezuela, Colombia, Panama, and, after 1739, Ecuador, with Bogotá as its administrative center; and La Plata, consisting of Argentina, Uruguay, and Paraguay, with Buenos Aires as the capital. Within each territory, the viceroy, or imperial governor, exercised broad military and civil authority as the direct representative of the sovereign in Madrid. The viceroy presided over the *audiencia,* a board of twelve to fifteen judges that served as his advisory council and the highest judicial body. The enlightened Spanish king Charles III (r. 1759–1788) introduced the system of *intendants.* These royal officials possessed broad military, administrative, and financial authority within their intendancy and were responsible not to the viceroy but to the monarchy in Madrid.

From the early sixteenth century to the beginning of the nineteenth, the Spanish monarchy acted on the mercantilist principle that the colonies existed for the financial benefit of the home country. The mining of gold and silver was always the most important industry in the colonies. The Crown claimed the **quinto,** one-fifth of all precious metals mined in South America. Gold and silver yielded the Spanish monarchy 25 percent of its total income. In return, it shipped manufactured goods to the Americas and discouraged the development of native industries.

The Portuguese governed their colony of Brazil in a similar manner. After the union of the Crowns of Portugal and Spain in 1580, Spanish administrative forms were introduced. Local officials called *corregidores* held judicial and military powers. Mercantilist policies placed severe restrictions on Brazilian industries that might compete with those of Portugal. In the seventeenth century, the use of black slave labor made possible the cultivation of coffee and cotton, and in the eighteenth century Brazil led the world in the production of sugar. The unique feature of colonial Brazil's culture and society was its thoroughgoing intermixture of Indians, whites, and blacks.

## Changing Attitudes

See DBQ 3

What were the cultural consequences of the religious wars and of the worldwide discoveries? What impact did the discoveries and wars have on Europeans' attitudes? The clash of traditional religious and geographical beliefs with the new knowledge provided by explorers—combined with decades of devastation and disorder within Europe—bred confusion, uncertainty, and insecurity. Geographical evidence based on verifiably scientific proofs contradicted the evidence of the Scriptures and of the classical authors.

The age of religious wars was one of extreme and violent contrasts. It was a deeply religious period in which people fought passionately for their beliefs; 70 percent of the books printed dealt with religious subjects. Yet the times saw the beginnings of religious skepticism. Europeans explored new continents, partly with the missionary aim of Christianizing the peoples they encountered. Yet the Spanish, Portuguese, Dutch, and English proceeded to dominate and enslave the Indians and blacks they found. While Europeans indulged in gross sensuality, the social status of women declined. The exploration of new continents reflected deep curiosity and broad intelligence, yet Europeans believed in witches and burned thousands at the stake. Sexism, racism, and skepticism had all originated in ancient times. But late in the sixteenth century, they began to take on their familiar modern forms.

### The Status of Women

Religious writers of the Reformation and early modern period did not express consistent views on women. Sometimes they were terribly negative, at other times very positive (see, for example, Luther's opinions on page 466). Some Reformation leaders, such as Calvin, addressed the subject of women only obliquely, in the context of some other topic; thus, interpretation of their views is difficult.

Although Protestant reformers rejected medieval Scholastic ideas on celibacy and marriage and broke with the institutional Catholic church, Protestants scarcely differed with Scholastics' notions about women. Luther, Calvin, Zwingli, and the English Puritans all held that women could merit salvation and that men and women were spiritually equal, but they also insisted that women were subordinate to men. Protestant reformers stressed the value of marriage. Marriage had three purposes: the procreation of children, the avoidance of sin, and mutual help and companionship. By "mutual help and companionship," however, they did not mean equality of husband and wife. Reformers urged everyone to marry. One Lutheran pastor held that "A man without a wife is only half a person and has only half a body and is a needy and miserable man who lacks help and assistance."[23] It was even more incumbent on women to marry. Reformers saw marriage as a woman's highest calling and believed that it freed women from sexual urges. They scorned unmarried women for upsetting the divine order, which they thought made women subject to men. While the reformers elevated marriage over celibacy, they did not elevate women as women. Sermons (in most parts of Europe people were required to go to church), pamphlets, and engravings reiterated these views, so women could not fail to know them.

Catholic thinkers upheld the traditional teaching that the celibate life was the highest form of Christian life. The institutional church vigorously enforced the Council of Trent's doctrine on a celibate clergy and removed candidates deemed unworthy. Church authorities recognized that most women would marry, and Catholic writings described the ideal wife in the same terms as Protestant manuals: she was obedient, silent, and pious.[24]

As for same-sex marriages, Protestants and Catholics would have agreed that lacking a scriptural basis such unions could not occur. When Maria of Antwerp (1719–1781) was arrested twice for marrying a woman, she claimed that she was a man in a woman's body. Perhaps we may infer she had no words to describe sexual love between two women. Male bias and general ignorance of the female anatomy led even educated people to insist that a woman could not achieve sexual satisfaction without a man.

Manuals emphasized the qualities expected of each partner. A husband was obliged to provide for the material welfare of his wife and children. He was directed to protect his family while remaining steady and self-controlled. Especially was a husband and father to rule his household firmly but justly. But he was not to behave as a tyrant, a guideline counselors repeated frequently. A wife should be a mature person, a good household manager, and a subservient and faithful spouse. The husband also owed fidelity, and both Protestant and Catholic moralists rejected the double standard of sexual morality as a threat to family unity. Counselors believed that marriage should be based on mutual respect and trust. While they discouraged impersonal unions arranged by parents, they did not think romantic attachments—based on physical attraction and emotional love—a sound basis for an enduring relationship.

Moralists held that the household was a woman's first priority. She might assist in her own or her husband's business and do charitable work. Involvement in social or public activities, however, was inappropriate because it distracted the wife from her primary responsibility, her household. If women suffered under their husbands' yokes, writers explained that submission was the punishment they had inherited from Eve, penance for man's fall, like the pain of childbearing. Moreover, they said, a woman's lot was no worse than a man's: he had to earn the family's bread by the sweat of his brow.[25]

Catholics viewed marriage as a sacramental union that, if validly entered into, could not be dissolved. Protestants saw marriage as a contract in which each partner promised the other support, companionship, and the sharing of mutual goods. Protestants recognized a mutual right to divorce and remarriage for various reasons, including adultery and irreparable breakdown.[26] Society in the early modern period was patriarchal. While women neither lost their identity nor lacked meaningful work, the pervasive assumption was that men ruled.

There were some remarkable success stories, however. Elizabeth Hardwick, the orphaned daughter of an obscure English country squire, made four careful marriages, each of which brought her more property and carried her higher up the social ladder. She managed her estates, amounting to more than 100,000 acres, with a degree of business sense rare in any age. The two great mansions she built, Chatsworth and Hardwick, stand today as monuments to her acumen. Having established several aristocratic dynasties, she died in 1608, past her eightieth year, one of the richest people in England.[27]

Artists' drawings of plump, voluptuous women and massive, muscular men revealed the contemporary standards of physical beauty. It was a sensual age that gloried in the delights of the flesh. Some people, such as humanist poet Aretino, found sexual satisfaction with both sexes. Reformers and public officials simultaneously condemned and condoned sexual "sins." The oldest profession had many practitioners, and when in 1566 Pope Pius IV expelled all the prostitutes from Rome, so many people left and the city suffered such a loss of revenue that in less than a month the pope was forced to rescind the order. Scholars debated Saint Augustine's notion that whores served a useful social function by preventing worse sins. Prostitution was common because poverty forced women and young men into it. Since the later Middle Ages, licensed houses of prostitution had been common in urban centers (see page 398). The general public took the matter for granted. Consequently, civil authorities in both Catholic and Protestant countries licensed houses of public prostitution. These establishments were intended, however, for the convenience of single men, and some Protestant cities, such as Geneva and Zurich, installed officials in the brothels with the express purpose of preventing married men from patronizing them.

Moralists naturally railed against prostitution. For example, Melchior Ambach, the Lutheran editor of many tracts against adultery and whoring, wrote in 1543 that if "houses of women" for single and married men were allowed, why not provide a "house of boys" for women who lacked husbands to service them? "Would whoring be any worse for the poor, needy female sex?"[28] Ambach, of course, was not being serious: by treating infidelity from the perspective of female, rather than male, customers, he was still insisting that prostitution destroyed the family and society.

Single women of the middle and working classes in the sixteenth and seventeenth centuries worked in many occupations and professions—as domestic servants, butchers, shopkeepers, nurses, goldsmiths, midwives, and workers in the weaving and printing industries. Married women normally assisted in their husbands' businesses. What became of the thousands of women who left convents and nunneries during the Reformation? Luther and the Protestant reformers believed that celibacy had no scriptural basis; they favored the suppression of women's religious houses and encouraged ex-nuns to marry. Marriage, the reformers maintained, freed women from clerical domination, cultural deprivation, and sexual repression.[29] Consequently, these women apparently passed from clerical domination to subservience to husbands.

If some nuns in the Middle Ages lacked a genuine religious vocation and if some religious houses witnessed financial mismanagement and moral laxness, convents nevertheless provided women of the upper classes with scope for their literary, artistic, medical, or administrative talents if they could not or would not marry. With the closing of convents, marriage became virtually the only occupation for upper-class Protestant women. This helps explain why Anglicans, Calvinists, and Lutherans established communities of religious women, such as the Lutheran one at Kaiserwerth in the Rhineland, in the eighteenth and nineteenth centuries.[30]

## The Great European Witch-hunt

The great European witch scare reveals something about contemporary attitudes toward women. The period of the religious wars witnessed a startling increase in the phenomenon of witch-hunting, whose prior history was long but sporadic. "A **witch**," according to Chief Justice Coke of England, "was a person who hath conference with the Devil to consult with him or to do some act." This definition by the highest legal authority in England demonstrates that educated as well as ignorant people believed in witches. Witches were thought to be individuals who could mysteriously injure other people or animals—by causing a person to become blind or impotent, for instance, or by preventing a cow from giving milk. Belief in witches predated Christianity. For centuries, tales had circulated about old women who made nocturnal travels on greased broomsticks to *sabbats,* or assemblies of witches, where they participated in sexual orgies and feasted on the flesh of infants. In the popular imagination, witches had definite characteristics. The vast majority were married women or widows between fifty and seventy years old, crippled or bent with age, with pockmarked skin. They often practiced midwifery or folk medicine, and most had sharp tongues and were quick to scold.

Religious reformers' extreme notions of the Devil's powers and the insecurity created by the religious wars contributed to the growth of belief in witches. The idea developed that witches made pacts with the Devil in return for the power to work mischief on their enemies. Since pacts with the Devil meant the renunciation of God, witchcraft was considered heresy. Persecution for witchcraft had actually begun in the later fourteenth century, when witchcraft was declared heresy. The century between 1560 and 1660, when mainstream Protestantism and Tridentine Catholicism had begun to settle into definite confessional blocs, saw witch-hunting on an unprecedented and virulent scale, touching every part of Europe from Iceland to Russia. Scholars currently estimate that during the sixteenth and seventeenth centuries between 100,000 and 200,000 people were officially tried for witchcraft, and between 50,000 and 100,000 were executed.

**Witches' Sabbat (1510)** Trained by the great German graphic artist and painter Albrecht Dürer at Nuremberg, Hans Baldung Grien (1484/5–1545) in this woodcut combines learned and stereotypical beliefs about witches: they traveled at night on broomsticks, met at sabbats (or assemblies), feasted on infants (in dish held high), concocted strange potions, and possessed an aged and debauched sensuality. *(Germanisches Nationalmuseum Nürnberg)*

Historians, sociologists, and anthropologists have presented a variety of explanations. Some scholars see witch-hunts as a consequence of the Reformation: rulers proved their piety and religious commitment either by religious wars or by cracking down on heretics or persons considered socially marginal. Some scholars attribute witch-hunts to socioeconomic factors: severe inflation; periodic famines due to poor harvests; wars; the enclosure of land, leading to the movement of the dispossessed and an increase in vagrants (beggars and homeless people)—all creating an atmosphere of instability and uncertainty in values. Still other writers blame demographic changes caused by late marriages and the increasing number of women who never married at all, women who were not under a man's supervision and thus highly suspect. Perhaps a number of causes—religious, intellectual, social, and economic—created the atmosphere that led to the deaths of so many.[31] Given the broad strand of misogyny (hatred of women) in Western religion, the long-held belief in the susceptibility of women (so-called weaker vessels) to the Devil's allurements, and the pervasive seventeenth-century belief about women's multiple and demanding orgasms and thus their sexual insatiability, it is not difficult to understand why women were accused of all sorts of mischief and witchcraft. As the most important capital crime for women in early modern times, witchcraft has considerable significance for the history and status of women.[32] Witch-hunting declined only in the eighteenth century, as fear of the Devil and his powers of malevolent sorcery waned among the educated ruling classes.

## European Slavery and the Origins of American Racism

Since ancient times, victors in battle have enslaved conquered peoples. Throughout the Middle Ages, slavery was deeply entrenched in southern Italy, Sicily, Crete, Iberia, and the Balkans. The bubonic plague, famines, and other epidemics created a severe shortage of agricultural and domestic workers throughout Europe, encouraging Italian merchants to buy slaves from the Balkans, Thrace, southern Russia, and central Anatolia for sale in the West. In 1364 the Florentine government allowed the unlimited importation of slaves so long as they were not Christians. Between 1414 and 1423, at least ten thousand slaves were sold in Venice alone. The slave trade represented one aspect of Italian business enterprise during the Renaissance: where profits were lucrative, papal threats of excommunication failed to stop Genoese slave traders (see page 436). The Genoese set up colonial stations in the Crimea and along the Black Sea, and according to an international authority on slavery, these outposts were "virtual laboratories" for the development of slave plantation agriculture in the New World.[33] This form of slavery had nothing to do with race; almost all slaves were white. How, then, did black African slavery enter the European picture and take root in South and then North America?

In 1453 the Ottoman capture of Constantinople halted the flow of white slaves from the Black Sea region and the Balkans. Mediterranean Europe, cut off from its traditional source of slaves, had no alternative source for

**African Slave and Indian Woman** A black slave approaches an Indian prostitute. Unable to explain what he wants, he points with his finger; she eagerly grasps for the coin. The Spanish caption above moralizes on the black man using stolen money—yet the Spaniards ruthlessly expropriated all South American mineral wealth. *(New York Public Library/Art Resource, NY)*

slave labor but sub-Saharan Africa. The centuries-old trans-Saharan trade was greatly stimulated by the existence of a ready market in the vineyards and sugar plantations of Sicily and Majorca. By the later fifteenth century, the Mediterranean had developed an "American" form of slavery before the discovery of America. (See the feature "Individuals in Society: Juan de Pareja.") Because slavery was sanctioned by the Bible and the ancient philosophers, few people thought it morally wrong.

Meanwhile, the Genoese and other Italians had colonized the Canary Islands in the eastern Atlantic. Prince Henry the Navigator's sailors (see page 502) discovered the Madeira Islands and made settlements there. In this stage of European expansion, "the history of slavery became inextricably tied up with the history of sugar." Though it was an expensive luxury that only the affluent could afford, population increases and monetary expansion in the fifteenth century led to an increasing demand for sugar. Resourceful Italians provided the capital, cane, and technology for sugar cultivation on plantations in southern Portugal, Madeira, and the Canary Islands. Meanwhile, in the period 1490 to 1530, the port of Lisbon saw between three hundred and two thousand black slaves arrive annually (see Map 15.4). From Lisbon, where African slaves performed most of the manual labor and constituted 10 percent of the city's population, slaves were transported to the sugar plantations of Madeira, the Azores, and the Cape Verde Islands. Sugar and the small Atlantic islands gave New World slavery its distinctive shape. Columbus himself, who spent a decade in Madeira, brought sugar plants on his voyages to "the Indies."[34]

As already discussed, European expansion across the Atlantic led to the economic exploitation of the Americas. In the New World, the major problem settlers faced was a shortage of labor. As early as 1495, the Spanish solved the problem by enslaving the native Indians. In the next two centuries, the Portuguese, Dutch, and English followed suit.

Although the Aztecs of Mexico and the Incas of Peru had various forms of servile labor, including domestic, agricultural, and industrial slavery, before European intrusion, Native American peoples were not accustomed to the harshness of Spanish exploitation. They could not endure panning for gold for twelve hours a day in the broiling sun. The Indians died "like fish in a bucket," one Spanish settler reported.[35] In 1515 a Spanish missionary, Bartolomé de las Casas (1474–1566), who had seen the evils of Indian slavery, urged the future emperor Charles V to end Indian slavery and to import blacks from Africa. Church law did not strictly forbid slavery, and Las Casas thought blacks could better survive under South American conditions. Charles agreed, and in 1518 the African slave trade began. (When the blacks arrived, Las Casas immediately regretted his suggestion.)

In Africa, where slavery was entrenched (as it was in the Islamic world, southern Europe, and China), African kings and dealers sold black slaves to European merchants who participated in the transatlantic trade. The Portuguese brought the first slaves to Brazil; by 1600, 4,000 were being imported annually. After its founding in 1621, the Dutch West India Company, with the full support of the government of the United Provinces,

# Individuals in Society

## Juan de Pareja

A marginal person is one who lives outside the mainstream of the dominant society, who is not fully assimilated into or accepted by that society, but from whose life and experience we learn about the values and ideals of the dominant group. Such a person was the Spanish religious and portrait painter Juan de Pareja.

Pareja was born in Antequera, an agricultural region and the old center of Muslim culture near Seville in southern Spain. Of his parents we know nothing. Because a rare surviving document calls him a "mulatto," one of his parents must have been white and the other must have had some African blood. The Spanish word *mulatto* derives from the Arabic *muwallad,* a person of mixed race, and some scholars, using religion to describe ethnic category, speak of Pareja's "Muslim descent." The region from which he came makes that possible, but we do not know whether he actually believed in or practiced Islam.

In 1630 Pareja applied to the mayor of Seville for permission to travel to Madrid to visit his brother and "to perfect his art." The document lists his occupation as "a painter in Seville." Since it mentions no other name, it is reasonable to assume that Pareja arrived in Madrid a free man. Sometime between 1630 and 1648, however, he came into the possession of the artist Diego Velázquez (1599–1660); Pareja became a slave.

In the twelfth century, Muslim slaves helped build the cathedral of Saint James at Santiago de Compostela, one of the great shrines of medieval Christendom. During the long wars of the reconquista, Muslims and Christians captured each other in battle and used the defeated as slaves. The fifteenth and sixteenth centuries had seen a steady flow of sub-Saharan Africans into the Iberian Peninsula. Thus early modern Spain was a slave-holding society.

How did Velázquez acquire Pareja? By purchase? As a gift? Had Pareja fallen into debt, or committed some crime, and thereby lost his freedom? We do not know. Velázquez, the greatest Spanish painter of the seventeenth century, had a large studio with many assistants. Pareja was set to grinding powders to make colors and to preparing canvases. He must have demonstrated ability because, when Velázquez went to Rome in 1648, he chose Pareja to accompany him.

In 1650, as practice for a portrait of Pope Innocent X, Velázquez painted Pareja. That same year, Velázquez signed the document that gave Pareja his freedom, to become effective in 1654. From 1654 until his death, Pareja worked in Madrid as an independent painter. Although he received recognition for his work, only one painting survives: *The Calling of Saint Matthew,* signed and dated 1661 (see page 522). Modern art historians dispute its merit. Some believe it shows a forceful baroque energy and considerable originality; others consider it derivative of Velázquez.

*Velázquez,* Juan de Pareja *(1650).* (The Metropolitan Museum of Art, Fletcher Fund, Rogers Fund, and Bequest of Miss Adelaide Milton de Groot (1876–1967), by exchange, supplemented by gifts from friends of the Museum, 1971. [1971.86]. Photograph © 1986 The Metropolitan Museum of Art)

What does the public career of this seventeenth-century marginal person tell us about the man and his world? After living in Seville and Madrid, he traveled widely, visiting Genoa, Venice, Rome, and Naples. Travel may have broadened him, producing a cosmopolitan man. Pareja's career suggests that a person of talent and ability could rise in Spanish society, despite the social and religious barriers that existed at the time. Jonathan Brown, the leading authority on Velázquez, describes Pareja's appearance in Velázquez's portrait as "self-confident." A more enthusiastic student writes, "The Metropolitan is probably the greatest museum in the world . . . and this [Velázquez's portrait of Pareja] is its greatest painting. . . . The man was technically a slave. . . . However, we can see from Velázquez's painting that the two were undeniably equals. That steady look of self-controlled power can even make us wonder which of the two had a higher opinion of himself."

### Questions for Analysis

1. Since slavery was an established institution in Spain, speculate on Velázquez's possible reasons for giving Pareja his freedom.
2. What issues of cultural diversity might Pareja have faced in seventeenth-century Spain?

*Sources:* Jonathan Brown, *Velázquez: Painter and Courtier* (New Haven, Conn.: Yale University Press, 1986); *Grove Dictionary of Art* (New York: Macmillan, 2000); *Sister Wendy Beckett's 1000 Masterpieces* (New York: Dorling Kindersley Inc., 1999).

*The* **history companion** *features additional information and activities related to this topic.*
**history.college.hmco.com/students**

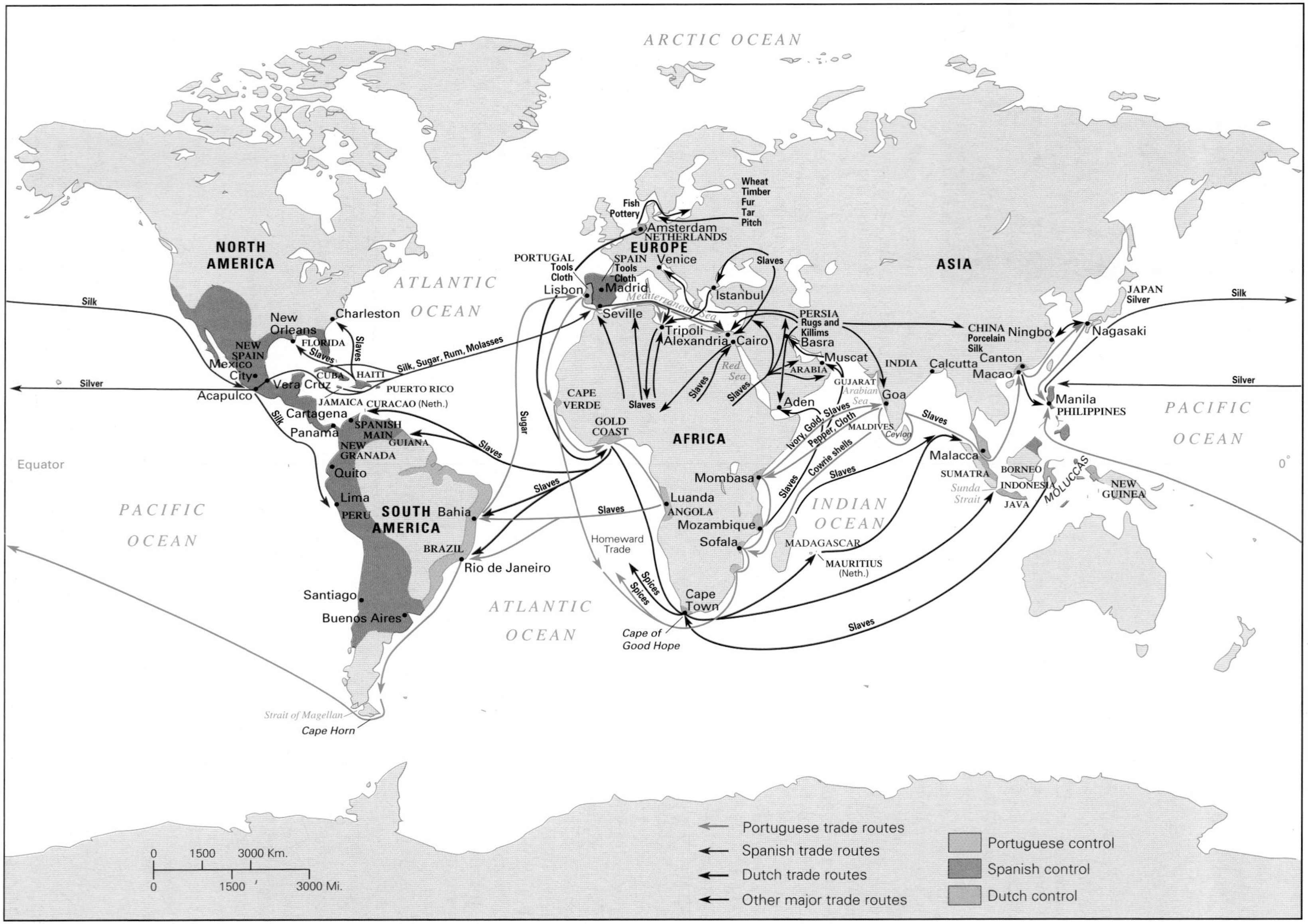


**MAP 15.4 The Worldwide Slave Trade** By the mid-seventeenth century, trade in spices, silk, sugar, and slaves linked all parts of the globe. The trans-Atlantic trade in African peoples was one aspect of global commerce, one facet of worldwide slavery.

transported thousands of Africans to Brazil and the Caribbean. In the late seventeenth century, with the chartering of the Royal African Company, the English got involved. Thereafter, large numbers of African blacks poured into the West Indies and North America. In 1790 there were 757,181 blacks in a total U.S. population of 3,929,625. When the first census was taken in Brazil in 1798, blacks numbered about 2 million in a total population of 3.25 million.

Settlers brought to the Americas the racial attitudes they had absorbed in Europe. Settlers' beliefs and attitudes toward blacks derived from two basic sources: Christian theological speculation (see page 438) and Arab ideas. In the sixteenth and seventeenth centuries, the English, for example, were extremely curious about Africans' lives and customs, and slavers' accounts were extraordinarily popular. Travel literature depicted Africans as savages because of their eating habits, morals, clothing, and social customs; as barbarians because of their language and methods of war; and as heathens because they were not Christian (nearly the identical language with which the English described the Irish—see page 404). Africans were believed to possess a potent sexuality. One seventeenth-century observer considered Africans "very lustful and impudent, . . . (for a Negroes hiding his members, their extraordinary greatness) is a token of their lust." African women were considered sexually aggressive, with a "temper hot and lascivious."[36]

"At the time when Columbus sailed to the New World, Islam was the largest world religion, and the only world religion that showed itself capable of expanding rapidly in areas as far apart and as different from each other as Senegal [in northwest Africa], Bosnia [in the Balkans], Java, and the Philippines."[37] Medieval Arabic literature spoke of blacks' physical repulsiveness, mental inferiority, and primitivism. In contrast to civilized peoples from the Mediterranean to China, some Arab writers absurdly claimed, sub-Saharan blacks were the only peoples who had produced no sciences or stable states. Though black kings, the Muslim historian Khaldun alleged, sold their subjects without even a pretext of crime or war, the victims bore no resentment because they gave no thought to the future and had "by nature few cares and worries; dancing and rhythm are for them inborn."[38] It is easy to see how such ridiculous myths developed into the stereotypes used to justify black slavery in South and North America in the seventeenth, eighteenth, and nineteenth centuries. Medieval Christians and Arabs had similar notions of blacks as primitive people ideally suited to enslavement. Perhaps centuries of commercial contacts between Middle Eastern and Mediterranean peoples had familiarized the latter with Arab racial attitudes. The racial beliefs that the Portuguese, Spanish, Dutch, and English brought to the New World, however, derived primarily from Christian theological speculation.

## Literature and Art

The age of religious wars and overseas expansion also witnessed an extraordinary degree of intellectual and artistic ferment. This effervescence can be seen in the development of the essay as a distinct literary genre; in other prose, poetry, and drama; in art; and in music. In many ways, literature, the visual arts, music, and the drama of the period mirrored the social and cultural conditions that gave rise to them.

### The Essay: Michel de Montaigne

Decades of religious fanaticism, bringing famine, civil anarchy, and death, led both Catholics and Protestants to doubt that any one faith contained absolute truth. The late sixteenth and seventeenth centuries witnessed the beginning of modern skepticism. Skepticism is a school of thought founded on doubt that total certainty or definitive knowledge is ever attainable. The skeptic is cautious and critical and suspends judgment. Perhaps the finest representative of early modern skepticism is Frenchman Michel de Montaigne (1533–1592).

Montaigne descended from a bourgeois family that had made a fortune selling salted herring and wine and in 1477 had purchased the title and property of Montaigne in Gascony; his mother came from a Jewish family that had been forced to flee Spain. Montaigne received a classical education, studied law, and secured a judicial appointment in 1554. He condemned the ancient nobility for being more concerned with war and sports than with the cultivation of the mind.

At the age of thirty-eight, Montaigne resigned his judicial post, retired to his estate, and devoted the rest of his life to study, contemplation, and an effort to understand himself. His wealth provided him with the leisure time to do so. A humanist, he believed that the object of life was to "know thyself," for self-knowledge teaches men and women how to live in accordance with nature and God. Montaigne developed a new literary genre, the essay—from the French *essayer,* meaning "to test or try"—to express his thoughts and ideas.

Montaigne's *Essays* provides insight into the mind of a remarkably civilized man. From the ancient authors, especially the Roman Stoic Seneca, Montaigne acquired a sense of calm, patience, tolerance, and broad-mindedness. Montaigne had grown up during the French civil wars, perhaps the worst kind of war. Religious ideology had set family against family, even brother against brother. He wrote:

*In this controversy . . . France is at present agitated by civil wars, the best and soundest side is undoubtedly that which maintains both the old religion and the old government of the country. However, among the good men who follow that side . . . we see many whom passion drives outside the bounds of reason, and makes them sometimes adopt unjust, violent, and even reckless courses.*[39]

Though he remained a Catholic, Montaigne possessed a detachment, an independence, an openness of mind, and a willingness to look at all sides of a question. As he wrote, "I listen with attention to the judgment of all men; but so far as I can remember, I have followed none but my own. Though I set little value upon my own opinion, I set no more on the opinions of others."

Montaigne's essay "On Cannibals" reflects the impact of overseas discoveries on Europeans' consciousness. His tolerant mind rejected the notion that one culture is superior to another:

*I long had a man in my house that lived ten or twelve years in the New World, discovered in these latter days, and in that part of it where Villegaignon landed [Brazil]. . . .*

*I find that there is nothing barbarous and savage in [that] nation, . . . excepting, that every one gives the title of barbarism to everything that is not in use in his own country. As, indeed, we have no other level of truth and reason, than the example and idea of the opinions and customs of the place wherein we live.*[40]

Montaigne's rejection of dogmatism, his secularism, and his skepticism thus represented a basic change. In his own time and throughout the seventeenth century, few would have agreed with him. The publication of his ideas, however, anticipated a basic shift in attitudes. Montaigne inaugurated an era of doubt. "Wonder," he said, "is the foundation of all philosophy, research is the means of all learning, and ignorance is the end."[41]

## Elizabethan and Jacobean Literature

In addition to the essay as a literary genre, the period fostered remarkable creativity in other branches of literature. England, especially in the latter part of Elizabeth's reign and in the first years of her successor, James I (r. 1603–1625), witnessed remarkable literary expression. The terms *Elizabethan* and *Jacobean* (referring to the reign of James) are used to designate the English music, poetry, prose, and drama of this period. The poetry of Sir Philip Sidney (1554–1586), such as *Astrophel* and *Stella,* strongly influenced later poetic writing. The *Faerie Queene* of Edmund Spenser (1552–1599) endures as one of the greatest moral epics in any language. The rare poetic beauty of the plays of Christopher Marlowe (1564–1593), such as *Tamburlaine* and *The Jew of Malta,* paved the way for the work of Shakespeare. Above all, the immortal dramas of William Shakespeare (1564–1616) and the stately prose of the Authorized, or King James, Bible marked the Elizabethan and Jacobean periods as the golden age of English literature.

William Shakespeare, the son of a successful glove manufacturer in Stratford-on-Avon, chose a career on the London stage. By 1592 he had gained recognition as an actor and playwright. He performed in Lord Chamberlain's Company and became co-owner of the Globe Theatre, which after 1603 presented his plays.

Shakespeare's genius lay in the originality of his characterizations, the diversity of his plots, his understanding of human psychology, and his unexcelled gift for language. Shakespeare was a Renaissance man in his deep appreciation for classical culture, individualism, and humanism. Such plays as *Julius Caesar, Pericles,* and *Antony and Cleopatra* deal with classical subjects and figures. Several of his comedies have Italian Renaissance settings. The nine history plays, including *Richard II, Richard III,* and *Henry IV,* enjoyed the greatest popularity among Shakespeare's contemporaries. Written during the decade after the defeat of the Spanish Armada, the history plays express English national consciousness. Lines such as these from *Richard II* reflect this sense of national greatness with unparalleled eloquence:

*This royal Throne of Kings, this sceptre'd Isle,*
*This earth of Majesty, this seat of Mars,*
*This other Eden, demi-paradise,*
*This fortress built by Nature for herself,*
*Against infection and the hand of war:*
*This happy breed of men, this little world,*
*This precious stone, set in the silver sea,*
*Which serves it in the office of a wall,*
*Or as a moat defensive to a house,*
*Against the envy of less happier Lands,*
*This blessed plot, this earth, this Realm, this England.*

Shakespeare's later plays, above all the tragedies *Hamlet, Othello,* and *Macbeth,* explore an enormous range of human problems and are open to an almost infinite variety of interpretations. *Othello* portrays an honorable man destroyed by a flaw in his own character and the satanic

**Titus Andronicus** With classical allusions, fifteen murders and executions, a Gothic queen who takes a black lover, and incredible violence, this early Shakespearean tragedy (1594) was a melodramatic thriller that enjoyed enormous popularity with the London audience. Modern critics believe that it foreshadowed *King Lear* with its emphasis on suffering and madness. *(Reproduced by permission of the Marquess of Bath, Longleat House, Warminster, Wilts)*

evil of his supposed friend Iago. *Macbeth*'s central theme is exorbitant ambition. Shakespeare analyzes the psychology of sin in the figures of Macbeth and Lady Macbeth, whose mutual love under the pressure of ambition leads to their destruction. The central figure in *Hamlet,* a play suffused with individuality, wrestles with moral problems connected with revenge and with the human being's relationship to life and death. The soliloquy in which Hamlet debates suicide is perhaps the most widely quoted passage in English literature:

*To be, or not to be: that is the question:*
*Whether 'tis nobler in the mind to suffer*
*The slings and arrows of outrageous fortune,*
*Or to take arms against a sea of troubles,*
*And by opposing end them?*

Hamlet's sad cry "There is nothing either good or bad but thinking makes it so" expresses the anguish and uncertainty of modern life. *Hamlet* has always enjoyed great popularity because in the title character's many-faceted personality people have seen an aspect of themselves.

Another great masterpiece of the Jacobean period was the Authorized Bible. At a theological conference in 1604, a group of Puritans urged James I to support a new translation of the Bible. The king in turn assigned the task to a committee of scholars, who published their efforts in 1611. Divided into chapters and verses, the Authorized Version is actually a revision of earlier Bibles more than an original work. Yet it provides a superb expression of the mature English vernacular in the early seventeenth century. Consider Psalm 37:

*Fret not thy selfe because of evill doers, neither bee thou envious against the workers of iniquitie.*
*For they shall soone be cut downe like the grasse; and wither as the greene herbe.*
*Trust in the Lord, and do good, so shalt thou dwell in the land, and verely thou shalt be fed.*

The Authorized Version, so called because it was produced under royal sponsorship—it had no official ecclesiastical endorsement—represented the Anglican and Puritan desire to encourage laypeople to read the Scriptures. It quickly achieved great popularity and displaced all earlier versions. British settlers carried this Bible to the North American colonies, where it became known as the King James Bible. For centuries the King James Bible has had a profound influence on the language and lives of English-speaking peoples.

## Baroque Art and Music

Throughout European history, the cultural tastes of one age have often seemed quite unsatisfactory to the next. So it was with the baroque. The term **baroque** itself may have come from the Portuguese word for an "odd-shaped, imperfect pearl" and was commonly used by late-eighteenth-century art critics as an expression of scorn for what they considered an overblown, unbalanced style. The hostility of these critics, who also scorned the Gothic style of medieval cathedrals in favor of a classicism inspired by antiquity and the Renaissance, has long since passed. Specialists now agree that the triumphs of the baroque marked one of the high points in the history of Western culture.

In the early development of the baroque, scholars stress the influence of Rome and the revitalized Catholic church of the later sixteenth century. The papacy and the Jesuits encouraged the growth of an intensely emotional,

**Juan de Pareja: The Calling of Saint Matthew** Using rich but subdued colors, Pareja depicts the biblical text (Mark 2:13–17), with Jesus in traditional first-century dress and the other figures, arranged around a table covered with an oriental carpet, in seventeenth-century apparel. Matthew, at Jesus' right hand, seems surprised by the "call." Pareja, following a long tradition, includes himself (*standing, rear center*). *(Museo Nacional del Prado, Madrid/The Bridgeman Art Library)*

**Rubens: The Horrors of War** With enormous intellectual and physical energy, as well as a large studio of assistants, Peter Paul Rubens was incredibly productive, the most influential figure in baroque art in northern Europe. In this dynamic allegory from 1638, Venus tries to restrain Mars (holding the torch); he is followed by disease and famine. The shrieking lady at left, clad in black, represents miserable Europe. *(Palazzo Pitti/The Bridgeman Art Library)*

exuberant art. These patrons wanted artists to go beyond the Renaissance focus on pleasing a small, wealthy, cultural elite. They wanted artists to appeal to the senses and thereby touch the souls and kindle the faith of ordinary churchgoers while proclaiming the power and confidence of the reformed Catholic church. In addition to this underlying religious emotionalism, the baroque drew its sense of drama, motion, and ceaseless striving from the Catholic Reformation. The interior of the famous Jesuit Church of Jesus in Rome—the Gesù—combined all these characteristics in its lavish, shimmering, wildly active decorations and frescoes.

Taking definite shape in Italy after 1600, the baroque style in the visual arts developed with exceptional vigor in Catholic countries—in Spain and Latin America, Austria, southern Germany, and Poland. Yet baroque art was more than just "Catholic art" in the seventeenth century and the first half of the eighteenth. True, neither Protestant England nor the Netherlands ever came fully under the spell of the baroque, but neither did Catholic France. And Protestants accounted for some of the finest examples of baroque style, especially in music. The baroque style spread partly because its tension and bombast spoke to an agitated age, which was experiencing great violence and controversy in politics and religion.

In painting, the baroque reached maturity early with Peter Paul Rubens (1577–1640), the most outstanding and representative of baroque painters. Studying in his native Flanders and in Italy, where he was influenced by masters of the High Renaissance such as Michelangelo, Rubens developed his own rich, sensuous, colorful style, which was characterized by animated figures, melodramatic contrasts, and monumental size. Rubens excelled in glorifying monarchs such as Queen Mother Marie de' Medici of France. He was also a devout Catholic; nearly half of his pictures treat Christian subjects. Yet one of

Rubens's trademarks was fleshy, sensual nudes, who populate his canvases as Roman goddesses, water nymphs, and remarkably voluptuous saints and angels.

Rubens was enormously successful. To meet the demand for his work, he established a large studio and hired many assistants to execute his rough sketches and gigantic murals. Sometimes the master artist added only the finishing touches. Rubens's wealth and position—on occasion he was given special diplomatic assignments by the Habsburgs—affirmed that distinguished artists continued to enjoy the high social status they had won in the Renaissance.

In music, the baroque style reached its culmination almost a century later in the dynamic, soaring lines of the endlessly inventive Johann Sebastian Bach (1685–1750), one of the greatest composers the Western world has ever produced. Organist and choirmaster of several Lutheran churches across Germany, Bach was equally at home writing secular concertos and sublime religious cantatas. Bach's organ music, the greatest ever written, combined the baroque spirit of invention, tension, and emotion in an unforgettable striving toward the infinite. Unlike Rubens, Bach was not fully appreciated in his lifetime, but since the early nineteenth century his reputation has grown steadily.

## Summary

European expansion and colonization took place against a background of religious conflict and rising national consciousness. Though the medieval religious framework had broken down, people still thought largely in religious terms. Europeans explained what they did politically and economically in terms of religious doctrine. Religious ideology served as a justification for a variety of goals, such as the French nobles' opposition to the Crown and the Dutch struggle for political and economic independence from Spain. In Germany, religious hatred and foreign ambition led to the Thirty Years' War. After 1648 the divisions between Protestant and Catholic tended to become permanent. Religious skepticism and racial attitudes were harbingers of developments to come. The essays of Montaigne, the plays of Marlowe and Shakespeare, the King James Bible, and the splendors of baroque art remain classic achievements of the Western cultural heritage.

In the sixteenth and seventeenth centuries, Europeans for the first time gained access to large parts of the globe. European peoples had the intellectual curiosity, driving ambition, and scientific technology to attempt feats that were as difficult and expensive then as going to the moon is today. Exploration and exploitation contributed to a more sophisticated standard of living, in the form of spices and Asian luxury goods, and to a terrible international inflation resulting from the influx of South American silver and gold. Governments, the upper classes, and the peasantry were badly hurt by the resulting inflation. Meanwhile, the middle class of bankers, shippers, financiers, and manufacturers prospered for much of the seventeenth century.

## Key Terms

Treaty of Cateau-Cambrésis
Huguenots
Saint Bartholomew's Day massacre
politiques
Edict of Nantes
bourse
Union of Utrecht
Escorial
Spanish Armada
Protestant Union
Peace of Westphalia
magnetic compass
astrolabe
*General History of the Indies*
Golden Century of Spain
price revolution
viceroyalties
quinto
witch
baroque

## Notes

1. G. Parker, *The Grand Strategy of Philip II* (New Haven, Conn.: Yale University Press, 2000), pp. 83–84.
2. J. H. Hale, "War and Public Opinion in the Fifteenth and Sixteenth Centuries," *Past and Present* 22 (July 1962): 18–32.
3. Quoted in J. L. Motley, *The Rise of the Dutch Republic* (Philadelphia: David McKay, 1898), 1.109.
4. Quoted in P. Smith, *The Age of the Reformation* (New York: Henry Holt, 1951), p. 248.
5. H. Kamen, *Philip of Spain* (New Haven, Conn.: Yale University Press, 1997), pp. 76–78; the quotations are on pp. 77 and 76, respectively.
6. Quoted ibid., p. 235.
7. Parker, *Grand Strategy of Philip II,* pp. 115–122; the quotation is on p. 119.
8. H. Kamen, "The Economic and Social Consequences of the Thirty Years' War," *Past and Present* 39 (April 1968): 44–61.
9. Quoted in C. M. Cipolla, *Guns, Sails, and Empires: Technological Innovation and the Early Phases of European Expansion, 1400–1700* (New York: Minerva Press, 1965), pp. 115–116.
10. J. H. Parry, *The Age of Reconnaissance* (New York: Mentor Books, 1963), chaps. 3 and 5.
11. See C. R. Phillips, *Ciudad Real, 1500–1750: Growth, Crisis, and Readjustment in the Spanish Economy* (Cambridge, Mass.: Harvard University Press, 1979), pp. 103–104, 115.

12. Quoted in Cipolla, *Guns, Sails, and Empires,* p. 132.
13. Quoted in F. H. Littell, *The Macmillan Atlas: History of Christianity* (New York: Macmillan, 1976), p. 75.
14. Quoted in Cipolla, *Guns, Sails, and Empires,* p. 133.
15. S. E. Morison, *Admiral of the Ocean Sea: A Life of Christopher Columbus* (Boston: Little, Brown, 1942), p. 339.
16. T. K. Rabb, "Columbus: Villain or Hero," *The Princeton Alumni Weekly,* October 14, 1992, p. 13.
17. J. M. Cohen, ed. and trans., *The Four Voyages of Christopher Columbus* (New York: Penguin Books, 1969), p. 37.
18. Quoted in R. L. Kagan, "The Spain of Ferdinand and Isabella," in *Circa 1492: Art in the Age of Exploration,* ed. J. A. Levenson (Washington, D.C.: National Gallery of Art, 1991), p. 60.
19. Quoted in F. Maddison, "Tradition and Innovation: Columbus' First Voyage and Portuguese Navigation in the Fifteenth Century," ibid., p. 69.
20. See W. D. Phillips and C. R. Phillips, *The Worlds of Christopher Columbus* (Cambridge: Cambridge University Press, 1992), p. 273.
21. A. W. Crosby, Jr., *The Columbian Exchange: Biological and Cultural Consequences of 1492* (Westport, Conn.: Greenwood, 1972), pp. 64–121.
22. Ibid., pp. 122–163.
23. See M. E. Wiesner, *Women and Gender in Early Modern Europe* (New York: Cambridge University Press, 1994), pp. 21–25; the quotation is on p. 22.
24. Ibid., pp. 23–24.
25. This passage is based heavily on S. Ozment, *When Fathers Ruled: Family Life in Reformation Europe* (Cambridge, Mass.: Harvard University Press, 1983), pp. 50–99.
26. Ibid., pp. 85–92.
27. See D. Durant, *Bess of Hardwick: Portrait of an Elizabethan Dynasty* (London: Weidenfeld & Nicolson, 1977).
28. Quoted in Ozment, *When Fathers Ruled,* p. 56.
29. Ibid., pp. 9–14.
30. See F. Biot, *The Rise of Protestant Monasticism* (Baltimore: Helicon Press, 1968), pp. 74–78.
31. Wiesner, *Women and Gender in Early Modern Europe,* pp. 220–223.
32. See E. W. Monter, "The Pedestal and the Stake: Courtly Love and Witchcraft," in *Becoming Visible: Women in European History,* ed. R. Bridenthal and C. Koonz (Boston: Houghton Mifflin, 1977), pp. 132–135; and A. Fraser, *The Weaker Vessel* (New York: Random House, 1985), pp. 100–103.
33. C. Verlinden, *The Beginnings of Modern Colonization*, trans. Y. Freccero (Ithaca, N.Y.: Cornell University Press, 1970), pp. 5–6, 80–97.
34. This section leans heavily on D. B. Davis, *Slavery and Human Progress* (New York: Oxford University Press, 1984), pp. 54–62; the quotation is on p. 58.
35. Quoted in D. P. Mannix, with M. Cowley, *Black Cargoes: A History of the Atlantic Slave Trade* (New York: Viking Press, 1968), p. 5.
36. Quoted ibid., p. 19.
37. See P. Brown, "Understanding Islam," *New York Review of Books,* February 22, 1979, pp. 30–33.
38. Quoted in Davis, *Slavery and Human Progress,* pp. 43–44.
39. D. M. Frame, trans., *The Complete Works of Montaigne* (Stanford, Calif.: Stanford University Press, 1958), pp. 175–176.
40. C. Cotton, trans., *The Essays of Michel de Montaigne* (New York: A. L. Burt, 1893), pp. 207, 210.
41. Ibid., p. 523.

## Suggested Reading

For the religious wars, in addition to the references in the Suggested Reading for Chapter 14 and the Notes to this chapter, see H. Kamen, *The Iron Century: Social Change in Europe, 1550–1660* (1971), a fundamental work; and G. Huppert, *After the Black Death: A Social History of Early Modern Europe* (1986), a lucidly written and highly recommended work for students. P. Roberts, *A City in Conflict: Troyes During the French Wars of Religion* (1996), provides a fascinating account of the bitter divisions the religious conflicts created among neighbors in one important French city. A. N. Galpern, *The Religions of the People in Sixteenth-Century Champagne* (1976), is a useful case study in religious anthropology, and W. A. Christian, Jr., *Local Religion in Sixteenth-Century Spain* (1981), traces the attitudes and practices of ordinary Spanish people. A. Cunningham and O. P. Grell, *The Four Horsemen of the Apocalypse: Religion, War, Famine and Death in Reformation Europe* (2000), explores the period 1490–1648 in terms of crises and the popular belief in the approaching Last Judgment.

For Spanish military operations in the Low Countries, see R. A. Stradling, *The Armada of Flanders: Spanish Maritime Policy and European War, 1568–1668* (1992). For the later phases of the Dutch-Spanish conflict, see J. I. Israel, *The Dutch Republic and the Hispanic World, 1606–1661* (1982), which treats the struggle in global perspective. Similarly, Geoffrey Parker, *The Grand Strategy of Philip II* (2000), treats Philip's attempts to rule a global empire.

The starting point for the study of England's great ruler is W. MacCaffrey, *Elizabeth I* (1993). N. Jones, *The Birth of the Elizabethan Age* (1993), brings to life the concerns of the English people. S. Frye, *Elizabeth I: The Competition for Representation* (1996), uses feminist analysis to describe the way Elizabeth built her public image and used her authority. C. Erickson, *The First Elizabeth* (1983), gives a psychologically resonant portrait, and C. Haight, *Elizabeth I* (1988), and J. E. Neale, *Queen Elizabeth I* (1957), remain helpful.

Nineteenth- and early-twentieth-century historians described the defeat of the Spanish Armada as a great victory for Protestantism, democracy, and capitalism, which those scholars tended to link together. More recent historians have treated the event in terms of its contemporary significance. H. Kamen, *Philip of Spain* (1971), offers a fine revisionist portrait of the ruler at the center of late-sixteenth-century international affairs. A. W. Lovett, *Early Habsburg Spain, 1517–1598* (1986), discusses many facets of Spanish culture. G. Mattingly, *The Armada* (1959), remains the most exciting and readable account of that event, but G. Parker and C. Martin, *The Spanish Armada* (1988), incorporates later literature.

R. G. Asch, *The Thirty Years War: The Holy Roman Empire and Europe* (1997), is an important revisionist study with

*(continued on page 528)*

# Listening to the Past

## Columbus Describes His First Voyage

*On his return voyage to Spain in January 1493, Christopher Columbus composed a letter intended for wide circulation and had copies of it sent ahead to Isabella and Ferdinand and others when the ship docked at Lisbon. Because the letter sums up Columbus's understanding of his achievements, it is considered the most important document of his first voyage. Remember that his knowledge of Asia rested heavily on Marco Polo's* Travels, *published around 1298.*

Since I know that you will be pleased at the great success with which the Lord has crowned my voyage, I write to inform you how in thirty-three days I crossed from the Canary Islands to the Indies, with the fleet which our most illustrious sovereigns gave me. I found very many islands with large populations and took possession of them all for their Highnesses; this I did by proclamation and unfurled the royal standard. No opposition was offered.

I named the first island that I found "San Salvador," in honour of our Lord and Saviour who has granted me this miracle. . . . When I reached Cuba, I followed its north coast westwards, and found it so extensive that I thought this must be the mainland, the province of Cathay.* . . . From there I saw another island eighteen leagues eastwards which I then named "Hispaniola."† . . .

Hispaniola is a wonder. The mountains and hills, the plains and meadow lands are both fertile and beautiful. They are most suitable for planting crops and for raising cattle of all kinds, and there are good sites for building towns and villages. The harbours are incredibly fine and there are many great rivers with broad channels and the majority contain gold.‡ The trees, fruits and plants are very different from those of Cuba. In Hispaniola there are many spices and large mines of gold and other metals. . . .§

The inhabitants of this island, and all the rest that I discovered or heard of, go naked, as their mothers bore them, men and women alike. A few of the women, however, cover a single place with a leaf of a plant or piece of cotton which they weave for the purpose. They have no iron or steel or arms and are not capable of using them, not because they are not strong and well built but because they are amazingly timid. All the weapons they have are canes cut at seeding time, at the end of which they fix a sharpened stick, but they have not the courage to make use of these, for very often when I have sent two or three men to a village to have conversation with them a great number of them have come out. But as soon as they saw my men all fled immediately, a father not even waiting for his son. And this is not because we have harmed any of them; on the contrary, wherever I have gone and been able to have conversation with them, I have given them some of the various things I had, a cloth and other articles, and received nothing in exchange. But they have still remained incurably timid. True, when they have been reassured and lost their fear, they are so ingenuous and so liberal with all their possessions that no one who has not seen them would believe it. If one asks for anything they have they never say no. On the contrary, they offer a share to anyone with demonstrations of

*Cathay is the old name for China. In the log-book and later in this letter Columbus accepts the native story that Cuba is an island which they can circumnavigate in something more than twenty-one days, yet he insists here and later, during the second voyage, that it is in fact part of the Asiatic mainland.

†Hispaniola is the second largest island of the West Indies; Haiti occupies the western third of the island, the Dominican Republic the rest.

‡This did not prove to be true.

§These statements are also inaccurate.

heartfelt affection, and they are immediately content with any small thing, valuable or valueless, that is given them. I forbade the men to give them bits of broken crockery, fragments of glass or tags of laces, though if they could get them they fancied them the finest jewels in the world.

I hoped to win them to the love and service of their Highnesses and of the whole Spanish nation and to persuade them to collect and give us of the things which they possessed in abundance and which we needed. They have no religion and are not idolaters; but all believe that power and goodness dwell in the sky and they are firmly convinced that I have come from the sky with these ships and people. In this belief they gave me a good reception everywhere, once they had overcome their fear; and this is not because they are stupid—far from it, they are men of great intelligence, for they navigate all those seas, and give a marvellously good account of everything—but because they have never before seen men clothed or ships like these. . . .

In all these islands the men are seemingly content with one woman, but their chief or king is allowed more than twenty. The women appear to work more than the men and I have not been able to find out if they have private property. As far as I could see whatever a man had was shared among all the rest and this particularly applies to food. . . . In another island, which I am told is larger than Hispaniola, the people have no hair. Here there is a vast quantity of gold, and from here and the other islands I bring Indians as evidence.

In conclusion, to speak only of the results of this very hasty voyage, their Highnesses can see that I will give them as much gold as they require, if they will render me some very slight assistance; also I will give them all the spices and cotton they want. . . . I will also bring them as much aloes as they ask and as many slaves, who will be taken from the idolaters. I believe also that I have found rhubarb and cinnamon and there will be countless other things in addition. . . .

So all Christendom will be delighted that our Redeemer has given victory to our most illustrious King and Queen and their renowned kingdoms, in this great matter. They should hold great celebrations and render solemn thanks to the Holy Trinity with many solemn prayers, for the great triumph which they will have, by the conversion of so many peoples to our holy faith and for the temporal benefits which will follow, for not only Spain, but all Christendom will receive encouragement and profit.

This is a brief account of the facts.

Written in the caravel off the Canary Islands.[||]

15 February 1493

At your orders
THE ADMIRAL

Christopher Columbus, by Ridolpho Ghirlandio. Friend of Raphael and teacher of Michelangelo, Ghirlandio (1483–1561) enjoyed distinction as a portrait painter, and so we can assume this is a good likeness of the older Columbus. *(Scala/Art Resource, NY)*

## Questions for Analysis

1. How did Columbus explain the success of his voyage?
2. What was Columbus's view of the Native Americans he met?
3. Evaluate his statements that the Caribbean islands possessed gold, cotton, and spices.
4. Why did Columbus cling to the idea that he had reached Asia?

[||]Actually, Columbus was off Santa Maria in the Azores.

*Source:* J. M. Cohen, ed. and trans., *The Four Voyages of Christopher Columbus* (Penguin Classics, 1958), pp. 115–123. Copyright © J. M. Cohen, 1958. Reproduced by permission of Penguin Books, Ltd.

valuable material on the role of war finance in domestic and international aspects of the conflict. G. Parker, *The Thirty Years' War* (1984), is important but densely written. A variety of opinions on the causes and results of the war are given in T. K. Rabb's anthology, *The Thirty Years' War* (1981).

A good starting point for the study of European society in the age of exploration is J. A. Levenson's anthology *Circa 1492: Art in the Age of Exploration* (1991), which treats geographical, nautical, political, and humanistic developments in a worldwide context. Parry, cited in the Notes, which addresses the causes and consequences of the voyage of discovery, and J. H. Parry, *The Discovery of South America* (1979), which examines Europeans' reactions to the maritime discoveries and the whole concept of discovery, are still valuable. The urbane studies of C. M. Cipolla, including the one cited in the Notes, *Clocks and Culture, 1300–1700* (1967), *Cristofano and the Plague: A Study in the History of Public Health in the Age of Galileo* (1973), and *Public Health and the Medical Profession in the Renaissance* (1976), present fascinating material on technological and sociological developments in a lucid style. The work of W. D. Phillips and C. R. Phillips, cited in the Notes, is strongly recommended. The advanced student should consult F. Braudel, *Civilization and Capitalism, 15th–18th Century,* vol. 1: *The Structures of Everyday Life* (1981); vol. 2: *The Wheels of Commerce* (1982); and vol. 3: *The Perspective of the World* (1984). These fat volumes combine vast erudition, a global perspective, and remarkable illustrations.

On witches and witchcraft, M. E. Wiesner, *Women and Gender in Early Modern Europe* (1994), contains sound material as well as an extensive bibliography. For women, marriage, and the family, see in addition to the title by Wiesner, L. Stone, *The Family, Sex, and Marriage in England, 1500–1800* (1977), a controversial work; D. Underdown, "The Taming of the Scold," and S. Amussen, "Gender, Family, and the Social Order," in *Order and Disorder in Early Modern England,* ed. A. Fletcher and J. Stevenson (1985); A. Macfarlane, *Marriage and Love in England: Modes of Reproduction, 1300–1848* (1986); C. R. Boxer, *Women in Iberian Expansion Overseas, 1415–1815* (1975), a helpful study of women's role in overseas migration; S. M. Wyntjes, "Women in the Reformation Era," in *Becoming Visible: Women in European History,* ed. R. Bridenthal and C. Koonz (1977), a quick survey of conditions in different countries; A. Clark, *The Working Life of Women in the Seventeenth Century* (1968); K. M. Wilson, ed., *Women Writers of the Renaissance and Reformation* (1987); M. J. M. Ezell, *The Patriarch's Wife: Literary Evidence and the History of the Family* (1987); and L. Pollock, *A Lasting Relationship: Parents and Children over Three Centuries* (1987). Ozment's work listed in the Notes is a seminal study concentrating on Germany and Switzerland.

As background to slavery and racism in North and South America, students should see J. L. Watson, ed., *Asian and African Systems of Slavery* (1980), a valuable collection of essays, as well as the works by Davis and by Mannix and Cowley mentioned in the Notes: Davis shows how slavery was viewed as a progressive force in the expansion of the Western world, and Mannix and Cowley provide a hideously fascinating account of the slave trade. For North American conditions, interested students should consult W. D. Jordan, *The White Man's Burden: Historical Origins of Racism in the United States* (1974). The excellent essays in G. M. Frederickson, *The Arrogance of Race: Historical Perspectives on Slavery, Racism, and Social Inequality* (1988), stress the social and economic circumstances associated with the rise of plantation slavery. For Caribbean and South American developments, see F. P. Bowser, *The African Slave in Colonial Peru* (1974); J. S. Handler and F. W. Lange, *Plantation Slavery in Barbados: An Archeological and Historical Investigation* (1978); and R. E. Conrad, *Children of God's Fire: A Documentary History of Black Slavery in Brazil* (1983).

The leading authority on Montaigne is D. M. Frame; see his *Montaigne's Discovery of Man* (1955) and his translation listed in the Notes. For baroque art, see V. L. Tapié, *The Age of Grandeur: Baroque Art and Architecture* (1961), and J. Montague, *Roman Baroque Sculpture: The Industry of Art* (1985), an original and entertaining study.

Pierre-Denis Martin, *View of the Chateau de Versailles,* 1722. With their classically harmonious, symmetrical, and geometric design, Versailles and its gardens nevertheless seem baroque in their vast size and extension. *(Châteaux de Versailles et de Trianon, Versailles/Réunion des Musées Nationaux/Art Resource, NY)*

chapter 16

# Absolutism and Constitutionalism in Western Europe (ca 1589–1715)

## chapter outline

- Absolutism
- Constitutionalism

The seventeenth century was a period of revolutionary transformation. That century witnessed agricultural and manufacturing crises that had profound political consequences. A colder and wetter climate throughout most of the period meant a shorter farming season. Grain yields declined. In an age when cereals constituted the bulk of the diet for most people everywhere, smaller harvests led to food shortages and starvation. Food shortages in turn meant population decline or stagnation. Industry also suffered. While the evidence does not permit broad generalizations, it appears that the output of woolen textiles, one of the most important manufactures, declined sharply in the first half of the century. This economic crisis was not universal: it struck various sections of Europe at different times and to different degrees. In the middle decades of the century, Spain, France, Germany, and England all experienced great economic difficulties; but these years saw the golden age of the Netherlands.

Meanwhile, governments increased their spending, primarily for state armies; in the seventeenth century, armies grew larger than they had been since the time of the Roman Empire. To pay for these armies, governments taxed. The greatly increased burden of taxation, falling on a population already existing at a subsistence level, triggered revolts. Peasant revolts were extremely common;[1] in France, urban disorders were so frequent an aspect of the social and political landscape as to be "a distinctive feature of life."[2]

Princes struggled to free themselves from the restrictions of powerful social groups or competing institutions. Spanish and French monarchs gained control of the major institution in their domains, the Roman Catholic church. Rulers of England and some of the German principalities set up national churches. In the German Empire, the Peace of Westphalia placed territorial sovereignty in the princes' hands. The kings of France, England, and Spain claimed the basic loyalty of their subjects. Monarchs made and enforced public laws, such as criminal law, which concerned the state and its rights and powers; but private or customary law, such as property law, which concerned relations between citizens, continued in the control of local elites, the nobility.

Monarchical power added up to something close to **sovereignty**. A state may be termed *sovereign* when it possesses a monopoly over the instruments of justice and the use of force within clearly defined boundaries. In a sovereign state, no system of courts, such as ecclesiastical tribunals, competes with state courts in the dispensation of justice; and private armies, such as those of feudal lords, present no threat to royal authority because the state's army is stronger. Royal law touches all persons within the country.

Sovereignty had been evolving during the late sixteenth century. Most seventeenth-century governments now needed to address the problem of *which* authority within the state would possess sovereignty—the Crown or privileged groups. In the period between roughly 1589 and 1715, two basic patterns of government emerged in Europe: absolute monarchy and the constitutional state. Almost all subsequent European governments have been modeled on one of these patterns.

- How did these forms of government differ from the feudal and dynastic monarchies of earlier centuries?
- In what sense were these forms "modern"?
- What social and economic factors limited absolute monarchs?
- Which Western countries most clearly illustrate the new patterns of political organization?
- Why is the seventeenth century considered the "golden age of the Netherlands"?

This chapter will explore these questions.

## Absolutism

See DBQ 4

In the Middle Ages, jurists held that as a consequence of kings' coronation and anointment with sacred oil, they ruled "by the grace of God." Law was given by God, kings discovered or "found" the law, and kings acknowledged that they must respect and obey the law. In contrast, in the *absolutist* state, kings claimed to rule "by divine right," meaning that they were responsible to God alone. In the seventeenth and eighteenth centuries, kings became legislators: they made law. Because they made the law, sovereignty was embodied in the person of the king. The seal of the king of France, showing him sitting in judgment, was intended to reveal his full power (the physical means to do something) and his authority (the legal right to do something).

Absolute rulers tried to control competing jurisdictions, institutions, or interest groups in their territories. They regulated religious sects. They abolished the liberties long held by certain areas, groups, or provinces. Absolute kings also secured the cooperation of the one class that historically had posed the greatest threat to monarchy, the nobility. Medieval governments, restrained by the church, the feudal nobility, and their own financial limitations, had been able to exert none of these controls.

In some respects, the key to the power and success of absolute monarchs lay in how they solved their financial problems. Medieval kings frequently had found temporary financial support through bargains with the nobility: the nobility agreed to an ad hoc grant of money in return for freedom from future taxation. In contrast, the absolutist solution was the creation of new state bureaucracies that directed the economic life of the country in the interests of the king, either forcing taxes ever higher or devising alternative methods of raising revenue.

Bureaucracies were composed of career officials appointed by and solely accountable to the king. The backgrounds of these civil servants varied. Absolute monarchs sometimes drew on the middle class, as in France, or utilized members of the nobility, as in Spain and eastern Europe. Where there was no middle class or an insignificant one, as in Austria, Prussia, Spain, and Russia, the government of the absolutist state consisted of an interlocking elite of monarchy, aristocracy, and bureaucracy.

Royal agents in medieval and Renaissance kingdoms had used their public offices and positions to benefit themselves and their families. In England, for example, Crown servants from Thomas Becket to Thomas Wolsey had treated their high offices as their private property and reaped considerable profit from them. Early modern bureaucrats continued to use their offices to enrich themselves.[3] The striking difference between seventeenth-century bureaucracies and their predecessors was that seventeenth-century civil servants served the state as represented by the king. Bureaucrats recognized that the offices they held were public, or state, positions. The state paid them salaries to handle revenues that belonged to the Crown. Bureaucrats gradually came to distinguish between public duties and private property.

Absolute monarchs also maintained permanent standing armies. Medieval armies had been raised by feudal lords for particular wars or campaigns, after which the troops were disbanded. In the seventeenth century, monarchs alone recruited and maintained armies—in peacetime as well as wartime. Kings deployed their troops both inside and outside the country in the interests of the monarchy. Armies became basic features of absolutist, and modern, states. Absolute rulers also invented new methods of compulsion. They concerned themselves with the private lives of potentially troublesome subjects, often through the use of secret police.

The word **absolutism** was coined in 1830, two centuries after the developments it attempts to classify occurred. Some scholars today deny that absolute monarchy

| 1575 | 1605 | 1635 | 1665 | 1695 | 1725 |
|---|---|---|---|---|---|

**POLITICAL/MILITARY**

- 1589–1610 Henry IV in France
- 1642–1649 English civil war ends with execution of Charles I
- 1643–1715 Louis XIV in France
- 1653–1658 Military rule in England under Oliver Cromwell
- 1659 Treaty of the Pyrenees marks end of Spanish imperial dominance
- 1660 Restoration of English monarchy under Charles II
- 1688–1689 Glorious Revolution in England
- 1701–1713 War of the Spanish Succession
- 1713 Peace of Utrecht

**SOCIAL/ECONOMIC**

- 1602 Dutch East India Company founded
- 1605–1715 Food riots common across Europe
- 1665–1683 Jean-Baptiste Colbert applies mercantilism to France

**INTELLECTUAL/RELIGIOUS**

- 1598 Edict of Nantes
- 1635 Birth of French Academy
- 1640–1680 Golden Age of Dutch art (Vermeer, Van Steen, Rembrandt)
- 1670 Charles II agrees to re-Catholicize England in secret agreement with Louis XIV
- 1685 Edict of Nantes revoked

was a stage in the evolution of the modern state between medieval feudal monarchies and the constitutional governments of recent centuries. As one student of early modern France writes, "I believe the prevailing historiographical concept of 'absolute monarchy' is a myth promulgated by the royal government and legitimized by historians."[4] Such historians prefer the term *administrative monarchy,* by which they mean that the French state in the seventeenth century became stronger in that it could achieve more of its goals, it was centralized from Paris, and its administrative bureaucracy greatly expanded. Although the administrative monarchy interfered in many aspects of the private individual's daily life, it did not have the consent of the governed, and it especially lacked the idea of the rule of law—law made by a representative body—the administrative monarchy was actually limited, or checked, in ways that traditional interpretations of absolute monarchy did not consider.[5]

The rule of absolute monarchs was not all-embracing because they lacked the financial and military resources and the technology to make it so. Thus the absolutist state was not the same as a totalitarian state. **Totalitarianism** was a twentieth-century phenomenon; it sought to direct all facets of a state's culture—art, education, religion, the economy, and politics—in the interests of the state. By definition, totalitarian rule is *total* regulation. By twentieth-century standards, the ambitions of absolute monarchs were quite limited: each ruler sought the exaltation of himself or herself as the embodiment of the state. Whether or not Louis XIV of France actually said, *"L'état, c'est moi!"* (I am the state!), the remark expresses his belief that he personified the French state. Perhaps over the course of his long life, however, he changed his mind. Louis is reputed to have said on his deathbed, "I am going, but the state remains," a remark suggesting that at the end of his life he drew a distinction between himself and the state. Scholars debate this issue but agree that absolutist states such as France did foreshadow recent totalitarian regimes in two fundamental respects: in the glorification of the state over all other aspects of the culture and in the use of war and an expansionist foreign policy to divert attention from domestic ills. France itself is aptly known as the model of absolute monarchy.

## The Foundations of French Absolutism: Henry IV, Sully, and Richelieu

In 1589 Henry IV (r. 1589–1610) inherited an enormous mess (see pages 490–492). Civil wars had wracked France since 1561. Catastrophically poor harvests meant that all across France peasants lived on the verge of starvation, fighting off wolves and bands of demobilized soldiers. Some provinces, such as Burgundy, suffered almost complete depopulation. Commercial activity had fallen to one-third its 1580 level. Nobles, officials, merchants, and peasants wanted peace, order, and stability. "Henri le Grand" (Henry the Great), as the king was called, promised "a chicken in every pot" and inaugurated a remarkable recovery. Henry may have been the first French ruler since Louis IX, in the thirteenth century, genuinely to care about his people, and he was the only king whose statue the Paris crowd did not tear down in the Revolution of 1789.

Henry converted to Catholicism and sought better relations with the pope. He tried to gain Protestant confidence by issuing the Edict of Nantes in 1598 (see page 492) and by appointing the devout Protestant Maximilien de Béthune, duke of Sully, as his chief minister. Aside from a short, successful war with Savoy in 1601, Henry kept France at peace. Maintaining that "if we are without compassion for the people, they must succumb and we all perish with them," Henry sharply lowered taxes on the overburdened peasants. In compensation for the lost revenues, in 1602–1604 he introduced the *paulette,* an annual fee paid by royal officials to guarantee heredity in their offices.

Sully proved to be an effective administrator. He combined the indirect taxes on salt, sales, and transit and leased their collection to financiers. Although the number of taxes declined, revenues increased because of the revival of trade.[6] One of the first French officials to appreciate the possibilities of overseas trade, Sully subsidized the Company for Trade with the Indies. He started a country-wide highway system and even dreamed of an international organization for the maintenance of peace.

In only twelve years, Henry IV and Sully restored public order in France and laid the foundations for economic prosperity. By the standards of the time, Henry IV's government was progressive and promising. His murder in 1610 by a crazed fanatic led to a severe crisis.

After the death of Henry IV, the queen-regent Marie de' Medici headed the government for the child-king Louis XIII (r. 1610–1643), but in fact feudal nobles and princes of the blood dominated the political scene. In 1624 Marie de' Medici secured the appointment of Armand Jean du Plessis—Cardinal Richelieu (1585–1642)—to the council of ministers. It was a remarkable appointment. The next year, Richelieu became president of the council, and after 1628 he was first minister of the French crown. Richelieu used his strong influence over King Louis XIII to exalt the French monarchy as the embodiment of the French state. One of the greatest servants of that state, Richelieu set in place the cornerstone of French absolutism, and his work served as the basis for France's cultural hegemony of Europe in the later seventeenth century.

Richelieu's policy was the total subordination of all groups and institutions to the French monarchy. The French nobility, with its selfish and independent interests, had long constituted the foremost threat to the centralizing goals of the Crown and to a strong national state. Therefore, Richelieu sought to curb the power of the nobility. In 1624 he succeeded in reshuffling the royal council, eliminating potential power brokers. Thereafter Richelieu dominated the council in an unprecedented way. He leveled castles, long the symbol of feudal independence, and crushed aristocratic conspiracies with quick executions. For example, when the duke of Montmorency, the first peer of France and godson of Henry IV, became involved in a revolt, he was summarily beheaded.

The constructive genius of Cardinal Richelieu is best reflected in the administrative system he established. He extended the use of the royal commissioners called intendants. France was divided into thirty-two *généralités* (districts), in each of which after 1634 a royal intendant held a commission to perform specific tasks, often financial but also judicial and policing. Intendants transmitted information from local communities to Paris and delivered

**Louis de Caulery: Ball in the Reign of Henry IV (detail)** Children dressed as adults imitate the courtly manners and aristocratic behavior of their parents. The vastness of space, the rich clothes, and the columns in the rear suggest the elegance and wealth of the French court. *(Musée de Beaux-Arts, Rennes/Giraudon/The Bridgeman Art Library)*

royal orders from the capital to their généralités. Almost always recruited from the newer judicial nobility, the *noblesse de robe,* intendants were appointed directly by the monarch, to whom they were solely responsible. They could not be natives of the districts where they held authority; thus they had no vested interest in their localities. The intendants recruited men for the army, supervised the collection of taxes, presided over the administration of local law, checked up on the local nobility, and regulated economic activities—commerce, trade, the guilds, marketplaces—in their districts. They were to use their power for two related purposes: to enforce royal orders in the généralités of their jurisdiction and to weaken the power and influence of the regional nobility. As the intendants' power increased under Richelieu, so did the power of the centralized French state.

In 1598 Henry IV's lawyers had drawn up the "Law of Concord." It had been published as the Edict of Nantes to create a temporary and provisional situation of religious toleration in order to promote *temporary* religious and civil concord between the Calvinist, Reformed, or Huguenot faith and Roman Catholicism. Full religious toleration of peoples of differing faiths in a pluralistic society developed only in the eighteenth century (see page 484). Meantime, all French people were theoretically reunited under the king's religion, Roman Catholicism. The Edict of Nantes named 150 towns throughout France; the king granted Protestants the right to practice their faith in those towns, and he gave the towns 180,000 écus to support the maintenance of their military garrisons. Huguenots numbered perhaps 10 percent of the total French population, most of them concentrated in the southwest. In 1627 Louis XIII, with the unanimous consent of the royal council, decided to end Protestant military and political independence, because, he said, it constituted "a state within a state." According to Louis, Huguenots demanded freedom of conscience but did not allow Catholics to worship in their cities. He interpreted this inequity as *political* disobedience.[7]

Attention focused on La Rochelle, fourth largest of the French Atlantic ports and a major commercial center with strong ties to the northern Protestant states of Holland and England. Louis intended to cut off English aid, and he personally supervised the siege of La Rochelle. The city fell in October 1628. Its municipal government was suppressed, and its walled fortifications were destroyed. Although Protestants retained the right of public worship, the king reinstated the Catholic liturgy, and Cardinal Richelieu himself celebrated the first Mass. The military fall of La Rochelle weakened the influence of aristocratic adherents of Calvinism and was one step in the evolution of a unified French state.

Louis XIII, Richelieu, and later Louis XIV also faced serious urban protests. Real or feared unemployment, high food prices, grain shortages, new taxes, and what ordinary townspeople perceived as oppressive taxation all triggered domestic violence. Major insurrections occurred at Dijon in 1630 and 1668, at Bordeaux in 1635 and 1675, at Montpellier in 1645, at Lyons in 1667–1668 and 1692, and at Amiens in 1685, 1695, 1704, and 1711. Sometimes rumor and misinformation sparked these riots. In any case, they were all characterized by deep popular anger, a vocabulary of violence, and what a recent historian calls "the culture of retribution"—that is, the punishment of royal "outsiders," officials who attempted to announce or to collect taxes. These officials often were seized, beaten, and hacked to death. For example, in 1673 Louis XIV's imposition of new taxes on legal transactions, tobacco, and pewterware provoked a major uprising in Bordeaux.

Municipal and royal authorities responded feebly. They lacked the means of strong action. They feared that stern repressive measures, such as sending in troops to fire on crowds, would create martyrs and further inflame the situation, while forcible full-scale military occupation of a city would be very expensive. Thus authorities allowed the crowds to "burn themselves out," as long as they did not do too much damage. Royal edicts were suspended, prisoners were released, and discussions were initiated. By the end of the century, municipal governments were better integrated into the national structure, and local authorities had the prompt military support of the Paris government. Those who publicly opposed government policies and taxes received swift and severe punishment.[8]

French foreign policy under Richelieu was aimed at the destruction of the fence of Habsburg territories that surrounded France. Consequently, Richelieu supported the Habsburgs' enemies. In 1631 he signed a treaty with the Lutheran king Gustavus Adolphus promising French support against the Catholic Habsburgs in what has been called the Swedish phase of the Thirty Years' War (see page 498). French influence became an important factor in the political future of the German Empire. Richelieu acquired for France extensive rights in Alsace in the east and Arras in the north.

Richelieu's efforts at centralization extended even to literature. In 1635 he gave official recognition to a group of philologists who were interested in grammar and rhetoric. Thus was born the French Academy. With Richelieu's encouragement, the French Academy began the preparation of a dictionary to standardize the French language; it was completed in 1694. The French Academy survives as a prestigious society, and its membership now includes people outside the field of literature.

All of these new policies, especially war, cost money. In his *Political Testament,* Richelieu wrote, "I have always said that finances are the sinews of the state." He meant that revenues determine a government's ability to inaugurate and enforce policies and programs. A state secures its revenues through taxation. But the political and economic structure of France greatly limited the government's ability to tax. Seventeenth-century France remained "a collection of local economies and local societies dominated by local elites." The rights of some assemblies in some provinces, such as Brittany, to vote their own taxes; the hereditary exemption from taxation of many wealthy members of the nobility and the middle class; and the royal pension system drastically limited the government's power to tax.

Richelieu and, later, Louis XIV temporarily solved their financial problems by securing the cooperation of local elites. The central government shared the proceeds of tax revenue with local powers. It never gained all the income it needed. Because the French monarchy could not tax at will, it never completely controlled the financial system. In practice, therefore, French absolutism was limited.[9]

In building the French state, Richelieu believed he had to resort to drastic measures against persons and groups within France and to conduct a tough anti-Habsburg foreign policy. He knew also that his approach sometimes seemed to contradict traditional Christian teaching. As a priest and bishop, how did he justify his policies? He developed his own **raison d'état** (reason of state): "Where the interests of the state are concerned, God absolves actions which, if privately committed, would be a crime."[10]

Richelieu's successor as chief minister and then regent for the boy-king Louis XIV was Cardinal Jules Mazarin (1602–1661). He continued Richelieu's centralizing policies, but his attempts to increase royal revenues led to the civil wars of 1648–1653 known as the **Fronde**.

The word *fronde* means "slingshot" or "catapult," and a *frondeur* was originally a street urchin who threw mud at the passing carriages of the rich. But the Fronde originated in the provinces, not Paris, and the term *frondeur* came to be applied to anyone who opposed the policies of the government. Many individuals and groups did so. Influential segments of the nobility resented the increased power of the monarchy under Louis XIII and what they perceived as their diminished role in government. Mazarin could not control them as Richelieu had done. Royal bureaucrats, judges in the parlements, and intendants who considered their positions the means to social and economic advancement felt that they were being manipulated by the Crown and their interests ignored.[11] The state's financial situation steadily weakened because entire regions of France refused to pay taxes. The French defeat of Spanish armies at Rocroi in 1643 marked the final collapse of Spanish military power in Europe; the victory also led the French people to believe that because peace was at hand, taxes were unnecessary. When a desperate government devised new taxes, the Parlement of Paris rejected them. Popular rebellions led by aristocratic factions broke out in the provinces and spread to Paris.[12] As rebellion continued, civil order broke down completely. A vast increase in the state bureaucracy, representing an expansion of royal power, and new means of extracting money from working people incurred the bitter opposition of peasants and urban artisans. Violence continued intermittently for the next twelve years.

The conflicts of the Fronde had three significant results for the future. First, it became apparent that the government would have to compromise with the bureaucrats and social elites that controlled local institutions and constituted the state bureaucracy. These groups were already largely exempt from taxation, and Louis XIV confirmed their privileged social status. Second, the French economy was badly disrupted and would take years to rebuild. Third, the Fronde had a traumatic effect on the young Louis XIV. The king and his mother were frequently threatened and sometimes treated as prisoners by aristocratic factions. On one occasion, a mob broke into the royal bedchamber to make sure the king was actually there; it succeeded in giving him a bad fright. Louis never forgot such humiliations. The period of the Fronde formed the cornerstone of his political education and of his conviction that the sole alternative to anarchy was absolute monarchy. The personal rule of Louis XIV represented the culmination of the process of centralization, but it also witnessed the institutionalization of procedures that would ultimately undermine the absolute monarchy.

## The Absolute Monarchy of Louis XIV

According to the court theologian Bossuet, the clergy at the coronation of Louis XIV in Reims Cathedral asked God to cause the splendors of the French court to fill all who beheld it with awe. God subsequently granted that prayer. In the reign of Louis XIV (r. 1643–1715), the longest in European history, the French monarchy reached the peak of absolutist development. In the magnificence of his court, in the brilliance of the culture that he presided over and that permeated all of Europe, and in his remarkably long life, the "Sun King" dominated his age. No wonder scholars have characterized the second half of the seventeenth century as the "Grand Century," the "Age of Magnificence," and, echoing the eighteenth-century philosopher Voltaire, the "Age of Louis XIV."

In old age, Louis claimed that he had grown up learning very little, but recent historians think he was being modest. True, he knew little Latin and only the rudiments of arithmetic and thus by Renaissance standards was not well educated. Nevertheless, he learned to speak Italian and Spanish fluently, he spoke and wrote elegant French, and he knew some French history and more European geography than the ambassadors accredited to his court. He imbibed the devout Catholicism of his mother, Anne of Austria, and throughout his long life scrupulously performed his religious duties. (Beginning in 1661, Louis attended Mass daily, but rather than paying attention to the liturgy, he said his rosary—to the scorn of his courtiers, who considered this practice "rustic.") Religion, Anne, and Mazarin all taught Louis that God had established kings as his rulers on earth. The royal coronation consecrated Louis to God's service, and he was certain—to use Shakespeare's phrase—that there was a divinity that doth hedge a king. Though kings were a race apart, they could not do as they pleased: they had to obey God's laws and rule for the good of the people.

Louis's education was more practical than formal. Under Mazarin's instruction, he studied state papers as they arrived, and he attended council meetings and sessions at which French ambassadors were dispatched abroad and foreign ambassadors received. He learned by direct experience and gained professional training in the work of government. Above all, the misery he suffered during the Fronde gave him an eternal distrust of the nobility and a profound sense of his own isolation. Accordingly, silence, caution, and secrecy became political tools for the achievement of his goals. His characteristic answer to requests of all kinds became the enigmatic *"Je verrai"* (I shall see).

Louis grew up with an absolute sense of his royal dignity. Contemporaries considered him tall (he was actually five feet five inches) and distinguished in appearance but inclined to heaviness because of the gargantuan meals in which he indulged. Louis XIV was a consummate actor, and his "terrifying majesty" awed all who saw him. He worked extremely hard and succeeded in being "every moment and every inch a king." Because he so relished the role of monarch, historians have had difficulty distinguishing the man from the monarch.

Historians have often said that Louis XIV introduced significant government innovations, the greatest of which was "the complete domestication of the nobility." By this phrase scholars mean that he exercised complete control over the powerful social class that historically had opposed the centralizing goals of the French monarchy. Recent research has suggested that notions of "domestication" represent an exaggeration. What Louis XIV actually achieved was the cooperation of the nobility. Throughout France the nobility agreed to participate in projects that both exalted the monarchy and reinforced the aristocrats' ancient prestige. Thus the relationship between the Crown and the nobility constituted collaboration rather than absolute control.

In the province of Languedoc, for example, Louis and his agents persuaded the notables to support the construction of the Canal des Deux Mers, a waterway linking the Mediterranean Sea and the Atlantic Ocean. Royal

**Luca Giordano: The Pasta Eater** In the seventeenth century, rich people carried a fork when they dined out, but its use spread very slowly from Italy and came into common use only about 1750. A German preacher damned the fork as a diabolical luxury: "God would not have given us fingers if he wanted us to use forks." So, if King Louis XIV could eat chicken stew with his fingers without spilling it, how can we fault this Neapolitan workingman for enjoying his pasta without a fork? *(The Art Museum, Princeton University Museum purchase, John Maclean Magie and Gertrude Magie Fund. Photo: Bruce White)*

encouragement for the manufacture of luxury draperies in Languedocian towns likewise tied provincial business people to national goals, although French cloths subsequently proved unable to compete with cheaper Dutch ones. Above all, in the campaign for the repression of the Huguenots, the interests of the monarchy and nobility coincided (see page 541). Through mutual collaboration, the nobility and the king achieved goals that neither could have won without the other. For his part, Louis won increased military taxation from the Estates of Languedoc. In return, Louis graciously granted the nobility and dignitaries privileged social status and increased access to his person, which meant access to the enormous patronage the king had to dispense. French government rested on the social and political structure of seventeenth-century France, a structure in which the nobility historically exercised great influence. In this respect, therefore, French absolutism was not so much modern as the last phase of a historical feudal society.[13]

Louis XIV installed his royal court at Versailles, a small town ten miles from Paris. He required all the great nobility of France, at the peril of social, political, and sometimes economic disaster, to come live at Versailles for at least part of the year. Today Versailles stands as the best surviving museum of a vanished society on earth. In the seventeenth century, it became a model of rational order, the center of France, and the perfect symbol of the king's power. (See the feature "Listening to the Past: The Court at Versailles" on pages 562–563.)

Louis XIII had begun Versailles as a hunting lodge, a retreat from a queen he did not like. His son's architects, Le Nôtre and Le Vau, turned what the duke of Saint-Simon called "the most dismal and thankless of sights" into a veritable paradise. Wings were added to the original building to make the palace U-shaped. Everywhere at Versailles the viewer had a sense of grandeur, vastness, and elegance. Enormous staterooms became display galleries for inlaid tables, Italian marble statuary, Gobelin tapestries woven at the state factory in Paris, silver ewers, and beautiful (if uncomfortable) furniture. If genius means attention to detail, Louis XIV and his designers had it: the decor was perfected down to the last doorknob and keyhole. In the gigantic Hall of Mirrors, later to reflect so much of German as well as French history, hundreds of candles illuminated the domed ceiling, where allegorical paintings celebrated the king's victories.

The art and architecture of Versailles served as fundamental tools of state policy under Louis XIV. The king used architecture to overawe his subjects and foreign visitors. Versailles was seen as a reflection of French genius. Thus the Russian tsar Peter the Great imitated Versailles in the construction of his palace, Peterhof, as did the Prussian emperor Frederick the Great in his palace at Potsdam outside Berlin.

As in architecture, so too in language. Beginning in the reign of Louis XIV, French became the language of polite society and the vehicle of diplomatic exchange. French also gradually replaced Latin as the language of international scholarship and learning. The wish of other kings to ape the courtly style of Louis XIV and the imitation of French intellectuals and artists spread the language all over Europe. The royal courts of Sweden, Russia, Poland, and Germany all spoke French. In the eighteenth century, the great Russian aristocrats were more fluent in French than in Russian. In England the first Hanoverian king, George I, spoke fluent French and only halting English. France inspired a cosmopolitan European culture in the late seventeenth century, and that culture was inspired by the king. The French today revere Louis XIV as one of their greatest national heroes because of the culture that he inspired and symbolized.

Against this background of magnificent splendor, Saint-Simon writes, Louis XIV

*reduced everyone to subjection, and brought to his court those very persons he cared least about. Whoever was old enough to serve did not dare demur. It was still another device to ruin the nobles by accustoming them to equality and forcing them to mingle with everyone indiscriminately. . . .*

*Louis XIV took great pains to inform himself on what was happening everywhere, in public places, private homes, and even on the international scene. . . . Spies and informers of all kinds were numberless.*[14]

Though this passage was written by one of Louis's severest critics, all agree that the king used court ceremonials to undermine the power of the great nobility. By excluding the highest nobles from his councils, he weakened their ancient right to advise the king and to participate in government; they became mere instruments of royal policy. Operas, fetes, balls, gossip, and trivia occupied the nobles' time and attention. Through painstaking attention to detail and precisely calculated showmanship, Louis XIV reduced the major threat to his power. He separated power from status and grandeur: he secured the nobles' cooperation, and the nobles enjoyed the status and grandeur in which they lived.

In government Louis utilized several councils of state, which he personally attended, and the intendants, who acted for the councils throughout France. A stream of questions and instructions flowed between local districts and Versailles, and under Louis XIV a uniform and centralized administration was imposed on the country. In 1685 France was the strongest and most highly centralized state in Europe.

Councilors of state came from the recently ennobled or the upper middle class. Royal service provided a means of social mobility. These professional bureaucrats served the state in the person of the king, but they did not share power with him. Louis stated that he chose bourgeois officials because he wanted "people to know by the rank of the men who served him that he had no intention of sharing power with them."[15] If great ones were the king's advisers, they would seem to share the royal authority; professional administrators from the middle class would not.

Throughout his long reign and despite increasing financial problems, he never called a meeting of the Estates General. The nobility therefore had no means of united expression or action. Nor did Louis have a first minister; he kept himself free from worry about the inordinate power of a Richelieu. Louis's use of spying and terror—a secret police force, a system of informers, and the practice of opening private letters—foreshadowed some of the devices of the modern state. French government remained highly structured, bureaucratic, centered at Versailles, and responsible to Louis XIV.

**The Spider and the Fly** In reference to the insect symbolism (*upper left*), the caption on the lower left side of this illustration states, "The noble is the spider, the peasant the fly." The other caption (*upper right*) notes, "The more people have, the more they want. The poor man brings everything—wheat, fruit, money, vegetables. The greedy lord sitting there ready to take everything will not even give him the favor of a glance." This satirical print summarizes peasant grievances. *(The New York Public Library, Art Resource, NY)*

## Financial and Economic Management Under Louis XIV: Colbert

Finance proved the grave weakness in Louis XIV's administration. An expanding professional bureaucracy, the court at Versailles, extensive military reform (see page 542), and war cost a great deal of money. English kings relied on one national assembly, Parliament, for consent to taxation for the entire country. French rulers had to consult local or provincial Estates for approval of taxes for particular regions. The reactions of the Estates of Burgundy to Louis's requests for revenue illustrate the king's relationship with the provincial Estates and his financial difficulties. That reaction also shows the limitations of royal absolutism. In 1658, 1662, 1665, and 1668, Louis called assemblies of deputies of Burgundy: the Estates legally consisted of the clergy, the nobility (the First and Second Estates), and representatives of all other people—merchants, artisans, and peasants (the Third Estate). Since the clergy and the nobility had many exemptions, the great burden of taxation fell on the Third Estate. At each of the assemblies, deputies pleaded their poverty, citing the crop failures of recent years; or they bargained for lower sums than the king asked for; or they asked that the taxes be postponed for a year or two; or if an assessment was grudgingly approved, they put off collecting it. Louis was never able to secure from the Estates of Burgundy all that he requested.[16]

In many parts of France the method of collecting taxes consistently failed to produce enough revenue. Tax farmers, agents who purchased from the Crown the right to collect taxes in a particular district, pocketed the difference between what they raked in and what they handed over to the state. Consequently, the tax farmers profited, while the government got far less than the people paid. In addition, by an old agreement between the Crown and the nobility, the king could freely tax the common people provided he did not tax the nobles. The nobility thereby relinquished a role in government: since nobles did not pay taxes, they could not legitimately claim a say in how taxes were spent. Louis, however, lost enormous potential revenue. The middle classes, moreover, secured many tax exemptions. With the rich and prosperous classes exempt, the tax burden fell heavily on those least able to pay, the poor peasants.

The king named Jean-Baptiste Colbert (1619–1683), the son of a wealthy merchant-financier of Reims, as controller general of finances. Colbert came to manage the entire royal administration and proved himself a financial genius. Colbert's central principle was that the wealth and the economy of France should serve the state. He did not invent the system called "mercantilism," but he rigorously applied it to France.

**Mercantilism** is a collection of governmental policies for the regulation of economic activities, especially commercial activities, by and for the state. In seventeenth- and eighteenth-century economic theory, a nation's international power was thought to be based on its wealth, specifically its gold supply. Because, mercantilist theory held, resources were limited, state intervention was needed to secure the largest part of a limited resource. To accumulate gold, a country always had to sell more goods abroad than it bought. Colbert believed that a successful economic policy meant more than a favorable balance of trade, however. He insisted that the French sell abroad and buy *nothing* back. France should be self-sufficient, able to produce within its borders everything the subjects of the French king needed. Consequently, the outflow of gold would be halted, debtor states would pay in bullion, and with the wealth of the nation increased, its power and prestige would be enhanced.

Colbert attempted to accomplish self-sufficiency through state support for both old industries and newly created ones. He subsidized the established cloth industries at Abbeville, Saint-Quentin, and Carcassonne. He granted special royal privileges to the rug and tapestry industries at Paris, Gobelin, and Beauvais. New factories at Saint-Antoine in Paris manufactured mirrors to replace Venetian imports. Looms at Chantilly and Alençon competed with lacemaking at Bruges in the Spanish Netherlands, and foundries at Saint-Étienne made steel and firearms that reduced Swedish imports. To ensure a high-quality finished product, Colbert set up a system of state inspection and regulation. To ensure order within every industry, he compelled all craftsmen to organize into guilds, and within every guild he gave the masters absolute power over their workers. Colbert encouraged skilled foreign craftsmen and manufacturers to immigrate to France, and he gave them special privileges. To improve communications, he built roads and canals, the most famous, the Canal des Deux Mers. To protect French goods, he abolished many domestic tariffs and enacted high foreign tariffs, which prevented foreign products from competing with French ones.

Colbert's most important work was the creation of a powerful merchant marine to transport French goods. He gave bonuses to French shipowners and shipbuilders and established a method of maritime conscription, arsenals, and academies for the training of sailors. In 1661 France possessed 18 unseaworthy vessels; by 1681 it had 276 frigates, galleys, and ships of the line.

Colbert hoped to make Canada—rich in untapped minerals and some of the best agricultural land in the world—part of a vast French empire. He gathered four thousand peasants from western France and shipped them to Canada, where they peopled the province of Quebec. (In 1608, one year after the English arrived at Jamestown, Virginia, Sully had established the city of Quebec, which became the capital of French Canada.) Subsequently, the Jesuit Jacques Marquette and the merchant Louis Joliet sailed down the Mississippi River and took possession of the land on both sides as far south as present-day Arkansas. In 1684 the French explorer Robert La Salle continued down the Mississippi to its mouth and claimed vast territories and the rich delta for Louis XIV. The area was called, naturally, "Louisiana."

How successful were Colbert's policies? His achievement in the development of manufacturing was prodigious. The textile industry, especially in woolens, expanded enormously, and "France . . . had become in 1683 the leading nation of the world in industrial productivity."[17] The commercial classes prospered, and between 1660 and 1700 their position steadily improved. The national economy, however, rested on agriculture. Although French peasants did not become serfs, as did the peasants of eastern Europe, they were mercilessly taxed. After 1685 other hardships afflicted them: poor harvests, continuing deflation of the currency, and fluctuation in the price of grain. Many peasants emigrated. With the decline in population and thus in the number of taxable people (the poorest), the state's resources fell. A totally inadequate tax base and heavy expenditure for war in the later years of Louis's reign made Colbert's goals unattainable.

## The Revocation of the Edict of Nantes

The absolutist state also attempted to control religion.

*We now see with the proper gratitude what we owe to God . . . for the best and largest part of our subjects of the so-called reformed religion have embraced Catholicism, and now that, to the extent that the execution of the Edict of Nantes remains useless, we have judged that we can do nothing better to wipe out the memory of the troubles, of the confusion, of the evils that the progress of this false religion has caused our kingdom . . . than to revoke entirely the said Edict.*[18]

With those words, in 1685 Louis XIV revoked the Edict of Nantes, by which his grandfather Henry IV had granted liberty of conscience to French Huguenots. The new law ordered the destruction of churches, the closing of schools, the Catholic baptism of Huguenots, and the exile of Huguenot pastors who refused to renounce their faith. Why? There had been so many mass conversions during previous years (many of them forced) that Madame de Maintenon, Louis's second wife, could say that "nearly all the Huguenots were converted." Some Huguenots had emigrated. Richelieu had already deprived French Calvinists of political rights. Why, then, did Louis, by revoking the edict, persecute some of his most loyal and industrially skilled subjects, force others to flee abroad, and provoke the outrage of Protestant Europe?

First, the French monarchy had never intended religious toleration to be permanent (see page 535); religious pluralism was not a seventeenth-century ideal. Although recent scholarship has convincingly shown that Louis XIV was basically tolerant, he considered religious unity politically necessary to realize his goal of "one king, one law, one faith." He hated division within the realm and insisted that religious unity was essential to his royal dignity and to the security of the state.

Second, while France in the early years of Louis's reign permitted religious liberty, it was not a popular policy. Aristocrats had long petitioned Louis to crack down on Protestants. But the revocation was solely the king's decision, and it won him enormous praise. "If the flood of congratulation means anything, it . . . was probably the one act of his reign that, at the time, was popular with the majority of his subjects."[19]

Although contemporaries applauded Louis XIV, later scholars damned him for the adverse impact that revocation of the Edict of Nantes had on the economy and foreign affairs. Tens of thousands of Huguenot craftsmen, soldiers, and business people emigrated, depriving France of their skills and tax revenues and carrying their bitterness to Holland, England, Prussia, and Cape Town in southern Africa. Modern scholarship, however, has greatly modified this picture: Huguenot settlers in northern Europe aggravated Protestant hatred for Louis, but revocation of the Edict of Nantes had only minor and scattered effects on French economic development.[20]

## French Classicism

Scholars characterize the art and literature of the age of Louis XIV as **French classicism.** By this they mean that the artists and writers of the late seventeenth century imitated the subject matter and style of classical antiquity, that their work resembled that of Renaissance Italy, and that French art possessed the classical qualities of discipline, balance, and restraint. Classicism was the official style of Louis's court. In painting, however, French classicism had already reached its peak before 1661, the beginning of the king's personal government.

Contemporaries said that Louis XIV never ceased playing the role of grand monarch on the stage of his court. If the king never fully relaxed from the pressures and intrigues of government, he did enjoy music and theater and used them as a backdrop for court ceremonials. Louis favored Jean-Baptiste Lully (1632–1687), whose orchestral works combined lively animation with the restrained austerity typical of French classicism. Lully also composed court ballets, and his operatic productions achieved a powerful influence throughout Europe. Louis supported François Couperin (1668–1733), whose harpsichord and organ works possessed the regal grandeur the king loved, and Marc-Antoine Charpentier (1634–1704), whose solemn religious music entertained him at meals. Charpentier received a pension for the *Te Deums,* hymns of thanksgiving, he composed to celebrate French military victories.

Louis XIV loved the stage, and in the plays of Molière and Racine his court witnessed the finest achievements in the history of the French theater. When Jean-Baptiste Poquelin (1622–1673), the son of a prosperous tapestry maker, refused to join his father's business and entered the theater, he took the stage name "Molière." As playwright, stage manager, director, and actor, Molière produced comedies that exposed the hypocrisies and follies of society through brilliant caricature. *Tartuffe* satirized the religious hypocrite, *Le Bourgeois Gentilhomme* (The Bourgeois Gentleman) attacked the social parvenu, and *Les Femmes Savantes* (The Learned Women) mocked the fashionable pseudo-intellectuals of the day. In structure Molière's plays followed classical models, but they were based on careful social observation. Molière made the bourgeoisie the butt of his ridicule; he stopped short of criticizing the nobility, reflecting the policy of his royal patron.

While Molière dissected social mores, his contemporary Jean Racine (1639–1699) analyzed the power of love. Racine based his tragic dramas on Greek and Roman legends, and his persistent theme was the conflict of good and evil. Several plays—*Andromaque, Bérénice, Iphigénie,* and *Phèdre*—bear the names of women and deal with the power of passion in women. Louis preferred *Mithridate* and *Britannicus* because of the "grandeur" of their themes. For simplicity of language, symmetrical structure, and calm restraint, the plays of Racine represent the finest examples of French classicism. His tragedies and Molière's comedies are still produced today.

## Louis XIV's Wars

On his deathbed, Louis XIV is reputed to have said, "I have gone to war too lightly and pursued it for vanity's sake." Perhaps he never actually said this. If he did, perhaps it was part of the confessional style of the time, which required that a penitent exaggerate his sins.[21] In any case, the course of Louis's reign suggests that he acted according to his observation that "the character of a conqueror is regarded as the noblest and highest of titles." In pursuit of the title of "conqueror," he kept France at war for thirty-three of the fifty-four years of his personal rule.

It is an axiom of history that war or the preparation for war is always a government's greatest expense. In 1635, when Richelieu became first minister of Louis XIII, the French army consisted of 25,000 men. In 1659, at the time of the Treaty of the Pyrenees, which ended the war with Spain, the army theoretically was composed of 250,000 men. In 1666 Louis appointed François le Tellier (later marquis de Louvois) secretary of state for war. Under the king's watchful eye, Louvois created a professional army that was modern in the sense that the French state, rather than private nobles, employed the soldiers. The king himself took command and directly supervised all aspects and details of military affairs.

Louvois utilized several methods in recruiting troops: dragooning, in which press gangs seized men off the streets, often drunks, bums, and criminals (this method was not popular); conscription; and, after 1688, lottery. Louvois also recruited regiments of foreign mercenaries. Under the strict direction of Jean Martinet (d. 1672), whose name became a byword in the French and English languages for absolute adherence to the rules, the foreign and native-born soldiers were turned into a tough, obedient military machine. A commissariat was established to feed the troops, taking the place of the ancient method of living off the countryside. An ambulance corps was designed to look after the wounded. Uniforms and weapons were standardized. A rational system of training and promotion was imposed. All this added up to a military revolution. A new military machine now existed that gave one national state, France, the potential to dominate the affairs of the continent for the first time in European history.

Louis continued on a broader scale the expansionist policy begun by Cardinal Richelieu. In 1667, using a dynastic excuse, he invaded Flanders, part of the Spanish Netherlands, and Franche-Comté in the east. In consequence, he acquired twelve towns, including the important commercial centers of Lille and Tournai (see Map 16.1). Five years later, Louis personally led an army of over 100,000 men into Holland, and the Dutch ultimately saved themselves only by opening the dikes and flooding the countryside. This war, which lasted six years and eventually involved the Holy Roman Empire and Spain, was concluded by the Treaty of Nijmegen (1678). Louis gained additional Flemish towns and all of Franche-Comté.

Encouraged by his successes, by the weakness of the German Empire, and by divisions among the other European powers, Louis continued his aggression. In 1681 he seized the city of Strasbourg, and three years later he sent his armies into the province of Lorraine. At that moment, the king seemed invincible. In fact, Louis had reached the limit of his expansion. The wars of the 1680s and 1690s brought him no additional territories.

Louis attempted to support an army of 200,000 men in several different theaters of war against the great nations of

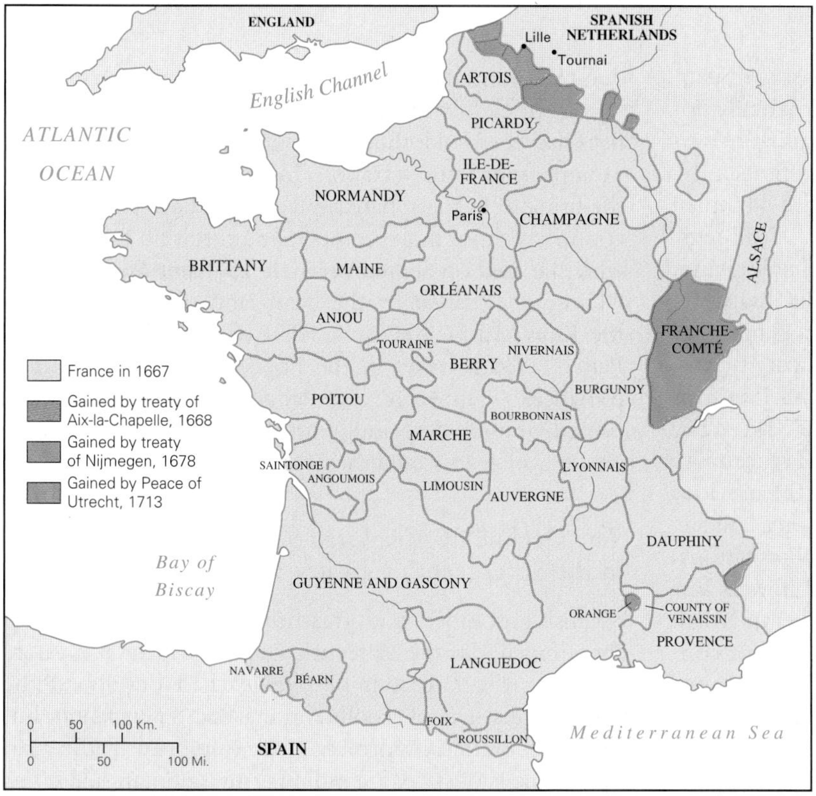


**MAP 16.1 The Acquisitions of Louis XIV, 1668–1713** The desire for glory and the weakness of his German neighbors encouraged Louis's expansionist policy, but he paid a high price for his acquisitions.

Europe, the powerful Bank of Amsterdam, and (after 1694) the Bank of England. This task far exceeded French resources, given the very inequitable system of taxation. The military revolution involving the reform and great expansion of the army required funding that the state could not meet. Claude Le Peletier, Colbert's successor as minister of finance, resorted to the devaluation of the currency (which hurt those who hoarded coins) and the old device of selling offices, tax exemptions, and titles of nobility. To raise revenue for the war effort, on December 14, 1689, Louis published a declaration ordering that all the nation's silverware be handed over to the mint. Setting an example, Louis sent off the silver furniture of Versailles. The royal apartments and the Hall of Mirrors looked like a house repossessed by sheriffs.[22] This action did little good. None of these measures produced enough revenue. So the weight of taxation fell on the already-overburdened peasants. They expressed their frustrations in widespread revolts that hit all parts of France in the 1690s.

A series of bad harvests between 1688 and 1694 brought catastrophe. Cold, wet summers reduced the harvests by an estimated one-third to two-thirds. The price of wheat skyrocketed. The result was widespread starvation, and in many provinces the death rate rose to several times the normal figure. Parish registers reveal that France buried at least one-tenth of its population in those years, perhaps 2 million in 1693 to 1694 alone. Rising grain prices, new taxes for war on top of old ones, a slump in manufacturing and thus in exports, and the constant nuisance of pillaging troops—all these meant great suffering for the French people. France wanted peace at any price. Louis XIV granted a respite for five years while he prepared for the conflict later known as the War of the Spanish Succession (1701–1713).

This war, provoked by the territorial disputes of the previous century, also involved the dynastic question of the succession to the Spanish throne. It was an open secret in Europe that the king of Spain, Charles II (r. 1665–1700), was mentally defective and sexually impotent. In 1698 the European powers, including France, agreed by treaty to partition, or divide, the vast Spanish possessions between the king of France and the Holy Roman emperor, who were Charles II's brothers-in-law. When Charles died in 1700, however, his will left the Spanish crown and the worldwide Spanish Empire to Philip of Anjou, Louis XIV's grandson. While the will specifically rejected union of the French and Spanish crowns, Louis was obviously the power in France, not his seventeen-year-old grandson. Louis reneged on the treaty and accepted the will.

The Dutch and the English would not accept French acquisition of the Spanish Netherlands and of the rich trade with the Spanish colonies. The union of the Spanish and French crowns, moreover, would have totally upset the European balance of power. Claiming that he was following both Spanish national interests and French dynastic and national interests, Louis presented Philip of Anjou to the Spanish ambassador saying, "You may salute him as your king." After a Mass of thanksgiving, the Spanish ambassador was heard to say, "What rapture! The Pyrenees no longer exist."[23] The possibility of achieving this goal provoked the long-anticipated crisis.

In 1701 the English, Dutch, Austrians, and Prussians formed the Grand Alliance against Louis XIV. They claimed that they were fighting to prevent France from becoming too strong in Europe, but during the previous half century, overseas maritime rivalry among France, Holland, and England had created serious international tension. The secondary motive of the allied powers was to check France's expanding commercial power in North America, Asia, and Africa. In the ensuing series of conflicts, two great soldiers dominated the alliance against France: Eugene, prince of Savoy, representing the Holy Roman Empire, and Englishman John Churchill, subsequently duke of Marlborough. Eugene and Churchill inflicted a severe defeat on Louis in 1704 at Blenheim in Bavaria. Marlborough followed with another victory at Ramillies near Namur in Brabant.

The war was finally concluded at Utrecht in 1713, where the principle of partition was applied. Louis's grandson, Philip, remained the first Bourbon king of Spain on the understanding that the French and Spanish crowns would never be united. France surrendered Newfoundland, Nova Scotia, and the Hudson Bay territory to England, which also acquired Gibraltar, Minorca, and control of the African slave trade from Spain. The Dutch gained little because Austria received the former Spanish Netherlands (see Map 16.2).

The **Peace of Utrecht** had important international consequences. It represented the balance-of-power principle in operation, setting limits on the extent to which any one power—in this case, France—could expand. The treaty completed the decline of Spain as a great power. It vastly expanded the British Empire. And it gave European powers experience in international cooperation.

The Peace of Utrecht marked the end of French expansionist policy. Louis's thirty-five-year quest for military glory had brought rights to all of Alsace, the gain of important cities in the north such as Lille, as well as Strasbourg. But at what price? Even revisionist historians, who portray the aging monarch as responsible in negotiation and moderate in his demands, acknowledge "that the widespread misery in France during the period was in part due to royal policies, especially the incessant wars."[24] To raise revenue for the wars, forty thousand additional offices had been sold, thus increasing the number of families exempt from future taxation. In 1714 France hovered on the brink of financial bankruptcy. Louis had exhausted the country without much compensation. It is no wonder that when he died on September 1, 1715, Saint-Simon wrote, "Those . . . wearied by the heavy and oppressive rule of the King and his ministers, felt a delighted freedom. . . . Paris . . . found relief in the hope of liberation. . . . The provinces . . . quivered with delight . . . [and] the people, ruined, abused, despairing, now thanked God for a deliverance which answered their most ardent desires."[25]

## The Decline of Absolutist Spain in the Seventeenth Century

Spanish absolutism and greatness had preceded those of the French. In the sixteenth century, Spain (or, more precisely, the kingdom of Castile) had developed the standard features of absolute monarchy: a permanent bureaucracy staffed by professionals employed in the various councils of state, a standing army, and national taxes, the *servicios,* which fell most heavily on the poor.

France depended on financial and administrative unification within its borders; Spain had developed an international absolutism on the basis of silver bullion from Peru. Spanish gold and silver, armies, and glory had dominated the continent for most of the sixteenth century, but by the 1590s the seeds of disaster were sprouting. The lack of a strong middle class, largely the result of the expulsion of the Jews and Moors (see page 510), the agricultural crisis and population decline, the failure to invest in productive enterprises, the intellectual isolation and psychological malaise—all combined to reduce Spain, by 1715, to a second-rate power.

The fabulous and seemingly inexhaustible flow of silver from Mexico and Peru, together with the sale of cloth, grain, oil, and wine to the colonies, greatly enriched Spain. In the early seventeenth century, however, the Dutch and English began to trade with the Spanish colonies, cutting into the revenues that had gone to Spain. Mexico and Peru themselves developed local industries, further lessening their need to buy from Spain. Between 1610 and 1650, Spanish trade with the colonies fell 60 percent.

At the same time, the native Indians and African slaves who worked the South American silver mines, under conditions that would have shamed the ancient Egyptian pharaohs, suffered frightful epidemics of disease. Moreover, the lodes started to run dry. Consequently, the quantity of metal produced for Spain steadily declined.

**Tiepolo: The Triumph of Spain** This painting is from the ceiling of the Royal Palace in Madrid. Arguably the greatest Italian painter of the eighteenth century, Giovanni Tiepolo depicted the Spanish Empire as the self-assured champion of Christian cultural values in Europe and America. Completed in 1764, a century after the empire had gone into irrevocable decline, this piece represents only an illusion of grandeur. *(Palacio Real de Madrid/The Bridgeman Art Library)*

But in Madrid royal expenditures constantly exceeded income. The remedies applied in the face of a mountainous state debt and declining revenues were devaluation of the coinage and declarations of bankruptcy. In 1596, 1607, 1627, 1647, and 1680, Spanish kings found no solution to the problem of an empty treasury other than to cancel the national debt. Given the frequency of cancellation, public confidence in the state deteriorated.

Spain, in contrast to the other countries of western Europe, had only a tiny middle class. Public opinion, taking its cue from the aristocracy, condemned moneymaking as vulgar and undignified. Those with influence or connections sought titles of nobility and social prestige. Thousands entered economically unproductive professions or became priests, monks, and nuns: there were said to be nine thousand monasteries in the province of Castile alone. The flood of gold and silver had produced severe inflation, pushing the costs of production in the textile industry higher and higher to the point that Castilian cloth could not compete in colonial and international markets. Many businessmen found so many obstacles in the way of profitable enterprise that they simply gave up.[26]

Spanish aristocrats, attempting to maintain an extravagant lifestyle they could no longer afford, increased the rents on their estates. High rents and heavy taxes in turn drove the peasants from the land. Agricultural production suffered, and the peasants departed for the large cities, where they swelled the ranks of unemployed beggars.

**MAP 16.2 Europe in 1715** The series of treaties commonly called the Peace of Utrecht (April 1713–November 1715) ended the War of the Spanish Succession and redrew the map of Europe. A French Bourbon king succeeded to the Spanish throne on the understanding that the French not attempt to unite the French and Spanish crowns. France surrendered to Austria the Spanish Netherlands (later Belgium), then in French hands, and France recognized the Hohenzollern rulers of Prussia. Spain ceded Gibraltar to Great Britain, for which it has been a strategic naval station ever since. Spain also granted to Britain the *asiento,* the contract for supplying African slaves to America.

Their most Catholic majesties, the kings of Spain, had no solutions to these dire problems. If one can discern personality from pictures, the portraits of Philip III (r. 1598–1622), Philip IV (r. 1622–1665), and Charles II (r. 1665–1700) hanging in the Prado, the Spanish national museum in Madrid, reflect the increasing weakness of the dynasty. Their faces—the small, beady eyes; the long noses; the jutting Habsburg jaws; the pathetically stupid expressions—tell a story of excessive inbreeding and decaying monarchy. The Spanish kings all lacked force of character. Philip III, a pallid, melancholy, and deeply pious man "whose only virtue appeared to reside in a total absence of vice," handed the government over to the lazy duke of Lerma, who used it to advance his personal and familial wealth. Philip IV left the management of his several kingdoms to Gaspar de Guzmán, count-duke of Olivares.

Olivares was an able administrator. He did not lack energy and ideas; he devised new sources of revenue. But he clung to the grandiose belief that the solution to Spain's difficulties rested in a return to the imperial tradition. Unfortunately, the imperial tradition demanded the revival of war with the Dutch at the expiration of a twelve-year truce in 1622 and a long war with France over Mantua (1628–1659). Spain thus became embroiled in the Thirty Years' War. These conflicts, on top of an empty treasury, brought disaster.

In 1640 Spain faced serious revolts in Catalonia and Portugal; in 1643 the French inflicted a crushing defeat on a Spanish army at Rocroi in what is now Belgium. By the Treaty of the Pyrenees of 1659, which ended the French-Spanish wars, Spain was compelled to surrender extensive territories to France. This treaty marked the end of Spain as a great power.

Seventeenth-century Spain was the victim of its past. It could not forget the grandeur of the sixteenth century and look to the future. The bureaucratic councils of state continued to function as symbols of the absolute Spanish monarchy. But because those councils were staffed by aristocrats, it was the aristocracy that held the real power. Spanish absolutism had been built largely on slave-produced gold and silver. When the supply of bullion decreased, the power and standing of the Spanish state declined.

The most cherished Spanish ideals were military glory and strong Roman Catholic faith. In the seventeenth century, Spain lacked the finances and the manpower to fight the expensive wars in which it got involved. Spain also ignored the new mercantile ideas and scientific methods because they came from heretical nations, Holland and England. The incredible wealth of South America destroyed what remained of the Spanish middle class and created contempt for business and manual labor.

The decadence of the Habsburg dynasty and the lack of effective royal councilors also contributed to Spanish failure. Spanish leaders seemed to lack the will to reform. Pessimism and fatalism permeated national life. In the reign of Philip IV, a royal council was appointed to plan

**Peeter Snayers: Spanish Troops (detail)** The long wars that Spain fought over Dutch independence, in support of Habsburg interests in Germany, and against France left the country militarily exhausted and financially drained by the mid-1600s. Here Spanish troops—thin, emaciated, and probably unpaid—straggle away from battle. *(Museo Nacional del Prado, Madrid. Photo: José Baztan y Alberto Otero)*

the construction of a canal linking the Tagus and Manzanares Rivers in Spain. After interminable debate, the committee decided that "if God had intended the rivers to be navigable, He would have made them so."

In the brilliant novel ***Don Quixote,*** Spanish writer Miguel de Cervantes (1547–1616) produced one of the great masterpieces of world literature. *Don Quixote* delineates the whole fabric of sixteenth-century Spanish society. The main character, Don Quixote, lives in a world of dreams, traveling about the countryside seeking military glory. From the title of the book, the English language has borrowed the word *quixotic*. Meaning "idealistic but impractical," the term characterizes seventeenth-century Spain. As a leading scholar has written, "The Spaniard convinced himself that reality was what he felt, believed, imagined. He filled the world with heroic reverberations. Don Quixote was born and grew."[27]

## Constitutionalism

The seventeenth century saw the appearance of the constitutional state. While France and, later, Prussia, Russia, and Austria solved the question of sovereignty with the absolutist state, England and Holland evolved toward the constitutional state. What is constitutionalism? Is it identical to democracy?

**Constitutionalism** is the limitation of government by law. Constitutionalism also implies a balance between the authority and power of the government, on the one hand, and the rights and liberties of the subjects, on the other.

A nation's constitution may be written or unwritten. It may be embodied in one basic document, occasionally revised by amendment or judicial decision, like the Constitution of the United States. Or it may be partly written and partly unwritten and include parliamentary statutes, judicial decisions, and a body of traditional procedures and practices, like the English, Canadian, and Dutch constitutions. Whether written or unwritten, a constitution gets its binding force from the government's acknowledgment that it must respect that constitution—that is, that the state must govern according to the laws. Likewise, in a constitutional state, the people look on the laws and the constitution as the protectors of their rights, liberties, and property.

Modern constitutional governments may take either a republican or a monarchical form. In a constitutional republic, the sovereign power resides in the electorate and is exercised by the electorate's representatives. In a constitutional monarchy, a king or queen serves as the head of state and possesses some residual political authority, but again the ultimate, or sovereign, power rests in the electorate.

A constitutional government is not, however, quite the same as a democratic government. In a complete democracy, *all* the people have the right to participate either directly or indirectly (through their elected representatives) in the government of the state. Democratic government, therefore, is intimately tied up with the *franchise* (the vote). Most men could not vote until the late nineteenth century. Even then, women—probably the majority in Western societies—lacked the franchise; they gained the right to vote only in the twentieth century. Consequently, although constitutionalism developed in the seventeenth century, full democracy was achieved only in recent times.

### The Decline of Royal Absolutism in England (1603–1649)

In 1588 Queen Elizabeth I of England exercised very great personal power; by 1689 the English monarchy was severely circumscribed. Change in England was anything but orderly. Seventeenth-century England displayed little political stability. It executed one king and experienced a bloody civil war; experimented with military dictatorship, then restored the son of the murdered king; and finally, after a bloodless revolution, established constitutional monarchy. Political stability came only in the 1690s. How do we account for the fact that after such a violent and tumultuous century, England laid the foundations for constitutional monarchy? What combination of political, socioeconomic, and religious factors brought on a civil war in 1642–1649 and then the constitutional settlement of 1688–1689?

The extraordinary success of Elizabeth I had rested on her political shrewdness and flexibility, her careful management of finances, her wise selection of ministers, her clever manipulation of Parliament, and her sense of royal dignity and devotion to hard work. The aging queen had always refused to discuss the succession. After her Scottish cousin James Stuart succeeded her as James I (r. 1603–1625), Elizabeth's strengths seemed even greater than they actually had been.

King James was well educated, learned, and, with thirty-five years' experience as king of Scotland, politically shrewd. But he was not as interested in displaying the majesty and mystique of monarchy as Elizabeth had been. He also lacked the common touch. Urged to wave at the crowds who waited to greet their new ruler, James complained that he was tired and threatened to drop his breeches "so they can cheer at my arse." The new king failed to live up to the role expected of him in England. Moreover, James, in contrast to Elizabeth, was a poor judge of character, and in a society already hostile to the

Scots and concerned about proper spoken English, James's Scottish accent was a disadvantage.[28]

James was devoted to the theory of the divine right of kings. He expressed his ideas about divine right in his essay "The Trew Law of Free Monarchy." According to James I, a monarch has a divine (or God-given) right to his authority and is responsible only to God. Rebellion is the worst of political crimes. If a king orders something evil, the subject should respond with passive disobedience but should be prepared to accept any penalty for noncompliance.

He went so far as to lecture the House of Commons: "There are no privileges and immunities which can stand against a divinely appointed King." This notion, implying total royal jurisdiction over the liberties, persons, and properties of English men and women, formed the basis of the Stuart concept of absolutism. Such a view ran directly counter to the long-standing English idea that a person's property could not be taken away without due process of law. James's expression of such views before the English House of Commons constituted a grave political mistake.

The House of Commons guarded the state's pocketbook, and James and later Stuart kings badly needed to open that pocketbook. Elizabeth had left James a sizable royal debt. Through prudent management, the debt could have been gradually reduced. Revisionist historians maintained that political calculations led James to lavish money on court favorites in the hope of building support. More recent scholars have reverted to the traditional view that James was adept at neither finances nor politics.[29]

Elizabeth had also left her Stuart successors a House of Commons that appreciated its own financial strength and intended to use that strength to acquire a greater say in the government of the state. The knights and burgesses who sat at Westminster in the late sixteenth and early seventeenth centuries wanted a voice in royal expenditures, religious reform, and foreign affairs. Essentially, the Commons wanted sovereignty.

Profound social changes had occurred since the sixteenth century. The English House of Commons during the reigns of James I and his son Charles I (r. 1625–1649) was very different from the assembly Henry VIII had manipulated into passing his Reformation legislation. The dissolution of the monasteries and the sale of monastic land had enriched many people. Agricultural techniques such as the draining of wasteland and the application of fertilizers had improved the land and its yield. In the seventeenth century, old manorial common land was enclosed and turned into sheep runs, breeding was carefully supervised, and the size of the flocks increased. In these activities, as well as in the renting and leasing of parcels of land, precise accounts were kept.

**Rubens: Ceiling of the Banqueting House, Whitehall Palace, London (1635)** King James I is raised by the allegorical figures of Justice, Religion, and Truth into the dazzling light of Heaven, perhaps a fitting memorial for the advocate of the divine right of kings. *(Whitehall, London/The Bridgeman Art Library)*

Many people invested in commercial ventures at home, such as the expanding cloth industry, and through partnerships and joint stock companies engaged in foreign enterprises. Many also made prudent marriages. These developments led to a great deal of social mobility. Both in commerce and in agriculture, the English in the late sixteenth and early seventeenth centuries were capitalists, investing their profits to make more money. Though the international inflation of the period hit everywhere, in England commercial and agricultural income rose faster than prices. Wealthy country gentry, rich city merchants, and financiers invested abroad.

The typical pattern was for the commercially successful to set themselves up as country gentry, thus creating an elite group that possessed a far greater proportion of land and of the national wealth in 1640 than had been the case in 1540. Small wonder that in 1640 someone could declare in the House of Commons, probably accurately, "We could buy the House of Lords three times over." Increased wealth had also produced a better-educated and more articulate House of Commons. Many members had acquired at least a smattering of legal knowledge, which they used to search for medieval precedents from which to argue against the king. The class that dominated the Commons wanted political power corresponding to its economic strength.

In England, unlike France, there was no social stigma attached to paying taxes. Members of the House of Commons were willing to tax themselves provided they had some say in the expenditure of those taxes and in the formulation of state policies. The Stuart kings, however, considered such ambitions intolerable presumption and a threat to their divine-right prerogative. Consequently, at every Parliament between 1603 and 1640, bitter squabbles erupted between the Crown and the wealthy, articulate, and legally minded Commons. Charles I's attempt to govern without Parliament (1629–1640) and to finance his government by arbitrary nonparliamentary levies, brought the country to a crisis.

## Religious Issues

An issue graver than royal extravagance and Parliament's desire to make law also disturbed the English and embittered relations between the king and the House of Commons. That problem was religion. In the early seventeenth century, increasing numbers of English people felt dissatisfied with the Church of England established by Henry VIII and reformed by Elizabeth. Many **Puritans** (see page 474) believed that the Reformation had not gone far enough. They wanted to "purify" the Anglican church of Roman Catholic elements—elaborate vestments and ceremonials, bishops, the position of the altar in the church, even the giving and wearing of wedding rings.

It is very difficult to establish what proportion of the English population was Puritan. According to the present scholarly consensus, the dominant religious groups in the early seventeenth century were Calvinist; their more zealous members were Puritans. It also seems clear that many English people were attracted by the socioeconomic implications of John Calvin's theology. Calvinism emphasized hard work, sobriety, thrift, competition, and postponement of pleasure, and it tended to link sin and poverty with weakness and moral corruption. These attitudes fit in precisely with the economic approaches and practices of many (successful) business people and farmers. These values have frequently been called the "Protestant ethic," "middle-class ethic," or "capitalist ethic." While it is hazardous to identify capitalism with Protestantism—there were many successful Catholic capitalists, for example—the "Protestant virtues" represented the prevailing values of members of the House of Commons.

Puritans wanted to abolish bishops in the Church of England, and when James I said, "No bishop, no king," he meant that the bishops were among the chief supporters of the throne. He was no Puritan, but he was Calvinist (see page 470) in doctrine. Yet James and his son Charles I both gave the impression of being sympathetic to Roman Catholicism. Charles supported the policies of William Laud (1573–1645), archbishop of Canterbury, who tried to impose elaborate ritual and rich ceremonials on all churches. Laud insisted on complete uniformity of church services and enforced that uniformity through an ecclesiastical court called the "Court of High Commission." People believed the country was being led back to Roman Catholicism. In 1637 Laud attempted to impose two new elements on church organization in Scotland: a new prayer book, modeled on the Anglican *Book of Common Prayer,* and bishoprics, which the Presbyterian Scots firmly rejected. The Scots therefore revolted. To finance an army to put down the Scots, King Charles was compelled to summon Parliament in November 1640.

Charles I was an intelligent man, but contemporaries found him deceitful, dishonest, and treacherous, and they did not trust him. After quarreling with Parliament over his right to collect customs duties on wine (tonnage) and wool (poundage), and over what the Commons perceived as religious innovations, Charles dissolved Parliament in 1629. From 1629 to 1640, he ruled without Parliament, financing his government through extraordinary stopgap levies considered illegal by most English people. For example, the king revived a medieval law requiring coastal districts to help pay the cost of ships for defense, but he levied the tax, called "ship money," on inland as well as coastal counties. When the issue was tested in the courts, the judges, having been suborned, decided in the king's favor.

Most members of Parliament believed that such taxation without consent amounted to arbitrary and absolute despotism. Consequently, they were not willing to trust the king with an army. Accordingly, this Parliament, called the "Long Parliament" because it sat from 1640 to 1660, proceeded to enact legislation that limited the power of the monarch and made arbitrary government impossible.

In 1641 the Commons passed the Triennial Act, which compelled the king to summon Parliament every three

**Puritan Occupations** These twelve engravings depict typical Puritan occupations and show that the Puritans came primarily from the artisan and lower middle classes. The governing classes and peasants adhered to the traditions of the Church of England.

years. The Commons impeached Archbishop Laud and abolished the Court of High Commission. It went further and threatened to abolish the institution of episcopacy. King Charles, fearful of a Scottish invasion—the original reason for summoning Parliament—accepted these measures. Understanding and peace were not achieved, however, partly because radical members of the Commons pushed increasingly revolutionary propositions, partly because Charles maneuvered to rescind those he had already approved. An uprising in Ireland precipitated civil war.

Ever since Henry II had conquered Ireland in 1171, English governors had mercilessly ruled the land, and English landlords had ruthlessly exploited the Irish people. The English Reformation had made a bad situation worse: because the Irish remained Catholic, religious differences became united with economic and political oppression. Without an army, Charles I could neither come to terms with the Scots nor put down the Irish rebellion, and the Long Parliament remained unwilling to place an army under a king it did not trust. Charles thus instigated military action against parliamentary forces. He recruited an army drawn from the nobility and its cavalry staff, the rural gentry, and mercenaries. The parliamentary army was composed of the militia of the city of London, country squires with business connections, and men with a firm belief in the spiritual duty of serving.

The English civil war (1642–1649) tested whether sovereignty in England was to reside in the king or in Parliament. The civil war did not resolve that problem, however, although it ended in 1649 with the execution of King Charles on the charge of high treason—a severe blow to the theory of divine-right monarchy. The period between 1649 and 1660, called the "Interregnum" because it separated two monarchical periods, witnessed England's solitary experience of military dictatorship.

## Puritanical Absolutism in England: Cromwell and the Protectorate

The problem of sovereignty was vigorously debated in the middle years of the seventeenth century. In *Leviathan,* English philosopher and political theorist Thomas Hobbes (1588–1679) maintains that sovereignty is ultimately derived from the people, who transfer it to the monarchy by implicit contract. The power of the ruler is absolute, but kings do not hold their power by divine right. This view pleased no one.

When Charles I was beheaded on January 30, 1649, the kingship was abolished. A *commonwealth,* or **republican government,** was proclaimed. Theoretically, legislative power rested in the surviving members of Parliament, and executive power was lodged in a council of state. In fact, the army that had defeated the royal forces controlled the government, and Oliver Cromwell controlled the army. Though called the "Protectorate," the rule of Cromwell (1653–1658) constituted military dictatorship.

The army had prepared a constitution, the Instrument of Government (1653), that invested executive power in a lord protector (Cromwell) and a council of state. The instrument provided for triennial parliaments and gave Parliament the sole power to raise taxes. But after repeated disputes, Cromwell tore the document up. He continued the standing army and proclaimed quasi-martial law. He divided England into twelve military districts, each governed by a major general. The major generals acted through the justices of the peace though sometimes overrode them. On the issue of religion, Cromwell favored toleration, and the Instrument of Government gave all Christians, except Roman Catholics, the right to practice their faith. Toleration meant state protection of many different Protestant sects, however, and most English people had no enthusiasm for such a notion; the idea was far ahead of its time. As for Irish Catholicism, Cromwell identified it with sedition. In 1649 he crushed a rebellion at Drogheda in Ireland with merciless savagery, leaving a

**Cartoon of 1649: "The Royall Oake of Brittayne"** Chopping down this tree signifies the end of royal authority, stability, Magna Carta (see page 344), and the rule of law. As pigs graze (representing the unconcerned common people), being fattened for slaughter, Oliver Cromwell, with his feet in Hell, quotes Scripture. This is a royalist view of the collapse of Charles I's government and the rule of Cromwell. *(Courtesy of the Trustees of the British Museum)*

legacy of Irish hatred for England that has not yet subsided. The state rigorously censored the press, forbade sports, and kept the theaters closed in England.

Cromwell's regulation of the nation's economy had features typical of seventeenth-century absolutism. The lord protector's policies were mercantilist, similar to those Colbert established in France. Cromwell enforced a Navigation Act (1651) requiring that English goods be transported on English ships. The navigation act was a great boost to the development of an English merchant marine and brought about a short but successful war with the commercially threatened Dutch. Cromwell also welcomed the immigration of Jews because of their skills, and they began to return to England after four centuries of absence.

Military government collapsed when Cromwell died in 1658. Fed up with military rule, the English longed for a return to civilian government, restoration of the common law, and social stability. Moreover, the strain of creating a community of puritanical saints proved too psychologically exhausting. Government by military dictatorship was an unfortunate experiment that the English never forgot or repeated. By 1660 they were ready to restore the monarchy.

## The Restoration of the English Monarchy

The Restoration of 1660 re-established the monarchy in the person of Charles II (r. 1660–1685), eldest son of Charles I. At the same time, both houses of Parliament were restored, together with the established Anglican church, the courts of law, and the system of local government through justices of the peace. The Restoration failed to resolve two serious problems, however. What was to be the attitude of the state toward Puritans, Catholics, and dissenters from the established church? And what was to be the constitutional position of the king—that is, what was to be the relationship between the king and Parliament?

About the first of these issues, Charles II, a relaxed, easygoing, and sensual man, was basically indifferent. He was not interested in doctrinal issues. Members of Parliament were, and they enacted a body of laws that sought to compel religious uniformity. Those who refused to receive the Eucharist of the Church of England could not vote, hold public office, preach, teach, attend the universities, or even assemble for meetings, according to the Test Act of 1673. But these restrictions could not be enforced. When the Quaker William Penn held a meeting of his Friends and was arrested, the jury refused to convict him.

In politics Charles II was determined "not to set out in his travels again," which meant that he intended to get along with Parliament. Charles II's solution to the problem of the relationship between the king and the House of Commons had profound importance for later constitutional development. Generally good rapport existed between the king and the strongly royalist Parliament that had restored him. This rapport was due largely to the king's appointment of a council of five men who served both as his major advisers and as members of Parliament, thus acting as liaison agents between the executive and the legislature. This body—known as the "Cabal" from the names of its five members (Clifford, Arlington, Buckingham, Ashley-Cooper, and Lauderdale)—was an ancestor of the later cabinet system (see page 555). Although its members sometimes disagreed and intrigued among themselves, it gradually came to be accepted that the Cabal was answerable in Parliament for the decisions of the king. This development gave rise to the concept of ministerial responsibility: royal ministers must answer to the Commons.

Harmony between the Crown and Parliament rested on the understanding that Charles would summon frequent parliaments and that Parliament would vote him sufficient revenues. But Parliament did not grant him an adequate income. Accordingly, in 1670 Charles entered into a secret agreement with Louis XIV. The French king would give Charles 200,000 pounds annually, and in return Charles would relax the laws against Catholics, gradually re-Catholicize England, support French policy against the Dutch, and convert to Catholicism himself.

When the details of this secret treaty leaked out, a great wave of anti-Catholic fear swept England. This fear was compounded by a crucial fact: although Charles had produced several bastards, he had no legitimate children. It therefore appeared that his brother and heir, James, duke of York, who had publicly acknowledged his Catholicism, would inaugurate a Catholic dynasty. A combination of hatred for the French absolutism embodied in Louis XIV, hostility to Roman Catholicism, and fear of a permanent Catholic dynasty produced virtual hysteria. The Commons passed an exclusion bill denying the succession to a Roman Catholic, but Charles quickly dissolved Parliament, and the bill never became law.

James II (r. 1685–1688) did succeed his brother. Almost at once the worst English anti-Catholic fears, already aroused by Louis XIV's revocation of the Edict of Nantes, were realized. In direct violation of the Test Act, James appointed Roman Catholics to positions in the army, the universities, and local government. When these actions were tested in the courts, the judges, whom James had appointed, decided for the king. The king was suspending the law at will and appeared to be reviving the absolutism of his father and grandfather. He went further. Attempting to broaden his base of support with Protestant dissenters and nonconformists, James issued a declaration of indulgence granting religious freedom to all.

Two events gave the signals for revolution. First, seven bishops of the Church of England petitioned the king that they not be forced to read the declaration of indulgence because of their belief that it was an illegal act. They were imprisoned in the Tower of London but subsequently acquitted amid great public enthusiasm. Second, in June 1688 James's second wife produced a male heir. A Catholic dynasty seemed ensured. The fear of a Roman Catholic monarchy supported by France and ruling outside the law prompted a group of eminent persons to offer the English throne to James's Protestant daughter, Mary, and her Dutch husband, Prince William of Orange. In December 1688 James II, his queen, and their infant son fled to France and became pensioners of Louis XIV. Early in 1689, William and Mary were crowned king and queen of England.

## The Triumph of England's Parliament: Constitutional Monarchy and Cabinet Government

The English call the events of 1688 to 1689 the "Glorious Revolution." The revolution was indeed glorious in the sense that it replaced one king with another with a minimum of bloodshed. It also represented the destruction, once and for all, of the idea of divine-right monarchy. William and Mary accepted the English throne from Parliament and in so doing explicitly recognized the supremacy of Parliament. The revolution of 1688 established the principle that sovereignty, the ultimate power in the state, was divided between king and Parliament and that the king ruled with the consent of the governed.

The men who brought about the revolution quickly framed their intentions in the Bill of Rights, the cornerstone of the modern British constitution. The basic

**Jan Vermeer: The Geographer (1668)** Vermeer is best known today for his quiet, contemplative scenes of women. The central figure here—surrounded by charts, maps, and atlases, and holding a pair of dividers—conveys the energetic curiosity of the Age of Discovery. *(Stadelsches Kunstinstitut, Frankfurt/akg-images)*

principles of the Bill of Rights were formulated in direct response to Stuart absolutism. Law was to be made in Parliament; once made, it could not be suspended by the Crown. Parliament had to be called at least every three years. Both elections to and debate in Parliament were to be free in the sense that the Crown was not to interfere in them (this aspect of the bill was widely disregarded in the eighteenth century). Judges would hold their offices "during good behavior," a provision that ensured the independence of the judiciary. No longer could the Crown get the judicial decisions it wanted by threats of removal. There was to be no standing army in peacetime—a limitation designed to prevent the repetition of Cromwellian military government. The Bill of Rights granted "that the subjects which are Protestants may have arms for their defense suitable to their conditions and as allowed by law,"[30] meaning that Catholics could not possess firearms because the Protestant majority feared them. Additional legislation granted freedom of worship to Protestant dissenters and nonconformists and required that the English monarch always be Protestant.

The Glorious Revolution found its best defense in political philosopher John Locke's ***Second Treatise of Civil Government*** (1690). Locke (1632–1704) maintained that people set up civil governments to protect life, liberty, and property. A government that oversteps its proper function—protecting the natural rights of life, liberty, and property—becomes a tyranny. (By "natural" rights, Locke meant rights basic to all men because all have the ability to reason.) Under a tyrannical government, the people have the natural right to rebellion. Such rebellion can be avoided if the government carefully respects the rights of citizens and if people zealously defend their liberty. Recognizing the close relationship between economic and political freedom, Locke linked economic liberty and private property with political freedom; his defense of property included a justification for a narrow franchise. Locke served as the great spokesman for the liberal English revolution of 1688 to 1689 and for representative government. His idea that there are natural or universal rights equally valid for all peoples and societies was especially popular in colonial America.

The events of 1688 to 1689 did not constitute a *democratic* revolution. The revolution placed sovereignty in Parliament, and Parliament represented the upper classes. The great majority of English people acquired no say in their government. The English revolution established a constitutional monarchy; it also inaugurated an age of aristocratic government, which lasted at least until 1832 and in many ways until 1928, when women received full voting rights.

In the course of the eighteenth century, the **cabinet system** of government evolved. The term *cabinet* derives from the small private room in which English rulers consulted their chief ministers. In a cabinet system, the leading ministers, who must have seats in and the support of a majority of the House of Commons, formulate common policy and conduct the business of the country. During the administration of one royal minister, Sir Robert Walpole, who led the cabinet from 1721 to 1742, the idea developed that the cabinet was responsible to the House of Commons. The Hanoverian king George I (r. 1714–1727) normally presided at cabinet meetings throughout his reign, but his son and heir, George II (r. 1727–1760), discontinued the practice. The influence of the Crown in decision making accordingly declined. Walpole enjoyed the favor of the monarchy and of the House of Commons and came to be called the king's first, or "prime," minister. In the English cabinet system, both legislative power and executive power are held by the leading ministers, who form the Government.

## The Dutch Republic in the Seventeenth Century

In the late sixteenth century, the seven northern provinces of the Netherlands fought for and won their independence from Spain as the Republic of United Provinces of the Netherlands—an independence that was confirmed by the Peace of Westphalia ending the Thirty Years' War in 1648 (see pages 498–499). The seventeenth century witnessed an unparalleled flowering of Dutch scientific, artistic, and literary achievement. In this period, often called the "golden age of the Netherlands," Dutch ideas and attitudes played a profound role in shaping a new and modern world-view. At the same time, the United Provinces was another model of the development of the modern constitutional state.

**Jan Steen: The Christening Feast** As the mother, surrounded by midwives, rests in bed (*rear left*) and the father proudly displays the swaddled child, thirteen other people, united by gestures and gazes, prepare the celebratory meal. Very prolific, Steen was a master of warm-hearted domestic scenes. In contrast to the order and cleanliness of many seventeenth-century Dutch genre paintings, Steen's more disorderly portrayals gave rise to the epithet "a Jan Steen household," meaning an untidy house. *(Wallace Collection, London/ The Bridgeman Art Library)*

**Room from Het Scheepje (The Little Ship)** A retired sea captain who became a successful brewer in Haarlem owned the house (adjacent to his brewery) that included this room. The brass chandelier, plates, tiles, Turkish rug on the table (probably from Transylvania in the Ottoman Empire), oak mantelpiece, and paneling make this a superb example of a Dutch domestic interior during the Golden Age. A bed, built into the wall paneling, was warmed at night by coals in the pan hanging by the fireplace. *(Room from Het Scheepje, Haarlem, The Netherlands, early 17th century. Philadelphia Museum of Art, Gift of Edward W. Bok. 1928-66-1)*

Within each province, an oligarchy of wealthy merchants called "regents" handled domestic affairs in the local Estates. The provincial Estates held virtually all the power. A federal assembly, or **States General,** handled matters of foreign affairs, such as war. But the States General did not possess sovereign authority since all issues had to be referred back to the local Estates for approval. The States General appointed a representative, the **stadholder,** in each province. As the highest executive there, the stadholder carried out ceremonial functions and was responsible for defense and good order. The sons of William the Silent, Maurice and William Louis, held the office of stadholder in all seven provinces. As members of the House of Orange, they were closely identified with Dutch patriotism. The regents in each province jealously guarded local independence and resisted efforts at centralization. Nevertheless, Holland, which had the largest navy and the most wealth, dominated the republic and the States General. Significantly, the Estates assembled at Holland's capital, The Hague.

The government of the United Provinces fit none of the standard categories of seventeenth-century political organization. The Dutch were not monarchical but fiercely republican. The government was controlled by wealthy merchants and financiers. Though rich, their values were not aristocratic but strongly middle-class. The Dutch republic was not a strong federation but a confederation—that is, a weak union of strong provinces. The provinces were a temptation to powerful neighbors, yet the Dutch resisted the long Spanish effort at reconquest and withstood both French and English attacks in the second half of the century.

The political success of the Dutch rested on the phenomenal commercial prosperity of the Netherlands. The moral and ethical bases of that commercial wealth were thrift, frugality, and religious toleration. John Calvin had written, "From where do the merchant's profits come except from his own diligence and industry?" This attitude encouraged a sturdy people who had waged a centuries-old struggle against the sea.

Alone of all European peoples in the seventeenth century, the Dutch practiced religious toleration. Peoples of all faiths were welcome within their borders. Although there is scattered evidence of anti-Semitism, Jews enjoyed a level of acceptance and assimilation in Dutch business and general culture unique in early modern Europe. (See the feature "Individuals in Society: Glückel of Hameln.") For example, Benedict Spinoza (1632–1677), a descendant of Spanish Jews who fled the Inquisition, passed his entire life in Amsterdam, supporting himself as a lens grinder while producing important philosophical treatises. The urbanity of Dutch society allowed a rare degree of religious

# Individuals in Society

## Glückel of Hameln

In 1690 a Jewish widow in the small German town of Hameln* in Lower Saxony sat down to write her autobiography. She wanted to distract her mind from the terrible grief she felt over the death of her husband and to provide her twelve children with a record "so you will know from what sort of people you have sprung, lest today or tomorrow your beloved children or grand-children came and know naught of their family." Out of her pain and heightened consciousness, Glückel (1646–1724) produced an invaluable source for scholars.

She was born in Hamburg two years before the end of the Thirty Years' War. In 1649 the merchants of Hamburg expelled the Jews, who moved to nearby Altona, then under Danish rule. When the Swedes overran Altona in 1657–1658, the Jews returned to Hamburg "purely at the mercy of the Town Council." Glückel's narrative proceeds against a background of the constant difficulties (harassment) to which Jews were subjected—special papers, permits, bribes—and in Hameln she wrote, "And so it has been to this day and, I fear, will continue in like fashion."

When Glückel was "barely twelve," her father betrothed her to Chayim Hameln. She married at age fourteen. She describes him as "the perfect pattern of the pious Jew," a man who stopped his work every day for study and prayer, fasted, and was scrupulously honest in his business dealings. Only a few years older than Glückel, Chayim earned his living dealing in precious metals and in making small loans on pledges (articles held on security). This work required his constant travel to larger cities, markets, and fairs, often in bad weather, always over dangerous roads. Chayim consulted his wife about all his business dealings. As he lay dying, a friend asked if he had any last wishes. "None," he replied. "My wife knows everything. She shall do as she has always done." For thirty years, Glückel had been his friend, full business partner, and wife. They had thirteen children, twelve of whom survived their father, eight then unmarried. As Chayim had foretold, Glückel succeeded in launching the boys in careers and in providing dowries for the girls.

Glückel's world was her family, the Jewish community of Hameln, and the Jewish communities into which her children married. Social and business activities took her to Amsterdam, Baiersdorf, Bamberg, Berlin, Cleves, Danzig, Metz, and Vienna, so her world was not a narrow or provincial one. She took great pride that Prince Frederick of Cleves, later king of Prussia, danced at the wedding of her eldest daughter. The rising prosperity of Chayim's businesses allowed the couple to maintain up to six servants. Jews, however, lived on the margins of Christian society, and traditional sociological categories cannot be applied to them.

*Gentleness and deep mutual devotion seem to pervade Rembrandt's* The Jewish Bride. (Rijksmuseum-Stichting Amsterdam)

Glückel was deeply religious, and her culture was steeped in Jewish literature, legends, and mystical and secular works. Above all, she relied on the Bible. Her language, heavily sprinkled with scriptural references, testifies to a rare familiarity with the basic book of Western civilization. The Scriptures were her consolation, the source of her great strength in a hostile world.

Students who would learn about business practices, the importance of the dowry in marriage, childbirth, the ceremony of bris, birthrates, family celebrations, even the meaning of life can gain a good deal from the memoirs of this extraordinary woman, who was, in the words of one of her descendants, the poet Heinrich Heine, "the gift of a world to me."

### Questions for Analysis

1. Consider the ways in which Glückel of Hameln was an ordinary woman of her times.
2. How was Glückel's life affected by the broad events and issues of the seventeenth century?

*Town immortalized by the Brothers Grimm. In 1284 the town contracted with the Pied Piper to rid it of rats and mice; he lured them away by playing his flute. When the citizens refused to pay, he charmed away their children in revenge.

*Source: The Memoirs of Glückel of Hameln,* trans. M. Lowenthal (New York: Schocken Books, 1977).

*The* **history companion** *features additional information and activities related to this topic.*
**history.college.hmco.com/students**

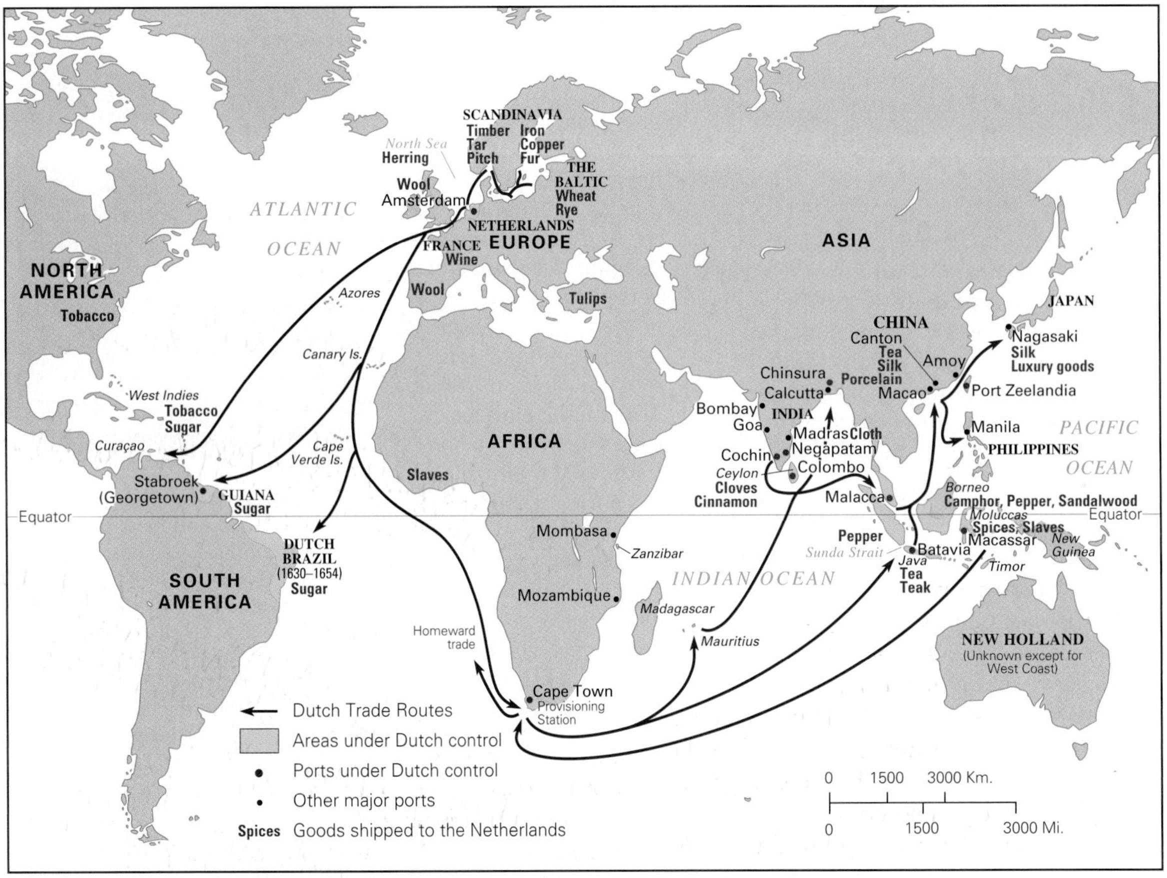


**MAP 16.3 Seventeenth-Century Dutch Commerce** Dutch wealth rested on commerce, and commerce depended on the huge Dutch merchant marine, manned by perhaps forty-eight thousand sailors. The fleet carried goods from all parts of the globe to the port of Amsterdam.

freedom. As long as business people conducted their religion in private, the government did not interfere with them.

In the Dutch Republic, toleration paid off: it attracted a great deal of foreign capital and investment. Deposits at the Bank of Amsterdam were guaranteed by the city council, and in the middle years of the century, the bank became Europe's best source of cheap credit and commercial intelligence and the main clearing-house for bills of exchange. People of all races and creeds traded in Amsterdam, at whose docks on the Amstel River five thousand ships were berthed. Joost van den Vondel, the poet of Dutch imperialism, exulted:

*God, God, the Lord of Amstel cried, hold every conscience free;*
*And Liberty ride, on Holland's tide, with billowing sails to sea,*
*And run our Amstel out and in; let freedom gird the bold,*
*And merchant in his counting house stand elbow deep in gold.*[31]

The fishing industry was the cornerstone of the Dutch economy. For half the year, from June to December, fishing fleets combed the dangerous English coast and the North Sea and raked in tiny herring. Profits from herring stimulated shipbuilding, and even before 1600 the Dutch were offering the lowest shipping rates in Europe. The Dutch merchant marine was the largest in Europe. In 1650 contemporaries estimated that the Dutch had sixteen thousand merchant ships, half the European total. All the wood for these ships had to be imported: the Dutch bought whole forests from Norway. They also bought entire vineyards from French growers before the grapes were harvested. They controlled the Baltic grain trade, buying entire wheat and rye crops in Poland, east

Prussia, and Swedish Pomerania. Because the Dutch dealt in bulk, nobody could undersell them. Foreign merchants coming to Amsterdam could buy anything from precision lenses for the microscope (recently invented by Dutchman Anton van Leeuwenhoek) to muskets for an army of five thousand. Although Dutch cities became famous for their exports—diamonds and linens from Haarlem, pottery from Delft—Dutch wealth depended less on exports than on transport.

In 1602 a group of the regents of Holland formed the **Dutch East India Company,** a joint stock company. The investors each received a percentage of the profits proportional to the amount of money they had put in. Within half a century, the Dutch East India Company had cut heavily into Portuguese trading in East Asia. The Dutch seized the Cape of Good Hope, Ceylon, and Malacca and established trading posts in each place. In the 1630s, the Dutch East India Company was paying its investors about a 35 percent annual return on their investments. The Dutch West India Company, founded in 1621, traded extensively with Latin America and Africa (see Map 16.3).

Trade and commerce brought the Dutch prodigious wealth. In the seventeenth century, the Dutch enjoyed the highest standard of living in Europe, perhaps in the world. Amsterdam and Rotterdam built massive granaries where the surplus of one year could be stored against possible shortages the next. Thus, excepting the 1650s, when bad harvests reduced supplies, food prices fluctuated very little. By the standards of Cologne, Paris, or London, salaries were high for all workers—except women, but even women's wages were high when compared with those of women in other parts of Europe. All classes of society, including unskilled laborers, ate well. The low price of bread meant that, compared to other places in Europe, a higher percentage of the worker's income could be spent on fish, cheese, butter, vegetables, even meat. A scholar has described the Netherlands as "an island of plenty in a sea of want." Consequently, the Netherlands experienced very few of the food riots that characterized the rest of Europe.[32]

Although the initial purpose of the Dutch East and West India Companies was commercial—the import of spices and silks to Europe—the Dutch found themselves involved in the imperialist exploitation of parts of East Asia and Latin America, with great success. In 1652 the Dutch founded Cape Town on the southern tip of Africa as a fueling station for ships planning to cross the Pacific. But war with France and England in the 1670s hurt the United Provinces. The long War of the Spanish Succession—in which the Dutch prince William of Orange utilized, as King William III of England, English wealth in the Dutch fight against Louis XIV—was a costly drain on Dutch labor and financial resources. The peace signed in 1713 to end the war marked the beginning of Dutch economic decline.

## Summary

According to Thomas Hobbes, the central drive in every human is "a perpetual and restless desire of Power, after Power, that ceaseth only in Death." The seventeenth century solved the problem of sovereign power in two fundamental ways: absolutism and constitutionalism. The France of Louis XIV witnessed the emergence of the fully absolutist state. The king commanded all the powers of the state: judicial, military, political, and, to a great extent, ecclesiastical. France developed a centralized bureaucracy, a professional army, and a state-directed economy, all of which Louis personally supervised. For the first time in history, all the institutions and powers of the national state were effectively controlled by a single person. The king saw himself as the representative of God on earth, and it has been said that "to the seventeenth century imagination God was a sort of image of Louis XIV."[33]

As Louis XIV personifies absolutism, so Stuart England exemplifies the evolution of the first modern constitutional state. The conflicts between Parliament and the first two Stuart rulers, James I and Charles I, tested where sovereign power would rest in the state. The resulting civil war did not solve the problem. The Instrument of Government provided for a balance of government authority and recognition of popular rights; as such, the Instrument has been called the first modern constitution. Unfortunately, it lacked public support. James II's absolutist tendencies brought on the Glorious Revolution of 1688 to 1689, and the people who made that revolution settled three basic issues. Sovereign power was divided between king and Parliament, with Parliament enjoying the greater share. Government was to be based on the rule of law. And the liberties of English people were made explicit in written form in the Bill of Rights.

The models of governmental power established by seventeenth-century England and France strongly influenced other states then and ever since. As American novelist William Faulkner wrote, "The past isn't dead; it's not even past."

## Key Terms

sovereignty
absolutism
totalitarianism
raison d'état
Fronde
mercantilism
French classicism
Peace of Utrecht

*Don Quixote*
constitutionalism
Puritans
republican government
*Second Treatise of Civil Government*
cabinet system
States General
stadholder
Dutch East India Company

## Notes


1. G. Parker and L. M. Smith, "Introduction," and N. Steensgaard, "The Seventeenth Century Crisis," in *The General Crisis of the Seventeenth Century,* ed. G. Parker and L. M. Smith (London: Routledge & Kegan Paul, 1985), pp. 1–53, esp. p. 12.
2. See W. Beik, *Urban Protest in Seventeenth-Century France: The Culture of Retribution* (New York: Cambridge University Press, 1997), p. 1.
3. See J. Bergin, *Cardinal Richelieu: Power and the Pursuit of Wealth* (New Haven, Conn.: Yale University Press, 1985), which describes how Richelieu made his vast wealth through his royal and ecclesiastical offices.
4. J. B. Collins, *The State in Early Modern France* (Cambridge: Cambridge University Press, 1995), p. 1.
5. Ibid., p. 3.
6. Ibid., pp. 22–26.
7. See M. Turchetti, "The Edict of Nantes," in *The Oxford Encyclopedia of the Reformation,* ed. H. J. Hillerbrand, vol. 3 (New York: Oxford University Press, 1996), pp. 126–128.
8. See Beik, *Urban Protest,* chaps. 1, 2, 3, and 11.
9. J. B. Collins, *Fiscal Limits of Absolutism: Direct Taxation in Early Seventeenth-Century France* (Berkeley: University of California Press, 1988), pp. 1, 3–4, 215–222.
10. Quoted in J. H. Elliott, *Richelieu and Olivares* (Cambridge: Cambridge University Press, 1984), p. 135; and in W. F. Church, *Richelieu and Reason of State* (Princeton, N.J.: Princeton University Press, 1972), p. 507.
11. D. Parker, *The Making of French Absolutism* (New York: St. Martin's Press, 1983), pp. 146–148.
12. Collins, *The State in Early Modern France,* pp. 65–78.
13. See W. Beik, *Absolutism and Society in Seventeenth-Century France: State Power and Provincial Aristocracy in Languedoc* (Cambridge: Cambridge University Press, 1985), pp. 279–302.
14. S. de Gramont, ed., *The Age of Magnificence: Memoirs of the Court of Louis XIV by the Duc de Saint Simon* (New York: Capricorn Books, 1964), pp. 141–145.
15. Quoted in J. Wolf, *Louis XIV* (New York: W. W. Norton, 1968), p. 146.
16. See J. Swann, *Provincial Power and Absolute Monarchy: The Estates General of Burgundy, 1661–1790* (New York: Cambridge University Press, 2003), pp. 154–162.
17. Quoted in A. Trout, *Jean-Baptiste Colbert* (Boston: Twayne, 1978), p. 128.
18. Quoted in Wolf, *Louis XIV,* p. 394.
19. Ibid.
20. See W. C. Scoville, *The Persecution of the Huguenots and French Economic Development: 1680–1720* (Berkeley: University of California Press, 1960).
21. F. Bluche, *Louis XIV,* trans. M. Greengrass (Oxford: Basil Blackwell, 1990), p. 607.
22. Ibid., p. 458.
23. Quoted ibid., p. 519.
24. W. F. Church, *Louis XIV in Historical Thought: From Voltaire to the Annales School* (New York: W. W. Norton, 1976), p. 92.
25. Quoted in Gramont, *The Age of Magnificence,* p. 183.
26. J. H. Elliott, *Imperial Spain, 1469–1716* (New York: Mentor Books, 1963), pp. 306–308.
27. B. Bennassar, *The Spanish Character: Attitudes and Mentalities from the Sixteenth to the Nineteenth Century,* trans. B. Keen (Berkeley: University of California Press, 1979), p. 125.
28. For a revisionist interpretation, see J. Wormald, "James VI and I: Two Kings or One?" *History* 62 (June 1983): 187–209.
29. See J. P. Sommerville's review of J. Cramsie, "Kingship and Crown Finance Under James VI and I, 1603–1625," *The American Historical Review* 109 (April 2004): 607–608.
30. C. Stephenson and G. F. Marcham, *Sources of English Constitutional History* (New York: Harper & Row, 1937), p. 601.
31. Quoted in D. Maland, *Europe in the Seventeenth Century* (New York: Macmillan, 1967), pp. 198–199.
32. S. Schama, *The Embarrassment of Riches: An Interpretation of Dutch Culture in the Golden Age* (New York: Alfred A. Knopf, 1987), pp. 165–170; quotation is on p. 167.
33. C. J. Friedrich and C. Blitzer, *The Age of Power* (Ithaca, N.Y.: Cornell University Press, 1957), p. 112.


## Suggested Reading

Students who wish to explore the problems presented in this chapter in greater depth will easily find a rich and exciting literature. The following surveys all provide good background material: H. Kamen, *The Iron Century: Social Change in Europe, 1550–1660* (1971); G. Parker, *Europe in Crisis, 1598–1618* (1980), a sound introduction to the social, economic, and religious tensions of the period; and R. S. Dunn, *The Age of Religious Wars, 1559–1715* (1979), which examines the period from the perspective of the confessional strife between Protestants and Catholics but contains material on absolutism and constitutionalism.

For the period of Louis XIII, Richelieu, and the Fronde, see L. Moote, *Louis XIII: The Just* (1989), an important biography; J. Bergin, *Richelieu: Power and the Pursuit of Wealth* (1989), a detailed study of how Richelieu used his various offices to acquire great wealth for himself and his family; and O. Ranum, *The Fronde* (1994), probably the best work in English on the Fronde. Two important studies of French local administration are J. B. Collins, *Classes, Estates, and Order in Early Modern Brittany* (1994), and R. Schneider, *Public Life in Toulouse, 1463–1789* (1989). K. Norberg, *Rich and Poor in Grenoble, 1600–1815* (1985), provides an interesting case study of the wretched conditions of the poor, while W. Beik, *Urban Protest in Seventeenth-Century France* (1997), explores the cultural significance of the widespread incidence of urban violence.

For the relationship between the army, finances, and state power, see J. B. Wood, *The King's Army: Warfare, Soldiers, and Society During the Wars of Religion in France, 1562–1576* (1996); J. Lynn, *Giant of the Grand Siècle: The French Army, 1610–1715* (1997); D. Parrott, *Richelieu's Army: War, Government and Society in France, 1624–1642* (2001); and G.

Rowlands, *The Dynastic State and the Army Under Louis XIV: Royal Service and Private Interest, 1661–1701* (2002).

The important work of P. K. Monod, *The Power of Kings: Monarchy and Religion in Europe, 1589–1715* (1999), provides a broad comparative study of the changes in monarchical authority and power and of the shift from medieval ideas of sacred kingship to "modern" ideas of the rational state.

Louis XIV and his age have predictably attracted the attention of many scholars. Bluche, although hagiographical, is an almost definitive study, and Wolf remains valuable; both are cited in the Notes. The excellent work of P. Burke, *The Fabrication of Louis XIV* (1992), explores the images or representations of the king in stone, bronze, paint, plays, operas, and rituals. For the court of Louis XIV, see also K. A. Hoffmann, *Society of Pleasures: Interdisciplinary Readings in Pleasure and Power During the Reign of Louis XIV* (1997), a sophisticated study of the uses of pleasure as a political tool; R. Chartier, *The Cultural Origins of the French Revolution* (1991); and J. F. Solnon, *La Cour de France* (1987). For Louis XIV's foreign policy and wars, see P. Sonnino, *Louis XIV and the Origins of the Dutch Wars* (1988), and H. Kamen, *The War of Succession in Spain, 1700–1715* (1969). R. Hatton, *Europe in the Age of Louis XIV* (1979), is a well-illustrated survey of many aspects of seventeenth-century European culture. O. Ranum, *Paris in the Age of Absolutism* (1968), describes the geographical, political, economic, and architectural significance of the cultural capital of Europe.

For Spain and Portugal, in addition to the works in the Notes, see H. Kamen, *Spain in the Later Seventeenth Century, 1665–1700* (1980); M. Defourneaux, *Daily Life in Spain in the Golden Age* (1976), highly useful for an understanding of ordinary people and of Spanish society; and C. R. Phillips, *Ciudad Real, 1500–1750: Growth, Crisis, and Readjustment in the Spanish Economy* (1979), a significant case study. A. Pagden, *Spanish Imperialism and the Political Imagination* (1990), explores Spanish ideas of empire, primarily in Italy and the Americas, and shows that the failure to revise ideas to meet changing circumstances led to the empire's decline.

The following works offer solid material on English political and social issues of the seventeenth century: J. P. Kenyon, *Stuart England* (1978), and K. Wrightson, *English Society, 1580–1680* (1982). Perhaps the most comprehensive treatments of Parliament are C. Russell, *Crisis of Parliaments, 1509–1660* (1971), and *Parliaments and English Politics, 1621–1629* (1979). On the background of the English civil war, L. Stone's *The Crisis of the Aristocracy* (1965) and *The Causes of the English Revolution* (1972) are standard works; both B. Manning, *The English People and the English Revolution* (1976), and D. Underdown, *Revel, Riot, and Rebellion* (1985), discuss the extent of popular involvement. For English intellectual currents, see J. O. Appleby, *Economic Thought and Ideology in Seventeenth-Century England* (1978). M. J. Braddick, *The Nerves of State: Taxation and the Financing of the English State, 1558–1714* (1996), surveys the evolution of parliamentary taxation as the means of financing state expenses, especially military ones. S. Porter, ed., *London and the Civil War* (1996), treats the city's choice of allegiance and contribution to the war effort.

C. Durston and J. Eales, eds., *The Culture of English Puritanism, 1560–1700* (1996), provides a revisionist definition of the term *Puritan* and explores topics such as Sabbatarianism and iconoclasm.

The excellent achievement of A. Woolrych, *Britain in Revolution, 1625–1660* (rev. ed. 2004), explores Scottish and Irish dynamics in the period in a lucid narrative.

For women, see R. Thompson, *Women in Stuart England and America* (1974), and A. Fraser, *The Weaker Vessel* (1985). For Cromwell and the Interregnum, see C. Firth, *Oliver Cromwell and the Rule of the Puritans in England* (1956); C. Hill, *God's Englishman* (1972); and A. Fraser, *Cromwell, the Lord Protector* (1973).

For the Restoration and the Glorious Revolution, see R. Hutton, *Charles II: King of England, Scotland and Ireland* (1989), and A. Fraser, *Royal Charles: Charles II and the Restoration* (1979), two highly readable biographies; R. Ollard, *The Image of the King: Charles I and Charles II* (1980), which examines the nature of monarchy; J. Miller, *James II: A Study in Kingship* (1977); J. Childs, *The Army, James II, and the Glorious Revolution* (1980); J. R. Jones, *The Revolution of 1688 in England* (1972); and L. G. Schwoerer, *The Declaration of Rights, 1689* (1981), a fine assessment of that fundamental document. For the continuation of an older system during the rise of the Whigs and Tories, see B. Hill, *The Early Parties and Politics in Britain, 1688–1832* (1996).

On Holland, the starting point for serious study is Schama, mentioned in the Notes, a brilliant and beautifully illustrated achievement. J. L. Price, *Culture and Society in the Dutch Republic During the Seventeenth Century* (1974), is a sound scholarly work. R. Boxer, *The Dutch Seaborne Empire* (1980), and the appropriate chapters of the Maland work cited in the Notes are useful for Dutch overseas expansion and the reasons for Dutch prosperity. The following works focus on the economic and cultural life of the leading Dutch city: V. Barbour, *Capitalism in Amsterdam in the Seventeenth Century* (1950), and D. Regin, *Traders, Artists, Burghers: A Cultural History of Amsterdam in the Seventeenth Century* (1977). J. M. Montias, *Artists and Artisans in Delft: A Socio-economic Study of the Seventeenth Century* (1982), examines another major city. The leading statesmen of the period may be studied in these biographies: H. H. Rowen, *John de Witt, Grand Pensionary of Holland, 1625–1672* (1978); S. B. Baxter, *William the III and the Defense of European Liberty, 1650–1702* (1966); and J. den Tex, *Oldenbarnevelt*, 2 vols. (1973).

Many facets of the lives of ordinary French, Spanish, English, and Dutch people are discussed in P. Burke, *Popular Culture in Early Modern Europe* (1978), a provocative study.

# Listening to the Past

## The Court at Versailles

*Although the Duc de Saint-Simon (1675–1755) was a soldier, courtier, and diplomat, his enduring reputation rests on his* Memoirs *(1788), an eyewitness account of the personality and court of Louis XIV. A nobleman of ancient lineage, Saint-Simon resented Louis's "domestication" of the nobility and his promotion of the bourgeoisie.* The Memoirs, *excerpted here, remains a monument of French literature and an indispensable historical source, partly for its portrait of the court at Versailles.*

Very early in the reign of Louis XIV the Court was removed from Paris, never to return. The troubles of the minority had given him a dislike to that city; his enforced and surreptitious flight from it still rankled in his memory; he did not consider himself safe there, and thought cabals would be more easily detected if the Court was in the country, where the movements and temporary absences of any of its members would be more easily noticed. . . . No doubt that he was also influenced by the feeling that he would be regarded with greater awe and veneration when no longer exposed every day to the gaze of the multitude.

His love-affair with Mademoiselle de la Vallière, which at first was covered as far as possible with a veil of mystery, was the cause of frequent excursions to Versailles. . . . The visits of Louis XIV becoming more frequent, he enlarged the *château* by degrees till its immense buildings afforded better accommodation for the Court than was to be found at St. Germain, where most of the courtiers had to put up with uncomfortable lodgings in the town. The Court was therefore removed to Versailles in 1682, not long before the Queen's death. The new building contained an infinite number of rooms for courtiers, and the King liked the grant of these rooms to be regarded as a coveted privilege.

He availed himself of the frequent festivities at Versailles, and his excursions to other places, as a means of making the courtiers assiduous in their attendance and anxious to please him; for he nominated beforehand those who were to take part in them, and could thus gratify some and inflict a snub on others. He was conscious that the substantial favours he had to bestow were not nearly sufficient to produce a continual effect; he had therefore to invent imaginary ones, and no one was so clever in devising petty distinctions and preferences which aroused jealousy and emulation. The visits to Marly later on were very useful to him in this way; also those to Trianon [Marly and Trianon were small country houses], where certain ladies, chosen beforehand, were admitted to his table. It was another distinction to hold his candlestick at his *coucher;* as soon as he had finished his prayers he used to name the courtier to whom it was to be handed, always choosing one of the highest rank among those present. . . .

Not only did he expect all persons of distinction to be in continual attendance at Court, but he was quick to notice the absence of those of inferior degree; at his *lever* [formal rising from bed in the morning], his *coucher* [preparations for going to bed], his meals, in the gardens of Versailles (the only place where the courtiers in general were allowed to follow him), he used to cast his eyes to right and left; nothing escaped him, he saw everybody. If any one habitually living at Court absented himself he insisted on knowing the reason; those who came there only for flying visits had also to give a satisfactory explanation; any one who seldom or never appeared there was certain to incur his displeasure. If asked to bestow a favour on such persons he would reply haughtily: "I do not know him";

of such as rarely presented themselves he would say, "He is a man I never see"; and from these judgements there was no appeal.

He always took great pains to find out what was going on in public places, in society, in private houses, even family secrets, and maintained an immense number of spies and tale-bearers. These were of all sorts; some did not know that their reports were carried to him; others did know it; there were others, again, who used to write to him directly, through channels which he prescribed; others who were admitted by the backstairs and saw him in his private room. Many a man in all ranks of life was ruined by these methods, often very unjustly, without ever being able to discover the reason; and when the King had once taken a prejudice against a man, he hardly ever got over it. . . .

No one understood better than Louis XIV the art of enhancing the value of a favour by his manner of bestowing it; he knew how to make the most of a word, a smile, even of a glance. If he addressed any one, were it but to ask a trifling question or make some commonplace remark, all eyes were turned on the person so honored; it was a mark of favour which always gave rise to comment. . . .

He loved splendour, magnificence, and profusion in all things, and encouraged similar tastes in his Court; to spend money freely on equipages [the king's horse carriages] and buildings, on feasting and at cards, was a sure way to gain his favour, perhaps to obtain the honour of a word from him. Motives of policy had something to do with this; by making expensive habits the fashion, and, for people in a certain position, a necessity, he compelled his courtiers to live beyond their income, and gradually reduced them to depend on his bounty for the means of subsistence. This was a plague which, once introduced, became a scourge to the whole country, for it did not take long to spread to Paris, and thence to the armies and the provinces; so that a man of any position is now estimated entirely according to his expenditure on his table and other luxuries. This folly, sustained by pride and ostentation, has already produced widespread confusion; it threatens to end in nothing short of ruin and a general overthrow.

Painting of Louis XIV by Mignard Pierre (1612–1695). *(Galleria Sabauda, Turin/Scala/Art Resource, NY)*

## Questions for Analysis

1. How would you define the French court? Why did Louis XIV move it to Versailles?
2. By what means did Louis control the nobility at Versailles? Why did he use those particular means?
3. Consider the role of ritual and ceremony in some modern governments, such as the U.S. government. How does it compare to Louis XIV's use of ceremony, as portrayed by Saint-Simon?
4. Saint-Simon faulted Louis for encouraging the nobles' extravagance. Is that a justifiable criticism?

*Source:* F. Arkwright, ed., *The Memoirs of the Duke de Saint-Simon,* vol. 5 (New York: Brentano's, n.d.), pp. 271–274, 276–278.

Peter the Great's magnificent new crown, created for his coronation in 1682 with his half-brother Ivan. *(State Museum of the Kremlin, Moscow)*

# chapter 17 Absolutism in Eastern Europe to 1740

**chapter outline**

- Lords and Peasants in Eastern Europe
- The Rise of Austria and Prussia
- The Development of Russia
- Absolutism and Baroque Architecture

The seventeenth century witnessed a struggle between constitutionalism and absolutism in eastern Europe, as it did in western Europe (see Chapter 16). But with the notable exception of the kingdom of Poland, monarchical absolutism was triumphant in eastern Europe; constitutionalism was decisively defeated. Absolute monarchies emerged in Austria, Prussia, and Russia. This development had significance for at least two reasons. First, these three monarchies exercised enormous influence until 1918, and they created an authoritarian tradition that lasted into the late twentieth century in eastern Europe. Second, the absolute monarchs of eastern Europe had a powerful impact on culture, encouraging a flowering of the baroque style in architecture and the arts.

Although the monarchs of eastern Europe were greatly impressed by Louis XIV and his model of royal absolutism, their states differed in several important ways from that of their French counterpart. Louis XIV built French absolutism on the foundation of a well-developed medieval monarchy and a strong royal bureaucracy. And when Louis XIV came to the throne, the powers of the nobility were already somewhat limited, the French middle class was relatively strong, and the peasants were generally free from serfdom. Eastern absolutism rested on a very different social reality: a powerful nobility, a weak middle class, and an oppressed peasantry composed of serfs.

These different conditions raise three questions:

- Why did the basic structure of society in eastern Europe move away from that of western Europe in the early modern period?
- How and why did the rulers of Austria, Prussia, and Russia, each in a different social environment, manage to build powerful absolute monarchies that proved more durable than that of Louis XIV?
- How did the absolute monarchs' interaction with artists and architects contribute to the splendid achievements of baroque culture?

These are the questions that this chapter will explore.

## Lords and Peasants in Eastern Europe

When absolute monarchy took shape in eastern Europe in the seventeenth century, it built on social and economic foundations laid between roughly 1400 and 1650. In those years, the princes and the landed nobility of eastern Europe—with the major exception of the Ottoman rulers in the Balkans—rolled back the gains made by the peasantry during the High Middle Ages and reimposed a harsh serfdom on the rural masses. The nobility also reduced the importance of the towns and the middle classes. This process differed profoundly from developments in western Europe, where peasants won greater freedom and the urban capitalistic middle class continued its rise.

### The Medieval Background

Between roughly 1400 and 1650, nobles and rulers re-established **serfdom** in the eastern lands of Bohemia, Silesia, Hungary, eastern Germany, Poland, Lithuania, and Russia. The east—the land east of the Elbe River in Germany, which historians often call "East Elbia"—gained a certain social and economic unity in the process. But eastern peasants lost their rights and freedoms. They became bound first to the land they worked and then, by degrading obligations, to the lords they served.

This development was a tragic reversal of trends in the High Middle Ages. The period from roughly 1050 to 1300 had been a time of general economic expansion characterized by the growth of trade, towns, and population. Expansion also meant clearing the forests and colonizing the frontier beyond the Elbe River. Anxious to attract German settlers to sparsely populated lands, the rulers and nobles of eastern Europe had offered potential newcomers economic and legal incentives. Large numbers of incoming settlers obtained land on excellent terms and gained much greater personal freedom. These benefits were also gradually extended to the local Slavic populations, even those of central Russia. Thus by 1300 a very general improvement in peasant conditions had occurred in eastern Europe; serfdom had all but disappeared. Peasants bargained freely with their landlords and moved about as they pleased. Opportunities and improvements east of the Elbe had a positive impact on western Europe, where the weight of serfdom was also reduced between 1100 and 1300. Thus fundamental social and economic developments moved in the same direction throughout Europe in the High Middle Ages, reinforcing a cultural and religious unity stretching all across Europe.

After about 1300, however, as Europe's population and economy both declined grievously, mainly because of the Black Death, the east and the west went in different directions. In both east and west, a many-sided landlord reaction occurred as lords sought to solve their tough economic problems by more heavily exploiting the peasantry. Yet this reaction generally failed in the west. In many western areas by 1500, almost all of the peasants were free, and in the rest of western Europe serf obligations had declined greatly. East of the Elbe, however, the landlords won. By 1500 eastern peasants were well on their way to becoming serfs again.

Throughout eastern Europe, as in western Europe, the drop in population and prices in the fourteenth and fifteenth centuries caused severe labor shortages and hard times for the nobles. Yet rather than offer better economic and legal terms to keep old peasants and attract new ones, eastern landlords used political and police power to turn the tables on peasants. They did this in two ways.

First, the lords made their kings and princes issue laws that restricted or eliminated the peasants' precious, time-honored right of free movement. Thus a peasant could no longer leave to take advantage of better opportunities elsewhere without the lord's permission, and the lord had no reason to make such concessions. In Prussian territories by 1500, the law required that runaway peasants be hunted down and returned to their lords; a runaway servant was to be nailed to a post by one ear and given a knife to cut himself loose. Until the middle of the fifteenth century, medieval Russian peasants had been free to move wherever they wished and seek the best landlord. Thereafter this freedom was gradually curtailed, so that by 1497 a Russian peasant had the right to move only during a two-week period after the fall harvest. Eastern peasants were losing their status as free and independent men and women.

Second, lords steadily took more and more of their peasants' land and imposed heavier and heavier labor obligations. Instead of being independent farmers paying reasonable, freely negotiated rents, peasants tended to become forced laborers on the lords' estates. By the early 1500s, lords in many territories could command their peasants to work for them without pay as many as six days a week.

The gradual erosion of the peasantry's economic position was bound up with manipulation of the legal system. The local lord was also the local prosecutor, judge, and jailer. As a matter of course, he ruled in his own favor in disputes with his peasants. There were no independent royal officials to provide justice or uphold the common law.

1400 1500 1600 1700 1800

POLITICAL/MILITARY

- 1462–1505 Reign of Ivan III in Russia
- 1533–1584 Reign of Ivan the Terrible in Russia
- 1620–1740 Growth of absolutism in Austria and Prussia
- 1640–1688 Reign of Frederick William in Prussia
- 1670–1671 Cossack revolt led by Razin
- 1683–1718 Habsburgs defend Vienna; win war with Ottoman Turks
- 1713–1740 Growth of Prussian military

SOCIAL/ECONOMIC

- ca 1400–1650 Re-emergence of serfdom in eastern Europe
- ca 1680–1750 Construction of baroque palaces
- 1702 Peter the Great founds St. Petersburg

INTELLECTUAL/RELIGIOUS

- 1620 Habsburgs crush Protestantism in Bohemia
- 1652 Nikon reforms Russian Orthodox church

## The Consolidation of Serfdom

Between 1500 and 1650, the social, legal, and economic conditions of peasants in eastern Europe continued to decline. Free peasants lost their freedom and became serfs. In Poland, for example, nobles gained complete control over their peasants in 1574, after which they could legally inflict the death penalty on their serfs whenever they wished. In Prussia in 1653, peasants were assumed to be tied to their lords in **hereditary subjugation**—bound to their lords from one generation to the next as well as to the land.

In Russia the right of peasants to move from a given estate was "temporarily" suspended in the 1590s and permanently abolished in 1603. In 1649 a new law code completed the process. The Russian tsar lifted the nine-year time limit on the recovery of runaways, who were to be returned to their lords whenever they were caught. Moreover, the new law code set no limits on the lords' authority over their peasants. Although the political development of the various eastern states differed, the legal re-establishment of permanent hereditary serfdom had become the common fate of peasants in the east by the middle of the seventeenth century.

This consolidation of serfdom was accompanied by the growth of estate agriculture, particularly in Poland and eastern Germany. In the sixteenth century, European economic expansion and population growth resumed after the great declines of the late Middle Ages. Prices for agricultural commodities also rose sharply as gold and silver flowed in from the New World. Thus Polish and German lords had powerful economic incentives to increase the production of their estates. And they did.

Lords seized more and more peasant land for their own estates and then demanded and received ever more unpaid serf labor on those enlarged estates. Even when the estates were inefficient and technically backward, as they generally were, the great Polish nobles and middle-rank German lords squeezed sizable, cheap, and thus very profitable surpluses out of their impoverished

**Estonia in the 1660s** The Estonians were conquered by German military nobility in the Middle Ages and reduced to serfdom. The German-speaking nobles ruled the Estonian peasants with an iron hand, and Peter the Great reaffirmed their domination when Russia annexed Estonia (see Map 17.3 on page 578). *(Mansell Collection/TimePix/Getty Images)*

peasants. Surpluses in wheat and timber were easily sold to big foreign merchants, who exported them to the growing cities of the west. Thus the poor east helped feed the wealthier west.

The re-emergence of serfdom in eastern Europe in the early modern period was clearly a momentous human development, and historians have advanced a variety of explanations for it. Some scholars have stressed the economic interpretation. Agricultural depression and population decline in the fourteenth and fifteenth centuries led to a severe labor shortage, they have argued, and thus eastern landlords naturally tied their precious peasants to the land. With the return of prosperity and the development of export markets in the sixteenth century, the landlords finished the job, grabbing the peasants' land and making them work as unpaid serfs within the framework of estate agriculture. This argument by itself is not very convincing, for almost identical economic developments "caused" the opposite result in the west.

It seems fairly clear, therefore, that political, rather than economic, factors were crucial in the simultaneous rise of serfdom in the east and decline of serfdom in the west. Specifically, eastern lords enjoyed much greater political power than their western counterparts. In the late Middle Ages, when much of eastern Europe experienced innumerable wars and general political chaos, the noble landlord class greatly increased its political power at the expense of the ruling monarchs. There were, for example, many disputed royal successions, so that weak kings were forced to grant political favors to win the support of the nobility. Thus while strong monarchs were rising in Spain, France, and England and providing effective central government, kings were generally losing power in the east. Such kings could not resist the demands of lords regarding peasants.

Moreover, most eastern monarchs did not want to resist even if they could. The typical king was only first among equals in the noble class. He, too, thought mainly in private, rather than public, terms. He, too, wanted to squeeze his peasants. The western concept and reality of sovereignty, as embodied in a king who protected the interests of all his people, was not well developed in eastern Europe before 1650.

The political power of the peasants was also weaker in eastern Europe and declined steadily after about 1400. Although there were occasional bloody peasant uprisings against the oppression of the landlords, they never succeeded. Nor did eastern peasants effectively resist day-by-day infringements on their liberties by their landlords. Part of the reason was that the lords, rather than the kings, ran the courts—one of the important concessions nobles extorted from weak monarchs.

Similarly, with the approval of weak kings, the landlords systematically undermined the medieval privileges of the towns and the power of the urban classes. Instead of selling products to local merchants in the towns, as required in the Middle Ages, the landlords sold directly to big foreign capitalists. For example, Dutch ships sailed up the rivers of Poland and eastern Germany to the loading docks of the great estates, completely short-circuiting the local towns. Moreover, "town air" no longer "made people free," for the eastern towns had lost their medieval right of refuge and were now compelled to return runaways to their lords. The population of the towns and the importance of the urban middle classes declined greatly. These developments both reflected and promoted the supremacy of noble landlords in most of eastern Europe in the sixteenth century.

Subsequently, in the eighteenth century, travelers and writers from western Europe became increasingly aware of real and even imagined differences that they observed in eastern Europe. Developing their ideas of refined society and gradual progress (see Chapter 18), westerners portrayed eastern Europe as being more "barbaric" and less "civilized" than their homelands.[1] Thus they expanded eastern Europe's undeniably harsher social and economic conditions to encompass a very debatable cultural and moral inferiority.

## The Rise of Austria and Prussia

See DBQ 4

Despite the strength of the nobility and the weakness of many monarchs before 1600, strong kings did begin to emerge in many lands in the course of the seventeenth century. War and the threat of war aided rulers greatly in their attempts to build absolute monarchies. There was also an endless struggle for power, as eastern rulers not only fought one another but also battled with armies of invaders from Asia. In this atmosphere of continual wartime emergency, monarchs reduced the political power of the landlord nobility. Cautiously leaving the nobles the unchallenged masters of their peasants, the would-be absolutist monarchs of eastern Europe gradually gained and monopolized political power in three key areas. First, they imposed and collected permanent taxes without consent. Second, they maintained permanent standing armies, which policed the country in addition to fighting abroad. Third, they conducted relations with other states as they pleased.

As with all general historical developments, there were important variations on the absolutist theme in eastern Europe. The royal **absolutism** created in Prussia was stronger and more effective than that established in Austria. This advantage gave Prussia a thin edge over Austria in the struggle for power in east-central Europe in the eighteenth century. That edge had great long-term political significance, for it was a rising Prussia that unified the German people in the nineteenth century and imposed on them a militaristic Prussian stamp.

### Austria and the Ottoman Turks

Like all the other peoples and rulers of central Europe, the Habsburgs of Austria emerged from the brutal Thirty Years' War, which lasted from 1618 to 1648, impoverished and exhausted. Their efforts to root out Protestantism in the German lands and to turn the weak Holy Roman Empire into a real state had failed utterly. The Habsburgs did remain the hereditary emperors of the ancient Holy Roman Empire, which was inhabited mainly by German-speakers and was more accurately called the German Empire. Real power in the German Empire lay in the hands of a bewildering variety of three hundred separate political jurisdictions, which included independent cities, small principalities, medium-size states such as Bavaria and Saxony, and some (but not all) of the territories of Prussia and the Habsburgs.

Defeat in central Europe opened new vistas for the Habsburgs. They were forced to turn inward and eastward in an attempt to fuse their diverse holdings into a strong unified state. An important step in this direction had actually been taken in Bohemia during the Thirty Years' War. Protestantism had been strong among the Czechs, a Slavic people concentrated in Bohemia. Indeed, the lesser Czech nobility was largely Protestant in 1600 and had considerable political power because it dominated the **Bohemian Estates**—the representative body of the different estates, or legal orders, in Bohemia. In 1618 the Bohemian Estates had risen up in defense of Protestant rights. This revolt was crushed in 1620 at the Battle of the White Mountain, a momentous turning point in Czech history. The victorious Habsburg king, Ferdinand II (r. 1619–1637), drastically reduced the power of the Bohemian Estates. Ferdinand also confiscated the landholdings of many Protestant nobles and gave them to a few great Catholic nobles who had remained loyal and to a motley band of aristocratic soldiers of fortune who had nothing in common with the Czech-speaking peasants. After 1650 a large portion of the Bohemian nobility was of recent foreign origin and owed everything to the Habsburgs.

With the help of this new nobility, the Habsburgs established strong direct rule over reconquered Bohemia. The condition of the enserfed peasantry worsened substantially: three days per week of unpaid labor—the *robot*—became the norm, and a quarter of the serfs worked for their lords every day but Sundays and religious holidays. Protestantism was also stamped out, in the course of which a growing unity of religion was brought about. The reorganization of Bohemia was a giant step toward absolutism.

After the Thirty Years' War, Ferdinand III (r. 1637–1657) centralized the government in the hereditary German-speaking provinces, most notably Austria, Styria, and the Tyrol, which formed the core area of the Habsburg holdings. For the first time, Ferdinand III's reign

**The Battle of Mohács, 1526** The *Süleymanname* (Book of Suleiman), a biography, contains these fascinating illustrations of the great Ottoman victory at Mohács, which enabled the Turks to add Hungary to their expanding empire. In the right panel, Suleiman in a white turban sits on a black horse surrounded by his personal guard, while his janissary soldiers fire their muskets and cannon at the enemy. In the left panel, the Europeans are in disarray, in contrast to the Turks' discipline and order. *(Topkapi Saray Museum)*

saw the creation of a permanent standing army ready to put down any internal opposition. The Habsburg monarchy was then ready to turn toward the plains of Hungary, which had long been divided and fought over by the Habsburgs and the Ottoman Turks.

The Ottomans had come out of Central Asia as conquering warriors, settled in Anatolia, in present-day Turkey, and created one of history's greatest military empires. At their peak in the middle of the sixteenth century under Sultan Suleiman the Magnificent (r. 1520–1566), they ruled the most powerful empire in the world. Their possessions stretched from western Persia across North Africa and up into the heart of central Europe (see Map 17.1). Followers of Islam, the Ottoman Turks were old and determined foes of the Catholic Habsburgs. Their armies had almost captured Vienna in 1529, and for more than 150 years thereafter the Ottomans ruled the many different ethnic groups living in the Balkans, almost all of Hungary, and part of southern Russia.

The Ottoman Empire was originally built on a fascinating and very non-European conception of state and society. There was an almost complete absence of private landed property. All the agricultural land of the empire was the personal hereditary property of the **sultan,** who exploited the land as he saw fit according to Ottoman political theory. There was therefore no security of land-

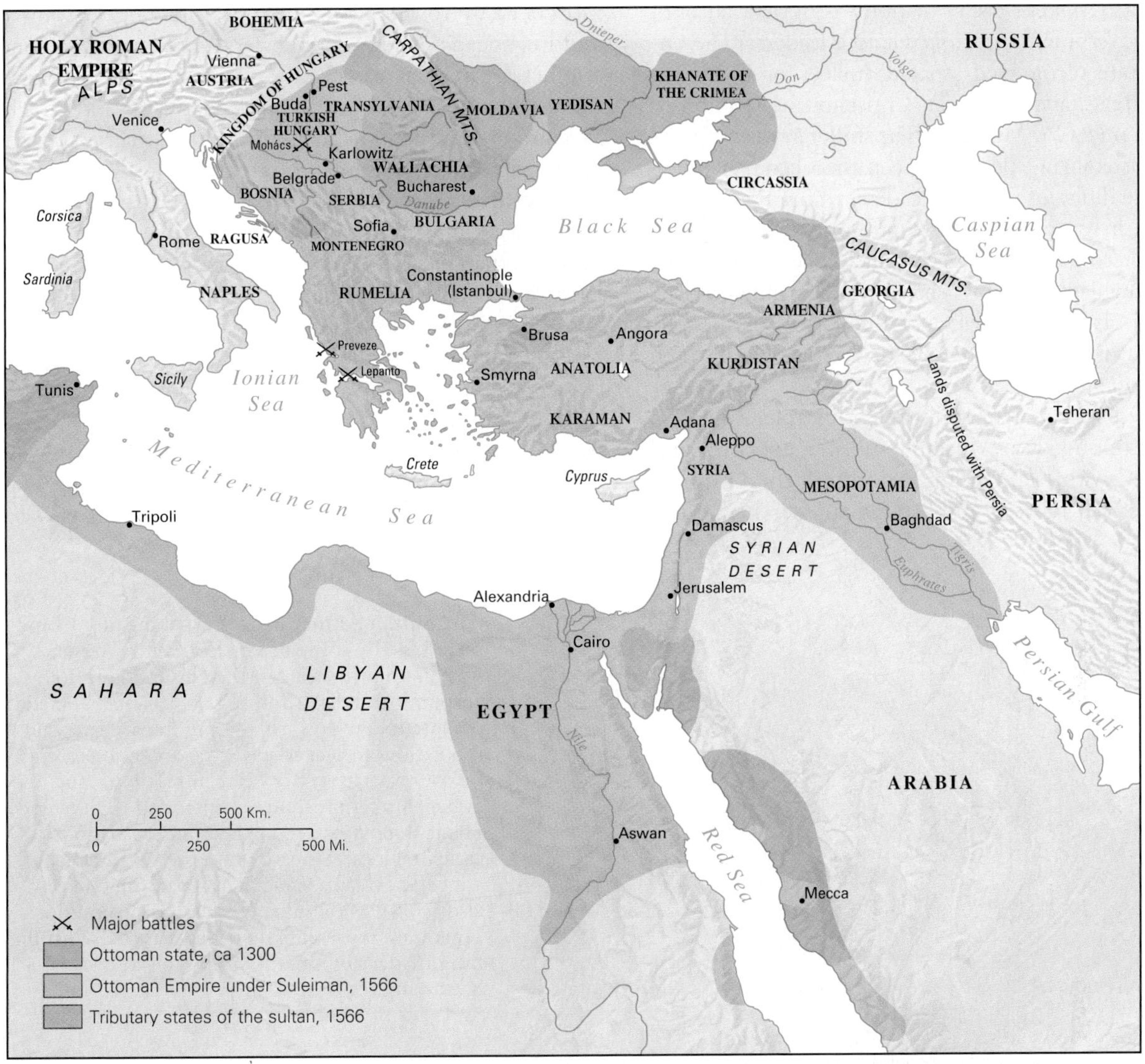


**MAP 17.1 The Ottoman Empire at Its Height, 1566** The Ottomans, like their great rivals the Habsburgs, rose to rule a vast dynastic empire encompassing many different peoples and ethnic groups. The army and the bureaucracy served to unite the disparate territories into a single state under an absolutist ruler.

holding and no hereditary nobility. The sultan also defended peasant communities from greedy officials, so that peasants could afford to pay their taxes and support the state.

The top ranks of the bureaucracy were staffed by the sultan's slave corps. Every year the sultan levied a "tax" of one to three thousand male children on the conquered Christian populations in the Balkans. These and other slaves were raised in Turkey as Muslims and trained to fight and to administer. The most talented slaves rose to the top of the bureaucracy; the less fortunate formed the brave and skillful core of the sultan's army, the so-called janissary corps. Lurid accounts of weeping Christian boys being carried off into Ottoman slavery did much to foster the idea of the brutal, fanatical Turk in the European mind.

In fact, the Ottomans were much more tolerant of religious differences than Europeans were. Building on the practices of the great Middle Eastern empires, the Ottomans divided their subjects into religious communities, whereby each *millet*—each "nation"—enjoyed autonomous self-government under its religious leaders. (The Ottoman Empire recognized separate millets for Orthodox Christians, Jews, and Armenian Christians, in addition to the Muslim millet for Muslims.) The **millet system** created a powerful stabilizing bond between the Ottoman ruling class and the different religious leaders, who supported the sultan's rule in return for extensive authority over the members of their communities. Each millet collected taxes for the state, regulated group behavior, and maintained law courts, schools, synagogues, and hospitals for its people. Individuals outside the ruling elite had status only through their millet membership.

Supported and reassured by religious toleration and cultural autonomy, non-Muslim minorities coexisted and commingled with the Muslim majority in the Ottoman Empire. Greek, Jewish, and Armenian merchants also moved easily to and from Europe, drawing Ottomans and Europeans closer together despite recurring war and conflict. Armenian merchants excelled as international silk merchants, Jews as textile manufacturers, and Greeks as mariners and shipowners, although all three groups participated in all Ottoman occupations in the sixteenth and seventeenth centuries.[2]

Following the death of Suleiman the Magnificent in 1566, monarchical absolutism and strong centralized rule gave way to palace intrigue, weak sultans, and the emergence of a powerful oligarchy of top officials. Temporary Muslim landowners became hard-to-control permanent oppressors, and the army lost its dedication and lagged behind its European foes in military innovation. The Ottoman Empire practically ceased to expand. Yet in the late seventeenth century, under vigorous reforming leadership, the Ottoman Empire succeeded in marshaling its forces for

**The Sultan Ahmet Mosque, Istanbul** Completed in 1614, the mosque of Sultan Ahmet I was built in the heart of the city and gracefully accommodated existing rug merchants, who still operate today. With six soaring minarets to call the faithful to prayer and semi-domes cascading on four axes from the vast central dome, the Sultan Ahmet mosque was intended to outshine Hagia Sophia, the renowned Greek Orthodox cathedral located nearby that the Ottomans had converted to a mosque. This beautiful edifice, also known as the Blue Mosque for its interior Iznik tiles, represents the culmination of Ottoman mosque development. *(Robert Frerck/Woodfin Camp & Associates)*

one last mighty attack on the Habsburgs. A huge Turkish army surrounded Vienna and laid siege to it in 1683. After holding out against great odds for two months, the city was relieved at the last minute by a mixed force of Habsburg, Saxon, Bavarian, and Polish troops, and the Ottomans were forced to retreat. Soon the retreat became a rout. As Russian and Venetian allies attacked on other fronts, the Habsburgs conquered almost all of Hungary and Transylvania (part of present-day Romania) by 1699 (see Map 17.2).

The Turkish wars and this great expansion strengthened the Habsburg army and promoted some sense of unity in the Habsburg lands. But Habsburg efforts to create a fully developed, highly centralized, absolutist state were only partly successful.

The Habsburg state was composed of three separate and distinct territories—the old "hereditary provinces" of Austria, the kingdom of Bohemia, and the kingdom of Hungary. These three parts were tied together primarily by their common ruler, the Habsburg monarch. Each part had its own laws and political life, for the noble-dominated Estates continued to exist in each territory, though with reduced powers. The Habsburgs themselves were well aware of the fragility of the union they had forged. In 1713 Charles VI (r. 1711–1740) proclaimed the so-called **Pragmatic Sanction,** which stated that the Habsburg possessions were never to be divided and were always to be passed intact to a single heir, who might be female since Charles was the last of all Habsburg males. Charles spent much of his reign trying to get this principle accepted by the various branches of the Habsburg family, by the three different Estates of the realm, and by the states of Europe. His fears turned out to be well founded.

The Hungarian nobility, despite its reduced strength, effectively thwarted the full development of Habsburg absolutism. Time and again throughout the seventeenth century, Hungarian nobles—the most numerous in Europe, making up 5 to 7 percent of the Hungarian population—rose in revolt against Vienna's attempts to impose absolute rule. They never triumphed decisively, but neither were they ever crushed, as the Czech nobility had been in 1620.

The Hungarians resisted because many of them remained Protestants, especially in the area long ruled by the more tolerant Turks, and hated the heavy-handed attempts of the conquering Habsburgs to re-Catholicize everyone. Moreover, until 1683 the lords of Hungary had a powerful military ally in Turkey. Finally, the Hungarian nobility, and even part of the Hungarian peasantry, had become attached to a national ideal long before most of the other peoples of eastern Europe did so. Hungarian nobles were determined to maintain as much independence and local control as possible. Thus when the Habsburgs were bogged down in the War of the Spanish Succession (see page 543), the Hungarians rose in one last patriotic rebellion under Prince Francis Rákóczy in 1703. Rákóczy and his forces were eventually defeated, but this time the Habsburgs had to accept a definitive compromise. Charles VI restored many of the traditional privileges of the Hungarian aristocracy in return for Hungarian acceptance of hereditary Habsburg rule. Thus Hungary, unlike Austria or Bohemia, never came close to being fully integrated into a centralized, absolute Habsburg state.

## Prussia in the Seventeenth Century

After 1400 the eastern German princes lost political power and influence, while a revitalized landed nobility became the undisputed ruling class. The Hohenzollern family, which ruled through its senior and junior branches as the imperial electors of Brandenburg and the dukes of Prussia, had little real princely power.

Nothing suggested that the Hohenzollern family and its princely territories would ever play an important role in European or even German affairs. The **elector of Brandenburg**'s right to help choose the Holy Roman emperor with six other electors bestowed prestige, but the elector had no military strength whatsoever. Moreover, Brandenburg, the area around Berlin and the elector's power base, was completely cut off from the sea (see Map 17.2). Brandenburg lacked defensible natural frontiers, and the land was poor, a combination of sand and swamp. Contemporaries contemptuously called Brandenburg the "sand-box of the Holy Roman Empire."[3]

Moreover, the territory of the elector's cousin, the duke of Prussia, was totally separated from Brandenburg and was part of Poland. Prussia had originally been conquered in the thirteenth century by the Germanic order of Teutonic Knights as part of a larger struggle between German conquerors and the indigenous Slavic populations. However, by 1600 Prussia's German-speaking peasants had much in common with Polish peasants in other provinces, for both ethnic groups had seen most of their freedoms reduced or revoked by their noble landlords. (Poland's numerous lesser nobility also dominated the Polish state, which was actually a constitutional republic headed by an elected king who had little real power.) In 1618 the junior branch of the Hohenzollern family died out, and Prussia reverted to the elector of Brandenburg.

The elector of Brandenburg was a helpless spectator in the Thirty Years' War, his territories alternately ravaged by Swedish and Habsburg armies. Population fell drastically, and many villages disappeared. Yet the devastation

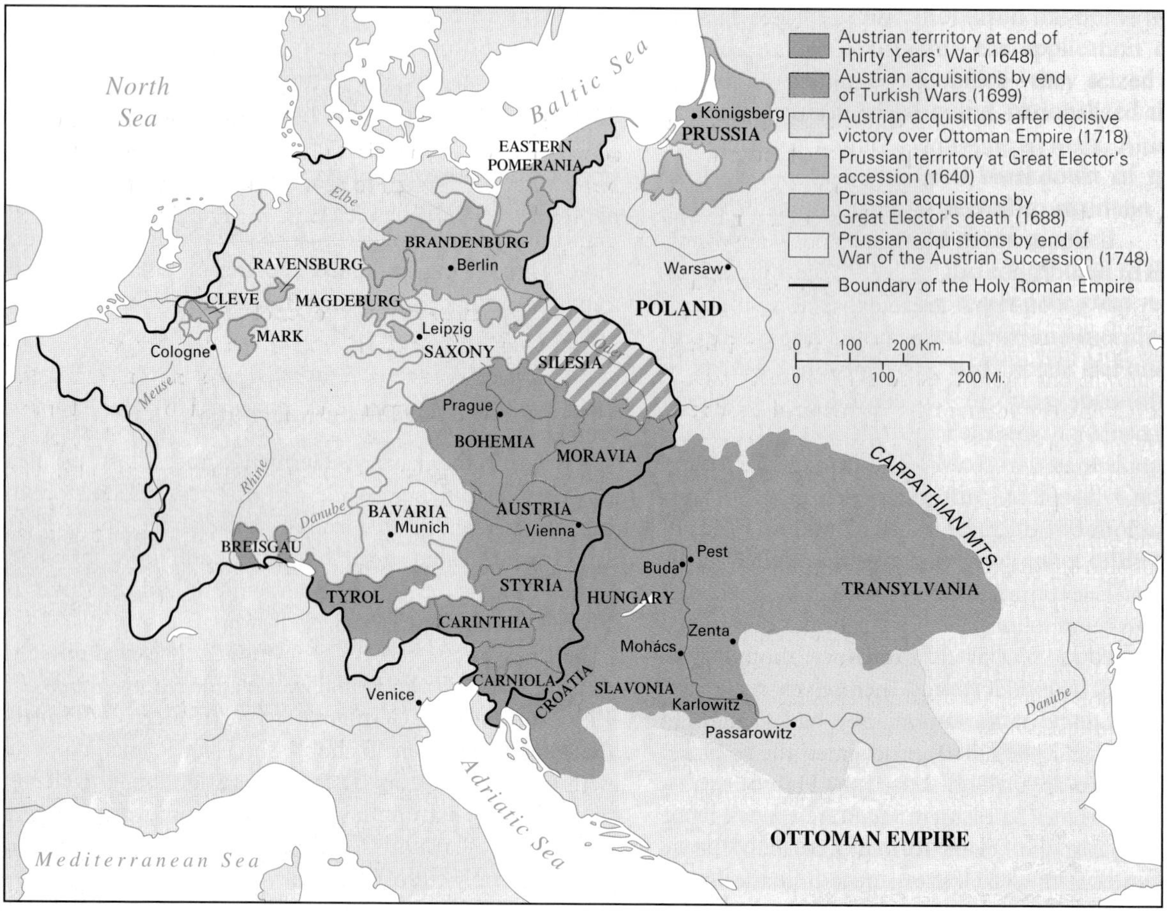


**MAP 17.2 The Growth of Austria and Brandenburg-Prussia to 1748** Austria expanded to the southwest into Hungary and Transylvania at the expense of the Ottoman Empire. It was unable to hold the rich German province of Silesia, however, which was conquered by Brandenburg-Prussia.

of Brandenburg and Prussia prepared the way for Hohenzollern absolutism because foreign armies dramatically weakened the political power of the Estates—the representative assemblies of the realm. This weakening of the Estates helped the very talented young elector Frederick William (r. 1640–1688), later known as the "Great Elector," to ride roughshod over traditional representative rights and to take a giant step toward royal absolutism. This constitutional struggle, often unjustly neglected by historians, was the most crucial in Prussian history for hundreds of years, until that of the 1860s.

When he came to power in 1640, the twenty-year-old Great Elector was determined to unify his three quite separate provinces and add to them by diplomacy and war. These provinces were Brandenburg itself; Prussia, inherited in 1618; and completely separate, scattered holdings along the Rhine in western Germany, inherited in 1614 (see Map 17.2). Each of the three provinces was inhabited by Germans, but each had its own Estates, whose power had increased until about 1600 as the power of the rulers declined. Although the Estates had not met regularly during the chaotic Thirty Years' War, they still had the power of the purse in their respective provinces. Taxes could not be levied without their consent. The Estates of Brandenburg and Prussia were dominated by the nobility and the landowning classes, known as the **Junkers.** But this was also the case in most European countries that had representative bodies, including the English Parliament before and after the civil war. Had the Estates successfully resisted the absolutist demands of the Great Elector, they, too, might have evolved toward more broadly based constitutionalism.

The struggle between the Great Elector and the provincial Estates was long, complicated, and intense. After the Thirty Years' War, representatives of the nobility zealously reasserted the right of the Estates to vote taxes, a right the Swedish armies of occupation had simply ignored. Yet first in Brandenburg in 1653 and then in Prussia between 1661 and 1663, the Great Elector eventually had his way.

To pay for the permanent standing army he first established in 1660, Frederick William forced the Estates to accept the introduction of permanent taxation without consent. The power of the Estates declined rapidly thereafter, for the Great Elector had both financial independence and superior force. The state's total revenue tripled during his reign. The size of the army leaped about tenfold. In 1688 a population of one million was supporting a peacetime standing army of thirty thousand.

In accounting for the Great Elector's fateful triumph, two factors appear central. First, as in the formation of every absolutist state, war was a decisive factor. The ongoing struggle between Sweden and Poland for control of the Baltic after 1648 and the wars of Louis XIV in western Europe created an atmosphere of permanent crisis. The wild Tartars of the Crimea in southern Russia swept through Prussia in the winter of 1656 to 1657, killing and carrying off as slaves more than fifty thousand people, according to an old estimate. This invasion softened up the Estates and strengthened the urgency of the Great Elector's demands for more money for more soldiers.

Second, the nobility had long dominated the government through the Estates, but it was unwilling to join the representatives of the towns in a consistent common front and was focused on its own rights and privileges. When, therefore, the Great Elector reconfirmed these privileges in 1653 and after, even while reducing the political power of the Estates, the nobility growled but did not bite. It accepted a compromise whereby the bulk of the new taxes fell on towns and royal authority stopped at the landlords' gates. The elector could and did use naked force to break the liberties of the towns. The main leader of the urban opposition in the key city of Königsberg, for example, was simply arrested and imprisoned for life without trial.

## The Consolidation of Prussian Absolutism

By the time of his death in 1688, the Great Elector had created a single state out of scattered principalities. But his new creation was still small and fragile. All the leading states of Europe had many more people, and strong monarchy was still a novelty. Moreover, the Great Elector's successor, Elector Frederick III, "the Ostentatious" (r. 1688–1713), was weak of body and mind, and he focused on imitating the style of Louis XIV, building an expensive palace and cultivating the arts. His main political accomplishment was winning a prestigious royal title and being crowned King Frederick I in 1701 as a reward for aiding the Holy Roman emperor in the War of the Spanish Succession.

This tendency toward luxury-loving, petty tyranny was completely reversed by Frederick William I, "the Soldiers' King" (r. 1713–1740). A crude, dangerous psychoneurotic, Frederick William I was nevertheless the most talented reformer ever produced by the Hohenzollern family. It was he who truly established Prussian absolutism and gave it a unique character. It was he who created the best army in Europe, for its size, and it was he who infused strict military values into a whole society. In the words of a famous historian of Prussia:

*For a whole generation, the Hohenzollern subjects were victimized by a royal bully, imbued with an obsessive bent for military organization and military scales of value. This left a deep mark upon the institutions of Prussiandom and upon the molding of the "Prussian spirit."*[4]

Frederick William's attachment to the army and military life was intensely emotional. He had, for example, a bizarre, almost pathological love for tall soldiers, whom he credited with superior strength and endurance. Like some fanatical modern-day basketball coach in search of a championship team, he sent his agents throughout Prussia and all of Europe to trick, buy, and kidnap top recruits. Neighboring princes sent him their giants as gifts to win his gratitude. Prussian mothers told their sons, "Stop growing or the recruiting agents will get you."[5]

Profoundly militaristic in temperament, Frederick William always wore an army uniform, and he lived the highly disciplined life of the professional soldier. He began his work by five or six in the morning; at ten he almost always went to the parade ground to drill or inspect his troops. A man of violent temper, Frederick William personally punished the most minor infractions on the spot: a missing button off a soldier's coat quickly provoked a savage beating with a heavy walking stick.

Frederick William's love of the army was also based on a hardheaded conception of the struggle for power and a dog-eat-dog view of international politics. Years later he summed up his life's philosophy in his instructions to his son: "A formidable army and a war chest large enough to make this army mobile in times of need can create great respect for you in the world, so that you can speak a word like the other powers."[6] This unshakable belief that the

**A Prussian Giant Grenadier** Frederick William I wanted tall, handsome soldiers. He dressed them in tight bright uniforms to distinguish them from the peasant population from which most soldiers came. He also ordered several portraits of his favorites from his court painter, J. C. Merk. Grenadiers wore the miter cap instead of an ordinary hat so that they could hurl their heavy grenades unimpeded by a broad brim. *(The Royal Collection © 2004, Her Majesty Queen Elizabeth II)*

welfare of king and state depended on the army above all else reinforced Frederick William's passion for the soldier's life.

The cult of military power provided the rationale for a great expansion of royal absolutism in Prussia. As the ruthless king himself put it: "I must be served with life and limb, with house and wealth, with honour and conscience, everything must be committed except eternal salvation—that belongs to God, but all else is mine."[7] To make good these extraordinary demands, Frederick William created a strong centralized bureaucracy. Meanwhile the last traces of the parliamentary Estates and local self-government vanished.

The king's grab for power brought him into considerable conflict with the noble landowners, the Junkers. In his early years, he even threatened to destroy them; yet, in the end, the Prussian nobility was not destroyed but enlisted—into the army. Responding to a combination of threats and opportunities, the Junkers became the officer caste. A new compromise had been worked out whereby the proud nobility imperiously commanded the peasantry in the army as well as on the estates.

Coarse and crude, penny-pinching and hard-working, Frederick William achieved results. Above all, he built a first-rate army, although he had only third-rate resources. The standing army increased from thirty-eight thousand to eighty-three thousand during his reign. Prussia, twelfth in Europe in population, had the fourth largest army by 1740. Moreover, soldier for soldier, the Prussian army became the best in Europe, astonishing foreign observers with its precision, skill, and discipline. For the next two hundred years, Prussia and then Prussianized Germany would usually win the crucial military battles.

Frederick William and his ministers also built an exceptionally honest and conscientious bureaucracy, which not only administered the country but also tried with some success to develop the country economically. Finally, like the miser he was known to be, living very frugally off the income of his own landholdings, the king loved his "blue boys" so much that he hated to "spend" them. This most militaristic of kings was, paradoxically, almost always at peace.

Nevertheless, the Prussian people paid a heavy and lasting price for the obsessions of their royal drillmaster. Civil society became rigid and highly disciplined. Prussia became the "Sparta of the North"; unquestioning obedience was the highest virtue. As a Prussian minister later summed up, "To keep quiet is the first civic duty."[8] Thus the policies of Frederick William I combined with harsh peasant bondage and Junker tyranny to lay the foundations for probably the most militaristic country of modern times.

# The Development of Russia

See DBQ 4

One of the favorite parlor games of nineteenth-century Russian (and non-Russian) intellectuals was debating whether Russia was a Western, European or a non-Western, Asiatic society. This question was particularly fascinating because it was unanswerable. To this day Russia differs fundamentally from the West in some basic ways, though Russian history has paralleled that of the West in other aspects.

Certainly Russian developments in the early medieval period had important parallels with those in the West. The eastern Slavs were converted by missionaries from the Byzantine Empire to Orthodox Christianity, which became the state religion of the powerful Kievan principality, in the territory of present-day Ukraine. **Eastern Orthodoxy** rejects the authority of the pope, but this is the main difference in religious and moral beliefs dividing it from Roman Catholicism. Also in the mainstream of European medieval civilization was the loose but real political unification of the eastern Slavic territories under a single prince and a single dynasty in the eleventh century. So, too, was the typical feudal division of the land-based society into a **boyard nobility** and a commoner peasantry. After the death of Great Prince Iaroslav the Wise (r. 1019–1054), the Kievan principality disintegrated into competing political units. But similar fragmentations of central authority occurred in many European kingdoms at various points in the Middle Ages, and a strong native ruler might have emerged in Russia eventually to resume the centralizing work of earlier Kievan monarchs.

Such was not the case, however. Brutally conquered and subjugated by a foreign invader, Russia created a system of rule that was nearly unknown in the West between about 1250 and 1690. Thus when absolute monarchy triumphed under the rough guidance of Peter the Great in the early eighteenth century, it was a quite different type of absolute monarchy from that of France or even Prussia.

## The Mongol Yoke and the Rise of Moscow

Like the Germans and the Italians, the eastern Slavs might have emerged from the Middle Ages weak and politically divided had it not been for the Mongol conquest of the Kievan principality. Nomadic tribes from present-day Mongolia, the Mongols were temporarily unified in the thirteenth century by Chinggis Khan (1162–1227), one of history's greatest conquerors. In five years his armies subdued all of China. His successors then turned westward, smashing everything in their path and reaching the plains of Hungary victorious before they pulled back in 1242. The Mongol army—the Golden Horde—was savage in the extreme, often slaughtering entire populations of cities before burning them to the ground. En route to Mongolia in 1245, Archbishop John of Plano Carpini, the papal ambassador to Mongolia, passed through Kiev, which the Mongols had sacked in 1242, and wrote an unforgettable eyewitness account:

*The Mongols went against Russia and enacted a great massacre in the Russian land. They destroyed towns and fortresses and killed people. They besieged Kiev, which had been the capital of Russia, and after a long siege they took it and killed the inhabitants of the city. For this reason, when we passed through that land, we found lying in the field countless heads and bones of dead people; for this city had been extremely large and very populous, whereas now it has been reduced to nothing: barely two hundred houses stand there, and those people are held in the harshest slavery.*[9]

Having devastated and conquered, the Mongols ruled the eastern Slavs for more than two hundred years, the so-called **Mongol Yoke.** They built their capital of Saray on the lower Volga (see Map 17.3). They forced all the bickering Slavic princes to submit to their rule and to give them tribute and slaves. If the conquered peoples rebelled, the Mongols were quick to punish with death and destruction. Thus the Mongols unified the eastern Slavs, for the Mongol khan was acknowledged by all as the supreme ruler.

The Mongol unification completely changed the internal political situation. Although the Mongols conquered, they were quite willing to use local princes as obedient servants and tax collectors. Therefore, they did not abolish the title of "great prince," bestowing it instead on the prince who served them best and paid them most handsomely.

Beginning with Alexander Nevsky in 1252, the previously insignificant princes of Moscow became particularly adept at serving the Mongols. They loyally put down popular uprisings and collected the khan's harsh taxes. By way of reward, the princes of Moscow emerged as hereditary great princes. Eventually the Muscovite princes were able to destroy their princely rivals and even replace the khan as supreme ruler. Ivan III (r. 1462–1505) completed this process of consolidating power around Moscow and won Novgorod, thereby almost reaching the Baltic Sea (see Map 17.3). The prince of Moscow had defeated all rivals to win complete princely authority.

Not only was the prince of Moscow the *unique* ruler, he was the *absolute* ruler, the autocrat, the *tsar*—the

**MAP 17.3 The Expansion of Russia to 1725** After the disintegration of the Kievan state and the Mongol conquest, the princes of Moscow and their descendants gradually extended their rule over an enormous territory. Ivan the Terrible acquired more territory than Peter the Great.

Slavic contraction for "caesar," with all its connotations. This imperious conception of absolute power and **autocracy** was powerfully reinforced by two developments. First, about 1480 Ivan III felt strong enough to stop acknowledging the khan as his supreme ruler. There is good evidence to suggest that Ivan and his successor saw themselves as khans, exercising unrestrained and unpredictable power.

Second, after the fall of Constantinople to the Turks in 1453, the tsars saw themselves as the heirs of both the caesars and Orthodox Christianity, the one true faith. All the other kings of Europe were heretics; only the tsars were rightful and holy rulers. The idea was promoted by Orthodox churchmen, who spoke of "holy Russia" as the "Third Rome." As the monk Pilotheus stated, "Two Romes have fallen, but the third stands, and a fourth there will not be."[10] Ivan's marriage to the daughter of the last Byzantine emperor further enhanced the aura of an imperial inheritance of Moscow.

As peasants had begun losing their freedom of movement in the fifteenth century, so had the noble boyars begun losing power and influence. For example, when

Ivan III conquered the principality of Novgorod in the 1480s, he confiscated fully 80 percent of the land, executing the previous owners or resettling them nearer Moscow. He then kept more than half of the confiscated land for himself and distributed the remainder to members of a newly emerging **service nobility,** who held the tsar's land on the explicit condition that they serve in the tsar's army.

## Tsar and People to 1689

The rise of the new service nobility accelerated under Ivan IV (r. 1533–1584), the famous "Ivan the Terrible." Having ascended the throne at age three, Ivan suffered insults and neglect at the hands of the haughty boyars after his mother mysteriously died, possibly poisoned, when he was just eight. At age sixteen he suddenly pushed aside his hated boyar advisers. In an awe-inspiring ceremony complete with gold coins pouring down on his head, he majestically crowned himself and officially took the august title of tsar for the first time.

Selecting the beautiful and kind Anastasia of the popular Romanov family for his wife and queen, the young tsar soon declared war on the remnants of Mongol power. He defeated the faltering khanates of Kazan and Astrakhan between 1552 and 1556, adding vast new territories to Russia. In the course of these wars, Ivan virtually abolished the old distinction between hereditary boyar private property and land granted temporarily for service. All nobles, old and new, had to serve the tsar in order to hold any land.

The process of transforming the entire nobility into a service nobility was completed in the second part of Ivan the Terrible's reign. In 1557 Ivan turned westward, and for the next twenty-five years Muscovy waged an exhausting, unsuccessful war primarily against the large Polish-Lithuanian state, which joined Poland with much of Ukraine in the sixteenth century. Quarreling with the boyars over the war and blaming them for the sudden death of his beloved Anastasia in 1560, the increasingly cruel and demented Ivan turned to strike down all who stood in his way.

Above all, he struck down the ancient Muscovite boyars with a reign of terror. Leading boyars, their relatives, and even their peasants and servants were executed en masse by a special corps of unquestioning servants. Dressed in black and riding black horses, they were forerunners of the modern dictator's secret police. Large estates were confiscated, broken up, and reapportioned to the lower service nobility. The great boyar families were severely reduced. The newer, poorer, more nearly equal service nobility, still less than 0.5 percent of the total population, was totally dependent on the autocrat.

**Ivan the Terrible** Ivan IV, the first to take the title Tsar of Russia, executed many Muscovite boyars and their peasants and servants. His ownership of all the land, trade, and industry restricted economic development. *(National Museum, Copenhagen, Denmark)*

Ivan also took giant strides toward making all commoners servants of the tsar. His endless wars and demonic purges left much of central Russia depopulated. As the service nobles demanded more from the remaining peasants, more and more peasants fled toward the wild, recently conquered territories to the east and south. There they formed free groups and outlaw armies known as **Cossacks,** who maintained a precarious independence beyond the tsar's reach. The solution to the problem of peasant flight was to complete the tying of the peasants to the land and to the noble landholders, who were bound in turn to serve the tsar.

In the time of Ivan the Terrible, urban traders and artisans were also bound to their towns and jobs so that the tsar could tax them more heavily. Ivan assumed that the tsar owned Russia's trade and industry, just as he owned all the land. The urban classes had no security in their

**Saint Basil's Cathedral, Moscow** With its sloping roofs and colorful onion-shaped domes, Saint Basil's is a striking example of powerful Byzantine influences on Russian culture. According to tradition, an enchanted Ivan the Terrible blinded the cathedral's architects to ensure that they would never duplicate their fantastic achievement, which still dazzles the beholder in today's Red Square. *(George Holton/Photo Researchers)*

work or property, and even the wealthiest merchants were basically dependent agents of the tsar. If a new commercial activity became important and profitable, it was often taken over by the tsar and made a royal monopoly. Royal monopolization and service obligations checked the growth of the Russian middle classes and stood in sharp contrast to developments in western Europe, where the capitalist middle classes were gaining strength and security in their private property.

Ivan the Terrible's system of autocracy and compulsory service struck foreign observers forcibly. Sigismund Herberstein, a German traveler to Russia, wrote in 1571: "All the people consider themselves to be *kholops,* that is, slaves of their Prince." At the same time, Jean Bodin, the French thinker who did so much to develop the modern concept of sovereignty, concluded that Russia's political system was fundamentally different from those of all other European monarchies and comparable only to that of the Ottoman Empire. In both the Ottoman Empire and Russia, "the prince is become lord of the goods and persons of his subjects . . . governing them as a master of a family does his slaves."[11] The Mongol inheritance weighed heavily on Russia.

As has so often occurred in Russia, the death of an iron-fisted tyrant—in this case, Ivan the Terrible in 1584—ushered in an era of confusion and violent struggles for power. Events were particularly chaotic after Ivan's son, Theodore, died in 1598 without an heir. The years 1598 to 1613 were aptly called the "Time of Troubles."

The close relatives of the deceased tsar intrigued against and murdered one another, alternately fighting and welcoming the invading Swedes and Poles, who even occupied Moscow. Most serious for the cause of autocracy, there was a great social upheaval. Cossack bands, led by a former slave named Ivan Bolotnikov, marched northward, rallying peasants and slaughtering nobles and officials. The mass of Cossacks and peasants called for the "true tsar," who would restore their freedom of movement, reduce their heavy taxes, and lighten the yoke imposed by the landlords.

This social explosion from below brought the nobles, big and small, to their senses. They put aside their quarrels and finally crushed the Cossack rebellion at the gates of Moscow. In 1613 the nobles elected Ivan the Terrible's sixteen-year-old grandnephew, Michael Romanov, the new hereditary tsar. Then they rallied around him in the face of common internal and external threats. Michael's election was a real restoration, and his reign saw the gradual re-establishment of tsarist autocracy. (See the feature "Listening to the Past: A Foreign Traveler in Russia" on pages 590–591.) Thus while peasants were completely enserfed in 1649, Ivan's heavy military obligations on the nobility were relaxed considerably. In the long reign of Michael's successor, the pious Alexis (r. 1645–1676), this asymmetry of obligations was accentuated.

The result was a second round of mass upheaval and protest. In the later seventeenth century, the unity of the Russian Orthodox church was torn apart by a great split. The initiating event was the religious reforms introduced in 1652 by the patriarch Nikon, a dogmatic purist who wished to bring "corrupted" Russian practices of worship into line with the Greek Orthodox model. The self-serving church hierarchy quickly went along, but the intensely religious common people resisted. They saw Nikon as the Antichrist, who was stripping them of the only thing they had—the true religion of "holy Russia."

Great numbers left the church and formed illegal communities of "Old Believers," who were hunted down and persecuted. As many as twenty thousand people burned themselves alive, singing the "hallelujah" in their chants three times rather than twice, as Nikon had demanded. After the great split, the Russian masses were alienated from the established church, which became dependent on the state for its authority.

Again the Cossacks revolted against the state, which was doggedly trying to catch up with them on the frontiers and reduce them to serfdom. Under Stenka Razin they moved up the Volga River in 1670 and 1671, attracting a great army of urban poor and peasants, killing landlords and government officials, and proclaiming freedom from oppression. This rebellion to overthrow the established order was finally defeated by the government. (See the feature "Individuals in Society: Stenka Razin, Russian Rebel.") In response, the thoroughly scared upper classes tightened the screws of serfdom even further. Holding down the peasants, and thereby maintaining the tsar, became almost the principal obligation of the nobility until 1689.

## The Reforms of Peter the Great

It is now possible to understand the reforms of Peter the Great (r. 1682–1725) and his kind of monarchical absolutism. Contrary to some historians' assertions, Peter was interested primarily in military power, not in some grandiose westernization plan. A giant for his time, at six feet seven inches, and possessing enormous energy and willpower, Peter was determined to redress the defeats the tsar's armies had occasionally suffered in their wars with Poland and Sweden since the time of Ivan the Terrible.

Peter was equally determined to continue the tsarist tradition of territorial expansion. After a long war, Russia had gained a large mass of Ukraine from weak and decentralized Poland in 1667 (see Map 17.3), and it completed the conquest of Siberia in the seventeenth century. After the seventeen-year-old Peter overturned the regency in 1689, the thirty-six years of his personal rule knew only one year of peace.

When Peter took control in 1689, the heart of his army still consisted of cavalry made up of boyars and service nobility. Foot soldiers played a secondary role, and the whole army served on a part-time basis. The Russian army was lagging behind the professional standing armies being formed in Europe in the seventeenth century. The core of such armies was a highly disciplined infantry that fired and refired muskets as it fearlessly advanced, until it charged with bayonets fixed. Such a large, permanent army would be enormously expensive, and thus Peter's military moves were cautious in the 1690s.

Maintaining an existing Russian alliance with Austria and Poland against the Ottoman Empire, Peter campaigned first against Turkish forts and Tartar vassals on the Black Sea. Learning from early mistakes, he conquered Azov in 1696. Fascinated by weapons and foreign technology, the confident tsar then led a group of 250 Russian officials and young nobles on an eighteen-month tour of western European capitals. Traveling unofficially as an ordinary Russian to avoid formal ceremonies, Peter

**Gustaf Cederstrom: The Swedish Victory at Narva (1701)** This poignant re-creation focuses on the contrast between the Swedish officers in handsome dress uniforms and the battered Russian soldiers laying down their standards in surrender. Charles XII of Sweden scored brilliant, rapid-fire victories over Denmark, Saxony, and Russia, but he failed to make peace with Peter while he was ahead and eventually lost Sweden's holdings on the Baltic coast. *(The National Museum of Fine Arts, Stockholm)*

worked with his hands at various crafts and met with foreign kings and experts. He was particularly impressed with the growing power of the Dutch and the English and considered how Russia could profit from their example.

Returning to Russia, Peter entered into a secret alliance with Denmark and the elector of Saxony, who was also the elected king of Poland, to wage a sudden war of aggression against Sweden. Sweden was then a leading power in northern Europe. Despite the country's small population and limited agricultural resources, Swedish rulers in the seventeenth century had developed a strong absolutist state and built an excellent standing army. Expanding beyond Sweden, they held substantial territory in northern Germany, Finland, and Estonia. Yet these possessions were scattered and appeared vulnerable. Above all, Peter and his allies believed that their combined forces could win easy victories because Sweden was in the hands of a new and inexperienced king. They were mistaken.

Eighteen-year-old Charles XII (1697–1718) surprised Peter when he showed daring military genius. Defeating Denmark quickly in 1700, Charles turned on Russia. In a blinding snowstorm, his well-trained professional army attacked and routed unsuspecting Russians besieging the Swedish fortress of Narva on the Baltic coast. Peter and the survivors fled in panic to Moscow. It was, for the

# Individuals in Society

## Stenka Razin, Russian Rebel

The Don Cossack Stenka Razin led the largest peasant rebellion in Europe in the seventeenth century, a century rich in peasant revolt. Who was this Cossack leader who challenged Moscow, this outlaw who grew into a social revolutionary?

Descended from fugitives who fled to the turbulent southern frontier in search of freedom, Razin epitomized the old Cossack spirit of liberty and self-rule. Sharing the Cossack love of fighting and adventure, Razin also felt great sympathy for northern "have-nots" who had lost out and could not escape their fate. Why this was so remains a mystery. His family belonged to the Cossack establishment, which had settled the lower Don Valley long ago and received annual payments from the tsar in return for friendship and defense. One folk story tells of a hatred kindled by a Russian prince who unjustly hanged an older brother leading a Cossack detachment in Poland. True or not, rebel leaders like Razin have often come from comfortable backgrounds. As Paul Avrich notes, "Seldom have the oppressed themselves led the way, but rather those who have been aroused by their suffering and degradation."*

Whatever his motivation, Stenka Razin was a born leader. A striking personality with violent emotions, he was also shrewd and generous. He understood the lower classes and how to move them. The crowds called him a magician—a magician who hated the privileged and whom they felt compelled to follow.

Razin was a seasoned warrior of about forty years of age when in 1667 he led his first campaign. With an armed band of poor and rootless Cossacks, recent fugitives living upstream from the well-settled Cossacks, Razin sailed down the Volga River and seized a rich convoy of Russian merchant ships. He reportedly told survivors they were free to go or join him as free Cossacks. "I have come to fight only the boyars and the wealthy lords. As for the poor and the plain folk, I shall treat them as brothers."† Moving on to plunder Persian commerce on the Caspian Sea, Razin's forces returned home loaded with booty, which they divided equally according to Cossack custom. Gaining immense popularity and responding to threats from Moscow, Razin and his movement changed. The gang of outlaws became a rebel army.

In early 1670, Razin marched north with seven thousand Don Cossacks. His leaflets proclaimed that he was entering Russia "to establish the Cossack way, so that all men will be equal." Shrewdly blaming treacherous nobles and officials, and not the divinely appointed tsar, for the exploitation of the people, Razin's agents infiltrated the fortified towns along the Volga. Some towns resisted, but many threw open their gates, as the urban poor rose up against the "traitors and bloodsuckers." Peasants joined the revolt, killing lords and burning manor houses.

*Stenka Razin in Cossack dress, from a contemporary engraving.* (Novosti)

Frightened but unified, Russia's tiny elite mobilized all its strength. In late 1670, crack cavalry units of service nobility finally repulsed the swollen, ill-equipped army of the poor at Simbirsk on the upper Volga. The insurgents had to retreat. Fighting until the end, Razin was captured, hideously tortured, and chopped into pieces on the execution block. His followers and sympathizers were slaughtered with ferocious cruelty.

A fearless leader in the struggle against tsarist absolutism, Stenka Razin nurtured a myth of rebellion that would inspire future generations with dreams of freedom. He became Russia's most celebrated folk hero. He lived in story and song, an immortal superman who would someday ride out of the forest and deliver the people from oppression.

### Questions for Analysis

1. What did Stenka Razin do? Why did his rebellion inspire future generations?
2. How would you interpret Razin? Was he a great hero, a common criminal, or something else?

*Paul Avrich, *Russian Rebels, 1600–1800* (New York: Schocken Books, 1972), p. 67. This account is based on Avrich's masterful study.

†Quoted ibid., p. 70.

*The* **history companion** *features additional information and activities related to this topic.*
**history.college.hmco.com/students**

**Peter the Great in 1723** This compelling portrait by Grigory Musikiysky captures the strength and determination of the warrior tsar after more than three decades of personal rule. In his hand Peter holds the scepter, symbol of royal sovereignty, and across his breastplate is draped an ermine fur, a mark of honor. In the background are the battleships of Russia's new Baltic fleet and the famous St. Peter and St. Paul Fortress that Peter built in St. Petersburg. *(The Bridgeman Art Library)*

Russians, a grim beginning to the long and brutal Great Northern War, which lasted from 1700 to 1721.

Suffering defeat and faced with a military crisis, the energetic Peter responded with a long series of practical but far-reaching measures designed to increase state power, strengthen his armies, and gain victory. In essence, Peter's solution was to tighten up Muscovy's old service system and really make it work. Every nobleman, great or small, was once again required to serve in the army or in the civil administration—for life. Since a more modern army and government required skilled technicians and experts, Peter created schools and even universities to produce them. One of his most hated reforms required five years of compulsory education away from home for every young nobleman. Peter established an interlocking military-civilian bureaucracy with fourteen ranks, and he decreed that all had to start at the bottom and work toward the top. Some people of non-noble origins rose to high positions in this embryonic meritocracy. Drawing on his experience abroad, Peter searched out talented foreigners and placed them in his service. These measures gradually combined to make the army and government more powerful and efficient.

Peter also greatly increased the service requirements of the commoners. In the wake of the disaster at Narva, he established a regular standing army of more than 200,000 soldiers, made up mainly of peasants commanded by officers from the nobility. In addition, special forces of Cossacks and foreigners numbered more than 100,000. The departure of a drafted peasant boy was celebrated by his family and village almost like a funeral, as indeed it was, since the recruit was drafted for life. The peasantry also served with its taxes, which increased threefold during Peter's reign. Serfs were arbitrarily assigned to work in the growing number of factories and mines. Most of these industrial enterprises were directly or indirectly owned by the state, and they were worked almost exclusively for the military. In general, Russian serfdom became more oppressive under the reforming tsar.

The constant warfare of Peter's reign consumed 80 to 85 percent of all revenues and brought only modest territorial expansion. Yet the Great Northern War with Sweden was crowned in the end by Russian victory. Mobilizing superior resources and a much larger population, Peter's new war machine crushed the smaller army of Sweden's Charles XII in Ukraine at Poltava in 1709, one of the most significant battles in Russian history. The war dragged on until 1721, but Sweden never really regained the offensive, and Russia eventually annexed Estonia and much of present-day Latvia (see Map 17.3), lands that had never before been under Russian rule. Russia became the dominant power on the Baltic Sea and very much a European Great Power. If victory or defeat is the ultimate historical criterion, Peter's reforms were a success.

There were other important consequences of Peter's reign. Because of his feverish desire to use modern technology to strengthen the army, many Westerners and Western ideas flowed into Russia for the first time. A new class of educated Russians began to emerge. At the same time, vast numbers of Russians, especially among the poor and weak, hated Peter's massive changes. The split between the enserfed peasantry and the educated nobility thus widened, even though all were caught up in the demands of the sovereign.

A new idea of state interest, as distinct from the tsar's personal interests, began to take hold. Peter himself claimed time and again to be serving the common good. For the first time, a Russian tsar attached explanations to his decrees in an attempt to gain the confidence and support of the populace. Yet as before, the tsar alone decided what the common good was. Here was a source of future tension between tsar and people.

Thus Peter built on the service obligations of old Muscovy. His monarchical absolutism was truly the culmination of the long development of a unique Russian civilization. Yet the creation of a more modern army and state introduced much that was new and Western to that civilization. This development paved the way for Russia to move much closer to the European mainstream in its thought and institutions during the Enlightenment, especially under Catherine the Great.

## Absolutism and Baroque Architecture

The rise of royal absolutism in eastern Europe had many consequences. Nobles served their powerful rulers in new ways, while the great inferiority of the urban middle classes and the peasants was reconfirmed. Armies became larger and more professional, while taxes rose and authoritarian traditions were strengthened. Nor was this all. Royal absolutism also interacted with baroque culture and art, baroque music and literature. Inspired in part by Louis XIV of France, the great and not-so-great rulers called on the artistic talent of the age to glorify their power and magnificence. This exaltation of despotic rule was particularly striking in the lavish masterpieces of architecture.

### Palaces and Power

**Baroque** culture and art grew out of the revitalized Catholic church of the later sixteenth century. The papacy and the Jesuits especially encouraged an emotional, exuberant art, which appealed to the senses of churchgoers and proclaimed the confidence and power of the Catholic Reformation. The baroque style then spread throughout Europe in the seventeenth century, for dramatic baroque palaces symbolized the age of absolutist power, as soaring Gothic cathedrals had expressed the idealized spirit of the High Middle Ages.

By 1700 palace building had become a veritable obsession for the rulers of central and eastern Europe. Their baroque palaces were clearly intended to overawe the people with the monarch's strength. The great palaces were also visual declarations of equality with Louis XIV and were therefore modeled after Versailles to a greater or lesser extent. One such palace was Schönbrunn, an enormous Viennese Versailles begun in 1695 by Emperor Leopold to celebrate Austrian military victories and Habsburg might. Charles XI of Sweden, having reduced the power of the aristocracy, ordered the construction in 1693 of his Royal Palace, which dominates the center of Stockholm to this day.

Petty princes in the German lands also contributed mightily to the palace-building mania. Frederick the Great of Prussia noted that every descendant of a princely family "imagines himself to be something like Louis XIV. He builds his Versailles, has his mistresses, and maintains his army."[12] The not-very-important elector-archbishop of Mainz, the ruling prince of that city, confessed apologetically that "building is a craze which costs much, but every fool likes his own hat."[13]

In central and eastern Europe, the favorite noble servants of royalty became extremely rich and powerful, and they, too, built grandiose palaces in the capital cities. These palaces were in part an extension of the monarch, for they surpassed the buildings of less favored nobles and showed all the high road to fame and fortune. Take, for example, the palaces of Prince Eugene of Savoy, a French nobleman who became Austria's most famous military hero. It was Eugene who led the Austrian army, smashed the Turks, fought Louis XIV to a standstill, and generally guided the triumph of absolutism in Austria. Rewarded with great wealth by his grateful royal employer, Eugene called on the leading architects of the day, J. B. Fischer von Erlach and Johann Lukas von Hildebrandt, to consecrate his glory in stone and fresco. Fischer built Eugene's Winter (or Town) Palace in Vienna, and he and Hildebrandt collaborated on the prince's Summer Palace on the city's outskirts (see accompanying illustration).

Palaces like those of Prince Eugene were magnificent examples of the baroque style. They expressed the baroque delight in bold, sweeping statements, which

**Prince Eugene's Summer Palace, Vienna** The prince's summer residence featured two baroque gems, the Lower Belvedere and the lovely Upper Belvedere, completed in 1722 and shown here. The building's interior is equally stunning, with crouching giants serving as pillars and a magnificent great staircase. Art and beauty convey a feeling of immense prestige and power. *(Erich Lessing/Art Resource, NY)*

were intended to provide a dramatic emotional experience. To create this experience, baroque masters dissolved the traditional artistic frontiers: the architect permitted the painter and the artisan to cover a building's undulating surfaces with wildly colorful paintings, graceful sculptures, and fanciful carvings. Space was used in a highly original way to blend everything together in a total environment. These techniques shone in all their glory in the churches of southern Germany and in the colossal halls of royal palaces. Artistic achievement and political statement reinforced each other.

## Royal Cities

Absolute monarchs and baroque architects were not content with fashioning ostentatious palaces. They remodeled existing capital cities, or even built new ones, to reflect royal magnificence and the centralization of political power. Karlsruhe, founded in 1715 as the capital city of a small German principality, is one extreme example. There broad, straight avenues radiated out from the palace so that all roads—like all power—were focused on the ruler. More typically, the monarch's architects added new urban areas alongside the old city; these areas then became the real heart of the expanding capital.

The distinctive features of these new additions were their broad avenues, their imposing government buildings, and their rigorous mathematical layout. Along these major thoroughfares nobles built elaborate baroque townhouses; stables and servants' quarters were built on the alleys behind. Wide avenues also facilitated the rapid movement of soldiers through the city to quell any disturbance (the king's planners had the needs of the military constantly in mind). Under the arcades along the avenues appeared smart and very expensive shops, the first department stores, with plate-glass windows and fancy displays.

The new avenues brought reckless speed to European cities all across the continent. Whereas everyone had walked through the narrow, twisting streets of the medieval town, the high and mighty now raced down the broad boulevards in their elegant carriages. A social gap opened between the wealthy riders and the gaping, dodging pedestrians. "Mind the carriages!" wrote one eighteenth-century observer in Paris:

*Here comes the black-coated physician in his chariot, the dancing master in his coach, the fencing master in his surrey—and the Prince behind six horses at the gallop as if he were in the open country. . . . The threatening wheels of the overbearing rich drive as rapidly as ever over stones stained with the blood of their unhappy victims.*[14]

Speeding carriages on broad avenues, an endless parade of power and position: here were the symbols and substance of the baroque city.

## The Growth of St. Petersburg

No city illustrates better than St. Petersburg the close ties among politics, architecture, and urban development in this period. In 1700, when the Great Northern War between Russia and Sweden began, the city did not exist. There was only a small Swedish fortress on one of the waterlogged islands at the mouth of the Neva River, where it flows into the Baltic Sea. In 1702 Peter the Great's armies seized this desolate outpost. Within a year the reforming tsar had decided to build a new city there and to make it, rather than ancient Moscow, his capital.

Since the first step was to secure the Baltic coast, military construction was the main concern for the next eight years. A mighty fortress was built on Peter Island, and a port and shipyards were built across the river on the mainland as a Russian navy came into being. The land was swampy and uninhabited, the climate damp and unpleasant. But Peter cared not at all: for him the inhospitable northern marshland was a future metropolis, gloriously bearing his name.

After the decisive Russian victory at Poltava in 1709 greatly reduced the threat of Swedish armies, Peter moved into high gear. In one imperious decree after another, he ordered his people to build a city that would equal any in the world. Such a city had to be Western and baroque, just as Peter's army had to be Western and permanent. From such a new city, his "window on Europe," Peter also believed it would be easier to reform the country militarily and administratively.

These general political goals matched Peter's architectural ideas, which had been influenced by his travels in western Europe. First, Peter wanted a comfortable, "modern" city. Modernity meant broad, straight, stone-paved avenues; houses built in a uniform line and not haphazardly set back from the street; large parks; canals for drainage; stone bridges; and street lighting. Second, all building had to conform strictly to detailed architectural regulations set down by the government. Finally, each social group—the nobility, the merchants, the artisans, and so on—was to live in a certain section of town. In short, the city and its population were to conform to a carefully defined urban plan of the baroque type.

**St. Petersburg, ca 1760** Rastrelli's remodeled Winter Palace, which housed the royal family until the Russian Revolution of 1917, stands on the left along the Neva River. The Navy Office with its famous golden spire and other government office buildings are nearby and across the river. Russia became a naval power and St. Petersburg a great port. *(Michael Holford)*

Peter used the traditional but reinforced methods of Russian autocracy to build his modern capital. The creation of St. Petersburg was just one of the heavy obligations he dictatorially imposed on all social groups in Russia. The peasants bore the heaviest burdens. Just as the government drafted peasants for the army, it also drafted twenty-five thousand to forty thousand men each summer to labor in St. Petersburg for three months without pay. Every ten to fifteen peasant households had to furnish one such worker each summer and then pay a special tax in order to feed that worker in St. Petersburg.

Peasants hated this forced labor in the capital, and each year one-fourth to one-third of those sent risked brutal punishment and ran away. Many peasant construction workers died each summer from hunger, sickness, and accidents. Thus beautiful St. Petersburg was built on the shoveling, carting, and paving of a mass of conscripted serfs.

Peter also drafted more privileged groups to his city, but on a permanent basis. Nobles were summarily ordered to build costly stone houses and palaces in St. Petersburg and to live in them most of the year. The more serfs a noble possessed, the bigger his dwelling had to be. Merchants and artisans were also commanded to settle and build in St. Petersburg. These nobles and merchants were then required to pay for the city's avenues, parks, canals, embankments, pilings, and bridges, all of which were very costly in terms of both money and lives because they were built on a swamp. The building of St. Petersburg was, in truth, an enormous direct tax levied on the wealthy, which in turn forced the peasantry to do most of the work. No wonder so many Russians hated Peter's new city.

Yet the tsar had his way. By the time of his death in 1725, there were at least six thousand houses and numerous impressive government buildings in St. Petersburg.

Under the remarkable women who ruled Russia throughout most of the eighteenth century, St. Petersburg blossomed fully as a majestic and well-organized city, at least in its wealthy showpiece sections. Peter's youngest daughter, the quick-witted Elizabeth (r. 1741–1762), named as her chief architect Bartolomeo Rastrelli, who had come to Russia from Italy as a boy of fifteen in 1715. Combining Italian and Russian traditions into a unique, wildly colorful St. Petersburg style, Rastrelli built many palaces for the nobility and all the larger government buildings erected during Elizabeth's reign. He also rebuilt the Winter Palace as an enormous, aqua-colored royal residence, now the Hermitage Museum. There Elizabeth established a flashy, luxury-loving, and slightly crude court, which Catherine the Great in turn made truly imperial. All the while St. Petersburg grew rapidly, and its almost 300,000 inhabitants in 1782 made it one of the world's largest cities. Peter and his successors had created out of nothing a magnificent and harmonious royal city, which unmistakably proclaimed the power of Russia's rulers and the creative potential of the absolutist state.

## Summary

From about 1400 to 1650, social and economic developments in eastern Europe increasingly diverged from those in western Europe. In the east, peasants and townspeople lost precious freedoms, while the nobility increased its power and prestige. It was within this framework of resurgent serfdom and entrenched nobility that Austrian and Prussian monarchs fashioned absolutist states in the seventeenth and early eighteenth centuries. These monarchs won absolutist control over standing armies, permanent taxes, and legislative bodies. But they did not question underlying social and economic relationships. Indeed, they enhanced the privileges of the nobility, which furnished the leading servitors for enlarged armies and growing state bureaucracies.

In Russia the social and economic trends were similar, but the timing of political absolutism was different. Mongol conquest and rule were a crucial experience, and a harsh, indigenous tsarist autocracy was firmly in place by the reign of Ivan the Terrible in the sixteenth century. More than a century later, Peter the Great succeeded in tightening up Russia's traditional absolutism and modernizing it by reforming the army, the bureaucracy, and the defense industry. In Russia and throughout eastern Europe, war and the needs of the state in time of war weighed heavily in the triumph of absolutism.

Triumphant absolutism interacted spectacularly with the arts. Baroque art, which had grown out of the Catholic Reformation's desire to move the faithful and exalt the true faith, admirably suited the secular aspirations of eastern European rulers. They built grandiose baroque palaces, monumental public squares, and even whole cities to glorify their power and majesty. Thus baroque art attained magnificent heights in eastern Europe, symbolizing the ideal and harmonizing with the reality of imperious royal absolutism.

## Key Terms

| | |
|---|---|
| serfdom | Junkers |
| hereditary subjugation | Eastern Orthodoxy |
| absolutism | boyard nobility |
| Bohemian Estates | Mongol Yoke |
| sultan | autocracy |
| millet system | service nobility |
| Pragmatic Sanction | Cossacks |
| elector of Brandenburg | baroque |

## Notes

1. See L. Wolff, *Inventing Eastern Europe: The Map of Civilization on the Mind of the Enlightenment* (Stanford, Calif.: Stanford University Press, 1994).
2. D. Goffman, *The Ottoman Empire and Early Modern Europe* (Cambridge: Cambridge University Press, 2002), pp. 9–18, 83–91.
3. Quoted in F. L. Carsten, *The Origins of Prussia* (Oxford: Clarendon Press, 1954), p. 175.
4. H. Rosenberg, *Bureaucracy, Aristocracy, and Autocracy: The Prussian Experience, 1660–1815* (Boston: Beacon Press, 1966), p. 38.
5. Quoted in R. Ergang, *The Potsdam Fuhrer: Frederick William I, Father of Prussian Militarism* (New York: Octagon Books, 1972), pp. 85, 87.
6. Ibid., p. 43.
7. Quoted in R. A. Dorwart, *The Administrative Reforms of Frederick William I of Prussia* (Cambridge, Mass.: Harvard University Press, 1953), p. 226.
8. Quoted in Rosenberg, *Bureaucracy, Aristocracy, and Autocracy,* p. 40.
9. Quoted in N. V. Riasanovsky, *A History of Russia* (New York: Oxford University Press, 1963), p. 79.
10. Quoted in I. Grey, *Ivan III and the Unification of Russia* (New York: Collier Books, 1967), p. 42.
11. Both quoted in R. Pipes, *Russia Under the Old Regime* (New York: Charles Scribner's Sons, 1974), pp. 65, 85.
12. Quoted in Ergang, *The Potsdam Fuhrer,* p. 13.
13. Quoted in J. Summerson, in *The Eighteenth Century: Europe in the Age of Enlightenment,* ed. A. Cobban (New York: McGraw-Hill, 1969), p. 80.
14. Quoted in L. Mumford, *The Culture of Cities* (New York: Harcourt Brace Jovanovich, 1938), p. 97.

*(continued on page 592)*

# Listening to the Past

## A Foreign Traveler in Russia

*Russia in the seventeenth century remained a remote and mysterious land for western and even central Europeans, who had few direct contacts with the tsar's dominion. Knowledge of Russia came mainly from occasional travelers who had visited Muscovy and sometimes wrote accounts of what they had seen.*

*The most famous of these accounts was by the German Adam Olearius (ca 1599–1671), who was sent to Moscow by the duke of Holstein on three diplomatic missions in the 1630s. These missions ultimately proved unsuccessful, but they provided Olearius with a rich store of information for his* Travels in Muscovy, *from which the following excerpts are taken. Published in German in 1647 and soon translated into several languages (but not Russian), Olearius's unflattering but well-informed study played a major role in shaping European ideas about Russia.*

The government of the Russians is what political theorists call a "dominating and despotic monarchy," where the sovereign, that is, the tsar or the grand prince who has obtained the crown by right of succession, rules the entire land alone, and all the people are his subjects, and where the nobles and princes no less than the common folk—townspeople and peasants—are his serfs and slaves, whom he rules and treats as a master treats his servants. . . .

If the Russians be considered in respect to their character, customs, and way of life, they are justly to be counted among the barbarians. . . . The vice of drunkenness is so common in this nation, among people of every station, clergy and laity, high and low, men and women, old and young, that when they are seen now and then lying about in the streets, wallowing in the mud, no attention is paid to it, as something habitual. If a cart driver comes upon such a drunken pig whom he happens to know, he shoves him onto his cart and drives him home, where he is paid his fare. No one ever refuses an opportunity to drink and to get drunk, at any time and in any place, and usually it is done with vodka. . . .

The Russians being naturally tough and born, as it were, for slavery, they must be kept under a harsh and strict yoke and must be driven to do their work with clubs and whips, which they suffer without impatience, because such is their station, and they are accustomed to it. Young and half-grown fellows sometimes come together on certain days and train themselves in fisticuffs, to accustom themselves to receiving blows, and, since habit is second nature, this makes blows given as punishment easier to bear. Each and all, they are slaves and serfs. . . .

Because of slavery and their rough and hard life, the Russians accept war readily and are well suited to it. On certain occasions, if need be, they reveal themselves as courageous and daring soldiers. . . .

Although the Russians, especially the common populace, living as slaves under a harsh yoke, can bear and endure a great deal out of love for their masters, yet if the pressure is beyond measure, then it can be said of them: "Patience, often wounded, finally turned into fury." A dangerous indignation results, turned not so much against their sovereign as against the lower authorities, especially if the people have been much oppressed by them and by their supporters and have not been protected by the higher authorities. And once they are aroused and enraged, it is not easy to appease them. Then, disregarding all dangers that may ensue, they resort to every kind of violence and behave like madmen. . . . They own little; most of them have no feather beds; they lie on cushions, straw, mats, or their clothes; they sleep on benches and, in winter, like the non-Germans [i.e., natives] in Livonia, upon the oven,

The brutality of serfdom is shown in this illustration from Olearius's *Travels in Muscovy. (University of Illinois Library, Champaign)*

which serves them for cooking and is flat on the top; here husband, wife, children, servants, and maids huddle together. In some houses in the countryside we saw chickens and pigs under the benches and the ovens. . . .

Russians are not used to delicate food and dainties; their daily food consists of porridge, turnips, cabbage, and cucumbers, fresh and pickled, and in Moscow mostly of big salt fish which stink badly, because of the thrifty use of salt, yet are eaten with relish. . . .

The Russians can endure extreme heat. In the bathhouse they stretch out on benches and let themselves be beaten and rubbed with bunches of birch twigs and wisps of bast (which I could not stand); and when they are hot and red all over and so exhausted that they can bear it no longer in the bathhouse, men and women rush outdoors naked and pour cold water over their bodies; in winter they even wallow in the snow and rub their skin with it as if it were soap; then they go back into the hot bathhouse. And since bathhouses are usually near rivers and brooks, they can throw themselves straight from the hot into the cold bath. . . .

Generally noble families, even the small nobility, rear their daughters in secluded chambers, keeping them hidden from outsiders; and a bridegroom is not allowed to have a look at his bride until he receives her in the bridal chamber. Therefore some happen to be deceived, being given a misshapen and sickly one instead of a fair one, and sometimes a kinswoman or even a maidservant instead of a daughter; of which there have been examples even among the highborn. No wonder therefore that often they live together like cats and dogs and that wife-beating is so common among Russians. . . .

In the Kremlin and in the city there are a great many churches, chapels, and monasteries, both within and without the city walls, over two thousand in all. This is so because every nobleman who has some fortune has a chapel built for himself, and most of them are of stone. The stone churches are round and vaulted inside. . . . They allow neither organs nor any other musical instruments in their churches, saying: Instruments that have neither souls nor life cannot praise God. . . .

In their churches there hang many bells, sometimes five or six, the largest not over two hundredweights. They ring these bells to summon people to church, and also when the priest during mass raises the chalice. In Moscow, because of the multitude of churches and chapels, there are several thousand bells, which during the divine service create such a clang and din that one unaccustomed to it listens in amazement.

## Questions for Analysis

1. In what ways were all social groups in Russia similar, according to Olearius?
2. How did Olearius characterize the Russians in general? What supporting evidence did he offer for his judgment?
3. Does Olearius's account help explain Stenka Razin's rebellion? In what ways?
4. On the basis of these representative passages, why do you think Olearius's book was so popular and influential in central and western Europe?

*Source:* G. Vernadsky and R. T. Fisher, Jr., eds., *A Source Book for Russian History from Early Times to 1917*, vol. 1 (New Haven: Yale University Press, 1972), pp. 249–251. Copyright © 1972 by Yale University Press. Reprinted by permission.

## Suggested Reading

All of the books cited in the Notes are recommended. Rosenberg remains the classic analysis of the social context of Prussian absolutism. In addition to Ergang's work, an exciting and critical biography of ramrod Frederick William I, D. McKay, *The Great Elector: Frederick William of Brandenburg-Prussia* (2001), examines the formative years of Prussian power. G. Craig, *The Politics of the Prussian Army, 1640–1945* (1964), expertly traces the great influence of the military on the Prussian state over three hundred years. A. Corvisier, *Armies and Societies in Europe, 1494–1789* (1979), places military organization in a broad social framework. A good general account is provided in D. McKay and H. Scott, *The Rise of the Great Powers, 1648–1815* (1983). J. Gagliardo, *Germany Under the Old Regime, 1600–1790* (1991), is an impressive survey of developments in all the German states and provides an excellent bibliography. M. Hughes, *Early Modern Germany, 1477–1802* (1992), is also recommended. R. J. Evans, *The Making of the Habsburg Empire, 1550–1700* (1979), is an impressive achievement. C. Ingrao, *The Habsburg Monarchy, 1618–1815* (1994), is a superior synthesis with an up-to-date bibliography. J. Stoye, *The Siege of Vienna* (1964), is a fascinating account of the last great Ottoman offensive. D. Goffman, cited in the Notes, is a superb reinterpretation of the Ottoman Empire. M. Greene, *A Shared World: Christians and Muslims in the Early Mediterranean* (2000), is a pioneering study of the two communities living together on the island of Crete. H. Inalcik and D. Quartaert, *Economic and Social History of the Ottoman Empire, 1300–1914* (1994), is an invaluable synthesis. On the Balkans, see T. Stoianovich, *Balkan Worlds: The First and Last Europe* (1994), and the innovative M. Todorova, *Imaging the Balkans* (1997). M. Pinson, ed., *The Muslims of Bosnia-Herzegovina: Their Historic Development from the Middle Ages to the Dissolution of Yugoslavia* (1993), is a good introduction.

On eastern European peasants and serfdom, D. Chirot, ed., *The Origins of Backwardness in Eastern Europe: Economics and Politics from the Middle Ages Until the Twentieth Century* (1989), is a wide-ranging introduction. W. Hagen, *Ordinary Prussians: Brandenburg Junkers and Villagers, 1500–1840* (2002), provides a fascinating and significant encounter with the people of a Prussian estate. S. Ogilve and B. Scribner, eds., *Germany: A New Economic and Social History, 1450–1800,* 2 vols. (1996), presents the fresh findings of today's scholars. T. Scott, ed., *The Peasants of Europe from the Fourteenth to the Eighteenth Centuries* (1998), examines a wide variety of regions and countries. Wolfe, cited in the Notes, argues provocatively that the French philosophes of the eighteenth century were the first to divide Europe into a backward east and a more advanced west. E. Levin, *Sex and Society in the World of the Orthodox Slavs, 900–1700* (1989), examines family history in eastern Europe. R. Mousnier, *Peasant Uprisings in Seventeenth-Century France, Russia, and China* (1970), is a classic comparative study. Another valuable comparative study, analyzing the political struggle between rulers and nobles in Poland, Hungary, Latvia, Moldavia, and Ukraine, is O. Subtelny, *Domination in Eastern Europe* (1986). Also see L. and M. Frey, *Societies in Upheaval: Insurrections in France, Hungary and Spain in the Early Eighteenth Century* (1989). J. Blum, *Lord and Peasant in Russia from the Ninth to the Nineteenth Century* (1961), provides a good look at conditions in rural Russia, and P. Avrich, *Russian Rebels, 1600–1800* (1972), treats some of the violent peasant upheavals those conditions produced. R. Hellie, *Enserfment and Military Change in Muscovy* (1971), is outstanding, as is A. Yanov's provocative *Origins of Autocracy: Ivan the Terrible in Russian History* (1981). In addition to the fine surveys by Pipes and Riasanovsky cited in the Notes, J. Billington, *The Icon and the Axe* (1970), is a stimulating history of early Russian intellectual and cultural developments, such as the great split in the church. M. Raeff, *Origins of the Russian Intelligentsia* (1966), skillfully probes the mind of the Russian nobility in the eighteenth century. James Cracraft, ed., *Peter the Great Transforms Russia,* 3d ed. (1991), groups interpretive essays by leading scholars, and B. Lincoln, *Sunlight at Midnight: St. Petersburg and the Rise of Modern Russia* (2001), captures the spirit of Peter's new northern capital. P. Buskovitch, *Peter the Great: The Struggle for Power, 1671–1725* (2001), is an outstanding, detailed biography, while B. H. Sumner, *Peter the Great and the Emergence of Russia* (1962), is still a useful brief introduction. N. Riasanovsky, *The Image of Peter the Great in Russian History and Thought* (1985), examines the tsar's place in the Russian imagination. G. Vernadsky and R. Fisher, eds., *A Source Book of Russian History from Early Times to 1917,* 3 vols. (1972), is an invaluable, highly recommended collection of documents and contemporary writings. S. Baron, ed., *The Travels of Olearius in Seventeenth-Century Russia* (1967), is also highly recommended. B. Engel, *Women in Russia, 1700–2000* (2004), is outstanding.

R. Harbison, *Reflections on the Baroque* (2001), is a well-illustrated and imaginative integration of ideas and the arts, while G. Hersey, *Architecture and Geometry in the Age of the Baroque* (2001), explores the link between architecture and scientific thinking. Also recommended on art and architecture are E. Hempel, *Baroque Art and Architecture in Central Europe* (1965), and N. Pevsner, *An Outline of European Architecture,* 6th ed. (1960). J. Cracraft has written an impressive two-volume study of the artistic and cultural transformation associated with Peter the Great, *The Petrine Revolution in Russian Architecture* (1988) and *The Petrine Revolution in Russian Imagery* (1997).

Voltaire, the renowned Enlightenment thinker, leans forward on the left to exchange ideas and witty conversation with Frederick the Great, king of Prussia. *(Bildarchiv Preussischer Kulturbesitz/Art Resource, NY)*

chapter

# 18 Toward a New World-view

**chapter outline**

- The Scientific Revolution
- The Enlightenment
- The Enlightenment and Absolutism

Most people are not philosophers, but they nevertheless have a basic outlook on life, a more or less coherent **world-view.** At the risk of oversimplification, one may say that the world-view of medieval and early modern Europe was primarily religious and theological. Not only did Christian or Jewish teachings form the core of people's spiritual and philosophical beliefs, but religious teachings also permeated all the rest of human thought and activity. Political theory relied on the divine right of kings, for example, and activities ranging from marriage and divorce to business and eating habits were regulated by churches and religious doctrines.

In the course of the eighteenth century, this religious and theological world-view underwent a fundamental transformation among the European upper and comfortable classes. Economically secure and increasingly well educated, these privileged groups of preindustrial Europe interacted with talented writers and as a result often came to see the world primarily in secular and scientific terms. And while few individuals abandoned religious beliefs altogether, the role of churches and religious thinking in earthly affairs and in the pursuit of knowledge was substantially reduced. Among many in the aristocracy and solid middle classes, a new critical, scientific, and very "modern" world-view took shape.

- Why did this momentous change occur?
- How did this new world-view affect the way people thought about society and human relations?
- What impact did this new way of thinking have on political developments and monarchical absolutism?

This chapter will focus on these questions.

See DBQ 5

## The Scientific Revolution

The foremost cause of the change in world-view was the scientific revolution. Modern science—precise knowledge of the physical world based on the union of experimental observations with sophisticated mathematics—crystallized in the seventeenth century. Whereas science had been secondary and subordinate in medieval intellectual life, it became independent and even primary for many educated people in the eighteenth century.

The emergence of modern science was a development of tremendous long-term significance. A noted historian has even said that the scientific revolution of the late sixteenth and seventeenth centuries "outshines everything since the rise of Christianity and reduces the Renaissance and Reformation to the rank of mere episodes, mere internal displacements, within the system of medieval Christendom." The scientific revolution was "the real origin both of the modern world and the modern mentality."[1] This statement is an exaggeration, but not much of one. Of all the great civilizations, only that of the West developed modern science. With the scientific revolution Western society began to acquire its most distinctive traits.

Though historians agree that the scientific revolution was enormously important, they approach it in quite different ways. Some scholars believe that the history of scientific achievement in this period had its own basic "internal" logic and that "nonscientific" factors had quite limited significance. These scholars write brilliant, often highly technical, intellectual studies, but they neglect the broader historical context. Other historians stress "external" economic, social, and religious factors, brushing over the scientific developments themselves. Historians of science now realize that these two approaches need to be brought together. Therefore, let us examine the milestones on the fateful march toward modern science first and then search for the nonscientific influences along the route.

## Scientific Thought in 1500

Since developments in astronomy and physics were at the heart of the scientific revolution, one must begin with the traditional European conception of the universe and movement within it. In the early 1500s, traditional European ideas about the universe were still based primarily on the ideas of Aristotle, the great Greek philosopher of the fourth century B.C. These ideas had gradually been recovered during the Middle Ages and then brought into harmony with Christian doctrines by medieval theologians. According to this revised Aristotelian view, a motionless earth was fixed at the center of the universe. Around it moved ten separate transparent crystal spheres. In the first eight spheres were embedded, in turn, the moon, the sun, the five known planets, and the fixed stars. Then followed two spheres added during the Middle Ages to account for slight changes in the positions of the stars over the centuries. Beyond the tenth sphere was Heaven, with the throne of God and the souls of the saved. Angels kept the spheres moving in perfect circles.

Aristotle's views, suitably revised by medieval philosophers, also dominated thinking about physics and motion on earth. Aristotle had distinguished sharply between the world of the celestial spheres and that of the earth—the sublunar world. The spheres consisted of a perfect, incorruptible "quintessence," or fifth essence. The sublunar world, however, was made up of four imperfect, changeable elements. The "light" elements (air and fire) naturally moved upward, while the "heavy" elements (water and earth) naturally moved downward. These natural directions of motion did not always prevail, however, for elements were often mixed together and could be affected by an outside force such as a human being. Aristotle and his followers also believed that a uniform force moved an object at a constant speed and that the object would stop as soon as that force was removed.

Aristotle's ideas about astronomy and physics were accepted with minor revisions for two thousand years, and with good reason. First, they offered an understandable, commonsense explanation for what the eye actually saw. Second, Aristotle's science as interpreted by Christian theologians fit neatly with Christian doctrines. It established a home for God and a place for Christian souls. It put human beings at the center of the universe and made them the critical link in a "great chain of being" that stretched from the throne of God to the most lowly insect on earth. Thus science was primarily a branch of theology, and it reinforced religious thought. At the same time, medieval "scientists" were already providing closely reasoned explanations of the universe, explanations they felt were worthy of God's perfect creation.

## The Copernican Hypothesis

The desire to explain and thereby glorify God's handiwork led to the first great departure from the medieval system. This departure was the work of the Polish clergyman and astronomer Nicolaus Copernicus (1473–1543). As a young man, Copernicus studied church law and astronomy in various European universities. He saw how professional astronomers still depended for their most accurate calculations on the work of Ptolemy, the last great ancient astronomer, who had lived in Alexandria in the second century A.D. Ptolemy's achievement had been to work out complicated rules to explain the minor irregularities in the movement of the planets. These rules enabled stargazers and astrologers to track the planets with

1540 1590 1640 1690 1740 1790

**POLITICAL/MILITARY**

- 1740–1786 Reign of Frederick the Great of Prussia
- ca 1750–1790 Enlightened absolutists
- 1762–1796 Reign of Catherine the Great of Russia
- 1780–1790 Reign of Joseph II of Austria

**SOCIAL/ECONOMIC**

- 1662 Royal Society of London founded
- 1700–1789 Growth of book publishing
- 1720–1780 Rococo style in art and decoration
- ca 1740–1780 Salons led by elite women

**INTELLECTUAL/RELIGIOUS**

- ca 1540–1690 Scientific revolution
- 1543 Copernicus, *On the Revolutions of the Heavenly Spheres*
- 1564–1642 Life of Galileo
- 1571–1630 Life of Kepler
- 1687 Newton, *Principia* and law of universal gravitation
- 1690 Locke, *Essay Concerning Human Understanding*
- ca 1690–1780 Enlightenment
- 1694–1778 Life of Voltaire
- 1751–1765 Diderot and d'Alembert, *Encyclopedia*
- 1762 Rousseau, *The Social Contract*

greater precision. Many people then (and now) believed that the changing relationships between planets and stars influenced and even determined the future.

The young Copernicus was uninterested in astrology and felt that Ptolemy's cumbersome and occasionally inaccurate rules detracted from the majesty of a perfect Creator. He preferred an old Greek idea being discussed in Renaissance Italy: that the sun, rather than the earth, was at the center of the universe. Finishing his university studies and returning to a church position in East Prussia, Copernicus worked on his hypothesis from 1506 to 1530. Never questioning the Aristotelian belief in crystal spheres or the idea that circular motion was most perfect and divine, Copernicus theorized that the stars and planets, including the earth, revolved around a fixed sun. Yet Copernicus was a cautious man. Fearing the ridicule of other astronomers, he did not publish his *On the Revolutions of the Heavenly Spheres* until 1543, the year of his death.

The **Copernican hypothesis** had enormous scientific and religious implications, many of which the conservative Copernicus did not anticipate. First, it put the stars at rest, their apparent nightly movement simply a result of the earth's rotation. Thus it destroyed the main reason for believing in crystal spheres capable of moving the stars around the earth. Second, Copernicus's theory suggested a universe of staggering size. If in the course of a year the earth moved around the sun and yet the stars appeared to remain in the same place, then the universe was unthinkably large or even infinite. Finally, by characterizing the earth as just another planet, Copernicus destroyed the basic idea of Aristotelian physics—that the earthly world was quite different from the heavenly one. Where, then, was the realm of perfection? Where were Heaven and the throne of God?

The Copernican hypothesis quickly brought sharp attacks from religious leaders, especially Protestants. Hearing of Copernicus's work even before it was published, Martin Luther spoke of him as the "new astrologer who wants to prove that the earth moves and goes round. . . . The fool wants to turn the whole art of astronomy upside down." Luther noted that "as the Holy Scripture tells us, so did Joshua bid the sun stand still and not the earth."[2] John Calvin also condemned Copernicus. Catholic reaction was milder at first. The Catholic church had never been hypnotized by literal interpretations of the Bible, and not until 1616 did it officially declare the Copernican hypothesis false.

This slow reaction also reflected the slow progress of Copernicus's theory for many years. Other events were almost as influential in creating doubts about traditional astronomical ideas. In 1572 a new star appeared and shone very brightly for almost two years. The new star, which was actually a distant exploding star, made an enormous impression on people. It seemed to contradict the idea that the heavenly spheres were unchanging and therefore perfect. In 1577 a new comet suddenly moved through the sky, cutting a straight path across the supposedly impenetrable crystal spheres. It was time, as a typical scientific writer put it, for "the radical renovation of astronomy."[3]

## From Brahe to Galileo

One astronomer who agreed was Tycho Brahe (1546–1601). Born into a leading Danish noble family and earmarked for a career in government, Brahe was at an early age tremendously impressed when a partial eclipse of the sun occurred exactly as expected. It seemed to him "something divine that men could know the motions of the stars so accurately that they were able a long time beforehand to predict their places and relative positions."[4] Completing his studies abroad and returning to Denmark, Brahe established himself as Europe's leading astronomer with his detailed observations of the new star of 1572. Aided by generous grants from the king of Denmark, Brahe built the most sophisticated observatory of his day. For twenty years he meticulously observed the stars and planets with the naked eye. An imposing man who had lost a piece of his nose in a duel and replaced it with a special bridge of gold and silver alloy, a noble who exploited his peasants arrogantly and approached the heavens humbly, Brahe's great contribution was his mass of data. His limited understanding of mathematics prevented him, however, from making much sense out of his data. Part Ptolemaic, part Copernican, he believed that all the planets revolved around the sun and that the entire group of sun and planets revolved in turn around the earth-moon system.

It was left to Brahe's brilliant young assistant, Johannes Kepler (1571–1630), to go much further. Kepler was a medieval figure in many ways. Coming from a minor German noble family and trained for the Lutheran ministry, he long believed that the universe was built on mystical mathematical relationships and a musical harmony of the heavenly bodies. Working and reworking Brahe's mountain of observations in a staggering sustained effort after the Dane's death, this brilliant mathematician eventually went beyond mystical intuitions.

Kepler formulated three famous laws of planetary motion. First, building on Copernican theory, he demonstrated in 1609 that the orbits of the planets around the sun are elliptical rather than circular. Second, he demonstrated that the planets do not move at a uniform speed in their orbits. Third, in 1619 he showed that the time a planet takes to make its complete orbit is precisely related to its distance from the sun. Kepler's contribution was monumental. Whereas Copernicus had speculated, Kepler proved mathematically the precise relations of a sun-centered (solar) system. His work demolished the old system of Aristotle and Ptolemy, and in his third law he came close to formulating the idea of universal gravitation.

While Kepler was unraveling planetary motion, a young Florentine named Galileo Galilei (1564–1642) was challenging all the old ideas about motion. Like so many early scientists, Galileo was a poor nobleman first marked for a religious career. However, he soon became fascinated by mathematics. A brilliant student, Galileo became a professor of mathematics in 1589 at age twenty-five. He proceeded to examine motion and mechanics in a new way. Indeed, his great achievement was the elaboration and consolidation of the **experimental method.** That is, rather than speculate about what might or should happen, Galileo conducted controlled experiments to find out what actually *did* happen.

In his famous acceleration experiment, he showed that a uniform force—in this case, gravity—produced a uniform acceleration. Here is how Galileo described his pathbreaking method and conclusion in his *Two New Sciences:*

> *A piece of wooden moulding . . . was taken; on its edge was cut a channel a little more than one finger in breadth. Having made this groove very straight, smooth and polished, and having lined it with parchment, also as smooth and polished as possible, we rolled along it a hard, smooth and very round bronze ball. . . . Noting . . . the time required to make the descent . . . we now rolled the ball only one-quarter the length of the channel; and having measured the time of its descent, we found it precisely one-half of the former. . . . In such experiments [over many distances], repeated a full hundred times, we always found that the spaces traversed were to each other as the squares of the times, and that this was true for all inclinations of the plane.*[5]

With this and other experiments, Galileo also formulated the **law of inertia.** Rest was not the natural state of objects. Rather, an object continues in motion forever unless stopped by some external force. Aristotelian physics was in a shambles.

In the tradition of Brahe, Galileo also applied the experimental method to astronomy. On hearing details about the invention of the telescope in Holland, Galileo made one for himself and trained it on the heavens. He quickly discovered the first four moons of Jupiter, which clearly suggested that Jupiter could not possibly be embedded

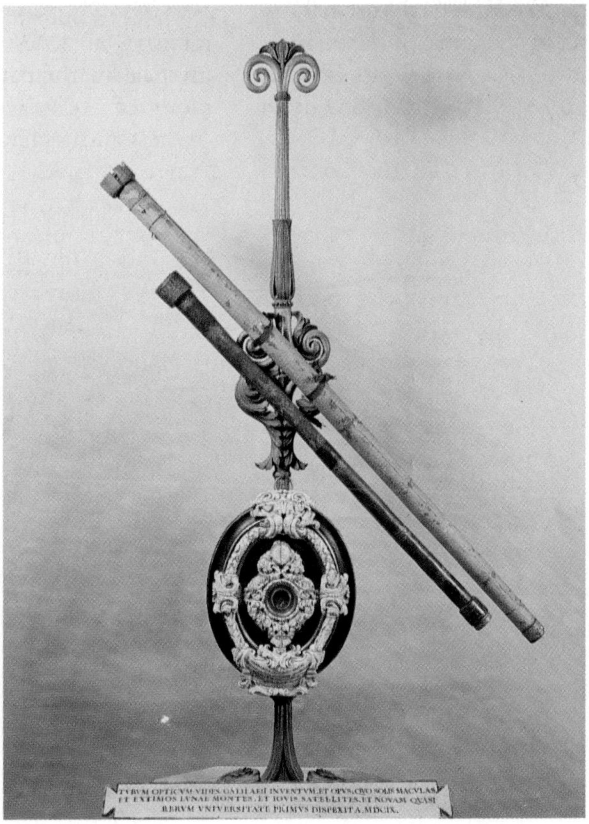

**Galileo's Paintings of the Moon** When Galileo published the results of his telescopic observations of the moon, he added these paintings to illustrate the marvels he had seen. Galileo made two telescopes, which are shown here. The larger one magnifies fourteen times, the smaller twenty times. *(Biblioteca Nazionale Centrale, Florence/Art Resource, NY; Museum of Science, Florence/Art Resource, NY)*

in any impenetrable crystal sphere. This discovery provided new evidence for the Copernican theory, in which Galileo already believed.

Galileo then pointed his telescope at the moon. He wrote in 1610 in *Siderus Nuncius:*

*I feel sure that the moon is not perfectly smooth, free from inequalities, and exactly spherical, as a large school of philosophers considers with regard to the moon and the other heavenly bodies. On the contrary, it is full of inequalities, uneven, full of hollows and protuberances, just like the surface of the earth itself, which is varied. . . . The next object which I have observed is the essence or substance of the Milky Way. By the aid of a telescope anyone may behold this in a manner which so distinctly appeals to the senses that all the disputes which have tormented philosophers through so many ages are exploded by the irrefutable evidence of our eyes, and we are freed from wordy disputes upon the subject. For the galaxy is nothing else but a mass of innumerable stars planted together in clusters.*[6]

Reading these famous lines, one feels a crucial corner in Western civilization being turned. The traditional religious and theological world-view, which rested on determining and accepting the proper established authority, was beginning to give way in certain fields to a critical, modern scientific method. This new method of learning and investigating was the greatest accomplishment of the entire scientific revolution, for it proved capable of great extension. A historian investigating documents of the past, for example, is not so different from a Galileo studying stars and rolling balls.

Galileo was employed in Florence by the Medici grand dukes of Tuscany, and his work eventually aroused the ire of some theologians. The issue was presented in 1624 to Pope Urban VIII, who permitted Galileo to write about

**Galileo Before the Papal Inquisition** Summoned to Rome in 1633 and charged with heresy for teaching that the sun, not the earth, was at the center of the universe, Galileo sits before his ecclesiastical judges in a packed courtroom in this anonymous painting. Galileo lost his battle with religious authority and was forced to renounce his scientific beliefs, but he inspired many who followed in the pursuit of intellectual freedom. *(Erich Lessing/Art Resource, NY)*

different possible systems of the world as long as he did not presume to judge which one actually existed. After the publication in Italian of his widely read *Dialogue on the Two Chief Systems of the World* in 1632, which openly lampooned the traditional views of Aristotle and Ptolemy and defended those of Copernicus, Galileo was tried for heresy by the papal Inquisition. Imprisoned and threatened with torture, the aging Galileo recanted, "renouncing and cursing" his Copernican errors. Of minor importance in the development of science, Galileo's trial later became for some writers the perfect symbol of the inherent conflict between religious belief and scientific knowledge.

## Newton's Synthesis

The accomplishments of Kepler, Galileo, and other scientists had taken effect by about 1640. The old astronomy and physics were in ruins, and several fundamental breakthroughs had been made. The new findings had not, however, been fused together in a new synthesis, a single explanatory system that would comprehend motion both on earth and in the skies. That synthesis, which prevailed until the twentieth century, was the work of Isaac Newton (1642–1727).

Newton was born into lower English gentry and attended Cambridge University. A genius who spectacularly united the experimental and theoretical-mathematical sides of modern science, Newton was also fascinated by alchemy. He sought the elixir of life and a way to change base metals into gold and silver. Not without reason did the twentieth-century economist John Maynard Keynes call Newton the "last of the magicians." Newton was also intensely religious. He was far from being the perfect rationalist so endlessly eulogized by writers in the eighteenth and nineteenth centuries.

Of his intellectual genius and incredible powers of concentration there can be no doubt, however. Arriving at some of his most basic ideas about physics in 1666 at age twenty-four, but unable to prove these theories mathematically, he attained a professorship and studied optics for many years. In 1684 Newton returned to physics for eighteen extraordinarily intensive months. For weeks on end he seldom left his room except to read his lectures. His meals were sent up, but he usually forgot to eat them, his mind fastened like a vise on the laws of the universe. He opened the third book of his immortal *Mathematical Principles of Natural Philosophy,* published in Latin in 1687 and generally known as the *Principia,* with these lines:

*In the preceding books I have laid down the principles of philosophy [that is, science]. . . . These principles are the laws of certain motions, and powers or forces, which chiefly have respect to philosophy. . . . It remains that from the same principles I now demonstrate the frame of the System of the World.*

**Isaac Newton** This portrait suggests the depth and complexity of the great genius. Is the powerful mind behind those piercing eyes thinking of science or of religion, or perhaps of both? *(Scala/Art Resource, NY)*

Newton made good his grandiose claim. His towering accomplishment was to integrate in a single explanatory system the astronomy of Copernicus, as corrected by Kepler's laws, with the physics of Galileo and his predecessors. Newton did this by means of a set of mathematical laws that explain motion and mechanics. These laws of dynamics are complex, and it took scientists and engineers two hundred years to work out all their implications. Nevertheless, the key feature of the Newtonian synthesis was the **law of universal gravitation.** According to this law, every body in the universe attracts every other body in the universe in a precise mathematical relationship, whereby the force of attraction is proportional to the quantity of matter of the objects and inversely proportional to the square of the distance between them. The whole universe—from Kepler's elliptical orbits to Galileo's rolling balls—was unified in one majestic system.

## Causes of the Scientific Revolution

With a charming combination of modesty and self-congratulation, Newton once wrote, "If I have seen further [than others], it is by standing on the shoulders of Giants."[7] Surely the path from Copernicus to Newton confirms the "internal" view of the scientific revolution as a product of towering individual genius. The problems of science were inherently exciting, and solution of those problems was its own reward for inquisitive, high-powered minds. Yet there were certainly broader causes as well.

First, the long-term contribution of medieval intellectual life and medieval universities to the scientific revolution was much more considerable than historians unsympathetic to the Middle Ages once believed. By the thirteenth century, permanent universities with professors and large student bodies had been established in western Europe to train the lawyers, doctors, and church leaders that society required. By 1300 philosophy had taken its place alongside law, medicine, and theology. Medieval philosophers developed a limited but real independence from theologians and a sense of free inquiry. They nobly pursued a body of knowledge and tried to arrange it meaningfully by means of abstract theories.

Within this framework, science was able to emerge as a minor but distinct branch of philosophy. In the fourteenth and fifteenth centuries, leading universities established new professorships of mathematics, astronomy, and physics (natural philosophy) within their faculties of philosophy. Although the prestige of the new fields was low among both professors and students, rational, critical thinking was applied to scientific problems by a permanent community of scholars. And an outlet existed for the talents of a Galileo or a Newton: all the great pathfinders either studied or taught at universities.

Second, the Renaissance also stimulated scientific progress. The recovery of the finest works of Greek mathematics—a byproduct of Renaissance humanism's ceaseless search for the knowledge of antiquity—greatly improved European mathematics well into the early seventeenth century. The recovery of more texts also showed that classical mathematicians had their differences; Europeans were thus forced to resolve, if possible, these ancient controversies by means of their own efforts. Finally, the Renaissance pattern of patronage, especially in Italy, was often scientific as well as artistic and humanistic. Various rulers and wealthy business people supported scientific investigations, as the Medicis of Florence supported those of Galileo.

The navigational problems of long sea voyages in the age of overseas expansion were a third factor in the scientific revolution. Ship captains on distant shores needed to be able to chart their positions as accurately as possible so that reliable maps could be drawn and the risks of international trade reduced. As early as 1484, the king of Portugal appointed a commission of mathematicians to perfect tables to help seamen find their latitude. This resulted in the first European navigation manual.

The problem of fixing longitude was much more difficult. In England the government and the great capitalistic trading companies turned to science and scientific education in an attempt to solve this pressing practical problem. When the famous Elizabethan financier Sir Thomas Gresham left a large amount of money to establish Gresham College in London, he stipulated that three of the college's seven professors had to concern themselves exclusively with scientific subjects. The professor of astronomy was directed to teach courses on the science of navigation. A seventeenth-century popular ballad took note of the new college's calling:

*This college will the whole world measure*
*Which most impossible conclude,*
*And navigation make a pleasure*
*By finding out the longitude.*[8]

At Gresham College scientists had, for the first time in history, an important, honored role in society. They enjoyed close ties with top officials of the Royal Navy and with leading merchants and shipbuilders. Gresham College became the main center of scientific activity in England in the first half of the seventeenth century. The close tie between practical men and scientists also led to the establishment in 1662 of the Royal Society of London, which published scientific papers and sponsored scientific meetings.

Navigational problems were also critical in the development of many new scientific instruments, such as the telescope, barometer, thermometer, pendulum clock, microscope, and air pump. Better instruments, which permitted more accurate observations, often led to important new knowledge. Galileo with his telescope was by no means unique.

Better instruments were part of a fourth factor in the scientific revolution, the development of better ways of obtaining knowledge about the world. Two important thinkers, Francis Bacon (1561–1626) and René Descartes (1596–1650), represented key aspects of this improvement in scientific methodology.

**The Observatory at Nuremberg** The quest for scientific knowledge in the seventeenth century was already an expensive undertaking that required teamwork and government support, as this encyclopedic illustration suggests. Nuremberg was a historic center of commerce and culture in southern Germany, and its observatory played a pioneering role in early astronomical advance. *(Kunstsammlungen der Veste Coburg)*

The English politician and writer Francis Bacon was the greatest early propagandist for the new experimental method. Rejecting the Aristotelian and medieval method of using speculative reasoning to build general theories, Bacon argued that new knowledge had to be pursued through empirical, experimental research. The researcher who wants to learn more about leaves or rocks should not speculate about the subject but rather collect a multitude of specimens and then compare and analyze them, he said. General principles will then emerge. Bacon's contribution was to formalize the empirical method, which had already been used by Brahe and Galileo, into the general theory of inductive reasoning known as **empiricism.**

Bacon claimed that the empirical method would result not only in more knowledge but also in highly practical, useful knowledge. According to Bacon, scientific discoveries like those so avidly sought at Gresham College would bring about much greater control over the physical environment and make people rich and nations powerful. Thus Bacon helped provide a radically new and effective justification for private and public support of scientific inquiry.

The French philosopher René Descartes was a true genius who made his first great discovery in mathematics. As a twenty-three-year-old soldier serving in the Thirty Years' War, he experienced on a single night in 1619 a life-changing intellectual vision. Descartes saw that there was a perfect correspondence between geometry and algebra and that geometrical, spatial figures could be expressed as algebraic equations and vice versa. A major step forward in the history of mathematics, Descartes's discovery of analytic geometry provided scientists with an important new tool.

Descartes's greatest achievement was to develop his initial vision into a whole philosophy of knowledge and science. He decided it was necessary to doubt everything that could reasonably be doubted and then, as in geometry, to use deductive reasoning from self-evident principles to ascertain scientific laws. Descartes's reasoning ultimately reduced all substances to "matter" and "mind"—that is, to the physical and the spiritual. His view of the world as consisting of two fundamental entities is known as **Cartesian dualism.** Descartes was a profoundly original and extremely influential thinker.

Bacon's inductive experimentalism and Descartes's deductive, mathematical reasoning are combined in the modern scientific method, which began to crystallize in the late seventeenth century. Neither man's extreme approach was sufficient by itself. Bacon's inability to appreciate the importance of mathematics and his obsession with practical results clearly showed the limitations of antitheoretical empiricism. Likewise, some of Descartes's positions—he believed, for example, that it was possible to deduce the whole science of medicine from first principles—demonstrated the inadequacy of rigid, dogmatic rationalism. Thus the modern scientific method has joined precise observations and experimentalism with the search for general laws that may be expressed in rigorously logical, mathematical language.

Finally, there is the question of the role of religion in the development of science. Just as some historians have argued that Protestantism led to the rise of capitalism, others have concluded that Protestantism was a fundamental factor in the rise of modern science. Protestantism, particularly in its Calvinist varieties, supposedly made scientific inquiry a question of individual conscience and not of religious doctrine. The Catholic church, in contrast, supposedly suppressed scientific theories that conflicted with its teachings and thus discouraged scientific progress.

The truth of the matter is more complicated. *All* religious authorities—Catholic, Protestant, and Jewish—opposed the Copernican system to a greater or lesser extent until about 1630, by which time the scientific revolution was definitely in progress. The Catholic church was initially less hostile than Protestant and Jewish religious leaders, and Italian scientists played a crucial role in scientific progress right up to the trial of Galileo in 1633. Thereafter, the Counter-Reformation church became more hostile to science, a change that helped account for the decline of science in Italy (but not in Catholic France) after 1640. At the same time, Protestant countries such as the Netherlands and Denmark became quite "proscience," especially if the country lacked a strong religious authority capable of imposing religious orthodoxy on scientific questions.

This was certainly the case with Protestant England after 1630. English religious conflicts became so intense that the authorities could not impose religious unity on anything, including science. Significantly, the forerunners of the Royal Society agreed to discuss only "neutral" scientific questions so as not to come to blows over closely related religious and political disputes. The work of Bacon's many followers during Oliver Cromwell's commonwealth helped solidify the neutrality and independence of science. Bacon advocated the experimental approach precisely because it was open-minded and independent of any preconceived religious or philosophical ideas. Neutral and useful, science became an accepted part of life and developed rapidly in England after about 1640.

## Some Consequences of the Scientific Revolution

The rise of modern science had many consequences, some of which are still unfolding. First, it went hand in hand with the rise of a new and expanding social group—the international scientific community. Members of this community were linked together by common interests and shared values as well as by journals and the learned scientific societies founded in many countries in the later seventeenth and the eighteenth centuries. Expansion of knowledge was the primary goal of this community, and scientists' material and psychological rewards depended on their success in this endeavor. Thus science became quite competitive, and even more scientific advance was inevitable.

**Finding Longitude** Not knowing their longitude, or how far east or west they were, sailors often ran aground and shipwrecked. In 1714 a motivated Parliament established a princely prize for the first person to solve the problem, and eventually a clock-making genius named John Harrison won with an amazingly accurate timepiece that permitted precise calculation of longitude at sea. Harrison's massive first effort, pictured here, was already the world's best shipboard clock. *(Courtesy, National Maritime Museum, London)*

Second, the scientific revolution introduced not only new knowledge about nature but also a new and revolutionary way of obtaining such knowledge—the modern scientific method. In addition to being both theoretical and experimental, this method was highly critical, and it differed profoundly from the old way of getting knowledge about nature. It refused to base its conclusions on tradition and established sources, on ancient authorities and sacred texts.

The scientific revolution had few consequences for economic life and the living standards of the masses until the late eighteenth century at the very earliest. True, improvements in the techniques of navigation facilitated overseas trade and helped enrich leading merchants. But science had relatively few practical economic applications, and the hopes of the early Baconians were frustrated. The close link between theoretical, or pure, science and applied technology, which we take for granted today, simply did not exist in the eighteenth century. Thus the scientific revolution of the seventeenth century was first and foremost an intellectual revolution. For more than a hundred years its greatest impact was on how people thought and believed.

## The Enlightenment

See DBQ 5

The scientific revolution was the single most important factor in the creation of the new world-view of the eighteenth-century **Enlightenment.** This world-view, which has played a large role in shaping the modern mind, grew out of a rich mix of ideas. These ideas were diverse and often conflicting, for the talented (and not-so-talented) writers who espoused them competed vigorously for the attention of a growing public of well-educated but fickle readers, who remained a small minority of the population. Despite this diversity, three central concepts stand at the core of Enlightenment thinking.

The most important and original idea of the Enlightenment was that the methods of natural science could and should be used to examine and understand all aspects of life. This was what intellectuals meant by *reason,* a favorite word of Enlightenment thinkers. Nothing was to be accepted on faith. Everything was to be submitted to the rational, critical, scientific way of thinking. This **rationalism** often brought the Enlightenment into a head-on conflict with established churches, which rested their beliefs on the special authority of the Bible and Christian theology. A second important Enlightenment concept was that the scientific method was capable of discovering the laws of human society as well as those of nature. Thus was social science born. Its birth led to the third key idea, that of **progress.** Armed with the proper method of discovering the laws of human existence, Enlightenment thinkers believed that it was at least possible for human beings to create better societies and better people. Their belief was strengthened by some modest improvements in economic and social life during the eighteenth century.

The Enlightenment was therefore profoundly secular. It revived and expanded the Renaissance concentration on worldly explanations. In the course of the eighteenth century, the Enlightenment had a profound impact on the thought and culture of the urban middle classes and the aristocracy. It did not, however, have much appeal for the urban poor and the peasants, who were preoccupied with the struggle for survival and who often resented the Enlightenment attack on traditional popular beliefs (see Chapters 19 and 20).

### The Emergence of the Enlightenment

Loosely united by certain key ideas, the European Enlightenment was a broad intellectual and cultural movement that gained strength gradually and did not reach its maturity until about 1750. Yet it was the generation that came of age between the publication of Newton's *Principia* in 1687 and the death of Louis XIV in 1715 that tied the crucial knot between the scientific revolution and a new outlook on life. Talented writers of that generation popularized hard-to-understand scientific achievements for the educated elite.

The most famous and influential popularizer was a versatile French man of letters, Bernard de Fontenelle (1657–1757). He set out to make science witty and entertaining for a broad nonscientific audience—as easy to read as a novel. This was a tall order, but Fontenelle largely succeeded. His most famous work, *Conversations on the Plurality of Worlds* (1686), begins with two elegant figures walking in the gathering shadows of a large park. One is a woman, a sophisticated aristocrat, and the other is her friend, perhaps even her lover. They gaze at the stars, and their talk turns to a passionate discussion of . . . astronomy! He confides that "each star may well be a different world," then gently stresses how error is giving way to truth. At one point he explains:

*There came on the scene . . . one Copernicus, who made short work of all those various circles, all those solid skies, which the ancients had pictured to themselves. . . . Fired with the noble zeal of a true astronomer, he took the earth and spun it very far away from the center of the universe, where it had*

**Popularizing Science** The frontispiece illustration of Fontenelle's *Conversations on the Plurality of Worlds* invites the reader to share the pleasures of astronomy with an elegant lady and an entertaining teacher. The drawing shows the planets revolving around the sun. *(By permission of the Syndics of Cambridge University Library)*

*been installed, and in that center he put the sun, which had a far better title to the honor.*[9]

Rather than despair at this dismissal of traditional understanding, Fontenelle's lady rejoices in the knowledge that the human mind is capable of making great progress.

This concept of progress was essentially a creation of the later seventeenth century. Medieval and Reformation thinkers had been concerned primarily with sin and salvation. The humanists of the Renaissance had emphasized worldly matters, but they had looked backward. They had believed it might be possible to equal the magnificent accomplishments of the ancients, but they did not ask for more. Fontenelle and like-minded writers had come to believe that at least in science and mathematics, their era had gone far beyond antiquity. Progress, at least intellectual progress, was very possible.

Fontenelle and other writers of his generation were also instrumental in bringing science into conflict with religion. This was a major innovation because many seventeenth-century scientists, both Catholic and Protestant, believed that their work exalted God. They did not draw antireligious implications from their scientific findings. The greatest scientist of them all, Isaac Newton, was a devout, if unorthodox, Christian who saw all of his studies as directed toward explaining God's message.

Fontenelle, in contrast, was skeptical about absolute truth and cynical about the claims of organized religion. Since such unorthodox views could not be stated openly in an absolute monarchy like Louis XIV's France, Fontenelle made his point through subtle editorializing about science. His depiction of the cautious Copernicus as a self-conscious revolutionary was typical. In *Eulogies of Scientists,* Fontenelle exploited with endless variations the fundamental theme of rational, progressive scientists versus prejudiced, reactionary priests.

The progressive and antireligious implications that writers such as Fontenelle drew from the scientific revolution reflected a very real crisis in European thought at the end of the seventeenth century. This crisis had its roots in several intellectual uncertainties and dissatisfactions, of which the demolition of Aristotelian-medieval science was only one.

A second uncertainty involved the whole question of religious truth. The destructive wars of religion that culminated in the Thirty Years' War (1618–1648) had been fought, in part, because religious freedom was an intolerable idea in Europe in the early seventeenth century. Both Catholics and Protestants had believed that religious truth was absolute and therefore worth fighting and dying for. Most Catholics and Protestants also believed that a strong state required unity in religious faith. Yet the disastrous results of the many attempts to impose such religious unity, such as Louis XIV's brutal expulsion of the French Huguenots in 1685, led some people to ask if ideological conformity in religious matters was really necessary. Others skeptically asked if religious truth could ever be known with absolute certainty and concluded that it could not.

The most famous of these skeptics was Pierre Bayle (1647–1706), a French Huguenot who despised Louis XIV and found refuge in the Netherlands. A teacher by profession and a crusading journalist by inclination, Bayle took full advantage of the toleration and intellectual freedom of his adopted land. He critically examined the religious beliefs and persecutions of the past in his *Historical and Critical Dictionary,* written in French and published in the Netherlands in 1697. Demonstrating that human beliefs had been extremely varied and very often mistaken, Bayle concluded that nothing can ever be known beyond all doubt. In religion as in philosophy, humanity's best hope was open-minded toleration. Bayle's **skepticism** was very influential. Reprinted frequently in the Netherlands and in England, his four-volume *Dictionary* was found in more private libraries of eighteenth-century France than any other book.

The rapidly growing travel literature on non-European lands and cultures was a third cause of uncertainty. In the wake of the great discoveries, Europeans were learning that the peoples of China, India, Africa, and the Americas all had their own very different beliefs and customs. Europeans shaved their faces and let their hair grow. Turks shaved their heads and let their beards grow. In Europe a man bowed before a woman to show respect. In Siam a man turned his back on a woman when he met her because it was disrespectful to look directly at her. Countless similar examples discussed in the travel accounts helped change the perspective of educated Europeans. They began to look at truth and morality in relative, rather than absolute, terms. If anything was possible, who could say what was right or wrong?

A fourth cause and manifestation of European intellectual turmoil was John Locke's epoch-making *Essay Concerning Human Understanding*. Published in 1690—the same year Locke published his famous *Second Treatise of Civil Government* (see page 554)—Locke's essay brilliantly set forth a new theory about how human beings learn and form their ideas. In doing so, he rejected the prevailing view of Descartes, who had held that all people are born with certain basic ideas and ways of thinking. Locke insisted that all ideas are derived from experience. The human mind at birth is like a blank tablet, or **tabula rasa,** on which the environment writes the individual's understanding and beliefs. Human development is therefore determined by education and social institutions, for good or for evil. Locke's *Essay Concerning Human Understanding* passed through many editions and translations. It was, along with Newton's *Principia,* one of the dominant intellectual inspirations of the Enlightenment.

## The Philosophes and the Public

By the time Louis XIV died in 1715, many of the ideas that would soon coalesce into the new world-view had been assembled. Yet Christian Europe was still strongly attached to its traditional beliefs, as witnessed by the powerful revival of religious orthodoxy in the first half of the eighteenth century (see pages 681–683). By the outbreak of the American Revolution in 1775, however, a large portion of western Europe's educated elite had embraced many of the new ideas. This acceptance was the work of one of history's most influential groups of intellectuals, the **philosophes.** It was the philosophes who proudly and effectively proclaimed that they, at long last, were bringing the light of knowledge to their ignorant fellow creatures in an Age of Enlightenment.

*Philosophe* is the French word for "philosopher," and it was in France that the Enlightenment reached its highest development. There were at least three reasons for this. First, French was the international language of the educated classes in the eighteenth century, and the education of the rich and the powerful across Europe often lay in the hands of French tutors espousing Enlightenment ideas. France's cultural leadership was reinforced by the fact that it was still the wealthiest and most populous country in Europe.

Second, after the death of Louis XIV, French absolutism and religious orthodoxy remained strong, but not too strong. Critical books were often banned by the censors, and their authors were sometimes jailed or exiled—but not tortured or burned. Intellectual radicals battled against powerful opposition in France, but they did not face the overwhelming restraints generally found in eastern and east-central Europe.

Third, the French philosophes were indeed philosophers, asking fundamental philosophical questions about the meaning of life, God, human nature, good and evil, and cause and effect. But in the tradition of Bayle and Fontenelle, they were not content with abstract arguments or ivory-tower speculations. They were determined to reach and influence all the French (and European) economic and social elites, many of which were joined together in the eighteenth-century concept of the educated or enlightened public, or simply **the public.**

As a wealth of recent scholarship has shown, the public was quite different from the great majority of the population, which was known as the common people, or simply "the people." French philosophe Jean le Rond d'Alembert (1717–1783) characteristically made a sharp distinction between "the truly enlightened public" and "the blind and noisy multitude."[10] A leading scholar has even concluded that the differences between the upper and comfortable middling groups that made up the French public were "insignificant" in comparison with the great gulf between the public and the common people.[11] Above all, the philosophes believed that the great majority of the common people were doomed to superstition and confusion because they lacked the money and leisure to look beyond their bitter struggle with grinding poverty (see pages 630–633).

Suspicious of the people but intensely committed to reason, reform, and slow, difficult progress, the great philosophes and their imitators were not free to write as they wished, since it was illegal in France to criticize openly either church or state. Their most radical works had to circulate in manuscript form. Knowing that direct attacks would probably be banned or burned, the philosophes wrote novels and plays, histories and philosophies, dictionaries and encyclopedias, all filled with satire and double meanings to spread their message to the public.

One of the greatest philosophes, the baron de Montesquieu (1689–1755), brilliantly pioneered this approach in *The Persian Letters,* an extremely influential social satire published in 1721. Montesquieu's work consisted of amusing letters supposedly written by Persian travelers, who see European customs in unique ways and thereby cleverly criticize existing practices and beliefs.

Having gained fame by using wit as a weapon against cruelty and superstition, Montesquieu settled down on his family estate to study history and politics. His interest was partly personal, for, like many members of the high French nobility, he was dismayed that royal absolutism had triumphed in France under Louis XIV. But Montesquieu was also inspired by the example of the physical sciences, and he set out to apply the critical method to the problem of government in *The Spirit of Laws* (1748). The result was a complex comparative study of republics, monarchies, and despotisms—a great pioneering inquiry in the emerging social sciences.

Showing that forms of government were shaped by history, geography, and customs, Montesquieu focused on the conditions that would promote liberty and prevent tyranny. He argued that despotism could be avoided if there was a **separation of powers,** with political power divided and shared by a variety of classes and legal estates holding unequal rights and privileges. A strong, independent upper class was especially important, according to Montesquieu, because in order to prevent the abuse of power, "it is necessary that by the arrangement of things, power checks power." Admiring greatly the English balance of power among the king, the houses of Parliament, and the independent courts, Montesquieu believed that in France the thirteen high courts—the *parlements*—were frontline defenders of liberty against royal despotism. Apprehensive about the uneducated poor, Montesquieu was clearly no democrat, but his theory of separation of powers had a great impact on France's wealthy, well-educated elite. The constitutions of the young United States in 1789 and of France in 1791 were based in large part on this theory.

The most famous and in many ways most representative philosophe was François Marie Arouet, who was known by the pen name Voltaire (1694–1778). In his long career, this son of a comfortable middle-class family wrote more than seventy witty volumes, hobnobbed with kings and queens, and died a millionaire because of shrewd business speculations. His early career, however, was turbulent. In 1717 Voltaire was imprisoned for eleven months in the Bastille in Paris for insulting the regent of France. In 1726 a barb from his sharp tongue led a great French nobleman to have him beaten and arrested. This experience made a deep impression on Voltaire. All his life he struggled against legal injustice and unequal treatment before the law. Released from prison after promising to leave the country, Voltaire lived in England for three years and came to share Montesquieu's enthusiasm for English institutions.

Returning to France and soon threatened again with prison in Paris, Voltaire had the great fortune of meeting Gabrielle-Emilie Le Tonnelier de Breteuil, marquise du Châtelet (1706–1749), an intellectually gifted woman from the high aristocracy with a passion for science. Inviting Voltaire to live in her country house at Cirey in Lorraine and becoming his long-time companion (under the eyes of her tolerant husband), Madame du Châtelet studied physics and mathematics and published scientific articles and translations.

Perhaps the finest representative of a small number of elite Frenchwomen and their scientific accomplishments during the Enlightenment, Madame du Châtelet suffered nonetheless because of her gender. Excluded on principle from the Royal Academy of Sciences and from stimulating interchange with other scientists because she was a woman, she depended on private tutors for instruction and became uncertain of her ability to make important scientific discoveries. Madame du Châtelet therefore concentrated on spreading the ideas of others, and her translation with an accompanying commentary of Newton's *Principia* into French for the first (and only) time was her greatest work. But she, who had patiently explained Newton's complex mathematical proofs to Europe's foremost philosophe, had no doubt that women's limited scientific contributions in the past were due to limited and unequal education. She once wrote that if she were a ruler, "I would reform an abuse which cuts off, so to speak, half the human race. I would make women participate in all the rights of humankind, and above all in those of the intellect."[12]

**Madame du Châtelet** The marquise du Châtelet was fascinated by the new world system of Isaac Newton. She helped to spread Newton's ideas in France by translating his *Principia* and by influencing Voltaire, her companion for fifteen years until her death. *(Giraudon/Art Resource, NY)*

While living at Cirey, Voltaire wrote various works praising England and popularizing English scientific progress. Newton, he wrote, was history's greatest man, for he had used his genius for the benefit of humanity. "It is," wrote Voltaire, "the man who sways our minds by the prevalence of reason and the native force of truth, not they who reduce mankind to a state of slavery by force and downright violence . . . that claims our reverence and admiration."[13] In the true style of the Enlightenment, Voltaire mixed the glorification of science and reason with an appeal for better individuals and institutions.

Yet like almost all of the philosophes, Voltaire was a reformer, not a revolutionary, in social and political matters. He was eventually appointed royal historian in 1743, and his *Age of Louis XIV* portrayed Louis as the dignified leader of his age. Voltaire also began a long correspondence with Frederick the Great and, after the death of his beloved Emilie, accepted Frederick's invitation to come brighten up the Prussian court in Berlin. The two men later quarreled, but Voltaire always admired Frederick as a free thinker and an enlightened monarch.

Unlike Montesquieu, Voltaire pessimistically concluded that the best one could hope for in the way of government was a good monarch, since human beings "are very rarely worthy to govern themselves." Nor did he believe in social and economic equality in human affairs. The idea of making servants equal to their masters was "absurd and impossible." The only realizable equality, Voltaire thought, was that "by which the citizen only depends on the laws which protect the freedom of the feeble against the ambitions of the strong."[14]

Voltaire's philosophical and religious positions were much more radical. In the tradition of Bayle, Voltaire's voluminous writings challenged, often indirectly, the Catholic church and Christian theology at almost every point. Though he was considered by many devout Christians to be a shallow blasphemer, Voltaire's religious views were influential and quite typical of the mature Enlightenment. Voltaire clearly believed in God, but his was a distant, deistic God, the great Clockmaker who built an orderly universe and then stepped aside and let it run. Above all, Voltaire and most of the philosophes hated all forms of religious intolerance, which they believed often led to fanaticism and savage, inhuman action. Simple piety and human kindness—as embodied in Christ's great commandments to "love God and your neighbor as yourself"—were religion enough, even Christianity enough, as may be seen in Voltaire's famous essay on religion. (See the feature "Listening to the Past: Voltaire on Religion" on pages 626–627.)

The ultimate strength of the French philosophes lay in their number, dedication, and organization. The philosophes felt keenly that they were engaged in a common undertaking that transcended individuals. Their greatest and most representative intellectual achievement was, quite fittingly, a group effort—the seventeen-volume *Encyclopedia: The Rational Dictionary of the Sciences, the Arts, and the Crafts,* edited by Denis Diderot (1713–1784) and Jean le Rond d'Alembert. Diderot and d'Alembert made a curious pair. Diderot began his career as a hack writer, first attracting attention with a skeptical tract on religion that was quickly burned by the judges of Paris. D'Alembert was one of Europe's leading scientists and mathematicians, the orphaned and illegitimate son of celebrated aristocrats. From different circles and with different interests, the two men set out to find coauthors who would examine the rapidly expanding whole of human knowledge. Even more fundamentally, they set out to teach people how to think critically and objectively about all matters. As Diderot said, he wanted the *Encyclopedia* to "change the general way of thinking."[15]

The editors of the *Encyclopedia* had to conquer innumerable obstacles. After the appearance in 1751 of the first volume, which dealt with such controversial subjects as atheism, the soul, and blind people (all words beginning with *a* in French), the government temporarily banned publication. The pope later placed the work on the Catholic church's index of forbidden works and pronounced excommunication on all who read or bought it. The timid publisher watered down some of the articles in the last ten volumes without the editors' consent in an attempt to appease the authorities. Yet Diderot's unwavering belief in the importance of his mission held the encyclopedists together for fifteen years, and the enormous work was completed in 1765. Hundreds of thousands of articles by leading scientists, famous writers, skilled workers, and progressive priests treated every aspect of life and knowledge.

Not every article was daring or original, but the overall effect was little short of revolutionary. Science and the industrial arts were exalted, religion and immortality questioned. Intolerance, legal injustice, and out-of-date social institutions were openly criticized. More generally, the writers of the *Encyclopedia* showed that human beings could use the process of reasoning to expand human knowledge. The encyclopedists were convinced that greater knowledge would result in greater human happiness, for knowledge was useful and made possible economic, social, and political progress. The *Encyclopedia* was widely read, especially in less expensive reprint editions published in Switzerland, and it was extremely influential in France and throughout western Europe as well. It summed up the new world-view of the Enlightenment.

## The Later Enlightenment

After about 1770, the harmonious unity of the philosophes and their thought began to break down. As the new world-view became increasingly accepted by the educated public, some thinkers sought originality by exaggerating certain Enlightenment ideas to the exclusion of others. These latter-day philosophes often built rigid, dogmatic systems.

In his *System of Nature* (1770) and other works, the wealthy German-born but French-educated Baron Paul d'Holbach (1723–1789) argued that human beings were machines completely determined by outside forces. Free will, God, and immortality of the soul were foolish myths. D'Holbach's aggressive atheism and determinism, which were coupled with deep hostility toward Christianity and all other religions, dealt the unity of the Enlightenment movement a severe blow. Deists such as Voltaire, who believed in God but not in established churches, were repelled by the inflexible atheism they found in the *System of Nature*. They saw in it the same dogmatic intolerance they had been fighting all their lives.

D'Holbach published his philosophically radical works anonymously in the Netherlands to avoid possible prosecution in France, and in his lifetime he was best known to

**Illustrating the *Encyclopedia:* "The Print Shop"** Diderot wanted to present all valid knowledge—that is, knowledge based on reason and the senses and not on tradition and authority. This plate, one of 3,000 detailed illustrations accompanying the 70,000 essays in the *Encyclopedia,* shows (*from left to right*) compositors setting type, arranging lines, and blocking down completed forms. Printed sheets dry above. *(Division of Rare & Manuscript Collections, Cornell University Library)*

the public as the generous patron and witty host of writers and intellectuals. At his twice-weekly dinner parties, an inner circle of regulars who knew the baron's secret exchanged ideas with aspiring philosophes and distinguished visitors. One of the most important was Scottish philosopher David Hume (1711–1776), whose carefully argued skepticism had a powerful long-term influence.

Building on Locke's teachings on learning, Hume argued that the human mind is really nothing but a bundle of impressions. These impressions originate only in sense experiences and our habits of joining these experiences together. Since our ideas ultimately reflect only our sense experiences, our reason cannot tell us anything about questions that cannot be verified by sense experience (in the form of controlled experiments or mathematics), such as the origin of the universe or the existence of God. Paradoxically, Hume's rationalistic inquiry ended up undermining the Enlightenment's faith in the power of reason.

Another French aristocrat, Marie-Jean Caritat, the marquis de Condorcet (1743–1794), transformed the Enlightenment belief in gradual, hard-won progress into fanciful utopianism. In his *Progress of the Human Mind,* written in 1793 during the French Revolution (see Chapter 21), Condorcet hypothesized and tracked nine stages of human progress that had already occurred and predicted that the tenth would bring perfection. Ironically, Condorcet wrote this work while fleeing for his life. Caught and condemned by revolutionary extremists, he preferred death by his own hand to the blade of the guillotine.

Other thinkers and writers after about 1770 began to attack the Enlightenment's faith in reason, progress, and moderation. The most famous of these was the Swiss Jean-Jacques Rousseau (1712–1778), a brilliant and difficult thinker, an appealing but neurotic individual. Born into a poor family of watchmakers in Geneva, Rousseau went to Paris and was greatly influenced by Diderot and Voltaire. Always extraordinarily sensitive and suspicious, Rousseau came to believe that his philosophe friends and the women of the Parisian salons were plotting against him. In the mid-1750s, he broke with them personally and intellectually, living thereafter as a lonely outsider with his uneducated common-law wife and going in his own highly original direction.

Like other Enlightenment thinkers, Rousseau was passionately committed to individual freedom. Unlike them, however, he attacked rationalism and civilization as destroying, rather than liberating, the individual. Warm, spontaneous feeling had to complement and correct cold intellect. Moreover, the basic goodness of the individual and the unspoiled child had to be protected from the cruel refinements of civilization. These ideas greatly influenced the early romantic movement (see pages 668–669), which rebelled against the culture of the Enlightenment in the late eighteenth century. They also had a powerful impact on the development of child psychology and modern education.

Rousseau's contribution to political theory in *The Social Contract* (1762) was equally significant. His contribution was based on two fundamental concepts: the general will and popular sovereignty. According to Rousseau, the **general will** is sacred and absolute, reflecting the common interests of all the people, who have displaced the monarch as the holder of sovereign power. The general will is not necessarily the will of the majority, however. At times the general will may be the authentic, long-term needs of the people as correctly interpreted by a farseeing minority. Little noticed before the French Revolution, Rousseau's concept of the general will appealed greatly to democrats and nationalists after 1789. The concept has also been used since 1789 by many dictators claiming that they, rather than some momentary majority of the voters, represent the general will and thus the true interests of democracy and the sovereign masses.

## Urban Culture and Public Opinion

The writings and press campaigns of the philosophes were part of a profound cultural transformation. The object of impressive ongoing research and scholarly debate in recent years, this transformation had several interrelated aspects.

Of great importance, the European market for books grew dramatically in the eighteenth century. In Germany the number of new titles appearing annually grew substantially and at an accelerating rate, from roughly six hundred new titles in 1700 to about eleven hundred in 1764 and about twenty-six hundred in 1780. Well-studied France, which was indicative of general European trends, witnessed an explosive growth in book consumption. A modest increase in literacy was partly responsible, as the popular classes bought more penny tracts and escapist stories (see pages 670–671). Yet the solid middle class, the clergy, and the aristocracy accounted for most of the change. The number of books in the hands of these privileged groups increased eightfold to tenfold between the 1690s and the 1780s, when the private library of the typical noble contained more than three hundred volumes. Moreover, a much more avid French reader purchased a totally transformed product. The number of religious and devotional books published legally in Paris declined precipitously, from one-half of the total in the 1690s to one-tenth of the total in the 1780s. History and law held constant, while the proportion of legally published books treating the arts and sciences surged.

Even these figures understate the shift in French taste because France's unpredictable but pervasive censorship caused many books to be printed abroad and then smuggled back into the country for "under-the-cloak" sale. Experts believe that perhaps the majority of French books produced between 1750 and 1789 came from publishing companies located outside France. These publishers, located primarily in the Netherlands and Switzerland but also in England and a few small west German principalities, also smuggled forbidden books in French and other languages into the absolutist states of central, southern, and eastern Europe. The recently discovered catalogues of some of these foreign publishers reveal a massive presence of the famous French philosophes, reaffirming the philosophes' central role in the spread of critical secular attitudes.

The illegal book trade in France also featured an astonishing growth of scandalmongering denunciations of high political figures and frankly pornographic works. These literary forms frequently came together in scathing pornographic accounts of the moral and sexual depravity of the French court, allegedly mired in luxury, perversion, and adultery. A favorite theme was the way that some beautiful but immoral aristocratic women used their sexual charms to gain power over weak rulers and high officials, thereby corrupting the process of government. Spurred by repeated royal directives, the French police did its best to stamp out this underground literature, but new slanders kept cropping up, like the wild tabloid fantasies at checkout counters in today's supermarkets.

**Selling Books, Promoting Ideas** This appealing bookshop with its intriguing ads for the latest works offers to put customers "Under the Protection of Minerva," the Roman goddess of wisdom. Large packets of books sit ready for shipment to foreign countries. Book consumption surged in the eighteenth century. *(Musée des Beaux-Arts, Dijon/Art Resource, NY)*

Reading more books on many more subjects, the educated public in France and throughout Europe increasingly approached reading in a new way. The result was what some German scholars have called a "reading revolution." The old style of reading in Europe had been centered on sacred texts, full of authority, inspiring reverence and teaching earthly duty and obedience to God. Reading had been patriarchal and communal, with the father of the family slowly reading the text aloud and the audience savoring each word. Now reading involved many texts, which were constantly changing and commanded no special respect. Reading became individual, silent, and rapid. The well-educated classes were reading insatiably, skeptically, and carelessly. Subtle but profound, the reading revolution was closely linked to the rise of a critical world-view.

As the reading public developed, it joined forces with the philosophes to call for the autonomy of the printed word. Immanuel Kant (1724–1804), a professor in East Prussia and the greatest German philosopher of the age, argued in 1784 that if serious thinkers were granted the freedom to exercise their reason publicly in print, then enlightenment would almost surely follow. Kant suggested that Prussia's Frederick the Great was an enlightened monarch precisely because he permitted such freedom of the press.

Outside of Prussia, the Netherlands, and Great Britain, however, the philosophes and the public resorted to discussion and social interchange in order to circumvent censorship and create an autonomous cultural sphere. Indeed, sparkling conversation in private homes spread Enlightenment ideas to Europe's upper middle class and aristocracy. Paris set the example, and other French and European cities followed. In Paris a number of talented and often rich women presided over regular social gatherings of the great and near-great in their elegant private drawing rooms, or **salons.** There they encouraged a d'Alembert and a Fontenelle to exchange witty, uncensored observations on literature, science, and philosophy with great aristocrats, wealthy middle-class financiers, high-ranking officials, and noteworthy foreigners. Thus talented hostesses brought the various French elites together and mediated the public's freewheeling examination of Enlightenment thought.

**Enlightenment Culture** Here the seven-year-old Austrian child prodigy Wolfgang Amadeus Mozart (1756–1791) plays his own composition at an "English tea" given by the Princess de Conti near Paris. Mozart's phenomenal creative powers lasted a lifetime and he produced a vast range of symphonies, operas, and chamber music. *(Réunion des Musées Nationaux/Art Resource, NY)*

Elite women also exercised an unprecedented feminine influence on artistic taste. Soft pastels, ornate interiors, sentimental portraits, and starry-eyed lovers protected by hovering cupids were all hallmarks of the style they favored. This style, known as rococo, was popular throughout Europe in the eighteenth century. It has been argued that feminine influence in the drawing room went hand in hand with the emergence of polite society and the general attempt to civilize a rough military nobility. Similarly, some philosophes championed greater rights and expanded education for women, claiming that the position and treatment of women were the best indicators of a society's level of civilization and decency.[16] To be sure, for these male philosophes greater rights for women did not mean equal rights, and the philosophes were not particularly disturbed by the fact that elite women remained legally subordinate to men in economic and political affairs. Elite women lacked many rights, but so did most men.

One of the most famous salons was that of Madame Geoffrin, the unofficial godmother of the *Encyclopedia*. Having lost her parents at an early age, the future Madame Geoffrin was married at fifteen by her well-meaning grandmother to a rich and boring businessman of forty-eight. After dutifully raising her children, Madame Geoffrin broke out of her gilded cage. With the aid of an aristocratic neighbor and in spite of her husband's loud protests, she developed a twice-weekly salon that counted Fontenelle and Montesquieu among its regular guests. Inheriting a large fortune after her husband's death, Madame Geoffrin gave the encyclopedists generous financial aid and helped save their enterprise from collapse. Corresponding with the king of Sweden and Catherine the Great of Russia, Madame Geoffrin remained her own woman, a practicing Christian who would not tolerate attacks on the church in her house.

The salons seem to have functioned as informal schools where established hostesses bonded with younger women and passed skills on to them. One talented young woman who received such help was Julie de Lespinasse. Eventually forming her own highly informal salon and attracting the keenest minds in France and Europe, Lespinasse epitomized the skills of the Enlightenment hostess. As one philosophe wrote:

*She could unite the different types, even the most antagonistic, sustaining the conversation by a well-aimed phrase, animating and guiding it at will. . . . Politics, religion, philosophy, news: nothing was excluded. Her circle met daily from five to nine. There one found men of all ranks in the State, the Church, and the Court, soldiers and foreigners, and the leading writers of the day.*[17]

As this passage suggests, the salons created an independent cultural realm freed from religious dogma and political censorship. There a diverse but educated public could debate issues and form its own ideas, its own *public opinion*. And all who were educated and civilized had equal rights in the elaboration of this new and powerful force. Thus the salons graciously united members of the intellectual, economic, and social elites. In such an atmosphere, the philosophes, the French nobility, and the prosperous middle classes intermingled and increasingly influenced one another. Thinking critically about almost any question became fashionable and flourished alongside hopes for human progress through greater knowledge and enlightened public opinion.

## The Enlightenment and Absolutism

See DBQ 5

How did the Enlightenment influence political developments? To this important question there is no easy answer. On the one hand, the French philosophes and kindred spirits in most continental countries were primarily interested in converting people to critical, scientific thinking and were not particularly concerned with politics. On the other hand, such thinking naturally led to political criticism and interest in political reform as both possible and desirable. Some Enlightenment thinkers, led by the nobleman Montesquieu, argued for curbs on monarchical power in order to promote liberty.

Until the American Revolution, however, most Enlightenment thinkers outside of England and the Netherlands believed that political change could best come from above—from the ruler—rather than from below, especially in central and eastern Europe. Royal absolutism was a fact of life, and the kings and queens of Europe's leading states clearly had no intention of giving up their great power. Therefore, the philosophes and their sympathizers realistically concluded that a benevolent absolutism offered the best opportunities for improving society. Critical thinking was turning the art of good government into an exact science. It was necessary only to educate and "enlighten" the monarch, who could then make good laws and promote human happiness. Enlightenment thinkers also turned toward rulers because rulers seemed to be listening, treating them with respect and seeking their advice. Finally, the philosophes distrusted "the people." They believed that the common people were deluded by superstitions and driven by violent passions, little children in need of firm parental guidance.

Encouraged and instructed by the philosophes, many absolutist rulers of the later eighteenth century tried to govern in an "enlightened" manner. Yet the actual programs and accomplishments of these rulers varied greatly. It is necessary to examine the evolution of monarchical absolutism at close range before trying to form any overall judgment regarding the Enlightenment's effect and the meaning of what historians have often called the **enlightened absolutism** of the later eighteenth century.

Enlightenment teachings inspired European rulers in small as well as large states in the second half of the eighteenth century. Absolutist princes and monarchs in several west German and Italian states, as well as in Scandinavia, Spain, and Portugal, proclaimed themselves more enlightened. A few smaller states were actually the most successful in making reforms, perhaps because their rulers were not overwhelmed by the size and complexity of their realms. Denmark, for example, carried out an extensive and progressive land reform in the 1780s that practically abolished serfdom and gave Danish peasants secure tenure on their farms. Yet by far the most influential of the new-style monarchs were in Prussia, Russia, and Austria, and they deserve primary attention.

### Frederick the Great of Prussia

Frederick II (r. 1740–1786), commonly known as Frederick the Great, built masterfully on the work of his father, Frederick William I (see pages 575–576). This was somewhat surprising, for, like many children with tyrannical parents, he rebelled against his family's wishes in his early years. Rejecting the crude life of the barracks, Frederick embraced culture and literature, even writing poetry and fine prose in French, a language his father detested. After trying unsuccessfully to run away in 1730 at age eighteen, he was virtually imprisoned and compelled to watch as his companion in flight was beheaded at his father's command. Yet like many other rebellious youths, Frederick eventually reached a reconciliation with his father, and by the time he came to the throne ten years later, Frederick was determined to use the splendid army that his father had left him.

Therefore, when the ruler of Austria, Charles VI, also died in 1740 and his young and charismatic daughter, Maria Theresa, inherited the Habsburg dominions, Frederick suddenly and without warning invaded her rich, mainly German province of Silesia. This action defied solemn Prussian promises to respect the Pragmatic Sanction, which guaranteed Maria Theresa's succession. Maria Theresa's ethnically diverse army was no match for Prussian precision. In 1742, as other greedy powers were falling on her lands in the general European War of the Austrian Succession (1740–1748), she was forced to cede almost all of Silesia to Prussia (see Map 17.2 on page 574). In one stroke Prussia doubled its population to six million people. Now Prussia unquestionably towered above all the other German states and stood as a European Great Power.

Though successful in 1742, Frederick had to spend much of his reign fighting against great odds to save Prussia from total destruction. Maria Theresa was determined to regain Silesia, and when the ongoing competition between Britain and France for colonial empire brought another great conflict in 1756 (see page 644), Austria fashioned an aggressive alliance with France and Russia. During the Seven Years' War (1756–1763), the aim of the alliance was to conquer Prussia and divide up its territory. Frederick led his army brilliantly, striking repeatedly at vastly superior forces invading from all sides. At times he believed all was lost, but he fought on with stoic courage. In the end, he was miraculously saved: Peter III came to the Russian throne in 1762 and called off the attack against Frederick, whom he greatly admired.

In the early years of his reign, Frederick II had kept his enthusiasm for Enlightenment culture strictly separated from a brutal concept of international politics. He wrote:

*Of all States, from the smallest to the biggest, one can safely say that the fundamental rule of government is the principle of extending their territories. . . . The passions of rulers have no other curb but the limits of their power. Those are the fixed laws of European politics to which every politician submits.*[18]

But the terrible struggle of the Seven Years' War tempered Frederick and brought him to consider how more humane policies for his subjects might also strengthen the state.

Thus Frederick went beyond a superficial commitment to Enlightenment culture for himself and his circle. He tolerantly allowed his subjects to believe as they wished in religious and philosophical matters. He promoted the advancement of knowledge, improving his country's schools and permitting scholars to publish their findings. Moreover, Frederick tried to improve the lives of his subjects more directly. As he wrote his friend Voltaire, "I must enlighten my people, cultivate their manners and morals, and make them as happy as human beings can be, or as happy as the means at my disposal permit." The legal system and the bureaucracy were Frederick's primary tools. Prussia's laws were simplified, torture of prisoners was abolished, and judges decided cases quickly and impartially. Prussian officials became famous for their hard work and honesty. After the Seven Years' War ended in 1763, Frederick's government energetically promoted the reconstruction of agriculture and industry in his war-torn country. Frederick himself set a good example. He worked hard and lived modestly, claiming that he was "only the first servant of the state." Thus Frederick justified monarchy in terms of practical results and said nothing of the divine right of kings.

Frederick's dedication to high-minded government went only so far, however. He never tried to change Prussia's existing social structure. True, he condemned serfdom in the abstract, but he accepted it in practice and did not even free the serfs on his own estates. He accepted and extended the privileges of the nobility, which he saw as his primary ally in the defense and extension of his realm. The Junker nobility remained the backbone of the army and the entire Prussian state.

Nor did Frederick listen to thinkers like Moses Mendelssohn (1729–1786), who urged that Jews be given freedom and civil rights. (See the feature "Individuals in Society: Moses Mendelssohn and the Jewish Enlightenment.") As in other German states, Jews in Prussia remained an oppressed group. The vast majority were confined to tiny, overcrowded ghettos, were excluded by law from most business and professional activities, and could be ordered out of the kingdom at a moment's notice. A very few Jews in Prussia did manage to succeed and obtain the right of permanent settlement, usually by performing some special service for the state. But they were the exception, and Frederick firmly opposed any general emancipation for the Jews, as he did for the serfs.

## Catherine the Great of Russia

Catherine the Great of Russia (r. 1762–1796) was one of the most remarkable rulers who ever lived, and the French philosophes adored her. Catherine was a German

# Individuals in Society

## Moses Mendelssohn and the Jewish Enlightenment

In 1743 a small, humpbacked Jewish boy with a stammer left his poor parents in Dessau in central Germany and walked eighty miles to Berlin, the capital of Frederick the Great's Prussia. According to one story, when the boy reached the Rosenthaler Gate, the only one through which Jews could pass, he told the inquiring watchman that his name was Moses and that he had come to Berlin "to learn." The watchman laughed and waved him through. "Go Moses, the sea has opened before you."* Embracing the Enlightenment and seeking a revitalization of Jewish religious thought, Moses Mendelssohn did point his people in a new and uncharted direction.

Turning in Berlin to a learned rabbi he had previously known in Dessau, the young Mendelssohn studied Jewish law and eked out a living copying Hebrew manuscripts in a beautiful hand. But he was soon fascinated by an intellectual world that had been closed to him in the Dessau ghetto. There, like most Jews throughout central Europe, he had spoken Yiddish—a mixture of German, Polish, and Hebrew. Now, working mainly on his own, he mastered German; learned Latin, Greek, French, and English; and studied mathematics and Enlightenment philosophy. Word of his exceptional abilities spread in Berlin's Jewish community (1,500 of the city's 100,000 inhabitants). He began tutoring the children of a wealthy Jewish silk merchant, and he soon became the merchant's clerk and later his partner. But his great passion remained the life of the mind and the spirit, which he avidly pursued in his off hours.

Gentle and unassuming in his personal life, Mendelssohn was a bold thinker. Reading eagerly in Western philosophy since antiquity, he was, as a pious Jew, soon convinced that Enlightenment teachings need not be opposed to Jewish thought and religion. Indeed, he concluded that reason could complement and strengthen religion, although each would retain its integrity as a separate sphere.† Developing his idea in his first great work, "On the Immortality of the Soul" (1767), Mendelssohn used the neutral setting of a philosophical dialogue between Socrates and his followers in ancient Greece to argue that the human soul lived forever. In refusing to bring religion and critical thinking into conflict, he was strongly influenced by contemporary German philosophers who argued similarly on behalf of Christianity. He reflected the way the German Enlightenment generally supported established religion, while the French Enlightenment attacked it. This was the most important difference in Enlightenment thinking between the two countries.

*Lavater* (right) *attempts to convert Mendelssohn, in a painting by Moritz Oppenheim of an imaginary encounter.* (Collection of the Judah L. Magnes Museum, Berkeley)

Mendelssohn's treatise on the human soul captivated the educated German public, which marveled that a Jew could have written a philosophical masterpiece. In the excitement, a Christian zealot named Lavater challenged Mendelssohn in a pamphlet to accept Christianity or to demonstrate how the Christian faith was not "reasonable." Replying politely but passionately, the Jewish philosopher affirmed that all his studies had only strengthened him in the faith of his fathers, although he certainly did not seek to convert anyone not born into Judaism. Rather, he urged toleration in religious matters. He spoke up courageously for his fellow Jews and decried the oppression they endured, and he continued to do so for the rest of his life.

Orthodox Jew and German philosophe, Moses Mendelssohn serenely combined two very different worlds. He built a bridge from the ghetto to the dominant culture over which many Jews would pass, including his novelist daughter Dorothea and his famous grandson, the composer Felix Mendelssohn.

### Questions for Analysis

1. How did Mendelssohn seek to influence Jewish religious thought in his time?
2. How do Mendelssohn's ideas compare with those of the French Enlightenment?

*H. Kupferberg, *The Mendelssohns: Three Generations of Genius* (New York: Charles Scribner's Sons, 1972), p. 3.
†D. Sorkin, *Moses Mendelssohn and the Religious Enlightenment* (Berkeley: University of California Press, 1996), pp. 8ff.

*The History Companion features additional information and activities related to this topic.*
**history.college.hmco.com/students**

**Catherine the Great as Equestrian** Catherine took advantage of her intelligence and good looks to overthrow her husband Peter III and became empress of Russia. Strongly influenced by the Enlightenment, she cultivated the French philosophes and instituted moderate reforms, only to reverse them in the aftermath of Pugachev's rebellion. Catherine's portrait hangs here above her throne in the palace throne room. *(Novosti)*

princess from Anhalt-Zerbst, a totally insignificant principality sandwiched between Prussia and Saxony. Her father commanded a regiment of the Prussian army, but her mother was related to the Romanovs of Russia, and that proved to be Catherine's chance.

Peter the Great had abolished the hereditary succession of tsars so that he could name his successor and thus preserve his policies. This move opened a period of palace intrigue and a rapid turnover of rulers until Peter's youngest daughter, Elizabeth, came to the Russian throne in 1741. A shrewd but crude woman—one of her official lovers was an illiterate shepherd boy—Elizabeth named her nephew Peter heir to the throne and chose Catherine to be his wife in 1744. It was a mismatch from the beginning. The fifteen-year-old Catherine was intelligent and attractive; her husband was stupid and ugly, his face badly scarred by smallpox. Ignored by her childish husband, Catherine carefully studied Russian, endlessly read writers such as Bayle and Voltaire, and made friends at court. Soon she knew what she wanted. "I did not care about Peter," she wrote in her *Memoirs,* "but I did care about the crown."[19]

As the old empress Elizabeth approached death, Catherine plotted against her unpopular husband. She selected as her new lover a tall, dashing young officer named Gregory Orlov, who with his four officer brothers commanded considerable support among the soldiers stationed in St. Petersburg. When Peter came to the throne in 1762, his decision to withdraw Russian troops from the coalition against Prussia alienated the army. At the end of six months, Catherine and her military conspirators deposed Peter III in a palace revolution. Then the Orlov brothers murdered him. The German princess became empress of Russia.

Catherine had drunk deeply at the Enlightenment well. Never questioning the common assumption that absolute monarchy was the best form of government, she set out to rule in an enlightened manner. She had three main goals. First, she worked hard to bring the sophisticated culture of western Europe to backward Russia. To do so, she imported Western architects, sculptors, musicians, and intellectuals. She bought masterpieces of Western art in wholesale lots and patronized the philosophes. An enthusiastic letter writer, she corresponded extensively with Voltaire and praised him as the "champion of the human race." When the French government banned the *Encyclopedia,* she offered to publish it in St. Petersburg. She sent money to Diderot when he needed it. With these and countless similar actions, Catherine won good press in the West for herself and for her country. Moreover, this intellectual ruler, who wrote plays and loved good talk, set the tone for the entire Russian nobility. Peter the Great westernized Russian armies, but it was Catherine who westernized the thinking of the Russian nobility.

Catherine's second goal was domestic reform, and she began her reign with sincere and ambitious projects. Better laws were a major concern. In 1767 she appointed a special legislative commission to prepare a new law code. No new unified code was ever produced, but Catherine did restrict the practice of torture and allowed limited religious toleration. She also tried to improve education and strengthen local government. The philosophes applauded these measures and hoped more would follow.

Such was not the case. In 1773 a common Cossack soldier named Emelian Pugachev sparked a gigantic uprising of serfs, very much as Stenka Razin had done a century earlier (see page 583). Proclaiming himself the true tsar, Pugachev issued "decrees" abolishing serfdom, taxes, and army service. Thousands joined his cause, slaughtering landlords and officials over a vast area of southwestern Russia. Pugachev's untrained hordes eventually proved no match for Catherine's noble-led regular army. Betrayed by his own company, Pugachev was captured and savagely executed.

Pugachev's rebellion was a decisive turning point in Catherine's domestic policy. On coming to the throne, she had condemned serfdom in theory, but Pugachev's rebellion put an end to any illusions she might have had about reforming the system. The peasants were clearly dangerous, and her empire rested on the support of the nobility. After 1775 Catherine gave the nobles absolute control of their serfs. She extended serfdom into new areas, such as Ukraine. In 1785 she formalized the nobility's privileged position, freeing nobles forever from taxes and state service. Under Catherine the Russian nobility attained its most exalted position, and serfdom entered its most oppressive phase.

Catherine's third goal was territorial expansion, and in this respect she was extremely successful. Her armies subjugated the last descendants of the Mongols, the Crimean Tartars, and began the conquest of the Caucasus. Her greatest coup by far was the partition of Poland (see Map 18.1). By 1700 Poland had become a weak and decentralized republic with an elected king (page 573), and Poland's fate in the late eighteenth century demonstrated the dangers of failing to build a strong absolutist state. All important decisions continued to require the unanimous agreement of all nobles elected to the Polish Diet, which meant that nothing could ever be done to strengthen the state. When, between 1768 and 1772, Catherine's armies scored unprecedented victories against the Turks and thereby threatened to disturb the balance of power between Russia and Austria in eastern Europe, Frederick of Prussia obligingly came forward with a deal. He proposed that Turkey be let off easily and that Prussia, Austria, and Russia each compensate itself by taking a gigantic slice of Polish territory. Catherine jumped at the chance. The first partition of Poland took place in 1772. Two more partitions, in 1793 and 1795, gave all three powers more Polish territory, and the ancient republic of Poland simply vanished from the map.

Expansion helped Catherine keep the nobility happy, for it provided her with vast new lands to give to her faithful servants and her many lovers. On all the official royal favorites she lavished large estates with many serfs, as if to make sure there were no hard feelings when her interest cooled. Until the end this remarkable woman—who always believed that, in spite of her domestic setbacks, she was slowly civilizing Russia—kept her zest for life. Fascinated by a new twenty-two-year-old flame when she was a roly-poly grandmother in her sixties, she happily reported her good fortune to a favorite former lover: "I have come back to life like a frozen fly; I am gay and well."[20]

## The Austrian Habsburgs

In Austria two talented rulers did manage to introduce major reforms, although traditional power politics was more important than Enlightenment teachings. One was Joseph II (r. 1780–1790), a fascinating individual. For an earlier generation of historians, he was the "revolutionary emperor," a tragic hero whose lofty reforms were undone by the landowning nobility he dared to challenge. More recent scholarship has revised this romantic interpretation and stressed how Joseph II continued the state-building work of his mother, the empress Maria Theresa (1740–1780), a remarkable but old-fashioned absolutist.

Emerging from the long War of the Austrian Succession in 1748 with only the serious loss of Silesia, Maria Theresa and her closest ministers were determined to introduce reforms that would make the state stronger and more efficient. Three aspects of these reforms were most important. First, Maria Theresa introduced measures aimed at limiting the papacy's political influence in her realm. Second, a whole series of administrative reforms

**MAP 18.1 The Partition of Poland and Russia's Expansion, 1772–1795** Though all three of the great eastern absolutist states profited from the division of large but weak Poland, Catherine's Russia gained the most. Russia's European border moved far to the west, and the Russian empire became a leading actor in European politics.

strengthened the central bureaucracy, smoothed out some provincial differences, and revamped the tax system, taxing even the lands of nobles without special exemptions. Third, the government sought to improve the lot of the agricultural population, cautiously reducing the power of lords over their hereditary serfs and their partially free peasant tenants.

Coregent with his mother from 1765 onward and a strong supporter of change, Joseph II moved forward rapidly when he came to the throne in 1780. He controlled the established Catholic church even more closely in an attempt to ensure that it produced better citizens. He granted religious toleration and civic rights to Protestants and Jews—a radical innovation that impressed his contemporaries. In even more spectacular peasant reforms, Joseph abolished serfdom in 1781, and in 1789 he decreed that all peasant labor obligations be converted into cash payments. This ill-conceived measure was violently rejected not only by the nobility but also by the peasants it was intended to help since their primitive barter economy was woefully lacking in money. When a disillusioned Joseph died prematurely at forty-nine, the entire Habsburg empire was in turmoil. His brother Leopold II (r. 1790–1792) was forced to cancel Joseph's radical edicts in order to re-establish order. Peasants once again were required to do forced labor for their lords.

## Absolutism in France

The Enlightenment's influence on political developments in France was complex. The monarchy maintained its absolutist claims, and some philosophes, such as

**Maria Theresa** The empress and her husband pose with eleven of their sixteen children at Schönbrunn palace in this family portrait by court painter Martin Meytens (1695–1770). Joseph, the heir to the throne, stands at the center of the star pattern. Wealthy women often had very large families, in part because they seldom nursed their babies as poor women usually did. *(Réunion des Musées Nationaux/Art Resource, NY)*

Voltaire, believed that the king was still the best source of needed reform. At the same time, discontented nobles and learned judges drew on thinkers such as Montesquieu for liberal arguments. They sought with some success to limit the king's power, as France diverged from the absolutist states just considered.

When Louis XIV finally died in 1715, to be succeeded by his five-year-old great-grandson, Louis XV (r. 1715–1774), the Sun King's elaborate system of absolutist rule was challenged in a general reaction. Favored by the duke of Orléans (1674–1723), who governed as regent until 1723, the nobility made a strong comeback.

Most important, in 1715 the duke restored to the high courts of France—the parlements—the ancient right to evaluate royal decrees publicly in writing before they were registered and given the force of law. The restoration of this right to evaluate, which had been suspended under Louis XIV, was a fateful step. The high court judges had originally come from the middle class. By the eighteenth century, however, these middle-class judges had risen to become hereditary nobles, thereby attaining the high social status that middle-class officials wanted. Moreover, these judicial positions became essentially private property, passed down from father to son. By allowing this well-entrenched and increasingly aristocratic group to evaluate the king's decrees before they became law, the duke of Orléans sanctioned a counterweight to absolute power.

These implications became clear when the heavy expenses of the War of the Austrian Succession plunged France into financial crisis. In 1748 Louis XV appointed a finance minister who decreed a 5 percent income tax on every individual regardless of social status. Exemption from most taxation had long been a hallowed privilege of the nobility, and other important groups—the clergy, the large towns, and some wealthy bourgeoisie—had also gained special tax advantages over time. The result was a vigorous protest from many sides, led by the influential Parlement of Paris. The monarchy retreated; the new tax was dropped.

Following the disastrously expensive Seven Years' War, the conflict re-emerged. The government tried to maintain emergency taxes after the war ended. The Parlement of Paris protested and even challenged the basis of royal authority, claiming that the king's power had to be limited to protect liberty. Once again the government caved in and withdrew the wartime taxes in 1764. The judicial opposition then asserted that the king could not levy taxes without the consent of the Parlement of Paris acting as the representative of the entire nation.

Indolent and sensual by nature, more interested in his many mistresses than in affairs of state, Louis XV finally roused himself for a determined defense of his absolutist inheritance. "The magistrates," he angrily told the Parlement of Paris in a famous face-to-face confrontation, "are my officers. . . . In my person only does the sovereign power rest."[21] In 1768 Louis appointed a tough career official named René de Maupeou as chancellor and ordered him to crush the judicial opposition.

Maupeou abolished the existing parlements and exiled the vociferous members of the Parlement of Paris to the provinces. He created a new and docile parlement of royal officials, and he began once again to tax the privileged groups. A few philosophes applauded these measures: the sovereign was using his power to introduce badly needed reforms that had been blocked by a self-serving aristocratic elite. Most philosophes and educated public opinion as a whole sided with the old parlements, however, and there was widespread criticism of "royal despotism." The illegal stream of scandalmongering, pornographic attacks on the king and his court became a torrent, and some scholars now believe these lurid denunciations ate away at the foundations of royal authority, especially among the common people in turbulent Paris. The king was being stripped of the sacred aura of God's anointed on earth and was being reinvented in the popular imagination as a loathsome degenerate. Yet the monarchy's power was still great enough for Maupeou simply to ride over the opposition, and Louis XV would probably have prevailed—if he had lived to a very ripe old age.

But Louis XV died in 1774. The new king, Louis XVI (r. 1774–1792), was a shy twenty-year-old with good intentions. Taking the throne, he is reported to have said, "What I should like most is to be loved."[22] The eager-to-please monarch decided to yield in the face of such strong criticism from so much of France's educated elite. He dismissed Maupeou and repudiated the strong-willed minister's work. All the old parlements were reinstated, as enlightened public opinion cheered and anticipated moves toward more representative government. But such moves were not forthcoming. Instead, a weakened but unreformed monarchy faced a judicial opposition that claimed to speak for the entire French nation. Increasingly locked in stalemate, the country was drifting toward renewed financial crisis and political upheaval.

## The Overall Influence of the Enlightenment

Having examined the evolution of monarchical absolutism in four leading states, we can begin to look for meaningful generalizations and evaluate the overall influence of Enlightenment thought on politics.

France clearly diverged from its eastern neighbors in its political development in the eighteenth century. The French monarch's capacity to govern in a truly absolutist manner declined substantially. The political resurgence of the French nobility after 1715 and the growth of judicial opposition drew crucial support from educated public opinion, which increasingly made the liberal critique of unregulated royal authority its own.

The situation in eastern and east-central Europe was different. The liberal critique of absolute monarchy remained an intellectual curiosity, and proponents of reform from above held sway. Moreover, despite differences, the leading eastern European monarchs of the later eighteenth century all claimed that they were acting on the principles of the Enlightenment. The philosophes generally agreed with this assessment and cheered them on. Beginning in the mid-nineteenth century, historians developed the idea of a common "enlightened despotism" or "enlightened absolutism," and they canonized Frederick, Catherine, and Joseph as its most outstanding examples. More recent research has raised doubts about this old interpretation and has led to a fundamental revaluation.

There is general agreement that these absolutists, especially Catherine and Frederick, did encourage and spread the cultural values of the Enlightenment. Perhaps this was their greatest achievement. Skeptical in religion and intensely secular in basic orientation, they unabashedly accepted the here and now and sought their happiness in the enjoyment of it. At the same time, they were proud of their intellectual accomplishments and good taste, and they supported knowledge, education, and the arts. No wonder the philosophes felt these monarchs were kindred spirits.

Historians also agree that the absolutists believed in change from above and tried to enact needed reforms. Yet the results of these efforts brought only very modest improvements, and the life of the peasantry remained very hard in the eighteenth century. Thus some historians have concluded that these monarchs were not really sincere in their reform efforts. Others disagree, arguing that powerful nobilities blocked the absolutists' genuine commitment to reform. (The old interpretation of Joseph II as the tragic revolutionary emperor forms part of this argument.)

The emerging answer to this controversy is that the later eastern absolutists were indeed committed to reform but that humanitarian objectives were of quite secondary importance. Above all, the absolutists wanted reforms that would strengthen the state and allow them to compete militarily with their neighbors. Modern scholarship has therefore stressed how Catherine, Frederick, and Joseph were in many ways simply continuing the state building of their predecessors, reorganizing armies and expanding bureaucracies to raise more taxes and troops. The reason for this continuation was simple. The international political struggle was brutal, and the stakes were high. First Austria under Maria Theresa and then Prussia under Frederick the Great had to engage in bitter fighting to escape dismemberment, while decentralized Poland was coldly divided and eventually liquidated.

Yet in this drive for more state power, the later absolutists were also innovators, and the idea of an era of enlightened absolutism retains a certain validity. Sharing the Enlightenment faith in critical thinking and believing that knowledge meant power, these absolutists really were more enlightened than their predecessors because they put state-building reforms in a new, broader perspective. Above all, the later absolutists considered how more humane laws and practices could help their populations become more productive and satisfied and thus able to contribute more substantially to the welfare of the state. It was from this perspective that they introduced many of their most progressive reforms, tolerating religious minorities, simplifying legal codes, and promoting practical education.

The primacy of state over individual interests also helps explain some puzzling variations in social policies. For example, Catherine the Great took measures that worsened the peasants' condition because she looked increasingly to the nobility as her natural ally and sought to strengthen it. Frederick the Great basically favored the status quo, limiting only the counterproductive excesses of his trusted nobility against its peasants. Joseph II believed that greater freedom for peasants was the means to strengthen his realm, and he acted accordingly. Each enlightened absolutist sought greater state power, but each believed a different policy would attain it.

The eastern European absolutists of the later eighteenth century combined old-fashioned state building with the culture and critical thinking of the Enlightenment. In doing so, they succeeded in expanding the role of the state in the life of society. Unlike the successors of Louis XIV, they perfected bureaucratic machines that were to prove surprisingly adaptive and capable of enduring into the twentieth century.

## Summary

This chapter has focused on the complex development of a new world-view in Western civilization. This new view was essentially critical and secular, drawing its inspiration from the scientific revolution and crystallizing in the Enlightenment.

Decisive breakthroughs in astronomy and physics in the seventeenth century, which demolished the imposing medieval synthesis of Aristotelian philosophy and Christian theology, had only limited practical consequences despite the expectations of scientific enthusiasts. Yet the impact of new scientific knowledge on intellectual life became great. Interpreting scientific findings and Newtonian laws in an antitraditional, antireligious manner, the French philosophes of the Enlightenment extolled the superiority of rational, critical thinking. This new method, they believed, promised not just increased knowledge but even the discovery of the fundamental laws of human society. Although they reached different conclusions when they turned to social and political realities, they did stimulate absolute monarchs to apply reason to statecraft and the search for useful reforms. Above all, the philosophes succeeded in shaping an emerging public opinion and spreading their radically new world-view. These were momentous accomplishments.

## Key Terms

| | |
|---|---|
| world-view | progress |
| Copernican hypothesis | skepticism |
| experimental method | tabula rasa |
| law of inertia | philosophes |
| law of universal gravitation | the public |
| empiricism | separation of powers |
| Cartesian dualism | general will |
| Enlightenment | salons |
| rationalism | enlightened absolutism |

## Notes

1. H. Butterfield, *The Origins of Modern Science* (New York: Macmillan, 1951), p. viii.
2. Quoted in A. G. R. Smith, *Science and Society in the Sixteenth and Seventeenth Centuries* (New York: Harcourt Brace Jovanovich, 1972), p. 97.
3. Quoted in Butterfield, *The Origins of Modern Science,* p. 47.
4. Quoted in Smith, *Science and Society,* p. 100.
5. Ibid., pp. 115–116.
6. Ibid., p. 120.
7. A. R. Hall, *From Galileo to Newton, 1630–1720* (New York: Harper & Row, 1963), p. 290.
8. Quoted in R. K. Merton, *Science, Technology and Society in Seventeenth-Century England,* rev. ed. (New York: Harper & Row, 1970), p. 164.
9. Quoted in P. Hazard, *The European Mind, 1680–1715* (Cleveland: Meridian Books, 1963), pp. 304–305.
10. Quoted in R. Chartier, *The Cultural Origins of the French Revolution* (Durham, N.C.: Duke University Press, 1991), p. 27.
11. J. Bosher, *The French Revolution* (New York: W. W. Norton, 1988), p. 31.
12. L. Schiebinger, *The Mind Has No Sex? Women in the Origins of Modern Science* (Cambridge, Mass.: Harvard University Press, 1989), p. 64.
13. Quoted in L. M. Marsak, ed., *The Enlightenment* (New York: John Wiley & Sons, 1972), p. 56.
14. Quoted in G. L. Mosse et al., eds., *Europe in Review* (Chicago: Rand McNally, 1964), p. 156.
15. Quoted in P. Gay, "The Unity of the Enlightenment," *History* 3 (1960): 25.
16. See E. Fox-Genovese, "Women in the Enlightenment," in *Becoming Visible: Women in European History,* 2d ed., ed. R. Bridenthal, C. Koonz, and S. Stuard (Boston: Houghton Mifflin, 1987), esp. pp. 252–259, 263–265.
17. Quoted in G. P. Gooch, *Catherine the Great and Other Studies* (Hamden, Conn.: Archon Books, 1966), p. 149.
18. Quoted in L. Krieger, *Kings and Philosophers, 1689–1789* (New York: W. W. Norton, 1970), p. 257.
19. Quoted in Gooch, *Catherine the Great,* p. 15.
20. Ibid., p. 53.
21. Quoted in R. R. Palmer, *The Age of Democratic Revolution,* vol. 1 (Princeton, N.J.: Princeton University Press, 1959), pp. 95–96.
22. Quoted in G. Wright, *France in Modern Times,* 4th ed. (New York: W. W. Norton, 1987), p. 34.

## Suggested Reading

The first three authors cited in the Notes—Butterfield, Smith, and Hall—have written excellent general interpretations of the scientific revolution. These may be compared with S. Shapin, *The Scientific Revolution* (2001), which is concise and well informed with an eye for the dramatic, and with M. Jacob, *The Cultural Meaning of the Scientific Revolution* (1988). M. Osler, ed., *Rethinking the Scientific Revolution* (2000), re-examines especially the impact of scientific discovery on religious belief. Schiebinger, cited in the Notes, provides a brilliant analysis of how the new science gradually excluded women interested in science. A. Debus, *Man and Nature in the Renaissance* (1978), is good on the Copernican revolution. D. Sobel, *Longitude: The True Story of a Lone Genius Who Solved the Greatest Scientific Problem of His Day* (1995), is an engrossing biography that became a bestseller. L. Jardine, *Ingenious Pursuits: Building the Scientific Revolution* (1999), is an engaging analysis of scientific institutions and English society. S. Drake, *Galileo* (1980), is a good short biography, while P. Machamer, ed., *The Cambridge Companion to Galileo* (1998), examines the many aspects of Galileo's enormous creativity. E. Andrade, *Sir Isaac Newton* (1958), is a good brief biography, which may be compared with R. Westfall, *Never at Rest: A Biography of Isaac Newton* (1993), and F. Manuel, *The Religion of Isaac Newton* (1974).

Hazard, listed in the Notes, is a classic study of the formative years of Enlightenment thought. R. Reill and E. Wilson, *Encyclopedia of the Enlightenment* (1996), is particularly helpful on culture and the leading philosophes. M. Jacob, *The Enlightenment: A Brief History with Documents* (2000), is also recommended. T. Munck, *The Enlightenment: A Comparative History* (2000), examines developments in different countries. Important studies from the cultural perspective include D. Goodman, *The Republic of Letters: A Cultural History of the Enlightenment* (1994), and A. Farge, *Subversive Worlds: Public Opinion in Eighteenth Century France* (1994). D. Roche, *France in the Enlightenment* (1998), is a distinguished scholar's bustling panorama of life and thought, action and wit. P. Gay has written several major studies on the Enlightenment: *Voltaire's Politics* (1959) and *The Party of Humanity* (1971) are two of the best. J. Sklar, *Montesquieu* (1987), is an engaging biography, and R. Riley, ed., *The Cambridge Companion to Rousseau* (2001), presents a useful, wide-ranging introduction. F. Baumer, *Religion and the Rise of Skepticism* (1969), and H. Payne, *The Philosophes and the People* (1976), are major studies. D. Van Kley, *The Religious Origins of the French Revolution* (1996), is a stimulating reinterpretation. The changing attitudes of the educated public are imaginatively analyzed by R. Chartier, *The Cultural Origins of the French Revolution* (1991) and *French Historical Studies* (Fall 1992). R. Danton, *The Forbidden Best-Sellers of Pre-Revolutionary France* (1995), explores the struggle between the government's censorship and the public's taste. On women, see the stimulating study by Fox-Genovese cited in the Notes, as well as the collected work by N. Davis and A. Farge, eds., *A History of Women: Renaissance and Enlightenment Paradoxes* (1993). More specialized studies include C. Hesse, *The Other Enlightenment: How French Women Became Modern* (2003), a brilliant social history of intellectual change; S. Spencer, ed., *French Women and the Age of Enlightenment* (1984); and K. Rogers, *Feminism in Eighteenth-Century England* (1982). J. Landes, *Women and the Public Sphere in the Age of the French Revolution* (1988), is a fascinating and controversial study of women and politics. S. Kale, *French Salons and Political Sociability from the Old Regime to the Revolution of 1848* (2004), examines the impact of salons from a fresh perspective, and S. Muthu, *Enlightenment Against Empire* (2003), is a pioneering study on the opposition of the leading philosophes to colonialism. Above all, one should read some of the philosophes and let them speak for themselves. Two good anthologies are C. Brinton, ed., *The Portable Age of Reason* (1956), and F. Manuel, ed., *The Enlightenment* (1951). Voltaire's most famous and very amusing novel, *Candide,* is highly recommended, as is Denis Diderot, *This Is Not a Story and Other Stories* (1991).

In addition to the works mentioned in the Suggested Reading for Chapters 16 and 17, the monarchies of Europe are carefully analyzed in H. Scott, *Enlightened Absolutism* (1990); C. Tilly, ed., *The Formation of National States in Western Europe* (1975); and J. Gagliardo, *Enlightened Despotism* (1967), all of which have useful bibliographies. M. Anderson, *Historians and Eighteenth-Century Europe* (1979), remains a valuable introduction to modern scholarship, and C. Behrens, *Society, Government, and the Enlightenment: The Experience of Eighteenth-Century France and Prussia* (1985), is a stimulating comparative study. J. Black, *Eighteenth-Century Europe, 1700–1789* (1990), is a fine survey, and E. Le Roy Ladurie, *The Ancien Régime* (1996), is an impressive synthesis by a well-known French historian. J. Lynch, *Bourbon Spain, 1700–1808* (1989), skillfully analyzes the impact of Enlightenment thought in Spain. Important works on Austria include C. Macartney, *Maria Theresa and the House of Austria* (1970); D. Beales, *Joseph II* (1987); and T. Blanning, *Joseph II and Enlightened Absolutism* (1970). There are several fine works on Russia. J. Alexander, *Catherine the Great: Life and Legend* (1989), is the best biography of the famous ruler, which may be compared with the empress's own story, *The Memoirs of Catherine the Great,* ed. D. Maroger (1961). I. de Madariaga, *Russia in the Age of Catherine the Great* (1981), is strongly recommended. G. MacDonagh, *Frederick the Great* (2001), is an outstanding biography, and H. Scott, *The Rise of the Eastern Powers, 1756–1775* (2001), carefully examines the growing importance of Prussia and Russia. Two excellent works on Moses Mendelssohn are the brilliant study by D. Sorkin, *Moses Mendelssohn and the Religious Enlightenment* (1996), and the popular biography of the family by H. Kupferberg, *The Mendelssohns: Three Generations of Genius* (1972). J. Israel, *European Jewry in the Age of Mercantilism, 1550–1750* (1985), is recommended.

The musical and artistic culture of the time may be approached through A. Cobban, ed., *The Eighteenth Century* (1969), a richly illustrated work with excellent essays; and C. B. Behrens, *The Ancien Régime* (1967). T. Crow, *Painters and Public Life in Eighteenth-Century Paris* (1985), examines artists and cultural politics. C. Rosen, *The Classical Style: Haydn, Mozart, Beethoven* (1972), brilliantly synthesizes music and society, as did Mozart himself in his great opera *The Marriage of Figaro,* where the count is the buffoon and his servant the hero.

# Listening to the Past

## Voltaire on Religion

*Voltaire was the most renowned and probably the most influential of the French philosophes. His biting, satirical novel* Candide *(1759) is still widely assigned in college courses, and his witty yet serious* Philosophical Dictionary *remains a source of pleasure and stimulation. The* Dictionary *consists of a series of essays on topics ranging from Adam to Zoroaster, from certainty to circumcision. The following passage is taken from the essay on religion.*

*Voltaire began writing the* Philosophical Dictionary *in 1752, at the age of fifty-eight, after arriving at the Prussian court in Berlin. Frederick the Great applauded Voltaire's efforts, but Voltaire put the project aside after leaving Berlin, and the first of several revised editions was published anonymously in 1764. It was an immediate, controversial success. Snapped up by an "enlightened" public, it was denounced by religious leaders as a threat to the Christian community and was burned in Geneva and Paris.*

I meditated last night; I was absorbed in the contemplation of nature; I admired the immensity, the course, the harmony of those infinite globes which the vulgar do not know how to admire.

I admired still more the intelligence which directs these vast forces. I said to myself: "One must be blind not to be dazzled by this spectacle; one must be stupid not to recognize its author; one must be mad not to worship the Supreme Being. What tribute of worship should I render Him? Should not this tribute be the same in the whole of space, since it is the same Supreme Power which reigns equally in all space?

"Should not a thinking being who dwells on a star in the Milky Way offer Him the same homage as a thinking being on this little globe of ours? Light is the same for the star Sirius as for us; moral philosophy must also be the same. If a feeling, thinking animal on Sirius is born of a tender father and mother who have been occupied with his happiness, he owes them as much love and care as we owe to our parents. If someone in the Milky Way sees a needy cripple, and if he can aid him and does not do so, then he is guilty toward all the globes.

"Everywhere the heart has the same duties: on the steps of the throne of God, if He has a throne; and in the depths of the abyss, if there is an abyss."

I was deep in these ideas when one of those genii who fill the spaces between the worlds came down to me. I recognized the same aerial creature who had appeared to me on another occasion to teach me that the judgments of God are different from our own, and how a good action is preferable to a controversy.

The genie transported me into a desert all covered with piles of bones. . . . He began with the first pile. "These," he said, "are the twenty-three thousand Jews who danced before a calf, together with the twenty-four thousand who were killed while fornicating with Midianitish women. The number of those massacred for such errors and offences amounts to nearly three hundred thousand.

"In the other piles are the bones of the Christians slaughtered by each other because of metaphysical disputes. They are divided into several heaps of four centuries each. One heap would have mounted right to the sky; they had to be divided."

"What!" I cried, "brothers have treated their brothers like this, and I have the misfortune to be of this brotherhood!"

"Here," said the spirit, "are the twelve million native Americans killed in their own land because they had not been baptized."

"My God! . . . Why assemble here all these abominable monuments to barbarism and fanaticism?"

"To instruct you. . . . Follow me now." [The genie takes Voltaire to the "heroes of humanity, who tried to banish violence and plunder from the world," and tells Voltaire to question them.]

[At last] I saw a man with a gentle, simple face, who seemed to me to be about thirty-five years old. From afar he looked with compassion upon those piles of whitened bones, through which I had been led to reach the sage's dwelling place. I was astonished to find his feet swollen and bleeding, his hands likewise, his side pierced, and his ribs laid bare by the cut of the lash. "Good God!" I said to him, "is it possible for a just man, a sage, to be in this state? I have just seen one who was treated in a very hateful way, but there is no comparison between his torture and yours. Wicked priests and wicked judges poisoned him; is it by priests and judges that you were so cruelly assassinated?"

With great courtesy he answered, "Yes."

"And who were these monsters?"

"They were hypocrites."

"Ah! that says everything; I understand by that one word that they would have condemned you to the cruelest punishment. Had you then proved to them, as Socrates did, that the Moon was not a goddess, and that Mercury was not a god?"

"No, it was not a question of planets. My countrymen did not even know what a planet was; they were all arrant ignoramuses. Their superstitions were quite different from those of the Greeks."

"Then you wanted to teach them a new religion?"

"Not at all; I told them simply: 'Love God with all your heart and your neighbor as yourself, for that is the whole of mankind's duty.' Judge yourself if this precept is not as old as the universe; judge yourself if I brought them a new religion." . . .

"But did you say nothing, do nothing that could serve them as a pretext?"

"To the wicked everything serves as pretext."

"Did you not say once that you were come not to bring peace, but a sword?"

"It was a scribe's error; I told them that I brought peace and not a sword. I never wrote anything; what I said can have been changed without evil intention."

"You did not then contribute in any way by your teaching, either badly reported or badly interpreted, to those frightful piles of bones which I saw on my way to consult with you?"

"I have only looked with horror upon those who have made themselves guilty of all these murders."

An impish Voltaire, by the French sculptor Houdon. *(Courtesy of Board of Trustees of the Victoria & Albert Museum)*

. . . [Finally] I asked him to tell me in what true religion consisted.

"Have I not already told you? Love God and your neighbor as yourself."

"Is it necessary for me to take sides either for the Greek Orthodox Church or the Roman Catholic?"

"When I was in the world I never made any difference between the Jew and the Samaritan."

"Well, if that is so, I take you for my only master." Then he made a sign with his head that filled me with peace. The vision disappeared, and I was left with a clear conscience.

## Questions for Analysis

1. Why did Voltaire believe in a Supreme Being? Does this passage reflect the influence of Isaac Newton's scientific system? If so, how?
2. Was Voltaire trying to entertain or teach, or do both? Was he effective? Why or why not?
3. If Voltaire was trying to convey serious ideas about religion and morality, what were those ideas? What was he attacking?
4. If a person today thought and wrote like Voltaire, would that person be called a defender or a destroyer of Christianity? Why?

*Source:* F. M. Arouet de Voltaire, *Oeuvres complètes,* vol. 8, trans. J. McKay (Paris: Firmin-Didot, 1875), pp. 188–190.

*The East India Dock, London* (detail), by Samuel Scott, a painting infused with the spirit of maritime expansion. *(© Board of Trustees of the Victoria & Albert Museum)*

chapter

# 19 The Expansion of Europe in the Eighteenth Century

**chapter outline**

- Agriculture and the Land
- The Beginning of the Population Explosion
- The Growth of Cottage Industry
- Building the Atlantic Economy

The world of absolutism and aristocracy, a combination of raw power and elegant refinement, was a world apart from that of the common people. For the overwhelming majority of the population in the eighteenth century, life remained a struggle with poverty and uncertainty, with the landlord and the tax collector. In 1700 peasants on the land and artisans in their shops lived little better than had their ancestors in the Middle Ages. Only in science and thought, and there only among a few intellectual elites and their followers, had Western society succeeded in going beyond the great achievements of the High Middle Ages, achievements that in turn owed so much to Greece and Rome.

Everyday life was a struggle because European societies, despite their best efforts, still could not produce very much by modern standards. Ordinary men and women might work like their beasts in the fields, and they often did, but there was seldom enough good food, warm clothing, and decent housing. Life went on; history went on. The wars of religion ravaged Germany in the seventeenth century; Russia rose to become a Great Power; the state of Poland simply disappeared; monarchs and nobles continually jockeyed for power and wealth. In 1700 or even 1750, the idea of progress, of substantial improvement in the lives of great numbers of people, was still only the dream of a small elite in fashionable salons.

Yet the economic basis of European life was beginning to change. In the course of the eighteenth century, the European economy emerged from the long crisis of the seventeenth century, responded to challenges, and began to expand once again. Population resumed its growth, while colonial empires developed and colonial elites prospered. Some areas were more fortunate than others. The rising Atlantic powers—Holland, France, and, above all, England—and their colonies led the way. The expansion of agriculture and industry, trade and population, marked the beginning of a surge comparable to that of the eleventh- and twelfth-century springtime of European civilization. But this time, broadly based expansion was not cut short. This time the response to new challenges led toward one of the most influential developments in human history, the Industrial Revolution, considered in Chapter 22.

- What were the causes of this renewed surge?
- Why were the fundamental economic underpinnings of European society beginning to change, and what were the dimensions of these changes?
- How did these changes affect people and their work?

These are the questions this chapter will address.

## Agriculture and the Land

At the end of the seventeenth century, the economy of Europe was agrarian, as it had been for several hundred years. With the possible exception of Holland, at least 80 percent of the people of all western European countries drew their livelihoods from agriculture. In eastern Europe the percentage was considerably higher. Men and women lavished their attention on the land, plowing fields and sowing seed, reaping harvests and storing grain. Yet even in a rich agricultural region such as the Po Valley in northern Italy, every bushel of wheat sown yielded on average only five or six bushels of grain at harvest during the seventeenth century. By modern standards, output was distressingly low.

In most regions of Europe in the sixteenth and seventeenth centuries, harvests were poor, or even failed completely, every eight or nine years. The vast majority of the population, which lived off the land, might survive a single bad harvest by eating less and drawing on their reserves of grain. But when the land's caprices combined with persistent bad weather—too much rain rotting the seed or drought withering the young stalks—the result was catastrophic. Meager grain reserves were soon exhausted, and the price of grain soared. Provisions from other areas with better harvests were hard to obtain.

In such crisis years, which periodically stalked Europe in the seventeenth and even into the early eighteenth century, a terrible tightening knot in the belly forced people to use substitutes—the **famine foods** of a desperate population. People gathered chestnuts and stripped bark in the forests, they cut dandelions and grass, and they ate these substitutes to escape starvation. Even cannibalism occurred in the seventeenth century.

Such unbalanced and inadequate food in famine years made people weak and extremely susceptible to illness and epidemics. Eating material unfit for human consumption, such as bark or grass, resulted in dysentery and intestinal ailments of many kinds. Influenza and smallpox preyed with particular savagery on populations weakened by famine. In famine years the number of deaths soared far above normal. A third of a village's population might disappear in a year or two. Indeed, the 1690s were as dismal as many of the worst periods of earlier times. One county in Finland, probably typical of the entire country, lost fully 28 percent of its inhabitants in 1696 and 1697.

### The Open-Field System

The greatest accomplishment of medieval agriculture was the **open-field system** of village farming developed by European peasants. That system divided the land to be cultivated by the peasants of a given village into several large fields, which were in turn cut up into long, narrow strips. The fields were open, and the strips were not enclosed into small plots by fences or hedges. Peasants farmed each large field as a community. Each family followed the same pattern of plowing, sowing, and harvesting in accordance with tradition and the village leaders.

The ever-present problem was exhaustion of the soil. When the community planted wheat year after year in a field, the nitrogen in the soil was soon depleted, and crop failure was certain. Since the supply of manure for fertilizer was limited, the only way for the land to recover its life-giving fertility was for a field to lie fallow for a period of time. In the early Middle Ages, a year of fallow was alternated with a year of cropping, but three-year rotations were introduced, especially on more fertile lands. This system permitted a year of wheat or rye to be followed by a year of oats or beans and only then by a year of fallow.

Traditional village rights reinforced the traditional pattern of farming. In addition to rotating field crops in a uniform way, villages maintained open meadows for hay and natural pasture. These lands were **common lands,** set aside primarily for the draft horses and oxen so necessary in the fields, but open to the cows and pigs of the village community as well. After the harvest, the men and women of the village also pastured their animals on the wheat or rye stubble. In many places such pasturing followed a brief period, also established by tradition, for the gleaning of grain. Poor women would go through the fields picking up the few single grains that had fallen to the ground in the course of the harvest.

In the age of absolutism and nobility, state and landlord continued to levy heavy taxes and high rents as a matter of course. In so doing, they stripped the peasants of much of their meager earnings. The level of exploitation varied.

Generally speaking, the peasants of eastern Europe were worst off. As we saw in Chapter 17, they were serfs bound to their lords in hereditary service. In much of eastern Europe, there were few limitations on the amount of forced labor the lord could require, and five or six days of unpaid work per week on the lord's land were not un-

1650 | 1700 | 1750 | 1800 | 1850

**POLITICAL/MILITARY**

- 1651–1663 British Navigation Acts
- 1652–1674 Anglo-Dutch wars; rise of British mercantilism
- 1701–1713 War of the Spanish Succession
- 1701–1763 Mercantilist wars of empire
- 1740–1748 War of the Austrian Succession
- 1756–1763 Seven Years' War
- 1759 Fall of Quebec
- 1760–1815 Height of parliamentary enclosure in England

**SOCIAL/ECONOMIC**

- ca 1650–1790 Growth of Atlantic economy
- ca 1650–1850 Agricultural improvement and revolution
- 1700–1790 Height of Atlantic slave trade
- 1700–1790 Expansion of rural industry in Europe
- 1720–1789 Growth of European population
- 1721–1722 Last of bubonic plague in Europe
- 1750–1790 Rise of economic liberalism
- 1807 British slave trade abolished

**INTELLECTUAL/RELIGIOUS**

- ca 1690–1780 Enlightenment
- 1776 Smith, *Wealth of Nations*

common. Well into the nineteenth century, individual Russian serfs and serf families were regularly sold with and without land.

Social conditions were better in western Europe. Peasants were generally free from serfdom. In France, western Germany, and the Low Countries, they owned land and could pass it on to their children. Yet life in the village was unquestionably hard, and poverty was the great reality for most people. For the Beauvais region of France at the beginning of the eighteenth century, it has been carefully estimated that in good years and bad only a tenth of the peasants could live satisfactorily off the fruits of their landholdings. And this was in a rich agricultural region in a country where peasants were comparatively well-off. The privileges of Europe's ruling elites weighed heavily on the people of the land.

## The Agricultural Revolution

One possible way for European peasants to improve their difficult position was to take land from those who owned but did not labor. Yet the social and political conditions that enabled the ruling elites to squeeze the peasants were ancient and deeply rooted, and powerful forces stood ready to crush any protest. Only with the coming of the French Revolution were European peasants, mainly in France, able to improve their position by means of radical mass action.

**Millet: The Gleaners** Poor French peasant women search for grains and stalks that the harvesters (*background*) have missed. The open-field system seen here could still be found in parts of Europe in 1857, when this picture was painted. Millet is known for his great paintings expressing social themes. *(Réunion des Musées Nationaux/Art Resource, NY)*

Technological progress offered another possibility. If peasants (and their noble landlords) could replace the idle fallow with crops, they could increase the land under cultivation by 50 percent. So remarkable were the possibilities and the results that historians have often spoken of the progressive elimination of the fallow, which occurred gradually throughout Europe from the mid-seventeenth century on, as an **agricultural revolution.** This agricultural revolution, which took longer than historians used to believe, was a great milestone in human development.

Because grain crops exhaust the soil and make fallowing necessary, the secret to eliminating the fallow lies in alternating grain with certain nitrogen-storing crops. The most important of these land-reviving crops are peas and beans, root crops such as turnips and potatoes, and clovers and grasses. As the eighteenth century went on, the number of crops that were systematically rotated grew. New patterns of organization allowed some farmers to develop increasingly sophisticated patterns of **crop rotation** to suit different kinds of soils. For example, farmers in French Flanders near Lille in the late eighteenth century used a ten-year rotation, alternating a number of grain, root, and hay crops in a given field on a ten-year schedule. Continual experimentation led to more scientific farming.

Improvements in farming had multiple effects. The new crops made ideal feed for animals. Because peasants and larger farmers had more fodder, hay, and root crops for the winter months, they could build up their small herds of cattle and sheep. More animals meant more meat and better diets for the people. More animals also meant more manure for fertilizer and therefore more grain for bread and porridge.

Advocates of the new crop rotations, who included an emerging group of experimental scientists, some government officials, and a few big landowners, believed that new methods were scarcely possible within the traditional framework of open fields and common rights. A farmer who wanted to experiment with new methods would have to get all the landholders in a village to agree to the plan. Advocates of improvement argued that innovating agriculturalists needed to enclose and consolidate their scattered holdings into compact, fenced-in fields in order to farm more effectively. In doing so, the innovators also needed to enclose their individual shares of the natural pasture, the common. According to proponents of this idea, known as **enclosure,** a revolution in village life and organization was the necessary price of technical progress.

That price seemed too high to many poor rural people, who held small, inadequate holdings or very little land at all. Common rights were precious to these poor peasants. Thus when the small landholders and the village poor could effectively oppose the enclosure of the open fields and the common pasture, they did so. Moreover, in many countries they usually found allies among the larger, predominately noble landowners, who were also wary of enclosure because it required large investments and posed risks for them as well. Only powerful social and political pressures could overcome such combined opposition.

The old system of unenclosed open fields and the new system of continuous rotation coexisted in Europe for a long time. It could also be found in much of France and Germany in the early years of the nineteenth century because peasants there had successfully opposed efforts to introduce the new techniques in the late eighteenth century. Indeed, until the end of the eighteenth century, the promise of the new system was extensively realized only in the Low Countries and in England.

## The Leadership of the Low Countries and England

The new methods of the agricultural revolution originated in the Low Countries. Seventeenth-century republican Holland, already the most advanced country in Europe in many areas of human endeavor (see pages 555–559), led the way.

By the middle of the seventeenth century, intensive farming was well established throughout much of the Low Countries. Enclosed fields, continuous rotation, heavy manuring, and a wide variety of crops—all these innovations were present. Agriculture was highly specialized and commercialized. One reason for early Dutch leadership in farming was that the Low Countries were one of the most densely populated areas in Europe. In order to feed themselves and provide employment, the Dutch were forced at an early date to seek maximum yields from their land and to increase the cultivated area through the steady draining of marshes and swamps. The pressure of population was connected with the second cause: the growth of towns and cities in the Low Countries. Stimulated by commerce and overseas trade, Amsterdam grew from 30,000 inhabitants to 200,000 in its golden seventeenth century. The growth of urban population provided Dutch peasants with good markets for all they could produce and allowed each region to specialize in what it did best. Thus the Dutch could develop their potential, and the Low Countries became "the Mecca of foreign agricultural experts who came . . . to see Flemish agriculture with their own eyes, to write about it and to propagate its methods in their home lands."[1]

The English were the best students. Drainage and water control were one subject in which they received instruction. Large parts of seventeenth-century Holland had once been sea and sea marsh, and the efforts of centuries had made the Dutch the world's leaders in the skills of drainage. In the first half of the seventeenth century, Dutch experts made a great contribution to draining the extensive marshes, or fens, of wet and rainy England.

The most famous of these Dutch engineers, Cornelius Vermuyden, directed one large drainage project in Yorkshire and another in Cambridgeshire. In the Cambridge fens, Vermuyden and his Dutch workers eventually reclaimed forty thousand acres, which were then farmed intensively in the Dutch manner. Swampy wilderness was converted into thousands of acres of some of the best land in England.

Jethro Tull (1674–1741), part crank and part genius, was an important English innovator. A true son of the early Enlightenment, Tull adopted a critical attitude toward accepted ideas about farming and tried to develop better methods through empirical research. He was especially enthusiastic about using horses, rather than slower-moving oxen, for plowing. He also advocated sowing seed with drilling equipment rather than scattering it by hand.

**Hendrick Sorgh: Vegetable Market (1662)** The wealth and well-being of the industrious, capitalistic Dutch shine forth in this winsome market scene. The market woman's baskets are filled with delicious fresh produce that ordinary citizens can afford—eloquent testimony to the responsive, enterprising character of Dutch agriculture. *(Historisch Museum, Rotterdam)*

Drilling distributed seed in an even manner and at the proper depth. There were also improvements in livestock, inspired in part by the earlier successes of English country gentlemen in breeding ever-faster horses for the races and fox hunts that were their passions. Selective breeding of ordinary livestock was a marked improvement over the old pattern, which has been graphically described as little more than "the haphazard union of nobody's son with everybody's daughter."

By the mid-eighteenth century, English agriculture was in the process of a long but radical transformation. The eventual result was that by 1870 English farmers were producing 300 percent more food than they had produced in 1700, although the number of people working the land had increased by only 14 percent. This great surge of agricultural production provided food for England's rapidly growing urban population. It was a tremendous achievement.

## The Cost of Enclosure

What was the cost of technical progress in England, and to what extent did its payment result in social injustice? Scholars agree that the impetus for enclosing the fields came mainly from the powerful ruling class, the English aristocracy. Owning large estates, the aristocracy benefited directly from higher yields that could support higher rents, and it was able and ready to make expensive investments in the new technology. Beyond these certainties, there are important differences of interpretation among historians.

Many historians stress the initiative and enterprise of the big English landowners, which they contrast with the inertia and conservatism of continental landowners, big and small. These historians also assert that the open fields were enclosed fairly, with both large and small owners receiving their fair share after the strips had been surveyed and consolidated.

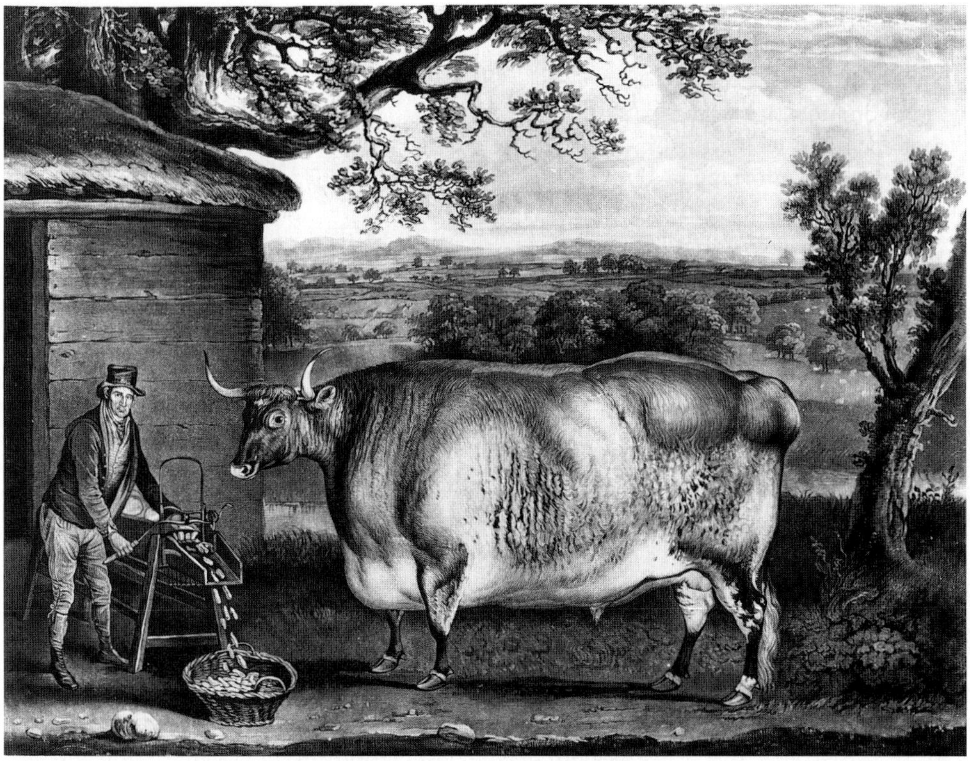

**Selective Breeding** New breeding practices meant bigger livestock and more meat on English tables. This gigantic champion, one of the new improved shorthorn breed, was known as the Newbus Ox. Such great fat beasts were pictured in the press and praised by poets. *(Institute of Agricultural History and Museum of English Rural Life, University of Reading)*

Other historians argue that fairness was more apparent than real. The large landowners controlled Parliament, which made the laws. They had Parliament pass hundreds of "enclosure acts," each of which authorized the fencing of open fields in a given village and the division of the common land in proportion to one's property in the open fields. The heavy legal and surveying costs of enclosure were also divided among the landowners. This meant that many peasants who had small holdings had to sell out to pay their share of the expenses. Similarly, landless cottagers lost their age-old access to the common pasture without any compensation whatsoever.

In assessing these conflicting interpretations, one must put eighteenth-century developments in a longer historical perspective. In the first place, as much as half of English farmland was already enclosed by 1750. Thus parliamentary enclosure, the great bulk of which occurred after 1760 and particularly during the Napoleonic wars early in the nineteenth century, only completed a process that was in full swing. Nor did an army of landless cottagers and farm laborers appear only in the last years of the eighteenth century. Much earlier, and certainly by 1700 because of the early enclosures for sheep runs, there were perhaps two landless agricultural workers in England for every independent farmer. In 1830, after the enclosures were complete, the proportion of landless laborers was not substantially greater.

By 1700 a highly distinctive pattern of landownership and production existed in England. At one extreme were a few large landowners; at the other, a large mass of landless cottagers who labored mainly for wages and who could graze only a pig or a cow on the village common. In between stood two other groups: small, independent peasant farmers who owned their own land and prosperous tenant farmers who rented land from the big landowners, hired wage laborers, and sold their output on a cash market. Yet the small, independent English peasant farmers had been declining in number since the early enclosures, and in the eighteenth century they could not compete with the rising group of profit-minded, market-oriented tenant farmers.

These tenant farmers, many of whom had formerly been independent owners, were the key to mastering the new methods of farming. Well financed by the large landowners, the tenant farmers fenced fields, built drains, and improved the soil with fertilizers. Such improvements actually increased employment opportunities for wage workers in some areas. So did new methods of farming, for land was farmed more intensively without the fallow, and new crops such as turnips required more care and effort. Thus enclosure did not force people off the land and into the towns by eliminating jobs, as has sometimes been claimed.

At the same time, by eliminating common rights and greatly reducing the access of poor men and women to the land, the eighteenth-century enclosure movement marked the completion of two major historical developments in England—the rise of market-oriented estate agriculture and the emergence of a landless rural proletariat. By 1815 a tiny minority of wealthy English (and Scottish) landowners held most of the land and pursued profits aggressively, leasing their holdings through agents at competitive prices to middle-size farmers, who relied on landless laborers for their workforce. These landless laborers worked very long hours, usually following a dawn-to-dusk schedule six days a week all year long. Moreover, landless laborers had lost that bit of independence and self-respect that common rights had provided and were completely dependent on cash wages. In no other European country had this **proletarianization**—this transformation of large numbers of small peasant farmers into landless rural wage earners—gone so far. And England's village poor found the cost of change heavy and unjust.

## The Beginning of the Population Explosion

See DBQ 6

Another factor that affected the existing order of life and forced economic changes in the eighteenth century was the remarkable growth of European population, the beginning of the "population explosion." This explosion continued in Europe until the twentieth century, by which time it was affecting nonwestern areas of the globe. What caused the growth of population, and what did the challenge of more mouths to feed and more hands to employ do to the European economy?

### Limitations on Population Growth

Many commonly held ideas about population in the past are wrong. One such mistaken idea is that people always married young and had large families. A related error is that population was always growing too fast. On the contrary, until 1700 the total population of Europe grew slowly much of the time, and it followed an irregular cyclical pattern (see Figure 19.1).

The cyclical pattern of European population growth had a great influence on many aspects of social and economic life over time, although striking local and regional differences often make generalization difficult. As we

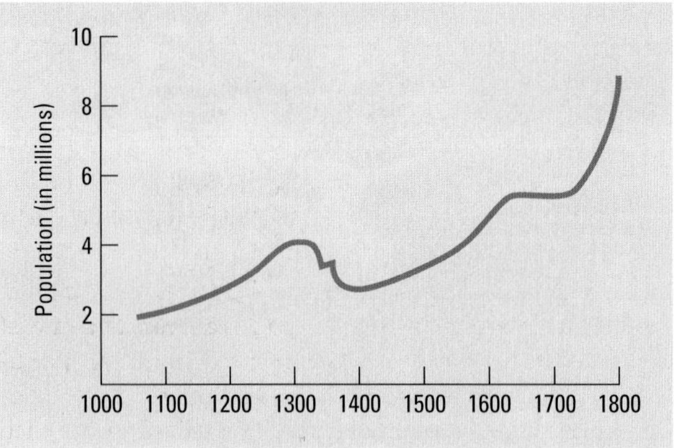


**FIGURE 19.1 The Growth of Population in England, 1000–1800** England is a good example of both the uneven increase of European population before 1700 and the third great surge of growth, which began in the eighteenth century. *(Source: E. A. Wrigley,* Population and History. *Copyright © 1969 by McGraw-Hill. Reprinted by permission of The McGraw-Hill Companies.)*

have seen, the terrible ravages of the Black Death caused a sharp drop in population and prices after 1350 and also created a labor shortage throughout Europe (see page 566). Lords in eastern Europe responded to this labor shortage by reversing the trend toward personal freedom and gradually reinstituting serfdom. This landlord reaction failed in western Europe, however, where serf obligations had declined or even disappeared by 1500. Moreover, the era of labor shortages and low food prices after the Black Death resulted in an increased standard of living for peasants and artisans. Some economic historians calculate that for those common people in western Europe who managed to steer clear of warfare and of power struggles within the ruling class, the later Middle Ages was an era of exceptional well-being.

But peasant and artisan well-being was eroded in the course of the sixteenth century. The second great surge of population growth (see Figure 19.1) outstripped the growth of agricultural production after about 1500. There was less food per person, and food prices rose more rapidly than wages, a development intensified by the inflow of precious metals from the Americas and a general, if uneven, European price revolution. The result was a substantial decline in living standards for the great majority of people throughout Europe. This decline especially aggravated the plight of both the urban and the rural poor. By 1600 the pressure of population on resources was severe in much of Europe, and widespread poverty was an undeniable reality.

For this reason, population growth slowed and stopped in seventeenth-century Europe. Births and deaths, fertility and mortality, were in a crude but effective balance. The birthrate—annual births as a proportion of the population—was fairly high but was far lower than it would have been if all women between ages fifteen and forty-five had been having as many children as biologically possible. The death rate in normal years was also high, though somewhat lower than the birthrate. As a result, the population grew modestly in normal years at a rate of perhaps 0.5 to 1 percent, or enough to double the population in 70 to 140 years. This is, of course, a generalization encompassing many different patterns. In areas such as Russia and colonial New England, where there was a great deal of frontier to be settled, the annual rate of natural increase, not counting in-migration, might well have exceeded 1 percent. In a country such as France, where the land had long been densely settled, the rate of increase might have been less than 0.5 percent.

Although population growth of even 1 percent per year is fairly modest by the standards of some African and Latin American countries today, it will produce a very large increase over a long period. An annual increase of even 1 percent will result in sixteen times as many people in three hundred years. Such gigantic increases simply did not occur in agrarian Europe before the eighteenth century. In certain abnormal years and tragic periods—the Black Death was only the most extreme and extensive example—many more people died than were born. Total population fell sharply, even catastrophically. A number of years of modest growth would then be necessary to make up for those who had died in an abnormal year. Such savage increases in deaths occurred periodically in the seventeenth century on a local and regional scale, and these demographic crises combined with birthrates far below the biological potential to check the growth of population until after 1700.

The grim reapers of demographic crisis were famine, epidemic disease, and war. Famine, the inevitable result of poor farming methods and periodic crop failures, was particularly murderous because it was accompanied by disease. With a brutal one-two punch, famine stunned and weakened a population, and disease finished it off. Disease could also ravage the population independently of famine.

War was another scourge. The indirect effects were more harmful than the organized killing. War spread disease. Soldiers and camp followers passed venereal disease throughout the countryside to scar and kill. Armies requisitioned scarce food supplies and disrupted the agricultural cycle. The Thirty Years' War witnessed all possible combinations of distress. In the German states, the number of inhabitants declined by more than *two-thirds* in some large areas and by at least one-third almost everywhere else.

## The New Pattern of the Eighteenth Century

In the eighteenth century, the population of Europe began to grow markedly. This increase in numbers occurred in all areas of Europe, western and eastern, northern and southern, dynamic and stagnant. Growth was especially dramatic after about 1750 (see Figure 19.2).

Although it is certain that Europe's population grew greatly, it is less clear why. Because population grew throughout Europe, it is best to look first for general factors. What caused fewer people to die or, possibly, more

**FIGURE 19.2 The Increase of Population in Europe in the Eighteenth Century** France's large population continued to support French political and intellectual leadership. Russia emerged as Europe's most populous state because natural increase was complemented by growth from territorial expansion.

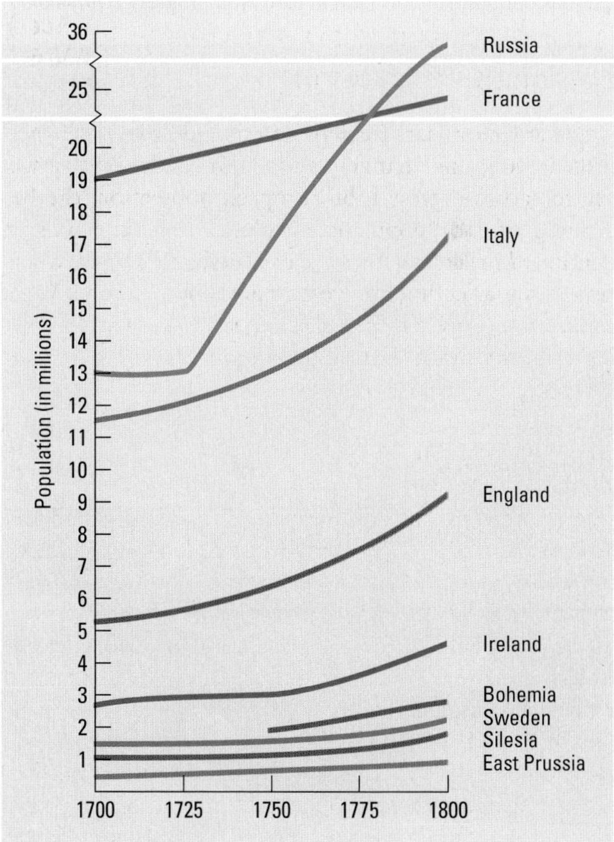

babies to be born? In some areas some women did have more babies than before because new opportunities for employment in rural industry allowed them to marry at an earlier age, as we shall see (see pages 664–666). But the basic cause for Europe as a whole was a decline in mortality—fewer deaths.

The bubonic plague mysteriously disappeared. Following the Black Death in the fourteenth century, plagues had remained a part of the European experience, striking again and again with savage force, particularly in towns. As late as 1721, a ship from Syria and the Levant, where plague was ever present, brought the disease to Marseilles. In a few weeks, forty thousand of the city's ninety thousand inhabitants died. The epidemic swept southern France, killing one-third, one-half, even three-fourths of those in the larger towns. Once again an awful fear swept across Europe. But the epidemic passed, and that was the last time plague fell on western and central Europe. Stricter measures of quarantine in Mediterranean ports and along the Austrian border with Turkey helped, as human carriers of plague were carefully isolated. Chance and plain good luck were more important, however.

It is now understood that bubonic plague is, above all, a disease of rats. More precisely, it is the black rat that spreads major epidemics, for the black rat's flea is the principal carrier of the plague bacillus. After 1600, for reasons unknown, a new rat of Asiatic origin—the brown, or wander, rat—began to drive out and eventually eliminate its black competitor. In the words of one authority, "This revolution in the animal kingdom must have gone far to break the lethal link between rat and man."[2] Although the brown rat also contracts the plague, another kind of flea is its main parasite. That flea carries the plague poorly and, for good measure, has little taste for human blood.

Advances in medical knowledge did not contribute much to reducing the death rate in the eighteenth century. The most important advance in preventive medicine

**Building a Royal Highway in France** An expanding system of all-weather roads improved French communications, promoted trade, and facilitated relief in time of famine. This majestic painting by Claude-Joseph Vernet (1714–1789) captures the spirit of the Enlightenment's cautious optimism and its faith in hard-won progress. *(Giraudon/The Bridgeman Art Library)*

in this period was inoculation against smallpox. This great improvement was long confined mainly to England and probably did little to reduce deaths throughout Europe until the latter part of the century. However, improvements in the water supply and sewerage, which were frequently promoted by strong absolutist monarchies, resulted in somewhat better public health and helped reduce such diseases as typhoid and typhus in some urban areas of western Europe. Improvements in water supply and the drainage of swamps also reduced Europe's large insect population. Filthy flies and mosquitoes played a major role in spreading serious epidemics and also in transmitting common diseases, especially those striking children and young adults. Thus early public health measures helped the decline in mortality that began with the disappearance of plague and continued into the early nineteenth century.

Human beings also became more successful in their efforts to safeguard the supply of food and protect against famine. The eighteenth century was a time of considerable canal and road building in western Europe. These advances in transportation, which were also among the more positive aspects of strong absolutist states, lessened the impact of local crop failure and famine. Emergency supplies could be brought in, and localized starvation became less frequent. Wars became more gentlemanly and less destructive than in the seventeenth century and spread fewer epidemics. New foods, particularly the potato from South America, were introduced. In short, population grew in the eighteenth century primarily because years of abnormal death rates were less catastrophic. Famines, epidemics, and wars continued to occur, but their severity moderated.

## The Growth of Cottage Industry

See DBQ 6

The growth of population increased the number of rural workers with little or no land, and this in turn contributed to the development of industry in rural areas. The poor in the countryside increasingly needed to supplement their earnings from agriculture with other types of work, and capitalists from the city were eager to employ them, often at lower wages than urban workers usually commanded. Manufacturing with hand tools in peasant cottages and work sheds grew markedly in the eighteenth century. Rural industry became a crucial feature of the European economy.

To be sure, peasant communities had always made some clothing, processed some food, and constructed some housing for their own use. But in the High Middle Ages, peasants did not produce manufactured goods on a large scale for sale in a market. By the eighteenth century, however, the pressures of rural poverty and the need to employ landless proletarians were overwhelming the efforts of urban artisans to maintain their traditional control over industrial production. A new system was expanding lustily.

The new system has had many names. It has often been called **cottage industry** or "domestic industry" to distinguish it from the factory industry that came later. In recent years, some scholars have preferred to speak of "protoindustrialization," by which they usually mean a stage of rural industrial development with wage workers and hand tools that necessarily preceded the emergence of large-scale factory industry. The focus on protoindustrialization has been quite valuable because it has sparked renewed interest in Europe's early industrial development and shown again that the mechanized factories grew out of a vibrant industrial tradition. However, the evolving concept of protoindustrialization also has different versions, some of which are rigid and unduly deterministic. Thus the phrase **putting-out system,** widely used by contemporaries to describe the key features of eighteenth-century rural industry, still seems a more appropriate term for the new form of industrial production.

### The Putting-Out System

The two main participants in the putting-out system were the merchant capitalist and the rural worker. The merchant loaned, or "put out," raw materials to several cottage workers, who processed the raw materials in their own homes and returned the finished product to the merchant. For example, a merchant would provide raw wool, and the workers would spin and weave the wool into cloth. The merchant then paid the outworkers for their work by the piece and proceeded to sell the finished product. There were endless variations on this basic relationship. Sometimes rural workers would buy their own materials and work as independent producers before they sold to the merchant. Sometimes several workers toiled together to perform a complicated process in a workshop. The relative importance of earnings from the land and from industry varied greatly for handicraft workers, although industrial wages usually became more important for a given family with time. In all cases, however, the putting-out system was a kind of capitalism. Merchants needed large amounts of capital, which they held in the form of goods being worked up and sold in distant markets. They sought to make profits and increase the capital in their businesses.

**The Weaver's Repose** This painting by Decker Cornelis Gerritz (1594–1637) captures the pleasure of release from long hours of toil in cottage industry. The loom realistically dominates the cramped living space and the family's modest possessions. *(Musées Royaux des Beaux-Arts, Brussels. Copyright A.C.I.)*

The putting-out system grew because it had competitive advantages. Underemployed labor was abundant, and poor peasants and landless laborers would work for low wages. Since production in the countryside was unregulated, workers and merchants could change procedures and experiment as they saw fit. Because they did not need to meet rigid guild standards, which maintained quality but discouraged the development of new methods, cottage industry became capable of producing many kinds of goods. Textiles; all manner of knives, forks, and housewares; buttons and gloves; clocks; and musical instruments could be produced quite satisfactorily in the countryside. Luxury goods for the rich, such as exquisite tapestries and fine porcelain, demanded special training, close supervision, and centralized workshops. Yet such goods were as exceptional as those who used them. The skills of rural industry were sufficient for everyday articles.

Rural manufacturing did not spread across Europe at an even rate. It appeared first in England and developed most successfully there, particularly for the spinning and weaving of woolen cloth. By 1500 half of England's textiles were being produced in the countryside. By 1700 English industry was generally more rural than urban and heavily reliant on the putting-out system. Continental countries developed rural industry more slowly.

In France at the time of Louis XIV, Colbert had revived the urban guilds and used them as a means to control the cities and collect taxes (see pages 540–541). But the pressure of rural poverty proved too great. In 1762 the special privileges of urban manufacturing were severely restricted in France, and the already developing rural industries were given free rein from then on. The royal government in France had come to believe that the best way to help the poor in the countryside was to encourage the growth of cottage manufacturing. Governments in Germany and the Low Countries also gradually reduced the power of guilds in the countryside. (See the feature "Listening to the Past: The Decline of the Guilds" on pages 658–659.) Thus the latter part of the eighteenth century witnessed a remarkable expansion of rural industry in certain densely populated regions of continental

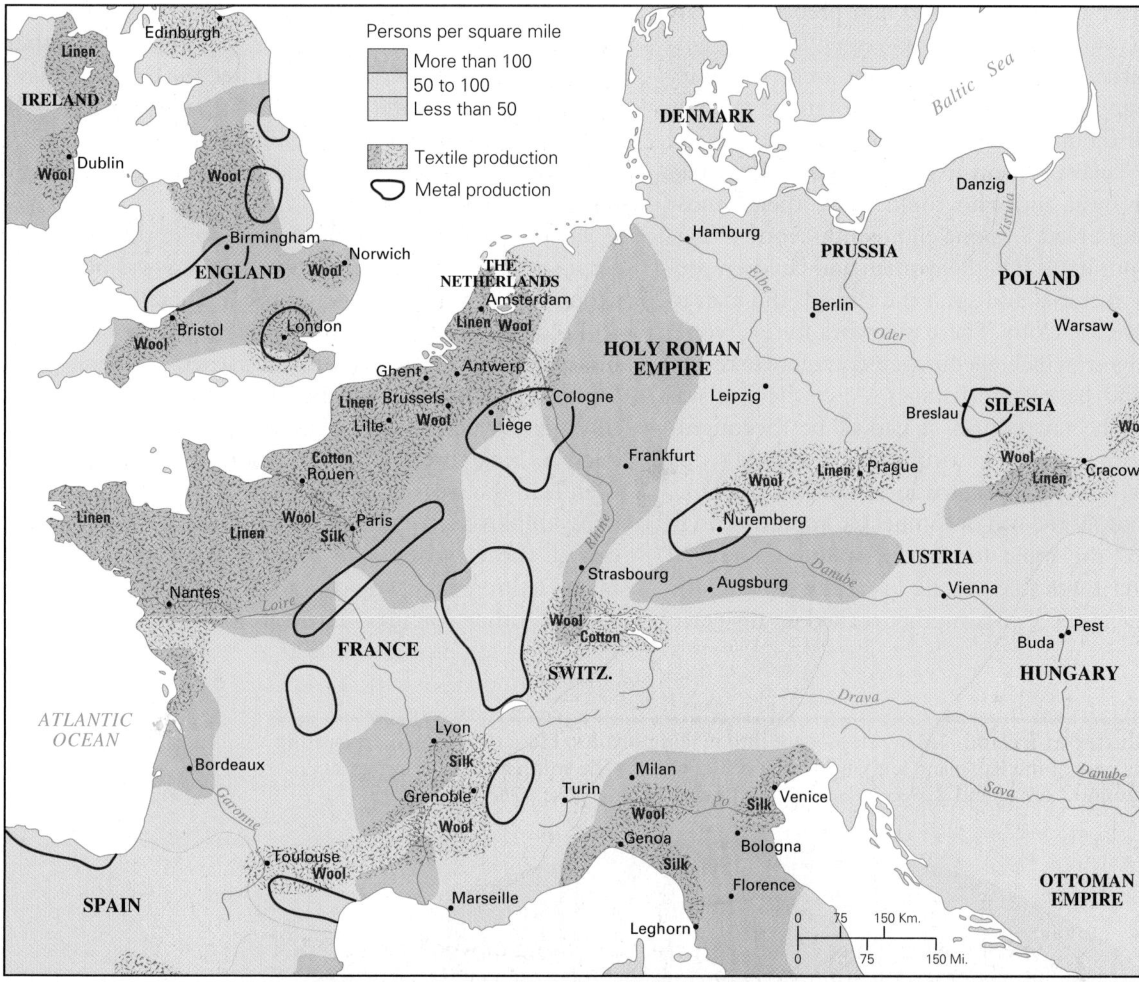


**MAP 19.1 Industry and Population in Eighteenth-Century Europe** The growth of cottage manufacturing in rural areas helped country people to increase their income and contributed to increases in the population. This putting-out system began in England, and much of the work was in the textile industry. Cottage industry was also strong in the Low Countries—modern-day Belgium and Holland.

Europe (see Map 19.1). The pattern established in England was spreading to the continent.

## The Textile Industry

Throughout most of history until at least the nineteenth century, the industry that has employed the most people has been textiles. The making of linen, woolen, and, eventually, cotton cloth was the typical activity of cottage workers engaged in the putting-out system. A look inside the cottage of the English rural textile worker illustrates a way of life as well as an economic system.

The rural worker lived in a small cottage with tiny windows and little space. Indeed, the worker's cottage was often a single room that served as workshop, kitchen, and bedroom. There were only a few pieces of furniture, of which the weaver's loom was by far the largest and most important. That loom had changed somewhat in the early eighteenth century, when John Kay's invention of the flying shuttle enabled the weaver to throw the shuttle back and forth between the threads with one hand. Aside from that improvement, however, the loom was as it had been for much of history. In the cottage there were also spinning wheels, tubs for dyeing cloth and washing raw wool, and carding pieces to comb and prepare the raw material.

These different pieces of equipment were necessary because cottage industry was first and foremost a family enterprise. All the members of the family helped in the work, so that "every person from seven to eighty (who retained their sight and who could move their hands) could earn their bread," as one eighteenth-century English observer put it.[3] While the women and children prepared the raw material and spun the thread, the man of the house wove the cloth. There was work for everyone, even the youngest, which encouraged cottage workers to marry early and have large families. After the dirt was beaten out of the raw cotton, it had to be thoroughly cleaned with strong soap in a tub, where a child's tiny feet functioned like the agitator in a washing machine. George Crompton, the son of Samuel Crompton, who in 1784 invented the mule for cotton spinning, recalled that "soon after I was able to walk I was employed in the cotton manufacture. . . . My mother tucked up my petticoats about my waist, and put me into the tub to tread upon the cotton at the bottom."[4] Slightly older children and aged relatives carded and combed the cotton or wool so that the mother and the older daughter she had taught could spin it into thread. Each member had a task. The very young and very old worked in the family unit as a matter of course.

There was always a serious imbalance in this family enterprise: the work of four or five spinners was needed to keep one weaver steadily employed. Therefore, the wife and the husband had to constantly find more thread and more spinners. Widows and unmarried women—those "spinsters" who spun for their living—were recruited by the wife. Or perhaps the weaver's son went off on horseback to seek thread. The need for more thread might even lead the weaver and his wife to become small capitalist employers. At the end of the week when they received the raw wool or cotton from the merchant manufacturer, they would put out some of this raw material to other cottages. The following week they would

**The Linen Industry in Ireland** Many steps went into making textiles. Here the women are beating away the woody part of the flax plant so that the man can comb out the soft part. The combed fibers will then be spun into thread and woven into cloth by this family enterprise. *(The Art Archive)*

return to pick up the thread and pay for the spinning, which would help keep the weaver busy for a week until the merchant came for the finished cloth.

Relations between workers and employers were often marked by sharp conflict. An English popular song written about 1700, called "The Clothier's Delight, or the Rich Men's Joy and the Poor Men's Sorrow," has the merchant boasting of the countless tricks he uses to "beat down wages":

*We heapeth up riches and treasure great store*
*Which we get by griping and grinding the poor.*
*And this is a way for to fill up our purse*
*Although we do get it with many a curse.*[5]

There were constant disputes over the weights of materials and the quality of the cloth. Merchants accused workers of stealing raw materials, and weavers complained that merchants delivered underweight bales. Suspicions abounded.

There was another problem, at least from the merchant capitalist's point of view. Rural labor was cheap, scattered, and poorly organized. For these reasons it was hard to control. Cottage workers tended to work in spurts. After they got paid on Saturday afternoon, the men in particular tended to drink and relax for two or three days. Indeed, Monday was called "holy Monday" because inactivity was so religiously observed. By the end of the week, the weaver was probably working feverishly to make his quota. But if he did not succeed, there was little the merchant could do. When times were good and the merchant could easily sell everything produced, the weaver and his family did fairly well and were particularly inclined to loaf—to the dismay of the capitalist. Thus the putting-out system in the textile industry had definite shortcomings from the employer's point of view. Ambitious merchant capitalists therefore intensified their search for ways to produce more efficiently and to squeeze still more work out of "undisciplined" cottage workers.

## Building the Atlantic Economy

See DBQ 6

In addition to agricultural improvement, population pressure, and growing cottage industry, the expansion of Europe in the eighteenth century was characterized by the growth of world trade. Spain and Portugal revitalized their empires and began drawing more wealth from renewed development. Yet once again the countries of northwestern Europe—the Netherlands, France, and, above all, Great Britain—benefited most. Great Britain, which was formed in 1707 by the union of England and Scotland in a single kingdom, gradually became the leading maritime power. Thus the British played the critical role in building a fairly unified Atlantic economy, which offered remarkable opportunities for them and their colonists.

### Mercantilism and Colonial Wars

Britain's commercial leadership in the eighteenth century had its origins in the mercantilism of the seventeenth century (see page 540). European **mercantilism** was a system of economic regulations aimed at increasing the power of the state. As practiced by a leading advocate such as Colbert under Louis XIV, mercantilism aimed particularly at creating a favorable balance of foreign trade in order to increase a country's stock of gold. A country's gold holdings served as an all-important treasure chest, to be opened periodically to pay for war in a violent age.

Early English mercantilists shared these views. What distinguished English mercantilism was the unusual idea that government economic regulations could and should serve the private interests of individuals and groups as well as the public needs of the state. As Josiah Child, a very wealthy brewer and director of the East India Company, put it, in the ideal economy "Profit and Power ought jointly to be considered."[6] By contrast, in France and other continental countries, seventeenth-century mercantilists generally put the needs of the state first, and they seldom saw a possible union of public and private interests for a common good.

The result of the English desire to increase both military power and private wealth was the mercantile system of the **Navigation Acts.** Oliver Cromwell established the first of these laws in 1651, and the restored monarchy of Charles II extended them further in 1660 and 1663; these Navigation Acts were not seriously modified until 1786. The acts required that most goods imported from Europe into England and Scotland be carried on British-owned ships with British crews or on ships of the country producing the article. Moreover, these laws gave British merchants and shipowners a virtual monopoly on trade with British colonies. The colonists were required to ship their products on British (or American) ships and to buy almost all of their European goods from Britain. It was believed that these economic regulations would help British merchants and workers as well as colonial plantation owners and farmers. And the emerging British Empire would develop a shipping industry with a large number of tough, experienced, deep-water seamen, who could be drafted when necessary into the Royal Navy to protect the island nation and its colonial possessions.

The Navigation Acts were a form of economic warfare. Their initial target was the Dutch, who were far ahead of the English in shipping and foreign trade in the mid-seventeenth century (see page 559). The Navigation Acts, in conjunction with three Anglo-Dutch wars between 1652 and 1674, did seriously damage Dutch shipping and commerce. The thriving Dutch colony of New Amsterdam was seized in 1664 and renamed "New York." By the late seventeenth century, the Netherlands was falling behind England in shipping, trade, and colonies.

Thereafter France stood clearly as England's most serious rival in the competition for overseas empire. Rich in natural resources, endowed with a population three or four times that of England, and allied with Spain, continental Europe's leading military power was already building a powerful fleet and a worldwide system of rigidly monopolized colonial trade. Thus from 1701 to 1763, Britain and France were locked in a series of wars to decide, in part, which nation would become the leading maritime power and claim the lion's share of the profits of Europe's overseas expansion (see Map 19.2).

The first round was the War of the Spanish Succession (see page 543), which started when Louis XIV declared his willingness to accept the Spanish crown willed to his grandson. Besides upsetting the continental balance of power, a union of France and Spain threatened to encircle and destroy the British colonies in North America (see Map 19.2). Defeated by a great coalition of states after twelve years of fighting, Louis XIV was forced in the Peace of Utrecht (1713) to cede Newfoundland, Nova Scotia, and the Hudson Bay territory to Britain. Spain was compelled to give Britain control of its West African slave trade—the so-called *asiento*—and to let Britain send one ship of merchandise into the Spanish colonies annually, through Porto Bello on the Isthmus of Panama.

France was still a mighty competitor. The War of the Austrian Succession (1740–1748), which started when Frederick the Great of Prussia seized Silesia from Austria's Maria Theresa (see page 636), gradually became a world war that included Anglo-French conflicts in India and North America. The war ended with no change in the territorial situation in North America.

This inconclusive standoff helped set the stage for the Seven Years' War (1756–1763). In central Europe, Austria's Maria Theresa sought to win back Silesia and crush Prussia, thereby re-establishing the Habsburgs' traditional leadership in German affairs. She almost succeeded (see page 616), but Prussia survived with its boundaries intact.

Inconclusive in Europe, the Seven Years' War was the decisive round in the Franco-British competition for colonial empire. The fighting began in North America. The population of New France was centered in Quebec and along the St. Lawrence River. But French soldiers and Canadian fur traders had also built forts and trading posts along the Great Lakes, through the Ohio country, and down the Mississippi to New Orleans (see Map 19.3). Allied with many Native American tribes, the French built more forts in 1753 in what is now western Pennsylvania to protect their claims. The following year, a Virginia force attacked a small group of French soldiers, and soon the war to conquer Canada was on.

Although the inhabitants of New France were greatly outnumbered—Canada counted 55,000 inhabitants, as opposed to 1.2 million in the thirteen English colonies—French and Canadian forces under the experienced marquis de Montcalm fought well and scored major victories until 1758. Then, led by their new chief minister, William Pitt, whose grandfather had made a fortune in India, the British diverted men and money from the war in Europe, which remained nevertheless the main focus for the French court at Versailles. The British concentrated instead on the struggle for empire, using superior sea power to destroy the French fleet and choke off French commerce around the world. In 1759 a combined British naval and land force laid siege to fortress Quebec. After four long months, they finally defeated Montcalm's army in a dramatic battle that sealed the fate of France in North America.

British victory on all colonial fronts was ratified in the Treaty of Paris (1763). France lost all its possessions on the mainland of North America. Canada and all French territory east of the Mississippi River passed to Britain, and France ceded Louisiana to Spain as compensation for Spain's loss of Florida to Britain. France also gave up most of its holdings in India, opening the way to British dominance on the subcontinent. By 1763 British naval power, built in large part on the rapid growth of the British shipping industry after the passage of the Navigation Acts, had triumphed decisively. Britain had realized its goal of monopolizing a vast trading and colonial empire for its exclusive benefit.

## Land and Labor in British America

As Britain built its empire in North America, it secured an important outlet for surplus population, so that migration abroad limited poverty in England, Scotland, and northern Ireland. The settlers also benefited, for they shared in the rights of European conquest and had privileged access

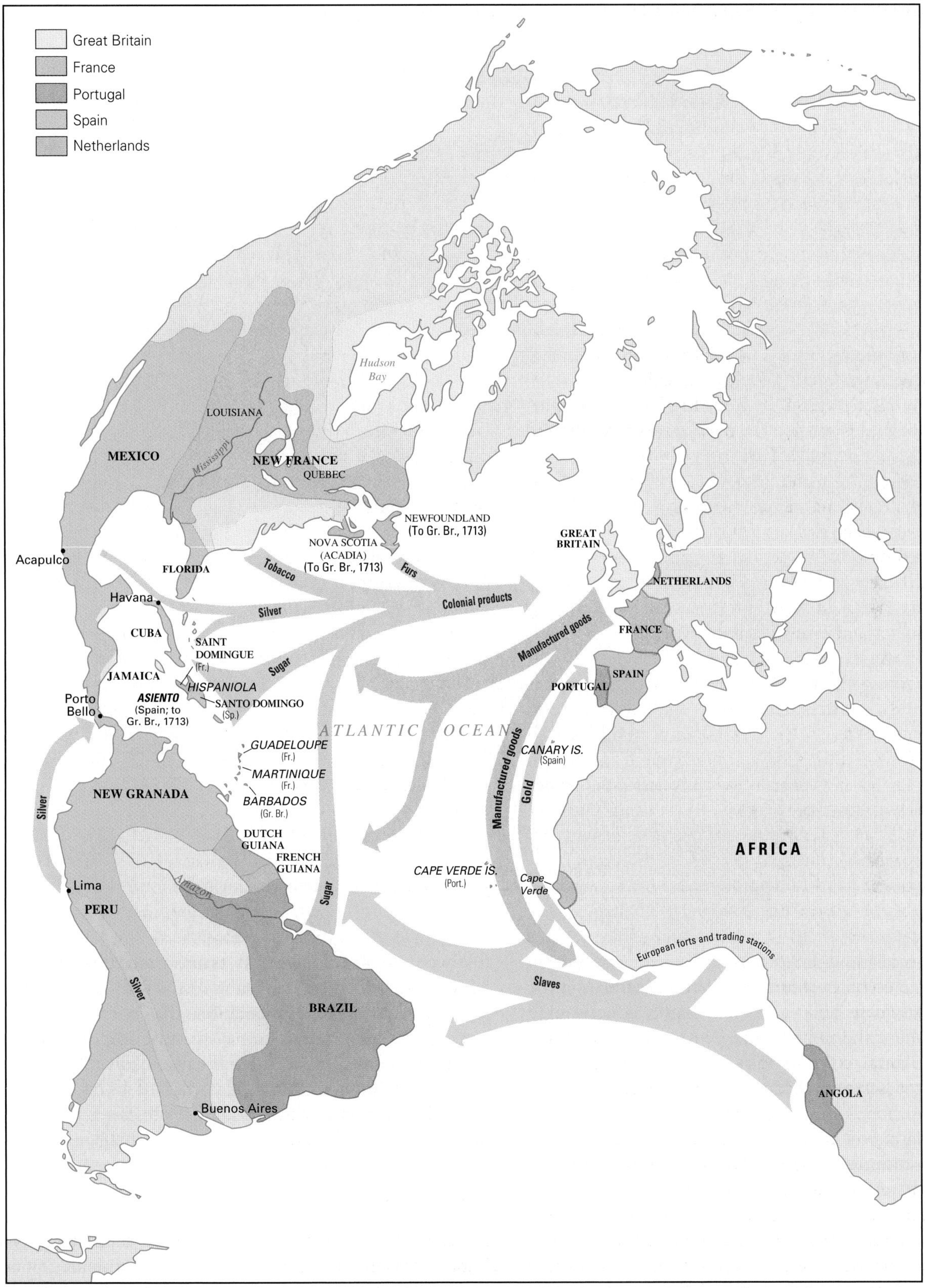


**MAP 19.2 The Atlantic Economy, 1701–1763** The growth of trade encouraged both economic development and military conflict in the Atlantic basin. Four continents were linked together by the exchange of goods and slaves.

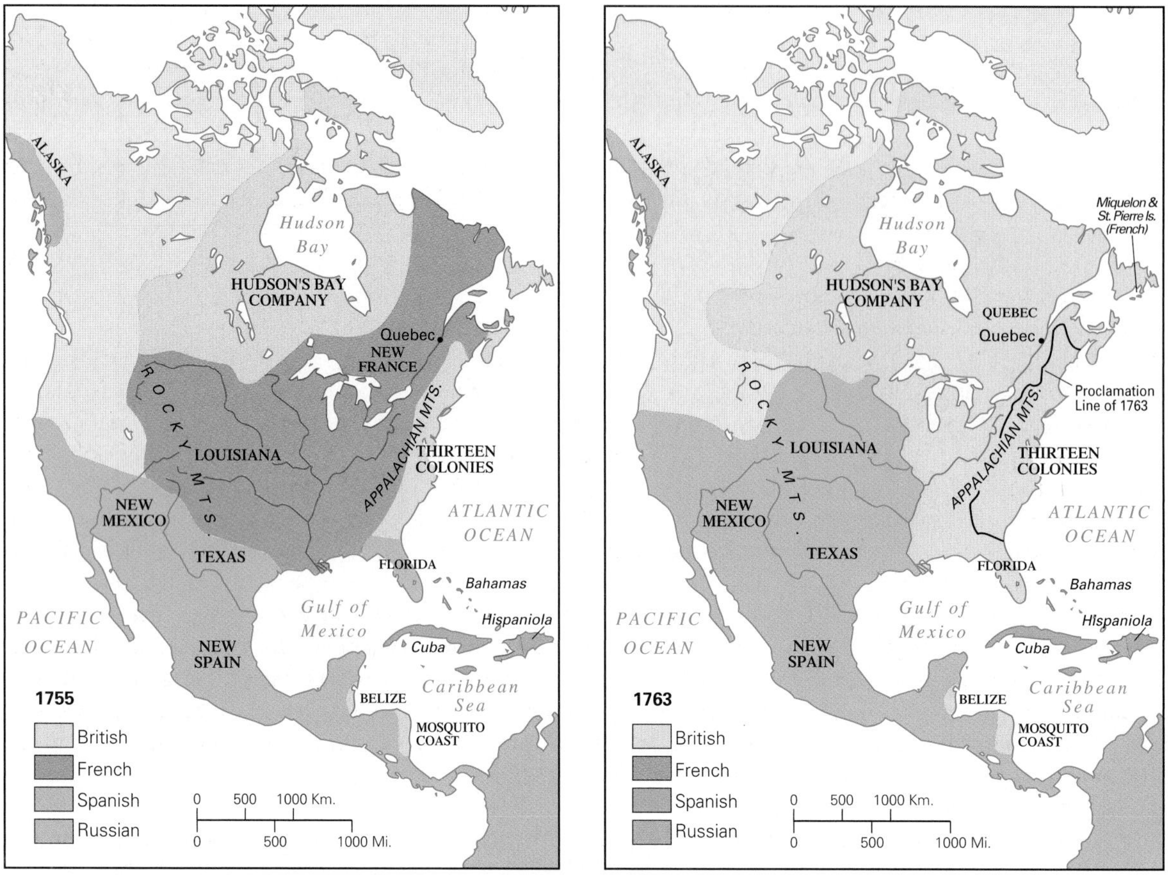


**MAP 19.3 European Claims in North America Before and After the Seven Years' War (1756–1763)** France lost its vast claims in North America, though the British government then prohibited colonists from settling west of the Appalachian Mountains in 1763. The British had raised taxes on themselves and the colonists to pay for the war, and they wanted to avoid costly conflicts with Native Americans living in the newly conquered territory.

to virtually free and unlimited land. Thus the situation in the American colonies contrasted sharply with that in the British Isles, where land was already highly concentrated in the hands of the nobility and gentry in 1700. White settlers who came to the colonies as free men and women, as indentured servants pledged to work seven years for their passage, or as prisoners and convicts could obtain their own farms on easy terms as soon as they had their personal freedom. And unlike the great majority of European peasants, American farmers could keep most of what they produced.

Cheap land and tremendous demand for scarce labor power were also critical factors in the growth of slavery in the British colonies. The Spanish and the Portuguese had introduced slavery into the Americas in the sixteenth century. In the seventeenth century, the Dutch aggressively followed their example and transported thousands of Africans, first to Brazil and then to the Caribbean. There slaves worked on sugar plantations that normally earned large profits for plantation owners and European traders. Most slaves came from Africa because Native Americans died in large numbers, especially when enslaved.

As England adopted mercantilist policies after 1650, big investors also established valuable sugar plantations in the Caribbean and brought slave laborers from Africa to work them. The small white farmers, who had settled the islands and grew tobacco, generally sold out and migrated to the mainland colonies. Black slaves then became the overwhelming majority of the population in Britain's Caribbean colonies. By 1700 the pattern of plantations based on slave exploitation had spread to the Virginia lowlands, which British indentured servants were carefully avoiding, and by 1730 the large plantations there were worked entirely by black slaves. The exploitation of slave labor permitted an astonishing tenfold increase in tobacco production between 1700 and 1774 and created a wealthy aristocratic planter class in Maryland and Virginia. In 1790, when the U.S. population was approaching 4 million, blacks accounted for almost 20 percent of the total.

Slavery was uncommon in New England and the middle colonies, and in the course of the eighteenth century these areas began to export ever more foodstuffs, primarily to the West Indies. There the owners of the sugar plantations came to depend on the mainland colonies for grain and dried fish to feed their slaves. The plantation owners, whether they grew tobacco in Virginia and Maryland or sugar in the West Indies, had the exclusive privilege of supplying the British Isles with their products. Thus white colonists, too, had their place in the protective mercantile system of the Navigation Acts.

The abundance of almost free land resulted in a rapid increase in the colonial population in the eighteenth century. In a mere three-quarters of a century after 1700, the white population of the mainland colonies multiplied a staggering ten times, as immigrants arrived and colonial couples raised large families. Rapid population growth did not reduce the white settlers to poverty. On the contrary, agricultural development resulted in fairly high standards of living, and on the eve of the American Revolution white men and women in the mainland British colonies probably had the highest average income and standard of living in the world.[7]

## The Growth of Foreign Trade

Britain and especially England, its most important part, also profited greatly from the mercantile system. Stimulated by trade and empire building, London grew in the eighteenth century into the West's largest and richest city. (See the feature "Images in Society: London: The Remaking of a Great City" on pages 648–649.) Above all, the rapidly growing and increasingly wealthy agricultural populations of the mainland colonies provided an expanding market for English manufactured goods. This situation was extremely fortunate, for England in the eighteenth century was gradually losing, or only slowly expanding, its sales to many of its traditional European markets. In the Americas merchant capitalists and manufacturers found new and exciting opportunities for profit and wealth.

Since the late Middle Ages, England had relied very heavily on the sale of woolen cloth in foreign markets. Indeed, as late as 1700, woolen cloth was the only important manufactured good exported from England, and fully 90 percent of it was sold to Europeans. In the course of the eighteenth century, the states of continental Europe were trying to develop their own cottage textile industries in an effort to deal with rural poverty and overpopulation. They adopted protectionist, mercantilist policies to exclude competing goods from abroad. By 1773 England was selling only about two-thirds as much woolen cloth to northern and western Europe as it had in 1700.

As trade with Europe stagnated, protected colonial markets came to the rescue. The markets of the Atlantic economy led the way (see Figure 19.3). English exports of manufactured goods to the Atlantic economy—primarily the mainland colonies of North America and the West Indian sugar islands, with an important assist from West Africa and Latin America—soared from £500,000 to £4.0 million. Sales to other colonies—Ireland and India—also rose substantially in the eighteenth century.

English exports became much more balanced and diversified. To America and Africa went large quantities of metal items—axes to frontier settlers, firearms, chains to slave owners. There were also clocks and coaches, buttons

**FIGURE 19.3 Exports of English Manufactured Goods, 1700–1774** While trade between England and Europe stagnated after 1700, English exports to Africa and the Americas boomed and greatly stimulated English economic development. *(Source: R. Davis, "English Foreign Trade, 1700–1774,"* Economic History Review, *2d ser., 15 (1962): 302–303.)*

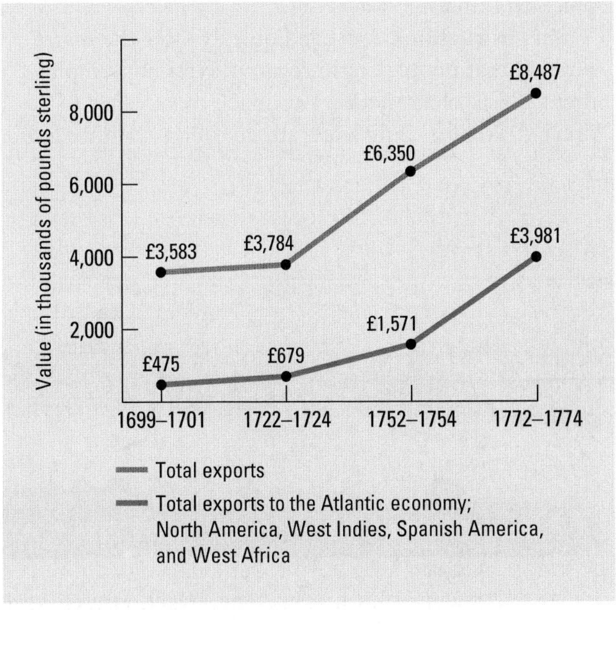

# *Images in Society*

## London: The Remaking of a Great City

Imperial capital and intercontinental trade center, London dominated Britain and astonished the visitor. Equal in population in 1650 to Paris with 400,000 inhabitants, the supercity of the West grew to 900,000 in 1801 while second-place Paris had 600,000. And as London grew, its citizens created a new urban landscape and style of living.

Image 1 shows the "true profile" of London and its built environment as viewed from the south before the Great Fire of 1666, which raged for four days and destroyed about 80 percent of the old, predominately wooden central city. With the River Thames flowing eastward toward the sea, one sees from left to right pre-Fire St. Paul's Cathedral, London Bridge crowded with houses, ships at the wharves, and the medieval Tower of London. Clearly visible in the distance are the open fields of the large estates surrounding London, while beyond view on the left are the royal palace and adjacent government buildings. Also missing is the famous London smog, the combination of fog and smoke from coal-burning fireplaces that already polluted the metropolis. How would you characterize pre-Fire London?

Reconstruction proceeded quickly after the Great Fire, so that people could regain shelter and employment. Brick construction was made mandatory to prevent fire, but only a few streets were straightened or widened. Thus social classes remained packed together in the rebuilt city. The rich merchant family in a first-class city residence (Image 2), built in the 1670s and still standing in 1939, shared a tiny courtyard and constantly rubbed shoulders with poor and "middling" people in everyday life.

As London rebuilt and kept growing, big noble landowners followed two earlier examples and sought to increase their incomes by setting up residential developments on their estates west of the city. A landowner would lay out a square with streets and building lots, which he (or she) would lease to speculative builders who put up fine houses for sale or rent. Soho Square, first laid out in the 1670s and shown in Image 3 as it appeared in 1731, was fairly typical. The spacious square with its gated park is surrounded by three-story row houses set on deep, narrow lots. Set in the country but close to the city, squares like Soho were a kind of elegant "village" with restrictive building codes that catered to aristocrats, officials, and successful professionals, who were served by artisans and shopkeepers living in alleys and side streets. Do you see a difference between the houses on the square and on the street behind? How would you compare Soho Square with the hills in the distance and with the old London of Images 1 and 2? The classy, new area, known as the West End, contrasted sharply with the shoddy rentals and makeshift shacks of laborers and sailors in the mushrooming East End, which artists rarely painted. Thus

**Image 1** London Before the Great Fire *(Hulton Archive/Getty Images)*

**Image 2** Merchant Family's Residence (built 1670–1680) *(English Heritage/NMR)*

**Image 3** Soho Square, 1731 *(Private Collection/The Stapleton Collection/The Bridgeman Art Library)*

**Image 4** Bloomsbury Square, 1787 *(The Art Archive)*

residential segregation by income level increased substantially in eighteenth-century London.

As the suburban villages grew and gradually merged together, the West End attracted increasingly the well-to-do from all over England. Rural landowners and provincial notables came for the social season from October to May. Operating out of comfortable second homes purchased or rented in the West End, they played the national market for mortgages, marriages, and recreation. Image 4, showing classy Bloomsbury Square in 1787 and the original country mansion of the enterprising noble developer, provides a glimpse into this well-born culture. How does Image 4 complement Image 3? What message is the artist conveying with the milkmaid and her cows? Finally, some historians believe London's West End was an important social innovation. Reconsidering these images, do you agree?

*The* **history companion** *features additional information and activities related to this topic.*
**history.college.hmco.com/students**

**Slaves Harvesting Sugar Cane** In this 1828 print a long line of hard-working slaves systematically harvests the ripe cane on the island of Antigua, while on the right more slaves load cut cane into wagons for refining at the plantation's central crushing mill. The manager on horseback may be ordering the overseer to quicken the work pace, always brutal and unrelenting at harvest time. Slave labor made high-intensity capitalist production of sugar possible in the Americas. *(John Carter Brown Library at Brown University)*

and saddles, china and furniture, musical instruments and scientific equipment, and a host of other things. By 1750 half the nails made in England were going to the colonies. Foreign trade became the bread and butter of some industries.

Thus the mercantilist system formed in the seventeenth century to attack the Dutch and to win power and profit for England achieved remarkable success in the eighteenth century. The English concentrated in their hands much of the trade flowing through the growing Atlantic economy. Of great importance, the pressure of demand from three continents on the cottage industry of one medium-size country heightened the efforts of English merchant capitalists to find new and improved ways to produce more goods. By the 1770s England stood on the threshold of the epoch-making industrial changes that will be described in Chapter 22.

## The Atlantic Slave Trade

Although the trade in African people was a worldwide phenomenon, the **Atlantic slave trade** became the most extensive and significant portion of it. In the words of a leading historian, by 1700 "it was impossible to imagine the Atlantic system without slavery and the slave trade."[8]

The forced migration of millions of Africans—so cruel, unjust, and tragic—remained a key element in the Atlantic system and western European economic expansion throughout the eighteenth century. Indeed, the brutal trade intensified dramatically after 1700, and especially after 1750. According to one authoritative estimate, European traders purchased and shipped 6.13 million African slaves across the Atlantic between 1701 and 1800—fully 52 percent of the estimated total of 11.7 million Africans transported between 1450 and 1900, not including an

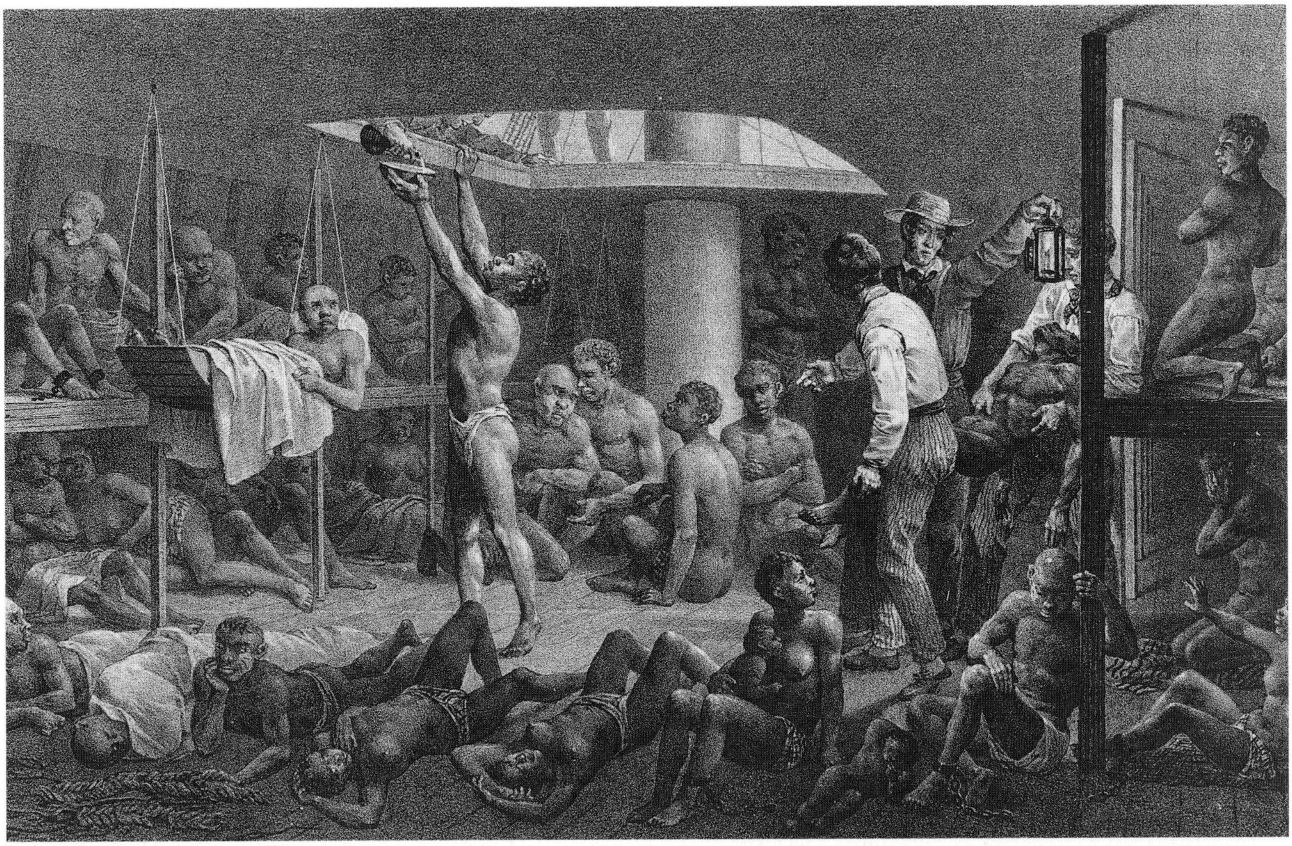

**A Slave Ship and Its Victims** This 1827 lithograph of slaves in a ship's hold bound for Brazil depicts the "scene of horror almost inconceivable" that Equiano encountered in crossing the Atlantic. Inhuman overcrowding of slaves resulted in shocking death rates. The man on the right will be thrown overboard. *(Houghton Library, Harvard University)*

additional 10 to 15 percent who died in procurement and transit.[9] By the peak decade of the 1780s, shipments of black men and women averaged about 80,000 per year, in an attempt to satisfy the constantly rising demand for labor power—and slave owner profits—in the Americas.

Taken to the Americas in chains, Africans made a decisive contribution to the development of the Atlantic economy. Above all, the labor of enslaved Africans made possible large-scale production of valuable commodities for sale in Europe, for Africans transported to the Americas could not go off and farm for themselves as white settlers did. Indeed, an important recent study concludes that in the years from 1761 to 1800 Africans and their descendants in Brazil, Spanish America, the Caribbean, and Britain's mainland slave colonies accounted for more than *four-fifths* of all the commodities produced in the Americas for sale in the Atlantic economy.[10] It was this flood of ever more, ever cheaper sugar, coffee, tobacco, rice, and (in the nineteenth century) cotton that generated hard cash in the Americas, cash that paid for manufactured goods and services from Britain and Europe, as well as for ever more slaves from Africa.

Intensification of the slave trade resulted in fundamental changes in its organization. Before 1700 European states waged costly wars with one another through monopolist trading companies, in hopes of controlling slave exports from Africa. European agents in fortified trading posts tapped into traditional African networks and markets for slaves, who were mainly captives taken in battles between African states, plus some Africans punished with slavery by local societies or secured through small-scale raiding. After 1700, as Britain became the undisputed leader in the slave trade, European governments and ship captains of different nationalities cut back on fighting between themselves and concentrated on commerce. They generally adopted the shore method of trading, which was less expensive. Thus European ships sent boats ashore or invited African dealers to bring traders and slaves out to their ships. This method allowed ships to move easily along the coast from market to market and to depart more quickly for the Americas.

Increasing demand resulted in rising prices for African slaves in the eighteenth century. Some African merchants and rulers who controlled exports profited, and some Africans secured foreign products that they found appealing because of price or quality. But generally such economic returns did not spread very far. The negative consequences of the expanding slave trade predominated.

Wars between Africans to obtain salable captives increased, and leaders purchased more guns and gunpowder and bought relatively fewer textiles and consumer goods. The kingdom of Dahomey, which entered the slave trade in the eighteenth century and made it a royal monopoly, built up its army, attacked far into the interior, and profited greatly as a major supplier of slaves. More common perhaps was the experience of the kingdom of the Congo in central Africa, where the perpetual Portuguese search for slaves undermined the monarchy, destroyed political unity, and led to constant disorder. All along Africa's western coast small-scale raiding for slaves also spread far into the interior. There kidnappers seized and enslaved men and women like Olaudah Equiano and his sister, whose tragic separation, exile, and exploitation personified the full horror and inhumanity of the Atlantic slave trade. (See the feature "Individuals in Society: Olaudah Equiano.") Africans who committed crimes had traditionally paid fines, but because of the urgent demand for slaves many misdemeanors became punishable by sale to slave dealers. Finally, while the population of Europe (and Asia) grew very substantially in the eighteenth century, that of Africa stagnated or possibly declined.

Until 1700, and perhaps even 1750, almost all Europeans considered the African slave trade a legitimate business activity. But shiploads of African slaves were never landed in northwestern Europe, partly because cheap labor abounded there. Blacks did arrive in England (and France) as personal slaves, but if a slave ran away, the courts and the poor often supported the slave, not the slave owner. Runaways merged into London's growing population of free and escaped blacks; unions between blacks and whites were not uncommon. In 1772 a high court ruling, though limited in scope, "clearly doomed the slave status in England."[11]

After 1775, a much broader campaign to abolish slavery developed in Britain, and according to some recent scholarship, between 1788 and 1792 it grew into the first peaceful mass political movement based on the mobilization of public opinion in British history. British women played a critical role in this mass movement. They denounced the immorality of human bondage and stressed the cruel and sadistic treatment of female slaves and slave families. These attacks put the defenders of slavery on the defensive. In 1807 Parliament abolished the British slave trade, although slavery continued for years in British colonies and the Americas.

## Revival in Colonial Latin America

When the last Spanish Habsburg, the feeble-minded Charles II, died in 1700 (see page 543), Spain's vast empire lay ready for dismemberment. Yet in one of those striking reversals with which history is replete, Spain revived. The empire held together and even prospered, while a European-oriented landowning aristocracy enhanced its position in colonial society.

Spain recovered in part because of better leadership. Louis XIV's grandson, who took the throne as Philip V (r. 1700–1746), brought new men and fresh ideas with him from France and rallied the Spanish people to his Bourbon dynasty in the long War of the Spanish Succession. When peace was restored, a series of reforming ministers reasserted royal authority, overhauling state finances and strengthening defense.

Revitalization in Madrid had positive results in the colonies. They succeeded in defending themselves from numerous British attacks and even increased in size. Spain received Louisiana from France in 1763, and missionaries and ranchers extended Spanish influence all the way to northern California.

Political success was matched by economic improvement. After declining markedly in the seventeenth century, silver mining recovered greatly, and in 1800 Spanish America accounted for half of the world's silver production. Silver mining also encouraged food production for large mining camps and gave the **Creoles**—people of Spanish blood born in America—the means to purchase more and more European luxuries and manufactured goods. A class of wealthy Creole merchants arose to handle this flourishing trade, which often relied on smuggled goods from Great Britain.

Rivaling the officials dispatched from Spain, Creole estate owners controlled much of the land and strove to become a genuine European aristocracy. Estate owners believed that work in the fields was the proper occupation of an impoverished peasantry. The defenseless Native Americans suited their needs. As the indigenous population recovered in numbers, slavery and periodic

# Individuals in Society

## Olaudah Equiano

The slave trade was a mass migration involving millions of human beings. It was also the sum of individual lives spent partly or entirely in slavery. Although most of those lives remain hidden to us, Olaudah Equiano (1745–1797) is an important exception.

Equiano was born in Benin (modern Nigeria) of Ibo ethnicity. His father, one of the village elders (or chieftains), presided over a large household that included "many slaves," prisoners captured in local wars. All people, slave and free, shared in the cultivation of family lands. One day, when all the adults were in the fields, two strange men and a woman broke into the family compound, kidnapped the eleven-year-old boy and his sister, tied them up, and dragged them into the woods. Brother and sister were separated and Olaudah was sold several times to various dealers before reaching the coast. As it took six months to walk there, his home must have been far inland.

The slave ship and the strange appearance of the white crew terrified the boy. Much worse was the long voyage from Benin to Barbados in the Caribbean, as Equiano later recounted. "The stench of the [ship's] hold . . . became absolutely pestilential . . . [and] brought on a sickness among the slaves, of which many died. . . . The shrieks of the women and the groans of the dying rendered the whole a scene of horror almost inconceivable." Placed on deck with the sick and dying, Equiano saw two and then three of his "enchained countrymen" escape somehow through the nettings and jump into the sea, "preferring death to such a life of misery."*

Equiano's new owner, an officer in the Royal Navy, took him to England and saw that the lad received some education. Engaged in bloody action in Europe for almost four years as a captain's boy in the Seven Years' War, Equiano hoped that his loyal service and Christian baptism would help to secure his freedom. He also knew that slavery was generally illegal in England. But his master deceived him. Docking in London, he and his accomplices forced a protesting and heartbroken Equiano onto a ship bound for the Caribbean.

There he was sold to Robert King, a Quaker merchant from Philadelphia who dealt in sugar and rum. Equiano developed his mathematical skills, worked hard to please as a clerk in King's warehouse, and became first mate on one of King's ships. Allowed to trade on the side for his own profit, Equiano amassed capital, repaid King his original purchase price, and received his deed of manumission at the age of twenty-one. King urged his talented former slave to stay on as a business partner, but Equiano hated the limitations and dangers of black freedom in the colonies—he was almost kidnapped back into slavery while loading a ship in Georgia—and could think only of England. Settling in London, Equiano studied, worked as a hairdresser, and went to sea periodically as a merchant seaman. He developed his ardent Christian faith and became a leading member of London's sizable black community.

*Olaudah Equiano, in an engraving from his autobiography.* (National Portrait Gallery, Smithsonian Institution/Art Resource, NY)

Equiano loathed the brutal slavery and the vicious exploitation that he saw in the West Indies and Britain's mainland colonies. A complex and sophisticated man, he also respected the integrity of Robert King and admired British navigational and industrial technologies. He encountered white oppressors and made white friends. He once described himself as "almost an Englishman." In the 1780s he joined with white and black activists in the antislavery campaign. He wrote his *Interesting Narrative,* a well-documented autobiographical indictment of slavery. Above all, he urged Christians to live by the principles they professed and to treat blacks equally as free human beings and children of God. With the success of his widely read book, he carried his message to large audiences across Britain and Ireland and inspired the growing movement to abolish slavery.

### Questions for Analysis

1. What aspects of Olaudah Equiano's life as a slave were typical? What aspects were atypical?
2. Describe Equiano's culture and personality. What aspects are most striking? Why?

*Olaudah Equiano, *The Interesting Narrative of the Life of Olaudah Equiano Written by Himself,* ed. with an introduction by Robert J. Allison (Boston: Bedford Books, 1995), pp. 56–57. Recent scholarship has re-examined Equiano's life and thrown some details of his identity into question.

*The* **History Companion** *features additional information and activities related to this topic.*
**history.college.hmco.com/students**

**Forming the Mexican People** This painting by an unknown eighteenth-century artist presents a naive but sympathetic view of interracial unions and marriages in colonial Mexico. On the left, the union of a Spanish man and a Native American woman has produced a racially mixed mestizo. The handsome group on the right features a mestizo woman and a Spaniard with their little daughter. *(Private Collection/Banco Nacional de Mexico)*

forced labor gave way to widespread **debt peonage** from 1600 on. Under this system, a planter or rancher would keep the estate's Christianized, increasingly Hispanicized Indians in perpetual debt bondage by periodically advancing food, shelter, and a little money. Debt peonage was a form of serfdom.

The large middle group in Spanish colonies consisted of racially mixed **mestizos,** the offspring of Spanish men and Indian women. The most talented mestizos realistically aspired to join the Creoles, for enough wealth and power could make one considered white. Thus by the end of the colonial era, roughly 20 percent of the population was classified as white and about 30 percent as mestizo. Pure-blooded Indians accounted for most of the remainder, but some black slaves were found in every part of Spanish America. Great numbers of blacks went in chains to work the enormous sugar plantations of Portuguese Brazil, and about half the Brazilian population in the early nineteenth century was of African origin. The people of Brazil intermingled sexually and culturally, and the population grew to include every color in the racial rainbow. South America occupied an important place in the expanding Atlantic economy.

## Adam Smith and Economic Liberalism

Although mercantilist policies strengthened both the Spanish and British colonial empires in the eighteenth century, a strong reaction against mercantilism ultimately set in. Creole merchants chafed at regulations imposed from Madrid. Small English merchants complained loudly about the injustice of handing over exclusive trading rights to great trading combines such as the East India Company. Wanting a bigger position in overseas commerce, independent merchants in many countries began campaigning against "monopolies" and calling for "free trade."

The general idea of freedom of enterprise in foreign trade was persuasively developed by Scottish professor of philosophy Adam Smith (1723–1790). Smith, whose *Inquiry into the Nature and Causes of the Wealth of Nations* (1776) established the basis for modern economics, was highly critical of eighteenth-century mercantilism. Mercantilism, he said, meant a combination of stifling government regulations and unfair privileges for state-approved monopolies and government favorites. Far preferable was free competition, which would best protect consumers from price gouging and give all citizens a fair and equal right to do what they did best. In keeping with his deep-seated fear of political oppression and with the "system of natural liberty" that he advocated, Smith argued that government should limit itself to "only three duties." It should provide a defense against foreign invasion, maintain civil order with courts and police protection, and sponsor certain indispensable public works and institutions that could never adequately profit private investors.

Often lampooned in the nineteenth and twentieth centuries as a mouthpiece for business interests, Smith was one of the Enlightenment's most original and characteristic thinkers. He relied on the power of reason to unlock the secrets of the secular world, and he believed that he spoke for truth, not for special interests. Thus unlike many disgruntled merchant capitalists, Smith applauded the modest rise in real wages of British workers in the eighteenth century and went on to say, "No society can surely be flourishing and happy, of which the far greater part of the members are poor and miserable." Quite realistically, Smith concluded that employers were "always and everywhere in a sort of tacit, but constant and uniform combination, not to raise the wages of labour above their actual rate" and sometimes entered "into particular combinations to sink the wages even below this rate."[12]

Yet Smith did not call for more laws and more police power to force people into proper economic behavior. Instead, he made the pursuit of self-interest in a competitive market the source of an underlying and previously unrecognized harmony, a harmony that would result in gradual progress.

According to Smith:

*[Every individual generally] neither intends to promote the public interest, nor knows how much he is promoting it. . . .*

**Adam Smith** Appointed professor at Glasgow University at age twenty-seven, Smith established an international reputation with his first book. He then became the well-paid tutor of a rich young lord and traveled widely before publishing *The Wealth of Nations,* the point of departure for modern economics. *(Special Collections/Glasgow University Library)*

*He is in this case, as in many cases, led by an invisible hand to promote an end which was no part of his intention. Nor is it always the worse for society that it was not part of it. I have never known much good done by those who affected to trade for the public good.*[13]

The "invisible hand" of free competition for one and for all disciplined the greed of selfish individuals and provided the most effective means of increasing the wealth of both rich and poor.

Smith's provocative work had a great international impact. Going through eight editions in English and translated into several languages within twenty years, it quickly emerged as the classic argument for **economic liberalism** and unregulated capitalism.

## Summary

While some European intellectual elites and parts of the educated public were developing a new view of the world in the eighteenth century, Europe as a whole was experiencing a gradual but far-reaching expansion. As agriculture began showing signs of modest improvement across the continent, first the Low Countries and then England launched changes that gradually revolutionized agriculture. Plague disappeared, and the populations of all countries grew significantly, thereby encouraging the growth of wage labor, cottage industry, and merchant capitalism.

Europeans also continued their overseas expansion, fighting for empire and profit and, in particular, consolidating their hold on the Americas. A revived Spain and its Latin American colonies participated fully in this expansion. As in agriculture and cottage industry, however, England and its empire proved most successful. The English concentrated much of the growing Atlantic trade in their hands, a development that challenged and enriched English industry and intensified interest in new methods of production and in an emerging economic liberalism. Thus by the 1770s, England was approaching an economic breakthrough as fully significant as the great political upheaval destined to develop shortly in neighboring France.

## Key Terms

famine foods
open-field system
common lands
agricultural revolution
crop rotation
enclosure
proletarianization
cottage industry
putting-out system
mercantilism
Navigation Acts
Atlantic slave trade
Creoles
debt peonage
mestizos
economic liberalism

## Notes

1. B. H. Slicher van Bath, *The Agrarian History of Western Europe, A.D. 500–1850* (New York: St. Martin's Press, 1963), p. 240.
2. Quoted in E. E. Rich and C. H. Wilson, eds., *The Cambridge Economic History of Europe,* vol. 4 (Cambridge: Cambridge University Press, 1967), p. 85.
3. Quoted in I. Pinchbeck, *Women Workers and the Industrial Revolution, 1750–1850* (New York: F. S. Crofts, 1930), p. 113.
4. Quoted in S. Chapman, *The Lancashire Cotton Industry* (Manchester, England: Manchester University Press, 1903), p. 13.
5. Quoted in P. Mantoux, *The Industrial Revolution in the Eighteenth Century* (New York: Harper & Row, 1961), p. 75.
6. Quoted in C. Wilson, *England's Apprenticeship, 1603–1763* (London: Longmans, Green, 1965), p. 169.
7. G. Taylor, "America's Growth Before 1840," *Journal of Economic History* 24 (December 1970): 427–444.
8. Seymour Drescher, "Free Labor vs. Slave Labor: The British and Caribbean Cases," in *Terms of Labor: Slavery, Serfdom, and Free Labor,* ed. Stanley L. Engerman (Stanford, Calif.: Stanford University Press, 1999), pp. 52–53.
9. P. E. Lovejoy, *Transformations in Slavery: A History of Slavery in Africa* (Cambridge: Cambridge University Press, 1983), p. 19.
10. J. Inikori, *Africans and the Industrial Revolution in England: A Study in International Trade and Economic Development* (Cambridge: Cambridge University Press, 2002), pp. 481–482.
11. Seymour Drescher, *Capitalism and Antislavery: British Mobilization in Comparative Perspective* (London: Macmillan, 1986), p. 38.
12. R. Heilbroner, ed., *The Essential Adam Smith* (New York: W. W. Norton, 1986), p. 196.
13. Ibid., p. 265.

## Suggested Reading

The work by Slicher van Bath listed in the Notes is a wide-ranging general introduction to the gradual transformation of European agriculture. J. Blum, *The End of the Old Order in Rural Europe* (1978), is an impressive comparative study. J. de Vries, *The Dutch Rural Economy in the Golden Age, 1500–1700* (1974), examines the causes of early Dutch leadership in farming, while J. de Vries and A. van der Woude, *The First Modern Economy: Success, Failure, and Perseverance of the Dutch Economy, 1500–1815* (1997), is a masterful extension of that investigation. M. Overton, *Agricultural Revolution in England* (1996), charts the path of agricultural progress in England. J. Neeson, *Commoners: Common Right, Enclosure and Social Change, 1700–1820* (1993), stresses popular resistance to enclosure and the losses it brought for the common people. J. Gargliardo, *From Pariah to Patriot: The Changing Image of the German Peasant, 1770–1840* (1969), examines the development of reforms designed to improve the lot of the peasantry in Germany. A. Goodwin, ed., *The European Nobility in the Eighteenth Century* (1967), is an excellent study on aristocrats in different countries. E. Le Roy Ladurie, *The Peasants of Languedoc* (1976), a brilliant and challenging study of rural life in southern France for several centuries, complements J. Goody et al., eds., *Family and Inheritance: Rural Society in Western Europe, 1200–1800* (1976). Important, more recent studies on population and disease include M. Oldstone, *Viruses, Plagues, and History* (1998), and C. Cipolla, *Miasmas and Disease:*

*Public Health and Environment in the Pre-Industrial Age* (1992). P. Allen, *The Wages of Sin: Sex and Disease, Past and Present* (2000), tells the long, sad story of sexually transmitted diseases with compassion. J. Brewer and R. Porter, eds., *Consumption and the World of Goods* (1993), is a fascinating collection of studies and reflects the growing historical interest in consumption as well as production. O. Hufton deals vividly and sympathetically with rural migration, work, women, and much more in *The Poor in Eighteenth-Century France* (1974).

S. Ogilvie and M. Cerman, eds., *European Proto-Industrialization* (1996), is a stimulating, up-to-date survey of several countries by leading scholars. An ambitious re-examination with extensive bibliographical references, M. Gutman, *Toward the Modern Economy: Early Modern Industry in Europe, 1500–1800* (1988), highlights the creativity of rural industry, as does J. Goodman and K. Honeyman, *Gainful Pursuits: The Making of Industrial Europe, 1600–1914* (1988). D. Landes, *The Unbound Prometheus* (1969), places more emphasis on the growing limitations of cottage production, as does S. Ogilvie, *State Corporatism and Proto-Industry: The Württemberg Black Forest, 1580–1797* (1997), which stresses the long life and intense conservatism of rural guilds in southern Germany. C. Crowston, *Fabricating Women: The Seamstresses of Old Regime France, 1675–1791* (2001), is a rich and important work. D. Hefter, ed., *European Women and Industrial Craft* (1995), and G. Gullickson, *Spinners and Weavers of Auffay: Rural Industry and the Sexual Division of Labor in a French Village, 1750–1850* (1986), are both valuable.

Two excellent multivolume series, one edited by Rich and Wilson and mentioned in the Notes, and the other edited by C. Cipolla, *The Fontana Economic History of Europe,* cover the sweep of economic developments from the Middle Ages to the present and have extensive bibliographies. So does R. Cameron and L. Neal, *A Concise Economic History of the World,* 4th ed. (2003), which deals mainly with Europe. F. Braudel, *Civilization and Capitalism, Fifteenth–Eighteenth Centuries* (1981, 1984), is a monumental and highly recommended three-volume synthesis. E. Rothschild, *Economic Sentiments: Adam Smith, Condorcet, and the Enlightenment* (2001), is a fascinating reconsideration of Smith and early liberalism. R. Porter, *London: A Social History* (1994), is a sparkling combination of fine scholarship and exciting popular history. J. Summerson, *Georgian London,* rev. ed. (2003), is a classic architectural study with intriguing illustrations. In the area of trade and colonial competition, V. Barbour, *Capitalism in Amsterdam* (1963), and C. R. Boxer, *The Dutch Seaborne Empire* (1970), are very interesting on Holland. R. Herr, *The Eighteenth-Century Revolution in Spain* (1958), studies economic policy and colonial revival. J. Brewer, *The Sinews of Power: War, Money, and the English State, 1688–1783* (1989), looks at English victories, and D. Ormrod, *The Rise of Commercial Empires: England and the Netherlands in the Age of Mercantilism, 1650–1770* (2003), examines the battle for supremacy in the North Sea. G. Parker, *The Military Revolution: Military Technology in the Rise of the West* (1988), a masterful, beautifully illustrated work, explores the roots of European power and conquest, and J. Black, *Cambridge Illustrated Atlas of Warfare: Renaissance to Revolution, 1492–1792* (1996), surveys war in a global perspective with dramatic pictures and outstanding maps. D. K. Fieldhouse, *The Colonial Empires* (1971), and R. Davies, *The Rise of Atlantic Economies* (1973), are valuable works on the struggle for empire. For slavery, see H. Klein, *The Atlantic Slave Trade* (1999), an excellent short synthesis, and P. Blackburn, *The Making of New World Slavery from the Baroque to the Modern, 1492–1800* (1997), a very impressive study. R. Harms, *The Diligent: A Voyage Through the Worlds of the Slave Trade* (2002), is the deeply moving history of a French slave ship and its victims. Inikori, cited in the Notes, shows the tremendous contribution of Africans to the development of the Atlantic economy. C. Midgley, *Women Against Slavery: The British Campaigns, 1780–1870* (1992), examines the major role of women abolitionists in Britain. J. Lamb, V. Smith, and N. Thomas, eds., *Exploration and Exchange: A South Seas Anthology, 1680–1900* (2001), is a collection of narratives by European visitors and a pleasure for the reader. W. J. Eccles, *France in America,* rev. ed. (1990), is outstanding and supersedes F. Parkman, *France and England in North America,* a multivolume classic and a famous example of nineteenth-century romantic history.

# Listening to the Past

## The Decline of the Guilds

*The growth of unregulated rural manufacturing in the eighteenth century put pressure on the guilds and contributed to their decline. Guilds, also known as trade corporations, were organized in a medieval hierarchy of masters (employers), journeymen (day workers), and apprentices, and they claimed that their rules guaranteed fair wages, high-quality goods, and community values. However, both French philosophes and liberal European officials increasingly disagreed. The first excerpt, from a 1776 law abolishing French guilds by the reform minister Jacques Turgot, is an important example of the liberal critique in action. The law was repealed when Turgot fell from office, but in 1791 French revolutionaries passed a similar measure. The second excerpt, from a letter by a Prussian official, explains what it meant "to work free" and testifies to the growth of the putting-out system alongside the guilds in the German states.*

### Edict Abolishing the Guilds in France

In nearly all the towns of our Kingdom the practice of different arts and crafts is concentrated in the hands of a small number of masters, united in a corporation, who alone have the exclusive right to manufacture and sell particular articles; so that those of our subjects who, through wish or necessity intend to practise in these fields, must have attained the mastership, to which they are admitted only after very long tests which are as difficult as they are useless, and after having satisfied rules or manifold exactions, which absorb part of the funds they need to set up in business or even to exist. . . .

God, in giving man needs, by making work necessary, has made the right to work a universal prerogative, and this is the first, the most sacred and the most indefeasible of all rights.

We regard it as one of the first duties of our law, and one of the acts most worthy of our charity, to free our subjects from all attacks against the inalienable right of mankind. Consequently, we wish to abolish these arbitrary institutions, which do not allow the poor man to earn his living; which reject a sex whose weakness has given it more needs and fewer resources, and which seem, in condemning it to an inevitable misery, to support seduction and debauchery; which destroy emulation and industry and nullify the talents of those whose circumstances have excluded them from membership of a corporation; which deprive the State and the arts of all the knowledge brought to them by foreigners; which retard the progress of these arts through the innumerable difficulties encountered by inventors with whom different corporations dispute the right to exploit their discoveries . . . which, by the huge expenses artisans are obliged to sustain to obtain the right to work, by their various exactions and frequent fines for alleged illegalities, by all kinds of expenditure, waste and interminable law suits, resulting from the respective claims of all these corporations on the extent of their exclusive privileges, burden industry with an oppressive tax, which bears heavily on the people, and is without benefit to the State; which finally, by the facility they provide for members of corporations to combine to force the poorest members to submit to the laws of the rich, become an instrument of privilege and encourage developments, the effect of which is to raise above their natural level the price of those goods which are most essential for the people.

### Breakdown of the Guilds in Germany

Following the repeated complaint of the woollen and worsted weaver named Ast, calling himself a manufacturer of woollen materials, about the runaway apprentice Leder, Your Majesty demanded on 10th and 21st inst. to be informed what the term "to work free" means. It is well known that the [free] woollen and worsted weavers in Germany and abroad are without a guild, that is to say, do not belong to a company which is governed by certain rules or privileges, but follow their trade as woollen and worsted weavers without regulation. For in an organized trade with its own Charter within which it has to operate and which has an assessor appointed whose task it is to see that it is observed, no apprentice may be taken on, unless he first proves by his birth certificate or patent of legitimacy that he was born in wedlock, or legitimized by royal patent. Further, according to the rules of apprenticeship, no apprentice may be given his freedom until his years of apprenticeship are ended according to the registry, and his master declares before the assembled trade when his indenture as journeyman is made out that he has an adequate knowledge of his craft. Similarly, no one can achieve the rights of mastership without having completed two years as journeyman as laid down, and produced the appropriate masterpiece.

All these regulations are omitted in the case of free weavers. For there are really no masters, journeymen and apprentices among them; but if a weaver is able and has resources to set up looms, he sets on workers, usually lads or those who have some knowledge of the trade, who may call themselves apprentices or journeymen, but are not recognized and esteemed as such by those within the guild, since the employer has not produced a masterpiece, the journeymen and apprentices have no indentures or birth certificates, they have no privileges, no assessor, and thus live without a regulation. Such a woollen or worsted weaver will then be called a "free worker." . . .

If such woollen weavers, who have mostly been attracted into the country by the large manufacturers, want to set up here on their own, although they have not been properly brought up within their company, and cannot be accepted as masters, they can receive permission, for themselves only, "to work free." Many of the weavers working "free" have felt the disadvantages of exclusion from their guild, so that some years ago, after some long-drawn-out disputes between the organized and unorganized weavers, they were granted the concession, on certain prescribed conditions, to be accepted as members of their guilds, whereby the number of unorganized ones has been much reduced, except for the large manufacturers and their workers, who are largely still unorganized.

Such outsiders as have risen to the level of manufacturers, by which it is meant that they man several, perhaps many, looms with unorganized workers, have never been granted this concession, but have, as the term goes, "worked free"; and since they cannot become masters and therefore are not allowed to use the term of master, have termed themselves woollen manufacturers, in order to distinguish themselves from the other excluded, but minor, weavers.

A German brush maker and guild member shows a customer his wares. *(The Fotomas Index/The Bridgeman Art Library)*

## Questions for Analysis

1. How did Turgot justify the abolition of French guilds? Do you think his reasons are valid? Why?
2. How were woolen weavers and their employers organized in Prussia?
3. Do guilds—and modern-day unions—help or hurt workers? Defend your position.

*Source:* S. Pollard and C. Holmes, eds., *Documents of European Economic History,* vol. 1: *The Process of Industrialization, 1750–1870* (New York: St. Martin's Press, 1968), pp. 53, 55–56. Copyright © S. Pollard and C. Holmes. Reprinted with permission of Palgrave.

A quack doctor uses a snake and a dog to sell a miraculous cure-all in an Italian village market, in a painting (detail) by Michele Graneri (1736–1778). *(Dagli Orti/Private Collection/The Art Archive)*

chapter

# 20 The Changing Life of the People

## chapter outline

- Marriage and the Family
- Children and Education
- Food and Medical Practice
- Religion and Popular Culture

The discussion of agriculture and industry in the last chapter showed the common people at work, straining to make ends meet within the larger context of population growth, gradual economic expansion, and ferocious political competition. Yet the world of work was only part of life. That life was embedded in a rich complex of family organization, community practices, everyday experiences, and collective attitudes.

In recent years, historians have intensively studied all these aspects of popular life. The challenge has been formidable because regional variations abounded and the common people left few written records. Yet despite many ongoing debates among specialists, imaginative research has resulted in major findings and much greater knowledge. It is now possible to follow the common people beyond the world of work and ask, "What about the rest of the human experience?"

- What changes occurred in marriage and the family in the course of the eighteenth century?
- What was life like for children, and how did attitudes toward children evolve?
- What did people eat, and how did changes in diet and medical care affect people's lives?
- What were the patterns of popular religion and culture? How did these patterns come into contact—and conflict—with the critical world-view of the educated public and thereby widen the cultural divide between rich and poor in the era of the Enlightenment?

Such questions help us better understand how the peasant masses and urban poor really lived in western Europe before the age of revolution opened at the end of the eighteenth century. These questions will be the focus of this chapter.

## Marriage and the Family

The basic unit of social organization is the family. It is within the structure of the family that human beings love, mate, and reproduce themselves. It is primarily the family that teaches the child, imparting values and customs that condition an individual's behavior for a lifetime. The family is also an institution woven into the web of history. It evolves and changes, assuming different forms in different times and places.

### Extended and Nuclear Families

In many traditional Asian and African societies, the typical family has often been an **extended family.** A newly married couple, instead of establishing a home, will go to live with either the bride's or the groom's family. The wife and husband raise their children while living under the same roof with their own brothers and sisters, who may also be married. The family is a big, three- or four-generation clan, headed by a patriarch or perhaps a matriarch, and encompassing everyone from the youngest infant to the oldest grandparent.

Extended families, it is often said, provide security for adults and children in traditional agrarian peasant economies. Everyone has a place within the extended family, from cradle to grave. Sociologists have frequently assumed that the extended family gives way to the conjugal, or nuclear, family with the advent of industrialization and urbanization. In a society characterized by nuclear families, couples establish their own households when they marry, and they raise their children apart from their parents. A similar process has indeed been occurring in much of Asia and Africa in recent times. And since Europe was once agrarian and preindustrial, it has often been believed that the extended family must also have prevailed in Europe before being destroyed by the Industrial Revolution.

In recent years, innovative historians, analyzing previously neglected parish registers of births, deaths, and marriages, have greatly increased knowledge about the details of family life for the great majority of people before the nineteenth century. It seems clear that the extended, three-generation family was a great rarity in western and central Europe by 1700. Indeed, the extended family may never have been common in Europe, although it is hard to know about the early Middle Ages because fewer records survive. When young European couples married, they normally established their own households and lived apart from their parents. When a three-generation household came into existence, it was usually a parent who moved in with a married child rather than a newly married couple moving in with either set of parents.

Most people did not marry young in the seventeenth and early eighteenth centuries. The average person, who was neither rich nor aristocratic, married surprisingly late, many years after reaching adulthood and many more after beginning to work. In one well-studied, apparently typical English village, both men and women married for the first time at an average age of twenty-seven or older in the seventeenth and eighteenth centuries. A similar pattern existed in early-eighteenth-century France. Moreover, a substantial portion of men and women never married at all.

The custom of late marriage combined with a nuclear-family household was a distinctive characteristic of European society. It seems likely that the aggressive dynamism and creativity that have characterized European society were due in large part to the pattern of marriage and family. This pattern of marriage normally joined a mature man and a mature woman—two adults who had already experienced a great deal of life and could transmit self-reliance and real skills to the next generation.

Why was marriage delayed? The main reason was that couples normally could not marry until they could support themselves economically. The land was still the main source of income. The peasant son often needed to wait until his father's death to inherit the family farm and marry his sweetheart. Similarly, the peasant daughter and her family needed to accumulate a small dowry to help her fiancé buy land or build a house.

There were also laws and community controls to temper impetuous love and physical attraction. In some areas, couples needed the legal permission or tacit approval of the local lord or landowner in order to marry. In Austria and Germany, there were legal restrictions on marriage, and well into the nineteenth century poor couples had particular difficulty securing the approval of local officials. These officials believed that freedom to marry for the lower classes would mean more landless paupers, more abandoned children, and more money for welfare. Village elders often agreed. Thus prudence, law, and custom combined to postpone the march to the altar. This pattern helped society maintain some kind of balance between the number of people and the available economic resources.

### Work Away from Home

Many young people worked within their families until they could start their own households. Boys plowed and

| 1700 | 1725 | 1750 | 1775 | 1800 | 1825 |
|---|---|---|---|---|---|

**POLITICAL/MILITARY**

- 1740–1780 Reign of Maria Theresa in Austria
- 1740–1786 Reign of Frederick the Great in Prussia
- 1789–1799 French Revolution
- 1775–1783 American Revolution
- 1799–1815 Napoleonic era

**SOCIAL/ECONOMIC**

- 1720–1780 Government-run foundling homes established
- 1750–1850 Illegitimacy explosion
- 1757 Madame du Coudray, *Manual on the Art of Childbirth*
- 1796 Jenner performs first smallpox vaccination

**INTELLECTUAL/RELIGIOUS**

- 1717 Attendance at elementary schools mandatory in Prussia
- 1750–1790 Wesley preaches revival in England
- 1762 Rousseau advocates child care in *Emile*
- 1763 Louis XV orders Jesuits out of France

wove; girls spun and tended the cows. Many others left home temporarily to work elsewhere. In the towns, a lad might be apprenticed to a craftsman for seven or fourteen years to learn a trade. During that time, he would not be permitted to marry. In most trades, he earned little and worked hard, but if he was lucky, he might eventually be admitted to a guild and establish his economic independence. More often, the young man would drift from one tough job to another: hired hand for a small farmer, wage laborer on a new road, carrier of water in a nearby town. He was always subject to economic fluctuations, and unemployment was a constant threat.

Girls also temporarily left their families to work, at an early age and in large numbers. The range of opportunities open to them was more limited, however. Service in another family's household was by far the most common job, and even middle-class families often sent their daughters into service. Thus a few years away from home as a servant were often a normal part of growing up.

The legions of young servant girls worked hard but had little real independence. Sometimes the employer paid the girl's wages directly to her parents. Constantly under the eye of her mistress, the servant girl found her tasks were many—cleaning, shopping, cooking, caring for the baby. Often the work was endless, for there were no laws to limit exploitation. Rarely were girls so brutalized that they snapped under the strain of such treatment like Varka—the Russian servant girl in Chekhov's chilling story "Sleepy"—who, driven beyond exhaustion, finally quieted her mistress's screaming child by strangling it in its cradle. But court records are full of complaints by servant girls of physical mistreatment by their mistresses. There were many others like the fifteen-year-old English girl in the early eighteenth century who told the judge that her mistress had not only called her "very opprobrious names, as Bitch, Whore and the like," but also "beat her without provocation and beyond measure."[1]

There was also the pressure of seducers and sexual attack. In theory, domestic service offered protection and security within a new family for a young girl leaving home. But in practice, she was often the easy prey of a lecherous master or his sons or friends. Indeed, "the evidence suggests that in all European countries, from Britain to Russia, the upper classes felt perfectly free to exploit sexually girls

**Chardin: The Scullery Maid** Charged with dirty kitchen work and cleaning pots and pans in the scullery, a room adjoining the kitchen, this young servant appears weary and pensive. Perhaps she yearns to return to her village and see her loved ones. A master of careful observation, Chardin specialized in everyday objects and simple domestic scenes. Contemporaries such as Diderot greatly admired the gentle poetry of his art. *(Hunterian Art Gallery, University of Glasgow/The Bridgeman Art Library)*

who were at their mercy."[2] If the girl became pregnant, she was quickly fired and thrown out in disgrace to make her own way. Prostitution and petty thievery were often the harsh consequences of unwanted pregnancy. "What are we?" exclaimed a bitter Parisian prostitute. "Most of us are unfortunate women, without origins, without education, servants and maids for the most part."[3]

## Premarital Sex and Community Controls

Did the plight of some former servant girls mean that late marriage in preindustrial Europe went hand in hand with premarital sex and many illegitimate children? For most of western and central Europe until at least 1750, the answer seems to have been no. English parish registers seldom listed more than one bastard out of every twenty children baptized. Some French parishes in the seventeenth century had extraordinarily low rates of illegitimacy, with less than 1 percent of the babies born out of wedlock. Illegitimate babies were apparently a rarity, at least as far as the official church records are concerned.

At the same time, premarital sex was clearly commonplace. In one well-studied English village, 33 percent of all first children were conceived before the couple was married, and many were born within three months of the marriage ceremony. In the mid-eighteenth century, 20 percent of the women in the French village of Auffay, in Normandy, were pregnant when they got married, although only 2 percent of all babies in the village were born to unwed mothers. No doubt many of these French and English couples were already betrothed, or at least "going steady," before they entered into an intimate relationship, and pregnancy simply set the marriage date once and for all.

But the combination of very low rates of illegitimate birth with large numbers of pregnant brides also reflected the powerful **community controls** of the traditional village, particularly the open-field village, with its pattern of cooperation and common action. That spirit of common action was rapidly mobilized by the prospect of an unwed (and therefore poor) mother with an illegitimate child, a condition inevitably viewed as a grave threat to the economic, social, and moral stability of the closely knit community. Irate parents and anxious village elders, indignant priests and authoritative landlords, all combined to pressure any young people who wavered about marriage in the face of unexpected pregnancy. These controls meant in the countryside that premarital sex was not entered into lightly and that it was generally limited to those contemplating marriage.

The concerns of the village and the family weighed heavily on most aspects of a couple's life, both before and after marriage. One leading authority describes the traditional French peasant household in these terms:

*The individuality of the couple, or rather, its tendency towards individuality, was crushed by the family institutions, and also by the social pressures exercised by the village community as a whole, and by the neighborhood in particular. Anything that might endanger the [couple's] household might also prejudice the village community, and the community reacted, occasionally violently, to punish those who contravened the rules. The intrusion of the community into every aspect of family life was very noticeable.*[4]

Whereas uninvolved individuals today are inclined to stay out of the domestic disputes and marital scandals of their neighbors, the people in peasant communities gave such affairs the loudest and most unfavorable publicity, either at the time of the event or during the Carnival season (see page 683). Relying on degrading public rituals, the young men of the village would typically gang up on the person they wanted to punish and force him or her to sit astride a donkey facing backward and holding up the donkey's tail. They would parade the overly brutal spouse-beating husband (or wife), or the couple whose adultery had been discovered, all around the village, loudly proclaiming the offender's misdeeds with scorn and ridicule. The donkey ride and similar colorful humiliations ranging from rotten vegetables splattered on the doorstep to obscene and insulting midnight serenades were common punishments throughout much of Europe. They epitomized the community's far-reaching effort to police personal behavior and maintain community standards.

Community controls did not extend to family planning, however. Once a couple married, it generally had several children. Birth control within marriage was not unknown in western and central Europe before the nineteenth century, but it was primitive and quite undependable. The most common method was *coitus interruptus*—withdrawal by the male before ejaculation. The French, who were apparently early leaders in contraception, were using this method extensively to limit family size by the end of the eighteenth century.

Mechanical and other means of contraception were also used in the eighteenth century, but mainly by certain sectors of the urban population. The "fast set" of London used the "sheath" regularly, although primarily to protect against venereal disease, not pregnancy. Prostitutes used various contraceptive techniques to prevent pregnancy, and such information was available in large towns if a person really sought it.

## New Patterns of Marriage and Illegitimacy

In the second half of the eighteenth century, the pattern of late marriage and few births out of wedlock began to change and break down. The number of illegitimate births soared between about 1750 and 1850 as much of Europe experienced an **illegitimacy explosion.** In Frankfurt, Germany, for example, illegitimate births rose steadily from about 2 percent of all births in the early 1700s to a peak of about 25 percent around 1850. In Bordeaux, France, 36 percent of all babies were being born out of wedlock by 1840. Small towns and villages experienced less startling climbs, but increases from a range of 1 to 3 percent initially to 10 to 20 percent between 1750 and 1850 were commonplace. Fewer young women were abstaining from premarital intercourse, and, more important, fewer young men were marrying the women they got pregnant. Thus a profound sexual and cultural transformation took place.

Historians are still debating the meaning of this transformation, but two interrelated ideas dominate most interpretations. First, the growth of cottage industry created new opportunities for earning a living, opportunities not tied to the land. Cottage industry tended to develop in areas where the land was poor in quality and divided into small, inadequate holdings. As cottage industry took hold in such areas, population grew rapidly because young people attained greater independence and did not have to wait to inherit a farm in order to get married and have children. A scrap of ground for a garden and a cottage for the loom and spinning wheel could be quite enough for a modest living. A contemporary observer of an area of rapidly growing cottage industry in Switzerland at the end of the eighteenth century described these changes:

*The increased and sure income offered by the combination of cottage manufacture with farming hastened and multiplied marriages and encouraged the division of landholdings, while enhancing their value; it also promoted the expansion and embellishment of houses and villages.*[5]

Cottage workers married not only at an earlier age but also for different reasons. Nothing could be so businesslike, so calculating, as a peasant marriage that was often dictated by the needs of the couple's families. After 1750, however, courtship became more extensive and freer as cottage industry grew. It was easier to yield to the attraction of the opposite sex and fall in love. Members of the older generation were often highly critical of the lack of responsibility they saw in the early marriages of the poor, the union of "people with only two spinning wheels and not even a bed." But such scolding did not stop cottage workers from marrying for love rather than for economic considerations as they blazed a path that factory workers would follow in the nineteenth century.

Second, the needs of a growing population sent many young villagers to towns and cities in search of temporary or permanent employment. Mobility in turn encouraged new sexual and marital relationships, which were less subject to village tradition and resulted in more illegitimate

**David Allan: The Penny Wedding (1795)** The spirited merry-making of a peasant wedding was a popular theme of European artists. In rural Scotland "penny weddings" like this one were common: guests paid a fee for the food and fun; the money left over went to the newlyweds to help them get started. Music, dancing, feasting, and drinking characterized these community parties, which led the Presbyterian church to oppose them and hasten their decline. *(National Galleries of Scotland)*

births. Yet most young women in urban areas found work only as servants or textile workers. Poorly paid, insecure, and with little possibility of truly independent, "liberated" lives, they looked mainly to marriage and family life as an escape from hard work and as the foundation of a satisfying life.

Promises of marriage from a man of the working girl's own class often led to sex, which was widely viewed as part of serious courtship. In one medium-size French city in 1787 to 1788, the great majority of unwed mothers stated that sexual intimacy had followed promises of marriage. Their sisters in rural Normandy reported again and again that they had been "seduced in anticipation of marriage."[6] Many soldiers, day laborers, and male servants were no doubt sincere in their proposals. But their lives were also insecure, and many hesitated to take on the heavy economic burdens of wife and child.

Thus it became increasingly difficult for a woman to convert pregnancy into marriage, and in a growing number of cases the intended marriage did not take place. The romantic, yet practical, dreams and aspirations of many young workingmen and workingwomen in towns and villages were frustrated by low wages, inequality, and changing economic and social conditions. Old patterns of marriage and family were breaking down among the common people. Only in the late nineteenth century would more stable patterns reappear.

## Children and Education

In the traditional framework of agrarian Europe, women married late but then began bearing children rapidly. If a woman married before she was thirty, and if both she and her husband lived to forty-five, the chances were roughly one in two that she would give birth to six or more children. The newborn child entered a dangerous world. Infant mortality was high. One in five was sure to die, and one in three was quite likely to in the poorer areas. Newborn children were very likely to catch mysterious infectious diseases of the chest and stomach, and many babies died of dehydration brought about by a bad bout of ordinary diarrhea. Even in rich families, little could be done for an ailing child. Childhood itself was dangerous because of adult indifference, neglect, and even abuse.

Schools and formal education played only a modest role in the lives of ordinary children, and many boys and many more girls never learned to read. Nevertheless, basic literacy was growing among the popular classes, whose reading habits have been intensively studied in recent years. Attempting to peer into the collective attitudes of the common people and compare them with those of the book-hungry cultivated public, historians have produced some fascinating insights.

## Child Care and Nursing

Women of the lower classes generally breast-fed their infants and for a much longer period than is customary today. Breast-feeding decreases the likelihood of pregnancy for the average woman by delaying the resumption of ovulation. By nursing their babies, women limited their fertility and spaced their children—from two to three years apart. If a newborn baby died, nursing stopped and a new life could be created. Nursing also saved lives: the breast-fed infant received precious immunity-producing substances with its mother's milk and was more likely to survive than when it was given any artificial food. In many areas of Russia, where the common practice was to give a new child a sweetened (and germ-laden) rag to suck on for its subsistence, half the babies did not survive the first year.

In contrast to the laboring poor, the women of the aristocracy and upper middle class seldom nursed their own children. The upper-class woman felt that breast-feeding was crude, common, and undignified. Instead, she hired a wet nurse to suckle her child. The urban mother of more modest means—the wife of a shopkeeper or an artisan—also commonly used a wet nurse in order to facilitate full-time work in the shop.

**Wet-nursing** was a very widespread and flourishing business in the eighteenth century, a dismal business within the framework of the putting-out system. The traffic was in babies rather than in wool and cloth, and two or three years often passed before the wet-nurse worker in the countryside finished her task. The wet nurse generally had little or no contact with the family that hired her, and she was expected to privilege the newcomer at the expense of her own nursing child.

Observers noted the flaws of wet-nursing. It was a common belief that with her milk a nurse passed her bad traits to a baby. When the child turned out poorly, it was assumed that "the nurse had changed it." Many observers charged that nurses were often negligent and greedy. They claimed that there were large numbers of **killing nurses** with whom no child ever survived. The nurse let the child die quickly so that she could take another child and another fee.

## Foundlings and Infanticide

In the ancient world it was not uncommon to allow or force newborn babies, particularly girl babies, to die when there were too many mouths to feed. To its great and eternal credit, the early medieval church, strongly influenced by Jewish law, denounced **infanticide** as a pagan practice and insisted that every human life was sacred. The willful destruction of newborn children became a crime punishable by death. And yet, as the previous reference to killing nurses suggests, direct and indirect methods of eliminating unwanted babies did not disappear. There were, for example, many cases of "overlaying"—parents rolling over and suffocating the child placed between them in their bed. Such parents claimed they had been drunk and had acted unintentionally. In Austria in 1784, suspicious authorities made it illegal for parents to take children under five into bed with them.

The young woman who could not provide for a child had few choices, especially if she were young and had no prospect of marriage. Abortions were illegal, dangerous, and apparently rare. Rather, the distraught mother could bundle up her newborn baby and leave it on the doorstep of a church, so that her child might at least be baptized. In the late seventeenth century, Saint Vincent de Paul was so distressed by the number of babies brought to the steps of Notre Dame in Paris that he established a home for foundlings. Others followed his example. Or, increasingly, the mother would give her baby to a foundling home, which would care for the abandoned child.

Foundling homes first took hold in Italy, Spain, and France, and after 1700 they spread to northern and central Europe. In eighteenth-century England, for example, the government acted on a petition calling for a foundling hospital "to prevent the frequent murders of poor, miserable infants at birth" and "to suppress the inhuman custom of exposing newborn children to perish in the streets." As new homes were established and old ones expanded in the eighteenth century, the number of foundlings being cared for surged. By the end of the century European foundling hospitals were admitting annually about 100,000 abandoned children, nearly all of them infants.

In much of Europe in the eighteenth century, foundling homes emerged as a favorite charity of the rich and powerful. Great sums were spent on them. In the early nineteenth century the foundling home in St. Petersburg had twenty-five thousand children in its care and was receiving five thousand new babies a year. At their best, foundling homes in the eighteenth century were a good example of Christian charity and social concern in an age of great poverty and inequality.

Yet the foundling home was no panacea. By the 1770s, one-third of all babies born in Paris were being immediately

**Abandoned Children** At this French foundlings' home a desperate, secretive mother could give up her baby without any questions, day or night. She placed her child on the revolving table and the nun on duty took it in. Similar practices existed in many countries. *(Archives Charmet/The Bridgeman Art Library)*

abandoned to the foundling home by their mothers. Moreover, fully one-third of all those foundlings were abandoned by married couples, a powerful commentary on the standard of living among the working poor, for whom an additional mouth to feed often meant tragedy. Indeed, scholars now believe that the tremendous increase in foundlings was not simply the result of the explosive growth of unwanted illegitimate children, but was also caused in large part by a growing tendency of desperately poor parents to abandon at least some of their children to the foundling home.[7]

Furthermore, great numbers of babies entered the foundling homes, but few left. Even in the best of these homes, 50 percent of the babies normally died within a year. In the worst, fully 90 percent did not survive. They succumbed to long journeys over rough roads, the intentional and unintentional neglect of their wet nurses, and the customary childhood illnesses. So great was the carnage that some contemporaries called the foundling hospitals "legalized infanticide."

## Attitudes Toward Children

What were the more typical circumstances of children's lives? Did the treatment of foundlings reflect the attitudes of normal parents? Although some scholars argue otherwise, it seems that the young child was often of minor concern to its parents and to society in the eighteenth century. This indifference toward children was found in all classes; rich children were by no means exempt. The practice of using wet nurses, who were casually selected and often negligent, is one example of how even the rich and the prosperous put the child out of sight and out of mind. One French moralist, writing in 1756 about how to improve humanity, observed that "one blushes to think of loving one's children." It has been said that the English gentleman of the period "had more interest in the diseases of his horses than of his children."[8]

Feelings toward children were greatly influenced by the terrible frequency of death among children of all classes. Doctors and clergymen urged parents not to become too emotionally involved with their children, who were so unlikely to survive. Mothers especially did not always heed such warnings, but the risk of emotional devastation was very real for them. The great eighteenth-century English historian Edward Gibbon (1737–1794) wrote that "the death of a new born child before that of its parents may seem unnatural but it is a strictly probable event, since of any given number the greater part are extinguished before the ninth year, before they possess the faculties of the mind and the body." Gibbon's father named all his boys Edward after himself, hoping that at least one of them would survive to carry his name. His prudence was not misplaced. Edward the future historian and eldest survived. Five brothers and sisters who followed him all died in infancy.

The medical establishment was seldom interested in the care of children. One contemporary observer quoted a famous doctor as saying that "he never wished to be called to a young child because he was really at a loss to know what to offer for it." The best hope for children was often treatment by women healers and midwives, who helped many women deliver their babies and provided advice on child care. Nevertheless, children were still caught in a vicious circle: they were neglected because they were very likely to die, and they were likely to die because they were neglected.

Emotional detachment from children often shaded off into abuse. When parents and other adults did turn toward children, it was normally to discipline and control them. The novelist Daniel Defoe (1659–1731), who was always delighted when he saw very young children work-

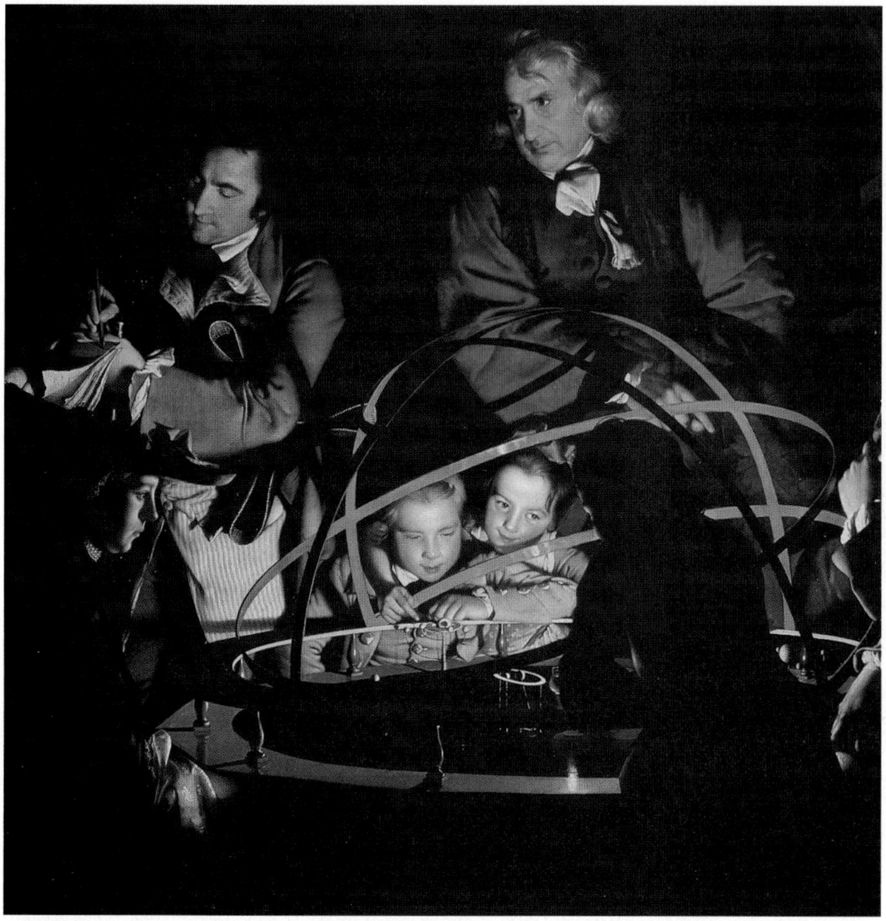

**Cultivating the Joy of Discovery** This English painting by Joseph Wright of Derby (1734–1797) reflects new attitudes toward child development and education, which advocated greater freedom and direct experience. The children rapturously watch a planetarium, which illustrates the movements and positions of the planets in the solar system. Wise teachers stand by, letting the children learn at their own pace. *(Derby Museum & Art Gallery/The Bridgeman Art Library)*

ing hard in cottage industry, coined the axiom "Spare the rod and spoil the child." He meant it. So did Susannah Wesley (1669–1742), mother of John Wesley, the founder of Methodism. According to her, the first task of a parent toward her children was "to conquer the will, and bring them to an obedient temper." She reported that her babies were "taught to fear the rod, and to cry softly; by which means they escaped the abundance of correction they might otherwise have had, and that most odious noise of the crying of children was rarely heard in the house."[9]

It was hardly surprising that when English parish officials dumped their paupers into the first factories late in the eighteenth century, the children were beaten and brutalized (see pages 744–746). That was part of the child-rearing pattern—considerable indifference, on the one hand, and strict physical discipline, on the other—that prevailed throughout most of the eighteenth century.

From the middle of the century, this pattern came under increasing attack and began to change. Critics, led by Jean-Jacques Rousseau in 1762 in his famous and influential treatise *Emile* (see the feature "Listening to the Past: Gender Constructions and Education for Girls" on pages 686–687), called for greater love and tenderness toward children and proposed imaginative new teaching methods that also constructed rigid gender differences. In addition to supporting foundling homes to discourage infanticide and urging wealthy women to nurse their own babies, these new voices ridiculed the practice of swaddling: wrapping youngsters in tight-fitting clothes and blankets was generally believed to form babies properly by "straightening them out." By the end of the eighteenth century, small children were often being dressed in simpler, more comfortable clothing, allowing much greater freedom of movement. More parents expressed a delight in the love and intimacy of the child and found real pleasure in raising their offspring. These changes were part of the general growth of humanitarianism and cautious optimism about human potential that characterized the eighteenth-century Enlightenment.

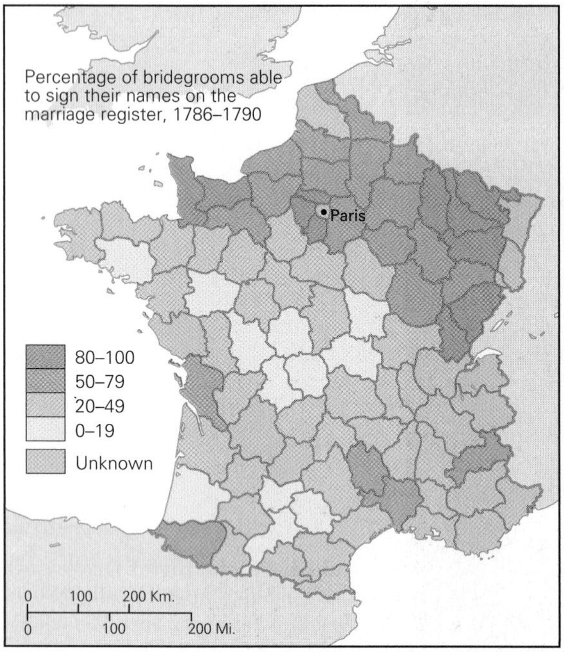


**MAP 20.1 Literacy in France on the Eve of the French Revolution** Literacy rates increased but still varied widely between and within states in eighteenth-century Europe. Northern France was clearly ahead of southern France.

## Schools and Popular Literature

The role of schools and formal education outside the home was also growing more important. The aristocracy and the rich had led the way in the sixteenth century with special colleges, often run by Jesuits. But schools charged specifically with elementary education of the children of the common people usually did not appear until the seventeenth century. These schools specialized in boys and girls from seven to twelve, who were taught basic literacy and religion.

Scholars generally agree that the religious struggle unleashed by the Protestant and Catholic Reformations served as the catalyst in promoting popular literacy between 1500 and 1800. Both Protestant and Catholic reformers pushed reading as a means of instilling their teachings more effectively. Thus literacy was often highest in border areas, such as eastern France, which were open to outside influences and to competition for believers from different churches. The growth of popular education quickened in the eighteenth century, but there was no revolutionary acceleration, and many common people received no formal education.

Prussia led the way in the development of universal education, inspired by the old Protestant idea that every believer should be able to read and study the Bible in the quest for personal salvation and by the new idea of a population capable of effectively serving the state. As early as 1717, Prussia made attendance at elementary schools compulsory, and more Protestant German states, such as Saxony and Württemberg, followed in the eighteenth century. Religious motives were also extremely important elsewhere. From the middle of the seventeenth century, Presbyterian Scotland was convinced that the path to salvation lay in careful study of the Scriptures, and it established an effective network of parish schools for rich and poor alike. The Church of England and the dissenting congregations established "charity schools" to instruct the children of the poor, and in 1682 France began setting up Christian schools to teach the catechism and prayers as well as reading and writing. France did less well than the Habsburg state, the only Catholic land to promote elementary education enthusiastically in the eighteenth century. Some elementary education was becoming a reality, and schools were of growing significance in the life of the child.

The result of these efforts was a remarkable growth in basic literacy between 1600 and 1800. Whereas in 1600 only one male in six was barely literate in France and Scotland, and one in four in England, by 1800 almost nine out of ten Scottish males, two out of three French males (see Map 20.1), and more than half of English males were literate. In all three countries, the bulk of the jump occurred in the eighteenth century. Women were also increasingly literate, although they lagged behind men in most countries.

The growth in literacy promoted a growth in reading, and historians have carefully examined what the common people read in an attempt to discern what they were thinking. One thing seems certain: the major philosophical works of the Enlightenment had little impact on peasants and workers, who could neither afford nor understand those favorites of the book-hungry educated public.

Although the Bible remained the overwhelming favorite, especially in Protestant countries, the staple of popular literature was short pamphlets known as chapbooks. Printed on the cheapest paper available, many chapbooks dealt with religious subjects. They featured Bible stories, prayers, devotions, and the lives of saints and exemplary Christians. Promising happiness after death, devotional literature was also intensely practical. It gave the believer moral teachings and a confidence in God that helped in daily living.

**A Peasant Family Reading the Bible** Praised by the philosophe Diderot for its moralistic message, this engraving of a painting by Jean-Baptiste Greuze (1725–1805) does capture the power of sacred texts and the spoken word. The peasant patriarch reads aloud from the massive family Bible and the close-knit circle of absorbed listeners concentrates on every word. Only the baby is distracted. *(Bibliothèque nationale de France/Giraudon/Art Resource, NY)*

Entertaining, often humorous stories formed a second element of popular literature. Fairy tales, medieval romances, fictionalized history, and fantastic adventures—these were some of the delights that filled the peddler's pack as he approached a village. Both heroes and villains possessed superhuman powers in this make-believe world, a world of danger and magic, of fairy godmothers and evil trolls. But the good fairies always triumphed over the evil ones in the story's marvelous resolution.

The significance of these entertaining stories for the peasant reader is debated. Many scholars see them reflecting a desire for pure escapism and a temporary flight from harsh everyday reality. Others see these tales reflecting ancient folk wisdom and counseling prudence in a world full of danger and evil, where wolves dress up like grandmothers and eat Little Red Riding Hoods.

Finally, some popular literature was highly practical, dealing with rural crafts, household repairs, useful plants, and similar matters. Much of such lore was stored in almanacs. With calendars listing secular, religious, and astrological events mixed in with agricultural schedules, bizarre bits of information, and jokes, the almanac was universal, noncontroversial, and highly appreciated, even by many in the comfortable classes. "Anyone who could would read an almanac."[10]

In general, however, the reading of the common people had few similarities with that of educated elites. Popular literature was simple and practical, both as devotional self-help and as how-to instruction. It was also highly escapist, not unlike the mass of inexpensive paperbacks sold in drugstores today. Neither the practical nor the escapist elements challenged the established order. Rather, the common people were apparently content with works that reinforced traditional values and did not foster social or religious criticism. These results fit well with the modest educational objectives of rulers and educated elites. They believed that carefully limited instruction stressing religion and morals was useful to the masses but that too much study would only disorient them and foster discontent.

## Food and Medical Practice

As we saw in Chapter 19, the European population increased rapidly in the eighteenth century. Plague and starvation gradually disappeared, and Europeans lived longer. What were the characteristics of diets and nutrition in this era of improving health and longevity? Although medical practice played only a small part, what was it like in the eighteenth century? What does a comparison of rich and poor reveal?

### Diets and Nutrition

At the beginning of the eighteenth century, ordinary men and women depended on grain as fully as they had in the past. Bread was quite literally the staff of life. Peasants in the Beauvais region of France ate two pounds of bread a day, washing it down with water, green wine, beer, or a little skim milk. Their dark bread was made from a mixture of roughly ground wheat and rye—the standard flour of the common people. The poor also ate grains in soup and gruel. In rocky northern Scotland, for example, people depended on oatmeal, which they often ate half-cooked so that it would swell in their stomachs and make them feel full.

Little wonder, then, that an adequate supply of grain and an affordable price of bread loomed large in the popular imagination. Even peasants normally needed to buy some grain for food, and, in full accord with landless laborers and urban workers, they believed in the old medieval idea of the **just price.** That is, they believed that prices should be "fair," protecting both consumers and producers and imposed by government decree if necessary.

**An English Food Riot** Nothing infuriated ordinary women and men more than the idea that merchants and landowners were withholding grain from the market in order to push high prices even higher. In this cartoon an angry crowd hands out rough justice to a rich farmer accused of hoarding. *(Courtesy of the Trustees of the British Museum)*

In the later eighteenth century, this traditional, moral view of prices and the economy clashed repeatedly with the emerging free-market philosophy of unregulated supply and demand, which was increasingly favored by government officials, large landowners, and economists led by Adam Smith (see page 655). In years of poor harvests and soaring prices, this clash often resulted in food riots and popular disturbances. Peasants and workers would try to stop wagons loaded with grain from leaving their region, or they would seize grain held by speculators and big merchants accused of hoarding and rigging the market. (Usually the tumultuous crowd paid what it considered to be a fair price for what it took.) Governments were keenly aware of the problem of adequate grain supplies, and they would sometimes try to control prices to prevent unrest in crisis years.

The rural and urban poor also ate a fair quantity of vegetables. Indeed, vegetables were considered "poor people's food." Peas and beans were probably the most common; grown as field crops in much of Europe since the Middle Ages, they were eaten fresh in late spring and summer. Dried, they became the basic ingredients in the soups and stews of the long winter months. In most regions, other vegetables appeared in season on the tables of the poor, primarily cabbages, carrots, and wild greens. Fruit was uncommon and limited to the summer months.

The common people of Europe loved meat and eggs, but they seldom ate their fill. Indeed, the poor ate less meat in 1700 than in 1500 because their general standard of living had declined as the population surged in the sixteenth century (see page 636) and meat became more expensive. In the eighteenth century, the beginnings of agricultural transformation (see page 632) increased per capita meat consumption only in Britain and the Low Countries. Moreover, in most European countries harsh game laws deprived the poor of the right to hunt and eat game such as rabbits, deer, and partridges. Only nobles and large landowners could legally kill game. Few laws were more bitterly resented—or more frequently broken—by ordinary people than those governing hunting. When the poor did eat meat—on a religious holiday or at a wedding or other festive occasion—it was most likely lamb or mutton. Sheep could survive on rocky soils and did not compete directly with humans for the slender resources of grain.

Milk was rarely drunk. Perhaps because some individuals do suffer seriously from dairy allergies, it was widely believed that milk caused sore eyes, headaches, and a variety of ills, except among the very young and very old. Milk was used primarily to make cheese and butter, which did not spoil as milk did and which the poor liked but could afford only occasionally. Medical and popular opinion considered whey, the watery liquid left after milk was churned, "an excellent temperate drink."

The diet of the rich—aristocrats, officials, and the comfortable bourgeoisie—was traditionally quite different from that of the poor. The upper classes were rapacious carnivores, and a truly elegant dinner consisted of one rich meat after another. Three separate meat courses might be followed by three fish courses laced with piquant sauces and complemented with sweets, cheeses, and nuts of all kinds. Fruits and vegetables were not often found on the tables of the rich.

There was also an enormous amount of overdrinking among the rich. The English squire, for example, who loved to hunt with his hounds, loved to drink with a similar passion. He became famous as the "four-bottle man." Sometimes he ended the evening under the table in a drunken stupor, but very often he did not. The wine and the meat were consumed together in long hours of sustained excess, permitting the gentleman and his guests to drink enormous quantities without getting stupefyingly drunk.

The diet of small traders, master craftsmen, minor bureaucrats—the people of the towns and cities—was generally less monotonous than that of the peasantry. The markets, stocked by market gardens on the outskirts, provided a substantial variety of meats, vegetables, and fruits, although bread and beans still formed the bulk of such families' diets.

There were also regional dietary differences in 1700. Generally speaking, northern, Atlantic Europe ate better than southern, Mediterranean Europe. The poor of England and the Netherlands probably ate best of all. Contemporaries on both sides of the Channel often contrasted the English citizen's consumption of meat with the French peasant's greater dependence on bread and vegetables.

## The Impact of Diet on Health

How were the poor and the rich served by their quite different diets? At first glance, the diet of the laboring poor, relying as it did on grains and vegetables, might seem low in protein. However, the whole-grain wheat or rye flour used in eighteenth-century bread retained most of the bran—the ground-up husk—and the all-important wheat germ, which contains higher proportions of some minerals, vitamins, and good-quality proteins than does the rest of the grain. In addition, the field peas and beans contained protein that complemented the proteins in whole-grain bread. The proteins in whey, cheese, and eggs, which the

**Royal Interest in the Potato** Frederick the Great of Prussia, shown here supervising cultivation of the potato, used his influence and position to promote the new food on his estates and throughout Prussia. Peasants could grow potatoes with the simplest hand tools, but it was backbreaking labor, as this painting by R. Warthmüller suggests. *(Private Collection, Hamburg/akg-images)*

poor ate at least occasionally, also supplemented the bread and vegetables.

The basic bread-and-vegetables diet of the poor *in normal times* was adequate. But a key dietary problem was getting enough green vegetables (or milk) to ensure adequate supplies of vitamins A and C. A severe deficiency of vitamin C produces scurvy, a disease that leads to rotting gums, swelling of the limbs, and great weakness. Before the season's first vegetables, many people experienced shortages of vitamin C and suffered from mild cases of scurvy. (Scurvy was an acute problem for sailors on long voyages and by the end of the sixteenth century was being controlled on ships by a daily ration of lime juice.)

The practice of gorging on meat, sweets, and spirits caused the rich their own nutritional problems. Because of their great disdain for fresh vegetables, they, too, were very often deficient in vitamins A and C. Gout was a common affliction of the overfed and underexercised rich. No wonder they were often caricatured as dragging their flabby limbs and bulging bellies to the table to stuff their swollen cheeks and poison their livers. People of moderate means, who could afford some meat and dairy products with fair regularity but who had not abandoned the bread and vegetables of the poor, were best off from a nutritional standpoint.

Patterns of food consumption changed rather markedly as the century progressed. More varied diets associated with new methods of farming were confined largely to the Low Countries and England, but a new food—the potato—came to the aid of the poor everywhere. Introduced into Europe from the Americas—along with corn, squash, tomatoes, and many other useful plants—the humble potato is actually an excellent food. Containing a good supply of carbohydrates, calories, and vitamins A and C, the potato offset the lack of vitamins from green vegetables in the poor person's winter and early-spring diet, and it provided a much higher caloric yield than grain for a given piece of land.

For some desperately poor peasants the potato replaced grain as the primary food in the eighteenth century. This happened first in Ireland, where English (Protestant) repression and exploitation forced large numbers of poor (Catholic) peasants to live off tiny scraps of rented ground. Elsewhere in Europe, potatoes took hold more slowly because many people did not like them. Thus, potatoes were first fed to pigs and livestock, and there was even debate over whether they were fit for humans. In Germany the severe famines caused by the Seven Years' War settled the matter: potatoes were edible and not just "famine food." By the end of the century, the potato had become an important dietary supplement in much of Europe.

There was also a general growth of market gardening, and a greater variety of vegetables appeared in towns and cities. In the course of the eighteenth century, the large towns and cities of maritime Europe began to receive semitropical fruits, such as oranges and lemons, from Portugal and the West Indies, although they were not cheap.

Bread also began to change, most noticeably for the English and for the comfortable groups on the European continent. Rising incomes and new tastes led to a shift from whole-grain black or brown bread to "bread as white as snow" and started a decline in bread's nutritional value. The high-roughage bran and some of the dark but high-vitamin germ were increasingly sifted out by millers. This foretold further "improvements" in the nineteenth century, which would leave bread perfectly white and greatly reduced in nutritional value.

Another sign of nutritional decline was the growing consumption of sugar. Initially a luxury, sugar dropped rapidly in price as slave-based production increased in the Americas and the sweetener was much more widely used in the eighteenth century. This development probably led to an increase in cavities and to other ailments as well, although the greater or lesser poverty of the laboring poor still protected most of them from the sugar-tooth virus of the rich and well-to-do.

## Medical Practitioners

Although sickness, pain, and disease—intractable challenges built into the human condition—permeated the European experience in the eighteenth century, medical science played a very small part in improving the health of most people. Yet the Enlightenment's growing focus on discovering the laws of nature and on human problems did give rise to a great deal of research and experimentation. The century also saw a remarkable rise in the number of medical practitioners. Therefore, when significant breakthroughs in knowledge came in the middle

**An Eighteenth-Century Pharmacy** In this lively painting a woman consults an apothecary in an elegant red suit while his assistants assemble drugs for new prescriptions. By 1700 apothecaries had emerged as a separate group of state-licensed medical professionals. They drew upon published lists and books describing the properties and dosages for their concoctions, but there were many different "recipes" and trade secrets. *(Civico Museo Bibliografico Musicale, Bologna, Italy/The Bridgeman Art Library)*

and late nineteenth century, they could be rapidly evaluated and diffused.

Care of the sick in the eighteenth century was the domain of several competing groups: faith healers, apothecaries (or pharmacists), physicians, surgeons, and midwives. Both men and women were prominent in the healing arts, as had been the case since the Middle Ages. But by 1700 the range of medical activities open to women was severely restricted, because women were generally denied admission to medical colleges male practitioners dominated and lacked the diplomas necessary for practice as physicians and surgeons. In the course of the eighteenth century, the position of women as midwives and healers further eroded.

Faith healers remained active. They and their patients believed that demons and evil spirits caused disease by lodging in people and that the proper treatment was to exorcise, or drive out, the offending devil. This demonic view of disease was strongest in the countryside, where popular belief placed great faith in the healing power of religious relics, prayer, and the laying on of hands. Faith healing was particularly effective in the treatment of mental disorders such as hysteria and depression, where the link between attitude and illness is most direct.

In the larger towns and cities, apothecaries sold a vast number of herbs, drugs, and patent medicines for every conceivable "temperament and distemper." Their prescriptions were incredibly complex—a hundred or more drugs might be included in a single prescription—and often very expensive. Some of the drugs and herbs undoubtedly worked. For example, strong laxatives were given to the rich for their constipated bowels, and regular **purging** of the bowels was considered essential for good health and the treatment of illness. In fact, only bloodletting was more effective in speeding patients to their graves. In the countryside, people often turned to midwives and women healers for herbs and folk remedies.

Physicians, who were invariably men, were apprenticed in their teens to a practicing physician for several years of on-the-job training. This training was then rounded out with hospital work or some university courses. Because such prolonged training was expensive, physicians continued to come mainly from prosperous families, and they usually concentrated on urban patients from similar social backgrounds. They had little contact with urban workers and less with peasants.

Physicians in the eighteenth century were increasingly willing to experiment with new methods, but time-honored practices lay heavily on them. Physicians, like apothecaries, laid great stress on purging. And bloodletting was still considered a medical cure-all. It was the way "bad blood," the cause of illness, was removed and the balance of humors necessary for good health was restored.

Surgeons, in contrast to physicians, made considerable medical and social progress in the eighteenth century. Long considered as ordinary male artisans comparable to butchers and barbers, surgeons began studying anatomy seriously and improved their art. With endless opportunities to practice, army surgeons on gory battlefields led the way. They learned that a soldier with an extensive wound, such as a shattered leg or arm, could perhaps be saved if the surgeon could obtain above the wound a flat surface that could be cauterized with fire. Thus if a soldier (or a civilian) had a broken limb and the bone stuck out, the surgeon amputated so that the remaining stump could be cauterized and the likelihood of death reduced.

The eighteenth-century surgeon (and patient) labored in the face of incredible difficulties. Almost all operations were performed without any painkiller, for the anesthesias of the day were hard to control and were believed too dangerous for general use. The terrible screams of people whose limbs were being sawed off echoed across battlefields and through hospitals. Many patients died from the agony and shock of such operations. Surgery was also performed in the midst of filth and dirt, for there simply was no knowledge of bacteriology and the nature of infection. The simplest wound treated by a surgeon could fester and lead to death.

Midwives, who were a special object of suspicion and persecution in the witch-hunt craze of the sixteenth and seventeenth centuries, continued to deliver the overwhelming majority of babies throughout the eighteenth century. The typical midwife was an older, often widowed woman of modest social origins and long professional experience. Trained initially by another woman practitioner, the midwife primarily assisted in labor and delivering babies. But the midwife also treated female problems, such as irregular menstrual cycles, breast-feeding difficulties, sterility, and venereal disease, and she ministered to small children.

The midwife orchestrated labor and birth in a woman's world, where friends and relatives offered the pregnant woman assistance and encouragement in the familiar surroundings of her own home. Excluded by tradition and modesty, the male surgeon (and the husband) rarely entered this world, because most births, then as now, were normal and spontaneous. Following the invention of the forceps, which might help in an exceptionally difficult birth, surgeon-physicians used their monopoly over this and other instruments to seek lucrative new business. Attacking midwives as ignorant and dangerous, they persuaded growing numbers of wealthy women of the supe-

Plate from Madame du Coudray's manual, illustrating "another incorrect method of delivery."
(Rare Books Division, Countway [Francis A.] Library of Medicine)

## Madame du Coudray, the Nation's Midwife

In 1751 a highly esteemed Parisian midwife left the capital for a market town in central France. Having accepted an invitation to instruct local women in the skills of childbirth, Madame Angelique Marguerite Le Boursier du Coudray soon demonstrated a marvelous ability to teach students and win their respect. The thirty-six-year-old midwife found her mission: she would become the nation's midwife.

For eight years Madame du Coudray taught young women from the impoverished villages of Auvergne. In doing so, she entered into the world of unschooled midwives, typically solid matrons with several children who relied on traditional birthing practices and folk superstitions. Trained in Paris through a rigorous three-year apprenticeship and imbued with an Enlightenment faith in the power of knowledge, du Coudray had little sympathy for these village midwives. Many peasant mothers told her about their difficult deliveries and their many uterine "infirmities," which they attributed to "the ignorance of the women to whom they had recourse, or to that of some inexperienced village [male] surgeons."* Du Coudray agreed. Botched deliveries by incompetents resulted in horrible deformities and unnecessary deaths.

Determined to raise standards, Madame du Coudray saw that her unlettered pupils learned through the senses, not through books. Thus she made, possibly for the first time in history, a life-size obstetrical model—a "machine"—out of fabric and stuffing for use in her classes. "I had . . . the students maneuver in front of me on a machine . . . which represented the pelvis of a woman, the womb, its opening, its ligaments, the conduit called the vagina, the bladder, and *rectum intestine*. I added a [toy] child of natural size, whose joints were flexible enough to be able to be put in different positions." Now du Coudray could demonstrate the problems of childbirth, and each student could practice on the model in the "lab session."

As her reputation grew, Madame du Coudray sought to reach a national audience. In 1757 she wrote and had published the first of several editions of her *Manual on the Art of Childbirth*. Handsomely and effectively illustrated (see the image above), the *Manual* incorporated her hands-on teaching method and served as a text and reference for students and graduates. In 1759 the government authorized Madame du Coudray to carry her instruction "throughout the realm" and promised financial support. Her reception was not always warm, for she was a self-assured and demanding woman, who could anger old midwives, male surgeons, and skeptical officials. But aided by servants, a niece, and her husband, this inspired and indefatigable woman took her course from town to town until her retirement in 1784. Typically her students were young peasant women on tiny stipends, who came into town from surrounding villages for two to three months of instruction. Classes met mornings and afternoons six days a week, with ample time to practice on the mannequin. After a recuperative break, Madame du Coudray and her entourage moved on.

Teaching thousands of fledgling midwives, Madame du Coudray may well have contributed to the decline in infant mortality and to the increase in population occurring in France in the eighteenth century—an increase she and her royal supporters fervently desired. Certainly she spread better knowledge about childbirth from the educated elite to the common people.

### Questions for Analysis

1. How do you account for Madame du Coudray's remarkable success?
2. Does Madame du Coudray's career reflect tensions between educated elites and the common people? If so, how?

*Quotes are from Nina Gelbart, *The King's Midwife: A History and Mystery of Madame du Coudray* (Berkeley: University of California Press, 1998), pp. 60–61. This definitive biography is excellent.

*The* **history companion** *features additional information and activities related to this topic.*
**history.college.hmco.com/students**

riority of their services and sought to undermine faith in midwives.

Recent research suggests that women practitioners successfully defended much but not all of their practice in the eighteenth century. In France one enterprising Parisian midwife secured royal financing for her campaign to teach better birthing techniques to village midwives, which reinforced the position of women practitioners. (See the feature "Individuals in Society: Madame du Coudray, the Nation's Midwife.") In northern Italy, state and church pressures led to major changes in midwife training and certification, but women remained dominant in the birthing trade. It appears that midwives generally lost no more babies than male doctors, who were still summoned to treat nonelite women only when a life-threatening situation required surgery.

While ordinary physicians were bleeding, apothecaries purging, surgeons sawing, faith healers praying, and midwives assisting, the leading medical thinkers were attempting to pull together and assimilate all the information and misinformation they had been accumulating. The attempt was ambitious: to systematize medicine around simple, basic principles, as Newton had done in physics. But the schools of thought resulting from such speculation and theorizing did little to improve medical care.

### Hospitals and Medical Experiments

Hospitals were terrible places throughout most of the eighteenth century. There was no isolation of patients. Operations were performed in a patient's bed. Nurses were old, ignorant, greedy, and often drunk women. Fresh air was considered harmful, and infections of every kind were rampant. Diderot's article in the *Encyclopedia* on the Hôtel-Dieu in Paris, the "richest and most terrifying of all French hospitals," vividly describes normal conditions of the 1770s:

*Imagine a long series of communicating wards filled with sufferers of every kind of disease who are sometimes packed three, four, five or even six into a bed, the living alongside the dead and dying, the air polluted by this mass of un-*

**Hospital Life** Patients crowded into hospitals like this one in Hamburg in 1746 had little chance of recovery. A priest by the window administers last rites, while in the center a surgeon coolly saws off the leg of a man who has received no anesthesia. *(Germanisches Nationalmuseum, Nuremberg)*

*healthy bodies, passing pestilential germs of their afflictions from one to the other, and the spectacle of suffering and agony on every hand. That is the Hôtel-Dieu.*

*The result is that many of these poor wretches come out with diseases they did not have when they went in, and often pass them on to the people they go back to live with. Others are half-cured and spend the rest of their days in an invalidism as hard to bear as the illness itself; and the rest perish, except for the fortunate few whose strong constitutions enable them to survive.*[11]

No wonder the poor of Paris hated hospitals and often saw confinement there as a plot to kill paupers.

In the last years of the century, the humanitarian concern already reflected in Diderot's description of the Hôtel-Dieu led to a movement for hospital reform throughout western Europe. Efforts were made to improve ventilation and eliminate filth on the grounds that bad air caused disease. The theory was wrong, but the results were beneficial, since the spread of infection was somewhat reduced.

Mental hospitals, too, were incredibly savage institutions. The customary treatment for mental illness was bleeding and cold water, administered more to maintain discipline than to effect a cure. Violent persons were chained to the wall and forgotten. A breakthrough of sorts occurred in the 1790s when William Tuke founded the first humane sanatorium in England. In Paris an innovative warden, Philippe Pinel, took the chains off the mentally disturbed in 1793 and tried to treat them as patients rather than as prisoners.

In the eighteenth century, all sorts of wildly erroneous ideas about mental illness circulated. One was that moonlight caused madness, a belief reflected in the word *lunatic*—someone harmed by lunar light. Another mid-eighteenth-century theory, which lasted until at least 1914, was that masturbation caused madness, not to mention acne, epilepsy, and premature ejaculation. Thus parents, religious institutions, and schools waged relentless war on masturbation by males, although they were uninterested in female masturbation.

In the second half of the eighteenth century, medicine in general turned in a more practical and experimental direction. Some of the experimentation was creative quackery involving the recently discovered phenomenon of electricity. One magnificent quack in London promoted sleep on a cure-all Celestial Bed, which was lavishly decorated with magnets and electrical devices. A single night on the bed cost a small fortune. Because so many expensive treatments were worthless or harmful, the common people were probably much less deprived by their reliance on faith healers and folk medicine than one might think.

Experimentation and the intensified search for solutions to human problems led to some real advances in medicine after 1750, however. The eighteenth century's greatest medical triumph was the conquest of smallpox. With the progressive decline of bubonic plague, smallpox became the most terrible of the infectious diseases, and it is estimated that 60 million Europeans died of it in the eighteenth century. Fully 80 percent of the population was stricken at some point in life.

The first step in the conquest of this killer in Europe came in the early eighteenth century. An English aristocrat whose beauty had been marred by the pox, Lady Mary Wortley Montagu, learned about the long-established practice of **smallpox inoculation** in the Muslim lands of western Asia while her husband was serving as British ambassador to the Ottoman Empire. She had her own son successfully inoculated with the pus from a smallpox victim and was instrumental in spreading the practice in England after her return in 1722. But inoculation was risky and widely condemned because about one person in fifty died from it. In addition, people who had been inoculated were infectious and often spread the disease.

Subsequent success in reducing the risks of inoculation and in finding cheaper methods led to something approaching mass inoculation in England in the 1760s. On the continent, the well-to-do were also inoculated, beginning with royal families and then spreading to the middle classes. By the later years of the century, smallpox inoculation was playing some part in the decline of the death rate and the general increase in European population.

The final breakthrough against smallpox came at the end of the century. Edward Jenner (1749–1823), a talented country doctor, noted that in the English countryside there was a long-standing belief that dairy maids who had contracted cowpox did not get smallpox. Cowpox produces sores on the cow's udder and on the hands of the milker. The sores resemble those of smallpox, but the disease is mild and not contagious.

For eighteen years Jenner practiced a kind of Baconian science, carefully collecting data on protection against smallpox by cowpox. Finally, in 1796 he performed his first vaccination on a young boy using matter taken from a milkmaid with cowpox. Performing more successful vaccinations, Jenner published his findings in 1798. The new method of treatment spread rapidly, and smallpox soon declined to the point of disappearance in Europe and then throughout the world. Jenner eventually received prizes totaling £30,000 from the British government for his great discovery, a fitting recompense for a man who made an enormous gift to humanity and helped lay the foundation for the science of immunology in the nineteenth century.

## Religion and Popular Culture

Though the critical spirit of the Enlightenment spread among the educated elite in the eighteenth century, the majority of ordinary men and women remained firmly committed to the Christian religion, especially in rural areas. Religious faith promised salvation and eternal life, and it gave comfort and courage in the face of sorrow and death. Religion also remained strong because it was usually embedded in local traditions, everyday social experience, and popular culture.

Yet the popular religion of village Europe was everywhere enmeshed in a larger world of church hierarchies and state power. These powerful outside forces sought to regulate religious life at the local level. Their efforts created tensions that helped set the scene for a vigorous religious revival in Germany and England. Similar tensions arose in Catholic countries, where powerful elites criticized and attacked popular religious practices that their increasingly rationalistic minds deemed foolish and superstitious.

### The Institutional Church

As in the Middle Ages, the local parish church remained the basic religious unit all across Europe. Still largely coinciding with the agricultural village, the parish fulfilled many needs. The parish church was the focal point of religious devotion, which went far beyond sermons and Holy Communion. The parish church organized colorful processions and pilgrimages to local shrines. Even in Protestant countries, where such activities were severely restricted, congregations gossiped and swapped stories after services, and neighbors came together in church for baptisms, marriages, funerals, and special events. Thus the parish church was woven into the very fabric of community life.

Moreover, the local church had important administrative tasks. Priests and parsons were truly the bookkeepers of agrarian Europe, and it is because parish registers were so complete that historians have learned so much about population and family life. Parishes also normally distributed charity to the destitute, looked after orphans, and provided whatever primary education was available for the common people.

The many tasks of the local church were usually the responsibility of a resident priest or pastor, a full-time professional working with assistants and lay volunteers. All clerics—whether Roman Catholic, Protestant, Greek Orthodox, or Russian Orthodox—also shared the fate of middlemen in a complicated institutional system. Charged most often with ministering to poor peasants, the priest or parson was the last link in a powerful church-state hierarchy that was everywhere determined to control religion down to the grassroots. However, the regulatory framework of belief, which went back at least to the fourth century when Christianity became the official religion of the Roman Empire, had undergone important changes since 1500.

The Protestant Reformation had burst forth as a culmination of medieval religiosity and a desire to purify Christian belief. Martin Luther, the most influential of the early reformers, preached that all men and women were saved from their sins and God's damnation only by personal faith in Jesus Christ. The individual could reach God directly, without need of priestly intermediaries.

As the Reformation gathered force, with peasant upheaval and doctrinal competition, German princes and monarchs in northern Europe put themselves at the head of official churches in their territories. Protestant authorities, with generous assistance from state-certified theologians like Luther, then proceeded to regulate their "territorial churches" strictly, selecting personnel and imposing detailed rules. They joined with Catholics to crush the Anabaptists, who, with their belief in freedom of conscience and separation of church and state, had become the real revolutionaries. Thus the Reformation, initially so radical in its rejection of Rome and its stress on individual religious experience, eventually resulted in a bureaucratization of the church and local religious life in Protestant Europe.

The Reformation era also increased the practical power of Catholic rulers over "their" churches, but it was only in the eighteenth century that some Catholic monarchs began to impose striking reforms. These reforms, which had their counterparts in Orthodox Russia, had a very "Protestant" aspect. They increased state control over the Catholic church, making it less subject to papal influence.

Spain, a deeply Catholic country with devout rulers, nevertheless took firm control of ecclesiastical appointments. Papal proclamations could not even be read in Spanish churches without prior approval from the government. Spain also asserted state control over the Spanish Inquisition, which pursued heresy as an independent agency under Rome's direction and went far toward creating a "national" Catholic church, as France had done earlier.

A more striking indication of state power and papal weakness was the fate of the Society of Jesus, or **Jesuits.** The well-educated Jesuits were extraordinary teachers, missionaries, and agents of the papacy. In many Catholic countries, the Jesuits exercised tremendous political influence, since individual members held high government positions and Jesuit colleges formed the minds of Europe's Catholic nobility. Yet by playing politics so effectively, the Jesuits eventually elicited a broad coalition of enemies. Bitter controversies led Louis XV to order the Jesuits out of France in 1763 and confiscate their property. France and Spain then pressured Rome to dissolve the Jesuits completely. In 1773 a reluctant pope caved in, although the order was revived after the French Revolution.

Some Catholic rulers also believed that the clergy in monasteries and convents should make a more practical contribution to social and religious life. Austria, a leader in controlling the church (see page 620) and promoting primary education, showed how far the process could go. Whereas Maria Theresa sharply restricted entry into "unproductive" orders, Joseph II recalled the radical initiatives of the Protestant Reformation. In his Edict on Idle Institutions, Joseph abolished contemplative orders, henceforth permitting only orders that were engaged in teaching, nursing, or other practical work. The state also expropriated the dissolved monasteries and used their wealth for charitable purposes and higher salaries for ordinary priests.

## Protestant Revival

In their attempt to recapture the vital core of the Christian religion, the Protestant reformers had rigorously suppressed all the medieval practices that they considered nonessential or erroneous. For example, they had taken very seriously the commandment "Thou shalt not make any graven image" (Exodus 20:4), and their radical reforms had reordered church interiors. Relics and crucifixes had been permanently removed from crypt and altar, while stained-glass windows had been smashed and walls and murals covered with whitewash. Processions and pilgrimages, saints and shrines—all such practices had been eliminated because they were not founded on Scripture. Such revolutionary changes had often troubled ordinary churchgoers, but by the late seventeenth century the vast reforms of the Reformation had been completed and thoroughly routinized in most Protestant churches.

Indeed, official Protestant churches had generally settled into a smug complacency. In the Reformation heartland, one concerned German minister wrote that the Lutheran church "had become paralyzed in forms of dead doctrinal conformity" and badly needed a return to its original inspiration.[12] This voice was one of many that would prepare

**A Midsummer Afternoon with a Methodist Preacher (detail)** This painting by de Loutherbourg suggests in a humorous manner how Wesley and his followers took their optimistic Christianity to the people of England. Methodist ministers championed open-air preaching and weeklong revivals. *(National Gallery of Canada, Ottawa)*

and then guide a powerful Protestant revival, which was largely successful because it answered the intense but increasingly unsatisfied needs of common people.

The Protestant revival began in Germany. It was known as **Pietism,** and three aspects helped explain its powerful appeal. First, Pietism called for a warm, emotional religion that everyone could experience. Enthusiasm—in prayer, in worship, in preaching, in life itself—was the key concept. "Just as a drunkard becomes full of wine, so must the congregation become filled with spirit," declared one exuberant writer. Another said simply, "The heart must burn."[13]

Second, Pietism reasserted the earlier radical stress on the priesthood of all believers, thereby reducing the large gulf between the official clergy and the Lutheran laity. Bible reading and study were enthusiastically extended to all classes, and this provided a powerful spur for popular education as well as individual religious development (see page 670). Finally, Pietists believed in the practical power of Christian rebirth in everyday affairs. Reborn Christians were expected to lead good, moral lives and come from all social classes.

Pietism had a major impact on John Wesley (1703–1791), who served as the catalyst for popular religious revival in England. Wesley came from a long line of ministers, and when he went to Oxford University to prepare for the clergy, he mapped a fanatically earnest "scheme of religion." Like some students during final-exam period, he organized every waking moment. After becoming a teaching fellow at Oxford, he organized a Holy Club for similarly minded students, who were soon known contemptuously as **Methodists** because they were so methodical in their devotion. Yet like the young Luther, Wesley remained intensely troubled about his own salvation, even after his ordination as an Anglican priest in 1728.

Wesley's anxieties related to grave problems of the faith in England. The Church of England was shamelessly used by the government to provide favorites with high-paying jobs and sinecures. Building of churches practically stopped while the population grew, and in many parishes there was a grave shortage of pews. Services and sermons had settled into an uninspiring routine. That the properly purified religion had been separated from local customs and social life was symbolized by church doors that were customarily locked on weekdays. Moreover, the skepticism of the Enlightenment was making inroads among the educated classes, and deism was becoming popular. Some bishops and church leaders acted as if they believed that doctrines such as the Virgin Birth were little more than particularly elegant superstitions.

Spiritual counseling from a sympathetic Pietist minister from Germany prepared Wesley for a mystical, emotional "conversion" in 1738. He described this critical turning point in his *Journal:*

*In the evening I went to a [Christian] society in Aldersgate Street where one was reading Luther's preface to the Epistle to the Romans. About a quarter before nine, while he was describing the change which God works in the heart through faith in Christ, I felt my heart strangely warmed. I felt I did trust in Christ, Christ alone for salvation; and an assurance was given me that he had taken away my sins, even mine, and saved me from the law of sin and death.*[14]

Wesley's emotional experience resolved his intellectual doubts. Moreover, he was convinced that any person, no matter how poor or uneducated, might have a similarly heartfelt conversion and gain the same blessed assurance.

Wesley took the good news to the people, traveling some 225,000 miles by horseback and preaching more than forty thousand sermons in fifty years. Since existing churches were often overcrowded and the church-state establishment was hostile, Wesley preached in open fields. People came in large numbers. Of critical importance was Wesley's rejection of Calvinist predestination—the doctrine of salvation granted only to a select few. Expanding on earlier Dutch theologians' views, he preached that *all* men and women who earnestly sought salvation might be saved. It was a message of hope and joy, of free will and universal salvation.

Wesley's ministry won converts, formed Methodist cells, and eventually resulted in a new denomination. And as Wesley had been inspired by Pietist revival in Germany, so evangelicals in the Church of England and the old dissenting groups now followed Wesley's example, giving impetus to an even broader awakening among the lower classes. In Protestant countries, religion remained a vital force in the lives of the people.

## Catholic Piety

Religion also flourished in Catholic Europe around 1700, but there were important differences with Protestant practice. First of all, the visual contrast was striking; baroque art had lavished rich and emotionally exhilarating figures and images on Catholic churches, just as Protestants had removed theirs. From almost every indication, people in Catholic Europe remained intensely religious. More than 95 percent of the population probably attended church for Easter Communion, the climax of the Catholic church year.

The tremendous popular strength of religion in Catholic countries reflected religion's integral role in community life and popular culture. Thus although Catholics reluctantly confessed their sins to priests, they enthusiastically joined together in religious festivals to celebrate the passage of the liturgical year. In addition to the great processional days—such as Palm Sunday, the joyful re-enactment of Jesus' triumphal entry into Jerusalem—each parish had its own saints' days, processions, and pilgrimages. Led by its priest, a congregation might march around the village or across the countryside to a local shrine or chapel. Before each procession or feast day, the priest explained its religious significance to kindle group piety. But processions were also folklore and tradition, an escape from work, and a form of recreation. A holiday atmosphere sometimes reigned on longer processions, with drinking and dancing and couples disappearing into the woods.

Indeed, devout Catholics held many religious beliefs that were marginal to the Christian faith, often of obscure or even pagan origin. On the Feast of Saint Anthony, for example, priests were expected to bless salt and bread for farm animals to protect them from disease. One saint's relics could help cure a child of fear, and there were healing springs for many ailments. The ordinary person combined a strong Christian faith with a wealth of time-honored superstitions.

Inspired initially by the fervor of the Catholic Counter-Reformation and then to some extent by the critical rationalism of the Enlightenment, parish priests and Catholic hierarchies sought increasingly to "purify" popular religious practice. Thus one parish priest in France lashed out at his parishioners, claiming that they were "more superstitious than devout . . . and sometimes appear as baptized idolators."[15] French priests particularly denounced the "various remnants of paganism" found in popular bonfire ceremonies during Lent, in which young men, "yelling and screaming like madmen," tried to jump over the bonfires in order to help the crops grow and protect themselves from illness. One priest saw rational Christians regressing into pagan animals—"the triumph of Hell and the shame of Christianity."[16]

In contrast with Protestant reformers, who had already used the power of the territorial state to crush such practices, many Catholic priests and hierarchies preferred a compromise between theological purity and the people's piety, perhaps realizing that the line between divine truth and mere superstition is not easily drawn. Thus the severity of the attack on popular Catholicism varied widely by country and region. Where authorities pursued purification vigorously, as in Austria under Joseph II, pious peasants saw only an incomprehensible attack on the true faith and drew back in anger. Their reaction dramatized the growing tension between the attitudes of educated elites and the common people.

**Good Friday Procession in Seville, Spain** This painting by Manuel Cabral suggests the strength of popular piety in Catholic countries. The entire community shares in the passion of the crucified Christ, adored by his weeping mother and flanked by the two thieves. The women in front with grotesque dunce caps represent the blindness and stupidity of those who killed Jesus and, by extension, the sinful nature of all human beings. *(Palacio Real, Madrid/Laurie Platt Winfrey)*

## Leisure and Recreation

The combination of religious celebration and popular recreation seen in festivals and processions was most strikingly displayed at **Carnival,** a time of reveling and excess in Catholic and Mediterranean Europe. Carnival preceded Lent—the forty days of fasting and penitence before Easter—and for a few exceptional days in February or March, a wild release of drinking, masquerading, and dancing reigned. Moreover, a combination of plays, processions, and rowdy spectacles turned the established order upside down. Peasants became nobles, fools turned into

**Cockfighting in England** This engraving by William Hogarth (1697–1764) satirizes the popular taste for blood sports, which Hogarth despised and lampooned in his famous *Four Stages of Cruelty*. The central figure in the wildly excited gathering is a blind nobleman, who actually existed and seldom missed a fight. Note the steel spurs on the birds' legs. *(Courtesy of Trustees of the British Museum)*

philosophers, and the rich were humbled. These once-a-year rituals gave people a much-appreciated chance to release their pent-up frustrations and aggressions before life returned to the usual pattern of leisure and recreation.

That pattern featured socializing in groups, for despite the spread of literacy, the culture of the common people was largely oral rather than written. In the cold, dark winter months, families gathered around the fireplace to talk, sing, tell stories, do craftwork, and keep warm. In some parts of Europe, women would gather together in groups in someone's cottage to chat, sew, spin, and laugh. Sometimes a few young men would be invited so that the daughters (and mothers) could size up potential suitors in a supervised atmosphere. A favorite recreation of men was drinking and talking with buddies in public places, and it was a sorry village that had no tavern. In addition to old favorites such as beer and wine, the common people turned with gusto toward cheap and potent hard liquor, which fell in price because of improved techniques for distilling grain in the eighteenth century.

Towns and cities offered a wide range of amusements. Many of these had to be paid for because the eighteenth century saw a sharp increase in the commercialization of leisure-time activities—a trend that continues to this day. Urban fairs featured prepared foods, acrobats, freak shows, open-air performances, optical illusions, and the like. Such entertainments attracted a variety of social classes. So did the growing number of commercial, profit-oriented spectator sports. These ranged from traveling circuses and horse races to boxing matches and bullfights. Modern sports heroes, such as brain-bashing heavyweight champions and haughty matadors, made their appearance on the historical scene.

**Blood sports,** such as bullbaiting and cockfighting, remained popular with the masses. In bullbaiting the bull, usually staked on a chain in the courtyard of an inn, was attacked by ferocious dogs for the amusement of the innkeeper's clients. Eventually the maimed and tortured animal was slaughtered by a butcher and sold as meat. In cockfighting two roosters, carefully trained by their owners and armed with razor-sharp steel spurs, slashed and clawed each other in a small ring until the victor won—and the loser died. An added attraction of cockfighting was that the screaming spectators could bet on the lightning-fast combat and its uncertain outcome.

In trying to place the vibrant popular culture of the common people in broad perspective, historians have stressed the growing criticism levied against it by the educated elites in the second half of the eighteenth century. These elites, which had previously shared the popular enthusiasm for religious festivals, Carnival, drinking in taverns, blood sports, and the like, now tended to see only superstition, sin, disorder, and vulgarity.[17] The resulting attack on popular culture, which had its more distant origins in the Protestant clergy's efforts to eliminate frivolity and superstition, was intensified as an educated public embraced the critical world-view of the Enlightenment. This shift in cultural attitudes drove a wedge between the common people and the educated public. The mutual hostility that this separation engendered played an important role in the emergence of sharp class conflict in the era of the French and the Industrial Revolutions.

## Summary

In the current generation, imaginative research has greatly increased the specialist's understanding of ordinary life and social patterns in the past. The human experience as recounted by historians has become richer and more meaningful, and many mistaken ideas have fallen by the wayside. This has been particularly true of eighteenth-century, predominately agrarian Europe, which combined a fascinating mixture of continuity and change.

To summarize, the life of the people remained primarily rural and oriented toward the local community. Tradition, routine, and well-established codes of behavior framed much of the everyday experience of the typical villager. Thus just as the three-field agricultural cycle and its pattern of communal rights had determined traditional patterns of grain production, so did community values in the countryside strongly encourage a late age of marriage, a low rate of illegitimate births, and a strict attitude toward children. Patterns of recreation and leisure, from churchgoing and religious festivals to sewing and drinking in groups within an oral culture, also reflected and reinforced community ties and values. Many long-standing ideas and beliefs, ranging from obscure religious customs to support for fair prices, remained strong forces and sustained continuity in popular life.

Yet powerful forces also worked for change. Many of these came from outside and above, from the aggressive capitalists, educated elites, and government officials discussed in the last two chapters. Closely knit villages began to lose control over families and marital practices, as could be seen in the earlier, more romantic marriages of cottage workers and in the beginning of the explosion in illegitimate births. Although the new, less rigorous attitudes toward children that were emerging in elite culture did not reach the people, the elite belief in the usefulness of some education did result in growing popular literacy. The grain-based diet became more varied with the grudging acceptance of the potato, and the benefits of the spectacular conquest of smallpox began to reach the common people in the late eighteenth century. Finally, the common people found that their beliefs and customs were being increasingly attacked by educated elites, who thought they knew better. The popular reaction to these attacks generally remained muted in the eighteenth century, but the common people and their advocates would offer vigorous responses and counterattacks in the revolutionary era.

## Key Terms

| | |
|---|---|
| extended family | purging |
| community controls | smallpox inoculation |
| illegitimacy explosion | Jesuits |
| wet-nursing | Pietism |
| killing nurses | Methodists |
| infanticide | Carnival |
| just price | blood sports |

## Notes

1. Quoted in J. M. Beattie, "The Criminality of Women in Eighteenth-Century England," *Journal of Social History* 8 (Summer 1975): 86.
2. W. L. Langer, "Infanticide: A Historical Survey," *History of Childhood Quarterly* 1 (Winter 1974): 357.
3. Quoted in R. Cobb, *The Police and the People: French Popular Protest, 1789–1820* (Oxford: Clarendon Press, 1970), p. 238.
4. M. Segalen, *Love and Power in the Peasant Family: Rural France in the Nineteenth Century* (New York: Basil Blackwell, 1983), p. 41. The passage as cited here has been edited to the past tense.
5. Quoted in D. S. Landes, ed., *The Rise of Capitalism* (New York: Macmillan, 1966), pp. 56–57.
6. G. Gullickson, *Spinners and Weavers of Auffay: Rural Industry and the Sexual Division of Labor in a French Village, 1750–1850* (Cambridge: Cambridge University Press, 1986), p. 186. See also L. A. Tilly, J. W. Scott, and M. Cohen, "Women's Work and European Fertility Patterns," *Journal of Interdisciplinary History* 6 (Winter 1976): 447–476.
7. P. Viazzo, "Mortality, Fertility, and Family," in *The History of the European Family*, ed. D. Kertzer and M. Barbagli, vol. 1 (New Haven: Yale University Press, 2001), pp. 176–178.
8. Quoted in B. W. Lorence, "Parents and Children in Eighteenth-Century Europe," *History of Childhood Quarterly* 2 (Summer 1974): 1–2.
9. Ibid., pp. 13, 16.
10. E. Kennedy, *A Cultural History of the French Revolution* (New Haven: Yale University Press, 1989), p. 47.
11. Quoted in R. Sand, *The Advance to Social Medicine* (London: Staples Press, 1952), pp. 86–87.
12. Quoted in K. Pinson, *Pietism as a Factor in the Rise of German Nationalism* (New York: Columbia University Press, 1934), p. 13.
13. Ibid., pp. 43–44.
14. Quoted in S. Andrews, *Methodism and Society* (London: Longmans, Green, 1970), p. 327.

*(continued on page 688)*

# Listening to the Past

## Gender Constructions and Education for Girls

*Emile, or On Education (1762), by Jean-Jacques Rousseau, is one of history's most original and influential books. Sometimes called a declaration of rights for children, it pleads for the humane treatment of children and lambasts widespread indifference and harsh discipline.*

*Rousseau's long, rambling work, part novel and part philosophical treatise, also had a powerful impact on theories of education.* Emile *argues that education must shield the unspoiled child from the corrupting influences of civilization and allow the child to develop naturally and spontaneously. Children should learn what they—not their teachers—find interesting and useful.*

*As this selection shows, Rousseau constructed sharp gender divisions. Girls and boys were basically equal as human beings, but sex made them both similar and different, intended by their natures for different occupations. Whereas Emile would eventually tackle academic subjects, Sophie, his future wife, would receive only lessons in household management, good mothering, and wifely obedience. The idea of educating girls and boys to operate "naturally" in their "separate spheres" would flourish in the nineteenth century.*

Sophie ought to be a woman as Emile is a man—that is to say, she ought to have everything which suits the constitution of her species and her sex in order to fill her place in the physical and moral order. Let us begin, then, by examining the similarities and the differences of her sex and ours.

In everything not connected with sex, woman is man. She has the same organs, the same needs, the same faculties. The machine is constructed in the same way; its parts are the same; the one functions as does the other; the form is similar; and in whatever respect one considers them, the difference between them is only one of more or less.

In everything connected with sex, woman and man are in every respect related and in every respect different. The difficulty of comparing them comes from the difficulty of determining what in their constitutions is due to sex and what is not. . . .

There is no parity between the two sexes in regard to the consequences of sex. The male is male only at certain moments. The female is female her whole life or at least during her whole youth. Everything constantly recalls her sex to her; and, to fulfill its functions well, she needs a constitution which corresponds to it. She needs care during her pregnancy; she needs rest at the time of childbirth; she needs a soft and sedentary life to suckle her children; she needs patience and gentleness, a zeal and an affection that nothing can rebuff in order to raise her children. She serves as the link between them and their father; she alone makes him love them and give them the confidence to call them his own. How much tenderness and care is required to maintain the union of the whole family! . . .

Once it is demonstrated that man and woman are not and ought not to be constituted in the same way in either character or temperament, it follows that they ought not to have the same education. In following nature's directions, man and woman ought to act in concert, but they ought not to do the same things. The goal of their labors is common, but their labors themselves are different, and consequently so are the tastes directing them. . . .

All the faculties common to the two sexes are not equally distributed between them; but taken together, they balance out. Woman is worth more as woman and less as man. Wherever she makes use of her rights, she has the advantage. Wherever she wants to usurp ours, she remains beneath us. . . .

To cultivate man's qualities in women and to neglect those which are proper to them is obviously to work to their detriment. . . . Believe me, judicious mother, do not make a decent man of your daughter, as though you would give nature the lie. Make a decent woman of her, and be sure that as a result she will be worth more for herself and for us.

Does it follow that she ought to be raised in ignorance of everything and limited to the housekeeping functions alone? Will man turn his companion into his servant? . . . Surely not. It is not thus that nature has spoken in giving women such agreeable and nimble minds. On the contrary, nature wants them to think, to judge, to love, to know, to cultivate their minds as well as their looks. These are the weapons nature gives them to take the place of the strength they lack and to direct others. They ought to learn many things but only those that are suitable for them to know. . . .

The children of both sexes have many common entertainments, and that ought to be so. Is this not also the case when they are grown up? They also have particular tastes which distinguish them. Boys seek movement and noise: drums, boots, little carriages. Girls prefer what presents itself to sight and is useful for ornamentation: mirrors, jewels, dresses, particularly dolls. The doll is the special entertainment of this sex. . . .

Observe a little girl spending the day around her doll. . . . [S]he puts all her coquetry into it. She will not always leave it there. She awaits the moment when she will be her own doll.

This is a very definite primary taste. You have only to follow and regulate it. It is certain that the little girl would want with all her heart to know how to adorn her doll, to make its bracelets, its scarf, its flounce, its lace. . . . In this way there emerges the reason for the first lessons she is given. They are not tasks prescribed to her, they are kindnesses done for her. In fact, almost all little girls learn to read and write with repugnance. But as for holding a needle, that they always learn gladly. They imagine themselves to be grown up and think with pleasure that these talents will one day be useful for adorning themselves.

Once this first path is opened, it is easy to follow. Sewing, embroidery, and lacemaking come by themselves. Tapestry is not much to their taste. . . .

Whatever humorists may say, good sense belongs equally to the two sexes. Girls are generally more docile than boys, and one should even use more authority with them, as I shall say a little later. But it does not follow that anything ought to be demanded from them whose utility they cannot see. The art of mothers is to show them the utility of everything they prescribe to them, and that is all the easier since intelligence is more precocious in girls than in boys. This rule banishes—for their sex

Jean-Jacques Rousseau (1712–1778), portrayed as a gentle teacher and a pensive philosopher. *(The Granger Collection, New York)*

as well as for ours—not only idle studies which lead to no good and do not even make those who have pursued them more attractive to others, but even those which are not useful at their age and whose usefulness for a more advanced age the child cannot foresee. If I do not want to push a boy to learn to read, all the more I do not want to force girls to before making them well aware of what the use of reading is. In the way this utility is ordinarily showed to them, we follow our own idea far more than theirs. After all, where is the necessity for a girl to know how to read and write so early? Will she so soon have a household to govern? There are very few girls who do abuse this fatal science more than they make good use of it. And all of them have too much curiosity not to learn it—without our forcing them to do so—when they have the leisure and the occasion. Perhaps girls ought to learn to do arithmetic before anything, for nothing presents a more palpable utility at all times, requires longer practice, and is so exposed to error as calculation. If the little girl were to get cherries for her snack only by doing an arithmetical operation, I assure you that she would soon know how to calculate.

## Questions for Analysis

1. What similarities and differences between women/girls and men/boys does Rousseau see? In your opinion, which appear more important to Rousseau? Why?
2. Were Rousseau's views on gender differences and education reactionary or progressive?

*Source:* Jean-Jacques Rousseau, *Emile, or On Education,* trans. Alan Bloom. Copyright © 1979 by Basic Books, Inc. Reprinted by permission of Basic Books, a member of Perseus Books, L.L.C.

15. Quoted in I. Woloch, *Eighteenth-Century Europe: Tradition and Progress, 1715–1789* (New York: W. W. Norton, 1982), p. 292.
16. Quoted in T. Tackett, *Priest and Parish in Eighteenth-Century France* (Princeton, N.J.: Princeton University Press, 1977), p. 214.
17. Woloch, *Eighteenth-Century Europe,* pp. 220–221; see also pp. 214–220 for this section.

## Suggested Reading

Among general introductions to the history of the family, women, and children, B. Gottlieb, *The Family in the Western World: From the Black Death to the Industrial Age* (1993), is recommended. D. Kertzer and M. Barbagli, cited in the Notes, and J. Ehmer, R. Wall, and T. Hareven, eds., *Family History Revisited: Comparative Perspectives* (2001), provide a rich feast of recent scholarly findings and ongoing debates. A. Imhof, *Lost Worlds: How Our European Ancestors Coped with Everyday Life and Why Life Is So Hard Today* (1996), sheds new light on family ties and attitudes toward death, which may be compared with P. Laslett, *The World We Have Lost* (1965), a pioneering investigation of England before the Industrial Revolution. R. Rudolph, ed., *The European Peasant Family and Society: Historical Studies* (1995), considers patterns of marriage and family dynamics; K. Lynch, *Individuals, Families, and Communities in Europe, 1200–1800* (2003), concentrates on urban families. L. Stone, *The Family, Sex and Marriage in England, 1500–1800* (1977), is a provocative general interpretation, and L. Tilly and J. Scott, *Women, Work and Family* (1978), remains an excellent introduction. Two valuable works on women, both with good bibliographies, are M. Boxer and J. Quataert, eds., *Connecting Spheres: European Women in a Globalizing World, 1500 to the Present,* 2d ed. (2000), and R. Bridenthal, S. Mosher Stuard, and M. Wiesner, eds., *Becoming Visible: Women in European History,* 3d ed. (1998). P. Aries, *Centuries of Childhood: A Social History of Family Life* (1962), is a famous pioneering study, which may be compared with the more recent synthesis by H. Cunningham, *Children and Childhood in Western Society Since 1500* (1995). J. Henderson and R. Walls, eds., *Poor Women and Children in the European Past* (1994), considers abandonment, illegitimacy, orphanages, and other topics in this chapter. M. Segalen, *Love and Power in the Peasant Family: Rural France in the Nineteenth Century* (1983), is an exceptionally fine study. A. MacFarlane, *Origins of English Individualism: The Family, Property and Social Transition* (1978), is a major work. B. Lorence-Kot, *Child-Rearing and Reform: A Study of Nobility in Eighteenth-Century Poland* (1985), stresses the harshness of parental discipline. Various aspects of sexual relationships are treated imaginatively by M. Foucault, *The History of Sexuality* (1981), and R. Wheaton and T. Hareven, eds., *Family and Sexuality in French History* (1980).

J. Burnett, *A History of the Cost of Living* (1969), has a great deal of interesting information about what people spent their money on in the past; K. Wrightson, *Earthly Necessities: Economic Lives in Early Modern Britain* (2000), examines the economics of everyday life with flair and understanding. J. C. Drummond and A. Wilbraham, *The Englishman's Food: A History of Five Centuries of English Diet,* 2d ed. (1958), remains a valuable and fascinating introduction. S. Mintz, *Sweetness and Power: The Place of Sugar in Modern History* (1985), examines the commodity with slavery and plantation agriculture. J. Knyveton, *Diary of a Surgeon in the Year 1751–1752* (1937), gives a contemporary's unforgettable picture of both eighteenth-century medicine and social customs, as does M. Romsey, *Professional and Popular Medicine in France, 1770–1830: The Social World of Medical Practice* (1988). Good introductions to the evolution of medical practices include Roy Porter, ed., *The Cambridge Illustrated History of Medicine* (1996), and A. Digby, *Making a Medical Living: Doctors and Patients in the English Market for Medicine, 1720–1991* (1994). A. Rusnock, *Vital Accounts: Quantifying Health and Population in Eighteenth-Century England and France* (2002), explores how physicians and officials learned to count diseases systematically, and J. Carrell, *The Speckled Monster: A Historical Tale of Battling Smallpox* (2003), is a lively popular account. M. Lindemann, *Health and Healing in Eighteenth-Century Germany* (1996), is a wide-ranging synthesis. H. Marland, ed., *The Art of Midwifery: Early Modern Midwives in Europe* (1993), discusses developments in several countries and complements L. Ulrich, *A Midwife's Tale: The Life of Martha Ballard, Based on Her Diary, 1785–1812* (1990), a superb reconstruction. W. Boyd, *History of Western Education* (1966), is a standard survey, whereas R. Houston, *Literacy in Early Modern Europe: Culture and Education, 1500–1800* (1988), is brief and engaging.

Among older studies of popular culture, M. George, *London Life in the Eighteenth Century* (1965), is a delight, whereas D. Roche, *The People of Paris: An Essay in Popular Culture in the Eighteenth Century* (1987), presents an unforgettable portrait of the Paris poor. I. Woloch, *Eighteenth-Century Europe: Tradition and Progress, 1715–1789* (1982), includes a survey of popular culture and a good bibliography. E. Kennedy, *A Cultural History of the French Revolution* (1989), beautifully captures rural and urban attitudes in France before and during the French Revolution. R. Malcolmson, *Popular Recreation in English Society, 1700–1850* (1973), provides a colorful account of boxers, bettors, bull-baiting, and more. L. Hunt, *The New Cultural History* (1989), provides an engaging discussion of conceptual issues. G. Rude, *The Crowd in History, 1730–1848* (1964), is an influential effort to see politics and popular protest from below. P. Burke, *Popular Culture in Early Modern Europe* (1978), is an excellent and influential study. J. Gillis, *For Better, for Worse: Marriage in Britain Since 1500* (1985), and R. Philips, *Untying the Knot: A Short History of Divorce* (1991), are good introductions to institutional changes.

Good works on religious life include J. Delumeau, *Catholicism Between Luther and Voltaire: A New View of the Counter-Reformation* (1977); B. Semmel, *The Methodist Revolution* (1973); and J. Bettey, *Church and Community: The Parish Church in English Life* (1979).

*The Planting of a Liberty Tree,* by Pierre Antoine Leseur.
*(Giraudon/Art Resource, NY)*

chapter

# 21 The Revolution in Politics, 1775–1815

**chapter outline**



The last years of the eighteenth century were a time of great upheaval. A series of revolutions and revolutionary wars challenged the old order of monarchs and aristocrats. The ideas of freedom and equality, ideas that have not stopped shaping the world since that era, flourished and spread. The revolutionary era began in North America in 1775. Then in 1789 France, the most influential country in Europe, became the leading revolutionary nation. It established first a constitutional monarchy, then a radical republic, and finally a new empire under Napoleon. The armies of France also joined forces with patriots and radicals abroad in an effort to establish new governments based on new principles throughout much of Europe. The world of modern domestic and international politics was born.

- What caused this era of revolution?
- What were the ideas and objectives of the men and women who rose up violently to undo the established system?
- What were the gains and losses for privileged groups and for ordinary people in a generation of war and upheaval?

These are the questions underlying this chapter's examination of the revolutionary era.

## Liberty and Equality

Two ideas fueled the revolutionary period in both America and Europe: **liberty and equality.** What did eighteenth-century politicians and other people mean by liberty and equality, and why were those ideas so radical and revolutionary in their day?

The call for liberty was first of all a call for individual human rights. Even the most enlightened monarchs customarily claimed that it was their duty to regulate what people wrote and believed. Liberals of the revolutionary era protested such controls from on high. They demanded freedom to worship according to the dictates of their consciences, an end to censorship, and freedom from arbitrary laws and from judges who simply obeyed orders from the government. The Declaration of the Rights of Man, issued at the beginning of the French Revolution, proclaimed, "Liberty consists in being able to do anything that does not harm another person." In the context of the monarchical and absolutist forms of government then dominating Europe, this was a truly radical idea.

The call for liberty was also a call for a new kind of government. Revolutionary liberals believed that the people had **sovereignty**—that is, that the people alone had the authority to make laws limiting an individual's freedom of action. In practice, this system of government meant choosing legislators who represented the people and were accountable to them.

Equality was a more ambiguous idea. Eighteenth-century liberals argued that, in theory, all citizens should have identical rights and civil liberties and that the nobility had no right to special privileges based on the accident of birth. However, liberals accepted some well-established distinctions.

First, most eighteenth-century liberals were *men* of their times, and they generally shared with other men the belief that equality between men and women was neither practical nor desirable. Women played an important political role in the French Revolution at several points, but the men of the French Revolution limited formal political rights—the right to vote, to run for office, to participate in government—to men.

Second, liberals never believed that everyone should be equal economically. Quite the contrary. As Thomas Jefferson wrote in an early draft of the American Declaration of Independence (before he changed "property" to the more noble-sounding "happiness"), everyone was equal in "the pursuit of property." Jefferson and other liberals certainly did not expect equal success in that pursuit. Great differences in wealth and income between rich and poor were perfectly acceptable to liberals. The essential point was that everyone should legally have an equal chance.

In eighteenth-century Europe, however, such equality of opportunity was a truly revolutionary idea. Society was still legally divided into groups with special privileges, such as the nobility and the clergy, and groups with special burdens, such as the peasantry. And in most countries, various middle-class groups—professionals, business people, townspeople, and craftsmen—enjoyed privileges that allowed them to monopolize all sorts of economic activity. Liberals criticized not economic inequality itself but this kind of economic inequality based on legal distinctions for different social groups.

Although the ideas of liberty and equality—the central ideas of classical liberalism—had deep roots in Western history dating back to ancient Greece and the Judeo-Christian tradition, classical liberalism first crystallized at the end of the seventeenth century and during the Enlightenment of the eighteenth century. Liberal ideas reflected the Enlightenment's stress on human dignity, personal liberty, and human happiness on earth and its faith in science, rationality, and progress.

Certain English and French thinkers were mainly responsible for joining the Enlightenment's concern for personal freedom and legal equality to a theoretical justification of liberal self-government. The two most important were John Locke and the baron de Montesquieu. Locke maintained that England's long political tradition rested on "the rights of Englishmen" and on representative government through Parliament. He argued that if a government oversteps its proper function of protecting the natural rights of life, liberty, and private property, it becomes a tyranny. Montesquieu was also inspired by English constitutional history. He, too, believed that powerful "intermediary groups"—such as the judicial nobility of which he was a proud member—offered the best defense of liberty against despotism.

The belief that representative institutions could defend their liberty and interests appealed powerfully to well-educated, prosperous, middle-class groups, which historians have traditionally labeled as the **bourgeoisie.** Yet liberal ideas about individual rights and political freedom also appealed to much of the hereditary nobility, at least in western Europe and as formulated by Montesquieu. **Representative government** did not mean democracy, which liberal thinkers tended to equate with mob rule. Rather, they envisioned voting for representatives as being restricted to those who owned property—those with "a stake in society." England had shown the way. After 1688 it had combined a parliamentary system and considerable individual liberty with a restricted franchise and unquestionable aristocratic pre-eminence. In the course of the eighteenth century, many leading French nobles, led by high-ranking noble judges, who were inspired by the doctrines of Montesquieu, were increasingly eager to follow the English example. Thus eighteenth-century liberalism in western Europe found broad support among the prosperous, well-educated elites in both the nobility and the bourgeoisie.

What liberalism lacked from the beginning was strong popular support, for at least two reasons. First, for common people, the great questions were not theoretical and political but immediate and economic; getting enough to eat was a crucial challenge. Second, some of the traditional practices and institutions that liberals wanted to abolish were dear to peasants and urban workers. Com-

1770 1780 1790 1800 1810 1820

**POLITICAL/MILITARY**

- 1773 Boston Tea Party
- 1775–1783 American Revolution
- 1789 Ratification of U.S. Constitution
- 1789 Storming of the Bastille
- 1789–1799 French Revolution
- 1793–1794 Robespierre's Reign of Terror
- 1793 Execution of Louis XVI
- 1794 Robespierre deposed and executed
- 1794–1799 Thermidorian reaction
- 1799–1815 Napoleonic era
- 1812 Napoleon invades Russia
- 1814–1815 Napoleon defeated and exiled

**SOCIAL/ECONOMIC**

- 1786–1789 Financial crisis in France
- 1789 Feudalism abolished in France
- 1793–1794 Economic controls to help poor in France

**INTELLECTUAL/RELIGIOUS**

- 1775 Paine, *Common Sense*
- 1790 Burke, *Reflections on the Revolution in France*
- 1792 Wollstonecraft, *A Vindication of the Rights of Woman*

fortable elites had already come into conflict with the people in the eighteenth century over the enclosure of common lands and the regulation of food prices. This conflict would sharpen in the revolutionary era as differences in outlook and well-being led to many misunderstandings and disappointments for both groups.

## The American Revolutionary Era, 1775–1789

The era of liberal political revolution began in the New World. The thirteen mainland colonies of British North America revolted against their home country and then succeeded in establishing a new, unified government.

Americans have long debated the meaning of their revolution. Some have even questioned whether it was a real revolution, as opposed to a war for independence. According to some scholars, the Revolution was conservative and defensive in that its demands were for the traditional liberties of English citizens; Americans were united against the British, but otherwise they were a satisfied people, not torn by internal conflict. Other scholars have argued that, on the contrary, the American Revolution was quite radical. It split families between patriots and Loyalists and divided the country. It achieved goals that were as fully advanced as those obtained by the French in their great Revolution a few years later.

How does one reconcile these positions? Both contain large elements of truth. The American revolutionaries did believe that they were demanding only the traditional rights of English men and women. But those traditional rights were liberal rights, and in the American context they had very strong democratic and popular overtones. Thus the American Revolution was fought in the name of established ideals that were still quite radical in the context of the times. And in founding a government firmly based on liberal principles, the Americans set an example that had a forceful impact on Europe and sped up political development there.

## The Origins of the Revolution

The American Revolution had its immediate origins in a squabble over increased taxes. The British government had fought and decisively won the Seven Years' War (see page 644) on the strength of its professional army and navy. The American colonists had furnished little real aid. The high cost of the war to the British, however, had led to a doubling of the British national debt. Anticipating further expense defending its recently conquered western lands from Native American uprisings, the British government in London set about reorganizing the empire with a series of bold, largely unprecedented measures. Breaking with tradition, the British decided to maintain a large army in North America after peace was restored in 1763 and to tax the colonies directly. In 1765 the government pushed through Parliament the Stamp Act, which levied taxes on a long list of commercial and legal documents, diplomas, pamphlets, newspapers, almanacs, dice, and playing cards. A stamp glued to each article indicated the tax had been paid.

**Toward Revolution in Boston** The Boston Tea Party was only one of many angry confrontations between British officials and Boston patriots. On January 27, 1774, an angry crowd seized a British customs collector and then tarred and feathered him. This French engraving of 1784 commemorates the defiant and provocative action. *(The Granger Collection, New York)*

This effort to increase taxes as part of a tightening up of the empire seemed perfectly reasonable to the British. Heavier stamp taxes had been collected in Great Britain for two generations, and Americans were being asked only to pay a share of their own defense costs. Moreover, Americans had been paying only very low local taxes. The Stamp Act would have doubled taxes to about 2 shillings per person per year, whereas the British paid the highest taxes in the Western world—26 shillings per person. The colonists protested the Stamp Act vigorously and violently, however, and after their rioting and boycotts against British goods, Parliament reluctantly repealed the new tax.

As the fury over the Stamp Act revealed, much more was involved than taxes. The key questions were political. To what extent could the home government refashion the empire and reassert its power while limiting the authority of colonial legislatures and their elected representatives? Accordingly, who should represent the colonies, and who had the right to make laws for Americans? The British government replied that Americans were represented in Parliament, albeit indirectly (like most British people themselves), and that the absolute supremacy of Parliament throughout the empire could not be questioned. Many Americans felt otherwise. As John Adams put it, "A Parliament of Great Britain can have no more rights to tax the colonies than a Parliament of Paris." Thus imperial reorganization and parliamentary supremacy came to appear as grave threats to Americans' existing liberties and time-honored institutions.

Americans had long exercised a great deal of independence. In British North America, unlike England and Europe, no powerful established church existed, and personal freedom in questions of religion was taken for granted. The colonial assemblies made the important laws, which were seldom overturned by the home government. The right to vote was much more widespread than in England. In many parts of colonial Massachusetts, for example, as many as 95 percent of the adult males could vote.

Moreover, greater political equality was matched by greater social and economic equality. Neither a hereditary nobility nor a hereditary serf population existed, although the slavery of the Americas consigned blacks to a legally oppressed caste. Independent farmers were the largest group in the country and set much of its tone. In short, the colonial experience had slowly formed a people who felt themselves separate and distinct from the home country, and the controversies over taxation intensified those feelings.

In 1773 the dispute over taxes and representation flared up again. The British government had permitted the financially hard-pressed East India Company to ship its tea from China directly to its agents in the colonies rather than through London middlemen who sold to independent merchants in the colonies. Thus the company secured a vital monopoly on the tea trade, and colonial merchants were suddenly excluded from a lucrative business. The colonists were quick to protest.

In Boston men disguised as Indians had a rowdy "tea party" and threw the company's tea into the harbor. This led to extreme measures. The so-called Coercive Acts closed the port of Boston, curtailed local elections and town meetings, and greatly expanded the royal governor's power. County conventions in Massachusetts protested vehemently and urged that the acts be "rejected as the attempts of a wicked administration to enslave America." Other colonial assemblies joined in the denunciations. In September 1774, the First Continental Congress met in Philadelphia, where the more radical members argued successfully against concessions to the Crown. Compromise was also rejected by the British Parliament, and in April 1775 fighting began at Lexington and Concord.

## Independence

The fighting spread, and the colonists moved slowly but inevitably toward open rebellion and a declaration of independence. The uncompromising attitude of the British government and its use of German mercenaries went a long way toward dissolving long-standing loyalties to the home country and rivalries among the separate colonies. *Common Sense* (1775), a brilliant attack by the recently arrived English radical Thomas Paine (1737–1809), also mobilized public opinion in favor of independence. A runaway bestseller with sales of 120,000 copies in a few months, Paine's tract ridiculed the idea of a small island ruling a great continent. In his call for freedom and republican government, Paine expressed Americans' growing sense of separateness and moral superiority.

On July 4, 1776, the Second Continental Congress adopted the Declaration of Independence. Written by Thomas Jefferson, the Declaration of Independence boldly listed the tyrannical acts committed by George III (r. 1760–1820) and confidently proclaimed the natural rights of mankind and the sovereignty of the American states. Sometimes called the world's greatest political editorial, the Declaration of Independence in effect universalized the traditional rights of English people and made them the rights of all mankind. It stated that "all men are created equal. . . . They are endowed by their Creator with certain unalienable rights. . . . Among these are life, liberty, and the pursuit of happiness." No other American political document has ever caused such excitement, either at home or abroad.

Many American families remained loyal to Britain; many others divided bitterly. After the Declaration of Independence, the conflict often took the form of a civil war pitting patriot against Loyalist. The Loyalists tended to be wealthy and politically moderate. Many patriots, too, were wealthy—individuals such as John Hancock and George Washington—but willingly allied themselves with farmers and artisans in a broad coalition. This coalition harassed the Loyalists and confiscated their property to help pay for the American war effort. The broad social base of the revolutionaries tended to make the liberal revolution democratic. State governments extended the right to vote to many more men (but not to any women) in the course of the war and re-established themselves as republics.

On the international scene, the French sympathized with the rebels and supplied guns and gunpowder from the beginning. The French wanted revenge for the humiliating defeats of the Seven Years' War. By 1777 French volunteers were arriving in Virginia, and a dashing young nobleman, the marquis de Lafayette (1757–1834), quickly became one of Washington's most trusted generals. In 1778 the French government offered a formal alliance to the American ambassador in Paris, Benjamin Franklin, and in 1779 and 1780 the Spanish and Dutch declared war on Britain. Catherine the Great of Russia helped organize the League of Armed Neutrality in order to protect neutral shipping rights, which Britain refused to recognize.

Thus by 1780 Great Britain was engaged in an imperial war against most of Europe as well as the thirteen colonies. In these circumstances, and in the face of severe reverses in India, in the West Indies, and at Yorktown in Virginia, a new British government decided to cut its losses. American negotiators in Paris were receptive. They feared that France wanted a treaty that would bottle up the new United States east of the Allegheny Mountains and give British holdings west of the Alleghenies to France's ally, Spain. Thus the American negotiators deserted their French allies and accepted the extraordinarily favorable terms Britain offered.

By the Treaty of Paris of 1783, Britain recognized the independence of the thirteen colonies and ceded all its

**The Signing of the Declaration of Independence, July 4, 1776** John Trumbull's famous painting shows the dignity and determination of America's revolutionary leaders. An extraordinarily talented group, they succeeded in rallying popular support without losing power to more radical forces in the process. *(The Granger Collection, New York)*

territory between the Allegheny Mountains and the Mississippi River to the Americans. Out of the bitter rivalries of the Old World, the Americans snatched dominion over a vast territory.

## Framing the Constitution

The liberal program of the American Revolution was consolidated by the federal Constitution, the Bill of Rights, and the creation of a national republic. Assembling in Philadelphia in the summer of 1787, the delegates to the Constitutional Convention were determined to end the period of economic depression, social uncertainty, and very weak central government that had followed independence. The delegates thus decided to grant the federal, or central, government important powers: regulation of domestic and foreign trade, the right to tax, and the means to enforce its laws.

Strong rule would be placed squarely in the context of representative self-government. Senators and congressmen would be the lawmaking delegates of the voters, and the president of the republic would be an elected official. The central government would operate in Montesquieu's framework of **checks and balances.** The executive, legislative, and judicial branches would systematically balance one another. The power of the federal government would in turn be checked by the powers of the individual states.

When the results of the secret deliberations of the Constitutional Convention were presented to the states for ratification, a great public debate began. The opponents of the proposed constitution—the Antifederalists—charged that the framers of the new document had taken too much power from the individual states and made the federal government too strong. Moreover, many Antifederalists feared for the personal liberties and individual freedoms for which they had just fought. In order to overcome these objections, the Federalists solemnly promised to spell out these basic freedoms as soon as the new Constitution was adopted. The result was the first ten amendments to the Constitution, which the first Congress passed shortly after it met in New York in March 1789. These amendments formed an effective bill of rights to safeguard the individual. Most of them—trial by jury, due process of law, right to assemble, freedom from unreasonable search—had their origins in English law and the English Bill of Rights of 1689. Other rights—the freedoms of speech, the press, and religion—reflected natural-law theory and the American experience.

The American Constitution and the Bill of Rights exemplified the great strengths and the limits of what came to be called **classical liberalism.** Liberty meant individual freedoms and political safeguards. Liberty also meant representative government but did not necessarily mean democracy, with its principle of one person, one vote. Equality—slaves excepted—meant equality before the law, not equality of political participation or wealth. The radicalism of liberal revolution in America was primarily legal and political, *not* economic or social.

### The Revolution's Impact on Europe

Hundreds of books, pamphlets, and articles analyzed and romanticized the American upheaval. Thoughtful Europeans noted, first of all, its enormous long-term implications for international politics. A secret report by the Venetian ambassador to Paris in 1783 stated what many felt: "If only the union of the Provinces is preserved, it is reasonable to expect that, with the favorable effects of time, and of European arts and sciences, it will become the most formidable power in the world."[1] More generally, American independence fired the imaginations of those aristocrats who were uneasy with their hereditary privileges and those commoners who yearned for legal equality. Many Europeans believed that the world was advancing and that America was leading the way.

Europeans who dreamed of a new era were fascinated by the political lessons of the American Revolution. The Americans had begun with a revolutionary defense against tyrannical oppression, and they had been victorious. They had then shown how rational beings could assemble together to exercise sovereignty and write a permanent constitution—a new social contract. All this gave greater reality to the concepts of individual liberty and representative government and reinforced one of the primary ideas of the Enlightenment: that a better world was possible.

## The French Revolution, 1789–1791

See DBQ 7

No country felt the consequences of the American Revolution more directly than France. Hundreds of French officers served in America and were inspired by the experience. The most famous of these, the young and impressionable marquis de Lafayette, left home as a great aristocrat determined only to fight France's traditional foe, England. He returned with a love of liberty and firm republican convictions. French intellectuals and publicists engaged in passionate analysis of the federal Constitution as well as the constitutions of the various states of the new United States. The American Revolution undeniably hastened upheaval in France.

Yet the French Revolution did not mirror the American example. It was more radical and more complex, more influential and more controversial, more loved and more hated. For Europeans and most of the rest of the world, it was the great revolution of the eighteenth century, *the* revolution that opened the modern era in politics.

### The Breakdown of the Old Order

Like the American Revolution, the French Revolution had its immediate origins in the financial difficulties of the government. The efforts of Louis XV's ministers to raise taxes had been thwarted by the high courts, led by the Parlement of Paris, which was strengthened in its opposition by widespread popular support (see page 622). When renewed efforts to reform the tax system met a similar fate in 1776, the government was forced to finance all of its enormous expenditures during the American war with borrowed money. As a result, the national debt and the annual budget deficit soared. By the 1780s, fully 50 percent of France's annual budget went for ever-increasing interest payments on the ever-increasing debt. Another 25 percent went to maintain the military, while 6 percent was absorbed by the costly and extravagant king and his court at Versailles. Less than 20 percent of the entire national budget was available for the productive functions of the state, such as transportation and general administration. This was an impossible financial situation.

**The Three Estates** In this political cartoon from 1789 a peasant of the third estate struggles under the crushing burden of a happy clergyman and a plumed nobleman. The caption—"Let's hope this game ends soon"—sets forth a program of reform that any peasant could understand. *(Réunion des Musées Nationaux/Art Resource, NY)*

One way out would have been for the government to declare partial bankruptcy, forcing its creditors to accept greatly reduced payments on the debt. The powerful Spanish monarchy had regularly repudiated large portions of its debt in earlier times, and France had done likewise after an attempt to establish a French national bank had ended in financial disaster in 1720. Yet by the 1780s, the French debt was being held by an army of aristocratic and bourgeois creditors, and the French monarchy, though absolute in theory, had become too weak for such a drastic and unpopular action.

Nor could the king and his ministers, unlike modern governments, print money and create inflation to cover their deficits. Unlike England and Holland, which had far larger national debts relative to their populations, France had no central bank, no paper currency, and no means of creating credit. French money was good gold coin. Therefore, when a depressed economy and a lack of public confidence made it increasingly difficult for the government to obtain new gold loans in 1786, it had no alternative but to try increasing taxes. And since France's tax system was unfair and out-of-date, increased revenues were possible only through fundamental reforms. Such reforms, which would affect all groups in France's complex and fragmented society, opened a Pandora's box of social and political demands. Thus historians have usually looked to social forces and social relationships in their efforts to understand the Revolution, as we shall now see.

## Legal Orders and Social Realities

As in the Middle Ages, France's 25 million inhabitants were still legally divided into three orders, or **estates**—the clergy, the nobility, and everyone else. As the nation's first estate, the clergy numbered about 100,000 and had important privileges. It owned about 10 percent of the land and paid only a "voluntary gift," rather than regular taxes, to the government every five years. Moreover, the church levied a tax (the tithe) on landowners, which averaged somewhat less than 10 percent. Much of the church's income was actually drained away from local parishes by political appointees and worldly aristocrats at the top of the church hierarchy—to the intense dissatisfaction of the poor parish priests.

The second legally defined estate consisted of some 400,000 noblemen and noblewomen—the descendants of "those who fought" in the Middle Ages. The nobles owned outright about 25 percent of the land in France, and they, too, were taxed very lightly. Moreover, nobles continued to enjoy certain **manorial rights,** or privileges of lordship, that dated back to medieval times and allowed them to tax the peasantry for their own profit. This was done by means of exclusive rights to hunt and fish, village monopolies on baking bread and pressing grapes for wine, fees for justice, and a host of other "useful privileges." In addition, nobles had "honorific privileges," such as the right to precedence on public occasions and the right to wear a sword. These rights conspicuously proclaimed the nobility's legal superiority and exalted social position.

Everyone else was a commoner, legally a member of the third estate. A few commoners—prosperous merchants or lawyers and officials—were well educated and rich, and might even buy up manorial rights as profitable investments. Many more commoners were urban artisans and unskilled day laborers. The vast majority of the third estate consisted of the peasants and agricultural workers in the countryside. Thus the third estate was a conglomeration of vastly different social groups united only by their shared legal status as distinct from the nobility and clergy.

In discussing the long-term origins of the French Revolution, historians have long focused on growing tensions between the nobility and the comfortable members of the third estate, usually known as the *bourgeoisie,* or middle class. A dominant historical interpretation, which held sway for at least two generations, maintained that the bourgeoisie was basically united by economic position and class interest. Aided by the general economic expansion discussed in Chapter 19, the middle class grew rapidly in the eighteenth century, tripling to about 2.3 million persons, or about 8 percent of France's population. Increasing in size, wealth, culture, and self-confidence, this rising bourgeoisie became progressively exasperated by archaic "feudal" laws restraining the economy and by the pretensions of a reactionary nobility, which was closing ranks against middle-class needs and aspirations. As a result, the French bourgeoisie eventually rose up to lead the entire third estate in a great social revolution, a revolution that destroyed feudal privileges and established a capitalist order based on individualism and a market economy.

In recent years, a flood of new research has challenged these accepted views. Above all, revisionist historians have questioned the existence of a growing social conflict between a progressive capitalistic bourgeoisie and a reactionary feudal nobility in eighteenth-century France. Instead, these historians see both bourgeoisie and nobility as highly fragmented, riddled with internal rivalries. The great nobility, for example, was profoundly separated from the lesser nobility by differences in wealth, education, and world-view. Differences within the bourgeoisie—between wealthy financiers and local lawyers, for example—were no less profound. Rather than standing as unified blocs against each other, nobility and bourgeoisie formed two parallel social ladders increasingly linked together at the top by wealth, marriage, and Enlightenment culture.

Revisionist historians stress three developments in particular. First, the nobility remained a fluid and relatively open order. Throughout the eighteenth century, substantial numbers of successful commoners continued to seek and obtain noble status through government service and purchase of expensive positions conferring nobility. Second, key sections of the nobility were no less liberal than the middle class, and until revolution actually began, both groups generally supported the judicial opposition to the government led by the Parlement of Paris. Third, the nobility and the bourgeoisie were not really at odds in the economic sphere. Both looked to investment in land and government service as their preferred activities, and the ideal of the merchant capitalist was to gain enough wealth to retire from trade, purchase estates, and live nobly as a large landowner. At the same time, wealthy nobles often acted as aggressive capitalists, investing especially in mining, metallurgy, and foreign trade.

The revisionists have clearly shaken the belief that the bourgeoisie and the nobility were inevitably locked in growing conflict before the Revolution. But in stressing the similarities between the two groups, especially at the top, revisionists have also reinforced the view, long maintained by historians, that the Old Regime had ceased to correspond with social reality by the 1780s. Legally, society was still based on rigid orders inherited from the Middle Ages. In reality, France had already moved far toward being a society based on wealth and education, where an emerging elite that included both aristocratic and bourgeois notables was frustrated by a bureaucratic monarchy that continued to claim the right to absolute power.

## The Formation of the National Assembly

The Revolution was under way by 1787, though no one could have realized what was to follow. Spurred by a depressed economy and falling tax receipts, Louis XVI's minister of finance revived old proposals to impose a general tax on all landed property as well as to form provincial assemblies to help administer the tax, and he convinced the king to call an assembly of notables to gain support for the idea. The assembled notables, who were mainly important noblemen and high-ranking clergy, were not in favor of it. In return for their support, they demanded that control over all government spending be given to the provincial assemblies. When the government refused, the notables responded that such sweeping tax changes required the approval of the Estates General, the representative body of all three estates, which had not met since 1614.

Facing imminent bankruptcy, the king tried to reassert his authority. He dismissed the notables and established new taxes by decree. In stirring language, the judges of the Parlement of Paris promptly declared the royal initiative null and void. When the king tried to exile the judges, a tremendous wave of protest swept the country. Frightened investors also refused to advance more loans to the state. Finally in July 1788, a beaten Louis XVI bowed to public opinion and called for a spring session of the Estates General. Absolute monarchy was collapsing.

What would replace it? Throughout the unprecedented election campaign of 1788 and 1789, that question excited France. All across the country, clergy, nobles, and commoners came together in their respective orders to draft petitions for change and to elect their respective delegates to the Estates General. The local assemblies of the clergy showed considerable dissatisfaction with the church hierarchy. The nobles were politically divided. A conservative majority was drawn from the poorer and more numerous provincial nobility, but fully one-third of the nobility's representatives were liberals committed to major changes.

As for the third estate, there was great popular participation in the elections. Almost all male commoners twenty-five years of age or older had the right to vote. However, voting required two stages, which meant that most of the representatives finally selected by the third estate were well-educated, prosperous members of the middle class. Most of them were not businessmen but lawyers and government officials. Social status and prestige were matters of particular concern to this economic elite. There were no delegates elected from the great mass of laboring poor—the peasants and urban artisans.

The petitions for change coming from the three estates showed a surprising degree of consensus on most issues. There was general agreement that royal absolutism should give way to constitutional monarchy, in which laws and taxes would require the consent of the Estates General meeting regularly. All agreed that individual liberties would have to be guaranteed by law, that the economic position of the parish clergy would have to be improved, and that economic development required reforms. The striking similarities in the grievance petitions of the clergy, nobility, and third estate reflected the broad commitment of France's educated elite to liberalism.

Yet an increasingly bitter quarrel undermined this consensus during the intense electoral campaign: *how* would the Estates General vote, and precisely *who* would lead in the political reorganization that was generally desired? The Estates General of 1614 had sat as three separate houses. Any action had required the agreement of at least two branches, a requirement that had virtually guaranteed control by the nobility and the clergy. Immediately after the victory over the king, the aristocratic Parlement of Paris, mainly out of respect for tradition but partly out of a desire to enhance the nobility's political position, ruled that the Estates General should once again sit separately. The ruling was quickly denounced by some middle-class intellectuals, who demanded instead a single assembly dominated by the third estate to ensure fundamental reforms. Reflecting increased political competition and a growing hostility toward aristocratic aspirations, the abbé Emmanuel Joseph Sieyès argued in 1789 in his famous pamphlet *What Is the Third Estate?* that the nobility was a tiny, overprivileged minority and that the neglected third estate constituted the true strength of the French nation. When the government agreed that the third estate should have as many delegates as the clergy and the nobility combined, but then rendered this act meaningless by upholding voting by separate order, middle-class leaders saw fresh evidence of an aristocratic conspiracy.

In May 1789, the twelve hundred delegates of the three estates paraded in medieval pageantry through the streets of Versailles to an opening session resplendent with feudal magnificence. The estates were almost immediately deadlocked. Delegates of the third estate refused to transact any business until the king ordered the clergy and nobility to sit with them in a single body. Finally, after a six-week war of nerves, a few parish priests began to go over to the third estate, which on June 17 voted to call itself the "National Assembly." On June 20, the delegates of the third estate, excluded from their hall because of "repairs," moved to a large indoor tennis court. There they swore the famous Oath of the Tennis Court, pledging not to disband until they had written a new constitution.

The king's actions were then somewhat contradictory. On June 23, he made a conciliatory speech urging reforms to a joint session, and four days later he ordered the three estates to meet together. At the same time, the vacillating and indecisive monarch apparently followed the advice of relatives and court nobles, who urged him to dissolve the Estates General by force. The king called an army of eighteen thousand troops toward Versailles, and on July 11 he dismissed his finance minister and his other more liberal ministers. Faced with growing opposition since 1787, Louis XVI had resigned himself to bankruptcy. Now he belatedly sought to reassert his historic "divine right" to rule. The middle-class delegates and their allies from the liberal nobility had done their best, but they were resigned to being disbanded at bayonet point. One third-estate delegate reassured a worried colleague, "You won't hang—you'll only have to go back home."[2]

## The Revolt of the Poor and the Oppressed

While the educated delegates of the third estate pressed for symbolic equality with the nobility and clergy in a single legislative body at Versailles, economic hardship gripped the common people of France in a tightening vise. Grain

**The Oath of the Tennis Court** This painting, based on an unfinished work by Jacques-Louis David (1748–1825), enthusiastically celebrates the revolutionary rupture of June 20, 1789. Locked out of their assembly hall at Versailles and joined by some sympathetic priests, the delegates of the third estate have moved to an indoor tennis court and are swearing never to disband until they have written a new constitution and put France on a firm foundation. *(Réunion des Musées Nationaux/Art Resource, NY)*

was the basis of the diet of ordinary people in the eighteenth century, and in 1788 the harvest had been extremely poor. The price of bread began to soar. In Paris, where bread was regularly subsidized by the government in an attempt to prevent popular unrest, the price rose to 4 sous. The poor could scarcely afford to pay 2 sous per pound, for even at that price a laborer with a wife and three children had to spend half of his wages to buy the family's bread.

Harvest failure and high bread prices unleashed a classic economic depression of the preindustrial age. With food so expensive and with so much uncertainty, the demand for manufactured goods collapsed. Thousands of artisans and small traders were thrown out of work. By the end of 1789, almost half of the French people would be in need of relief. One person in eight was a pauper living in extreme want. In Paris perhaps 150,000 of the city's 600,000 people were without work in July 1789.

Against this background of poverty and ongoing political crisis, the people of Paris entered decisively onto the revolutionary stage. They believed in a general, though ill-defined, way that the economic distress had human causes. They believed that they should have steady work and enough bread at fair prices to survive. Specifically, they feared that the dismissal of the king's moderate finance minister would put them at the mercy of aristocratic landowners and grain speculators. Rumors that the king's troops would sack the city began to fill the air.

**The Surrender of the Bastille** In this contemporary painting the governor of the medieval fort, long since converted into a prison, is led out under arrest by the French Guards and armed citizens who had stormed the fortress. The crowd soon slaughtered the governor and his officers. Parisians celebrated wildly the taking of the Bastille, and they immediately started to demolish this grim symbol of oppression and royal despotism. July 14—Bastille Day—is France's most important national holiday. *(The Bridgeman Art Library)*

Angry crowds formed, and passionate voices urged action. On July 13, the people began to seize arms for the defense of the city as the king's armies moved toward Paris, and on July 14 several hundred people marched to the Bastille to search for weapons and gunpowder.

A medieval fortress with walls ten feet thick and eight great towers each one hundred feet high, the Bastille had long been used as a prison. It was guarded by eighty retired soldiers and thirty Swiss mercenaries. The governor of the fortress-prison refused to hand over the powder, panicked, and ordered his men to fire, killing ninety-eight people attempting to enter. Cannon were brought to batter the main gate, and fighting continued until the prison surrendered. The governor of the prison was later hacked to death, and his head was stuck on a pike and paraded through the streets. The next day a committee of citizens appointed the marquis de Lafayette commander of the city's armed forces. Paris was lost to the king, who was forced to recall the finance minister and disperse his troops. The popular uprising had broken the power monopoly of the royal army and thereby saved the National Assembly.

As the delegates resumed their long-winded and inconclusive debates at Versailles, the countryside sent them a radical and unmistakable message. Throughout France, peasants began to rise in spontaneous, violent, and effective insurrection against their lords, ransacking manor houses and burning feudal documents that recorded the peasants' obligations. Neither middle-class landowners, who often owned manors and village monopolies, nor the larger, more prosperous farmers were spared. In some areas, peasants reinstated traditional village practices, undoing recent enclosures and reoccupying old common lands. Peasants seized forests, and taxes went unpaid. Fear of vagabonds and outlaws—called the **Great Fear** by contemporaries—seized the countryside and fanned the flames of rebellion. The long-suffering peasants were doing their best to free themselves from manorial rights and exploitation.

Faced with chaos, yet afraid to call on the king to restore order, some liberal nobles and middle-class delegates at Versailles responded to peasant demands with a surprise maneuver on the night of August 4, 1789. The duke of Aiguillon, also notably one of France's greatest noble landowners, declared that

*in several provinces the whole people forms a kind of league for the destruction of the manor houses, the ravaging of the lands, and especially for the seizure of the archives where the title deeds to feudal properties are kept. It seeks to throw off at last a yoke that has for many centuries weighted it down.*[3]

He urged equality in taxation and the elimination of feudal dues. In the end, all the old exactions imposed on the peasants—serfdom where it still existed, exclusive hunting rights for nobles, fees for justice, village monopolies, the right to make peasants work on the roads, and a host of other dues—were abolished, generally without compensation. Though a clarifying law passed a week later was less generous, the peasants ignored the "fine print." They never paid feudal dues again. Thus the French peasantry, which already owned about 30 percent of all the land, achieved an unprecedented victory in the early days of revolutionary upheaval. Henceforth, the French peasants would seek mainly to protect and consolidate their revolutionary triumph. As the Great Fear subsided in the countryside, they became a force for order and stability.

## A Limited Monarchy

The National Assembly moved forward. On August 27, 1789, it issued the Declaration of the Rights of Man, which stated, "Men are born and remain free and equal in rights." The declaration also maintained that mankind's natural rights are "liberty, property, security, and resistance to oppression" and that "every man is presumed innocent until he is proven guilty." As for law, "it is an expression of the general will; all citizens have the right to concur personally or through their representatives in its formation. . . . Free expression of thoughts and opinions is one of the most precious rights of mankind: every citizen may therefore speak, write, and publish freely." In short, this clarion call of the liberal revolutionary ideal guaranteed equality before the law, representative government for a sovereign people, and individual freedom. This revolutionary credo, only two pages long, was propagandized throughout France and Europe and around the world.

Moving beyond general principles to draft a constitution proved difficult. The questions of how much power the king should retain and whether he could permanently veto legislation led to another deadlock. Once again the decisive answer came from the poor—in this instance, the poor women of Paris.

Women customarily bought the food and managed the poor family's slender resources. In Paris great numbers of women also worked for wages, often within the putting-out system, making garments and luxury items destined for an aristocratic and international clientele. Immediately after the fall of the Bastille, many of France's great court nobles began to leave Versailles for foreign lands, so that a plummeting demand for luxuries intensified the general economic crisis; international markets also declined. The church was no longer able to give its traditional grants of food and money to the poor. Increasing unemployment and hunger put tremendous pressure on household managers, and the result was another popular explosion.

On October 5 some seven thousand desperate women marched the twelve miles from Paris to Versailles to demand action. A middle-class deputy looking out from the Assembly saw "multitudes arriving from Paris including fishwives and bullies from the market, and these people wanted nothing but bread." This great crowd invaded the Assembly, "armed with scythes, sticks and pikes." One tough old woman directing a large group of younger women defiantly shouted into the debate, "Who's that talking down there? Make the chatterbox shut up. That's not the point: the point is that we want bread."[4] Hers was the genuine voice of the people, essential to any understanding of the French Revolution.

The women invaded the royal apartments, slaughtered some of the royal bodyguards, and furiously searched for the queen, Marie Antoinette, who was widely despised for her frivolous and supposedly immoral behavior. "We are going to cut off her head, tear out her heart, fry her liver, and that won't be the end of it," they shouted, surging through the palace in a frenzy. It seems likely that only the intervention of Lafayette and the National Guard saved the royal family. But the only way to calm the disorder was for the king to go and live in Paris, as the crowd demanded.

The next day, the king, the queen, and their son left for Paris in the midst of a strange procession. The heads of two aristocrats, stuck on pikes, led the way. They were followed by the remaining members of the royal bodyguard, unarmed and mocked by fierce men holding sabers and pikes. A mixed and victorious multitude surrounded the carriage of the captured royal family, hurling crude insults at the queen. There was drinking and eating among the women, who had clearly emerged as a major element in the Parisian revolutionary crowd.[5]

The National Assembly followed the king to Paris, and the next two years, until September 1791, saw the consolidation of the liberal revolution. Under middle-class leadership, the National Assembly abolished the French nobility as a legal order and pushed forward with the creation of a **constitutional monarchy,** which Louis XVI reluctantly agreed to accept in July 1790. In the final constitution, the king remained the head of state, but all lawmaking power was placed in the hands of the National Assembly, elected by the economic upper half of French males.

New laws broadened women's rights to seek divorce, to inherit property, and to obtain financial support from fathers for illegitimate children. But women were not allowed to vote or hold political office for at least two reasons. First, the great majority of comfortable, well-educated males in the National Assembly believed that women should be limited to child rearing and domestic duties and should leave politics and most public activities to men, as Rousseau had advocated in his influential *Emile* (see pages 686–687). Second, the delegates to the National Assembly were convinced that political life in absolutist France had been profoundly corrupt and that a prime example of this corruption was the way that some talented but immoral aristocratic women had used their sexual charms to manipulate weak rulers and their ministers. Thus delegates argued that excluding women from politics would help create the civic virtue that had been missing: pure, home-focused wives would raise the high-minded sons needed to govern the nation.

The National Assembly replaced the complicated patchwork of historic provinces with eighty-three departments of approximately equal size. The jumble of weights and measures that varied from province to province was reformed, leading to the introduction of the simple, uniform metric system in 1793. The National Assembly promoted the liberal concept of economic freedom. Monopolies, guilds, and workers combinations were prohibited, and barriers to trade within France were abolished in the name of economic liberty. Thus the National Assembly applied the critical spirit of the Enlightenment to reform France's laws and institutions completely.

The Assembly also imposed a radical reorganization on the country's religious life. It granted religious freedom to the tiny minority of French Jews and Protestants. Of greater impact, it then nationalized the Catholic church's property and abolished monasteries as useless relics of a distant past. The government used all former church property as collateral to guarantee a new paper currency, the *assignats,* and then sold these properties in an attempt to put the state's finances on a solid footing. Although the church's land was sold in large blocks, peasants eventually purchased much when it was subdivided. These purchases strengthened their attachment to the new revolutionary order in the countryside.

The religious reorganization of France brought the new government into conflict with the Catholic church and many sincere Christians, especially in the countryside. Many delegates to the National Assembly, imbued with the rationalism and skepticism of the eighteenth-century philosophes, harbored a deep distrust of popular piety and "superstitious religion." Thus they established a national church, with priests chosen by voters. In the face of widespread resistance, the National Assembly then required the Catholic clergy to take a loyalty oath to the new government and become just so many more employees of the state. The pope formally condemned this attempt to subjugate the church, and only half the priests of France took the oath of allegiance. The result was a deep division within both the country and the clergy on the religious question; confusion and hostility among French Catholics were pervasive. The attempt to remake the Catholic church, like the Assembly's abolition of guilds and workers combinations, sharpened the conflict between the educated classes and the common people that had been emerging in the eighteenth century. This policy toward the church was the revolutionary government's first important failure.

## World War and Republican France, 1791–1799

See DBQ 7

When Louis XVI accepted the final version of the completed constitution in September 1791, a young and still obscure provincial lawyer and member of the National Assembly named Maximilien Robespierre (1758–1794) evaluated the work of two years and concluded, "The Revolution is over." Robespierre was both right and wrong. He was right in the sense that the most constructive and lasting reforms were in place. Nothing substantial in the way of liberty and useful reform would be gained in the next generation. He was wrong in the sense that a much more radical stage lay ahead. New heroes and new ideologies were to emerge in revolutionary wars and international conflict.

## Foreign Reactions and the Beginning of War

The outbreak and progress of revolution in France produced great excitement and a sharp division of opinion in Europe and the United States. Liberals and radicals saw a mighty triumph of liberty over despotism. In Great Britain especially, they hoped that the French example would lead to a fundamental reordering of Parliament, which was in the hands of the aristocracy and a few wealthy merchants. After the French Revolution began, conservative leaders such as Edmund Burke (1729–1797) were deeply troubled by the aroused spirit of reform. In 1790 Burke published *Reflections on the Revolution in France,* one of the great intellectual defenses of European conservatism. He defended inherited privileges in general and those of the English monarchy and aristocracy. He glorified the unrepresentative Parliament and predicted that thoroughgoing reform like that occurring in France would lead only to chaos and tyranny. Burke's work sparked much debate.

One passionate rebuttal came from a young writer in London, Mary Wollstonecraft (1759–1797). Born into the middle class, Wollstonecraft was schooled in adversity by a mean-spirited father who beat his wife and squandered his inherited fortune. Determined to be independent in a society that generally expected women of her class to become homebodies and obedient wives, she struggled for years to earn her living as a governess and teacher—practically the only acceptable careers for single, educated women—before attaining success as a translator and author. Incensed by Burke's book, Wollstonecraft immediately wrote a blistering, widely read attack, *A Vindication of the Rights of Man* (1790).

Then she made a daring intellectual leap. She developed for the first time the logical implications of natural-law philosophy in her masterpiece, *A Vindication of the Rights of Woman* (1792). To fulfill the still-unrealized potential of the French Revolution and to eliminate the sexual inequality she had felt so keenly, she demanded that

*the Rights of Women be respected . . . [and] JUSTICE for one-half of the human race. . . . It is time to effect a revolution in female manners, time to restore to them their lost dignity, and make them, as part of the human species, labor, by reforming themselves, to reform the world.*

Setting high standards for women—"I wish to persuade women to endeavor to acquire strength, both of mind and body"—Wollstonecraft broke with those who had a low opinion of women's intellectual potential. She advocated rigorous coeducation, which would make women better wives and mothers, good citizens, and even economically independent people. Women could manage businesses and enter politics if only men would give them the chance. Men themselves would benefit from women's rights, for Wollstonecraft believed that "the two sexes mutually corrupt and improve each other."[6] Wollstonecraft's analysis testified to the power of the Revolution to excite and inspire outside of France. Paralleling ideas put forth independently in France by Olympe de Gouges (1748–1793), a self-taught writer and woman of the people (see the feature "Listening to the Past: Revolution and Women's Rights" on pages 722–723), Wollstonecraft's work marked the birth of the modern women's movement for equal rights, and it was ultimately very influential.

The kings and nobles of continental Europe, who had at first welcomed the revolution in France as weakening a competing power, began to feel no less threatened than Burke and his supporters. When Louis XVI and Marie Antoinette were arrested and returned to Paris after trying unsuccessfully to slip out of France in June 1791, the monarchs of Austria and Prussia issued the Declaration of Pillnitz. This carefully worded statement declared their willingness to intervene in France in certain circumstances and was expected to have a sobering effect on revolutionary France without causing war.

But the crowned heads of Europe misjudged the revolutionary spirit in France. When the National Assembly disbanded, it sought popular support by decreeing that none of its members would be eligible for election to the new Legislative Assembly. This meant that when the new representative body convened in October 1791, it had a different character. The great majority of the legislators were still prosperous, well-educated, middle-class men, but they were younger and less cautious than their predecessors. Many of the deputies were loosely allied and called **Jacobins,** after the name of their political club.

The new representatives to the Assembly were passionately committed to liberal revolution and distrustful of monarchy after Louis's attempted flight. They increasingly lumped "useless aristocrats" and "despotic monarchs" together, and they easily whipped themselves into a patriotic

**The Capture of Louis XVI, June 1791** This painting commemorates a dramatic turning point in the French Revolution, the midnight arrest of Louis XVI and the royal family as they tried to flee France in disguise and reach counter-revolutionaries in the Austrian Netherlands. Recognized and stopped at Varennes, just 40 miles from the border, the king still nearly succeeded, telling municipal officers that dangerous mobs controlled Paris and securing promises of safe passage. But within hours the local leaders reversed themselves and by morning Louis XVI was headed back to Paris. *(Bibliothèque nationale de France)*

fury with bombastic oratory. If the courts of Europe were attempting to incite a war of kings against France, then "we will incite a war of people against kings. . . . Ten million Frenchmen, kindled by the fire of liberty, armed with the sword, with reason, with eloquence would be able to change the face of the world and make the tyrants tremble on their thrones."[7] Only Robespierre and a very few others argued that people would not welcome liberation at the point of a gun. Such warnings were brushed aside. France would "rise to the full height of her mission," as one deputy urged. In April 1792, France declared war on Francis II, the Habsburg monarch.

France's crusade against tyranny went poorly at first. Prussia joined Austria in the Austrian Netherlands (present-day Belgium), and French forces broke and fled at their first encounter with armies of this First Coalition. The road to Paris lay open, and it is possible that only conflict between the eastern monarchs over the division of Poland saved France from defeat.

Military reversals and patriotic fervor led the Legislative Assembly to declare the country in danger. Volunteer armies from the provinces streamed through Paris, fraternizing with the people and singing patriotic songs like the stirring "Marseillaise," later the French national anthem.

In this supercharged wartime atmosphere, rumors of treason by the king and queen spread in Paris. On August 10, 1792, a revolutionary crowd attacked the royal palace at the Tuileries, capturing it after heavy fighting with the Swiss Guards. The king and his family fled for their lives to the nearby Legislative Assembly, which suspended the king from all his functions, imprisoned him, and called for a new National Convention to be elected by universal male suffrage. Monarchy in France was on its deathbed, mortally wounded by war and popular upheaval.

## The Second Revolution

The fall of the monarchy marked a rapid radicalization of the Revolution, a phase that historians often call the **second revolution.** Louis's imprisonment was followed by the September Massacres. Wild stories seized the city that imprisoned counter-revolutionary aristocrats and priests were plotting with the allied invaders. As a result, angry crowds invaded the prisons of Paris and summarily slaughtered half the men and women they found. In late September 1792, the new, popularly elected National Convention proclaimed France a republic.

The republic sought to create a new popular culture, fashioning compelling symbols that broke with the past and glorified the new order. It adopted a brand-new revolutionary calendar, which eliminated saints' days and renamed the days and the months after the seasons of the year. Citizens were expected to address each other with the friendly "thou" of the people rather than with the formal "you" of the rich and powerful. The republic energetically promoted broad, open-air, democratic festivals. These spectacles brought the entire population together and sought to redirect the people's traditional enthusiasm for Catholic religious celebrations to secular holidays instilling republican virtue and a love of nation. These spectacles were less successful in villages than in cities, where popular interest in politics was greater and Catholicism was weaker.

All of the members of the National Convention were republicans, and at the beginning almost all belonged to the Jacobin club of Paris. But control of the Convention was increasingly contested by two bitterly competitive groups—the **Girondists,** named after a department in southwestern France, and **the Mountain,** led by Robespierre and another young lawyer, Georges Jacques Danton. The Mountain was so called because its members sat on the uppermost left-hand benches of the assembly hall. A majority of the indecisive Convention members, seated in the "Plain" below, floated back and forth between the rival factions.

This division was clearly apparent after the National Convention overwhelmingly convicted Louis XVI of treason. By a narrow majority, the Convention then sentenced him to death in January 1793. Louis died with tranquil dignity on the newly invented guillotine. One of his last statements was "I am innocent and shall die without fear. I would that my death might bring happiness to the French, and ward off the dangers which I foresee."[8]

Both the Girondists and the Mountain were determined to continue the "war against tyranny." The Prussians had been stopped at the Battle of Valmy on September 20, 1792, one day before the republic was proclaimed. French armies then invaded Savoy and captured Nice, moved into the German Rhineland, and by November 1792 were occupying the entire Austrian Netherlands. Everywhere they went, French armies of occupation chased the princes, "abolished feudalism," and found support among some peasants and middle-class people.

But the French armies also lived off the land, requisitioning food and supplies and plundering local treasures. The liberators looked increasingly like foreign invaders. International tensions mounted. In February 1793, the National Convention, at war with Austria and Prussia, declared war on Britain, Holland, and Spain as well. Republican France was now at war with almost all of Europe, a great war that would last almost without interruption until 1815.

As the forces of the First Coalition drove the French from the Austrian Netherlands, peasants in western France revolted against being drafted into the army. They were supported and encouraged in their resistance by devout Catholics, royalists, and foreign agents.

In Paris the quarrelsome National Convention found itself locked in a life-and-death political struggle between the Girondists and the Mountain. Both groups were sincere republicans, hating privilege and wanting to temper economic liberalism with social concern. Yet personal hatreds ran deep. The Girondists feared a bloody dictatorship by the Mountain, and the Mountain was no less convinced that the more moderate Girondists would turn to conservatives and even royalists in order to retain power. With the middle-class delegates so bitterly divided, the laboring poor of Paris emerged as the decisive political factor.

The laboring men and women of Paris always constituted—along with the peasantry in the summer of 1789—the elemental force that drove the Revolution forward. It was the artisans, day laborers, market women, and garment workers who had stormed the Bastille, marched on Versailles, driven the king from the Tuileries, and carried out the September Massacres. The laboring poor and the petty traders were often known as the **sans-culottes,** "without breeches," because sans-culottes men wore trousers instead of the knee breeches of the aristocracy and the solid middle class. The immediate interests of the sans-culottes were mainly economic, and in the spring of 1793 rapid inflation, unemployment, and food shortages were again weighing heavily on poor families.

Moreover, by the spring of 1793, the sans-culottes had become keenly interested in politics. Encouraged by the so-called angry men, such as the passionate young expriest and journalist Jacques Roux, sans-culottes men and women were demanding radical political action to guarantee them their daily bread. At first the Mountain joined the Girondists in rejecting these demands. But in the face of military defeat, peasant revolt, and hatred of the Girondists, the Mountain and especially Robespierre became more sympathetic. The Mountain joined with sans-culottes activists in the city government to engineer a popular uprising, which forced the Convention to arrest thirty-one Girondist deputies for treason on June 2. All power passed to the Mountain.

Robespierre and others from the Mountain joined the recently formed Committee of Public Safety, to which the Convention had given dictatorial power to deal with the national emergency. These developments in Paris triggered revolt in leading provincial cities, such as Lyons and Marseilles, where moderates denounced Paris and demanded a decentralized government. The peasant revolt spread, and the republic's armies were driven back on all fronts. By July 1793, only the areas around Paris

**Contrasting Visions of the Sans-Culottes** The woman on the left, with her playful cat and calm simplicity, suggests how the French sans-culottes saw themselves as democrats and virtuous citizens. The ferocious sans-culotte harpy on the right, a creation of wartime England's vivid counter-revolutionary imagination, screams for more blood, more death: "I am the Goddess of Liberty! Long live the guillotine!" *(Bibliothèque nationale de France)*

and on the eastern frontier were firmly held by the central government. Defeat seemed imminent.

## Total War and the Terror

A year later, in July 1794, the Austrian Netherlands and the Rhineland were once again in the hands of conquering French armies, and the First Coalition was falling apart. This remarkable change of fortune was due to the revolutionary government's success in harnessing, for perhaps the first time in history, the explosive forces of a planned economy, revolutionary terror, and modern nationalism in a total war effort.

Robespierre and the Committee of Public Safety advanced with implacable resolution on several fronts in 1793 and 1794. First, they collaborated with the fiercely patriotic and democratic sans-culottes, who retained the common people's traditional faith in fair prices and a moral economic order and who distrusted most wealthy capitalists and all aristocrats. Thus Robespierre and his coworkers established, as best they could, a **planned economy** with egalitarian social overtones. Rather than let supply and demand determine prices, the government set maximum allowable prices for key products. Though the state was too weak to enforce all its price regulations, it did fix the price of bread in Paris at levels the poor could afford. Rationing was introduced, and bakers were permitted to make only the "bread of equality"—a brown bread made of a mixture of all available flours. White bread and pastries were outlawed as luxuries. The poor of Paris may not have eaten well, but at least they ate.

They also worked, mainly to produce arms and munitions for the war effort. The government told craftsmen what to produce, nationalized many small workshops, and requisitioned raw materials and grain from the peasants. Sometimes planning and control did not go beyond

## The French Revolution

| | |
|---|---|
| **May 5, 1789** | Estates General convene at Versailles. |
| **June 17, 1789** | Third estate declares itself the National Assembly. |
| **June 20, 1789** | Oath of the Tennis Court is sworn. |
| **July 14, 1789** | Storming of the Bastille occurs. |
| **July–August 1789** | Great Fear ravages the countryside. |
| **August 4, 1789** | National Assembly abolishes feudal privileges. |
| **August 27, 1789** | National Assembly issues Declaration of the Rights of Man. |
| **October 5, 1789** | Women march on Versailles and force royal family to return to Paris. |
| **November 1789** | National Assembly confiscates church lands. |
| **July 1790** | Civil Constitution of the Clergy establishes a national church.<br>Louis XVI reluctantly agrees to accept a constitutional monarchy. |
| **June 1791** | Royal family is arrested while attempting to flee France. |
| **August 1791** | Austria and Prussia issue the Declaration of Pillnitz. |
| **April 1792** | France declares war on Austria. |
| **August 1792** | Parisian mob attacks the palace and takes Louis XVI prisoner. |
| **September 1792** | September Massacres occur.<br>National Convention declares France a republic and abolishes monarchy. |
| **January 1793** | Louis XVI is executed. |
| **February 1793** | France declares war on Britain, Holland, and Spain.<br>Revolts take place in some provincial cities. |
| **March 1793** | Bitter struggle occurs in the National Convention between Girondists and the Mountain. |
| **April–June 1793** | Robespierre and the Mountain organize the Committee of Public Safety and arrest Girondist leaders. |
| **September 1793** | Price controls are instituted to aid the sans-culottes and mobilize the war effort. |
| **1793–1794** | Reign of Terror darkens Paris and the provinces. |
| **Spring 1794** | French armies are victorious on all fronts. |
| **July 1794** | Robespierre is executed.<br>Thermidorian reaction begins. |
| **1795–1799** | Directory rules. |
| **1795** | Economic controls are abolished, and suppression of the sans-culottes begins. |
| **1797** | Napoleon defeats Austrian armies in Italy and returns triumphant to Paris. |
| **1798** | Austria, Great Britain, and Russia form the Second Coalition against France. |
| **1799** | Napoleon overthrows the Directory and seizes power. |

**The Last Roll Call** Prisoners sentenced to death by revolutionary courts listen to an official solemnly reading the names of those selected for immediate execution. After being bound, the prisoners will ride standing up in a small cart through the streets of Paris to the nearby guillotine. As this painting highlights, both women and men were executed for political crimes under the Terror. *(Mansell/Time Pictures/Getty Images)*

orders to meet the latest emergency: "Ten thousand soldiers lack shoes. You will take the shoes of all the aristocrats in Strasbourg and deliver them ready for transport to headquarters at 10 A.M. tomorrow." But failures to control and coordinate were failures of means and not of desire. The second revolution and the ascendancy of the sans-culottes had produced an embryonic emergency socialism, which thoroughly frightened Europe's propertied classes and had great influence on the subsequent development of socialist ideology.

Second, while radical economic measures supplied the poor with bread and the armies with weapons, the **Reign of Terror** (1793–1794) used revolutionary terror to solidify the home front. Special revolutionary courts responsible only to Robespierre's Committee of Public Safety tried rebels and "enemies of the nation" for political crimes. Drawing on popular, sans-culottes support centered in the local Jacobin clubs, these local courts ignored normal legal procedures and judged severely. Some 40,000 French men and women were executed or died in prison. Another 300,000 suspects crowded the prisons and often brushed close to death in a revolutionary court.

Robespierre's Reign of Terror was one of the most controversial phases of the French Revolution. Most historians now believe that the Reign of Terror was not directed against any single class. Rather, it was a political weapon directed impartially against all who might oppose the revolutionary government. For many Europeans of the time, however, the Reign of Terror represented a frightening perversion of the generous ideals of 1789. It strengthened the belief that France had foolishly replaced a weak king with a bloody dictatorship.

The third and perhaps most decisive element in the French republic's victory over the First Coalition was its ability to draw on the explosive power of patriotic dedication to a national state and a national mission. An essential part of modern **nationalism,** this commitment was something new in history. With a common language and a common tradition newly reinforced by the ideas of popular sovereignty and democracy, large numbers of French people were stirred by a common loyalty. They developed an intense emotional commitment to the defense of the nation, and they imagined the nation as a great loving family that included all right-thinking patriots.

In such circumstances, war was no longer the gentlemanly game of the eighteenth century, but rather total war, a life-and-death struggle between good and evil. Everyone had to participate in the national effort. According to a famous decree of August 23, 1793:

*The young men shall go to battle and the married men shall forge arms. The women shall make tents and clothes, and shall serve in the hospitals; children shall tear rags into lint. The old men will be guided to the public places of the cities to kindle the courage of the young warriors and to preach the unity of the Republic and the hatred of kings.*

Like the wars of religion, war in 1793 was a crusade. This war, however, was fought for a secular, rather than a religious, ideology.

The all-out mobilization of French resources under the Terror combined with the fervor of modern nationalism to create an awesome fighting machine. After August 1793, all unmarried young men were subject to the draft, and by January 1794 the French had about 800,000 soldiers on active duty in fourteen armies. A force of this size was unprecedented in the history of European warfare, and recent research concludes that the French armed forces outnumbered their enemies almost four to one.[9] Well trained, well equipped, and constantly indoctrinated, the enormous armies of the republic were led by young, impetuous generals. These generals often had risen from the ranks, and they personified the opportunities the Revolution seemed to offer gifted sons of the people. Following orders from Paris to attack relentlessly, French generals used mass assaults at bayonet point to overwhelm the enemy. "No maneuvering, nothing elaborate," declared the fearless General Hoche. "Just cold steel, passion and patriotism."[10] By the spring of 1794, French armies were victorious on all fronts. The republic was saved.

## The Thermidorian Reaction and the Directory, 1794–1799

The success of the French armies led Robespierre and the Committee of Public Safety to relax the emergency economic controls, but they extended the political Reign of Terror. Their lofty goal was increasingly an ideal democratic republic where justice would reign and there would be neither rich nor poor. Their lowly means were unrestrained despotism and the guillotine, which struck down any who might seriously question the new order. In March 1794, to the horror of many sans-culottes, Robespierre's Terror wiped out many of the angry men who had been criticizing Robespierre for being soft on the wealthy and who were led by the radical social democrat Jacques Hébert. Two weeks later, several of Robespierre's long-standing collaborators, led by the famous orator Danton, marched up the steps to the guillotine. A strange assortment of radicals and moderates in the Convention, knowing that they might be next, organized a conspiracy. They howled down Robespierre when he tried to speak to the National Convention on 9 Thermidor (July 27, 1794). On the following day, it was Robespierre's turn to be shaved by the revolutionary razor.

As Robespierre's closest supporters followed their leader, France unexpectedly experienced a thorough reaction to the despotism of the Reign of Terror. In a general way, this **Thermidorian reaction** recalled the early days of

**The Execution of Robespierre** The guillotine was painted red and completely wooden except for the heavy iron blade. Large crowds witnessed the executions in a majestic public square in central Paris, then known as the Place de la Revolution and now called the Place de la Concorde (Harmony Square). *(Musée Carnavalet/Edimedia)*

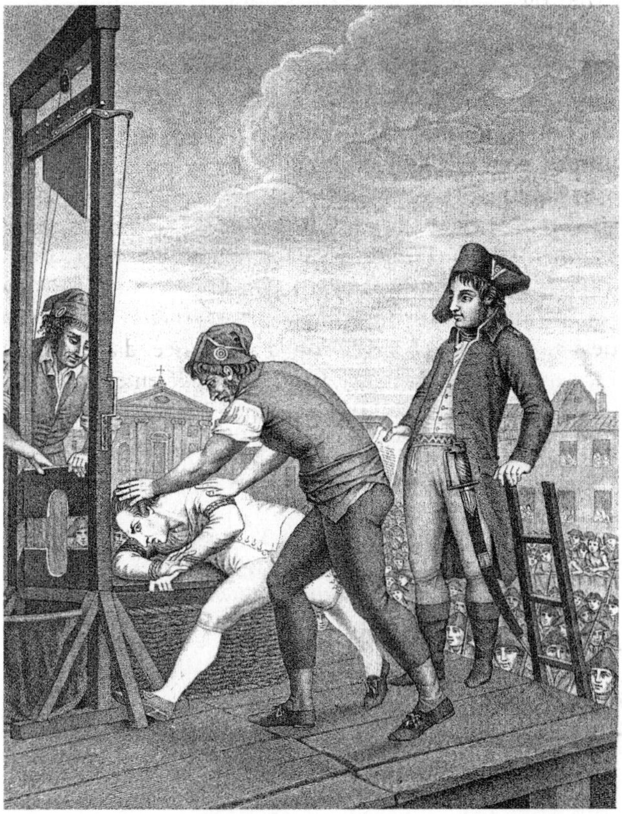

the Revolution. The respectable middle-class lawyers and professionals who had led the liberal revolution of 1789 reasserted their authority, drawing support from their own class, the provincial cities, and the better-off peasants. The National Convention abolished many economic controls, let prices rise sharply, and severely restricted the local political organizations where the sans-culottes had their strength. And all the while, wealthy bankers and newly rich speculators celebrated the sudden end of the Terror with an orgy of self-indulgence and ostentatious luxury, an orgy symbolized by the shockingly low-cut gowns that quickly became the rage among their wives and mistresses.

The collapse of economic controls, coupled with runaway inflation, hit the working poor very hard. The gaudy extravagance of the rich wounded their pride. The sans-culottes accepted private property, but they believed passionately in small business, decent wages, and economic justice. Increasingly disorganized after Robespierre purged radical leaders, the common people of Paris finally revolted against the emerging new order in early 1795. The Convention quickly used the army to suppress these insurrections and made no concessions to the poor. In the face of all these reversals, the revolutionary fervor of the laboring poor in Paris finally subsided. Excluded and disillusioned, the urban poor would have little interest in and influence on politics until 1830.

In villages and small towns there arose a great cry for peace and a turning toward religion, especially from women, who had seldom experienced the political radicalization of sans-culottes women in the big cities. Instead, these women had tenaciously defended their culture and religious beliefs against the often heavy-handed attacks of antireligious revolutionary officials after 1789. As the government began to retreat on the religious question from 1796 to 1801, the women of rural France brought back the Catholic church and the open worship of God. In the words of a leading historian, these women worked for a return to a normal and structured lifestyle:

> *Peacefully but purposefully, they sought to re-establish a pattern of life punctuated by a pealing bell and one in which the rites of passage—birth, marriage, and death—were respected and hallowed. The state had intruded too far and women entered the public arena to push it back and won. It was one of the most resounding political statements made by the populace in the entire history of the Revolution.*[11]

As for the middle-class members of the National Convention, in 1795 they wrote yet another constitution, which they believed would guarantee their economic position and political supremacy. As in previous elections, the mass of the population voted only for electors, whose number was cut back to men of substantial means. Electors then elected the members of a reorganized legislative assembly, as well as key officials throughout France. The new assembly also chose a five-man executive—the Directory.

The Directory continued to support French military expansion abroad. War was no longer so much a crusade as a means to meet ever-present, ever-unsolved economic problems. Large, victorious French armies reduced unemployment at home and were able to live off the territories they conquered and plundered.

The unprincipled action of the Directory reinforced widespread disgust with war and starvation. This general dissatisfaction revealed itself clearly in the national elections of 1797, which returned a large number of conservative and even monarchist deputies who favored peace at almost any price. The members of the Directory, fearing for their skins, used the army to nullify the elections and began to govern dictatorially. Two years later, Napoleon Bonaparte ended the Directory in a *coup d'état* and substituted a strong dictatorship for a weak one. The effort to establish stable representative government had failed.

## The Napoleonic Era, 1799–1815

See DBQ 7

For almost fifteen years, from 1799 to 1814, France was in the hands of a keen-minded military dictator of exceptional ability. One of history's most fascinating leaders, Napoleon Bonaparte (1769–1821) realized the need to put an end to civil strife in France, in order to create unity and consolidate his rule. And he did. But Napoleon saw himself as a man of destiny, and the glory of war and the dream of universal empire proved irresistible. For years he spiraled from victory to victory, but in the end he was destroyed by a mighty coalition united in fear of his restless ambition.

### Napoleon's Rule of France

In 1799 when he seized power, young General Napoleon Bonaparte was a national hero. Born in Corsica into an impoverished noble family in 1769, Napoleon left home and became a lieutenant in the French artillery in 1785. After a brief and unsuccessful adventure fighting for Corsican independence in 1789, he returned to France as a French patriot and a dedicated revolutionary. Rising rapidly in the new army, Napoleon was placed in command of French forces in Italy and won brilliant victories there in 1796 and 1797. His next campaign, in Egypt, was a failure, but Napoleon returned to France before the fiasco was generally known. His reputation remained intact.

## The Napoleonic Era

| | |
|---|---|
| November 1799 | Napoleon overthrows the Directory. |
| December 1799 | French voters overwhelmingly approve Napoleon's new constitution. |
| 1800 | Napoleon founds the Bank of France. |
| 1801 | France defeats Austria and acquires Italian and German territories in the Treaty of Lunéville.<br>Napoleon signs the Concordat with the pope. |
| 1802 | France signs the Treaty of Amiens with Britain. |
| December 1804 | Napoleon crowns himself emperor. |
| October 1805 | Britain defeats the French and Spanish fleet at the Battle of Trafalgar. |
| December 1805 | Napoleon defeats Austria and Russia at the Battle of Austerlitz. |
| 1807 | Napoleon redraws the map of Europe in the treaties of Tilsit. |
| 1810 | The Grand Empire is at its height. |
| June 1812 | Napoleon invades Russia with 600,000 men. |
| Fall–Winter 1812 | Napoleon makes a disastrous retreat from Russia. |
| March 1814 | Russia, Prussia, Austria, and Britain form the Quadruple Alliance to defeat France. |
| April 1814 | Napoleon abdicates and is exiled to Elba. |
| February–June 1815 | Napoleon escapes from Elba and rules France until he is defeated at the Battle of Waterloo. |

Napoleon soon learned that some prominent members of the legislature were plotting against the Directory. The dissatisfaction of these plotters stemmed not so much from the fact that the Directory was a dictatorship as from the fact that it was a weak dictatorship. Ten years of upheaval and uncertainty had made firm rule much more appealing than liberty and popular politics to these disillusioned revolutionaries. The abbé Sieyès personified this evolution in thinking. In 1789 he had written that the nobility was grossly overprivileged and that the entire people should rule the French nation. Now Sieyès's motto was "Confidence from below, authority from above."

Like the other members of his group, Sieyès wanted a strong military ruler. The flamboyant thirty-year-old Napoleon was ideal. Thus the conspirators and Napoleon organized a takeover. On November 9, 1799, they ousted the Directors, and the following day soldiers disbanded the legislature at bayonet point. Napoleon was named first consul of the republic, and a new constitution consolidating his position was overwhelmingly approved in a plebiscite in December 1799. Republican appearances were maintained, but Napoleon was already the real ruler of France.

The essence of Napoleon's domestic policy was to use his great and highly personal powers to maintain order and end civil strife. He did so by working out unwritten agreements with powerful groups in France whereby these groups received favors in return for loyal service. Napoleon's bargain with the solid middle class was codified in the famous Civil Code of 1804, which reasserted two of the fundamental principles of the liberal and essentially moderate revolution of 1789: equality of all male citizens before the law and absolute security of wealth and private property. Napoleon and the leading bankers of Paris established the privately owned Bank of France, which loyally served the interests of both the state and the financial oligarchy. Napoleon's defense of the new economic order also appealed successfully to the peasants, who had gained both land and status from the revolutionary changes. Thus Napoleon reconfirmed the gains of the peasantry and reassured the solid middle class, which had lost a large number of its revolutionary illusions in the face of social upheaval.

At the same time, Napoleon accepted and strengthened the position of the French bureaucracy. Building on the solid foundations that revolutionary governments had inherited from the Old Regime, he perfected a thoroughly centralized state. As recent scholarship shows, Napoleon consolidated his rule by recruiting disillusioned revolutionaries for the network of ministers, prefects, and centrally appointed mayors that depended on him and came to serve him well. Only former revolutionaries who leaned too far to the left or to the right were pushed to the sidelines.[12] Nor were members of the old nobility slighted. In 1800 and again in 1802, Napoleon granted amnesty to 100,000 émigrés on the condition that they return to France and take a loyalty oath. Members of this returning elite soon ably occupied many high posts in the expanding centralized state. Only one thousand die-hard monarchists were exempted and remained abroad. Napoleon also created a new imperial nobility in order to reward his most talented generals and officials.

Napoleon's skill in gaining support from important and potentially hostile groups is illustrated by his treatment of the Catholic church in France. In 1800 the French clergy was still divided into two groups: those who had taken an oath of allegiance to the revolutionary government and those in exile or hiding who had refused to do so. Personally uninterested in religion, Napoleon wanted to heal the religious division so that a united Catholic church in France could serve as a bulwark of order and social peace. After arduous negotiations, Napoleon and Pope Pius VII (1800–1823) signed the Concordat of 1801. The pope gained for French Catholics the precious right to practice their religion freely, but Napoleon gained political power: his government now nominated bishops, paid the clergy, and exerted great influence over the church in France.

The domestic reforms of Napoleon's early years were his greatest achievement. Much of his legal and administrative reorganization has survived in France to this day. More generally, Napoleon's domestic initiatives gave the great majority of French people a welcome sense of stability and national unity.

Order and unity had their price: Napoleon's authoritarian rule. Women, who had often participated in revolutionary politics without having legal equality, lost many of the gains they had made in the 1790s. Under the law of the new Napoleonic Code, women were dependents of either their fathers or their husbands, and they could not make contracts or even have bank accounts in their own names. Indeed, Napoleon and his advisers aimed at re-establishing a **family monarchy,** where the power of the husband and father was as absolute over the wife and the children as that of Napoleon was over his subjects.

Free speech and freedom of the press were continually violated. By 1811 only four newspapers were left, and they were little more than organs of government propaganda. The occasional elections were a farce. Later laws prescribed harsh penalties for political offenses.

These changes in the law were part of the creation of a police state in France. Since Napoleon was usually busy making war, this task was largely left to Joseph Fouché, an unscrupulous opportunist who had earned a reputation for brutality during the Reign of Terror. As minister of police, Fouché organized a ruthlessly efficient spy system, which kept thousands of citizens under continual police surveillance. People suspected of subversive activities were arbitrarily detained, placed under house arrest, or consigned to insane asylums. After 1810 political suspects were held in state prisons, as they had been during the Terror. There were about twenty-five hundred such political prisoners in 1814.

## Napoleon's Wars and Foreign Policy

Napoleon was above all a military man, and a great one. After coming to power in 1799, he sent peace feelers to Austria and Great Britain, the two remaining members of the Second Coalition, which had been formed against France in 1798. When these overtures were rejected, French armies led by Napoleon decisively defeated the Austrians. In the Treaty of Lunéville (1801), Austria accepted the loss of almost all its Italian possessions, and German territory on the west bank of the Rhine was incorporated into France. Once more, as in 1797, the British were alone, and war-weary, like the French.

Still seeking to consolidate his regime domestically, Napoleon concluded the Treaty of Amiens with Great Britain in 1802. France remained in control of Holland, the Austrian Netherlands, the west bank of the Rhine, and most of the Italian peninsula. Napoleon was free to reshape the German states as he wished. The Treaty of Amiens was clearly a diplomatic triumph for Napoleon, and peace with honor and profit increased his popularity at home.

In 1802 Napoleon was secure but unsatisfied. Ever a romantic gambler as well as a brilliant administrator, he

**The Coronation of Napoleon, 1804 (detail)** In this grandiose painting by Jacques-Louis David, Napoleon prepares to crown his beautiful wife, Josephine, in an elaborate ceremony in Notre Dame Cathedral. Napoleon, the ultimate upstart, also crowned himself. Pope Pius VII, seated glumly behind the emperor, is reduced to being a spectator. *(Louvre/Réunion des Musées Nationaux/Art Resource, NY)*

could not contain his power drive. Aggressively redrawing the map of Germany so as to weaken Austria and attract the secondary states of southwestern Germany toward France, Napoleon tried to restrict British trade with all of Europe. Deciding to renew war with Britain in May 1803, Napoleon concentrated his armies in the French ports on the Channel in the fall of 1803 and began making preparations to invade England. Yet Great Britain remained dominant on the seas. When Napoleon tried to bring his Mediterranean fleet around Gibraltar to northern France, a combined French and Spanish fleet was, after a series of mishaps, virtually annihilated by Lord Nelson at the Battle of Trafalgar on October 21, 1805. Invasion of England was henceforth impossible. Renewed fighting had its advantages, however, for the first consul used the wartime atmosphere to have himself proclaimed emperor in late 1804.

Austria, Russia, and Sweden joined with Britain to form the Third Coalition against France shortly before the Battle of Trafalgar. Actions such as Napoleon's assumption of the Italian crown had convinced both Alexander I of Russia and Francis II of Austria that Napoleon was a threat to their interests and to the European balance of power. Yet the Austrians and the Russians were no match for Napoleon, who scored a brilliant victory over them at the Battle of Austerlitz in December 1805. Alexander I decided to pull back, and Austria accepted large territorial losses in return for peace as the Third Coalition collapsed.

Victorious at Austerlitz, Napoleon proceeded to reorganize the German states to his liking. In 1806 he

**MAP 21.1 Napoleonic Europe in 1810** Only Great Britain remained at war with Napoleon at the height of the Grand Empire. Many British goods were smuggled through Helgoland, a tiny but strategic British possession off the German coast.

abolished many of the tiny German states as well as the ancient Holy Roman Empire. Napoleon established by decree the German Confederation of the Rhine, a union of fifteen German states minus Austria, Prussia, and Saxony. Naming himself "protector" of the confederation, Napoleon firmly controlled western Germany.

Napoleon's intervention in German affairs alarmed the Prussians, who mobilized their armies after more than a decade of peace with France. Napoleon attacked and won two more brilliant victories in October 1806 at Jena and Auerstädt, where the Prussians were outnumbered two to one. The war with Prussia, now joined by Russia, continued into the following spring, and after Napoleon's larger armies won another victory, Alexander I of Russia wanted peace.

For several days in June 1807, the young tsar and the French emperor negotiated face to face on a raft anchored in the middle of the Niemen River. All the while, the helpless Frederick William III of Prussia rode back and forth on the shore anxiously awaiting the results. As the German poet Heinrich Heine said later, Napoleon had but to whistle and Prussia would have ceased to exist. In the subsequent treaties of Tilsit, Prussia lost half of its population, while Russia accepted Napoleon's reorganization of western and central Europe and promised to enforce Napoleon's economic blockade against British goods.

Increasingly Napoleon saw himself as the emperor of Europe and not just of France. The so-called Grand Empire he built had three parts. The core, or first part, was an ever-expanding France, which by 1810 included Belgium, Holland, parts of northern Italy, and much German territory on the east bank of the Rhine. Beyond French borders Napoleon established the second part: a number of dependent satellite kingdoms, on the thrones of which he placed (and replaced) the members of his large family. The third part comprised the independent but allied states of Austria, Prussia, and Russia. Both satellites and allies were expected after 1806 to support Napoleon's continental system and cease trade with Britain.

The impact of the Grand Empire on the peoples of Europe was considerable. In the areas incorporated into France and in the satellites (see Map 21.1), Napoleon introduced many French laws, abolishing feudal dues and serfdom where French revolutionary armies had not already done so. Some of the peasants and middle class benefited from these reforms. Yet Napoleon had to put the prosperity and special interests of France first in order to safeguard his power base. Levying heavy taxes in money and men for his armies, Napoleon came to be regarded more as a conquering tyrant than as an enlightened liberator. Thus French rule sparked patriotic upheavals and encouraged the growth of reactive nationalisms, for individuals in different lands learned to identify emotionally with their own embattled national families, as the French had done earlier.

The first great revolt occurred in Spain. In 1808 a coalition of Catholics, monarchists, and patriots rebelled against Napoleon's attempts to make Spain a French satellite with a Bonaparte as its king. French armies occupied Madrid, but the foes of Napoleon fled to the hills and waged uncompromising guerrilla warfare. Spain was a clear warning: resistance to French imperialism was growing.

Yet Napoleon pushed on, determined to hold his complex and far-flung empire together. In 1810, when the Grand Empire was at its height, Britain still remained at war with France, helping the guerrillas in Spain and Portugal. The continental system, organized to exclude British goods from the continent and force that "nation of shopkeepers" to its knees, was a failure. Instead, it was France that suffered from Britain's counter-blockade, which created hard times for French artisans and the middle class. Perhaps looking for a scapegoat, Napoleon turned on Alexander I of Russia, who in 1811 openly repudiated Napoleon's war of prohibitions against British goods.

Napoleon's invasion of Russia began in June 1812 with a force that eventually numbered 600,000, probably the largest force yet assembled in a single army. Only one-third of this Great Army was French, however; nationals of all the satellites and allies were drafted into the operation. (See the feature "Individuals in Society: Jakob Walter, German Draftee with Napoleon.") Originally planning to winter in the Russian city of Smolensk if Alexander did not sue for peace, Napoleon reached Smolensk and recklessly pressed on toward Moscow. The great Battle of Borodino that followed was a draw, and the Russians retreated in good order. Alexander ordered the evacuation of Moscow, which then burned in part, and he refused to negotiate. Finally, after five weeks in the abandoned city, Napoleon ordered a retreat. That retreat was one of the great military disasters in history. The Russian army, the Russian winter, and starvation cut Napoleon's army to pieces. When the frozen remnants staggered into Poland and Prussia in December, 370,000 men had died and another 200,000 had been taken prisoner.[13]

Leaving his troops to their fate, Napoleon raced to Paris to raise yet another army. Possibly he might still have saved his throne if he had been willing to accept a France reduced to its historical size—the proposal offered by Austria's foreign minister, Prince Klemens von Metternich. But Napoleon refused. Austria and Prussia deserted Napoleon and joined Russia and Great Britain in the Fourth Coalition. All across Europe, patriots called for a "war of

**The War in Spain** This unforgettable etching by the Spanish painter Francisco Goya (1746–1828) comes from his famous collection "The Disasters of the War." A French firing squad executes captured Spanish rebels almost as soon as they are captured, an everyday event in a war of atrocities on both sides. Do you think these rebels are "terrorists," or "freedom fighters"? *(Foto Marburg/Art Resource, NY)*

liberation" against Napoleon's oppression, and the well-disciplined regular armies of Napoleon's enemies closed in for the kill. This time the coalition held together, cemented by the Treaty of Chaumont, which created a Quadruple Alliance intended to last for twenty years. Less than a month later, on April 4, 1814, a defeated Napoleon abdicated his throne. After this unconditional abdication, the victorious allies granted Napoleon the island of Elba off the coast of Italy as his own tiny state. Napoleon was even allowed to keep his imperial title, and France was required to pay him a yearly income of 2 million francs.

The allies also agreed to the restoration of the Bourbon dynasty, in part because demonstrations led by a few dedicated French monarchists indicated some support among the French people for that course of action. The new monarch, Louis XVIII (r. 1814–1824), tried to consolidate that support by issuing the Constitutional Charter, which accepted many of France's revolutionary changes and guaranteed civil liberties. Indeed, the charter gave France a constitutional monarchy roughly similar to that established in 1791, although far fewer people had the right to vote for representatives to the resurrected Chamber of Deputies. Moreover, in an attempt to strengthen popular support for Louis XVIII's new government, France was treated leniently by the allies, which agreed to meet in Vienna to work out a general peace settlement.

Yet Louis XVIII—old, ugly, and crippled by gout—totally lacked the glory and magic of Napoleon. Hearing of political unrest in France and diplomatic tensions in Vienna, Napoleon staged a daring escape from Elba in February 1815. Landing in France, he issued appeals for support and marched on Paris with a small band of followers. French officers and soldiers who had fought so long for their emperor responded to the call. Louis XVIII fled, and once more Napoleon took command. But Napoleon's gamble was a desperate long shot, for the allies were united against him. At the end of a frantic period known as the Hundred Days, they crushed his forces at Waterloo on June 18, 1815, and imprisoned him on the rocky island of St. Helena, far off the western coast of Africa. Old Louis XVIII returned again—this time "in the baggage of the allies," as his detractors scornfully put it—and recommenced his reign. The allies now dealt more harshly with the apparently incorrigible French. As for Napoleon, he took revenge by writing his memoirs, skillfully nurturing the myth that he had been Europe's revolutionary liberator, a romantic hero whose lofty work had been undone by oppressive reactionaries. An era had ended.

# *Individuals in Society*

*The retreat from Moscow; detail of an engraving by G. Küstler. Soldiers strip the sick of their blankets and boots, leaving them to die in the cold.*
(The New York Public Library/Art Resource, NY)

## Jakob Walter, German Draftee with Napoleon

In January 1812, a young German named Jakob Walter (1788–1864) was recalled to active duty in the army of Württemberg, a Napoleonic satellite in the Confederation of the Rhine. Stonemason and common draftee, Walter later wrote a rare enlisted man's account of the Russian campaign, a personal history that testified to the terrible price paid by the common people for a generation of war.

Napoleon's invasion of Russia was a desperate gamble from the beginning. French armies were accustomed to living off well-developed local economies, but this strategy did not work well in poor, sparsely populated eastern Europe. Scrounging for food dominated Walter's recollection of earlier fighting in Poland, and now, in 1812, the food situation was much worse. Crossing into Russia, Walter and his buddies found the nearby villages half-burned and stripped of food. Running down an occasional hog, they greedily tore it to pieces and ate it raw. Strangled by dust and thirst and then pelted for days by cold rain, the Great Army raced to catch the retreating Russians and force them into battle. When the famished troops stopped, the desperate search for food began.

In mid-August Walter's company helped storm the city of Smolensk in heavy fighting. From there onward, the road was littered with men, horses, and wagons, and all the towns and villages had been burned by the Russians to deprive the enemy of supplies. Surrounded by all these horrors, Walter almost lost his nerve, but he drew on his Catholic faith and found the courage "to go on trustingly to meet my fate."* Fighting at the great Battle of Borodino, "where the death cries and the shattering gunfire seemed a hell," he and the allied troops entered a deserted and fire-damaged Moscow in mid-September. But food, liquor, and fancy silks were there for the taking, and the weather was warm.

On October 18, the reprieve was over, and the retreating allied infantrymen re-entered Hell. Yet Walter, "still alert and spirited," was asked by an officer to be his attendant and received for his services a horse to ride. The horse proved a lifesaver. It allowed Walter to forage for food farther off the highway, to flee from approaching Cossacks, and to conserve his strength as vicious freezing winter weather set in. Yet food found at great peril could be quickly lost. Once Walter fought off some French soldiers with the help of some nearby Germans, who then robbed him of his bread. But what, he reflected later, could one expect? The starving men had simply lost their humanity. "I myself could look cold-bloodedly into the lamenting faces of the wounded, the freezing, and the burned," he wrote. When his horse was stolen as he slept, he silently stole someone else's. Struggling on in this brutal every-man-for-himself environment, Walter reached Poland in late December and hobbled home, a rare survivor. He went on to recover, marry, and have ten children.

Why did Jakob Walter survive? Pure chance surely played a large part. So did his robust constitution and street smarts. His faith in God also provided strength to meet each day's challenges. The beautiful vision of returning home and seeing his family offered equal encouragement. Finally, he lacked hatred and animosity, whether toward the Russians, the French, or whomever. He accepted the things he could not change and concentrated on those he could.

### Questions for Analysis

1. Why was obtaining food such a problem for Jakob Walter and his fellow soldiers?
2. What impresses you most about Walter's account of the Russian campaign?

*Jakob Walter, *The Diary of a Napoleonic Foot Soldier,* ed. with an introduction by M. Raeff (New York: Penguin Books, 1993), p. 53. Also pp. 54, 66.

*The* **history companion** *features additional information and activities related to this topic.*
**history.college.hmco.com/students**

## Summary

The French Revolution left a compelling and many-sided political legacy. This legacy included, most notably, liberalism, assertive nationalism, radical democratic republicanism, embryonic socialism, and self-conscious conservatism. It also left a rich and turbulent history of electoral competition, legislative assemblies, and even mass politics. Thus the French Revolution and conflicting interpretations of its significance presented a whole range of political options and alternative visions of the future. For this reason, it was truly the revolution in modern European politics.

The revolution that began in America and spread to France was a liberal revolution. Revolutionaries on both sides of the Atlantic wanted to establish civil liberties and equality before the law within the framework of representative government, and they succeeded. In France liberal nobles and an increasingly class-conscious middle class overwhelmed declining monarchical absolutism and feudal privilege, thanks to the intervention of the common people—the sans-culottes and the peasants. Featuring electoral competition and civil equality, the government established by the Declaration of the Rights of Man and the French constitution of 1791 was remarkably similar to that created in America by the federal Constitution and the Bill of Rights. France's new political system reflected a social structure based increasingly on wealth and achievement rather than on tradition and legal privileges.

After the establishment of the republic, the radical phase of the Revolution during the Terror, and the fall of Robespierre, the educated elites and the solid middle class reasserted themselves under the Directory. And though Napoleon sharply curtailed representative institutions and individual rights, he effectively promoted the reconciliation of old and new, of centralized bureaucracy and careers open to talent, of noble and bourgeois in a restructured property-owning elite. Louis XVIII had to accept the commanding position of this restructured elite, and in granting representative government and civil liberties to facilitate his restoration to the throne in 1814, he submitted to the rest of the liberal triumph of 1789 to 1791. The liberal core of the French Revolution had successfully survived a generation of war and dictatorship.

Revolution in France, as opposed to in the United States, also left a multiplicity of legacies that extended well beyond the triumphant liberalism of 1789. Indeed, the lived experience of the French Revolution and the wars that went with it exercised a pervasive influence on politics and the political imagination in the nineteenth century, not only in France but throughout Europe and even the rest of the world. First, there was the radical legacy of the embattled republic of 1793 and 1794, with its sans-culottes democratic republicanism and its egalitarian ideology and embryonic socialism. This legacy would inspire republicans, democrats, and early socialists. Second, there was the legacy of a powerful and continuing reaction to the French Revolution and to aggressive French nationalism. Monarchists and traditionalists now believed that 1789 had been a tragic mistake. They concluded that democratic republicanism and sans-culottes activism led only to war, class conflict, and savage dictatorship. And even though revolutionary upheaval encouraged generations of radicals to believe that political revolution might remake society and even create a new humanity, conservatives and many comfortable moderates were profoundly disillusioned by the revolutionary era. They looked with nostalgia toward the supposedly ordered world of benevolent monarchy, firm government, and respectful common people.

## Key Terms

| | |
|---|---|
| liberty and equality | Jacobins |
| sovereignty | second revolution |
| bourgeoisie | Girondists |
| representative government | the Mountain |
| checks and balances | sans-culottes |
| classical liberalism | planned economy |
| estates | Reign of Terror |
| manorial rights | nationalism |
| Great Fear | Thermidorian reaction |
| constitutional monarchy | family monarchy |

## Notes

1. Quoted in R. R. Palmer, *The Age of the Democratic Revolution,* vol. 1 (Princeton, N.J.: Princeton University Press, 1959), p. 239.
2. G. Lefebvre, *The Coming of the French Revolution* (New York: Vintage Books, 1947), p. 81.
3. P. H. Beik, ed., *The French Revolution* (New York: Walker, 1970), p. 89.
4. G. Pernoud and S. Flaisser, eds., *The French Revolution* (Greenwich, Conn.: Fawcett, 1960), p. 61.
5. O. Hufton, *Women and the Limits of Citizenship in the French Revolution* (Toronto: University of Toronto Press, 1992), pp. 3–22.
6. Quotations from Wollstonecraft are drawn from E. W. Sunstein, *A Different Face: The Life of Mary Wollstonecraft* (New York: Harper & Row, 1975), pp. 208, 211; and H. R. James, *Mary Wollstonecraft: A Sketch* (London: Oxford University Press, 1932), pp. 60, 62, 69.
7. Quoted in L. Gershoy, *The Era of the French Revolution, 1789–1799* (New York: Van Nostrand, 1957), p. 150.
8. Pernoud and Flaisser, *The French Revolution,* pp. 193–194.
9. T. Blanning, *The French Revolutionary Wars, 1787–1802* (London: Arnold, 1996), pp. 116–128.
10. Quoted ibid., p. 123.
11. Hufton, *Women and the Limits of Citizenship,* p. 130.

12. I. Woloch, *Napoleon and His Collaborators: The Making of a Dictatorship* (New York: W. W. Norton, 2001), pp. 36–65.
13. D. Sutherland, *France, 1789–1815: Revolution and Counterrevolution* (New York: Oxford University Press, 1986), p. 420.

## Suggested Reading

For fascinating eyewitness reports on the French Revolution, see the edited works by Beik and by Pernoud and Flaisser mentioned in the Notes. In addition, A. Young, *Travels in France During the Years 1787, 1788 and 1789* (1969), offers an engrossing contemporary description of France and Paris on the eve of revolution. E. Burke, *Reflections on the Revolution in France,* first published in 1790, is the classic conservative indictment. The intense passions the French Revolution has generated may be seen in nineteenth-century French historians, notably the enthusiastic J. Michelet, *History of the French Revolution;* the hostile H. Taine; and the judicious A. de Tocqueville, whose masterpiece, *The Old Regime and the French Revolution,* was first published in 1856. Modern classics on the entire period include the work by Palmer, cited in the Notes, which paints a comparative international picture, and E. J. Hobsbawm, *The Age of Revolution, 1789–1848* (1962). P. Schroeder, *The Transformation of European Politics, 1763–1848* (1994), is a masterful synthesis and reinterpretation that includes detailed treatment of the revolutionary era.

Revisionist scholarship has created a wealth of new scholarship and interpretation. A. Cobban, *The Social Interpretation of the French Revolution* (1964), and F. Furet, *Interpreting the French Revolution* (1981), are major reassessments of long-dominant ideas, which are admirably presented in N. Hampson, *A Social History of the French Revolution* (1963), and in the volume by Lefebvre listed in the Notes. F. Furet, *Revolutionary France, 1770–1880* (1995), is an extended development of the author's revisionist interpretations. E. Kennedy, *A Cultural History of the French Revolution* (1989), beautifully written and handsomely illustrated, and W. Doyle, *Origins of the French Revolution,* 3d ed. (1988), are excellent on long-term developments. Among valuable studies, which generally are often quite critical of revolutionary developments, several are noteworthy: J. Bosher, *The French Revolution* (1988); S. Schama, *Citizens: A Chronicle of the French Revolution* (1989); and D. Sutherland, *France, 1789–1815: Revolution and Counterrevolution* (1986).

Two excellent anthologies concisely presenting a range of interpretations are F. Kafker and J. Laux, eds., *The French Revolutions: Conflicting Interpretations,* 4th ed. (1989), and G. Best, ed., *The Permanent Revolution: The French Revolution and Its Legacy, 1789–1989* (1988). G. Rudé makes the men and women of the great days of upheaval come alive in *The Crowd in the French Revolution* (1959). Four other particularly interesting, detailed works are B. Shapiro, *Revolutionary Justice in Paris, 1789–1790* (1993); D. Jordan, *The Revolutionary Career of Maximilien Robespierre* (1985); J. P. Bertaud, *The Army of the French Revolution: From Citizen-Soldier to Instrument of Power* (1988); and C. L. R. James, *The Black Jacobins* (1938, 1980), on black slave revolt in Haiti. Other significant studies on aspects of revolutionary France include P. Jones's pathbreaking *The Peasantry in the French Revolution* (1988); W. Sewell Jr.'s imaginative *Work and Revolution in France: The Language of Labor from the Old Regime to 1848* (1980); and L. Hunt's innovative *The Family Romance of the French Revolution* (1992). M. Ozouf, *Festivals and the French Revolution* (1988), is a pioneering cultural study focusing on revolutionary symbols. Two major studies on the era's continuous wars are Blanning, cited in the Notes, and O. Connelly, *Blundering to Glory: Napoleon's Military Campaigns* (1987).

Studies on women in the French Revolution present conflicting interpretations. This may be seen by comparing two particularly important works: J. Landes, *Women and the Public Sphere in the Age of the French Revolution* (1988), and Hufton, listed in the Notes. A. de Baecque, *The Body Politic: Corporeal Metaphor in Revolutionary France* (1993), and J. Landes, *Visualizing the Nation: Gender, Representation, and Revolution in Eighteenth-Century France* (2001), provide innovative analyses of the gender-related aspects of revolutionary imagery and are recommended. H. Applewhite and D. Levy, eds., *Women and Politics in the Age of Democratic Revolution* (1990), compares developments in leading countries, while K. Offen, *European Feminisms, 1700–1950: A Political History* (2000), considers the French Revolution and women's political aspirations. Mary Wollstonecraft's dramatic life is the subject of several good biographies, including those by Sunstein and James, cited in the Notes.

P. Higonnet, *Goodness Beyond Virtue: Jacobins During the French Revolution* (1998), is an important reassessment, and T. Tackett, *When the King Took Flight* (2003), is an exciting re-creation of the king's effort to escape from Paris. D. Bell, *The Cult of the Nation in France: Inventing Nationalism, 1680–1800* (2001), traces early French nationalism through its revolutionary culmination. E. Morgan, *Inventing the People: The Rise of Popular Sovereignty in England and America* (1988), is a major work.

I. Woloch, cited in the Notes, examines former revolutionaries who supported the Napoleonic takeover, while L. Bergeron, *France Under Napoleon* (1981), remains an excellent synthesis. E. Arnold Jr., ed., *A Documentary Survey of Napoleonic France* (1994), includes political and cultural selections. K. Kafker and J. Laux, eds., *Napoleon and His Times: Selected Interpretations* (1989), is an interesting collection of articles that may be compared with R. Jones, *Napoleon: Man and Myth* (1977). M. Broers, *Europe Under Napoleon* (2002), probes the conflicted reactions of conquered peoples to Napoleon's rule. Good biographies are J. Thompson, *Napoleon Bonaparte: His Rise and Fall* (1952); P. Johnson, *Napoleon* (2002); and V. Cronin, *Napoleon Bonaparte* (1972). Wonderful novels inspired by the period include Raphael Sabatini's *Scaramouche,* a swashbuckler of revolutionary intrigue with accurate historical details; Charles Dickens's fanciful *A Tale of Two Cities;* and Leo Tolstoy's monumental saga of Napoleon's invasion of Russia (and much more), *War and Peace.*

# Listening to the Past

## Revolution and Women's Rights

*The 1789 Declaration of the Rights of Man was a revolutionary call for legal equality, representative government, and individual freedom. But the new rights were strictly limited to men; Napoleon tightened further the subordination of French women.*

*Among those who saw the contradiction in granting supposedly universal rights to only half the population was Marie Gouze (1748–1793), known to history as Olympe de Gouges. The daughter of a provincial butcher and peddler, she pursued a literary career in Paris after the death of her husband. Between 1790 and 1793, she wrote more than two dozen political pamphlets under her new name. De Gouges's great work was her "Declaration of the Rights of Woman" (1791). Excerpted here, de Gouges's manifesto went beyond the 1789 Rights of Man. It called on males to end their oppression of women and give women equal rights. A radical on women's issues, de Gouges sympathized with the monarchy and criticized Robespierre in print. Convicted of sedition, she was guillotined in November 1793.*

. . . Man, are you capable of being just? . . . Tell me, what gives you sovereign empire to oppress my sex? Your strength? Your talents? Observe the Creator in his wisdom . . . and give me, if you dare, an example of this tyrannical empire. Go back to animals, consult the elements, study plants . . . and distinguish, if you can, the sexes in the administration of nature. Everywhere you will find them mingled; everywhere they cooperate in harmonious togetherness in this immortal masterpiece.

Man alone has raised his exceptional circumstances to a principle. . . . [H]e wants to command as a despot a sex which is in full possession of its intellectual faculties; he pretends to enjoy the Revolution and to claim his rights to equality in order to say nothing more about it.

DECLARATION OF THE RIGHTS OF WOMAN AND THE FEMALE CITIZEN

For the National Assembly to decree in its last sessions, or in those of the next legislature:

Preamble

Mothers, daughters, sisters and representatives of the nation demand to be constituted into a national assembly. Believing that ignorance, omission, or scorn for the rights of woman are the only causes of public misfortunes and of the corruption of governments, [the women] have resolved to set forth in a solemn declaration the natural, inalienable, and sacred rights of woman. . . .

. . . the sex that is as superior in beauty as it is in courage during the sufferings of maternity recognizes and declares in the presence and under the auspices of the Supreme Being, the following Rights of Woman and of Female Citizens:

I. Woman is born free and lives equal to man in her rights. Social distinctions can be based only on the common utility.

II. The purpose of any political association is the conservation of the natural and imprescriptible rights of woman and man; these rights are liberty, property, security, and especially resistance to oppression.

III. The principle of all sovereignty rests essentially with the nation, which is nothing but the union of woman and man. . . .

IV. Liberty and justice consist of restoring all that belongs to others; thus, the only limits on the exercise of the natural rights of woman are perpetual male tyranny; these limits are to be reformed by the laws of nature and reason.

V. Laws of nature and reason proscribe all acts harmful to society. . . .

VI. The law must be the expression of the general will; all female and male citizens must contribute either personally or through their representatives to its formation; it must be the same for all: male and female citizens, being equal in the eyes of the law, must be equally admitted to all honors, positions, and public employment according to their capacity and without other distinctions besides those of their virtues and talents.

VII. No woman is an exception; she is accused, arrested, and detained in cases determined by law. Women, like men, obey this rigorous law.

VIII. The law must establish only those penalties that are strictly and obviously necessary. . . .

IX. Once any woman is declared guilty, complete rigor is [to be] exercised by the law.

X. No one is to be disquieted for his very basic opinions; woman has the right to mount the scaffold; she must equally have the right to mount the rostrum, provided that her demonstrations do not disturb the legally established public order.

XI. The free communication of thoughts and opinions is one of the most precious rights of woman, since that liberty assures the recognition of children by their fathers. Any female citizen thus may say freely, I am the mother of a child which belongs to you, without being forced by a barbarous prejudice to hide the truth. . . .

XIII. For the support of the public force and the expenses of administration, the contributions of woman and man are equal; she shares all the duties . . . and all the painful tasks; therefore, she must have the same share in the distribution of positions, employment, offices, honors, and jobs. . . .

XIV. Female and male citizens have the right to verify, either by themselves or through their representatives, the necessity of the public contribution. This can only apply to women if they are granted an equal share, not only of wealth, but also of public administration. . . .

XV. The collectivity of women, joined for tax purposes to the aggregate of men, has the right to demand an accounting of his administration from any public agent.

XVI. No society has a constitution without the guarantee of rights and the separation of powers; the constitution is null if the majority of individuals comprising the nation have not cooperated in drafting it.

XVII. Property belongs to both sexes whether united or separate; for each it is an inviolable and sacred right. . . .

Olympe de Gouges in 1784; aquatint by Madame Aubry (1748–1793). *(Musée de la Ville de Paris, Musée Carnavalet, Paris, France/The Bridgeman Art Library)*

Postscript

Women, wake up. . . . Discover your rights. . . . Oh, women, women! When will you cease to be blind? What advantage have you received from the Revolution? A more pronounced scorn, a more marked disdain. . . . [If men persist in contradicting their revolutionary principles,] courageously oppose the force of reason to the empty pretensions of superiority . . . and you will soon see these haughty men, not groveling at your feet as servile adorers, but proud to share with you the treasure of the Supreme Being. Regardless of what barriers confront you; it is in your power to free yourselves; you have only to want to. . . .

## Questions for Analysis

1. On what basis did de Gouges argue for gender equality? Did she believe in natural law?
2. What consequences did "scorn for the rights of woman" have for France, according to de Gouges?
3. Did de Gouges stress political rights at the expense of social and economic rights? If so, why?

*Source:* Olympe de Gouges, "Declaration of the Rights of Woman," in Darline G. Levy, Harriet B. Applewhite, and Mary D. Johnson, eds., *Women in Revolutionary Paris, 1789–1795* (Urbana: University of Illinois Press, 1979), pp. 87–96. Copyright © 1979 by the Board of Trustees, University of Illinois. Used with permission.

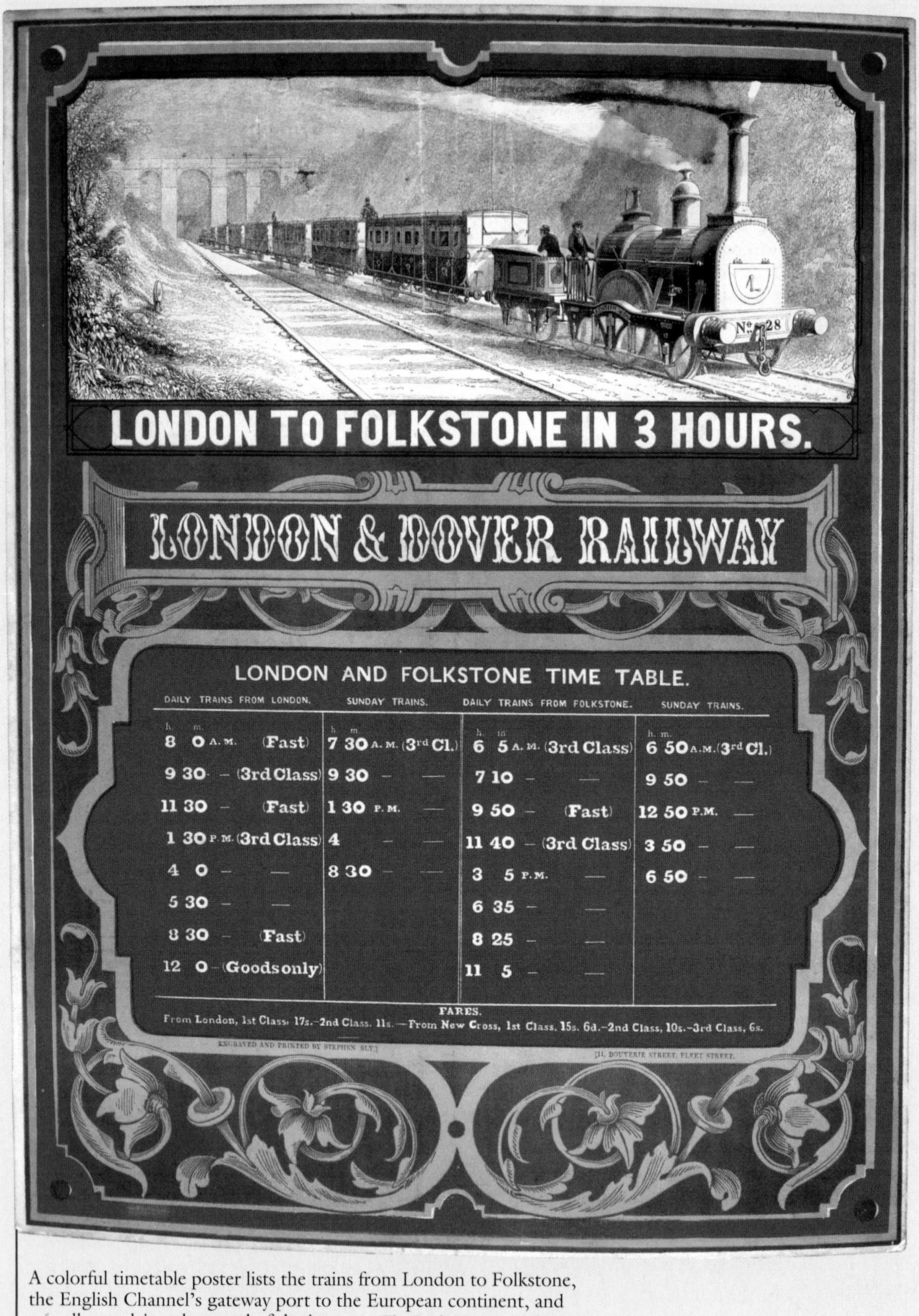


A colorful timetable poster lists the trains from London to Folkstone, the English Channel's gateway port to the European continent, and proudly proclaims the speed of the journey. *(The Bridgeman Art Library)*

chapter

# 22 The Revolution in Energy and Industry

## chapter outline

- The Industrial Revolution in Britain
- Industrialization in Continental Europe
- Capital and Labor

While the revolution in France was opening a new political era, another revolution was beginning to transform economic and social life. This was the Industrial Revolution, which began in Great Britain around the 1780s and started to influence continental Europe after 1815. Because the Industrial Revolution was less dramatic than the French Revolution, some historians see industrial development as basically moderate and evolutionary. But from a longer perspective, it was rapid and brought about numerous radical changes. Quite possibly only the development of agriculture during Neolithic times had a comparable impact and significance.

The Industrial Revolution profoundly modified much of human experience. It changed patterns of work, transformed the social class structure and the way people thought about class, and eventually even altered the international balance of political power. The Industrial Revolution also helped ordinary people gain a higher standard of living as the widespread poverty of the preindustrial world was gradually reduced.

Unfortunately, the improvement in the European standard of living was quite limited until about 1850 for at least two reasons. First, even in Britain, only a few key industries experienced a technological revolution. Many more industries continued to use old methods, especially on the continent, and this held down the increase in total production. Second, the increase in total population, which began in the eighteenth century (see page 637), continued all across Europe as the era of the Industrial Revolution unfolded. As a result, the rapid growth in population threatened to eat up the growth in production and to leave most individuals poorer than ever. As a consequence, rapid population growth provided a somber background for European industrialization and made the wrenching transformation all the more difficult.

- What, then, characterized the Industrial Revolution?
- What were its origins, and how did it develop?
- How did the changes it brought affect people and society in an era of continued rapid population growth?

These are some of the questions this chapter will seek to answer.

# The Industrial Revolution in Britain

The Industrial Revolution began in Great Britain, that historic union of Scotland, Wales, and England—the wealthiest and the dominant part of the country. It was something new in history, and it was quite unplanned. With no models to copy and no idea of what to expect, Britain had to pioneer not only in industrial technology but also in social relations and urban living. Between 1793 and 1815, these formidable tasks were complicated by almost constant war with France. As the trailblazer in economic development, as France was in political change, Britain must command special attention.

**MAP 22.1 Cottage Industry and Transportation in Eighteenth-Century England** England had an unusually good system of navigable rivers. From about 1770 to 1800 a canal-building boom linked these rivers together and greatly improved inland transportation.

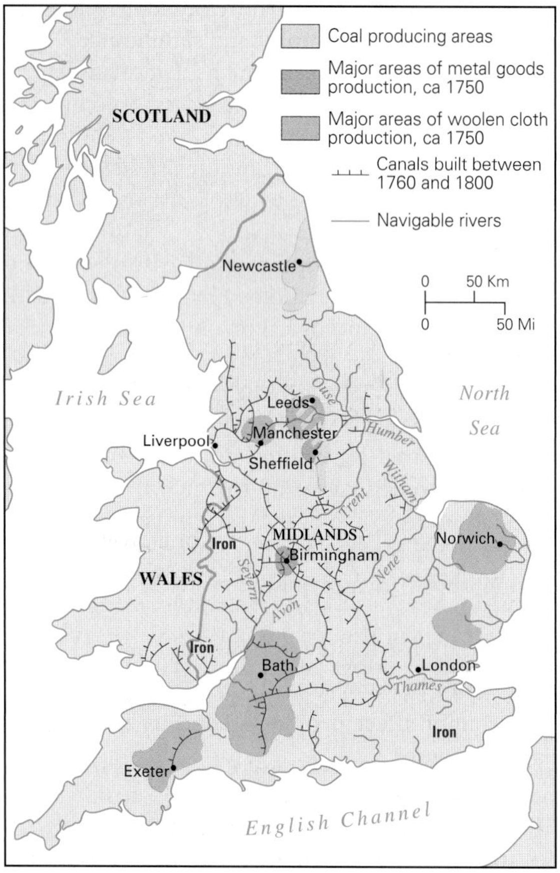


## Eighteenth-Century Origins

Although many aspects of the British Industrial Revolution are still matters for scholarly debate, it is generally agreed that the industrial changes that did occur grew out of a long process of development. First, the expanding Atlantic economy of the eighteenth century served mercantilist Britain remarkably well. The colonial empire that Britain aggressively built, augmented by a strong position in Latin America and in the African slave trade, provided a growing market for British manufactured goods. So did the domestic market. In an age when it was much cheaper to ship goods by water than by land, no part of England was more than twenty miles from navigable water. Beginning in the 1770s, a canal-building boom greatly enhanced this natural advantage (see Map 22.1). Rivers and canals provided easy movement of England's and Wales's enormous deposits of iron and coal, resources that would be critical raw materials in Europe's early industrial age. Nor were there any tariffs within the country to hinder trade, as there were in France before 1789 and in politically fragmented Germany.

Second, agriculture played a central role in bringing about the Industrial Revolution in Britain. English farmers in particular were second only to the Dutch in productivity in 1700, and they were continually adopting new methods of farming as the century went on. The result, especially before 1760, was a period of bountiful crops and low food prices. The ordinary English family did not have to spend almost everything it earned just to buy bread. It could spend more on, for example, manufactured goods—leather shoes or a razor for the man, a bonnet or a shawl for the woman, toy soldiers for the son, and a doll for the daughter. Thus demand for goods within the country complemented the demand from the colonies.

Third, Britain had other assets that helped give rise to industrial leadership. Unlike eighteenth-century France, Britain had an effective central bank and well-developed credit markets. The monarchy and the aristocratic oligarchy, which had jointly ruled the country since 1688, provided stable and predictable government. At the same time, the government let the domestic economy operate with few controls, encouraging personal initiative, technical change, and a free market. Finally, Britain had long had a large class of hired agricultural laborers, rural proletarians whose numbers were further increased by the second great round of enclosures in the late eighteenth century. These rural wage earners were relatively mobile—compared to village-bound peasants in France and western Germany, for example—and along with cottage workers they formed a potential industrial labor force for capitalist entrepreneurs.

1765 | 1780 | 1795 | 1810 | 1825 | 1840 | 1855

POLITICAL/MILITARY

1775–1783 American Revolution

1789–1799 French Revolution

1799 Combination Acts passed

1810 Strike of Manchester cotton spinners

1824 Combination Acts repealed

1833 Factory Act

1842 Mines Act

SOCIAL/ECONOMIC

ca 1765 Hargreaves invents spinning jenny

1769 Watt creates modern steam engine

1780–1851 Population boom in England

1780s–1830 Industrial Revolution

1830 Stephenson's *Rocket;* first important railroad

1851 Great Exhibition held at Crystal Palace

INTELLECTUAL/RELIGIOUS

1798 Malthus, *Essay on the Principle of Population*

1841 List, *National System of Political Economy*

1844 Engels, *The Condition of the Working Class in England*

All these factors combined to initiate the **Industrial Revolution,** a term first coined by awed contemporaries in the 1830s to describe the burst of major inventions and technical changes they had witnessed in certain industries. This technical revolution went hand in hand with an impressive quickening in the annual rate of industrial growth in Britain. Whereas industry had grown at only 0.7 percent between 1700 and 1760 (before the Industrial Revolution), it grew at the much higher rate of 3 percent between 1801 and 1831 (when industrial transformation was in full swing).[1] The decisive quickening of growth probably came in the 1780s, after the American War of Independence and just before the French Revolution.

Therefore, the great economic and political revolutions that shaped the modern world occurred almost simultaneously, though they began in different countries. The Industrial Revolution was, however, a longer process than the political upheavals. It was not complete in Britain until 1850 at the earliest, and it had no real impact on continental countries until after 1815.

## The First Factories

The pressure to produce more goods for a growing market was directly related to the first decisive breakthrough of the Industrial Revolution—the creation of the world's first large factories in the British cotton textile industry. Technological innovations in the manufacture of cotton cloth led to a new system of production and social relationships. Since no other industry experienced such a rapid or complete transformation before 1830, these trailblazing developments deserve special consideration.

Although the putting-out system of merchant capitalism (see page 641) was expanding all across Europe in the

**Woman Working a Hargreaves's Spinning Jenny** The loose cotton strands on the slanted bobbins passed up to the sliding carriage and then on to the spindles in back for fine spinning. The worker, almost always a woman, regulated the sliding carriage with one hand and with the other she turned the crank on the wheel to supply power. By 1783 one woman could spin by hand a hundred threads at a time on an improved model. *(Mary Evans Picture Library)*

eighteenth century, this pattern of rural industry was most fully developed in Britain. There, under the pressure of growing demand, the system's limitations began to outweigh its advantages for the first time. This was especially true in the British textile industry after about 1760.

A constant shortage of thread in the textile industry focused attention on ways of improving spinning. Many a tinkering worker knew that a better spinning wheel promised rich rewards. It proved hard to spin the traditional raw materials—wool and flax—with improved machines, but cotton was different. Cotton textiles had first been imported into Britain from India by the East India Company, and by 1760 there was a tiny domestic industry in northern England. After many experiments over a generation, a gifted carpenter and jack-of-all-trades, James Hargreaves, invented his cotton-spinning jenny about 1765. At almost the same moment, a barber-turned-manufacturer named Richard Arkwright invented (or possibly pirated) another kind of spinning machine, the water frame. These breakthroughs produced an explosion in the infant cotton textile industry in the 1780s, when it was increasing the value of its output at an unprecedented rate of about 13 percent each year. By 1790 the new machines were producing ten times as much cotton yarn as had been made in 1770.

Hargreaves's **spinning jenny** was simple and inexpensive. In early models, from six to twenty-four spindles were mounted on a sliding carriage, and each spindle spun a fine, slender thread. The woman moved the carriage back and forth with one hand and turned a wheel to supply power with the other. Now it was the male weaver who could not keep up with the vastly more efficient female spinner.

Arkwright's **water frame** employed a different principle. It quickly acquired a capacity of several hundred spindles and demanded much more power—waterpower. The water frame thus required large specialized mills, factories that employed as many as one thousand workers from the very beginning. The water frame could spin only coarse, strong thread, which was then put out for respinning on hand-powered cottage jennies. Around 1790 an alternative technique invented by Samuel Crompton also began to require more power than the human arm could supply. After that time, all cotton spinning was gradually concentrated in factories.

The first consequences of these revolutionary developments were more beneficial than is generally believed. Cotton goods became much cheaper, and they were bought and treasured by all classes. In the past, only the wealthy could afford the comfort and cleanliness of underwear, which was called **body linen** because it was made from expensive linen cloth. Now millions of poor people, who had earlier worn nothing underneath their coarse, filthy outer garments, could afford to wear cotton slips and underpants as well as cotton dresses and shirts.

Families using cotton in cottage industry were freed from their constant search for adequate yarn from scattered, part-time spinners, since all the thread needed could be spun in the cottage on the jenny or obtained from a nearby factory. The wages of weavers, now hard-pressed to keep up with the spinners, rose markedly until about 1792. Weavers were among the best-paid workers in England. They were known to walk proudly through the streets with 5-pound notes stuck in their hatbands, and they dressed like the middle class. As a result, large numbers of agricultural laborers became hand-loom weavers, while mechanics and capitalists sought to invent a power loom to save on labor costs. This Edmund Cartwright achieved in 1785. But the power looms of the factories worked poorly at first, and hand-loom weavers continued to receive good wages until at least 1800.

Working conditions in the early factories were less satisfactory than those of cottage weavers and spinners, and people were reluctant to work in them. Therefore, factory owners often turned to young children who had been abandoned by their parents and put in the care of local parishes. Parish officers often "apprenticed" such unfortunate foundlings to factory owners. The parish thus saved money, and the factory owners gained workers over whom they exercised almost the authority of slave owners.

Apprenticed as young as five or six years of age, boy and girl workers were forced by law to labor for their "masters" for as many as fourteen years. Housed, fed, and locked up nightly in factory dormitories, the young workers received little or no pay. Hours were appalling—commonly thirteen or fourteen hours a day, six days a week. Harsh physical punishment maintained brutal discipline. To be sure, poor children typically worked long hours and frequently outside the home for brutal masters. But the wholesale coercion of orphans as factory apprentices constituted exploitation on a truly unprecedented scale. This exploitation ultimately piqued the conscience of reformers and reinforced more humanitarian attitudes toward children and their labor in the early nineteenth century.

The creation of the world's first modern factories in the British cotton textile industry in the 1770s and 1780s, which grew out of the putting-out system of cottage production, was a major historical development. Both symbolically and substantially, the big new cotton mills marked the beginning of the Industrial Revolution in Britain. By 1831 the largely mechanized cotton textile industry towered above all others, accounting for fully 22 percent of the country's entire industrial production.

## The Problem of Energy

The growth of the cotton textile industry might have been stunted or cut short, however, if water from rivers and streams had remained the primary source of power for the new factories. But this did not occur. Instead, an epoch-making solution was found to the age-old problem of energy and power. This solution permitted continued rapid development in cotton textiles, the gradual generalization of the factory system, and the triumph of the Industrial Revolution in Britain.

Human beings, like all living organisms, require energy. Adult men and women need two thousand to four thousand calories (units of energy) daily simply to fuel their bodies, work, and survive. Prehistoric people relied on plants and plant-eating animals as their sources of energy. With the development of agriculture, early civilizations were able to increase the number of useful plants and thus the supply of energy. Some plants could be fed to domesticated animals, such as the horse. Stronger than human beings, these animals converted the energy in the plants into work.

Human beings have long used their toolmaking abilities to construct machines that convert one form of energy into another for their own benefit. In the medieval period, people began to develop water mills to grind their grain and windmills to pump water and drain swamps. More efficient use of water and wind in the sixteenth and seventeenth centuries enabled human beings to accomplish more; intercontinental sailing ships were a prime example. Nevertheless, even into the eighteenth century, society continued to rely for energy mainly on plants, and human beings and animals continued to perform most work. This dependence meant that Western civilization remained poor in energy and power.

Lack of power lay at the heart of the poverty that afflicted the large majority of people. The man behind the plow and the woman at the spinning wheel could employ only horsepower and human muscle in their labor. No matter how hard they worked, they could not produce very much. What people needed were new sources of energy and more power at their disposal.

The shortage of energy had become particularly severe in Britain by the eighteenth century. Because of the growth of population, most of the great forests of medieval Britain had long ago been replaced by fields of grain and hay.

**Manchester, England, 1851** The development of the steam engine enabled industry to concentrate in towns and cities. Manchester mushroomed from a town of 20,000 in 1750 into "Cottonopolis," cotton city, with 400,000 inhabitants in 1850. In this painting the artist contrasts the smoky city and its awesome power with the idealized beauty of the suburbs, where the new rich settled and built their mansions. *(The Royal Collection, © 2004 Her Majesty Queen Elizabeth II)*

Wood was in ever-shorter supply, yet it remained tremendously important. It served as the primary source of heat for all homes and industries and as a basic raw material. Processed wood (charcoal) was the fuel that was mixed with iron ore in the blast furnace to produce pig iron. The iron industry's appetite for wood was enormous, and by 1740 the British iron industry was stagnating. Vast forests enabled Russia to become the world's leading producer of iron, much of which was exported to Britain. But Russia's potential for growth was limited, too, and in a few decades Russia would reach the barrier of inadequate energy that was already holding England back.

## The Steam Engine Breakthrough

As this early energy crisis grew worse, Britain looked toward its abundant and widely scattered reserves of coal as an alternative to its vanishing wood. Coal was first used in Britain in the late Middle Ages as a source of heat. By 1640 most homes in London were heated with it, and it also provided heat for making beer, glass, soap, and other products. Coal was not used, however, to produce mechanical energy or to power machinery. It was there that coal's potential was enormous, as a simple example shows.

A hard-working miner can dig out 500 pounds of coal a day using hand tools. Even an extremely inefficient converter, which transforms only 1 percent of the heat energy in coal into mechanical energy, will produce 27 horsepower-hours of work from that 500 pounds of coal. The miner, by contrast, produces only about 1 horsepower-hour in the course of a day. Early steam engines were powerful but still inefficient converters of energy.

As more coal was produced, mines were dug deeper and deeper and were constantly filling with water. Mechanical pumps, usually powered by animals walking in circles at the surface, had to be installed. At one mine, fully five hundred horses were used in pumping. Such power was expensive and bothersome. In an attempt to overcome these disadvantages, Thomas Savery in 1698 and Thomas Newcomen in 1705 invented the first primitive **steam engines.** Both engines were extremely inefficient. Both burned coal to produce steam, which was then used to operate a pump. However, by the early 1770s, many of the Savery engines and hundreds of the Newcomen engines were operating successfully, though inefficiently, in English and Scottish mines.

In the early 1760s, a gifted young Scot named James Watt (1736–1819) was drawn to a critical study of the steam engine. Watt was employed at the time by the University of Glasgow as a skilled craftsman making scientific instruments. The Scottish universities were pioneers in practical technical education, and in 1763 Watt was called on to repair a Newcomen engine being used in a physics course. After a series of observations, Watt saw that the Newcomen engine's waste of energy could be reduced by adding a separate condenser. This splendid invention, patented in 1769, greatly increased the efficiency of the steam engine.

To invent something in a laboratory is one thing; to make it a practical success is quite another. Watt needed skilled workers, precision parts, and capital, and the relatively advanced nature of the British economy proved essential. A partnership with a wealthy English toymaker provided risk capital and a manufacturing plant. In the craft tradition of locksmiths, tinsmiths, and millwrights, Watt found skilled mechanics who could install, regulate, and repair his sophisticated engines. From ingenious manufacturers such as the cannonmaker John Wilkinson, Watt was gradually able to purchase precision parts. This support allowed him to create an effective vacuum and regulate a complex engine. In more than twenty years of constant effort, Watt made many further improvements. By the late 1780s, the steam engine had become a practical and commercial success in Britain.

The steam engine of Watt and his followers was the Industrial Revolution's most fundamental advance in technology. For the first time in history, humanity had, at least for a few generations, almost unlimited power at its disposal. For the first time, inventors and engineers could devise and implement all kinds of power equipment to aid people in their work. For the first time, abundance was at least a possibility for ordinary men and women.

The steam engine was quickly put to use in several industries in Britain. It drained mines and made possible

**James Nasmyth's Mighty Steam Hammer** Nasmyth's invention was the forerunner of the modern pile driver, and its successful introduction in 1832 epitomized the rapid development of steam power technology in Britain. In this painting by the inventor himself, workers manipulate a massive iron shaft being hammered into shape at Nasmyth's foundry near Manchester. *(Science & Society Picture Library, London)*

the production of ever more coal to feed steam engines elsewhere. The steam-power plant began to replace waterpower in the cotton-spinning mills during the 1780s, contributing greatly to that industry's phenomenal rise. Steam also took the place of waterpower in flour mills, in the malt mills used in breweries, in the flint mills supplying the china industry, and in the mills exported by Britain to the West Indies to crush sugar cane.

Steam power promoted important breakthroughs in other industries. The British iron industry was radically transformed. The use of powerful, steam-driven bellows in blast furnaces helped ironmakers switch over rapidly from limited charcoal to unlimited **coke** (which is made from coal) in the smelting of pig iron after 1770. In the 1780s, Henry Cort developed the puddling furnace, which allowed pig iron to be refined in turn with coke. Strong, skilled ironworkers—the puddlers—"cooked" molten pig iron in a great vat, raking off globs of refined iron for further processing. Cort also developed heavy-duty, steam-powered rolling mills, which were capable of spewing out finished iron in every shape and form.

The economic consequence of these technical innovations was a great boom in the British iron industry. In 1740 annual British iron production was only 17,000 tons. With the spread of coke smelting and the first impact of Cort's inventions, production reached 68,000 tons in 1788, 125,000 tons in 1796, and 260,000 tons in 1806. In 1844 Britain produced 3 million tons of iron. This was a truly amazing expansion. Once scarce and expensive, iron became the cheap, basic, indispensable building block of the economy.

## The Coming of the Railroads

The second half of the eighteenth century saw extensive construction of hard and relatively smooth roads, particularly in France before the Revolution. Yet it was passenger traffic that benefited most from this construction. Overland shipment of freight, relying solely on horsepower, was still quite limited and frightfully expensive; shippers used rivers and canals for heavy freight whenever possible. It was logical, therefore, that inventors would try to use steam power.

As early as 1800, an American ran a "steamer on wheels" through city streets. Other experiments followed. In the 1820s, English engineers created steam cars capable of carrying fourteen passengers at ten miles an hour—as fast as the mail coach. But the noisy, heavy steam automobiles frightened passing horses and damaged themselves as well as the roads with their vibrations. For the rest of the century, horses continued to reign on highways and city streets.

The coal industry had long been using plank roads and rails to move coal wagons within mines and at the surface. Rails reduced friction and allowed a horse or a human being to pull a heavier load. Thus once a rail capable of supporting a heavy locomotive was developed in 1816, all sorts of experiments with steam engines on rails went forward. In 1825 after ten years of work, George Stephenson built an effective locomotive. In 1830 his ***Rocket*** sped down the track of the just-completed Liverpool and Manchester Railway at sixteen miles per hour. This was the world's first important railroad, fittingly steaming in the heart of industrial England. The line from Liverpool to Manchester was a financial as well as a technical success, and many private companies were quickly organized to build more rail lines. Within twenty years, they had completed the main trunk lines of Great Britain. Other countries were quick to follow.

The significance of the railroad was tremendous. The railroad dramatically reduced the cost and uncertainty of shipping freight overland. This advance had many economic consequences. Previously, markets had tended to be small and local; as the barrier of high transportation costs was lowered, markets became larger and even nationwide. Larger markets encouraged larger factories with more sophisticated machinery in a growing number of industries. Such factories could make goods more cheaply and gradually subjected most cottage workers and many urban artisans to severe competitive pressures.

In all countries, the construction of railroads created a strong demand for unskilled labor and contributed to the growth of a class of urban workers. Hard work on construction gangs was done in the open air with animals and hand tools. Many landless farm laborers and poor peasants, long accustomed to leaving their villages for temporary employment, went to build railroads. By the time the work was finished, life back home in the village often seemed dull and unappealing, and many men drifted to towns in search of work. By the time they sent for their wives and sweethearts to join them, they had become urban workers.

The railroad changed the outlook and values of the entire society. The last and culminating invention of the Industrial Revolution, the railroad dramatically revealed the power and increased the speed of the new age. Racing down a track at sixteen miles per hour or, by 1850, at a phenomenal fifty miles per hour was a new and awesome experience. As a French economist put it after a ride on the Liverpool and Manchester in 1833, "There are certain impressions that one cannot put into words!"

**The Saltash Bridge** Railroad construction presented innumerable challenges, such as the building of bridges to span rivers and gorges. Civil engineers responded with impressive feats, and their profession bounded ahead. This painting portrays the inauguration of I. K. Brunel's Saltash Bridge, where the railroad crosses the Tamar River into Cornwall in southwest England. The high spans allow large ships to pass underneath. *(Elton Collection, Ironbridge Gorge Museum Trust)*

Some great painters, notably Joseph M. W. Turner (1775–1851) and Claude Monet (1840–1926), succeeded in expressing this sense of power and awe. So did the massive new train stations, the cathedrals of the industrial age. Leading railway engineers such as Isambard Kingdom Brunel and Thomas Brassey, whose tunnels pierced mountains and whose bridges spanned valleys, became public idols—the astronauts of their day. Everyday speech absorbed the images of railroading. After you got up a "full head of steam," you "highballed" along. And if you didn't "go off the track," you might "toot your own whistle." The railroad fired the imagination.

## Industry and Population

In 1851 London was the site of a famous industrial fair. This Great Exhibition was held in the newly built **Crystal Palace,** an architectural masterpiece made entirely of glass and iron, both of which were now cheap and abundant. For the millions who visited, one fact stood out: the little island of Britain was the "workshop of the world." It alone produced two-thirds of the world's coal and more than one-half of its iron and cotton cloth. More generally, it has been carefully estimated that in 1860 Britain produced a truly remarkable 20 percent of the entire world's output of industrial goods, whereas it had produced only about 2 percent of the world total in 1750.[2] Experiencing revolutionary industrial change, Britain became the first industrial nation (see Map 22.2).

As the British economy significantly increased its production of manufactured goods, the gross national product (GNP) rose roughly fourfold at constant prices between 1780 and 1851. In other words, the British people as a whole increased their wealth and their national income dramatically. At the same time, the population of Britain boomed, growing from about 9 million in 1780 to almost

**The Crystal Palace** The Great Exhibition of 1851 attracted more than six million visitors, many of whom journeyed to London on the newly built railroads. Countries and companies from all over the world displayed their products and juries awarded prizes in the strikingly modern Crystal Palace, an architectural marvel built using the cheap iron and glass of the industrial age. In this illustration visitors stroll through the domed hall and peruse the 1500 exhibits. *(Courtesy of the Trustees of the British Museum)*

21 million in 1851. Thus growing numbers consumed much of the increase in total production. According to one important study, average consumption per person increased by only 75 percent between 1780 and 1851, as the growth in the total population ate up a large part of the fourfold increase in GNP in those years.[3]

Although the question is still debated, many economic historians now believe that rapid population growth in Great Britain was not harmful because it facilitated industrial expansion. More people meant a more mobile labor force, with a wealth of young workers in need of employment and ready to go where the jobs were. Contemporaries were much less optimistic. In his famous and influential *Essay on the Principle of Population* (1798), Thomas Malthus (1766–1834) argued that population would always tend to grow faster than the food supply. In Malthus's opinion, the only hope of warding off such "positive checks" to population growth as war, famine, and disease was "prudential restraint." That is, young men and women had to limit the growth of population by the old tried-and-true means of marrying late in life. But Malthus was not optimistic about this possibility. The powerful attraction of the sexes would cause most people to marry early and have many children.

Wealthy English stockbroker and leading economist David Ricardo (1772–1823) coldly spelled out the pessimistic implications of Malthus's thought. Ricardo's depressing **iron law of wages** posited that because of the pressure of population growth, wages would always sink to subsistence level. That is, wages would be just high

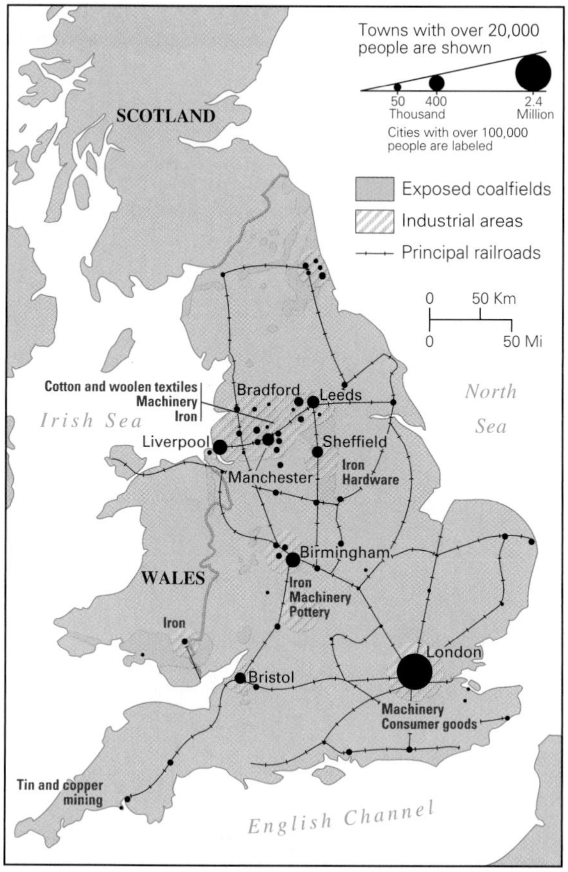


**MAP 22.2 The Industrial Revolution in England, ca 1850** Industry concentrated in the rapidly growing cities of the north and the Midlands, where rich coal and iron deposits were in close proximity.

enough to keep workers from starving. With Malthus and Ricardo setting the tone, economics was soon dubbed "the dismal science."

Malthus, Ricardo, and their many followers were proved wrong—in the long run. However, until the 1820s, or even the 1840s, contemporary observers might reasonably have concluded that the economy and the total population were racing neck and neck, with the outcome very much in doubt. The closeness of the race added to the difficulties inherent in the journey toward industrial civilization.

There was another problem as well. Perhaps workers, farmers, and ordinary people did not get their rightful share of the new wealth. Perhaps only the rich got richer, while the poor got poorer or made no progress. We will turn to this great issue after looking at the process of industrialization in continental countries.

## Industrialization in Continental Europe

The new technologies developed in the British Industrial Revolution were adopted rather slowly by businesses in continental Europe. Yet by the end of the nineteenth century, several European countries as well as the United States had also industrialized their economies to a considerable but variable degree. This meant that the process of Western industrialization proceeded gradually, with uneven jerks and national (and regional) variations.

Scholars are still struggling to explain these variations, especially since good answers may offer valuable lessons in our own time for poor countries seeking to improve their material condition through industrialization and economic development. The latest findings on the Western experience are encouraging. They suggest that there were alternative paths to the industrial world in the nineteenth century and that, today as then, there was no need to follow a rigid, predetermined British model.

### National Variations

European industrialization, like most economic developments, requires some statistical analysis as part of the effort to understand it. Comparative data on industrial production in different countries over time help give us an overview of what happened. One set of data, the work of a Swiss scholar, compares the level of industrialization on a per capita basis in several countries from 1750 to 1913. These data are far from perfect because there are gaps in the underlying records. But they reflect basic trends and are presented in Table 22.1 for closer study.

As the heading of Table 22.1 makes clear, this is a per capita comparison of levels of industrialization—a comparison of how much industrial product was available, on average, to each person in a given country in a given year. Therefore, all the numbers in Table 22.1 are expressed in terms of a single index number of 100, which equals the per capita level of industrial goods in Great Britain (and Ireland) in 1900. Every number is thus a percentage of the 1900 level in Britain and is directly comparable. The countries are listed in roughly the order that they began to use large-scale, power-driven technology.

What does this overview of European industrialization tell us? First, and very significantly, one sees that in 1750 all countries were fairly close together and that Britain was only slightly ahead of its archenemy, France. Second, Britain had opened up a noticeable lead over all continental

**Table 22.1 Per Capita Levels of Industrialization, 1750–1913**

| | 1750 | 1800 | 1830 | 1860 | 1880 | 1900 | 1913 |
|---|---|---|---|---|---|---|---|
| Great Britain | 10 | 16 | 25 | 64 | 87 | 100 | 115 |
| Belgium | 9 | 10 | 14 | 28 | 43 | 56 | 88 |
| United States | 4 | 9 | 14 | 21 | 38 | 69 | 126 |
| France | 9 | 9 | 12 | 20 | 28 | 39 | 59 |
| Germany | 8 | 8 | 9 | 15 | 25 | 52 | 85 |
| Austria-Hungary | 7 | 7 | 8 | 11 | 15 | 23 | 32 |
| Italy | 8 | 8 | 8 | 10 | 12 | 17 | 26 |
| Russia | 6 | 6 | 7 | 8 | 10 | 15 | 20 |
| China | 8 | 6 | 6 | 4 | 4 | 3 | 3 |
| India | 7 | 6 | 6 | 3 | 2 | 1 | 2 |

*Note:* All entries are based on an index value of 100, equal to the per capita level of industrialization in Great Britain in 1900. Data for Great Britain are actually for the United Kingdom, thereby including Ireland with England, Wales, and Scotland.

*Source:* P. Bairoch, "International Industrialization Levels from 1750 to 1980," *Journal of European Economic History* 11 (Spring 1982): 294. Reprinted with permission.

countries by 1800, and that gap progressively widened as the British Industrial Revolution accelerated to 1830 and reached full maturity by 1860. The British level of per capita industrialization was twice the French level in 1830, for example, and more than three times the French level in 1860. All other large countries (except the United States) had fallen even further behind Britain than France had at both dates. Sophisticated quantitative history confirms the primacy and relative rapidity of Britain's Industrial Revolution.

Third, variations in the timing and in the extent of industrialization in the continental powers and the United States are also apparent. Belgium, independent in 1831 and rich in iron and coal, led in adopting Britain's new technology. France developed factory production more gradually, and most historians now detect no burst in French mechanization and no acceleration in the growth of overall industrial output that may accurately be called revolutionary. They stress instead France's relatively good pattern of early industrial growth, which was unjustly tarnished by the spectacular rise of Germany and the United States after 1860. By 1913 Germany was rapidly closing in on Britain, while the United States had already passed the first industrial nation in per capita production.

Finally, all European states (as well as the United States, Canada, and Japan) managed to raise per capita industrial levels in the nineteenth century. These continent-wide increases stood in stark contrast to the large and tragic decreases that occurred at the same time in most non-Western countries, most notably in China and India. European countries industrialized to a greater or lesser extent even as most of the non-Western world *de*-industrialized. Thus differential rates of wealth- and power-creating industrial development, which heightened disparities within Europe, also greatly magnified existing inequalities between Europe and the rest of the world. We shall return to this momentous change in Chapter 26.

## The Challenge of Industrialization

The different patterns of industrial development suggest that the process of industrialization was far from automatic. Indeed, building modern industry was an awesome challenge. To be sure, throughout Europe the eighteenth century was an era of agricultural improvement, population increase, expanding foreign trade, and growing cottage industry. Thus when the pace of British industry began to accelerate in the 1780s, continental businesses began to adopt the new methods as they proved their profitability. British industry enjoyed clear superiority, but at first the continent was close behind.

By 1815, however, the situation was quite different. In spite of wartime difficulties, British industry maintained the momentum of the 1780s and continued to grow and improve between 1789 and 1815. On the continent, the upheavals that began with the French Revolution had another effect: they disrupted trade, created runaway inflation, and fostered social anxiety. War severed normal communications between Britain and the continent, severely handicapping continental efforts to use new British machinery and technology. Moreover, the years from 1789 to 1815 were, even for the privileged French economy receiving special favors from Napoleon, a time of "national catastrophe"—in the graphic words of a famous French scholar.[4] Thus France and the rest of Europe were further behind Britain in 1815 than in 1789.

This widening gap made it more difficult, if not impossible, for other countries to follow the British pattern in energy and industry after peace was restored in 1815. Above all, in the newly mechanized industries, British goods were being produced very economically, and these goods had come to dominate world markets completely while the continental states were absorbed in war between 1792 and 1815. In addition, British technology had become so advanced and complicated that very few engineers or skilled technicians outside England understood it. Moreover, the technology of steam power had grown much more expensive. It involved large investments in the iron and coal industries and, after 1830, required the existence of railroads, which were very costly. Continental business people had great difficulty finding the large sums of money the new methods demanded, and there was a shortage of laborers accustomed to working in factories. Landowners and government officials were often so suspicious of the new form of industry and the changes it brought that they did little at first to encourage it. All these disadvantages slowed the spread of modern industry (see Map 22.3).

After 1815, however, when continental countries began to face up to the British challenge, they had at least three important advantages. First, most continental countries had a rich tradition of putting-out enterprise, merchant capitalists, and skilled urban artisans. Such a tradition gave continental firms the ability to adapt and survive in the face of new market conditions. Second, continental capitalists did not need to develop their own advanced technology. Instead, they could simply "borrow" the new methods developed in Great Britain, as well as engineers and some of the financial resources these countries lacked. European countries such as France and Russia also had a third asset that many non-Western areas lacked in the nineteenth century. They had strong independent governments, which did not fall under foreign political control. These governments could fashion economic policies to serve their own interests, as they proceeded to do. They would eventually use the power of the state to promote industry and catch up with Britain.

## Agents of Industrialization

The British realized the great value of their technical discoveries and tried to keep their secrets to themselves. Until 1825 it was illegal for artisans and skilled mechanics to leave Britain; until 1843 the export of textile machinery and other equipment was forbidden. Many talented, ambitious workers, however, slipped out of the country illegally and introduced the new methods abroad.

One such man was William Cockerill, a Lancashire carpenter. He and his sons began building cotton-spinning equipment in French-occupied Belgium in 1799. In 1817 the most famous son, John Cockerill, purchased the old summer palace of the deposed bishops of Liège in southern Belgium. Cockerill converted the palace into a large industrial enterprise, which produced machinery, steam engines, and then railway locomotives. He also established modern ironworks and coal mines.

Cockerill's plants in the Liège area became an industrial nerve center, continually gathering new information and transmitting it across Europe. Many skilled British workers came illegally to work for Cockerill, and some went on to found their own companies throughout Europe. Newcomers brought the latest plans and secrets, so Cockerill could boast that ten days after an industrial advance occurred in Britain, he knew all about it in Belgium. Thus British technicians and skilled workers were a powerful force in the spread of early industrialization.

A second agent of industrialization were talented entrepreneurs such as Fritz Harkort, a business pioneer in the German machinery industry. Serving in England as a Prussian army officer during the Napoleonic wars, Harkort was impressed and enchanted with what he saw. He concluded that Germany had to match all these English achievements as quickly as possible. Setting up shop in an abandoned castle in the still-tranquil Ruhr Valley, Harkort felt an almost religious calling to build steam engines and become the "Watt of Germany."

Harkort's basic idea was simple, but it was enormously difficult to carry out. Lacking skilled laborers to do the job, Harkort turned to England for experienced, though expensive, mechanics. Getting materials also posed a

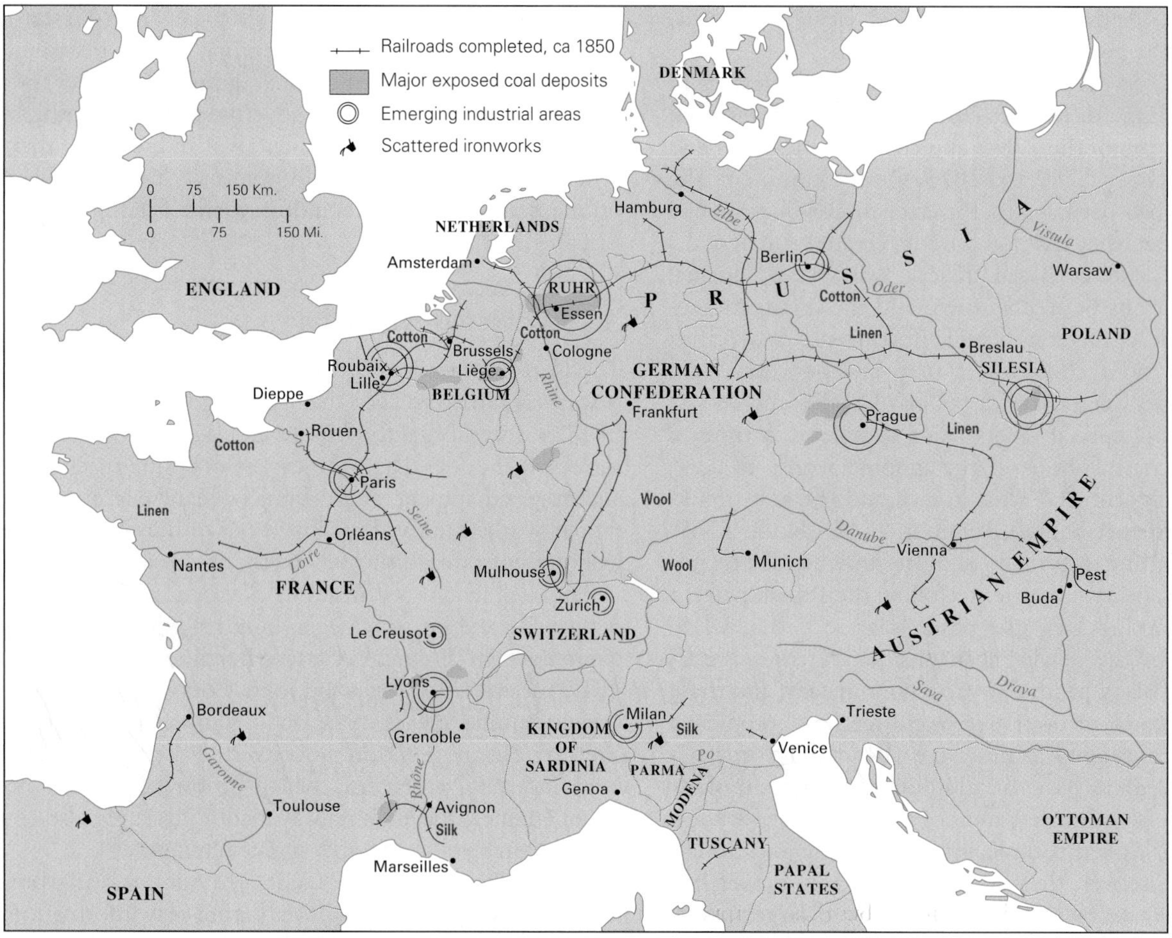


**MAP 22.3 Continental Industrialization, ca 1850** Although continental countries were beginning to make progress by 1850, they still lagged far behind Britain. For example, continental railroad building was still in an early stage, whereas the British rail system was essentially complete.

great problem. He had to import the thick iron boilers that he needed from England at great cost. In spite of all these problems, Harkort built and sold engines, winning fame and praise. His ambitious efforts over sixteen years also resulted in large financial losses for himself and his partners, and in 1832 he was forced out of his company by his financial backers, who cut back operations to reduce losses. His career illustrates both the great efforts of a few important business leaders to duplicate the British achievement and the difficulty of the task.

Entrepreneurs like Harkort were obviously exceptional. Most continental businesses adopted factory technology slowly, and handicraft methods lived on. Indeed, as recent research on France has shown, continental industrialization usually brought substantial but uneven expansion of handicraft industry in both rural and urban areas for a time. Artisan production of luxury items grew in France as the rising income of the international middle class created foreign demand for silk scarfs, embroidered needlework, perfumes, and fine wines.

A third force for industrialization was government, which often helped business people in continental countries to overcome some of their difficulties. **Tariff protection** was one such support. For example, after Napoleon's wars ended in 1815, France was suddenly flooded with cheaper and better British goods. The French government responded by laying high tariffs on many British imports in order to protect the French economy. After 1815 continental governments bore the cost of building roads and canals to improve transportation.

**A German Ironworks, 1850** This big business enterprise has mastered the new British method of smelting iron with coke. Germany, and especially the state of Prussia, was well endowed with both iron and coal, and the rapid exploitation of these resources after 1840 transformed a poor agricultural country into an industrial powerhouse. *(Deutsches Museum Munich)*

They also bore to a significant extent the cost of building railroads. Belgium led the way in the 1830s and 1840s. In an effort to tie the newly independent nation together, the Belgian government decided to construct a state-owned system. Built rapidly as a unified network, Belgium's state-owned railroads stimulated the development of heavy industry and made the country an early industrial leader. Several of the smaller German states also built state systems.

The Prussian government provided another kind of invaluable support. It guaranteed that the state treasury would pay the interest and principal on railroad bonds if the closely regulated private companies in Prussia were unable to do so. Thus railroad investors in Prussia ran little risk, and capital was quickly raised. In France the state shouldered all the expense of acquiring and laying roadbed, including bridges and tunnels. Finished roadbed was leased to a carefully supervised private company, which usually benefited from a state guarantee of its debts. In short, governments helped pay for railroads, the all-important leading sector in continental industrialization.

The career of German journalist and thinker Friedrich List (1789–1846) reflects government's greater role in industrialization on the continent than in England. List considered the growth of modern industry of the utmost importance because manufacturing was a primary means of increasing people's well-being and relieving their poverty. Moreover, List was a dedicated nationalist. He wrote that the "wider the gap between the backward and advanced nations becomes, the more dangerous it is to remain behind." For an agricultural nation was not only poor but also weak, increasingly unable to defend itself and maintain its political independence. To promote industry was to defend the nation.

The practical policies that List focused on in articles and in his influential *National System of Political Economy* (1841) were railroad building and the tariff. List supported the formation of a customs union, or *Zollverein,* among the separate German states. Such a tariff union came into being in 1834, allowing goods to move between the German member states without tariffs, while erecting a single uniform tariff against other nations. List wanted a high protective tariff, which would encourage infant industries, allowing them to develop and eventually hold their own against their more advanced British counterparts. List denounced the British doctrine of free trade as little more than Britain's attempt "to make the rest of the world, like the Hindus, its serfs in all industrial and commercial relations." By the 1840s List's **economic nationalism** had become increasingly popular in Germany and elsewhere.

Finally, banks, like governments, also played a larger and more creative role on the continent than in Britain. Previously, almost all banks in Europe had been private, organized as secretive partnerships. Because of the possibility of unlimited financial loss, the partners of private banks tended to be quite conservative and were content to deal with a few rich clients and a few big merchants. They generally avoided industrial investment as being too risky.

In the 1830s, two important Belgian banks pioneered in a new direction. They received permission from the growth-oriented government to establish themselves as corporations enjoying limited liability. That is, a stockholder could lose only his or her original investment in the bank's common stock and could not be assessed for any additional losses. Publicizing the risk-reducing advantage of limited liability, these Belgian banks were able to attract many shareholders, large and small. They mobilized impressive resources for investment in big companies, became industrial banks, and successfully promoted industrial development.

Similar corporate banks became important in France and Germany in the 1850s and 1860s. Usually working in collaboration with governments, they established and developed many railroads and many companies working in heavy industry, which were increasingly organized as limited liability corporations. The most famous such bank was the Crédit Mobilier of Paris, founded by Isaac and Emile Pereire, two young Jewish journalists from Bordeaux. The Crédit Mobilier advertised extensively. It used the savings of thousands of small investors as well as the resources of big ones. The activities of the bank were far-reaching; it built railroads all over France and Europe. As Emile Pereire had said in 1835, "It is not enough to outline gigantic programs on paper. I must write my ideas on the earth."

The combined efforts of skilled workers, entrepreneurs, governments, and industrial banks meshed successfully between 1850 and the financial crash of 1873. This was a period of unprecedentedly rapid economic growth on the continent. In Belgium, Germany, and France, key indicators of modern industrial development—such as railway mileage, iron and coal production, and steam-engine capacity—increased at average annual rates of 5 to 10 percent. As a result, rail networks were completed in western and much of central Europe, and the leading continental countries mastered the industrial technologies that had first been developed in Great Britain. In the early 1870s, Britain was still Europe's most industrial nation, but a select handful of countries were closing the gap that had been opened up by the Industrial Revolution.

## Capital and Labor

See DBQ 8

Industrial development brought new social relations and intensified long-standing problems between capital and labor in both urban workshops and cottage industry (see pages 639–643). A new group of factory owners and industrial capitalists arose. These men and women and their families strengthened the wealth and size of the middle class, which had previously been made up mainly of merchants and professional people. The nineteenth century became the golden age of the middle class. Modern industry also created a much larger group, the factory workers. For the first time, large numbers of men, women, and children came together under one roof to work with complicated machinery for a single owner or a few partners in large companies.

The growth of new occupational groups in industry stimulated new thinking about social relations. Often combined with reflections on the French Revolution, this thinking led to the development of a new overarching interpretation—a new paradigm—regarding social relationships (see Chapter 23). Briefly, this paradigm argued, with considerable success, that individuals were members of economically determined classes, which had conflicting interests. Accordingly, the comfortable, well-educated "public" of the eighteenth century came increasingly to see itself as the backbone of the middle class (or the middle classes), and the "people" gradually transformed themselves into the modern working class (or working classes). And if the new class interpretation was more of a deceptive simplification than a fundamental truth for some critics, it appealed to many because it seemed to explain what was happening. Therefore, conflicting classes existed, in part, because many individuals came to believe

**Ford Maddox Brown: Work** This midcentury painting provides a rich visual representation of the new concepts of social class that became common by 1850. The central figures are the colorful laborers, endowed by the artist with strength and nobility. Close by, a poor girl minds her brother and sister for her working mother. On the right, a middle-class minister and a social critic observe and do intellectual work. What work does the couple on horseback perform? *(Birmingham Museums and Art Gallery/The Bridgeman Art Library)*

they existed and developed an appropriate sense of class feeling—what Marxists call **class-consciousness.**

What, then, was the relationship between capital and labor in the early Industrial Revolution? Did the new industrial middle class ruthlessly exploit the workers, as Karl Marx and others have charged?

## The New Class of Factory Owners

Early industrialists operated in a highly competitive economic system. As the careers of Watt and Harkort illustrate, there were countless production problems, and success and large profits were by no means certain. Manufacturers therefore waged a constant battle to cut their production costs and stay afloat. Much of the profit had to go back into the business for new and better machinery. "Dragged on by the frenzy of this terrible life," according to one of the dismayed critics, the struggling manufacturer had "no time for niceties. He must conquer or die, make a fortune or drown himself."[5]

Most early industrialists drew upon their families and friends for labor and capital, but they came from a variety of backgrounds. Many, such as Harkort, were from well-established merchant families, which provided a rich network of contacts and support. Others, such as Watt and Cockerill, were of modest means, especially in the early days. Artisans and skilled workers of exceptional ability had unparalleled opportunities. Members of ethnic and religious groups who had been discriminated against in the traditional occupations controlled by the landed aristocracy jumped at the new chances and often helped each other. Scots, Quakers, and other Protestant dissenters were tremendously important in Britain; Protestants and Jews dominated banking in Catholic France. Many of the industrialists were newly rich, and, not surprisingly, they were very proud and self-satisfied.

As factories and firms grew larger, opportunities declined, at least in well-developed industries. It became considerably harder for a gifted but poor young mechanic to start a small enterprise and end up as a wealthy manufacturer. Formal education (for sons and males) became more important as a means of success and advancement, and formal education at the advanced level was expensive. In Britain by 1830 and in France and Germany by 1860, leading industrialists were more likely to have inherited their well-established enterprises, and they were financially much more secure than their struggling fathers and mothers had been. They also had a greater sense of class-consciousness, fully aware that ongoing industrial development had widened the gap between themselves and their workers.

The wives and daughters of successful businessmen also found fewer opportunities for active participation in Europe's increasingly complex business world. Rather than contributing as vital partners in a family-owned enterprise, as so many middle-class women such as Elizabeth Strutt had done (see the feature "Individuals in Society: The Strutt Family"), these women were increasingly valued for their ladylike gentility. By 1850 some influential women writers and most businessmen assumed that middle-class wives and daughters should steer clear of undignified work in offices and factories. Rather, a middle-class lady should protect and enhance her femininity. She should concentrate on her proper role as wife and mother, preferably in an elegant residential area far removed from ruthless commerce and the volatile working class.

## The New Factory Workers

The social consequences of the Industrial Revolution have long been hotly debated. The condition of British workers during the transformation has always generated the most controversy among historians because Britain was the first country to industrialize and because the social consequences seemed harshest there. Before 1850 other countries had not proceeded very far with industrialization, and almost everyone agrees that the economic conditions of European workers improved after 1850. Thus the experience of British workers to about 1850 deserves special attention. (Industrial growth also promoted rapid urbanization, with its own awesome problems, as will be shown in Chapter 24.)

From the beginning, the Industrial Revolution in Britain had its critics. Among the first were the romantic poets. William Blake (1757–1827) called the early factories "satanic mills" and protested against the hard life of the London poor. William Wordsworth (1770–1850) lamented the destruction of the rural way of life and the pollution of the land and water. Some handicraft workers—notably the **Luddites,** who attacked whole factories in northern England in 1812 and after—smashed the new machines, which they believed were putting them out of work. Doctors and reformers wrote eloquently of problems in the factories and new towns, while Malthus and Ricardo concluded that workers would earn only enough to stay alive.

This pessimistic view was accepted and reinforced by Friedrich Engels (1820–1895), the future revolutionary and colleague of Karl Marx. After studying conditions in northern England, this young middle-class German published in 1844 *The Condition of the Working Class in England,* a blistering indictment of the middle classes. "At the bar of world opinion," he wrote, "I charge the English middle classes with mass murder, wholesale robbery, and all the other crimes in the calendar." The new poverty of industrial workers was worse than the old poverty of cottage workers and agricultural laborers, according to Engels. The culprit was industrial capitalism, with its relentless competition and constant technical change. Engels's extremely influential charge of middle-class exploitation and increasing worker poverty was embellished by Marx and later socialists.

Meanwhile, other observers believed that conditions were improving for the working people. Andrew Ure wrote in 1835 in his study of the cotton industry that conditions in most factories were not harsh and were even quite good. Edwin Chadwick, a great and conscientious government official well acquainted with the problems of the working population, concluded that the "whole mass of the laboring community" was increasingly able "to buy more of the necessities and minor luxuries of life."[6] Nevertheless, if all the contemporary assessments had been counted up, those who thought conditions were getting worse for working people would probably have been the majority.

In an attempt to go beyond the contradictory judgments of contemporaries, some historians have looked at different kinds of sources. Statistical evidence is one such source. If working people suffered a great economic decline, as Engels and later socialists asserted, then the pur-

# Individuals in Society

## The Strutt Family

For centuries economic life in Europe revolved around hundreds of thousands of small family enterprises. These family enterprises worked farms, crafted products, and traded goods. They built and operated the firms and factories of the early industrial era, with the notable exceptions of the capital-hungry railroads and a few big banks. Indeed, until late in the nineteenth century, close-knit family groups continued to control most successful businesses, including those organized as corporations.

One successful and fairly well-documented family enterprise began with the marriage of Jedediah Strutt (1726–1797) and Elizabeth Woollat (1729–1774) in Derbyshire in northern England in 1755. The son of a farmer, Jedediah fell in love with Elizabeth when he was apprenticed away from home as a wheelwright and lodged with her parents. Both young people grew up in the close-knit dissenting Protestant community, which did not accept the doctrines of the state-sponsored Church of England, and the well-educated Elizabeth worked in a local school for dissenters and then for a dissenter minister in London. Indecisive and self-absorbed, Jedediah inherited in 1754 a small stock of animals from an uncle and finally married Elizabeth the following year.

Aided by Elizabeth, who was "obviously a very capable woman" and who supplied some of the drive her husband had previously lacked, Jedediah embarked on a new career.* He invented a machine to make handsome, neat-fitting ribbed silk stockings, which had previously been made by hand. He secured a patent, despite strong opposition from competitors, and went into production. Elizabeth helped constantly in the enterprise, which was nothing less than an informal partnership between husband and wife.†

In 1757, for example, when Jedediah was fighting to uphold his patent in the local court, Elizabeth left her son of nine months and journeyed to London to seek a badly needed loan from her former employer. She also canvassed her London relatives and dissenter friends for orders for stockings and looked for sales agents and sources of capital. Elizabeth's letters reveal a detailed knowledge of ribbed stockings and the prices and quality of different kinds of thread. The family biographers, old-line economic historians writing without a trace of feminist concerns, conclude that her husband "owed much of his success to her energy and counsel." Elizabeth was always "active in the business—a partner in herself."‡ Historians have often overlooked such invaluable contributions from wives like Elizabeth, partly because the legal rights and consequences of partnership were denied to married women in Britain and Europe in the eighteenth and nineteenth centuries.

*Jedediah Strutt (ca 1790), by Joseph Wright of Derby.* (Derby Museum & Art Gallery/The Bridgeman Art Library)

The Strutt enterprise grew and gradually prospered, but it always retained its family character. The firm built a large silk mill and then went into cotton spinning in partnership with Richard Arkwright, the inventor of the water frame (see page 728). The brothers of both Jedediah and Elizabeth worked for the firm, and their eldest daughter worked long hours in the warehouse. Bearing three sons, Elizabeth fulfilled yet another vital task because the typical family firm looked to its own members for managers and continued success. All three sons entered the business and became cotton textile magnates. Elizabeth never saw these triumphs. The loyal and talented wife in the family partnership died suddenly at age forty-five while in London with Jedediah on a business trip.

### Questions for Analysis

1. How and why did the Strutts succeed?
2. What does Elizabeth's life tell us about the role of British women in the early Industrial Revolution?

*R. Fitton and A. Wadsworth, *The Strutts and the Arkwrights, 1758–1830: A Study of the Early Factory System* (Manchester, England: Manchester University Press, 1958), p. 23.

† See the excellent discussion by C. Hall, "Strains in the 'Firm of Wife, Children and Friends'? Middle-Class Women and Employment in Early Nineteenth-Century England," in P. Hudson and W. Lee, eds., *Women's Work and the Family Economy in Historical Perspective* (Manchester, England: Manchester University Press, 1990), pp. 106–132.

‡ Fitton and Wadsworth, *The Strutts,* pp. 110–111.

*The* **history companion** *features additional information and activities related to this topic.*
**history.college.hmco.com/students**

chasing power of the working person's wages must have declined drastically.

Scholarly statistical studies have weakened the idea that the condition of the working class got much worse with industrialization. But the most recent studies also confirm the view that the early years of the Industrial Revolution were hard ones for British workers. There was little or no increase in the purchasing power of the average British worker from about 1780 to about 1820. The years from 1792 to 1815, a period of almost constant warfare with France, were particularly difficult. Food prices rose faster than wages, and the living conditions of the laboring poor declined. Only after 1820, and especially after 1840, did real wages rise substantially, so that the average worker earned and consumed roughly 50 percent more in real terms in 1850 than in 1770.[7] In short, there was considerable economic improvement for workers throughout Great Britain by 1850, but that improvement was hard won and slow in coming.

This important conclusion must be qualified, however. First, the hours in the average workweek increased; to a large extent, workers earned more simply because they worked more. Indeed, significant recent research shows that in England nonagricultural workers labored about 250 days per year in 1760 as opposed to 300 days per year in 1830, while the normal workday remained an exhausting eleven hours throughout the entire period. In 1760 nonagricultural workers still observed many religious and public holidays by not working, and Monday was popularly known as "Saint Monday" because so many workers took the day off. These days of leisure and relaxation declined rapidly after 1760, and by 1830 nonagricultural workers had joined landless agricultural laborers in toiling six rather than five days a week.[8]

Second, the wartime decline in the average worker's standard of living was very important. The difficult war years were formative years for the new factory labor force, and they colored the early experience of modern industrial life in somber tones.

Another way to consider the workers' standard of living is to look at the goods that they purchased. Again the evidence is somewhat contradictory. Speaking generally, workers ate somewhat more food of higher nutritional quality as the Industrial Revolution progressed, except during wartime. Diets became more varied; people ate more potatoes, dairy products, fruits, and vegetables. Clothing improved, but housing for working people probably deteriorated somewhat. In short, per capita use of specific goods supports the position that the standard of living of the working classes rose, at least moderately, after the long wars with France.

## Conditions of Work

What about working conditions? Did workers eventually earn more only at the cost of working longer and harder? Were workers exploited harshly by the new factory owners?

The first factories were cotton mills, which began functioning along rivers and streams in the 1770s. Cottage workers, accustomed to the putting-out system, were reluctant to work in the new factories even when they received relatively good wages because factory work was unappealing. In the factory, workers had to keep up with the machine and follow its tempo. They had to show up every day and work long, monotonous hours. Factory workers had to adjust their daily lives to the shrill call of the factory whistle.

Cottage workers were not used to that kind of life and discipline. All members of the family worked hard and long, but in spurts, setting their own pace. They could interrupt their work when they wanted to. Women and children could break up their long hours of spinning with other tasks. On Saturday afternoon the head of the family delivered the week's work to the merchant manufacturer and got paid. Saturday night was a time of relaxation and drinking, especially for the men. Recovering from his hangover on Tuesday, the weaver bent to his task on Wednesday and then worked frantically to meet his deadline on Saturday. Like some students today, he might "pull an all-nighter" on Thursday or Friday in order to get his work in.

Also, early factories resembled English poorhouses, where totally destitute people went to live at public expense. Some poorhouses were industrial prisons, where the inmates had to work in order to receive their food and lodging. The similarity between large brick factories and large stone poorhouses increased the cottage workers' fear of factories and their hatred of factory discipline.

It was cottage workers' reluctance to work in factories that prompted the early cotton mill owners to turn to abandoned and pauper children for their labor. As we have seen, these owners contracted with local officials to employ large numbers of these children, who had no say in the matter. Pauper children were often badly treated and terribly overworked in the mills, as they were when they were apprenticed as chimney sweeps, market girls, shoemakers, and so forth. In the eighteenth century,

**Workers at a Large Cotton Mill** This 1833 engraving shows adult women operating power looms under the supervision of a male foreman, and it accurately reflects both the decline of family employment and the emergence of a gender-based division of labor in many English factories. The jungle of belts and shafts connecting the noisy looms to the giant steam engine on the ground floor created a constant din. *(Time Life Pictures/Getty Images)*

semiforced child labor seemed necessary and was socially accepted. From our modern point of view, it was cruel exploitation and a blot on the record of the new industrial system.

By 1790 the early pattern was rapidly changing. The use of pauper apprentices was in decline, and in 1802 it was forbidden by Parliament. Many more factories were being built, mainly in urban areas, where they could use steam power rather than waterpower and attract a workforce more easily than in the countryside. The need for workers was great. Indeed, people came from near and far to work in the cities, both as factory workers and as laborers, builders, and domestic servants. Yet as they took these new jobs, working people did not simply give in to a system of labor that had formerly repelled them. Rather, they helped modify the system by carrying over old, familiar working traditions.

For one thing, they often came to the mills and the mines as family units. This was how they had worked on farms and in the putting-out system. The mill or mine owner bargained with the head of the family and paid him or her for the work of the whole family. In the cotton mills, children worked for their mothers or fathers, collecting scraps and "piecing" broken threads together. In the mines, children sorted coal and worked the ventilation equipment. Their mothers hauled coal in the tunnels below the surface, while their fathers hewed with pick and shovel at the face of the seam.

The preservation of the family as an economic unit in the factories from the 1790s on made the new surroundings more tolerable, both in Great Britain and in other countries, during the early stages of industrialization. Parents disciplined their children, making firm measures socially acceptable, and directed their upbringing. The presence of the whole family meant that children and adults worked the same long hours (twelve-hour shifts were normal in cotton mills in 1800). In the early years, some very young children were employed solely to keep the family together. For example, Jedediah Strutt (see page 743) believed children should be at least ten years old to work in his mills, but he reluctantly employed seven-year-olds to satisfy their parents. Adult workers were not particularly interested in limiting the minimum working age or hours of their children as long as family members worked side by side. Only when technical changes threatened to place control and discipline in the hands of impersonal managers and overseers did adult workers protest against inhuman conditions in the name of their children.

Some enlightened employers and social reformers in Parliament definitely felt otherwise. They argued that more humane standards were necessary, and they used widely circulated parliamentary reports to influence public opinion. For example, Robert Owen (1771–1858), a very successful manufacturer in Scotland, testified in 1816 before an investigating committee on the basis of his experience. He stated that "very strong facts" demonstrated that employing children under ten years of age as factory workers was "injurious to the children, and not beneficial to the proprietors." The parliamentary committee asked him to explain, and the testimony proceeded as follows:

*"Seventeen years ago, a number of individuals, with myself, purchased the New Lanark establishment from the late Mr Dale, of Glasgow. At that period I find that there were 500 children, who had been taken from poor-houses, chiefly in Edinburgh. . . . The hours of work at that time were thirteen, inclusive of meal times, and an hour and a half was allowed for meals. I very soon discovered that although those children were very well fed, well clothed, well lodged, and very great care taken of them when out of the mills, their growth and their minds were materially injured by being employed at those ages within the cotton mills for eleven and a half hours per day. . . . Their limbs were generally deformed, their growth was stunted, and although one of the best school-masters upon the old plan was engaged to instruct those children every night, in general they made but a very slow progress, even in learning the common alphabet. . . ."*

*"Do you think the age of ten the best period for the admission of children into full and constant employment for ten or eleven hours per day, within woollen, cotton, and other mills or manufactories?"*

*"I do not."*

*"What other period would you recommend for their full admission to full work?"*

*"Twelve years."*[9]

Owen's testimony rang true because he had already raised the age of employment in his mills and was promoting education for young children. Workers also provided graphic testimony at such hearings as the reformers pressed Parliament to pass corrective laws. They scored some important successes.

Their most significant early accomplishment was the **Factory Act of 1833.** It limited the factory workday for children between nine and thirteen to eight hours and that of adolescents between fourteen and eighteen to twelve hours, although the act made no effort to regulate the hours of work for children at home or in small businesses. Children under nine were to be enrolled in the elementary schools that factory owners were required to establish. The employment of children declined rapidly. Thus the Factory Act broke the pattern of whole families working together in the factory because efficiency required standardized shifts for all workers.

Ties of blood and kinship were important in other ways in Great Britain in the formative years between about 1790 and 1840. Many manufacturers and builders hired workers through subcontractors. They paid the subcontractors on the basis of what the subcontractors and their crews produced—for smelting so many tons of pig iron or moving so much dirt or gravel for a canal or roadbed. Subcontractors in turn hired and fired their own workers, many of whom were friends and relations. The subcontractor might be as harsh as the greediest capitalist, but the relationship between subcontractor and work crew was close and personal. This kind of personal relationship had traditionally existed in cottage industry and in urban crafts, and it was more acceptable to many workers than impersonal factory discipline. This system also provided people with an easy way to find a job. Even today, a friend or relative who is a supervisor is frequently worth a host of formal application forms.

Ties of kinship were particularly important for newcomers, who often traveled great distances to find work. Many urban workers in Great Britain were from Ireland. Forced out of rural Ireland by population growth and deteriorating economic conditions from 1817 on, Irish in search of jobs could not be choosy; they took what they could get. As early as 1824, most of the workers in the Glasgow cotton mills were Irish; in 1851 one-sixth of the population of Liverpool was Irish. Like many other immigrant groups held together by ethnic and religious ties, the Irish worked together, formed their own neighborhoods, and not only survived but also thrived.

## The Sexual Division of Labor

The era of the Industrial Revolution witnessed major changes in the sexual division of labor. In preindustrial Europe most people generally worked in family units. By tradition, certain jobs were defined by gender—women and girls for milking and spinning, men and boys for plowing and weaving—but many tasks might go to either sex. Family employment carried over into early factories and subcontracting, but it collapsed as child labor was restricted and new attitudes emerged. A different sexual division of labor gradually arose to take its place. The man emerged as the family's primary wage earner, while the woman found only limited job opportunities. Generally denied good jobs at good wages in the growing urban economy, women were expected to concentrate on unpaid housework, child care, and craftwork at home.

This new pattern of "separate spheres" had several aspects. First, all studies agree that married women from the working classes were much less likely to work full-time for wages outside the house after the first child arrived, although they often earned small amounts doing putting-out handicrafts at home and taking in boarders. Second, when married women did work for wages outside the house, they usually came from the poorest families, where the husbands were poorly paid, sick, unemployed, or missing. Third, these poor married (or widowed) women were joined by legions of young unmarried women, who worked full-time but only in certain jobs. Fourth, all women were generally confined to low-paying, dead-end jobs. Virtually no occupation open to women paid a wage sufficient for a person to live independently. Men predominated in the better-paying, more promising employments. Evolving gradually, but largely in place by 1850, the new sexual division of labor in Britain constituted a major development in the history of women and of the family.

If the reorganization of paid work along gender lines is widely recognized, there is no agreement on its causes. One school of scholars sees little connection with industrialization and finds the answer in the deeply ingrained sexist attitudes of a "patriarchal tradition," which predated the economic transformation. These scholars stress the role of male-dominated craft unions in denying working women access to good jobs and relegating them to unpaid housework. Other scholars, stressing that the gender roles of women and men can vary enormously with time and culture, look more to a combination of economic and biological factors in order to explain the emergence of a sex-segregated division of labor.

Three ideas stand out in this more recent interpretation. First, the new and unfamiliar discipline of the clock and the machine was especially hard on married women of the laboring classes. Above all, relentless factory discipline conflicted with child care in a way that labor on the farm or in the cottage had not. A woman operating ear-splitting spinning machinery could mind a child of seven or eight working beside her (until such work was outlawed), but she could no longer pace herself through pregnancy or breast-feed her baby on the job. Thus a working-class woman had strong incentives to concentrate on child care within her home if her family could afford it.

Second, running a household in conditions of primitive urban poverty was an extremely demanding job in its own right. There were no supermarkets or public transportation. Everything had to be done on foot. Shopping and feeding the family constituted a never-ending challenge. The woman marched from one tiny shop to another, dragging her tired children (for who was to watch them?) and struggling valiantly with heavy sacks and tricky shopkeepers. Yet another brutal job outside the house—a "second shift"—had limited appeal for the average married woman. Thus women might well have accepted the emerging division of labor as the best available strategy for family survival in the industrializing society.[10]

Third, why were the women who did work for wages outside the home segregated and confined to certain "women's jobs"? No doubt the desire of males to monopolize the best opportunities and hold women down provides part of the answer. Yet as some feminist scholars have argued, sex-segregated employment was also a collective response to the new industrial system. Previously, at least in theory, young people worked under a watchful parental eye. The growth of factories and mines brought unheard-of opportunities for girls and boys to mix on the job, free of familial supervision. Continuing to mix after work, they were "more likely to form liaisons, initiate courtships, and respond to advances."[11] Such intimacy also led to more unplanned pregnancies and fueled the illegitimacy explosion that had begun in the late eighteenth century and that gathered force until at least 1850 (see pages 665–666). Thus segregation of jobs by gender was partly an effort by older people to help control the sexuality of working-class youths.

Investigations into the British coal industry before 1842 provide a graphic example of this concern. (See the feature "Listening to the Past: The Testimony of Young Mine Workers" on pages 752–753.) The middle-class men leading the inquiry, who expected their daughters and wives to pursue ladylike activities, often failed to appreciate the physical effort of the girls and women who dragged with belt and chain the unwheeled carts of coal along narrow underground passages. But they professed horror at the sight of girls and women working without shirts, which was a common practice because of the heat, and they quickly assumed the prevalence of licentious sex with the male miners, who also wore very little clothing. In fact, most girls and married women worked for related males in a family unit that provided considerable protection and restraint. Yet many witnesses from the working class also believed that "blackguardism and debauchery" were common and that "they are best out of the pits, the lasses." Some miners stressed particularly the danger of sexual aggression for girls working past puberty. As one explained:

*I consider it a scandal for girls to work in the pits. Till they are 12 or 14 they may work very well but after that it's an abomination. . . . The work of the pit does not hurt them, it is the effect on their morals that I complain of, and after 14 they should not be allowed to go. . . . After that age it is dreadful for them.*[12]

The **Mines Act of 1842** prohibited underground work for all women as well as for boys under ten.

Some women who had to support themselves protested against being excluded from coal mining, which paid higher wages than most other jobs open to working-class women. But provided they were part of families that could manage economically, the girls and the women who had worked underground were generally pleased with the law. In explaining her satisfaction in 1844, one mother of four provided a real insight into why many women accepted the emerging sexual division of labor:

*While working in the pit I was worth to my [miner] husband seven shillings a week, out of which we had to pay 2½ shillings to a woman for looking after the younger children. I used to take them to her house at 4 o'clock in the morning, out of their own beds, to put them into hers. Then there was one shilling a week for washing; besides, there was mending to pay for, and other things. The house was not guided. The other children broke things; they did not go to school when they were sent; they would be playing about, and get ill-used by other children, and their clothes torn. Then when I came home in the evening, everything was to do after the day's labor, and I was so tired I had no heart for it; no fire lit, nothing cooked, no water fetched, the house dirty, and nothing comfortable for my husband. It is all far better now, and I wouldn't go down again.*[13]

## The Early Labor Movement in Britain

Many kinds of employment changed slowly during and after the Industrial Revolution in Great Britain. In 1850 more British people still worked on farms than in any other occupation. The second-largest occupation was domestic service, with more than one million household servants, 90 percent of whom were women. Thus many old, familiar jobs outside industry lived on and provided alternatives for individual workers. This helped ease the transition to industrial civilization.

Within industry itself, the pattern of artisans working with hand tools in small shops remained unchanged in many trades, even as some others were revolutionized by technological change. For example, as in the case of cotton and coal, the British iron industry was completely dominated by large-scale capitalist firms by 1850. Many large ironworks had more than one thousand people on their payrolls. Yet the firms that fashioned iron into small metal goods, such as tools, tableware, and toys, employed on average fewer than ten wage workers, who used time-honored handicraft skills. Only gradually after 1850 did some owners find ways to reorganize some handicraft industries with new machines and new patterns of work. The survival of small workshops gave many workers an alternative to factory employment.

Working-class solidarity and class-consciousness developed in small workshops as well as in large factories. In the northern factory districts, where thousands of "hired hands" looked across at a tiny minority of managers and owners, anticapitalist sentiments were frequent by the 1820s. Commenting in 1825 on a strike in the woolen center of Bradford and the support it had gathered from other regions, one paper claimed with pride that "it is all the workers of England against a few masters of Bradford."[14] Modern technology had created a few versus a many.

The transformation of some traditional trades by organizational changes, rather than technological innovations, could also create ill will and class feeling. The liberal concept of economic freedom gathered strength in the late eighteenth and early nineteenth centuries. As in France

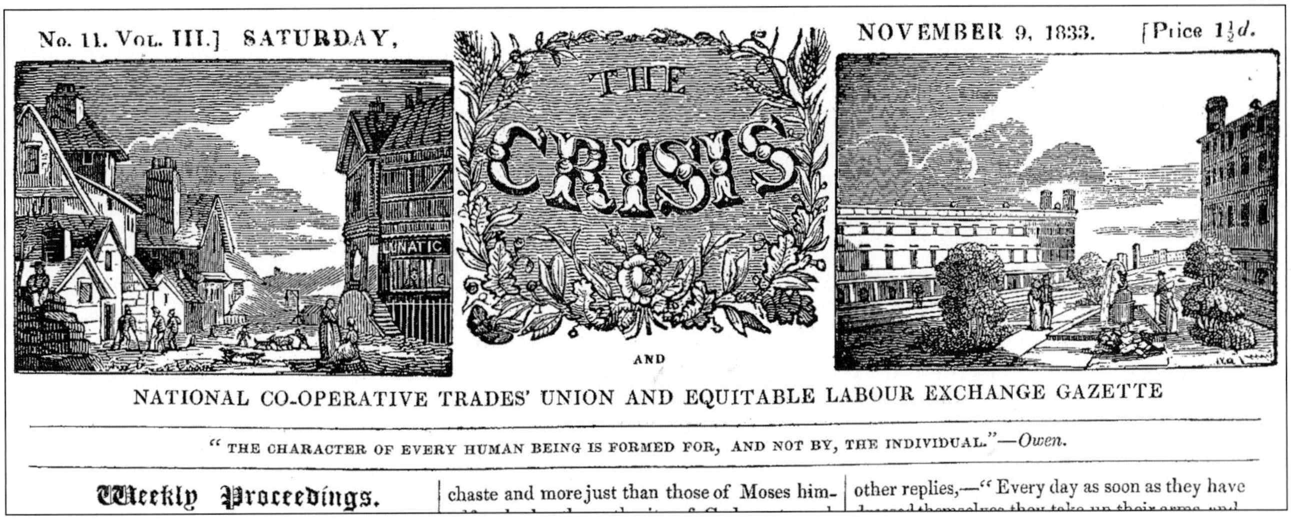
No. 11. Vol. III.] SATURDAY, NOVEMBER 9, 1833. [Price $1\frac{1}{2}d$.

THE CRISIS

AND

NATIONAL CO-OPERATIVE TRADES' UNION AND EQUITABLE LABOUR EXCHANGE GAZETTE

"THE CHARACTER OF EVERY HUMAN BEING IS FORMED FOR, AND NOT BY, THE INDIVIDUAL."—*Owen.*

Weekly Proceedings. | chaste and more just than those of Moses him- | other replies,—"Every day as soon as they have



**The Working-Class Press** *The Crisis,* an influential newspaper inspired by the teachings of Robert Owen, summed up its analysis of Britain's problems with two images at the top of the first page. Degrading poverty for the many and superfluous wealth for the few equaled national crisis. Newspapers helped to strengthen and channel the British labor movement. *(Private Collection/The Bridgeman Art Library)*

during the French Revolution, the British government attacked monopolies, guilds, and workers combinations in the name of individual liberty. In 1799 Parliament passed the **Combination Acts,** which outlawed unions and strikes. In 1813 and 1814, Parliament repealed the old and often disregarded law of 1563 regulating the wages of artisans and the conditions of apprenticeship. As a result of these and other measures, certain skilled artisan workers, such as bootmakers and high-quality tailors, found aggressive capitalists ignoring traditional work rules and flooding their trades with unorganized women workers and children to beat down wages.

The liberal capitalist attack on artisan guilds and work rules was bitterly resented by many craftworkers, who subsequently played an important part in Great Britain and in other countries in gradually building a modern labor movement to improve working conditions and to serve worker needs. The Combination Acts were widely disregarded by workers. Printers, papermakers, carpenters, tailors, and other such craftsmen continued to take collective action, and societies of skilled factory workers also organized unions. Unions sought to control the number of skilled workers, limit apprenticeship to members' own children, and bargain with owners over wages. They were not afraid to strike; there was, for example, a general strike of adult cotton spinners in Manchester in 1810. In the face of widespread union activity, Parliament repealed the Combination Acts in 1824, and unions were tolerated, though not fully accepted, after 1825.

The next stage in the development of the British trade-union movement was the attempt to create a single large national union. This effort was led not so much by working people as by social reformers such as Robert Owen. Owen, a self-made cotton manufacturer (see page 746), had pioneered in industrial relations by combining firm discipline with concern for the health, safety, and hours of his workers. After 1815 he experimented with cooperative and socialist communities, including one at New Harmony, Indiana. Then in 1834 Owen organized one of the largest and most visionary of the early national unions, the **Grand National Consolidated Trades Union.** When this and other grandiose schemes collapsed, the British labor movement moved once again after 1851 in the direction of craft unions. The most famous of these "new model unions" was the Amalgamated Society of Engineers, which represented skilled machinists. These unions won real benefits for members by fairly conservative means and thus became an accepted part of the industrial scene.

British workers also engaged in direct political activity in defense of their own interests. After the collapse of Owen's national trade union, many working people went into the Chartist movement, which sought political democracy. The key Chartist demand—that all men be given the right to vote—became the great hope of millions of aroused people. Workers were also active in campaigns to limit the workday in factories to ten hours and to permit duty-free importation of wheat into Great Britain to secure cheap bread. Thus working people developed a sense of their own identity and played an active role in shaping the new industrial system. They were neither helpless victims nor passive beneficiaries.

## Summary

Western society's industrial breakthrough grew out of a long process of economic and social change in which the rise of capitalism, overseas expansion, and the growth of rural industry stood out as critical preparatory developments. Eventually taking the lead in all of these developments, and also profiting from stable government, abundant natural resources, and a flexible labor force, Britain experienced between the 1780s and the 1850s an epoch-making transformation, one that is still aptly termed the Industrial Revolution.

Building on technical breakthroughs, power-driven equipment, and large-scale enterprise, the Industrial Revolution in England greatly increased output in certain radically altered industries, stimulated the large handicraft and commercial sectors, and speeded up overall economic growth. Rugged Scotland industrialized at least as fast as England, and Great Britain became the first industrial nation. By 1850 the level of British per capita industrial production was surpassing continental levels by a growing margin, and Britain savored a near monopoly in world markets for mass-produced goods.

Continental countries inevitably took rather different paths to the urban industrial society. They relied more on handicraft production in both towns and villages. Only in the 1840s did railroad construction begin to create the strong demand for iron, coal, and railway equipment that speeded up the process of industrialization in the 1850s and 1860s.

The rise of modern industry had a profound impact on people and their lives. In the early stages, Britain again led the way, experiencing in a striking manner the long-term social changes accompanying the economic transformation. Factory discipline and Britain's stern capitalist economy weighed heavily on working people, who, however, actively fashioned their destinies and refused to be passive victims. Improvements in the standard of living came slowly, but they were substantial by 1850. The era of industrialization fostered new attitudes toward child labor, encouraged protective factory legislation, and called forth a new sense of class feeling and an assertive labor movement. It also promoted a more rigid division of roles and responsibilities within the family that was detrimental to women, another gradual but profound change of revolutionary proportions.

## Key Terms

Industrial Revolution
spinning jenny
water frame
body linen
steam engines
coke
*Rocket*
Crystal Palace
iron law of wages
tariff protection
economic nationalism
class-consciousness
Luddites
Factory Act of 1833
Mines Act of 1842
Combination Acts
Grand National Consolidated Trades Union

## Notes


1. N. F. R. Crafts, *British Economic Growth During the Industrial Revolution* (Oxford: Oxford University Press, 1985), p. 32.
2. P. Bairoch, "International Industrialization Levels from 1750 to 1980," *Journal of European Economic History* 11 (Spring 1982): 269–333.
3. Crafts, *British Economic Growth,* pp. 45, 95–102.
4. M. Lévy-Leboyer, *Les banques européennes et l'industrialisation dans la première moitié du XIXe siècle* (Paris: Presses Universitaires de France, 1964), p. 29.
5. J. Michelet, *The People,* trans. with an introduction by J. P. McKay (Urbana: University of Illinois Press, 1973; original publication, 1846), p. 64.
6. Quoted in W. A. Hayek, ed., *Capitalism and the Historians* (Chicago: University of Chicago Press, 1954), p. 126.
7. Crafts, *British Economic Growth,* p. 95.
8. H-J. Voth, *Time and Work in England, 1750–1830* (Oxford: Oxford University Press, 2000), pp. 268–270; also pp. 118–133.
9. Quoted in E. R. Pike, *"Hard Times": Human Documents of the Industrial Revolution* (New York: Praeger, 1966), p. 109.
10. See especially J. Brenner and M. Rama, "Rethinking Women's Oppression," *New Left Review* 144 (March–April 1984): 33–71, and sources cited there.
11. J. Humphries, ". . . 'The Most Free from Objection' . . . : The Sexual Division of Labor and Women's Work in Nineteenth-Century England," *Journal of Economic History* 47 (December 1987): 948.
12. Ibid., p. 941; Pike, *"Hard Times,"* p. 266.
13. Pike, *"Hard Times,"* p. 208.
14. Quoted in D. Geary, ed., *Labour and Socialist Movements in Europe Before 1914* (Oxford: Berg, 1989), p. 29.


## Suggested Reading

There is a vast and exciting literature on the Industrial Revolution. R. Cameron and L. Neal, *A Concise Economic History of the World,* 4th ed. (2003), provides an introduction to the issues and has a carefully annotated bibliography. J. Goodman and K. Honeyman, *Gainful Pursuits: The Making of Industrial Europe, 1600–1914* (1988); D. S. Landes, *The Unbound Prometheus: Technological Change and Industrial Development in Western Europe from 1750 to the Present* (1969); and S. Pollard, *Peaceful Conquest: The Industrialization of Europe* (1981), are excellent general treatments of European industrial growth. These studies also suggest the range of issues and interpretations. R. Sylla and G. Toniolo, eds., *Patterns of European Industrialization* (1991), is an important collection by specialists. T. Kemp, *Industrialization in Europe,* 2d ed. (1985), is also useful. S. King and G. Timmins, *Making Sense of the Industrial Revolution* (2001); P. Hudson, *The Industrial Revolution* (1992); and M. Berg, *The Age of Manufactures: Industry, Innovation and Work in Britain, 1700–1820* (1985), admirably discuss the various aspects of the British breakthrough and offer good bibliographies, as does the work by Crafts mentioned in the Notes. E. A. Wrigley, *Continuity, Chance and Change: The Character of the Industrial Revolution in England* (1994), is an important reconsideration stressing resources and population. K. Pomeranz, *The Great Divergence: China, Europe, and the Making of the Modern World Economy* (2000), is a sophisticated reconsideration of why western Europe achieved this industrial breakthrough and China did not. P. Stearns, *The Industrial Revolution in World History* (1998), is a useful brief survey.

W. Walton, *France and the Crystal Palace: Bourgeois Taste and Artisan Manufacture in the 19th Century* (1992), and H. Kirsh, *From Domestic Manufacturing to Industrial Revolution: The Case of the Rhineland Textile Districts* (1989), examine the gradual transformation of handicraft techniques and their persistent importance in the international economy. R. Cameron, *France and the Economic Development of Europe, 1800–1914* (1961), traces the spread of railroads and industry across Europe. A. S. Milward and S. B. Saul, *The Economic Development of Continental Europe, 1780–1870* (1973) and *The Development of the Economies of Continental Europe, 1850–1914* (1977), may be compared with J. Clapham's old-fashioned classic, *Economic Development of France and Germany* (1963). C. Heywood, *The Economic Development of France, 1750–1914* (1992), introduces the main issues and provides an up-to-date bibliography. Other important works on industrial developments are G. Tortella, *The Development of Modern Spain* (2000); L. Schofer, *The Formation of a Modern Labor Force* (1975), which focuses on the Silesian part of Germany; and W. Blackwell, *The Industrialization of Russia,* 2d ed. (1982). M. Wintle, *An Economic and Social History of the Netherlands: Demographic, Economic and Social Transitions* (2000), and L. Magnusson, *An Economic History of Sweden* (2000), are excellent surveys of developments in two smaller countries. L. Moch, *Paths to the City: Regional Migration in Nineteenth-Century France* (1983), and W. Schivelbusch, *Disenchanted Night: The Industrialization of Light in the Nineteenth Century* (1983), imaginatively analyze quite different aspects of industrialization's many consequences.

The debate between "optimists" and "pessimists" about the consequences of industrialization in Britain goes on. Two excellent studies with a gender perspective revitalize the debate: D. Valenze, *The First Industrial Woman* (1995); P. Hudson and W. Lee, eds., *Women's Work and the Family Economy in Historical Perspective* (1990). A. Clarke, *The Struggle for the Breeches: Gender and the Making of the British Working Class* (1995), is a masterful examination of working-class marriages and gender politics. P. Taylor, ed., *The Industrial Revolution: Triumph or Disaster?* (1970), is a useful introduction to older studies. It is also fascinating to compare Engels's classic condemnation, *The Condition of the Working Class in England* (1844), with Andrew Ure's optimistic defense, *The Philosophy of Manufactures,* first published in 1835 and often reprinted. J. Rule, *The Labouring Classes in Early Industrial England, 1750–1850* (1987), is a recommended synthesis. E. P. Thompson continues and enriches the Engels tradition in *The Making of the English Working Class* (1963), an exciting book rich in detail and early working-class lore. Pike's documentary collection, cited in the Notes, provides fascinating insights into the lives of working people, as does the detailed investigation by C. Tuttle, *Hard Work in Factories and Mines: The Economics of Child Labor During the Industrial Revolution* (1999). Voth, cited in the Notes, is a fundamental contribution. L. Davidoff and C. Hall, *Family Fortunes: Men and Women of the English Middle Class, 1750–1850,* rev. ed. (2003), examines both economic activities and cultural beliefs with great skill. D. Winch, *Riches and Poverty: An Intellectual History of Political Economy in Britain, 1750–1834* (1996), provides an excellent survey of early English economists. F. Klingender, *Art and the Industrial Revolution,* rev. ed. (1968), is justly famous, and M. Ignatieff, *A Just Measure of Pain* (1980), is an engrossing study of prisons during British industrialization.

Among general studies, G. S. R. Kitson Clark, *The Making of Victorian England* (1967), is particularly imaginative. M. Bentley, *Politics Without Democracy, 1815–1914* (1984), is a fine general history of Britain. H. Ausubel discusses a major reformer in *John Bright* (1966), and B. Harrison skillfully illuminates the problem of heavy drinking in *Drink and the Victorians* (1971). The most famous contemporary novel dealing with the new industrial society is Charles Dickens's *Hard Times,* an entertaining but exaggerated story. *Mary Barton* and *North and South* by Elizabeth Gaskell are more realistic portrayals, and both are highly recommended.

# Listening to the Past

## The Testimony of Young Mine Workers

*The use of child labor in British industrialization quickly attracted the attention of humanitarians and social reformers. This interest led to investigations by parliamentary commissions, which resulted in laws limiting the hours and the ages of children working in large factories. Designed to build a case for remedial legislation, parliamentary inquiries gave large numbers of workers a rare chance to speak directly to contemporaries and to historians.*

*The moving passages that follow are taken from testimony gathered in 1841 and 1842 by the Ashley Mines Commission. Interviewing employers and many male and female workers, the commissioners focused on the physical condition of the youth and on the sexual behavior of workers far underground. The subsequent Mines Act of 1842 sought to reduce immoral behavior and sexual bullying by prohibiting underground work for all women (and for boys younger than ten).*

**Mr. Payne, coal master:**

That children are employed generally at nine years old in the coal pits and sometimes at eight. In fact, the smaller the vein of coal is in height, the younger and smaller are the children required; the work occupies from six to seven hours per day in the pits; they are not ill-used or worked beyond their strength; a good deal of depravity exists but they are certainly not worse in morals than in other branches of the Sheffield trade, but upon the whole superior; the morals of this district are materially improving; Mr. Bruce, the clergyman, has been zealous and active in endeavoring to ameliorate their moral and religious education. . . .

**Ann Eggley, hurrier, 18 years old:**

I'm sure I don't know how to spell my name. We go at four in the morning, and sometimes at half-past four. We begin to work as soon as we get down. We get out after four, sometimes at five, in the evening. We work the whole time except an hour for dinner, and sometimes we haven't time to eat. I hurry [move coal wagons underground] by myself, and have done so for long. I know the corves [small coal wagons] are very heavy, they are the biggest corves anywhere about. The work is far too hard for me; the sweat runs off me all over sometimes. I am very tired at night. Sometimes when we get home at night we have not power to wash us, and then we go to bed. Sometimes we fall asleep in the chair. Father said last night it was both a shame and a disgrace for girls to work as we do, but there was naught else for us to do. I began to hurry when I was seven and I have been hurrying ever since. I have been 11 years in the pits. The girls are always tired. I was poorly twice this winter; it was with headache. I hurry for Robert Wiggins; he is not akin to me. . . . We don't always get enough to eat and drink, but we get a good supper. I have known my father go at two in the morning to work . . . and he didn't come out till four. I am quite sure that we work constantly 12 hours except on Saturdays. We wear trousers and our shifts in the pit and great big shoes clinkered and nailed. The girls never work naked to the waist in our pit. The men don't insult us in the pit. The conduct of the girls in the pit is good enough sometimes and sometimes bad enough. I never went to a day-school. I went a little to a Sunday-school, but I soon gave it over. I thought it too bad to be confined both Sundays and week-days. I walk about and get the fresh air on Sundays. I have not learnt to read. I don't know my letters. I never learnt naught. I never go to church or chapel; there is no church or chapel at Gawber, there is none nearer than a mile. . . . I have never heard that a good man came into the world who was God's son to save sinners. I never heard of Christ

This illustration of a girl dragging a coal wagon was one of several that shocked public opinion and contributed to the Mines Act of 1842. *(The British Library)*

at all. Nobody has ever told me about him, nor have my father and mother ever taught me to pray. I know no prayer; I never pray.

**Patience Kershaw, aged 17:**

My father has been dead about a year; my mother is living and has ten children, five lads and five lasses; the oldest is about thirty, the youngest is four; three lasses go to mill; all the lads are colliers, two getters and three hurriers; one lives at home and does nothing; mother does nought but look after home.

All my sisters have been hurriers, but three went to the mill. Alice went because her legs swelled from hurrying in cold water when she was hot. I never went to day-school; I go to Sunday-school, but I cannot read or write; I go to pit at five o'clock in the morning and come out at five in the evening; I get my breakfast of porridge and milk first; I take my dinner with me, a cake, and eat it as I go; I do not stop or rest any time for the purpose; I get nothing else until I get home, and then have potatoes and meat, not every day meat. I hurry in the clothes I have now got on, trousers and ragged jacket; the bald place upon my head is made by thrusting the corves; my legs have never swelled, but sisters' did when they went to mill; I hurry the corves a mile and more under ground and back; they weigh 300; I hurry 11 a day; I wear a belt and chain at the workings to get the corves out; the putters [miners] that I work for are *naked* except their caps; they pull off all their clothes; I see them at work when I go up; sometimes they beat me, if I am not quick enough, with their hands; they strike me upon my back; the boys take liberties with me, sometimes, they pull me about; I am the only girl in the pit; there are about 20 boys and 15 men; all the men are naked; I would rather work in mill than in coal-pit.

**Isabel Wilson, 38 years old, coal putter:**

When women have children thick [fast] they are compelled to take them down early. I have been married 19 years and have had 10 bairns [children]; seven are in life. When on Sir John's work was a carrier of coals, which caused me to miscarry five times from the strains, and was gai [very] ill after each. Putting is no so oppressive; last child was born on Saturday morning, and I was at work on the Friday night.

Once met with an accident; a coal brake my cheek-bone, which kept me idle some weeks.

I have wrought below 30 years, and so has the guid man; he is getting touched in the breath now.

None of the children read, as the work is no regular. I did read once, but no able to attend to it now; when I go below lassie 10 years of age keeps house and makes the broth or stir-about.

## Questions for Analysis

1. To what extent are the testimonies of Ann Eggley and Patience Kershaw in harmony with that of Payne?
2. Describe the work of Eggley and Kershaw. What do you think of their work? Why?
3. What strikes you most about the lives of these workers?
4. The witnesses were responding to questions from middle-class commissioners. What did the commissioners seem interested in? Why?

*Source:* J. Bowditch and C. Ramsland, eds., *Voices of the Industrial Revolution*. Copyright © 1961, 1989 by the University of Michigan. Reprinted by permission.

*Revolutionaries in Transylvania.* Ana Ipatescu, of the first group of revolutionaries in Transylvania against Russia, 1848. *(National Historical Museum, Bucharest/The Art Archive)*

chapter

# 23 Ideologies and Upheavals, 1815–1850

## chapter outline

- The Peace Settlement
- Radical Ideas and Early Socialism
- The Romantic Movement
- Reforms and Revolutions
- The Revolutions of 1848

The momentous economic and political transformation of modern times began in the late eighteenth century with the Industrial Revolution in England and then the French Revolution. Until about 1815, these economic and political revolutions were separate, involving different countries and activities and proceeding at very different paces. After peace returned in 1815, the situation changed. Economic and political changes tended to fuse, reinforcing each other and bringing about what historian Eric Hobsbawm has incisively called the **dual revolution.** For instance, the growth of the industrial middle class encouraged the drive for representative government, and the demands of the French sans-culottes in 1793 and 1794 inspired many socialist thinkers. Gathering strength, the dual revolution rushed on to alter completely first Europe and then the rest of the world. Much of world history in the past two centuries can be seen as the progressive unfolding of the dual revolution.

In Europe in the nineteenth century, as in Asia and Africa in more recent times, the interrelated economic and political transformation was built on complicated histories, strong traditions, and highly diverse cultures. Radical change was eventually a constant, but the particular results varied enormously. In central and eastern Europe especially, the traditional elites—the monarchs, noble landowners, and bureaucrats—proved capable of defending their privileges and eventually using nationalism as a way to respond to the dual revolution and to serve their interests, as we shall see in Chapter 25.

The dual revolution also posed a tremendous intellectual challenge. The meanings of the economic, political, and social changes that were occurring, as well as the ways they would be shaped by human action, were anything but clear. These changes fascinated observers and stimulated the growth of new ideas and powerful ideologies. The most important of these were conservatism, liberalism, nationalism, and socialism.

- How did thinkers develop these ideas to describe and shape the transformation going on before their eyes?
- How did the artists and writers of the romantic movement also reflect and influence changes in this era?

**MAP 23.1 Europe in 1815** Europe's leaders re-established a balance of political power after the defeat of Napoleon. Prussia gained territory on the Rhine and in Saxony and consolidated its position as a Great Power.

1810 | 1820 | 1830 | 1840 | 1850 | 1860

**POLITICAL/MILITARY**

- 1809–1848 Metternich serves as Austrian foreign minister
- 1815 Holy Alliance formed
- 1819 Carlsbad Decrees issued by German Confederation
- 1830 Greece wins independence from Turks
- 1830–1848 Reign of Louis Philippe in France
- 1832 Reform Bill in Britain
- 1848 Revolutions in France, Austria, and Prussia

**SOCIAL/ECONOMIC**

- 1815 Revision of Corn Laws in Britain
- 1845–1851 Great Famine in Ireland
- 1847 Ten Hours Act in Britain

**INTELLECTUAL/RELIGIOUS**

- 1790s–1840s Romantic movement in literature and the arts
- 1810 Staël, *On Germany*
- 1839 Blanc, *Organization of Work*
- 1848 Marx and Engels, *The Communist Manifesto*

- How did the political revolution, derailed in France and resisted by European monarchs, eventually break out again after 1815?
- Why did the revolutionary surge triumph briefly in 1848 and then fail almost completely?

These are the questions this chapter will explore.

## The Peace Settlement

The eventual triumph of revolutionary economic and political forces was by no means certain as the Napoleonic era ended. Quite the contrary. The conservative, aristocratic monarchies of Russia, Prussia, Austria, and Great Britain had finally defeated France and reaffirmed their determination to hold France in line. But many other international questions were outstanding, and the allies agreed to meet at the **Congress of Vienna** to fashion a general peace settlement.

Most people felt a profound longing for peace. The great challenge for political leaders in 1814 was to construct a settlement that would last and not sow the seeds of another war. Their efforts were largely successful and contributed to a century unmarred by destructive, generalized war (see Map 23.1).

### The European Balance of Power

The allied powers were concerned first and foremost with the defeated enemy, France. Agreeing to the restoration of the Bourbon dynasty (see page 718), the allies were quite lenient toward France after Napoleon's abdication. The first Peace of Paris gave to France the boundaries it possessed in 1792, which were larger than those of 1789, and France did not have to pay any war reparations. Thus the victorious powers did not foment a spirit of injustice and revenge in the defeated country.

When the four allies of the Quadruple Alliance met together at the Congress of Vienna, assisted in a minor way by a host of delegates from the smaller European states, they also agreed to raise a number of formidable barriers against renewed French aggression. The Low Countries—Belgium and Holland—were united under an enlarged Dutch monarchy capable of opposing France more effectively. Above all, Prussia received considerably more

**Adjusting the Balance** The Englishman on the left uses his money to counterbalance the people that the Prussian and the fat Metternich are gaining in Saxony and Italy. Alexander I sits happily on his prize, Poland. This cartoon captures the essence of how most people thought about balance-of-power diplomacy at the Congress of Vienna. *(Bibliothèque nationale de France)*

territory on France's eastern border so as to stand as the "sentinel on the Rhine" against France. In these ways, the Quadruple Alliance combined leniency toward France with strong defensive measures.

In their moderation toward France, the allies were motivated by self-interest and traditional ideas about the balance of power. To Klemens von Metternich and Robert Castlereagh, the foreign ministers of Austria and Great Britain, respectively, as well as their French counterpart, Charles Talleyrand, the balance of power meant an international equilibrium of political and military forces that would discourage aggression by any combination of states or, worse, the domination of Europe by any single state.

The Great Powers—Austria, Britain, Prussia, Russia, and France—used the balance of power to settle their own dangerous disputes at the Congress of Vienna. There was general agreement among the victors that each of them should receive compensation in the form of territory for their successful struggle against the French. Great Britain had already won colonies and strategic outposts during the long wars. Metternich's Austria gave up territories in Belgium and southern Germany but expanded greatly elsewhere, taking the rich provinces of Venetia and Lombardy in northern Italy as well as former Polish possessions and new lands on the eastern coast of the Adriatic (see Map 23.1).

One ticklish question almost led to renewed war in January 1815, however. The vaguely progressive, impetuous Tsar Alexander I of Russia wanted to restore the ancient kingdom of Poland, on which he expected to bestow the benefits of his rule. The Prussians agreed, provided they could swallow up the large and wealthy kingdom of Saxony, their German neighbor to the south. These demands were too much for Castlereagh and Metternich, who feared an unbalancing of forces in central Europe. In an astonishing about-face, they turned for diplomatic support to the wily Talleyrand and the defeated France he represented, signing a secret alliance directed against Russia and Prussia. War seemed imminent.

But the threat of war caused the rulers of Russia and Prussia to moderate their demands. Russia accepted a small Polish kingdom, and Prussia took only part of Saxony (see Map 23.1). This compromise was very much within the framework of balance-of-power ideology. And it enabled France to regain its Great Power status and end its diplomatic isolation.

Unfortunately for France, Napoleon suddenly escaped from his "comic kingdom" on the island of Elba. Yet the second Peace of Paris, concluded after Napoleon's final defeat at Waterloo, was still relatively moderate toward France. Fat old Louis XVIII was restored to his throne for a second time. France lost only a little territory, had to pay an indemnity of 700 million francs, and had to support a large army of occupation for five years.

The rest of the settlement already concluded at the Congress of Vienna was left intact. The members of the Quadruple Alliance, however, did agree to meet periodically to discuss their common interests and to consider appropriate measures for the maintenance of peace in Europe. This agreement marked the beginning of the European "congress system," which lasted long into the nineteenth century and settled many international crises through international conferences and balance-of-power diplomacy.

### Intervention and Repression

There was also a domestic political side to the reestablishment of peace. Within their own countries, the leaders of the victorious states were much less flexible. In 1815 under Metternich's leadership, Austria, Prussia, and Russia embarked on a crusade against the ideas and politics of the dual revolution. This crusade lasted until 1848. The first step was the **Holy Alliance,** formed by Austria, Prussia, and Russia in September 1815. First proposed by Russia's Alexander I, the alliance soon became a symbol of the repression of liberal and revolutionary movements all over Europe.

In 1820 revolutionaries succeeded in forcing the monarchs of Spain and the southern Italian kingdom of the Two Sicilies to grant liberal constitutions against their wills. Metternich was horrified: revolution was rising once again. Calling a conference at Troppau in Austria under the provisions of the Quadruple Alliance, he and Alexander I proclaimed the principle of active intervention to maintain all autocratic regimes whenever they were threatened. Austrian forces then marched into Naples in 1821 and restored Ferdinand I to the throne of the Two Sicilies, while French armies likewise restored the Spanish regime.

In the following years, Metternich continued to battle against liberal political change. Sometimes he could do little, as in the case of the new Latin American republics that broke away from Spain. Nor could he undo the dynastic changes of 1830 and 1831 in France and Belgium. Nonetheless, until 1848 Metternich's system proved quite effective in central Europe, where his power was the greatest.

Metternich's policies dominated not only Austria and the Italian peninsula but also the entire German Confederation, which the peace settlement of Vienna had called into being. The confederation was composed of thirty-eight independent German states, including Prussia and Austria. These states met in complicated assemblies dominated by Austria, with Prussia a willing junior partner in the execution of repressive measures.

It was through the German Confederation that Metternich had the infamous **Carlsbad Decrees** issued in 1819. These decrees required the thirty-eight German member states to root out subversive ideas in their universities and newspapers. The decrees also established a permanent committee with spies and informers to investigate and punish any liberal or radical organizations.

### Metternich and Conservatism

Metternich's determined defense of the status quo made him a villain in the eyes of most progressive, optimistic historians of the nineteenth century. Yet rather than denounce the man, we can try to understand him and the general conservatism he represented.

Born into the middle ranks of the landed nobility of the Rhineland, Prince Klemens von Metternich (1773–1859) was an internationally oriented aristocrat who made a brilliant diplomatic career in Austria. Austrian foreign minister from 1809 to 1848, the cosmopolitan Metternich always remained loyal to his class and jealously defended its rights and privileges. Like most other conservatives of his time, he did so with a clear conscience. The nobility was one of Europe's most ancient institutions, and conservatives regarded tradition as the basic source of human institutions. In their view, the proper state and society remained those of pre-1789 Europe, which rested on a judicious blend of monarchy, bureaucracy, aristocracy, and respectful commoners.

Metternich firmly believed that liberalism, as embodied in revolutionary America and France, had been responsible for a generation of war with untold bloodshed and suffering. Like many other conservatives then and

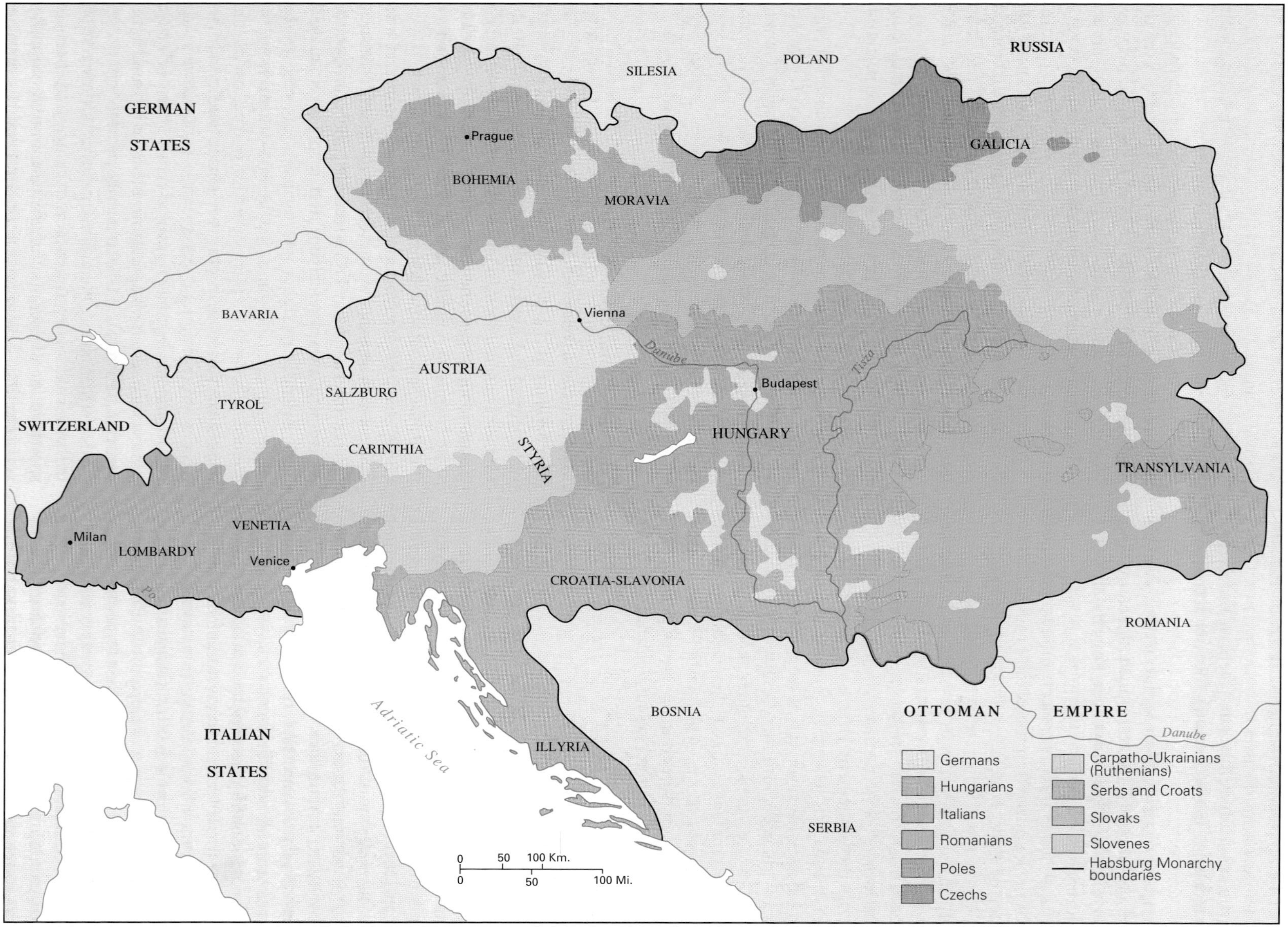


**MAP 23.2 Peoples of the Habsburg Monarchy, 1815** The old dynastic state was a patchwork of nationalities. Note the widely scattered pockets of Germans and Hungarians.

**Metternich** This portrait by Sir Thomas Lawrence reveals much about Metternich the man. Handsome, refined, and intelligent, Metternich was a great aristocrat who was passionately devoted to the defense of his class and its interests. *(The Royal Collection, © 2004 Her Majesty Queen Elizabeth II)*

since, Metternich blamed liberal middle-class revolutionaries for stirring up the lower classes, which he believed desired nothing more than peace and quiet.

The threat of liberalism appeared doubly dangerous to Metternich because it generally went with national aspirations. Liberals believed that each people, each national group, had a right to establish its own independent government and seek to fulfill its own destiny. The idea of national self-determination was repellent to Metternich. It not only threatened the primacy of the aristocracy but also threatened to destroy the Austrian Empire and revolutionize central Europe.

The vast Austrian Empire of the Habsburgs was a great dynastic state. Formed over centuries by war, marriage, and luck, it was made up of many peoples (see Map 23.2). The Germans had long dominated the empire, yet they accounted for only one-fourth of the population. The Magyars (Hungarians), a substantially smaller group, dominated the kingdom of Hungary, though they did not account for a majority of the population in that part of the Austrian Empire.

The Czechs, the third major group, were concentrated in Bohemia and Moravia. There were also large numbers of Italians, Poles, and Ukrainians as well as smaller groups of Slovenes, Croats, Serbs, Ruthenians, and Romanians. The various Slavic peoples, together with the Italians and the Romanians, represented a widely scattered and completely divided majority in an empire dominated by Germans and Hungarians. Different ethnic groups often lived in the same provinces and even in the same villages. Thus the different parts and provinces of the empire differed in languages, customs, and institutions.

The multiethnic state Metternich served was both strong and weak. It was strong because of its large population and vast territories; it was weak because of its many and potentially dissatisfied nationalities. In these circumstances, Metternich virtually had to oppose liberalism and nationalism, for Austria was simply unable to accommodate these ideologies of the dual revolution.

## Radical Ideas and Early Socialism

In the years following the peace settlement of 1815 intellectuals and social observers sought to understand the revolutionary changes that had occurred and were still taking place. These efforts led to ideas that still motivate the world.

Almost all of these basic ideas were radical. In one way or another, they rejected the old, deeply felt conservatism, with its stress on tradition, a hereditary monarchy, a strong and privileged landowning aristocracy, and an official church. Instead, they developed and refined alternative visions—alternative ideologies—and tried to convince society to act on them. With time, they were very successful.

### Liberalism

The principal ideas of **liberalism**—liberty and equality—were by no means defeated in 1815. First realized successfully in the American Revolution and then achieved in part in the French Revolution, this political and social philosophy continued to pose a radical challenge to revived conservatism. Liberalism demanded representative government as opposed to autocratic monarchy, equality before the law as opposed to legally separate classes. The idea of liberty also meant specific individual freedoms:

freedom of the press, freedom of speech, freedom of assembly, and freedom from arbitrary arrest. In Europe only France with Louis XVIII's Constitutional Charter and Great Britain with its Parliament and historic rights of English men and women had realized much of the liberal program in 1815. Even in those countries, liberalism had not fully succeeded.

Although liberalism retained its cutting edge, it was seen by many as being a somewhat duller tool than it had been. The reasons for this were that liberalism faced more radical ideological competitors in the early nineteenth century. Opponents of liberalism especially criticized its economic principles, which called for unrestricted private enterprise and no government interference in the economy. This philosophy was popularly known as the doctrine of **laissez faire.** (This form of liberalism is often called "classical" liberalism in the United States in order to distinguish it sharply from modern American liberalism, which usually favors more government programs to meet social needs and to regulate the economy.)

The idea of a free economy had first been persuasively formulated by Scottish philosophy professor Adam Smith, whose *Inquiry into the Nature and Causes of the Wealth of Nations* (1776) founded modern economics. Smith was highly critical of eighteenth-century mercantilism and its attempt to regulate trade and economic activity. Far preferable were free competition and the "invisible hand" of the self-regulating market, which would give all citizens a fair and equal opportunity to do what they did best. Smith argued effectively that freely competitive private enterprise would result in greater income for everyone, not just the rich.

In early-nineteenth-century Britain this economic liberalism, which promoted continued economic growth in the Industrial Revolution, was embraced most enthusiastically by business groups and became a doctrine associated with business interests. Businessmen used the doctrine to defend their right to do as they wished in their factories. Labor unions were outlawed because they supposedly restricted free competition and the individual's "right to work."

In the early nineteenth century, liberal political ideals also became more closely associated with narrow class interests. Early nineteenth-century liberals favored representative government, but they generally wanted property qualifications attached to the right to vote. In practice, this meant limiting the vote to well-to-do aristocratic landowners, substantial businessmen, and successful members of the professions. Workers and peasants, as well as the lower middle class of shopkeepers, clerks, and artisans, did not own the necessary property and thus could not vote.

As liberalism became increasingly identified with the middle class after 1815, some intellectuals and foes of conservatism felt that liberalism did not go nearly far enough. Inspired by memories of the French Revolution and the example of Jacksonian democracy in the young American republic, they called for universal voting rights, at least for males, and for democracy. These democrats and republicans were more radical than the liberals, and they were more willing than most liberals to endorse violent upheaval to achieve goals. All of this meant that liberals and radical, democratic republicans could join forces against conservatives only up to a point.

## Nationalism

**Nationalism** was a second radical idea in the years after 1815—an idea destined to have an enormous influence in the modern world. Nationalism had its immediate origins in the French Revolution and the Napoleonic wars, and there were already hints of its remarkable ability to spread and develop.

Early advocates of the "national idea" argued that each people had its own genius and its own *cultural* unity. For nationalists this cultural unity was basically self-evident, manifesting itself especially in a common language, history, and territory. In fact, in the early nineteenth century such cultural unity was more a dream than a reality as far as most nationalities were concerned. Within each ethnic grouping only an elite spoke a standardized written language. Local dialects abounded, and peasants from nearby villages often failed to understand each other. As for historical memory, it divided the inhabitants of the different German or Italian states as much as it unified them. Moreover, a variety of ethnic groups shared the territory of most states.

Despite these basic realities, sooner or later European nationalists usually sought to turn the cultural unity that they perceived into a *political* reality. They sought to make the territory of each people coincide with well-defined boundaries in an independent nation-state. It was this political goal that made nationalism so explosive in central and eastern Europe after 1815, when there were either too few states (Austria, Russia, and the Ottoman Empire) or too many (the Italian peninsula and the German Confederation) and when different peoples overlapped and intermingled.

In recent years scholars have been trying to understand how the nationalist vision, often fitting so poorly with existing conditions and promising so much upheaval, was so successful in the long run. Certain interrelated ideas stand out.

Of fundamental importance in the rise of nationalism was the epoch-making development of complex industrial and urban society, which required much better communication between individuals and groups.[1] These communication needs promoted the use of a standardized national language within many countries, creating at least a superficial cultural unity as it eventually encompassed the entire population through mass education. When a minority population was large and concentrated, the nationalist campaign for a standardized language often led to a push for a separate nation-state.

Many scholars also argue that nations are recent creations, the product of the new, self-conscious nationalist ideology. Thus nation-states emerged in the nineteenth century as "imagined communities," communities seeking to bind millions of strangers together around the abstract concept of an all-embracing national identity. This meant bringing citizens together with emotionally charged symbols and ceremonies, such as independence holidays and patriotic parades. On such fleeting occasions the imagined nation of spiritual equals might celebrate its most hallowed traditions, which were often recent inventions.[2]

Historians also stress the dynamic, ever-changing character of nationalism. Industrialism and mass education, so important in the later nineteenth century, played only a minor role before 1850. In those years the faith in nationhood was fresh, idealistic, and progressive.

Between 1815 and 1850 most people who believed in nationalism also believed in either liberalism or radical, democratic republicanism. A common faith in the creativity and nobility of the people was perhaps the single most important reason for the linking of these two concepts. Liberals and especially democrats saw the people as the ultimate source of all government. Yet liberals and nationalists agreed that the benefits of self-government would be possible only if the people were united by common traditions that transcended local interests and even class differences.

**Creating Nationalism** Festivals and patriotic celebrations helped build a feeling of belonging to a large invisible community. This illustration from May 1848 depicts "the Solemn Entry of Archduke Johann of Austria into Frankfurt," when cannon sounded and dignitaries proclaimed the opening of a new era. The revolutionary assembly in Frankfurt had named Johann regent of the unified Germany that it was hoping to establish. In May 1849 the assembly offered the imperial crown to the king of Prussia. *(Germanisches Nationalmuseum, Nürnberg)*

Early nationalists usually believed that every nation, like every citizen, had the right to exist in freedom and to develop its character and spirit. They were confident that a symphony of nations would promote the harmony and ultimate unity of all peoples. As the French historian Jules Michelet put it in *The People* in 1846, each citizen "learns to recognize his country . . . as a note in the grand concert; through it he himself participates and loves the world." Similarly, the great Italian patriot Giuseppe Mazzini believed that "in laboring according to the true principles of our country we are laboring for Humanity." (See the feature "Listening to the Past: Faith in Democratic Nationalism" on pages 784–785.) Thus the liberty of the individual and the love of a free nation overlapped greatly in the early nineteenth century.

Yet early nationalists also stressed the differences among peoples. Even early nationalism developed a strong sense of "we" and "they." To this "we-they" outlook, it was all too easy for nationalists to add two highly volatile ingredients: a sense of national mission and a sense of national superiority. Even Michelet, so alive to the aspirations of other peoples, could not help speaking in 1846 of the "superiority of France"; the principles espoused in the French Revolution had made France the "salvation of mankind."

German and Spanish nationalists had a very different opinion of France. In the narratives they constructed, the French often seemed oppressive, as the Germans did to the Czechs and as the Russians did to the Poles. Thus "they" often emerged as the enemy.

Early nationalism was ambiguous. Its main thrust was liberal and democratic. But below the surface lurked ideas of national superiority and national mission that could lead to aggression and conflict.

## French Utopian Socialism

**Socialism,** the new radical doctrine after 1815, began in France, despite the fact that France lagged far behind Great Britain in developing modern industry. Early French socialist thinkers were acutely aware that the political revolution in France, the rise of laissez faire, and the emergence of modern industry in Britain were transforming society. They were disturbed because they saw these developments as fomenting selfish individualism and splitting the community into isolated fragments. There was, they believed, an urgent need for a further reorganization of society to establish cooperation and a new sense of community.

Early French socialists believed in economic planning. Inspired by the emergency measures of 1793 and 1794 in France, they argued that the government should rationally organize the economy and not depend on destructive competition to do the job. Early socialists also shared an intense desire to help the poor, and they preached that the rich and the poor should be more nearly equal economically. Finally, socialists believed that private property should be strictly regulated by the government or that it should be abolished and replaced by state or community ownership. Planning, greater economic equality, and state regulation of property—these were the key ideas of early French socialism and of all socialism since.

One of the most influential early socialist thinkers was a nobleman, Count Henri de Saint-Simon (1760–1825). Saint-Simon optimistically proclaimed the tremendous possibilities of industrial development: "The age of gold is before us!" The key to progress was proper social organization. Such an arrangement of society required the **parasites**—the court, the aristocracy, lawyers, and churchmen—to give way, once and for all, to the **doers**—the leading scientists, engineers, and industrialists. The doers would carefully plan the economy and guide it forward by undertaking vast public works projects and establishing investment banks. Saint-Simon also stressed in highly moralistic terms that every social institution ought to have as its main goal improved conditions for the poor.

After 1830 the socialist critique of capitalism became sharper. Charles Fourier (1772–1837), a lonely, saintly man with a tenuous hold on reality, envisaged a socialist utopia of mathematically precise, self-sufficient communities, each made up of 1,620 people. Fourier was also an early proponent of the total emancipation of women. Extremely critical of middle-class family life, Fourier believed that most marriages were only another kind of prostitution. According to Fourier, young single women were shamelessly "sold" to their future husbands for dowries and other financial considerations. Therefore, Fourier called for the abolition of marriage, free unions based only on love, and sexual freedom. Many middle-class men and women found these ideas, which were shared and even practiced by some followers of Saint-Simon, shocking and immoral. The socialist program for the liberation of women as well as workers appeared to them as doubly dangerous and revolutionary.

Louis Blanc (1811–1882), a sharp-eyed, intelligent journalist, focused on practical improvements. In his *Organization of Work* (1839), he urged workers to agitate for universal voting rights and to take control of the state peacefully. Blanc believed that the state should set up government-backed workshops and factories to guarantee full employment. The right to work had to become as sacred as any other right.

Finally, there was Pierre Joseph Proudhon (1809–1865), a self-educated printer who wrote a pamphlet in 1840 titled *What Is Property?* His answer was that it was nothing but theft. Property was profit that was stolen from the worker, who was the source of all wealth. Unlike most socialists, Proudhon feared the power of the state and was often considered an anarchist.

Of great importance, the message of French utopian socialists interacted with the experiences of French urban workers. Workers cherished the memory of the radical phase of the French Revolution, and they became violently opposed to laissez-faire laws that denied workers the right to organize. Developing a sense of class in the process, workers favored collective action and government intervention in economic life. Thus the aspirations of workers and utopian theorists reinforced each other, and a genuine socialist movement emerged in Paris in the 1830s and 1840s. To Karl Marx was left the task of establishing firm foundations for modern socialism.

**Karl Marx** Active in the revolution of 1848, Marx fled from Germany in 1849 and settled in London. There he wrote *Capital,* the weighty exposition of his socialist theories, and worked to organize the working class. Marx earned a modest living as a journalist, supplemented by financial support from his coauthor, Friedrich Engels. *(The Granger Collection, New York)*

## The Birth of Marxian Socialism

In 1848 the thirty-year-old Karl Marx (1818–1883) and the twenty-eight-year-old Friedrich Engels (1820–1895) published *The Communist Manifesto,* which became the bible of socialism. The son of a Jewish lawyer who had converted to Christianity, the atheistic young Marx had studied philosophy at the University of Berlin before turning to journalism and economics. He read widely in French socialist thought, and like Fourier he looked forward to the emancipation of women and the abolition of the family. By the time Marx was twenty-five, he was developing his own socialist ideas.

Early French socialists often appealed to the middle class and the state to help the poor. Marx ridiculed such appeals as naive. He argued that the interests of the middle class and those of the industrial working class were inevitably opposed to each other. Indeed, according to the *Manifesto,* the "history of all previously existing society is the history of class struggles." In Marx's view, one class had always exploited the other, and with the advent of modern industry, society was split more clearly than ever before: between the middle class (the **bourgeoisie**) and the modern working class (the **proletariat**).

Just as the bourgeoisie had triumphed over the feudal aristocracy, Marx predicted that the proletariat would conquer the bourgeoisie in a violent revolution. While a tiny minority owned the means of production and grew richer, the ever-poorer proletariat was constantly growing in size and in class-consciousness. In this process, the proletariat was aided, according to Marx, by a portion of the bourgeoisie who had gone over to the proletariat and who (like Marx and Engels) "had raised themselves to the level of comprehending theoretically the historical moment." The critical moment, Marx thought, was very near. "Let the ruling classes tremble at a Communist revolution. The proletarians have nothing to lose but their chains. They have a world to win. WORKING MEN OF ALL COUNTRIES, UNITE!" So ends *The Communist Manifesto.*

Marx's ideas united sociology, economics, and all human history in a vast and imposing edifice. He synthesized in his socialism not only French utopian schemes but also English classical economics and German philosophy—the major intellectual currents of his day.

Marx's debt to England was great. He was the last of the classical economists. Following David Ricardo, who had taught that labor was the source of all value, Marx went on to argue that profits were really wages stolen from the workers. Moreover, Marx incorporated Engels's charges of terrible oppression of the new class of factory workers in England; thus Marx's doctrines seemed to be based on hard facts.

Marx's theory of historical evolution was built on the philosophy of the German Georg Hegel (1770–1831). Hegel believed that each age is characterized by a dominant set of ideas, which produces opposing ideas and eventually a new synthesis. The idea of being had been dominant initially, for example, and it had produced its antithesis, the idea of nonbeing. This idea in turn had resulted in the synthesis of becoming. Thus history has pattern and purpose.

Marx retained Hegel's view of history as a dialectic process of change but made economic relationships between classes the driving force. This dialectic explained the decline of agrarian feudalism and the rise of industrial capitalism. Marx stressed repeatedly that the "bourgeoisie, historically, has played a most revolutionary part. . . . During its rule of scarcely one hundred years the bourgeoisie has created more massive and more colossal productive forces than have all preceding generations together." Marx's next idea, that it was now the bourgeoisie's turn to give way to the socialism of revolutionary workers, appeared to many the irrefutable capstone of a brilliant interpretation of humanity's long development. Thus Marx pulled together powerful ideas and insights to create one of the great secular religions out of the intellectual ferment of the early nineteenth century.

## The Romantic Movement

Radical concepts of politics and society were accompanied by comparable changes in literature and other arts during the dual revolution. The early nineteenth century marked the acme of the romantic movement, which profoundly influenced the arts and enriched European culture immeasurably.

The romantic movement was in part a revolt against classicism and the Enlightenment. Classicism was essentially a set of artistic rules and standards that went hand in glove with the Enlightenment's belief in rationality, order, and restraint. The classicists believed that the ancient Greeks and Romans had discovered eternally valid aesthetic rules and that playwrights and painters should continue to follow them. Classicists could enforce these rules in the eighteenth century because they dominated the courts and academies for which artists worked.

Forerunners of the romantic movement appeared from about 1750 on. Of these, Rousseau (see page 612)—the passionate advocate of feeling, freedom, and natural goodness—was the most influential. Romanticism then crystallized fully in the 1790s, primarily in England and Germany. The French Revolution kindled the belief that radical reconstruction was also possible in cultural and artistic life (even though many early English and German romantics became disillusioned with events in France and turned from liberalism to conservatism in politics). Romanticism gained strength until the 1840s.

### Romanticism's Tenets

**Romanticism** was characterized by a belief in emotional exuberance, unrestrained imagination, and spontaneity in both art and personal life. In Germany early romantics of the 1770s and 1780s called themselves the **Sturm und Drang** ("Storm and Stress"), and many romantic artists of the early nineteenth century lived lives of tremendous emotional intensity. Suicide, duels to the death, madness, and strange illnesses were not uncommon among leading romantics. Romantic artists typically led bohemian lives, wearing their hair long and uncombed in preference to powdered wigs and living in cold garrets rather than frequenting stiff drawing rooms. They rejected materialism and sought to escape to lofty spiritual heights through their art. Great individualists, the romantics believed the full development of one's unique human potential to be the supreme purpose in life.

Nowhere was the break with classicism more apparent than in romanticism's general conception of nature. Classicism was not particularly interested in nature. In the words of the eighteenth-century English author Samuel Johnson, "A blade of grass is always a blade of grass; men and women are my subjects of inquiry." Nature was portrayed by classicists as beautiful and chaste, like an eighteenth-century formal garden. The romantics, in contrast, were enchanted by nature. For some it was awesome and tempestuous, while others saw nature as a source of spiritual inspiration. As the great English landscape artist John Constable declared, "Nature is Spirit visible."

Most romantics saw the growth of modern industry as an ugly, brutal attack on their beloved nature and on the human personality. They sought escape—in the un-

**Nature and the Meaning of Life** Caspar David Friedrich (1774–1840) was Germany's greatest romantic painter, and his *Traveler Looking over a Sea of Fog* (1815) is a representative masterpiece. Friedrich's paintings often focus on dark, silhouetted figures silently contemplating an eerie landscape. Friedrich came to believe that humans were only an insignificant part of an all-embracing higher unity. *(Bildarchiv Preussischer Kulturbesitz/Art Resource, NY)*

spoiled Lake District of northern England, in exotic North Africa, in an idealized Middle Ages.

Fascinated by color and diversity, the romantic imagination turned toward history with a passion. Beautiful, exciting, and important, history was the art of change over time—the key to a universe that was now perceived to be organic and dynamic, not mechanical and static as the Enlightenment had believed. Historical studies promoted the growth of national aspirations, fanning the embers of memory and encouraging entire peoples to seek in the past their special destinies.

## Literature

Britain was the first country where romanticism flowered fully in poetry and prose, and the British romantic writers were among the most prominent in Europe. Wordsworth, Coleridge, and Scott were all active by 1800, to be followed shortly by Byron, Shelley, and Keats. All were poets: romanticism found its distinctive voice in poetry, as the Enlightenment had in prose.

A towering leader of English romanticism, William Wordsworth (1770–1850) traveled in France after his graduation from Cambridge. There he fell passionately in love with a Frenchwoman, who bore him a daughter. Deeply influenced by Rousseau and the spirit of the early French Revolution, Wordsworth returned to England and settled in the countryside with his sister, Dorothy, and Samuel Taylor Coleridge (1772–1834). In 1798 the two poets published their *Lyrical Ballads,* which abandoned flowery classical conventions for the language of ordinary speech and endowed simple subjects with the loftiest majesty.

One of the best examples of Wordsworth's romantic credo and genius is "Daffodils":

*I wandered lonely as a cloud*
*That floats on high o'er vales and hills,*
*When all at once I saw a crowd,*
*A host, of golden daffodils;*
*Beside the lake, beneath the trees,*
*Fluttering and dancing in the breeze.*

. . . . . . . . . . . . . .

*The waves beside them danced, but they*
*Out-did the sparkling waves in glee:*
*A poet could not but be gay,*
*In such a jocund company:*
*I gazed—and gazed—but little thought*
*What wealth the show to me had brought:*

*For oft, when on my couch I lie*
*In vacant or in pensive mood,*
*They flash upon that inward eye*
*Which is the bliss of solitude;*
*And then my heart with pleasure fills,*
*And dances with the daffodils.*

Here indeed are simplicity and love of nature in commonplace forms, which could be appreciated by everyone. Wordsworth's conception of poetry as the "spontaneous overflow of powerful feeling recollected in tranquility" is well illustrated by the last stanza.

Born in Edinburgh, Walter Scott (1771–1832) personified the romantic movement's fascination with history. Raised on his grandfather's farm, Scott fell under the spell of the old ballads and tales of the Scottish border. He was also deeply influenced by German romanticism, particularly by the immortal poet and dramatist Johann Wolfgang von Goethe (1749–1832). Scott translated Goethe's famous *Gotz von Berlichingen,* a play about a sixteenth-century knight who revolted against centralized authority and championed individual freedom—at least in Goethe's romantic drama. A natural storyteller, Scott composed long narrative poems and a series of historical novels. Scott excelled in re-creating the spirit of bygone ages and great historical events, especially those of Scotland.

Classicism remained strong in France under Napoleon and inhibited the growth of romanticism there. In 1813 Germaine de Staël (1766–1817), a Franco-Swiss writer living in exile, urged the French to throw away their worn-out classical models. Her study *On Germany* (1810) extolled the spontaneity and enthusiasm of German writers and thinkers, and it had a powerful impact on the post-1815 generation in France. (See the feature "Individuals in Society: Germaine de Staël.") Between 1820 and 1850, the romantic impulse broke through in the poetry and prose of Lamartine, de Vigny, Hugo, Dumas, and Sand. Of these, Victor Hugo (1802–1885) was the greatest in both poetry and prose.

Son of a Napoleonic general, Hugo achieved an amazing range of rhythm, language, and image in his lyric poetry. His powerful novels exemplified the romantic fascination with fantastic characters, exotic historical settings, and human emotions. The hero of Hugo's famous *Hunchback of Notre Dame* (1831) is the great cathedral's deformed bell-ringer, a "human gargoyle" overlooking the teeming life of fifteenth-century Paris. Renouncing his early conservatism, Hugo equated freedom in literature with liberty in politics and society. Hugo's political evolution was thus exactly the opposite of Wordsworth's, in whom youthful radicalism gave way to middle-aged caution. As the contrast between the two artists suggests, romanticism was a cultural movement compatible with many political beliefs.

Amandine Aurore Lucie Dupin (1804–1876), generally known by her pen name, George Sand, defied the narrow conventions of her time in an unending search for self-fulfillment. After eight years of unhappy marriage she abandoned her husband and took her two children to Paris to pursue a career as a writer. There Sand soon achieved fame and wealth, eventually writing over eighty novels on a variety of romantic and social themes. George Sand's striking individualism went far beyond her flamboyant preference for men's clothing and her notorious affairs. Her semi-autobiographical novel *Lélia* was shockingly modern, delving deeply into her tortuous quest for sexual and personal freedom.

In central and eastern Europe, literary romanticism and early nationalism often reinforced each other. Seeking a unique greatness in every people, well-educated romantics plumbed their own histories and cultures. Like modern anthropologists, they turned their attention to peasant life and transcribed the folk songs, tales, and proverbs that the cosmopolitan Enlightenment had disdained. The brothers Jacob and Wilhelm Grimm were

# Individuals in Society

## Germaine de Staël

Rich, intellectual, passionate, and assertive, Germaine Necker de Staël (1766–1817) astonished contemporaries and still fascinates historians. She was strongly influenced by her parents, poor Swiss Protestants who soared to the top of prerevolutionary Parisian society. Her brilliant but rigid mother filled Germaine's head with knowledge, and each week the precocious child listened, wide-eyed and attentive, to illustrious writers and philosophers performing at her mother's salon. At age twelve, she suffered a physical and mental breakdown. Only then was she allowed to have a playmate and romp and run on the family estate. Her adoring father was Jacques Necker, a banker who made an enormous fortune and became France's reform-minded minister of finance before the Revolution. Worshiping her father in adolescence, Germaine also came to love politics.

Accepting at nineteen an arranged marriage with Baron de Staël-Holstein, a womanizing Swedish diplomat bewitched by her dowry, Germaine began her life's work. She opened an intellectual salon and began to write and publish. Her wit and exuberance attracted foreigners and liberal French aristocrats, one of whom became the first of many lovers as her marriage soured and she searched unsuccessfully for the happiness of her parents' union. Fleeing Paris in 1792 and returning after the Thermidorian reaction, she subsequently angered Napoleon by criticizing his dictatorial rule. In 1803 he permanently banished her from Paris.

Retiring again to her isolated estate in Switzerland and skillfully managing her inherited wealth, Staël fought insomnia with opium and boredom with parties that attracted luminaries from all over Europe. Always seeking stimulation for her restless mind, she traveled widely in Italy and Germany and drew upon these experiences in her novel *Corinne* (1807) and her study *On Germany* (1810). Both works summed up her romantic faith and enjoyed enormous success.

Staël urged creative individuals to abandon traditional rules and classical models. She encouraged them to embrace experimentation, emotion, and enthusiasm. Enthusiasm, which she had in abundance, was the key, the royal road to creativity, personal fulfillment, and human improvement. Thrilling to music, for example, she felt that only an enthusiastic person could really appreciate this gift of God, this wordless message that "unifies our dual nature and blends senses and spirit in a common rapture."*

*Germaine de Staël, by J.-B. Isabey.* (Réunion des Musées Nationaux/Art Resource, NY)

Yet a profound sadness runs through her writing. This sadness, so characteristic of the romantic temperament, grew in part out of disappointments in love and prolonged exile. But it also grew out of the insoluble predicament of being an enormously gifted woman in an age of intense male chauvinism. Little wonder that uneasy male competitors and literary critics took delight in ridiculing and defaming her as a neurotic and masculine woman, a mediocre and unnatural talent who had foolishly dared to enter the male world of serious thought and action. Even her supporters could not accept her for what she was. The admiring poet Lord Byron recognized her genius and called her "the most eminent woman author of this, or perhaps of any century." But he quickly added that "she should have been born a man."†

Buffeted and saddened by scorn and condescension because of her gender, Staël advocated equal rights for women throughout her life. Only with equal rights and duties—in education and careers, in love and marital relations—could an exceptional woman like herself, or indeed any woman, ever hope to realize her intellectual and emotional potential. Practicing what she preached as best she could, Germaine de Staël was a trailblazer in the struggle for women's rights.

### Questions for Analysis

1. In what ways did Germaine de Staël's life and thought reflect basic elements of the romantic movement?
2. Why did male critics often attack Staël? What do these criticisms tell us about gender relations in the early nineteenth century?

*Quoted in G. R. Besser, *Germaine de Staël Revisited* (New York: Twayne Publishers, 1994), p. 106. Enhanced by a feminist perspective, this is the best recent study.
†Quoted ibid., p. 139.

*The* **history companion** *features additional information and activities related to this topic.*
**history.college.hmco.com/students**

particularly successful at rescuing German fairy tales from oblivion. In the Slavic lands, romantics played a decisive role in converting spoken peasant languages into modern written languages. The greatest of all Russian poets, Aleksander Pushkin (1799–1837), rejecting eighteenth-century attempts to force Russian poetry into a classical straitjacket, used his lyric genius to mold the modern literary language.

### Art and Music

The greatest and most moving romantic painter in France was Eugène Delacroix (1798–1863), probably the illegitimate son of French foreign minister Talleyrand. Delacroix was a master of dramatic, colorful scenes that stirred the emotions. He was fascinated with remote and exotic subjects, whether lion hunts in Morocco or dreams of languishing, sensuous women in a sultan's harem. Yet he was also a passionate spokesman for freedom. His masterpiece, *Liberty Leading the People,* celebrated the nobility of popular revolution in general and revolution in France in particular.

In England the most notable romantic painters were Joseph M. W. Turner (1775–1851) and John Constable (1776–1837). Both were fascinated by nature, but their interpretations of it contrasted sharply, aptly symbolizing the tremendous emotional range of the romantic movement. Turner depicted nature's power and terror; wild storms and sinking ships were favorite subjects. Constable painted gentle Wordsworthian landscapes in which human beings were at one with their environment, the comforting countryside of unspoiled rural England.

It was in music that romanticism realized most fully and permanently its goals of free expression and emotional intensity. Abandoning well-defined structures, the great romantic composers used a wide range of forms to create a thousand musical landscapes and evoke a host of powerful emotions. Romantic composers also transformed the small classical orchestra, tripling its size by adding wind instruments, percussion, and more brass and strings. The crashing chords evoking the surge of the masses in Chopin's Revolutionary Etude, and the bottomless despair of the funeral march in Beethoven's Third Symphony—such were the modern orchestra's musical paintings that plumbed the depths of human feeling.

This range and intensity gave music and musicians much greater prestige than in the past. Music no longer simply complemented a church service or helped a nobleman digest his dinner. Music became a sublime end in itself, most perfectly realizing the endless yearning of the soul. The unbelievable one-in-a-million performer—the great virtuoso who could transport the listener to ecstasy and hysteria—became a cultural hero. People swooned for Franz Liszt (1811–1886), the greatest pianist of his age, as they scream for rock stars today.

Though romanticism dominated music until late in the nineteenth century, no composer ever surpassed its first great master, Ludwig van Beethoven (1770–1827). Extending and breaking open classical forms, Beethoven used contrasting themes and tones to produce dramatic conflict and inspiring resolutions. As one contemporary admirer wrote, "Beethoven's music sets in motion the lever of fear, of awe, of horror, of suffering, and awakens just that infinite longing which is the essence of Romanticism." Beethoven's range and output were tremendous. At the peak of his fame, he began to lose his hearing. He considered suicide but eventually overcame despair: "I will take fate by the throat; it will not bend me completely to its will."[3] Beethoven continued to pour out immortal music, although his last years were silent, spent in total deafness.

## Reforms and Revolutions

See DBQ 9

While the romantic movement was developing, liberal, national, and socialist forces battered against the conservatism of 1815. In some countries, change occurred gradually and peacefully. Elsewhere, pressure built up like steam in a pressure cooker without a safety valve and eventually caused an explosion in 1848. Three important countries—Greece, Great Britain, and France—experienced variations on this basic theme.

### National Liberation in Greece

National, liberal revolution, frustrated in Italy and Spain by conservative statesmen, succeeded first after 1815 in Greece. Since the fifteenth century, the Greeks had been living under the domination of the Ottoman Turks. In spite of centuries of foreign rule, the Greeks had survived as a people, united by their language and the Greek Orthodox religion. It was perfectly natural that the general growth of national aspirations and a desire for independence would inspire some Greeks in the early nineteenth century. This rising national movement led to the formation of secret societies and then to revolt in 1821, led by Alexander Ypsilanti, a Greek patriot and a general in the Russian army.

The Great Powers, particularly Metternich, were opposed to all revolution, even revolution against the Islamic Turks. They refused to back Ypsilanti and supported the

**Delacroix: Massacre at Chios** The Greek struggle for freedom and independence won the enthusiastic support of liberals, nationalists, and romantics. The Ottoman Turks were portrayed as cruel oppressors who were holding back the course of history, as in this moving masterpiece by Delacroix. *(Réunion des Musées Nationaux/Art Resource, NY)*

Ottoman Empire. Yet for many Europeans, the Greek cause became a holy one. Educated Americans and Europeans were in love with the culture of classical Greece; Russians were stirred by the piety of their Orthodox brethren. Writers and artists, moved by the romantic impulse, responded enthusiastically to the Greek national struggle.

The Greeks, though often quarreling among themselves, battled on against the Turks and hoped for the eventual support of European governments. In 1827 Great Britain, France, and Russia responded to popular demands at home and directed Turkey to accept an armistice. When the Turks refused, the navies of these three powers trapped the Turkish fleet at Navarino and destroyed it. Russia then declared another of its periodic wars of expansion against the Turks. This led to the establishment of a Russian protectorate over much of present-day Romania, which had also been under Turkish rule. Great Britain, France, and Russia finally declared Greece independent in 1830 and installed a German prince as king of the new country in 1832. In the end, the Greeks had won: a small nation had gained its independence in a heroic war against a foreign empire.

## Liberal Reform in Great Britain

Eighteenth-century British society had been both flexible and remarkably stable. It was dominated by the landowning aristocracy, but that class was neither closed nor rigidly defined. Successful business and professional people could buy land and become gentlefolk, while the common people had more than the usual opportunities of the preindustrial world. Basic civil rights for all were balanced by a tradition of deference to one's social superiors. Parliament was manipulated by the king and was thoroughly undemocratic. Only about 8 percent of the population could vote for representatives to Parliament, and by the 1780s there was growing interest in some kind of political reform.

But the French Revolution threw the British aristocracy into a panic for a generation, making it extremely hostile to any attempts to change the status quo. The Tory party, completely controlled by the landed aristocracy, was particularly fearful of radical movements at home and abroad. After 1815 the aristocracy defended its ruling position by repressing every kind of popular protest.

The first step in this direction began with revision of the **Corn Laws** in 1815. Corn Laws to regulate the foreign grain trade had long existed, but they were not needed during a generation of war with France because the British had been unable to import cheap grain from eastern Europe. As shortages occurred and agricultural prices skyrocketed, a great deal of marginal land had been brought under cultivation, fattening the landed aristocracy's rent rolls. Peace meant that grain could be imported again and that the price of wheat and bread would go down, benefiting almost everyone except the aristocracy. The aristocracy, however, rammed far-reaching changes in the Corn Laws through Parliament. The new regulation prohibited the importation of foreign grain unless the price at home rose to improbable levels. Seldom has a class legislated more selfishly for its own narrow economic advantage or done more to promote a class-based view of political action.

The change in the Corn Laws, coming as it did at a time of widespread unemployment and postwar economic distress, resulted in protests and demonstrations by urban laborers, who were supported by radical intellectuals. In 1817 the Tory government responded by temporarily suspending the traditional rights of peaceable assembly and habeas corpus. Two years later, Parliament passed the infamous Six Acts, which, among other things, placed controls on a heavily taxed press and practically eliminated all mass meetings. These acts followed an enormous but orderly protest, at Saint Peter's Fields in Manchester, that had been savagely broken up by armed cavalry. Nicknamed the **Battle of Peterloo,** in scornful reference to the British victory at Waterloo, this incident demonstrated the government's determination to repress and stand fast.

Strengthened by ongoing industrial development, the new manufacturing and commercial groups insisted on a place for their new wealth alongside the landed wealth of the aristocracy in the framework of political power and social prestige. They called for many kinds of liberal reform: reform of town government, organization of a new police force, more rights for Catholics and dissenters, and reform of the Poor Laws that provided aid to some low-paid workers. In the 1820s, a less frightened Tory government moved in the direction of better urban administration, greater economic liberalism, and civil equality for Catholics. The prohibition on imports of foreign grain was replaced by a heavy tariff. These actions encouraged the middle classes to press on for reform of Parliament so they could have a larger say in government and perhaps repeal the latest revision of the Corn Laws, that symbol of aristocratic domination.

The Whig party, though led like the Tories by great aristocrats, had by tradition been more responsive to commercial and manufacturing interests. In 1830 a Whig ministry introduced "an act to amend the representation of the people of England and Wales." Defeated, then passed by the House of Commons, this reform bill was rejected by the House of Lords. But when in 1832 the Whigs got the king to promise to create enough new peers to pass the law, the House of Lords reluctantly gave in rather than see its snug little club ruined by upstart manufacturers and plutocrats. A mighty surge of popular protest had helped the king and lords make up their minds.

The Reform Bill of 1832 had profound significance. The House of Commons had emerged as the all-important legislative body. In the future, an obstructionist House of Lords could always be brought into line by the threat of creating new peers. The new industrial areas of the country gained representation in the Commons, and many old "rotten boroughs"—electoral districts that had very few voters and that the landed aristocracy had bought and sold—were eliminated.

**Hayter: The House of Commons, 1833** This collective portrait of the first parliament elected after the Reform Bill of 1832 was painted over several years. The arrangement of the members reflects Britain's historic two-party system, with the majority on one side and the "loyal opposition" on the other. Most European countries developed multiparty systems and coalition politics, with competing groups seated in a large half circle. *(Trustees of the National Portrait Gallery, London)*

The redistribution of seats reflected the shift in population to the northern manufacturing counties and the gradual emergence of an urban society. As a result of the Reform Bill of 1832, the number of voters increased by about 50 percent, giving about 12 percent of adult men in Britain and Ireland the right to vote. Comfortable middle-class groups in the urban population, as well as some substantial farmers who leased their land, received the vote. Thus the pressures building in Great Britain were successfully—though only temporarily—released. A major reform had been achieved peacefully, without revolution or civil war. More radical reforms within the system appeared difficult but not impossible. Legislation could solve problems and improve social conditions.

The principal radical program was embodied in the "People's Charter" of 1838 and the Chartist movement (see page 749). Partly inspired by the economic distress of the working class in the 1830s and 1840s, the Chartists' core demand was universal male (but not female) suffrage. They saw complete political democracy and rule by the common people as the means to a good and just society. Hundreds of thousands of people signed gigantic petitions calling on Parliament to grant all men the right to vote, first and most seriously in 1839, again in 1842, and yet again in 1848. Parliament rejected all three petitions. In the short run, the working poor failed with their Chartist demands, but they learned a valuable lesson in mass politics.

While calling for universal male suffrage, many working-class people joined with middle-class manufacturers in the Anti–Corn Law League, founded in Manchester in 1839. Mass participation made possible a popular crusade led by fighting liberals, who argued that lower food prices and more jobs in industry depended on repeal of the Corn Laws. Much of the working class agreed. When Ireland's potato crop failed in 1845, famine prices for food and even famine itself also seemed likely in England. To avert the impending catastrophe, Tory prime minister Robert Peel joined with the Whigs and a minority of his

## The Prelude to 1848

| | |
|---|---|
| **March 1814** | Russia, Prussia, Austria, and Britain form the Quadruple Alliance to defeat France. |
| **April 1814** | Napoleon abdicates. |
| **May–June 1814** | Bourbon monarchy is restored; Louis XVIII issues the Constitutional Charter providing for civil liberties and representative government.<br>First Peace of Paris: allies combine leniency with a defensive posture toward France. |
| **October 1814–June 1815** | Congress of Vienna peace settlement establishes balance-of-power principle and creates the German Confederation. |
| **February 1815** | Napoleon escapes from Elba and marches on Paris. |
| **June 1815** | Napoleon defeated at the Battle of Waterloo. |
| **September 1815** | Austria, Prussia, and Russia form the Holy Alliance to repress liberal and revolutionary movements. |
| **November 1815** | Second Peace of Paris and renewal of Quadruple Alliance punish France and establish the European "congress system." |
| **1819** | In Carlsbad Decrees, Metternich imposes harsh measures throughout the German Confederation. |
| **1820** | Revolution occurs in Spain and the kingdom of the Two Sicilies.<br>At the Congress of Troppau, Metternich and Alexander I of Russia proclaim the principle of intervention to maintain autocratic regimes. |
| **1821** | Austria crushes a liberal revolution in Naples and restores the Sicilian autocracy.<br>Greeks revolt against the Ottoman Turks. |
| **1823** | French armies restore the Spanish regime. |
| **1824** | Reactionary Charles X succeeds Louis XVIII in France. |
| **1830** | Charles X repudiates the Constitutional Charter; insurrection and collapse of the government follow. Louis Philippe succeeds to the throne and maintains a narrowly liberal regime until 1848.<br>Greece wins independence from the Ottoman Empire. |
| **1832** | Reform Bill expands British electorate and encourages the middle class. |
| **1839** | Louis Blanc publishes *Organization of Work*. |
| **1840** | Pierre Joseph Proudhon publishes *What Is Property?* |
| **1846** | Jules Michelet publishes *The People*. |
| **1848** | Karl Marx and Friedrich Engels publish *The Communist Manifesto*. |

own party to repeal the Corn Laws in 1846 and allow free imports of grain. England escaped famine. Thereafter the liberal doctrine of free trade became almost sacred dogma in Great Britain.

The following year, the Tories passed a bill designed to help the working classes, but in a different way. The Ten Hours Act of 1847 limited the workday for women and young people in factories to ten hours. Tory aristocrats continued to champion legislation regulating factory conditions. They were competing vigorously with the middle class for the support of the working class. This healthy competition between a still-vigorous aristocracy and a strong middle class was a crucial factor in Great Britain's peaceful evolution. The working classes could make temporary alliances with either competitor to better their own conditions.

## Ireland and the Great Famine

The people of Ireland did not benefit from the political competition in Britain. The great mass of the population (outside of the northern counties of Ulster, which were partly Presbyterian) were Irish Catholics, who rented their land from a tiny minority of Church of England Protestants, many of whom lived in England. These landlords lacked the improving zeal of their English counterparts and were content to use their power to grab as much as possible.

The result was that the condition of the Irish peasantry around 1800 was abominable. The typical peasant lived in a wretched cottage and could afford neither shoes nor stockings. Hundreds of shocking accounts describe hopeless poverty. Yet in spite of terrible conditions, population growth sped onward. The 3 million of 1725 reached 4 million in 1780 and doubled to 8 million by 1840. Between 1780 and 1840, 1.75 million people left Ireland for Britain and America.

The population grew so quickly for three reasons: extensive cultivation of the potato, early marriage, and exploitation of peasants by landlords. The cultivation of the potato, introduced into Ireland (and all of Europe) in the late sixteenth century, was originally a response to the pressure of numbers. Once peasants began to cultivate potatoes, many more people could exist. A single acre of land spaded and planted with potatoes could feed a family of six for a year, whereas two to four acres of grain and pasture were needed to feed the same number. The potato also could thrive on boggy wastelands.

Needing only a big potato patch to survive, Irish men and women married early. Setting up housekeeping was easy, for a cabin of mud and stone could be slapped together with the help of friends and relatives in a few days. A mat for a bed, chairs and a table, and an iron pot to boil potatoes were easily acquired. To be sure, the young couple was embracing a life of extreme poverty. They would literally live on potatoes—ten pounds a day for an average male—moistened at best with a cup of milk.

Yet the decision to marry and have large families made sense. Landlords only leased land for short periods. Peasants had no incentive to make permanent improvements because anything beyond what was needed for survival would quickly be taken by higher rent. Rural poverty was inescapable and better shared with a spouse, while a dutiful son or a loving daughter was an old person's best hope of escaping destitution.

As population and potato dependency grew, conditions became more precarious. From 1820 onward deficiencies and diseases in the potato crop became more common. In 1845 and 1846, and again in 1848 and 1851, the potato crop failed in Ireland.

The result was unmitigated disaster—the **Great Famine.** Blight attacked the young plants, the leaves withered, and the tubers rotted. Widespread starvation and mass fever epidemics followed. Yet the British government, committed to rigid laissez-faire ideology and hoping that the repeal of the Corn Laws would alleviate the food shortage, was slow to act. When it did, its relief efforts were tragically inadequate. Moreover, the government continued to collect taxes, and landlords demanded their rents. Tenants who could not pay were evicted and their homes destroyed. Famine or no, Ireland remained the conquered jewel of foreign landowners.

The Great Famine shattered the pattern of Irish population growth. Fully 1 million emigrants fled the famine between 1845 and 1851, and at least 1.5 million died or went unborn because of the disaster. Alone among the countries of Europe, Ireland experienced a declining population in the nineteenth century, from about 8 million in 1845 to 4.4 million in 1911. Ireland became a land of continuous out-migration, late marriage, and widespread celibacy.

The Great Famine also intensified anti-British feeling and promoted Irish nationalism, for the bitter memory of starvation, exile, and British inaction was burned deeply into the popular consciousness. Patriots could call on powerful collective emotions in their campaigns for land reform, home rule, and, eventually, Irish independence.

## The Revolution of 1830 in France

Louis XVIII's Constitutional Charter of 1814—theoretically a gift from the king but actually a response to political pressures—was basically a liberal constitution (see page

**Daniel McDonald: The Discovery of the Potato Blight** Although the leaves of diseased plants usually shriveled and died, they could also look deceptively healthy. This Irish family has dug up its potato harvest and just discovered to its horror that the blight has rotted the crop. Like thousands of Irish families, this family now faces the starvation and the mass epidemics of the Great Famine. (*Department of Irish Folklore, University College, Dublin*)

718). The economic and social gains made by sections of the middle class and the peasantry in the French Revolution were fully protected, great intellectual and artistic freedom was permitted, and a parliament with upper and lower houses was created. Immediately after Napoleon's abortive Hundred Days, the moderate, worldly king refused to bow to the wishes of die-hard aristocrats such as his brother Charles, who wished to sweep away all the revolutionary changes and return to a bygone age of royal absolutism and aristocratic pretension. Instead, Louis appointed as his ministers moderate royalists, who sought and obtained the support of a majority of the representatives elected to the lower Chamber of Deputies between 1816 and Louis's death in 1824.

Louis XVIII's charter was anything but democratic. Only about 100,000 of the wealthiest males out of a total population of 30 million had the right to vote for the deputies who, with the king and his ministers, made the laws of the nation. Nonetheless, the "notable people" who did vote came from very different backgrounds. There were wealthy businessmen, war profiteers, successful professionals, ex-revolutionaries, large landowners from the old aristocracy and the middle class, Bourbons, and Bonapartists.

The old aristocracy, with its pre-1789 mentality, was a minority within the voting population. It was this situation that Louis's successor, Charles X (r. 1824–1830), could not abide. Crowned in a lavish, utterly medieval, five-hour ceremony in the cathedral of Reims in 1824, Charles was a true reactionary. He wanted to re-establish the old order in France. Increasingly blocked by the opposition of the deputies, Charles's government turned in 1830 to military adventure in an effort to rally French nationalism and gain popular support. A long-standing economic and diplomatic dispute with Muslim Algeria, a vassal state of the Ottoman Empire, provided the opportunity.

In June 1830, a French force of 37,000 crossed the Mediterranean, landed to the west of Algiers, and took the capital city in three short weeks. Victory seemed complete, but in 1831 tribes in the interior revolted and waged a fearsome war until 1847, when French armies finally subdued the country. Bringing French, Spanish, and Italian settlers to Algeria and leading to the expropriation of large tracts of Muslim land, the conquest of Algeria marked the rebirth of French colonial expansion.

Emboldened by the good news from Algeria, which actually had limited impact in Paris, Charles repudiated the Constitutional Charter in an attempted coup in July 1830.

**The Fall of Algiers, July 1830** France assembled more than six hundred ships for its attack on the Ottoman dependency of Algeria, and this contemporary engraving depicts the ferocious naval bombardment that destroyed the capital's last remaining fortifications. However, after the surrender French soldiers rampaged through the city, and news of this brutal behavior encouraged Muslims in the interior to revolt and fight on until 1847. *(Musée de la Ville de Paris, Musée Carnavalet, Paris, France/Lauros/Giraudon/The Bridgeman Art Library)*

He issued decrees stripping much of the wealthy middle class of its voting rights, and he censored the press. The immediate reaction, encouraged by journalists and lawyers, was an insurrection in the capital by printers, other artisans, and small traders. In "three glorious days," the government collapsed. Paris boiled with revolutionary excitement, and Charles fled. Then the upper middle class, which had fomented the revolt, skillfully seated Charles's cousin, Louis Philippe, duke of Orléans, on the vacant throne.

Louis Philippe (r. 1830–1848) accepted the Constitutional Charter of 1814; adopted the red, white, and blue flag of the French Revolution; and admitted that he was merely the "king of the French people." In spite of such symbolic actions, the situation in France remained fundamentally unchanged. Casimir Périer, a wealthy banker and Louis Philippe's new chief minister, bluntly told a deputy who complained when the vote was extended only from 100,000 to 170,000 citizens, "The trouble with this country is that there are too many people like you who imagine that there has been a revolution in France."[4] The wealthy notable elite actually tightened its control as the old aristocracy retreated to the provinces to sulk harmlessly. For the upper middle class, there had been a change in dynasty in order to protect the status quo and the narrowly liberal institutions of 1815. Republicans, democrats, social reformers, and the poor of Paris were bitterly disappointed. They had made a revolution, but it seemed for naught.

# The Revolutions of 1848

In 1848 revolutionary political and social ideologies combined with severe economic crisis and the romantic impulse to produce a vast upheaval across Europe. Only the most advanced and the most backward major countries—reforming Great Britain and immobile Russia—escaped untouched. Governments toppled; monarchs and ministers bowed or fled. National independence, liberal-democratic constitutions, and social reform: the lofty aspirations of a generation seemed at hand. Yet in the end, the revolutions failed. Why was this so?

## A Democratic Republic in France

The late 1840s in Europe were hard economically and tense politically. The potato famine in Ireland in 1845 and in 1846 had many echoes on the continent. Bad harvests jacked up food prices and caused misery and unemployment in the cities. "Prerevolutionary" outbreaks occurred all across Europe: an abortive Polish revolution in the northern part of Austria in 1846, a civil war between radicals and conservatives in Switzerland in 1847, and an armed uprising in Naples, Italy, in January 1848. Revolution was almost universally expected, but it took revolution in Paris—once again—to turn expectations into realities.

Louis Philippe's "bourgeois monarchy" had been characterized by stubborn inaction and complacency. There was a glaring lack of social legislation, and politics was dominated by corruption and selfish special interests. With only the rich voting for deputies, many of the deputies were docile government bureaucrats.

The government's stubborn refusal to consider electoral reform heightened a sense of class injustice among middle-class shopkeepers, skilled artisans, and unskilled working people, and it eventually touched off a popular revolt in Paris. Barricades went up on the night of February 22, 1848, and by February 24 Louis Philippe had abdicated in favor of his grandson. But the common people in arms would tolerate no more monarchy. This refusal led to the proclamation of a provisional republic, headed by a ten-man executive committee and certified by cries of approval from the revolutionary crowd.

A generation of historians and journalists had praised the First French Republic, and their work had borne fruit: the revolutionaries were firmly committed to a republic (as

**The Triumph of Democratic Republics** This French illustration constructs a joyous, optimistic vision of the initial revolutionary breakthrough in 1848. The peoples of Europe, joined together around their respective national banners, are achieving republican freedom, which is symbolized by the statue of liberty and the discarded crowns. The woman wearing pants—very radical attire—represents feminist hopes for liberation. (*Archive of Arnoldo Mondadori Editore, Milan*)

opposed to any form of constitutional monarchy), and they immediately set about drafting a constitution for France's Second Republic. Moreover, they wanted a truly popular and democratic republic so that the healthy, life-giving forces of the common people—the peasants, the artisans, and the unskilled workers—could reform society with wise legislation. In practice, building such a republic meant giving the right to vote to every adult male, and this was quickly done. Revolutionary compassion and sympathy for freedom were expressed in the freeing of all slaves in French colonies, the abolition of the death penalty, and the establishment of a ten-hour workday for Paris.

Yet there were profound differences within the revolutionary coalition in Paris. On the one hand, there were the moderate, liberal republicans of the middle class. They viewed universal male suffrage as the ultimate concession to be made to popular forces, and they strongly opposed any further radical social measures. On the other hand, there were radical republicans and hard-pressed artisans. Influenced by a generation of utopian socialists, and appalled by the poverty and misery of the urban poor, the radical republicans were committed to some kind of socialism. So were many artisans, who hated the unrestrained competition of cutthroat capitalism and who advocated a combination of strong craft unions and worker-owned businesses.

Worsening depression and rising unemployment brought these conflicting goals to the fore in 1848. Louis Blanc, who along with a worker named Albert represented the republican socialists in the provisional government, pressed for recognition of a socialist right to work. Blanc asserted that permanent government-sponsored cooperative workshops should be established for workers. Such workshops would be an alternative to capitalist employment and a decisive step toward a new, noncompetitive social order.

The moderate republicans wanted no such thing. They were willing to provide only temporary relief. The resulting compromise set up national workshops—soon to become little more than a vast program of pick-and-shovel public works—and established a special commission under Blanc to "study the question." This satisfied no one. The national workshops were, however, better than nothing. An army of desperate poor from the French provinces and even from foreign countries streamed into Paris to sign up. As the economic crisis worsened, the number enrolled in the workshops soared from 10,000 in March to 120,000 by June, and another 80,000 were trying unsuccessfully to join.

While the workshops in Paris grew, the French masses went to the election polls in late April. Voting in most cases for the first time, the people of France elected to the new Constituent Assembly about five hundred moderate republicans, three hundred monarchists, and one hundred radicals who professed various brands of socialism. One of the moderate republicans was the author of *Democracy in America,* Alexis de Tocqueville (1805–1859), who had predicted the overthrow of Louis Philippe's government. To this brilliant observer, socialism was the most characteristic aspect of the revolution in Paris.

This socialist revolution was evoking a violent reaction not only among the frightened middle and upper classes but also among the bulk of the population—the peasants. The French peasants owned land, and according to Tocqueville, "private property had become with all those who owned it a sort of bond of fraternity."[5] The countryside, Tocqueville wrote, had been seized with a universal hatred of radical Paris. Returning from Normandy to take his seat in the new Constituent Assembly, Tocqueville saw that a majority of the members were firmly committed to the republic and strongly opposed to the socialists and their artisan allies, and he shared their sentiments.

This clash of ideologies—of liberal capitalism and socialism—became a clash of classes and arms after the elections. The new government's executive committee dropped Blanc and thereafter included no representative of the Parisian working class. Fearing that their socialist hopes were about to be dashed, artisans and unskilled workers invaded the Constituent Assembly on May 15 and tried to proclaim a new revolutionary state. But the government was ready and used the middle-class National Guard to squelch this uprising. As the workshops continued to fill and grow more radical, the fearful but powerful propertied classes in the Assembly took the offensive. On June 22, the government dissolved the national workshops in Paris, giving the workers the choice of joining the army or going to workshops in the provinces.

The result was a spontaneous and violent uprising. Frustrated in attempts to create a socialist society, masses of desperate people were now losing even their life-sustaining relief. As a voice from the crowd cried out when the famous astronomer François Arago counseled patience, "Ah, Monsieur Arago, you have never been hungry!"[6] Barricades sprang up in the narrow streets of Paris, and a terrible class war began. Working people fought with the courage of utter desperation, but the government had the army and the support of peasant France. After three terrible "June Days" and the death or injury of more than ten thousand people, the republican army under General Louis Cavaignac stood triumphant in a sea of working-class blood and hatred.

The revolution in France thus ended in spectacular failure. The February coalition of the middle and working classes had in four short months become locked in mortal combat. In place of a generous democratic republic, the Constituent Assembly completed a constitution featuring a strong executive. This allowed Louis Napoleon, nephew of Napoleon Bonaparte, to win a landslide victory in the election of December 1848. The appeal of his great name as well as the desire of the propertied classes for order at any cost had produced a semi-authoritarian regime.

## The Austrian Empire in 1848

Throughout central Europe, the first news of the upheaval in France evoked feverish excitement and eventually revolution. Liberals demanded written constitutions, representative government, and greater civil liberties from authoritarian regimes. When governments hesitated, popular revolts followed. Urban workers and students served as the shock troops, but they were allied with middle-class liberals and peasants. In the face of this united front, monarchs collapsed and granted almost everything. The popular revolutionary coalition, having secured great and easy victories, then broke down as it had in France. The traditional forces—the monarchy, the aristocracy, and the regular army—recovered their nerve, reasserted their authority, and took back many, though not all, of the concessions. Reaction was everywhere victorious.

The revolution in the Austrian Empire began in Hungary, where nationalistic Hungarians demanded national autonomy, full civil liberties, and universal suffrage. When the monarchy in Vienna hesitated, Viennese students and workers took to the streets, and peasant disorders broke out in parts of the empire. The Habsburg emperor Ferdinand I (r. 1835–1848) capitulated and promised reforms and a liberal constitution. Metternich fled in disguise toward London. The old absolutist order seemed to be collapsing with unbelievable rapidity.

The coalition of revolutionaries was not stable, however. The Austrian Empire was overwhelmingly agricultural, and serfdom still existed. On March 20, as part of its capitulation before upheaval, the monarchy abolished serfdom, with its degrading forced labor and feudal services. Feeling they had won a victory reminiscent of that in France in 1789, newly free men and women of the land then lost interest in the political and social questions agitating the cities. Meanwhile, the coalition of urban revolutionaries also broke down. When artisan workers and the urban poor rose in arms and presented their own demands for socialist workshops and universal voting rights for men, the prosperous middle classes recoiled in alarm.

The coalition of March was also weakened, and ultimately destroyed, by conflicting national aspirations. In March the Hungarian revolutionary leaders pushed through an extremely liberal, almost democratic, constitution. But the Hungarian revolutionaries also sought to transform the mosaic of provinces and peoples that was the kingdom of Hungary into a unified, centralized, Hungarian nation. To the minority groups that formed half of the population—the Croats, Serbs, and Romanians—such unification was completely unacceptable. Each felt entitled to political autonomy and cultural independence. The Habsburg monarchy in Vienna exploited the fears of the minority groups, and they were soon locked in armed combat with the new Hungarian government. In a somewhat similar way, Czech nationalists based in Bohemia and the city of Prague came into conflict with German nationalists. Thus conflicting national aspirations within the Austrian Empire enabled the monarchy to play off one group against the other.

Finally, the conservative aristocratic forces gathered around Emperor Ferdinand I regained their nerve and reasserted their great strength. The archduchess Sophia, a conservative but intelligent and courageous Bavarian princess married to the emperor's brother, provided a rallying point. Deeply ashamed of the emperor's collapse before a "mess of students," she insisted that Ferdinand, who had no heir, abdicate in favor of her son, Francis Joseph.[7] Powerful nobles who held high positions in the government, the army, and the church agreed completely. They organized around Sophia in a secret conspiracy to reverse and crush the revolution.

Their first breakthrough came when the army bombarded Prague and savagely crushed a working-class revolt there on June 17. Other Austrian officials and nobles began to lead the minority nationalities of Hungary against the revolutionary government proclaimed by the Hungarian patriots. At the end of October, the well-equipped, predominately peasant troops of the regular Austrian army attacked the student and working-class radicals in Vienna and retook the city at the cost of more than four thousand casualties. Thus the determination of the Austrian aristocracy and the loyalty of its army were the final ingredients in the triumph of reaction and the defeat of revolution.

When Francis Joseph (r. 1848–1916) was crowned emperor of Austria immediately after his eighteenth birthday in December 1848, only Hungary had yet to be brought under control. But another determined conservative, Nicholas I of Russia (r. 1825–1855), obligingly lent his iron hand. On June 6, 1849, 130,000 Russian troops poured into Hungary and subdued the country after bitter fighting. For a number of years, the Habsburgs ruled Hungary as a conquered territory.

## Prussia and the Frankfurt Assembly

After Austria, Prussia was the largest and most influential German kingdom. Prior to 1848, the goal of middle-class Prussian liberals had been to transform absolutist Prussia into a liberal constitutional monarchy, which would lead the thirty-eight states of the German Confederation into the liberal, unified nation desired by liberals throughout the German states. The agitation following the fall of Louis Philippe encouraged Prussian liberals to press their demands. When the artisans and factory workers in Berlin exploded in March and joined temporarily with the middle-class liberals in the struggle against the monarchy, the autocratic yet paternalistic Frederick William IV (r. 1840–1861) vacillated and finally caved in. On March 21, he promised to grant Prussia a liberal constitution and to merge Prussia into a new national German state that was to be created. But urban workers wanted much more and the Prussian aristocracy wanted much less than the moderate constitutional liberalism

**Street Fighting in Frankfurt, 1848** Workers and students could tear up the cobblestones, barricade a street, and make it into a fortress. But urban revolutionaries were untrained and poorly armed. They were no match for professional soldiers led by tough officers who were sent against them after frightened rulers had recovered their nerve. *(The Granger Collection, New York)*

the king conceded. The workers issued a series of democratic and vaguely socialist demands that troubled their middle-class allies, and the conservative clique gathered around the king to urge counter-revolution.

As an elected Prussian Constituent Assembly met in Berlin to write a constitution for the Prussian state, a self-appointed committee of liberals from various German states successfully called for a national assembly to begin writing a federal constitution for a unified German state. Meeting in Frankfurt in May, the National Assembly was a curious revolutionary body. It was a really serious middle-class body of lawyers, professors, doctors, officials, and businessmen.

Convened to write a constitution, the learned body was soon absorbed in a battle with Denmark over the provinces of Schleswig and Holstein, an extremely complicated issue from a legal point of view. The provinces were inhabited primarily by Germans but were ruled by the king of Denmark, although Holstein was a member of the German Confederation. When Frederick VII, the new nationalistic king of Denmark, tried to integrate both provinces into the rest of his state, the Germans in these provinces revolted. Hypnotized by this conflict, the National Assembly at Frankfurt debated ponderously and finally called on the Prussian army to oppose Denmark in the name of the German nation. Prussia responded and began war with Denmark. As the Schleswig-Holstein issue demonstrated, the national ideal was a crucial factor motivating the German middle classes in 1848.

In March 1849, the National Assembly finally completed its drafting of a liberal constitution and elected King Frederick William of Prussia emperor of the new German national state (minus Austria and Schleswig-Holstein). By early 1849, however, reaction had been successful almost everywhere. Frederick William had reasserted his royal authority, disbanded the Prussian Constituent Assembly, and granted his subjects a limited, essentially conservative constitution. Reasserting that he ruled by divine right, Frederick William contemptuously refused to accept the "crown from the gutter." Bogged down by their preoccupation with nationalist issues, the reluctant revolutionaries in Frankfurt had waited too long and acted too timidly.

When Frederick William, who really wanted to be emperor but only on his own authoritarian terms, tried to get the small monarchs of Germany to elect him emperor, Austria balked. Supported by Russia, Austria forced Prussia to renounce all its schemes of unification in late 1850. The German Confederation was re-established. Attempts to unite the Germans—first in a liberal national state and then in a conservative Prussian empire—had failed completely.

## Summary

In 1814 the victorious allied powers sought to restore peace and stability in Europe. Dealing moderately with France and wisely settling their own differences, the allies laid the foundations for beneficial international cooperation throughout much of the nineteenth century. Led by Metternich, the conservative powers also sought to prevent the spread of subversive ideas and radical changes in domestic politics. Yet European thought has seldom been more powerfully creative than after 1815, and ideologies of liberalism, nationalism, and socialism all developed to challenge the existing order in this period of early industrialization and rapid population growth. The romantic movement, breaking decisively with the dictates of classicism, reinforced the spirit of change and revolutionary anticipation.

All of these forces culminated in the liberal and nationalistic revolutions of 1848. Political, economic, and social pressures that had been building since 1815 exploded dramatically, but the upheavals of 1848 were abortive, and very few revolutionary goals were realized. The moderate, nationalistic middle classes were unable to consolidate their initial victories in France or elsewhere in Europe. Instead, they drew back when artisans, factory workers, and radical socialists rose up to present their own much more revolutionary demands. This retreat facilitated the efforts of dedicated aristocrats in central Europe and made possible the crushing of Parisian workers by a coalition of solid bourgeoisie and landowning peasantry in France. A host of fears, a sea of blood, and a torrent of disillusion had drowned the lofty ideals and utopian visions of a generation. The age of romantic revolution was over.

## Key Terms

dual revolution
Congress of Vienna
Holy Alliance
Carlsbad Decrees
liberalism
laissez faire
nationalism
socialism
parasites
doers
bourgeoisie
proletariat
romanticism
Sturm und Drang
Corn Laws
Battle of Peterloo
Great Famine

## Notes

1. E. Gellner, *Nations and Nationalism* (Oxford: Basil Blackwell, 1983), especially pp. 19–39.
2. This paragraph draws on the influential views of B. Anderson, *Imagined Communities: Reflections on the Origins and Spread of*

*Nationalism,* rev. ed. (London/New York: Verso, 1991), and E. J. Hobsbawm and T. Ranger, eds., *The Invention of Tradition* (Cambridge: Cambridge University Press, 1983).

3. Quoted in F. B. Artz, *From the Renaissance to Romanticism: Trends in Style in Art, Literature, and Music, 1300–1830* (Chicago: University of Chicago Press, 1962), pp. 276, 278.
4. Quoted in G. Wright, *France in Modern Times,* 4th ed. (Chicago: Rand McNally, 1987), p. 145.
5. A. de Tocqueville, *Recollections* (New York: Columbia University Press, 1949), p. 94.
6. M. Agulhon, *1848* (Paris: Éditions du Seuil, 1973), pp. 68–69.
7. W. L. Langer, *Political and Social Upheaval, 1832–1852* (New York: Harper & Row, 1969), p. 361.

## Suggested Reading

The works cited in the Notes are highly recommended. Among general studies, R. Gildea, *Barricades and Borders: Europe, 1800–1914,* 2d ed. (1996), is recommended. C. Morazé, *The Triumph of the Middle Classes* (1968), a wide-ranging procapitalist interpretation, may be compared with E. J. Hobsbawm's flexible Marxism in *The Age of Revolution, 1789–1848* (1962). For English history, W. Rubinstein, *Britain's Century: A Political and Social History, 1815–1905* (1998), is excellent. C. Ó Gráda, *Black '47 and Beyond: The Irish Famine in History, Economy, and Memory* (1999), is an outstanding and imaginative treatment of the Great Famine. R. Price, *A Social History of Nineteenth-Century France* (1987), is a fine synthesis. D. Blackbourn, *The Long Nineteenth Century: A History of Germany, 1780–1918* (1998), and J. Sheehan, *Germany, 1770–1866* (1989), are stimulating general histories that skillfully incorporate recent research. Two important reconsiderations of nationalism are B. Anderson, *Imagined Communities,* 2d ed. (1991), and E. Hobsbawm and T. Ranger, *The Invention of Tradition* (1990). R. Brubaker, *Citizenship and Nationhood in France and Germany* (1992), is an important comparative study, and A. Greene, *Fatherlands: State-Building and Nationhood in Nineteenth-Century Germany* (2001), is a brilliant discussion of the smaller German states. E. Kedourie, *Nationalism* (1960), is an influential historical critique of the new faith. T. Chapman, *Congress of Vienna: Origins, Processes, and Results* (1998), is a good introduction, which may be compared with H. Nicolson's entertaining *The Congress of Vienna* (1946). On 1848, J. Sperber, *The European Revolutions, 1848–1851* (1993), is a solid recent synthesis. M. Agulhon, *The Republican Experiment, 1848–1852* (1983), is outstanding. I. Deak, *The Lawful Revolution: Louis Kossuth and the Hungarians, 1848–49* (1979), is a noteworthy study of an interesting figure.

On early socialism and Marxism, see A. Lindemann's stimulating survey, *A History of European Socialism* (1983), and W. Sewell Jr., *Work and Revolution in France: The Language of Labor from the Old Regime to 1848* (1980), as well as G. Lichtheim's high-powered *Marxism* (1961). J. Seigel, *Marx's Fate: The Shape of a Life* (1978), is a major biography. P. Stock-Morton, *The Life of Marie d'Agoult, Alias Daniel Stern* (2000), is a fascinating biography of the French romantic novelist, and J. Margadant, ed., *The New Biography: Performing Femininity in Nineteenth-Century France* (2000), is an innovative collection on the images leading writers created for themselves. P. Pilbeam, *French Socialists Before Marx: Workers, Women, and the Social Question* (2000), shows the large role of women in utopian socialism. Also highly recommended are B. Taylor, *Eve and the New Jerusalem: Socialism and Feminism in the Nineteenth Century* (1983), which explores fascinating English attempts to emancipate workers and women at the same time, and B. Anderson, *Joyous Greetings: The First International Women's Movement* (2000), which stresses the importance of 1848. On liberalism, see R. Heilbroner's entertaining *The Worldly Philosophers* (1967) and G. de Ruggiero's classic *History of European Liberalism* (1959). D. Brown, *Romanticism* (2001), an engaging, lavishly illustrated feast, and M. Cranston, *The Romantic Movement* (1994), skillfully discuss romanticism. A. Brookner, *Romanticism and Its Discontents* (2000), is a stimulating reconsideration of French painters and writers. J. Seigel, *Bohemian Paris: Culture, Politics, and the Boundaries of Bourgeois Life* (1986), imaginatively places romantic aspirations in a broad cultural framework. R. Stromberg, *An Intellectual History of Modern Europe,* 3d ed. (1981), is a valuable survey. The important place of religion in nineteenth-century thought is considered from different perspectives in H. McLeod, *Religion and the People of Western Europe* (1981), and O. Chadwick, *The Secularization of the European Mind in the Nineteenth Century* (1976). Two good church histories with useful bibliographies are J. Altholz, *The Churches in the Nineteenth Century* (1967), and A. Vidler, *The Church in an Age of Revolution: 1789 to the Present Day* (1961).

The thoughtful reader is strongly advised to delve into the incredibly rich writing of contemporaries. J. Bowditch and C. Ramsland, eds., *Voices of the Industrial Revolution* (1961), is an excellent starting point, with well-chosen selections from leading economic thinkers and early socialists. H. Hugo, ed., *The Romantic Reader,* is another fine anthology. Mary Shelley's *Frankenstein,* a great romantic novel, draws an almost lovable picture of the famous monster and is highly recommended. Jules Michelet's compassionate masterpiece *The People,* a famous historian's anguished examination of French social divisions on the eve of 1848, draws one into the heart of the period and is highly recommended. Alexis de Tocqueville covers some of the same ground less romantically in his *Recollections,* which may be compared with Karl Marx's white-hot "instant history," *Class Struggles in France, 1848–1850.* Great novels that accurately portray aspects of the times are Victor Hugo, *Les Misérables,* an exciting story of crime and passion among France's poor; Honoré de Balzac, *La Cousine Bette* and *Le Père Goriot;* and Thomas Mann, *Buddenbrooks,* a wonderful historical novel that traces the rise and fall of a prosperous German family over three generations during the nineteenth century.

# Listening to the Past

## Faith in Democratic Nationalism

*Early advocates of the national ideal usually believed that progress for one people would also contribute to the progress of all humanity. They believed that a Europe of independent nation-states would provide the proper framework for securing freedom, democracy, social justice, and even international peace.*

*This optimistic faith guided Giuseppe Mazzini (1805–1872), the leading prophet of Italian nationalism and unification. Banished from Italy in 1830, the exiled Mazzini founded a secret society called Young Italy to fight for Italian unification and a democratic republic. Mazzini's group inspired numerous local insurrections and then led Italy's radicals in the unsuccessful revolutions of 1848. Italy was united a decade later, but by other means.*

*Mazzini's best-known work was* The Duties of Man, *a collection of essays. The following famous selection, titled "Duties Towards Your Country," was written in 1858 and addressed to Italian workingmen.*

Your first Duties . . . are to Humanity. . . . But what can each of you, with his isolated powers, do for the moral improvement, for the progress of Humanity? . . .

God gave you the means of multiplying your forces and your powers of action indefinitely when he gave you a Country, when, like a wise overseer of labor, who distributes the different parts of the work according to the capacity of the workmen, he divided Humanity into distinct groups upon the face of our globe, and thus planted the seeds of nations. Evil governments have disfigured the design of God, which you may see clearly marked out, as far, at least, as regards Europe, by the courses of the great rivers, by the lines of the lofty mountains, and by other geographical conditions; they have disfigured it by conquest, by greed, by jealousy of the just sovereignty of others; disfigured it so much that today there is perhaps no nation except England and France whose confines correspond to this design.

[These evil governments] did not, and they do not, recognize any country except their own families and dynasties, the egoism of caste. But the divine design will infallibly be fulfilled. Natural divisions, the innate spontaneous tendencies of the peoples will replace the arbitrary divisions sanctioned by evil governments. The map of Europe will be remade. The Countries of the People will rise, defined by the voice of the free, upon the ruins of the Countries of Kings and privileged castes. Between these Countries there will be harmony and brotherhood. And then the work of Humanity for the general amelioration, for the discovery and application of the real law of life, carried on in association and distributed according to local capacities, will be accomplished by peaceful and progressive development.

Then each of you, strong in the affections and in the aid of many millions of men speaking the same language, endowed with the same tendencies, and educated by the same historic tradition, may hope by your personal effort to benefit the whole of Humanity.

Without Country you have neither name, voice, nor rights, no admission as brothers into the fellowship of the Peoples. You are the bastards of Humanity. Soldiers without a banner, . . . you will find neither faith nor protection. . . . Do not beguile yourselves with the hope of emancipation from unjust social conditions if you do not first conquer a Country for yourselves; where there is no Country there is no common agreement to which you can appeal; the egoism of self-interest rules alone, and he who has the upper hand keeps it, since there is no common safeguard for the interests of all. . . .

O my Brothers! love your Country. Our Country is our home, the home which God has given us, placing therein a numerous family which we love and are loved by. . . . In labouring according to true principles for our Country we are labouring for Humanity; our Country is the fulcrum of the lever which we have to wield for the common good. If we give up this fulcrum we run the risk of becoming useless to our Country and to Humanity. . . .

There is no true Country without a uniform law. There is no true Country where the uniformity of that law is violated by the existence of caste, privilege, and inequality, where the powers and faculties of a large number of individuals are suppressed or dormant, where there is no common principle accepted, recognized, and developed by all. In such a state of things there can be no Nation, no People, but only a multitude, a fortuitous agglomeration of men whom circumstances have brought together and different circumstances will separate. In the name of your love for your Country you must combat without truce the existence of every privilege, every inequality, upon the soil which has given you birth. . . .

Your Country should be your Temple. God at the summit, a People of equals at the base. Do not accept any other formula, any other moral law, if you do not want to dishonour your Country and yourselves. Let the secondary laws for the gradual regulation of your existence be the progressive application of this supreme law.

And in order that they should be so, it is necessary that *all* should contribute to the making of them. The laws made by one fraction of the citizens only can never by the nature of things and men do otherwise than reflect the thoughts and aspirations and desires of that fraction; they represent, not the whole Country, but a third, a fourth part, a class, a zone of the Country. The law must express the general aspiration, promote the good of all, respond to a beat of the nation's heart. The whole nation therefore should be, directly or indirectly, the legislator. By yielding this mission to a few men, you put the egoism of one class in the place of the Country, which is the union of *all* the classes.

A Country is not a mere territory; the particular territory is only its foundation. The Country is the idea which rises upon that foundation; it is the sentiment of love, the sense of fellowship which binds together all the sons of that territory.

So long as a single one of your brothers is not represented by his own vote in the development of the national life—so long as a single one vegetates uneducated among the educated—so long as a single one able and willing to work languishes in poverty for want of work—you have not got a Country such as it ought to be, the Country of all and for all.

*Votes, education, work* are the three main pillars of the nation; do not rest until your hands have solidly erected them.

Portrait of Giuseppe Mazzini, from the Museo del Risorgimento, Milan. *(Museo del Risorgimento/ Scala/ Art Resource, NY)*

## Questions for Analysis

1. What did Mazzini mean by "evil governments"? Why are they evil?
2. What are the characteristics of the "true Country"?
3. What form of government is best? Why?
4. Why, according to Mazzini, should poor workingmen have been interested in the political unification of Italy?
5. How might a woman today criticize Mazzini's program? Debate how Mazzini might respond to such criticism.

*Source:* Slightly adapted from J. Mazzini, *The Duties of Man and Other Essays* (London: J. M. Dent and Sons, 1907), pp. 51–57.

John Perry, *A Bill-poster's Fantasy* (1855), explores the endless diversity of big-city entertainment. *(dunhill Museum & Archive, 48 Germyn Street, St. James's, London)*

chapter

# 24 Life in the Emerging Urban Society

**chapter outline**

- Taming the City
- Rich and Poor and Those in Between
- The Changing Family
- Science and Thought

The era of intellectual and political upheaval that culminated in the revolutions of 1848 was also an era of rapid urbanization. After 1848 Western political development veered off in a novel and uncharted direction, but the growth of towns and cities rushed forward with undiminished force. Thus Western society was urban and industrial in 1900 as surely as it had been rural and agrarian in 1800. The urbanization of society was both a result of the Industrial Revolution and a reflection of its enormous long-term impact.

- What was life like in the cities, and how did it change?
- What did the emergence of urban industrial society mean for rich and poor and those in between?
- How did families change as they coped with the challenges and the opportunities of the developing urban civilization?
- What changes in science and thought reflected and influenced this new civilization?

These are the questions this chapter will investigate.

## Taming the City

The growth of industry posed enormous challenges for all elements of Western society, from young factory workers confronting relentless discipline to aristocratic elites maneuvering to retain political power. As we saw in Chapter 22, the early consequences of economic transformation were mixed and far-reaching and by no means wholly negative. By 1850 at the latest, working conditions were improving and real wages were rising for the mass of the population, and they continued to do so until 1914. Thus given the poverty and uncertainty of preindustrial life, some historians maintain that the history of industrialization in the nineteenth century is probably better written in terms of increasing opportunities than in terms of greater hardships.

Critics of this relatively optimistic view of industrialization claim that it neglects the quality of life in urban areas. They stress that the new industrial towns and cities were awful places where people, especially poor people, suffered from bad housing, lack of sanitation, and a sense of hopelessness. They ask if these drawbacks did not more than cancel out higher wages and greater opportunity. An examination of the development of cities in the nineteenth century provides some answers to this complex question.

## Industry and the Growth of Cities

Since the Middle Ages, European cities had been centers of government, culture, and large-scale commerce. They had also been congested, dirty, and unhealthy. People were packed together almost as tightly as possible within the city limits. The typical city was a "walking city": for all but the wealthiest classes, walking was the only available form of transportation.

Infectious disease spread with deadly speed in cities, and people were always more likely to die in the city than in the countryside. In the larger towns, more people died each year than were born, on average, and urban populations were able to maintain their numbers only because newcomers were continually arriving from rural areas. Little could be done to improve these conditions, given the pervasive poverty, absence of urban transportation, lack of medical knowledge, and deadly overcrowding.

Clearly, deplorable urban conditions did not originate with the Industrial Revolution. What the Industrial Revolution did was to reveal those conditions more nakedly than ever before. The steam engine freed industrialists from dependence on the energy of fast-flowing streams and rivers so that by 1800 there was every incentive to build new factories in urban areas. Cities had better shipping facilities than the countryside and thus better supplies of coal and raw materials. There were also many hands wanting work in the cities, for cities drew people like a magnet. And it was a great advantage for a manufacturer to have other factories nearby to supply the business's needs and buy its products. Therefore, as industry grew, there was also a rapid expansion of already overcrowded and unhealthy cities.

The challenge of the urban environment was felt first and most acutely in Great Britain. The number of people living in cities of 20,000 or more in England and Wales jumped from 1.5 million in 1801 to 6.3 million in 1851 and reached 15.6 million in 1891. Such cities accounted for 17 percent of the total English population in 1801, 35 percent as early as 1851, and fully 54 percent in 1891. Other countries duplicated the English pattern as they industrialized (see Map 24.1). An American observer was hardly exaggerating when he wrote in 1899 that "the most remarkable social phenomenon of the present century is the concentration of population in cities."[1]

In the 1820s and 1830s, people in Britain and France began to worry about the condition of their cities. In those years, the populations of a number of British cities

**MAP 24.1 European Cities of 100,000 or More, 1800 and 1900** There were more large cities in Great Britain in 1900 than in all of Europe in 1800. Northwestern Europe was the most urbanized area.

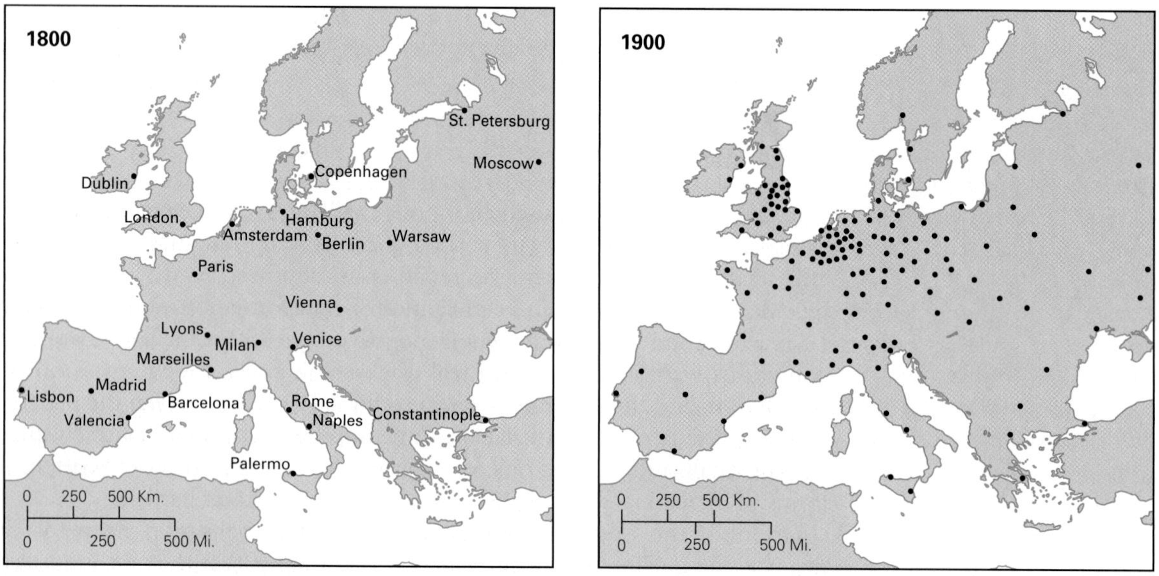

1850 | 1865 | 1880 | 1895 | 1910

**POLITICAL/MILITARY**

- 1861–1865 U.S. Civil War
- 1859–1870 Unification of Italy
- 1866 Austro-Prussian War
- 1870–1871 Franco-Prussian War

**SOCIAL/ECONOMIC**

- 1850–1914 Condition of working classes improves
- ca 1850–1870 Modernization of Paris
- 1880–1913 Birthrate steadily declines in Europe
- 1890s Electric streetcars introduced in Europe

**INTELLECTUAL/RELIGIOUS**

- 1854 Pasteur studies fermentation and develops pasteurization
- 1854–1870 Development of germ theory
- 1880–1881 Dostoevski, *The Brothers Karamazov*
- 1857 Flaubert, *Madame Bovary*
- 1859 Darwin, *On the Origin of Species*
- 1869 Mendeleev creates periodic table

were increasing by 40 to 70 percent each decade. With urban areas expanding at such previously undreamed-of rates, people's fatalistic acceptance of overcrowded, unsanitary urban living conditions began to give way to active concern. Something urgently needed to be done.

On one point everyone could agree: except on the outskirts, each town or city was using every scrap of land to the fullest extent. Parks and open areas were almost nonexistent. Buildings were erected on the smallest possible lots in order to pack the maximum number of people into a given space. Narrow houses were built wall to wall in long rows. These row houses had neither front nor back yards, and only a narrow alley in back separated one row from the next. Or buildings were built around tiny courtyards completely enclosed on all four sides. Many people lived in extremely small, often overcrowded cellars or attics. "Six, eight, and even ten occupying one room is anything but uncommon," wrote a doctor from Aberdeen in Scotland for a government investigation in 1842.

These highly concentrated urban populations lived in extremely unsanitary and unhealthy conditions. Open drains and sewers flowed alongside or down the middle of unpaved streets. Toilet facilities were primitive in the extreme. In parts of Manchester, as many as two hundred people shared a single outhouse. Such privies filled up rapidly, and since they were infrequently emptied, sewage often overflowed and seeped into cellar dwellings. Moreover, some courtyards in poorer neighborhoods became dunghills, collecting excrement that was sometimes sold as fertilizer. By the 1840s there was among the better-off classes a growing, shocking "realization that, to put it as mildly as possible, millions of English men, women, and children were living in shit."[2]

Who or what was responsible for these awful conditions? The crucial factors were the tremendous pressure of more people and the *total* absence of public transportation. People simply had to jam themselves together if they were to be able to walk to shops and factories. Another factor was that government in Great Britain, both local and national, was slow to provide sanitary facilities and establish adequate building codes. This slow pace was probably attributable more to a need to explore and identify

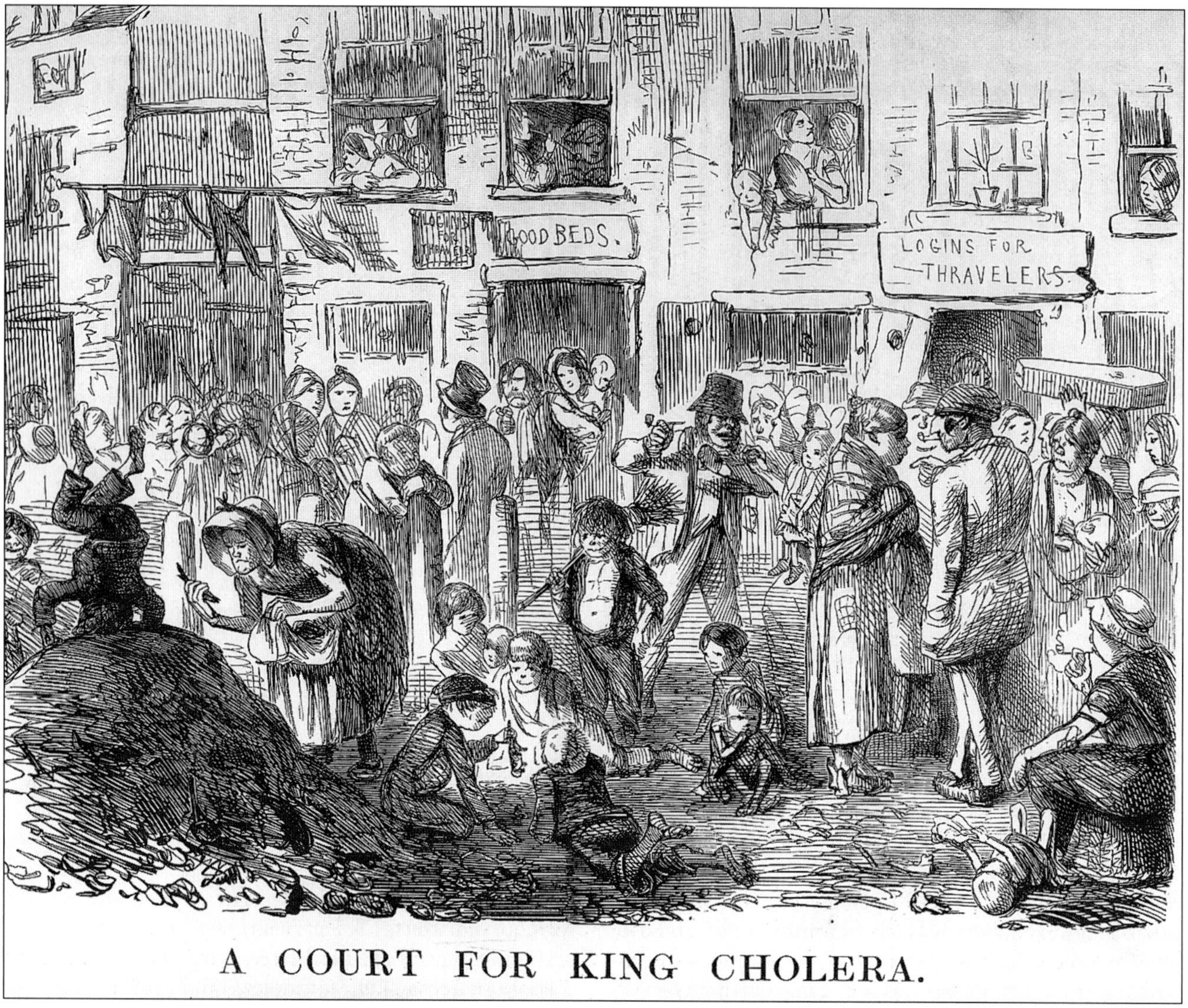


**Filth and Disease** This 1852 drawing from *Punch* tells volumes about the unhealthy living conditions of the urban poor. In the foreground children play with a dead rat and a woman scavenges a dungheap. Cheap rooming houses provide shelter for the frightfully overcrowded population. *(The British Library)*

what precisely should be done than to rigid middle-class opposition to government action. Certainly, Great Britain had no monopoly on overcrowded and unhealthy urban conditions; many continental cities with stronger traditions of municipal regulation were every bit as bad.

Most responsible of all was the sad legacy of rural housing conditions in preindustrial society combined with appalling ignorance. As one authority concludes, "the decent cottage was the exception, the hovel the rule."[3] Thus housing was far down on the newcomer's list of priorities, and ordinary people generally took dirt and filth for granted. One English miner told an investigator, "I do not think it usual for the lasses [in the coal mines] to wash their bodies; my sisters never wash themselves." As for the men, "their legs and bodies are as black as your hat."[4]

## Public Health and the Bacterial Revolution

Although cleanliness was not next to godliness in most people's eyes, it was becoming so for some reformers. The most famous of these was Edwin Chadwick, one of the commissioners charged with the administration of relief to paupers under Britain's revised Poor Law of 1834. Chadwick was a good **Benthamite**—that is, a follower of radical philosopher Jeremy Bentham (1748–1832). Bentham had taught that public problems ought to be dealt with on a rational, scientific basis and according to the "greatest good for the greatest number." Applying these principles, Chadwick soon became convinced that disease and death actually caused poverty simply because a sick worker was an unemployed worker and orphaned children were poor children. Most important, Chadwick believed that disease could be prevented by cleaning up the urban environment. That was his "sanitary idea."

Chadwick collected detailed reports from local Poor Law officials on the "sanitary conditions of the laboring population" and published his hard-hitting findings in 1842. This mass of widely publicized evidence proved that disease was related to filthy environmental conditions, which were in turn caused largely by lack of drainage, sewers, and garbage collection.

Chadwick correctly believed that the stinking excrement of communal outhouses could be dependably carried off by water through sewers at less than one-twentieth the cost of removing it by hand. The cheap iron pipes and tile drains of the industrial age would provide running water and sewerage for all sections of town, not just the wealthy ones. In 1848, with the cause strengthened by the cholera epidemic of 1846, Chadwick's report became the basis of Great Britain's first public health law, which created a national health board and gave cities broad authority to build modern sanitary systems.

The public health movement won dedicated supporters in the United States, France, and Germany from the 1840s on. Governments accepted at least limited responsibility for the health of all citizens, and their programs broke decisively with the age-old fatalism of urban populations in the face of shockingly high mortality. By the 1860s and 1870s, European cities were making real progress toward adequate water supplies and sewerage systems, city dwellers were beginning to reap the reward of better health, and death rates began to decline (see Figure 24.1).

Still, effective control of communicable disease required a great leap forward in medical knowledge and biological theory. Early reformers such as Chadwick were seriously handicapped by the prevailing **miasmatic theory** of disease—the belief that people contract disease when they breathe the bad odors of decay and putrefying excrement. Keen observation by doctors and public health officials in the 1840s and 1850s pinpointed the role of bad drinking water in the transmission of disease and suggested that contagion was *spread through* filth and not caused by it, thus weakening the miasmatic idea.

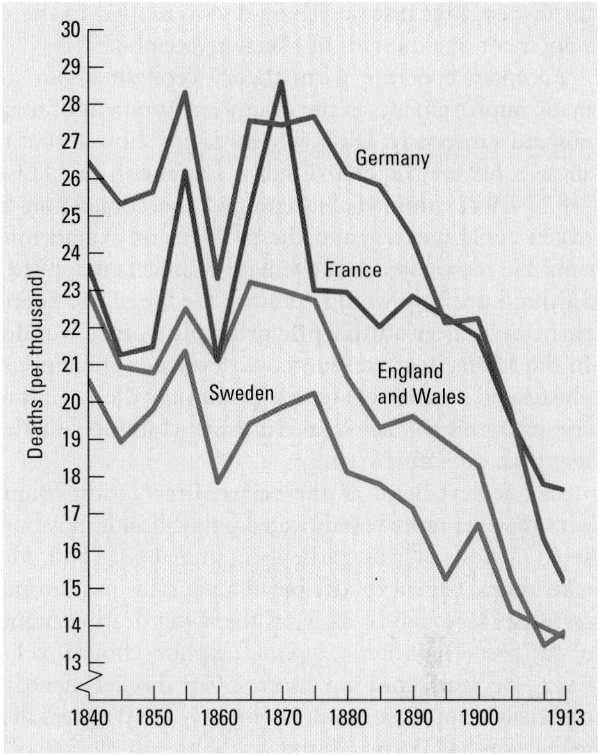


**FIGURE 24.1 The Decline of Death Rates in England and Wales, Germany, France, and Sweden, 1840–1913** A rising standard of living, improvements in public health, and better medical knowledge all contributed to the dramatic decline of death rates in the nineteenth century.

The breakthrough was the development of the **germ theory** of disease by Louis Pasteur (1822–1895), a French chemist who began studying fermentation in 1854 at the request of brewers. Using his microscope to develop a simple test that brewers could use to monitor the fermentation process and avoid spoilage, Pasteur found that fermentation depended on the growth of living organisms and that the activity of these organisms could be suppressed by heating the beverage—by **pasteurization.** The breathtaking implication was that specific diseases were caused by specific living organisms—germs—and that those organisms could be controlled in people as well as in beer, wine, and milk.

By 1870 the work of Pasteur and others had demonstrated the general connection between germs and disease. When, in the middle of the 1870s, German country doctor Robert Koch and his coworkers developed pure cultures of harmful bacteria and described their life cycles, the dam broke. Over the next twenty years, researchers—mainly Germans—identified the organisms responsible for disease after disease. These discoveries led to the development of a number of effective vaccines.

Acceptance of the germ theory brought about dramatic improvements in the deadly environment of hospitals and surgery. In 1865, when Pasteur showed that the air was full of bacteria, English surgeon Joseph Lister (1827–1912) immediately grasped the connection between aerial bacteria and the problem of wound infection. He reasoned that a chemical disinfectant applied to a wound dressing would "destroy the life of the floating particles." Lister's **antiseptic principle** worked wonders. In the 1880s, German surgeons developed the more sophisticated practice of sterilizing not only the wound but also everything—hands, instruments, clothing—that entered the operating room.

The achievements of the bacterial revolution coupled with the ever more sophisticated public health movement saved millions of lives, particularly after about 1880. Mortality rates began to decline dramatically in European countries (see Figure 24.1) as the awful death sentences of the past—diphtheria, typhoid, typhus, cholera, yellow fever—became vanishing diseases. City dwellers benefited especially from these developments. By 1910 a great silent revolution had occurred: the death rates for people of all ages in urban areas were generally no greater than those for people in rural areas, and sometimes they were less.

## Urban Planning and Public Transportation

More effective urban planning was one of the keys to improving the quality of urban life. Urban planning was in decline by the early nineteenth century, but after 1850 its practice was revived and extended. France took the lead during the rule of Napoleon III (r. 1848–1870), who sought to stand above class conflict and promote the welfare of all his subjects through government action. He believed that rebuilding much of Paris would provide employment, improve living conditions, and testify to the power and glory of his empire. In the baron Georges Haussmann (1809–1884), an aggressive, impatient Alsatian whom he placed in charge of Paris, Napoleon III found an authoritarian planner capable of bulldozing both buildings and opposition. In twenty years, Paris was transformed.

The Paris of 1850 was a labyrinth of narrow, dark streets, the results of desperate overcrowding. In a central city not twice the size of New York's Central Park lived more than one-third of the city's 1 million inhabitants. Terrible slum conditions and extremely high death rates were facts of life. There were few open spaces and only two public parks for the entire metropolis. Public transportation played a very small role in this enormous walking city.

Haussmann and his fellow planners proceeded on many interrelated fronts. With a bold energy that often shocked their contemporaries, they razed old buildings in order to cut broad, straight, tree-lined boulevards through the center of the city as well as in new quarters on the outskirts (see Map 24.2). These boulevards, designed in part to prevent the easy construction and defense of barricades by revolutionary crowds, permitted traffic to flow freely and afforded impressive vistas. Their creation also demolished some of the worst slums. New streets stimulated the construction of better housing, especially for the middle classes. Small neighborhood parks and open spaces were created throughout the city, and two very large parks suitable for all kinds of holiday activities were developed—one on the wealthy west side and one on the poor east side of the city. The city also improved its sewers, and a system of aqueducts more than doubled the city's supply of good fresh water.

Rebuilding Paris provided a new model for urban planning and stimulated modern urbanism throughout Europe, particularly after 1870. In city after city, public authorities mounted a coordinated attack on many of the interrelated problems of the urban environment. As in Paris, improvements in public health through better water supply and waste disposal often went hand in hand with new boulevard construction. Cities such as Vienna and Cologne followed the Parisian example of tearing down old walled fortifications and replacing them with broad, circular boulevards on which office buildings, town halls, theaters, opera houses, and museums were erected. These ring roads and the new boulevards that radiated out from them toward the outskirts eased movement and encouraged urban expansion (see Map 24.2). Zoning expropriation laws, which allowed a majority of the owners of land in a given quarter of the city to impose major street or sanitation improvements on a reluctant minority, were an important mechanism of the new urbanism.

The development of mass public transportation was also of great importance in the improvement of urban living conditions. In the 1870s, many European cities authorized private companies to operate horse-drawn streetcars, which had been developed in the United States, to carry riders along the growing number of major thoroughfares. Then in the 1890s, the real revolution occurred: European countries adopted another American transit innovation, the electric streetcar.

Electric streetcars were cheaper, faster, more dependable, and more comfortable than their horse-drawn counterparts. Service improved dramatically. Millions of

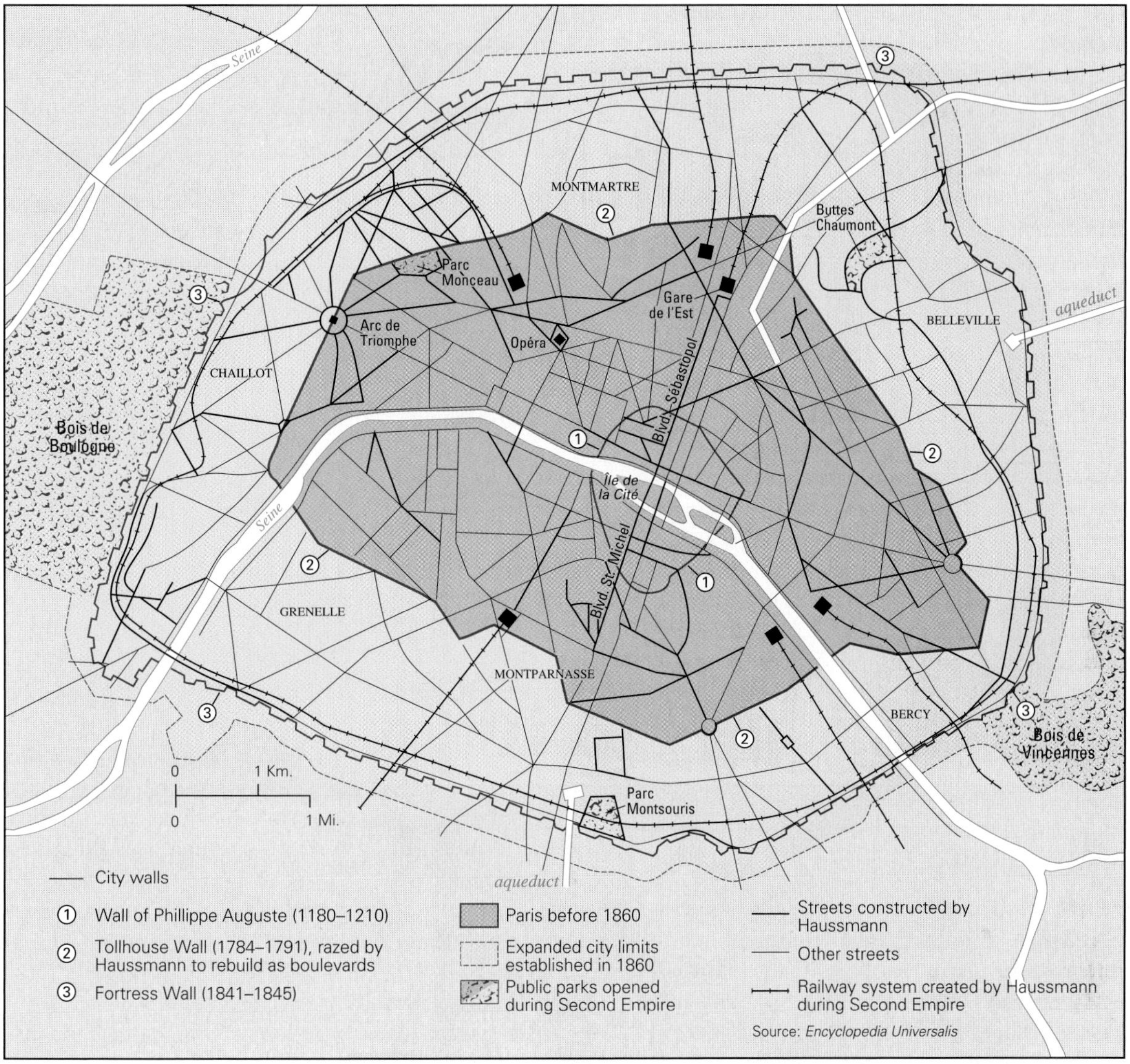


**MAP 24.2 The Modernization of Paris, ca 1850–1870** Broad boulevards, large parks, and grandiose train stations transformed Paris. The cutting of the new north-south axis—known as the Boulevard Saint-Michel—was one of Haussmann's most controversial projects. It razed much of Paris's medieval core and filled the Île de la Cité with massive government buildings.

Europeans—workers, shoppers, schoolchildren—hopped on board during the workweek. And on weekends and holidays, streetcars carried millions on happy outings to parks and countryside, racetracks and music halls. In 1886 the horse-drawn streetcars of Austria-Hungary, France, Germany, and Great Britain were carrying about 900 million riders. By 1910 electric streetcar systems in the four countries were carrying 6.7 billion riders.[5] Each man, woman, and child was using public transportation four times as often in 1910 as in 1886.

Good mass transit helped greatly in the struggle for decent housing. The new boulevards and horse-drawn streetcars had facilitated a middle-class move to better housing in the 1860s and 1870s; after 1890 electric streetcars gave people of modest means access to new, improved housing. The still-crowded city was able to expand and become less congested. In England in 1901, only 9 percent of the urban population was "overcrowded" in terms of the official definition of more than two persons per room. On the continent, many city governments in

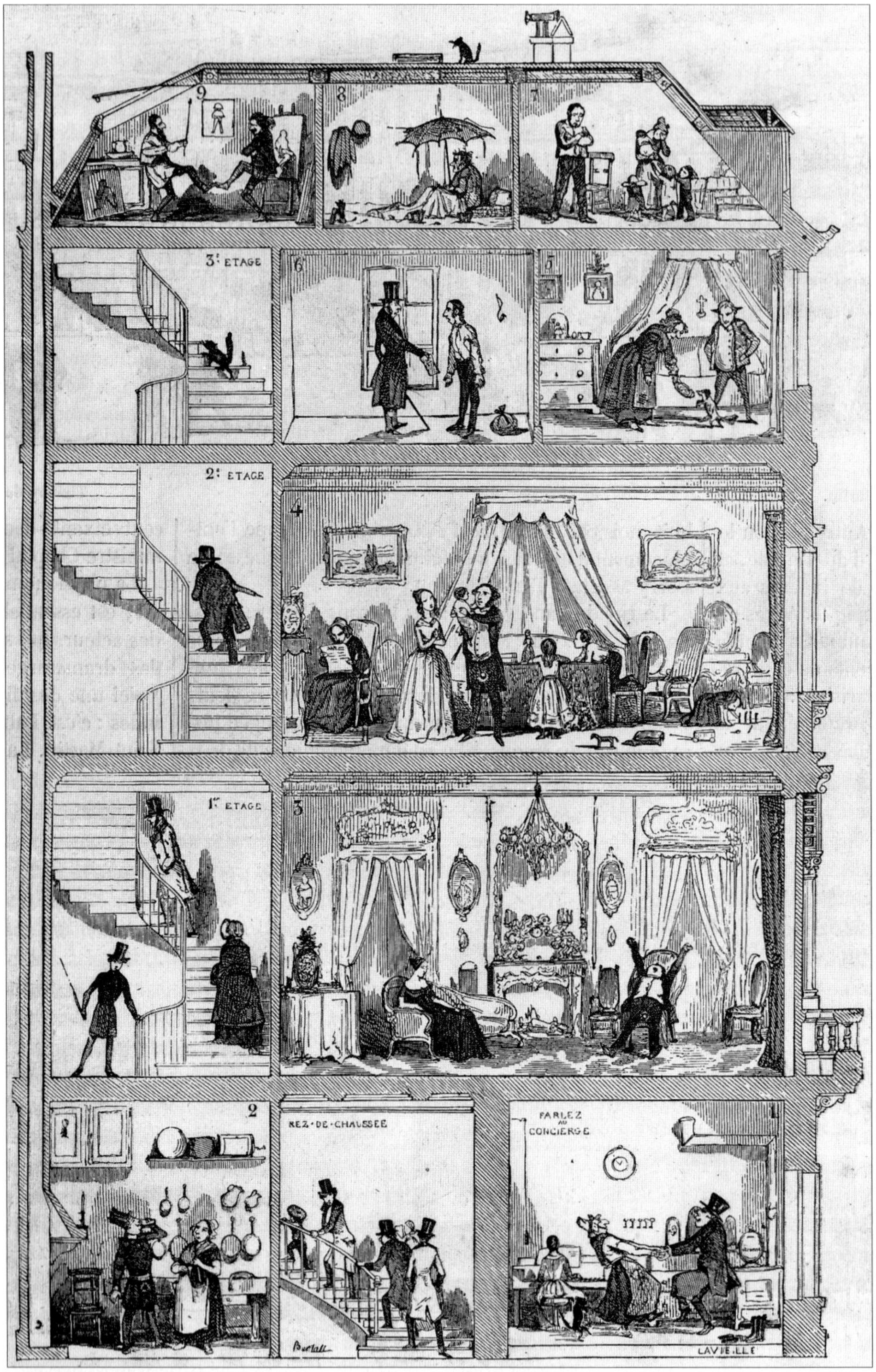


**Apartment Living in Paris** This drawing shows how different social classes lived close together in European cities in about 1850. Passing the middle-class family on the first floor (American second floor), the economic condition of the tenants declined until one reached abject poverty in the garret. *(Bibliothèque nationale de France)*

**The Urban Landscape: Madrid in 1900** This wistful painting of a Spanish square on a rainy day, by Enrique Martinez Cubells y Ruiz (1874–1917), includes a revealing commentary on public transportation. Coachmen wait atop their expensive hackney cabs for a wealthy clientele, while modern electric streetcars that carry the masses converge on the square from all directions. *(Museo Municipal, Madrid/The Bridgeman Art Library)*

the early twentieth century were building electric streetcar systems that provided transportation to new public and private housing developments in outlying areas of the city for the working classes.

## Rich and Poor and Those in Between

General improvements in health and in the urban environment had beneficial consequences for all kinds of people. Yet differences in living conditions among social classes remained gigantic.

### Social Structure

How much did the almost-completed journey to an urban, industrialized world change the social framework of rich and poor and those in between? The first great change was a substantial and undeniable increase in the standard of living for the average person. The real wages of British workers, for example, which had already risen by 1850, almost doubled between 1850 and 1906. Similar increases occurred in continental countries as industrial development quickened after 1850. Ordinary people took a major step forward in the centuries-old battle

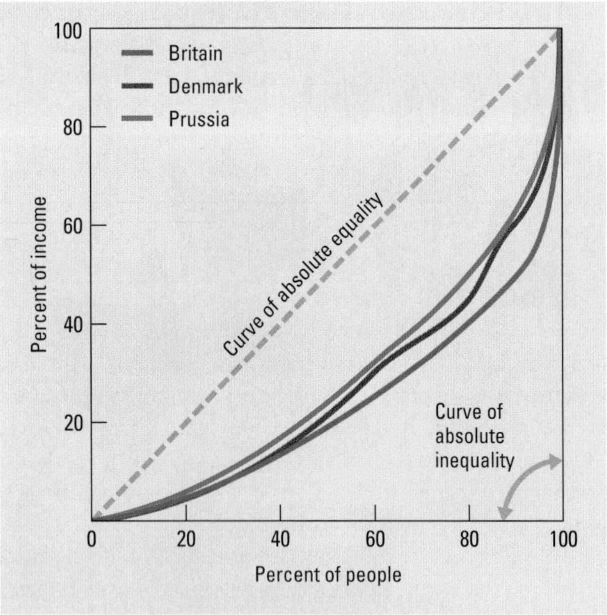


**Distribution of Income**

| | Richest 5% | Richest 10% | Richest 20% | Poorest 60% |
|---|---|---|---|---|
| Britain | 43% | | 59% | |
| Denmark | 30% | 39% | 55% | 31% |
| Prussia | 30% | | 50% | 33% |

**FIGURE 24.2 The Distribution of Income in Britain, Denmark, and Prussia in 1913** The so-called Lorenz curve is useful for showing the degree of economic inequality in a given society. The closer the actual distribution of income lies to the (theoretical) curve of absolute equality, where each 20 percent of the population receives 20 percent of all income, the more incomes are nearly equal. European society was very far from any such equality before World War I. Notice that incomes in Prussia were somewhat more equal than those in Britain. *(Source: S. Kuznets,* Modern Economic Growth, *pp. 208–209. Copyright © 1966 by Yale University Press. Reprinted by permission.)*

against poverty, reinforcing efforts to improve many aspects of human existence.

There is another side to the income coin, however. Greater economic rewards for the average person did *not* eliminate hardship and poverty, nor did they make the wealth and income of the rich and the poor significantly more equal. In almost every advanced country around 1900, the richest 5 percent of all households in the population received 33 percent of all national income. The richest 20 percent of households received anywhere from 50 to 60 percent of all national income, while the entire bottom 80 percent received only 40 to 50 percent. Moreover, the bottom 30 percent of households received 10 percent or less of all income. These enormous differences are illustrated in Figure 24.2.

The middle classes, smaller than they are today, accounted for less than 20 percent of the population; thus the statistics show that the upper and middle classes alone received more than 50 percent of all income. The poorest 80 percent—the working classes, including peasants and agricultural laborers—received less altogether than the two richest classes. Moreover, income taxes on the wealthy were light or nonexistent. Thus the gap between rich and poor remained enormous at the beginning of the twentieth century. It was probably almost as great as it had been in the age of agriculture and aristocracy before the Industrial Revolution.

The great gap between rich and poor endured, in part, because industrial and urban development made society more diverse and less unified. By no means did society split into two sharply defined opposing classes, as Marx had predicted. Instead, economic specialization enabled society to produce more effectively and in the process created more new social groups than it destroyed. There developed an almost unlimited range of jobs, skills, and earnings; one group or subclass shaded off into another in a complex, confusing hierarchy. Thus the tiny elite of the very rich and the sizable mass of the dreadfully poor were separated from each other by a range of subclasses, each filled with individuals struggling to rise or at least to hold their own in the social order. In this atmosphere of competition and hierarchy, neither the middle classes nor the working classes acted as a unified force. This social and occupational hierarchy developed enormous variations, but the age-old pattern of great economic inequality remained firmly intact.

## The Middle Classes

By the beginning of the twentieth century, the diversity and range within the urban middle class were striking. Indeed, it is more meaningful to think of a confederation of middle classes loosely united by occupations requiring mental, rather than physical, skill.

At the top stood the upper middle class, composed mainly of the most successful business families from banking, industry, and large-scale commerce. As people in the upper middle class gained in income and progressively lost all traces of radicalism after the trauma of 1848, they were almost irresistibly drawn toward the aristocratic lifestyle. And although the genuine hereditary aristocracy constituted only a tiny minority in every European country, it retained imposing wealth, unrivaled social prestige, and substantial political influence. This was especially true in central and eastern Europe, where the monarch—the highest-ranking noble of them all—continued to hold great political power.

As the aristocracy had long divided the year between palatial country estates and lavish townhouses during "the season," so the upper middle class purchased country places or built beach houses for weekend and summer use. The number of servants was an important indicator of wealth and standing for the middle class, as it had always been for the aristocracy. Private coaches and carriages, ever-expensive items in the city, were also signs of rising social status.

The topmost reaches of the upper middle class tended to shade off into the old aristocracy to form a new upper class of at most 5 percent of the population. Much of the aristocracy welcomed this development. Having experienced a sharp decline in its relative income in the course of industrialization, the landed aristocracy had met big business coming up the staircase and was often delighted to trade titles, country homes, and snobbish elegance for good hard cash. Some of the best bargains were made through marriages to American heiresses. Correspondingly, wealthy aristocrats tended increasingly to exploit their agricultural and mineral resources as if they were business people. Bismarck was not the only proud nobleman to make a fortune distilling brandy on his estates.

Below the wealthy upper middle class were much larger, much less wealthy, and increasingly diversified middle-class groups. Here one found the moderately successful industrialists and merchants as well as professionals in law and medicine. This was the middle middle class, solid and quite comfortable but lacking great wealth. Below it were independent shopkeepers, small traders, and tiny manufacturers—the lower middle class. Both of these traditional elements of the middle class expanded modestly in size with economic development.

Meanwhile, the traditional middle class was gaining two particularly important additions. The expansion of industry and technology created a growing demand for experts with specialized knowledge. The most valuable of the specialties became solid middle-class professions. Engineering, for example, emerged from the world of skilled labor as a full-fledged profession of great importance, considerable prestige, and many branches. Architects, chemists, accountants, and surveyors, to name only a few, first achieved professional standing in this period. They established criteria for advanced training and certification and banded together in organizations to promote and defend their interests.

Management of large public and private institutions also emerged as a kind of profession as governments provided more services and as very large corporations such as railroads came into being. Government officials and many private executives were not capitalists in the sense that they owned business enterprises. But public and private managers did have specialized knowledge and the capacity to earn a good living. And they shared most of the values of the business-owning entrepreneurs and the older professionals.

Industrialization also expanded and diversified the lower middle class. The number of independent, property-owning shopkeepers and small business people grew, and so did the number of white-collar employees—a mixed group of traveling salesmen, bookkeepers, store managers, and clerks who staffed the offices and branch stores of large corporations. White-collar employees were propertyless and often earned no more than the better-paid skilled or semiskilled workers did. Yet white-collar workers were fiercely committed to the middle class and to the ideal of moving up in society. In the Balkans, for example, clerks let their fingernails grow very long to distinguish themselves from people who worked with their hands. The tie, the suit, and soft, clean hands were no-less-subtle marks of class distinction than wages.

Relatively well educated but without complex technical skills, many white-collar groups aimed at achieving professional standing and the accompanying middle-class status. Elementary school teachers largely succeeded in this effort. From being miserably paid part-time workers in the early nineteenth century, teachers rode the wave of mass education to respectable middle-class status and income. Nurses also rose from the lower ranks of unskilled labor to precarious middle-class standing. Dentistry was taken out of the hands of working-class barbers and placed in the hands of highly trained (and middle-class) professionals.

## Middle-Class Culture

In spite of growing occupational diversity and conflicting interests, the middle classes were loosely united by a certain style of life and culture. Food was the largest item in the household budget, for middle-class people liked to eat very well. The European middle classes consumed meat in abundance, and a well-off family might spend 10 percent of its substantial earnings on meat and fully 25 percent of its income on food and drink. Spending on food was also great because the dinner party was this class's favored social occasion. A wealthy family might give a lavish party for eight to twelve almost every week,

**"A Corner of the Table"** With photographic precision, the French academic artist Paul-Émile Chabas (1869–1937) idealizes the elegance and intimacy of a sumptuous dinner party. Throughout Europe, such dinners were served in eight or nine separate courses, beginning with appetizers and ending with coffee and liqueurs. *(Archives Charmet/The Bridgeman Art Library)*

whereas more modest households would settle for once a month.

The middle-class wife could cope with this endless procession of meals, courses, and dishes because she had both servants and money at her disposal. Indeed, the employment of at least one enormously helpful full-time maid to cook and clean was the best single sign that a family had crossed the cultural divide separating the working classes from what some contemporary observers called the "servant-keeping classes." The greater a family's income, the greater the number of servants it employed. Food and servants together absorbed about 50 percent of income at all levels of the middle class.

Well fed and well served, the middle classes were also well housed by 1900. Many quite prosperous families rented, rather than owned, their homes. Apartment living, complete with tiny rooms for servants under the eaves of the top floor, was commonplace, and wealthy investors and speculative builders found good profits in middle-class housing. By 1900 the middle classes were also quite clothes-conscious. The factory, the sewing machine, and the department store had all helped reduce the cost and expand the variety of clothing. Middle-class women were particularly attentive to the fickle dictates of fashion. (See the feature "Images in Society: Class and Gender Boundaries in Women's Fashion, 1850–1914" on pages 800–801.)

Education was another growing expense, as middle-class parents tried to provide their children with ever more crucial advanced education. The keystones of culture and leisure were books, music, and travel. The long realistic novel, the heroics of composers Wagner and Verdi, the diligent striving of the dutiful daughter at the piano, and the packaged tour to a foreign country were all sources of middle-class pleasure.

Finally, the middle classes were loosely united by a shared code of expected behavior and morality. This code was strict and demanding. It laid great stress on hard work, self-discipline, and personal achievement. Men and women who fell into crime or poverty were generally assumed to be responsible for their own circumstances. Traditional Christian morality was reaffirmed by this code and was preached tirelessly by middle-class people. Drunkenness and gambling were denounced as vices; sexual purity and fidelity were celebrated as virtues. In short, the middle-class person was supposed to know right from wrong and was expected to act accordingly.

## The Working Classes

About four out of five people belonged to the working classes at the turn of the century. Many members of the working classes—that is, people whose livelihoods depended on physical labor and who did not employ domestic servants—were still small landowning peasants and hired farm hands. This was especially true in eastern Europe. In western and central Europe, however, the typical worker had left the land. In Great Britain, less than 8 percent of the people worked in agriculture, and in rapidly industrializing Germany only 25 percent were employed in agriculture and forestry. Even in less industrialized France, less than 50 percent of the people depended on the land in 1900.

The urban working classes were even less unified and homogeneous than the middle classes. In the first place, economic development and increased specialization expanded the traditional range of working-class skills, earnings, and experiences. Meanwhile, the old sharp distinction between highly skilled artisans and unskilled manual workers gradually broke down. To be sure, highly skilled printers and masons as well as unskilled dockworkers and common laborers continued to exist. But between these extremes there appeared ever more semiskilled groups, many of which were composed of factory workers and machine tenders (see Figure 24.3).

In the second place, skilled, semiskilled, and unskilled workers developed widely divergent lifestyles and cultural values, and their differences contributed to a keen sense of social status and hierarchy within the working classes. The result was great variety and limited class unity.

Highly skilled workers, who made up about 15 percent of the working classes, became a real **labor aristocracy.** These workers earned only about two-thirds of the income of the bottom ranks of the servant-keeping classes, but that was fully twice as much as the earnings of unskilled workers. The most "aristocratic" of the highly skilled workers were construction bosses and factory foremen, men who had risen from the ranks and were fiercely proud of their achievement. The labor aristocracy also included members of the traditional highly skilled handicraft trades that had not been mechanized or placed in factories, like cabinetmakers, jewelers, and printers.

This group as a whole was under constant long-term pressure. Irregularly but inexorably, factory methods were being extended to more crafts, and many skilled artisans were being replaced by lower-paid semiskilled factory workers. Traditional woodcarvers and watchmakers virtually disappeared, for example, as the making of furniture and timepieces now took place in the factory. At the same time, the labor aristocracy was consistently being enlarged by new kinds of skilled workers such as shipbuilders and railway locomotive engineers. Thus the labor elite remained in a state of flux as individuals and whole crafts moved in and out of it.

To maintain this precarious standing, the upper working class adopted distinctive values and strait-laced, almost puritanical behavior. Like the middle classes, the labor aristocracy was strongly committed to the family and to economic improvement. Families in the upper working class saved money regularly, worried about their children's education, and valued good housing. Despite these similarities, skilled workers viewed themselves not as aspirants to the middle class but as the pacesetters and natural leaders of all the working classes. Well aware of the degradation not so far below them, they practiced self-discipline and stern morality.

The upper working class in general frowned on heavy drinking and sexual permissiveness. An organized temperance movement was strong in the countries of northern Europe. As one German labor aristocrat somberly warned, "The path to the brothel leads through the tavern" and from there quite possibly to drastic decline or total ruin for person and family.[6] Men and women of the labor aristocracy were also quick to find fault with those below them who failed to meet their standards. Finally, many members of the labor aristocracy had definite political and

**FIGURE 24.3 The Urban Social Hierarchy**

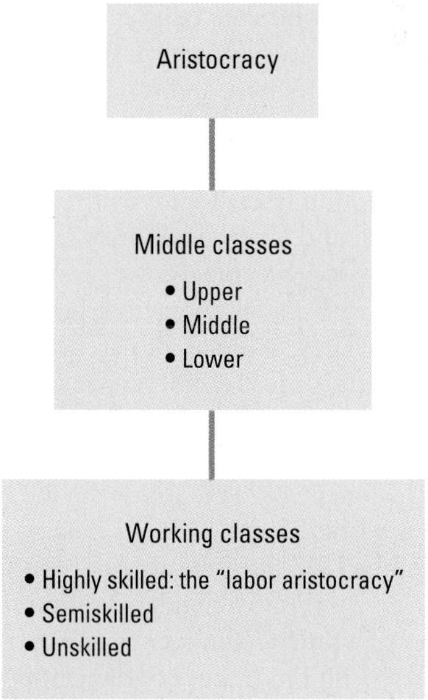

# Images in Society

## Class and Gender Boundaries in Women's Fashion, 1850–1914

Women's fashion was big business in the nineteenth century. Long the dominant industrial pursuit in human history, the production of textiles took off with the Industrial Revolution. In the later nineteenth century fashionable clothing, especially for middle-class women, became the first modern consumer industry as careful buyers snapped up the constantly changing ready-to-wear goods sold by large department stores.

In the nineteenth century, before society fragmented into many different groups expressing themselves in many dress styles, clothing patterns focused mainly on perceived differences in class and gender. The four illustrations presented here allow one to analyze the social information communicated through women's clothing. As you study these illustrations, note the principal characteristics and then try to draw out the larger implications. What does the impractical, restrictive clothing in these images reveal about society's view of women during this period? What is the significance of the emergence of alternative styles of well-groomed dress?

Most changes in women's fashion originated in Paris in the nineteenth century. Image 1 shows the attire worn by French aristocratic and wealthy middle-class women in the 1850s and 1860s. Note that these expensive dresses, flawlessly tailored by an army of skilled seamstresses, abound in elaborate embroidery, rich velvety materials, and fancy accessories. The circular spread of these floor-sweeping gowns is due to the crinoline, a slip with metal hoops that holds the skirt out on all sides. These women also are wearing the corset, the century's most characteristic women's undergarment, which was laced up tightly in back and pressed unmercifully from the breasts to the hips. What does this image tell you about the life of these women (their work, leisure activities, and so on)?

The intriguing 1875 painting by Atkinson Grimshaw, *Summer* (Image 2), shows a middle-class interior and the evolution of women's summer fashion two decades later. The corset still binds, but crinoline hoops have given way to the bustle, a cotton fan with steel reinforcement that pushes the dress out in back and exaggerates gender differences. The elaborate costume of the wealthy elite, available in cheaper ready-to-wear versions sold through department stores and mail-order catalogues throughout Europe, had become the standard for middle-class women. Emulating the elite in style, conventional middle-class women shopped carefully, scouting for sales, and drew a boundary separating themselves from working-class women in their simple cotton clothes. What implications, if any, do you see this having on class distinctions?

The young middle-class Englishwoman in an 1893 photo (Image 3) has chosen a woman's tailored suit, the only major English innovation in nineteenth-century women's fashion. This "alternative dress" combines the tie, suit jacket, vest, and straw hat—all

**Image 1** Crinoline Dresses, Paris, 1859. *(The Illustrated London News Picture Library)*

**Image 2** Summer Dress with Bustle, England, 1875. *(Roy Miles, Esq./The Bridgeman Art Library)*

**Image 3** Alternative Fashion, England, 1893. *(Manchester City Art Galleries)*

**Image 4** Loose-fitting Dress, France, 1910. *(© Corbis)*

initially items of male attire—with typical feminine elements, such as the skirt and gloves. This practical, socially accepted alternative dress appealed to the growing number of women in paid employment in the 1890s. The historian Diana Crane has argued that this departure from the dominant style can be seen as a symbolic, nonverbal assertion of independence and equality with men.* Do you agree with this? If so, what was the significance of the pre-1914 turn from stifling corset to the more flexible brassiere and the mainstream embrace of loose-fitting garments, such as the 1910 dress in Image 4? Did the greater freedom of movement in clothing reflect the emerging emancipation of Western women? Or was the coquettish femininity of these loose, flowing dresses only a repackaging of the dominant culture's sharply defined gender boundaries?

*Diana Crane, *Fashion and Its Social Agendas: Class, Gender, and Identity in Clothing* (Chicago: University of Chicago Press, 2000), pp. 99–114.

*The* ***history companion*** *features additional information and activities related to this topic.*
**history.college.hmco.com/students**

**The Labor Aristocracy** This group of British foremen is attending the International Exhibition in Paris in 1862. Their "Sunday best" includes the silk top hats and long morning coats of the propertied classes, but they definitely remain workers, the proud leaders of laboring people. *(© The Board of Trustees of the Victoria & Albert Museum)*

philosophical beliefs, which further strengthened their firm moral code.

Below the labor aristocracy stood semiskilled and unskilled urban workers. The enormous complexity of this sector of the world of labor is not easily summarized. Workers in the established crafts—carpenters, bricklayers, pipe fitters—stood near the top of the semiskilled hierarchy, often flirting with (or sliding back from) the labor elite. A large number of the semiskilled were factory workers who earned highly variable but relatively good wages and whose relative importance in the labor force was increasing.

Below the semiskilled workers was a larger group of unskilled workers that included day laborers such as longshoremen, wagon-driving teamsters, teenagers, and every kind of "helper." Many of these people had real skills and performed valuable services, but they were unorganized and divided, united only by the common fate of meager earnings. The same lack of unity characterized street vendors and market people—self-employed workers who competed savagely with each other and with the established shopkeepers of the lower middle class.

One of the largest components of the unskilled group was domestic servants, whose numbers grew steadily in the nineteenth century. In advanced Great Britain, for example, one out of every seven employed persons was a domestic servant in 1911. The great majority were women; indeed, one out of every three girls in Britain between the ages of fifteen and twenty was a domestic servant. Throughout Europe and America, a great many female domestics in the cities were recent migrants from rural areas. As in earlier times, domestic service was still

**A School for Servants** Although domestic service was poorly paid, there was always plenty of competition for the available jobs. Schools sprang up to teach young women the manners and the household skills that employers in the "servant-keeping classes" demanded. *(Corporation of London: London Metropolitan Archives)*

hard work at low pay with limited personal independence and the danger of sexual exploitation. For the full-time general maid in a lower-middle-class family, there was an unending routine of baby-sitting, shopping, cooking, and cleaning. In the great households, the girl was at the bottom of a rigid hierarchy of status-conscious butlers and housekeepers.

Nonetheless, domestic service had real attractions for "rough country girls" with strong hands and few specialized skills. Marriage prospects were better, or at least more varied, in the city. And though wages were low, they were higher and more regular than in hard agricultural work. Finally, as one London observer noted, young girls and other migrants were drawn to the city by

*the contagion of numbers, the sense of something going on, the theaters and the music halls, the brightly lighted streets and busy crowds—all, in short, that makes the difference between the Mile End fair on a Saturday night, and a dark and muddy country lane, with no glimmer of gas and with nothing to do.*[7]

Many young domestics from the countryside made a successful transition to working-class wife and mother. Yet with an unskilled or unemployed husband and a growing family, such a woman often had to join the broad ranks of workingwomen in the "sweated industries." These industries flowered after 1850 and resembled the old putting-out and cottage industries of earlier times. The women normally worked at home, paid by the piece and not by the hour. They and their young daughters, for whom organization and collective action were virtually impossible, earned pitiful wages and lacked any job security.

Some women did hand-decorating of every conceivable kind of object; the majority, however, made clothing, especially after the advent of the sewing machine. By 1900 only a few such tailors lingered on in high-priced "tailor-made" shops. An army of poor women accounted for the bulk of the inexpensive "ready-made" clothes displayed on department store racks and in tiny shops.

## Working-Class Leisure and Religion

Notwithstanding the rise and fall of groups and individuals, the urban working classes sought fun and recreation, and they found both. Across the face of Europe, drinking remained unquestionably the favorite leisure-time activity of working people. For many middle-class moralists as well as moralizing historians since, love of drink has been a curse of the modern age—a sign of social dislocation and popular suffering. Certainly, drinking was deadly serious business. One English slum dweller recalled that "drunkenness was by far the commonest cause of dispute and misery in working class homes. On account of it one saw many a decent family drift down through poverty into total want."[8]

Generally, however, heavy "problem" drinking declined in the late nineteenth century as it became less and less socially acceptable. This decline reflected in part the moral leadership of the upper working class. At the same time, drinking became more public and social. Cafés and pubs became increasingly bright, friendly places. Working-class political activities, both moderate and radical, were also concentrated in taverns and pubs. Moreover, social drinking in public places by married couples and sweethearts became an accepted and widespread practice for the first time. This greater participation by women undoubtedly helped civilize the world of drink and hard liquor.

The two other leisure-time passions of the working classes were sports and music halls. A great decline in "cruel sports," such as bullbaiting and cockfighting, had occurred throughout Europe by the late nineteenth century. Their place was filled by modern spectator sports, of which racing and soccer were the most popular. There was a great deal of gambling on sports events, and for many a working person a desire to decipher racing forms provided a powerful incentive toward literacy. Music halls and vaudeville theaters, the working-class counterparts of middle-class opera and classical theater, were enormously popular throughout Europe. In 1900 there were more than fifty such halls and theaters in London alone. Music hall audiences were thoroughly mixed, which may account for the fact that drunkenness, sexual intercourse and pregnancy before marriage, marital difficulties, and problems with mothers-in-law were favorite themes of broad jokes and bittersweet songs.

In more serious moments, religion and Christian churches continued to provide working people with solace and meaning. The eighteenth-century vitality of popular religion in Catholic countries and the Protestant rejuvenation exemplified by German Pietism and English Methodism (see pages 681–682) carried over into the nineteenth century. Indeed, many historians see the early nineteenth century as an age of religious revival. Yet historians also recognize that by the last two or three decades of the nineteenth century, a considerable decline in both church attendance and church donations was occurring in most European countries. And it seems clear that this decline was greater for the urban working classes than for their rural counterparts or for the middle classes.

What did the decline in working-class church attendance really mean? Some have argued that it accurately reflected a general decline in faith and religious belief. Others disagree, noting correctly that most working-class families still baptized their children and considered themselves Christians. Although more research is necessary, it appears that the urban working classes in Europe did become more secular and less religious in the late nineteenth and early twentieth centuries. They rarely repudiated the Christian religion, but it tended to play a diminishing role in their daily lives.

Part of the reason for this change was that the construction of churches failed to keep up with the rapid growth of urban population, especially in new working-class neighborhoods. Thus the vibrant, materialistic urban environment undermined popular religious impulses, which were poorly served in the cities. Equally important, however, was the fact that throughout the nineteenth century both Catholic and Protestant churches were normally seen as they saw themselves—as conservative institutions defending social order and custom. Therefore, as the European working classes became more politically conscious, they tended to see the established (or quasi-established) "territorial church" as defending what they wished to change and as allied with their political opponents. Especially the men of the urban working classes developed vaguely antichurch attitudes, even though they remained neutral or positive toward religion. They tended to regard regular church attendance as "not our kind of thing"—not part of urban working-class culture.

The pattern was different in the United States. There, most churches also preached social conservatism in the nineteenth century. But because church and state had always been separate and because there was always a host of competing denominations and even different religions, working people identified churches much less with the political and social status quo. Instead, individual churches in the United States were often closely identified with an ethnic group rather than with a social class, and churches thrived, in part, as a means of asserting ethnic identity. This same process did occur in Europe if the church or synagogue had never been linked to the state and served as a focus for ethnic cohesion. Irish Catholic churches in Protestant Britain and Jewish synagogues in Russia were outstanding examples.

## The Changing Family

Urban life wrought many fundamental changes in the family. Although much is still unknown, it seems clear that in the second half of the nineteenth century the family had stabilized considerably after the disruption of the late eighteenth and early nineteenth centuries. The home became more important for both men and women. The role of women and attitudes toward children underwent substantial change, and adolescence emerged as a distinct stage of life. These are but a few of the transformations that affected all social classes in varying degrees.

### Premarital Sex and Marriage

By 1850 the preindustrial pattern of lengthy courtship and mercenary marriage was pretty well dead among the working classes. In its place, the ideal of romantic love had triumphed. Couples were ever more likely to come from different, even distant, towns and to be more nearly the same age, further indicating that romantic sentiment was replacing tradition and financial considerations.

Economic considerations in marriage remained more important to the middle classes than to the working classes after 1850. In France dowries and elaborate legal marriage contracts were common practice among the middle classes in the later nineteenth century, and marriage was for many families one of life's most crucial financial transactions. A popular author advised young Frenchmen that "marriage is in general a means of increasing one's credit and one's fortune and of insuring one's success in the world."[9] This preoccupation with money led many middle-class men in France and elsewhere to marry late, after they had been established economically, and to choose women considerably younger than themselves. These differences between husband and wife became a source of tension in many middle-class marriages.

A young woman of the middle class found her romantic life carefully supervised by her well-meaning mother, who schemed for a proper marriage and guarded her daughter's virginity like the family's credit. (See the feature "Listening to the Past: Middle-Class Youth and Sexuality" on pages 820–821.) After marriage, middle-class morality sternly demanded fidelity.

Middle-class boys were watched, too, but not as vigilantly. By the time they reached late adolescence, they had usually attained considerable sexual experience with maids or prostitutes.

In the early nineteenth century, sexual experimentation before marriage also triumphed, as did illegitimacy. There was an **illegitimacy explosion** between 1750 and 1850 (see page 665). By the 1840s, one birth in three was occurring outside of wedlock in many large cities of western, northern, and central Europe. In Vienna and Stockholm, one out of every two births was illegitimate. Although poverty and economic uncertainty undoubtedly prevented many lovers from marrying, there were also many among the poor and propertyless who saw little wrong with having illegitimate offspring. Thus the pattern of romantic ideals, premarital sexual activity, and widespread illegitimacy was firmly established by midcentury among the urban working classes.

Some regions, especially those little touched by industrialization and urbanization, did not experience an illegitimacy explosion. Neither did certain churches and religious communities that strictly prohibited premarital sex. "The Catholic Church in Ireland and many southern European regions, Calvinist communities in the Netherlands, Moslems in the Balkans, and Jewish communities throughout Europe seem to have been successful in enforcing this norm."[10] Although these religious groups exercised strict external control, they succeeded in large part because their young people internalized the values they were taught and acted accordingly.

In western, northern, and central Europe, the rising rate of illegitimacy was reversed in the second half of the nineteenth century: more babies were born to married mothers. Some observers have argued that this shift reflected the growth of puritanism and a lessening of sexual permissiveness among the unmarried. This explanation, however, is unconvincing.

The percentage of brides who were pregnant continued to be high and showed little or no tendency to decline after 1850. In many parts of urban Europe around 1900, as many as one woman in three was going to the altar an expectant mother. Moreover, unmarried people almost certainly used the cheap condoms and diaphragms the industrial age had made available to prevent pregnancy, at least in predominately Protestant countries.

Thus unmarried young people were probably engaging in just as much sexual activity as their parents and grandparents who had created the illegitimacy explosion of 1750 to 1850. But in the later nineteenth century, pregnancy for a young single woman led increasingly to marriage and the establishment of a two-parent household. This important development reflected the growing respectability of the working classes as well as their gradual economic improvement. Skipping out was less acceptable, and marriage was less of an economic challenge. Thus the urban working-class couple became more stable, and that stability strengthened the family as an institution.

## Prostitution

In Paris alone, 155,000 women were registered as prostitutes between 1871 and 1903, and 750,000 others were suspected of prostitution in the same years. Men of all classes visited prostitutes, but the middle and upper classes supplied much of the motivating cash. Thus, though many middle-class men abided by the publicly professed code of stern puritanical morality, others indulged their appetites for prostitutes and sexual promiscuity.

*My Secret Life,* the anonymous eleven-volume autobiography of an English sexual adventurer from the servant-keeping classes, provides a remarkable picture of such a man. Beginning at an early age with a maid, the author becomes progressively obsessed with sex and devotes his life to living his sexual fantasies. In almost every one of his innumerable encounters all across Europe, this man of wealth simply buys his pleasure. Usually meetings are

**Inside a Paris Brothel** In *The Reception Room in the Brothel on the Rue des Moulins,* a biting ironic painting by Henri de Toulouse-Lautrec (1864–1901), the aging madame maintains a prim and proper decorum while the women working for her lounge about on the couches. Wealthy nobleman by birth and tragically disabled by an accident in childhood, Toulouse-Lautrec combined stupendous creativity and dedicated debauchery in his short life. His work focused on music halls, circuses, and the bizarre individuals who made Paris nightlife the scandal of Europe. *(The Bridgeman Art Library)*

arranged in a businesslike manner: regular and part-time prostitutes quote their prices; working-class girls are corrupted by hot meals and baths.

At one point, he offers a young girl a sixpence for a kiss and gets it. Learning that the pretty, unskilled working girl earns nine pence a day, he offers her the equivalent of a week's salary for a few moments of fondling. When she finally agrees, he savagely exults that "*her* want was my opportunity." Later he offers more money for more gratification, and when she refuses, he tries unsuccessfully to rape her in a hackney cab. On another occasion he takes a farm worker by force.[11]

Obviously atypical in its excesses, *My Secret Life* does reveal the dark side of sex and class in urban society. Frequently thinking of their wives largely in terms of money, family, and social position, the men of the comfortable classes often purchased sex and even affection from poor girls both before and after marriage. Moreover, the great continuing differences between rich and poor made for every kind of debauchery and sexual exploitation. Brutal sexist behavior was part of life—a part the sternly moral women (and men) of the upper working class detested and tried to shield their daughters from. For many poor young women, prostitution, like domestic service, was a stage of life and not a permanent employment. Having done it for a while in their twenties, they went on to marry (or live with) men of their own class and establish homes and families.

## Kinship Ties

Within working-class homes, ties to relatives after marriage—kinship ties—were in general much stronger than many social observers have recognized. Most newlyweds tried to live near their parents, though not in the same house. Indeed, for many married couples in later-nineteenth-century cities, ties to mothers and fathers, uncles and aunts, were more important than ties to nonrelated acquaintances.

People turned to their families for help in coping with sickness, unemployment, death, and old age. Although governments were generally providing more welfare services by 1900, the average couple and its children inevitably faced crises. Funerals, for example, brought sudden demands, requiring a large outlay for special clothes, carriages, and burial services. Unexpected death or desertion could leave the bereaved or abandoned, especially widows and orphans, in need of financial aid or perhaps a foster home. Relatives responded hastily to such cries, knowing full well that their own time of need and repayment would undoubtedly come.

Relatives were also valuable at less tragic moments. If a couple was very poor, an aged relation often moved in to cook and mind the children so that the wife could earn badly needed income outside the home. Sunday dinners were often shared, as were outgrown clothing and useful information. Often the members of a large family group all lived in the same neighborhood.

## Gender Roles and Family Life

Industrialization and the growth of modern cities brought great changes to the lives of European women. These changes were particularly consequential for married women, and most women did marry in the nineteenth century.

After 1850 the work of most wives became increasingly distinct and separate from that of their husbands. Husbands became wage earners in factories and offices, while wives tended to stay home and manage households and care for children. The preindustrial pattern among both peasants and cottage workers, in which husbands and wives worked together and divided up household duties and child rearing, declined. Only in a few occupations, such as retail trade, did married couples live where they worked and struggle together to make their mom-and-pop operations a success. Factory employment for married women also declined as the early practice of hiring entire families in the factory disappeared.

As economic conditions improved, most men expected married women to work outside the home only in poor families. One old English worker recalled that "the boy wanted to get into a position that would enable him to keep a wife and family, as it was considered a thoroughly unsatisfactory state of affairs if the wife had to work to help maintain the home."[12] The ideal became a strict division of labor by gender and rigidly constructed **separate spheres:** the wife as mother and homemaker, the husband as wage earner.

This rigid gender division of labor meant that married women faced great injustice when they needed—or wanted—to move into the man's world of employment outside the home. Husbands were unsympathetic or hostile. Well-paying jobs were off-limits to women, and a woman's wage was almost always less than a man's, even for the same work.

Moreover, married women were subordinated to their husbands by law and lacked many basic legal rights. In England the situation in the early nineteenth century was summed up in a famous line from jurist William Blackstone: "In law husband and wife are one person, and the husband is that person." Thus a wife in England had no legal identity and hence no right to own property in her own name. Even the wages she might earn belonged to her husband. In France the Napoleonic Code (see pages 713–714) also enshrined the principle of female subordination and gave the wife few legal rights regarding property, divorce, and custody of the children. Legal inferiority for women permeated Western society.

With all women facing discrimination in education and employment and with middle-class women suffering especially from a lack of legal rights, there is little wonder that some women rebelled and began the long-continuing fight for equality of the sexes and the rights of women. Their struggle proceeded on two main fronts. First, following in the steps of women such as Mary Wollstonecraft (see page 705), organizations founded by middle-class feminists campaigned for equal legal rights for women as well as access to higher education and professional employment. These middle-class feminists argued that unmarried women and middle-class widows with inadequate incomes simply had to have more opportunities to support themselves. Middle-class feminists also recognized that paid (as opposed to unpaid) work could relieve the monotony that some women found in their sheltered middle-class existence and put greater meaning into their lives.

In the later nineteenth century, these organizations scored some significant victories, such as the 1882 law giving English married women full property rights. More women found professional and white-collar employment, especially after about 1880. But progress was slow and hard won. For example, in Germany before 1900, women were not admitted as fully registered students at a single university, and it was virtually impossible for a woman to receive certification and practice as a lawyer or doctor. (See the feature "Individuals in Society: Franziska Tiburtius.") In the years before 1914, middle-class feminists increasingly focused their attention on political action and fought for the right to vote for women.

Women inspired by utopian and especially Marxian socialism blazed a second path. Often scorning the programs of middle-class feminists, socialist women leaders argued that the liberation of working-class women would come only with the liberation of the entire working class through revolution. In the meantime, they championed the cause of workingwomen and won some practical improvements, especially in Germany, where the socialist movement was most effectively organized. In a general way, these different approaches to women's issues reflected the diversity of classes in urban society.

If the ideology and practice of rigidly separate spheres undoubtedly narrowed women's horizons and caused some women to rebel, there was a brighter side to the same coin. As home and children became the typical wife's main concerns in the late nineteenth century, her control and influence there apparently became increasingly strong throughout Europe. Among the English working classes, it was the wife who generally determined how the family's money was spent. In many families, the husband gave all his earnings to his wife to manage, whatever the law might read. She returned to him only a small allowance for carfare, beer, tobacco, and union dues. All the major domestic decisions, from the children's schooling and religious instruction to the selection of new furniture or a new apartment, were hers. In France women had even greater power in their assigned domain. One English feminist noted in 1908 that "though legally women occupy a much inferior status than men [in France], in practice they constitute the superior sex. They are the power behind the throne."[13]

Women ruled at home partly because running the urban household was a complicated, demanding, and valuable task. Twice-a-day food shopping, penny-pinching, economizing, and the growing crusade against dirt—not to mention child rearing—were a full-time occupation. Nor were there any laborsaving appliances to help, and even when servants were present, they had to be carefully watched and supervised. Working yet another job for wages outside the home had limited appeal for most married women unless such earnings were essential for family survival. Many married women in the working classes did make a monetary contribution to family income by taking in boarders or doing piecework at home in the sweated industries (see page 804).

The wife also guided the home because a good deal of her effort was directed toward pampering her husband as he expected. In countless humble households, she saw that he had meat while she ate bread, that he relaxed by the fire while she did the dishes.

The woman's guidance of the household went hand in hand with the increased emotional importance of home and family. The home she ran was idealized as a warm shelter in a hard and impersonal urban world. For a child of the English slums in the early 1900s,

*home, however poor, was the focus of all love and interests, a sure fortress against a hostile world. Songs about its beauties were ever on people's lips. "Home, sweet home," first heard in the 1870s, had become "almost a second national anthem." Few walls in lower-working-class houses lacked "mottoes"—colored strips of paper, about nine inches wide and eighteen inches in length, attesting to domestic joys: EAST, WEST, HOME'S BEST; BLESS OUR HOME; GOD*

# Individuals in Society

## Franziska Tiburtius

Why did a small number of women in the late nineteenth century brave great odds and embark on a professional career? And how did a few of those manage to reach their objectives? The career and personal reflections of Franziska Tiburtius, a pioneer in German medicine, suggest that talent, determination, and economic necessity were critical ingredients.*

Like many women of her time who would study and pursue a professional career, Franziska Tiburtius (1843–1927) was born into a property-owning family of modest means. The youngest of nine children on a small estate in northeastern Germany, the sensitive child wilted with a harsh governess but flowered with a caring teacher and became an excellent student.

Graduating at sixteen and needing to support herself, Tiburtius had few opportunities. A young woman from a "proper" background could work as a governess or a teacher without losing her respectability and spoiling her matrimonial prospects, but that was about it. She tried both avenues. Working for six years as a governess in a noble family and no doubt learning that poverty was often one's fate in this genteel profession, she then turned to teaching. Called home from her studies in Britain in 1871 to care for her brother, who had contracted typhus as a field doctor in the Franco-Prussian War, she found her calling. She decided to become a medical doctor.

Supported by her family, Tiburtius's decision was truly audacious. In all Europe, only the University of Zurich in republican Switzerland accepted female students. Moreover, if it became known that she had studied medicine and failed, she would never get a job as a teacher. No parent would entrust a daughter to an "emancipated" radical who had carved up dead bodies!

Although the male students at the university sometimes harassed the women with crude pranks, Tiburtius thrived. The revolution of the microscope and the discovery of microorganisms was rocking Zurich, and she was fascinated by her studies. She became close friends with a fellow female medical student from Germany, Emilie Lehmus, with whom she would form a lifelong partnership in medicine. She did her internship with families of cottage workers around Zurich and loved her work.

Graduating at age thirty-three in 1876, Tiburtius went to stay with her brother the doctor in Berlin. Though well qualified to practice, she ran into pervasive discrimination. She was not even permitted to take the state medical exams and could practice only as an unregulated (and unprofessional) "natural healer." But after persistent fighting with the bureaucrats, she was able to display her diploma and practice as "Franziska Tiburtius, M.D. University of Zurich." She and Lehmus were in business.

*Franziska Tiburtius, pioneering woman physician in Berlin.* (Ullstein Bilderdienst)

Soon the two women realized their dream and opened a clinic, subsidized by a wealthy industrialist, for women factory workers. The clinic filled a great need and was soon treating many patients. A room with beds for extremely sick women was later expanded into a second clinic.

Tiburtius and Lehmus became famous. For fifteen years, they were the only women doctors in all Berlin. An inspiration for a new generation of women, they added the wealthy to their thriving practice. But Tiburtius's clinics always concentrated on the poor, providing them with subsidized and up-to-date treatment. Talented, determined, and working with her partner, Tiburtius experienced the joys of personal achievement and useful service, joys that women and men share in equal measure.

### Questions for Analysis

1. How does Franziska Tiburtius's life reflect both the challenges and the changing roles of middle-class women in the later nineteenth century?
2. In what ways was Tiburtius's career related to improvements in health in urban society and to the expansion of the professions?

*This portrait draws on Conradine Lück, *Frauen: Neun Lebensschicksale* (Reutlingen: Ensslin & Laiblin, n.d.), pp. 153–185.

*The* **history companion** *features additional information and activities related to this topic.* **history.college.hmco.com/students**

*IS MASTER OF THIS HOUSE; HOME IS THE NEST WHERE ALL IS BEST.*[14]

By 1900 home and family were what life was all about for millions of people of all classes.

Married couples also developed stronger emotional ties to each other. Even in the comfortable classes, marriages in the late nineteenth century were based more on sentiment and sexual attraction than they had been earlier in the century, as money and financial calculation declined in importance. Affection and eroticism became more central to the couple after marriage. Gustave Droz, whose bestseller *Mr., Mrs., and Baby* went through 121 editions between 1866 and 1884, saw love within marriage as the key to human happiness. He condemned men who made marriage sound dull and practical, men who were exhausted by prostitutes and rheumatism and who wanted their young wives to be little angels. He urged women to follow their hearts and marry a man more nearly their own age:

*A husband who is stately and a little bald is all right, but a young husband who loves you and who drinks out of your glass without ceremony, is better. Let him, if he ruffles your dress a little and places a kiss on your neck as he passes. Let him, if he undresses you after the ball, laughing like a fool. You have fine spiritual qualities, it is true, but your little body is not bad either and when one loves, one loves completely. Behind these follies lies happiness.*[15]

Many French marriage manuals of the late 1800s stressed that women had legitimate sexual needs, such as the "right to orgasm." Perhaps the French were a bit more enlightened in these matters than other nationalities. But the rise of public socializing by couples in cafés and music halls as well as franker affection within the family suggests a more erotic, pleasurable intimate life for women throughout Western society. This, too, helped make the woman's role as mother and homemaker acceptable and even satisfying.

## Child Rearing

One striking sign of deepening emotional ties within the family was the growing love and concern that mothers gave their tiny infants. Because so many babies died so early in life, mothers in preindustrial Western society often avoided making a strong emotional commitment to a newborn in order to shield themselves from recurrent heartbreak. Early emotional bonding and a willingness to make real sacrifices for the welfare of the infant were beginning to spread among the comfortable classes by the end of the eighteenth century, but the ordinary mother of modest means adopted new attitudes only as the nineteenth century progressed. The baby became more important, and women became better mothers.

Mothers increasingly breast-fed their infants, for example, rather than paying wet nurses to do so. Breastfeeding involved sacrifice—a temporary loss of freedom, if nothing else. Yet in an age when there was no good alternative to mother's milk, it saved lives. This surge of maternal feeling also gave rise to a wave of specialized books on child rearing and infant hygiene, such as Droz's phenomenally successful book. Droz urged fathers to get into the act and pitied those "who do not know how to roll around on the carpet, play at being a horse and a great wolf, and undress their baby."[16] Another sign, from France, of increased affection is that fewer illegitimate babies were abandoned as foundlings after about 1850. Moreover, the practice of swaddling disappeared completely. Instead, ordinary mothers allowed their babies freedom of movement and delighted in their spontaneity.

The loving care lavished on infants was matched by greater concern for older children and adolescents. They, too, were wrapped in the strong emotional ties of a more intimate and protective family. For one thing, European women began to limit the number of children they bore in order to care adequately for those they had. It was evident by the end of the nineteenth century that the birthrate was declining across Europe, as Figure 24.4 shows, and it continued to do so until after World War II. The Englishwoman who married in the 1860s, for example, had an average of about six children; her daughter marrying in the 1890s had only four; and her granddaughter marrying in the 1920s had only two or possibly three.

The most important reason for this revolutionary reduction in family size, in which the comfortable and well-educated classes took the lead, was parents' desire to improve their economic and social position and that of their children. Children were no longer an economic asset in the later nineteenth century. By having fewer youngsters, parents could give those they had valuable advantages, from music lessons and summer vacations to long, expensive university educations and suitable dowries. A young German skilled worker with only one child spoke for many in his class when he said, "We want to get ahead, and our daughter should have things better than my wife and sisters did."[17] Thus the growing tendency of couples in the late nineteenth century to use a variety of contraceptive methods—rhythm method, withdrawal method, and mechanical devices—certainly reflected increased concern for children.

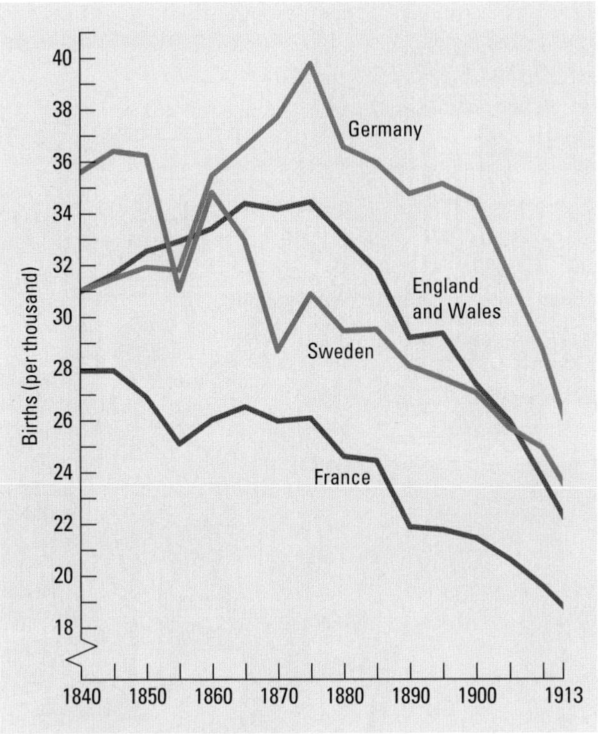


**FIGURE 24.4 The Decline of Birthrates in England and Wales, France, Germany, and Sweden, 1840–1913** Women had fewer babies for a variety of reasons, including the fact that their children were increasingly less likely to die before reaching adulthood. Compare with Figure 24.1 on page 791.

Indeed, many parents, especially in the middle classes, probably became *too* concerned about their children, unwittingly subjecting them to an emotional pressure cooker of almost unbearable intensity. The result was that many children and especially adolescents came to feel trapped and in need of greater independence.

Prevailing biological and medical theories led parents to believe in the possibility that their own emotional characteristics were passed on to their offspring and that they were thus directly responsible for any abnormality in a child. The moment the child was conceived was thought to be of enormous importance. "Never run the risk of conception when you are sick or over-tired or unhappy," wrote one influential American woman. "For the bodily condition of the child, its vigor and magnetic qualities, are much affected by conditions ruling this great moment."[18] So might the youthful "sexual excess" of the father curse future generations. Although this was true in the case of syphilis, which could be transmitted to unborn children, the rigid determinism of such views left little scope for the child's individual development.

Another area of excessive parental concern was the sexual behavior of the child. Masturbation was viewed with horror, for it represented an act of independence and even defiance. Diet, clothing, games, and sleeping were carefully regulated. Girls were discouraged from riding horses and bicycling because rhythmic friction simulated masturbation. Boys were dressed in trousers with shallow and widely separated pockets. Between 1850 and 1880, there were surgical operations for children who persisted in masturbating. Thereafter until about 1905, various restraining apparatuses were more often used.

These and less blatant attempts to repress the child's sexuality were a source of unhealthy tension, often made worse by the rigid division of gender roles within the family. It was widely believed that mother and child loved each other easily but that relations between father and child were necessarily difficult and often tragic. The father was a stranger; his world of business was far removed from the maternal world of spontaneous affection. Moreover, the father was demanding, often expecting the child to succeed where he himself had failed and making his love conditional on achievement. Little wonder that the imaginative literature of the late nineteenth century came to deal with the emotional and destructive elements of father-son relationships. In the Russian Feodor Dostoevski's great novel *The Brothers Karamazov* (1880–1881), for example, four sons work knowingly or unknowingly to destroy their father. Later at the murder trial, one of the brothers claims to speak for all mankind and screams out, "Who doesn't wish his father dead?"

Sigmund Freud (1856–1939), the Viennese founder of psychoanalysis, formulated the most striking analysis of the explosive dynamics of the family, particularly the middle-class family in the late nineteenth century. A physician by training, Freud began his career treating mentally ill patients. He noted that the hysteria of his patients appeared to originate in bitter early-childhood experiences wherein the child had been obliged to repress strong feelings. When these painful experiences were recalled and reproduced under hypnosis or through the patient's free association of ideas, the patient could be brought to understand his or her unhappiness and eventually deal with it.

One of Freud's most influential ideas concerned the Oedipal tensions resulting from the son's instinctive competition with the father for the mother's love and affection. More generally, Freud postulated that much of human behavior is motivated by unconscious emotional needs whose nature and origins are kept from conscious

**A Working-Class Home, 1875** Emotional ties within ordinary families grew stronger in the nineteenth century. Parents gave their children more love and better care. *(Illustrated London News Library)*

awareness by various mental devices he called **defense mechanisms.** Freud concluded that much unconscious psychological energy is sexual energy, which is repressed and precariously controlled by rational thinking and moral rules. If Freud exaggerated the sexual and familial roots of adult behavior, that exaggeration was itself a reflection of the tremendous emotional intensity of family life in the late nineteenth century.

The working classes probably had more avenues of escape from such tensions than did the middle classes. Unlike their middle-class counterparts, who remained economically dependent on their families until a long education was finished or a proper marriage secured, working-class boys and girls went to work when they reached adolescence. Earning wages on their own, they could bargain with their parents for greater independence within the household by the time they were sixteen or seventeen. If they were unsuccessful, they could and did leave home to live cheaply as paying lodgers in other working-class homes. Thus the young person from the working classes broke away from the family more easily when emotional ties became oppressive. In the twentieth century, middle-class youths would follow this lead.

## Science and Thought

Major changes in Western science and thought accompanied the emergence of urban society. Two aspects of these complex intellectual developments stand out as especially significant. First, scientific knowledge expanded rapidly, influencing the Western world-view even more profoundly than ever before and spurring the creation of new products and whole industries. Second, between about the 1840s and the 1890s, European literature underwent a shift from soaring romanticism to tough-minded realism.

## The Triumph of Science

As the pace of scientific advance quickened and as theoretical advances resulted in great practical benefits, science exercised growing influence on human thought. The intellectual achievements of the scientific revolution had resulted in few such benefits, and theoretical knowledge had also played a relatively small role in the Industrial Revolution in England. But breakthroughs in industrial technology enormously stimulated basic scientific inquiry, as researchers sought to explain theoretically how such things as steam engines and blast furnaces actually worked. The result was an explosive growth of fundamental scientific discoveries from the 1830s onward. And in contrast to earlier periods, these theoretical discoveries were increasingly transformed into material improvements for the general population.

A perfect example of the translation of better scientific knowledge into practical human benefits was the work of Louis Pasteur and his followers in biology and the medical sciences. Another was the development of the branch of physics known as **thermodynamics.** Building on Isaac Newton's laws of mechanics and on studies of steam engines, thermodynamics investigated the relationship between heat and mechanical energy. By midcentury, physicists had formulated the fundamental laws of thermodynamics, which were then applied to mechanical engineering, chemical processes, and many other fields. The *law of conservation of energy* held that different forms of energy—such as heat, electricity, and magnetism—could be converted but neither created nor destroyed. Nineteenth-century thermodynamics demonstrated that the physical world was governed by firm, unchanging laws.

Chemistry and electricity were two other fields characterized by extremely rapid scientific progress. And in both fields, "science was put in the service of industry," as the influential economist Alfred Marshall (1842–1924) argued at the time.

Chemists devised ways of measuring the atomic weight of different elements, and in 1869 the Russian chemist Dmitri Mendeleev (1834–1907) codified the rules of chemistry in the periodic law and the periodic table. Chemistry was subdivided into many specialized branches, such as **organic chemistry**—the study of the compounds of carbon. Applying theoretical insights gleaned from this new field, researchers in large German chemical companies discovered ways of transforming the dirty, useless coal tar that accumulated in coke ovens into beautiful, expensive synthetic dyes for the world of fashion. The basic discoveries of Michael Faraday (1791–1867) in electromagnetism in the 1830s and 1840s resulted in the first dynamo (generator) and opened the way for the subsequent development of the telegraph, electric motor, electric light, and electric streetcar.

The successful application of scientific research in the fast-growing electrical and organic chemical industries promoted solid economic growth between 1880 and 1913 and provided a model for other industries. Systematic "R & D"—research and development—was born in the late nineteenth century.

The triumph of science and technology had at least three more significant consequences. First, though ordinary citizens continued to lack detailed scientific knowledge, everyday experience and innumerable popularizers impressed the importance of science on the popular mind.

Second, as science became more prominent in popular thinking, the philosophical implications of science formulated in the Enlightenment spread to broad sections of the population. Natural processes appeared to be determined by rigid laws, leaving little room for either divine intervention or human will. Yet scientific and technical advances had also fed the Enlightenment's optimistic faith in human progress, which now appeared endless and automatic to many middle-class minds.

Third, the methods of science acquired unrivaled prestige after 1850. For many, the union of careful experiment and abstract theory was the only reliable route to truth and objective reality. The "unscientific" intuitions of poets and the revelations of saints seemed hopelessly inferior.

## Social Science and Evolution

From the 1830s onward, many thinkers tried to apply the objective methods of science to the study of society. In some ways, these efforts simply perpetuated the critical thinking of the philosophes. Yet there were important differences. The new "social scientists" had access to the massive sets of numerical data that governments had begun to collect on everything from children to crime, from population to prostitution. In response, social scientists developed new statistical methods to analyze these facts "scientifically" and supposedly to test their theories. And the systems of the leading nineteenth-century social scientists were more unified, all-encompassing, and dogmatic than those of the philosophes. Marx was a prime example (see pages 765–766).

Another extremely influential system builder was French philosopher Auguste Comte (1798–1857). Initially a disciple of the utopian socialist Saint-Simon (see page 764), Comte wrote the six-volume *System of Positive Philosophy* (1830–1842), which was largely overlooked during the romantic era. But when the political

**MR. BERGH TO THE RESCUE.**

THE DEFRAUDED GORILLA. "That *Man* wants to claim my Pedigree. He says he is one of my Descendants."

MR. BERGH. "Now, MR. DARWIN, how could you insult him so?"

**Satirizing Darwin's Ideas** The heated controversies over Darwin's theory of evolution also spawned innumerable jokes and cartoons. This cartoon is by Darwin's contemporary, the American Thomas Nast. *(Culver Pictures)*

failures of 1848 completed the swing to realism, Comte's philosophy came into its own. Its influence has remained great to this day.

Comte postulated that all intellectual activity progresses through predictable stages:

*The great fundamental law . . . is this:—that each of our leading conceptions—each branch of our knowledge—passes successively through three different theoretical conditions: the Theological, or fictitious; the Metaphysical, or abstract; and the Scientific, or positive. . . . The first is the necessary point of departure of human understanding, and the third is the fixed and definitive state. The second is merely a transition.*[19]

By way of example, Comte noted that the prevailing explanation of cosmic patterns had shifted, as knowledge of astronomy developed, from the will of God (the theological) to the will of an orderly nature (the metaphysical) to the rule of unchanging laws (the scientific). Later, this same intellectual progression took place in increasingly complex fields—physics, chemistry, and, finally, the study of society. Comte believed that by applying the scientific method, also called the **positivist method,** his new discipline of sociology would soon discover the eternal laws of human relations. This colossal achievement would in turn enable expert social scientists to impose a disciplined harmony and well-being on less enlightened citizens. Dismissing the "fictions" of traditional religions, Comte became the chief priest of the religion of science and rule by experts.

Comte's stages of knowledge exemplify the nineteenth-century fascination with the idea of **evolution** and dynamic development. Thinkers in many fields, such as the romantic historians and "scientific" Marxists, shared and applied this basic concept. In geology, Charles Lyell (1797–1875) effectively discredited the long-standing view that the earth's surface had been formed by short-lived cataclysms, such as biblical floods and earthquakes. Instead, according to Lyell's principle of uniformitarianism, the same geological processes that are at work today slowly formed the earth's surface over an immensely long time. The evolutionary view of biological development, first proposed by the Greek Anaximander in the sixth century B.C., re-emerged in a more modern form in the work of Jean Baptiste Lamarck (1744–1829). Lamarck asserted that all forms of life had arisen through a long process of continuous adjustment to the environment.

Lamarck's work was flawed—he believed that the characteristics parents acquired in the course of their lives could be inherited by their children—and was not accepted, but it helped prepare the way for Charles Darwin (1809–1882), the most influential of all nineteenth-century evolutionary thinkers. As the official naturalist on a five-year scientific cruise to Latin America and the South Pacific beginning in 1831, Darwin carefully collected specimens of the different animal species he encountered on the voyage. Back in England, convinced by fossil evidence and by his friend Lyell that the earth and life on it were immensely ancient, Darwin came to doubt the general belief in a special divine creation of each species of animal. Instead, he concluded, all life had gradually evolved from a common ancestral origin in an unending "struggle for survival." After long hesitation, Darwin published his research, which immediately attracted wide attention.

Darwin's great originality lay in suggesting precisely *how* biological evolution might have occurred. His theory is summarized in the title of his work *On the Origin of Species by the Means of Natural Selection* (1859). Decisively influenced by Thomas Malthus's gloomy theory that populations naturally grow faster than their food supplies (see page 734), Darwin argued that chance differences among the members of a given species help some survive while others die. Thus the variations that prove useful in the struggle for survival are selected naturally and gradually spread to the entire species through reproduction. Darwin did not explain why such variations occurred in the first place, and not until the early twentieth century did the study of genetics and the concept of mutation provide some answers.

As the capstone of already-widespread evolutionary thinking, Darwin's theory had a powerful and many-sided influence on European thought and the European middle classes. Darwin was hailed as the great scientist par excellence, the "Newton of biology," who had revealed once again the powers of objective science. Darwin's findings also reinforced the teachings of secularists such as Comte and Marx, who scornfully dismissed religious belief in favor of agnostic or atheistic materialism. In the great cities especially, religion was on the defensive. Finally, many writers applied the theory of biological evolution to human affairs. Herbert Spencer (1820–1903), an English disciple of Auguste Comte, saw the human race as driven forward to ever-greater specialization and progress by the brutal economic struggle. According to Spencer, this unending struggle efficiently determined the "survival of the fittest." The poor were the ill-fated weak; the prosperous were the chosen strong. Understandably, Spencer and other **Social Darwinists** were especially popular with the upper middle class.

## Realism in Literature

In 1868 Emile Zola (1840–1902), the giant of the realist movement in literature, defended his violently criticized first novel against charges of pornography and corruption of morals. Such accusations were meaningless, Zola claimed: he was only a purely objective scientist using

*the modern method, the universal instrument of inquiry of which this age makes such ardent use to open up the future. . . . I chose characters completely dominated by their nerves and their blood, deprived of free-will, pushed to each action of their lives by the fatality of their flesh. . . . I have simply done on living bodies the work of analysis which surgeons perform on corpses.*[20]

Zola's literary manifesto articulated the key themes of **realism,** which had emerged in the 1840s and continued to dominate Western culture and style until the 1890s. Realist writers believed that literature should depict life exactly as it was. Forsaking poetry for prose and the personal, emotional viewpoint of the romantics for strict, scientific objectivity, the realists simply observed and recorded—content to let the facts speak for themselves.

The major realist writers focused their extraordinary powers of observation on contemporary everyday life. Emphatically rejecting the romantic search for the exotic

**Manet: Emile Zola** The young novelist's sensitivity and strength of character permeate this famous portrait by the great French painter Edouard Manet. Focusing on nuances and subtle variations, Manet was at first denounced by the critics, and after Zola lost a newspaper job defending Manet they became close friends. Manet was strongly influenced by Japanese prints, seen in the background. *(Erich Lessing/Art Resource, NY)*

and the sublime, they energetically pursued the typical and the commonplace. Beginning with a dissection of the middle classes, from which most of them sprang, many realists eventually focused on the working classes, especially the urban working classes, which had been neglected in imaginative literature before this time. The realists put a microscope to many unexplored and taboo subjects—sex, strikes, violence, alcoholism—and hastened to report that slums and factories teemed with savage behavior. Many shocked middle-class critics denounced realism as ugly sensationalism wrapped provocatively in pseudoscientific declarations and crude language.

The realists' claims of objectivity did not prevent the elaboration of a definite world-view. Unlike the romantics, who had gloried in individual freedom and an unlimited universe, realists such as Zola were strict determinists. Human beings, like atoms, were components of the physical world, and all human actions were caused by unalterable natural laws. Heredity and environment determined human behavior; good and evil were merely social conventions.

The realist movement began in France, where romanticism had never been completely dominant, and three of its greatest practitioners—Balzac, Flaubert, and Zola—were French. Honoré de Balzac (1799–1850) spent thirty years writing a vastly ambitious panorama of postrevolutionary French life. Known collectively as *The Human Comedy,* this series of nearly one hundred books vividly portrays more than two thousand characters from virtually all sectors of French society. Balzac pictures urban society as grasping, amoral, and brutal, characterized by a Darwinian struggle for wealth and power. In *Le Père Goriot* (1835), the hero, a poor student from the provinces, eventually surrenders his idealistic integrity to feverish ambition and society's pervasive greed.

*Madame Bovary* (1857), the masterpiece of Gustave Flaubert (1821–1880), is far narrower in scope than Balzac's work but unparalleled in its depth and accuracy of psychological insight. Unsuccessfully prosecuted as an outrage against public morality and religion, Flaubert's carefully crafted novel tells the ordinary, even banal, story of a frustrated middle-class housewife who has an adulterous love affair and is betrayed by her lover. Without moralizing, Flaubert portrays the provincial middle class as petty, smug, and hypocritical.

Zola was most famous for his seamy, animalistic view of working-class life. But he also wrote gripping, carefully researched stories featuring the stock exchange, the big department store, and the army, as well as urban slums and bloody coal strikes. Like many later realists, Zola sympathized with socialism, a sympathy evident in his overpowering novel *Germinal* (1885).

Realism quickly spread beyond France. In England, Mary Ann Evans (1819–1880), who wrote under the pen name George Eliot, brilliantly achieved a more deeply felt, less sensational kind of realism. "It is the habit of my imagination," George Eliot wrote, "to strive after as full a vision of the medium in which a character moves as one of the character itself." Her great novel *Middlemarch: A Study of Provincial Life* (1871–1872) examines masterfully the ways in which people are shaped by their social medium as well as their own inner strivings, conflicts, and moral choices. Thomas Hardy (1840–1928) was more in the Zola tradition. His novels, such as *Tess of the D'Urbervilles* (1891) and *The Return of the Native* (1878), depict men and women frustrated and crushed by fate and bad luck.

**"Life Is Everywhere"** The simple but profound joys of everyday life infuse this outstanding example of Russia's powerful realist tradition. Painted in 1888 by N. A. Yaroshenko, this representation of the mother and child and adoring men also draws on the classic theme of the infant Jesus and the holy family. *(Sovfoto)*

The greatest Russian realist, Count Leo Tolstoy (1828–1910), combined realism in description and character development with an atypical moralizing, which came to dominate his later work. Tolstoy's greatest work is *War and Peace* (1864–1869), a monumental novel set against the historical background of Napoleon's invasion of Russia in 1812. Tolstoy probed deeply into the lives of a multitude of unforgettable characters, such as the ill-fated Prince Andrei; the shy, fumbling Pierre; and the enchanting, level-headed Natasha. Tolstoy went to great pains to develop his fatalistic theory of history, which regards free will as an illusion and the achievements of even the greatest leaders as only the channeling of historical necessity. Yet Tolstoy's central message is one that most of the people discussed in this chapter would have readily accepted: human love, trust, and everyday family ties are life's enduring values.

Thoroughgoing realism (or "naturalism," as it was often called) arrived late in the United States, most arrestingly in the work of Theodore Dreiser (1871–1945). His first novel, *Sister Carrie* (1900), a story of an ordinary farm girl who does well going wrong in Chicago, so outraged conventional morality that the publisher withdrew the book. The United States subsequently became a bastion of literary realism in the twentieth century after the movement had faded away in Europe.

## Summary

The revolution in industry had a decisive influence on the urban environment. The populations of towns and cities grew rapidly because it was economically advantageous to locate factories and offices in urban areas. This rapid growth worsened long-standing overcrowding and unhealthy living conditions and posed a frightening challenge for society. Eventually government leaders, city planners, reformers, scientists, and ordinary citizens responded. They took effective action in public health and provided themselves with other badly needed urban services. Gradually they tamed the ferocious savagery of the traditional city.

As urban civilization emerged, there were major changes in family life. Especially among the working classes, family life became more stable, more loving, and less mercenary. These improvements had a price, however. Gender roles for men and women became sharply defined and rigidly separate. Women especially tended to be locked into a subordinate and stereotypical role. Nonetheless, on balance, the quality of family life improved for all family members. Better, more stable family relations reinforced the benefits for the masses of higher real wages, increased social security, political participation, and education.

While the quality of urban and family life improved, the class structure became more complex and diversified than before. Urban society featured many distinct social groups, which existed in a state of constant flux and competition. The gap between rich and poor remained enormous and really quite traditional in mature urban society, although there were countless gradations between the extremes. Large numbers of poor women in particular continued to labor as workers in sweated industries, as domestic servants, and as prostitutes in order to satisfy the demands of their masters in the servant-keeping classes. Urban society in the late nineteenth century represented a long step forward for humanity, but it remained very unequal.

Inequality was a favorite theme of realist novelists such as Balzac and Zola. More generally, literary realism reflected Western society's growing faith in science, material progress, and evolutionary thinking. The emergence of urban, industrial civilization accelerated the secularization of the Western world-view.

## Key Terms

Benthamite
miasmatic theory
germ theory
pasteurization
antiseptic principle
labor aristocracy
illegitimacy explosion
separate spheres
defense mechanisms
thermodynamics
organic chemistry
positivist method
evolution
Social Darwinists
realism

## Notes


1. A. Weber, *The Growth of Cities in the Nineteenth Century* (New York: Columbia University Press, 1899), p. 1.
2. S. Marcus, "Reading the Illegible," in *The Victorian City: Images and Realities,* ed. H. J. Dyos and Michael Wolff, vol. 1 (London: Routledge & Kegan Paul, 1973), p. 266.
3. E. Gauldie, *Cruel Habitations: A History of Working-Class Housing, 1780–1918* (London: George Allen & Unwin, 1974), p. 21.
4. Quoted in E. Chadwick, *Report on the Sanitary Condition of the Labouring Population of Great Britain,* ed. M. W. Flinn (Edinburgh: University of Edinburgh Press, 1965; original publication, 1842), pp. 315–316.
5. J. P. McKay, *Tramways and Trolleys: The Rise of Urban Mass Transport in Europe* (Princeton, N.J.: Princeton University Press, 1976), p. 81.
6. Quoted in R. P. Neuman, "The Sexual Question and Social Democracy in Imperial Germany," *Journal of Social History* 7 (Winter 1974): 276.
7. Quoted in J. A. Banks, "The Contagion of Numbers," in *The Victorian City: Images and Realities,* ed. H. J. Dyos and Michael Wolff, vol. 1 (London: Routledge & Kegan Paul, 1973), p. 112.
8. Quoted in R. Roberts, *The Classic Slum: Salford Life in the First Quarter of the Century* (Manchester, England: University of Manchester Press, 1971), p. 95.
9. Quoted in T. Zeldin, *France, 1848–1945,* vol. 1 (Oxford: Clarendon Press, 1973), p. 288.
10. J. Ehmer, "Marriage," in *The History of the European Family,* ed. D. Kertzer and M. Barbagli, vol. 2 (New Haven: Yale University Press, 2002), p. 319.
11. S. Marcus, *The Other Victorians: A Study of Sexuality and Pornography in Mid-Nineteenth-Century England* (New York: Basic Books, 1966), p. 142.
12. Quoted in G. S. Jones, "Working-Class Culture and Working-Class Politics in London, 1870–1900: Notes on the Remaking of a Working Class," *Journal of Social History* 7 (Summer 1974): 486.
13. Quoted in Zeldin, *France,* p. 346.
14. Roberts, *The Classic Slum,* p. 35.
15. Quoted in Zeldin, *France,* p. 295.
16. Quoted ibid., p. 328.
17. Quoted in Neuman, "The Sexual Question," p. 281.
18. Quoted in S. Kern, "Explosive Intimacy: Psychodynamics of the Victorian Family," *History of Childhood Quarterly* 1 (Winter 1974): 439.
19. A. Comte, *The Positive Philosophy of Auguste Comte,* trans. H. Martineau, vol. 1 (London: J. Chapman, 1853), pp. 1–2.
20. Quoted in G. J. Becker, ed., *Documents of Modern Literary Realism* (Princeton, N.J.: Princeton University Press, 1963), p. 159.


## Suggested Reading

All of the books and articles cited in the Notes are highly recommended. Ehmer, cited in the Notes, is one of many excellent contributions to Kertzer and Barbagli, eds., an important new three-volume history of the European family from 1500 to the present. T. Zeldin, *France, 1848–1945,* 2 vols. (1973, 1977), is a pioneering social history that opens many doors, as is the ambitious synthesis by T. Hamerow, *The Birth of a New Europe: State and Society in the Nineteenth Century* (1983). F. Thompson, *The Rise of Respectable Society: A Social History of Victorian Britain, 1830–1900* (1986), is a laudable survey.

On the European city, D. Harvey, *Consciousness and the Urban Experience* (1985), is provocative. D. Silverman, *Art Nouveau in Fin-de-Siècle France: Politics, Psychology, and Style* (1989), and D. Pickney, *Napoleon III and the Rebuilding of Paris* (1972), are major studies. Also recommended are P. Fritzsche, *Reading Berlin in 1900* (1996), an imaginative cultural investigation; O. Olsen, *The City as a Work of Art: London, Paris, and Vienna* (1986), an architectural feast; and M. Hamm, ed., *The City in Russian History* (1976), which still has no equal. G. Crossick and S. Jaumain, eds., *Cathedrals of Consumption: The European Department Store, 1850–1939* (1999), and M. Jacobs and P. Scholliers, eds., *Eating Out in Europe: Picnics, Gourmet Dining, and Snacks Since the Eighteenth Century* (2003), consider major aspects of urban consumerism in important studies. The outstanding study by J. Schmiechen, *Sweated Industries and Sweated Labor: The London Clothing Trades* (1984), complements H. Mayhew's wonderful contemporary study, *London Labour and the Labouring Poor* (1861), reprinted recently. D. Crane, *Fashion and Its Social Agendas: Class, Gender, and Identity* (2000), is an innovative and extremely helpful historical investigation. L. Tiersten, *Marianne in the Market: Envisioning Consumer Society in Fin-de-Siècle France* (2001), is a subtle treatment of women as consumers. E. Johnson, *Urbanization and Crime: Germany, 1871–1914* (1995), presents a portrait of a police state zealously defending property rights. J. P. Goubert, *The Conquest of Water: The Advent of Health in the Industrial Age* (1989), and A. Corbin, *The Foul and the Fragrant: Odor and the French Social Imagination of Public Health* (1986), are excellent introductions to sanitary developments and attitudes toward smells. B. Gottlieb, *The Family in the Western World* (1993), is a wide-ranging synthesis. J. Laver's handsomely illustrated *Manners and Morals in the Age of Optimism, 1848–1914* (1966) investigates the urban underworld and relations between the sexes. Sexual attitudes are also examined in J. Walkowitz, *Prostitution and Victorian Society: Women, Class and State* (1980), and L. Engelstein, *The Key to Happiness: Sex and the Search for Modernity in Fin-de-Siècle Russia* (1992). P. Allen, *The Wages of Sin: Sex and Disease, Past and Present* (2000), is the best history of sexually transmitted diseases. P. Mainard, *Husbands, Wives, and Lovers: Marriage and Its Discontents in Nineteenth-Century France* (2003), carefully explores attitudes toward marriage and adultery.

Studies on women continue to expand rapidly. In addition to the general works by Stone and Tilly and Scott cited in Chapter 20, B. Anderson and J. Zinsser, *A History of Their Own: Women in Europe from Prehistory to the Present,* vol. 2, rev. ed. (2000), is an excellent, wide-ranging survey. U. Frevert, *Women in German History: From Bourgeois Emancipation to Sexual Liberation* (1990), is recommended, and M. Perrot, ed., *A History of Private Life* (1990), is a fascinating multivolume work. Eye-opening specialized investigations include L. Davidoff, *The Best Circles* (1973), and P. Jalland, *Women, Marriage and Politics, 1860–1914* (1986), on upper-class society types; B. Engel, *Between the Fields and the City: Women, Work and Family in Russia, 1861–1914* (1994); and P. Smith, *Feminism in the Third Republic* (1996). M. J. Peterson, *Love and Work in the Lives of Victorian Gentlewomen* (1989); J. Coffin, *The Politics of Women's Work: The Paris Garment Trades, 1750–1914* (1996); and M. Vicinus, *Independent Women: Work and Community for Single Women, 1850–1920* (1985), examine women at work. M. Vicinus, ed., *Suffer and Be Still* (1972) and *A Widening Sphere* (1981), are far-ranging collections of essays on women's history, as is R. Bridenthal, S. Mosher Stuard, and M. Wiesner, eds., *Becoming Visible: Women in European History,* 3d ed. (1998). Feminism is treated perceptively in C. Moses, *French Feminism in the Nineteenth Century* (1984). L. Tickner, *The Spectacle of Women: Imagery of the Suffrage Campaign, 1907–1914* (1988), discusses Britain. J. Tosh, *A Man's Place: Masculinity and the Middle-Class Home in Victorian Britain* (1999), is a major work, exploring fatherhood and the cult of the home. J. Gillis, *Youth and History* (1974), is a good introduction.

Among studies on the working classes, M. Maynes, *Taking the Hard Road: Life Course in French and German Workers' Biographies in the Era of Industrialization* (1995), provides fascinating stories and shows how workers saw themselves. Everyday life in a great city comes wonderfully alive in W. S. Haine, *The World of the Paris Café: Sociability Among the French Working Class, 1789–1914* (1996). A. Davin, *Growing Up Poor: Home, School, and Street in London, 1870–1914* (1996), and J. Wegs, *Growing Up Working Class: Continuity and Change Among Viennese Youth, 1890–1938* (1989), are recommended and make for interesting comparisons. Two good studies on the middle classes are P. Pillbeam, *The Middle Classes in Europe, 1789–1914: France, Germany, Italy, and Russia* (1990), a stimulating introduction, and J. Kocka and A. Mitchell, eds., *Bourgeois Society in Nineteenth-Century Europe* (1993), a collection by leading specialists. Two fine recent studies on the professions are A. Digby, *Making a Medical Living: Doctors and Patients in the English Market for Medicine, 1720–1922* (1994), and A. Quartaro, *Women Teachers and Popular Education in Nineteenth-Century France* (1995). Servants and their employers receive excellent treatment in T. McBride, *The Domestic Revolution: The Modernization of Household Service in England and France, 1820–1912* (1976), and B. Smith, *Ladies of the Leisure Class: The Bourgeoises of Northern France in the Nineteenth Century* (1981), which may be compared with the innovative study by M. Miller, *The Bon Marché: Bourgeois Culture and the Department Store, 1869–1920* (1981). J. Schmiechen and K. Carls, *The British Market Hall: A Social and Architectural History* (1999), is a fascinating and beautiful study of Britain's enclosed markets, which revolutionized the sale of food and proclaimed civic pride. T. Griffiths, *The Lancashire Working Classes, c. 1880–1930* (2001), reexamines both class and gender relationships, emphasizing the enduring centrality of family ties.

On Darwin and evolution, J. Weiner, *The Beak of the Finch: The Story of Evolution in Our Time* (1994), is a prizewinning, highly readable account. M. Ruse, *The Darwinian Revolution* (1979), and P. Bowler, *Evolution: The History of an Idea,* rev. ed. (1989), are also recommended. O. Chadwick, *The Secularization of the European Mind in the Nineteenth Century* (1976), analyzes the impact of science (and other factors) on religious belief. M. Teich and R. Porter, eds., *Fin de Siècle and Its Legacy* (1990), is a fascinating collection of essays, ranging widely from industry and cars to sports and painting. The masterpieces of the great realist social novelists remain among the best and most memorable introductions to nineteenth-century culture and thought. In addition to the novels discussed in this chapter and those cited in the Suggested Reading for Chapters 22 and 23, Ivan Turgenev's *Fathers and Sons* and Emile Zola's *The Dram-Shop* are especially recommended.

# Listening to the Past

## Middle-Class Youth and Sexuality

*Growing up in Vienna in a prosperous Jewish family, Stephan Zweig (1881–1942) became an influential voice calling for humanitarian values and international culture in early-twentieth-century Europe. Passionately opposed to the First World War, Zweig wrote poetry, plays, and novels. But he was most famous for many outstanding biographies, which featured shrewd psychological portraits of intriguing historical figures such as Magellan and Marie Antoinette. After Hitler came to power in Germany in 1933, Zweig lived in exile until his death in 1942.*

*Zweig's last work was* The World of Yesterday *(1943), one of the truly fascinating autobiographies of the twentieth century. In the following passage taken from that work, Zweig recalls and also interprets the romantic experiences and the sexual separation of middle-class youth before the First World War.*

During the eight years of our higher schooling [beyond grade school], something had occurred which was of great importance to each one of us: we ten-year-olds had grown into virile young men of sixteen, seventeen, and eighteen, and Nature began to assert its rights. . . . It did not take us long to discover that those authorities in whom we had previously confided—school, family, and public morals—manifested an astonishing insincerity in this matter of sex. But what is more, they also demanded secrecy and reserve from us in this connection. . . .

This "social morality," which on the one hand privately presupposed the existence of sexuality and its natural course, but on the other would not recognize it openly at any price, was doubly deceitful. While it winked one eye at a young man and even encouraged him with the other "to sow his wild oats," as the kindly language of the home put it, in the case of a woman it studiously shut both eyes and acted as if it were blind. That a man could experience desires, and was permitted to experience them, was silently admitted by custom. But to admit frankly that a woman could be subject to similar desires, or that creation for its eternal purposes also required a female polarity, would have transgressed the conception of the "sanctity of womanhood." In the pre-Freudian era, therefore, the axiom was agreed upon that a female person could have no physical desires as long as they had not been awakened by man, and that, obviously, was officially permitted only in marriage. But even in those moral times, in Vienna in particular, the air was full of dangerous erotic infection, and a girl of good family had to live in a completely sterilized atmosphere, from the day of her birth until the day when she left the altar on her husband's arm. In order to protect young girls, they were not left alone for a single moment. . . . Every book which they read was inspected, and above all else, young girls were constantly kept busy to divert their attention from any possible dangerous thoughts. They had to practise the piano, learn singing and drawing, foreign languages, and the history of literature and art. They were educated and overeducated. But while the aim was to make them as educated and as socially correct as possible, at the same time society anxiously took great pains that they should remain innocent of all natural things to a degree unthinkable today. A young girl of good family was not allowed to have any idea of how the male body was formed, or to know how children came into the world, for the angel was to enter into matrimony not only physically untouched, but completely "pure" spiritually as well. "Good breeding," for a young girl of that time, was identical with ignorance of life; and this ignorance ofttimes lasted for the rest of their lives. . . .

What possibilities actually existed for a young man of the middle-class world? In all the others, in the so-called lower classes, the problem was no problem at all. . . . In most of our Alpine villages the number of natural children greatly exceeded the legitimate ones. Among the proletariat, the worker, before he could get married, lived with another worker in free love. . . . It was only in our middle-class society that such a remedy as an early marriage was scorned. . . . And so there was an artificial interval of six, eight, or ten years between actual manhood and manhood as society accepted it; and in this interval the young man had to take care of his own "affairs" or adventures.

Those days did not give him too many opportunities. Only a very few particularly rich young men could afford the luxury of keeping a mistress, that is, taking an apartment and paying her expenses. And only a very few fortunate young men achieved the literary ideal of love of the times—the only one which it was permitted to describe in novels—an affair with a married woman. The others helped themselves for the most part with shopgirls and waitresses, and this offered little inner satisfaction. . . . But, generally speaking, prostitution was still the foundation of the erotic life outside of marriage; in a certain sense it constituted a dark underground vault over which rose the gorgeous structure of middle-class society with its faultless, radiant façade.

The present generation has hardly any idea of the gigantic extent of prostitution in Europe before the [First] World War. Whereas today it is as rare to meet a prostitute on the streets of a big city as it is to meet a wagon in the road, then the sidewalks were so sprinkled with women for sale that it was more difficult to avoid than to find them. To this was added the countless number of "closed houses," the night clubs, the cabarets, the dance parlours with their dancers and singers, and the bars with their "come-on" girls. At that time female wares were offered for sale at every hour and at every price. . . . And this was the same city, the same society, the same morality, that was indignant when young girls rode bicycles, and declared it a disgrace to the dignity of science when Freud in his calm, clear, and penetrating manner established truths that they did not wish to be true. The same world that so pathetically defended the purity of womanhood allowed this cruel sale of women, organized it, and even profited thereby.

We should not permit ourselves to be misled by sentimental novels or stories of that epoch. It was a bad time for youth. The young girls were hermetically locked up under the control of the family, hindered in their free bodily as well as intellectual development. The young men were forced to secrecy and reticence by a morality which fundamentally no one believed or obeyed. Unhampered, honest relationships—in other words, all that could have made youth happy and joyous according to the laws of Nature—were permitted only to the very few.

An elegant ball for upper-class youth, with debutantes, junior officers, and vigilant chaperons watching in the background. *(State Russian Museum, St. Petersburg, Russia/The Bridgeman Art Library)*

## Questions for Analysis

1. According to Zweig, how did the sex lives of young middle-class women and young middle-class men differ? What accounted for these differences?
2. Was there nonetheless a basic underlying unity in the way society treated both the young men and the young women of the comfortable middle class? If so, what was that unity?
3. Zweig ends this passage with a value judgment: "It was a bad time for youth." Do you agree or disagree? Why?

*Source: The World of Yesterday* by Stephan Zweig, translated by Helmut Ripperger. Translation copyright 1943 by the Viking Press, Inc. Used with permission of Viking Penguin, a division of Penguin Group (USA) Inc.

France's Napoleon III and Empress Eugénie greet Britain's Queen Victoria and Prince Albert in a dazzling ceremony in Paris in 1855.
*(The Royal Collection, © 2004 Her Majesty Queen Elizabeth II)*

chapter

# 25 The Age of Nationalism, 1850–1914

**chapter outline**

- Napoleon III in France
- Nation Building in Italy and Germany
- Nation Building in the United States
- The Modernization of Russia
- The Responsive National State, 1871–1914
- Marxism and the Socialist Movement

The revolutions of 1848 closed one era and opened another. Urban industrial society began to take a strong hold on the continent and in the young United States, as it already had in Great Britain. Internationally, the repressive peace and diplomatic stability of Metternich's time were replaced by a period of war and rapid change. In thought and culture, exuberant romanticism gave way to hardheaded realism. In the Atlantic economy, the hard years of the 1840s were followed by good times and prosperity throughout most of the 1850s and 1860s. Perhaps most important of all, Western society progressively developed, for better or worse, a new and effective organizing principle capable of coping with the many-sided challenge of the dual revolution and the emerging urban civilization. That principle was nationalism—dedication to an identification with the nation-state.

The triumph of nationalism is an enormously significant historical development that was by no means completely predictable. After all, nationalism had been a powerful force since at least 1789. Yet it had repeatedly failed to realize its goals, most spectacularly so in 1848.

- Why, then, did nationalism become in one way or another an almost universal faith in Europe and in the United States between 1850 and 1914?
- More specifically, how did nationalism evolve so that it appealed not only to predominately middle-class liberals but also to the broad masses of society?

These are the questions this chapter will seek to answer.

## Napoleon III in France

Early nationalism was generally liberal and idealistic and often democratic and radical as well. The ideas of nationhood and popular sovereignty posed a fearful revolutionary threat to conservatives like Metternich. Yet from the vantage point of the twenty-first century, it is clear that nationalism wears many masks: it may be narrowly liberal or democratic and radical, as it was for Mazzini and Michelet, but it can also flourish in dictatorial states, which may be conservative, fascist, or communist. Napoleon I's France had already combined national feeling with authoritarian rule. Significantly, it was Napoleon's nephew,

Louis Napoleon, who revived and extended this merger. He showed how governments could reconcile popular and conservative forces in an authoritarian nationalism. In doing so, he provided a model for political leaders elsewhere.

## The Second Republic and Louis Napoleon

Although Louis Napoleon Bonaparte had played no part in French politics before 1848, universal male suffrage gave him three times as many votes as the four other presidential candidates combined in the French presidential election of December 1848. This outcome occurred for several reasons. First, Louis Napoleon had the great name of his uncle, whom romantics had transformed from a dictator into a demigod as they created a Napoleonic legend after 1820. Second, as Karl Marx stressed at the time, middle-class and peasant property owners feared the socialist challenge of urban workers, and they wanted a tough ruler to provide protection. Third, in late 1848 Louis Napoleon had a positive "program" for France, which was to guide him through most of his long reign. This program had been elaborated earlier in two pamphlets, *Napoleonic Ideas* and *The Elimination of Poverty,* which he had written while imprisoned for an attempt to overthrow Louis Philippe's government. Prior to the presidential election, these pamphlets had been widely circulated.

Above all, Louis Napoleon believed that the government should represent the people and that it should try hard to help them economically. But how were these tasks to be done? Parliaments and political parties were not the answer, according to Louis Napoleon. French politicians

**Paris in the Second Empire** The flash and glitter of unprecedented prosperity in the Second Empire come alive in this vibrant contemporary painting. Writers and intellectuals chat with elegant women and trade witticisms with financiers and government officials at the Café Tortoni, a favorite rendezvous for fashionable society. Horse-drawn omnibuses with open top decks mingle with cabs and private carriages on the broad new boulevard. *(Lauros/Giraudon/The Bridgeman Art Library)*

1850 | 1865 | 1880 | 1895 | 1910

**POLITICAL/MILITARY**

- 1852–1871 Reign of Napoleon III in France
- 1859–1870 Unification of Italy
- 1861–1865 U.S. Civil War
- 1866 Austro-Prussian War
- 1870–1871 Franco-Prussian War
- 1905 "Bloody Sunday" in Russia

**SOCIAL/ECONOMIC**

- 1860–1900 Industrialization of Russia
- 1861 Freeing of Russian serfs
- 1883 First social security laws to help workers in Germany

**INTELLECTUAL/RELIGIOUS**

- 1859 Mill, *On Liberty*
- 1870–1878 Kulturkampf, Bismarck's attack on Catholic church
- 1880s Educational reforms affect Catholic schools in France

represented special-interest groups, particularly middle-class ones. The answer was a strong, even authoritarian, national leader, like the first Napoleon, who would serve all the people, rich and poor. This leader would be linked to each citizen by direct democracy, his sovereignty uncorrupted by politicians and legislative bodies. These political ideas went hand in hand with Louis Napoleon's vision of national unity and social progress. The state and its leader had a sacred duty to provide jobs and stimulate the economy. All classes would benefit by such action.

Louis Napoleon's political and social ideas were at least vaguely understood by large numbers of French peasants and workers in December 1848. To many common people, he appeared to be a strong man *and* a forward-looking champion of their interests, and that is why they voted for him.

Elected to a four-year term, President Louis Napoleon had to share power with a conservative National Assembly. But in 1851, after the Assembly failed to change the constitution so he could run for a second term, Louis Napoleon began to conspire with key army officers. On December 2, 1851, he illegally dismissed the Assembly and seized power in a coup d'état. There was some armed resistance in Paris and widespread insurrection in the countryside in southern France, but these protests were crushed by the army. Restoring universal male suffrage, Louis Napoleon called on the French people, as his uncle had done, to legalize his actions. They did: 92 percent voted to make him president for ten years. A year later, 97 percent in a plebiscite made him hereditary emperor; for the third time, and by the greatest margin yet, the authoritarian Louis Napoleon was overwhelmingly elected to lead the French nation.

## Napoleon III's Second Empire

Louis Napoleon—now proclaimed Emperor Napoleon III—experienced both success and failure between 1852 and 1870. His greatest success was with the economy, particularly in the 1850s. His government encouraged the new investment banks and massive railroad construction that were at the heart of the Industrial Revolution on the continent. The government also fostered general economic expansion through an ambitious program of public works, which included the rebuilding of Paris to improve the urban environment (see page 792). The profits of business people soared with prosperity, and unemployment declined greatly.

Louis Napoleon always hoped that economic progress would reduce social and political tensions. This hope was at least partially realized. Until the mid-1860s there was considerable support from France's most dissatisfied group, the urban workers. Napoleon III's regulation of pawnshops and his support of credit unions and better housing for the working classes were evidence of positive concern in the 1850s. In the 1860s, he granted workers the right to form unions and the right to strike—important economic rights denied by earlier governments.

At first, political power remained in the hands of the emperor. He alone chose his ministers, and they had great freedom of action. At the same time, Napoleon III restricted but did not abolish the Assembly. Members were elected by universal male suffrage every six years, and Louis Napoleon and his government took the parliamentary elections very seriously. They tried to entice notable people, even those who had opposed the regime, to stand as government candidates in order to expand the base of support. Moreover, the government used its officials and appointed mayors to spread the word that the election of the government's candidates—and the defeat of the opposition—was the key to roads, tax rebates, and a thousand other local concerns.

In 1857 and again in 1863, Louis Napoleon's system worked brilliantly and produced overwhelming electoral victories. Yet in the 1860s, Napoleon III's electoral system gradually disintegrated. A sincere nationalist, Napoleon had wanted to reorganize Europe on the principle of nationality and gain influence and territory for France and himself in the process. Instead, problems in Italy and the rising power of Prussia led to increasing criticism at home from his Catholic and nationalist supporters. With increasing effectiveness, the middle-class liberals who had always wanted a less authoritarian regime continued to denounce his rule.

Napoleon was always sensitive to the public mood. Public opinion, he once said, always wins the last victory. Thus in the 1860s, he progressively liberalized his empire. He gave the Assembly greater powers and the opposition candidates greater freedom, which they used to good advantage. In 1869 the opposition, consisting of republicans, monarchists, and liberals, polled almost 45 percent of the vote.

The next year, a sick and weary Louis Napoleon again granted France a new constitution, which combined a basically parliamentary regime with a hereditary emperor as chief of state. In a final great plebiscite on the eve of the disastrous war with Prussia, 7.5 million Frenchmen voted in favor of the new constitution, and only 1.5 million opposed it. Napoleon III's attempt to reconcile a strong national state with universal male suffrage was still evolving and was doing so in a democratic direction.

## Nation Building in Italy and Germany

See DBQ 9

Louis Napoleon's triumph in 1848 and his authoritarian rule in the 1850s provided the old ruling classes of Europe with a new model in politics. To what extent might the expanding urban middle classes and even portions of the growing working classes rally to a strong and essentially conservative national state? This was one of the great political questions in the 1850s and 1860s. In central Europe, a resounding answer came with the national unification of Italy and Germany.

### Italy to 1850

Italy had never been united prior to 1850. Part of Rome's great empire in ancient times, the Italian peninsula was divided in the Middle Ages into competing city-states that led the commercial and cultural revival of the West with amazing creativity. A battleground for great powers after 1494, Italy was reorganized in 1815 at the Congress of Vienna. The rich northern provinces of Lombardy and Venetia were taken by Metternich's Austria. Sardinia and Piedmont were under the rule of an Italian monarch, and Tuscany, with its famous capital Florence, shared north-central Italy with several smaller states. Central Italy and Rome were ruled by the papacy, which had always considered an independent political existence necessary to fulfill its spiritual mission. Naples and Sicily were ruled, as they had been for almost a hundred years, by a branch of the Bourbons. Metternich was not wrong in dismissing Italy as "a geographical expression" (see Map 25.1).

Between 1815 and 1848, the goal of a unified Italian nation captured the imaginations of many Italians. There were three basic approaches. The first was the radical program of the idealistic patriot Giuseppe Mazzini, who preached a centralized democratic republic based on universal male suffrage and the will of the people (see page 764). The second was that of Vincenzo Gioberti, a Catholic priest who called for a federation of existing states under the presidency of a progressive pope. The third was the program of those who looked for leadership to the autocratic kingdom of Sardinia-Piedmont, much as many Germans looked to Prussia.

**MAP 25.1 The Unification of Italy, 1859–1870** The leadership of Sardinia-Piedmont and nationalist fervor were decisive factors in the unification of Italy.

The third alternative was strengthened by the failures of 1848, when Austria smashed Mazzini's republicanism. Almost by accident, Sardinia's monarch, Victor Emmanuel, retained the liberal constitution granted under duress in March 1848. This constitution provided for a fair degree of civil liberties and real parliamentary government, with deputies elected by a limited franchise based on income. To the Italian middle classes, Sardinia appeared to be a liberal, progressive state ideally suited to achieve the goal of national unification. By contrast,

Mazzini's brand of democratic republicanism seemed quixotic and too radical.

As for the papacy, the initial cautious support by Pius IX (r. 1846–1878) for unification had given way to fear and hostility after he was temporarily driven from Rome during the upheavals of 1848. For a long generation, the papacy would stand resolutely opposed not only to national unification but also to most modern trends. In 1864 in the *Syllabus of Errors,* Pius IX strongly denounced rationalism, socialism, separation of church and state, and religious liberty, denying that "the Roman pontiff can and ought to reconcile and align himself with progress, liberalism, and modern civilization."

## Cavour and Garibaldi in Italy

Sardinia had the good fortune of being led by a brilliant statesman, Count Camillo Benso di Cavour, the dominant figure in the Sardinian government from 1850 until his death in 1861. Indicative of the coming tacit alliance between the aristocracy and the solid middle class under the banner of the strong nation-state, Cavour came from a noble family and embraced the economic doctrines and business activities associated with the prosperous middle class. Before entering politics, he made a substantial fortune in sugar mills, steamships, banks, and railroads. Cavour's national goals were limited and realistic. Until 1859 he sought unity only for the states of northern and perhaps central Italy in a greatly expanded kingdom of Sardinia.

In the 1850s, Cavour worked to consolidate Sardinia as a liberal constitutional state capable of leading northern Italy. His program of highways and railroads, of civil liberties and opposition to clerical privilege, increased support for Sardinia throughout northern Italy. Yet Cavour realized that Sardinia could not drive Austria out of Lombardy and Venetia and unify northern Italy under Victor Emmanuel without the help of a powerful ally. Accordingly, he worked for a secret diplomatic alliance with Napoleon III against Austria.

Finally, in July 1858 Cavour succeeded and goaded Austria into attacking Sardinia in 1859. Napoleon III came to Sardinia's defense. Then after the victory of the combined Franco-Sardinian forces, Napoleon III did a sudden about-face. Deciding it was not in his interest to have too strong a state on his southern border and criticized by French Catholics for supporting the pope's declared enemy, Napoleon III abandoned Cavour. He made a compromise peace with the Austrians at Villafranca in July 1859. Sardinia would receive only Lombardy, the area around Milan. The rest of the map of Italy would remain essentially unchanged. Cavour resigned in a rage.

Yet Cavour's plans were salvaged by the skillful maneuvers of his allies in the moderate nationalist movement. While the war against Austria had raged in the north, pro-Sardinian nationalists in central Italy had fanned popular revolts and driven out their easily toppled princes. Using and controlling the popular enthusiasm, the middle-class nationalist leaders in central Italy called for fusion with Sardinia. This was not at all what France and the other Great Powers wanted, but the nationalists held firm. Cavour returned to power in early 1860 and gained Napoleon III's support by ceding Savoy and Nice to France. The people of central Italy then voted overwhelmingly to join a greatly enlarged kingdom of Sardinia. Cavour had achieved his original goal of a northern Italian state (see Map 25.1).

For superpatriots such as Giuseppe Garibaldi (1807–1882), the job of unification was still only half done. The son of a poor sailor, Garibaldi personified the romantic, revolutionary nationalism and republicanism of Mazzini and 1848. Leading a corps of volunteers against Austria in 1859, Garibaldi emerged in 1860 as an independent force in Italian politics.

Partly to use him and partly to get rid of him, Cavour secretly supported Garibaldi's bold plan to "liberate" the kingdom of the Two Sicilies. Landing on the shores of Sicily in May 1860, Garibaldi's guerrilla band of a thousand **Red Shirts** captured the imagination of the Sicilian peasantry. Outwitting the twenty-thousand-man royal army, the guerrilla leader won battles, gained volunteers, and took Palermo. Then he and his men crossed to the mainland, marched triumphantly toward Naples, and prepared to attack Rome and the pope. But the wily Cavour quickly sent Sardinian forces to occupy most of the Papal States (but not Rome) and to intercept Garibaldi.

Cavour realized that an attack on Rome would bring about war with France, and he also feared Garibaldi's radicalism and popular appeal. Thus he immediately organized a plebiscite in the conquered territories. Despite the urging of some radical supporters, the patriotic Garibaldi did not oppose Cavour, and the people of the south voted to join Sardinia. When Garibaldi and Victor Emmanuel rode through Naples to cheering crowds, they symbolically sealed the union of north and south, of monarch and nation-state.

Cavour had succeeded. He had controlled Garibaldi and had turned popular nationalism in a conservative direction. The new kingdom of Italy, which expanded to include Venice in 1866 and Rome in 1870, was a parlia-

**Garibaldi and Victor Emmanuel** The historic meeting in Naples between the leader of Italy's revolutionary nationalists and the king of Sardinia sealed the unification of northern and southern Italy in a unitary state. With only the sleeve of his red shirt showing, Garibaldi offers his hand—and his conquests—to the uniformed king and his moderate monarchical government. *(Scala/Art Resource, NY)*

mentary monarchy under Victor Emmanuel, neither radical nor democratic. Despite political unity, only a small minority of Italian males had the right to vote. The propertied classes and the common people were divided. A great and growing social and cultural gap separated the progressive, industrializing north from the stagnant, agrarian south. The new Italy was united on paper, but profound divisions remained.

## Germany Before Bismarck

In the aftermath of 1848, the German states were locked in a political stalemate. After Austria and Russia blocked Frederick William's attempt to unify Germany "from above," tension grew between Austria and Prussia as each power sought to block the other within the German Confederation (see pages 759 and 781–782). Stalemate also prevailed in the domestic politics of the individual states in the 1850s.

At the same time, powerful economic forces were undermining the political status quo. Modern industry grew rapidly within the German customs union, or **Zollverein,** founded in 1834 to stimulate trade and increase the revenues of member states. The Zollverein had not included Austria, and after 1848 this exclusion became a crucial factor in the Austro-Prussian rivalry.

The Zollverein's tariff duties were substantially reduced so that Austria's highly protected industry could not bear to join. In retaliation, Austria tried to destroy the Zollverein, but without success. Indeed, by the end of 1853 all the German states except Austria had joined the customs union. A new Germany excluding Austria was becoming an economic reality. Middle-class and business groups in the Zollverein were enriching themselves and finding solid economic reasons to bolster their idealistic support of national unification. Prussia's leading role within the Zollverein gave it a valuable advantage in its struggle against Austria's supremacy in German political affairs.

The national uprising in Italy in 1859 made a profound impression in the German states. In Prussia great political change and war—perhaps with Austria, perhaps with France—seemed quite possible. Along with his top military advisers, the tough-minded William I of Prussia (r. 1861–1888), who had replaced the unstable Frederick William IV as regent in 1858 and become king himself in 1861, was convinced of the need for major army reforms. William I wanted to double the size of the highly disciplined regular army. Army reforms meant a bigger defense budget and higher taxes.

Prussia had emerged from 1848 with a parliament of sorts, which was in the hands of the liberal middle class by 1859. The wealthy middle class, like the landed aristocracy, was greatly overrepresented by the Prussian electoral system, and it wanted society to be less, not more, militaristic. Above all, middle-class representatives wanted to establish once and for all that the parliament, not the king, had the ultimate political power. They also wanted to ensure that the army was responsible to Prussia's elected representatives and was not a "state within a state." These demands were popular. The parliament rejected the military budget in 1862, and the liberals triumphed completely in new elections. King William then called on Count Otto von Bismarck to head a new ministry and defy the parliament. This was a momentous choice.

## Bismarck and the Austro-Prussian War, 1866

The most important figure in German history between Luther and Hitler, Otto von Bismarck (1815–1898) has been the object of enormous interest and debate. A great hero to some, a great villain to others, Bismarck was above all a master of politics. Born into the Prussian landowning aristocracy, the young Bismarck was a wild and tempestuous student given to duels and drinking. Proud of his Junker heritage and always devoted to his Prussian sovereign, Bismarck had a strong personality and an unbounded desire for power. Yet in his drive to secure power for himself and for Prussia, Bismarck was extraordinarily flexible and pragmatic. "One must always have two irons in the fire," he once said. He kept his options open, pursuing one policy and then another as he moved with skill and cunning toward his goal.

Bismarck first honed his political skills as a high-ranking diplomat for the Prussian government. When he took office as chief minister in 1862, he made a strong but unfavorable impression. His speeches were a sensation and a scandal. Declaring that the government would rule without parliamentary consent, Bismarck lashed out at the middle-class opposition: "The great questions of the day will not be decided by speeches and resolutions—that was the blunder of 1848 and 1849—but by blood and iron." Denounced for this view that "might makes right," Bismarck had the Prussian bureaucracy go right on collecting taxes, even though the parliament refused to approve the budget. Bismarck reorganized the army. And for four years, from 1862 to 1866, the voters of Prussia continued to express their opposition by sending large liberal majorities to the parliament.

Opposition at home spurred the search for success abroad. The ever-knotty question of Schleswig-Holstein provided a welcome opportunity. In 1864, when the Danish king tried again, as in 1848, to bring the provinces into a more centralized Danish state against the will of the German Confederation, Prussia joined Austria in a short and successful war against Denmark. However, Bismarck was convinced that Prussia had to control completely the northern, predominately Protestant part of the German Confederation, which meant expelling Austria from German affairs. After the victory over Denmark, Bismarck's skillful maneuvering had Prussia in a position to force Austria out by war, if necessary. Bismarck knew that a war with Austria would have to be a localized one that would not provoke a mighty alliance against Prussia. By skillfully neutralizing Russia and France, he was in a position to engage in a war of his own making.

The Austro-Prussian War of 1866 lasted only seven weeks. Utilizing railroads to mass troops and the new breechloading needle gun to achieve maximum firepower, the reorganized Prussian army overran northern Germany and defeated Austria decisively at the Battle of Sadowa in Bohemia. Anticipating Prussia's future needs, Bismarck offered Austria realistic, even generous, peace terms. Austria paid no reparations and lost no territory to Prussia, although Venetia was ceded to Italy. But the German Confederation was dissolved, and Austria agreed to withdraw from German affairs. The states north of the Main River were grouped in the new North German Confederation, led by an expanded Prussia. The mainly Catholic states of the south remained independent while forming alliances with Prussia. Bismarck's fundamental goal of Prussian expansion was being realized (see Map 25.2).

**MAP 25.2 The Unification of Germany, 1866–1871** This map deserves careful study. Note how Prussian expansion, Austrian expulsion from the old German Confederation, and the creation of a new German empire went hand in hand. Austria lost no territory, but Prussia's neighbors in the north suffered grievously or simply disappeared. The annexation of Alsace-Lorraine turned France into a lasting enemy of Germany before 1914.

## The Taming of the Parliament

Bismarck had long been convinced that the old order he so ardently defended should make peace, on its own terms, with the liberal middle class and the nationalist movement. He realized that nationalism was not necessarily hostile to conservative, authoritarian government. Moreover, Bismarck believed that because of the events of 1848, the German middle class could be led to prefer the reality of national unity under conservative leadership to a long, uncertain battle for truly liberal institutions. During the constitutional struggle over army reform and parliamentary authority, he had delayed but not abandoned this goal. Thus during the attack on Austria in 1866, he increasingly identified Prussia's fate with the "national development of Germany."

In the aftermath of victory, Bismarck fashioned a federal constitution for the new North German Confederation. Each state retained its own local government, but the king of Prussia became president of the confederation, and the chancellor—Bismarck—was responsible only to the president. The federal government—William I and Bismarck—controlled the army and foreign affairs. There was also a legislature consisting of two houses that shared equally in the making of laws. Delegates to the upper house were appointed by the different states, but members of the lower house were elected by universal, single-class, male suffrage. With this radical innovation, Bismarck opened the door to popular participation and the possibility of going over the head of the middle class directly to the people, much as Napoleon III had done in France. All the while, however, ultimate power rested in the hands of Prussia and its king and army.

In Prussia itself, Bismarck held out an olive branch to the parliamentary opposition. Marshaling all his diplomatic skill, Bismarck asked the parliament to pass a special indemnity bill to approve after the fact all the government's spending between 1862 and 1866. Most of the liberals jumped at the chance to cooperate. For four long years, they had opposed and criticized Bismarck's "illegal" measures. Yet Bismarck, the king, and the army with its aristocratic leadership had succeeded beyond the wildest dreams of the liberal middle class. In 1866 German unity was in sight, and the people were to be allowed to participate actively in the new state.

Many liberals repented their "sins," and none repented more ardently than Hermann Baumgarten, a thoroughly decent history professor and member of the liberal opposition. In 1866 he confessed in an essay, "We thought that by agitation we could transform Germany. . . . Yet we have experienced a miracle almost without parallel. The victory of our principles would have brought us misery, whereas the defeat of our principles has brought boundless salvation."[1] The constitutional struggle was over. The German middle class was bowing respectfully before Bismarck and the monarchical authority and aristocratic superiority he represented. In the years before 1914, the values of the aristocratic Prussian army officer increasingly replaced those of the middle-class liberal in public esteem and set the social standard.[2]

## The Franco-Prussian War, 1870–1871

The final act in the drama of German unification followed quickly. Bismarck realized that a patriotic war with France would drive the south German states into his arms. The French obligingly played their part. The apparent issue—whether a distant relative of Prussia's William I (and France's Napoleon III) might become king of Spain—was only a diplomatic pretext. By 1870 the French leaders of the Second Empire, goaded by Bismarck and alarmed by their powerful new neighbor on the Rhine, had decided on a war to teach Prussia a lesson.

As soon as war against France began in 1870, Bismarck had the wholehearted support of the south German states. With other governments standing still—Bismarck's generosity to Austria in 1866 was paying big dividends—German forces under Prussian leadership decisively defeated the main French army at Sedan on September 1, 1870. Louis Napoleon himself was captured and humiliated. Three days later, French patriots in Paris proclaimed yet another French republic and vowed to continue fighting. But after five months, in January 1871, a starving Paris surrendered, and France went on to accept Bismarck's harsh peace terms. By this time, the south German states had agreed to join a new German empire. The victorious William I was proclaimed emperor of Germany in the Hall of Mirrors in the palace of Versailles. Europe had a nineteenth-century German "sun king." As in the 1866 constitution, the king of Prussia and his ministers had ultimate power in the new German Empire, and the lower house of the legislature was elected by universal male suffrage.

Bismarck and the German Empire imposed a harsh peace on France. France was forced to pay a colossal indemnity of 5 billion francs and to cede the rich eastern province of Alsace and part of Lorraine to Germany. The German general staff asserted that this annexation would enhance military security, and German nationalists claimed that the Alsacians, who spoke a German dialect as well as French, wanted to rejoin the fatherland after more than two hundred years. But both cases were weak, and revenge for France's real and imagined aggression in the past was probably the decisive factor. In any event, French men and women of all classes viewed the seizure of Alsace and Lorraine as a terrible crime. They could never forget and never forgive, and thus relations between France and Germany after 1871 were tragically poisoned.

The Franco-Prussian War, which Europeans generally saw as a test of nations in a pitiless Darwinian struggle for existence, released an enormous surge of patriotic feeling in Germany. Bismarck's genius, the invincible Prussian

**Proclaiming the German Empire, January 1871** This commemorative painting by Anton von Werner testifies to the nationalistic intoxication in Germany after the victory over France. William I of Prussia stands on a platform surrounded by princes and generals in the famous Hall of Mirrors in the palace of Versailles, while officers from all the units around a besieged Paris cheer and salute him with uplifted swords as emperor of a unified Germany. Bismarck, like a heroic white knight, stands between king and army. *(akg-images)*

army, the solidarity of king and people in a unified nation—these and similar themes were trumpeted endlessly during and after the war. The weakest of the Great Powers in 1862 (after Austria, Britain, France, and Russia), Prussia had become, with fortification by the other German states, the most powerful state in Europe in less than a decade. Most Germans were enormously proud, blissfully imagining themselves the fittest and best of the European species. Semi-authoritarian nationalism and a "new conservatism," which was based on an alliance of the propertied classes and sought the active support of the working classes, had triumphed in Germany.

## Nation Building in the United States

Closely linked to European developments in the nineteenth century, the United States experienced the full drama of separatist nationalism and bloody nation building. The "United" States was divided by slavery from its birth, as economic development in the young republic carried free and slaveholding states in very different directions. Northerners extended family farms westward and began building English-model factories in the Northeast. By 1850 an industrializing, urbanizing North was also building a system of canals and railroads and attracting most of the European immigrants. In the South, industry and cities did not develop, and newcomers avoided the region. And even though three-quarters of all Southern white families were small farmers and owned no slaves in 1850, plantation owners holding twenty or more slaves dominated the economy and the society. These profit-minded slave owners used gangs of black slaves to claim a vast new kingdom across the Deep South where cotton was king (see Map 25.3). By 1850, this kingdom produced 5 million bales a year and satisfied an apparently insatiable demand from textile mills in Europe and New England.

The rise of the cotton empire revitalized slave-based agriculture, spurred exports, and played a key role in igniting rapid U.S. economic growth. The large profits flowing from cotton also led influential Southerners to

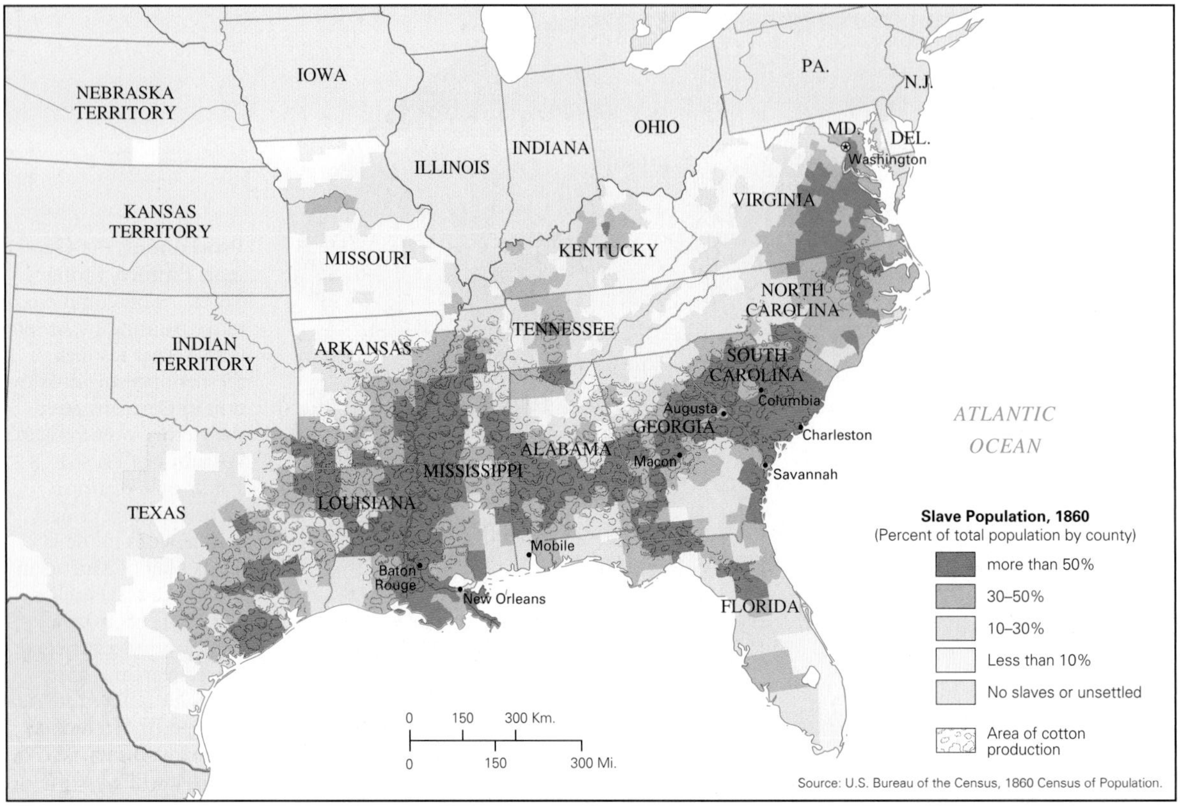


**MAP 25.3 Slavery in the United States, 1860** This map illustrates the nation on the eve of the Civil War. Although many issues contributed to the developing opposition between North and South, slavery was the fundamental, enduring force that underlay all others. Lincoln's prediction, "I believe this government cannot endure permanently half slave and half free," tragically proved correct. *(Source: Carol Berkin et al.,* Making America: A History of the United States, *2nd ed., p. 322. Copyright © 1999 by Houghton Mifflin Company. Reprinted with permission.)*

defend slavery, and Southern whites came to see themselves as a closely knit "we" distinct from the Northern "they." Northern whites viewed their free-labor system as being no less economically and morally superior. Thus regional antagonisms intensified.

These antagonisms came to a climax after 1848 when a defeated Mexico ceded to the United States a vast area stretching from west Texas to the Pacific Ocean. Debate over the extension of slavery in this new territory caused attitudes to harden on both sides. In Abraham Lincoln's famous words, the United States was a "house divided."

Lincoln's election as president in 1860 gave Southern "fire-eaters" the chance they had been waiting for. Eventually eleven states left the Union, determined to win their own independence and forming the Confederate States of America. When Southern troops fired on a Union fort in South Carolina's Charleston harbor, war began.

The long Civil War (1861–1865) was the bloodiest conflict in all of American history, but in the end the South was decisively defeated and the Union preserved. The vastly superior population, industry, and transportation of the North placed the South at a great, probably fatal, disadvantage. The enormous gap between the slave-owning elite and the poor whites also made it impossible for the South to build effectively on the patriotism of 1861. As the war ground on, many ordinary whites felt that the burden of war was falling mainly on their shoulders. Desertions from Southern armies mounted rapidly from 1863 on as soldiers became disillusioned.

In the North, by contrast, many people prospered during the war years. Enthusiasm remained high, and certain dominant characteristics of American life and national culture took shape. Powerful business corporations emerged, steadfastly supported by the Republican party during and after the war. The **Homestead Act** of 1862, which gave western land to settlers, and the Thirteenth Amendment of 1865, which ended slavery, reinforced the concept of free labor taking its chances in a market economy. Finally, the success of Lincoln and the North in holding the Union together seemed to confirm that the "manifest destiny" of the United States was indeed to straddle a continent as a great world power. Thus a new American nationalism grew out of the war aimed at preventing Southern nationhood.

Northern victory also led to a "national" policy of sorts toward American blacks. Congress at first guaranteed the legal freedom of blacks, but Northern whites lost interest in continued sectional struggle, and Southern whites regained control of the state governments. Moreover, freed blacks were generally forced to continue laboring for white landowners in the unfair arrangement called sharecropping. Thus as a result of war and reunification, the life of blacks in the Southern states moved much closer to that of the small number of blacks in the North, who had long been free but unequal citizens.

## The Modernization of Russia

Russia also experienced a profound midcentury crisis of nation building. This crisis was unlike those occurring in Italy and Germany, for Russia had no need to build a single state out of a jumble of principalities. The Russian empire was already an enormous multinational state that contained all the ethnic Russians and many other nationalities as well. Thus Russia's rulers saw national self-determination as a subversive ideology in the early nineteenth century, and they tried with some success to limit its development among their non-Russian subjects.

Then, after 1853, old autocratic Russia found itself in serious trouble. It became clear to Russia's leaders that the country had to embrace the process of **modernization,** defined narrowly and usefully as the changes that enable a country to compete effectively with the leading countries at a given time. This limited conception of modernization fits Russia after the Crimean War particularly well.

### The "Great Reforms"

In the 1850s, Russia was a poor agrarian society with a rapidly growing population. Industry was little developed, and almost 90 percent of the population lived on the land. Agricultural techniques were backward: the ancient open-field system reigned supreme. Serfdom was still the basic social institution. Bound to the lord on a hereditary basis, the peasant serf was little more than a slave. Individual serfs and serf families were regularly sold, with and without land, in the early nineteenth century. Serfs were obliged to furnish labor services or money payments as the lord saw fit. Moreover, the lord could choose freely among the serfs for army recruits, who had to serve for twenty-five years, and he could punish a serf with deportation to Siberia. Sexual exploitation of female serfs by their lords was common.

Serfdom had become the great moral and political issue for the government by the 1840s. Then the Crimean War of 1853 to 1856, arising out of a dispute with France over who should protect certain Christian shrines in the Ottoman Empire, brought crisis. Because the fighting was concentrated in the Crimean peninsula on the Black Sea, Russia's transportation network of rivers and wagons failed to supply the distant Russian armies adequately. France and Great Britain, aided by Sardinia and the Ottoman Empire, inflicted a humiliating defeat on Russia.

This military defeat marked a turning point in Russian history because it demonstrated that Russia had fallen behind the rapidly industrializing nations of western Europe in many areas. At the very least, Russia needed railroads, better armaments, and reorganization of the army if it was to maintain its international position. Moreover, the disastrous war had caused hardship and raised the specter of massive peasant rebellion. Reform of serfdom was imperative. And as the new tsar, Alexander II (r. 1855–1881), told the serf owners, it would be better if reform came from above. Military disaster thus forced Alexander II and his ministers along the path of rapid social change and general modernization.

The first and greatest of the reforms was the freeing of the serfs in 1861. Human bondage was abolished forever, and the emancipated peasants received, on average, about half of the land. Yet they had to pay fairly high prices for their land, and because the land was owned collectively, each peasant village was jointly responsible for the payments of all the families in the village. The government hoped that collective responsibility would strengthen the peasant village as a social unit and prevent the development of a class of landless peasants. In practice, collective ownership and responsibility made it very difficult for individual peasants to improve agricultural methods or leave their villages. Old patterns of behavior predominated, and Russia's peasant population continued to increase rapidly. Thus the effects of the reform were limited.

Most of the later reforms were also halfway measures. In 1864 the government established a new institution of local government, the **zemstvo.** Members of this local assembly were elected by a three-class system of towns, peasant villages, and noble landowners. A zemstvo executive council dealt with local problems. Russian liberals hoped that this reform would lead to an elected national parliament, but they were soon disappointed. The local zemstvo remained subordinate to the traditional bureaucracy and the local nobility. More successful was reform of the legal system, which established independent courts and equality before the law. Education and policies toward Russian Jews were also liberalized somewhat, and censorship was relaxed but not removed.

## The Industrialization of Russia

Until the twentieth century, Russia's greatest strides toward modernization were economic rather than political. Industry and transport, both so vital to the military, were transformed in two industrial surges. The first of these came after 1860. The government encouraged and subsidized private railway companies, and construction boomed. In 1860 the empire had only about 1,250 miles of railroads; by 1880 it had about 15,500 miles. The railroads enabled agricultural Russia to export grain and thus earn money for further industrialization. Industrial suburbs grew up around Moscow and St. Petersburg, and a class of modern factory workers began to take shape.

Industrial development strengthened Russia's military forces and gave rise to territorial expansion to the south and east. Imperial expansion greatly excited many ardent Russian nationalists and superpatriots, who became some of the government's most enthusiastic supporters. Industrial development also contributed mightily to the spread of Marxian thought and the transformation of the Russian revolutionary movement after 1890.

In 1881 Alexander II was assassinated by a small group of terrorists. The era of reform came to an abrupt end, for the new tsar, Alexander III (r. 1881–1894), was a de-

**The Fruits of Terrorism, 1881** In the late 1870s a small group of revolutionaries believed that killing the tsar could destroy the Russian state. Succeeding in blowing up the reforming Alexander II after several near misses, the five assassins, including one woman, were quickly caught and hung. Russia entered an era of reaction and harsh authoritarian rule. *(Illustrated London News, 1881)*

termined reactionary. Russia, and indeed all of Europe, experienced hard times economically in the 1880s. Political modernization remained frozen until 1905, but economic modernization sped forward in the massive industrial surge of the 1890s. Nationalism played a decisive role, as it had after the Crimean War. The key leader was Sergei Witte, the tough, competent minister of finance from 1892 to 1903. Inspired by the writings of Friedrich List (see pages 739–740), Witte believed that the harsh reality of industrial backwardness was threatening Russia's power and greatness.

Therefore, under Witte's leadership the government built state-owned railroads rapidly, doubling the network to thirty-five thousand miles by the end of the century. The gigantic trans-Siberian line connecting Moscow with Vladivostok on the Pacific Ocean five thousand miles away was Witte's pride. Witte established high protective tariffs to build Russian industry, and he put the country on the gold standard of the "civilized world" in order to strengthen Russian finances.

Witte's greatest innovation, however, was to use the West to catch up with the West. He aggressively encouraged foreigners to use their abundant capital and advanced technology to build great factories in backward Russia. As he told the tsar, "The inflow of foreign capital is . . . the only way by which our industry will be able to supply our country quickly with abundant and cheap products."[3] This policy was brilliantly successful, especially in southern Russia. There, in eastern Ukraine, foreign capitalists and their engineers built an enormous and very modern steel and coal industry almost from scratch in little more than a decade. By 1900 only the United States, Germany, and Great Britain were producing more steel than Russia. The Russian petroleum industry had even pulled up alongside that of the United States and was producing and refining half the world's oil. Peasants still constituted the great majority of the population, but a fiercely autocratic and independent Russia was industrializing and catching up with the advanced nations of the West.

**"Freedom!"** So reads the red "socialist" banner of this peasant woman, who appears as the symbol of radical demands in the Russian countryside in the revolution of 1905. This vibrant drawing is on the first page of a new review featuring political cartoons from the rapidly growing popular press. *(The New York Public Library/Art Resource, NY)*

## The Revolution of 1905

Catching up partly meant vigorous territorial expansion, for this was the age of Western imperialism. By 1903 Russia had established a sphere of influence in Chinese Manchuria and was casting greedy eyes on northern Korea. When the diplomatic protests of equally imperialistic Japan were ignored, the Japanese launched a surprise attack in February 1904. To the amazement of self-confident Europeans, Japan scored repeated victories, and Russia was forced in September 1905 to accept a humiliating defeat.

As is often the case, military disaster abroad brought political upheaval at home. The business and professional classes had long wanted to match economic with political modernization. Their minimal goal was to turn the last of Europe's absolutist monarchies into a liberal, representative regime. Factory workers, strategically concentrated in the large cities, had all the grievances of early industrialization and were organized in a radical and still illegal labor movement. Peasants had gained little from the era of reforms and were suffering from poverty and overpopulation. At the same time, nationalist sentiment was emerging among the empire's minorities. The politically and culturally dominant ethnic Russians were only about 45 percent of the population, and by 1900 some intellectuals among the subject nationalities were calling for self-rule and autonomy. Separatist nationalism was strongest among the Poles and Ukrainians. With the army pinned down in Manchuria, all these currents of discontent converged in the **revolution of 1905.**

The beginning of the revolution pointed up the incompetence of the government. On a Sunday in January 1905, a massive crowd of workers and their families converged peacefully on the Winter Palace in St. Petersburg to present a petition to the tsar. The workers were led by a trade-unionist priest named Father Gapon, who had been secretly supported by the police as a preferable alternative to more radical unions. Carrying icons and respectfully singing "God save the tsar," the workers did not know Nicholas II had fled the city. Suddenly troops opened fire, killing and wounding hundreds. The **Bloody Sunday** massacre turned ordinary workers against the tsar and produced a wave of general indignation.

Outlawed political parties came out into the open, and by the summer of 1905 strikes, peasant uprisings, revolts among minority nationalities, and troop mutinies were sweeping the country. The revolutionary surge culminated in October 1905 in a great paralyzing general strike, which forced the government to capitulate. The tsar issued the **October Manifesto,** which granted full civil rights and promised a popularly elected duma (parliament) with real legislative power. The manifesto split the opposition. Frightened middle-class leaders helped the government repress the uprising and survive as a constitutional monarchy.

On the eve of the opening of the first **Duma** in May 1906, the government issued the new constitution, the Fundamental Laws. The tsar retained great powers. The Duma, elected indirectly by universal male suffrage, and a largely appointive upper house could debate and pass laws, but the tsar had an absolute veto. As in Bismarck's Germany, the emperor appointed his ministers, who did not need to command a majority in the Duma.

The disappointed, predominately middle-class liberals, the largest group in the newly elected Duma, saw the Fundamental Laws as a step backward. Efforts to cooperate with the tsar's ministers soon broke down. The tsar then dismissed the Duma, only to find that a more hostile and radical opposition was elected in 1907. After three months of deadlock, the tsar dismissed the second Duma. Thereupon he and his reactionary advisers unilaterally rewrote the electoral law so as to increase greatly the weight of the propertied classes at the expense of workers, peasants, and national minorities.

The new law had the intended effect. With landowners assured half the seats in the Duma, the government secured a loyal majority in 1907 and again in 1912. Thus armed, the tough, energetic chief minister, Peter Stolypin, pushed through important agrarian reforms designed to break down collective village ownership of land and encourage the more enterprising peasants—his "wager on the strong." In 1914, Russia was partially modernized, a conservative constitutional monarchy with a peasant-based but industrializing economy.

## The Responsive National State, 1871–1914

See DBQ 9

For central and western Europe, the unification of Italy and Germany by "blood and iron" marked the end of a dramatic period of nation building. After 1871 the heartland of Europe was organized into strong national states. Only on the borders of Europe—in Ireland and Russia, in Austria-Hungary and the Balkans—did subject peoples still strive for political unity and independence. Despite national differences, European domestic politics after 1871 had a common framework, the firmly established national state. The common themes within that framework were the emergence of mass politics and growing mass loyalty toward the national state.

For good reason, ordinary people—the masses of an industrializing, urbanizing society—felt increasing loyalty to their governments. More people could vote. By 1914 universal male suffrage had become the rule rather than the exception. This development had as much psychological as political significance. Ordinary men were no longer denied the right to vote because they lacked wealth or education. They felt that they counted; they could influence the government to some extent. They were becoming "part of the system."

Women also began to demand the right to vote. The women's suffrage movement achieved its first success in the western United States, and by 1913 women could vote in twelve states. Europe, too, moved slowly in this direction. In 1914 Norway gave the vote to most women. Elsewhere, women such as the English Emmeline Pankhurst were very militant in their demands. They heckled politicians and held public demonstrations. These efforts generally failed before 1914, but they prepared the way for the triumph of the women's suffrage movement immediately after World War I.

As the right to vote spread, politicians and parties in national parliaments represented the people more responsively. The multiparty system prevailing in most countries

**"Votes for Women!"** The long-simmering campaign for women's suffrage in England came to a rapid boil after 1903, as militants took to the streets, disrupted political meetings, and tried to storm Parliament. Manhandled by the police and often jailed, some activists responded by damaging public property and going on hunger strikes in prison. This 1908 illustration shows demonstrators giving a hero's welcome to Mary Leigh, the first suffragette imprisoned for property damage after she threw rocks through the windows of the prime minister's house. *(The Art Archive)*

meant that parliamentary majorities were built on shifting coalitions of different parties, and this gave individual parties leverage to obtain benefits for their supporters. Governments also passed laws to alleviate general problems, thereby acquiring greater legitimacy and appearing more worthy of support.

There was a less positive side to building support for strong nation-states after 1871. Governments found that they could manipulate national feeling to create a sense of unity and to divert attention away from underlying class conflicts. Conservative and moderate leaders found that workers who voted socialist would rally around the flag in a diplomatic crisis or cheer when distant territory of doubtful value was seized in Africa or Asia (see Chapter 26). Therefore, after 1871 governing elites frequently used antiliberal and militaristic policies to help manage domestic conflicts, but at the expense of increasing the international tensions that erupted in 1914 in cataclysmic war and revolution (see Chapter 27).

In these same years some fanatics and demagogic political leaders also sought to build extreme nationalist movements by whipping up popular animosity toward imaginary enemies, especially the Jews. The growth of modern anti-Semitism after 1880 epitomized the most negative aspects of European nationalism before the First World War.

## The German Empire

Politics in Germany after 1871 reflected many of the general developments. The new German Empire was a federal union of Prussia and twenty-four smaller states. Much of the everyday business of government was conducted by the separate states, but there was a strong national government with a chancellor—until 1890, Bismarck—and a popularly elected lower house, called the **Reichstag.** Although Bismarck refused to be bound by a parliamentary majority, he tried nonetheless to maintain one. This situation gave the political parties opportunities. Until 1878 Bismarck relied mainly on the National Liberals, who had rallied to him after 1866. They supported legislation useful for further economic and legal unification of the country.

Less wisely, they backed Bismarck's attack on the Catholic church, the so-called **Kulturkampf,** or "struggle for civilization." Like Bismarck, the middle-class National Liberals were particularly alarmed by Pius IX's declaration of papal infallibility in 1870. That dogma seemed to ask German Catholics to put loyalty to their church above loyalty to their nation. Only in Protestant Prussia did the Kulturkampf have even limited success. Catholics throughout the country generally voted for the Catholic Center party, which blocked passage of national laws hostile to the church. Finally, in 1878 Bismarck abandoned his attack. Indeed, he and the Catholic Center party entered into an uneasy but mutually advantageous alliance. Their reasons for doing so were largely economic.

In 1873 there was a worldwide financial crash, which put European agriculture in an increasingly difficult position. Wheat prices plummeted as cheap grain poured in from the United States, Canada, and Russia, where new lands were opening up. More railroads and technical improvements in shipping cut freight rates for grain drastically. European peasants, with their smaller, less efficient farms, could not compete in cereal production, especially in western and southern Germany. The peasantry there was largely Catholic, and the Catholic Center party was thus converted to higher tariffs to protect the economic interests of its supporters.

The same competitive pressures caused the Protestant Junkers, who owned large estates in eastern Germany, to embrace the cause of higher tariffs. These noble landowners were joined by some of the iron and steel magnates of the Prussian Rhineland and Westphalia who had previously favored free trade. With three such influential groups lobbying energetically, Bismarck was happy to go along with a new protective tariff in 1879. In doing so, he won new supporters in the Reichstag—the Center party of the Catholics and the Conservative party of the Prussian landowners—and he held on to most of the National Liberals.

Bismarck had been looking for a way to increase taxes, and the solution he chose was higher tariffs. Many other governments acted similarly. The 1880s and 1890s saw a widespread return to protectionism. France, in particular, established very high tariffs to protect agriculture and industry, peasants and manufacturers, from foreign competition. Thus the German government and other governments responded effectively to a major economic problem and won greater loyalty. The general rise of protectionism in this period was also an outstanding example of the dangers of self-centered nationalism: new tariffs led to international name-calling and nasty trade wars.

As for socialism, Bismarck tried to stop its growth in Germany because he genuinely feared its revolutionary language and allegiance to a movement transcending the nation-state. In 1878, after two attempts on the life of William I by radicals (though not socialists), Bismarck used a carefully orchestrated national outcry to ram through the Reichstag a law that strictly controlled socialist meetings and publications and outlawed the Social Democratic party, which was thereby driven underground. However, German socialists displayed a discipline and organization worthy of the Prussian army itself. Bismarck decided to try another tack.

Thus Bismarck's essentially conservative nation-state pioneered with social measures designed to win the support of working-class people. In 1883 he pushed through the Reichstag the first of several modern social security laws to help wage earners. The laws of 1883 and 1884 established national sickness and accident insurance; the law of 1889 established old-age pensions and retirement benefits. Henceforth sick, injured, and retired workers could look forward to some regular benefits from the state. This national social security system, paid for through compulsory contributions by wage earners and employers as well as grants from the state, was the first of its kind anywhere. Bismarck's social security system did not wean workers from voting socialist, but it did give them a small stake in the system and protect them from some of the uncertainties of the complex urban industrial world. This enormously significant development was a product of political competition and government efforts to win popular support.

Increasingly, the great issues in German domestic politics were socialism and the Marxian Social Democratic party. In 1890 the new emperor, the young, idealistic, and unstable William II (r. 1888–1918), opposed Bismarck's attempt to renew the law outlawing the Social Democratic party. Eager to rule in his own right and to earn the support of the workers, William II forced Bismarck to resign. After the "dropping of the pilot," German foreign policy changed profoundly and mostly for the worse, but the government did pass new laws to aid workers and to legalize socialist political activity.

Yet William II was no more successful than Bismarck in getting workers to renounce socialism. Indeed, socialist ideas spread rapidly, and more and more Social Democrats were elected to the Reichstag in the 1890s. After opposing a colonial war in German Southwest Africa in 1906 that led to important losses in the general elections of 1907, the German Social Democratic party broadened its base and adopted a more patriotic tone. In 1912 the party scored a great electoral victory, becoming the largest single party in the Reichstag. This victory shocked aristocrats and their wealthy conservative middle-class allies, heightening the fears of an impending socialist upheaval in both groups. Yet the "revolutionary" socialists were actually becoming less radical in Germany. In the years before World War I, the strength of socialist opposition to greater military spending and imperialist expansion declined substantially, for example. German socialists identified increasingly with the German state, and they concentrated on gradual social and political reform.

## Republican France

Although Napoleon III's reign made some progress in reducing antagonisms between classes, the war with Prussia undid these efforts, and in 1871 France seemed hopelessly divided once again. The patriotic republicans who proclaimed the Third Republic in Paris after the military disaster at Sedan refused to admit defeat. They defended Paris with great heroism for weeks, living off rats and zoo animals until they were starved into submission by German armies in January 1871. When national elections then sent a large majority of conservatives and monarchists to the National Assembly and France's new leaders decided they had no choice but to surrender Alsace and Lorraine to Germany, the traumatized Parisians exploded in patriotic frustration and proclaimed the Paris Commune in March 1871. Vaguely radical, the leaders of the Commune wanted to govern Paris without interference from the conservative French countryside. The National Assembly, led by aging politician Adolphe Thiers, would hear none of it. The Assembly ordered the French army into Paris and brutally crushed the Commune. Twenty thousand people died in the fighting. As in June 1848, it was Paris against the provinces, French against French.

Out of this tragedy, France slowly formed a new national unity, achieving considerable stability before 1914. How is one to account for this? Luck played a part. Until 1875 the monarchists in the "republican" National Assembly had a majority but could not agree who should be king. The compromise Bourbon candidate refused to rule except under the white flag of his ancestors—a completely unacceptable condition. In the meantime, Thiers's destruction of the radical Commune and his other firm measures showed the fearful provinces and the middle class that the Third Republic might be moderate and socially conservative. France therefore retained the republic, though reluctantly. As President Thiers cautiously said, this was "the government which divides us least."

Another stabilizing factor was the skill and determination of the moderate republican leaders in the early years. The most famous of these was Léon Gambetta, the son of an Italian grocer, a warm, easygoing, unsuccessful lawyer who had turned professional politician. A master of emerging mass politics, Gambetta combined eloquence with the personal touch as he preached a republic of truly equal opportunity. Gambetta was also instrumental in establishing absolute parliamentary supremacy between 1877 and 1879, when the deputies challenged Marshall MacMahon and forced the somewhat autocratic president of the republic to resign. By 1879 the great majority of members of both the upper and the lower houses of the National Assembly were republicans. Although these republicans were split among many parliamentary groups and later among several parties—a situation that led to constant coalition politics and the rapid turnover of ministers—the Third Republic had firm foundations after almost a decade.

The moderate republicans sought to preserve their creation by winning the hearts and minds of the next generation. Trade unions were fully legalized, and France acquired a colonial empire. More important, under the leadership of Jules Ferry, the moderate republicans of small towns and villages passed a series of laws between 1879 and 1886 establishing free compulsory elementary education for both girls and boys. At the same time, they greatly expanded the state system of public tax-supported schools. Thus France shared fully in the general expansion of public education, which served as a critical nation-building tool throughout the Western world in the late nineteenth century.

In France most elementary and much secondary education had traditionally been in the parochial schools of the Catholic church, which had long been hostile to republics and to much of secular life. Free compulsory elementary education in France became secular republican education. The pledge of allegiance and the national anthem replaced the catechism and the "Ave Maria." Young male and female teachers carried the ideology of patriotic republicanism into every corner of France and sought to win the loyalty of the young citizens to the republic.

Unlike most Western countries, which insisted on the total "purity" of their female teachers and would not hire married women, the Third Republic actively encouraged young teachers to marry and guaranteed that both partners would teach in the same location. There were three main reasons for this unusual policy. First, married female (and male) teachers with their own children provided a vivid contrast to celibate nuns (and priests), who had for generations stood for most primary education in the popular mind. Second, the republican leaders believed that married women (and men) would better cope with the potential loneliness and social isolation of unfamiliar towns and villages, especially where the local Catholic school was strong. Third, French politicians and opinion leaders worried continually about France's very low birthrate after 1870, and they believed that women combining teaching careers and motherhood would provide the country with a good example. Hiring married schoolteachers was part of an effort to create a whole new culture of universal, secular, and republican education. This illustrates a larger truth—that truly lasting political change must usually be supported by changes in the underlying culture.

Although the educational reforms of the 1880s disturbed French Catholics, many of them rallied to the republic in the 1890s. The limited acceptance of the modern world by the more liberal Pope Leo XIII (1878–1903) eased tensions between church and state. Unfortunately, the **Dreyfus affair** changed all that.

Alfred Dreyfus, a Jewish captain in the French army, was falsely accused and convicted of treason. His family never doubted his innocence and fought to reopen the case, enlisting the support of prominent republicans and intellectuals such as novelist Emile Zola. In 1898 and 1899, the case split France apart. On one side was the army, which had manufactured evidence against Dreyfus, joined by anti-Semites and most of the Catholic establishment. On the other side stood the civil libertarians and most of the more radical republicans.

**Captain Alfred Dreyfus** Leaving an 1899 reconsideration of his original court martial, Dreyfus receives an insulting "guard of dishonor" from soldiers whose backs are turned. Top army leaders were determined to brand Dreyfus as a traitor. *(Roger-Viollet/Getty Images)*

This battle, which eventually led to Dreyfus's being declared innocent, revived republican feeling against the church. Between 1901 and 1905, the government severed all ties between the state and the Catholic church after centuries of close relations. The salaries of priests and bishops were no longer paid by the government, and all churches were given to local committees of lay Catholics. Catholic schools were put on their own financially and soon lost a third of their students. The state school system's power of indoctrination was greatly strengthened. In France only the growing socialist movement, with its very different and thoroughly secular ideology, stood in opposition to patriotic, republican nationalism.

**"No Home Rule"** Posters like this one helped to foment pro-British, anti-Catholic sentiment in the northern Irish counties of Ulster before the First World War. The rifle raised defiantly and the accompanying rhyme are a thinly veiled threat of armed rebellion and civil war. *(Reproduced with the kind permission of the Trustees of the National Museums & Galleries of Northern Ireland)*

## Great Britain and Ireland

Britain in the late nineteenth century has often been seen as a shining example of peaceful and successful political evolution. Germany was stuck with a manipulated parliament that gave an irresponsible emperor too much power; France had a quarrelsome parliament that gave its presidents too little power. Great Britain, in contrast, seemed to enjoy an effective two-party parliament that skillfully guided the country from classical liberalism to full-fledged democracy with hardly a misstep.

This view of Great Britain is not so much wrong as it is incomplete. After the right to vote was granted to males of the solid middle class in 1832, opinion leaders and politicians wrestled with the uncertainties of a further expansion of the franchise. In his famous essay *On Liberty,* published in 1859, philosopher John Stuart Mill (1806–1873), the leading heir to the Benthamite tradition (see page 791), probed the problem of how to protect the rights of individuals and minorities in the emerging age of mass electoral participation. Mill pleaded eloquently for the practical and moral value inherent in safeguarding individual differences and unpopular opinions. In 1867 Benjamin Disraeli and the Conservatives extended the vote to all middle-class males and the best-paid workers. The son of a Jewish stockbroker and himself a novelist and urban dandy, the ever-fascinating Disraeli (1804–1881) was willing to risk this "leap in the dark" in order to broaden the Conservative party's traditional base of aristocratic and landed support. After 1867 English political parties and electoral campaigns became more modern, and the "lower orders" appeared to vote as responsibly as their "betters." Hence the Third Reform Bill of 1884 gave the vote to almost every adult male.

While the House of Commons was drifting toward democracy, the House of Lords was content to slumber nobly. Between 1901 and 1910, however, that bastion of aristocratic conservatism tried to reassert itself. Acting as supreme court of the land, it ruled against labor unions in two important decisions. And after the Liberal party came to power in 1906, the Lords vetoed several measures passed by the Commons, including the so-called **People's Budget,** which was designed to increase spending on social welfare services. The Lords finally capitulated, as they had done in 1832, when the king threatened to create enough new peers to pass the bill.

Aristocratic conservatism yielded to popular democracy once and for all. The result was that extensive social welfare measures, slow to come to Great Britain, were passed in a spectacular rush between 1906 and 1914. During those years, the Liberal party, inspired by the fiery Welshman David Lloyd George (1863–1945), substantially raised taxes on the rich as part of the People's Budget. This income helped the government pay for national health insurance, unemployment benefits, old-age pensions, and a host of other social measures. The state was integrating the urban masses socially as well as politically.

This record of accomplishment was only part of the story, however. On the eve of World War I, the unanswered question of Ireland brought Great Britain to the brink of civil war. The terrible Irish famine fueled an Irish revolutionary movement. Thereafter, the English slowly granted concessions, such as the abolition of the privileges of the Anglican church and rights for Irish peasants. Liberal prime minister William Gladstone (1809–1898), who had proclaimed twenty years earlier that "my mission is to pacify Ireland," introduced bills to give Ireland self-government in 1886 and in 1893. They failed to pass. After two decades of relative quiet, Irish nationalists in the British Parliament saw their chance. They supported the Liberals in their battle for the People's Budget and received a home-rule bill for Ireland in return.

Thus Ireland, the emerald isle, was on the brink of achieving self-government. Yet Ireland was composed of two peoples. As much as the Irish Catholic majority in the southern counties wanted home rule, precisely that much did the Irish Protestants of the northern counties of Ulster come to oppose it. Motivated by the accumulated fears and hostilities of generations, the Protestants of Ulster refused to submerge themselves in a Catholic Ireland, just as Irish Catholics had refused to submit to a Protestant Britain.

The Ulsterites vowed to resist home rule in northern Ireland. By December 1913 they had raised 100,000 armed volunteers, and they were supported by much of English public opinion. Thus in 1914 the Liberals in the House of Lords introduced a compromise home-rule bill that did not apply to the northern counties. This bill, which openly betrayed promises made to Irish nationalists, was rejected, and in September the original home-rule bill was passed but simultaneously suspended for the duration of the hostilities—the momentous Irish question had been overtaken by an earth-shattering world war in August 1914.

Irish developments illustrated once again the power of national feeling and national movements in the nineteenth century. Moreover, they were proof that governments could not elicit greater loyalty unless they could capture and control that elemental current of national feeling. Though Great Britain had much going for it—power, Parliament, prosperity—none of these availed in the face of the conflicting nationalisms created by Catholics and Protestants in northern Ireland. Similarly, progressive Sweden was powerless to stop the growth of the Norwegian national movement, which culminated in Norway's breaking away from Sweden and becoming a fully independent nation in 1905. In this light, one can also see how hopeless was the case of the Ottoman Empire in Europe in the later nineteenth century. It was only a matter of time before the Serbs, Bulgarians, and Romanians would break away, and they did.

## The Austro-Hungarian Empire

The dilemma of conflicting nationalisms in Ireland also helps one appreciate how desperate the situation in the Austro-Hungarian Empire had become by the early twentieth century. In 1849 Magyar nationalism had driven Hungarian patriots to declare an independent Hungarian republic, which was savagely crushed by Russian and Austrian armies (see page 780). Throughout the 1850s, Hungary was ruled as a conquered territory, and Emperor Francis Joseph and his bureaucracy tried hard to centralize the state and Germanize the language and culture of the different nationalities.

Then in the wake of defeat by Prussia in 1866, a weakened Austria was forced to strike a compromise and establish the so-called dual monarchy. The empire was divided in two, and the nationalistic Magyars gained virtual independence for Hungary. Henceforth each half of the empire agreed to deal with its own "barbarians"—its own minorities—as it saw fit. The two states were joined only by a shared monarch and common ministries for finance, defense, and foreign affairs.

In Austria ethnic Germans were only one-third of the population, and in 1895 many Germans saw their traditional dominance threatened by Czechs, Poles, and other Slavs. A particularly emotional issue in the Austrian parliament was the language used in government and elementary education at the local level. From 1900 to 1914 the parliament was so divided that ministries generally could not obtain a majority and ruled instead by decree. Efforts by both conservatives and socialists to defuse national antagonisms by stressing economic issues that cut across ethnic lines were largely unsuccessful.

In Hungary the Magyar nobility in 1867 restored the constitution of 1848 and used it to dominate both the Magyar peasantry and the minority populations until

**The Language Ordinances of 1897** The ordinances, which were intended to satisfy the Czechs by establishing equality between German and the local language in non-German districts of Austria, produced a powerful backlash among Germans. This wood engraving shows troops dispersing German protesters of the new law before the parliament building. *(Österreichische Nationalbibliothek)*

1914. Only the wealthiest one-fourth of adult males had the right to vote, making the parliament the creature of the Magyar elite. Laws promoting the use of the Magyar (Hungarian) language in schools and government were rammed through and bitterly resented, especially by the Croatians and Romanians. While Magyar extremists campaigned loudly for total separation from Austria, the radical leaders of the subject nationalities dreamed in turn of independence from Hungary. Unlike most major countries, which harnessed nationalism to strengthen the state after 1871, the Austro-Hungarian Empire was progressively weakened and destroyed by it.

## Jewish Emancipation and Modern Anti-Semitism

Revolutionary changes in political principles and the triumph of the nation-state brought equally revolutionary changes in Jewish life in western and central Europe. Beginning in France in 1791, Jews gradually gained their civil rights, although the process was slow and uneven. The decisive turning point came in 1848, when Jews formed part of the revolutionary vanguard in Vienna and Berlin and the Frankfurt Assembly endorsed full rights for German Jews. Important gains in 1848 survived the conservative reaction, and throughout the 1850s and 1860s liberals in Austria, Italy, and Prussia pressed successfully for legal equality. In 1871 the constitution of the new German Empire consolidated the process of Jewish emancipation in central Europe. It abolished all restrictions on Jewish marriage, choice of occupation, place of residence, and property ownership. Exclusion from government employment and discrimination in social relations remained. However, according to one leading historian, by 1871 "it was widely accepted in Central Europe that the gradual disappearance of anti-Jewish prejudice was inevitable."[4]

The process of emancipation presented Jews with challenges and opportunities. Traditional Jewish occupations, such as court financial agent, village moneylender, and peddler, were undermined by free-market reforms, but careers in business, the professions, and the arts were opening to Jewish talent. Many Jews responded energetically and successfully. Active in finance and railroad building, European Jews excelled in wholesale and retail trade, consumer industries, journalism, medicine, and law. By 1871 a majority of Jewish people in western and central Europe had improved their economic situation and entered the middle classes. Most Jewish people also identified strongly with their respective nation-states and with good reason saw themselves as patriotic citizens.

Vicious anti-Semitism reappeared after the stock market crash of 1873, beginning in central Europe. Drawing on long traditions of religious intolerance, ghetto exclusion, and periodic anti-Jewish riots and expulsions, this anti-Semitism was also a modern development. It built on the general reaction against liberalism and its economic and political policies. Modern anti-Semitism whipped up resentment against Jewish achievement and Jewish "financial control," while fanatics claimed that the Jewish race (rather than the Jewish religion) posed a biological threat to the German people. Anti-Semitic beliefs were particularly popular among conservatives, extremist nationalists, and people who felt threatened by Jewish competition, such as small shopkeepers, officeworkers, and professionals.

Anti-Semites also created modern political parties to attack and degrade Jews. In 1893, the prewar electoral high point in Germany, small anti-Semitic parties secured 2.9 percent of the votes cast. However, in Austrian Vienna in the early 1890s, Karl Lueger and his "Christian socialists" won striking electoral victories, spurring Theodor Herzl to turn from German nationalism and advocate political **Zionism** and the creation of a Jewish state. (See the feature "Individuals in Society: Theodor Herzl.") Lueger, the popular mayor of Vienna from 1897 to 1910, combined fierce anti-Semitic rhetoric with municipal ownership of basic services, and he appealed especially to the German-speaking lower middle class—and an unsuccessful young artist named Adolf Hitler.

Before 1914 anti-Semitism was most oppressive in eastern Europe, where Jews also suffered from terrible poverty. In the Russian empire, where there was no Jewish emancipation and 4 million of Europe's 7 million Jewish people lived in 1880, officials used anti-Semitism to channel popular discontent away from the government and onto the Jewish minority. Russian Jews were denounced as foreign exploiters who corrupted national traditions, and in 1881–1882 a wave of violent pogroms commenced in southern Russia. The police and the army stood aside for days while peasants looted and destroyed Jewish property. Official harassment continued in the following decades, and quotas were placed on Jewish residency, education, and participation in the professions. As a result, some Russian Jews turned toward self-emancipation and the vision of a Zionist settlement in Palestine. Large numbers also emigrated to western Europe and the United States. About 2.75 million Jews left eastern Europe between 1881 and 1914.

## Marxism and the Socialist Movement

Nationalism served, for better or worse, as a new unifying principle. But what about socialism? Did the rapid growth of socialist parties, which were generally Marxian parties dedicated to an international proletarian revolution, mean that national states had failed to gain the support of workers? Certainly, many prosperous and conservative citizens were greatly troubled by the socialist movement. And numerous historians have portrayed the years before 1914 as a time of increasing conflict between revolutionary socialism, on the one hand, and a nationalist alliance of the conservative aristocracy and the prosperous middle class, on the other. This question requires close examination.

### The Socialist International

Socialism appealed to large numbers of workingmen and workingwomen in the late nineteenth century, and the growth of socialist parties after 1871 was phenomenal. (See the feature "Listening to the Past: The Making of a Socialist" on pages 852–853.) Neither Bismarck's antisocialist laws nor his extensive social security system checked the growth of the German Social Democratic party, which espoused the Marxian ideology. By 1912 it had millions of followers and was the largest party in the Reichstag. Socialist parties also grew in other countries, though nowhere else with such success. In 1883 Russian exiles in Switzerland founded the Russian Social Democratic party, which grew rapidly after 1890 despite internal disputes. In France various socialist parties re-emerged in the 1880s after the carnage of the Paris Commune. They were finally unified in 1905 in an increasingly powerful Marxian party called the French Section of the Workers International. Belgium and Austria-Hungary also had strong socialist parties.

As the name of the French party suggests, Marxian socialist parties were eventually linked together in an international organization. As early as 1848, Marx had laid out his intellectual system in *The Communist Manifesto* (see pages 765–766). He had declared that "the working men have no country," and he had urged proletarians of all nations to unite against their governments. Joining the flood of radicals and republicans who fled continental Europe for England and America after the unsuccessful revolutions of 1848, Marx settled in London. Poor

# Individuals in Society

## Theodor Herzl

In September 1897, only days after his vision and energy had called into being the First Zionist Congress in Basel, Switzerland, Theodor Herzl (1860–1904) assessed the results in his diary: "If I were to sum up the Congress in a word—which I shall take care not to publish—it would be this: At Basel I founded the Jewish state. If I said this out loud today I would be greeted by universal laughter. In five years perhaps, and certainly in fifty years, everyone will perceive it."* Herzl's buoyant optimism, which so often carried him forward, was prophetic. Leading the Zionist movement until his death at age forty-four in 1904, Herzl guided the first historic steps toward modern Jewish political nationhood and the creation of Israel in 1948.

Theodor Herzl was born in Budapest, Hungary, into an upper-middle-class, German-speaking Jewish family. When Herzl was eighteen, his family moved to Vienna, where he studied law. As a university student, he soaked up the liberal beliefs of most well-to-do Viennese Jews, who also championed the assimilation of German culture. Wrestling with his nonreligious Jewishness and his strong pro-German feeling, Herzl embraced German nationalism and joined a German dueling fraternity. There he discovered that full acceptance required openly anti-Semitic attitudes and a repudiation of all things Jewish. This Herzl could not tolerate, and he resigned. After receiving his law degree, he embarked on a literary career. In 1889 Herzl married into a wealthy Viennese Jewish family, but he and his socialite wife were mismatched and never happy together.

Herzl achieved considerable success as both a journalist and a playwright. His witty comedies focused on the bourgeoisie, including Jewish millionaires trying to live like aristocrats. Accepting many German stereotypes, Herzl sometimes depicted eastern Jews as uneducated and grasping. But as a dedicated, highly educated liberal, he mainly believed that the Jewish shortcomings he perceived were the results of age-old persecution and would disappear through education and assimilation. Herzl also took a growing pride in Jewish steadfastness in the face of victimization and suffering. He savored memories of his early Jewish education and going with his father to the synagogue.

The emergence of modern anti-Semitism shocked Herzl, as it did many acculturated Jewish Germans. Moving to Paris in 1891 as the correspondent for Vienna's leading liberal newspaper, Herzl studied politics and pondered recent historical developments. He then came to a bold conclusion, published in 1896 as *The Jewish State: An Attempt at a Modern Solution to the Jewish Question.* According to Herzl, Jewish assimilation had failed, and attempts to combat anti-Semitism would never succeed. Only by building an independent Jewish state could the Jewish people achieve dignity and renewal. As recent scholarship shows, Herzl developed his political nationalism, or Zionism, before the anti-Jewish agitation accompanying the Dreyfus affair, which only strengthened his faith in his analysis.

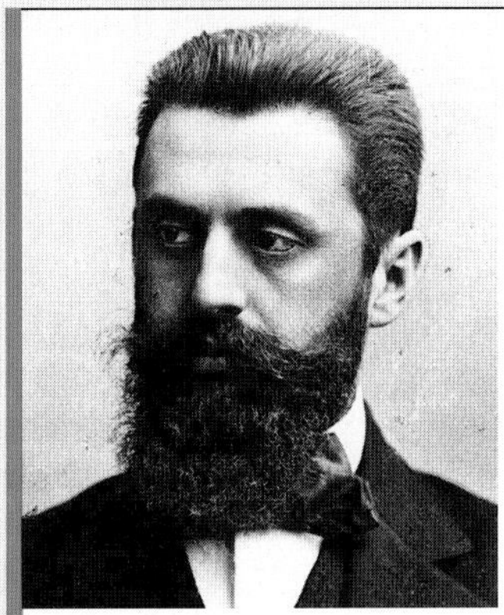

*Theodor Herzl, ca 1900.* (akg-images)

Generally rebuffed by skeptical Jewish elites in western and central Europe, Herzl turned for support to youthful idealists and the poor Jewish masses. He became an inspiring man of action, rallying the delegates to the annual Zionist congresses, directing the growth of the worldwide Zionist organization, and working himself to death. Herzl also understood that national consciousness required powerful emotions and symbols, such as a Jewish flag. Flags build nations, he said, because people "live and die for a flag."

Putting the Zionist vision before non-Jews and world public opinion, Herzl believed in international diplomacy and political agreements. He traveled constantly to negotiate with European rulers and top officials, seeking their support in securing territory for a Jewish state, usually in the Ottoman Empire. Aptly described by an admiring contemporary as "the first Jewish statesman since the destruction of Jerusalem," Herzl proved most successful in Britain. He paved the way for the 1917 Balfour Declaration, which solemnly pledged British support for a "Jewish homeland" in Palestine.

### Questions for Analysis

1. Describe Theodor Herzl's background and early beliefs. Do you see a link between Herzl's early German nationalism and his later Zionism?
2. How did Herzl work as a leader to turn his Zionist vision into a reality?

*Quotes are from Theodor Herzl, *The Diaries of Theodor Herzl,* trans. and ed. with an introduction by Marvin Lowenthal (New York: Grosset & Dunlap, 1962), pp. 224, 22, xxi.

*The* **history companion** *features additional information and activities related to this topic.*
**history.college.hmco.com/students**

**"Greetings from the May Day Festival"** Workers participated enthusiastically in the annual one-day strike on May 1 to honor internationalist socialist solidarity, as this postcard from a happy woman visitor to her cousin suggests. Speeches, picnics, and parades were the order of the day, and workers celebrated their respectability and independent culture. Picture postcards developed with railroads and mass travel. *(AKG London)*

and depressed, he lived on his meager earnings as a journalist and on the gifts of his friend Friedrich Engels. Marx never stopped thinking of revolution. Digging deeply into economics and history, he concluded that revolution follows economic crisis and tried to prove this in his greatest theoretical work, *Capital* (1867).

The bookish Marx also excelled as a practical organizer. In 1864 he played an important role in founding the First International of socialists—the International Working Men's Association. In the following years, he battled successfully to control the organization and used its annual meetings as a means of spreading his realistic, "scientific" doctrines of inevitable socialist revolution. Then Marx enthusiastically embraced the passionate, vaguely radical patriotism of the Paris Commune and its terrible conflict with the French National Assembly as a giant step toward socialist revolution. This impetuous action frightened many of his early supporters, especially the more moderate British labor leaders. The First International collapsed.

Yet international proletarian solidarity remained an important objective for Marxists. In 1889, as the individual parties in different countries grew stronger, socialist leaders came together to form the Second International, which lasted until 1914. The International was only a federation of national socialist parties, but it had a great psychological impact. Every three years, delegates from the different parties met to interpret Marxian doctrines and plan coordinated action. May 1 (May Day) was declared an annual international one-day strike, a day of marches and demonstrations. A permanent executive for the International was established. Many feared and many others rejoiced in the growing power of socialism and the Second International.

## Unions and Revisionism

Was socialism really radical and revolutionary in these years? On the whole, it was not. Indeed, as socialist parties grew and attracted large numbers of members, they looked more and more toward gradual change and steady improvement for the working class and less and less toward revolution. The mainstream of European socialism became militantly moderate; that is, socialists increasingly combined radical rhetoric with sober action.

Workers themselves were progressively less inclined to follow radical programs. There were several reasons for this. As workers gained the right to vote and to participate politically in the nation-state, they focused their attention more on elections than on revolutions. And as workers won real, tangible benefits, this furthered the process. Workers were also not immune to patriotic education and indoctrination during military service, and many responded positively to drum-beating parades and aggressive foreign policy as they loyally voted for socialists. Nor were workers a unified social group.

Perhaps most important of all, workers' standard of living rose gradually but substantially after 1850 as the promise of the Industrial Revolution was at least partially realized. In Great Britain, for example, workers could buy almost twice as much with their wages in 1906 as in 1850, and most of the increase came after 1870. Workers experienced similar gradual increases in most continental countries after 1850, though much less strikingly in late-developing Russia. Improvement in the standard of living was much more than merely a matter of higher wages. The quality of life improved dramatically in urban areas. For all these reasons, workers tended more and more to become militantly moderate: they demanded gains, but they were less likely to take to the barricades in pursuit of them.

The growth of labor unions reinforced this trend toward moderation. In the early stages of industrialization, modern unions were generally prohibited by law. A famous law of the French Revolution had declared all guilds and unions illegal in the name of "liberty" in 1791. In Great Britain, attempts by workers to unite were considered criminal conspiracies after 1799. Other countries had similar laws, and these obviously hampered union development. In France, for example, about two hundred workers were imprisoned each year between 1825 and 1847 for taking part in illegal combinations. Unions were considered subversive bodies, only to be hounded and crushed.

From this sad position workers struggled to escape. Great Britain led the way in 1824 and 1825 when unions won the right to exist but (generally) not the right to strike. After the collapse of Robert Owen's attempt to form one big union in the 1830s (see page 749), new and more practical kinds of unions appeared. Limited primarily to highly skilled workers such as machinists and carpenters, the "new model unions" avoided both radical politics and costly strikes. Instead, their sober, respectable leaders concentrated on winning better wages and hours for their members through collective bargaining and compromise. This approach helped pave the way to full acceptance in Britain in the 1870s, when unions won the right to strike without being held legally liable for the financial damage inflicted on employers. After 1890 unions for unskilled workers developed, and between 1901 and 1906 the legal position of British unions was further strengthened.

Germany was the most industrialized, socialized, and unionized continental country by 1914. German unions were not granted important rights until 1869, and until the antisocialist law was repealed in 1890, they were frequently harassed by the government as socialist fronts. Nor were socialist leaders particularly interested in union activity, believing as they did in the iron law of low wages and the need for political revolution. The result was that as late as 1895, there were only about 270,000 union members in a male industrial workforce of nearly 8 million. Then, with German industrialization still storming ahead and almost all legal harassment eliminated, union membership skyrocketed, reaching roughly 3 million in 1912.

This great expansion both reflected and influenced the changing character of German unions. Increasingly, unions in Germany focused on bread-and-butter issues—wages, hours, working conditions—rather than on the dissemination of pure socialist doctrine. Genuine collective bargaining, long opposed by socialist intellectuals as a "sellout," was officially recognized as desirable by the German Trade Union Congress in 1899. When employers proved unwilling to bargain, a series of strikes forced them to change their minds.

Between 1906 and 1913, successful collective bargaining gained a prominent place in German industrial relations. In 1913 alone, over ten thousand collective bargaining agreements affecting 1.25 million workers were signed. Gradual improvement, not revolution, was becoming the primary goal of the German trade-union movement.

The German trade unions and their leaders were in fact, if not in name, thoroughgoing revisionists. **Revisionism**—that most awful of sins in the eyes of militant Marxists in the twentieth century—was an effort by various socialists to update Marxian doctrines to reflect the realities of the time. Thus the socialist Edward Bernstein (1850–1932) argued in 1899 in his *Evolutionary Socialism* that Marx's predictions of ever-greater poverty for workers and ever-greater concentration of wealth in ever-fewer hands had been proved false. Therefore, Bernstein suggested, socialists should reform their doctrines and tactics. They should combine with other progressive forces to win gradual evolutionary gains for workers through legislation, unions, and further economic development. These views were denounced as heresy by the German Social Democratic party and later by the entire Second International. Yet the revisionist, gradualist approach continued to gain the tacit acceptance of many German socialists, particularly in the trade unions.

Moderation found followers elsewhere. In France the great socialist leader Jean Jaurès (1859–1914) formally repudiated revisionist doctrines in order to establish a unified socialist party, but he remained at heart a gradualist and optimistic secular humanist. Questions of revolution split Russian Marxists.

Socialist parties before 1914 had clear-cut national characteristics. Russians and socialists in the Austro-Hungarian Empire tended to be the most radical. The German party talked revolution and practiced reformism, greatly influenced by its enormous trade-union movement. The French party talked revolution and tried to practice it, unrestrained by a trade-union movement that was both very weak and very radical. In England the socialist but non-Marxian Labour party, reflecting the well-established union movement, was formally committed to gradual reform. In Spain and Italy, Marxian socialism was very weak. There anarchism, seeking to smash the state rather than the bourgeoisie, dominated radical thought and action.

In short, socialist policies and doctrines varied from country to country. Socialism itself was to a large extent "nationalized" behind the imposing façade of international unity. This helps explain why when war came in 1914, almost all socialist leaders supported their governments.

## Summary

From the mid-nineteenth century on, Western society became nationalistic as well as urban and industrial. Nation-states gradually enlisted widespread popular support and gave men and women a greater sense of belonging. Even socialism became increasingly national in orientation, gathering strength as a champion of working-class interests in domestic politics. Yet even though nationalism served to unite peoples, it also drove them apart—obvious not only in the United States before the Civil War and in Austria-Hungary and Ireland, but also throughout Europe. There the universal national faith, which usually reduced social tensions within states, promoted a bitter, almost Darwinian, competition between states and thus threatened the progress and unity it had helped to build.

## Key Terms

Red Shirts
Zollverein
Homestead Act
modernization
zemstvo
revolution of 1905
Bloody Sunday
October Manifesto
Duma
Reichstag
Kulturkampf
Dreyfus affair
People's Budget
Zionism
revisionism

## Notes

1. Quoted in H. Kohn, *The Mind of Germany: The Education of a Nation* (New York: Charles Scribner's Sons/Macmillan, 1960), p. 159.
2. H. Schulze, *States, Nations and Nationalism: From the Middle Ages to the Present* (Oxford: Blackwell, 1994), pp. 222–223, 246–247.
3. Quoted in J. McKay, *Pioneers for Profit: Foreign Entrepreneurship and Russian Industrialization, 1885–1913* (Chicago: University of Chicago Press, 1970), p. 11.
4. R. Seltzer, *Jewish People, Jewish Thought: The Jewish Experience in History* (New York: Macmillan, 1980), p. 533.

## Suggested Reading

In addition to the general works mentioned in the Suggested Reading for Chapter 23, R. Gildea, *Barricades and Borders: Europe, 1800–1914,* 2d ed. (1996), and T. Blanning, *The Cambridge Illustrated History of Europe* (1996), provide useful surveys of the entire nineteenth century. E. Hobsbawm, *The Age of Empire, 1875–1914* (1987), and B. Moore, *Social Origins of Dictatorship and Democracy* (1966), remain outstanding interpretative works.

R. Tombs, *France, 1814–1914* (1996), is an impressive recent survey with an up-to-date bibliography, and R. Anderson, *France, 1870–1914* (1977), provides a clear introduction. K. Marx, *The Eighteenth Brumaire of Louis Napoleon,* is a famous denunciation of the coup d'état, and D. Harvey, *Paris, Capital of Modernity* (2004), is handsomely illustrated and captures the spirit of the great city in the late nineteenth century. G. Gullickson, *Unruly Women of Paris: Images of the Commune* (1996), is an exciting portrait of contested images of radical women in the Paris Commune, and E. Accampo, R. Fuchs, and M. Stewart, *Gender and the Politics of Social Reform in*

*France, 1870–1914* (1995), shows how views of women influenced social legislation. E. Weber, *Peasants into Frenchmen* (1976), stresses the role of education and modern communications in the transformation of rural France after 1870. E. Cahm, *The Dreyfus Affair in French Society and Politics* (1996), and G. Chapman, *The Dreyfus Case: A Reassessment* (1955), are careful examinations of the famous case. In *Jean Barois,* Nobel Prize winner Roger Du Gard accurately re-creates in novel form the Dreyfus affair, and Emile Zola's novel *The Debacle* treats the Franco-Prussian War realistically.

The resurgence of European nationalism since the fall of communism has led to important new studies; particularly recommended are H. Schulze, *States, Nations and Nationalism: From the Middle Ages to the Present* (1996), and R. Brubaker, *Citizenship and Nationhood in France and Germany* (1992). D. M. Smith has written widely on Italy, and his *Mazzini* (1994) is an engaging biography. R. Ridley, *Garibaldi* (2001), is a thorough study of the world-renowned revolutionary nationalist. In addition to the classic study on Germany by O. Pflanze, *Bismarck and the Development in Germany: The Period of Unification, 1815–1871* (1963), see D. Williamson, *Bismarck and Germany, 1862–1890* (1994), and A. Green, *Fatherlands: State-Building and Nationhood in Nineteenth-Century Germany* (2001), a superb comparative history of the German states after 1815. H. Wehler, *The German Empire, 1871–1918* (1985), stresses the strength of the landed nobility and the weakness of the middle class in an influential synthesis, which is challenged by D. Blackbourn and G. Eley, *The Peculiarities of German History: Bourgeois Society and Politics in Nineteenth-Century Germany* (1984). M. Kitchen, *The Cambridge Illustrated History of Germany* (1996), features handsome pictures and a readable text. F. Stern, *Gold and Iron* (1977), is a fascinating examination of relations between Bismarck and his financial adviser, the Jewish banker Bleichröder. L. Cecil, *Wilhelm II: Prince and Emperor, 1859–1900* (1989), probes the character and politics of Germany's ruler. K. McAleer, *Dueling: The Cult of Honor in Fin-de-Siècle Germany* (1994), and E. Spencer, *Management and Labor in Imperial Germany: Ruhr Industrialists as Employers* (1984), are valuable in-depth investigations. H. Glasser, ed., *The German Mind in the Nineteenth Century* (1981), is an outstanding anthology, as are R. E. Joeres and M. Maynes, eds., *German Women in the Eighteenth and Nineteenth Centuries* (1986), and P. Mendes-Flohr, ed., *The Jew in the Modern World: A Documentary History* (1980). D. Vital, *A People Apart: The Jews in Europe, 1789–1939* (1999), is an engaging and judicious survey. C. Schorske, *Fin de Siècle Vienna: Politics and Culture* (1980), and P. Gay, *Freud, Jews, and Other Germans* (1978), are brilliant on aspects of modern culture. I. Berend, *History Derailed: Central and Eastern Europe in the Long Nineteenth Century* (2003), focuses on industrialization and consequences, and A. Sked, *The Decline and Fall of the Habsburg Empire, 1815–1918,* 2d ed. (2001), highlights the nationality problem in Austria-Hungary. Southern nationalism in the United States has been interpreted from different perspectives by P. Escott, *After Secession: Jefferson Davis and the Failure of Confederate Nationalism* (1974), and D. Faust, *The Creation of Confederate Nationalism* (1988). E. Foner, *A Short History of Reconstruction* (1989), is recommended.

In addition to the fundamental study on Russian industrial development by T. von Laue, *Sergei Witte and the Industrialization of Russia* (1963), McKay cited in the Notes, P. Gatrell, *The Tsarist Economy, 1850–1917* (1986), and A. Rieber, *Merchants and Entrepreneurs in Imperial Russia* (1982), are recommended. Among fine studies on Russian development, see especially H. Rogger, *Russia in the Age of Modernization and Revolution, 1881–1917* (1983), which has an excellent bibliography; T. Emmons, *The Russian Landed Gentry and the Peasant Emancipation of 1861* (1968); and H. Troyat, *Daily Life in Russia Under the Last Tsar* (1962). T. Friedgut, *Iuzovka and Revolution: Life and Work in Russia's Donbass, 1869–1924* (1989), and R. Johnson, *Peasant and Proletarian: The Working Class of Moscow at the End of the Nineteenth Century* (1979), skillfully treat different aspects of working-class life and politics. T. Clyman and J. Vowles, eds., *Russia Through Women's Eyes: Autobiographies from Tsarist Russia* (1996), is an exciting collection. A. Asher, *P. A. Stolypin: The Search for Political Stability in Late Imperial Russia* (2001), is a sympathetic biography of tsarist Russia's last great statesman. A. Geifman, *Thou Shalt Kill: Revolutionary Terrorism in Russia* (1993), probes the politics of violence in a pioneering study. J. Le Donne, *The Russian Empire and the World, 1700–1917: The Geopolitics of Expansion and Containment* (1996), is an important reconsideration of Russian foreign affairs.

G. Dangerfield, *The Strange Death of Liberal England* (1961), brilliantly examines social tensions in Ireland as well as Englishwomen's struggle for the vote before 1914. P. Gurney, *Co-operative Culture and the Politics of Consumption in England, 1870–1930* (1996), breaks new ground and is recommended. D. Boyce, *Nationalism in Ireland,* 2d ed. (1991), provides an excellent account of the Irish struggle for nationhood. The theme of aristocratic strength and survival is expanded in A. Mayer's provocative *Persistence of the Old Regime: Europe to the Great War* (1981). J. Seigel, *Marx's Fate: The Shape of a Life* (1978), is an outstanding biography. G. Steenson, *Not One Man! Not One Penny!: German Social Democracy, 1863–1913* (1999), is an up-to-date survey, while C. Schorske, *German Social Democracy, 1905–1917* (1955), is a modern classic. V. Lidtke, *The Alternative Culture: Socialist Labor in Imperial Germany* (1985), and J. Quataert, *Reluctant Feminists in German Social Democracy, 1885–1917* (1979), are also recommended for the study of the German socialists. H. Goldberg, *The Life of Jean Jaurès* (1962), is a sympathetic account of the great French socialist leader. Two excellent collections by specialists are L. Berlanstein, ed., *Rethinking Labor History* (1993), and D. Geary, ed., *Labour and Socialist Movements in Europe Before 1914* (1989), which examines several different countries.

# Listening to the Past

## The Making of a Socialist

*Nationalism and socialism appeared locked in bitter competition in Europe before 1914, but they actually complemented each other in many ways. Both faiths were secular as opposed to religious, and both fostered political awareness. A working person who became interested in politics and developed nationalist beliefs might well convert to socialism at a later date.*

*This was the case for Adelheid Popp (1869–1939), a self-taught workingwoman who became an influential socialist leader. Born into a desperately poor working-class family in Vienna and remembering only a "hard and gloomy childhood," she was forced by her parents to quit school at age ten to begin full-time work. She struggled with low-paying piecework for years before she landed a solid factory job, as she recounts in the following selection from her widely read autobiography.*

*Always an avid reader, Popp became the editor of a major socialist newspaper for German workingwomen. She then told her life story so that all workingwomen might share her truth: "Socialism could change and strengthen others, as it did me."*

[Finally] I found work again; I took everything that was offered me in order to show my willingness to work, and I passed through much. But at last things became better. [At age fifteen] I was recommended to a great factory which stood in the best repute. Three hundred girls and about fifty men were employed. I was put in a big room where sixty women and girls were at work. Against the windows stood twelve tables, and at each sat four girls. We had to sort the goods which had been manufactured, others had to count them, and a third set had to brand on them the mark of the firm. We worked from 7 A.M. to 7 P.M. We had an hour's rest at noon, half-an-hour in the afternoon. . . . I had never yet been paid so much. . . .

I seemed to myself to be almost rich. . . . [Yet] from the women of this factory one can judge how sad and full of deprivation is the lot of a factory worker. In none of the neighbouring factories were the wages so high; we were envied everywhere. Parents considered themselves fortunate if they could get their daughters of fourteen in there on leaving school. . . . And even here, in this paradise, all were badly nourished. Those who stayed at the factory for the dinner hour would buy themselves for a few pennies a sausage or the leavings of a cheese shop. . . . In spite of all the diligence and economy, every one was poor, and trembled at the thought of losing her work. All humbled themselves, and suffered the worst injustice from the foremen, not to risk losing this good work, not to be without food. . . .

I did not only read novels and tales; I had begun . . . to read the classics and other good books. I also began to take an interest in public events. . . . I was not democratically inclined. I was full of enthusiasm then for emperors, and kings and highly placed personages played no small part in my fancies. . . . I bought myself a strict Catholic paper, that criticised very adversely the workers' movement, which was attracting notice. Its aim was to educate in a patriotic and religious direction. . . . I took the warmest interest in the events that occurred in the royal families, and I took the death of the Crown Prince of Austria so much to heart that I wept a whole day. . . . Political events [also] held me in suspense. The possibility of a war with Russia roused my patriotic enthusiasm. I saw my brother already returning from the battlefield covered with glory. . . .

When a particularly strong anti-Semitic feeling was noticeable in political life, I sympathised with it for a time. A broad sheet, "How Israel Attained Power and Sovereignty over all the Nations of the Earth," fascinated me. . . .

About this time an Anarchist group was active. Some mysterious murders which had taken place were ascribed to the Anarchists, and the police made use of them to oppress the rising workmen's movement. . . . I followed the trial of the Anarchists with passionate sympathy. I read all the speeches, and because, as always happens, Social Democrats, whom the authorities really wanted to attack, were among the accused, I learned their views. I became full of enthusiasm. Every single Social Democrat . . . seemed to me a hero. . . .

There was unrest among the workers . . . and demonstrations of protest followed. When these were repeated the military entered the "threatened" streets. . . . In the evenings I rushed in the greatest excitement from the factory to the scene of the disturbance. The military did not frighten me; I only left the place when it was "cleared."

Later on my mother and I lived with one of my brothers who had married. Friends came to him, among them some intelligent workmen. One of these workmen was particularly intelligent, and . . . could talk on many subjects. He was the first Social Democrat I knew. He brought me many books, and explained to me the difference between Anarchism and Socialism. I heard from him, also for the first time, what a republic was, and in spite of my former enthusiasm for royal dynasties, I also declared myself in favour of a republican form of government. I saw everything so near and so clearly, that I actually counted the weeks which must still elapse before the revolution of state and society would take place.

From this workman I received the first Social Democratic party organ. . . . I first learned from it to understand and judge of my own lot. I learned to see that all I had suffered was the result not of a divine ordinance, but of an unjust organization of society. . . .

In the factory I became another woman. . . . I told my [female] comrades all that I had read of the workers' movement. Formerly I had often told stories when they had begged me for them. But instead of narrating . . . the fate of some queen, I now held forth on oppression and exploitation. I told of accumulated wealth in the hands of a few, and introduced as a contrast the shoemakers who had no shoes and the tailors who had no clothes. On breaks I read aloud the articles in the Social Democratic paper and explained what Socialism was as far as I understood it. . . . [While I was reading] it often happened that one of the clerks passing by shook his head and said to another clerk: "The girl speaks like a man."

1890 engraving of a meeting of workers in Berlin. *(Bildarchiv Preussischer Kulturbesitz/Art Resource, NY)*

## Questions for Analysis

1. How did Popp describe and interpret work in the factory?
2. To what extent did her socialist interpretation of factory life fit the facts she described?
3. What were Popp's political interests before she became a socialist?
4. How and why did she become a Social Democrat?
5. Was this account likely to lead other workingwomen to socialism? Why or why not?

*Source:* Slightly adapted from A. Popp, *The Autobiography of a Working Woman,* trans. E. C. Harvey (Chicago: F. G. Browne, 1913), pp. 29, 34–35, 39, 66–69, 71, 74, 82–90.

Africans in Madagascar transport a French diplomat in 1894, shortly before France annexed the island. *(Snark/Art Resource, NY)*

chapter

# 26 The West and the World

## chapter outline



While industrialization and nationalism were transforming urban life and Western society, Western society itself was reshaping the world. At the peak of its power and pride, the West entered the third and most dynamic phase of the aggressive expansion that had begun with the Crusades and continued with the great discoveries and the rise of seaborne colonial empires. An ever-growing stream of products, people, and ideas flowed out of Europe in the nineteenth century. Hardly any corner of the globe was left untouched. The most spectacular manifestations of Western expansion came in the late nineteenth century when the leading European nations established or enlarged their far-flung political empires. The political annexation of territory in the 1880s—the "new imperialism," as it is often called by historians—was the capstone of a profound underlying economic and technological process.

- How and why did this many-sided, epoch-making expansion occur in the nineteenth century?
- What were some of its consequences for the West?
- How did Western expansion affect the rest of the world?

These are the questions this chapter will examine.

## Industrialization and the World Economy

The Industrial Revolution created, first in Great Britain and then in continental Europe and North America, a growing and tremendously dynamic economic system. In the course of the nineteenth century, that system was extended across the face of the earth. Some of this extension into non-Western areas was peaceful and beneficial for all concerned, for the West had many products and techniques the rest of the world desired. If peaceful methods failed, however, Europeans did not stand on ceremony. They used their superior military power to force non-Western nations to open their doors to Western economic interests. In general, Westerners fashioned the global economic system so that the largest share of the ever-increasing gains from trade, technology, and migration flowed to the West and its propertied classes.

## The Rise of Global Inequality

The Industrial Revolution in Europe marked a momentous turning point in human history. Indeed, only by placing Europe's economic breakthrough in a global perspective can one truly appreciate its revolutionary implications and consequences.

From such a global perspective, the ultimate significance of the Industrial Revolution was that it allowed those regions of the world that industrialized in the nineteenth century to increase their wealth and power enormously in comparison to those that did not. As a result, a gap between the industrializing regions (mainly Europe and North America) and the nonindustrializing ones (mainly Africa, Asia, and Latin America) opened up and grew steadily throughout the nineteenth century. Moreover, this pattern of uneven global development became institutionalized, or built into the structure of the world economy. Thus we evolved a "lopsided world," a world of rich lands and poor.

In recent years historical economists have begun to chart the long-term evolution of this gap with some precision. Figure 26.1 summarizes the important findings of one such study. It compares the long-term evolution of average income per person in today's "developed" (or industrialized) regions—defined as Europe, North America, and Japan—with that found in Africa, Asia, and Latin America, also often known as the **Third World.** To get these individual income figures, researchers estimate a country's gross national product (GNP) at different points in time, convert those estimates to some common currency, and divide by the total population.

**FIGURE 26.1 The Growth of Average Income per Person in the Third World, Developed Countries, and Great Britain, 1750–1970** Growth is given in 1960 U.S. dollars and prices. *(Source: P. Bairoch and M. Lévy-Leboyer, eds.,* Disparities in Economic Development Since the Industrial Revolution. *Copyright © 1981. Reprinted by permission of Palgrave Macmillan, UK.)*

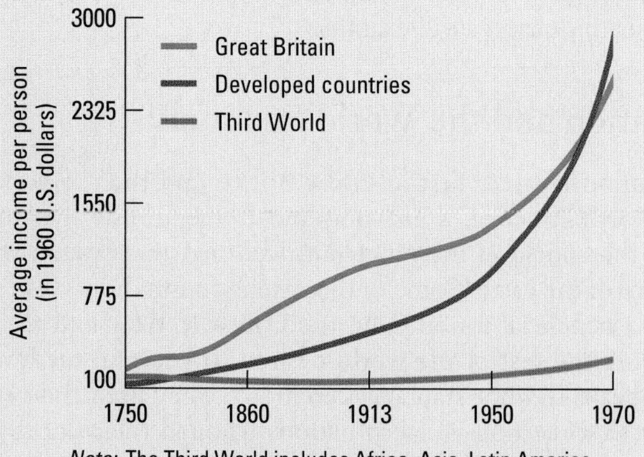


*Note:* The Third World includes Africa, Asia, Latin America, and Oceania. Developed countries include all European countries, Canada, the United States, and Japan.

Figure 26.1 highlights three main points. First, in 1750 the average standard of living was no higher in Europe as a whole than in the rest of the world. In 1750 Europe was still a poor agricultural society. By 1970, however, the average person in the wealthiest countries had an income fully twenty-five times as great as that received by the average person in the poorest countries of Africa and Asia.

Second, it was industrialization that opened the gaps in average wealth and well-being among countries and regions. One sees that Great Britain had jumped well above the European average by 1830, when the first industrial nation was well in advance of its continental competitors. One also sees how Great Britain's lead gradually narrowed as other European countries and the United States successfully industrialized in the course of the nineteenth century.

Third, income per person stagnated in the Third World before 1913, in striking contrast to the industrializing regions. Only after 1945, in the era of political independence and decolonization, did Third World countries finally make some real economic progress, beginning in their turn the critical process of industrialization.

The rise of these enormous income disparities, which are poignant indicators of equal disparities in food and clothing, health and education, life expectancy and general material well-being, has generated a great deal of debate. One school of interpretation stresses that the West used science, technology, capitalist organization, and even its critical world-view to create its wealth and greater physical well-being. Another school argues that the West used its political and economic power to steal much of its riches, continuing in the nineteenth (and twentieth) century the rapacious colonialism born of the era of expansion.

These issues are complex, and there are few simple answers. As noted in Chapter 22, the wealth-creating potential of technological improvement and more intensive capitalist organization was indeed great. At the same time, those breakthroughs rested, in part, on Great Britain's having already used political force to dominate part of the world economy by the late eighteenth century. In the nineteenth century other industrializing countries joined with Britain to extend Western domination over the entire world economy. Wealth—unprecedented wealth—was indeed created, but the lion's share of that new wealth flowed to the West and its propertied classes.

1850 | 1865 | 1880 | 1895 | 1910

**POLITICAL/MILITARY**

- 1863–1879 Reign of Ismail in Egypt
- 1865–1909 Reign of Leopold II in Belgium
- 1867 Meiji Restoration in Japan
- 1898 United States takes over Philippines
- 1898 "Hundred days of reform" in China

**SOCIAL/ECONOMIC**

- 1853 Perry "opens" Japan for trade
- 1869 Completion of Suez Canal

**INTELLECTUAL/RELIGIOUS**

- 1899 Kipling, "The White Man's Burden"
- 1902 Conrad, *Heart of Darkness*
- 1902 Hobson, *Imperialism*

## The World Market

Commerce between nations has always been a powerful stimulus to economic development. Never was this more true than in the nineteenth century, when world trade grew prodigiously. In 1913 the value of world trade was roughly $38 billion, or about *twenty-five* times what it had been in 1800, even though prices of both manufactured goods and raw materials were lower in 1913 than in 1800. In a general way, the enormous increase in international commerce summed up the growth of an interlocking world economy centered in and directed by Europe.

Great Britain played a key role in using trade to tie the world together economically. In 1815 Britain already had a colonial empire, for India, Canada, Australia, and other scattered areas remained British possessions after American independence. The technological breakthroughs of the Industrial Revolution allowed Britain to manufacture cotton textiles, iron, and other goods more cheaply and to far outstrip domestic demand for such products. Thus British manufacturers sought export markets first in Europe and then around the world.

Take the case of cotton textiles. By 1820 Britain was exporting 50 percent of its production. Europe bought 50 percent of these cotton textile exports, while India bought only 6 percent. Then as European nations and the United States erected protective tariff barriers and promoted domestic industry, British cotton textile manufacturers aggressively sought and found other foreign markets in non-Western areas. By 1850 India was buying 25 percent and Europe only 16 percent of a much larger total. As a British colony, India could not raise tariffs to protect its ancient cotton textile industry, and thousands of Indian weavers lost their livelihoods.

After the repeal of the Corn Laws in 1846 (see page 773), Britain became the world's single best market. Until 1914 Britain remained the world's emporium, where not only agricultural products and raw materials but also manufactured goods entered freely. Free access to Britain's market stimulated the development of mines and plantations in many non-Western areas.

The growth of trade was facilitated by the conquest of distance. The earliest railroad construction occurred in Europe (including Russia) and in America north of the Rio Grande; other parts of the globe saw the building of rail lines after 1860. By 1920 more than one-quarter of the world's railroads were in Latin America, Asia, Africa, and Australia. Wherever railroads were built, they drastically

**British Ships and Shipbuilders** The British continued to dominate international trade before the First World War. This handsome membership certificate of the British shipbuilders union features the vessels that drew the world together and were Britain's pride. Britain's thriving shipbuilding industry was concentrated in southern Scotland along the Clyde. *(Trade Union Congress, London/The Bridgeman Art Library)*

reduced transportation costs, opened new economic opportunities, and called forth new skills and attitudes. Much of the railroad construction undertaken in Latin America, Asia, and Africa connected seaports with inland cities and regions, as opposed to linking and developing cities and regions within a given country. Thus railroads dovetailed admirably with Western economic interests, facilitating the inflow and sale of Western manufactured goods and the export and the development of local raw materials.

The power of steam revolutionized transportation by sea as well as by land. Steam power, long used to drive paddle wheelers on rivers, particularly in Russia and North America, finally began to supplant sails on the oceans of the world in the late 1860s. Lighter, stronger, cheaper steel replaced iron, which had replaced wood. Screw propellers superseded paddle wheels, while mighty compound steam engines cut fuel consumption by half. Passenger and freight rates tumbled, and the intercontinental shipment of low-priced raw materials became feasible.

An account of an actual voyage by a typical tramp freighter highlights nineteenth-century developments in global trade. The ship left England in 1910 carrying rails and general freight to western Australia. From there it carried lumber to Melbourne in southeastern Australia, where it took on harvester combines for Argentina. In Buenos Aires it loaded wheat for Calcutta, and in Calcutta it took on jute for New York. From New York it carried a variety of industrial products to Australia before returning to England with lead, wool, and wheat after a voyage of approximately seventy-two thousand miles to six continents in seventeen months.

The revolution in land and sea transportation helped European pioneers open up vast new territories and produce agricultural products and raw materials there for sale in Europe. Improved transportation enabled Asia, Africa, and Latin America to ship not only the traditional tropical products—spices, tea, sugar, coffee—but also new raw materials for industry, such as jute, rubber, cotton, and coconut oil.

Intercontinental trade was enormously facilitated by the Suez and Panama Canals. Of great importance, too, was large and continual investment in modern port facilities, which made loading and unloading cheaper, faster, and more dependable. Finally, transoceanic telegraph cables inaugurated rapid communications among the financial centers of the world. While a British tramp freighter steamed from Calcutta to New York, a broker in London was arranging by telegram for it to carry an American cargo to Australia. World commodity prices were also instantaneously conveyed by the same network of communications.

The growth of trade and the conquest of distance encouraged the expanding European economy to make massive foreign investments beginning about 1840. By the outbreak of World War I in 1914, Europeans had invested more than $40 billion abroad. Great Britain, France, and Germany were the principal investing countries, although by 1913 the United States was emerging as a substantial foreign investor. The sums involved were enormous (see Map 26.1). In the decade before 1914, Great Britain was investing 7 percent of its annual national income abroad, or slightly more than it was invest-

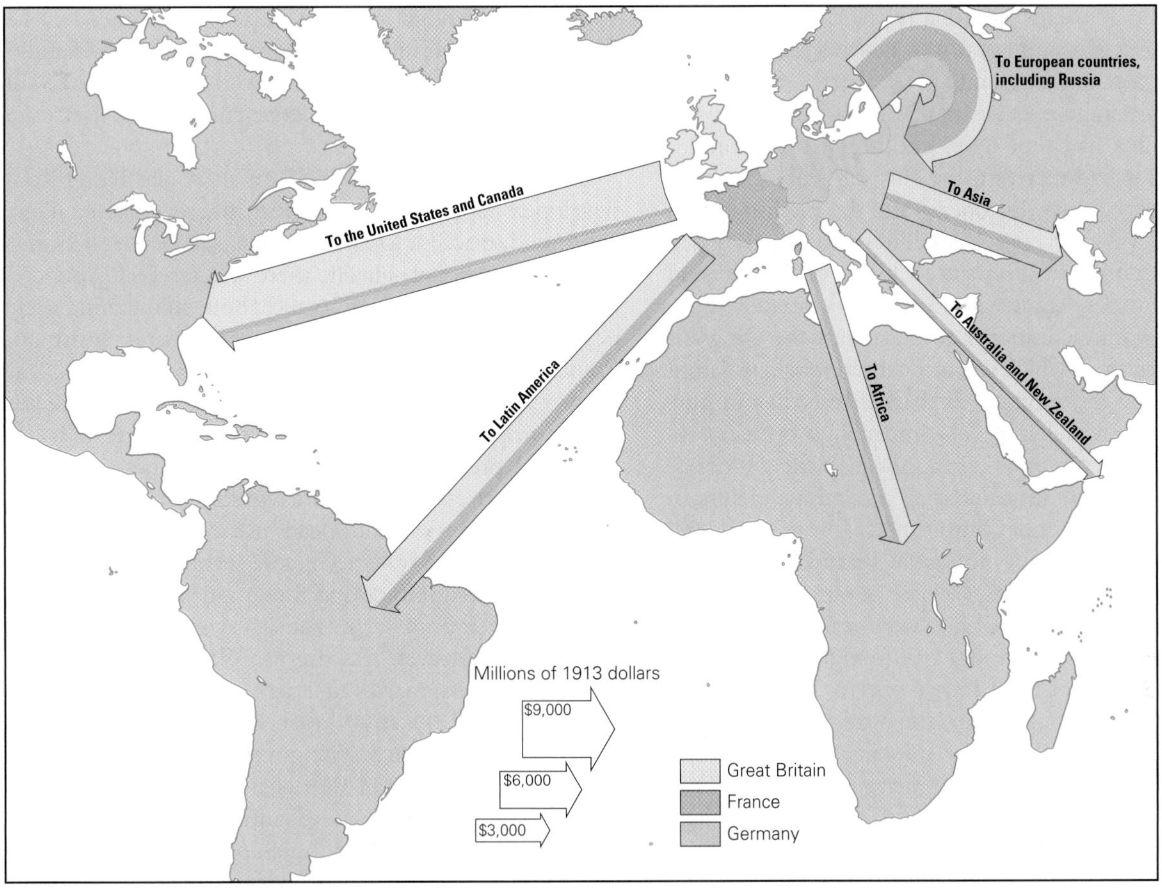


**MAP 26.1 European Investment to 1914** Foreign investment grew rapidly after 1850, and Britain, France, and Germany were the major investing nations. As this map suggests, most European investment was not directed to the African and Asian areas seized by the "new imperialism" after 1880.

ing in its entire domestic economy. The great gap between rich and poor within Europe meant that the wealthy and moderately well-to-do could and did send great sums abroad in search of interest and dividends.

Most of the capital exported did not go to European colonies or protectorates in Asia and Africa. About three-quarters of total European investment went to other European countries, the United States and Canada, Australia and New Zealand, and Latin America. Europe found its most profitable opportunities for investment in construction of the railroads, ports, and utilities that were necessary to settle and develop the almost-vacant lands in such places as Australia and the Americas. By lending money for a foreign railroad, Europeans also enabled white settlers to buy European rails and locomotives and developed sources of cheap food and raw materials. Much of this investment was peaceful and mutually beneficial for lenders and borrowers. The victims were Native American Indians and Australian aborigines, who were decimated by the diseases, liquor, and weapons of an aggressively expanding Western society.

## The Opening of China and Japan

Europe's relatively peaceful development of robust offshoots in sparsely populated North America, Australia, and much of Latin America absorbed huge quantities of goods, investments, and migrants. From a Western point of view, that was the most important aspect of Europe's global thrust. Yet Europe's economic and cultural penetration of old, densely populated civilizations was also profoundly significant, especially for the non-European peoples affected by it. With such civilizations Europeans also increased their trade and profit. Moreover, as had been the case ever since Vasco da Gama and Christopher Columbus, the expanding Western society was prepared to use force, if necessary, to attain its desires. This was what happened in China and Japan, two crucial examples of the general pattern of intrusion into non-Western lands.

Traditional Chinese civilization was self-sufficient. For centuries China had sent more goods and inventions to Europe than it had received, and this was still the case in the eighteenth century. Europeans and the English in particular had developed a taste for Chinese tea, but they had to pay for it with hard silver since China was uninterested in European wares. Trade with Europe was carefully regulated by the Chinese imperial government—the Qing (or Manchu) Dynasty—which was more interested in isolating and controlling the strange "sea barbarians" than in pursuing commercial exchange. The imperial government refused to establish diplomatic relations with the "inferior" European states, and it required all foreign merchants to live in the southern city of Canton and to buy from and sell to only the local merchant monopoly. Practices considered harmful to Chinese interests, such as the sale of opium and the export of silver from China, were strictly forbidden.

For years the little community of foreign merchants in Canton had to accept the Chinese system. By the 1820s, however, the dominant group, the British, were flexing their muscles. Moreover, in the smoking of opium—that "destructive and ensnaring vice" denounced by Chinese decrees—they had found something the Chinese really wanted. Grown legally in British-occupied India, opium was smuggled into China by means of fast ships and bribed officials. The more this rich trade developed, the greedier British merchants became. By 1836 the aggressive goal of the British merchants in Canton was an independent British colony in China and "safe and unrestricted liberty" in trade. Spurred on by economic motives, they pressured the British government to take decisive action and enlisted the support of British manufacturers with visions of vast Chinese markets to be opened.

At the same time, the Qing government decided that the **opium trade** had to be stamped out. It was ruining the people and stripping the empire of its silver, which was going to British merchants to pay for the opium. The government began to prosecute Chinese drug dealers vigorously and in 1839 sent special envoy Lin Tse-hsü to Canton. Lin Tse-hsü ordered the foreign merchants to obey China's laws, "for our great unified Manchu Empire regards itself as responsible for the habits and morals of its subjects and cannot rest content to see any of them become victims of a deadly poison."[1] The British merchants refused and were expelled, whereupon war soon broke out.

Using troops from India and being in control of the seas, the British occupied several coastal cities and forced China to surrender. In the Treaty of Nanking in 1842, the imperial government was forced to cede the island of Hong Kong to Britain forever, pay an indemnity of $100 million, and open up four large cities to foreign trade with low tariffs.

Thereafter the opium trade flourished, and Hong Kong developed rapidly as an Anglo-Chinese enclave. China continued to accept foreign diplomats in Beijing (Peking), the imperial capital. Finally, there was a second round of foreign attack between 1856 and 1860, culminating in the occupation of Beijing by seventeen thousand British and French troops and the intentional burning of the emperor's summer palace. Another round of harsh treaties gave European merchants and missionaries greater privileges and protection and forced the Chinese to accept trade and investment on unfavorable terms for several more cities. Thus did Europeans use military aggression to blow a hole in the wall of Chinese seclusion and open the country to foreign trade and foreign ideas.

China's neighbor Japan had its own highly distinctive civilization and even less use for Westerners. European traders and missionaries first arrived in Japan in the sixteenth century. By 1640 Japan had reacted quite negatively to their presence. The government decided to seal off the country from all European influences in order to preserve traditional Japanese culture and society. When American and British whaling ships began to appear off Japanese coasts almost two hundred years later, the policy of exclusion was still in effect. An order of 1825 commanded Japanese officials to "drive away foreign vessels without second thought."[2]

Japan's unbending isolation seemed hostile and barbaric to the West, particularly to the United States. It complicated the practical problems of shipwrecked American sailors and the provisioning of whaling ships and China traders sailing in the eastern Pacific. It also thwarted the hope of trade and profit. Moreover, Americans shared the self-confidence and dynamism of expanding Western society, and they felt destined to play a great role in the Pacific. To Americans it seemed the duty of the United States to force the Japanese to share their ports and behave as a "civilized" nation.

After several unsuccessful American attempts to establish commercial relations with Japan, Commodore Matthew Perry steamed into Edo (now Tokyo) Bay in 1853 and demanded diplomatic negotiations with the emperor. Japan entered a grave crisis. Some Japanese warriors urged resistance, but senior officials realized how defenseless their cities were against naval bombardment. Shocked and humiliated, they reluctantly signed a treaty

**Britain and China at War, 1841** Britain capitalized on its overwhelming naval superiority, and this British aquatint celebrates a dramatic moment in a crucial battle near Guangzhou. Having received a direct hit from a steam-powered British ironclad, a Chinese sailing ship explodes into a wall of flame. The Chinese lost eleven ships and five hundred men in the two-hour engagement; the British suffered only minor damage. *(National Maritime Museum, London)*

with the United States that opened two ports and permitted trade. Over the next five years, more treaties spelled out the rights and privileges of the Western nations and their merchants in Japan. Japan was "opened." What the British had done in China with war, the Americans had done in Japan with only the threat of war.

## Western Penetration of Egypt

Egypt's experience illustrates not only the explosive power of the expanding European economy and society but also their seductive appeal in non-Western lands. European involvement in Egypt also led to a new model of formal political control, which European powers applied widely in Africa and Asia after 1882.

Of great importance in African and Middle Eastern history, the ancient land of the pharaohs had since 525 B.C. been ruled by a succession of foreigners, most recently by the Ottoman Turks. In 1798 French armies under young General Napoleon Bonaparte invaded the Egyptian part of the Ottoman Empire and occupied the territory for three years. Into the power vacuum left by the French withdrawal stepped an extraordinary Albanian-born Turkish general, Muhammad Ali (1769–1849).

First appointed governor of Egypt by the Turkish sultan, Muhammad Ali soon disposed of his political rivals and set out to build his own state on the strength of a large, powerful army organized along European lines. He drafted for the first time the illiterate, despised peasant masses of Egypt, and he hired French and Italian army officers to train these raw recruits and their Turkish officers. The government was also reformed, new lands were cultivated, and communications were improved. By the time of his death in 1849, Muhammad Ali had established a strong and virtually independent Egyptian state, to be ruled by his family on a hereditary basis within the Turkish empire.

**The Opening of the Suez Canal** A long procession of eighty ships passed through the Suez Canal when it was opened in November 1869, and thousands of spectators lined the shores and joined in the celebrations. The building of the hundred-mile canal was a momentous event, cutting in half the length of the journey between Europe and Asia. *(Archives Charmet/The Bridgeman Art Library)*

Muhammad Ali's policies of modernization attracted large numbers of Europeans to the banks of the Nile. As one Arab sheik of the Ottoman Empire remarked in the 1830s, "Englishmen are like ants; if one finds a bit of meat, hundreds follow."[3] The port city of Alexandria had more than fifty thousand Europeans by 1864. Europeans served not only as army officers but also as engineers, doctors, government officials, and police officers. Others found their "meat" in trade, finance, and shipping.

To pay for his ambitious plans, Muhammad Ali encouraged the development of commercial agriculture. This development had profound implications. Egyptian peasants were poor but largely self-sufficient, growing food for their own consumption on state-owned lands allotted to them by tradition. Faced with the possibility of export agriculture, high-ranking officials and members of Muhammad Ali's family began carving large private landholdings out of the state domain. The new landlords made the peasants their tenants and forced them to grow cash crops geared to European markets. Thus Egyptian landowners "modernized" agriculture, but to the detriment of peasant well-being.

These trends continued under Muhammad Ali's grandson Ismail, who in 1863 began his sixteen-year rule as Egypt's **khedive,** or prince. Educated at France's leading military academy, Ismail was a westernizing autocrat. The large irrigation networks he promoted caused cotton production and exports to Europe to boom, and with his support the Suez Canal was completed by a French company in 1869. The Arabic of the masses replaced the Turkish of the conquerors as the official language. Young Egyptians educated in Europe spread new skills, and Cairo acquired modern boulevards and Western hotels. As Ismail proudly declared, "My country is no longer in Africa, we now form part of Europe."[4]

Yet Ismail was too impatient and reckless. His projects were enormously expensive, and the sale of his stock in the Suez Canal to the British government did not relieve the situation. By 1876 Egypt owed foreign bondholders a colossal debt that it could not pay. Rather than let Egypt go bankrupt and repudiate its loans, the governments of France and Great Britain intervened politically to protect the European bondholders. They forced Ismail to appoint French and British commissioners to oversee Egyptian finances so that the Egyptian debt would be paid in full. This momentous decision implied direct European political control and was a sharp break with the previous pattern of trade and investment. Throughout most of the nineteenth century, Europeans had used military might and political force primarily to make sure that non-Western lands would accept European trade and investment. Now Europeans were going to determine the state budget and effectively rule Egypt.

Foreign financial control evoked a violent nationalistic reaction among Egyptian religious leaders, young intellectuals, and army officers. In 1879, under the leadership of Colonel Ahmed Arabi, they formed the Egyptian Nationalist party. Continuing diplomatic pressure, which forced Ismail to abdicate in favor of his weak son, Tewfiq (r. 1879–1892), resulted in bloody anti-European riots in Alexandria in 1882. A number of Europeans were killed, and Tewfiq and his court had to flee to British ships for safety. When the British fleet bombarded Alexandria, more riots swept the country, and Colonel Arabi led a revolt. But a British expeditionary force put down the rebellion and occupied all of Egypt.

The British said their occupation was temporary, but British armies remained in Egypt until 1956. They maintained the façade of the khedive's government as an autonomous province of the Ottoman Empire, but the khedive was a mere puppet. British rule did result in tax reforms and somewhat better conditions for peasants, while foreign bondholders received their interest and Egyptian nationalists nursed their injured pride.

British rule in Egypt provided a new model for European expansion in densely populated lands. Such expansion was based on military force, political domination, and a self-justifying ideology of beneficial reform. This model was to predominate until 1914. Thus did Europe's Industrial Revolution lead to tremendous political as well as economic expansion throughout the world.

## The Great Migration

A poignant human drama was interwoven with economic expansion: millions of people pulled up stakes and left their ancestral lands in the course of history's greatest migration. To millions of ordinary people, for whom the opening of China and the interest on the Egyptian debt had not the slightest significance, this great movement was the central experience in the saga of Western expansion. It was, in part, because of this **great migration** that the West's impact on the world in the nineteenth century was so powerful and many-sided.

### The Pressure of Population

In the early eighteenth century, the growth of European population entered its third and decisive stage, which continued unabated until the twentieth century (see Chapter 19). Birthrates eventually declined in the nineteenth century, but so did death rates, mainly because of the rising standard of living and secondarily because of the medical revolution. Thus the population of Europe (including Asiatic Russia) more than doubled, from approximately 188 million in 1800 to roughly 432 million in 1900.

These figures actually understate Europe's population explosion, for between 1815 and 1932 more than 60 million people left Europe. These migrants went primarily to the "areas of European settlement"—North and South America, Australia, New Zealand, and Siberia—where they contributed to a rapid growth in numbers. Since population grew more slowly in Africa and Asia than in Europe and the Americas, as Figure 26.2 shows,

**FIGURE 26.2 The Increase of European and World Populations, 1750–1980** *(Sources: W. Woodruff,* Impact of Western Man: A Study of Europe's Role in the World Economy. *St. Martin's Press, New York, 1967, p. 103; United Nations,* Statistical Yearbook, 1982, *1985, pp. 2–3.)*

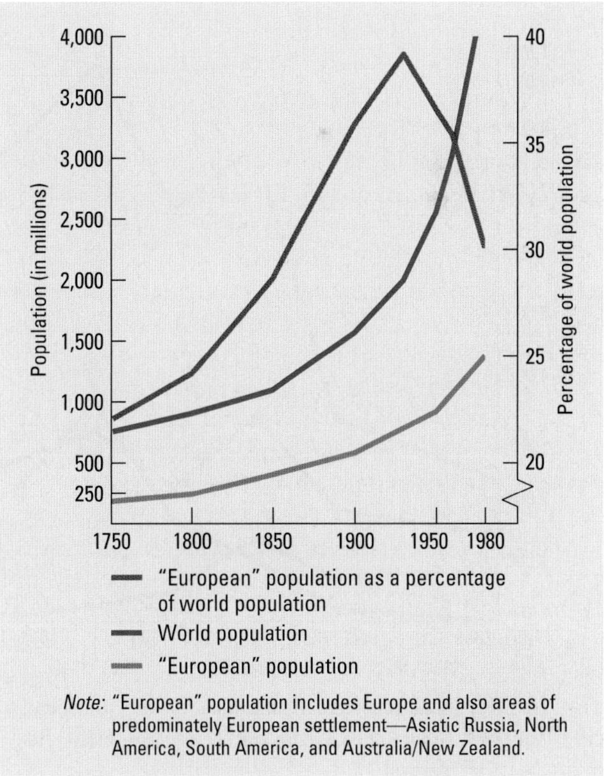

Europeans and people of predominately European origin jumped from about 22 percent of the world's total to about 38 percent on the eve of World War I.

The growing number of Europeans provided further impetus for Western expansion. It was a driving force behind emigration. As in the eighteenth century, the rapid increase in numbers put pressure on the land and led to land hunger and relative overpopulation in area after area. In most countries, migration increased twenty years after a rapid growth in population, as many children of the baby boom grew up, saw little available land and few opportunities, and migrated. This pattern was especially prevalent when rapid population increase predated extensive industrial development, which offered the best long-term hope of creating jobs within the country and reducing poverty. Thus millions of country folk went abroad as well as to nearby cities in search of work and economic opportunity.

Before looking at the people who migrated, let us consider three facts. First, the number of men and women who left Europe increased rapidly before World War I. As Figure 26.3 shows, more than 11 million left in the first decade of the twentieth century, over five times the number departing in the 1850s. The outflow of migrants was clearly an enduring characteristic of European society for the entire period.

Second, different countries had very different patterns of movement. As Figure 26.3 also shows, people left Britain and Ireland (which are not distinguished in the British figures) in large numbers from the 1840s on. This emigration reflected not only rural poverty but also the movement of skilled, industrial technicians and the preferences shown to British migrants in the British Empire. Ultimately, about one-third of all European migrants between 1840 and 1920 came from the British Isles. German migration was quite different. It grew irregularly after about 1830, reaching a first peak in the early 1850s and another in the early 1880s. Thereafter it declined rapidly, for Germany's rapid industrialization was providing adequate jobs at home. This pattern contrasted sharply with that of Italy. More and more Italians left the country right up to 1914, reflecting severe problems in Italian villages and relatively slow industrial growth. Thus migration patterns mirrored social and economic conditions in the various European countries and provinces.

Third, although the United States absorbed the largest number of European migrants, less than half of all migrants went to the United States. Asiatic Russia, Canada,

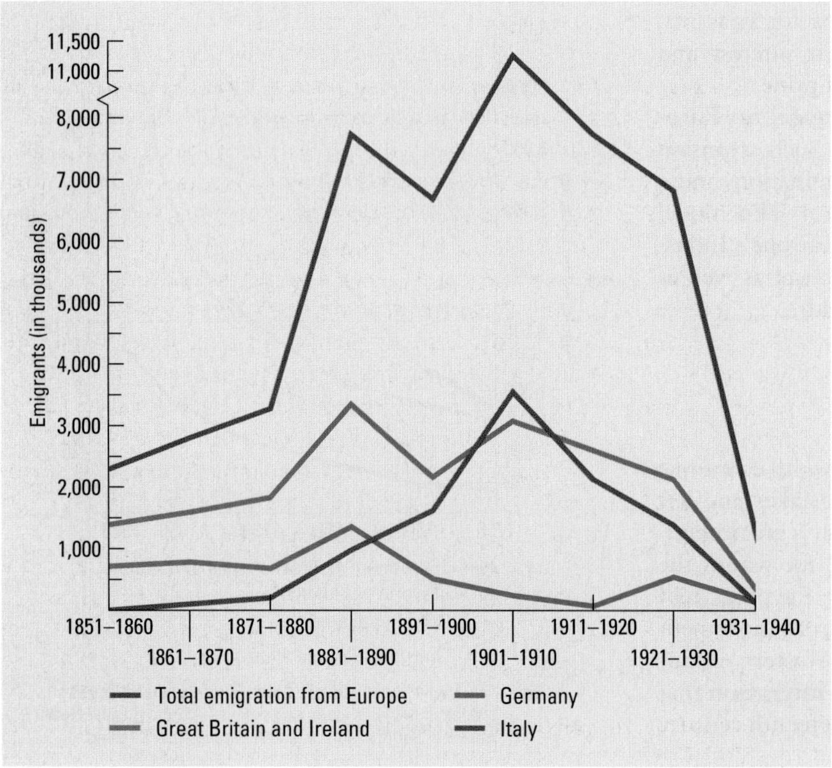


**FIGURE 26.3 Emigration from Europe by Decades, 1851–1940**
*(Source: Copyright © W. Woodruff, from* Impact of Western Man, *by W. Woodruff, 1982. Reprinted with permission of University Press of America.)*

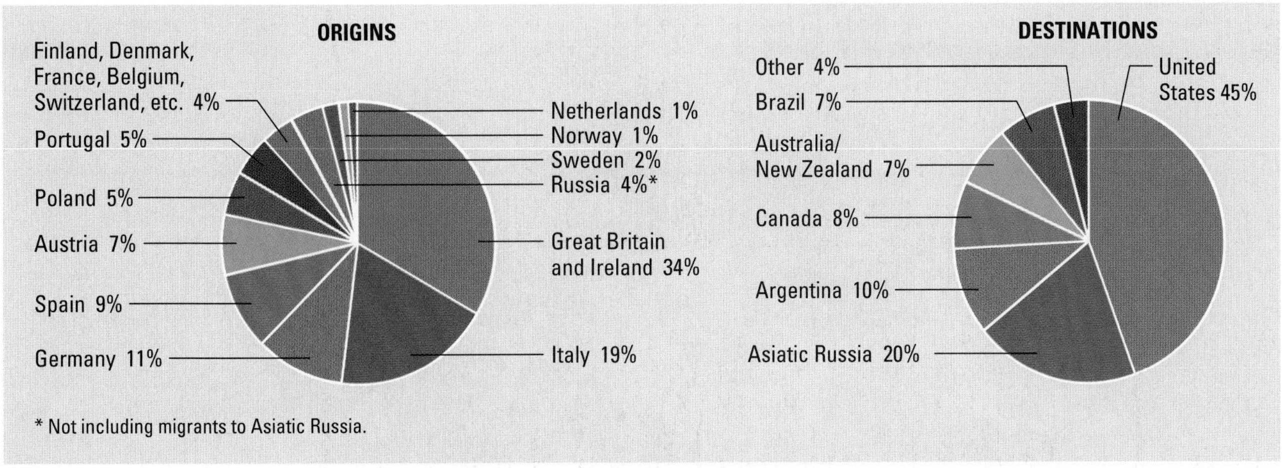


**FIGURE 26.4 Origin and Destination of European Emigrants, 1851–1960** *(Source: Copyright © W. Woodruff, from* Impact of Western Man, *by W. Woodruff, 1982. Reprinted with permission of University Press of America.)*

Argentina, Brazil, Australia, and New Zealand also attracted large numbers, as Figure 26.4 shows. Moreover, migrants accounted for a larger proportion of the total population in Argentina, Brazil, and Canada than in the United States. The common American assumption that European migration meant migration to the United States is quite inaccurate.

## European Migrants

What kind of people left Europe, and what were their reasons for doing so? The European migrant was most often a small peasant landowner or a village craftsman whose traditional way of life was threatened by too little land, estate agriculture, and cheap, factory-made goods. German peasants who left the Rhineland and southwestern Germany between 1830 and 1854, for example, felt trapped by what Friedrich List called the "dwarf economy," with its tiny landholdings and declining craft industries. Selling out and moving to buy much cheaper land in the American Midwest became a common response. Thus the European migrant was generally an energetic small farmer or skilled artisan trying hard to stay ahead of poverty, not a desperately impoverished landless peasant or urban proletarian.

Determined to maintain or improve their status, migrants were a great asset to the countries that received them. This was doubly so because the vast majority were young and very often unmarried. They came in the prime of life and were ready to work hard in the new land, at least for a time. Many Europeans moved but remained within Europe, settling temporarily or permanently in another European country. Jews from eastern Europe and peasants from Ireland migrated to Great Britain, Russians and Poles sought work in Germany, and Latin peoples from Spain, Portugal, and Italy entered France. Many Europeans were truly migrants as opposed to immigrants—that is, they returned home after some time abroad. One in two migrants to Argentina and probably one in three to the United States eventually returned to their native land.

The likelihood of repatriation varied greatly by nationality. People who migrated from the Balkans, for instance, were much more likely to return to their countries than people from Ireland and eastern European Jews. Once again, the possibility of buying land in the old country was of central importance. In Ireland (as well as in England and Scotland) land was tightly held by large, often absentee landowners, and little land was available for purchase. In Russia most land was held by non-Jews. Therefore, when Russian Jewish artisans began in the 1880s to escape both factory competition and oppression by migrating, it was basically a once-and-for-all departure. Non-Jewish migrants from Russia had access to land and returned much more frequently to their peasant villages in central Russia, Poland, and Ukraine.

The mass movement of Italians illustrates many of the characteristics of European migration. As late as the 1880s, which was for Italians, as for Russian Jews, the first decade of substantial exodus, three of every four Italians depended on agriculture. With the influx of cheap North American wheat, the long-standing problems of the Italian village became more acute. With industry failing to

**The Jewish Market, New York, 1900** The center of economic and social life in the Lower East Side was the market. Jewish immigrants could usually find work with Jewish employers, and New York's Jewish population soared from 73,000 in 1880 to 1.1 million in 1910. *(The Granger Collection, New York)*

provide enough jobs for the rapidly growing population, many small landowning peasants whose standard of living was falling began to leave their country. Migration provided them with an escape valve and possible income to buy more land. Landless laborers from areas dominated by large estates tended to stay in Italy and turned increasingly toward radical politics.

Many Italians went to the United States, but before 1900 more went to Argentina and Brazil. In Brazil the large coffee planters, faced with the collapse of black slavery, attracted Italians to their plantations with subsidized travel and promises of relatively high wages. France was also a favorite destination for Italians. In 1911 the Italian-born population of France was roughly a third as large as that in the United States.

Many Italians had no intention of settling abroad permanently. Some called themselves **swallows.** After harvesting their own wheat and flax in Italy, they "flew" to Argentina to harvest wheat between December and April. Returning to Italy for the spring planting, they repeated this exhausting process. This was a very hard life, but a frugal worker could save $250 to $300 in the course of a season.

Ties of family and friendship played a crucial role in the movement of peoples. Many people from a given province or village settled together in rural enclaves or tightly knit urban neighborhoods thousands of miles away. Very often a strong individual—a businessman, a religious leader—would blaze the way and others would follow, forming a "migration chain."

Many landless young European men and women were spurred to leave by a spirit of revolt and independence. In Sweden and in Norway, in Jewish Russia and in Italy, these young people felt frustrated by the small privileged classes, which often controlled both church and government and resisted demands for change and greater opportunity. Many a young Norwegian seconded the passionate cry of Norway's national poet, Martinius Bjørnson: "Forth will I! Forth! I will be crushed and consumed if I stay."[5]

Many young Jews wholeheartedly agreed with a spokesman of Kiev's Jewish community in 1882, who declared, "Our human dignity is being trampled upon, our wives and daughters are being dishonored, we are looted and pillaged: either we get decent human rights or else let us go wherever our eyes may lead us."[6] Thus for many, migration was a radical way to "get out from under." Migration slowed down when the people won basic political and social reforms, such as the right to vote and social security.

## Asian Migrants

Not all migration was from Europe. A substantial number of Chinese, Japanese, Indians, and Filipinos—to name only four key groups—responded to rural hardship with temporary or permanent migration. At least 3 million Asians (as opposed to more than 60 million Europeans) moved abroad before 1920. Most went as indentured laborers to work under incredibly difficult conditions on

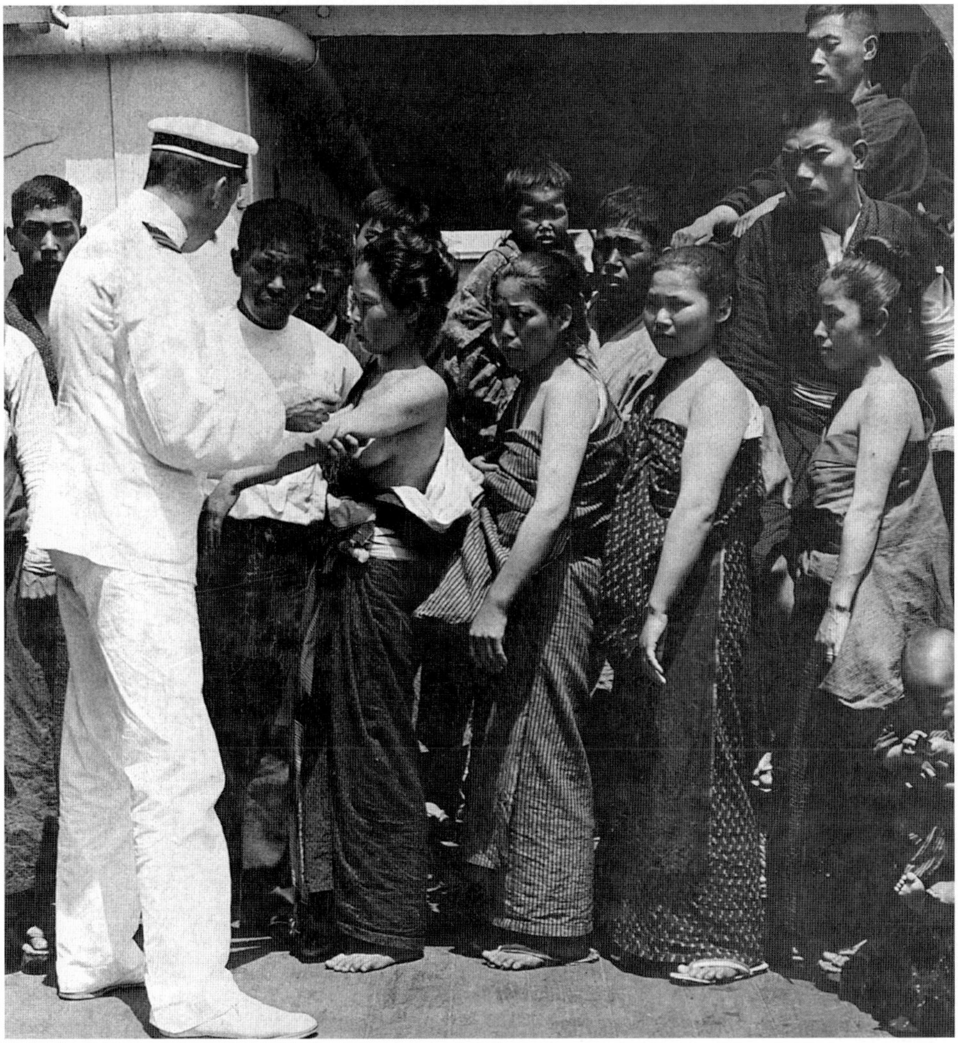

**Vaccinating Migrants Bound for Hawaii, 1904** First Chinese, then Japanese, and finally Koreans and Filipinos went in large numbers across the Pacific to labor in Hawaii on American-owned sugar plantations in the late nineteenth century. The native Hawaiians had been decimated by disease, preparing the way for the annexation of Hawaii by the United States in 1898. *(Corbis)*

**MAP 26.2 The Partition of Africa** European nations carved up Africa after 1880 and built vast political empires. What African states remained independent?

the plantations or in the gold mines of Latin America, southern Asia, Africa, California, Hawaii, and Australia. White estate owners very often used Asians to replace or supplement blacks after the suppression of the slave trade.

In the 1840s, for example, there was a strong demand for field hands in Cuba, and the Spanish government actively recruited Chinese laborers. Between 1853 and 1873, when such migration was stopped, more than 130,000 Chinese laborers went to Cuba. The majority spent their lives as virtual slaves. The great landlords of Peru also brought in more than 100,000 workers from China in the nineteenth century, and there were similar movements of Asians elsewhere.

Such migration from Asia would undoubtedly have grown to much greater proportions if planters and mine owners in search of cheap labor had been able to hire as many Asian workers as they wished. But they could not. Asians fled the plantations and gold mines as soon as possible, seeking greater opportunities in trade and towns. There they came into conflict with local populations, whether in Malaya, East Africa, or areas settled by Europeans.

These European settlers demanded a halt to Asian migration. One Australian brutally summed up the typical view: "The Chinaman knows nothing about Caucasian civilization. . . . It would be less objectionable to drive a flock of sheep to the poll than to allow Chinamen to vote."[7] By the 1880s, Americans and Australians were building **great white walls**—discriminatory laws designed to keep Asians out. Thus a final, crucial factor in the migrations before 1914 was the general policy of "whites only" in the open lands of possible permanent settlement. This, too, was part of Western dominance in the increasingly lopsided world. Largely successful in monopolizing the best overseas opportunities, Europeans and people of European ancestry reaped the main benefits from the great migration. By 1913 people in Australia, Canada, and the United States all had higher average incomes than people in Great Britain, still Europe's wealthiest nation.

# Western Imperialism

The expansion of Western society reached its apex between about 1880 and 1914. In those years, the leading European nations not only continued to send massive streams of migrants, money, and manufactured goods around the world, but also rushed to create or enlarge vast *political* empires abroad. This political empire building contrasted sharply with the economic penetration of non-Western territories between 1816 and 1880, which had left a China or a Japan "opened" but politically independent. By contrast, the empires of the late nineteenth century recalled the old European colonial empires of the seventeenth and eighteenth centuries and led contemporaries to speak of the **new imperialism.**

Characterized by a frantic rush to plant the flag over as many people and as much territory as possible, the new imperialism had momentous consequences. It resulted in new tensions among competing European states, and it led to wars and rumors of war with non-European powers. The new imperialism was aimed primarily at Africa and Asia. It put millions of black, brown, and yellow peoples directly under the rule of whites. How and why did this happen?

## The Scramble for Africa

The most spectacular manifestation of the new imperialism was the seizure of Africa, which broke sharply with previous patterns and fascinated contemporary Europeans and Americans. As late as 1880, European nations controlled only 10 percent of the African continent, and their possessions were hardly increasing. The French had begun conquering Algeria in 1830, and by 1880 substantial numbers of French, Italian, and Spanish colonists had settled among the overwhelming Arab majority.

At the other end of the continent, in South Africa, the British had taken possession of the Dutch settlements at Cape Town during the wars with Napoleon I. This takeover had led disgruntled Dutch cattle ranchers and farmers in 1835 to make their so-called Great Trek into the interior, where they fought the Zulu and Xhosa peoples for land. After 1853, while British colonies such as Canada and Australia were beginning to evolve toward self-government, the Boers, or **Afrikaners** (as the descendants of the Dutch in the Cape Colony were beginning to call themselves), proclaimed their political independence and defended it against British armies. By 1880 Afrikaner and British settlers, who detested each other, had wrested control of much of South Africa from the Zulu, Xhosa, and other African peoples.

European trading posts and forts dating back to the Age of Discovery and the slave trade dotted the coast of West Africa. The Portuguese proudly but ineffectively held their old possessions in Angola and Mozambique. Elsewhere over the great mass of the continent, Europeans did not rule.

Between 1880 and 1900, the situation changed drastically. Britain, France, Germany, and Italy scrambled for African possessions as if their national livelihoods depended on it (see Map 26.2). By 1900 nearly the whole continent had been carved up and placed under European rule: only

Ethiopia in northeast Africa, which repulsed Italian invaders, and Liberia on the West African coast remained independent. In the years before 1914, the European powers tightened their control and established colonial governments to rule their gigantic empires.

The Dutch settler republics also succumbed to imperialism, but the final outcome was quite different. The British, led by Cecil Rhodes in the Cape Colony, leapfrogged over the Afrikaner states in the early 1890s and established protectorates over Bechuanaland (now Botswana) and Rhodesia (now Zimbabwe and Zambia), named in honor of its freelance imperial founder. Trying unsuccessfully to undermine the stubborn Afrikaners in the Transvaal, where English-speaking capitalists like Rhodes were developing fabulously rich gold mines, the British conquered their white rivals in the bloody South African War (1899–1902). In 1910 their territories were united with the old Cape Colony and the eastern province of Natal in a new Union of South Africa, established—unlike any other territory in Africa—as a largely "self-governing" colony. This enabled the defeated Afrikaners to use their numerical superiority over the British settlers to gradually take political power, as even the most educated nonwhites lost the right to vote outside the Cape Colony. (See the feature "Individuals in Society: Cecil Rhodes.")

In the complexity of the European seizure of Africa, certain events and individuals stand out. Of enormous importance was the British occupation of Egypt in 1882, which established the new model of formal political control. There was also the role of Leopold II of Belgium (r. 1865–1909), an energetic, strong-willed monarch with a lust for distant territory. "The sea bathes our coast, the world lies before us," he had exclaimed in 1861. "Steam and electricity have annihilated distance, and all the nonappropriated lands on the surface of the globe can become the field of our operations and of our success."[8] By 1876 Leopold was focusing on central Africa. Subsequently, he formed a financial syndicate under his personal control to send Henry M. Stanley, a sensation-seeking journalist and part-time explorer, to the Congo basin. Stanley was able to establish trading stations, sign "treaties" with African chiefs, and plant Leopold's flag. Leopold's actions alarmed the French, who quickly sent out an expedition under Pierre de Brazza. In 1880 de Brazza signed a treaty of protection with the chief of the large Teke tribe and began to establish a French protectorate on the north bank of the Congo River.

Leopold's buccaneering intrusion into the Congo area raised the question of the political fate of Africa. By 1882 Europe had caught "African fever." There was a gold rush mentality, and the race for territory was on.

To lay down some basic rules for this new and dangerous game of imperialist competition in sub-Saharan Africa, Jules Ferry of France and Otto von Bismarck of Germany arranged an international conference on Africa in Berlin in 1884 and 1885. The conference established the principle that European claims to African territory had to rest on "effective occupation" in order to be recognized by other states. This meant that Europeans would push relentlessly into interior regions from all sides and that no single European power would be able to claim the entire continent. The conference recognized Leopold's personal rule over a neutral Congo free state and agreed to work to stop slavery and the slave trade in Africa.

The **Berlin conference** coincided with Germany's sudden emergence as an imperial power. Prior to about 1880, Bismarck, like many other European leaders at the time, had seen little value in colonies. Colonies reminded him, he said, of a poor but proud nobleman who wore a fur coat when he could not afford a shirt underneath. Then in 1884 and 1885, as political agitation for expansion increased, Bismarck did an abrupt about-face, and Germany established protectorates over a number of small African kingdoms and tribes in Togo, Cameroons, southwest Africa, and, later, East Africa. In acquiring colonies, Bismarck cooperated against the British with France's Ferry, who was as ardent for empire as he was for education. With Bismarck's tacit approval, the French pressed southward from Algeria, eastward from their old forts on the Senegal coast, and northward from their protectorate on the Congo River.

Meanwhile, the British began enlarging their West African enclaves and impatiently pushing northward from the Cape Colony and westward from Zanzibar. Their thrust southward from Egypt was blocked in the Sudan by fiercely independent Muslims, who massacred a British force at Khartoum in 1885.

A decade later, another British force, under General Horatio H. Kitchener, moved cautiously and more successfully up the Nile River, building a railroad to supply arms and reinforcements as it went. Finally, in 1898 these British troops met their foe at Omdurman (see Map 26.2), where Muslim tribesmen armed with spears charged time and time again only to be cut down by the recently invented machine gun. For one smug participant, the young British officer Winston Churchill, it was "like a pantomime scene" in a play. "These extraordinary foreign figures . . . march up one by one from the darkness of Barbarism to the footlights of civilization . . . and their conquerors, taking their possessions, forget even their names." For another, more somber English observer, "It was not a battle but an execution. The bodies were

# Individuals in Society

*Cecil Rhodes, after crushing the last African revolt in Rhodesia in 1896.* (Brown Brothers)

## Cecil Rhodes

Cecil Rhodes (1853–1902) epitomized the dynamism and the ruthlessness of the new imperialism. He built a corporate monopoly, claimed vast tracts in Africa, and established the famous Rhodes scholarships to develop colonial (and American) leaders who would love and strengthen the British Empire. But to Africans, he left a bitter legacy.

Rhodes came from a large middle-class family and at seventeen went to southern Africa to seek his fortune. He soon turned to diamonds, newly discovered at Kimberley, picked good partners, and was wealthy by 1876. But Rhodes, often called a dreamer, wanted more. He entered Oxford University, while returning periodically to Africa, and his musings crystallized in a belief in progress through racial competition and territorial expansion. "I contend," he wrote, "that we [English] are the finest race in the world and the more of the world we inhabit the better it is for the human race."*

Rhodes's belief in British expansion never wavered. In 1880 he formed the De Beers Mining Company, and by 1888 his firm monopolized southern Africa's diamond production and earned fabulous profits. Rhodes also entered the Cape Colony's legislature and became the all-powerful prime minister from 1890 to 1896. His main objective was to dominate the Afrikaner republics and to impose British rule on as much land as possible beyond their northern borders. Working through a state-approved private company financed in part by De Beers, Rhodes's agents forced and cajoled African kings to accept British "protection," then put down rebellions with Maxim machine guns. Britain thus obtained a great swath of empire on the cheap.

But Rhodes, like many high achievers obsessed with power and personal aggrandizement, went too far. He backed, and then in 1896 failed to call back, a failed invasion of the Transvaal, which was designed to topple the Dutch-speaking republic. Repudiated by top British leaders who had encouraged his plan, Rhodes had to resign as prime minister. In declining health, he continued to agitate against the Afrikaner republics. He died at age forty-nine as the South African War (1899–1902) ended.

In accounting for Rhodes's remarkable but flawed achievements, both sympathetic and critical biographers stress his imposing size, enormous energy, and powerful personality. His ideas were commonplace, but he believed in them passionately, and he could persuade and inspire others to follow his lead. Rhodes the idealist was nonetheless a born negotiator, a crafty dealmaker who believed that everyone could be had for a price. According to his best biographer, Rhodes's homosexuality—discreet, partially repressed, and undeniable—was also "a major component of his magnetism and his success."† Never comfortable with women, he loved male companionship. He drew together a "band of brothers," both gay and straight, to share in the pursuit of power.

Rhodes cared nothing for the rights of blacks. Ever a combination of visionary and opportunist, he looked forward to an eventual reconciliation of Afrikaners and British in a united white front. Therefore, as prime minister of the Cape Colony, he broke with the colony's liberal tradition and supported Afrikaner demands to reduce drastically the number of black voters and limit black freedoms. This helped lay the foundation for the Union of South Africa's brutal policy of racial segregation known as *apartheid* after 1948.

### Questions for Analysis

1. How did Rhodes relate to Afrikaners and to black Africans? How do you account for the differences and the similarities?
2. In what ways does Rhodes's career throw additional light on the debate over the causes of the new imperialism?

*Robert Rotberg, *The Founder: Cecil Rhodes and the Pursuit of Power* (New York: Oxford University Press, 1988), p. 150.
†Ibid., p. 408.

*The* **history companion** *features additional information and activities related to this topic.*
**history.college.hmco.com/students**

not in heaps . . . but they spread evenly over acres and acres."[9] In the end, eleven thousand brave Muslim tribesmen lay dead, while only twenty-eight Britons had been killed.

Continuing up the Nile after the Battle of Omdurman, Kitchener's armies found that a small French force had already occupied the village of Fashoda. Locked in imperial competition with Britain ever since the British occupation of Egypt, France had tried to beat the British to one of Africa's last unclaimed areas—the upper reaches of the Nile. The result was a serious diplomatic crisis and even the threat of war. Eventually, wracked by the Dreyfus affair (see page 842) and unwilling to fight, France backed down and withdrew its forces, allowing the British to take over.

The British conquest of the Sudan exemplifies the general process of empire building in Africa. The fate of the Muslim force at Omdurman was eventually inflicted on all native peoples who resisted European rule: they were blown away by vastly superior military force. But however much the European powers squabbled for territory and privilege around the world, they always had the sense to stop short of actually fighting each other. Imperial ambitions were not worth a great European war.

**European Imperialism at its Worst** This 1908 English cartoon, "Leopold, King of the Congo, in his native dress," focuses on the barbaric practice of cutting off the hands and feet of Africans who refused to gather as much rubber as Leopold's company demanded. In 1908 an international human rights campaign forced the Belgian king to cede his personal fief to the Belgian state. *(Archive of Arnoldo Mondadori Editore, Milan)*

## Imperialism in Asia

Although the sudden division of Africa was more spectacular, Europeans also extended their political control in Asia. In 1815 the Dutch ruled little more than the island of Java in the East Indies. Thereafter they gradually brought almost all of the three-thousand-mile archipelago under their political authority, though—in good imperialist fashion—they had to share some of the spoils with Britain and Germany. In the critical decade of the 1880s, the French under the leadership of Ferry took Indochina. India, Japan, and China also experienced a profound imperialist impact (see Map 26.3).

Two other great imperialist powers, Russia and the United States, also acquired rich territories in Asia. Russia moved steadily forward on two fronts throughout the nineteenth century. Russians conquered Muslim areas to the south in the Caucasus and in Central Asia and also proceeded to nibble greedily on China's outlying provinces in the Far East, especially in the 1890s.

The United States' great conquest was the Philippines, taken from Spain in 1898 after the Spanish-American War. When it quickly became clear that the United States had no intention of granting independence, Philippine patriots rose in revolt and were suppressed only after long, bitter fighting. Some Americans protested the taking of the Philippines, but to no avail. Thus another great Western power joined the imperialist ranks in Asia.

## Causes of the New Imperialism

Many factors contributed to the late-nineteenth-century rush for territory and empire, which was in turn one aspect of Western society's generalized expansion in the age of industry and nationalism. It is little wonder that controversies have raged over interpretation of the new imperialism, especially since authors of every persuasion have often exaggerated particular aspects in an attempt to prove their own theories. Yet despite complexity and controversy, basic causes are clearly identifiable.

Economic motives played an important role in the extension of political empires, especially the British Empire. By the late 1870s, France, Germany, and the United States were industrializing rapidly behind rising tariff barriers. Great Britain was losing its early lead and facing increasingly tough competition in foreign markets. In this new economic situation, Britain came to value old possessions, such as India and Canada, more highly. The days when a leading free-trader such as Richard Cobden could denounce the "bloodstained fetish of Empire" and statesman Benjamin Disraeli could call colonies a "millstone round our necks" came to an abrupt end. When continental powers began to grab territory in the 1880s, the British followed suit immediately. They feared that France and Germany would seal off their empires with high tariffs and restrictions and that future economic opportunities would be lost forever.

Actually, the overall economic gains of the new imperialism proved quite limited before 1914. The new colonies were simply too poor to buy much, and they offered few immediately profitable investments. Nonetheless, even the poorest, most barren desert was jealously prized, and no territory was ever abandoned. Colonies became important for political and diplomatic reasons. Each leading country saw colonies as crucial to national security, military power, and international prestige. For instance, safeguarding the Suez Canal played a key role in the British occupation of Egypt, and protecting Egypt in turn led to the bloody conquest of the Sudan. Far-flung possessions guaranteed ever-growing navies the safe havens and the dependable coaling stations they needed in time of crisis or war.

Many people were convinced that colonies were essential to great nations. "There has never been a great power without great colonies," wrote one French publicist in 1877. "Every virile people has established colonial power," echoed the famous nationalist historian of Germany, Heinrich von Treitschke. "All great nations in the fullness of their strength have desired to set their mark upon barbarian lands and those who fail to participate in this great rivalry will play a pitiable role in time to come."[10]

Treitschke's harsh statement reflects not only the increasing aggressiveness of European nationalism after Bismarck's wars of German unification but also Social Darwinian theories of brutal competition among races. As one prominent English economist argued, the "strongest nation has always been conquering the weaker . . . and the strongest tend to be best." Thus European nations, which were seen as racially distinct parts of the dominant white race, had to seize colonies to show they were strong and virile. Moreover, since racial struggle was nature's inescapable law, the conquest of "inferior" peoples was just. "The path of progress is strewn with the wreck . . . of inferior races," wrote one professor in 1900. "Yet these dead peoples are, in very truth, the stepping stones on which mankind has risen to the higher intellectual and deeper emotional life of today."[11] Social Darwinism and harsh racial doctrines fostered imperialist expansion.

So did the industrial world's unprecedented technological and military superiority. Three aspects were crucial. First, the rapidly firing machine gun, so lethal at Omdurman in the Sudan, was an ultimate weapon in many another unequal battle. Second, newly discovered quinine proved no less effective in controlling attacks of malaria, which had previously decimated whites in the tropics whenever they left breezy coastal enclaves and dared to venture into mosquito-infested interiors. Third, the combination of the steamship and the international telegraph permitted Western powers to quickly concentrate their firepower in a given area when it was needed. Never before—and never again after 1914—would the technological gap between the West and non-Western regions of the world be so great.

Social tensions and domestic political conflicts also contributed mightily to overseas expansion, according to a prominent interpretation of recent years. Certainly in Germany, in Russia, and in other countries to a lesser extent, contemporary critics of imperialism charged conservative political leaders with manipulating colonial issues in order to divert popular attention from the class struggle at home and to create a false sense of national unity. Thus imperial propagandists relentlessly stressed that colonies benefited workers as well as capitalists, providing jobs and cheap raw materials that raised workers' standard of living. Government leaders and their allies in the tabloid press successfully encouraged the masses to savor foreign triumphs and glory in the supposed increase in national prestige. In short, conservative leaders

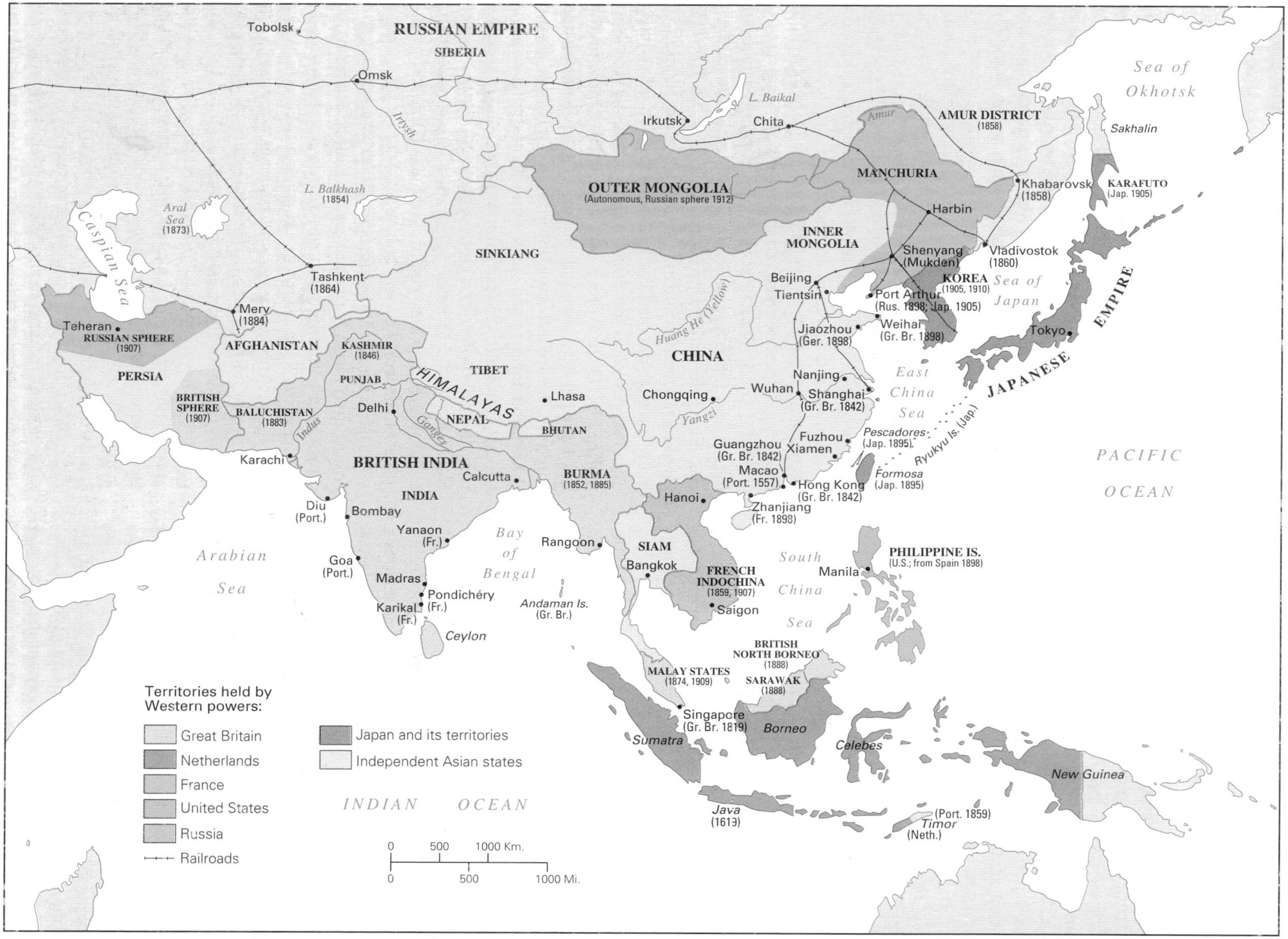


**MAP 26.3 Asia in 1914** India remained under British rule, while China precariously preserved its political independence. The Dutch empire in modern-day Indonesia was old, but French control of Indochina was a product of the new imperialism.

defined imperialist development as a national necessity, which they used to justify the status quo and their hold on power.

Finally, certain special-interest groups in each country were powerful agents of expansion. Shipping companies wanted lucrative subsidies. White settlers demanded more land and greater protection. Missionaries and humanitarians wanted to spread religion and stop the slave trade. Military men and colonial officials, whose role has often been overlooked, foresaw rapid advancement and high-paid positions in growing empires. The actions of such groups pushed the course of empire forward.

Western society did not rest the case for empire solely on naked conquest and a Darwinian racial struggle or on power politics and the need for naval bases on every ocean. Imperialists developed additional arguments in order to satisfy their consciences and answer their critics.

A favorite idea was that Europeans could and should "civilize" more primitive, nonwhite peoples. According to this view, nonwhites would eventually receive the benefits of modern economies, cities, advanced medicine, and higher standards of living. In time, they might be ready for self-government and Western democracy. Thus the French spoke of their sacred "civilizing mission." In

**A Missionary School** A Swahili schoolboy leads his classmates in a reading lesson in Dar es Salaam in German East Africa before 1914, as portraits of Emperor William II and his wife look down on the classroom. Europeans argued that they were spreading the benefits of a superior civilization with schools like this one, which is unusually solid because of its strategic location in the capital city. *(Ullstein Bilderdienst)*

1899 Rudyard Kipling (1865–1936), who wrote masterfully of Anglo-Indian life and was perhaps the most influential British writer of the 1890s, exhorted Europeans (and Americans in the United States) to unselfish service in distant lands:

*Take up the White Man's Burden—*
*Send forth the best ye breed—*
*Go bind your sons to exile*
*To serve your captives' need,*
*To wait in heavy harness,*
*On fluttered folk and wild—*
*Your new-caught, sullen peoples*
*Half-devil and half-child.*[12]

Many Americans accepted the ideology of the **white man's burden.** It was an important factor in the decision to rule, rather than liberate, the Philippines after the Spanish-American War. Like their European counterparts, these Americans sincerely believed that their civilization had reached unprecedented heights and that they had unique benefits to bestow on all "less advanced" peoples. Another argument was that imperial government protected natives from tribal warfare as well as cruder forms of exploitation by white settlers and business people.

Peace and stability under European control also facilitated the spread of Christianity. In Africa Catholic and Protestant missionaries competed with Islam south of the Sahara, seeking converts and building schools to spread the Gospel. Many Africans' first real contact with whites was in mission schools. Some peoples, such as the Ibo in Nigeria, became highly Christianized.

Such occasional successes in black Africa contrasted with the general failure of missionary efforts in India, China, and the Islamic world. There Christians often preached in vain to peoples with ancient, complex religious beliefs. Yet the number of Christian believers around the world did increase substantially in the nineteenth century, and missionary groups kept trying. Unfortunately, "many missionaries had drunk at the well of European racism," and this probably prevented them from doing better.[13]

## Critics of Imperialism

The expansion of empire aroused sharp, even bitter, critics. A forceful attack was delivered in 1902, after the unpopular South African War, by radical English economist J. A. Hobson (1858–1940) in his *Imperialism,* a work that influenced Lenin and others. Hobson contended that the rush to acquire colonies was due to the economic needs of unregulated capitalism, particularly the need of the rich to find outlets for their surplus capital. Yet, Hobson argued, imperial possessions did not pay off economically for the country as a whole. Only unscrupulous special-interest groups profited from them, at the expense of both the European taxpayer and the natives. Moreover, Hobson argued that the quest for empire diverted popular attention away from domestic reform and the need to reduce the great gap between rich and poor. These and similar arguments were not very persuasive, however. Most people then (and now) were sold on the idea that imperialism was economically profitable for the homeland, and a broad and genuine enthusiasm for empire developed among the masses.

Hobson and many other critics struck home, however, with their moral condemnation of whites imperiously ruling nonwhites. They rebelled against crude Social Darwinian thought. "O Evolution, what crimes are committed in thy name!" cried one foe. Another sardonically coined a new beatitude: "Blessed are the strong, for they shall prey on the weak."[14] Kipling and his kind were lampooned as racist bullies whose rule rested on brutality, racial contempt, and the Maxim machine gun. Henry Labouchère, a member of Parliament and prominent spokesman for this position, mocked Kipling's famous poem:

*Pile on the Brown Man's burden!*
*And if ye rouse his hate,*
*Meet his old-fashioned reasons*
*With Maxims up to date,*
*With shells and Dum-Dum bullets*
*A hundred times plain*
*The Brown Man's loss must never*
*Imply the White Man's gain.*[15]

Similarly, in 1902 in *Heart of Darkness* Polish-born novelist Joseph Conrad (1857–1924) castigated the "pure selfishness" of Europeans in "civilizing" Africa; the main character, once a liberal scholar, turns into a savage brute.

Critics charged Europeans with applying a degrading double standard and failing to live up to their own noble ideals. At home Europeans had won or were winning representative government, individual liberties, and a certain equality of opportunity. In their empires, Europeans imposed military dictatorships on Africans and Asians; forced them to work involuntarily, almost like slaves; and discriminated against them shamelessly. Only by renouncing imperialism, its critics insisted, and giving captive peoples the freedoms Western society had struggled for since the French Revolution would Europeans be worthy of their traditions. Europeans who denounced the imperialist tide provided colonial peoples with a Western ideology of liberation.

## Responses to Western Imperialism

See DBQ 10

To peoples in Africa and Asia, Western expansion represented a profoundly disruptive assault. Everywhere it threatened traditional ruling classes, traditional economies, and traditional ways of life. Christian missionaries and European secular ideologies challenged established beliefs and values. Non-Western peoples experienced a crisis of identity, one made all the more painful by the power and arrogance of the white intruders.

The initial response of African and Asian rulers was to try driving the unwelcome foreigners away. This was the case in China, Japan, and the upper Sudan, as we have seen. Violent antiforeign reactions exploded elsewhere again and again, but the superior military technology of the industrialized West almost invariably prevailed. Beaten in battle, many Africans and Asians concentrated on preserving their cultural traditions at all costs. Others found themselves forced to reconsider their initial hostility. Some (such as Ismail of Egypt) concluded that the West was indeed superior in some ways and that it was therefore necessary to reform their societies and copy European achievements. Thus it is possible to think of responses to the Western impact as a spectrum, with "traditionalists" at one end, "westernizers" or "modernizers" at the other, and many shades of opinion in between. Both before and after European domination, the struggle among these groups was often intense. With time, however, the modernizers tended to gain the upper hand.

When the power of both the traditionalists and the modernizers was thoroughly shattered by superior force, the great majority of Asians and Africans accepted imperial rule. Political participation in non-Western lands was historically limited to small elites, and the masses were used to doing what their rulers told them. In these circumstances Europeans, clothed in power and convinced of their righteousness, governed smoothly and effectively. They received considerable support from both traditionalists (local chiefs, landowners, religious leaders) and modernizers (Western-educated professional classes and civil servants).

Nevertheless, imperial rule was in many ways an imposing edifice built on sand. Support for European rule among the conforming and accepting millions was shallow and weak. Thus the conforming masses followed with greater or lesser enthusiasm a few determined personalities who came to oppose the Europeans. Such leaders always arose, both when Europeans ruled directly and when they manipulated native governments, for at least two basic reasons.

First, the nonconformists—the eventual anti-imperialist leaders—developed a burning desire for human dignity. They came to feel that such dignity was incompatible with foreign rule. Second, potential leaders found in the Western world the ideologies and justification for their protest. They discovered liberalism, with its credo of civil liberty and political self-determination. They echoed the demands of anti-imperialists in Europe and America that the West live up to its own ideals. Above all, they found themselves attracted to modern nationalism, which asserted that every people had the right to control its own destiny. After 1917 anti-imperialist revolt would find another weapon in Lenin's version of Marxian socialism. Thus the anti-imperialist search for dignity drew strength from Western culture, as is apparent in the development of three major Asian countries—India, Japan, and China.

### Empire in India

India was the jewel of the British Empire, and no colonial area experienced a more profound British impact. Unlike Japan and China, which maintained a real or precarious independence, and unlike African territories, which were annexed by Europeans only at the end of the nineteenth century, India was ruled more or less absolutely by Britain for a very long time.

Arriving in India on the heels of the Portuguese in the seventeenth century, the British East India Company had conquered the last independent native state by 1848. The last "traditional" response to European rule—the attempt by the established ruling classes to drive the white man out by military force—was broken in India in 1857 and 1858. Those were the years of the **Great Rebellion** (which the British called a "mutiny"), when an insurrection by Muslim and Hindu mercenaries in the British army spread throughout northern and central India before it was finally crushed, primarily by loyal native troops from southern India. Thereafter Britain ruled India directly.

After 1858 India was ruled by the British Parliament in London and administered by a tiny, all-white civil service in India. In 1900 this elite consisted of fewer than 3,500 top officials, for a population of 300 million. The white elite, backed by white officers and native troops, was competent and generally well-disposed toward the welfare of the Indian peasant masses. Yet it practiced strict job discrimination and social segregation, and most of its members quite frankly considered the jumble of Indian peoples and castes to be racially inferior. As Lord Kitchener, one of the most distinguished top military commanders in India, stated:

*It is this consciousness of the inherent superiority of the European which has won for us India. However well educated*

**Imperial Complexities in India** Britain permitted many native princes to continue their rule, if they accepted British domination. This photo shows a road-building project designed to facilitate famine relief in a southern native state. Officials of the local Muslim prince and their British "advisers" watch over workers drawn from the Hindu majority. *(Nizam's Good Works Project-Famine Relief: Road Building, Aurangabad 1895–1902, from Judith Mara Gutman,* Through Indian Eyes. *Courtesy, Private Collection)*

*and clever a native may be, and however brave he may prove himself, I believe that no rank we can bestow on him would cause him to be considered an equal of the British officer.*[16]

British women played an important part in the imperial enterprise, especially after the opening of the Suez Canal in 1869 made it much easier for civil servants and businessmen to bring their wives and children with them to India. These British families tended to live in their own separate communities, where they occupied large houses with well-shaded porches, handsome lawns, and a multitude of servants. It was the wife's responsibility to manage this complex household. Many officials' wives learned to relish their duties, and they directed their households and servants with the same self-confident authoritarianism that characterized British political rule in India. (See the feature "Listening to the Past: A British Woman in India" on pages 884–885.)

A small minority of British women—many of them feminists, social reformers, or missionaries, both married and single—sought to go further and shoulder the "white women's burden" in India, as one historian has described it.[17] These women tried especially to improve the lives of Indian women, both Hindu and Muslim, and to move them closer through education and legislation to the better conditions that they believed Western women had attained. Their greatest success was educating some elite Hindu women who took up the cause of reform.

With British men and women sharing a sense of mission as well as strong feelings of racial and cultural superiority, the British acted energetically and introduced many desirable changes to India. Realizing that they needed well-educated Indians to serve as skilled subordinates in the government and army, the British established a modern system of progressive secondary education in which all instruction was in English. Thus through education and government service, the British offered some Indians excellent opportunities for both economic and social advancement. High-caste Hindus, particularly quick to respond, emerged as skillful intermediaries between the British rulers and the Indian people, and soon they formed a new elite profoundly influenced by Western thought and culture.

This new bureaucratic elite played a crucial role in modern economic development, which was a second result of British rule. Irrigation projects for agriculture, the world's third-largest railroad network for good communications, and large tea and jute plantations geared to the world economy were all developed. Unfortunately, the lot of the Indian masses improved little, for the increase in production was eaten up by population increase.

Finally, with a well-educated, English-speaking Indian bureaucracy and modern communications, the British created a unified, powerful state. They placed under the same general system of law and administration the different Hindu and Muslim peoples and the vanquished kingdoms of the entire subcontinent—groups that had fought each other for centuries and had been repeatedly conquered by Muslim and Mongol invaders. It was as if Europe, with its many states and varieties of Christianity, had been conquered and united in a single great empire.

In spite of these achievements, the decisive reaction to European rule was the rise of nationalism among the Indian elite. No matter how anglicized and necessary a member of the educated classes became, he or she could never become the white ruler's equal. The top jobs, the best clubs, the modern hotels, and even certain railroad compartments were sealed off to brown-skinned Indians. The peasant masses might accept such inequality as the latest version of age-old oppression, but the well-educated, English-speaking elite eventually could not. For the elite, racial discrimination meant injured pride and bitter injustice. It flagrantly contradicted those cherished Western concepts of human rights and equality. Moreover, it was based on dictatorship, no matter how benign.

By 1885, when educated Indians came together to found the predominately Hindu Indian National Congress, demands were increasing for the equality and self-government that Britain had already granted white-settler colonies, such as Canada and Australia. By 1907, emboldened in part by Japan's success (see the next section), the radicals in the Indian National Congress were calling for complete independence. Even the moderates were demanding home rule for India through an elected parliament. Although there were sharp divisions between Hindus and Muslims, Indians were finding an answer to the foreign challenge. The common heritage of British rule and Western ideals, along with the reform and revitalization of the Hindu religion, had created a genuine movement for national independence.

## The Example of Japan

When Commodore Matthew Perry arrived in Japan in 1853 with his crude but effective gunboat diplomacy, Japan was a complex feudal society. At the top stood a figurehead emperor, but real power was in the hands of a hereditary military governor, the **shogun.** With the help of a warrior nobility known as **samurai,** the shogun governed a country of hard-working, productive peasants and city dwellers. Often poor and restless, the intensely proud samurai were humiliated by the sudden American intrusion and the unequal treaties with Western countries.

When foreign diplomats and merchants began to settle in Yokohama, radical samurai reacted with a wave of antiforeign terrorism and antigovernment assassinations between 1858 and 1863. The imperialist response was swift and unambiguous. An allied fleet of American, British, Dutch, and French warships demolished key forts, further weakening the power and prestige of the shogun's government. Then in 1867, a coalition led by patriotic samurai seized control of the government with hardly any bloodshed and restored the political power of the emperor. This was the Meiji Restoration, a great turning point in Japanese development.

The immediate, all-important goal of the new government was to meet the foreign threat. The battle cry of the

**The Rapid Modernization of the Japanese Army** This woodcut from about 1870 shows Japanese soldiers outfitted in Western uniforms and marching in Western formation. Japanese reformers, impressed by Prussian discipline and success on the battlefield, looked to Germany for their military models. *(Ryogoku Tsuneo Tamba Collection/Laurie Platt Winfrey)*

Meiji reformers was "Enrich the state and strengthen the armed forces." Yet how were these tasks to be done? In an about-face that was one of history's most remarkable chapters, the young but well-trained, idealistic but flexible leaders of Meiji Japan dropped their antiforeign attacks. Convinced that Western civilization was indeed superior in its military and industrial aspects, they initiated from above a series of measures to reform Japan along modern lines. In the broadest sense, the Meiji leaders tried to harness the power inherent in Europe's dual revolution in order to protect their country and catch up with the West.

In 1871 the new leaders abolished the old feudal structure of aristocratic, decentralized government and formed a strong unified state. Following the example of the French Revolution, they dismantled the four-class legal system and declared social equality. They decreed freedom of movement in a country where traveling abroad had been a most serious crime. They created a free, competitive, government-stimulated economy. Japan began to build railroads and modern factories. Thus the new generation adopted many principles of a free, liberal society, and, as in Europe, such freedom resulted in a tremendously creative release of human energy.

Yet the overriding concern of Japan's political leadership was always a powerful state, and to achieve this, more than liberalism was borrowed from the West. A powerful modern navy was created, and the army was completely reorganized along European lines, with three-year military service for all males and a professional officer corps. This army of draftees effectively put down disturbances in the countryside, and in 1877 it was used to crush a major rebellion by feudal elements protesting the loss of their privileges. Japan also borrowed rapidly and adapted skillfully the West's science and modern technology, particularly in industry, medicine, and education. Many Japanese were encouraged to study abroad, and the government paid large salaries to attract foreign experts. These experts were always carefully controlled, however, and replaced by trained Japanese as soon as possible.

By 1890, when the new state was firmly established, the wholesale borrowing of the early restoration had given way to more selective emphasis on those things foreign that were in keeping with Japanese tradition. Following the model of the German Empire, Japan established an authoritarian constitution and rejected democracy. The power of the emperor and his ministers was vast; that of the legislature, limited.

Japan successfully copied the imperialism of Western society. Expansion not only proved that Japan was strong; it also cemented the nation together in a great mission. Having "opened" Korea with the gunboat diplomacy of imperialism in 1876, Japan decisively defeated China in a war over Korea in 1894 and 1895 and took Formosa (modern-day Taiwan). In the next years, Japan competed aggressively with the leading European powers for influence and territory in China, particularly Manchuria. There Japanese and Russian imperialism met and collided. In 1904 Japan attacked Russia without warning, and after a bloody war, Japan emerged with a valuable foothold in China, Russia's former protectorate over Port Arthur (see Map 26.3). By 1910, with the annexation of Korea, Japan had become a major imperialist power.

Japan became the first non-Western country to use an ancient love of country to transform itself and thereby meet the many-sided challenge of Western expansion. Moreover, Japan demonstrated convincingly that a modern Asian nation could defeat and humble a great Western power. Many Chinese nationalists were fascinated by Japan's achievement. A group of patriots in French-ruled southern Vietnam sent Vietnamese students to Japan to learn the island empire's secret of success. Japan provided patriots throughout Asia and Africa with an inspiring example of national recovery and liberation.

## Toward Revolution in China

In 1860 the two-hundred-year-old Qing Dynasty in China appeared on the verge of collapse. Efforts to repel foreigners had failed, and rebellion and chaos wracked the country. Yet the government drew on its traditional strengths and made a surprising comeback that lasted more than thirty years.

Two factors were crucial in this reversal. First, the traditional ruling groups temporarily produced new and effective leadership. Loyal scholar-statesmen and generals quelled disturbances such as the great Tai Ping rebellion. The empress dowager Tzu Hsi, a truly remarkable woman, governed in the name of her young son and combined shrewd insight with vigorous action to revitalize the bureaucracy.

Second, destructive foreign aggression lessened, for the Europeans had obtained their primary goal of commercial and diplomatic relations. Indeed, some Europeans contributed to the dynasty's recovery. A talented Irishman effectively reorganized China's customs office and increased the government tax receipts, while a sympathetic American diplomat represented China in foreign lands and helped strengthen the central government. Such efforts dovetailed with the dynasty's efforts to adopt some aspects of Western government and technology while maintaining traditional Chinese values and beliefs.

The parallel movement toward domestic reform and limited cooperation with the West collapsed under the blows of Japanese imperialism. The Sino-Japanese War of 1894 to 1895 and the subsequent harsh peace treaty revealed China's helplessness in the face of aggression, triggering a rush for foreign concessions and protectorates in China. At the high point of this rush in 1898, it appeared that the European powers might actually divide China among themselves, as they had recently divided Africa. Probably only the jealousy each nation felt toward its imperialist competitors saved China from partition, although the U.S. Open Door policy, which opposed formal annexation of Chinese territory, may have helped tip the balance.

**The Empress Dowager Tzu Hsi (1835–1908)** Tzu Hsi drew on conservative forces, like the court eunuchs surrounding her here, to maintain her power. Three years after her death in 1908, a revolution broke out and forced the last Chinese emperor, a boy of six, to abdicate. *(Freer Gallery of Art and Arthur M. Sackler Gallery Archives, Smithsonian Institution. Photographer: Hsun-ling. Negative no. 261)*

In any event, the tempo of foreign encroachment greatly accelerated after 1894.

So, too, did the intensity and radicalism of the Chinese reaction. Like the leaders of the Meiji Restoration, some modernizers saw salvation in Western institutions. In 1898 the government launched a desperate **hundred days of reform** in an attempt to meet the foreign challenge. More radical reformers, such as the revolutionary Sun Yat-sen (1866–1925), who came from the peasantry and was educated in Hawaii by Christian missionaries, sought to overthrow the dynasty altogether and establish a republic.

On the other side, some traditionalists turned back toward ancient practices, political conservatism, and fanatical hatred of the "foreign devils." "Protect the country, destroy the foreigner" was their simple motto. Such conservative, antiforeign patriots had often clashed with foreign missionaries, whom they charged with undermining reverence for ancestors and thereby threatening the Chinese family and the entire society. In the agony of defeat and unwanted reforms, secret societies such as the Boxers rebelled. In northeastern China, more than two hundred foreign missionaries and several thousand Chinese Christians were killed. Once again the imperialist response was swift and harsh. Peking was occupied and plundered by foreign armies. A heavy indemnity was imposed.

The years after the Boxer Rebellion (1900–1903) were ever more troubled. Anarchy and foreign influence spread as the power and prestige of the Qing Dynasty declined still further. Antiforeign, antigovernment revolutionary groups agitated and plotted. Finally in 1912, a spontaneous uprising toppled the Qing Dynasty. After thousands of years of emperors and empires, a loose coalition of revolutionaries proclaimed a Western-style republic and called for an elected parliament. The transformation of China under the impact of expanding Western society entered a new phase, and the end was not in sight.

## Summary

In the nineteenth century, the industrializing West entered the third and most dynamic phase of its centuries-old expansion into non-Western lands. In so doing, Western nations profitably subordinated those lands to their economic interests, sent forth millions of emigrants, and established political influence in Asia and vast political empires in Africa. The reasons for this culminating surge were many, but the economic thrust of robust industrial capitalism, an ever-growing lead in technology, and the competitive pressures of European nationalism were particularly important.

Western expansion had far-reaching consequences. For the first time in human history, the world became in many ways a single unit. Moreover, European expansion diffused the ideas and techniques of a highly developed civilization. Yet the West relied on force to conquer and rule, and it treated non-Western peoples as racial inferiors. Thus non-Western elites, often armed with Western doctrines, gradually responded to the Western challenge. They launched a national, anti-imperialist struggle for dignity, genuine independence, and modernization. This struggle would emerge as a central drama of world history after the great European civil war of 1914 to 1918, which reduced the West's technological advantage and shattered its self-confidence and complacent moral superiority.

## Key Terms

Third World
opium trade
khedive
great migration
swallows
great white walls
new imperialism
Afrikaners
Berlin conference
white man's burden
Great Rebellion
shogun
samurai
hundred days of reform

## Notes


1. Quoted in A. Waley, *The Opium War Through Chinese Eyes* (New York: Macmillan, 1958), p. 29.
2. Quoted in J. W. Hall, *Japan, from Prehistory to Modern Times* (New York: Delacorte Press, 1970), p. 250.
3. Quoted in R. Hallett, *Africa to 1875* (Ann Arbor: University of Michigan Press, 1970), p. 109.
4. Quoted in Earl of Cromer, *Modern Egypt* (London, 1911), p. 48.
5. Quoted in T. Blegen, *Norwegian Migration to America,* vol. 2 (Northfield, Minn.: Norwegian-American Historical Association, 1940), p. 468.
6. Quoted in I. Howe, *World of Our Fathers* (New York: Harcourt Brace Jovanovich, 1976), p. 25.
7. Quoted in C. A. Price, *The Great White Walls Are Built: Restrictive Immigration to North America and Australia, 1836–1888* (Canberra: Australian National University Press, 1974), p. 175.
8. Quoted in W. L. Langer, *European Alliances and Alignments, 1871–1890* (New York: Vintage Books, 1931), p. 290.
9. Quoted in J. Ellis, *The Social History of the Machine Gun* (New York: Pantheon Books, 1975), pp. 86, 101.
10. Quoted in G. H. Nadel and P. Curtis, eds., *Imperialism and Colonialism* (New York: Macmillan, 1964), p. 94.
11. Quoted in W. L. Langer, *The Diplomacy of Imperialism,* 2d ed. (New York: Alfred A. Knopf, 1951), pp. 86, 88.
12. Rudyard Kipling, *The Five Nations* (London, 1903).
13. E. H. Berman, "African Responses to Christian Mission Education," *African Studies Review* 17 (1974): 530.
14. Quoted in Langer, *The Diplomacy of Imperialism,* p. 88.
15. Quoted in Ellis, *The Social History of the Machine Gun,* pp. 99–100.

16. Quoted in K. M. Panikkar, *Asia and Western Dominance: A Survey of the Vasco da Gama Epoch of Asian History* (London: George Allen & Unwin, 1959), p. 116.
17. A. Burton, "The White Women's Burden: British Feminists and 'The Indian Women,' 1865–1915," in *Western Women and Imperialism: Complicity and Resistance,* ed. N. Chauduri and M. Strobel (Bloomington: Indiana University Press, 1992), pp. 137–157.

## Suggested Reading

General interpretations of European expansion in a broad perspective include K. Pomeranz, *The Great Divergence: China, Europe, and the Making of the Modern World Economy* (2000), and T. Smith, *The Patterns of Imperialism* (1981). Valuable documentary collections include A. Conklin, ed., *European Imperialism, 1830–1930* (1999), and B. Smith, ed., *Imperialism: A Collection of Documents* (2000). Two important works by D. Chakrabarty, *Provincializing Europe: Postcolonial Thought and National Difference* (2000) and *Habitations of Modernity: Essays in the Wake of Subaltern Studies* (2002), introduce imaginative new research on colonized peoples. D. K. Fieldhouse has written two fine surveys, *Economics and Empire, 1830–1914* (1970) and *Colonialism, 1870–1945* (1981). J. A. Hobson's classic *Imperialism* (1902) is readily available, and the Marxist-Leninist case is effectively presented in V. G. Kieran, *Marxism and Imperialism* (1975). Among the cultural studies probing the minds of imperialists and non-Europeans, E. Said, *Orientalism* (1978), is a very influential interpretation. T. Ballantyne, *Orientalism and Race: Aryanism and the British Empire* (2002), is a major work on imperial racial thinking.

Britain's leading position in European imperialism is examined in a lively way by G. Goodlad, *British Foreign and Imperial Policy, 1865–1919* (2000); B. Porter, *The Lion's Share* (1976); and P. Cain and A. Hopkins, *British Imperialism: Innovation and Expansion, 1688–1914* (1993). P. Marshall, ed., *Cambridge Illustrated History of the British Empire* (1996), and D. Judd, *The Victorian Empire* (1970), are stunning pictorial histories. G. Stocking, *Victorian Anthropology* (1987), is a brilliant analysis of the cultural and racial implications of Western expansion. R. Aldrich, *Greater France: A History of French Overseas Expansion* (1996), and W. Baumgart, *Imperialism: The Idea and Reality of British and French Colonial Expansion* (1982), are well-balanced studies. A. Conklin, *A Mission to Civilize: The French Republican Ideal and West Africa, 1895–1930* (1997), is outstanding, and H. Brunschwig, *French Colonialism, 1871–1914* (1966), is a classic short study. A. Hochshild, *King Leopold's Ghost: A Story of Greed, Terror, and Heroism in Colonial Africa, 1895–1930* (1997), tells the chilling story of Belgian imperialism in the Congo, and S. Cook, *Colonial Encounters in the Age of High Imperialism* (1996), is a very readable account of the explorer Stanley and central Africa. R. Rotberg, *The Founder: Cecil Rhodes and the Pursuit of Power* (1988), examines the imperialist's mind and times with great skill, and B. Roberts, *Cecil Rhodes: Flawed Colossus* (1987), is engaging and entertaining. A. Blunt, *Travel, Gender, and Imperialism: Mary Kingsley and West Africa* (1994), analyzes a complicated woman whose travels made her into a powerful critic of British expansion. D. Lievan, *The Russian Empire and Its Rivals* (2001), ably considers Russian imperialism. D. Headrick looks at the diffusion of Western technology in *The Tentacles of Progress: Technology Transfer in the Age of Imperialism, 1850–1940* (1988), and P. Curtin, *Death by Migration: Europe's Encounter with the Tropical World in the Nineteenth Century* (1989), ably charts the medical revolution in the tropics. R. Vecoli and S. Sinke, eds., *A Century of European Migrations, 1830–1930* (1991), and L. Moch, *Moving Europeans: Migration in Europe Since 1650* (1993), are valuable general studies. Howe and Blegen, cited in the Notes, provide dramatic accounts of Jewish and Norwegian migration to the United States. M. Walker, *Germany and the Emigration, 1816–1885* (1964), and W. Adams, *Ireland and Irish Emigration to the New World* (reissued 1967), are outstanding.

E. Wolf, *Europe and the People Without History* (1982), considers, with skill and compassion, the impact of imperialism on non-Western peoples. F. Fanon, *Wretched of the Earth* (1965), is a famous attack on white racism by a black psychologist active in the Algerian revolution. B. Smith, *European Vision and the South Pacific* (1988), is an original and influential work combining art history and intellectual development. In addition to Chauduri and Strobel, cited in the Notes, J. Clancey-Smith and F. Gouda, eds., *Domesticating the Empire: Race, Gender, and Family in French and Dutch Colonialism* (1998), V. Ware, *Beyond the Pale: White Women, Racism and History* (1992), and C. Midgley, ed., *Gender and Imperialism* (1998), examine the complex questions related to European women and imperialism. Novels also bring the psychological and human dimensions of imperialism alive. Rudyard Kipling, the most famous writer of European expansion, is at his stirring best in *Kim* and *Soldiers Three.* Joseph Conrad unforgettably probes European motives in *Heart of Darkness*. William Boyd, *An Ice-Cream War,* a good story of British and Germans fighting each other in Africa during the First World War, is a favorite with students.

P. Ebrey, *The Cambridge Illustrated History of China* (1996), is a lively and beautiful work by a leading specialist. J. Spence, *The Search for Modern China* (1990), is also recommended. I. Hsü, *The Rise of Modern China,* 5th ed. (1995), is a fine history with many suggestions for further reading. E. Reischauer's topical survey, *Japan: The Story of a Nation* (1981), is recommended, as are T. Huber, *The Revolutionary Origins of Modern Japan* (1981), and Y. Fukuzawa, *Autobiography* (1966), the account of a leading intellectual who saw the birth of modern Japan.

G. Perry, *The Middle East: Fourteen Islamic Centuries* (1983), concisely surveys nineteenth-century developments. P. Curtin et al., *African History: From Earliest Times to Independence,* 2d ed. (1995), is an excellent brief introduction to Africa in the age of imperialism. J. D. Fage, *A History of Africa,* 3d ed. (1995), is also recommended. A classic study of Western expansion from an Indian viewpoint is Panikkar's volume mentioned in the Notes. S. Wolpert, *A New History of India,* 5th ed. (1997), incorporates recent scholarship in a wide-ranging study that is highly recommended.

# Listening to the Past

## A British Woman in India

*Guides for housekeeping became popular in Europe in the nineteenth century as middle-class women funneled great energy into their homes. A British woman in India probably consulted* The Complete Indian Housekeeper and Cook *by Flora Annie Steel and Grace Gardiner, a bestseller published in 1888 and frequently updated.*

*Steel (1847–1929) moved to India in 1867 with her husband, a civil engineer, and lived there until the family returned to England in 1889. Accustomed to directing a large household with several Indian servants, Steel believed herself well qualified to offer advice "to English girls to whom fate may assign the task of being house-mothers in our Eastern empire." The following passage focuses on how the British mistress should manage her Indian servants, and along with practical suggestions it lays bare some basic attitudes and assumptions of Europeans in colonial settings. Steel subsequently wrote books on India, education, and women's issues.*

Housekeeping in India, when once the first strangeness has worn off, is a far easier task in many ways than it is in England, though it none the less requires time, and, in this present transitional period, an almost phenomenal patience. . . .

And, first it must be distinctly understood that it is not necessary, or in the least degree desirable, that an educated woman should waste the best years of her life in scolding and petty supervision. Life holds higher duties, and it is indubitable that friction and over-zeal is a sure sign of a bad housekeeper. . . .

Easy, however, as the actual housekeeping is in India, the personal attention of the mistress is quite as much needed here as at home. The Indian servant, it is true, learns more readily, and is guiltless of the sniffiness with which Mary Jane [the servant in England] receives suggestions, but a few days of absence or neglect on the part of the mistress, results in the servants falling into their old habits with the inherited conservatism of dirt. This is, of course, disheartening, but it has to be faced as a necessary condition of life, until a few generations of training shall have started the Indian servant on a new inheritance of habit. It must never be forgotten that at present those mistresses who aim at anything beyond keeping a good table are in the minority, and that pioneering is always arduous work.

The first duty of a mistress is, of course, to be able to give intelligible orders to her servants; therefore it is necessary she should learn to speak Hindustani. No sane Englishwomen would dream of living, say, for twenty years, in Germany, Italy, or France, without making the *attempt,* at any rate, to learn the language. . . .

The next duty is obviously to insist on her orders being carried out. And here we come to the burning question: "How is this to be done?" Certainly, there is at present very little to which we can appeal in the average Indian servant, but then, until it is implanted by training, there is very little sense of duty in a child; yet in some well-regulated nurseries obedience is a foregone conclusion. The secret lies in making rules, and *keeping to them.* The Indian servant is a child in everything save age, and should be treated as a child; that is to say, kindly, but with the greatest firmness. The laws of the household should be those of the Medes and Persians, and first faults should never go unpunished. By overlooking a first offence, we lose the only opportunity we have of preventing it becoming a habit.

But it will be asked, How are we to punish our servants when we have no hold either on their minds or bodies? . . .

In their own experience the authors have found a system of rewards and punishments perfectly easy of attainment. One of them has for years adopted the plan of engaging her servants at so much a month—the lowest rate at which such servant is obtainable—and so much extra as *buksheesh* [a bonus], conditional on good service. For instance, a *khitmutgâr* [male table servant] is engaged permanently on Rs. 9 a month, but the additional rupee which makes the wage up to that usually demanded by good servants is a fluctuating assessment! . . . That plan has never been objected to, and . . . the household quite enters into the spirit of the idea, infinitely preferring it to volcanic eruptions of fault-finding. . . .

In regard to actual housekeeping, the authors emphatically deny the common assertion that it must necessarily run on different lines to what it does in England. Economy, prudence, efficiency are the same all over the world, and because butcher meat is cheap, that is no excuse for its being wasted. Some modification, of course, there must be, *but as little as possible.* . . .

A good mistress in India will try to set a good example to her servants in routine, method, and tidiness. Half-an-hour after breakfast should be sufficient for the whole arrangements for the day; but that half-hour should be given as punctually as possible. An untidy mistress invariably has *untidy,* a weak one, *idle* servants. It should never be forgotten that—though it is true in both hemispheres that if you want a thing done you should do it yourself—still, having to do it is a distinct confession of failure in your original intention. Anxious housewifes are too apt to accept defeat in this way; the result being that the lives of educated women are wasted in doing the work of lazy servants.

The authors' advice is therefore—

*"Never do work which an ordinarily good servant ought to be able to do. If the one you have will not or cannot do it, get another who can."* . . .

Having thus gone generally into the duties of the mistress, we may detail what in our opinion should be the daily routine.

The great object is to secure three things—smooth working, quick ordering, and subsequent peace and leisure to the mistress. It is as well, therefore, with a view to the preservation of temper, to eat your breakfast in peace before venturing into the pantry and cookroom; it is besides a mistake to be constantly on the worry.

Inspection parade should begin, then, immediately after breakfast, or as near ten o'clock as circumstances will allow. The cook should be waiting—in clean raiment—with a pile of plates, and his viands for the day spread out on a table. With everything *en evidence,* it will not take five minutes to decide on what is best, while a very constant occurrence at Indian tables—the serving up of stale, sour, and unwholesome food—will be avoided. It is perhaps *not* pleasant to go into such details, but a good mistress will remember the breadwinner who requires blood-forming nourishment, and the children whose constitutions are being built up day by day, sickly or healthy, according to the food given them; and bear in mind the fact that, in India especially, half the comfort of life depends on clean, wholesome, digestible food. . . .

We do not wish to advocate an unholy haughtiness; but an Indian household can no more be governed peacefully, without dignity and prestige, than an Indian Empire. For instance, if the mistress wishes to teach the cook a new dish, let her give the order for everything, down to charcoal, to be ready at a given time, and the cook in attendance; and let her do nothing herself that the servants can do, if only for this reason, that the only way of teaching is to *see* things done, not to let others see *you* do them.

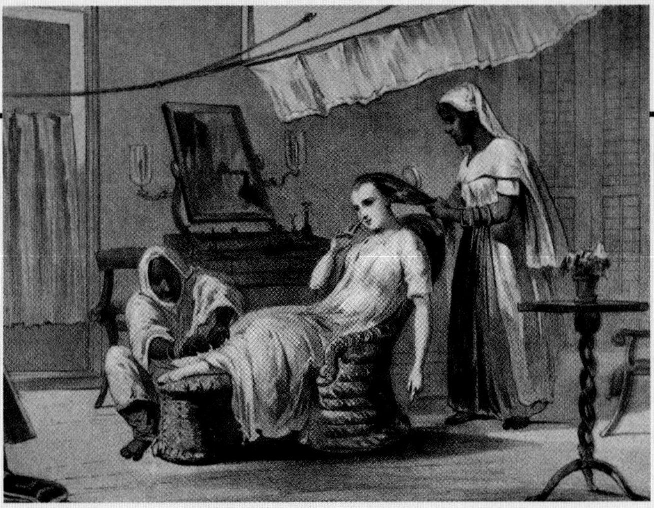

An English lady attended by her Indian servants and pampered from head to toe. *(Mary Evans Picture Library)*

## Questions for Analysis

1. What challenges does the British housekeeper face in India? How, according to Steel, should she meet them?
2. In what ways do Steel's comments and housekeeping policies reflect the attitudes of European imperialism?

*Source:* F. A. Steel and G. Gardiner, *The Complete Indian Housekeeper and Cook* (London: William Heinemann, 1902), chap. 1. Reprinted in L. DiCaprio and M. Wiesner, eds., *Lives and Voices: Sources in European Women's History* (Boston: Houghton Mifflin, 2001), pp. 323–328.

French soldiers in the trenches man a machine gun, the weapon that killed so many, in this chilling work by Christopher Nevinson. *(Tate Gallery, London/Art Resource, NY)*

chapter

# 27 The Great Break: War and Revolution

**chapter outline**

- The First World War
- The Home Front
- The Russian Revolution
- The Peace Settlement

In the summer of 1914, the nations of Europe went willingly to war. They believed they had no other choice. Moreover, both peoples and governments confidently expected a short war leading to a decisive victory. Such a war, they believed, would "clear the air," and European society would be able to go on as before.

These expectations were almost totally mistaken. The First World War was long, indecisive, and tremendously destructive. To the shell-shocked generation of survivors, it was known simply as the Great War: the war of unprecedented scope and intensity. From today's perspective, it is clear that the First World War marked a great break in the course of Western historical development since the French and Industrial Revolutions. A noted British political scientist has gone so far as to say that even in victorious and relatively fortunate Great Britain, the First World War was *the* great turning point in government and society, "as in everything else in modern British history. . . . There's a much greater difference between the Britain of 1914 and, say, 1920, than between the Britain of 1920 and today."[1] This strong statement contains a great amount of truth, for all of Europe as well as for Britain.

- What caused the Great War?
- How did the war lead to revolution and the fall of empires?
- How and why did war and revolution have such enormous and destructive consequences?
- How did the years of trauma and bloodshed form elements of today's world, many of which people now accept and even cherish?

These are the questions this chapter will address and try to answer.

## The First World War

The First World War was so long and destructive because it involved all the Great Powers and because it quickly degenerated into a senseless military stalemate. Like evenly matched boxers in a championship bout, the two sides tried to wear each other down. But there was no referee to call a draw, only the blind hammering of a life-or-death struggle. What were the roots of this terrible ordeal?

## The Bismarckian System of Alliances

The Franco-Prussian War and the founding of the German Empire opened a new era in international relations. France was decisively defeated in 1871 and forced to pay a large war indemnity and give up Alsace-Lorraine. In ten short years, from 1862 to 1871, Bismarck had made Prussia-Germany—traditionally the weakest of the Great Powers—the most powerful nation in Europe (see pages 829–833). Yet, as Bismarck never tired of repeating after 1871, Germany was a "satisfied" power. Within Europe, Germany had no territorial ambitions and wanted only peace.

But how was peace to be preserved? Bismarck's first concern was to keep an embittered France diplomatically isolated and without military allies. His second concern

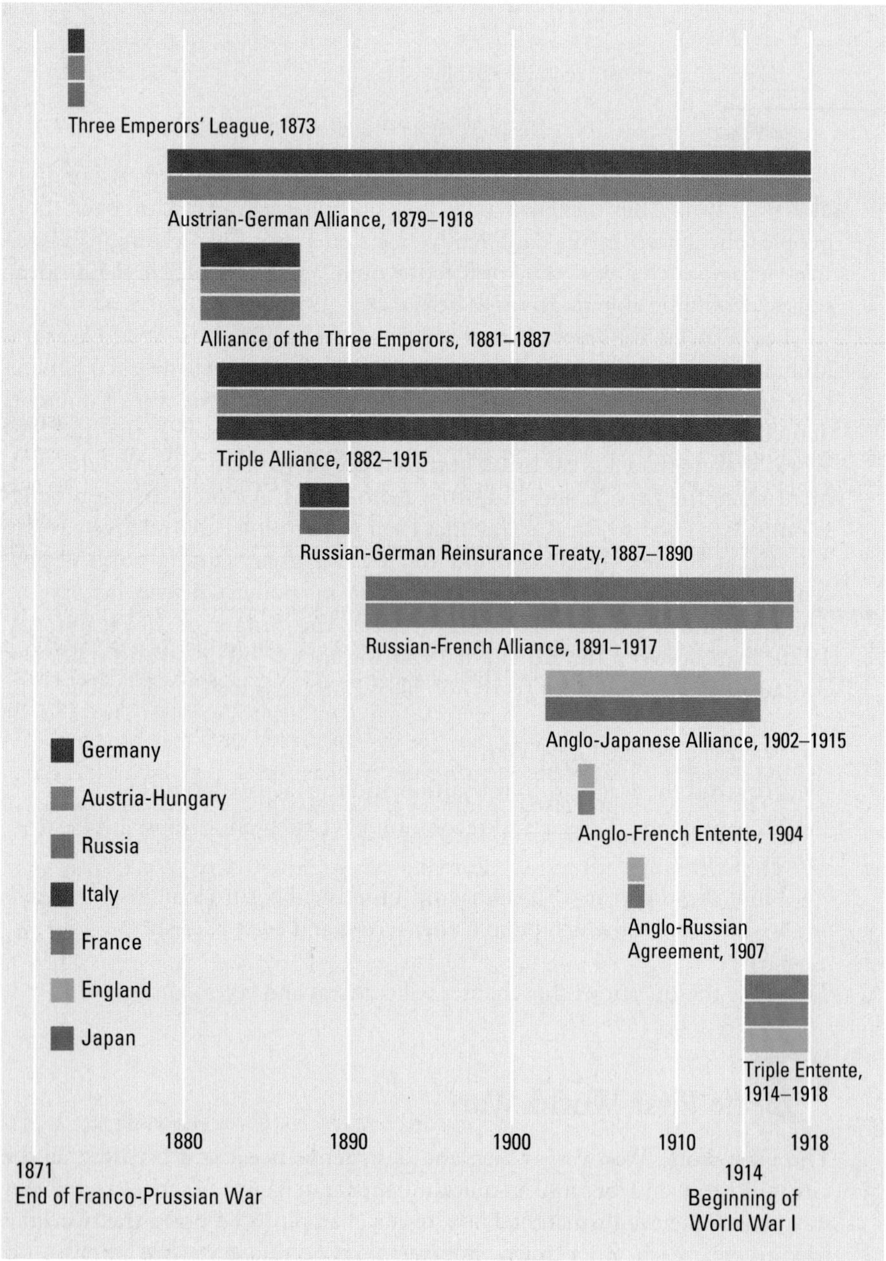


**FIGURE 27.1 The Alliance System After 1871** Bismarck's subtle diplomacy maintained reasonably good relations among the eastern monarchies—Germany, Russia, and Austria-Hungary—and kept France isolated. The situation changed dramatically in 1891, when the Russian-French Alliance divided the Great Powers into two fairly equal military blocs.

1912 | 1914 | 1916 | 1918 | 1920

**POLITICAL/MILITARY**

- 1912 First Balkan War
- 1914 Assassination of Archduke Francis Ferdinand
- 1914–1918 World War I
- 1915 Italy and Bulgaria enter World War I
- 1916 Rasputin murdered
- 1917 Russian Revolution
- 1919 Treaty of Versailles

**SOCIAL/ECONOMIC**

- 1915 Ministry of Munitions established in Britain
- 1916 German males between seventeen and sixty required to work only for war effort

**INTELLECTUAL/RELIGIOUS**

- 1916–1918 Growth of antiwar movement throughout Europe

was the threat to peace posed from the east, from Austria-Hungary and from Russia. Those two enormous multinational empires had many conflicting interests, particularly in the Balkans, where the Ottoman Empire—the "sick man of Europe"—was ebbing fast. There was a real threat that Germany might be dragged into a great war between the two rival empires. Bismarck's solution was a system of alliances (see Figure 27.1) to restrain both Russia and Austria-Hungary, to prevent conflict between them, and to isolate a hostile France, which could never forget the loss of Alsace-Lorraine.

A first step was the creation in 1873 of the conservative **Three Emperors' League,** which linked the monarchs of Austria-Hungary, Germany, and Russia in an alliance against radical movements. In 1877 and 1878, when Russia's victories in a war with the Ottoman Empire threatened the balance of Austrian and Russian interests in the Balkans and the balance of British and Russian interests in the Middle East, Bismarck played the role of sincere peacemaker. But his balancing efforts at the Congress of Berlin in 1878 infuriated Russian nationalists, and this led Bismarck to conclude a defensive military alliance with Austria against Russia in 1879. This alliance lasted until 1918 and the end of World War I. Motivated by tensions with France, Italy joined Germany and Austria in 1882, thereby forming what became known as the Triple Alliance.

Bismarck continued to work for peace in eastern Europe, seeking to neutralize tensions between Austria-Hungary and Russia. In 1881 he capitalized on their mutual fears and cajoled them both into a secret alliance with Germany. This Alliance of the Three Emperors lasted until 1887.

Bismarck also maintained good relations with Britain and Italy, while encouraging France in Africa but keeping France isolated in Europe. In 1887 Russia declined to renew the Alliance of the Three Emperors because of new tensions in the Balkans. Bismarck craftily substituted the Russian-German Reinsurance Treaty, by which both states promised neutrality if the other was attacked.

Bismarck's accomplishments in foreign policy after 1871 were great. For almost a generation, he maintained German leadership in international affairs, and he worked successfully for peace by managing conflicts and by restraining Austria-Hungary and Russia with defensive alliances.

## The Rival Blocs

In 1890 the young, impetuous Emperor William II dismissed Bismarck, in part because of the chancellor's friendly policy toward Russia since the 1870s. William then adamantly refused to renew the Russian-German Reinsurance Treaty, in spite of Russian willingness to do

**German Warships Under Full Steam** As these impressive ships engaged in battle exercises in 1907 suggest, Germany did succeed in building a large modern navy. But Britain was equally determined to maintain its naval superiority, and the spiraling arms race helped poison relations between the two countries. *(Archives Charmet/Bibliothèque des Arts Décoratifs/Jean-Loup Charmet/The Bridgeman Art Library)*

so. This fateful departure in foreign affairs prompted long-isolated republican France to court absolutist Russia, offering loans, arms, and friendship. In both countries, there were enthusiastic public demonstrations, and in 1891 in St. Petersburg harbor, the autocratic Alexander III stood bareheaded on a French battleship while a band played the "Marseillaise," the hymn of the Revolution. A preliminary agreement between the two countries was reached in 1891, and in early 1894 France and Russia became military allies. This alliance (see Figure 27.1) was to remain in effect as long as the Triple Alliance of Austria, Germany, and Italy existed. As a result, continental Europe was dangerously divided into two rival blocs.

Great Britain's foreign policy became increasingly crucial. Long content with "splendid isolation" and no permanent alliances, Britain after 1891 was the only uncommitted Great Power. Could Britain afford to remain isolated, or would it feel compelled to take sides? Alliance with France or Russia certainly seemed highly unlikely. With a vast and rapidly expanding empire, Britain was often in serious conflict with these countries around the world.

Britain also squabbled with Germany, but many Germans and some Britons felt that a "natural alliance" united the advanced, racially related Germanic and Anglo-Saxon peoples. However, the generally good relations that had prevailed between Prussia and Great Britain ever since the mid-eighteenth century, and certainly under Bismarck, gave way to a bitter Anglo-German rivalry.

There were several reasons for this tragic development. Commercial rivalry in world markets between Germany and Great Britain increased sharply in the 1890s, and William II's tactless public statements and Germany's pursuit of world power unsettled the British. Above all, Germany's decision in 1900 to expand greatly its battle fleet posed a challenge to Britain's long-standing naval supremacy. This decision coincided with the hard-fought South African War (1899–1902) between the British and the tiny Dutch republics of southern Africa, which had a major impact on British policy. British political leaders saw that Britain was overextended around the world. The South African War also brought into the open widespread anti-British feeling, as editorial writers in many nations denounced this latest manifestation of British imperialism. Thus British leaders prudently set about shoring up their exposed position with alliances and agreements.

Britain improved its often-strained relations with the United States and in 1902 concluded a formal alliance with Japan (see Figure 27.1). Britain then responded favorably to the advances of France's skillful foreign minister, Théophile Delcassé, who wanted better relations with Britain and was willing to accept British rule in Egypt in return for British support of French plans to dominate Morocco. The resulting Anglo-French Entente of 1904 settled all outstanding colonial disputes between Britain and France.

Frustrated by Britain's turn toward France in 1904, Germany's leaders decided to test the strength of the entente. Rather than accept the typical territorial payoff of imperial competition—a slice of French jungle somewhere in Africa or a port in Morocco—in return for French primacy in Morocco, the Germans foolishly rattled their swords by insisting in 1905 on an international conference on the whole Moroccan question. Germany's crude bullying forced France and Britain closer together, and Germany left the resulting Algeciras Conference of 1906 empty-handed and isolated (except for Austria-Hungary).

The result of the Moroccan crisis and the Algeciras Conference was something of a diplomatic revolution. Britain, France, Russia, and even the United States began to see Germany as a potential threat, a would-be intimidator that might seek to dominate all Europe. At the same time, German leaders began to see sinister plots to "encircle" Germany and block its development as a world power. In 1907 Russia, battered by its disastrous war with Japan and the revolution of 1905, agreed to settle its quarrels with Great Britain in Persia and Central Asia with the Anglo-Russian Agreement (see Figure 27.1). As a result of that agreement, Germany's blustering paranoia increased, as did Britain's thinly disguised hostility.

Germany's decision to add a large, enormously expensive fleet of big-gun battleships to its already expanding navy also heightened tensions after 1907. German nationalists, led by the extremely persuasive Admiral Alfred von Tirpitz, saw a large navy as the legitimate mark of a great world power and as a source of pride and patriotic unity. But British leaders such as David Lloyd George saw it as a detestable military challenge, which forced them to spend the "People's Budget" (see page 844) on battleships rather than social welfare. Unscrupulous journalists and special-interest groups in both countries also portrayed healthy competition in foreign trade and investment as a form of economic warfare.

Many educated shapers of public opinion and ordinary people in Britain and Germany were increasingly locked in a fateful "love-hate" relationship between the two countries. Proud nationalists in both countries simultaneously admired and feared the power and accomplishments of their nearly equal rival. In 1909 the mass-circulation London *Daily Mail* hysterically informed its readers in a series of reports that "Germany is deliberately preparing to destroy the British Empire."[2] By then Britain was psychologically, if not officially, in the Franco-Russian camp. The leading nations of Europe were divided into two hostile blocs, both ill-prepared to deal with upheaval on Europe's southeastern frontier.

## The Outbreak of War

In the early years of the twentieth century, war in the Balkans was as inevitable as anything can be in human history. The reason was simple: nationalism was destroying the Ottoman Empire in Europe and threatening to break up the Austro-Hungarian Empire. The only questions were what kinds of wars would occur and where they would lead.

Greece had long before led the struggle for national liberation, winning its independence in 1832. In 1875 widespread nationalist rebellion in the Ottoman Empire had resulted in Turkish repression, Russian intervention, and Great Power tensions. Bismarck had helped resolve this crisis at the 1878 Congress of Berlin, which worked out the partial division of Turkish possessions in Europe. Austria-Hungary obtained the right to "occupy and administer" Bosnia and Herzegovina. Serbia and Romania won independence, and a part of Bulgaria won local autonomy. The Ottoman Empire retained important Balkan holdings, for Austria-Hungary and Russia each feared the other's domination of totally independent states in the area (see Map 27.1).

By 1903, however, Balkan nationalism was on the rise once again. Serbia led the way, becoming openly hostile toward both Austria-Hungary and the Ottoman Empire. The Serbs, a Slavic people, looked to Slavic Russia for support of their national aspirations. To block Serbian expansion and to take advantage of Russia's weakness

**MAP 27.1 The Balkans After the Congress of Berlin, 1878** The Ottoman Empire suffered large territorial losses but remained a power in the Balkans.

**MAP 27.2 The Balkans in 1914** Ethnic boundaries did not follow political boundaries, and Serbian national aspirations threatened Austria-Hungary.

after the revolution of 1905, Austria in 1908 formally annexed Bosnia and Herzegovina, with their large Serbian, Croatian, and Muslim populations. The kingdom of Serbia erupted in rage but could do nothing without Russian support.

Then, in 1912, in the First Balkan War, Serbia joined Greece and Bulgaria to attack the Ottoman Empire and then quarreled with Bulgaria over the spoils of victory—a dispute that led in 1913 to the Second Balkan War. Austria intervened in 1913 and forced Serbia to give up Albania. After centuries, nationalism had finally destroyed the Ottoman Empire in Europe (see Map 27.2). This sudden but long-awaited event elated the Balkan nationalists and dismayed the leaders of multinational Austria-Hungary. The former hoped and the latter feared that Austria might be next to be broken apart.

Within this tense context, Archduke Francis Ferdinand, heir to the Austrian and Hungarian thrones, and his wife, Sophie, were assassinated by Serbian revolutionaries living in Bosnia on June 28, 1914, during a state visit to the Bosnian capital of Sarajevo. After some hesitation, the leaders of Austria-Hungary concluded that Serbia was implicated and had to be severely punished once and for all. On July 23 Austria-Hungary finally presented Serbia with an unconditional ultimatum. The Serbian government had forty-eight hours in which to agree to demands that would amount to ceding control of the Serbian state. When Serbia replied moderately but evasively, Austria began to mobilize and then declared war on Serbia on July 28. Thus a desperate multinational Austria-Hungary deliberately chose war in a last-ditch attempt to stem the rising tide of hostile nationalism within its borders and save the existing state. The "Third Balkan War" had begun.

Of prime importance in Austria-Hungary's fateful decision was Germany's unconditional support. Emperor William II and his chancellor, Theobald von Bethmann-Hollweg, gave Austria-Hungary a "blank check" and urged aggressive measures in early July, even though they realized that war between Austria and Russia was the most probable result. They knew Russian pan-Slavs saw Russia not only as the protector but also as the eventual liberator of southern Slavs. A resurgent Russia could not stand by, as in the Bosnian crisis, and simply watch the Serbs be crushed. Yet Bethmann-Hollweg apparently hoped that while Russia (and therefore France) would go to war, Great Britain would remain neutral, unwilling to fight for "Russian aggression" in the distant Balkans.

In fact, the diplomatic situation was already out of control. Military plans and timetables began to dictate policy. Russia, a vast country, would require much longer to mobilize its armies than Germany and Austria-Hungary. On July 28, as Austrian armies bombarded Belgrade, Tsar Nicholas II ordered a partial mobilization against Austria-Hungary. Almost immediately he found that this was impossible. All the complicated mobilization plans of the Russian general staff had assumed a war with both Austria and Germany: Russia could not mobilize against one without mobilizing against the other. Therefore, on July 29 Russia ordered full mobilization and in effect declared general war.

The same tragic subordination of political considerations to military strategy descended on Germany. The German general staff had also thought only in terms of a

**Nationalist Opposition in the Balkans** This band of well-armed and determined guerrillas from northern Albania was typical of groups fighting against Ottoman rule in the Balkans. Balkan nationalists succeeded in driving the Ottoman Turks out of most of Europe, but their victory increased tensions with Austria-Hungary and among the Great Powers. *(Roger-Viollet/Getty Images)*

"**Never Forget!**" This 1915 French poster with its passionate headline dramatizes Germany's brutal invasion of Belgium in 1914. Neutral Belgium is personified as a traumatized mother, assaulted and ravished by savage outlaws. The "rape of Belgium" featured prominently—and effectively—in anti-German propaganda. *(Mary Evans Picture Library)*

two-front war. The staff's plan for war called for knocking out France first with a lightning attack through neutral Belgium before turning on Russia. So on August 2, 1914, General Helmuth von Moltke, "acting under a dictate of self-preservation," demanded that Belgium permit German armies to pass through its territory. Belgium, whose neutrality had been solemnly guaranteed in 1839 by all the great states including Prussia, refused. Germany attacked. Thus Germany's terrible, politically disastrous response to a war in the Balkans was an all-out invasion of France by way of the plains of neutral Belgium on August 3. In the face of this act of aggression, Great Britain joined France and declared war on Germany the following day. The First World War had begun.

## Reflections on the Origins of the War

In reflecting on the origins of the First World War, it seems clear that Austria-Hungary deliberately started the Third Balkan War. A war for the right to survive was Austria-Hungary's desperate, though understandable, response to the aggressive, yet understandable, revolutionary drive of Serbian nationalists to unify their people in a single state. Moreover, in spite of Russian intervention in the quarrel, it is clear that from the beginning of the crisis, Germany not only pushed and goaded Austria-Hungary but also was responsible for turning a little war into the Great War by means of a sledgehammer attack on Belgium and France. Why Germany was so aggressive in 1914 is less certain.

Diplomatic historians stress that German leaders lost control of the international system after Bismarck's resignation in 1890. They felt increasingly that Germany's status as a world power was declining, while that of Britain, France, Russia, and the United States was growing. Indeed, the powers of what officially became in August 1914 the **Triple Entente**—Great Britain, France, and Russia—were checking Germany's vague but real aspirations as well as working to strangle Austria-Hungary, Germany's only real ally. Germany's aggression in 1914 reflected the failure of all European leaders, not just those in Germany, to incorporate Bismarck's mighty empire permanently and peacefully into the international system.

A more controversial interpretation argues that domestic conflicts and social tensions lay at the root of German aggression. While Germany industrialized and urbanized rapidly after 1870 and established a popularly elected parliament, political power remained concentrated in the hands of the monarchy, the army, and the Prussian nobility. Determined to hold on to power and frightened by the rising socialist movement and a powerful wave of strikes in 1914, the German ruling class was willing to take chances. It was willing to gamble on diplomatic victory and even on war as the means of rallying the masses to its side and preserving its privileged position. Historians have also discerned similar, if less clear-cut, behavior in Great Britain, where leaders faced civil war in northern Ireland, and in Russia, where the revolution of 1905 had brought tsardom to its knees.

This debate over social tensions and domestic political factors correctly suggests that the triumph of nationalism was a crucial underlying precondition of the Great War. Nationalism was at the heart of the Balkan wars, in the form of Serbian aspirations and the grandiose pan-German versus pan-Slavic racism of some fanatics. Nationalism also drove the spiraling arms race. Broad popular commitment to "my country right or wrong" weakened groups that thought in terms of international communities and consequences. Thus the big international bankers, who were frightened by the prospect of war in July 1914, and the extreme-left socialists, who believed that the enemy was at home and not abroad, were equally out of step with national feeling. In each country, the great majority of the population enthusiastically embraced the outbreak of war in August 1914. In each country, people believed that their country had been wronged, and they rallied to defend it. Patriotic nationalism brought unity in the short run.

In all of this, the wealthy governing classes certainly underestimated the risk of war to themselves in 1914. They had forgotten that great wars and great social revolutions very often go hand in hand. Metternich's alliance of conservative forces in support of international peace and the social status quo had become only a distant memory.

## Stalemate and Slaughter

When the Germans invaded Belgium in August 1914, they and everyone else believed that the war would be short, for urban society rested on the food and raw materials of the world economy: "The boys will be home by Christmas." The Belgian army heroically defended its homeland, however, and fell back in good order to join a rapidly landed British army corps near the Franco-Belgian border. Instead of quickly capturing Paris in a vast encircling movement, by the end of August dead-tired German soldiers were advancing along an enormous front in the scorching summer heat.

On September 6 the French attacked a gap in the German line at the Battle of the Marne. For three days, France threw everything into the attack. At one point, the French government desperately requisitioned all the taxis of Paris to rush reserves to the troops at the front. Finally, the Germans fell back. Paris and France had been miraculously saved (see Map 27.3 on page 898).

Soon, with the armies stalled, both sides began to dig trenches to protect themselves from machine-gun fire. By November 1914, an unbroken line of trenches extended from the Belgian ports through northern France, past the fortress of Verdun, and on to the Swiss frontier. In the face of this unexpected stalemate, slaughter on the western front began in earnest. The defenders on both sides dug in behind rows of trenches, mines, and barbed wire. For days and even weeks, ceaseless shelling by heavy artillery supposedly "softened up" the enemy in a given area (and also signaled the coming attack). Then young draftees and their junior officers went "over the top" of the trenches in frontal attacks on the enemy's line.

The cost in lives of this **trench warfare** was staggering, the gains in territory minuscule. The massive French and British offensives during 1915 never gained more than 3 miles of blood-soaked earth from the enemy. In the Battle of the Somme in the summer of 1916, the British and French gained an insignificant 125 square miles at the cost of 600,000 dead or wounded, while the Germans lost 500,000 men. In that same year the unsuccessful German campaign against Verdun cost 700,000 lives on both sides. British poet Siegfried Sassoon (1886–1967) wrote of the Somme offensive, "I am staring at a sunlit picture of Hell."

The year 1917 was equally terrible. The hero of Erich Remarque's great novel *All Quiet on the Western Front* (1929) describes one attack:

*We see men living with their skulls blown open; we see soldiers run with their two feet cut off. . . . Still the little piece of convulsed earth in which we lie is held. We have yielded no more than a few hundred yards of it as a prize to the enemy. But on every yard there lies a dead man.*

Such was war on the western front.

Trench warfare shattered an entire generation of young men. Millions who could have provided political creativity and leadership after the war were forever missing. Moreover, those who lived through the slaughter were maimed, shell-shocked, embittered, and profoundly disillusioned. The young soldiers went to war believing in the world of their leaders and elders—the pre-1914 world of order, progress, and patriotism. Then, in Remarque's words, the "first bombardment showed us our mistake, and under it the world as they had taught it to us broke in pieces."

## The Widening War

On the eastern front, slaughter did not degenerate into suicidal trench warfare. With the outbreak of the war, the "Russian steamroller" immediately moved into eastern Germany. Very badly damaged by the Germans under Generals Paul von Hindenburg and Erich Ludendorff at the Battles of Tannenberg and the Masurian Lakes in August and September 1914, Russia never threatened Germany again. On the Austrian front, enormous armies seesawed back and forth, suffering enormous losses. Austro-Hungarian armies were repulsed twice by Serbia in bitter fighting. But with the help of German forces, they reversed the Russian advances of 1914 and forced the Russians to retreat deep into their own territory in the eastern campaign of 1915. A staggering 2.5 million Russians were killed, wounded, or taken prisoner that year.

**The Tragic Absurdity of Trench Warfare** Soldiers charge across a scarred battlefield and overrun an enemy trench. The dead defender on the right will fire no more. But this is only another futile charge that will yield much blood and little land. A whole generation is being decimated by the slaughter. *(By courtesy of the Trustees of the Imperial War Museum)*

These changing tides of victory and hopes for territorial gains brought neutral countries into the war (see Map 27.3). Italy, a member of the Triple Alliance since 1882, had declared its neutrality in 1914 on the grounds that Austria had launched a war of aggression. Then in May 1915, Italy joined the Triple Entente of Great Britain, France, and Russia in return for promises of Austrian territory. In October 1914 the Ottoman Empire joined with Austria and Germany, by then known as the Central Powers. The following September Bulgaria decided to follow the Ottoman Empire's lead in order to settle old scores with Serbia. The Balkans, with the exception of Greece, came to be occupied by the Central Powers.

The entry of the Ottoman Turks carried the war into the Middle East. Heavy fighting between the Ottomans and the Russians saw battle lines seesawing back and forth and enveloping the Armenians, who lived on both sides of the border and had experienced brutal repression by the Turks in 1909 (see Map 27.5 on page 915). When in 1915 some Armenians welcomed Russian armies as liberators, the Ottoman government ordered a genocidal mass deportation of its Armenian citizens from their homeland. A million Armenians died from murder, starvation, and disease during World War I. In 1915 British forces tried to take the Dardanelles and Constantinople from the Ottomans but were badly defeated.

**Otto Dix: War** Returning to Germany after the war, Dix was haunted by the horrors he had seen. This vivid expressionist masterpiece, part of a triptych painted in 1929–1932, probes the tormented memory of endless days in muddy trenches and dugouts, living with rats and lice and the constant danger of exploding shells, snipers, and all-out attack. Many who escaped death or dismemberment were mentally wounded forever by their experiences. *(Staatliche Kunstsammlungen Dresden, © 2004 Artists Rights Society [ARS], New York/VG Bild-Kunst, Bunn)*

The British were more successful at inciting the Arabs to revolt against their Turkish overlords. An enigmatic British colonel, soon known to millions as Lawrence of Arabia, helped lead the Arab revolt in early 1917. In 1918 British armies from Egypt smashed the Ottoman Empire once and for all, drawing primarily on forces from Australia, New Zealand, and India. Thus war brought revolutionary change to the Middle East.

War also spread to some parts of East Asia and Africa. Instead of revolting as the Germans hoped, the colonial subjects of the British and French generally supported their foreign masters, providing crucial supplies and fighting in Europe and the Ottoman Empire. They also helped local British and French commanders seize Germany's colonies around the globe. The Japanese, allied in Asia with the British since 1902, similarly used the war to grab German outposts in the Pacific Ocean and on the Chinese mainland, infuriating Chinese patriots and heightening long-standing tensions between China and Japan. More than a million Africans and Asians served in the various armies of the warring powers; more than double that number served as porters to carry equipment. The French, facing a shortage of young men, made especially heavy use of colonial troops.

**MAP 27.3 The First World War in Europe** Trench warfare on the western front was concentrated in Belgium and northern France, while the war in the east encompassed an enormous territory.

**The Armenian Atrocities** When in 1915 some Armenians welcomed Russian armies as liberators after years of persecution, the Ottoman government ordered a genocidal mass deportation of its Armenian citizens from their homeland in the empire's eastern provinces. This photo, taken in Kharpert in 1915 by a German businessman from his hotel window, shows Turkish guards marching Armenian men off to a prison, where they will be tortured to death. A million Armenians died from murder, starvation, and disease during World War I. *(Courtesy of the Armenian Library, Watertown, Mass.)*

In April 1917 the United States declared war on Germany, another crucial development in the expanding conflict. American intervention grew out of the war at sea, sympathy for the Triple Entente, and the increasing desperation of total war. At the beginning of the war, Britain and France had established a total naval blockade to strangle the Central Powers. No neutral ship was permitted to sail to Germany with any cargo. The blockade annoyed Americans, but effective propaganda about German atrocities in occupied Belgium as well as lush profits from selling war supplies to Britain and France blunted American indignation.

Moreover, in early 1915 Germany launched a counter-blockade using the murderously effective submarine, a new weapon that violated traditional niceties of fair warning under international law. In May 1915, after sinking about ninety ships in the British war zone, a German submarine sank the British passenger liner ***Lusitania,*** which was also carrying arms and munitions. More than 1,000 lives, among them 139 Americans, were lost. President Woodrow Wilson protested vigorously. Germany was forced to relax its submarine warfare for almost two years; the alternative was almost certain war with the United States.

Early in 1917, the German military command—confident that improved submarines could starve Britain into submission before the United States could come to its rescue—resumed unrestricted submarine warfare. Like the invasion of Belgium, this was a reckless gamble. "German submarine warfare against commerce," President Wilson had told a sympathetic Congress and people, "is a warfare against mankind." Thus the last uncommitted great nation, as fresh and enthusiastic as Europe had been in 1914, entered the world war in April 1917, almost three years after it began. Eventually the United States was to tip the balance in favor of the Triple Entente and its allies.

## The Home Front

See DBQ 11

Before looking at the last year of the Great War, let us turn our attention to the people on the home front. They were tremendously involved in the titanic struggle. War's impact on them was no less massive than on the men crouched in the trenches. (See the feature "Listening to the Past: The Experience of War" on pages 918–919.)

### Mobilizing for Total War

In August 1914, most people greeted the outbreak of hostilities enthusiastically. In every country, the masses believed that their nation was in the right and defending itself from aggression. With the exception of a few extreme left-wingers, even socialists supported the war. Everywhere the support of the masses and working class contributed to national unity and an energetic war effort.

By mid-October generals and politicians had begun to realize that more than patriotism would be needed to win the war, whose end was not in sight. Each country experienced a relentless, desperate demand for men and weapons. In each country, economic life and organization had to change and change fast to keep the war machine from sputtering to a stop. And change they did.

In each country, a government of national unity began to plan and control economic and social life in order to wage **total war.** Free-market capitalism was abandoned, at least "for the duration." Instead, government planning boards established priorities and decided what was to be produced and consumed. Rationing, price and wage controls, and even restrictions on workers' freedom of movement were imposed by government. Only through such regimentation could a country make the greatest possible military effort. Thus, though there were national variations, the great nations all moved toward planned economies commanded by the established political leadership.

The economy of total war blurred the old distinction between soldiers on the battlefield and civilians at home. The war was a war of whole peoples and entire populations. Based on tremendously productive industrial economies not confined to a single nation, total war yielded an effective—and therefore destructive—war effort on all sides.

However awful the war was, the ability of governments to manage and control highly complicated economies strengthened the cause of socialism. With the First World War, state socialism became for the first time a realistic economic blueprint rather than a utopian program. Germany illustrates the general trend. It also went furthest in developing a planned economy to wage total war.

As soon as war began, Walter Rathenau, the talented, foresighted Jewish industrialist in charge of Germany's largest electric company, convinced the government to set up the **War Raw Materials Board** to ration and distribute raw materials. Under Rathenau's direction, every useful material from foreign oil to barnyard manure was inventoried and rationed. Moreover, the board launched successful attempts to produce substitutes such as synthetic rubber and synthetic nitrates, needed to make explosives and essential to the blockaded German war machine. An aggressive recycling campaign, including everything from fruit peels to women's hair, augmented these efforts.

Food was also rationed in accordance with physical need. Men and women doing hard manual work were given extra rations. During the last two years of the war, only children and expectant mothers received milk rations. At the same time, Germany failed to tax the war profits of private firms heavily enough. This failure contributed to massive deficit financing, inflation, the growth of a black market, and the eventual re-emergence of class conflict.

Following the terrible Battles of Verdun and the Somme in 1916, Chancellor Bethmann-Hollweg was driven from office in 1917 by military leaders Hindenburg and Ludendorff, who became the real rulers of Germany. They decreed the ultimate mobilization for total war. Germany, said Hindenburg, could win only "if all the treasures of our soil that agriculture and industry can produce are used exclusively for the conduct of War. . . . All other considerations must come second."[3] Thus in December 1916, military leaders rammed through the Reichstag the Auxiliary Service Law, which required all males between seventeen and sixty to work only at jobs considered critical to the war effort.

Although women and children were not specifically mentioned, this forced-labor law was also aimed at them. Many women already worked in war factories, mines, and steel mills, where they labored, like men, at the heaviest and most dangerous jobs. With the passage of the Auxiliary Service Law, many more women followed. People averaged little more than one thousand calories a day. Thus in Germany total war led to the establishment of history's first "totalitarian" society, and war production increased while some people starved to death.

Great Britain mobilized for total war less rapidly and less completely than Germany, for it could import materi-

**Hair for the War Effort** Blockaded and cut off from overseas supplies, Germany mobilized effectively to find substitutes at home. This poster calls on German women—especially young women with long flowing tresses—to donate their hair, which was used to make rope. Children were organized by their teachers into garbage brigades to collect every scrap of useful material. *(akg-images)*

als from its empire and from the United States. By 1915, however, a serious shortage of shells had led to the establishment of the Ministry of Munitions under David Lloyd George. The ministry organized private industry to produce for the war, controlled profits, allocated labor, fixed wage rates, and settled labor disputes. By December 1916, when Lloyd George became prime minister, the British economy was largely planned and regulated. More than two hundred factories and 90 percent of all imports were bought and allocated directly by the state. Great Britain had followed successfully in Germany's footsteps.

## The Social Impact

The social impact of total war was no less profound than the economic impact, though again there were important national variations. The millions of men at the front and the insatiable needs of the military created a tremendous demand for workers. Jobs were available for everyone. This situation—seldom, if ever, seen before 1914, when unemployment and poverty had been facts of urban life—brought about momentous changes.

One such change was greater power and prestige for labor unions. Having proved their loyalty in August 1914, labor unions cooperated with war governments on work rules, wages, and production schedules in return for real participation in important decisions. This entry of labor leaders and unions into policymaking councils paralleled the entry of socialist leaders into the war governments.

The role of women changed dramatically. In every country, large numbers of women left home and domestic service to work in industry, transportation, and offices. By 1917 women formed fully 43 percent of the labor force in Russia. Moreover, women became highly visible—not only as munitions workers but as bank tellers, mail carriers, even police officers. Women also served as nurses and doctors at the front. (See the feature "Individuals in Society: Vera Brittain.") In general, the war greatly expanded the range of women's activities and changed attitudes toward women. As a direct result of women's many-sided war effort, Britain, Germany, and Austria granted women the right to vote immediately after the war. Women also showed a growing spirit of independence during the war, as they started to bob their hair, shorten their skirts, and smoke in public.

War promoted greater social equality, blurring class distinctions and lessening the gap between rich and poor. This blurring was most apparent in Great Britain, where wartime hardship was never extreme. In fact, the bottom third of the population generally lived *better* than they ever had, for the poorest gained most from the severe shortage of labor. English writer Robert Roberts recalled how his parents' tiny grocery store in the slums of Manchester thrived during the war as never before when people who had scrimped to buy bread and soup bones were able to afford fancy cakes and thick steaks. In continental countries, greater equality was reflected in full employment, rationing according to physical needs, and a sharing of hardships. There, too, society became more uniform and more egalitarian, in spite of some war profiteering.

Finally, death itself had no respect for traditional social distinctions. It savagely decimated the young aristocratic officers who led the charge, and it fell heavily on the mass

**Waging Total War** A British war plant strains to meet the insatiable demand for trench-smashing heavy artillery shells. Quite typically, many of these defense workers are women. *(By courtesy of the Trustees of the Imperial War Museum)*

of drafted peasants and unskilled workers who followed. Yet death often spared the aristocrats of labor, the skilled workers and foremen. Their lives were too valuable to squander at the front, for they were needed to train the newly recruited women and older unskilled men laboring valiantly in war plants at home.

## Growing Political Tensions

During the first two years of war, most soldiers and civilians supported their governments. Even in Austria-Hungary—the most vulnerable of the belligerents, with its competing nationalities—loyalty to the state and monarchy remained astonishingly strong through 1916. Belief in a just cause, patriotic nationalism, the planned economy, and a sharing of burdens united peoples behind their various national leaders.

Each government employed rigorous censorship to control public opinion, and each used both crude and subtle propaganda to maintain popular support. German propaganda hysterically pictured black soldiers from France's African empire raping German women, while German atrocities in Belgium and elsewhere were ceaselessly recounted and exaggerated by the French and British. Patriotic posters and slogans, slanted news, and biased editorials inflamed national hatreds and helped sustain superhuman efforts.

By the spring of 1916, however, people were beginning to crack under the strain of total war. In April 1916, Irish nationalists in Dublin tried to take advantage of this situation and rose up against British rule in their great Easter Rebellion. A week of bitter fighting passed before the rebels were crushed and their leaders executed. On May 1, 1916, several thousand demonstrators in Berlin heard the radical socialist leader Karl Liebknecht (1871–1919) shout, "Down with the government! Down with the war!" Liebknecht was immediately arrested and imprisoned, but his daring action electrified Europe's far

# Individuals in Society

## Vera Brittain

Although the Great War upended millions of lives, it struck Europe's young people with the greatest force. For Vera Brittain (1893–1970), as for so many in her generation, the war became life's defining experience, which she captured forever in her famous autobiography, *Testament of Youth* (1933).

Brittain grew up in a wealthy business family in northern England, bristling at small-town conventions and discrimination against women. Very close to her brother Edward, two years her junior, Brittain read voraciously and dreamed of being a successful writer. Finishing boarding school and beating down her father's objections, she prepared for Oxford's rigorous entry exams and won a scholarship to its women's college. Brittain also fell in love with Roland Leighton, an equally brilliant student from a literary family and her brother's best friend. All three, along with two more close friends, Victor Richardson and Geoffrey Thurlow, confidently prepared to enter Oxford in late 1914.

When war suddenly approached in July 1914, Brittain shared with millions of Europeans a thrilling surge of patriotic support for her government, a pro-war enthusiasm she later played down in her published writings. She wrote in her diary that her "great fear" was that England would declare its neutrality and commit the "grossest treachery" toward France.* She seconded Roland's decision to enlist, agreeing with her sweetheart's glamorous view of war as "very ennobling and very beautiful." Later, exchanging anxious letters in 1915 with Roland in France, Vera began to see the conflict in personal, human terms. She wondered if any victory or defeat could be worth Roland's life.

Struggling to quell her doubts, Brittain redoubled her commitment to England's cause and volunteered as an army nurse. For the next three years she served with distinction in military hospitals in London, Malta, and northern France, repeatedly torn between the vision of noble sacrifice and the reality of human tragedy. She lost her sexual inhibitions caring for mangled male bodies, and she longed to consummate her love with Roland. Awaiting his return on leave on Christmas Day in 1915, she was greeted instead with a telegram: Roland had been killed two days before.

Roland's death was the first of the devastating blows that eventually overwhelmed Brittain's idealistic patriotism. In 1917, first Geoffrey and then Victor died from gruesome wounds. In early 1918, as the last great German offensive covered the floors of her war-zone hospital with maimed and dying German prisoners, the bone-weary Vera felt a common humanity and saw only more victims. A few weeks later brother Edward—her last hope—died in action. When the war ended, she was, she said, a "complete automaton," with "my deepest emotions paralyzed if not dead."

*Vera Brittain, marked forever by her wartime experiences.* (Vera Brittain Archive, William Ready Division of Archives and Research Collections, McMaster University Library)

Returning to Oxford and finishing her studies, Brittain gradually recovered. She formed a deep, restorative friendship with another talented woman writer, Winifred Holtby, published novels and articles, and became a leader in the feminist campaign for gender equality. She also married and had children. But her wartime memories were always there. Finally, Brittain succeeded in coming to grips with them in *Testament of Youth,* her powerful antiwar autobiography. The unflinching narrative spoke to the experiences of an entire generation and became a runaway bestseller. Above all perhaps, Brittain captured the ambivalent, contradictory character of the war, when millions of young people found excitement, courage, and common purpose but succeeded only in destroying their lives with their superhuman efforts and futile sacrifices. Becoming ever more committed to pacifism, Brittain opposed England's entry into World War II.

### Questions for Analysis

1. What were Brittain's initial feelings toward the war? How did they change as the conflict continued? Why did they change?
2. Why did Brittain volunteer as a nurse, as many women did? Judging from her account, how might wartime nursing have influenced women of her generation?
3. In portraying the ambivalent, contradictory character of World War I for Europe's youth, was Brittain describing the contradictory character of all modern warfare?

*Quoted in the excellent study by P. Berry and M. Bostridge, *Vera Brittain: A Life* (London: Virago Press, 2001), p. 59; additional quotes are from pp. 80 and 136. This work is highly recommended.

*The* **history companion** *features additional information and activities related to this topic.*
**history.college.hmco.com/students**

left. Strikes and protest marches over inadequate food began to flare up on every home front.

Soldiers' morale also began to decline. Italian troops mutinied. Numerous French units refused to fight after the disastrous French offensive of May 1917. Only tough military justice for leaders and a tacit agreement with the troops that there would be no more grand offensives enabled the new general in chief, Henri Philippe Pétain, to restore order. A rising tide of war-weariness and defeatism also swept France's civilian population before Georges Clemenceau emerged as a ruthless and effective wartime leader in November 1917. Clemenceau (1841–1929) established a virtual dictatorship, pouncing on strikers and jailing without trial journalists and politicians who dared to suggest a compromise peace with Germany.

The strains were worse for the Central Powers. In October 1916, the chief minister of Austria was assassinated by a young socialist crying, "Down with Absolutism! We want peace!"[4] The following month, when feeble old Emperor Francis Joseph died, a symbol of unity disappeared. In spite of absolute censorship, political dissatisfaction and conflicts among nationalities grew. In April 1917, Austria's chief minister summed up the situation in the gloomiest possible terms. The country and army were exhausted. Another winter of war would bring revolution and disintegration. "If the monarchs of the Central Powers cannot make peace in the coming months," he wrote, "it will be made for them by their peoples."[5] Both Czech and Yugoslav leaders demanded autonomous democratic states for their peoples. The British blockade kept tightening; people were starving.

The strain of total war and of the Auxiliary Service Law was also evident in Germany. In the winter of 1916 to 1917, Germany's military position appeared increasingly desperate. Stalemates and losses in the west were matched by temporary Russian advances in the east: hence the military's insistence on an all-or-nothing gamble of unrestricted submarine warfare when the Triple Entente refused in December 1916 to consider peace on terms favorable to the Central Powers.

Also, the national political unity of the first two years of war was collapsing as the social conflict of prewar Germany re-emerged. A growing minority of moderate socialists in the Reichstag began to vote against war credits. With little taste for violent upheaval and civil war, they called for a compromise "peace without annexations or reparations." In July 1917, a coalition of socialists and Catholics passed a resolution in the Reichstag to that effect. Such a peace was unthinkable for conservatives and military leaders. So also was the surge in revolutionary agitation and strikes by war-weary workers that occurred in early 1917. When the bread ration was further reduced in April, more than 200,000 workers struck and demonstrated for a week in Berlin, returning to work only under the threat of prison and military discipline. Thus militaristic Germany, like its ally Austria-Hungary (and its enemy France), was beginning to crack in 1917. Yet it was Russia that collapsed first and saved the Central Powers—for a time.

## The Russian Revolution

The Russian Revolution of 1917 was one of modern history's most momentous events. Directly related to the growing tensions of World War I, it had a significance far beyond the wartime agonies of a single European nation. The Russian Revolution opened a new era. For some, it was Marx's socialist vision come true; for others, it was the triumph of dictatorship. To all, it presented a radically new prototype of state and society.

### The Fall of Imperial Russia

Like its allies and its enemies, Russia embraced war with patriotic enthusiasm in 1914. At the Winter Palace, while throngs of people knelt and sang, "God save the tsar," Tsar Nicholas II (r. 1894–1917) repeated the oath Alexander I had sworn in 1812 and vowed never to make peace as long as the enemy stood on Russian soil. Russia's lower house, the Duma, voted war credits. Conservatives anticipated expansion in the Balkans, while liberals and most socialists believed alliance with Britain and France would bring democratic reforms. For a moment, Russia was united.

Unprecedented artillery barrages used up Russia's supplies of shells and ammunition, and better-equipped German armies inflicted terrible losses. In 1915 substantial numbers of Russian soldiers were sent to the front without rifles; they were told to find their arms among the dead. There were 2 million Russian casualties in 1915 alone. Nevertheless, Russia's battered peasant army did not collapse but continued to fight courageously, and Russia moved toward full mobilization on the home front. The Duma and organs of local government took the lead, setting up special committees to coordinate defense, industry, transportation, and agriculture. These efforts improved the military situation. Yet there were many failures, and Russia mobilized less effectively for total war than the other warring nations.

The great problem was leadership. Under the constitution resulting from the revolution of 1905 (see pages 837–838), the tsar had retained complete control over the bureaucracy and the army. Legislation proposed by the Duma, which was weighted in favor of the wealthy and conservative classes, was subject to the tsar's veto. Moreover, Nicholas II fervently wished to maintain the sacred inheritance of supreme royal power, which, with the Orthodox church, was for him the key to Russia's greatness. A kindly, slightly stupid man, of whom a friend said he "would have been an ideal country gentleman, devoting his life to wife and children, his farms and his sport," Nicholas failed to form a close partnership with his citizens in order to fight the war more effectively. He came to rely instead on the old bureaucratic apparatus, distrusting the moderate Duma, rejecting popular involvement, and resisting calls to share power.

As a result, the Duma, the educated middle classes, and the masses became increasingly critical of the tsar's leadership. Following Nicholas's belated dismissal of the incompetent minister of war, demands for more democratic and responsive government exploded in the Duma in the summer of 1915. In September parties ranging from conservative to moderate socialist formed the Progressive bloc, which called for a completely new government responsible to the Duma instead of the tsar. In answer, Nicholas temporarily adjourned the Duma and announced that he was traveling to the front in order to lead and rally Russia's armies.

His departure was a fatal turning point. With the tsar in the field with the troops, control of the government was taken over by the hysterical empress, Tsarina Alexandra, and a debauched adventurer and self-proclaimed holy man, Rasputin. A minor German princess and granddaughter of England's Queen Victoria, Nicholas's wife was a devoted mother with a sick child, a strong-willed woman with a hatred of parliaments. Having constantly urged her husband to rule absolutely, Alexandra tried to do so herself in his absence. She seated and unseated the top ministers. Her most trusted adviser was "our Friend Grigori," an uneducated Siberian preacher who was appropriately nicknamed "Rasputin"—the "Degenerate."

Rasputin began his career with a sect noted for mixing sexual orgies with religious ecstasies, and his influence rested on mysterious healing powers. Alexis, Alexandra's fifth child and heir to the throne, suffered from the rare blood disease hemophilia. The tiniest cut meant uncontrollable bleeding, terrible pain, and possible death. Medical science could do nothing. Only Rasputin could miraculously stop the bleeding, perhaps through hypnosis. The empress's faith in Rasputin was limitless. "Believe more in our Friend," she wrote her husband in 1916. "He lives for you and Russia." In this atmosphere of unreality, the government slid steadily toward revolution.

**"The Russian Ruling House"** This wartime cartoon captures the ominous, spellbinding power of Rasputin over Tsar Nicholas II and his wife, Alexandra. Rasputin's manipulations disgusted Russian public opinion and contributed to the monarchy's collapse. *(Stock Montage)*

In a desperate attempt to right the situation and end unfounded rumors that Rasputin was the empress's lover, three members of the high aristocracy murdered Rasputin in December 1916. The empress went into semipermanent shock, her mind haunted by the dead man's prophecy: "If I die or you desert me, in six months you will lose your son and your throne."[6] Food shortages in the cities worsened; morale declined. On March 8, women calling for bread in Petrograd (formerly St. Petersburg) started riots, which spontaneously spread to the factories and then elsewhere throughout the city. From the front, the tsar ordered troops to restore order, but discipline broke down, and the soldiers joined the revolutionary crowd.

The Duma responded by declaring a provisional government on March 12, 1917. Three days later, Nicholas abdicated.

## The Provisional Government

The March revolution was the result of an unplanned uprising of hungry, angry people in the capital, but it was joyfully accepted throughout the country. The patriotic upper and middle classes rejoiced at the prospect of a more determined and effective war effort, while workers happily anticipated better wages and more food. All classes and political parties called for liberty and democracy. They were not disappointed. As Vladimir Lenin said, Russia became the freest country in the world. After generations of arbitrary authoritarianism, the provisional government quickly established equality before the law; freedom of religion, speech, and assembly; the right of unions to organize and strike; and the rest of the classic liberal program.

Yet both liberal and moderate socialist leaders of the provisional government rejected social revolution. The reorganized government formed in May 1917 included the fiery agrarian socialist Alexander Kerensky, who became prime minister in July. He refused to confiscate large landholdings and give them to peasants, fearing that such drastic action in the countryside would only complete the disintegration of Russia's peasant army. For the patriotic Kerensky, as for other moderate socialists, the continuation of war was still the all-important national duty. There would be plenty of time for land reform later, and thus all the government's efforts were directed toward a last offensive in July. Human suffering and war-weariness grew, sapping the limited strength of the provisional government.

From its first day, the provisional government had to share power with a formidable rival—the **Petrograd Soviet** (or council) of Workers' and Soldiers' Deputies. Modeled on the revolutionary soviets of 1905, the Petrograd Soviet was a huge, fluctuating mass meeting of two thousand to three thousand workers, soldiers, and socialist intellectuals. Seeing itself as a true grassroots revolutionary democracy, this counter- or half-government suspiciously watched the provisional government and issued its own radical orders, further weakening the provisional government. Most famous of these was **Army Order No. 1,** issued to all Russian military forces as the provisional government was forming.

Army Order No. 1 stripped officers of their authority and placed power in the hands of elected committees of common soldiers. Designed primarily to protect the revolution from some counter-revolutionary Bonaparte on horseback, the order instead led to a total collapse of army discipline. Many an officer was hanged for his sins. Meanwhile, following the foolhardy summer offensive, masses of peasant soldiers began "voting with their feet," to use Lenin's graphic phrase. That is, they began returning to their villages to help their families get a share of the land, which peasants were simply seizing as they settled old scores in a great agrarian upheaval. All across the country, liberty was turning into anarchy in the summer of 1917. It was an unparalleled opportunity for the most radical and most talented of Russia's many socialist leaders, Vladimir Ilyich Lenin (1870–1924).

## Lenin and the Bolshevik Revolution

From his youth, Lenin's whole life had been dedicated to the cause of revolution. Born into the middle class, Lenin became an implacable enemy of imperial Russia when his older brother was executed for plotting to kill the tsar in 1887. As a law student, Lenin began searching for a revolutionary faith. He found it in Marxian socialism, which began to win converts among radical intellectuals as industrialization surged forward in Russia in the 1890s. Exiled to Siberia for three years because of socialist agitation, Lenin studied Marxian doctrines with religious intensity. After his release, this young priest of socialism joined fellow believers in western Europe. There he lived for seventeen years and developed his own revolutionary interpretations of the body of Marxian thought.

Three interrelated ideas were central for Lenin. First, like other eastern European radical socialists after 1900, he turned to the early fire-breathing Marx of 1848 and *The Communist Manifesto* for inspiration. Thus Lenin stressed that capitalism could be destroyed only by violent revolution. He tirelessly denounced all revisionist theories of a peaceful evolution to socialism as betraying Marx's message of unending class conflict. Lenin's second, more original idea was that under certain conditions a socialist revolution was possible even in a relatively backward country like Russia. There the industrial working class was small, but peasants were poor and thus potential revolutionaries.

Lenin believed that at a given moment revolution was determined more by human leadership than by vast historical laws. Thus was born his third basic idea: the necessity of a highly disciplined workers' party, strictly controlled by a dedicated elite of intellectuals and full-time revolutionaries like Lenin himself. Unlike ordinary workers and trade-union officials, this elite would never be seduced by short-term gains. It would not stop until revolution brought it to power.

Lenin's theories and methods did not go unchallenged by other Russian Marxists. At meetings of the Russian

## The Russian Revolution

| | |
|---|---|
| **1914** | Russia enthusiastically enters the First World War. |
| **1915** | Russia suffers 2 million casualties.<br>Progressive bloc calls for a new government responsible to the Duma rather than to the tsar.<br>Tsar Nicholas adjourns the Duma and departs for the front; Alexandra and Rasputin exert a strong influence on the government. |
| **December 1916** | Rasputin is murdered. |
| **March 8, 1917** | Bread riots take place in Petrograd (St. Petersburg). |
| **March 12, 1917** | Duma declares a provisional government. |
| **March 15, 1917** | Tsar Nicholas abdicates without protest. |
| **April 3, 1917** | Lenin returns from exile and denounces the provisional government. |
| **May 1917** | Reorganized provisional government, including Kerensky, continues the war.<br>Petrograd Soviet issues Army Order No. 1, granting military power to committees of common soldiers. |
| **Summer 1917** | Agrarian upheavals: peasants seize estates; peasant soldiers desert the army to participate. |
| **October 1917** | Bolsheviks gain a majority in the Petrograd Soviet. |
| **November 6, 1917** | Bolsheviks seize power; Lenin heads the new "provisional workers' and peasants' government." |
| **November 1917** | Lenin accepts peasant seizure of land and worker control of factories; all banks are nationalized. |
| **January 1918** | Lenin permanently disbands the Constituent Assembly. |
| **February 1918** | Lenin convinces the Bolshevik Central Committee to accept a humiliating peace with Germany in order to safeguard the revolution. |
| **March 1918** | Treaty of Brest-Litovsk: Russia loses one-third of its population.<br>Trotsky as war commissar begins to rebuild the Russian army.<br>Government moves from Petrograd to Moscow. |
| **1918–1920** | Great civil war takes place. |
| **Summer 1918** | Eighteen regional governments compete for power.<br>White armies oppose the Bolshevik Revolution. |
| **1919** | White armies are on the offensive but divided politically; they receive little benefit from Allied intervention. |
| **1920** | Lenin and the Red Army are victorious, retaking Belorussia and Ukraine. |

Social Democratic Labor party in London in 1903, matters came to a head. Lenin demanded a small, disciplined, elitist party, while his opponents wanted a more democratic party with mass membership. The Russian party of Marxian socialism promptly split into two rival factions. Lenin's camp was called **Bolsheviks,** or "majority group"; his opponents were *Mensheviks,* or "minority group." Lenin's majority did not last, but Lenin did not care. He kept the fine-sounding name Bolshevik and developed the party he wanted: tough, disciplined, revolutionary.

Unlike most other socialists, Lenin did not rally round the national flag in 1914. Observing events from neutral Switzerland, he saw the war as a product of imperialistic rivalries and as a marvelous opportunity for class war and socialist upheaval. After the March revolution the German government provided the impatient Lenin, his wife, and about twenty trusted colleagues with safe passage across Germany and back into Russia in April 1917. The Germans hoped that Lenin would undermine the sagging war effort of the world's freest society. They were not disappointed.

Arriving triumphantly at Petrograd's Finland Station on April 3, Lenin attacked at once. To the great astonishment of the local Bolsheviks, he rejected all cooperation with the "bourgeois" provisional government of the liberals and moderate socialists. His slogans were radical in the extreme: "All power to the soviets"; "All land to the peasants"; "Stop the war now." Never a slave to Marxian determinism, the brilliant but not unduly intellectual Lenin was a superb tactician. The moment was now.

Yet Lenin almost overplayed his hand. An attempt by the Bolsheviks to seize power in July collapsed, and Lenin fled and went into hiding. He was charged with being a German agent, and indeed he and the Bolsheviks were getting money from Germany.[7] But no matter. Intrigue between Kerensky, who became prime minister in July, and his commander in chief, General Lavr Kornilov, a popular war hero "with the heart of a lion and the brains of a sheep," resulted in Kornilov's leading a feeble attack against the provisional government in September. In the face of this rightist "counter-revolutionary" threat, the Bolsheviks were rearmed and redeemed. Kornilov's forces disintegrated, but Kerensky lost all credit with the army, the only force that might have saved him and democratic government in Russia.

## Trotsky and the Seizure of Power

Throughout the summer, the Bolsheviks had appealed very effectively to the workers and soldiers of Petrograd, markedly increasing their popular support. Party membership had soared from 50,000 to 240,000, and in October the Bolsheviks gained a fragile majority in the Petrograd Soviet. It was now Lenin's supporter Leon Trotsky (1879–1940), a spellbinding revolutionary orator and independent radical Marxist, who brilliantly executed the Bolshevik seizure of power.

Painting a vivid but untruthful picture of German and counter-revolutionary plots, Trotsky first convinced the Petrograd Soviet to form a special military-revolutionary committee in October and make him its leader. Military power in the capital passed into Bolshevik hands. Trotsky's second master stroke was to insist that the Bolsheviks reduce opposition to their coup by taking power in the name not of the Bolsheviks but of the more popular and democratic soviets, which were meeting in Petrograd from all over Russia in early November. On the night of November 6, militants from Trotsky's committee joined with trusty Bolshevik soldiers to seize government buildings and pounce on members of the provisional government. Then they went on to the congress of soviets. There a Bolshevik majority—roughly 390 of 650 turbulent delegates—declared that all power had passed to the soviets and named Lenin head of the new government.

The Bolsheviks came to power for three key reasons. First, by late 1917 democracy had given way to anarchy: power was there for those who would take it. Second, in Lenin and Trotsky the Bolsheviks had an utterly determined and truly superior leadership, which both the tsarist government and the provisional government lacked. Third, in 1917 the Bolsheviks succeeded in appealing to many soldiers and urban workers, people who were exhausted by war and eager for socialism. With time, many workers would become bitterly disappointed, but for the moment they had good reason to believe that they had won what they wanted.

## Dictatorship and Civil War

History is full of short-lived coups and unsuccessful revolutions. The truly monumental accomplishment of Lenin, Trotsky, and the rest of the Bolsheviks was not taking power but keeping it. In the next four years, the Bolsheviks went on to conquer the chaos they had helped create, and they began to build their kind of dictatorial socialist society. The conspirators became conquerors. How was this done?

Lenin had the genius to profit from developments over which he and the Bolsheviks had no control. Since summer, a peasant revolution had been sweeping across Russia as the tillers of the soil invaded and divided among themselves the estates of the landlords and the church. Peasant seizure of the land—a Russian 1789—was not very Marxian, but it was quite unstoppable in 1917. Thus Lenin's first law, which supposedly gave land to the peasants, actually merely approved what peasants were already doing. Urban workers' great demand in November was direct control of individual factories by local workers committees. This, too, Lenin ratified with a decree in November.

Unlike many of his colleagues, Lenin acknowledged that Russia had lost the war with Germany and that the only realistic goal was peace at any price. That price was very high. Germany demanded in December 1917 that the Soviet government give up all its western territories. These areas were inhabited by Poles, Finns, Lithuanians, and other non-Russians—all those people who had been conquered by the tsars over three centuries and put into the "prisonhouse of nationalities," as Lenin had earlier called the Russian empire.

At first, Lenin's fellow Bolsheviks would not accept such great territorial losses. But when German armies resumed their unopposed march into Russia in February 1918, Lenin had his way in a very close vote in the Central Committee of the party. "Not even his greatest enemy can deny that at this moment Lenin towered like a giant over his Bolshevik colleagues."[8] A third of old Russia's population was sliced away by the German meat ax in the Treaty of Brest-Litovsk in March 1918. With peace, Lenin had escaped the certain disaster of continued war and could pursue his goal of absolute political power for the Bolsheviks—now renamed Communists—within Russia.

In November 1917, the Bolsheviks had cleverly proclaimed their regime only a "provisional workers' and peasants' government," promising that a freely elected **Constituent Assembly** would draw up a new constitution. But free elections produced a stunning setback for the Bolsheviks, who won less than one-fourth of the elected delegates. The Socialist Revolutionaries—the peasants' party—had a clear majority. The Constituent Assembly met for only one day, on January 18, 1918. It was then permanently disbanded by Bolshevik soldiers acting under Lenin's orders. Thus even before the peace with Germany, Lenin was forming a one-party government.

The destruction of the democratically elected Constituent Assembly helped feed the flames of civil war. People who had risen up for self-rule in November saw that once again they were getting dictatorship from the capital. For the next three years, "Long live the [democratic] soviets; down with the Bolsheviks" was to be a popular slogan. The officers of the old army took the lead in organizing the so-called White opposition to the Bolsheviks in southern Russia, Ukraine, Siberia, and west of Petrograd. The Whites came from many social groups and were united only by their hatred of the Bolsheviks—the Reds.

**Lenin Rallies Worker and Soldier Delegates** At a midnight meeting of the Petrograd Soviet, the Bolsheviks rise up and seize power on November 6, 1917. This painting from the 1940s idealizes Lenin, but his great talents as a revolutionary leader are undeniable. In this re-creation Stalin, who actually played only a small role in the uprising, is standing behind Lenin, already his trusty right-hand man. *(Sovfoto)*

By the summer of 1918, fully eighteen self-proclaimed regional governments—several of which represented minority nationalities—were competing with Lenin's Bolsheviks in Moscow. By the end of the year, White armies were on the attack. In October 1919, it appeared they might triumph, as they closed in on Lenin's government from three sides. Yet they did not. By the spring of 1920, the White armies had been almost completely defeated, and the Bolshevik Red Army had retaken Belorussia and Ukraine. The following year, the Communists also reconquered the independent nationalist governments of the Caucasus. The civil war was over; Lenin had won.

Lenin and the Bolsheviks won for several reasons. Strategically, they controlled the center, while the Whites were always on the fringes and disunited. Moreover, the poorly defined political program of the Whites was vaguely conservative, and it did not unite all the foes of the Bolsheviks

**"You! Have You Volunteered?"** A Red Army soldier makes a compelling direct appeal to the ordinary citizen and demands all-out support for the Bolshevik cause in this 1920 poster by Dmitri Moor, a popular Soviet artist. Lenin recognized the importance of visual propaganda in a vast country with limited literacy, and mass-produced posters like this one were everywhere during the civil war of 1918–1921. *(Stephen White, University of Glasgow)*

under a progressive, democratic banner. Most important, the Communists quickly developed a better army, an army for which the divided Whites were no match.

Once again, Trotsky's leadership was decisive. The Bolsheviks had preached democracy in the army and elected officers in 1917. But beginning in March 1918, Trotsky as war commissar re-established the draft and the most drastic discipline for the newly formed Red Army. Soldiers deserting or disobeying an order were summarily shot. Moreover, Trotsky made effective use of former tsarist army officers, who were actively recruited and given unprecedented powers of discipline over their troops. In short, Trotsky formed a disciplined and effective fighting force.

The Bolsheviks also mobilized the home front. Establishing **war communism**—the application of the total war concept to a civil conflict—they seized grain from peasants, introduced rationing, nationalized all banks and industry, and required everyone to work. Although these measures contributed to a breakdown of normal economic activity, they also served to maintain labor discipline and to keep the Red Army supplied.

"Revolutionary terror" also contributed to the Communist victory. The old tsarist secret police was re-established as the **Cheka,** which hunted down and executed thousands of real or supposed foes, such as the tsar and his family and other "class enemies." At one point shortly after the government moved from Petrograd to Moscow in March 1918, a circus clown in Moscow was making fun of the Bolsheviks to an appreciative audience. Chekists in the crowd quickly pulled out their guns and shot several laughing people. Moreover, people were shot or threatened with being shot for minor nonpolitical failures. The terror caused by the secret police became a tool of the government. The Cheka sowed fear, and fear silenced opposition.

Finally, foreign military intervention in the civil war ended up helping the Communists. After Lenin made peace with Germany, the Allies (United States, Britain, Japan) sent troops to Archangel and Vladivostok to prevent war materiel they had sent the provisional government from being captured by the Germans. After the Soviet government nationalized all foreign-owned factories without compensation and refused to pay all of Russia's foreign debts, Western governments, particularly France, began to support White armies in the south and west. Yet these efforts were small and halfhearted. In 1919 Western peoples were sick of war, and few Western politicians believed in a military crusade against the Bolsheviks. Thus Allied intervention in the civil war did not aid the Whites effectively, though it did permit the Communists to appeal to the patriotic nationalism of ethnic Russians, in particular former tsarist army officers. Allied intervention was both too little and too much.

Together, the Russian Revolution and the Bolshevik triumph were one of the reasons the First World War was such a great turning point in modern history. A radically new government, based on socialism and one-party dictatorship, came to power in a great European state, maintained power, and eagerly encouraged worldwide revolution. Although halfheartedly constitutional monarchy in Russia was undoubtedly headed for some kind of political crisis before 1914, it is hard to imagine the triumph of the most radical proponents of change and reform except in a situation of total collapse. That was precisely what happened to Russia in the First World War.

## The Peace Settlement

Victory over revolutionary Russia boosted sagging German morale, and in the spring of 1918 the Germans launched their last major attack against France. Yet this offensive failed, just as those before it had. With breathtaking rapidity, the United States, Great Britain, and France decisively defeated Germany militarily. The guns of world war finally fell silent. Then as civil war spread in Russia and as chaos engulfed much of eastern Europe, the victorious Western Allies came together in Paris to establish a lasting peace.

Expectations were high; optimism was almost unlimited. The Allies labored intensively and soon worked out terms for peace with Germany and for the creation of the peacekeeping League of Nations. Nevertheless, the hopes of peoples and politicians were soon disappointed, for the peace settlement of 1919 turned out to be a failure. Rather than creating conditions for peace, it sowed the seeds of another war. Surely this was the ultimate tragedy of the Great War, a war that directly and indirectly cost $332 billion and left 10 million dead and another 20 million wounded. How did this tragedy happen? Why was the peace settlement unsuccessful?

### The End of the War

In early 1917, the strain of total war was showing everywhere. After the Russian Revolution in March, there were major strikes in Germany. In July a coalition of moderates passed a "peace resolution" in the Reichstag, calling for peace without territorial annexations. To counter this moderation born of war-weariness, the German military established a virtual dictatorship. The military also aggressively exploited the collapse of Russian armies, winning great concessions in the Treaty of Brest-Litovsk in March 1918.

With victory in the east quieting German moderates, General Ludendorff and company fell on France once more in the great spring offensive of 1918. For a time, German armies pushed forward, coming within thirty-five miles of Paris. But Ludendorff's exhausted, overextended forces never broke through. They were decisively stopped in July at the second Battle of the Marne, where 140,000 fresh American soldiers saw action. Adding 2 million men in arms to the war effort by August, the late but massive American intervention decisively tipped the scales in favor of Allied victory.

By September British, French, and American armies were advancing steadily on all fronts, and a panicky General Ludendorff realized that Germany had lost the war. Yet he insolently insisted that moderate politicians shoulder the shame of defeat, and on October 4 the emperor formed a new, more liberal German government to sue for peace. As negotiations over an armistice dragged on, an angry and frustrated German people finally rose up. On November 3, sailors in Kiel mutinied, and throughout northern Germany soldiers and workers began to establish revolutionary councils on the Russian soviet model. The same day, Austria-Hungary surrendered to the Allies and began breaking apart. Revolution broke out in Germany, and masses of workers demonstrated for peace in Berlin. With army discipline collapsing, the emperor abdicated and fled to Holland. Socialist leaders in Berlin proclaimed a German republic on November 9 and simultaneously agreed to tough Allied terms of surrender. The armistice went into effect on November 11, 1918. The war was over.

### Revolution in Germany

Military defeat brought political revolution to Germany and Austria-Hungary, as it had to Russia. In Austria-Hungary the revolution was primarily nationalistic and republican in character. Having started the war to preserve an antinationalistic dynastic state, the Habsburg empire had perished in the attempt. In its place, independent Austrian, Hungarian, and Czechoslovakian republics were proclaimed, while a greatly expanded Serbian monarchy united the South Slavs and took the name Yugoslavia. The prospect of firmly establishing the new national states overrode class considerations for most people in east-central Europe.

The German Revolution of November 1918 resembled the Russian Revolution of March 1917. In both cases, a genuine popular uprising welled up from below, toppled an authoritarian monarchy, and brought the establishment of a liberal provisional republic. In both countries, liberals and moderate socialists took control of the central government, while workers' and soldiers' councils formed a counter-government. In Germany, however, the moderate socialists and their liberal allies won, and the Lenin-like radical revolutionaries in the councils lost. In communist terms, the liberal, republican revolution in Germany in 1918 was only half a revolution: a bourgeois political revolution without a communist second installment. It was Russia without Lenin's Bolshevik triumph.

There were several reasons for the German outcome. The great majority of Marxian socialist leaders in the Social Democratic party were, as before the war, really pink and not red. They wanted to establish real political democracy and civil liberties, and they favored the gradual elimination of capitalism. They were also German nationalists, appalled by the prospect of civil war and revolutionary terror. Moreover, there was less popular support among workers, soldiers, and peasants.

Of crucial importance was the fact that the moderate German Social Democrats, unlike Kerensky and company, accepted defeat and ended the war the day they took power. This act ended the decline in morale among soldiers and prevented the regular army, with its conservative officer corps, from disintegrating. When radicals headed by Karl Liebknecht and Rosa Luxemburg and their supporters in the councils tried to seize control of the government in Berlin in January, the moderate socialists called on the army to crush the uprising. Liebknecht and Luxemburg were arrested and then brutally murdered by army leaders. Their murders, widely believed to have had government support, caused many working-class activists in the Social Democratic party to break away in anger and join the pro-Lenin German Communist party that Liebknecht's group had just founded. Finally, even if the moderate socialists had followed Liebknecht and Luxemburg on the Leninist path, it is very unlikely they would have succeeded. Civil war in Germany would certainly have followed. And the Allies, who were already occupying western Germany according to the terms of the armistice, would have marched on to Berlin and ruled Germany directly.

**The Allied Leaders at Versailles** The old tiger, Clemenceau of France, gestures with his walking stick to the scholarly Woodrow Wilson, as the strong-willed Lloyd George strides forward on the left. The negotiations at Versailles were difficult and often bitter, but the Allies reached a compromise agreement and imposed it on Germany. *(Corbis)*

## The Treaty of Versailles

The peace conference opened in Paris in January 1919 with seventy delegates representing twenty-seven victorious nations. There were great expectations. A young British diplomat later wrote that the victors "were convinced that they would never commit the blunders and iniquities of the Congress of Vienna [of 1815]." Then the "misguided, reactionary, pathetic aristocrats" had cynically shuffled populations; now "we believed in nationalism, we believed in the self-determination of peoples." Indeed, "we were journeying to Paris . . . to found a new order in Europe. We were preparing not Peace only, but Eternal Peace."[9] This general optimism and idealism had been greatly strengthened by President Wilson's January 1918 peace proposal, the Fourteen Points, which stressed national self-determination and the rights of small countries.

The real powers at the conference were the United States, Great Britain, and France, for Germany was not allowed to participate and Russia was locked in civil war and did not attend. Italy was considered part of the Big Four, but its role was quite limited. Almost immediately the three great Allies began to quarrel. President Wilson, who was wildly cheered by European crowds as the spokesman for a new idealistic and democratic international cooperation, was almost obsessed with creating the **League of Nations.** Wilson insisted that this question come first, for he passionately believed that only a permanent international organization could protect member states from aggression and avert future wars. Wilson had his way, although Lloyd George of Great Britain and especially Clemenceau of France were unenthusiastic. They were primarily concerned with punishing Germany.

Playing on British nationalism, Lloyd George had already won a smashing electoral victory in December on the popular platform of making Germany pay for the war. "We shall," he promised, "squeeze the orange until the pips squeak." Personally inclined to make a somewhat moderate peace with Germany, Lloyd George was to a considerable extent a captive of demands for a total victory worthy of the sacrifices of total war against a totally depraved enemy. As Kipling summed up the general British feeling at the end of the war, the Germans were "a people with the heart of beasts."[10]

France's Georges Clemenceau, "the Tiger" who had broken wartime defeatism and led his country to victory,

**MAP 27.4 Shattered Empires and Territorial Changes After World War I** The Great War brought tremendous changes in eastern Europe. New nations were established, and a dangerous power vacuum was created between Germany and Soviet Russia.

wholeheartedly agreed. Like most French people, Clemenceau wanted old-fashioned revenge. He also wanted lasting security for France. This, he believed, required the creation of a buffer state between France and Germany, the permanent demilitarization of Germany, and vast German reparations. He feared that sooner or later Germany with its 60 million people would attack France with its 40 million unless the Germans were permanently weakened. Moreover, France had no English Channel (or Atlantic Ocean) as a reassuring barrier against German aggression. Wilson, supported by Lloyd George, would hear none of this. Clemenceau's demands seemed vindictive, violating morality and the principle of national self-determination. By April the countries attending the conference were deadlocked on the German question, and Wilson packed his bags to go home.

In the end, convinced that France could not afford to face Germany alone in the future, Clemenceau agreed to a compromise. He gave up the French demand for a Rhineland buffer state in return for a formal defensive alliance with the United States and Great Britain. Under the terms of this alliance, both Wilson and Lloyd George promised that their countries would come to France's aid in the event of a German attack. Thus Clemenceau appeared to win his goal of French security, as Wilson had won his of a permanent international organization. The Allies moved quickly to finish the settlement, believing that any adjustments would later be possible within the dual framework of a strong Western alliance and the League of Nations (see Map 27.4).

The **Treaty of Versailles** between the Allies and Germany was the key to the settlement, and the terms were not unreasonable as a first step toward re-establishing international order. Had Germany won, it seems certain that France and Belgium would have been treated with greater severity, as Russia had been at Brest-Litovsk. Germany's colonies were given to France, Britain, and Japan as League of Nations mandates. Germany's territorial losses within Europe were minor, thanks to Wilson. Alsace-Lorraine was returned to France. Parts of Germany inhabited primarily by Poles were ceded to the new Polish state, in keeping with the principle of national self-determination. Predominately German Danzig was also placed within the Polish tariff lines, but as a self-governing city under League of Nations protection. Germany had to limit its army to 100,000 men and agree to build no military fortifications in the Rhineland.

More harshly, the Allies declared that Germany (with Austria) was responsible for the war and had therefore to pay reparations equal to all civilian damages caused by the war. This unfortunate and much-criticized clause expressed inescapable popular demands for German blood, but the actual figure was not set, and there was the clear possibility that reparations might be set at a reasonable level in the future when tempers had cooled.

When presented with the treaty, the German government protested vigorously. But there was no alternative, especially considering that Germany was still starving because the Allies had not yet lifted their naval blockade. On June 28, 1919, German representatives of the ruling moderate Social Democrats and the Catholic party signed the treaty in the Sun King's Hall of Mirrors at Versailles, where Bismarck's empire had been joyously proclaimed almost fifty years before.

Separate peace treaties were concluded with the other defeated European powers—Austria, Hungary, and Bulgaria. For the most part, these treaties merely ratified the existing situation in east-central Europe following the breakup of the Austro-Hungarian Empire. Like Austria, Hungary was a particularly big loser, as its "captive" nationalities (and some interspersed Hungarians) were ceded to Romania, Czechoslovakia, Poland, and Yugoslavia. Italy got some Austrian territory.

The changes imposed on what had been the Ottoman Empire were truly radical and became very controversial. Basically, the Ottoman Empire was broken up, Britain and France expanded their power and influence in the Middle East, and Arab nationalists felt cheated and betrayed.

The British government had encouraged the wartime Arab revolt against the Ottoman Turks (see page 897) and had even made vague promises of an independent Arab kingdom. However, when the fighting stopped, the British and the French chose instead to honor their secret wartime agreements to divide and rule the Ottoman lands. President Wilson proved willing to compromise on his earlier call for national self-determination in the Ottoman Empire, for Britain and France were determined to control Syria, Iraq, Palestine, and Transjordan but were also willing to use the smoke screen of League of Nations mandates (see Map 27.5). Thus when Arab nationalists in Syria called for independence, a French army attacked Damascus and took over in July 1920. Meanwhile, British troops crushed a bloody uprising in Iraq and took control of the newly created country. After heavy fighting, only the Turks won independence, which they denied to the Kurds and to the Armenians.

The British mandate for the old Ottoman province of Palestine also angered Arab nationalists. The **Balfour Declaration** of November 1917, made by the British foreign secretary Arthur Balfour, had declared that Britain favored a "National Home for the Jewish People" in Palestine, but without prejudicing the civil and religious rights of the existing non-Jew communities. Some members of the British cabinet believed the declaration would appeal to German, Austrian, and American Jews and thus help the British war effort. Others sincerely supported the Zionist vision of a Jewish homeland (pages 846, 847), which they hoped would also help Britain maintain control of the Suez Canal. In any event, Palestinian Arabs were dismayed, believing that a Jewish homeland would be incompatible with majority rule and chafing under a British colonial administration. National self-determination remained a reality only for Europeans and their offspring in the self-governing colonies. Western imperialism appeared to have replaced Turkish rule in the Middle East.

### American Rejection of the Versailles Treaty

The rapidly concluded Versailles Treaty of early 1919 was not perfect, but within the context of war-shattered Europe it was an acceptable beginning. The principle of national self-determination, which had played such a large role in starting the war, was accepted for Europe and served as an organizing framework. Germany had been punished but not dismembered. A new world organiza-

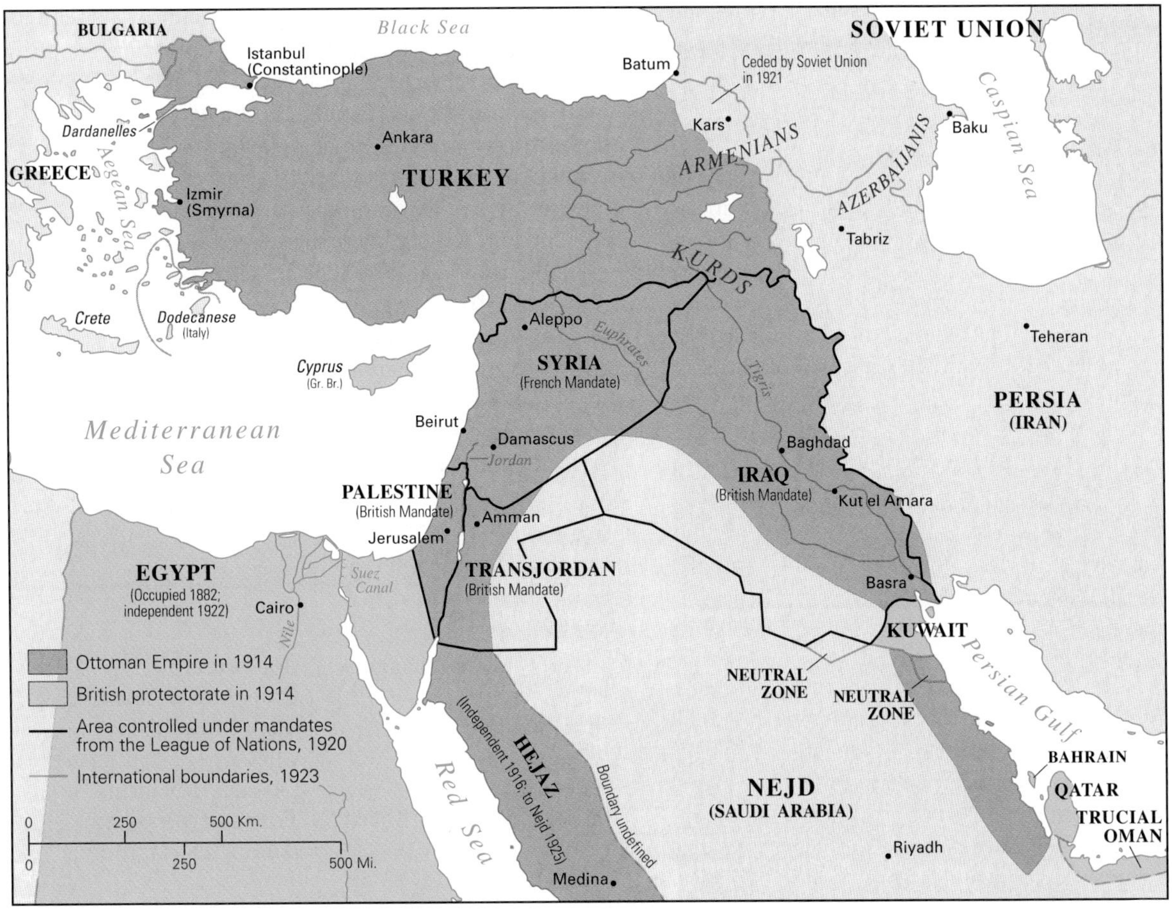


**MAP 27.5 The Partition of the Ottoman Empire, 1914–1923** By 1914 the Ottoman Turks had been pushed out of the Balkans, and their Arab provinces were on the edge of revolt. That revolt, in alliance with the British, erupted in the First World War and contributed greatly to the Ottomans' defeat. Refusing to grant independence to the Arabs, the Allies established League of Nations mandates and replaced Ottoman rulers in Syria, Iraq, Transjordan, and Palestine.

tion complemented a traditional defensive alliance of satisfied powers. The serious remaining problems could be worked out in the future. Moreover, Allied leaders had seen speed as essential for another reason: they detested Lenin and feared that his Bolshevik Revolution might spread. They realized that their best answer to Lenin's unending calls for worldwide upheaval was peace and tranquillity for war-weary peoples.

There were, however, two great interrelated obstacles to such peace: Germany and the United States. Plagued by communist uprisings, reactionary plots, and popular disillusionment with losing the war at the last minute, Germany's moderate socialists and their liberal and Catholic supporters faced an enormous challenge. Like French republicans after 1871, they needed time (and luck) if they were to establish firmly a peaceful and democratic republic. Progress in this direction required understanding but firm treatment of Germany by the victorious Western Allies, particularly by the United States.

However, the U.S. Senate and, to a lesser extent, the American people rejected Wilson's handiwork. Republican senators led by Henry Cabot Lodge refused to ratify the Treaty of Versailles without changes in the articles creating the League of Nations. The key issue was the League's power—more apparent than real—to require member states to take collective action against aggression. Lodge and others believed that this requirement gave away Congress's constitutional right to declare war. In failing health, Wilson, with narrow-minded self-righteousness, rejected all attempts at compromise. In doing so, he ensured that the treaty would never be ratified by the United States in any form and that the United States would never join the League of Nations. Moreover, the Senate refused to ratify Wilson's treaties forming a defensive alliance with France and Great Britain. America turned its back on Europe.

The Wilson-Lodge fiasco and the newfound gospel of isolationism represented a tragic and cowardly renunciation of America's responsibility. Using America's action as an excuse, Great Britain, too, refused to ratify its defensive alliance with France. Bitterly betrayed by its allies, France stood alone. Very shortly France was to take actions against Germany that would feed the fires of German resentment and seriously undermine democratic forces in the new republic. The great hopes of early 1919 had turned to ashes by the end of the year. The Western alliance had collapsed, and a grandiose plan for permanent peace had given way to a fragile truce. For this and for what came later, the United States must share a large part of the guilt.

## Summary

Why did World War I have such revolutionary consequences? Why was it such a great break with the past? World War I was, first of all, a war of committed peoples. In France, Britain, and Germany in particular, governments drew on genuine popular support. This support reflected not only the diplomatic origins of the war but also the way western European society had been unified under the nationalist banner in the later nineteenth century, despite the fears that the growing socialist movement aroused in conservatives. The relentlessness of total war helps explain why so many died, why so many were crippled physically and psychologically, and why Western civilization would in so many ways never be the same again. More concretely, the war swept away monarchs and multinational empires. National self-determination apparently triumphed across Europe, not only in Austria-Hungary but also in many of Russia's western borderlands. Except in Ireland and parts of Soviet Russia, the revolutionary dream of national unity, born of the French Revolution, had finally come true.

Two other revolutions were products of the war. In Russia the Bolsheviks established a radical regime, smashed existing capitalist institutions, and stayed in power with a new kind of authoritarian rule. Whether the new Russian regime was truly Marxian or socialist was questionable, but it indisputably posed a powerful, ongoing revolutionary challenge to Europe and its colonial empires.

More subtle but quite universal in its impact was an administrative revolution. This revolution, born of the need to mobilize entire societies and economies for total war, greatly increased the power of government. And after the guns grew still, government planning and wholesale involvement in economic and social life did not disappear in Europe. Liberal market capitalism and a well-integrated world economy were among the many casualties of the administrative revolution, and greater social equality was everywhere one of its results. Thus even in European countries where a communist takeover never came close to occurring, society still experienced a great revolution.

Finally, the "war to end war" did not bring peace—only a fragile truce. In the West, the Allies failed to maintain their wartime solidarity. Germany remained unrepentant and would soon have more grievances to nurse. Moreover, the victory of national self-determination in eastern Europe created small, weak states and thus a power vacuum between a still-powerful Germany and a potentially mighty communist Russia. A vast area lay open to military aggression from two sides.

## Key Terms

Three Emperors' League
Triple Entente
trench warfare
*Lusitania*
total war
War Raw Materials Board
Petrograd Soviet
Army Order No. 1
Bolsheviks
Constituent Assembly
war communism
Cheka
League of Nations
Treaty of Versailles
Balfour Declaration

## Notes

1. M. Beloff, quoted in *U.S. News & World Report,* March 8, 1976, p. 53.
2. Quoted in J. Remak, *The Origins of World War I* (New York: Holt, Rinehart & Winston, 1967), p. 84.
3. Quoted in F. P. Chambers, *The War Behind the War, 1914–1918* (London: Faber & Faber, 1939), p. 168.
4. Quoted in R. O. Paxton, *Europe in the Twentieth Century* (New York: Harcourt Brace Jovanovich, 1975), p. 109.
5. Quoted in Chambers, *The War Behind the War,* p. 378.
6. Quoted ibid., pp. 302, 304.
7. A. B. Ulam, *The Bolsheviks* (New York: Collier Books, 1968), p. 349.
8. Ibid., p. 405.
9. H. Nicolson, *Peacemaking 1919* (New York: Grosset & Dunlap Universal Library, 1965), pp. 8, 31–32.
10. Quoted ibid., p. 24.

## Suggested Reading

E. Hobsbawm, *The Age of Extremes: A History of the World, 1914–1991* (1996), is a provocative interpretation by a famous historian, with a good discussion of war and revolution. O. Hale, *The Great Illusion, 1900–1914* (1971), is a thorough account of the prewar era. Remak's volume cited in the

Notes, J. Joll, *The Origins of the First World War* (1992), and L. Lafore, *The Long Fuse* (1971), are recommended studies of the causes of the First World War. V. Steiner, *Britain and the Origins of the First World War* (1978), and E. Brose, *The Kaiser's Army, 1870–1914: Technological, Tactical, and Operational Dilemmas in Germany During the Machine Age* (2001), are also major contributions. K. Jarausch, *The Enigmatic Chancellor* (1973), is an important study on Bethmann-Hollweg and German policy in 1914. M. Gilbert, *The First World War: A Complete History* (1994), is comprehensive, while M. Howard, *The First World War* (2002), is a fine brief introduction. B. Tuchman, *The Guns of August* (1962), is a marvelous account of the dramatic first month of the war and the beginning of military stalemate. J. Winter, *The Experience of World War I* (1988), is a strikingly illustrated history of the war, and I. Ousby, *The Road to Verdun: World War I's Most Momentous Battle and the Folly of Nationalism* (2002), is a moving reconsideration of the famous siege. J. Ellis, *Eye-Deep in Hell* (1976), is a vivid account of trench warfare, and P. Leese, *Shell Shock: Traumatic Neurosis and the British Soldiers of the First World War* (2002), is a carefully crafted study of a neglected topic. L. Zuckerman, *The Rape of Belgium: The Untold Story of World War I* (2004), is a poignant examination of German atrocities. D. Gorham, *Vera Brittain: A Feminist Life* (1996), is a major study of Brittain's life. A. Marwick, *War and Change in Twentieth-Century Europe* (1990), is a useful synthesis.

F. L. Carsten, *War Against War* (1982), considers radical movements in Britain and Germany. The comprehensive and exciting study by Chambers mentioned in the Notes is still very useful. M. Higonnet, J. Jensen, and M. Weitz, eds., *Behind the Lines: Gender and the Two World Wars* (1987), examines the changes that the war brought for women and for relations between the sexes. S. Hynes, *A War Imagined: The First World War and English Culture* (1990), examines intellectual and cultural reactions. Two important studies on France are M. Hanna, *The Mobilization of Intellect: French Scholars and Writers in the Great War* (1996), and J. Keiger, *Raymond Poincaré* (1997), an excellent reconsideration of one of France's most important leaders before, during, and after the First World War. H. Herwig, *The First World War: Germany and Austria, 1914–1918* (1997), ably follows the hard road to defeat and collapse, while B. Davis, *Home Fires Burning: Food, Politics, and Everyday Life in Berlin in World War I* (2000), shows women struggling to feed their families. An excellent collection of essays, R. Wall and J. Winter, eds., *The Upheaval of War: Family, Work, and Welfare in Europe, 1914–1918* (1988), probes the enormous consequences of the war for people and society. The debate over Germany's guilt and aggression may be approached through G. Feldman, ed., *German Imperialism, 1914–1918* (1972), and A. Hillgruber, *Germany and the Two World Wars* (1981). R. Abraham, *Rosa Luxemburg: A Life for the International* (1989), is an excellent biography. In addition to Erich Maria Remarque's great novel *All Quiet on the Western Front* (1928), Henri Barbusse, *Under Fire* (1917), and Jules Romains, *Verdun* (1939), are highly recommended for their fictional yet realistic re-creations of the war. P. Fussell, *The Great War and Modern Memory* (1975), probes all the powerful literature inspired by the war. M. Eckstein, *Rites of Spring: The Great War and the Birth of the Modern Age* (1989), is an imaginative cultural investigation that has won critical acclaim.

C. Read, *From Tsar to Soviets: The Russian People and Their Revolution, 1917–1921* (1996), is highly recommended. S. Fitzpatrick, *The Russian Revolution* (1982), is an older provocative interpretation. R. Suny and A. Adams, eds., *The Russian Revolution and Bolshevik Victory* (1990), presents a wide range of interpretations. Ulam's work cited in the Notes, which focuses on Lenin, is a classic introduction to the Russian Revolution, whereas D. Volkogonov, *Lenin: A New Biography* (1994), is a lively study with some new revelations by a well-known post-Communist Russian historian. B. Wolfe, *Three Who Made a Revolution* (1955), an old but good collective biography of Lenin, Trotsky, and Stalin, and R. Conquest, *V. I. Lenin* (1972), are recommended. L. Trotsky himself wrote the colorful and exciting *History of the Russian Revolution* (1932), which may be compared with the classic eyewitness account of the young, pro-Bolshevik American J. Reed, *Ten Days That Shook the World* (1919). D. Koenker, W. Rosenberg, and R. Suny, eds., *Party, State and Society in the Russian Civil War* (1989), probes the social foundations of Bolshevik victory. A. Wildman, *The End of the Russian Imperial Army* (1980), is a fine account of the soldiers' revolt, and G. Leggett, *The Cheka: Lenin's Secret Police* (1981), shows revolutionary terror in action. S. Volkov, *St. Petersburg: A Cultural History* (1997), is particularly moving on the great city's tragic moments in the twentieth century. Boris Pasternak's justly celebrated *Doctor Zhivago* is a great historical novel of the revolutionary era. R. Massie, *Nicholas and Alexandra* (1971), is a moving popular biography of Russia's last royal family and the terrible health problem of the heir to the throne. Nicolson's study listed in the Notes captures the spirit of the Versailles settlement. W. Widenor, *Henry Cabot Lodge and the Search for an American Foreign Policy* (1981), is recommended. A. Mayer, *The Politics and Diplomacy of Peacemaking* (1969), stresses the influence of domestic social tensions and widespread fear of further communist revolt. D. Fromkin, *A Peace to End All Peace* (1989), is a brilliant account of the collapse of the Ottoman Empire and its division by the Allies. M. Yapp, *The Near East Since the First World War* (1991), is an excellent survey of major developments, and B. Lewis, *The Shaping of the Modern Middle East* (1993), is a stimulating synthesis by a distinguished scholar.

# *Listening to the Past*

## The Experience of War

*World War I was a "total" war: it enlisted the efforts of men, women, and children, both at home and on the battlefield. It was a terrifying and painful experience for all those involved. To be sure, it was not the romantic endeavor it was purported to be. The documents below offer two different wartime experiences. The first excerpt is from a letter written by a German soldier fighting in the trenches. The second is from the diary of a Viennese woman. As you read both passages, think about the different ways war and its consequences were made real for these two people.*

### A German Soldier Writes from the Trenches, March 1915

*Souchez, March 11th, 1915*

"So fare you well, for we must now be parting," so run the first lines of a soldier-song which we often sang through the streets of the capital. These words are truer than ever now, and these lines are to bid farewell to you, to all my nearest and dearest, to all who wish me well or ill, and to all that I value and prize.

Our regiment has been transferred to this dangerous spot, Souchez. No end of blood has already flowed down this hill. A week ago the 142nd attacked and took four trenches from the French. It is to hold these trenches that we have been brought here. There is something uncanny about this hill-position. Already, times without number, other battalions of our regiment have been ordered here in support, and each time the company came back with a loss of twenty, thirty or more men. In the days when we had to stick it out here before, we had 22 killed and 27 wounded. Shells roar, bullets whistle; no dug-outs, or very bad ones; mud, clay, filth, shell-holes so deep that one could bathe in them.

This letter has been interrupted no end of times. Shells began to pitch close to us—great English 12-inch ones—and we had to take refuge in a cellar. One such shell struck the next house and buried four men, who were got out from the ruins horribly mutilated. I saw them and it was ghastly!

Everybody must be prepared now for death in some form or other. Two cemeteries have been made up here, the losses have been so great. I ought not to write that to you, but I do so all the same, because the newspapers have probably given you quite a different impression. They tell only of our gains and say nothing about the blood that has been shed, of the cries of agony that never cease. The newspaper doesn't give any description either of *how* the "heroes" are laid to rest, though it talks about "heroes' graves" and writes poems and such-like about them. Certainly in Lens I have attended funeral-parades where a number of dead were buried in one large grave with pomp and circumstance. But up here it is pitiful the way one throws the dead bodies out of the trench and lets them lie there, or scatters dirt over the remains of those which have been torn to pieces by shells.

I look upon death and call upon life. I have not accomplished much in my short life, which has been chiefly occupied with study. I have commended my soul to the Lord God. It bears His seal and is altogether His. Now I am free to dare anything. My future life belongs to God, my present one to the Fatherland, and I myself still possess happiness and strength.

### A Viennese Woman Remembers Home Front Life

Ten dekagrammes [3½ ounces] of horse-flesh per head are to be given out to-day for the week. The cavalry horses held in reserve by the military authorities are being slaughtered for lack of fodder, and the people of Vienna are for a change to get a few mouthfuls of meat of which they have so long been deprived. Horse-flesh! I should like to know whether my instinctive repugnance to horse-flesh as food is personal, or whether my dislike is shared by many other housewives. My loathing of it is based, I believe, not on a physical but on a psychological prejudice.

I overcame my repugnance, rebuked myself for being sentimental, and left the house. A soft, steady rain was falling, from which I tried to protect myself with galoshes, waterproof, and umbrella. As I left the house before seven o'clock and the meat distribution did not begin until nine o'clock, I hoped to get well to the front of the queue.

No sooner had I reached the neighbourhood of the big market hall than I was instructed by the police to take a certain direction. I estimated the crowd waiting here for a meagre midday meal at two thousand at least. Hundreds of women had spent the night here in order to be among the first and make sure of getting their bit of meat. Many had brought with them improvised seats—a little box or a bucket turned upside down. No one seemed to mind the rain, although many were already wet through. They passed the time chattering, and the theme was the familiar one: What have you had to eat? What are you going to eat? One could scent an atmosphere of mistrust in these conversations: they were all careful not to say too much or to betray anything that might get them into trouble.

At length the sale began. Slowly, infinitely slowly, we moved forward. The most determined, who had spent the night outside the gates of the hall, displayed their booty to the waiting crowd: a ragged, quite freshly slaughtered piece of meat with the characteristic yellow fat. [Others] alarmed those standing at the back by telling them that there was only a very small supply of meat and that not half the people waiting would get a share of it. The crowd became very uneasy and impatient, and before the police on guard could prevent it, those standing in front organized an attack on the hall which the salesmen inside were powerless to repel. Everyone seized whatever he could lay his hands on, and in a few moments all the eatables had vanished. In the confusion stands were overturned, and the police forced back the aggressors and closed the gates. The crowds waiting outside, many of whom had been there all night and were soaked through, angrily demanded their due, whereupon the mounted police made a little charge, provoking a wild panic and much screaming and cursing. At length I reached home, depressed and disgusted, with a broken umbrella and only one galosh.

Germans wait in line for their meager rations, as pictured on a ration coupon used in the city of Eisenberg. *(akg-images)*

We housewives have during the last four years grown accustomed to standing in queues; we have also grown accustomed to being obliged to go home with empty hands and still emptier stomachs. Only very rarely do those who are sent away disappointed give cause for police intervention. On the other hand, it happens more and more frequently that one of the pale, tired women who have been waiting for hours collapses from exhaustion. The turbulent scenes which occurred to-day inside and outside the large market hall seemed to me perfectly natural. In my dejected mood the patient apathy with which we housewives endure seemed to me blameworthy and incomprehensible.

## Questions for Analysis

1. How did the soldier see the war he was in? Was it a grand patriotic effort? Or was it a story of senseless bloodshed and loss of life?
2. How did the soldiers cope with the reality of war in the trenches?
3. How did the experience of the Viennese woman differ from the soldier's?
4. Were the women who pillaged the food hall "blameworthy" or "reprehensible," as the Viennese woman says?

*Sources:* Alfons Ankenbrand, in *German Students' War Letters,* ed. A. F. Wedd (London: Methuen, 1929), pp. 72–73; *Blockade: The Diary of an Austrian Middle-Class Woman, 1914–1924,* trans. Winifred Ray (New York: Ray Long & Richard Smith, 1932), pp. 63–68.

This detail of George Grosz's *Draussen und Drinnen* (Outside and Inside) captures the uncertainty and anxiety of the 1920s. *(akg-images)*

chapter

# 28 The Age of Anxiety

**chapter outline**

- Uncertainty in Modern Thought
- Modern Art and Music
- Movies and Radio
- The Search for Peace and Political Stability
- The Great Depression, 1929–1939

When Allied diplomats met in Paris in early 1919 with their optimistic plans for building a lasting peace, most people looked forward to happier times. They hoped that life would return to normal after the terrible trauma of total war. They hoped that once again life would make sense in the familiar prewar terms of peace, prosperity, and progress. These hopes were in vain. The Great Break—the First World War and the Russian Revolution—had mangled too many things beyond repair. Life would no longer fit neatly into the old molds.

Instead, great numbers of men and women felt themselves increasingly adrift in a strange, uncertain, and uncontrollable world. They saw themselves living in an age of anxiety, an age of continual crisis (this age lasted until at least the early 1950s). In almost every area of human experience, people went searching for ways to put meaning back into life.

- What did such doubts and searching mean for Western thought, art, and culture?
- How did leaders deal with the political dimensions of uncertainty and try to re-establish real peace and prosperity between 1919 and 1939?
- Why did those leaders fail?

These are the questions this chapter will explore.

See DBQ 12

## Uncertainty in Modern Thought

A complex revolution in thought and ideas was under way before the First World War, but only small, unusual groups were aware of it. After the war, these new and upsetting ideas began to spread through the entire population. Western society as a whole began to question and even abandon many cherished values and beliefs that had guided it since the eighteenth-century Enlightenment and the nineteenth-century triumph of industrial development, scientific advances, and evolutionary thought.

Before 1914 most people still believed in progress, reason, and the rights of the individual. Progress was a daily reality, apparent in the rising standard of living, the taming of the city, and the steady increase in popular education.

**Kollwitz: The Grieving Parents** After the renowned German artist Kathe Kollwitz learned in October 1914 that her son Peter had died in battle, the heartbroken mother conceived of a sculpture to honor his memory. Yet her efforts were repeatedly overwhelmed by sorrow. Only in 1931 could she complete this graveside memorial in a military cemetery, a telling indication of the war's ongoing devastation for millions. The grieving father and mother are finally reunited with their son, and they beg forgiveness for the mad war their generation inflicted on its children. *(John Parker, Photographer)*

Such developments also encouraged the comforting belief in the logical universe of Newtonian physics as well as faith in the ability of a rational human mind to understand that universe through intellectual investigation. And just as there were laws of science, so were there laws of society that rational human beings could discover and then wisely act on. At the same time, the rights of the individual were not just taken for granted; they were actually increasing. Well-established political rights were gradually spreading to women and workers, and new "social rights," such as old-age pensions, were emerging. In short, before World War I most Europeans had a moderately optimistic view of the world, and with good reason.

Nevertheless, since the 1880s, a small band of serious thinkers and creative writers had been attacking these well-worn optimistic ideas. These critics rejected the general faith in progress and the power of the rational human mind. An expanding chorus of thinkers echoed and enlarged their views after the experience of history's most destructive war—a war that suggested to many that human beings were a pack of violent, irrational animals quite capable of tearing the individual and his or her rights to shreds. Disorientation and pessimism were particularly acute in the 1930s, when the rapid rise of harsh dictatorships and the Great Depression transformed old certainties into bitter illusions.

No one expressed this state of uncertainty better than French poet and critic Paul Valéry (1871–1945) in the early 1920s. Speaking of the "crisis of the mind," Valéry noted that Europe was looking at its future with dark foreboding:

*The storm has died away, and still we are restless, uneasy, as if the storm were about to break. Almost all the affairs of men remain in a terrible uncertainty. We think of what has disappeared, and we are almost destroyed by what has been destroyed; we do not know what will be born, and we fear the future, not without reason. . . . Doubt and disorder are in us and with us. There is no thinking man, however shrewd or learned he may be, who can hope to dominate this anxiety, to escape from this impression of darkness.*[1]

In the midst of economic, political, and social disruptions, Valéry saw the "cruelly injured mind," besieged by doubts and suffering from anxieties. This was the general intellectual crisis of the twentieth century, which touched almost every field of thought. The implications of new

1919 | 1924 | 1929 | 1934 | 1939

**POLITICAL/MILITARY**

- 1919 Treaty of Versailles
- 1923 French and Belgian armies occupy the Ruhr
- 1926 Germany joins League of Nations
- 1928 Kellogg-Briand Pact
- 1932 Franklin Roosevelt elected U.S. president
- 1935 Creation of WPA as part of New Deal
- 1936 Formation of Popular Front in France

**SOCIAL/ECONOMIC**

- 1919 Keynes, *Economic Consequences of the Peace*
- 1920s–1930s Dadaism and surrealism (artistic movements)
- 1924 Dawes Plan
- 1925 Berg's opera *Wozzeck* first performed
- 1929–1939 Great Depression
- 1930 van der Rohe becomes director of Bauhaus
- 1934 Riefenstahl's documentary film *The Triumph of the Will*

**INTELLECTUAL/RELIGIOUS**

- 1919 Rutherford splits the atom
- 1919 Freudian psychology gains popular attention
- 1920s Existentialism gains prominence
- 1922 Wittgenstein writes on logical empiricism
- 1922 Woolf, *Jacob's Room*
- 1922 Joyce, *Ulysses*
- 1922 Eliot, *The Waste Land*
- 1925 Kafka, *The Trial*
- 1927 Heisenberg's principle of uncertainty
- 1929 Faulkner, *The Sound and the Fury*

ideas and discoveries in philosophy, physics, psychology, and literature played a central role in this crisis, disturbing "thinking people" everywhere.

## Modern Philosophy

Among the small band of thinkers in the late nineteenth century who challenged the belief in progress and the general faith in the rational human mind, German philosopher Friedrich Nietzsche (1844–1900) was particularly influential. The son of a Lutheran minister, Nietzsche rejected Christianity and became a professor of classical languages until ill health forced him to retire at an early age. Never a systematic philosopher, Nietzsche wrote as a prophet in a provocative and poetic style. His first great work in 1872 argued that ever since classical Athens, the West had overemphasized rationality and stifled the passion and animal instinct that drive human activity and true creativity. Nietzsche went on to question all values. He claimed that Christianity embodied a "slave morality" that glorified

**Friedrich Nietzsche** This colored photograph of the German philosopher was taken in 1882, when he was at the height of his creative powers. A brilliant iconoclast, Nietzsche debunked European values and challenged the optimistic faith in human rationality before World War I. *(akg-images)*

weakness, envy, and mediocrity. In Nietzsche's most famous line, a wise fool proclaims that "God is dead," dead because he has been murdered by lackadaisical modern Christians who no longer really believe in him. Nietzsche viewed the pillars of conventional morality—reason, democracy, progress, respectability—as outworn social and psychological constructs whose influence was suffocating self-realization and excellence.

Nietzsche painted a dark world, foreshadowing perhaps his loss of sanity in 1889. The West was in decline; false values had triumphed. The death of God left people disoriented and depressed. The only hope for the individual was to accept the meaninglessness of human existence and then make that very meaninglessness a source of self-defined personal integrity and hence liberation. This would at least be possible for a few superior individuals, who could free themselves from the humdrum thinking of the masses and become true heroes. Little read during his active years, Nietzsche attracted growing attention in the early twentieth century, especially from German radicals who found inspiration in Nietzsche's ferocious assault on the conventions of pre-1914 imperial Germany. Subsequent generations have each discovered new Nietzsches, and his influence remains enormous to this day.

This growing dissatisfaction with established ideas before 1914 was apparent in other important thinkers. In the 1890s, French philosophy professor Henri Bergson (1859–1941) convinced many young people through his writing that immediate experience and intuition were as important as rational and scientific thinking for understanding reality. Indeed, according to Bergson, a religious experience or a mystical poem was often more accessible to human comprehension than a scientific law or a mathematical equation.

Another thinker who agreed about the limits of rational thinking was French socialist Georges Sorel (1847–1922). Sorel frankly characterized Marxian socialism as an inspiring but unprovable religion rather than a rational scientific truth. Socialism would come to power, he believed, through a great, general strike of all working people, which would shatter capitalist society. Sorel rejected democracy and believed that the masses of the new socialist society would have to be tightly controlled by a small revolutionary elite.

The First World War accelerated the revolt against established certainties in philosophy, but that revolt went in two very different directions. In English-speaking countries, the main development was the acceptance of logical empiricism (or logical positivism) in university circles. In continental countries, the primary development in philosophy was existentialism.

**Logical empiricism** was truly revolutionary. It quite simply rejected most of the concerns of traditional philosophy, from the existence of God to the meaning of happiness, as nonsense and hot air. This outlook began primarily with Austrian philosopher Ludwig Wittgenstein (1889–1951), who later immigrated to England, where he trained numerous disciples.

Wittgenstein argued in his pugnacious *Tractatus Logico-Philosophicus* (Essay on Logical Philosophy) in 1922 that philosophy is only the logical clarification of thoughts, and therefore it becomes the study of language, which expresses thoughts. The great philosophical issues of the ages—God, freedom, morality, and so on—are quite literally senseless, a great waste of time, for statements about them can be neither tested by scientific experiments nor demonstrated by the logic of mathematics. Statements about such matters reflect only the personal preferences of a given individual. As Wittgenstein put it in the famous last sentence of his work, "Of what one cannot speak, of that one must keep silent." Logical empiricism, which has remained dominant in England and the United States to this day, drastically reduced the scope of philosophical inquiry. Anxious people could find few, if any, answers in this direction.

Some looked for answers in **existentialism.** Highly diverse and even contradictory, existential thinkers were loosely united in a courageous search for moral values in a world of terror and uncertainty. Theirs were true voices of the age of anxiety.

Most existential thinkers in the twentieth century were atheists. Often inspired by Nietzsche, who had already proclaimed the death of God and called for new values, they did not believe a supreme being had established humanity's fundamental nature and given life its meaning. In the words of the famous French existentialist Jean-Paul Sartre (1905–1980), human beings simply exist: "They turn up, appear on the scene." Only after they "turn up" do they seek to define themselves. Honest human beings are terribly alone, for there is no God to help them. They are hounded by despair and the meaninglessness of life. The crisis of the existential thinker epitomized the modern intellectual crisis—the shattering of beliefs in God, reason, and progress.

Existentialists did recognize that human beings, unless they kill themselves, must act. Indeed, in the words of Sartre, "man is condemned to be free." There is therefore the possibility—indeed, the necessity—of giving meaning to life through actions, of defining oneself through choices. To do so, individuals must become "engaged" and choose their own actions courageously and consistently and in full awareness of their inescapable responsibility for their own behavior. In the end, existentialists argued, human beings can overcome life's absurdity.

Modern existentialism first attained prominence in Germany in the 1920s when philosophers Martin Heidegger and Karl Jaspers found a sympathetic audience among disillusioned postwar university students. But it was in France during and immediately after World War II that existentialism came of age. The terrible conditions of the war (see Chapter 29) reinforced the existential view of and approach to life. On the one hand, the armies of the German dictator Hitler had conquered most of Europe and unleashed a hideous reign of barbarism. On the other, men and women had more than ever to define themselves by their actions. Specifically, each individual had to choose whether to join the resistance against Hitler or accept and even abet tyranny. The writings of Sartre, who along with Albert Camus (1913–1960) was the leading French existentialist, became enormously influential. Himself active in the French resistance, Sartre and his colleagues offered a powerful answer to profound moral issues and the contemporary crisis.

## The Revival of Christianity

The loss of faith in human reason and in continual progress also led to a renewed interest in the Christian view of the world. Christianity and religion in general had been on the defensive in intellectual circles since the Enlightenment. In the years before 1914, some theologians, especially Protestant ones, had felt the need to interpret Christian doctrine and the Bible so that they did not seem to contradict science, evolution, and common sense. Christ was therefore seen primarily as the greatest moral teacher, and the "supernatural" aspects of his divinity were strenuously played down. Indeed, some modern theologians were embarrassed by the miraculous, unscientific aspects of Christianity and turned away from them.

Especially after World War I, a number of thinkers and theologians began to revitalize the fundamentals of Christianity. Sometimes described as Christian existentialists because they shared the loneliness and despair of atheistic existentialists, they stressed human beings' sinful nature, the need for faith, and the mystery of God's forgiveness. The revival of fundamental Christian belief after World War I was fed by rediscovery of the work of nineteenth-century Danish religious philosopher Søren Kierkegaard (1813–1855), whose ideas became extremely influential. Having rejected formalistic religion, Kierkegaard had eventually resolved his personal anguish over his imperfect nature by making a total religious commitment to a remote and majestic God.

Similar ideas were brilliantly developed by Swiss Protestant theologian Karl Barth (1886–1968), whose many influential writings after 1920 sought to re-create the religious intensity of the Reformation. For Barth, the basic fact about human beings is that they are imperfect, sinful creatures whose reason and will are hopelessly flawed. Religious truth is therefore made known to human beings only through God's grace. People have to accept God's word and the supernatural revelation of Jesus Christ with awe, trust, and obedience. Lowly mortals should not expect to "reason out" God and his ways.

Among Catholics, the leading existential Christian thinker was Gabriel Marcel (1887–1973). Born into a cultivated French family, where his atheistic father was "gratefully aware of all that . . . art owed to Catholicism but regarded Catholic thought itself as obsolete and tainted with absurd superstitions,"[2] Marcel found in the Catholic church an answer to what he called the postwar "broken world." Catholicism and religious belief provided the hope, humanity, honesty, and piety for which he hungered. Flexible and gentle, Marcel and his countryman Jacques Maritain (1882–1973) denounced anti-Semitism and supported closer ties with non-Catholics.

After 1914 religion became much more relevant and meaningful to thinking people than it had been before the war. In addition to Marcel and Maritain, many other illustrious individuals turned to religion between about 1920 and 1950. Poets T. S. Eliot and W. H. Auden, novelists Evelyn Waugh and Aldous Huxley, historian Arnold Toynbee, Oxford professor C. S. Lewis, psychoanalyst Karl Stern, physicist Max Planck, and philosopher Cyril Joad were all either converted to religion or attracted to it for the first time. Religion, often of a despairing, existential variety, was one meaningful answer to terror and anxiety. In the words of a famous Roman Catholic convert, English novelist Graham Greene, "One began to believe in heaven because one believed in hell."[3]

## The New Physics

Ever since the scientific revolution of the seventeenth century, scientific advances and their implications had greatly influenced the beliefs of thinking people. By the late nineteenth century, science was one of the main pillars supporting Western society's optimistic and rationalistic view of the world. The Darwinian concept of evolution had been accepted and assimilated in most intellectual circles. Progressive minds believed that science, unlike religion and philosophical speculation, was based on hard facts and controlled experiments. Science seemed to have achieved an unerring and almost complete picture of reality. Unchanging natural laws seemed to determine physical processes and permit useful solutions to more and more problems. All this was comforting, especially to people who were no longer committed to traditional religious beliefs. And all this was challenged by the new physics.

An important first step toward the new physics was the discovery at the end of the nineteenth century that atoms were not like hard, permanent little billiard balls. They were actually composed of many far-smaller, fast-moving particles, such as electrons and protons. Polish-born physicist Marie Curie (1867–1934) and her French husband, Pierre, discovered that radium constantly emits subatomic particles and thus does not have a constant atomic weight. Building on this and other work in radiation, German physicist Max Planck (1858–1947) showed in 1900 that subatomic energy is emitted in uneven little spurts, which Planck called "quanta," and not in a steady stream, as previously believed. Planck's discovery called into question the old sharp distinction between matter and energy; the implication was that matter and energy might be different forms of the same thing. The old view of atoms as the stable, basic building blocks of nature, with a different kind of unbreakable atom for each of the ninety-two chemical elements, was badly shaken.

In 1905 the German-Jewish genius Albert Einstein (1879–1955) went further than the Curies and Planck in undermining Newtonian physics. His famous theory of special relativity postulated that time and space are relative to the viewpoint of the observer and that only the speed of light is constant for all frames of reference in the universe. In order to make his revolutionary and paradoxical idea somewhat comprehensible to the nonmathematical layperson, Einstein later used analogies involving moving trains. For example, if a woman in the middle of a moving car got up and walked forward to the door, she had gone, relative to the train, a half car length. But relative to an observer on the embankment, she had gone farther. The closed framework of Newtonian physics was quite limited compared to that of Einsteinian physics, which unified an apparently infinite universe with the incredibly small, fast-moving subatomic world. Moreover, Einstein's theory stated clearly that matter and energy are interchangeable and that even a particle of matter contains enormous levels of potential energy.

The 1920s opened the "heroic age of physics," in the apt words of one of its leading pioneers, Ernest Rutherford (1871–1937). Breakthrough followed breakthrough. In 1919 Rutherford showed that the atom could be split. By 1944 seven subatomic particles had been identified, of which the most important was the **neutron.** The neutron's capacity to pass through other atoms allowed for even more intense experimental bombardment of matter, leading to chain reactions of unbelievable force. This was the road to the atomic bomb.

Although few nonscientists understood this revolution in physics, the implications of the new theories and discoveries, as presented by newspapers and popular writers, were disturbing to millions of men and women in the 1920s and 1930s. The new universe was strange and troubling. It lacked any absolute objective reality. Everything was "relative," that is, dependent on the observer's frame of reference. Moreover, the universe was uncertain and undetermined, without stable building blocks. In 1927 German physicist Werner Heisenberg (1901–1976) formulated the "principle of uncertainty," which postu-

**Unlocking the Power of the Atom** Many of the fanciful visions of science fiction came true in the twentieth century, although not exactly as first imagined. This 1927 cartoon satirizes a professor who has split the atom and unwittingly destroyed his building and neighborhood in the process. In the Second World War the professors harnessed the atom in bombs and decimated faraway cities and foreign civilians. *(Mary Evans Picture Library)*

lates that because it is impossible to know the position and speed of an individual electron, it is therefore impossible to predict its behavior. Instead of Newton's dependable, rational laws, there seemed to be only tendencies and probabilities in an extraordinarily complex and uncertain universe.

Moreover, a universe described by abstract mathematical symbols seemed to have little to do with human experience and human problems. When, for example, Planck was asked what science could contribute to resolving conflicts of values, his response was simple: "Science is not qualified to speak to this question." Physics, the queen of the sciences, no longer provided people easy, optimistic answers—for that matter, it did not provide any answers at all.

## Freudian Psychology

With physics presenting an uncertain universe so unrelated to ordinary human experience, questions regarding the power and potential of the human mind assumed special significance. The findings and speculations of leading psychologist Sigmund Freud (see page 811) were particularly disturbing.

**Giorgio de Chirico: The Song of Love** De Chirico strongly influenced the surrealist painters of the 1920s and 1930s, who saw civilization in crisis and found inspiration in Freudian theories of human thought and action. In this 1914 painting De Chirico tightly groups unrelated images—a classical head, a glove, a ball, a building—in a fantastic, dreamlike combination that fascinates and puzzles. What mysterious significance, if any, lies behind this reordering of everyday reality? *(Digital image © The Museum of Modern Art/Licensed by Scala/Art Resource, NY)*

Before Freud, poets and mystics had probed the unconscious and irrational aspects of human behavior. But most professional, "scientific" psychologists assumed that a single, unified conscious mind processed sense experiences in a rational and logical way. Human behavior in turn was the result of rational calculation—of "thinking"—by the conscious mind. Basing his insights on the analysis of dreams and of hysteria, Freud developed a very different view of the human psyche beginning in the late 1880s.

According to Freud, human behavior is basically irrational. The key to understanding the mind is the primitive, irrational unconscious, which he called the **id.** The unconscious is driven by sexual, aggressive, and pleasure-seeking desires and is locked in a constant battle with the other parts of the mind: the rationalizing conscious (the **ego**), which mediates what a person *can* do, and ingrained moral values (the **superego**), which specify what a person *should* do. Human behavior is a product of a fragile compromise between instinctual drives and the controls of rational thinking and moral values. Since the instinctual drives are extremely powerful, the ever-present danger for individuals and whole societies is that unacknowledged drives will overwhelm the control mechanisms in a violent, distorted way. Yet Freud also agreed with Nietzsche that the mechanisms of rational thinking and traditional moral values can be too strong. They can repress sexual desires too effectively, crippling individuals and entire peoples with guilt and neurotic fears.

Freudian psychology and clinical psychiatry had become an international movement by 1910, but only after 1918 did they receive popular attention, especially in the Protestant countries of northern Europe and in the United States. Many opponents and even some enthusiasts interpreted Freud as saying that the first requirement for mental health is an uninhibited sex life. Thus after the First World War, the popular interpretation of Freud reflected and encouraged growing sexual experimentation, particularly among middle-class women. For more serious students, the psychology of Freud and his followers drastically undermined the old, easy optimism about the rational and progressive nature of the human mind.

## Twentieth-Century Literature

The general intellectual climate of pessimism, relativism, and alienation was also articulated in literature. Novelists developed new techniques to express new realities. The great nineteenth-century novelists had typically written as all-knowing narrators, describing realistic characters and their relationship to an understandable, if sometimes harsh, society. In the twentieth century, most major writers adopted the limited, often confused viewpoint of a single individual. Like Freud, these novelists focused their attention on the complexity and irrationality of the human mind, where feelings, memories, and desires are forever scrambled. The great French novelist Marcel Proust (1871–1922), in his semi-autobiographical *Remembrance of Things Past* (1913–1927), recalled bittersweet memories of childhood and youthful love and tried to discover their innermost meaning. To do so, Proust lived like a hermit in a soundproof Paris apartment for ten years, withdrawing from the present to dwell on the past.

Serious novelists also used the **stream-of-consciousness technique** to explore the psyche. In *Jacob's Room* (1922), Virginia Woolf (1882–1941) created a novel made up of a series of internal monologues, in which ideas and emotions from different periods of time bubble up as randomly as from a patient on a psychoanalyst's couch. William Faulkner (1897–1962), perhaps America's greatest twentieth-century novelist, used the same technique in *The Sound and the Fury* (1929), much of whose intense drama is confusedly seen through the eyes of an idiot. The most famous stream-of-consciousness novel—and surely the most disturbing novel of its generation—is *Ulysses,* which Irish novelist James Joyce (1882–1941) published in 1922. Into an account of an ordinary day in the life of an ordinary man, Joyce weaves an extended ironic parallel between his hero's aimless wanderings through the streets and pubs of Dublin and the adventures of Homer's hero Ulysses on his way home from Troy. Abandoning conventional grammar and blending foreign words, puns, bits of knowledge, and scraps of memory together in bewildering confusion, the language of *Ulysses* is intended to mirror modern life itself: a gigantic riddle waiting to be unraveled.

**Virginia Woolf** Her novels, like impressionist paintings, captured sensations, and her home attracted a circle of artists and writers known as the Bloomsbury Group. Many of Woolf's essays dealt with women's issues and urged greater opportunity for women's creativity. *(Gisèle Freund/Photo Researchers, Inc.)*

As creative writers turned their attention from society to the individual and from realism to psychological relativity, they rejected the idea of progress. Some even described "anti-utopias," nightmare visions of things to come. In 1918 an obscure German high school teacher named Oswald Spengler (1880–1936) published *The Decline of the West,* which quickly became an international sensation. According to Spengler, every culture experiences a life cycle of growth and decline. Western civilization, in Spengler's opinion, was in its old age, and death was approaching in the form of conquest by the yellow race. T. S. Eliot (1888–1965), in his famous poem *The Waste Land* (1922), depicts a world of growing desolation, although after his conversion to Anglo-Catholicism in 1927, Eliot came to hope cautiously for humanity's salvation. No such hope appears in the work of Franz Kafka (1883–1924), whose novels *The Trial* (1925) and *The Castle* (1926), as well as several of his greatest short stories, portray helpless individuals crushed by inexplicably hostile forces. The German-Jewish Kafka died young, at forty-one, and so did not see the world of his nightmares materialize in the Nazi state.

Englishman George Orwell (1903–1950), however, had seen both that reality and its Stalinist counterpart by 1949, when he wrote perhaps the ultimate in anti-utopian literature: *1984.* Orwell set the action in the future, in 1984. Big Brother—the dictator—and his totalitarian state use a new kind of language, sophisticated technology, and psychological terror to strip a weak individual of his last shred of human dignity. The supremely self-confident chief of the Thought Police tells the tortured, broken, and framed Winston Smith, "If you want a picture of the future, imagine a boot stamping on a human face—forever."[4] A phenomenal bestseller, *1984* spoke to millions of people in the closing years of the age of anxiety.

## Modern Art and Music

See DBQ 12

Throughout the twentieth century, there was considerable unity in the arts. Even today the "modernism" of the immediate prewar years and the 1920s still seems strikingly modern. Like the scientists and creative artists who were partaking of the same culture, creative artists rejected old forms and old values. Modernism in art and music meant constant experimentation and a search for new kinds of expression. And though many people find the numerous and varied modern visions of the arts strange, disturbing, and even ugly, the twentieth century, so dismal in many respects, will probably stand as one of Western civilization's great artistic eras.

### Architecture and Design

Modernism in the arts was loosely unified by a revolution in architecture. This revolution intended nothing less than a transformation of the physical framework of urban society according to a new principle: **functionalism.** Buildings, like industrial products, should be useful and "functional"—that is, they should serve, as well as possible, the purpose for which they were made. Thus architects and designers had to work with engineers, town planners, and even sanitation experts. Moreover, they had to throw away useless ornamentation and find beauty and aesthetic pleasure in the clean lines of practical constructions and efficient machinery. Franco-Swiss genius Le Corbusier (1887–1965) insisted that "a house is a machine for living in."[5]

The United States, with its rapid urban growth and lack of rigid building traditions, pioneered in the new architecture. In the 1890s, the Chicago school of architects, led by Louis H. Sullivan (1856–1924), used cheap steel, reinforced concrete, and electric elevators to build skyscrapers and office buildings lacking almost any exterior ornamentation. In the first decade of the twentieth century, Sullivan's student Frank Lloyd Wright (1869–1959) built a series of radically new and truly modern houses featuring low lines, open interiors, and mass-produced building materials. Europeans were inspired by these and other American examples of functional construction, like the massive, unadorned grain elevators of the Midwest.

In Europe architectural leadership centered in German-speaking countries until Hitler took power in 1933. In 1911 twenty-eight-year-old Walter Gropius (1883–1969) broke sharply with the past in his design of the Fagus shoe factory at Alfeld, Germany—a clean, light, elegant building of glass and iron. After the First World War, Gropius merged the schools of fine and applied arts at Weimar into a single, interdisciplinary school, the **Bauhaus.** The Bauhaus brought together many leading modern architects, designers, and theatrical innovators. Working as an effective, inspired team, they combined the study of fine art, such as painting and sculpture, with the study of applied art in the crafts of printing, weaving, and furniture making. Throughout the 1920s, the Bauhaus, with its stress on functionalism and good design for everyday life, attracted enthusiastic students from all over the world. It had a great and continuing impact.

Another leader in the "international" style, Ludwig Mies van der Rohe (1886–1969), followed Gropius as director of the Bauhaus in 1930 and immigrated to the United States in 1937. His classic Lake Shore Apartments in Chicago, built between 1948 and 1951, symbolized the triumph of steel-frame and glass-wall modern architecture in the great building boom after the Second World War.

### Modern Painting

Modern painting grew out of a revolt against French impressionism. The *impressionism* of such French painters as Claude Monet (1840–1926), Pierre Auguste Renoir (1841–1919), and Camille Pissarro (1830–1903) was, in part, a kind of "superrealism." Leaving exact copying of objects to photography, these artists sought to capture the momentary overall feeling, or impression, of light falling on a real-life scene before their eyes. By 1890, when impressionism was finally established, a few artists known as *postimpressionists,* or sometimes as *expressionists,* were already striking out in new directions. After 1905 art increasingly took on a nonrepresentational, abstract character, a development that reached its high point after World War II.

**Frank Lloyd Wright: The "Falling Water" House** Often considered Wright's masterpiece, Falling Water combines modern architectural concepts with close attention to a spectacular site. Anchored to a high rock ledge by means of reinforced concrete, the house soars out over a cascading waterfall at Bear Run in western Pennsylvania. Built in 1937 for a Pittsburgh businessman, Falling Water is now open to the public and attracts 70,000 visitors each year. *(Western Pennsylvania Conservancy/Art Resource, NY/© 2004 Artists Rights Society [ARS], New York)*

Though individualistic in their styles, postimpressionists were united in their desire to know and depict worlds other than the visible world of fact. Like the early-nineteenth-century romantics, they wanted to portray unseen, inner worlds of emotion and imagination. Like modern novelists, they wanted to express a complicated psychological view of reality as well as an overwhelming emotional intensity. In *The Starry Night* (1889), for example, the great Dutch expressionist Vincent van Gogh (1853–1890) painted the moving vision of his mind's eye (see the illustration on page 932). Paul Gauguin (1848–1903), the French stockbroker-turned-painter, pioneered in expressionist techniques, though he used them to infuse his work with tranquillity and mysticism. In 1891 he fled to the South Pacific in search of unspoiled beauty and a primitive way of life. Gauguin believed that the form and design of a picture were important in themselves and that the painter need not try to represent objects on canvas as the eye actually saw them.

**Van Gogh: The Starry Night** Van Gogh absorbed impressionism in Paris, but under the burning sun of southern France he went beyond the portrayal of external reality. In *The Starry Night* (1889) flaming cypress trees, exploding stars, and a comet-like Milky Way swirl together in one great cosmic rhythm. Painting an inner world of intense emotion and wild imagination, van Gogh contributed greatly to the rise of expressionism in modern art. *(Digital Image © The Museum of Modern Art/Licensed by Scala/Art Resource, NY)*

Fascination with form, as opposed to light, was characteristic of postimpressionism and expressionism. Paul Cézanne (1839–1906), who had a profound influence on twentieth-century painting, was particularly committed to form and ordered design. He told a young painter, "You must see in nature the cylinder, the sphere, and the cone."[6] As Cézanne's later work became increasingly abstract and nonrepresentational, it also moved away from the traditional three-dimensional perspective toward the two-dimensional plane, which has characterized so much of modern art. The expressionism of a group of painters led by Henri Matisse (1869–1954) was so extreme that an exhibition of their work in Paris in 1905 prompted shocked critics to call them *les fauves*—"the wild beasts." Matisse and his followers still painted real objects, but their primary concern was the arrangement of color, line, and form as an end in itself.

In 1907 a young Spaniard in Paris, Pablo Picasso (1881–1973), founded another movement—*cubism*. (See the feature "Images in Society: Pablo Picasso and Modern Art" on pages 934–935.) Cubism concentrated on a complex geometry of zigzagging lines and sharply angled, overlapping planes. About three years later came the ultimate stage in the development of abstract, nonrepresentational art. Artists such as the Russian-born Wassily Kandinsky (1866–1944) turned away from nature completely. "The observer," said Kandinsky, "must learn to look at [my] pictures . . . as form and color combinations . . . as a representation of mood and not as a representation of *objects.*"[7] On the eve of the First World War, extreme expressionism and abstract painting were developing rapidly not only in Paris but also in Russia and Germany. Modern art had become international.

In the 1920s and 1930s, the artistic movements of the prewar years were extended and consolidated. The most notable new developments were *dadaism* and *surrealism.* **Dadaism** attacked all accepted standards of art and behavior, delighting in outrageous conduct. Its name, from the French word *dada,* meaning "hobbyhorse," is deliberately nonsensical. A famous example of dadaism is a reproduction of Leonardo da Vinci's *Mona Lisa* in which the famous woman with the mysterious smile sports a mustache and is ridiculed with an obscene inscription. After 1924 many dadaists were attracted to surrealism, which became very influential in art in the late 1920s and 1930s. Surrealists painted a fantastic world of wild dreams and complex symbols, where watches melted and giant metronomes beat time in precisely drawn but impossible alien landscapes. Refusing to depict ordinary visual reality, surrealist painters made powerful statements about the age of anxiety.

### Modern Music

Developments in modern music were strikingly parallel to those in painting. Composers, too, were attracted by the emotional intensity of expressionism. The ballet *The Rite of Spring* by composer Igor Stravinsky (1882–1971) practically caused a riot when it was first performed in Paris in 1913 by Sergei Diaghilev's famous Russian dance company. The combination of pulsating, dissonant rhythms from the orchestra pit and an earthy representation of lovemaking by the dancers on the stage seemed a shocking, almost pornographic enactment of a primitive fertility rite.

After the experience of the First World War, when irrationality and violence seemed to pervade the human experience, expressionism in opera and ballet flourished. One of the most famous and powerful examples was the opera *Wozzeck,* by Alban Berg (1885–1935), first performed in Berlin in 1925. Blending a half-sung, half-spoken kind of dialogue with harsh, atonal music, *Wozzeck* is a gruesome tale of a soldier driven by Kafka-like inner terrors and vague suspicions of unfaithfulness to murder his mistress.

Some composers turned their backs on long-established musical conventions. As abstract painters arranged lines and color but did not draw identifiable objects, so modern composers arranged sounds without creating recognizable harmonies. Led by Viennese composer Arnold Schönberg (1874–1951), they abandoned traditional harmony and tonality. The musical notes in a given piece were no longer united and organized by a key; instead they were independent and unrelated. Schönberg's twelve-tone music of the 1920s arranged all twelve notes of the scale in an abstract, mathematical pattern, or "tone row." This pattern sounded like no pattern at all to the ordinary listener and could be detected only by a highly trained eye studying the musical score. Accustomed to the harmonies of classical and romantic music, audiences generally resisted modern atonal music. Only after the Second World War did it begin to win acceptance.

## Movies and Radio

Until after World War II at the earliest, these revolutionary changes in art and music appealed mainly to a minority of "highbrows" and not to the general public. That public was primarily and enthusiastically wrapped up in movies and radio. The long-declining traditional arts and amusements of people in villages and small towns almost vanished, replaced by standardized, commercial entertainment.

Moving pictures were first shown as a popular novelty in naughty peepshows—"What the Butler Saw"—and penny arcades in the 1890s, especially in Paris. The first movie houses date from an experiment in Los Angeles in 1902. They quickly attracted large audiences and led to the production of short, silent action films such as the eight-minute *Great Train Robbery* of 1903. American directors and business people then set up "movie factories," at first in the New York area and then after 1910 in Los Angeles. These factories churned out two short films each week. On the eve of the First World War, full-length feature films such as the Italian *Quo Vadis* and the American *Birth of a Nation,* coupled with improvements in the quality of pictures, suggested the screen's vast possibilities.

During the First World War, the United States became the dominant force in the rapidly expanding silent-film industry. In the 1920s, Mack Sennett (1884–1960) and his zany Keystone Kops specialized in short, slapstick comedies noted for frantic automobile chases, custard-pie battles, and gorgeous bathing beauties. Screen stars such as Mary Pickford and Lillian Gish, Douglas Fairbanks and Rudolf Valentino, became household names, with their own "fan

# Images in Society

## Pablo Picasso and Modern Art

Pablo Picasso (1881–1973) was probably the most significant artist of the early twentieth century. For more than seventy years, he personified the individuality, freedom, and revolutionary creativity of the modern artist.

Born at Málaga in southern Spain, Picasso quickly demonstrated a precocious talent. At nineteen he headed for Paris, Europe's art capital. Suffering from poverty and falling into depression, he painted the weak and the poor in somber blue and purple tones. These pessimistic paintings of Picasso's "Blue Period" (1901–1904) are masterpieces in the tradition of Spanish realism.

Yet the young Picasso soon sought a new visual reality. In 1907 his arduous struggle to create a new style resulted in *Les Demoiselles d'Avignon* (Image 1), a painting originating in memories of a brothel scene in Barcelona. This work was considered a revolutionary upheaval in art. Since the Renaissance, artists had been expected to follow established rules, seeing objects in an orderly perspective from a single viewpoint and creating "beauty" and unified human forms. Do the faces of the central figures in this work conform to these rules? Regard the figures on either side, who were painted later. Notice how the light fails to combine with the shadow to create bodies with continuous, three-dimensional contours. The figures appear broken into large, flat planes with heads that are twisted, fractured dislocations. Do you see the magical violence of a pictorial breakthrough or a grotesque, ugly departure?

Picasso extended his revolutionary experiments, and after 1910 he was joined by others. A critic called the new school cubism because these artists used many geometric forms in intersecting planes. Objects, viewed from many shifting viewpoints, often emerged as purely abstract designs.

*Three Musicians* (Image 2), painted in 1921, represents mature cubism. Many people believe that it marks the culmination of Picasso's cubist style. What similarities and differences do you see between this picture and Image 1? Notice the limited number of viewpoints, with the white clown, the harlequin, the monk, their instruments, and the

**Image 1 Les Demoiselles d'Avignon** (1907). *(Digital image © The Museum of Modern Art/Licensed by Scala/Art Resource, NY/© 2004 Estate of Pablo Picasso/Artists Rights Society [ARS], New York)*

**Image 2 Three Musicians** (1921). *(Digital image © The Museum of Modern Art/Licensed by Scala/Art Resource, NY/© 2004 Estate of Pablo Picasso/Artists Rights Society [ARS], New York)*

table in front cut up into rectangular shapes and reassembled in recognizable form on a shallow series of planes. What is the effect of the bright primary colors and the harmonious, decorative order? Picasso had been making the sets for Sergei Diaghilev's famous Russian dance company in Paris, and these three jagged figures from traditional Italian comedy seem to convey the atmosphere of the theater and the dissonant, syncopated rhythm of modern music. Picasso always drew back from pure abstraction because he began with real objects and used models.

Picasso's passionate involvement in his times infuses his immense painting *Guernica* (Image 3), often considered his greatest work. Painted for the Spanish pavilion at the Paris International Exhibition in 1937, this mural, with its mournful white, black, and blue colors, was inspired by the Spanish civil war and the deadly terror bombing of Guernica by fascist planes in a single night. In this complex work, a shrieking woman falls from a burning house on the far right. On the left, a woman holds a dead child, while toward the center are fragments of a warrior and a screaming horse pierced by a spear. Do cubist techniques heighten the effect? Picasso also draws on other aspects of the modernist revolution here. Compare *Guernica* with the expressionist work on pages 897 and 932. Surrealists were fascinated with grotesque subject matter and apparently unrelated objects in surprising situations. Are these elements also present here? Picasso wanted his painting to be an unforgettable attack on "brutality and darkness." Did he succeed? How do the works presented here enhance your understanding of modern art?

*The* **history companion** *features additional information and activities related to this topic.*
**history.college.hmco.com/students**

**Image 3 Guernica** (1937). *(Bridgeman-Giraudon/Art Resource, NY/© 2004 Estate of Pablo Picasso/Artists Rights Society [ARS], New York)*

**The Great Dictator** In 1940 the renowned actor and director Charlie Chaplin abandoned the Little Tramp role to satirize the "great dictator," Adolf Hitler. Chaplin had strong political views and made a number of films with political themes as the escapist fare of the Great Depression gave way to the reality of the Second World War. *(The Museum of Modern Art/Still Film Archives)*

clubs." Yet Charlie Chaplin (1889–1978), a funny little Englishman working in Hollywood, was unquestionably the king of the "silver screen" in the 1920s. In his enormously popular role as the lonely Little Tramp, complete with baggy trousers, battered derby, and an awkward, shuffling walk, Chaplin symbolized the "gay spirit of laughter in a cruel, crazy world."[8] Chaplin also demonstrated that in the hands of a genius, the new medium could combine mass entertainment and artistic accomplishment.

The early 1920s were also the great age of German films. Protected and developed during the war, the large German studios excelled in bizarre expressionist dramas, beginning with *The Cabinet of Dr. Caligari* in 1919. Unfortunately, their period of creativity was short-lived. By 1926 American money was drawing the leading German talents to Hollywood and consolidating America's international domination. Film making was big business, and European theater owners were forced to book whole blocks of American films to get the few pictures they really wanted. This system put European producers at a great disadvantage until "talkies" permitted a revival of national film industries in the 1930s, particularly in France.

Whether foreign or domestic, motion pictures became the main entertainment of the masses until after the Second World War. In Great Britain one in every four adults went to the movies twice a week in the late 1930s, and two in five went at least once a week. Continental countries had similar figures. The greatest appeal of motion pictures was that they offered ordinary people a temporary escape from the hard realities of everyday life. The appeal of escapist entertainment was especially strong during the Great Depression. Millions flocked to musical comedies featuring glittering stars such as Ginger Rogers and Fred Astaire and to the fanciful cartoons of Mickey Mouse and his friends.

Radio became possible with the transatlantic "wireless" communication of Guglielmo Marconi (1874–1937) in 1901 and the development of the vacuum tube in 1904, which permitted the transmission of speech and music. But only in 1920 were the first major public broadcasts of special events made in Great Britain and the United States. Lord Northcliffe, who had pioneered in journalism with the inexpensive, mass-circulation *Daily Mail,* sponsored a broadcast of "only one artist . . . the world's very best, the soprano Nellie Melba."[9] Singing from London in English, Italian, and French, Melba was heard simultaneously all over Europe on June 16, 1920. This historic event captured the public's imagination. The meteoric career of radio was launched.

Every major country quickly established national broadcasting networks. In the United States such networks were privately owned and financed by advertising. In Great Britain Parliament set up an independent, public corporation, the British Broadcasting Corporation (BBC), supported by licensing fees. Elsewhere in Europe the typical pattern was direct control by the government.

Whatever the institutional framework, radio became popular and influential. By the late 1930s, more than three out of every four households in both democratic Great Britain and dictatorial Germany had at least one cheap, mass-produced radio.

Radio in unscrupulous hands was particularly well suited for political propaganda. Dictators such as Mussolini and

Hitler controlled the airwaves and could reach enormous national audiences with their frequent, dramatic speeches. In democratic countries, politicians such as President Franklin Roosevelt and Prime Minister Stanley Baldwin effectively used informal "fireside chats" to bolster their support.

Motion pictures also became powerful tools of indoctrination, especially in countries with dictatorial regimes. Lenin himself encouraged the development of Soviet film making, believing that the new medium was essential to the social and ideological transformation of the country. Beginning in the mid-1920s, a series of epic films, the most famous of which were directed by Sergei Eisenstein (1898–1948), brilliantly dramatized the communist view of Russian history.

In Germany Hitler turned to a young and immensely talented woman film maker, Leni Riefenstahl (1902–2003), for a masterpiece of documentary propaganda, *The Triumph of the Will,* based on the Nazi party rally at Nuremberg in 1934. Riefenstahl combined stunning aerial photography, joyful crowds welcoming Hitler, and mass processions of young Nazi fanatics. Her film was a brilliant and all-too-powerful documentary of Germany's "Nazi rebirth." The new media of mass culture were potentially dangerous instruments of political manipulation.

## The Search for Peace and Political Stability

As established patterns of thought and culture were challenged and mangled by the ferocious impact of World War I, so also was the political fabric stretched and torn by the consequences of the great conflict. The Versailles settlement had established a shaky truce, not a solid peace. Thus national leaders faced a gigantic task as they struggled with uncertainty and sought to create a stable international order within the general context of intellectual crisis and revolutionary artistic experimentation.

The pursuit of real and lasting peace proved difficult for many reasons. Germany hated the Treaty of Versailles. France was fearful and isolated. Britain was undependable, and the United States had turned its back on European problems. Eastern Europe was in ferment, and no one could predict the future of communist Russia. Moreover, the international economic situation was poor and greatly complicated by war debts and disrupted patterns of trade. Yet for a time, from 1925 to late 1929, it appeared that peace and stability were within reach. When the subsequent collapse of the 1930s mocked these hopes, the disillusionment of liberals in the democracies was intensified.

### Germany and the Western Powers

Germany was the key to lasting peace. Yet to Germans of all political parties, the Treaty of Versailles represented a harsh, dictated peace, to be revised or repudiated as soon as possible. The treaty had neither broken nor reduced Germany, which was potentially still the strongest country in Europe. Thus the treaty had fallen between two stools: too harsh for a peace of reconciliation, too soft for a peace of conquest.

Moreover, with ominous implications for the future, France and Great Britain did not see eye to eye on Germany. By the end of 1919, France wanted to stress the harsh elements in the Treaty of Versailles. Most of the war in the west had been fought on French soil, and the expected costs of reconstruction, as well as repaying war debts to the United States, were staggering. Thus French politicians believed that massive reparations from Germany were a vital economic necessity. Also, having compromised with President Wilson only to be betrayed by America's failure to ratify the treaty, many French leaders saw strict implementation of all provisions of the Treaty of Versailles as France's last best hope. Large reparation payments could hold Germany down indefinitely, and France would realize its goal of security.

The British soon felt differently. Prewar Germany had been Great Britain's second-best market in the entire world, and after the war a healthy, prosperous Germany appeared to be essential to the British economy. Indeed, many English people agreed with the analysis of the young English economist John Maynard Keynes (1883–1946), who eloquently denounced the Treaty of Versailles in his famous *Economic Consequences of the Peace* (1919). According to Keynes's interpretation, astronomical reparations and harsh economic measures would impoverish Germany and also increase economic hardship in all countries. Only a complete revision of the foolish treaty could save Germany—and Europe. Keynes's attack exploded like a bombshell and became very influential. It stirred deep guilt feelings about Germany in the English-speaking world, feelings that often paralyzed English and American leaders in their relations with Germany and its leaders between the First and Second World Wars.

The British were also suspicious of France's army—the largest in Europe, and authorized at Versailles to occupy the German Rhineland until 1935—and France's foreign policy. Ever since 1890, France had looked to Russia as a powerful ally against Germany. But with Russia hostile and communist, and with Britain and the United States unwilling to make any firm commitments, France turned to the newly formed states of eastern Europe for diplomatic support. In 1921 France signed a mutual defense pact with Poland and associated itself closely with the so-called Little Entente, an alliance that joined Czechoslovakia, Romania, and Yugoslavia against defeated and bitter Hungary.

While French and British leaders drifted in different directions, the Allied reparations commission completed its work. In April 1921, it announced that Germany had to pay the enormous sum of 132 billion gold marks ($33 billion) in annual installments of 2.5 billion gold marks. Facing possible occupation of more of its territory, the young German republic—generally known as the Weimar Republic—made its first payment in 1921. Then in 1922, wracked by rapid inflation and political assassinations and motivated by hostility and arrogance as well, the Weimar Republic announced its inability to pay more. It proposed a moratorium on reparations for three years, with the clear implication that thereafter reparations would be either drastically reduced or eliminated entirely.

**"Hands Off the Ruhr"** The French occupation of the Ruhr to collect reparations payments raised a storm of patriotic protest in Germany. This anti-French poster of 1923 turns Marianne, the personification of French republican virtue, into a vicious harpy. *(International Instituut voor Sociale Geschiedenis)*

The British were willing to accept a moratorium on reparations, but the French were not. Led by their tough-minded prime minister, Raymond Poincaré (1860–1934), they decided they had to either call Germany's bluff or see the entire peace settlement dissolve to France's great disadvantage. So, despite strong British protests, in early January 1923, armies of France and its ally Belgium moved out of the Rhineland and began to occupy the Ruhr district, the heartland of industrial Germany, creating the most serious international crisis of the 1920s. If forcible collection proved impossible, France would use occupation to paralyze Germany and force it to accept the Treaty of Versailles.

Strengthened by a wave of patriotism, the German government ordered the people of the Ruhr to stop working and start passively resisting the French occupation. The coal mines and steel mills of the Ruhr grew silent, leaving 10 percent of Germany's total population in need of relief. The French answer to passive resistance was to seal off the Ruhr and the entire Rhineland from the rest of Germany, letting in only enough food to prevent starvation.

By the summer of 1923, France and Germany were engaged in a great test of wills. French armies could not collect reparations from striking workers at gunpoint. But French occupation was indeed paralyzing Germany and its economy and had turned rapid German inflation into runaway inflation. Faced with the need to support the striking Ruhr workers and their employers, the German government began to print money to pay its bills. Prices soared. People went to the store with a big bag of paper money; they returned home with a handful of groceries. German money rapidly lost all value.

Runaway inflation brought about a social revolution. The accumulated savings of many retired and middle-class people were wiped out. Catastrophic inflation cruelly mocked the old middle-class virtues of thrift, caution, and self-reliance. Many Germans felt betrayed. They hated and blamed the Western governments, their own government, big business, the Jews, the workers, and the communists for their misfortune. They were psychologically prepared to follow radical leaders in a crisis.

In August 1923, as the mark fell and political unrest grew throughout Germany, Gustav Stresemann (1878–1929) assumed leadership of the government. Stresemann adopted a compromising attitude. He called off passive resistance in the Ruhr and in October agreed in principle to pay reparations but asked for a re-examination of

Germany's ability to pay. Poincaré accepted. His hard line was becoming increasingly unpopular with French citizens, and it was hated in Britain and the United States. (See the feature "Individuals in Society: Gustav Stresemann.")

More generally, in both Germany and France, power was finally passing to the moderates, who realized that continued confrontation was a destructive, no-win situation. Thus after five long years of hostility and tension, culminating in a kind of undeclared war in the Ruhr in 1923, Germany and France decided to give compromise and cooperation a try. The British, and even the Americans, were willing to help. The first step was a reasonable agreement on the reparations question.

## Hope in Foreign Affairs, 1924–1929

The reparations commission appointed an international committee of financial experts headed by American banker Charles G. Dawes to re-examine reparations from a broad perspective. The resulting **Dawes Plan** (1924) was accepted by France, Germany, and Britain. Germany's yearly reparations were reduced and depended on the level of German economic prosperity. Germany would also receive large loans from the United States to promote German recovery. In short, Germany would get private loans from the United States and pay reparations to France and Britain, thus enabling those countries to repay the large sums they owed the United States.

This circular flow of international payments was complicated and risky, but for a while it worked. The German republic experienced a spectacular economic recovery. With prosperity and large, continual inflows of American capital, Germany easily paid about $1.3 billion in reparations in 1927 and 1928, enabling France and Britain to pay the United States. In this way the Americans belatedly played a part in the general economic settlement that, though far from ideal, facilitated the worldwide recovery of the late 1920s.

This economic settlement was matched by a political settlement. In 1925 the leaders of Europe signed a number of agreements at Locarno, Switzerland. Germany and France solemnly pledged to accept their common border, and both Britain and Italy agreed to fight either France or Germany if one invaded the other. Stresemann also agreed to settle boundary disputes with Poland and Czechoslovakia by peaceful means, and France promised those countries military aid if Germany attacked them. For years, a "spirit of Locarno" gave Europeans a sense of growing security and stability in international affairs.

Other developments also strengthened hopes. In 1926 Germany joined the League of Nations, where Stresemann continued his "peace offensive." In 1928 fifteen countries signed the Kellogg-Briand Pact, initiated by French prime minister Aristide Briand and U.S. secretary of state Frank B. Kellogg. This multinational pact "condemned and renounced war as an instrument of national policy." The signing states agreed to settle international disputes peacefully. Often seen as idealistic nonsense because it made no provisions for action in case war actually occurred, the pact was still a positive step. It fostered the cautious optimism of the late 1920s and also encouraged the hope that the United States would accept its responsibilities as a great world power and contribute to European stability.

## Hope in Democratic Government

Domestic politics also offered reason to hope. During the occupation of the Ruhr and the great inflation, republican government in Germany had appeared on the verge of collapse. In 1923 communists momentarily entered provincial governments, and in November an obscure nobody named Adolf Hitler leaped onto a table in a beer hall in Munich and proclaimed a "national socialist revolution." But Hitler's plot to seize control of the government was poorly organized and easily crushed, and Hitler was sentenced to prison, where he outlined his theories and program in his book ***Mein Kampf*** (My Struggle). Throughout the 1920s, Hitler's National Socialist party attracted support only from a few fanatical anti-Semites, ultranationalists, and disgruntled ex-servicemen. In 1928 his party had an insignificant twelve seats in the Reichstag. Indeed, after 1923 democracy seemed to take root in Weimar Germany. A new currency was established, and the economy boomed.

The moderate businessmen who tended to dominate the various German coalition governments were convinced that economic prosperity demanded good relations with the Western powers, and they supported parliamentary government at home. Stresemann himself was a man of this class, and he was the key figure in every government until his death in 1929. Elections were held regularly, and republican democracy appeared to have growing support among a majority of the Germans.

There were, however, sharp political divisions in the country. Many unrepentant nationalists and monarchists populated the right and the army. Members of Germany's recently formed Communist party were noisy and active on the left. The Communists, directed from Moscow, reserved their greatest hatred and sharpest barbs for their cousins the Social Democrats, whom they endlessly accused of

**American Jazz in Paris** This woodcut from a 1928 French book on cafés and nightclubs suggests how black musicians took Europe by storm, although the blacks are represented stereotypically. One French critic concluded that American blacks had attained a "pre-eminent" place in music since the war, "for they have impressed the entire world with their vibrating or melancholy rhythms." *(akg-images)*

betraying the revolution. The working classes were divided politically, but a majority supported the nonrevolutionary but socialist Social Democrats.

The situation in France had numerous similarities to that in Germany. Communists and Socialists battled for the support of the workers. After 1924 the democratically elected government rested mainly in the hands of coalitions of moderates, and business interests were well represented. France's great accomplishment was rapid rebuilding of its war-torn northern region. The expense of this undertaking led, however, to a large deficit and substantial inflation. By early 1926, the franc had fallen to 10 percent of its prewar value, causing a severe crisis. Poincaré was recalled to office, while Briand remained minister for foreign affairs. The Poincaré government proceeded to slash spending and raise taxes, restoring confidence in the economy. The franc was "saved," stabilized at about one-fifth of its prewar value. Good times prevailed until 1930.

Despite political shortcomings, France attracted artists and writers from all over the world in the 1920s. Much of the intellectual and artistic ferment of the times flourished in Paris. As writer Gertrude Stein (1874–1946), a leader of the large colony of American expatriates living in Paris, later recalled, "Paris was where the twentieth century was."[10] More generally, France appealed to foreigners and the French as a harmonious combination of small businesses and family farms, of bold innovation and solid traditions.

Britain, too, faced challenges after 1920. The wartime trend toward greater social equality continued, however, helping maintain social harmony. The great problem was unemployment. Many of Britain's best markets had been lost during the war. In June 1921, almost 2.2 million people—23 percent of the labor force—were out of work, and throughout the 1920s unemployment hovered around 12 percent. Yet the state provided unemployment benefits of equal size to all those without jobs and supplemented those payments with subsidized housing, medical aid, and increased old-age pensions. These and other measures kept living standards from seriously declining, defused class tensions, and pointed the way toward the welfare state Britain established after World War II.

Relative social harmony was accompanied by the rise of the Labour party as a determined champion of the working classes and of greater social equality. Committed to the kind of moderate, "revisionist" socialism that had emerged before World War I (see pages 849–850), the Labour party replaced the Liberal party as the main opposition to the Conservatives. The new prominence of the Labour party reflected the decline of old liberal ideals of competitive capitalism, limited government control, and individual responsibility. In 1924 and 1929, the Labour party under Ramsay MacDonald (1866–1937) governed the country with the support of the smaller Liberal party. Yet Labour moved toward socialism gradually and democratically, so that the middle classes were not overly frightened as the working classes won new benefits.

The Conservatives under Stanley Baldwin (1867–1947) showed the same compromising spirit on social issues. The last line of Baldwin's greatest speech in March 1925 summarized his international and domestic programs: "Give us peace in our time, O Lord." In spite of such conflicts as the 1926 strike by hard-pressed coal miners, which ended in an unsuccessful general strike, social unrest in Britain was

# Individuals in Society

## Gustav Stresemann

The German foreign minister Gustav Stresemann (1878–1929) is a controversial historical figure. Hailed by many as a hero of peace, he was denounced as a traitor by radical German nationalists and then by Hitler's Nazis. After World War II, revisionist historians stressed Stresemann's persistent nationalism and cast doubt on his peaceful intentions. Weimar Germany's most renowned leader is a fascinating example of the restless quest for convincing historical interpretation.

Stresemann's origins were modest. His parents were Berlin innkeepers and retailers of bottled beer, and only Gustav of their five children was able to attend high school. Attracted first to literature and history, Stresemann later turned to economics, earned a doctoral degree, and quickly reached the top as a manager and director of German trade associations. A highly intelligent extrovert with a knack for negotiation, Stresemann entered the Reichstag in 1907 as a business-oriented liberal and nationalist. When World War I erupted, he believed, like most Germans, that Germany had acted defensively and was not at fault. He emerged as a strident nationalist and urged German annexation of conquered foreign territories. Germany's collapse in defeat and revolution devastated Stresemann. He seemed a prime candidate for the hateful extremism of the far right.

Yet although Stresemann opposed the Treaty of Versailles as an unjust and unrealistic imposition, he turned back toward the center. He accepted the new Weimar Republic and played a growing role in the Reichstag as the leader of his own small probusiness party. His hour came in the Ruhr crisis, when French and Belgian troops occupied the district. Named chancellor in August 1923, he called off passive resistance and began talks with the French. His government also quelled communist uprisings; put down rebellions in Bavaria, including Hitler's attempted coup; and ended runaway inflation with a new currency. Stresemann fought to preserve German unity, and he succeeded.

Voted out as chancellor in November 1923, Stresemann remained as foreign minister in every government until his death in 1929. Proclaiming a policy of peace and agreeing to pay reparations, he achieved his greatest triumph in the Locarno agreements of 1925 (see page 939). But the interlocking guarantees of existing French and German borders (and the related agreements to resolve peacefully all disputes with Poland and Czechoslovakia) did not lead the French to make any further concessions that might have disarmed Stresemann's extremist foes. Working himself to death, he made little additional progress in achieving international reconciliation and sovereign equality for Germany.

*Foreign Minister Gustav Stresemann of Germany* (right) *leaves a meeting with Aristide Briand, his French counterpart.* (Corbis)

Stresemann was no fuzzy pacifist. Historians debunking his "legend" are right in seeing an enduring love of nation in his defense of German interests. But Stresemann, like his French counterpart Aristide Briand, was a statesman of goodwill who wanted peace through mutually advantageous compromise. A realist trained by business and politics in the art of the possible, Stresemann also reasoned that Germany had to be a satisfied and equal partner if peace was to be secure. His unwillingness to guarantee Germany's eastern borders (see Map 27.4 on page 913), which is often criticized, reflects his conviction that keeping some Germans under Polish and Czechoslovak rule created a ticking time bomb in Europe. Stresemann was no less convinced that war on Poland would almost certainly re-create the Allied coalition that had crushed Germany in 1918.* His insistence on the necessity of peace in the east as well as the west was prophetic. Hitler's 1939 invasion of Poland resulted in an even mightier coalition that almost annihilated Germany in 1945.

### Questions for Analysis

1. What did Gustav Stresemann do to promote reconciliation in Europe? How did his policy toward France differ from that toward Poland and Czechoslovakia?
2. What is your interpretation of Stresemann? Does he arouse your sympathy or your suspicion and hostility? Why?

*Robert Grathwol, "Stresemann: Reflections on His Foreign Policy," *Journal of Modern History* 45 (March 1973): 52–70.

*The* **history companion** *features additional information and activities related to this topic.*
**history.college.hmco.com/students**

limited in the 1920s and in the 1930s as well. In 1922 Britain granted southern, Catholic Ireland full autonomy after a bitter guerrilla war, thereby removing another source of prewar friction. Thus developments in both international relations and the domestic politics of the leading democracies gave cause for optimism in the late 1920s.

## The Great Depression, 1929–1939

Like the Great War, the **Great Depression** must be spelled with capital letters. Economic depression was nothing new. Depressions occurred throughout the nineteenth century with predictable regularity, as they recur in the form of recessions and slumps to this day. What was new about this depression was its severity and duration. It struck the entire world with ever-greater intensity from 1929 to 1933, and recovery was uneven and slow. Only with the Second World War did the depression disappear in much of the world.

The social and political consequences of prolonged economic collapse were enormous. The depression shattered the fragile optimism of political leaders in the late 1920s. Mass unemployment and failing farms made insecurity a reality for millions of ordinary people, who had paid little attention to the intellectual crisis or to new directions in art and ideas (see Map 28.1). In desperation, people looked for leaders who would "do something." They were willing to support radical attempts to deal with the crisis by both democratic leaders and dictators.

### The Economic Crisis

There is no agreement among historians and economists about why the Great Depression was so deep and lasted so long. Thus it is best to trace the course of the great collapse before trying to identify what caused it.

Though economic activity was already declining moderately in many countries by early 1929, the crash of the stock market in the United States in October of that year triggered the collapse into the Great Depression. The American economy had prospered in the late 1920s, but there were large inequalities in income and a serious imbalance between "real" investment and stock market speculation. Thus net investment—in factories, farms, equipment, and the like—actually fell from $3.5 billion in 1925 to $3.2 billion in 1929. In the same years, as money flooded into stocks, the value of shares traded on the exchanges soared from $27 billion to $87 billion. As a financial historian concluded in an important study, "It should have been clear to everybody concerned that a crash was inevitable under such conditions."[11] Of course it was not. Irving Fisher, one of America's most brilliant economists, was highly optimistic in 1929 and fully invested in stocks. He then lost his entire fortune and would have been forced from his house if his university had not bought it and rented it to him.

The American stock market boom was built on borrowed money. Many wealthy investors, speculators, and people of modest means had bought stocks by paying only a small fraction of the total purchase price and borrowing the remainder from their stockbrokers. Such buying "on margin" was extremely dangerous. When prices started falling, the hard-pressed margin buyers either had to put up more money, which was often impossible, or sell their shares to pay off their brokers. Thus thousands of people started selling all at once. The result was a financial panic. Countless investors and speculators were wiped out in a matter of days or weeks.

The general economic consequences were swift and severe. Stripped of wealth and confidence, battered investors and their fellow citizens started buying fewer goods. Prices fell, production began to slow down, and unemployment began to rise. Soon the entire American economy was caught in a vicious, spiraling decline.

The financial panic in the United States triggered a worldwide financial crisis, and that crisis resulted in a drastic decline in production in country after country. Throughout the 1920s, American bankers and investors had lent large amounts of capital to many countries. Many of these loans were short-term, and once panic broke, New York bankers began recalling them. Gold reserves thus began to flow out of European countries, particularly Germany and Austria, toward the United States. It became very hard for European business people to borrow money, and the panicky public began to withdraw its savings from the banks. These banking problems eventually led to the crash of the largest bank in Austria in 1931 and then to general financial chaos. The recall of private loans by American bankers also accelerated the collapse in world prices, as business people around the world dumped industrial goods and agricultural commodities in a frantic attempt to get cash to pay what they owed.

The financial crisis led to a general crisis of production: between 1929 and 1933, world output of goods fell by an estimated 38 percent. As this happened, each country turned inward and tried to go it alone. In 1931, for example, Britain went off the gold standard, refusing to convert bank notes into gold, and reduced the value of its money. Britain's goal was to make its goods cheaper and therefore more salable in the world market. But because more than twenty nations, including the United States in 1934, also

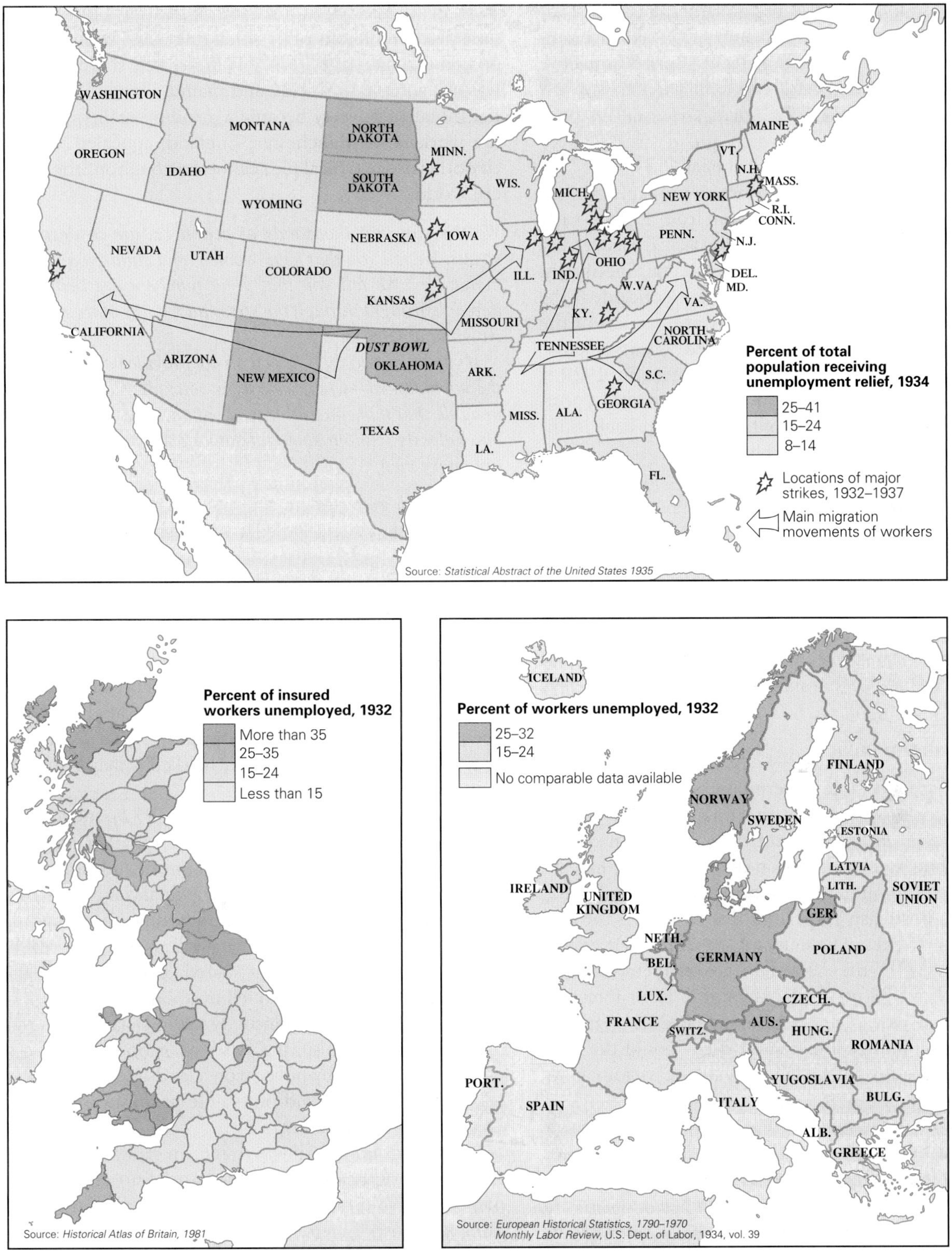


**MAP 28.1 The Great Depression in the United States, Britain, and Europe** National and regional differences were substantial. Germany, industrial northern Britain, and the American Midwest were particularly hard hit.

went off the gold standard, few countries gained a real advantage. Similarly, country after country followed the example of the United States when in 1930 it raised protective tariffs to their highest levels ever and tried to seal off shrinking national markets for American producers only. Within this context of fragmented and destructive economic nationalism, recovery finally began in 1933.

Although opinions differ, two factors probably best explain the relentless slide to the bottom from 1929 to early 1933. First, the international economy lacked a leadership able to maintain stability when the crisis came. Specifically, as a noted American economic historian concluded, the seriously weakened British, the traditional leaders of the world economy, "couldn't and the United States wouldn't" stabilize the international economic system in 1929.[12] The United States, which had momentarily played a positive role after the occupation of the Ruhr, cut back its international lending and erected high tariffs.

The second factor was poor national economic policy in almost every country. Governments generally cut their budgets and reduced spending when they should have run large deficits in an attempt to stimulate their economies. After World War II, such a "counter-cyclical policy," advocated by John Maynard Keynes, became a well-established weapon against downturn and depression. But in the 1930s, Keynes's prescription was generally regarded with horror by orthodox economists.

## Mass Unemployment

The need for large-scale government spending was tied to mass unemployment. As the financial crisis led to cuts in production, workers lost their jobs and had little money to buy goods. In Britain unemployment had averaged 12 percent in the 1920s; between 1930 and 1935, it averaged more than 18 percent. Far worse was the case of the United States, where unemployment had averaged only 5 percent in the 1920s. In 1932 unemployment soared to about 33 percent of the entire labor force: 14 million people were out of work (see Map 28.1). Only by pumping new money into the economy could the government increase demand and break the vicious cycle of decline.

Along with economic effects, mass unemployment posed a great social problem. Poverty increased dramatically, although in most countries unemployed workers generally received some kind of meager unemployment benefits or public aid that prevented starvation. (See the feature "Listening to the Past: Life on the Dole in Great Britain" on pages 950–951.) Millions of people lost their spirit, condemned to an apparently hopeless search for work or to idle boredom. Homes and ways of life were disrupted in millions of personal tragedies. Young people postponed marriages, and birthrates fell sharply. There was an increase in suicide and mental illness. Poverty or the threat of poverty became a grinding reality. In 1932 the workers of Manchester, England, appealed to their city officials—a typical plea echoed throughout the Western world:

*We tell you that thousands of people . . . are in desperate straits. We tell you that men, women, and children are going hungry. . . . We tell you that great numbers are being rendered distraught through the stress and worry of trying to exist without work. . . .*

*If you do not do this—if you do not provide useful work for the unemployed—what, we ask, is your alternative? Do not imagine that this colossal tragedy of unemployment is going on endlessly without some fateful catastrophe. Hungry men are angry men.*[13]

Only strong government action could deal with mass unemployment, a social powder keg preparing to explode.

## The New Deal in the United States

Of all the major industrial countries, only Germany was harder hit by the Great Depression, or reacted more radically to it, than the United States. Depression was so traumatic in the United States because the 1920s had been a period of complacent optimism. The Great Depression and the response to it marked a major turning point in American history.

President Herbert Hoover (1895–1972) and his administration initially reacted to the stock market crash and economic decline with dogged optimism and limited action. But when the full force of the financial crisis struck Europe in the summer of 1931 and boomeranged back to the United States, people's worst fears became reality. Banks failed; unemployment soared. Between 1929 and 1932, industrial production fell by about 50 percent.

In these tragic circumstances, Franklin Delano Roosevelt (1882–1945), an inspiring wheelchair-bound aristocrat previously crippled by polio, won a landslide electoral victory in 1932 with grand but vague promises of a "**New Deal** for the forgotten man."

Roosevelt's basic goal was to reform capitalism in order to preserve it. Roosevelt rejected socialism and government ownership of industry in 1933. To right the situation, he chose forceful government intervention in the economy. In this choice, Roosevelt was flexible, pragmatic, and willing to experiment. He and his "brain trust" of advisers adopted policies echoing the American experi-

**Isaac Soyer: Employment Agency (1937)** The frustration and agony of looking for work against long odds are painfully evident in this American masterpiece. The time-killing, pensive resignation and dejection seen in the three figures are only aspects of the larger problem. One of three talented brothers born in Russia and trained as artists in New York, Isaac Soyer worked in the tradition of American realism and concentrated on people and the influence of their environment. *(Oil on canvas, 34¼ × 45 in. Whitney Museum of American Art, New York; Purchase 37.44)*

ence in World War I, when the American economy had been thoroughly planned and regulated.

Innovative programs promoted agricultural recovery, a top priority. Almost half of the American population still lived in rural areas, and American farmers were hard hit by the depression. Roosevelt's decision to leave the gold standard and devalue the dollar was designed to raise American prices and rescue farmers. The Agricultural Adjustment Act of 1933 also aimed at raising prices and farm income by limiting production. These planning measures worked for a while, and farmers repaid Roosevelt in 1936 with overwhelming support.

The most ambitious attempt to control and plan the economy was the National Recovery Administration (NRA). Intended to reduce competition and fix prices and wages for everyone's benefit, the NRA broke with the cherished American tradition of free competition and aroused conflicts among business people, consumers, and bureaucrats. It did not work well and was declared unconstitutional in 1935.

Roosevelt and his advisers then attacked the key problem of mass unemployment directly. The federal government accepted the responsibility of employing directly as many people as financially possible. New agencies were created to undertake a vast range of projects. The most famous of these was the Works Progress Administration (**WPA**), set up in 1935. One-fifth of the entire labor force worked for the WPA at some point in the 1930s, constructing public buildings, bridges, and highways. The WPA was enormously popular, and the hope of a government job helped check the threat of social revolution in the United States.

Relief programs like the WPA were part of the New Deal's most fundamental commitment, the commitment to use the federal government to provide for the welfare of all Americans. This commitment marked a profound shift from the traditional stress on family support and community responsibility. Embraced by a large majority in the 1930s, this shift in attitudes proved to be one of the New Deal's most enduring legacies.

Other social measures aimed in the same direction. Following the path blazed by Germany's Bismarck in the 1880s, the U.S. government in 1935 established a national social security system, with old-age pensions and unemployment benefits, to protect many workers against some of life's uncertainties. The National Labor Relations Act of 1935 gave union organizers the green light by declaring collective bargaining to be the policy of the United States. Union membership more than doubled, from 4 million in 1935 to 9 million in 1940. In general, between 1935 and 1938 government rulings and social reforms chipped away at the privileges of the wealthy and tried to help ordinary people.

Yet despite undeniable accomplishments in social reform, the New Deal was only partly successful as a response to the Great Depression. At the height of the recovery in May 1937, 7 million workers were still unemployed, as opposed to a high of 15 million in 1933. The economic situation then worsened seriously in the recession of 1937 and 1938, and unemployment was still a staggering 10 million when war broke out in Europe in September 1939. The New Deal never did pull the United States out of the depression.

## The Scandinavian Response to the Depression

Of all the Western democracies, the Scandinavian countries under Social Democratic leadership responded most successfully to the challenge of the Great Depression. Having grown steadily in number in the late nineteenth century, the **Social Democrats** became the largest political party in Sweden and then in Norway after the First World War. In

**Oslo Breakfast** Scandinavian socialism championed cooperation and practical welfare measures, playing down strident rhetoric and theories of class conflict. The Oslo Breakfast exemplified the Scandinavian approach. It provided every schoolchild in the Norwegian capital with a good breakfast free of charge. *(Courtesy, Directorate for Health and Social Affairs, Oslo)*

the 1920s, they passed important social reform legislation for both peasants and workers, gained practical administrative experience, and developed a unique kind of socialism. Flexible and nonrevolutionary, Scandinavian socialism grew out of a strong tradition of cooperative community action. Even before 1900, Scandinavian agricultural cooperatives had shown how individual peasant families could join together for everyone's benefit. Labor leaders and capitalists were also inclined to work together.

When the economic crisis struck in 1929, socialist governments in Scandinavia built on this pattern of cooperative social action. Sweden in particular pioneered in the use of large-scale deficits to finance public works and thereby maintain production and employment. Scandinavian governments also increased social welfare benefits, from old-age pensions and unemployment insurance to subsidized housing and maternity allowances. All this spending required a large bureaucracy and high taxes, first on the rich and then on practically everyone. Yet both private and cooperative enterprise thrived, as did democracy. Some observers saw Scandinavia's welfare socialism as an appealing "middle way" between sick capitalism and cruel communism or fascism.

## Recovery and Reform in Britain and France

In Britain MacDonald's Labour government and then, after 1931, the Conservative-dominated coalition government followed orthodox economic theory. The budget was balanced, but unemployed workers received barely enough welfare to live. Despite government lethargy, the economy recovered considerably after 1932. By 1937 total production was about 20 percent higher than in 1929. In fact, for Britain the years after 1932 were actually somewhat better than the 1920s had been, quite the opposite of the situation in the United States and France.

This good but by no means brilliant performance reflected the gradual reorientation of the British economy. After going off the gold standard in 1931 and establishing protective tariffs in 1932, Britain concentrated increasingly on the national, rather than the international, market. The old export industries of the Industrial Revolution, such as textiles and coal, continued to decline, but new industries, such as automobiles and electrical appliances, grew in response to British home demand. Moreover, low interest rates encouraged a housing boom. By the end of the decade, there were highly visible differences between the old, depressed industrial areas of the north and the new, growing areas of the south. These developments encouraged Britain to look inward and avoid unpleasant foreign questions.

Because France was relatively less industrialized and more isolated from the world economy, the Great Depression came late. But once the depression hit France, it stayed and stayed. Decline was steady until 1935, and a short-lived recovery never brought production or employment back up to predepression levels. Economic stagnation both reflected and heightened an ongoing political crisis. There was no stability in government. As before 1914, the French parliament was made up of many political parties, which could never cooperate for very long. In 1933, for example, five coalition cabinets formed and fell in rapid succession.

The French lost the underlying unity that had made government instability bearable before 1914. Fascist-type organizations agitated against parliamentary democracy and looked to Mussolini's Italy and Hitler's Germany for inspiration (see Chapter 29). In February 1934, French fascists and semifascists rioted and threatened to overturn the republic. At the same time, the Communist party and many workers opposed to the existing system were looking to Stalin's Russia for guidance. The vital center of moderate republicanism was sapped from both sides.

Frightened by the growing strength of the fascists at home and abroad, the Communists, the Socialists, and the Radicals formed an alliance—the **Popular Front**—for the national elections of May 1936. Their clear victory reflected the trend toward polarization. The number of Communists in the parliament jumped dramatically from 10 to 72, while the Socialists, led by Léon Blum, became the strongest party in France, with 146 seats. The really quite moderate Radicals slipped badly, and the conservatives lost ground to the semifascists.

In the next few months, Blum's Popular Front government made the first and only real attempt to deal with the social and economic problems of the 1930s in France. Inspired by Roosevelt's New Deal, the Popular Front encouraged the union movement and launched a far-reaching program of social reform, complete with paid vacations and a forty-hour workweek. Popular with workers and the lower middle class, these measures were quickly sabotaged by rapid inflation and cries of revolution from fascists and frightened conservatives. Wealthy people sneaked their money out of the country, labor unrest grew, and France entered a severe financial crisis. Blum was forced to announce a "breathing spell" in social reform.

The fires of political dissension were also fanned by civil war in Spain. Communists demanded that France support the Spanish republicans, while many French conservatives would gladly have joined Hitler and Mussolini in aiding the attack of Spanish fascists. Extremism grew, and France itself was within sight of civil war. Blum was forced to resign in

June 1937, and the Popular Front quickly collapsed. An anxious and divided France drifted aimlessly once again, preoccupied by Hitler and German rearmament.

## Summary

After the First World War, Western society entered a complex and difficult era—truly an age of anxiety. Intellectual life underwent a crisis marked by pessimism, uncertainty, and fascination with irrational forces. Ceaseless experimentation and rejection of old forms characterized art and music, while motion pictures and radio provided a new, standardized entertainment for the masses. Intellectual and artistic developments that had been confined to small avant-garde groups before 1914, along with the insecure state of mind they expressed, gained wider currency.

Politics and economics were similarly disrupted. In the 1920s, political leaders groped to create an enduring peace and rebuild the prewar prosperity, and for a brief period late in the decade, they even seemed to have succeeded. Then the Great Depression shattered that fragile stability. Uncertainty returned with redoubled force in the 1930s. The international economy collapsed, and unemployment struck millions worldwide. The democracies turned inward as they sought to cope with massive domestic problems and widespread disillusionment. Generally speaking, they were not very successful, although relief measures and social concern eased distress and prevented revolutions in the leading Western nations. The old liberal ideals of individual rights and responsibilities, elected government, and economic freedom declined and seemed outmoded to many. And in many countries of central and eastern Europe, these ideas were abandoned completely, as we shall see in the next chapter.

## Key Terms

| | |
|---|---|
| logical empiricism | dadaism |
| existentialism | Dawes Plan |
| neutron | *Mein Kampf* |
| id, ego, and superego | Great Depression |
| stream-of-consciousness technique | New Deal |
| functionalism | WPA |
| Bauhaus | Social Democrats |
| | Popular Front |

## Notes

1. P. Valéry, *Variety,* trans. M. Cowley (New York: Harcourt Brace, 1927), pp. 27–28.
2. Quoted in S. Hughes, *The Obstructed Path: French Social Thought in the Years of Desperation, 1930–1960* (New York: Harper & Row, 1967), p. 82.
3. G. Greene, *Another Mexico* (New York: Viking Press, 1939), p. 3.
4. G. Orwell, *1984* (New York: New American Library, 1950), p. 220.
5. C. E. Jeanneret-Gris (Le Corbusier), *Towards a New Architecture* (London: J. Rodker, 1931), p. 15.
6. Quoted in A. H. Barr Jr., *What Is Modern Painting?* 9th ed. (New York: Museum of Modern Art, 1966), p. 27.
7. Quoted ibid., p. 25.
8. R. Graves and A. Hodge, *The Long Week End: A Social History of Great Britain, 1918–1939* (New York: Macmillan, 1941), p. 131.
9. Quoted in A. Briggs, *The Birth of Broadcasting,* vol. 1 (London: Oxford University Press, 1961), p. 47.
10. Quoted in R. J. Sontag, *A Broken World, 1919–1939* (New York: Harper & Row, 1971), p. 129.
11. Dietmar Rothermund, *The Global Impact of the Great Depression, 1929–1939* (London: Routledge, 1996), p. 50.
12. C. P. Kindleberger, *The World in Depression, 1929–1939* (Berkeley: University of California Press, 1973), p. 292.
13. Quoted in S. B. Clough et al., eds., *Economic History of Europe: Twentieth Century* (New York: Harper & Row, 1968), pp. 243–245.

## Suggested Reading

A. Bullock, ed., *The Twentieth Century* (1971), is particularly noteworthy because it is a lavish visual feast combined with penetrating essays on major developments. Two excellent accounts of contemporary history—one with a liberal and the other with a conservative point of view—are R. Paxton, *Europe in the Twentieth Century,* 3d ed. (1997), and P. Johnson, *Modern Times: The World from the Twenties to the Eighties* (1983). I. Cawood, *Britain in the Twentieth Century* (2004), and J. McMillan, *Twentieth-Century France: Politics and Society, 1898–1991* (1992), are two recommended national surveys. Crucial changes in thought before and after World War I are discussed in three rewarding intellectual histories: J. Burrow, *The Crisis of Reason: European Thought, 1848–1914* (2000); W. Everdell, *The First Moderns: Profiles in the Origins of Twentieth-Century Thought* (1997); and M. Berman, *All That Is Solid Melts into Air: The Experience of Modernity* (1982). B. Smith, *Modernism's History: A Study in Twentieth-Century Thought and Ideas* (1998), is admirably straightforward with a global perspective, and J. Winders, *European Culture Since 1848: From Modernism to Postmodern and Beyond* (1998), is lively and accessible. S. Aschheim, *The Nietzsche Legacy in Germany, 1890–1990* (1992), considers the range of responses to the pioneering philosopher.

N. Cantor, *The American Century: Varieties of Culture in Modern Times* (1997), is a pugnacious and stimulating survey. J. Winter, *Sites of Memory, Sites of Meaning: The Great War in European Cultural History* (1995), is an excellent study of the war's influence on literature, art, and society. J. Rewald, *The History of Impressionism* (1961), and R. Golan, *Modernity and Nostalgia: Art and Politics in France Between the Wars* (1995), are excellent and also reflect changing tastes in art history. H. Jaffé, *Pablo Picasso* (1982), is a visual feast and highly recommended. Barr, cited in the Notes, is helpful. P. Collaer, *A History of Modern Music* (1961), and H. R. Hitchcock, *Architecture: Nineteenth and Twentieth Centuries* (1958), are good introductions, whereas T. Wolfe, *From Bauhaus to My House* (1981), is a lively critique of modern architecture. L. Barnett, *The Universe and Dr. Einstein* (1952), is a fascinating study of the new physics. A. Storr, *Freud* (1989), and P. Rieff, *Freud* (1956), consider the man and how his theories have stood the test of time. S. Freud, *Civilization and Its Discontents* (1930), which is highly recommended, explores Freud's theory of instinct and repression, arguing that society's necessary repression of instinctual drives will always leave people unhappy. M. White, ed., *The Age of Analysis* (1955), opens up basic questions of twentieth-century psychology and philosophy. T. Judt, *The Burden of Responsibility: Blum, Camus, Aron, and the French Twentieth Century* (1998), probes the moral and intellectual issues of the modern age. H. Liebersohn, *Fate and Utopia in German Sociology* (1988), analyzes developments in German social science. D. Kertzer and M. Barbagli, eds., *The History of the European Family, Vol. 3: Family Life in the Twentieth Century* (2003), is a distinguished collection of essays by experts. M. Marrus, ed., *Emergence of Leisure* (1974), is a pioneering inquiry into an important aspect of mass culture. H. Daniels-Rops, *A Fight for God,* 2 vols. (1966), is a sympathetic history of the Catholic church between 1870 and 1939.

G. Ambrosius and W. Hibbard, *A Social and Economic History of Twentieth-Century Europe* (1989), and F. Tipton and R. Aldrich, *An Economic and Social History of Europe, 1890–1939* (1987), are recommended and interesting to compare. P. Fritzsche, *Rehearsals for Fascism: Populism and Political Mobilization in Weimar Germany* (1990), and R. Kuisel, *Capital and State in Modern France: Renovation and Economic Management* (1982), are two important studies on aspects of the postwar challenge. J. Jacobson, *Locarno Diplomacy: Germany and the West, 1925–1929* (1972), is a superb study of Stresemann and enduring tensions after the Locarno breakthrough. B. Martin, *France and the Après Guerre: Illusions and Disillusionments* (1999), is a solid work with masterful portraits of key figures. S. Reynolds, *France Between the Wars: Gender and Politics* (1996), and J. Keiger, *Raymond Poincaré* (1996), are major reconsiderations of French politics from different perspectives. R. McRibben, *Classes and Cultures: England, 1918–1951* (2000), is recommended. I. Berend, *Decades of Crisis: Central and Eastern Europe Before World War II* (2001), is a stimulating, up-to-date study of the complex region. M. Childs, *Sweden: The Middle Way* (1961), applauds Sweden's efforts at social reform. O. and L. Handlin, *Liberty in America Since 1600,* vol. 4 (1994), argues that the United States has erred in moving from equality of opportunity to equality of results since 1920. The crisis of the interwar period comes alive in R. Crossman, ed., *The God That Failed* (1950), in which famous Western writers tell why they were attracted to and later repelled by communism; J. Ortega y Gasset's renowned *The Revolt of the Masses* (1932); and F. A. Hayek's *The Road to Serfdom* (1944), a famous warning of the dangers to democratic freedoms.

In addition to Rothermund's and Kindleberger's excellent studies of the Great Depression cited in the Notes, P. Temin, *Lessons from the Great Depression* (1987), is a judicious evaluation by an outstanding economic historian. J. Garraty, *Unemployment in History* (1978), is noteworthy, though novels best portray the human tragedy of economic decline. W. Holtby, *South Riding* (1936), and W. Greenwood, *Love on the Dole* (1933), are moving stories of the Great Depression in England. Hans Fallada, *Little Man, What Now?* (1932), is the classic counterpart for Germany. Also highly recommended as commentaries on English life between the wars are N. Gray, *The Worst of Times: An Oral History of the Great Depression in Britain* (1985), and George Orwell, *The Road to Wigan Pier* (1937). Among French novelists, André Gide painstakingly examines the French middle class and its values in *The Counterfeiters;* Albert Camus, the greatest of the existential novelists, is at his unforgettable best in *The Stranger* (1942) and *The Plague* (1947).

# Listening to the Past

## Life on the Dole in Great Britain

*Periodic surges in unemployment were an old story in capitalist economies, but the long-term joblessness of millions in the Great Depression was something new and unexpected. In Britain especially, where the depression followed a weak postwar recovery, large numbers suffered involuntary idleness for years at a time. Whole families lived "on the dole," the weekly welfare benefits paid by the government.*

*One of the most insightful accounts of unemployed workers was written by the British journalist and novelist George Orwell (1903–1950), who studied the conditions in northern England and wrote* The Road to Wigan Pier *(1937). An independent socialist who distrusted rigid Marxism, Orwell believed that socialism could triumph in Britain if it came to mean "justice and liberty" for a commonsense majority. Orwell's disillusionment with authoritarian socialism and communism pervades his most famous work,* 1984 *(1949).*

When you see the unemployment figures quoted at two millions, it is fatally easy to take this as meaning that two million people are out of work and the rest of the population is comparatively comfortable. . . . [Adding in the destitute,] you might take the number of underfed people in England (for *everyone* on the dole or thereabouts is underfed) as being, at the very most, five millions.

This is an enormous under-estimate, because, in the first place, the only people shown on unemployment figures are those actually drawing the dole—that is, in general, heads of families. An unemployed man's dependants do not figure on the list unless they too are drawing a separate allowance. . . . In addition there are great numbers of people who are in work but who, from a financial point of view, might equally be unemployed, because they are not drawing anything that can be described as a living wage. Allow for these and their dependants, throw in as before the old-age pensioners, the destitute and other nondescripts, and you get an *underfed* population of well over ten millions. . . .

Take the figures for Wigan, which is typical enough of the industrial and mining districts. . . . The total population of Wigan is a little under 87,000; so that at any moment more than one person in three out of the whole population—not merely the registered workers—is either drawing or living on the dole. . . .

Nevertheless, in spite of the frightful extent of unemployment, it is a fact that poverty—extreme poverty—is less in evidence in the industrial North than it is in London. Everything is poorer and shabbier, there are fewer motor-cars and fewer well-dressed people; but also there are fewer people who are obviously destitute. . . . In the industrial towns the old communal way of life has not yet broken up, tradition is still strong and almost everyone has a family—potentially, therefore, a home. In a town of 50,000 or 100,000 inhabitants there is no casual and as it were unaccounted-for population; nobody sleeping in the streets, for instance. Moreover, there is just this to be said for the unemployment regulations, that they do not discourage people from marrying. A man and wife on twenty-three shillings a week are not far from the starvation line, but they can make a home of sorts; they are vastly better off than a single man on fifteen shillings. . . .

But there is no doubt about the deadening, debilitating effect of unemployment upon everybody, married or single, and upon men more than upon women. . . . Everyone who saw Greenwood's play *Love on the Dole* must remember that dreadful moment when the poor, good, stupid working man beats on the table and cries out, "O God, send me some work!" This was not dramatic exaggeration, it was a touch from life. That cry must have been uttered, in almost those words, in tens of thousands, perhaps hundreds of thousands of English homes, during the past fifteen years.

But, I think not again—or at least, not so often. . . . When people live on the dole for years at a time they grow used to it, and drawing the dole, though it remains unpleasant, ceases to be shameful. Thus the old, independent, workhouse-fearing tradition is undermined. . . .

So you have whole populations settling down, as it were, to a lifetime of the P.A.C. . . . Take, for instance, the fact that the working class think nothing of getting married on the dole. . . . Life is still fairly normal, more normal than one really has the right to expect. Families are impoverished, but the family-system has not broken up. The people are in effect living a reduced version of their former lives. Instead of raging against their destiny they have made things tolerable by lowering their standards.

But they don't necessarily lower their standards by cutting out luxuries and concentrating on necessities; more often it is the other way about—the more natural way, if you come to think of it. Hence the fact that in a decade of unparalleled depression, the consumption of all cheap luxuries has increased. The two things that have probably made the greatest difference of all are the movies and the mass-production of cheap smart clothes since the war. The youth who leaves school at fourteen and gets a blind-alley job is out of work at twenty, probably for life; but for two pounds ten on the hire-purchase system he can buy himself a suit which, for a little while and at a little distance, looks as though it had been tailored in Savile Row. The girl can look like a fashion plate at an even lower price. . . . You can stand on the street corner, indulging in a private daydream of yourself as Clark Gable or Greta Garbo, which compensates you for a great deal. . . .

Trade since the war has had to adjust itself to meet the demands of underpaid, underfed people, with the result that a luxury is nowadays almost always cheaper than a necessity. One pair of plain solid shoes costs as much as two ultra-smart pairs. . . . And above all there is gambling, the cheapest of all luxuries. Even people on the verge of starvation can buy a few days' hope ("Something to live for," as they call it) by having a penny on a sweepstake. . . . Twenty million people are underfed but literally everyone in England has access to a radio. What we have lost in food we have gained in electricity. Whole sections of the working class who have been plundered of all they really need are being compensated, in part, by cheap luxuries which mitigate the surface of life.

Poster used in the election campaign of 1931, when unemployment rose to a new record high. *(Conservative Research Department/The Bridgeman Art Library)*

Do you consider all this desirable? No, I don't. But it may be that the psychological adjustment which the working class are visibly making is the best they could make in the circumstances. They have neither turned revolutionary nor lost their self-respect; merely they have kept their tempers and settled down to make the best of things on a fish-and-chip standard. The alternative would be God knows what continued agonies of despair; or it might be attempted insurrections which, in a strongly governed country like England, could only lead to futile massacres and a régime of savage repression.

## Questions for Analysis

1. According to Orwell, "extreme poverty" was less visible in the northern industrial towns than in London. Were family relations important in this regard?
2. What were the consequences of long-term unemployment for English workers? Were some of the consequences surprising?
3. Judging from Orwell's description, did radical revolution seem likely in England in the Great Depression? Why or why not?

*Source:* Excerpts from Chapter V in *The Road to Wigan Pier* by George Orwell, copyright © 1958 and renewed 1986 by the Estate of Sonia B. Orwell. Reprinted by permission of Harcourt, Inc.

Hugo Jager's photograph of a crowd of enthusiastic Hitler supporters. *(Time Life Pictures/Getty Images)*

chapter

# 29 Dictatorships and the Second World War

## chapter outline

- Authoritarian States
- Stalin's Soviet Union
- Mussolini and Fascism in Italy
- Hitler and Nazism in Germany
- Nazi Expansion and the Second World War

The era of anxiety and economic depression was also a time of growing strength for political dictatorship. Popularly elected governments and basic civil liberties declined drastically in Europe. On the eve of the Second World War, liberal democratic governments were surviving only in Great Britain, France, the Low Countries, the Scandinavian nations, and Switzerland. Elsewhere in Europe, various kinds of "strongmen" ruled. Dictatorship seemed the wave of the future. Thus the intellectual and economic crisis discussed in Chapter 28 and the decline in liberal political institutions and rise of dictatorship to be considered in this chapter were interrelated elements in the general crisis of European civilization.

The era of dictatorship is a highly disturbing chapter in the history of Western civilization. The key development was not only the resurgence of authoritarian rule but also the rise of a particularly ruthless and dynamic tyranny. This new kind of tyranny reached its full realization in the Soviet Union and Nazi Germany in the 1930s. Stalin and Hitler mobilized their peoples for enormous undertakings and ruled with unprecedented severity. Hitler's mobilization was ultimately directed toward racial aggression and territorial expansion, and his sudden attack on Poland in 1939 started World War II.

Nazi armies were defeated by a great coalition, and today we want to believe that the era of totalitarian dictatorship was a terrible accident, that Stalin's slave-labor camps and Hitler's gas chambers "can't happen again." Yet the cruel truth is that horrible atrocities continue to plague the world in our time. The Khmer Rouge inflicted genocide on its people in Kampuchea, and civil war in Bosnia and in Rwanda led to racially motivated atrocities recalling the horrors of World War II. And there are other examples. Thus it is all the more vital that we understand Europe's era of brutal and aggressive dictatorship in order to guard against the possibility of its recurrence in the future.

- What was the nature of twentieth-century dictatorship and authoritarian rule?
- How did people live in the most extreme states—the Soviet Union and Nazi Germany?
- How did the rise of aggressive dictatorships result in another world war?

These are among the questions this chapter will seek to answer.

## Authoritarian States

Both conservative and radical dictatorships swept through Europe in the 1920s and 1930s. Although these two types of dictatorship shared some characteristics and sometimes overlapped in practice, they were in essence profoundly different. Conservative authoritarian regimes were an old story in Europe. Radical, totalitarian dictatorships were a new and frightening development.

### Conservative Authoritarianism

The traditional form of antidemocratic government in European history was conservative authoritarianism. Like Catherine the Great in Russia and Metternich in Austria, the leaders of such governments tried to prevent major changes that would undermine the existing social order. To do so, they relied on obedient bureaucracies, vigilant police departments, and trustworthy armies. Popular participation in government was forbidden or limited to such natural allies as landlords, bureaucrats, and high church officials. Liberals, democrats, and socialists were persecuted as subversive radicals, often finding themselves in jail or exile.

Yet old-fashioned authoritarian governments were limited in their power and in their objectives. They had neither the ability nor the desire to control many aspects of their subjects' lives. Nor did they wish to do so. Preoccupied with the goal of mere survival, these governments largely limited their demands to taxes, army recruits, and passive acceptance. As long as the people did not try to change the system, they often had considerable personal independence.

After the First World War, this kind of authoritarian government revived, especially in the less-developed eastern part of Europe. There the parliamentary regimes that had been founded on the wreckage of empires in 1918 fell one by one. By early 1938, only economically and socially advanced Czechoslovakia remained true to liberal political ideals. Conservative dictators also took over in Spain and Portugal.

There were several reasons for this development. These lands lacked a strong tradition of self-government, with its necessary restraint and compromise. Moreover, many of these new states, such as Yugoslavia, were torn by ethnic conflicts that threatened their very existence. Dictatorship appealed to nationalists and military leaders as a way to repress such tensions and preserve national unity. Large landowners and the church were still powerful forces in these largely agrarian areas, and they often looked to dictators to save them from progressive land reform or communist agrarian upheaval. So did some members of the middle class, which was small and weak in eastern Europe. Finally, though some kind of democracy managed to stagger through the 1920s in Austria, Bulgaria, Romania, Greece, Estonia, and Latvia, the Great Depression delivered the final blow to those countries by 1936.

Although some of the conservative authoritarian regimes adopted certain Hitlerian and fascist characteristics in the 1930s, their general aims were limited. They were concerned more with maintaining the status quo than with forcing society into rapid change or war. This tradition continued into the twenty-first century, especially in some of the military dictatorships that ruled in Latin America until the late 1980s.

### Radical Totalitarian Dictatorships

Conservative authoritarianism predominated in the smaller states of central and eastern Europe by the mid-1930s, but a new kind of radical dictatorship emerged in the Soviet Union, Germany, and, to a lesser extent, Italy. Almost all scholars agree that the leaders of these radical dictatorships violently rejected parliamentary restraint and liberal values. Scholars also agree that these dictatorships exercised unprecedented control over the masses and sought to mobilize them for action. However, there has always been controversy over the interpretation of these regimes.

One extremely useful approach relates the radical dictatorships to the rise of modern totalitarianism. The concept of **totalitarianism** emerged in the 1920s and 1930s, although it is frequently and mistakenly seen as developing only after 1945 as part of anti-Soviet propaganda during the cold war. In 1924 Benito Mussolini spoke of the "fierce totalitarian will" of his movement in Italy. In the 1930s more and more British, American, and German exiled writers used the concept of totalitarianism to describe what they saw happening before their eyes. They linked Italian and especially German fascism with Soviet communism in "a 'new kind of state' that could be called totalitarian." With the alliance between Hitler and Stalin in 1939, "all doubts" about the totalitarian nature of both dictatorships "were swept away for most Americans."[1]

Early writers believed that modern totalitarian dictatorship burst on the scene with the revolutionary total war effort of 1914–1918. The war called forth a ten-

| 1920 | 1926 | 1932 | 1938 | 1944 | 1950 |
|---|---|---|---|---|---|

**POLITICAL/MILITARY**

- 1922 Mussolini seizes power in Italy
- 1924–1929 Buildup of Nazi party in Germany
- 1927 Stalin comes to power in U.S.S.R.
- 1928 Stalin's first five-year plan
- 1933 Hitler appointed chancellor in Germany
- 1934 Sergei Kirov, Stalin's number-two man, is murdered
- 1935 Mussolini invades Ethiopia
- 1936 Start of great purges under Stalin
- 1939 Germany occupies Czech lands
- 1939 Germany invades Poland; Britain and France declare war on Germany
- 1941 Germany invades Soviet Union; bombing of Pearl Harbor; U.S. enters war
- 1944 Allied invasion at Normandy
- 1945 Atomic bombs dropped on Japan; end of war

**SOCIAL/ECONOMIC**

- 1921 New Economic Policy (NEP) in U.S.S.R.
- 1929 Start of collectivization in Soviet Union
- 1929–1939 Great Depression
- 1932–1933 Famine in Ukraine
- 1941 SS stops Jewish emigration from Europe
- 1941–1945 Six million Jews killed in death camps

**INTELLECTUAL/RELIGIOUS**

- 1929 Lateran Agreement
- 1933 Nazis begin to control intellectual life and blacklist authors
- 1936 Halévy, *The Era of Tyrannies,* analyzes totalitarianism

dency to subordinate all institutions and all classes to the state in order to achieve one supreme objective: victory. As the French thinker Elie Halévy put it in 1936 in his influential *The Era of Tyrannies,* the varieties of modern totalitarian tyranny—fascism, Nazism, and communism—could be thought of as "feuding brothers" with a common father: the nature of modern war.[2]

Writers such as Halévy believed that the crucial experience of World War I was carried further by Lenin and the Bolsheviks during the Russian civil war. Lenin showed how a dedicated minority could achieve victory over a less determined majority and subordinate institutions and human rights to the needs of a single group—the Communist party—and its leader. Providing a model for single-party dictatorship, Lenin inspired imitators, including Adolf Hitler. The modern totalitarian state reached maturity in the 1930s in the Stalinist U.S.S.R. and Nazi Germany.

Embellishing on early insights, numerous Western political scientists and historians argued in the 1950s and 1960s that the totalitarian state used modern technology and communications to exercise complete political power. But it did not stop there. Increasingly, the state took over

**Nazi Mass Rally, 1936** This picture captures the essence of the totalitarian interpretation of dynamic modern dictatorship. The uniformed members of the Nazi party have willingly merged themselves into a single force and await the command of the godlike leader. *(Wide World Photos)*

and tried to control just as completely the economic, social, intellectual, and cultural aspects of people's lives. Deviation from the norm, even in art or family behavior, could become a crime. In theory, nothing was politically neutral; nothing was outside the scope of the state.

This vision of total state represented a radical revolt against liberalism. Classical liberalism (see page 762) sought to limit the power of the state and protect the rights of the individual. Moreover, liberals stood for rationality, peaceful progress, economic freedom, and a strong middle class. All of that disgusted totalitarians as sentimental slop. They believed in willpower, preached conflict, and worshiped violence. The individual was infinitely less valuable than the state, and there were no lasting rights, only temporary rewards for loyal and effective service.

Unlike old-fashioned authoritarianism, modern totalitarianism was based not on an elite but on people who had already become engaged in the political process, most notably through commitment to nationalism and socialism. Thus totalitarian societies were fully mobilized societies moving toward some goal and possessing boundless dynamism. As soon as one goal was achieved at the cost of enormous sacrifice, another arose at the leader's command to take its place. Thus totalitarianism was a *permanent* revolution, an *unfinished* revolution, in which rapid, profound change imposed from on high went on forever.

In developing the concept of totalitarianism, scholars recognized that there were major differences between Stalin's communist U.S.S.R. and Hitler's Nazi Germany. Soviet communism, growing out of Marxian socialism, seized all private property (except personal property) for the state and crushed the middle classes. Nazi Germany, growing out of extreme nationalism and racism, criticized big landowners and industrialists, but both private property and the middle classes survived. This difference in property and class relations led some scholars to speak of "totalitarianism of the left"—Stalinist Russia—and "totalitarianism of the right"—Nazi Germany.

A second group of writers in the 1930s approached radical dictatorships outside the Soviet Union through the concept of **fascism.** A term of pride for Mussolini and Hitler, who used it to describe the supposedly "total" and revolutionary character of their movements, fascism was severely criticized by these writers and linked to decaying capitalism and domestic class conflict. Orthodox Marxists, generally sympathetic to the Soviet Union and the socialism it established, argued that fascism was the way powerful capitalists sought to create a mass movement capable of destroying the revolutionary working class and thus protect their enormous profits.

Scholarly interest in fascism declined in the 1950s but revived thereafter. Comparative studies of fascist movements all across Europe showed that they shared many characteristics, including extreme, often expansionist nationalism; an antisocialism aimed at destroying working-class movements; alliances with powerful capitalists and landowners; a dynamic and violent leader; and glorification of war and the military. Yet these studies also highlighted how fascist movements generally failed to gain political power.

In recent years, many historians have tended to adopt a third approach, emphasizing the uniqueness of developments in each country. This is especially true for Hitler's Germany, where some elements of the totalitarian interpretation have been nuanced and revised, as we shall see. A similar revaluation of Stalin's U.S.S.R. is in progress now that the fall of communism has opened the former Soviet Union's archives to new research. For many of today's historians, the differences within broad historical patterns often seem more important than the similarities.

In summary, these conclusions seem appropriate. First, although the concept of totalitarianism has been questioned, it remains a valuable tool for historical understanding. It correctly highlights that both Hitler's Germany and Stalin's Soviet Union made an unprecedented "total claim" on the belief and behavior of their respective citizens, as a noted scholar has recently concluded.[3] Second, antidemocratic, antisocialist fascist movements sprang up all over Europe, but only in Italy and Germany (and some would say Spain) were they able to take power. Studies of fascist movements seeking to gain power locate important common elements, but they do not explain what fascist governments in Italy and Germany actually did. Finally, it is important to remember that the problem of Europe's radical dictatorships is complex and that there are few easy answers.

## Stalin's Soviet Union

See DBQ 13

Lenin's harshest critics claim that he established the basic outlines of a modern totalitarian dictatorship after the Bolshevik Revolution and during the Russian civil war. If this is so, then Joseph Stalin (1879–1953) certainly finished the job. A master of political infighting, Stalin cautiously consolidated his power and eliminated his enemies in the mid-1920s. Then in 1928, as undisputed leader of the ruling Communist party, he launched the first **five-year plan**—the "revolution from above," as he so aptly termed it.

The five-year plans were extremely ambitious. Often incorrectly considered a mere set of economic measures to speed up the Soviet Union's industrial development, the five-year plans actually marked the beginning of a renewed attempt to mobilize and transform Soviet society along socialist lines. The ultimate goal of the plans was to generate new attitudes, new loyalties, and a new socialist humanity. The means Stalin and the small Communist party elite chose in order to do so were constant propaganda, enormous sacrifice by the people, and the concentration of all power in party hands. Thus the Soviet Union in the 1930s became a dynamic, modern totalitarian state.

### From Lenin to Stalin

By spring 1921, Lenin and the Bolsheviks had won the civil war, but they ruled a shattered and devastated land. Many farms were in ruins, and food supplies were exhausted. In southern Russia, drought combined with the ravages of war to produce the worst famine in generations. By 1920, according to the government, from 50 to 90 percent of the population in seventeen provinces was starving. Industrial production also broke down completely. In 1921, for example, output of steel and cotton textiles was only about 4 percent of what it had been in 1913. The Bolsheviks had destroyed the economy as well as their foes.

In the face of economic disintegration, riots by peasants and workers, and an open rebellion by previously pro-Bolshevik sailors at Kronstadt, the tough but ever-flexible Lenin changed course. In March 1921, he announced the **New Economic Policy (NEP),** which re-established

**Kazimir Malevich: Suprematism, ca 1917** Russian artists occupied a prominent position in the international avant-garde in the early twentieth century, and the Ukrainian-born Malevich is widely recognized as a leading figure in the development of modern abstract art. Malevich originated the theory of suprematism, whereby he abandoned images from nature and painted pure forms that were beautiful in themselves, as in this outstanding example. When the Bolsheviks condemned abstraction and demanded "socialist realism," Malevich returned to more recognizable forms and taught design. *(Erich Lessing/Art Resource, NY)*

limited economic freedom in an attempt to rebuild agriculture and industry. During the civil war, the Bolsheviks had simply seized grain without payment. Now peasant producers were permitted to sell their surpluses in free markets, and private traders and small handicraft manufacturers were allowed to reappear. Heavy industry, railroads, and banks, however, remained wholly nationalized.

The NEP was shrewd and successful both politically and economically. Politically, it was a necessary but temporary compromise with the Soviet Union's overwhelming peasant majority. Realizing that his government was not strong enough to take land from the peasants and turn them into state workers, Lenin made a deal with the only force capable of overturning his government. Economically, the NEP brought rapid recovery. In 1926 industrial output surpassed the level of 1913, and Soviet peasants were producing almost as much grain as before the war. Counting shorter hours and increased social benefits, urban workers as well as peasants were living somewhat better than they had in the past.

As the economy recovered and the government partially relaxed its censorship and repression, an intense struggle for power began in the inner circles of the Communist party, for Lenin had left no chosen successor when he died in 1924. The principal contenders were the stolid Stalin and the flamboyant Trotsky.

The son of a shoemaker, Joseph Dzhugashvili—later known as Stalin—studied for the priesthood but was expelled from his theological seminary, probably for rude rebelliousness. By 1903 he had joined the Bolsheviks. In the years before the First World War, he engaged in many revolutionary activities in the southern Transcaucasian area of the multinational Russian empire, including a daring bank robbery to get money for the Bolsheviks. This raid gained Lenin's attention and approval.

Stalin was a good organizer but a poor speaker and writer, with no experience outside of Russia. Trotsky, a great and inspiring leader who had planned the 1917 takeover (see page 908) and then created the victorious Red Army, appeared to have all the advantages. Yet it was

Stalin who succeeded Lenin. Stalin won because he was more effective at gaining the all-important support of the party, the only genuine source of power in the one-party state. Rising to general secretary of the party's Central Committee just before Lenin's first stroke in 1922, Stalin used his office to win friends and allies with jobs and promises.

The practical Stalin also won because he appeared better able than the brilliant Trotsky to relate Marxian teaching to Soviet realities in the 1920s. Stalin developed a theory of "socialism in one country" that was more appealing to the majority of communists than Trotsky's doctrine of "permanent revolution." Stalin argued that the Russian-dominated Soviet Union had the ability to build socialism on its own. Trotsky maintained that socialism in the Soviet Union could succeed only if revolution occurred quickly throughout Europe. To many Russian communists, Trotsky's views seemed to sell their country short and to promise risky conflicts with capitalist countries by recklessly encouraging revolutionary movements around the world. Stalin's willingness to break with the NEP and "build socialism" at home appealed to young militants in the party, who detested the capitalist-appearing NEP.

With cunning skill, Stalin gradually achieved supreme power between 1922 and 1927. First, he allied with Trotsky's personal enemies to crush Trotsky, who was expelled from the Soviet Union in 1929 and eventually was murdered in Mexico in 1940, undoubtedly on Stalin's order. Second, Stalin aligned with the moderates, who wanted to go slow at home, to suppress Trotsky's radical followers. Third, having defeated all the radicals, he turned against his allies, the moderates, and destroyed them as well. Stalin's final triumph came at the party congress of December 1927, which condemned all "deviation from the general party line" formulated by Stalin. The dictator and his followers were then ready to launch the revolution from above—the real revolution for millions of ordinary citizens.

## The Five-Year Plans

The party congress of 1927, which ratified Stalin's consolidation of power, marked the end of the NEP and the beginning of the era of socialist five-year plans. Building on planning models developed by Soviet economists in the 1920s, the first five-year plan had staggering economic objectives. In just five years, total industrial output was to increase by 250 percent. Heavy industry, the preferred sector, was to grow even faster. Agricultural production was slated to increase by 150 percent, and one-fifth of the peasants in the Soviet Union were scheduled to give up their private plots and join socialist collective farms. By 1930 economic and social change was sweeping the country.

Stalin unleashed his "second revolution" for a variety of interrelated reasons. There were, first of all, ideological considerations. Like Lenin, Stalin and his militant supporters were deeply committed to socialism as they understood it. They feared a gradual restoration of capitalism, and they burned to stamp out the NEP's private traders, independent artisans, and property-owning peasants. Purely economic motivations were also important. Although the economy had recovered, it seemed to have stalled in 1927 and 1928. A new socialist offensive seemed necessary if industry and agriculture were to grow rapidly.

Political considerations were most important. Internationally, there was the old problem, remaining from prerevolutionary times, of catching up with the advanced and presumably hostile capitalist nations of the West. Stalin said in 1931, when he pressed for ever-greater speed and sacrifice, "We are fifty or a hundred years behind the advanced countries. We must make good this distance in ten years. Either we do it, or we shall go under." (See the feature "Listening to the Past: Stalin Justifies the Five-Year Plan" on pages 986–987.)

Domestically, there was what communist writers of the 1920s called the "cursed problem"—the problem of the peasants. For centuries the peasants had wanted to own the land, and finally they had it. Sooner or later, the communists reasoned, the peasants would become conservative little capitalists and pose a threat to the regime. At the same time, the mainly urban communists believed that the feared and despised "class enemy" in the villages could be squeezed to provide the enormous sums needed for all-out industrialization. Thus Stalin decided on a war against the peasantry in order to bring it under the control of the state and to make it pay the costs of the new socialist offensive.

That war was **collectivization**—the forcible consolidation of individual peasant farms into large, state-controlled enterprises. Beginning in 1929, peasants all over the Soviet Union were ordered to give up their land and animals and become members of collective farms, although they continued to live in their own homes. As for the **kulaks,** the better-off peasants, Stalin instructed party workers to "liquidate them as a class." Stripped of land and livestock, the kulaks were generally not even permitted to join the collective farms. Many starved or were deported to forced-labor camps for "re-education."

Since almost all peasants were in fact poor, the term *kulak* soon meant any peasant who opposed the new

**Life in a Forced-Labor Camp** This rare photo from about 1933 shows the reality of deported peasants and other political prisoners building the Stalin–White Sea Canal in far northern Russia, with their bare hands and under the most dehumanizing conditions. In books and plays Stalin's followers praised the project as a model for the regeneration of "reactionaries" and "kulak exploiters" through the joys of socialist work. *(David King Collection)*

system. Whole villages were often attacked. One conscience-stricken colonel in the secret police confessed to a foreign journalist,

*I am an old Bolshevik. I worked in the underground against the Tsar and then I fought in the Civil War. Did I do all that in order that I should now surround villages with machine guns and order my men to fire indiscriminately into crowds of peasants? Oh, no, no!*[4]

Forced collectivization of the peasants led to economic and human disaster. Large numbers of peasants slaughtered their animals and burned their crops in sullen, hopeless protest. Between 1929 and 1933, the number of horses, cattle, sheep, and goats in the Soviet Union fell by at least half. Nor were the state-controlled collective farms more productive. The output of grain barely increased between 1928 and 1938, when it was almost identical to that of 1913. Moreover, the state had to invest heavily in agriculture, building thousands of tractors to replace slaughtered draft horses. Collectivized agriculture was unable to make any substantial financial contribution to Soviet industrial development in the first five-year plan.

The human dimension of the tragedy was absolutely staggering. As one leading historian writes in outrage, "The number dying in Stalin's war against the peasants was higher than the total deaths of all the countries in World War I." Yet, he notes, in Stalin's war only one side was armed and the other side bore almost all the casualties, many of whom were women, children, and the old.[5] Stalin himself confided to Winston Churchill at Yalta in 1945 that 10 million people had died in the course of collectivization.

In Ukraine the drive against peasants snowballed into a general assault on Ukrainians as reactionary nationalists and enemies of socialism. Thus in 1932, as collectivization and deportations continued, Stalin and his associates set levels of grain deliveries for the Ukrainian collective at excessively high levels, and they refused to relax those quotas or even allow food relief when Ukrainian communist leaders reported that starvation was occurring. The result was a terrible man-made famine in Ukraine in 1932 and 1933, which probably claimed 6 million lives. Stalin denied completely the existence of famine, and for years the party successfully suppressed much of the truth at home and abroad.

Collectivization, justly called the "second serfdom," was a cruel but real victory for communist ideologues. By the end of 1932, fully 60 percent of peasant families had been herded onto collective farms; by 1938, 93 percent. Regimented as employees of the state and dependent on the state-owned tractor stations, the collectivized peasants were no longer even a potential political threat to Stalin and the Communist party. Moreover, the state paid very low prices for grain to guarantee cheap bread for urban workers, who were much more important politically than the peasants.

Yet, as recent research shows, peasants fought back with indirect daily opposition and forced the supposedly all-powerful state to make modest compromises. Peasants secured the right to limit a family's labor on the state-run farms and to cultivate tiny family plots, which provided them with much of their food. In 1938 these family plots produced 22 percent of all Soviet agricultural produce on only 4 percent of all cultivated land, eloquent testimony to the inefficiency of collectivized agriculture and the quiet resistance of the weak in the countryside.

The industrial side of the five-year plans was more successful—indeed, quite spectacular. Soviet industry produced about four times as much in 1937 as it had in 1928. No other major country had ever achieved such rapid industrial growth. Heavy industry led the way; consumer industry grew quite slowly. A new heavy industrial complex was built almost from scratch in western Siberia. Industrial growth also went hand in hand with urban development, and more than 25 million people migrated to cities during the 1930s.

The great industrialization drive, concentrated between 1928 and 1937, was an awe-inspiring achievement purchased at enormous sacrifice. The sudden creation of dozens of new factories required a great increase in total investment. Although few nations had ever invested more than one-sixth of their yearly net national income, Soviet planners decreed that more than one-third of net income go for investment. This meant that only two-thirds of everything being produced could be consumed by the people *and* the increasingly voracious military. The money for investment was collected from the people by means of heavy, hidden sales taxes.

Two other factors contributed importantly to rapid industrialization: firm labor discipline and foreign engineers. Between 1930 and 1932, trade unions lost most of their power. The government could assign workers to any job anywhere in the country, and individuals could not move without the permission of the police. When factory managers needed more hands, they called on their counterparts on the collective farms, who sent them millions of "unneeded" peasants over the years.

Foreign engineers were hired to plan and construct many of the new factories. Highly skilled American engineers, hungry for work in the depression years, were particularly important until newly trained Soviet experts began to replace them after 1932. The gigantic mills of the new Siberian steel industry were modeled on America's best. Thus Stalin's planners harnessed even the skill and technology of capitalist countries to promote the surge of socialist industry.

## Life and Culture in Soviet Society

The aim of Stalin's five-year plans was to create a new kind of society and human personality as well as a strong industrial economy and a powerful army. Stalin and his helpers were good Marxian economic determinists. Once everything was owned by the state, they believed, a socialist society and a new kind of human being would inevitably emerge. Their utopian vision of a new humanity floundered, but they did build a new society, whose broad outlines existed into the mid-1980s. Life in this society had both good and bad aspects.

Because consumption was reduced to pay for investment, there was no improvement in the average standard of living. Indeed, the most careful studies show that the average nonfarm wage apparently purchased only about half as many goods in 1932 as in 1928. After 1932 real wages rose slowly, so that in 1937 workers could buy about 60 percent of what they had bought in 1928 and less than in 1913. Collectivized peasants experienced greater declines.

Life was hard in Stalin's Soviet Union. The masses of people lived primarily on black bread and wore old, shabby clothing. There were constant shortages in the stores, although very heavily taxed vodka was always readily available. A shortage of housing was a particularly serious problem. Millions were moving into the cities, but the government built few new apartments. In 1940 there were approximately 4 people per room in every urban dwelling, as opposed to 2.7 per room in 1926. A relatively lucky

**"Let's All Get to Work, Comrades!"** Art in the Stalinist era generally followed the official doctrine of socialist realism, representing objects in a literal style and celebrating Soviet achievements. Characteristically, this poster glorifies the working class, women's equality (in hard labor at least), mammoth factories, and the Communist Party (represented by the hammer and sickle by the woman's foot). Assailed by propaganda, Soviet citizens often found refuge in personal relations and deep friendships. *(From* Art of the October Revolution, *Mikhail Guerman [Aurora Publishers, Leningrad]. Reproduced by permission of V/O Vneshtorgizdat)*

family received one room for all its members and shared both a kitchen and a toilet with others on the floor. Less fortunate workers, kulaks, and class enemies built scrap-lumber shacks or underground dugouts in shantytowns.

Life was hard but by no means hopeless. Idealism and ideology had real appeal for many communists, who saw themselves heroically building the world's first socialist society while capitalism crumbled in a worldwide depression and degenerated into fascism in the West. This optimistic belief in the future of the Soviet Union also attracted many disillusioned Westerners to communism in the 1930s.

On a more practical level, Soviet workers did receive some important social benefits, such as old-age pensions, free medical services, free education, and day-care centers for children. Unemployment was almost unknown. Finally, there was the possibility of personal advancement.

The keys to improving one's position were specialized skills and technical education. Rapid industrialization required massive numbers of trained experts, such as skilled workers, engineers, and plant managers. Thus the Stalinist state broke with the egalitarian policies of the 1920s and provided tremendous incentives to those who could serve its needs. It paid the mass of unskilled workers and collective farmers very low wages, but it dangled high salaries and many special privileges before its growing technical and managerial elite. This elite joined with the political and artistic elites in a new upper class, whose members were rich, powerful, and insecure. Thus millions struggled for an education. One young man summed it up: "In Soviet Russia there is no capital except education. If a person does not want to become a collective farmer or just a cleaning woman, the only means you have to get something is through education."[6]

The radical transformation of Soviet society had a profound impact on women's lives. Marxists had traditionally believed that both capitalism and the middle-class husband exploited women. The Russian Revolution of 1917 immediately proclaimed complete equality of rights for women. In the 1920s, divorce and abortion were made easily available, and women were urged to work outside the home and liberate themselves sexually. The most prominent Bolshevik feminist, Alexandra Kollontai, went so far as to declare that the sex act had no more significance than "drinking a glass of water."[7] After Stalin came to power, sexual and familial liberation was played down, and the most lasting changes for women involved work and education.

Young women were constantly told that they had to be fully equal to men. Peasant women in Russia had long experienced the equality of backbreaking physical labor in the countryside, and with the advent of the five-year plans, millions of women also toiled in factories and in heavy construction, building dams, roads, and steel mills in summer heat and winter frost. Many of the opportunities open to men through education were also open to women. Determined women pursued their studies and entered the ranks of the better-paid specialists in industry and science. Medicine practically became a woman's profession. By 1950, 75 percent of all doctors in the Soviet Union were women.

Soviet society also demanded great sacrifices from women. The vast majority of women simply *had* to work outside the home. Wages were so low that it was almost impossible for a family or couple to live only on the husband's earnings. Men continued to dominate the very best jobs. Finally, rapid change and economic hardship led to many broken families, creating further physical and emotional strains for women. In any event, the massive mobilization of women was a striking characteristic of the Soviet state.

Culture lost its autonomy in the 1930s and became thoroughly politicized through constant propaganda and indoctrination. Party activists lectured workers in factories and peasants on collective farms, while newspapers, films, and radio broadcasts endlessly recounted socialist achievements and capitalist plots. Whereas the 1920s had seen considerable experimentation in modern art and theater, intellectuals were ordered by Stalin to become "engineers of human minds." Writers and artists who could effectively combine genuine creativity and political propaganda became the darlings of the regime. It became increasingly important for the successful writer and artist to glorify Russian nationalism. Russian history was rewritten so that early tsars such as Ivan the Terrible and Peter the Great became worthy forerunners of the greatest Russian leader of all—Stalin.

Stalin seldom appeared in public, but his presence was everywhere—in portraits, statues, books, and quotations from his "sacred" writings. Although the government persecuted religion and turned churches into "museums of atheism," the state had both an earthly religion and a high priest—Marxism-Leninism and Joseph Stalin.

## Stalinist Terror and the Great Purges

In the mid-1930s, the great offensive to build socialism and a new socialist personality culminated in ruthless police terror and a massive purging of the Communist party. First used by the Bolsheviks in the civil war to maintain their power, terror as state policy was revived in the collectivization drive against the peasants. The top members of the party and government publicly supported Stalin's initiatives, but there was some grumbling in the party. At a small gathering in November 1932, even Stalin's wife complained bitterly about the misery of the people and the horrible famine in Ukraine. Stalin showered her with insults, and she died that same night, apparently by her own hand. In late 1934, Stalin's number-two man, Sergei Kirov, was suddenly and mysteriously murdered. Although Stalin himself probably ordered Kirov's murder, he used the incident to launch a reign of terror.

In August 1936, sixteen prominent Old Bolsheviks confessed to all manner of plots against Stalin in spectacular public trials in Moscow. Then in 1937 the secret police arrested a mass of lesser party officials and newer members, also torturing them and extracting more confessions for more show trials. In addition to the party faithful, union officials, managers, intellectuals, army officers, and countless ordinary citizens were struck down. In all, at least 8 million people were probably arrested, and millions of these were executed or never returned from prisons and forced-labor camps.

Stalin and the remaining party leadership recruited 1.5 million new members to take the place of those purged. Thus more than half of all Communist party members in 1941 had joined since the purges. "These new men were 'thirty-something' products of the Second Revolution of the 1930s, Stalin's upwardly mobile yuppies, so to speak."[8] Often sons (and daughters) of workers, they had usually studied in the new technical schools, and they soon proved capable of managing the government and large-scale production. A product of the great purges, this new generation of Stalin-formed communists would serve the leader effectively until his death in 1953, and they would govern the Soviet Union until the early 1980s.

Stalin's mass purges remain baffling, for almost all historians believe that those purged posed no threat and confessed to crimes they had not committed. Certainly the highly publicized purges sent a warning to the people: no one was secure; everyone had to serve the party and its leader with redoubled devotion. Some Western scholars have also argued that the terror reflected a fully developed totalitarian state, which must always be fighting real or imaginary enemies.

The long-standing Western interpretation that puts the blame for the great purges on Stalin, which became very popular in Russia after the fall of communism, has nevertheless been challenged in recent years. Some historians now argue that Stalin's fears were exaggerated but real. Moreover, these fears and suspicions were shared by many in the party and in the general population. Bombarded with ideology and political slogans, the population responded energetically to Stalin's directives. Investigations and trials snowballed into a mass hysteria, a new witch-hunt that claimed millions of victims.[9] In short, in this view of the 1930s, a deluded Stalin found large numbers of willing collaborators for crime as well as for achievement.

## Mussolini and Fascism in Italy

See DBQ 13

Mussolini's movement and his seizure of power in 1922 were important steps in the rise of dictatorships in Europe between the two world wars. Like all the future dictators, the young Mussolini hated liberalism and wanted to destroy it in Italy. But although Mussolini began as a revolutionary socialist, like Stalin, he turned against the working class and successfully sought the support of conservatives. At the same time, Mussolini and his supporters were the first to call themselves "fascists"—revolutionaries determined to create a certain kind of totalitarian state. Yet few scholars today would argue that Mussolini succeeded. His dictatorship was brutal and theatrical, but it remained a halfway house between conservative authoritarianism and dynamic totalitarianism.

### The Seizure of Power

In the early twentieth century, Italy was a liberal state with civil rights and a constitutional monarchy. On the eve of the First World War, the parliamentary regime finally granted universal male suffrage, and Italy appeared to be moving toward democracy. But there were serious problems. Much of the Italian population was still poor, and many peasants were more attached to their villages and local interests than to the national state. Moreover, the papacy, many devout Catholics, conservatives, and landowners remained strongly opposed to liberal institutions and to the heirs of Cavour and Garibaldi—the middle-class lawyers and politicians who ran the country largely for their own benefit. Relations between church and state were often tense. Class differences were also extreme, and a powerful revolutionary socialist movement had developed. Only in Italy among the main European countries did the radical left wing of the Socialist party gain the leadership as early as 1912, and only in Italy did the Socialist party unanimously oppose the war from the very beginning.[10]

The war worsened the political situation. Having fought on the side of the Allies almost exclusively for purposes of territorial expansion, the parliamentary government bitterly disappointed Italian nationalists with Italy's modest gains at Versailles. Workers and peasants also felt cheated: to win their support during the war, the government had promised social and land reform, which it did not deliver after the war.

The Russian Revolution inspired and energized Italy's revolutionary socialist movement. The Socialist party quickly lined up with the Bolsheviks, and radical workers and peasants began occupying factories and seizing land in 1920. These actions scared and mobilized the property-owning classes. Moreover, after the war the pope lifted his ban on participation by Catholics in Italian politics, and a strong Catholic party quickly emerged. Thus by 1921 revolutionary socialists, antiliberal conservatives, and frightened property owners were all opposed—though for different reasons—to the liberal parliamentary government.

Into these crosscurrents of unrest and fear stepped the blustering, bullying Benito Mussolini (1883–1945). Son of a village schoolteacher and a poor blacksmith, Mussolini began his political career as a Socialist party leader and radical newspaper editor before World War I. In 1914, powerfully influenced by antidemocratic cults of violent action, the young Mussolini urged that Italy join the Allies, a stand for which he was expelled from the Italian Socialist party. Later Mussolini fought at the front and was wounded in 1917. Returning home, he began organizing bitter war veterans like himself into a band of fascists—from the Italian word for "a union of forces."

At first Mussolini's program was a radical combination of nationalist and socialist demands, including territorial expansion, benefits for workers, and land reform for peasants. As such, it competed directly with the well-organized Socialist party and failed to get off the ground. When Mussolini saw that his violent verbal assaults on rival Socialists won him growing support from conservatives and the frightened middle classes, he shifted gears in 1920. In thought and action, Mussolini was a striking example of the turbulent uncertainty of the age of anxiety.

Mussolini and his growing private army of **Black Shirts** began to grow violent. Typically, a band of fascist toughs would roar off in trucks at night and swoop down on a few isolated Socialist organizers, beating them up and force-feeding them almost deadly doses of castor oil. Few people were killed, but socialist newspapers, union halls, and local Socialist party headquarters were destroyed. Mussolini's toughs pushed Socialists out of the city governments of northern Italy.

A skillful politician, Mussolini allowed his followers to convince themselves that they were not just opposing the "Reds" but also making a real revolution of their own, forging a strong, dynamic movement that would help the little people against the established interests. With the government breaking down in 1922, largely because of the chaos created by his direct-action bands, Mussolini stepped forward as the savior of order and property. Striking a conservative note in his speeches and gaining the sympathetic neutrality of army leaders, Mussolini demanded the resignation of the existing government and his own appointment

**Hitler and Mussolini in Italy, May 1938** At first Mussolini distrusted Hitler, but Mussolini's conquest of Ethiopia in 1936 and Hitler's occupation of the Rhineland brought the two dictators together in a close alliance. State visits by Mussolini to Berlin in 1937 and by Hitler to Rome in 1938 included gigantic military reviews, which were filmed to impress the whole world. Uniformed Italian fascists accompany this motorcade. *(Time Life Pictures/Getty Images)*

by the king. In October 1922, to force matters, a large group of fascists marched on Rome to threaten the king and force him to call on Mussolini. The threat worked. Victor Emmanuel III (r. 1900–1946), who had no love for the old liberal politicians, asked Mussolini to form a new cabinet. Thus, after widespread violence and a threat of armed uprising, Mussolini seized power "legally." He was immediately granted dictatorial authority for one year by the king and the parliament.

## The Regime in Action

Mussolini became dictator on the strength of Italians' rejection of parliamentary government coupled with fears of Soviet-style revolution. Yet what he intended to do with his power was by no means clear until 1924. Some of his dedicated supporters pressed for a "second revolution." Mussolini's ministers, however, included old conservatives, moderates, and even two reform-minded Socialists. A new electoral law was passed giving two-thirds of the representatives in the parliament to the party that won the most votes, a change that allowed the Fascist party and its allies to win an overwhelming majority in 1924. Shortly thereafter, five of Mussolini's thugs kidnapped and murdered Giacomo Matteotti, the leader of the Socialists in the parliament. In the face of this outrage, the opposition demanded that Mussolini's armed squads be dissolved and all violence be banned.

Although Mussolini may or may not have ordered Matteotti's murder, he stood at the crossroads of a severe political crisis. After some hesitation, he charged forward. Declaring his desire to "make the nation Fascist," he imposed a series of repressive measures. Freedom of the press was abolished, elections were fixed, and the government ruled by decree. Mussolini arrested his political opponents, disbanded all independent labor unions, and put dedicated Fascists in control of Italy's schools. Moreover, he created a fascist youth movement, fascist labor unions, and many other fascist organizations. Mussolini trumpeted his goal in a famous slogan of 1926: "Everything in the state, nothing outside the state, nothing against the state." By the end of that year, Italy was a one-party dictatorship under Mussolini's unquestioned leadership.

Mussolini, however, did not complete the establishment of a modern totalitarian state. His Fascist party never became all-powerful. It never destroyed the old power structure, as the Communists did in the Soviet Union, or succeeded in dominating it, as the Nazis did in Germany. Membership in the Fascist party was more a sign of an Italian's respectability than a commitment to radical change. Interested primarily in personal power, Mussolini was content to compromise with the old conservative classes that controlled the army, the economy, and the state. He never tried to purge these classes or even move very vigorously against them. He controlled and propagandized labor but left big business to regulate itself, profitably and securely. There was no land reform.

Mussolini also drew increasing support from the Catholic church. In the **Lateran Agreement** of 1929, he recognized the Vatican as a tiny independent state, and he agreed to give the church heavy financial support. The pope expressed his satisfaction and urged Italians to support Mussolini's government.

Nothing better illustrates Mussolini's unwillingness to harness everyone and everything for dynamic action than his treatment of women. He abolished divorce and told women to stay at home and produce children. To promote that goal, he decreed a special tax on bachelors in 1934. In 1938 women were limited by law to a maximum of 10 percent of the better-paying jobs in industry and government. Italian women appear not to have changed their attitudes or behavior in any important way under fascist rule.

Mussolini's government did not pass racial laws until 1938 and did not persecute Jews savagely until late in the Second World War, when Italy was under Nazi control. Nor did Mussolini establish a truly ruthless police state. Only twenty-three political prisoners were condemned to death between 1926 and 1944. In spite of much pompous posing by the chauvinist leader and in spite of mass meetings, salutes, and a certain copying of Hitler's aggression in foreign policy after 1933, Mussolini's fascist Italy, though repressive and undemocratic, was never really totalitarian.

## Hitler and Nazism in Germany

See DBQ 13

The most frightening dictatorship developed in Nazi Germany. A product of Hitler's evil genius as well as of Germany's social and political situation and the general attack on liberalism and rationality in the age of anxiety, the Nazi movement shared some of the characteristics of Mussolini's Italian model and was a form of fascism. But Nazi dictatorship smashed or took over most independent organizations, mobilized the economy, and violently persecuted the Jewish population. Thus Nazism asserted an unlimited claim over German society and proclaimed the ultimate power of its endlessly aggressive leader—Adolf Hitler. The aspirations of Nazism were truly totalitarian.

### The Roots of Nazism

**Nazism** grew out of many complex developments, of which the most influential were extreme nationalism and racism. These two ideas captured the mind of the young Hitler, and it was he who dominated Nazism for as long as it lasted.

Born the fourth child of a successful Austrian customs official and an indulgent mother, Adolf Hitler (1889–1945) spent his childhood in small towns in Austria. A good student in grade school, Hitler did poorly on reaching high school and dropped out at age fourteen following the death of his father. After four years of unfocused loafing, Hitler finally left for Vienna, where he lived a comfortable, lazy life on his generous orphan's pension and found most of the perverted beliefs that guided his life.

In Vienna Hitler soaked up extreme German nationalism, which was particularly strong there. Austro-German nationalists believed Germans to be a superior people and the natural rulers of central Europe. They often advocated union with Germany and violent expulsion of "inferior" peoples as the means of maintaining German domination of the Austro-Hungarian Empire.

Hitler was deeply impressed by Vienna's mayor, Karl Lueger (1844–1910). With the help of the Catholic trade unions, Lueger had succeeded in winning the support of the little people of Vienna, and he showed Hitler the enormous potential of anticapitalist and antiliberal propaganda. From Lueger and others, Hitler eagerly absorbed virulent anti-Semitism, racism, and hatred of Slavs. He developed an unshakable belief in the crudest, most exaggerated distortions of the Darwinian theory of survival, the superiority of Germanic races, and the inevitability of racial conflict. Thus anti-Semitism and racism became Hitler's most passionate convictions, his explanation for everything. The Jews, he claimed, directed an international conspiracy of finance capitalism and Marxian socialism against German culture, German unity, and the German race. Hitler's belief was totally irrational, but he never doubted it.

Although he moved to Munich in 1913 to avoid being drafted in the Austrian army, the lonely Hitler greeted the outbreak of the First World War as a salvation. He later wrote in his autobiography, *Mein Kampf,* that, "overcome by passionate enthusiasm, I fell to my knees and thanked heaven out of an overflowing heart." The struggle and discipline of war gave life meaning, and Hitler served bravely as a dispatch carrier on the western front.

When Germany was suddenly defeated in 1918, Hitler's world was shattered. Not only was he a fanatical nationalist, but war was also his reason for living. Convinced that Jews and Marxists had "stabbed Germany in the back," he vowed to fight on.

In late 1919, Hitler joined a tiny extremist group in Munich called the German Workers' party. In addition to denouncing Jews, Marxists, and democrats, the German Workers' party promised unity under a uniquely German "national socialism" that would abolish the injustices of capitalism and create a mighty "people's community." By 1921 Hitler had gained absolute control of this small but growing party. He was already a master of mass propaganda and political showmanship. His most effective tool was the mass rally, where he often worked his audience into a frenzy with wild, demagogic attacks on the Versailles treaty, the Jews, the war profiteers, and Germany's Weimar Republic.

Party membership multiplied tenfold after early 1922. In late 1923, the Weimar Republic seemed on the verge of collapse, and Hitler, inspired by Mussolini's recent easy victory, decided on an armed uprising in Munich. Despite the failure of the poorly organized plot and Hitler's arrest, Nazism had been born.

### Hitler's Road to Power

At his trial, Hitler violently denounced the Weimar Republic, and he gained enormous publicity and attention. Moreover, he learned from his unsuccessful revolt. Hitler concluded that he had to undermine, rather than overthrow, the government and come to power legally through electoral competition. He forced his more violent supporters to accept his new strategy. He also used his brief prison term to dictate *Mein Kampf.* There he expounded on his basic themes: "race," with a stress on anti-Semitism; "living space," with a sweeping vision of war and conquered territory; and the leader-dictator (**Führer**), with unlimited, arbitrary power.

In the years of prosperity and relative stability between 1924 and 1929, Hitler concentrated on building his National Socialist German Workers' party, or Nazi party. By 1928 the party had 100,000 highly disciplined members under Hitler's absolute control. To appeal to the middle-class voters, Hitler de-emphasized the anticapitalist elements of national socialism and vowed to fight Bolshevism. Yet the Nazis remained a small splinter group in 1928, when they received only 2.6 percent of the vote in the general elections and twelve seats in the Reichstag. There the Nazi deputies pursued the legal strategy of using democracy to destroy democracy.

The Great Depression, shattering economic prosperity from 1929 on, presented Hitler with a fabulous opportunity. Unemployment jumped from 1.3 million in 1929 to 5 million in 1930. By the end of 1932, an incredible 43 percent of the labor force was unemployed. Industrial production fell by one-half between 1929 and 1932. No factor contributed more to Hitler's success than the economic crisis. Never very interested in economics before, Hitler began promising German voters economic as well as political and international salvation.

Above all, Hitler rejected free-market capitalism and advocated government programs to bring recovery. Hitler pitched his speeches especially to middle- and lower-middle-class groups—small business people, officeworkers, artisans, and peasants—as well as to skilled workers striving for middle-class status. Seized by panic as bankruptcies increased, unemployment soared, and the Communists made dramatic election gains, great numbers of middle- and lower-middle-class people "voted their pocketbooks"[11] and deserted the conservative and moderate parties for the Nazis. In the election of 1930, the Nazis won 6.5 million votes and 107 seats, and in July 1932 they gained 14.5 million votes—38 percent of the total—and became the largest party in the Reichstag.

The appeal to pocketbook interests was particularly effective in the early 1930s because Hitler appeared more mainstream, playing down his anti-Jewish hatred and racist nationalism. A master of mass propaganda and psychology, he had written in *Mein Kampf* that the masses were the "driving force of the most important changes in this world" and were themselves driven by fanaticism and not by knowledge. To arouse such hysterical fanaticism, he believed that all propaganda had to be limited to a few simple, endlessly repeated slogans. But now when he harangued vast audiences with wild oratory and simple slogans, he featured "national rebirth" and the "crimes" of the Versailles treaty. And many uncertain individuals, surrounded by thousands of enthralled listeners, found a sense of belonging as well as hope for better times.

Hitler and the Nazis also appealed strongly to German youth. Indeed, in some ways the Nazi movement was a mass movement of young Germans. Hitler himself was only forty in 1929, and he and most of his top aides were much younger than other leading German politicians.

**"The Officers of Tomorrow"** The Nazis tried hard to win the support of young people. After they came to power, the Nazis put boys in the uniform of the Hitler Youth, shown here in a German historical museum. The Hitler Youth preached Nazi values and militarism, the message of the poster and its caption. *(akg-images)*

"National Socialism is the organized will of the youth," proclaimed the official Nazi slogan, and the battle cry of Gregor Strasser, a leading Nazi organizer, was "Make way, you old ones."[12] In 1931 almost 40 percent of Nazi party members were under thirty, compared with 20 percent of Social Democrats. National recovery, exciting and rapid change, and personal advancement were the appeals of Nazism to millions of German youths.

Another reason Hitler came to power was that normal democratic government broke down as early as May 1930. Unable to gain the support of a majority in the Reichstag, Chancellor (chief minister) Heinrich Brüning convinced the president, the aging war hero General Hindenburg, to authorize rule by decree. Intending to use this emergency measure indefinitely, Brüning was determined to overcome the economic crisis by cutting back government spending and ruthlessly forcing down prices and wages. Brüning's ultra-orthodox policies not only intensified the economic collapse in Germany but also convinced many voters that the country's republican leaders were stupid and corrupt, thereby adding to Hitler's appeal.

The continuation of the struggle between the Social Democrats and the Communists, right up until the moment Hitler took power, was another aspect of the breakdown of democratic government. The Communists refused to cooperate with the Social Democrats, even though the two parties together outnumbered the Nazis in the Reichstag, even after the elections of 1932. German Communists (and the still complacent Stalin) were blinded by hatred of socialists and by ideology: the Communists believed that Hitler's fascism represented the last agonies of monopoly capitalism and that a communist revolution would soon follow his taking power. Disunity on the left was undoubtedly another nail in the republic's coffin.

Finally, Hitler excelled in the dirty, backroom politics of the decaying Weimar Republic. That, in fact, brought him to power. In complicated infighting in 1932, he cleverly succeeded in gaining additional support from key people in the army and big business. These people thought they could use Hitler for their own advantage to get increased military spending, fat contracts, and tough measures against workers. Many conservative and nationalistic politicians thought similarly. They thus accepted Hitler's demand to join the government only if he became chancellor. There would be only two other National Socialists and nine solid conservatives as ministers, and in such a coalition government, they reasoned, Hitler could be used and controlled. On January 30, 1933, Adolf Hitler, leader of the largest party in Germany, was legally appointed chancellor by Hindenburg.

## The Nazi State and Society

Hitler moved rapidly and skillfully to establish an unshakable dictatorship. Continuing to maintain legal appearances, he immediately called for new elections. In the midst of a violent electoral campaign, the Reichstag building was partly destroyed by fire. Hitler screamed that the Communist party was responsible, and he convinced President Hindenburg to sign dictatorial emergency acts that practically abolished freedom of speech and assembly as well as most personal liberties.

When the Nazis won only 44 percent of the vote in the elections, Hitler immediately outlawed the Communist party and arrested its parliamentary representatives. Then on March 23, 1933, the Nazis pushed through the Reichstag the so-called **Enabling Act,** which gave Hitler absolute dictatorial power for four years. Armed with the Enabling Act, Hitler and the Nazis moved to smash or control all independent organizations. Their deceitful stress on legality, coupled with divide-and-conquer techniques, disarmed the opposition until it was too late for effective resistance.

Germany soon became a one-party state. Only the Nazi party was legal. Elections were farces. The Reichstag was jokingly referred to as the most expensive glee club in the country, for its only function was to sing hymns of praise to the Führer. Hitler and the Nazis took over the government bureaucracy intact, installing many Nazis in top positions. At the same time, they created a series of overlapping Nazi party organizations responsible solely to Hitler.

**Reaching a National Audience** This poster ad promotes the VE-301 receiver, "the world's cheapest radio," and claims that "All Germany listens to the Führer on the people's receiver." Constantly broadcasting official views and attitudes, the state-controlled media also put the Nazis' favorite entertainment—gigantic mass meetings that climaxed with Hitler's violent theatrical speeches—on an invisible stage for millions. *(Bundesarchiv Koblenz Plak 003-022-025)*

As research in recent years shows, the resulting system of dual government was riddled with rivalries, contradictions, and inefficiencies. Thus the Nazi state was sloppy and often disorganized, lacking the all-encompassing unity that its propagandists claimed. Yet this fractured system suited Hitler and his purposes. He could play the established bureaucracy against his private, personal "party government" and maintain his freedom of action. Hitler could concentrate on general principles and the big decisions, which he always made.

In the economic sphere, one big decision outlawed strikes and abolished independent labor unions, which were replaced by the Nazi Labor Front. Professional people—doctors and lawyers, teachers and engineers—also saw their previously independent organizations swallowed up by Nazi associations. Publishing houses were put under Nazi control, and universities and writers were quickly brought into line. Democratic, socialist, and Jewish literature was put on ever-growing blacklists. Passionate students and pitiful professors burned forbidden books in public squares. Modern art and architecture were ruthlessly prohibited. Life became violently anti-intellectual. As the cynical Joseph Goebbels put it, "When I hear the word 'culture' I reach for my gun."[13] By 1934 a brutal dictatorship characterized by frightening dynamism and obedience to Hitler was already largely in place.

Only the army retained independence, and Hitler moved brutally and skillfully to establish his control there, too. The Nazi storm troopers (the SA), the quasi-military band of 3 million toughs in brown shirts who had fought communists and beaten up Jews before the Nazis took power, expected top positions in the army and even talked of a "second revolution" against capitalism. Hitler decided that the SA leaders had to be eliminated. Needing to preserve good relations with the army as well as with big business, he struck on the night of June 30, 1934. Hitler's elite personal guard—the SS—arrested and shot without trial roughly a thousand SA leaders and assorted political enemies. Shortly thereafter army leaders swore a binding oath of "unquestioning obedience . . . to the Leader of the German State and People, Adolf Hitler." The SS grew rapidly. Under its methodical, inhuman leader, Heinrich Himmler (1900–1945), the SS joined with the political police, the Gestapo, to expand its network of special courts and concentration camps. Nobody was safe.

From the beginning, Jews were a special object of Nazi persecution. By the end of 1934, most Jewish lawyers, doctors, professors, civil servants, and musicians had lost their jobs and the right to practice their professions. In 1935 the infamous Nuremberg Laws classified as Jewish anyone having one or more Jewish grandparents and deprived Jews of all rights of citizenship. By 1938 roughly 150,000 of Germany's half a million Jews had emigrated, sacrificing almost all their property in order to leave Germany.

In late 1938, the attack on the Jews accelerated. A well-organized wave of violence, known to history as "Kristallnacht," smashed windows, looted shops, and destroyed homes and synagogues. German Jews were then rounded up and made to pay for the damage. Another 150,000 Jews fled Germany. Some Germans privately opposed these outrages, but most went along or looked the other way. This lack of opposition reflected anti-Semitism to a degree still being debated by historians, but it certainly reflected the strong popular support Hitler's government enjoyed.

## Hitler's Popularity

Hitler had promised the masses economic recovery—"work and bread"—and he delivered. Breaking with Brüning's do-nothing policies, Hitler launched a large public works program to help pull Germany out of the depression. Work began on superhighways, offices, gigantic sports stadiums, and public housing. Hitler also appointed as Germany's central banker a well-known conservative named Hjalmar Schacht, who skillfully restored credit and business. In 1936 an openly aggressive Hitler broke with Schacht, and Germany turned decisively toward rearmament and preparation for war. As a result of these policies (and plain good luck), unemployment dropped steadily, from 6 million in January 1933 to about 1 million in late 1936. By 1938 there was a shortage of workers, as unemployment fell to 2 percent, and women began to take jobs previously denied them by the antifeminist Nazis. Thus between 1932 and 1938, the standard of living for the average employed worker increased moderately. The profits of business rose sharply. For millions of people, economic recovery was tangible evidence that Nazi promises were more than show and propaganda.

For the masses of ordinary German citizens who were not Jews, Slavs, Gypsies, Jehovah's Witnesses, communists, or homosexuals, Hitler's government meant greater equality and more opportunities. In 1933 the position of the traditional German elites—the landed aristocracy, the wealthy capitalists, and the well-educated professional classes—was still very strong. Barriers between classes were generally high. Hitler's rule introduced changes that lowered these barriers. For example, stiff educational requirements, which favored the well-to-do, were relaxed. The new Nazi elite included many young and poorly educated dropouts, rootless lower-middle-class people like Hitler who rose to the top with breathtaking speed. More generally, the Nazis tolerated privilege and wealth only as long as they served the needs of the party. Even big business was constantly ordered around.

Yet few historians today believe that Hitler and the Nazis brought about a real social revolution, as an earlier generation of scholars often argued. Millions of modest middle-class and lower-middle-class people *felt* that Germany was becoming more open and equal, as Nazi propagandists constantly claimed. But quantitative studies show that the well-educated classes held on to most of their advantages and that only a modest social leveling occurred in the Nazi years. It is significant that the Nazis shared with the Italian fascists the stereotypic view of women as housewives and mothers. Only under the relentless pressure of war did they reluctantly mobilize large numbers of German women for work in offices and factories.

Hitler's rabid nationalism, which had helped him gain power, continued to appeal to Germans after 1933. Ever since the wars against Napoleon, many Germans had believed in a special mission for a superior German nation. The successes of Bismarck had furthered such feelings, and near-victory in World War I made nationalists eager for renewed expansion in the 1920s. Thus when Hitler went from one foreign triumph to another and a great German empire seemed within reach, the majority of the population was delighted and kept praising the Führer's actions well into the war.

Not all Germans supported Hitler, however, and a number of German groups actively resisted him after 1933. Tens of thousands of political enemies were imprisoned, and thousands were executed. But opponents of the Nazis pursued various goals, and they were never unified, a fact that helps account for their ultimate lack of success. In the first years of Hitler's rule, the principal resisters were the communists and the socialists in the trade unions. But the expansion of the SS system of terror after 1935 smashed most of these leftists. A second group of opponents arose in the Catholic and Protestant churches. However, their efforts were directed primarily at preserving genuine religious life, not at overthrowing Hitler. Finally in 1938 (and again in 1942–1944), some high-ranking army officers, who feared the consequences of Hitler's reckless aggression, plotted against him, unsuccessfully.

# Nazi Expansion and the Second World War

Although economic recovery and somewhat greater opportunity for social advancement won Hitler support, they were only byproducts of the Nazi regime. The guiding and unique concepts of Nazism remained space and race—the territorial expansion of the superior German race. As Germany regained its economic strength and as independent organizations were brought under control, Hitler formed alliances with other dictators and began expanding. German expansion was facilitated by the uncertain and divided Western democracies, which tried to buy off Hitler to avoid war.

Yet war inevitably broke out, in both the West and the East, for Hitler's ambitions were essentially unlimited. On both war fronts, Nazi soldiers scored enormous successes until late 1942, establishing a vast empire of death and destruction. Hitler's reckless aggression also raised a mighty coalition determined to smash the Nazi order. Led by Britain, the United States, and the Soviet Union, the Grand Alliance—to use Winston Churchill's favorite term—functioned quite effectively in military terms. By the summer of 1943, the tide of battle had turned. Two years later, Germany and its allies lay in ruins, utterly defeated. Thus the terrible Nazi empire proved short-lived.

## Aggression and Appeasement, 1933–1939

Hitler's tactics in international politics after 1933 strikingly resembled those he had used in domestic politics between 1924 and 1933. When Hitler was weak, he righteously proclaimed that he intended to overturn the "unjust system" established by the Treaties of Versailles and Locarno—but only by legal means. As he grew stronger, and as other leaders showed their willingness to compromise, he increased his demands and finally began attacking his independent neighbors (see Map 29.1).

Hitler realized that his aggressive policies had to be carefully camouflaged at first, for Germany's army was limited by the Treaty of Versailles to only 100,000 men. As he told a group of army commanders in February 1933, the early stages of his policy of "conquest of new living space in the East and its ruthless Germanization" had serious dangers. If France had real leaders, Hitler said, it would "not give us time but attack us, presumably with its eastern satellites."[14] To avoid such threats to his plans, Hitler loudly proclaimed his peaceful intentions to all the world. Nevertheless, he felt strong enough to walk out of a sixty-nation disarmament conference and withdraw from the League of Nations in October 1933. Gustav Stresemann's policy of peaceful cooperation (see pages 938–939) was dead; the Nazi determination to rearm was out in the open.

Following this action, Hitler sought to incorporate independent Austria into a greater Germany. But a worried Mussolini, who had initially greeted Hitler as a fascist little brother, massed his troops on Brenner Pass and threatened to fight. When in March 1935 Hitler established a general military draft and declared the "unequal" disarmament clauses of the Treaty of Versailles null and void, other countries appeared to understand the danger. With France taking the lead, Italy and Great Britain protested strongly and warned against future aggressive actions.

**MAP 29.1 The Growth of Nazi Germany, 1933–1939** Until March 1939, Hitler brought ethnic Germans into the Nazi state; then he turned on the Slavic peoples he had always hated. He stripped Czechoslovakia of its independence and prepared for an attack on Poland in September 1939.

Yet the emerging united front against Hitler quickly collapsed. Of crucial importance, Britain adopted a policy of **appeasement,** granting Hitler everything he could reasonably want (and more) in order to avoid war. The first step was an Anglo-German naval agreement in June 1935 that broke Germany's isolation. The second step came in March 1936 when Hitler suddenly marched his armies into the demilitarized Rhineland, brazenly violating the Treaties of Versailles and Locarno. This was the last good chance to stop the Nazis, for Hitler had ordered his troops to retreat if France resisted militarily. But an uncertain France would not move without British support, and the occupation of German soil by German armies seemed right and just to Britain. With a greatly improved strategic position, Germany handed France a tremendous psychological defeat.

## Events Leading to World War II

| | |
|---|---|
| 1919 | Treaty of Versailles is signed; J. M. Keynes publishes *Economic Consequences of the Peace.* |
| 1919–1920 | U.S. Senate rejects the Treaty of Versailles. |
| 1921 | Germany is billed $33 billion in reparations. |
| 1922 | Mussolini seizes power in Italy; Germany proposes a moratorium on reparations. |
| January 1923 | France and Belgium occupy the Ruhr; Germany orders passive resistance to the occupation. |
| October 1923 | Stresemann agrees to reparations based on Germany's ability to pay. |
| 1924 | Dawes Plan: German reparations are reduced and put on a sliding scale. Large U.S. loans to Germany are recommended to promote German recovery; Adolf Hitler dictates *Mein Kampf.* |
| 1924–1929 | Spectacular German economic recovery occurs; circular flow of international funds enables sizable reparations payments. |
| 1925 | Treaties of Locarno promote European security and stability. |
| 1926 | Germany joins the League of Nations. |
| 1928 | Kellogg-Briand Pact renounces war as an instrument of international affairs. |
| 1929 | U.S. stock market crashes and triggers worldwide financial crisis. |
| 1929–1939 | Great Depression rages. |
| 1931 | Japan invades Manchuria. |
| 1932 | Nazis become the largest party in the Reichstag. |
| January 1933 | Hitler is appointed chancellor of Germany. |
| March 1933 | Reichstag passes the Enabling Act, granting Hitler absolute dictatorial power. |
| October 1933 | Germany withdraws from the League of Nations. |
| 1935 | Nuremberg Laws deprive Jews of all rights of citizenship. |
| March 1935 | Hitler announces German rearmament. |
| June 1935 | Anglo-German naval agreement is signed. |
| October 1935 | Mussolini invades Ethiopia and receives Hitler's support. |
| March 1936 | German armies move unopposed into the demilitarized Rhineland. |
| July 1936 | Civil war breaks out in Spain. |
| 1937 | Japan invades China; Rome-Berlin Axis in effect. |
| March 1938 | Germany annexes Austria. |
| September 1938 | Munich Conference: Britain and France agree to German seizure of the Sudetenland from Czechoslovakia. |
| March 1939 | Germany occupies the rest of Czechoslovakia; appeasement ends in Britain. |
| August 1939 | Nazi-Soviet nonaggression pact is signed. |
| September 1, 1939 | Germany invades Poland. |
| September 3, 1939 | Britain and France declare war on Germany. |

British appeasement, which practically dictated French policy, lasted far into 1939. It was motivated by British feelings of guilt toward Germany and the pacifism of a population still horrified by the memory of the First World War. As in Germany, many powerful conservatives in Britain underestimated Hitler. They believed that Soviet communism was the real danger and that Hitler could be used to stop it. A leading member of Britain's government personally told Hitler in November 1937 that it was his conviction that Hitler "not only had accomplished great things in Germany itself, but that through the total destruction of Communism in his own country . . . Germany rightly had to be considered as a Western bulwark against Communism."[15] Such rigid anticommunist feelings made an alliance between the Western powers and Stalin unlikely.

As Britain and France opted for appeasement and the Soviet Union watched all developments suspiciously, Hitler found powerful allies. In 1935 the bombastic Mussolini decided that imperial expansion was needed to revitalize Italian fascism. From Italian colonies on the east coast of Africa, he attacked the independent African kingdom of Ethiopia. The Western powers and the League of Nations piously condemned Italian aggression, but Hitler supported Italy energetically and overcame Mussolini's lingering doubts about the Nazis. The result in late 1936 was an agreement on close cooperation between Italy and Germany, the so-called Rome-Berlin Axis. Japan, which had been expanding into Manchuria since 1931, soon joined the Axis alliance.

At the same time, Germany and Italy intervened in the long, complicated Spanish civil war, which broke out in July 1936. German and Italian support eventually helped General Francisco Franco's fascist movement defeat republican Spain. Only the Soviet Union gave aid to the leftist government that Franco fought, for public opinion in Britain and especially in France was hopelessly divided on the Spanish question.

In late 1937, while proclaiming peaceful intentions to the British and their gullible prime minister, Neville Chamberlain, Hitler told his generals his real plans. His "unshakable decision" was to crush Austria and Czechoslovakia at the earliest possible moment as the first step in his long-contemplated drive to the east for living space. By threatening Austria with invasion, Hitler forced the Austrian chancellor in March 1938 to put local Nazis in control of the government. The next day, German armies moved in unopposed, and Austria became two more provinces of Greater Germany (see Map 29.1).

Simultaneously, Hitler began demanding that the pro-Nazi, German-speaking minority of western Czechoslovakia—the Sudetenland—be turned over to Germany. Yet democratic Czechoslovakia was prepared to defend itself. Moreover, France had been Czechoslovakia's ally since 1924; and if France fought, the Soviet Union was pledged

**Hitler's Success with Aggression** This biting criticism of appeasing leaders by the cartoonist David Low appeared shortly after Hitler remilitarized the Rhineland. Appeasement also appealed to millions of ordinary citizens in Britain and France, who wanted to avoid at any cost another great war. *(London Evening/Solo Standard Ltd.)*

to help. War appeared inevitable, but appeasement triumphed again. In September 1938, Chamberlain flew to Germany three times in fourteen days. In these negotiations, to which the U.S.S.R. was deliberately not invited, Chamberlain and the French agreed with Hitler that the Sudetenland should be ceded to Germany immediately. Returning to London from the Munich Conference, Chamberlain told cheering crowds that he had secured "peace with honor . . . peace for our time." Sold out by the Western powers, Czechoslovakia gave in.

Confirmed once again in his opinion of the Western democracies as weak and racially degenerate, Hitler accelerated his aggression. In a shocking violation of his solemn assurances that the Sudetenland was his last territorial demand, Hitler's armies occupied the Czech lands in March 1939, while Slovakia became a puppet state. The effect on Western public opinion was electrifying. For the first time, there was no possible rationale of self-determination for Nazi aggression since Hitler was seizing Czechs and Slovaks as captive peoples. Thus when Hitler used the question of German minorities in Danzig as a pretext to confront Poland, a suddenly militant Chamberlain declared that Britain and France would fight if Hitler attacked his eastern neighbor. Hitler did not take these warnings seriously and decided to press on.

In an about-face that stunned the world, Hitler offered and Stalin signed a ten-year Nazi-Soviet nonaggression pact in August 1939. Each dictator promised to remain neutral if the other became involved in war. An attached secret protocol, which became known only after the war, ruthlessly divided eastern Europe into German and Soviet zones, "in the event of a political territorial reorganization." The nonaggression pact itself was enough to make Britain and France cry treachery, for they, too, had been negotiating with Stalin. But Stalin had remained distrustful of Western intentions, and Hitler had offered immediate territorial gain.

For Hitler, everything was set. He told his generals on the day of the nonaggression pact, "My only fear is that at the last moment some dirty dog will come up with a mediation plan." On September 1, 1939, German armies and warplanes smashed into Poland from three sides. Two days later, Britain and France, finally true to their word, declared war on Germany. The Second World War had begun.

### Hitler's Empire, 1939–1942

Using planes, tanks, and trucks in the first example of a **blitzkrieg,** or "lightning war," Hitler's armies crushed Poland in four weeks. While the Soviet Union quickly took its part of the booty—the eastern half of Poland and the independent Baltic states of Lithuania, Estonia, and Latvia—French and British armies dug in in the west. They expected another war of attrition and economic blockade.

In spring 1940, the lightning war struck again. After occupying Denmark, Norway, and Holland, German motorized columns broke through southern Belgium, split the Franco-British forces, and trapped the entire British army on the beaches of Dunkirk. By heroic efforts, the British withdrew their troops but not their equipment.

France was taken by the Nazis. Aging marshal Henri-Philippe Pétain formed a new French government—the so-called Vichy government—to accept defeat, and German armies occupied most of France. By July 1940, Hitler ruled practically all of western continental Europe; Italy was an ally, and the Soviet Union and Spain were friendly neutrals. Only Britain, led by the uncompromising Winston Churchill (1874–1965), remained unconquered. Churchill proved to be one of history's greatest wartime leaders, rallying the British with stirring speeches, infectious confidence, and bulldog determination.

Germany sought to gain control of the air, the necessary first step toward an amphibious invasion of Britain. In the Battle of Britain, up to a thousand German planes attacked British airfields and key factories in a single day, dueling with British defenders high in the skies. Losses were heavy on both sides. Then in September Hitler angrily and foolishly changed his strategy, turning from military objectives to indiscriminate bombing of British cities in an attempt to break British morale. British aircraft factories increased production, anti-aircraft defense improved with the help of radar, and the heavily bombed people of London defiantly dug in. In September and October 1940, Britain was beating Germany three to one in the air war. There was no possibility of an immediate German invasion of Britain.

In these circumstances, the most reasonable German strategy would have been to attack Britain through the eastern Mediterranean, taking Egypt and the Suez Canal and pinching off Britain's supply of oil. By April 1941, Germany had already moved to the southeast, conquering Greece and Yugoslavia and forcing Hungary, Romania, and Bulgaria into alliances. But Hitler was not a reasonable person. His lifetime obsession with a vast eastern European empire for the "master race" dictated policy. So in June 1941, German armies suddenly attacked the Soviet Union along a vast front (see Map 29.2). By October 1941, Leningrad was practically surrounded, Moscow was besieged, and most of Ukraine had been overrun. But with Britain still unconquered, Hitler's decision was a wild, irrational gamble epitomizing the violent, unlimited, and ultimately self-destructive ambitions of Nazism. The Soviets did not collapse, and when a

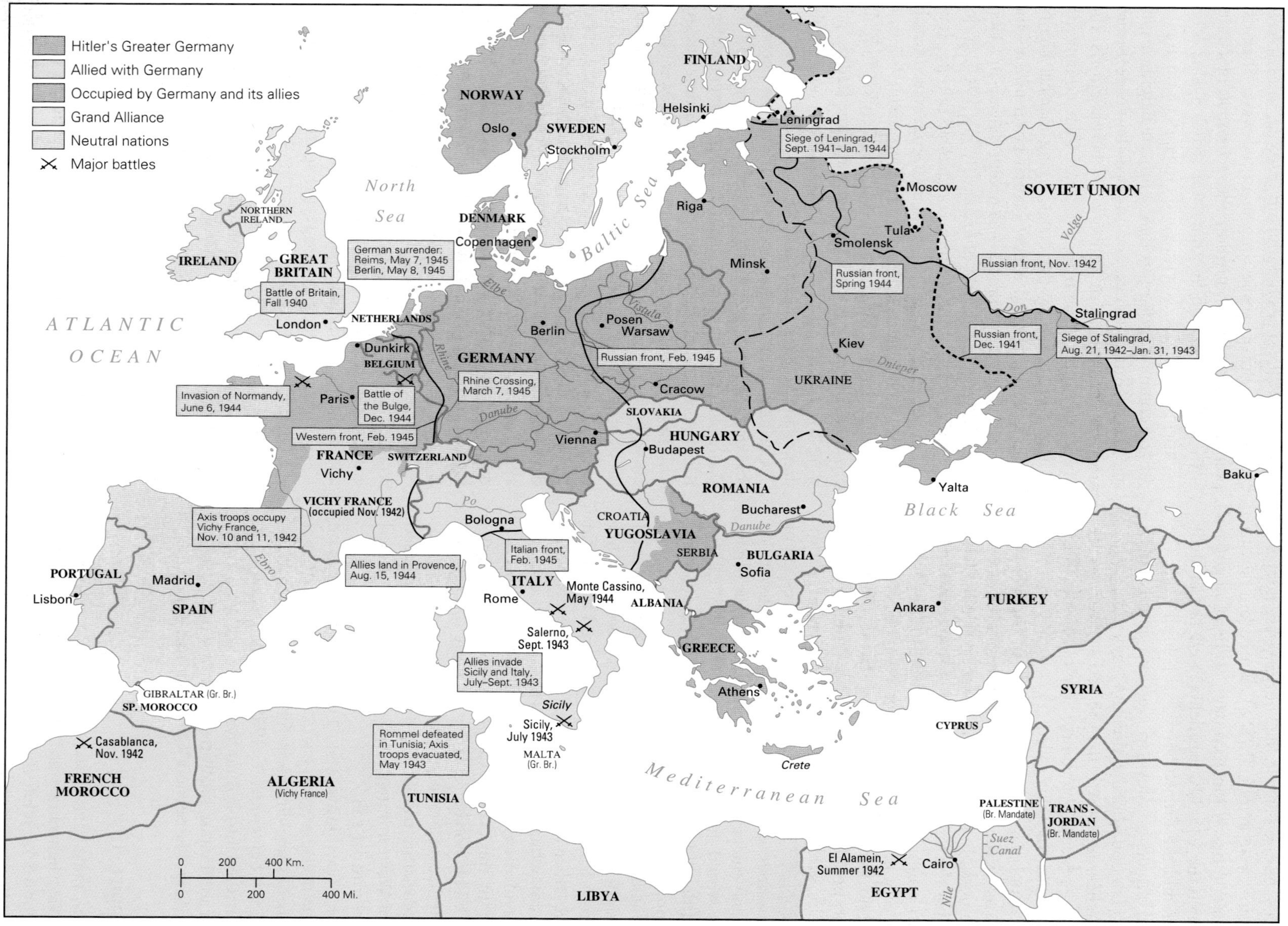


**MAP 29.2 World War II in Europe** The map shows the extent of Hitler's empire at its height, before the Battle of Stalingrad in late 1942 and the subsequent advances of the Allies until Germany surrendered on May 7, 1945.

**London, 1940** Hitler believed that his relentless terror bombing of London—the "blitz"—could break the will of the British people. He was wrong. The blitz caused enormous destruction, but Londoners went about their business with courage and calm determination, as this unforgettable image of a milkman in the rubble suggests. *(Corbis)*

severe winter struck German armies outfitted in summer uniforms, the invaders were stopped.

While Hitler's armies dramatically expanded the war in Europe, his Japanese allies did the same in Asia. Engaged in a general but undeclared war against China since 1937, Japan's rulers had increasingly come into diplomatic conflict with the Pacific basin's other great power, the United States. When the Japanese occupied French Indochina in July 1941, the United States retaliated by cutting off sales of vital rubber, scrap iron, oil, and aviation fuel. Tension mounted further, and on December 7, 1941, Japan attacked the U.S. naval base at Pearl Harbor in Hawaii. Hitler immediately declared war on the United States, and Japanese forces advanced swiftly into Southeast Asia (see Map 29.3 on page 982).

Meanwhile, though stalled in Russia, Hitler ruled over a vast European empire stretching from the outskirts of Moscow to the English Channel. Hitler, the Nazi leadership, and the loyal German army were positioned to greatly accelerate construction of their "New Order" in Europe, and they continued their efforts until their final collapse in 1945. In doing so, they showed what Nazi victory would have meant.

Hitler's **New Order** was based firmly on the guiding principle of Nazi totalitarianism: racial imperialism. Within this New Order, the Nordic peoples—the Dutch, Norwegians, and Danes—received preferential treatment, for they were racially related to the master race, the Germans. The French, an "inferior" Latin people, occupied a middle position. They were heavily taxed to support the Nazi war effort but were tolerated as a race. Once Nazi reverses began to mount in late 1942, however, all the occupied territories of western and northern Europe were exploited with increasing intensity. Material shortages and both mental and physical suffering afflicted millions of people.

Slavs in the conquered territories to the east were treated with harsh hatred as "subhumans." At the height of his success in 1941 and 1942, Hitler set the tone. He painted for his intimate circle the fantastic vision of a vast eastern colonial empire where Poles, Ukrainians, and Russians would be enslaved and forced to die out, while Germanic peasants resettled the resulting abandoned lands. But he needed countless helpers and many ambitious initiators to turn his dreams into reality. These accomplices came forth.

Himmler and the elite corps of SS volunteers shared Hitler's ideology of barbarous racial imperialism, and they rarely wavered in their efforts to realize his goals.[16] Supported (or condoned) by military commanders and German policemen in the occupied territories, the SS corps pressed relentlessly to implement this program of destruction even before victory was secured. In western Poland, the SS arrested and evacuated Polish peasants to cleanse the region and create a "mass settlement space" for Germans. Polish workers and Soviet prisoners of war were transported to Germany, where conditions of slave labor were so harsh that four out of five Soviet prisoners did not survive the war.

Finally, the Nazi state condemned all European Jews to extermination, along with many Gypsies, Jehovah's Witnesses, and captured communists. After the fall of Warsaw, the Nazis stepped up their expulsion campaign and began deporting all German Jews to occupied Poland. There they and Jews from all over Europe were concentrated in ghettos, compelled to wear the Jewish star, and turned into slave laborers.

In 1941, as part of the "war of annihilation" in the Soviet Union, expulsion spiraled into extermination. On the Russian front, Himmler's special SS killing squads and also regular army units forced Soviet Jews to dig giant pits, which became mass graves as the victims were lined up on the edge and cut down by machine guns. Then in late 1941, Hitler and the Nazi leadership, in some still-debated combination, ordered the SS to stop all Jewish emigration from Europe and speeded up planning for mass murder. As one German diplomat put it, "The Jewish Question must be resolved in the course of the war, for only so can it be solved without a worldwide outcry."[17] The "final solution of the Jewish question"—the murder of every single Jew—had begun. Jews were systematically arrested, packed like cattle onto freight trains, and dispatched to extermination camps. Many Jews could hardly imagine the enormity of the crime that lay before them.

Arriving at their destination, small numbers of Jews were sent to nearby slave labor camps, where they were starved and systematically worked to death. (See the feature "Individuals in Society: Primo Levi.") But most of the victims were moved immediately to the death camps, where they were taken by force or deception to "shower rooms" that were actually gas chambers. These gas chambers, first perfected in the quiet, efficient execution of seventy thousand mentally ill Germans between 1938 and 1941, permitted rapid, hideous, and thoroughly bureaucratized mass murder. For fifteen to twenty minutes came the terrible screams and gasping sobs of men, women, and children choking to death on poison gas. Then, only silence. Special camp workers quickly yanked the victims' gold teeth from their jaws, and the bodies were then cremated or sometimes boiled for oil to make soap. At Auschwitz-Birkenau, the most infamous of the Nazi death factories, as

**Prelude to Murder** This photo captures the terrible inhumanity of Nazi racism. Frightened and bewildered families from the soon-to-be-destroyed Warsaw Ghetto are being forced out of their homes by German soldiers for deportation to concentration camps. There they face murder in the gas chambers. *(Hulton Archive/Getty Images)*

# Individuals in Society

## Primo Levi

Most Jews deported to Auschwitz were murdered as soon as they arrived, but the Nazis made some prisoners into slave laborers and a few of these survived. Primo Levi (1919–1987), an Italian Jew, became one of the most influential witnesses to the Holocaust and its death camps.

Like much of Italy's small Jewish community, Levi's family belonged to the urban professional classes. The young Primo graduated in 1941 from the University of Turin with highest honors in chemistry. But since 1938, when Italy introduced racial laws, he had faced growing discrimination, and two years after graduation he joined the antifascist resistance movement. Quickly captured, he was deported to Auschwitz with 650 Italian Jews in February 1944. Stone-faced SS men picked only ninety-six men and twenty-nine women to work in their respective labor camps. Primo was one of them.

Nothing prepared Levi for what he encountered. The Jewish prisoners were kicked, punched, stripped, branded with tattoos, crammed into huts, and worked unmercifully. Hoping for some sign of prisoner solidarity in this terrible environment, Levi found only a desperate struggle of each against all and enormous status differences among prisoners. Many stunned and bewildered newcomers, beaten and demoralized by their bosses—the most privileged prisoners—simply collapsed and died. Others struggled to secure their own privileges, however small, because food rations and working conditions were so abominable that ordinary Jewish prisoners perished in two to three months.

Sensitive and noncombative, Levi found himself sinking into oblivion. But instead of joining the mass of the "drowned," he became one of the "saved"—a complicated surprise with moral implications that he would ponder all his life. As Levi explained in *Survival in Auschwitz* (1947), the usual road to salvation in the camps was some kind of collaboration with German power.* Savage German criminals were released from prison to become brutal camp guards; non-Jewish political prisoners competed for jobs entitling them to better conditions, and, especially troubling for Levi, a small number of Jewish men plotted and struggled for the power of life and death over other Jewish prisoners. Though not one of these Jewish bosses, Levi believed that he himself, like almost all survivors, had entered the "gray zone" of moral compromise. Only a very few superior individuals, "the stuff of saints and martyrs," survived the death camps without shifting their moral stance.

*Primo Levi, who never stopped thinking, writing, and speaking about the Holocaust.* (Giansanti/Corbis Sygma)

For Levi, compromise and salvation came from his profession. Interviewed by a German technocrat for the camp's synthetic rubber program, Levi performed brilliantly in scientific German and savored his triumph as a Jew over Nazi racism. Work in the warm camp laboratory offered Levi opportunities to pilfer equipment that could then be traded for food and necessities with other prisoners. Levi also gained critical support from three saintly prisoners, who refused to do wicked and hateful acts. And he counted "luck" as essential for his survival: in the camp infirmary with scarlet fever in February 1945 as advancing Russian armies prepared to liberate the camp, Levi was not evacuated by the Nazis and shot to death like most Jewish prisoners.

After the war Primo Levi was forever haunted by the nightmare that the Holocaust would be ignored or forgotten. Always ashamed that so many people whom he considered better than himself had perished, he wrote and lectured tirelessly to preserve the memory of Jewish victims and guilty Nazis. Wanting the world to understand the Jewish genocide in all its complexity so that never again would people tolerate such atrocities, he grappled tirelessly with his vision of individual choice and moral compromise in a hell designed to make the victims collaborate and persecute each other.

### Questions for Analysis

1. Describe Levi's experience at Auschwitz. How did camp prisoners treat each other? Why?
2. What does Levi mean by the "gray zone"? How is this concept central to his thinking?
3. Will a vivid historical memory of the Holocaust help to prevent future genocide?

*Primo Levi, *Survival in Auschwitz: The Nazi Assault on Humanity,* rev. ed. 1958 (London: Collier Books, 1961), pp. 79–84, and *The Drowned and the Saved* (New York: Summit Books, 1988). These powerful testimonies are highly recommended.

*The* **history companion** *features additional information and activities related to this topic.*
**history.college.hmco.com/students**

many as twelve thousand human beings were slaughtered each day. The extermination of European Jews was the ultimate monstrosity of Nazi racism and racial imperialism. By 1945, 6 million Jews had been murdered.

Who was responsible for this terrible crime? An older generation of historians usually laid most of the guilt on Hitler and the Nazi leadership. Ordinary Germans had little knowledge of the extermination camps, it was argued, and those who cooperated had no alternative given the brutality of Nazi terror and totalitarian control. But in recent years, many studies have revealed a much broader participation of German people in the Holocaust and popular indifference (or worse) to the fate of the Jews. Yet exactly why so many perpetrated or condoned Nazi crimes has remained unclear.

In a controversial work, the American historian Daniel Goldhagen has reignited discussion of Nazi crimes by arguing that, above all, the extreme anti-Semitism of "ordinary Germans" led them to respond to Hitler and to become his "willing executioners" in World War II.[18] Yet in most occupied countries, local non-German officials also cooperated in the arrest and deportation of Jews to a large extent. As in Germany, only a few exceptional bystanders did not turn a blind eye. Thus some scholars have concluded that the key for most Germans (and most people in occupied countries) was that they felt no personal responsibility for Jews and therefore were not prepared to help them. This meant that many individuals, conditioned by Nazi racist propaganda but also influenced by peer pressure and brutalizing wartime violence, were psychologically prepared to join the SS ideologues and perpetrate ever-greater crimes. They were ready to plumb the depths of evil and to spiral downward from mistreatment to arrest to mass murder.

## The Grand Alliance

While the Nazis built their savage empire, the Allies faced the hard fact that chance, rather than choice, had brought them together. Stalin had been cooperating fully with Hitler between August 1939 and June 1941, and only the Japanese attack on Pearl Harbor in December 1941 and Hitler's immediate declaration of war had overwhelmed powerful isolationism in the United States. The Allies' first task was to overcome their mutual suspicions and build an unshakable alliance on the quicksand of accident. By means of three interrelated policies, they succeeded.

First, President Roosevelt accepted Churchill's contention that the United States should concentrate first on defeating Hitler. Only after victory in Europe was achieved would the United States turn toward the Pacific for an all-out attack on Japan, the lesser threat. The promise of huge military aid under America's policy of **Europe first** helped solidify the anti-Hitler coalition.

Second, within the European framework, the Americans and the British put immediate military needs first. They consistently postponed tough political questions relating to the eventual peace settlement and thereby avoided conflicts that might have split the alliance until after the war.

Third, to further encourage mutual trust, the Allies adopted the principle of the "unconditional surrender" of Germany and Japan. This policy cemented the Grand Alliance because it denied Hitler any hope of dividing his foes. It probably also discouraged Germans and Japanese who might have tried to overthrow their dictators in order to make a compromise peace. Of great importance for the postwar shape of Europe, it meant that Soviet and Anglo-American armies would almost certainly come together to divide all of Germany, and most of the continent, among the victorious allies.

The military resources of the Grand Alliance were awesome. The strengths of the United States were its mighty industry, its large population, and its national unity. Even before Pearl Harbor, President Roosevelt had called America the "arsenal of democracy" and given military aid to Britain and the Soviet Union. Now the United States geared up rapidly for all-out war production and drew heavily on a generally cooperative Latin America for resources. It not only equipped its own armies but also eventually gave its allies about $50 billion in arms and equipment. Britain received by far the most, but about one-fifth of the total went to the Soviet Union in the form of badly needed trucks, planes, and munitions.

Too strong to lose and too weak to win standing alone, Britain continued to make a great contribution as well. The British economy was totally and effectively mobilized, and the sharing of burdens through rationing and heavy taxes on war profits maintained social harmony. Moreover, by early 1943 the Americans and the British were combining small aircraft carriers with radar-guided bombers to rid the Atlantic of German submarines. Britain, the impregnable floating fortress, became a gigantic frontline staging area for the decisive blow to the heart of Germany.

As for the Soviet Union, so great was its strength that it might well have defeated Germany without Western help. In the face of the German advance, whole factories and populations were successfully evacuated to eastern Russia and Siberia. There war production was reorganized and expanded, and the Red Army was increasingly well supplied. The Red Army was also well led, for a new generation of talented military leaders quickly arose to replace those so recently purged. Most important of all, Stalin drew on the massive support and heroic determi-

**Raoul Auger: The Normandy Invasion** Airborne paratroopers landed behind German coastal fortifications around midnight, and American and British troops hit the beaches at daybreak as Allied ships and bombers provided cover. The heaviest fighting was at Omaha Beach, where American troops secured full control by nightfall at the cost of three thousand casualties. The Allies tricked the Germans into thinking the long-awaited invasion would come near the Belgian border, and Allied air power prevented the Germans from bringing up their reserves and counterattacking. *(Archives Charmet/The Bridgeman Art Library)*

nation of the Soviet people, especially those in the central Russian heartland. Broad-based Russian nationalism, as opposed to narrow communist ideology, became the powerful unifying force in what was appropriately called the "Great Patriotic War of the Fatherland."

Finally, the United States, Britain, and the Soviet Union were not alone. They had the resources of much of the world at their command. And, to a greater or lesser extent, they were aided by a growing resistance movement against the Nazis throughout Europe, even in Germany. Thus although Ukrainian peasants sometimes welcomed the Germans as liberators, the barbaric occupation policies of the Nazis quickly drove them to join and support behind-the-lines guerrilla forces. More generally, after the U.S.S.R. was invaded in June 1941, communists throughout Europe took the lead in the underground resistance, joined by a growing number of patriots and Christians. Anti-Nazi leaders from occupied countries established governments-in-exile in London, like that of the "Free French" under the intensely proud General Charles de Gaulle. These governments gathered valuable secret information from resistance fighters and even organized armies to help defeat Hitler.

## The Tide of Battle

Barely halted at the gates of Moscow and Leningrad in 1941, the Germans renewed their offensive against the Soviet Union in July 1942, driving toward the southern city of Stalingrad and occupying most of the city in a month of incredibly savage house-to-house fighting.

Then, in November 1942, Soviet armies counterattacked. They rolled over Romanian and Italian troops to the north and south of Stalingrad, quickly closing the trap and surrounding the entire German Sixth Army of 300,000 men. The surrounded Germans were systematically destroyed, until by the end of January 1943 only

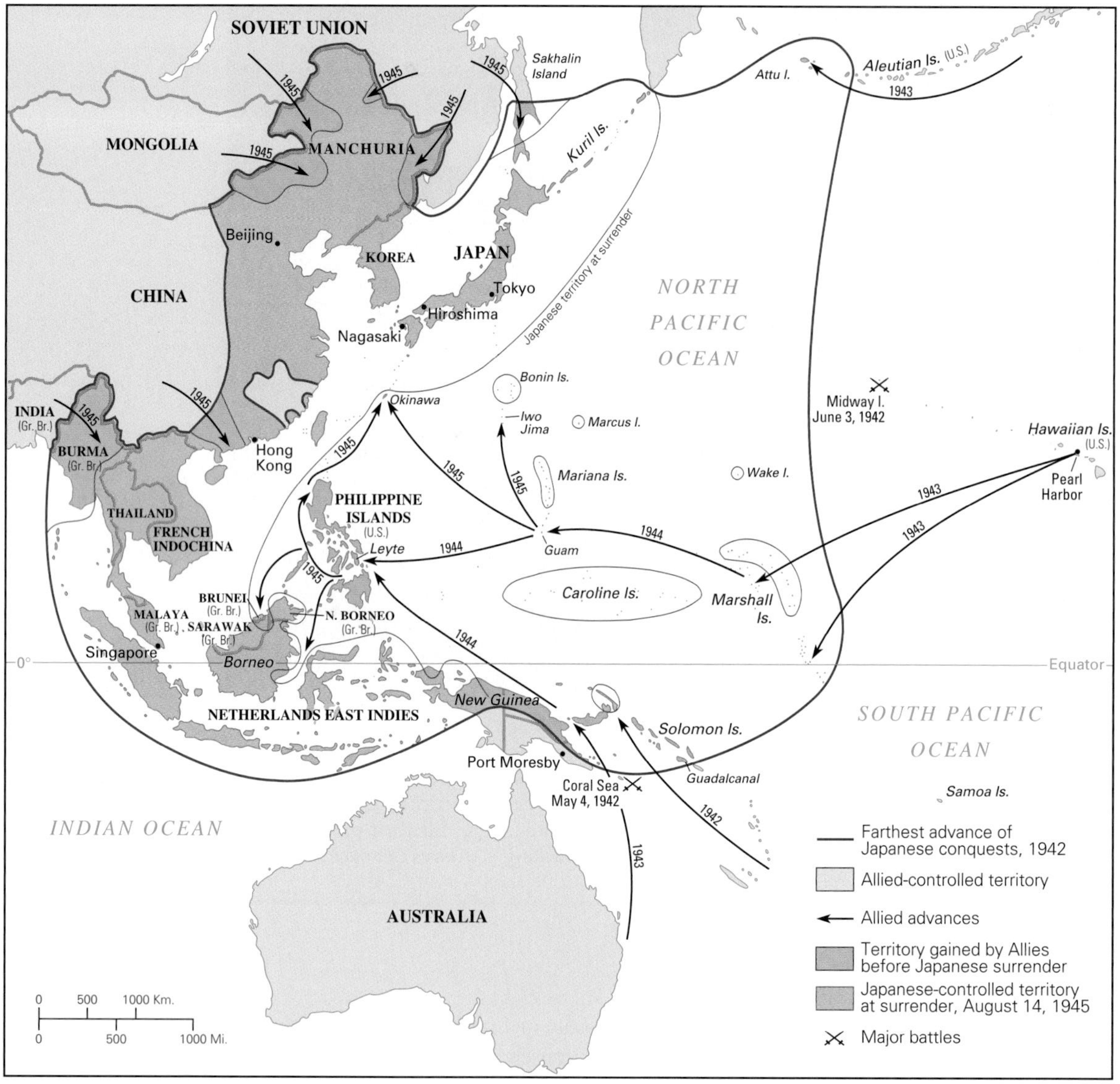


**MAP 29.3 World War II in the Pacific** Japanese forces overran an enormous amount of territory in 1942, which the Allies slowly recaptured in a long, bitter struggle. As this map shows, Japan still held a large Asian empire in August 1945, when the unprecedented devastation of atomic warfare suddenly forced it to surrender.

123,000 soldiers were left to surrender. Hitler, who had refused to allow a retreat, had suffered a catastrophic defeat. In the summer of 1943, the larger, better-equipped Soviet armies took the offensive and began moving forward (see Map 29.2).

In late 1942, the tide also turned in the Pacific and in North Africa. By late spring 1942, Japan had established a great empire in East Asia (see Map 29.3). Unlike the Nazis, the Japanese made clever appeals to local nationalists, who hated European imperial domination and preferred Japan's so-called Greater Asian Co-prosperity Sphere.

Then in the Battle of the Coral Sea in May 1942, Allied naval and air power stopped the Japanese advance and also relieved Australia from the threat of invasion. This victory was followed by the Battle of Midway Island, in which American pilots sank all four of the attacking Japanese aircraft carriers and established American naval superiority in the Pacific. In August 1942, American marines attacked Guadalcanal in the Solomon Islands. Badly hampered by the policy of "Europe first"—only 15 percent of Allied resources were going to fight the war in the Pacific in early 1943—the Americans and the Australians nevertheless began "island hopping" toward Japan. Japanese forces were on the defensive.

In North Africa the war had been seesawing back and forth since 1940 (see Map 29.2). In May 1942, combined German and Italian armies were finally defeated by British forces at the Battle of El Alamein, only seventy miles from Alexandria. In October the British counterattacked in Egypt, and almost immediately thereafter an Anglo-American force landed in Morocco and Algeria. These French possessions, which were under the control of Pétain's Vichy government, quickly went over to the side of the Allies.

Having driven the Axis powers from North Africa by the spring of 1943, Allied forces maintained the initiative by invading Sicily and then mainland Italy. Mussolini was deposed by a war-weary people, and the new Italian government publicly accepted unconditional surrender in September 1943. Italy, it seemed, was liberated. Yet German commandos rescued Mussolini in a daring raid and put him at the head of a puppet government. German armies seized Rome and all of northern Italy. Fighting continued in Italy.

Indeed, bitter fighting continued in Europe for almost two years. Germany, less fully mobilized for war than Britain in 1941, applied itself to total war in 1942 and enlisted millions of German women and millions of prisoners of war and slave laborers from all across occupied Europe in that effort. Between early 1942 and July 1944, German war production actually tripled. Although British and American bombing raids killed many German civilians, these raids were surprisingly ineffective from a military point of view. Also, German resistance against Hitler failed. After an unsuccessful attempt on Hitler's life in July 1944, SS fanatics brutally liquidated thousands of Germans. Terrorized at home and frightened by the prospect of unconditional surrender, the Germans fought on with suicidal stoicism.

On June 6, 1944, American and British forces under General Dwight Eisenhower landed on the beaches of Normandy, France, in history's greatest naval invasion. In a hundred dramatic days, more than 2 million men and almost half a million vehicles pushed inland and broke through German lines. Rejecting proposals to strike straight at Berlin in a massive attack, Eisenhower moved forward cautiously on a broad front. Not until March 1945 did American troops cross the Rhine and enter Germany.

**A Hiroshima Survivor Remembers** Yasuko Yamagata was seventeen when she saw the brilliant blue-white "lightning flash" that became a fiery orange ball consuming everything that would burn. Thirty years later Yamagata painted this scene, her most unforgettable memory of the atomic attack. An incinerated woman, poised as if running with her baby clutched to her breast, lies near a water tank piled high with charred corpses. *(From a public exhibition assembled by the Japan Broadcasting Corporation)*

The Soviets, who had been advancing steadily since July 1943, reached the outskirts of Warsaw by August 1944. For the next six months, they moved southward into Romania, Hungary, and Yugoslavia. In January 1945, the Red Army again moved westward through Poland, and on April 26 it met American forces on the Elbe River. The Allies had closed their vise on Nazi Germany and overrun Europe. As Soviet forces fought their way into Berlin, Hitler committed suicide in his bunker, and on May 7 the remaining German commanders capitulated.

Three months later, the United States dropped atomic bombs on Hiroshima and Nagasaki in Japan. Mass bombing of cities and civilians, one of the terrible new practices of World War II, had ended in the final nightmare—unprecedented human destruction in a single blinding flash. On August 14, 1945, the Japanese announced their surrender. The Second World War, which had claimed the lives of more than 50 million soldiers and civilians, was over.

## Summary

The Second World War marked the climax of the tremendous practical and spiritual maladies of the age of anxiety, which led in many lands to the rise of dictatorships. Many of these dictatorships were variations on conservative authoritarianism, but there was also a fateful innovation—a new kind of dictatorship that was dynamic and theoretically unlimited in its actions.

When apprehensive middle-class liberals in the West faced the rise of these new dictatorships, they often focused on their perceived similarities. Liberals fastened on the violent, profoundly antiliberal, and apparently totalitarian character of these brutal challengers, linking the one-party socialism of Lenin and Stalin with the one-party fascism of Mussolini and Hitler. In contrast, the political left often insisted on the differences between the revolutionary socialist tradition—triumphing, however imperfectly, in the Bolsheviks' Soviet Union—and the reactionary and capitalist nature of European fascist movements and fascist governments in Italy and Germany.

As the dramatic struggles of the 1930s and the Second World War (and early cold war) fall into a longer perspective and as more historians concentrate on the specific developments in each regime, Hitler's Nazism appears increasingly as a uniquely evil and nihilistic system. Nazism had fascist origins, but German fascism in power ultimately presented only superficial similarities with fascism in Italy. As for Hitler's Germany and Stalin's U.S.S.R., both asserted a total claim on the lives of their citizens, posed ambitious goals, and found enthusiastic supporters. This combination gave both dictatorships their awesome power and dynamism. That dynamism was, however, channeled in quite different directions. Stalin and the Communist party aimed at building their kind of socialism and a new socialist personality at home. Hitler and the Nazi elite aimed at unlimited territorial and racial aggression on behalf of a master race; domestic recovery was only a means to that end.

Nazi racism and unlimited aggression made war inevitable, first with the western European democracies, then with hated eastern neighbors, and finally with the United States. Plunging Europe into the ultimate nightmare, unlimited aggression unwittingly forged a mighty coalition that smashed the racist Nazi empire and its leader. In the words of the ancient Greeks, he whom the gods would destroy, they first make mad.

## Key Terms

totalitarianism
fascism
five-year plan
New Economic Policy (NEP)
collectivization
kulaks
Black Shirts
Lateran Agreement
Nazism
Führer
Enabling Act
appeasement
blitzkrieg
New Order
Europe first

## Notes


1. A. Gleason, *Totalitarianism: The Inner History of the World War* (New York: Oxford University Press, 1995), p. 50.
2. E. Halévy, *The Era of Tyrannies* (Garden City, N.Y.: Doubleday, 1965), pp. 265–316, esp. p. 300.
3. I. Kershaw, *The Nazi Dictatorship: Problems and Perspectives of Interpretation,* 2d ed. (London: Edward Arnold, 1989), p. 34.
4. Quoted in I. Deutscher, *Stalin: A Political Biography,* 2d ed. (New York: Oxford University Press, 1967), p. 325.
5. R. Conquest, *The Harvest of Sorrow: Soviet Collectivization and the Terror-Famine* (New York: Oxford University Press, 1986), pp. 4, 303.
6. Quoted in H. K. Geiger, *The Family in Soviet Russia* (Cambridge, Mass.: Harvard University Press, 1968), p. 156.
7. Quoted in B. Rosenthal, "Women in the Russian Revolution and After," in *Becoming Visible: Women in European History,* ed. R. Bridenthal and C. Koonz (Boston: Houghton Mifflin, 1976), p. 383.
8. M. Malia, *The Soviet Tragedy: A History of Socialism in Russia* (New York: Free Press, 1994), p. 248.
9. R. Thurston, *Life and Terror in Stalin's Russia, 1934–1941* (New Haven, Conn.: Yale University Press, 1996), esp. pp. 16–106; also Malia, *The Soviet Tragedy,* pp. 227–270.
10. R. Vivarelli, "Interpretations on the Origins of Fascism," *Journal of Modern History* 63 (March 1991): 41.
11. W. Brustein, *The Logic of Evil: The Social Origins of the Nazi Party, 1925–1933* (New Haven, Conn.: Yale University Press, 1996), pp. 52, 182.
12. Quoted in K. D. Bracher, *The German Dictatorship: The Origins, Structure and Effects of National Socialism* (New York: Praeger, 1970), pp. 146–147.
13. Quoted in R. Stromberg, *An Intellectual History of Modern Europe* (New York: Appleton-Century-Crofts, 1966), p. 393.
14. Quoted in Bracher, *The German Dictatorship,* p. 289.
15. Quoted ibid., p. 306.
16. R. Allen, *The Business of Genocide: The SS, Slave Labor, and the Concentration Camps* (Chapel Hill: University of North Carolina Press, 2002), pp. 270–285.
17. Quoted in M. Marrus, *The Holocaust in History* (Hanover, N.H.: University Press of New England, 1987), p. 28.
18. D. Goldhagen, *Hitler's Willing Executioners: Ordinary Germans and the Holocaust* (New York: Vintage Books, 1997).


## Suggested Reading

The historical literature on fascist and totalitarian dictatorships is rich and fascinating. Kershaw's work, cited in the Notes, provides an excellent survey of this literature, includes extensive bibliographical references, and is highly recommended. P. Brooker, *Twentieth-Century Dictatorships: The Ideological One-Party State* (1995), compares leading examples throughout the world, and Gleason, cited in the Notes, is an important recent study. H. Arendt, *The Origins of Totalitarianism* (1951), is a classic interpretation. F. L. Carsten, *The Rise of Fascism* (1982), and W. Laqueur, ed., *Fascism* (1976), are also recommended. Z. Sternhell, *Neither Right nor Left: Fascist Ideology in France* (1986), is important and stimulating, stressing the antiliberal and antisocialist origins of fascist thinking in France.

Malia's work, cited in the Notes, is a provocative reassessment of Soviet history and an excellent introduction to scholarly debates. It may be compared with the fine synthesis of M. Lewin, *The Making of the Soviet System* (1985). R. Stites, *The Women's Liberation Movement in Russia: Feminism, Nihilism, and Bolshevism, 1860–1930* (1978), and the works by Geiger and Deutscher, cited in the Notes, are highly recommended. R. Service, *Lenin: A Biography* (2002), is a major work using new sources. D. Volkogonov, *Autopsy for an Empire: The Seven Leaders Who Built the Soviet Union* (1998), is an engrossing collective biography by a leading Russian historian. R. Conquest, *The Great Terror: A Reassessment* (1990), is an excellent account of Stalin's purges of the 1930s, and A. Solzhenitsyn, *The Gulag Archipelago* (1964), passionately condemns Soviet police terror. Three important reconsiderations of Soviet purges, women, and urban life are Thurston's revisionist work, cited in the Notes; S. Fitzpatrick and Y. Slezkine, eds., *In the Shadow of Revolution: Life Stories of Russian Women from 1917 to the Second World War* (2000); and S. Kotkin, *Magnetic Mountain: Stalinism as Civilization* (1995). S. Marks, *How Russia Shaped the Modern World: From Art to Anti-Semitism, Ballet to Bolshevism* (2004), is an ambitious but clear history of Russian ideas and their impact in many fields. D. Ransel, *Village Mothers: Three Generations of Change in Russia and Tartaria* (2000), is a pathbreaking study based on oral histories made in the 1990s. Arthur Koestler, *Darkness at Noon* (1956), is a famous fictional account of Stalin's trials of the Old Bolsheviks. J. Scott, *Behind the Urals* (1973), is a remarkable eyewitness account of an American steelworker in the Soviet Union in the 1930s.

A. De Grand, *Italian Fascism: Its Origins and Development* (1989), and A. Lyttelton, *The Seizure of Power: Fascism in Italy, 1919–1929,* 2d ed. (1987), are excellent studies of Italy under Mussolini. D. Mack Smith, *Mussolini* (1982), is authoritative. Ignazio Silone, *Bread and Wine* (1937), is a moving novel by a famous opponent of dictatorship in Italy. E. Morante, *History* (1978), a fictional account of one family's divergent reactions to Mussolini's rule, is recommended. Two excellent books on Spain are H. Thomas, *The Spanish Civil War* (1977), and E. Malefakis, *Agrarian Reform and Peasant Revolution in Spain* (1970). R. Paxton, *Vichy France* (1973), tells a controversial story extremely well.

On Germany, F. Stern, *The Politics of Cultural Despair* (1963), and W. Smith, *The Ideological Origins of Nazi Imperialism* (1986), are fine complementary studies on the origins of Nazism. M. Burleigh, *The Third Reich: A New History* (2000), is a splendid accomplishment that includes a refurbishing of the concept of totalitarianism. Two major studies by influential German historians are M. Brozat, *The Nazi State* (1981), and H. Mommsen, *From Weimar to Auschwitz* (1991). W. Shirer, *The Rise and Fall of the Third Reich* (1960), is a famous popular account of an American journalist who experienced Nazi Germany firsthand. A. Bullock, *Hitler and Stalin* (1993), is a fascinating comparison by a master biographer, while I. Kershaw, *The "Hitler Myth": Image and Reality in the Third Reich* (1987), is a provocative reassessment of Hitler's power. R. Gellately, *Backing Hitler: Consent and Coercion* (2001), is a major reexamination by a leading historian, and M. Mayer, *They Thought They Were Free* (1955), probes the minds of ten ordinary Nazis who supported Hitler. R. Allen, cited in the Notes, is outstanding scholarship, showing how Nazi ideology united the SS engineers who ran the slave labor camps. C. Koonz, *Mothers in the Fatherland: Women, the Family, and Nazi Politics* (1987), and D. Peukert, *Inside Nazi Germany: Conformity, Opposition, and Racism in Everyday Life* (1987), are pioneering forays into the social history of the Nazi era. Moving accounts of the Holocaust include Y. Bauer, *A History of the Holocaust* (1982); C. Browning, *The Origins of the Final Solution: The Evolution of Nazi Jewish Policy, September 1939–March 1942* (2004), a definitive work drawing on the latest research; and R. Hilberg, *The Destruction of the European Jews, 1933–1945,* 3 vols., rev. ed. (1985), a monumental scholarly achievement. M. Marrus, *The Holocaust in History* (1987), is an excellent interpretive survey, and I. Clendinnen, *Reading the Holocaust* (1999), is an imaginative reconsideration of victims and perpetrators. Goldhagen's widely debated study, cited in the Notes, may be compared with C. Browning, *Ordinary Men: Reserve Police Battalion 101 and the Final Solution in Poland,* 2d ed. (2001). E. Staub, *The Roots of Evil: The Origins of Genocide and Other Group Violence* (1989), is a profound study by a noted psychologist with a gift for history. Especially recommended are E. Weisel, *Night* (1961), a brief and compelling autobiographical account of a young Jew in a Nazi concentration camp, and A. Frank, *The Diary of Anne Frank,* a remarkable personal account of a Jewish girl in hiding during the Nazi occupation of Holland. R. Gellately and N. Stolzfus, eds., *Social Outsiders in Nazi Germany* (2001), studies other groups that were oppressed in addition to the Jews, and A. Fraser, *The Gypsies* (1992), considers a misunderstood people decimated by Nazi terror.

J. Campbell, *The Experience of World War II* (1989), is attractively illustrated and captures the drama of global conflict, as does G. Keegan, *The Second World War* (1990). G. Wright, *The Ordeal of Total War, 1939–1945* (1990), and C. Emsley, *World War II and Its Consequences* (1990), are also recommended. G. Weinberg, *World at Arms: A Global History of World War II* (1994), is a masterful interconnected overview. Two dramatic studies of special aspects of the war are A. Dallin, *German Rule in Russia, 1941–1945* (1981), which analyzes the effects of Nazi occupation policies on the Soviet population, and L. Collins and D. La Pierre, *Is Paris Burning?* (1965), a best-selling account of the liberation of Paris and Hitler's plans to destroy the city.

# Listening to the Past

## Stalin Justifies the Five-Year Plan

*On February 4, 1931, Joseph Stalin delivered the following address, entitled "No Slowdown in Tempo!," to the First Conference of Soviet Industrial Managers. Published the following day in* Pravda, *the newspaper of the Communist party, and widely publicized at home and abroad, Stalin's speech reaffirmed the leader's commitment to the breakneck pace of industrialization and collectivization set forth in the first five-year plan. Arguing that more sacrifices were necessary, Stalin sought to rally the people and generate support for the party's program. His address captures the spirit of Soviet public discourse in the early 1930s.*

*Stalin's concluding idea, that Bolsheviks needed to master technology and industrial management, reflected another major development. The Soviet Union was training a new class of communist engineers and technicians, who were beginning to replace foreign engineers and "bourgeois specialists," Russian engineers trained in tsarist times who were grudgingly tolerated after the revolution.*

It is sometimes asked whether it is not possible to slow down the tempo somewhat, to put a check on the movement. No, comrades, it is not possible! The tempo must not be reduced! On the contrary, we must increase it as much as is within our powers and possibilities. This is dictated to us by our obligations to the workers and peasants of the U.S.S.R. This is dictated to us by our obligations to the working class of the whole world.

To slacken the tempo would mean falling behind. And those who fall behind get beaten. But we do not want to be beaten. No, we refuse to be beaten! One feature of the history of old Russia was the continual beatings she suffered because of her backwardness. She was beaten by the Mongol khans, . . . the Turkish beys, . . . and the Japanese barons. All beat her—because of her backwardness, cultural backwardness, political backwardness, industrial backwardness, agricultural backwardness. They beat her because to do so was profitable and could be done with impunity. . . . Such is the law of the exploiters—to beat the backward and the weak. It is the jungle law of capitalism. You are backward, you are weak—therefore you are wrong; hence you can be beaten and enslaved. You are mighty—therefore you are right; hence we must be wary of you.

That is why we must no longer lag behind.

In the past we had no fatherland, nor could we have had one. But now that we have overthrown capitalism and power is in our hands, in the hands of the people, we have a fatherland, and we will uphold its independence. Do you want our socialist fatherland to be beaten and to lose its independence? If you do not want this, you must put an end to its backwardness in the shortest possible time and develop a genuine Bolshevik tempo in building up its socialist economy. There is no other way. That is why Lenin said on the eve of the October Revolution: "Either perish, or overtake and outstrip the advanced capitalist countries."

We are fifty or a hundred years behind the advanced countries. We must make good this distance in ten years. Either we do it, or we shall go under.

That is what our obligations to the workers and peasants of the U.S.S.R. dictate to us.

But we have yet other, more serious and more important, obligations. They are our obligations to the world proletariat. . . . We achieved victory not solely through the efforts of the working class of the U.S.S.R., but also thanks to the support of the working class of the world. Without this support we would have been torn to pieces long ago. . . . Why does the international proletariat support us? How did we merit this support? By the fact that we were the first to hurl ourselves into the battle against capitalism, we were the first to establish working-class state power, we were the first to begin building socialism. By the fact that we are engaged on a cause which, if successful, will transform the whole world and free the entire working class. But what is needed for success? The elimination of our backwardness, the development of a high Bolshevik tempo of construction. We must march forward in such a way that the working class of the whole world, looking at us, may say: There you have my advanced detachment, my shock brigade, my working-class state power, my fatherland; they are engaged on their cause, *our* cause, and they are working well; let us support them against the capitalists and promote the cause of the world revolution. Must we not justify the hopes of the world's working class, must we not fulfill our obligations to them? Yes, we must if we do not want to utterly disgrace ourselves.

Such are our obligations, internal and international.

As you see, they dictate to us a Bolshevik tempo of development.

I will not say that we have accomplished nothing in regard to management of production during these years. In fact, we have accomplished a good deal. . . . But we could have accomplished still more if we had tried during this period really to master production, the technique of production, the financial and economic side of it.

In ten years at most we must make good the distance that separates us from the advanced capitalist countries. We have all the "objective" possibilities for this. The only thing lacking is the ability to make proper use of these possibilities. And that depends on us. *Only* on us! . . . If you are a factory manager—interfere in all the affairs of the factory, look into everything, let nothing escape you, learn and learn again. Bolsheviks must master technique. It is time Bolsheviks themselves became experts. . . .

It is said that it is hard to master technique. That is not true! There are no fortresses that Bolsheviks cannot capture. We have solved a number of most difficult problems. We have overthrown capitalism. We have assumed power. We have built up a huge socialist industry. We have transferred the middle peasants on the path of socialism. We have already accomplished what is most important from the point of view of construction. What remains to be done is not so much: to study technique, to master science. And when we have done that we shall develop a tempo of which we dare not even dream at present.

And we shall do it if we really want to.

"Our program is realistic," Stalin proclaims on this poster, "because it is you and me working together." *(David King Collection)*

## Questions for Analysis

1. What reasons does Stalin give to justify an unrelenting "Bolshevik" tempo of industrial and social change? In the light of history, which reason seems most convincing? Why?
2. Imagine that the year is 1931 and you are a Soviet student reading Stalin's speech. Would Stalin's determination inspire you, frighten you, or leave you cold? Why?
3. Some historians argue that Soviet socialism was a kind of utopianism—that zealots believed that the economy, the society, and even human beings could be completely remade and perfected. What utopian elements do you see in Stalin's declaration?

*Source:* Joseph Stalin, "No Slowdown in Tempo!," *Pravda,* February 5, 1931.

The youth revolution. London, ca 1980.
*(Wellcome Photo Library/Anthea Seiveking)*

chapter

# 30 Cold War Conflicts and Social Transformations, 1945–1985

## chapter outline

- The Division of Europe
- The Western Renaissance, 1945–1968
- Soviet Eastern Europe, 1945–1968
- Postwar Social Transformations, 1945–1968
- Conflict and Challenge in the Late Cold War, 1968–1985

The total defeat of the Nazis and their allies in 1945 laid the basis for one of Western civilization's most remarkable recoveries. A battered western Europe dug itself out from under the rubble and fashioned a great renaissance, building strong democracies, vibrant economies, and new societies. The United States also made solid progress, and the Soviet Union became more humane and less dictatorial. Yet there was also a tragic setback. The Grand Alliance against Hitler gave way to an apparently endless cold war in which tension between East and West threatened world peace.

In the late 1960s and early 1970s, the postwar Western renaissance came to an end. First, as cold war competition again turned very hot in Vietnam, postwar certainties such as domestic political stability and social harmony evaporated, and several countries experienced major crises. Second, the astonishing postwar economic advance came to a halt, and this had serious social consequences. Third, new roles for women after World War II led to a powerful "second wave" of feminist thought and action in the 1970s, resulting in major changes for women and gender relations. Thus the long cold war created an underlying unity for the years 1945–1985, but the first half of the cold war era was quite different from the second.

- What were the causes of the cold war?
- How and why, in spite of the cold war, did western Europe recover so successfully from the ravages of war and Nazism?
- To what extent did communist eastern Europe and the United States also experience such a recovery?
- How did political crisis strike many countries from the late 1960s on?
- Why, after a generation, did the economy shift into reverse gear, and what were some of the social consequences of the reversal?
- How did women's lives change and promote a revitalized women's movement?

These are the questions this chapter will seek to answer.

## The Division of Europe

In 1945 triumphant American and Russian soldiers came together and embraced on the banks of the Elbe River in the heart of vanquished Germany. At home, in the United States and in the Soviet Union, the soldiers' loved ones erupted in joyous celebration. Yet victory was flawed. The Allies could not cooperate politically in peacemaking. Motivated by different goals and hounded by misunderstandings, the United States and the Soviet Union soon found themselves at loggerheads. By the end of 1947, Europe was rigidly divided. It was West versus East in a cold war that was waged around the world for forty years.

### The Origins of the Cold War

The most powerful allies in the wartime coalition—the Soviet Union and the United States—began to quarrel almost as soon as the unifying threat of Nazi Germany disappeared. A tragic disappointment for millions of people, the hostility between the Eastern and Western superpowers was the sad but logical outgrowth of military developments, wartime agreements, and long-standing political and ideological differences.

In the early phases of the Second World War, the Americans and the British made military victory their highest priority. They consistently avoided discussion of Stalin's war aims and the shape of the eventual peace settlement. Stalin received only a military alliance and no postwar commitments. Yet the United States and Britain did not try to take advantage of the Soviet Union's precarious position in 1942, because they feared that hard bargaining would encourage Stalin to consider making a separate peace with Hitler. They focused instead on the policy of unconditional surrender to solidify the alliance.

By late 1943, discussion about the shape of the postwar world could no longer be postponed. The conference that Stalin, Roosevelt, and Churchill held in the Iranian capital of Teheran in November 1943 thus proved of crucial importance in determining subsequent events. There, the **Big Three** jovially reaffirmed their determination to crush Germany and searched for the appropriate military strategy. Churchill, fearful of the military dangers of a direct attack, argued that American and British forces should follow up their Italian campaign with an

**The Big Three** In 1945 a triumphant Winston Churchill, an ailing Franklin Roosevelt, and a determined Joseph Stalin met at Yalta in southern Russia to plan for peace. Cooperation soon gave way to bitter hostility. *(F.D.R. Library)*

1945 | 1955 | 1965 | 1975 | 1985

**POLITICAL/MILITARY**

- 1945–1960s Decolonization of Asia and Africa
- 1947 Truman Doctrine
- 1949 Formation of NATO
- 1950–1953 Korean War
- 1953–1964 De-Stalinization of Soviet Union
- 1961 Building of Berlin Wall
- 1962 Cuban missile crisis
- 1964–1973 U.S. involvement in Vietnam War
- 1968 Soviet invasion of Czechoslovakia
- 1972 Watergate break-in
- 1979 Margaret Thatcher becomes British prime minister

**SOCIAL/ECONOMIC**

- 1947 Marshall Plan
- 1957 Formation of Common Market
- 1964 Civil Rights Act in the U.S.
- 1966 Formation of National Organization for Women (NOW)
- 1968 Student protests in Paris
- 1973 OPEC oil embargo

**INTELLECTUAL/RELIGIOUS**

- 1945–1962 U.S. takes lead in Big Science
- 1949 Beauvoir, *The Second Sex*
- 1949 Stalin launches verbal attack on Soviet Jews
- 1956 Pasternak, *Doctor Zhivago*
- 1962 Solzhenitsyn, *One Day in the Life of Ivan Denisovich*
- 1969 First Apollo moon landing

indirect attack on Germany through the Balkans. Roosevelt, however, agreed with Stalin that an American-British frontal assault through France would be better. This agreement was part of Roosevelt's general effort to meet Stalin's wartime demands whenever possible, and it had momentous political implications. It meant that the Soviet and the American-British armies would come together in defeated Germany along a north-south line and that only Soviet troops would liberate eastern Europe. Thus the basic shape of postwar Europe was emerging even as the fighting continued.

When the Big Three met again in February 1945 at Yalta on the Black Sea in southern Russia, advancing Soviet armies were within a hundred miles of Berlin. The Red Army had occupied not only Poland but also Bulgaria, Romania, Hungary, part of Yugoslavia, and much of Czechoslovakia. The temporarily stalled American-British forces had yet to cross the Rhine into Germany. Moreover, the United States was far from defeating Japan. In short, the Soviet Union's position was strong and America's weak.

There was little the increasingly sick and apprehensive Roosevelt could do but double his bet on Stalin's peaceful intentions. It was agreed at Yalta that Germany would be divided into zones of occupation and would pay heavy reparations to the Soviet Union. At American insistence, Stalin agreed to declare war on Japan after Germany was defeated. As for Poland and eastern Europe—"that Pandora's Box of infinite troubles," according to American secretary of state Cordell Hull—the Big Three struggled to reach an ambiguous compromise at Yalta: eastern European governments were to be freely elected but pro-Russian. As Churchill put it at the time, "The Poles will have their future in their own hands, with the single limitation that they must honestly follow in harmony with their allies, a policy friendly to Russia."[1]

The Yalta compromise over eastern Europe broke down almost immediately. Even before the Yalta Conference, Bulgaria and Poland were controlled by communists who arrived home with the Red Army. Elsewhere in eastern Europe, pro-Soviet "coalition" governments of several parties were formed, but the key ministerial posts were reserved for Moscow-trained communists.

At the postwar Potsdam Conference of July 1945, the long-avoided differences over eastern Europe finally surged to the fore. The compromising Roosevelt had died and been succeeded by the more determined President Harry Truman, who demanded immediate free elections throughout eastern Europe. Stalin refused point-blank. "A freely elected government in any of these East European countries would be anti-Soviet," he admitted simply, "and that we cannot allow."[2]

Here, then, is the key to the much-debated origins of the cold war. American ideals, pumped up by the crusade against Hitler, and American politics, heavily influenced by millions of voters from eastern Europe, demanded free elections in Soviet-occupied eastern Europe. Stalin, who had lived through two enormously destructive German invasions, wanted absolute military security from Germany and its potential Eastern allies. Suspicious by nature, he believed that only communist states could be truly dependable allies, and he realized that free elections would result in independent and possibly hostile governments on his western border. Moreover, by the middle of 1945, there was no way short of war that the United States could determine political developments in eastern Europe, and war was out of the question. Stalin was bound to have his way.

### West Versus East

The American response to Stalin's exaggerated conception of security was to "get tough." In May 1945, Truman abruptly cut off all aid to the U.S.S.R. In October he declared that the United States would never recognize any government established by force against the free will of its people. In March 1946, former British prime minister Churchill ominously informed an American audience that an "iron curtain" had fallen across the continent, dividing Germany and all of Europe into two antagonistic camps. Emotional, moralistic denunciations of Stalin and communist Russia emerged as part of American political life. Yet the United States also responded to the popular desire to "bring the boys home" and demobilized its troops with great speed. Some historians have argued that American leaders believed that the atomic bomb gave the United States all the power it needed, but "getting tough" really meant "talking tough."

Stalin's agents quickly reheated what they viewed as the "ideological struggle against capitalist imperialism." The large, well-organized Communist parties of France and Italy obediently started to uncover "American plots" to take over Europe and challenged their own governments with violent criticisms and large strikes. The Soviet Union also put pressure on Iran, Turkey, and Greece, while a bitter civil war raged in China. By the spring of 1947, it appeared to many Americans that Stalin was determined to export communism by subversion throughout Europe and around the world.

The United States responded to this challenge with the Truman Doctrine, which was aimed at "containing" communism to areas already occupied by the Red Army. Truman told Congress in March 1947, "I believe it must be the policy of the United States to support free people who are resisting attempted subjugation by armed minorities or by outside pressure." To begin, Truman asked Congress for military aid to Greece and Turkey, countries that Britain, weakened by war and financially overextended, could no longer protect. Then, in June, Secretary of State George C. Marshall offered Europe economic aid—the **Marshall Plan**—to help it rebuild.

Stalin refused Marshall Plan assistance for all of eastern Europe. He purged the last remaining noncommunist elements from the coalition governments of eastern Europe and established Soviet-style, one-party communist dictatorships. The seizure of power in Czechoslovakia in February 1948 was particularly antidemocratic, and it greatly strengthened Western fears of limitless communist expansion. Thus, when Stalin blocked all traffic through the Soviet zone of Germany to Berlin, the former capital, which the occupying powers had also divided into sectors at the end of the war, the Western allies acted firmly but not provocatively. Hundreds of planes began flying over the Soviet roadblocks around the clock, supplying provisions to the people of West Berlin and thwarting Soviet efforts to swallow up the West Berliners. After 324 days, the Soviets backed down: containment seemed to work. In 1949, therefore, the United States formed an anti-Soviet military alliance of Western governments: the North Atlantic Treaty Organization (**NATO**). Stalin countered by tightening his hold on his satellites, later united in the Warsaw Pact. Europe was divided into two hostile blocs.

In late 1949, the communists triumphed in China, frightening and angering many Americans, who saw new evidence of a powerful worldwide communist conspiracy. When the Russian-backed communist army of North Korea invaded South Korea in 1950, President Tru-

**The Berlin Airlift** Standing in the rubble of their bombed-out city, a German crowd in the American sector awaits the arrival of a U.S. transport plane flying in over the Soviet blockade in 1948. The crisis over Berlin was a dramatic indication of growing tensions among the Allies, which resulted in the division of Europe into two hostile camps. *(Time Life Pictures/Getty Images)*

man acted swiftly. American-led United Nations forces under General Douglas MacArthur intervened. Initially, the North Koreans almost conquered the entire peninsula, but the South Koreans and the Americans rallied and advanced until China suddenly entered the war. The bitter, bloody contest then seesawed back and forth near where it had begun, as President Truman rejected General MacArthur's call to attack China and fired him instead. In 1953 a fragile truce was negotiated, and the fighting stopped. Thus the United States extended its policy of containment to Asia but drew back from an attack on communist China and possible nuclear war.

The rapid descent from victorious Grand Alliance to bitter **cold war** was directly connected to the tragic fate of eastern Europe. After 1933, when the eastern European power vacuum invited Nazi racist imperialism, the appeasing Western democracies mistakenly did nothing. They did, however, have one telling insight: how, they asked themselves, could they unite with Stalin to stop Hitler without giving Stalin great gains on his western borders? After Hitler's invasion of the Soviet Union, the Western powers preferred to ignore this question and hope for the best. But when Stalin later began to claim the spoils of victory, the United States began to protest and professed outrage. This belated opposition quite possibly encouraged even more aggressive measures by the always-suspicious Stalin, and it helped explode the quarrel over eastern Europe into a global confrontation. Thus the Soviet-American confrontation became institutionalized and formed the bedrock of the long cold war era, which lasted until the mid-1980s despite intermittent periods of relaxation.

## The Western Renaissance, 1945–1968

As the cold war divided Europe into two blocs, the future appeared bleak on both sides of the iron curtain. European economic conditions were the worst in generations, and Europe was weak and divided, a battleground for cold war ambitions. Moreover, western European empires were crumbling in the face of nationalism in Asia and Africa. Yet Europe recovered, and the nations of western

**MAP 30.1 The Results of World War II in Europe** Millions of refugees fled westward because of war and territorial changes. The Soviet Union and Poland took land from Germany, which the Allies partitioned into occupation zones. Those zones subsequently formed the basis of the East and West German states, as the iron curtain fell to divide both Germany and Europe. Austria was detached from Germany, but the Soviets subsequently permitted Austria to reunify as a neutral state.

Europe led the way. In less than a generation, western Europe achieved unprecedented economic prosperity and peaceful social transformation, while the United States boomed and eventually experienced a wholesome social revolution. It was an amazing rebirth—a true renaissance.

## The Postwar Challenge

After the war, economic conditions in western Europe were terrible. Runaway inflation and black markets testified to severe shortages and hardships. Many people believed that Europe was quite simply finished.

Suffering was most intense in defeated Germany. The major territorial change of the war had moved the Soviet Union's border far to the west. Poland was in turn compensated for this loss to the Soviets with land taken from Germany (see Map 30.1). To solidify these changes in boundaries, 13 million Germans were driven from their homes and forced to resettle in a greatly reduced Germany. The Russians were also seizing factories and equipment as reparations in their zone, even tearing up railroad tracks and sending the rails to the Soviet Union.

In 1945 and 1946, conditions were not much better in the Western zones, for the Western allies also treated the German population with severity at first. Countless Germans sold prized possessions to American soldiers to buy food. By the spring of 1947, refugee-clogged, hungry, prostrate Germany was on the verge of total collapse and threatening to drag down the rest of Europe. Yet western Europe was not finished. The Nazi occupation and the war had discredited old ideas and old leaders. All over Europe, many people were willing to change and experiment, and new groups and new leaders were coming to the fore to guide these aspirations. Progressive Catholics and revitalized Catholic political parties—the **Christian Democrats**—were particularly influential.

In Italy the Christian Democrats emerged as the leading party in the first postwar elections in 1946, and in early 1948 they won an absolute majority in the parliament in a landslide victory. Their very able leader was Alcide De Gasperi, a courageous antifascist firmly committed to political democracy, economic reconstruction, and moderate social reform. In France, too, the Catholic party also provided some of the best postwar leaders after January 1946, when General Charles de Gaulle, the inspiring wartime leader of the Free French, resigned after having re-established the free and democratic Fourth Republic. As Germany was partitioned by the cold war, a purified Federal Republic of Germany (as West Germany was officially known) found new and able leadership among its Catholics. In 1949 Konrad Adenauer, the former mayor of Cologne and a long-time anti-Nazi, began his long, highly successful democratic rule; the Christian Democrats became West Germany's majority party for a generation. In providing effective leadership for their respective countries, the Christian Democrats were inspired and united by a common Christian and European heritage. They steadfastly rejected authoritarianism and narrow nationalism and placed their faith in democracy and cooperation.

The socialists and the communists, active in the resistance against Hitler, also emerged from the war with increased power and prestige, especially in France and Italy. They, too, provided fresh leadership and pushed for social change and economic reform. In the immediate postwar years, welfare measures such as family allowances, health insurance, and increased public housing were enacted throughout continental Europe. Britain followed the same trend, as the newly elected socialist Labour party established a "welfare state." Many British industries were nationalized, and the government provided free medical service. Thus all across Europe, social reform complemented political transformation, creating solid foundations for a great European renaissance.

The United States also supplied strong and creative leadership, providing western Europe with both massive economic aid and ongoing military protection. Economic aid was channeled through the Marshall Plan, and military security was provided through NATO, which featured American troops stationed permanently in Europe and the American nuclear umbrella. Thus the United States assumed the international responsibilities it had shunned after 1919.

As Marshall Plan aid poured in, the battered economies of western Europe began to turn the corner in 1948. The outbreak of the Korean War in 1950 further stimulated economic activity, and Europe entered a period of rapid economic progress that lasted into the late 1960s. Never before had the European economy grown so fast. There were many reasons for western Europe's brilliant economic performance. American aid helped the process get off to a fast start. Moreover, economic growth became a basic objective of all western European governments, for leaders and voters were determined to avoid a return to the dangerous and demoralizing stagnation of the 1930s. Thus governments generally accepted Keynesian economics (see pages 937 and 944) and sought to stimulate their economies. They also adopted a variety of imaginative and successful strategies.

In postwar West Germany, Minister of Economy Ludwig Erhard, a roly-poly, cigar-smoking former professor, broke decisively with the straitjacketed Nazi economy.

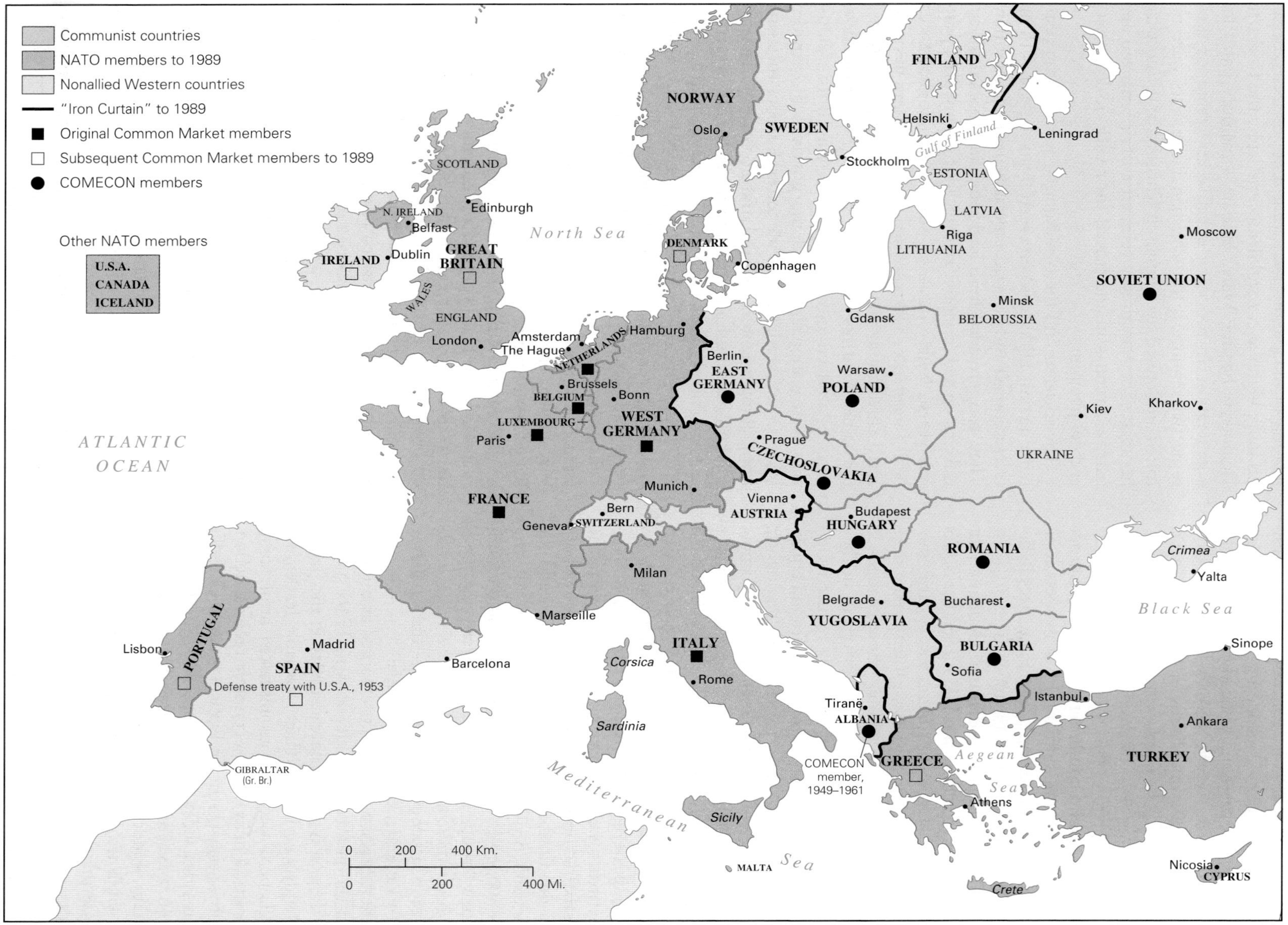


**MAP 30.2 European Alliance Systems, 1949–1989** After the cold war divided Europe into two hostile military alliances, six western European countries formed the Common Market in 1957. The Common Market grew later to include most of western Europe. The communist states organized their own economic association—COMECON.

Erhard bet on the free-market economy while maintaining the extensive social welfare network inherited from the Hitler era. He and his teachers believed not only that capitalism was more efficient but also that political and social freedom could thrive only if there were real economic freedom. Erhard's first step was to reform the currency and abolish rationing and price controls in 1948. He boldly declared, "The only ration coupon is the Mark."[3] West Germany's success renewed respect for free-market capitalism.

The French innovation was a new kind of planning. Under the guidance of Jean Monnet, an economic pragmatist and apostle of European unity, a planning commission set ambitious but flexible goals for the French economy and used the nationalized banks to funnel money into key industries. Thus France combined flexible planning and a "mixed" state and private economy to achieve the most rapid economic development in its long history.

In most countries, there were many people ready to work hard for low wages and the hope of a better future. Moreover, although many consumer products had been invented or perfected since the late 1920s, few Europeans had been able to buy them. In 1945 the electric refrigerator, the washing machine, and the automobile were rare luxuries. There was a great potential demand, which the economic system moved to satisfy. Finally, western European nations abandoned protectionism and gradually created a large unified market known as the "Common Market." This historic action, which certainly stimulated the economy, was part of a larger search for European unity.

## Toward European Unity

Western Europe's political recovery was spectacular in the generation after 1945. Republics were re-established in France, West Germany, and Italy. Constitutional monarchs were restored in Belgium, Holland, and Norway. Democratic governments, often within the framework of multiparty politics and shifting parliamentary coalitions, took root again and thrived. National self-determination was accompanied by civil liberties and individual freedom.

A similarly extraordinary achievement was the march toward a united Europe. The Christian Democrats, with their shared Catholic heritage, were particularly committed to "building Europe," and other groups shared their dedication. Many Europeans believed that only unity in a new "European nation" could reassert western Europe's influence in world affairs.

The close cooperation among European states required by the Americans for Marshall Plan aid led to the creation of both the Organization of European Economic Cooperation (OEEC) and the Council of Europe in 1948. European federalists hoped that the Council of Europe would quickly evolve into a true European parliament with sovereign rights, but this did not happen. Britain, with its empire and its "special relationship" with the United States, consistently opposed giving any real political power—any sovereignty—to the council. Many continental nationalists and communists felt similarly.

Frustrated in the direct political approach, European federalists turned toward economics as a way of working toward genuine unity. Two far-seeing French statesmen, the planner Jean Monnet and Foreign Minister Robert Schuman, took the lead in 1950 and called for a special international organization to control and integrate all European steel and coal production. West Germany, Italy, Belgium, the Netherlands, and Luxembourg accepted the French idea in 1952; the British would have none of it. The immediate economic goal—a single steel and coal market without national tariffs or quotas—was rapidly realized. The more far-reaching political goal was to bind the six member nations so closely together economically that war among them would eventually become unthinkable and virtually impossible.

In 1957 the six nations of the Coal and Steel Community signed the Treaty of Rome, which created the European Economic Community, generally known as the **Common Market** (see Map 30.2). The first goal of the treaty was a gradual reduction of all tariffs among the six in order to create a single market almost as large as that of the United States. Other goals included the free movement of capital and labor and common economic policies and institutions. The Common Market was a great success, encouraging companies and regions to specialize in what they did best.

The development of the Common Market fired imaginations and encouraged hopes of rapid progress toward political as well as economic union. In the 1960s, however, these hopes were frustrated by a resurgence of more traditional nationalism. France took the lead. Mired in a bitter colonial war in Algeria, the French turned in 1958 to General de Gaulle, who established the Fifth Republic and ruled as its president until 1969. De Gaulle was at heart a romantic nationalist, and he viewed the United States as the main threat to genuine French (and European) independence. He withdrew all French military forces from the "American-controlled" NATO, developed France's own nuclear weapons, and vetoed the scheduled advent of majority rule within the Common Market. Thus throughout the 1960s, the Common Market thrived economically but remained a union of sovereign states.

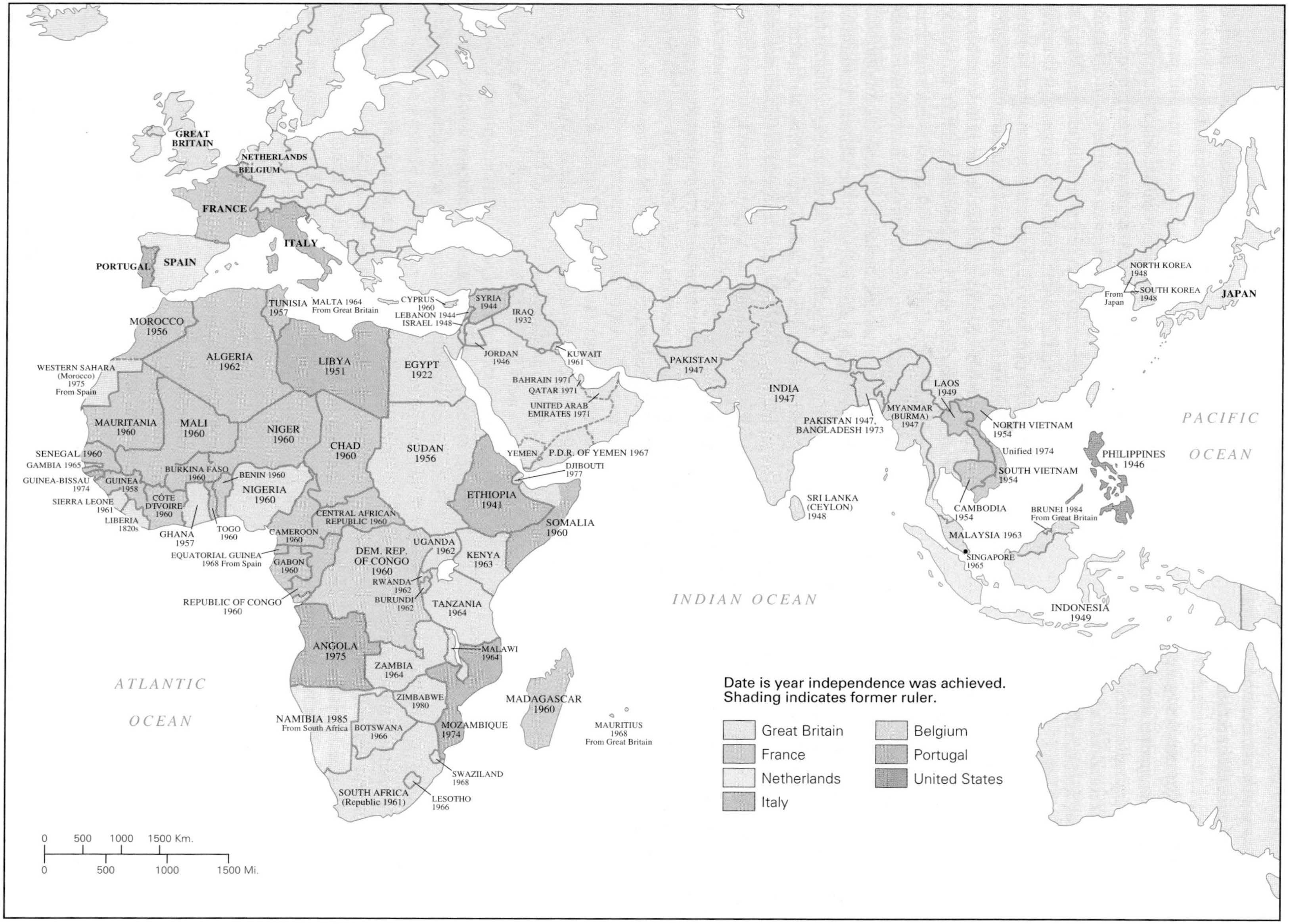


**MAP 30.3 The New States in Africa and Asia** Divided primarily along religious lines into two states, British India led the way to political independence in 1947. Most African territories achieved statehood by the mid-1960s, as European empires passed away, unlamented.

**Gandhi Arrives in Delhi, October 1939** A small frail man, Gandhi possessed enormous courage and determination. His campaign of nonviolent resistance to British rule inspired the Indian masses and nurtured national identity and self-confidence. Here he arrives for talks with the British viceroy after the outbreak of World War II. *(Corbis)*

## Decolonization

In the postwar era, Europe's long-standing overseas expansion was dramatically reversed. Future generations will almost certainly see this rolling back of Western expansion as one of world history's great turning points (see Map 30.3).

The most basic cause of imperial collapse—what Europeans called **decolonization**—was the rising demand of Asian and African peoples for national self-determination, racial equality, and personal dignity. This demand spread from intellectuals to the masses in nearly every colonial territory after the First World War. As a result, colonial empires had already been shaken by 1939, and the way was prepared for the eventual triumph of independence movements.

European empires had been based on an enormous power differential between the rulers and the ruled, a difference that had greatly declined by 1945. Not only was western Europe poor and battered immediately after the war, but imperial rulers had been driven from large parts of South Asia by the Japanese, and in these areas Europeans now faced strong nationalist movements that had developed under the Japanese occupation.

Many Europeans also regarded their empires very differently after 1945 than before 1914, or even before 1939. Empire had rested on self-confidence and self-righteousness; Europeans had believed their superiority to be not only technical and military but also spiritual and moral. The horrors of the Second World War destroyed such complacent arrogance and gave opponents of imperialism much greater influence in Europe. With their political power and moral authority in tatters in 1945, many Europeans had little taste for bloody colonial wars and wanted to concentrate on rebuilding at home.

India, Britain's oldest, largest, and most lucrative nonwhite possession, played a key role in decolonization. Nationalist opposition to British rule coalesced after the First World War under the leadership of British-educated lawyer Mohandas "Mahatma" Gandhi (1869–1948), one of the twentieth century's most significant and influential figures. In the 1920s and 1930s Gandhi built a mass movement preaching nonviolent "noncooperation" with the British. In 1935 Gandhi wrested from the frustrated and unnerved British a new constitution that was practically a blueprint for independence. When the Labour party came to power in Great Britain in 1945, it was ready to relinquish sovereignty. British socialists had always been critical of imperialism, and the heavy cost of governing India had become a large financial burden. The obstacle to India's independence posed by conflict between India's Hindu and Muslim populations was resolved in 1947 through the creation of two states, predominately Hindu India and Muslim Pakistan.

If Indian nationalism drew on Western parliamentary liberalism, Chinese nationalism developed and triumphed in the framework of Marxist-Leninist ideology. In the turbulent early 1920s, a broad alliance of nationalist forces within the Soviet-supported Guomindang (Kuomintang, or National People's party) was dedicated to unifying China and abolishing European concessions. But in 1927 Chiang Kai-shek (1887–1975), successor to Sun Yat-sen (see page 882) and leader of the Guomindang, broke with his more radical communist allies, headed by Mao Zedong (Mao Tse-tung), and tried to destroy them.

In 1931, to escape Guomindang armies closing in for the kill, Mao (1893–1976) led his followers on an incredible 5,000-mile march to remote northern China and built up an independent power base there. Even war could not force Mao and Chiang to cooperate. By late 1945 their long-standing quarrel had erupted in civil war. Stalin gave Mao some aid, and the Americans gave Chiang much more. Winning the support of the peasantry by promising to expropriate the big landowners, the tougher, better-organized communists forced the Nationalists to withdraw to the island of Taiwan in 1949.

Mao and the communists united China's 550 million inhabitants in a strong centralized state, expelled foreigners, and began building a new society along Soviet lines, with mass arrests, forced-labor camps, and ceaseless propaganda. The peasantry was collectivized, and the inevitable five-year plans concentrated successfully on the expansion of heavy industry.

Most Asian countries followed the pattern of either India or China. In 1946 the Philippines achieved independence peacefully from the United States. Britain quickly granted Sri Lanka (Ceylon) and Burma independence in 1948. However, Indonesian nationalists had to beat off attempts by the Dutch to reconquer the Dutch East Indies before Indonesia emerged in 1949 as a sovereign state.

The French also tried their best to re-establish colonial rule in Indochina, but despite American aid, they were defeated in 1954 by forces under the communist and nationalist guerrilla leader Ho Chi Minh (1890–1969), who was supported by the Soviet Union and China. But Indochina was not unified and two independent Vietnamese states came into being, which led to civil war and subsequent intervention by the United States (see page 1015).

In the Middle East, the movement toward political independence continued after World War II (see Map 30.3). In 1944 the French gave up their League of Nations mandates in Syria and Lebanon. In British-mandated Palestine, where after 1918 the British government established a Jewish homeland alongside the Arab population, violence and terrorism mounted on both sides. In 1947 the frustrated British decided to leave Palestine, and the United Nations then voted in a nonbinding resolution to divide Palestine into two states—one Arab and one Jewish, which became Israel. The Jews accepted the plan but the Arabs did not, and in 1948 they attacked the Jewish state as soon as it was proclaimed. The Israelis drove off the invaders and conquered more territory, as roughly 900,000 Arabs fled or were expelled. Holocaust survivors from Europe streamed into Israel, as Theodor Herzl's Zionist dream came true (see page 847). The next fifty years saw four more wars between the Israelis and the Arab states and innumerable clashes between the Israelis and the Palestinians.

The Arab defeat in 1948 triggered a powerful nationalist revolution in Egypt in 1952, where a young army officer named Gamal Abdel Nasser (1918–1970) drove out the pro-Western king. In 1956 Nasser abruptly nationalized the foreign-owned Suez Canal Company, the last symbol and substance of Western power in the Middle East. Infuriated, the British and the French, along with the Israelis, invaded Egypt. This was, however, the dying gasp of traditional imperial power: the moralistic Americans joined with the Soviets to force the British, French, and Israelis to withdraw. Nasser and anti-Western Egyptian nationalism triumphed.

The failure of Britain and France to unseat Nasser in 1956 encouraged Arab nationalists in Algeria. The country's large French population considered colonial Algeria an integral part of France and was determined to stay in Algeria and continue dominating the Arab majority. This settler determination made the Algerian war for independence long, bloody, and dirty, with systematic torture and numerous atrocities on both sides. In the end, General de Gaulle, who had returned to power as part of the movement to keep Algeria French, accepted the principle of Algerian self-determination. In 1962, after more than

**Nationalizing the Suez Canal** Nasser's 1956 takeover of the Suez Canal, cheered here by a huge crowd in Cairo, was wildly popular throughout Egypt and the Arab world. Jubilation quickly turned to humiliation as invading forces from Israel, Britain, and France crushed the Egyptian army, and a shell-shocked Nasser offered to resign. But the Egyptian masses demanded he stay, enabling the charismatic Nasser to emerge triumphant with American support. *(Hulton-Deutsch Collection/Corbis)*

a century of French rule, Algeria became independent and its European population quickly fled to France.

In much of Africa south of the Sahara, decolonization proceeded much more smoothly. Beginning in 1957, Britain's colonies achieved independence with little or no bloodshed and then entered a very loose association with Britain as members of the British Commonwealth of Nations. In 1958 the clever de Gaulle offered the leaders of French black Africa the choice of a total break with France or immediate independence within a kind of French commonwealth. All but one of the new states chose association with France. African leaders did so because they identified with French culture and because they wanted aid from France. The French were eager to help—provided their former colonies would accept close ties with France on French terms. As in the past, the French and their Common Market partners, who helped foot the bill, saw themselves as continuing their civilizing mission in sub-Saharan Africa. More important, they saw in Africa untapped markets for their industrial goods, raw materials for their factories, outlets for profitable investment, and good temporary jobs for their engineers and teachers. The British acted somewhat similarly.

As a result, western European countries actually managed to increase their economic and cultural ties with their former African colonies in the 1960s and 1970s. Above all, they used the lure of special trading privileges and heavy investment in French- and English-language education to enhance a powerful Western presence in the new African states. This situation led a variety of leaders and scholars to charge that western Europe (and the United States) had imposed a system of neocolonialism on the former colonies. According to this view, **neocolonialism** was a system designed to perpetuate Western economic domination and undermine the promise of political independence, thereby extending to Africa (and much of Asia) the economic subordination that the United States had established in Latin America in the nineteenth century. At the very least, enduring influence in sub-Saharan Africa testified to western Europe's resurgent economic and political power in international relations.

## America's Civil Rights Revolution

The Second World War cured the depression in the United States and brought about an economic boom. Despite fears that peace would bring renewed depression, conversion to a peacetime economy went smoothly. As in western Europe, the U.S. economy proceeded to advance fairly steadily for a long generation.

Belatedly and reluctantly, postwar America did experience a genuine social revolution. After a long struggle, African Americans (and their white supporters) threw off a deeply entrenched system of segregation, discrimination, and repression. Eloquent lawyers challenged school segregation and in 1954 won a landmark decision in the Supreme Court, which ruled in *Brown v. Board of Education* that "separate educational facilities are inherently unequal." Blacks effectively challenged institutionalized inequality with bus boycotts, sit-ins, and demonstrations. As civil rights leader Martin Luther King, Jr. (1929–1968), told the white power structure, "We will not hate you, but we will not obey your evil laws."[4]

In key northern states, African Americans used their growing political power to gain the support of the liberal wing of the Democratic party. A liberal landslide elected Lyndon Johnson (1908–1973) president in 1964. The Civil Rights Act of 1964 prohibited discrimination in public services and on the job; the Voting Rights Act of 1965 guaranteed all blacks the right to vote. By the 1970s, substantial numbers of blacks had been elected to public and private office throughout the southern states,

**The March on Washington, August 1963** The march marked a dramatic climax in the civil rights struggle. More than 200,000 people gathered at the Lincoln Memorial to hear the young Martin Luther King, Jr., deliver his greatest address, the "I have a dream" speech. *(Time Life Pictures/Getty Images)*

proof positive that dramatic changes had occurred in American race relations.

President Johnson also declared "unconditional war on poverty," and Congress and the administration created a host of antipoverty programs intended to aid all poor Americans and bring greater economic equality. Thus the United States promoted in the mid-1960s the kind of fundamental social reform that western Europe had embraced immediately after the Second World War. The United States became more of a welfare state, as government spending for social benefits rose dramatically and approached European levels.

## Soviet Eastern Europe, 1945–1968

See DBQ 14

While western Europe surged ahead economically after the Second World War and increased its political power as American influence gradually waned, eastern Europe followed a different path. The Soviet Union first tightened its grip on the "liberated" nations of eastern Europe under Stalin and then refused to let go. Thus postwar economic recovery in eastern Europe proceeded along Soviet lines, and political and social developments were strongly influenced by changes in the Soviet Union.

### Stalin's Last Years, 1945–1953

Americans were not the only ones who felt betrayed by Stalin's postwar actions. The "Great Patriotic War of the Fatherland" had fostered Russian nationalism and a relaxation of dictatorial terror. It also had produced a rare but real unity between Soviet rulers and most Russian people. Having made a heroic war effort, the vast majority of the Soviet people hoped in 1945 that a grateful party and government would grant greater freedom and democracy. Such hopes were soon crushed.

Even before the war ended, Stalin was moving his country back toward rigid dictatorship. As early as 1944, the leading members of the Communist party were being given a new motivating slogan: "The war on Fascism ends, the war on capitalism begins."[5] By early 1946, Stalin was publicly singing the old tune that war was inevitable as long as capitalism existed. Stalin's new foreign foe in the West provided an excuse for re-establishing a harsh dictatorship. Many returning soldiers and ordinary citizens were purged in 1945 and 1946, as Stalin revived the terrible forced-labor camps of the 1930s.

Culture and art were also purged in violent campaigns that reimposed rigid anti-Western ideological conformity. Many artists were denounced, including the composers Sergei Prokofiev and Dimitri Shostakovich and the film director Sergei Eisenstein. In 1949 Stalin launched a savage verbal attack on Soviet Jews, accusing them of being pro-Western and antisocialist.

In the political realm, Stalin reasserted the Communist party's complete control of the government and his absolute mastery of the party. Five-year plans were reintroduced to cope with the enormous task of economic reconstruction. Once again, heavy industry and the military were given top priority, and consumer goods, housing, and collectivized agriculture were neglected. Everyday life was very hard. In short, it was the 1930s all over again in the Soviet Union, although police terror was less intense.

Stalin's prime postwar innovation was to export the Stalinist system to the countries of eastern Europe. The Communist parties of eastern Europe had established one-party states by 1948, thanks to the help of the Red Army and the Russian secret police. Rigid ideological indoctrination, attacks on religion, and a lack of civil liberties were soon facts of life. Industry was nationalized, and the middle class was stripped of its possessions. Economic life was then faithfully recast in the Stalinist mold. Forced industrialization lurched forward without regard for human costs. The collectivization of agriculture began.

Only Josip Broz Tito (1892–1980), the resistance leader and Communist chief of Yugoslavia, was able to resist Soviet domination successfully. Tito stood up to Stalin in 1948, and since there was no Russian army in Yugoslavia, he got away with it. Yugoslavia prospered as a multiethnic state until it began to break apart in the 1980s (see page 1005). Tito's proclamation of independence infuriated Stalin. Popular Communist leaders who, like Tito, had led the resistance against Germany were purged as Stalin sought to create absolutely obedient instruments of domination in eastern Europe. (See the feature "Individuals in Society: Tito and the Rise of Independent Communism.")

### Reform and De-Stalinization, 1953–1964

In 1953 the aging Stalin finally died, and the dictatorship that he had built began to change. Even as Stalin's heirs struggled for power, they realized that reforms were necessary because of the widespread fear and hatred of Stalin's political terrorism. The power of the secret police was curbed, and many of the forced-labor camps were gradually closed. Change was also necessary for economic reasons. Moreover, Stalin's belligerent foreign policy had led directly to a strong Western alliance, which isolated the Soviet Union.

**Sergei Eisenstein: Ivan the Terrible** Eisenstein's final masterpiece—one of the greatest films ever—was filmed during the Second World War and released in two parts in 1946. In this chilling scene, the crafty paranoid tyrant, who has saved Russia from foreign invaders, invites the unsuspecting Prince Vladimir to a midnight revel that will lead to his murder. The increasingly demonic Ivan seemed to resemble Stalin, and Eisenstein was censored and purged. *(David King Collection)*

On the question of just how much change should be permitted in order to preserve the system, the Communist leadership was badly split. Conservatives wanted to make as few changes as possible. Reformers, who were led by Nikita Khrushchev, argued for major innovations. Khrushchev (1894–1971), who had joined the party as an uneducated coal miner in 1918 and risen to a high-level position in the 1930s, emerged as the new ruler in 1955.

To strengthen his position and that of his fellow reformers within the party, Khrushchev launched an all-out attack on Stalin and his crimes at a closed session of the Twentieth Party Congress in 1956. In gory detail, he described to the startled Communist delegates how Stalin had tortured and murdered thousands of loyal Communists, how he had trusted Hitler completely and bungled the country's defense, and how he had "supported the glorification of his own person with all conceivable methods." Khrushchev's "secret speech" was read at Communist party meetings held throughout the country, and it strengthened the reform movement.

The liberalization—or **de-Stalinization,** as it was called in the West—of the Soviet Union was genuine. The Communist party jealously maintained its monopoly on political power, but Khrushchev shook up the party and brought in new members. Some resources were shifted from heavy industry and the military toward consumer goods and agriculture, and Stalinist controls over workers were relaxed. The Soviet Union's very low standard of living finally began to improve and continued to rise substantially throughout the booming 1960s.

De-Stalinization created great ferment among writers and intellectuals who hungered for cultural freedom. The poet Boris Pasternak (1890–1960) finished his great novel *Doctor Zhivago* in 1956. Published in the West but not in Russia, *Doctor Zhivago* is both a literary masterpiece and a powerful challenge to communism. It tells the story of a prerevolutionary intellectual who rejects the violence and brutality of the revolution of 1917 and the Stalinist years. Even as he is destroyed, he triumphs because of his humanity and Christian spirit. Pasternak was denounced—but he was not shot. Other talented writers followed Pasternak's lead, and courageous editors let the sparks fly.

The writer Aleksandr Solzhenitsyn (b. 1918) created a sensation when his *One Day in the Life of Ivan Denisovich* was published in the Soviet Union in 1962. Solzhenitsyn's novel portrays in grim detail life in a Stalinist concentration camp—a life to which Solzhenitsyn himself had been unjustly condemned—and is a damning indictment of the Stalinist past.

Khrushchev also de-Stalinized Soviet foreign policy. "Peaceful coexistence" with capitalism was possible, he argued, and great wars were not inevitable. Khrushchev even made concessions, agreeing in 1955 to real independence for a neutral Austria after ten long years of Allied occupation. Thus there was considerable relaxation

# Individuals in Society

## Tito and the Rise of Independent Communism

Josip Tito (1892–1980) was always a dedicated communist. But after fighting the Nazis and bringing revolution to Yugoslavia, he experienced Stalin's wrath. He then built an independent communist state and achieved remarkable influence as a world leader.

Tito was born into a peasant family of mixed ethnic background in northwest Croatia, in what was then Austria-Hungary. Leaving home as a teenager for work in towns, he became a communist labor organizer in the 1920s. Imprisoned for five years in the 1930s, Tito went to Moscow and in 1937 was charged by the Soviets to reorganize the Communist party of Yugoslavia and then to lead the resistance to Nazi and Italian occupation.

Communist revolution was always Tito's main goal. His guerrilla forces fought as much against the competing noncommunist resistance movement, centered in the Serbian region of Yugoslavia and loyal to the deposed monarchy, as against the Nazis and Italians and their collaborators in Croatia, Bosnia, and Serbia. Yet Tito played down his revolutionary objectives and appealed with some success to all ethnic groups in Yugoslavia. He promised "brotherhood and unity" when the carnage ended. Liberating Yugoslavia in 1945 in coordination with Stalin's Red Army, which moved on in pursuit of the retreating Germans, Tito and his followers quickly established the first Stalinist regime in eastern Europe. Yugoslavia's peasants were exploited to pay for heavy industry. Tito's picture was everywhere, and the Communists held all power.

Yet Stalin grew dissatisfied with his ally. Tito bubbled with revolutionary enthusiasm. He supported the Greek communists in their civil war, called for a communist federation in the Balkans, and enraged U.S. public opinion by shooting down an American "spy plane" over Yugoslavia. Stalin preferred cautious moderation in relations with the West, which would, he hoped, facilitate Soviet consolidation in eastern Europe and encourage a division of the world into spheres of influence. Above all, he demanded absolutely obedient Communist leaders. In 1948 he suddenly denounced Tito as a heretic and called on Yugoslavia's Communist party to oust him. Tito later described the rupture as his most traumatic experience, but he stayed calm, rallied party stalwarts, and survived.

At first, Tito's independent communism remained strictly Stalinist, imprisoning opponents and proclaiming its Marxist-Leninist orthodoxy. But Tito soon steered a middle course between East and West. He approved the introduction of "workers' self-management" in Yugoslavia, which loosened the state's hold on the economy and was trumpeted internationally as a radical step toward genuine communism. In the 1950s and 1960s, Tito's one-party dictatorship allowed greater personal freedom and presented would-be communist reformers in eastern Europe with an intriguing model.

*Marshal Tito in 1940, planning operations for the liberation of Yugoslavia.* (Corbis)

Yugoslavia's independent, "nonaligned" communism became an influential model in world politics. Tito adroitly negotiated indispensable military commitments from the United States to keep Stalin's armies at bay, and he received massive U.S. aid. But he also reestablished generally good relations with the Soviet Union after Stalin's death. Finally, Tito joined with India's Jawaharlal Nehru and Egypt's Gamal Abdel Nasser to lead and inspire the movement of nonaligned, newly independent countries. Pressing his case on many fronts, Tito strengthened the idea that Third World nations should avoid crippling cold war alliances and concentrate instead on building independent socialist states like his.

### Questions for Analysis

1. Does the rupture between Tito and Stalin throw light on the origins of the cold war? In what ways?
2. What were the characteristics of Tito's independent communism? How did it enhance his status as a leader?

*The* **history companion** *features additional information and activities related to this topic.*
**history.college.hmco.com/students**

of cold war tensions between 1955 and 1957. At the same time, Khrushchev began wooing the new nations of Asia and Africa—even if they were not communist—with promises and aid.

De-Stalinization stimulated rebelliousness in the eastern European satellites. Having suffered in silence under Stalin, communist reformers and the masses were quickly emboldened to seek much greater liberty and national independence. Poland took the lead in 1956, when extensive rioting brought a new government that managed to win greater autonomy.

Hungary experienced a real and tragic revolution. Led by students and workers—the classic urban revolutionaries—the people of Budapest installed a liberal communist reformer as their new chief in October 1956. Soviet troops were forced to leave the country. But after the new government promised free elections and renounced Hungary's military alliance with Moscow, the Russian leaders ordered an invasion and crushed the national and democratic revolution. Fighting was bitter until the end, for the Hungarians hoped that the United States would come to their aid. When this did not occur, most people in eastern Europe concluded that their only hope was to strive for small domestic gains while following Russia obediently in foreign affairs.

## The End of Reform

By late 1962, opposition in party circles to Khrushchev's policies was strong, and in 1964 Khrushchev fell in a bloodless palace revolution. Under Leonid Brezhnev (1906–1982), the Soviet Union began a period of stagnation and limited "re-Stalinization." The basic reason for this development was that Khrushchev's Communist colleagues saw de-Stalinization as a dangerous, two-sided threat. How could Khrushchev denounce the dead dictator without eventually denouncing and perhaps even arresting his still-powerful henchmen? Moreover, the widening campaign of de-Stalinization posed a clear threat to the dictatorial authority of the party. The party had to tighten up considerably while there was still time. Khrushchev had to go.

Another reason for conservative opposition was that Khrushchev's policy toward the West was erratic and ultimately unsuccessful. In 1958 he ordered the Western allies to evacuate West Berlin within six months. In response, the allies reaffirmed their unity in West Berlin, and Khrushchev backed down. Then in 1961, as relations with communist China deteriorated dramatically, Khrushchev ordered the East Germans to build a wall between East and West Berlin, thereby sealing off West Berlin in clear violation of existing access agreements between the Great Powers. The recently elected U.S. president, John F. Kennedy, acquiesced to the construction of the Berlin Wall. Emboldened and seeing a chance to change the balance of military power decisively, Khrushchev ordered missiles with nuclear warheads installed in Fidel Castro's communist Cuba in 1962. President Kennedy countered with a naval blockade of Cuba. After a tense diplomatic crisis, Khrushchev agreed to remove the Soviet missiles in return for American pledges not to disturb Castro's regime. Khrushchev looked like a bumbling buffoon; his influence, already slipping, declined rapidly after the Cuban fiasco.

After Brezhnev and his supporters took over in 1964, they started talking quietly of Stalin's "good points" and ignoring his crimes. This change informed Soviet citizens that further liberalization could not be expected at home. Soviet leaders, determined never to suffer Khrushchev's humiliation in the face of American nuclear superiority, also launched a massive arms buildup. Yet Brezhnev and company proceeded cautiously in the mid-1960s and avoided direct confrontation with the United States.

In the wake of Khrushchev's reforms, the 1960s brought modest liberalization and more consumer goods to eastern Europe, as well as somewhat greater national autonomy, especially in Poland and Romania. In January 1968, the reform elements in the Czechoslovak Communist party gained a majority and voted out the long-time Stalinist leader in favor of Alexander Dubček (1921–1992), whose new government launched dramatic reforms.

Educated in Moscow, Dubček was a dedicated Communist. But he and his allies believed that they could reconcile genuine socialism with personal freedom and internal party democracy. Thus local decision making by trade unions, managers, and consumers replaced rigid bureaucratic planning, and censorship was relaxed. The reform program proved enormously popular.

Although Dubček remembered the lesson of the Hungarian revolution and constantly proclaimed his loyalty to the Warsaw Pact, the determination of the Czechoslovak reformers to build what they called "socialism with a human face" frightened hard-line Communists. These fears were particularly strong in Poland and East Germany, where leaders knew full well that they lacked popular support. Moreover, the Soviet Union feared that a liberalized Czechoslovakia would eventually be drawn to neutrality or even to the democratic West. Thus the Eastern bloc countries launched a concerted campaign of intimidation against the Czechoslovak leaders, and in August 1968, 500,000 Russian and allied eastern European troops sud-

**The Invasion of Czechoslovakia** Armed with Czechoslovakian flags, courageous Czechs in downtown Prague try to stop a Soviet tank and repel the invasion and occupation of their country by the Soviet Union and its eastern European allies. This dramatic confrontation marked a high point, because the Czechs and the Slovaks realized that military resistance would be suicidal. *(AP/Wide World Photos)*

denly occupied Czechoslovakia. The Czechoslovaks made no attempt to resist militarily, and the arrested leaders surrendered to Soviet demands. The reform program was abandoned, and the Czechoslovak experiment in humanizing communism came to an end. Shortly after the invasion of Czechoslovakia, Brezhnev declared the so-called **Brezhnev Doctrine,** according to which the Soviet Union and its allies had the right to intervene in any socialist country whenever they saw the need.

The 1968 invasion of Czechoslovakia was the crucial event of the Brezhnev era, which really lasted beyond the aging leader's death in 1982 until the emergence in 1985 of Mikhail Gorbachev. The invasion demonstrated the determination of the ruling elite to maintain the status quo in the Soviet bloc. In the U.S.S.R. that determination resulted in further repression, but the Soviet Union appeared quite stable in the 1970s and early 1980s.

## Postwar Social Transformations, 1945–1968

While Europe staged its astonishing political and economic recovery from the Nazi nightmare, the patterns of everyday life and the structure of Western society were changing no less rapidly and remarkably. Epoch-making inventions and new technologies profoundly affected human existence. Important groups in society formulated new attitudes and demands, which were closely related to the changing class structure and social reforms. An international youth culture took shape and rose to challenge established lifestyles and even governments.

## Science and Technology

Ever since the scientific revolution of the seventeenth century and the Industrial Revolution at the end of the eighteenth century, scientific and technical developments had powerfully influenced attitudes, society, and everyday life. Never was this influence stronger than after about 1940. Science and technology proved so productive and influential because, for the first time in history, "pure theoretical" science and "practical" technology (or "applied" science) were effectively joined together on a massive scale.

With the advent of the Second World War, pure science lost its impractical innocence. Most leading university scientists went to work on top-secret projects to help their governments fight the war. The development by British scientists of radar to detect enemy aircraft was a particularly important outcome of this new kind of sharply focused research. A radically improved radar system played a key role in Britain's victory in the battle for air supremacy in 1940. The air war also greatly stimulated the development of jet aircraft and spurred further research on electronic computers, which calculated the complex mathematical relationships between fast-moving planes and anti-aircraft shells to increase the likelihood of a hit.

The most spectacular result of directed scientific research during the war was the atomic bomb. In August 1939, physicist Albert Einstein wrote to President Franklin Roosevelt that recent work in physics suggested that "it may become possible to set up a nuclear chain reaction in a large mass of uranium" and to construct "extremely powerful bombs of a new type."[6] This letter and ongoing experiments by nuclear physicists led to the top-secret Manhattan Project, which ballooned into a mammoth crash program. After three years of intensive effort, the first atomic bomb was successfully tested in July 1945. In August 1945, two bombs were dropped on Hiroshima and Nagasaki, thereby ending the war with Japan.

The atomic bomb showed the world both the awesome power and the heavy moral responsibilities of modern science and its high priests. As one Los Alamos scientist exclaimed as he watched the first mushroom cloud rise over the American desert, "We are all sons-of-bitches now!"[7]

The spectacular results of directed research during World War II inspired a new model for science—**Big Science.** By combining theoretical work with sophisticated engineering in a large organization, Big Science could attack extremely difficult problems, from better products for consumers to new and improved weapons for the military. Big Science was extremely expensive, requiring large-scale financing from governments and large corporations.

Populous, victorious, and wealthy, the United States took the lead in Big Science after World War II. Between 1945 and 1965, spending on scientific research and development in the United States grew five times as fast as the national income, and by 1965 such spending took 3 percent of all U.S. income. It was generally accepted that government should finance science heavily in both the "capitalist" United States and the "socialist" Soviet Union.

One reason for the parallel between the two countries was that science was not demobilized in either country after the war. Scientists remained a critical part of every major military establishment, and a large portion of all postwar scientific research went for "defense." New weapons such as rockets, nuclear submarines, and spy satellites demanded breakthroughs no less remarkable than those of radar and the first atomic bomb. After 1945 roughly one-quarter of all men and women trained in science and engineering in the West—and perhaps more in the Soviet Union—were employed full-time in the production of weapons to kill other humans.

Sophisticated science, lavish government spending, and military needs all came together in the space race of the 1960s. In 1957 the Soviets used long-range rockets developed in their nuclear weapons program to put a satellite in orbit. In 1961 they sent the world's first cosmonaut circling the globe. Embarrassed by Soviet triumphs, President Kennedy made an all-out U.S. commitment to catch up with the Soviets and land a crewed spacecraft on the moon "before the decade was out." Harnessing pure science, applied technology, and up to $5 billion a year, the Apollo Program achieved its ambitious objective in 1969. Four more moon landings followed by 1972.

The rapid expansion of government-financed research in the United States attracted many of Europe's best scientists during the 1950s and 1960s. Thoughtful Europeans lamented this "brain drain" and feared that Europe was falling hopelessly behind the United States in science and technology. In fact, a revitalized Europe was already responding to the American challenge, with countries pooling their efforts on such Big Science projects as the Concorde supersonic passenger airliner and the peaceful uses of atomic energy.

The rise of Big Science and of close ties between science and technology greatly altered the lives of scientists. The scientific community grew much larger than ever before. There were about four times as many scientists in Europe and North America in 1975 as in 1945. Scientists, technologists, engineers, and medical specialists counted after 1945, in part because there were so many of them.

One consequence of the growth of science was its high degree of specialization, for no one could possibly master a broad field such as physics or medicine. Intense specialization in new disciplines and subdisciplines increased the rates at which both basic knowledge was acquired and practical applications were made.

Highly specialized modern scientists and technologists normally had to work as members of a team, which completely changed the work and lifestyle of modern scientists. A great deal of work therefore went on in large bureaucratic organizations, where the individual was very often a small cog in a great machine. The growth of large scientific bureaucracies in government and private enterprise suggested how scientists and technologists permeated the entire society and many aspects of life.

Modern science became highly, even brutally, competitive. This competitiveness is well depicted in Nobel Prize winner James Watson's fascinating book *The Double Helix,* which tells how in 1953 Watson and an Englishman, Francis Crick, discovered the structure of DNA, the molecule of heredity. A brash young American Ph.D. in his twenties, Watson seemed almost obsessed by the idea that some other research team would find the solution first and thereby deprive him of the fame and fortune he desperately wanted. With so many thousands of like-minded researchers in the wealthy countries of the world, scientific and technical knowledge rushed forward in the postwar era.

## The Changing Class Structure

Rapid economic growth went a long way toward creating a new society in Europe after the Second World War. European society became more mobile and more democratic. Old class barriers relaxed, and class distinctions became fuzzier.

Changes in the structure of the middle class were particularly influential in the general drift toward a less rigid class structure. In the nineteenth and early twentieth centuries, the model for the middle class had been the independent, self-employed individual who owned a business or practiced a liberal profession such as law or medicine. Ownership of property—very often inherited property—and strong family ties had often been the keys to wealth and standing within the middle class. After 1945 this pattern declined drastically in western Europe. A new breed of managers and experts replaced traditional property owners as the leaders of the middle class. Ability to serve the needs of a big organization largely replaced inherited property and family connections in determining an individual's social position in the middle and upper middle classes. At the same time, the middle class grew massively and became harder to define.

There were several reasons for these developments. Rapid industrial and technological expansion created in large corporations and government agencies a powerful demand for technologists and managers. Moreover, the old propertied middle class lost control of many family-owned businesses, and many small businesses (including family farms) simply passed out of existence as their former owners joined the ranks of salaried employees.

Top managers and ranking civil servants therefore represented the model for a new middle class of salaried specialists. Well paid and highly trained, often with backgrounds in engineering or accounting, these experts increasingly came from all social classes, even the working class. Pragmatic and realistic, they were primarily concerned with efficiency and practical solutions to concrete problems. Managers and technocrats, of whom a small but growing number were women (see pages 1010–1012), could pass on the opportunity for all-important advanced education to their children, but only in rare instances could they pass on the positions they had attained. Thus the new middle class, which was based largely on specialized skills and high levels of education, was more open, democratic, and insecure than the old propertied middle class.

The structure of the lower classes also became more flexible and open. There was a mass exodus from farms and the countryside, as one of the most traditional and least mobile groups in European society drastically declined. Meanwhile, the industrial working class ceased to expand, and job opportunities for white-collar and service employees grew rapidly. Such employees bore a greater resemblance to the new middle class of salaried specialists than to industrial workers, who were also better educated and more specialized.

European governments were reducing class tensions with a series of social security reforms. Many of these reforms—such as increased unemployment benefits and more extensive old-age pensions—simply strengthened social security measures first pioneered in Bismarck's Germany before the First World War (see pages 840–841). Other programs were new, like comprehensive national health systems directed by the state. Most countries also introduced family allowances—direct government grants to parents to help them raise their children. These allowances helped many poor families make ends meet. Most European governments also gave maternity grants and built inexpensive public housing for low-income families and individuals. These and other social reforms provided a humane floor of well-being. Reforms also promoted

**Consumers on the Move** In the early postwar years the Italians had their motor scooters and the French their motorbikes. This ad promises young people that "sooner or later" they will have a "Velo," and it subtly assures housewives that the bike is safe. In small towns and villages the slow-moving motorbike could be a godsend for errands and daily shopping. *(Roger Perrin/The Bridgeman Art Library)*

greater equality because they were expensive and were paid for in part by higher taxes on the rich.

The rising standard of living and the spread of standardized consumer goods also worked to level Western society, as the percentage of income spent on food and drink declined substantially. For example, the European automobile industry expanded phenomenally after lagging far behind the United States since the 1920s. In 1948 there were only 5 million cars in western Europe, but in 1965 there were 44 million. Car ownership was democratized and came within the range of better-paid workers.

Europeans took great pleasure in the products of the "gadget revolution" as well. Like Americans, Europeans filled their houses and apartments with washing machines, vacuum cleaners, refrigerators, dishwashers, radios, TVs, and stereos. The purchase of consumer goods was greatly facilitated by installment purchasing, which allowed people to buy on credit. With the expansion of social security safeguards, reducing the need to accumulate savings for hard times, ordinary people were increasingly willing to take on debt. This change had far-reaching consequences.

Leisure and recreation occupied an important place in consumer societies. The most astonishing leisure-time development was the blossoming of mass travel and tourism. With month-long paid vacations required by law in most European countries and widespread automobile ownership, beaches and ski resorts came within the reach of the middle class and much of the working class. By the late 1960s, packaged tours with cheap group flights and bargain hotel accommodations had made even distant lands easily accessible. A French company grew rich building imitation Tahitian paradises around the world. At Swedish nudist colonies on secluded West African beaches, officeworkers from Stockholm fleetingly worshiped the sun in the middle of the long northern winter. Truly, consumerism had come of age.

## New Roles for Women

A growing emancipation of women in Europe and North America was unquestionably one of the most significant transformations of the cold war era. This historic development grew out of long-term changes in the basic patterns of motherhood and paid work outside the home. These changing patterns altered women's experiences and expectations, preparing the way for the success of a new generation of feminist thinkers and a militant women's movement in the 1970s and 1980s (see pages 1017–1018).

Before the Industrial Revolution, most Europeans married late. Once a woman was married, however, she usually had children as long as she was fertile, and she bore several children, of whom one-third to one-half would not survive to adulthood. With the growth of industry, people began to marry earlier, death rates fell, and population grew rapidly. By the late nineteenth century, improved diet, higher incomes, and the use of contraception within marriage were producing the demographic transition from high birthrates and death rates to low birthrates and death rates.

These trends continued in the twentieth century. In the 1950s and 1960s, the typical woman in the West married early and bore her children quickly. The postwar baby boom did make for larger families and a fairly rapid popu-

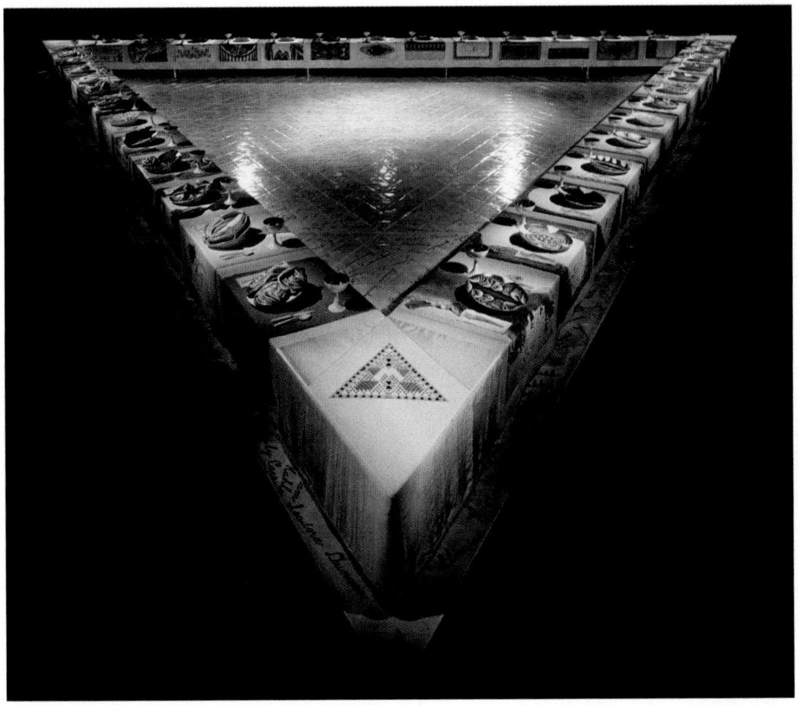

**Celebrating Women's History** Judy Chicago's multimedia creation *The Dinner Party* features thirty-nine handcrafted placemats and ceramic plates, each embellished with a painted motif associated with the woman being honored. Begun in 1974 and completed in 1978 with the participation of more than one hundred women, *The Dinner Party* was intended to represent the "historic struggle of women to participate in all the aspects of society." It attracted enormous crowds. *(© Judy Chicago, 1979; mixed media, 48′ × 42′ × 3′. Photo: © Donald Woodman)*

lation growth of 1 to 1.5 percent per year in many European countries. However, in the 1960s the long-term decline in birthrates resumed, and from the mid-1970s on in many European countries, the total population practically stopped growing from natural increase, with limited subsequent growth coming mainly from immigation.

The postwar culmination of the trends toward early marriage, early childbearing, and small family size in wealthy urban societies had revolutionary implications for women. Above all, pregnancy and child care occupied a much smaller portion of a woman's life than in earlier times. By the early 1970s, about half of Western women were having their last baby by the age of twenty-six or twenty-seven. When the youngest child trooped off to kindergarten, the average mother had more than forty years of life in front of her.

This was a momentous change. Throughout history male-dominated society insisted on defining most women as mothers or potential mothers, and motherhood was very demanding. In the postwar years, however, motherhood no longer absorbed the energies of a lifetime, and more and more married women looked for new roles in the world of work outside the family.

For centuries before the Industrial Revolution, ordinary women worked hard and long on farms and in home industries while caring for their large families. With the growth of modern industry and much more rigid gender roles, few middle-class women worked outside the home for wages, although charity work was socially acceptable. Young unmarried women continued to work as wage earners, but poor married women typically earned their money at home in low-paid crafts as they looked after their children.

In the twentieth century and especially after World War II, the ever-greater complexity of the modern economy meant that almost all women had to go outside the home to find cash income. Three major forces helped women searching for jobs. First, the economy boomed from about 1950 to 1973 and created a strong demand for labor. Second, the economy continued its gradual shift away from the old, male-dominated heavy industries, such as coal, steel, and shipbuilding, to the more dynamic, "white-collar" service industries, such as government, education, trade, and health care. Women had always worked in these service fields. Third, young Western women shared fully in the postwar education revolution and could take advantage of the growing need for officeworkers and well-trained professionals. Thus more and more married women became full-time and part-time wage earners.

The trend went the furthest in communist eastern Europe, where women accounted for almost half of all employed persons. In noncommunist western Europe and North America, there was a good deal of variation, with the percentage of married women in the workforce rising from a range of roughly 20 to 25 percent in 1950 to a range of 40 to 70 percent in the early 1980s.

Rising employment for married women went hand in hand with the decline of the birthrate (see Figure 30.1). Women who worked outside the home had significantly fewer children than women of the same age who did not. Raising a family while holding down a full-time job was a tremendous challenge and often resulted in a woman's being grossly overworked. The multiple demands of job, motherhood, and marriage became more manageable with fewer children.

Married women entering (or re-entering) the labor force faced widespread, long-established discrimination in pay, advancement, and occupational choice in comparison to men. Moreover, many women could find only part-time work. As the divorce rate rose in the 1960s, part-time work, with its low pay and scanty benefits, meant poverty for many women with teenage children. Finally, in the best of circumstances, married working women still carried most of the child-raising and housekeeping responsibilities. A reason for many to accept part-time employment, this gendered imbalance meant an exhausting "double day"—on the job and at home—for the full-time worker.

The injustices that married women encountered as wage earners contributed greatly to the subsequent movement for women's equality and emancipation. A young unmarried woman of seventy or a hundred years ago was more likely to accept such problems as temporary nuisances because she looked forward to marriage and motherhood for fulfillment. In the postwar era, a married wage earner in her thirties gradually developed a very different perspective. She saw employment as a permanent condition within which she, like her male counterpart, sought not only income but also psychological satisfaction. Sexism and discrimination in the workplace—and in the home—grew loathsome and evoked the sense of injustice that drives revolutions and reforms. When powerful voices arose to challenge the system, they found support among working women.

**FIGURE 30.1 The Decline of the Birthrate and the Increase of Married Working Women in the United States, 1952–1979** The challenge of working away from home encouraged American wives to prefer fewer children and helped to lower the birthrate.

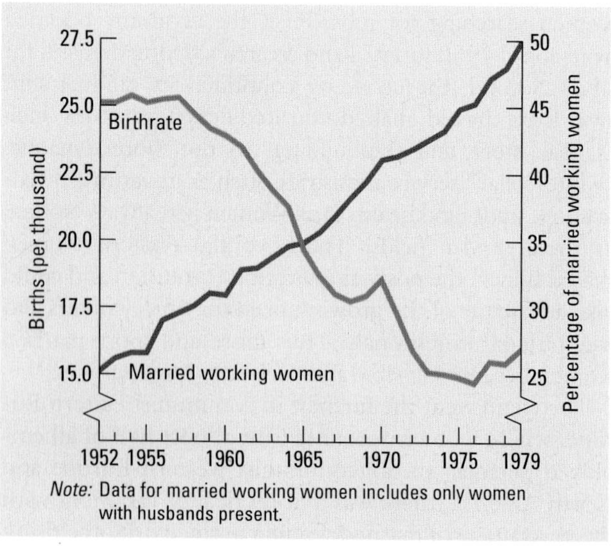


## Youth and the Counterculture

Economic prosperity and a more democratic class structure had a powerful impact on youth throughout the Western world. The bulging cohort of youth born after World War II developed a distinctive and very international youth culture, which eventually became a "counterculture" that rebelled against parents, authority figures, and the status quo.

Young people in the United States took the lead. American college students in the 1950s were often dismissed as the "Silent Generation," but by the late 1950s the "beat" movement was stoking the fires of revolt in selected urban enclaves, such as the Near North Side of Chicago. There the young (and the not-so-young) fashioned a highly publicized subculture that blended radical politics, unbridled personal experimentation (with drugs and communal living, for example), and new artistic styles. This subculture quickly spread to major American and western European cities. The young folksinger Bob Dylan summed up the increasingly radical political and cultural aspirations of the "younger generation" in lyrics that became a rallying cry, "the times they are a'changing."[8]

Certainly the sexual behavior of young people appeared to change dramatically in the 1960s and into the 1970s. More young people engaged in sexual intercourse, and they did so at an earlier age, in part because the discovery of safe and effective contraceptive pills could eliminate the risk of unwanted pregnancy. A 1973 study reported that only 4.5 percent of West German youths born in 1945 and 1946 had experienced sexual relations before their seventeenth birthday but that 32 percent of those born in 1953 and 1954 had done so.[9] Perhaps even more significant was the growing tendency of young unmarried people to live together in a separate household on a semipermanent basis, with little thought of getting married or having children. Thus many youths, especially middle-class youths, defied social custom, claiming in effect that the long-standing monopoly of married couples on legitimate sexual unions was dead.

Several factors contributed to the emergence of the international youth culture in the 1960s. First, mass communications and youth travel linked countries and continents together. Second, the postwar baby boom meant that young people became an unusually large part of the population and could therefore exercise exceptional influence on society as a whole. Third, postwar prosperity and greater equality gave young people more purchasing power than ever before. This enabled them to set their own trends and patterns of consumption, which fostered generational loyalty. Finally, prosperity meant that good jobs were readily available. Students and young job seekers had little need to fear punishment from strait-laced employers for unconventional behavior.

The youth culture practically fused with the counterculture in opposition to the established order in the late 1960s. Student protesters embraced romanticism and revolutionary idealism, dreaming of complete freedom and simpler, purer societies. The materialistic West was hopelessly rotten, but better societies were being built in the newly independent countries of Asia and Africa, or so many young radicals believed. Thus the Vietnam War took on special significance. Many politically active students believed that the older generation was fighting an immoral and imperialistic war against a small and heroic people. As the war in Vietnam intensified, so did worldwide student opposition to it.

Student protests in western Europe also highlighted more general problems of youth, education, and a society of specialists. In contrast to the United States, high school and university educations in Europe had been limited for centuries to a small elite. Whereas 22 percent of the American population was going on to some form of higher education in 1950, only 3 to 4 percent of western European youths were doing so. Then enrollments skyrocketed. By 1960 at least three times as many students were going to some kind of university as had attended before the war, and the number continued to rise sharply until the 1970s. Reflecting the development of a more democratic class structure and a growing awareness that higher education was the key to success, European universities gave more scholarships and opened their doors to more students from the lower middle and lower classes.

The rapid expansion of higher education meant that classes were badly overcrowded. Competition for grades became intense. Moreover, although more practical areas of study were gradually added, many students felt that they were not getting the kind of education they needed

**Woodstock, 1969** The brainchild of four young entrepreneurs, Woodstock snowballed into the world's biggest rock concert, a three-day bash in a pasture in upstate New York that drew 450,000 guests and caused twenty-mile traffic jams. Standout performers included the guitarist Jimi Hendrix, Janis Joplin, and Joe Cocker, whose back-up band faces the crowd in this photo. A high point for the youth culture, with antiwar and free love overtones, Woodstock spawned many myths and conflicting interpretations. *(Elliot Landy/Magnum Photos)*

**Student Rebellion in Paris** These rock-throwing students in the Latin Quarter of Paris are trying to force education reforms and even to topple de Gaulle's government. Throughout May 1968 students clashed repeatedly with France's tough riot police in bloody street fighting. De Gaulle remained in power, but a major reform of French education did follow. *(Bruno Barbey/Magnum Photos)*

for jobs in the modern world. At the same time, some reflective students warned of the dangers of narrowly trained experts. They feared that universities would soon do nothing but turn out docile technocrats both to stock and to serve "the establishment."

The many tensions within the exploding university population came to a head in the late 1960s and early 1970s. As in the United States, European university students rose to challenge their university administrations and even their governments. The most far-reaching of these revolts occurred in France in 1968. Students occupied buildings and took over the University of Paris, which led to violent clashes with police. Most students demanded both changes in the curriculum and a real voice in running the university. Some student radicals went further, attacking capitalism and appealing to France's industrial workers for help. Rank-and-file workers ignored the advice of their cautious union officials, and a more or less spontaneous general strike spread across France in May 1968. It seemed certain that President de Gaulle's Fifth Republic would collapse.

In fact, de Gaulle stiffened, like an irate father. Declaring that he was in favor of university reforms and higher minimum wages but would oppose the "bed-wetting" of undisciplined students and workers, he moved troops toward Paris and called for new elections. Thoroughly frightened by the student-sparked upheaval and fearing an eventual communist takeover, the masses of France voted overwhelmingly for de Gaulle's party and a return to law and order. Workers went back to work, and the mini-revolution collapsed. Yet the proud de Gaulle and the postwar European renaissance that he represented had been shaken, and within a year he resigned. Growing out of the counterculture and youthful idealism, the student rebellion of 1968 signaled the end of an era and the return of unrest and uncertainty in the 1970s and early 1980s.

## Conflict and Challenge in the Late Cold War, 1968–1985

Similar to but more important than the student upheaval in France and the crushing of socialist reform in Czechoslovakia, the Vietnam War marked the beginning of a new era of challenges and uncertainties in the late 1960s. The Vietnam War and its aftermath divided the people of the

United States, shook the ideology of containment, and weakened the Western alliance. A second major challenge appeared when the great postwar economic boom came to a close in 1973, opening a long period of economic stagnation, widespread unemployment, and social dislocation.

## The United States and Vietnam

President Johnson wanted to go down in history as a master reformer and a healer of old wounds. Instead, he opened new ones with the Vietnam War.

Although many student radicals believed that imperialism was the main cause, American involvement in Vietnam was more clearly a product of the cold war and the policy of containment (see page 992). From the late 1940s on, most Americans and their leaders viewed the world in terms of a constant struggle to stop the spread of communism. As western Europe began to revive and China established a communist government in 1949, efforts to contain communism shifted to Asia. The bloody Korean War (1950–1953) ended in stalemate, but the United States did succeed in preventing a communist victory in South Korea. After the defeat of the French in Vietnam in 1954, the Eisenhower administration refused to sign the Geneva Accords that temporarily divided the country into two zones pending national unification by means of free elections. President Eisenhower then acquiesced in the refusal of the anticommunist South Vietnamese government to accept the verdict of elections and provided it with military aid. President Kennedy greatly increased the number of American "military advisers" to sixteen thousand.

After winning the 1964 election on a peace platform, President Johnson greatly expanded the American role in the Vietnam conflict. American strategy was to "escalate" the war sufficiently to break the will of the North Vietnamese and their southern allies without resorting to "overkill," which might risk war with the entire Communist bloc. Thus South Vietnam received massive military aid, American forces in the South gradually grew to half a million men, and the United States bombed North Vietnam with ever-greater intensity. But there was no invasion of the North or naval blockade. In the end, the American strategy of limited warfare backfired. It was the American people who grew weary and the American leadership that cracked.

The undeclared war in Vietnam, fought nightly on American television, eventually divided the nation. Initial support was strong. The politicians, the media, and the population as a whole saw the war as part of a legitimate defense against communist totalitarianism in all poor countries. But an antiwar movement quickly emerged on

**Seymour Chwast: End Bad Breath** Antiwar messages came in every shape and form as opposition to the Vietnam War heated up. This vibrant poster assumes, quite reasonably, that the American viewer is steeped in the popular culture of the mass media. It ridicules American military involvement with a sarcastic parody of familiar television commercials. *(Library of Congress)*

college campuses, where the prospect of being drafted to fight savage battles in Asian jungles made male stomachs churn. In October 1965, student protesters joined forces with old-line socialists, New Left intellectuals, and pacifists in antiwar demonstrations in fifty American cities. By 1967 a growing number of critics denounced the war as a criminal intrusion into a complex and distant civil war.

Criticism reached a crescendo after the Vietcong Tet Offensive in January 1968. This, the communists' first comprehensive attack with conventional weapons on major cities in South Vietnam, failed militarily: the Vietcong suffered heavy losses, and the attack did not spark a mass uprising. But Washington had been claiming that victory in South Vietnam was in sight, and U.S. critics of the Vietnam War quickly interpreted the bloody combat as a decisive

American defeat. America's leaders lost heart. In 1968, after a narrow victory in the New Hampshire primary, President Johnson called for negotiations with North Vietnam and announced that he would not stand for re-election.

Elected by a razor-slim margin in 1968, President Richard Nixon (1913–1994) sought to gradually disengage America from Vietnam and the accompanying national crisis. Intensifying the continuous bombardment of the enemy while simultaneously pursuing peace talks with the North Vietnamese, Nixon suspended the draft, so hated on college campuses, and cut American forces in Vietnam from 550,000 to 24,000 in four years. The cost of the war dropped dramatically. Moreover, President Nixon launched a flank attack in diplomacy. He journeyed to China in 1972 and reached a spectacular if limited reconciliation with the People's Republic of China. In doing so, Nixon took advantage of China's growing fears of the Soviet Union and undermined North Vietnam's position.

Fortified by the overwhelming endorsement of the voters in his 1972 electoral triumph, President Nixon and Secretary of State Henry Kissinger finally reached a peace agreement with North Vietnam. The agreement allowed remaining American forces to complete their withdrawal, and the United States reserved the right to resume bombing if the accords were broken. Fighting declined markedly in South Vietnam, where the South Vietnamese army appeared to hold its own against the Vietcong. The storm of crisis in the United States seemed to have passed.

On the contrary, the country reaped the **Watergate** whirlwind. Like some other recent American presidents, Nixon authorized spying activities that went beyond the law. Going further than his predecessors, he allowed special units to use various illegal means to stop the leaking of government documents to the press. One such group broke into the Democratic party headquarters in Washington's Watergate complex in June 1972 and was promptly arrested. Nixon and many of his assistants then tried to hush up the bungled job, but the media and the machinery of congressional investigation eventually exposed the administration's web of lies and lawbreaking. In 1974 a beleaguered Nixon was forced to resign in disgrace.

The consequences of renewed political crisis flowing from the Watergate affair were profound. First, Watergate resulted in a major shift of power away from the presidency and toward Congress, especially in foreign affairs. Therefore, as American aid to South Vietnam diminished in 1973 and as an emboldened North Vietnam launched a general invasion against South Vietnamese armies in early 1974, Congress refused to permit any American military response. A second consequence of the U.S. crisis was that after more than thirty-five years of battle, the Vietnamese communists unified their country in 1975 as a harsh dictatorial state. Third, the belated fall of South Vietnam in the wake of Watergate shook America's postwar confidence and left the country divided and uncertain about its proper role in world affairs.

## Détente or Cold War?

One alternative to the badly damaged policy of containing communism was the policy of **détente,** or the progressive piecemeal relaxation of cold war tensions. Thus while the cold war continued to rage outside Europe and generally defined superpower relations between the Soviet Union and the United States, West Germany took a major step toward genuine peace in Europe.

West German chancellor Willy Brandt (1913–1992) took the lead when in December 1970 he flew to Poland for the signing of a historic treaty of reconciliation. In a dramatic moment rich in symbolism, Brandt laid a wreath at the tomb of the Polish unknown soldier and another at the monument commemorating the armed uprising of Warsaw's Jewish ghetto against occupying Nazi armies. Standing before the ghetto memorial, a somber Brandt fell to his knees and knelt as if in prayer. "I wanted," Brandt said later, "to ask pardon in the name of our people for a million-fold crime which was committed in the misused name of the Germans."[10]

Brandt's gesture at the Warsaw Ghetto memorial and the treaty with Poland were part of his policy of reconciliation with eastern Europe. Indeed, Brandt aimed at nothing less than a comprehensive peace settlement for central Europe and the two German states established after 1945. The Federal Republic of Germany (West Germany) had long claimed that the communist German Democratic Republic (East Germany) lacked free elections and hence any legal or moral basis. West Germany also refused to accept the loss of German territory taken by Poland and the Soviet Union after 1945. But Brandt, the popular socialist mayor of West Berlin when the Berlin Wall was built in 1961, believed that the wall showed the painful limitations of West Germany's official hard line toward communist eastern Europe. A new foreign policy was needed.

Winning the chancellorship in 1969, Brandt negotiated treaties with the Soviet Union, Poland, and Czechoslovakia that formally accepted existing state boundaries in return for a mutual renunciation of force or the threat of force. Using the imaginative formula of "two German states within one German nation," Brandt's government also broke decisively with the past and entered into direct relations with East Germany. He aimed for modest practical improvements rather than reunification, which at that point was completely impractical.

The policy of détente reached its high point when all European nations (except isolationist Albania), the United States, and Canada signed the Final Act of the Helsinki Conference in 1975. The thirty-five nations participating agreed that Europe's existing political frontiers could not be changed by force. They also solemnly accepted numerous provisions guaranteeing the human rights and political freedoms of their citizens.

Optimistic hopes for détente in international relations gradually faded in the later 1970s. Brezhnev's Soviet Union ignored the human rights provisions of the Helsinki agreement, and East-West political competition remained very much alive outside Europe. Many Americans became convinced that the Soviet Union was taking advantage of détente, steadily building up its military might and pushing for political gains and revolutions in Africa, Asia, and Latin America. The Soviet invasion of Afghanistan in December 1979, which was designed to save an increasingly unpopular Marxist regime, was especially alarming. Many Americans feared that the oil-rich states of the Persian Gulf would be next, and once again they looked to the Atlantic alliance and military might to thwart communist expansion.

President Jimmy Carter (b. 1924), elected in 1976, tried to lead the Atlantic alliance beyond verbal condemnation and urged economic sanctions against the Soviet Union. Yet only Great Britain among the European allies supported the American initiative. The alliance showed the same lack of concerted action when the Solidarity movement rose in Poland. Some observers concluded that the alliance had lost the will to think and act decisively in dealing with the Soviet bloc.

The Atlantic alliance endured, however. The U.S. military buildup launched by Carter in his last years in office was greatly accelerated by President Ronald Reagan (1911–2004), who was swept into office in 1980 by a wave of patriotism and economic discontent. The new American leadership acted as if the military balance had tipped in favor of the Soviet Union, which Reagan anathematized as the "evil empire." Increasing defense spending enormously, the Reagan administration concentrated on nuclear arms and an expanded navy as keys to American power in the post-Vietnam age.

A broad swing in the historical pendulum toward greater conservatism in the 1980s gave Reagan invaluable allies in western Europe. In Great Britain a strong-willed Margaret Thatcher worked well with Reagan and was a forceful advocate for a revitalized Atlantic alliance. After a strongly pro-American Helmut Kohl (b. 1930) came to power with the conservative Christian Democrats in 1982, West Germany and the United States once again effectively coordinated military and political policy toward the Soviet bloc.

Passing in the 1970s and early 1980s from détente to confusion to regeneration, the Atlantic alliance bent, but it did not break. In maintaining the alliance, the Western nations gave indirect support to ongoing efforts to liberalize authoritarian communist eastern Europe and probably helped convince the Soviet Union's Mikhail Gorbachev that endless cold war conflict was foolish and dangerous.

### The Women's Movement

The 1970s marked the birth of a broad-based feminist movement devoted to securing genuine gender equality and promoting the general interests of women. Three basic reasons accounted for this major development. First, ongoing changes in underlying patterns of motherhood and paid work created novel conditions and new demands (see pages 1010–1012). Second, a vanguard of feminist intellectuals articulated a powerful critique of gender relations, which stimulated many women to rethink their assumptions and challenge the status quo. Third, taking a lesson from the civil rights movement in the United States and worldwide student protest against the Vietnam War, dissatisfied individuals recognized that they had to band together if they were to influence politics and secure fundamental reforms.

One of the most influential works produced by this new feminist wave was *The Second Sex* (1949) by the French writer and philosopher Simone de Beauvoir (1908–1986). Characterizing herself as a "dutiful daughter" of the bourgeoisie in childhood, the adolescent Beauvoir came to see her pious and submissive mother as foolishly renouncing any self-expression outside of home and marriage and showing Beauvoir the dangers of a life she did not want. A brilliant university student, Beauvoir began at the Sorbonne a complex relationship with Jean-Paul Sartre, the future philosopher who became her lifelong intellectual companion and sometime lover.

Beauvoir analyzed the position of women within the framework of existential thought (see pages 924–925). She argued that women—like all human beings—were in essence free but that they had almost always been trapped by particularly inflexible and limiting conditions. (See the feature "Listening to the Past: A Feminist Critique of Marriage" on pages 1024–1025.) Only by means of courageous action and self-assertive creativity could a woman become a completely free person and escape the role of the inferior "other" that men had constructed for her gender. Drawing on history, philosophy, psychology,

**Italian Feminists** These women demonstrate in Rome in 1981 for the passage of legislation legalizing abortion, which the pope and the Catholic church have steadfastly opposed. This woman's provocative sign says that she does not want the pope in her bed. *(Giansanti/Corbis Sygma)*

biology, and literature, Beauvoir's massive investigation inspired a generation of women intellectuals.

One such woman was Betty Friedan (b. 1924), who played a key role in reopening a serious discussion of women's issues in the United States. Unlike Beauvoir, who believed that each woman had to chart her own course, Friedan reflected the American faith in group action and political solutions. As a working wife and the mother of three small children in the 1950s, Friedan became acutely aware of the conflicting pressures of career and family. Conducting an in-depth survey of her classmates at Smith College fifteen years after their graduation, she concluded that many well-educated women shared her growing dissatisfaction. In her pathbreaking study *The Feminine Mystique* (1963), Friedan identified this dissatisfaction as the "problem that has no name." According to Friedan, the cause of this nameless problem was a crisis of identity. Women were not permitted to become mature adults and genuine human beings. Instead, they were expected to conform to a false, infantile pattern of femininity and live (like Beauvoir's mother) for their husbands and children. In short, women faced what feminists would soon call *sexism,* a pervasive social problem that required drastic reforms.

When long-standing proposals to treat sex discrimination as seriously as race discrimination fell again on deaf ears, Friedan took the lead in 1966 in founding the National Organization for Women (NOW) to press for women's rights. NOW flourished, growing from seven hundred members in 1967 to forty thousand in 1974. Many other women's organizations of varying persuasions rose to follow NOW in Europe and the United States. Throughout the 1970s, a proliferation of publications, conferences, and institutions devoted to women's issues reinforced the emerging international movement.

Although national peculiarities abounded, this movement generally shared the common strategy of entering the political arena and changing laws regarding women. First, advocates of women's rights pushed for new statutes in the workplace: laws against discrimination, "equal pay for equal work," and measures such as maternal leave and affordable day care designed to help women combine careers and family responsibilities. Second, the movement concentrated on gender and family questions, including the right to divorce (in some Catholic countries), legalized abortion, the needs of single mothers, and protection from rape and physical violence. In almost every country, the effort to decriminalize abortion served as a catalyst in mobilizing an effective, self-conscious women's movement (and in creating an opposition to it, as in the United States).

In countries that had long placed women in a subordinate position, the legal changes were little less than revolutionary. In Italy, for example, new laws abolished restrictions on divorce and abortion, which had been strengthened by Mussolini and defended energetically by the Catholic church in the postwar era. By 1988 divorce and abortion were common in Italy, which had the lowest birthrate in Europe. More generally, the sharply focused women's movement of the 1970s won new rights for women. Subsequently, the movement became more diffuse, a victim of both its successes and the resurgence of an antifeminist opposition.

The accomplishments of the women's movement encouraged mobilization by many other groups. Gay men and lesbian women pressed their own demands, organizing politically and calling for an end to legal discrimination and social harassment. People with physical disabilities joined together to promote their interests. Thus many subordinate groups challenged the dominant majorities, and the expansion and redefinition of human liberty—one of the great themes of modern Western and world history—continued.

## The Troubled Economy

For twenty years after 1945, most Europeans were preoccupied with the possibilities of economic progress and consumerism. The more democratic class structure also helped to reduce social tension, and ideological conflict went out of style. In the late 1960s, sharp criticism and social conflict re-emerged, however, marking the passing of postwar stability.

Yet it was the reappearance of economic crisis in the early 1970s that brought the most serious challenges for the average person. The postwar international monetary system was based on the American dollar, valued in gold at $35 an ounce. Giving foreign aid and fighting foreign wars, the United States sent billions abroad. By early 1971, it had only $11 billion in gold left, and Europe had accumulated U.S. $50 billion. Foreigners then panicked and raced to exchange their dollars for gold. President Richard Nixon responded by stopping the sale of American gold. The value of the dollar fell sharply, and inflation accelerated worldwide. Fixed rates of exchange were abandoned, and great uncertainty replaced postwar predictability in international trade and finance.

Even more damaging was the dramatic reversal in the price and availability of energy. The great postwar boom was fueled by cheap oil from the Middle East, which permitted energy-intensive industries—automobiles, chemicals, and electric power—to expand rapidly and lead other sectors of the economy forward. By 1971 the Arab-led Organization of Petroleum Exporting Countries (**OPEC**) had watched the price of crude oil decline consistently compared with the rising price of manufactured goods and had decided to reverse that trend by presenting a united front against the oil companies. The stage was set for a revolution in energy prices during the fourth Arab-Israeli war in October 1973, when Egypt and Syria launched a surprise attack on Israel. OPEC then declared an embargo on oil shipments to the United States, Israel's ally, and within a year crude oil prices quadrupled. Western nations realized that the rapid price rise was economically destructive, but they did nothing. Thus governments, industry, and individuals had no other choice than to deal piecemeal with the so-called oil shock—a "shock" that turned out to be an earthquake.

Coming on the heels of upheaval in the international monetary system, the revolution in energy prices plunged the world into its worst economic decline since the 1930s. The energy-intensive industries that had driven the economy up in the 1950s and 1960s now dragged it down. Unemployment rose; productivity and living standards declined. By 1976 a modest recovery was in progress. But when a fundamentalist Islamic revolution struck Iran and oil production collapsed in that country, the price of crude oil doubled in 1979 and the world economy succumbed to its second oil shock. Unemployment and inflation rose dramatically before another uneven recovery began in 1982. In 1985 the unemployment rate in western Europe rose to its highest level since the Great Depression. Nineteen million people were unemployed.

One telling measure of the troubled economy was the **misery index,** which combined rates of inflation and unemployment in a single, powerfully emotional number. Figure 30.2 shows a comparison of misery indexes for the United States, Japan, and the Common Market countries between 1970 and 1986. "Misery" increased on both sides of the Atlantic, but the increase was substantially greater in western Europe, where these hard times were often referred to simply as "the crisis." Japan did better than both Europe and the United States in this period.

Throughout the 1970s and 1980s, anxious observers, recalling the disastrous consequences of the Great Depression, worried that the Common Market would disintegrate in the face of severe economic dislocation and that economic nationalism would halt steps toward European unity. Yet the Common Market—now officially known as the European Economic Community—continued to attract new members. In 1973 Denmark and Iceland, in addition to Britain, finally joined. Greece joined in 1981, and Portugal and Spain entered in 1986. The nations of the European Economic Community also cooperated more closely in international undertakings, and the movement toward unity for western Europe stayed alive.

## Society in a Time of Economic Uncertainty

The most pervasive consequences of economic stagnation in the 1970s and early 1980s were probably psychological and attitudinal. Optimism gave way to pessimism; romantic utopianism yielded to sober realism. This drastic change in mood—a complete surprise only to those who had never

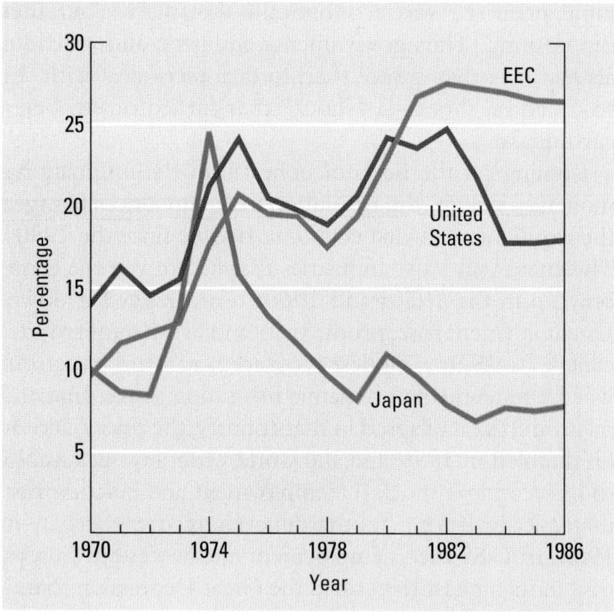


**FIGURE 30.2 The Misery Index, 1970–1986** Combining rates of unemployment and inflation provided a simple but effective measure of economic hardship. This particular index represents the sum of two times the unemployment rate plus the inflation rate, reflecting the widespread belief that joblessness causes more suffering than higher prices. EEC = European Economic Community, or Common Market countries. *(Source: OECD data, as given in* The Economist, *June 15, 1985, p. 69.)*

studied history—affected states, institutions, and individuals in countless ways.

To be sure, there were heartbreaking human tragedies—lost jobs, bankruptcies, homelessness, and mental breakdowns. But on the whole, the welfare system fashioned in the postwar era prevented mass suffering and degradation through extended benefits for the unemployed, pensions for the aged, free medical care and special allowances for the needy, and a host of lesser supports. The responsive, socially concerned national state undoubtedly contributed to the preservation of political stability and democracy in the face of economic difficulties that might have brought revolution and dictatorship in earlier times.

The energetic response of governments to social needs helps explain the sharp increase in total government spending in most countries during the 1970s and early 1980s. In 1982 western European governments spent an average of more than 50 percent of all national income, as compared to only 37 percent fifteen years earlier. In all countries, people were much more willing to see their governments increase spending than raise taxes. This imbalance contributed to the rapid growth of budget deficits, national debts, and inflation. By the late 1970s, a powerful reaction against government's ever-increasing role had set in, however, and Western governments were gradually forced to introduce austerity measures to slow the growth of public spending and the welfare state.

Part of a broad cultural shift toward greater conservatism, growing voter dissatisfaction with government and government spending helped bring Margaret Thatcher (b. 1925) to power in Britain in 1979. Thatcher had some success in slowing government spending and in "privatizing" industry—that is, in selling off state-owned companies to private investors. Thatcher's Conservative government also encouraged low- and moderate-income renters in state-owned housing projects to buy their apartments at rock-bottom prices. This privatization initiative created a whole new class of property owners, thereby eroding the electoral base of Britain's socialist Labour party.

President Ronald Reagan's success in the United States was more limited. With widespread popular support and the agreement of most congressional Democrats as well as Republicans, Reagan in 1981 pushed through major cuts in income taxes all across the board. But Reagan and Congress failed to cut government spending, which increased as a percentage of national income in the course of his presidency. Reagan's massive military buildup was partly responsible, but spending on social programs also grew rapidly. The harsh recession of the early 1980s required that the government spend more on unemployment benefits, welfare benefits, and medical treatment for the poor. Moreover, Reagan's antiwelfare rhetoric mobilized the liberal opposition and eventually turned many moderates against him. Thus the budget deficit soared and the U.S. government debt tripled in a decade.

The striking but temporary exception to the trend toward greater frugality was François Mitterrand (1916–1996) of France. After his election as president in 1981, Mitterrand led his Socialist party on a lurch to the left, launching a vast program of nationalization and public investment designed to spend France out of economic stagnation. By 1983 this attempt had clearly failed. Mitterrand's Socialist government was then compelled to impose a wide variety of austerity measures and to maintain those policies for the rest of the decade.

When governments were forced to restrain spending, large scientific projects were often singled out for cuts. These reductions reinforced the ongoing computer revolution. This new scientific revolution thrived on the diffusion of ever-cheaper computational and informational capacity to small research groups and private businesses, which were both cause and effect of the revolution itself. Big organizations lost some of their advantages over small firms.

Individuals felt the impact of austerity at an early date, for unlike governments, they could not pay their bills by printing money and going ever further into debt. The energy crisis of the 1970s forced them to re-examine not only their fuel bills but also the whole pattern of self-indulgent materialism in the postwar years. A growing number of experts and citizens concluded that the world was running out of resources and decried wasteful industrial practices and environmental pollution. In West Germany young activists known as the Greens in 1979 founded a political party to fight for environmental causes. The German Green movement elected some national and local representatives, and similar parties developed throughout Europe as environmentalism became a leading societal concern.

Another consequence of austerity in both Europe and North America was a leaner, tougher lifestyle in the 1970s and early 1980s, featuring more attention to nutrition and a passion for exercise. Correspondingly, there was less blind reliance on medical science for good health and a growing awareness that individuals had to accept a large portion of the responsibility for illness and disease. More people began to realize that they could substantially increase their life spans simply by eating regular meals, sleeping seven or eight hours each night, exercising two or three times a week, maintaining moderate weight, forgoing smoking, and using alcohol only in moderation. In the late 1970s, a forty-five-year-old American male who practiced three or fewer of these habits could expect to live to be sixty-seven; one who adhered to five or six could expect to live eleven years more, to age seventy-eight.

Economic troubles also strengthened the new trends within the family. Men and women were encouraged to postpone marriage until they had put their careers on a firm foundation, so the age of marriage rose sharply for both sexes in many Western countries. Indeed, the very real threat of unemployment—or "underemployment" in a dead-end job—seemed to shape the outlook of a

**German Greens Supporting Poland's Solidarity** Best known for its passionate commitment to the environment, the German Green party has also supported many progressive causes and campaigned against militarism and communism. These Greens are protesting in 1982 against the crackdown on Solidarity, the trade union movement that challenged Communist rule in Poland in the 1980s. The Greens are now Germany's third-largest political party, and they exercise real influence. *(Time Life Pictures/Getty Images)*

whole generation. College students of the 1980s were serious, practical, and often conservative. As one young woman at a French university told a reporter in 1985, "Jobs are the big worry now, so everyone wants to learn something practical."[11] In France as elsewhere, the shift away from the romantic visions and the political activism of the late 1960s was astonishing.

Harder times also help explain why ever more women entered or remained in the workforce after they did marry. Although attitudes related to personal fulfillment were one reason for the continuing increase—especially for well-educated, upper-middle-class women—many wives in poor and middle-class families simply had to work outside the home because of economic necessity. As in preindustrial Europe, the wife's earnings provided the margin of survival for millions of hard-pressed families.

## Summary

The recovery of western Europe after World War II was one of the most striking chapters in the long, uneven course of Western civilization. Although the dangerous tensions of the cold war frustrated hopes for a truly peaceful international order, the transition from imperialism to decolonization proceeded rapidly, surprisingly smoothly, and without serious damage to western Europe. Genuine political democracy gained unprecedented strength in western Europe, and rapid economic progress marked a generation.

Fundamental social changes accompanied the political recovery and economic expansion after World War II. Pure science combined with applied technology to achieve remarkable success. The triumphs of applied science contributed not only to economic expansion but also to a more fluid, less antagonistic class structure, in which specialized education was the high road to advancement for men and women. Married women entered the labor force in growing numbers.

Postwar developments in eastern Europe displayed both similarities to and differences from developments in western Europe and North America. Perhaps the biggest difference was that Stalin imposed harsh one-party rule in the lands occupied by his armies, which led to the bitter cold war. Nevertheless, the Soviet Union became less dictatorial under Khrushchev, and the standard of living in the Soviet Union improved markedly in the 1950s and 1960s.

In the late 1960s and early 1970s, Europe and North America entered a time of crisis. Many nations, from France to Czechoslovakia to the United States, experienced major political difficulties, as cold war conflicts and ideological battles divided peoples and shook governments. Beginning with the oil shocks of the 1970s, severe economic problems added to the turmoil and brought real hardship to millions of people. Yet in western Europe and North America, the welfare system held firm, and both democracy and the movement toward European unity successfully passed through the storm. The women's movement also mobilized effectively and won expanded rights in the best tradition of Western civilization. Finally, efforts to achieve détente in central Europe while still maintaining a strong Atlantic alliance met some success. This modest progress helped lay the foundations for the sudden end of the cold war and the opening of a new era.

## Key Terms

Big Three
Marshall Plan
NATO
cold war
Christian Democrats
Common Market
decolonization
neocolonialism
de-Stalinization
Brezhnev Doctrine
Big Science
Watergate
détente
OPEC
misery index

## Notes

1. Quoted in N. Graebner, *Cold War Diplomacy, 1945–1960* (Princeton, N.J.: Van Nostrand, 1962), p. 17.
2. Quoted ibid.
3. Quoted in J. Hennessy, *Economic "Miracles"* (London: Andre Deutsch, 1964), p. 5.
4. Quoted in S. E. Morison et al., *A Concise History of the American Republic* (New York: Oxford University Press, 1977), p. 697.
5. Quoted in D. Treadgold, *Twentieth Century Russia,* 5th ed. (Boston: Houghton Mifflin, 1981), p. 442.
6. Quoted in J. Ziman, *The Force of Knowledge: The Scientific Dimension of Society* (Cambridge: Cambridge University Press, 1976), p. 128.
7. Quoted in S. Toulmin, *The Twentieth Century: A Promethean Age,* ed. A. Bullock (London: Thames & Hudson, 1971), p. 294.
8. Quoted in N. Cantor, *Twentieth-Century Culture: Modernism to Deconstruction* (New York: Peter Lang, 1988), p. 252.
9. M. Mitterauer, *The History of Youth* (Oxford: Basil Blackwell, 1992), p. 40.
10. Quoted in Kessing's Research Report, *Germany and East Europe Since 1945: From the Potsdam Agreement to Chancellor Brandt's "Ostpolitik"* (New York: Charles Scribner's Sons, 1973), pp. 284–285.
11. *Wall Street Journal,* June 28, 1985, p. 1.

## Suggested Reading

M. Eksteins, *Walking Since Daybreak: A Story of Eastern Europe, World War II, and the Heart of Our Century* (1999), is a powerful, partly autobiographical account that is highly recommended. Three valuable general studies with extensive bibliographies are W. Hitchcock, *The Struggle for Europe:*

*The Turbulent History of a Divided Continent, 1945 to the Present* (2003); W. Laqueur, *Europe in Our Time: A History, 1945–1992* (1992); and C. Black, *Rebirth: A History of Europe Since World War II* (1992). Winston Churchill and Charles de Gaulle both wrote histories of the war in the form of memoirs. Other interesting memoirs are those of Dwight Eisenhower, *Crusade in Europe* (1948), and Dean Acheson, *Present at the Creation* (1969), a defense of American foreign policy in the early cold war. K. Sainsbury, *Churchill and Roosevelt at War: The War They Fought and the Peace They Hoped to Make* (1994), is an excellent, very readable introduction. Valuable works on the cold war include A. Winkler, *The Cold War: A Collection of Documents* (2000); P. de Senarclens, *From Yalta to the Iron Curtain: The Great Powers and the Origins of the Cold War* (1995); and M. Walker, *The Cold War: A History* (1993).

J. Gillingham, *European Integration, 1950–2003: Superstate or New Market Economy?* (2003), is a brilliant interpretive history, and D. Urwin, *The Community of Europe: A History of European Integration,* 2d ed. (1995), traces the steps toward western European unity. W. Leuchtenberg, *In the Shadow of FDR: From Harry Truman to Ronald Reagan* (1989), ably discusses developments in the United States. Postwar economic and social developments are analyzed in G. Ambrosius and W. Hibbard, *A Social and Economic History of Twentieth-Century Europe* (1989), and F. Tipton and R. Aldrich, *An Economic and Social History of Europe from 1939 to the Present* (1986).

Two outstanding works on France are K. Ross, *Fast Cars, Clean Bodies: Decolonization and the Reordering of French Culture* (1995), and S. Bernstein, *The Republic of de Gaulle, 1958–1969* (1993). On postwar West Germany, H. Turner, *The Two Germanies Since 1945: East and West* (1987), and W. Patterson and G. Smith, eds., *The West German Model: Perspectives on a Stable State* (1981), are good introductions. R. Dahrendorf, *Society and Democracy in Germany* (1971), is a classic interpretation. The spiritual dimension of West German recovery is probed by Günter Grass in his world-famous novel *The Tin Drum* (1963), as well as in the novels of Heinrich Böll. A. Marwick, *British Society Since 1945* (1982), and A. H. Halsey, *Change in British Society* (1981), are good on postwar developments. M. Chamberlain, *Decolonialization: The Fali of European Empires,* 2d ed. (1999), is a clear, up-to-date account. R. Betts, *Decolonization,* 2d ed. (2003), is a wide-ranging useful introduction, and J. Le Sueur, ed., *The Decolonization Reader* (2003), is a valuable collection of recent research.

Z. Brzezinski, *The Grand Failure: The Birth and Death of Communism in the Twentieth Century* (1989), is a readable overview by a leading American scholar. Two important studies of Soviet decline are S. Kotkin, *Armageddon Averted: The Soviet Collapse, 1970–2000* (2001), and W. Odum, *The Collapse of the Soviet Military* (1999). L. Johnson, *Central Europe: Enemies, Neighbors, Friends* (1996), is a stimulating synthesis discussing major developments. J. Ridley, *Tito* (1994), is lively and learned. P. Zinner, *Revolution in Hungary* (1962), is excellent on the tragic events of 1956.

R. Guha, *Environmentalism: A Global History* (2000), is a concise description of environmental movements around the world. A. Bramwell, *Ecology in the Twentieth Century: A History* (1989), examines negative aspects of technical and industrial development. Two more stimulating works on postwar technology are J. J. Servan-Schreiber, *The World Challenge* (1981), and H. Jacoby, *The Bureaucratization of the World* (1973).

Mitterauer and Cantor, both cited in the Notes, are excellent on the youth culture and the trends that made it possible. L. Wylie, *Village in the Vauclause* (1964), and P. J. Hélias, *The Horse of Pride* (1980), provide fascinating pictures of life in the French village before prosperity arrived. A. Kriegel, *The French Communists* (1972) and *Eurocommunism* (1978), are also recommended. D. Caute, *The Year of the Barricades: A Journey Through 1968* (1988), is a high-energy account that brings the upheavals of 1968 to life, while C. Fink et al., *1968: The World Transformed* (1998), is a stimulating reconsideration. Two outstanding works on the Vietnam War are R. Mann, *A Grand Delusion: America's Descent into Vietnam* (2001), and A. Short, *The Origins of the Vietnam War* (1989). Among the many books to come out of the Czechoslovak experience in 1968, Z. Zeman, *Prague Spring* (1969), is particularly recommended.

M. Boxer and J. Quartaert, *Connecting Spheres: European Women in a Globalizing World, 1500 to the Present,* 2d ed. (2000), is an excellent survey with up-to-date bibliographies. E. Sullerot, *Women, Society and Change* (1971), is a pioneering analysis of women's evolving roles after 1945. Two extremely influential books on women and their new awareness are S. de Beauvoir, *The Second Sex* (1949), and B. Friedan, *The Feminine Mystique* (1963). V. de Grazia and E. Furlough, eds., *The Sex of Things: Gender and Consumption in Historical Perspective* (1996), is an important, influential study on consumerism and gender relations.

J. Scott, *Only Paradoxes to Offer* (2000), is an up-to-date and important study of feminism and the women's movement. J. Lovenduski, *Women and European Politics: Contemporary Feminism and Public Policy* (1986), provides an extremely useful comparative study of similar developments in different countries. C. Duchen, *Feminism in France: From May '68 to Mitterrand* (1986), is also recommended. L. Appignanesi, *Simone de Beauvoir* (1988), is a readable study of the life and thought of the famous thinker. Good studies on British women include E. Wilson, *Only Halfway to Paradise: Women in Postwar Britain, 1945–1968* (1980), and M. Barrett, *Women's Opposition Today* (1980). U. Frevert, *Women in German History: From Bourgeois Emancipation to Sexual Liberation* (1989), is both learned and engaging. Two good studies on Soviet women before the collapse of communism are F. DuPlessix Gray, *Soviet Women* (1989), and T. Mamonova, ed., *Women and Russia* (1986).

# Listening to the Past

## A Feminist Critique of Marriage

*Having grown up in Paris in a middle-class family and become a teacher, novelist, and intellectual, Simone de Beauvoir (1908–1986) turned increasingly to feminist concerns after World War II. Her most influential work was* The Second Sex *(1949), a massive declaration of independence for contemporary women.*

*As an existentialist, Beauvoir believed that all individuals must accept responsibility for their lives and strive to overcome the tragic dilemmas they face. Studying the experience of women since antiquity, Beauvoir argued that men had generally used education and social conditioning to create a dependent "other," a negative nonman who was not permitted to grow and strive for freedom.*

*Marriage—on men's terms—was part of this unjust and undesirable process. Beauvoir's conclusion that some couples could establish free and equal unions was based in part on her experience with philosopher Jean-Paul Sartre, Beauvoir's encouraging companion and sometime lover.*

Every human existence involves transcendence and immanence at the same time; to go forward, each existence must be maintained, for it to expand toward the future it must integrate the past, and while intercommunicating with others it should find self-confirmation. These two elements—maintenance and progression—are implied in any living activity, and for *man* marriage permits precisely a happy synthesis of the two. In his occupation and his political life he encounters change and progress, he senses his extension through time and the universe; and when he is tired of such roaming, he gets himself a home, a fixed location, and an anchorage in the world. At evening he restores his soul in the home, where his wife takes care of his furnishings and children and guards the things of the past that she keeps in store. But she has no other job than to maintain and provide for life in pure and unvarying generality; she perpetuates the species without change, she ensures the even rhythm of the days and the continuity of the home, seeing to it that the doors are locked. But she is allowed no direct influence upon the future nor upon the world; she reaches out beyond herself toward the social group only through her husband as intermediary.

Marriage today still retains, for the most part, this traditional form. . . . The male is called upon for action, his vocation is to produce, fight, create, progress, to transcend himself toward the totality of the universe and the infinity of the future; but traditional marriage does not invite woman to transcend herself with him; it confines her in immanence, shuts her up within the circle of herself. She can thus propose to do nothing more than construct a life of stable equilibrium in which the present as a continuance of the past avoids the menaces of tomorrow—that is, construct precisely a life of happiness. . . .

In domestic work, with or without the aid of servants, woman makes her home her own, finds social justification, and provides herself with an occupation, an activity, that deals usefully and satisfyingly with material objects—shining stoves, fresh, clean clothes, bright copper, polished furniture—but provides no escape from immanence and little affirmation of individuality. . . . Few tasks are more like the torture of Sisyphus than housework, with its endless repetition: the clean becomes soiled, the soiled is made clean, over and over, day after day. The housewife wears herself out marking time: she makes nothing, simply perpetuates the present. She never senses conquest of a positive Good, but rather indefinite struggle against negative Evil. . . . Washing, ironing, sweeping, ferreting out rolls of lint from under wardrobes—all this halting of decay is also the denial of life; for time simultaneously creates and destroys, and only its negative aspect concerns the housekeeper. . . .

Thus woman's work within the home gives her no autonomy; it is not directly useful to society, it does not open out on the future, it produces nothing. It takes on meaning and dignity only as it is linked with existent beings who reach out beyond themselves, transcend themselves, toward society in production and action. That is, far from freeing the matron, her occupation makes her dependent upon husband and children; she is justified through them; but in their lives she is only an inessential intermediary. . . .

The tragedy of marriage is not that it fails to assure woman the promised happiness—there is no such thing as assurance in regard to happiness—but that it mutilates her; it dooms her to repetition and routine. The first twenty years of woman's life are extraordinarily rich, as we have seen; she discovers the world and her destiny. At twenty or thereabouts mistress of a home, bound permanently to a man, a child in her arms, she stands with her life virtually finished forever. Real activities, real work, are the prerogative of her man: she has mere things to occupy her which are sometimes tiring but never fully satisfying. . . .

Marriage should be a combining of two whole, independent existences, not a retreat, an annexation, a flight, a remedy. . . . The couple should not be regarded as a unit, a close cell; rather each individual should be integrated as such in society at large, where each (whether male or female) could flourish without aid; then attachments could be formed in pure generosity with another individual equally adapted to the group, attachments that would be founded upon the acknowledgment that both are free.

This balanced couple is not a utopian fancy: such couples do exist, sometimes even within the frame of marriage, most often outside it. Some mates are united by a strong sexual love that leaves them free in their friendships and in their work; others are held together by a friendship that does not preclude sexual liberty; more rare are those who are at once lovers and friends but do not seek in each other their sole reasons for living. Many nuances are possible in the relations between a man and a woman: in comradeship, pleasure, trust, fondness, co-operation, and love, they can be for each other the most abundant source of joy, richness, and power available to human beings.

Simone de Beauvoir as a teacher in 1947, when she was writing *The Second Sex. (Hulton-Deutsch Collection/Corbis)*

## Questions for Analysis

1. How did Beauvoir analyze marriage and marriage partners in terms of existential philosophy?
2. To what extent does a married woman benefit from a "traditional" marriage, according to Beauvoir? Why?
3. What was Beauvoir's solution to the situation she described? Was her solution desirable? Realistic?
4. What have you learned about the history of women that supports or challenges Beauvoir's analysis? Include developments since World War II and your own reflections.

*Source:* Simone de Beauvoir, *The Second Sex,* trans. H. M. Parshley. Copyright © 1952 and renewed 1980 by Alfred A. Knopf, a division of Random House, Inc. Used by permission of Alfred A. Knopf, a division of Random House, Inc.

The European Parliament, Strasbourg.
*(Stuart Franklin/Magnum Photos)*

chapter

# 31 Revolution, Rebuilding, and New Challenges: 1985 to the Present

## chapter outline

- The Decline of Communism in Eastern Europe
- The Revolutions of 1989
- Building a New Europe in the 1990s
- New Challenges in the Twenty-first Century
- The Future in Perspective

In the late twentieth century, massive changes swept through eastern Europe and opened a new era in human history. Efforts in the late 1980s to reform and revitalize the communist system in the Soviet Union snowballed out of control, and in 1989 revolutions swept away communist rule throughout the entire Soviet bloc. The cold war came to a spectacular end, West Germany absorbed East Germany, and the Soviet Union broke into fifteen independent countries. Thus after forty years of cold war division, Europe regained an underlying unity, as faith in democratic government and some kind of market economy became the common European creed. In 1991 hopes for peaceful democratic progress throughout Europe were almost universal.

The post–cold war years saw the realization of some of these hopes, but the new era brought its own problems and tragedies. The cold war division of Europe had kept a lid on ethnic conflicts and nationalism, which suddenly burst into the open and led to a disastrous civil war in the former Yugoslavia. Moreover, most western European economies were plagued by high unemployment and struggling to adapt to the wide-open global economy, which undermined cherished social benefits and complicated the task of working together with the former communist states. Thus in eastern Europe, the process of rebuilding shattered societies was more difficult than optimists had envisioned in 1991, and in western Europe, the road toward greater integration and eastward expansion proved bumpy. Nevertheless, the will to undo the cold war division prevailed, and in 2004 eight former communist countries as well as the islands of Cyprus and Malta joined the European Union—a historic achievement.

The new century brought a growing awareness of a new set of fundamental challenges, which were related to the prospect of population decline, the reality of large-scale immigration, the promotion of human rights, and the future of Western cooperation in world affairs. These challenges promised to preoccupy Western society for years to come.

- Why did efforts to reform the communist system fail and result in successful anticommunist revolutions throughout eastern Europe?
- What were the consequences of these revolutions and the end of the cold war?

- How, in the 1990s, did the different parts of a unifying Europe meet the challenges of postcommunist reconstruction, resurgent nationalism, and economic union?
- What new challenges are facing Europe in the twenty-first century, and how did war in Iraq split the West?

These are the fundamental questions that this chapter will address.

## The Decline of Communism in Eastern Europe

See DBQ 14

The Soviet bloc perplexed Western observers in the 1970s and early 1980s, and with good reason. On the one hand, attempts to liberalize the system continued, and the brutality of the Stalinist era was never re-established after Nikita Khrushchev fell from power in 1964. These changes encouraged Western hopes of gradual liberalization and of a more democratic, less threatening Soviet eastern Europe.

On the other hand, hard facts frequently intervened to undermine these hopes. In addition to periodic threats and military action, the Soviet Union repeatedly demonstrated that it remained a harsh and aggressive dictatorship that paid only lip service to egalitarian ideology and was determined to uphold its rule throughout eastern Europe. Periodic efforts to achieve fundamental political change were doomed to failure sooner or later—or so it seemed to most Western experts into the mid-1980s.

And then Mikhail Gorbachev burst on the scene. The new Soviet leader opened an era of reform that was as sweeping as it was unexpected. Although many believed that Gorbachev would soon fall from power, his reforms rapidly transformed Soviet culture and politics, and they drastically reduced cold war tensions. But communism, which Gorbachev wanted so desperately to revitalize in order to save it, continued to decline as a functioning system throughout the Soviet bloc.

### The Soviet Union to 1985

The 1968 invasion of Czechoslovakia (see pages 1006–1007) was the crucial event of the Brezhnev era, a period that actually lasted beyond the aging leader's death in 1982 until the emergence in 1985 of Gorbachev. The invasion demonstrated the intense conservatism of the Soviet Union's ruling elite and its determination to maintain the status quo in the Soviet bloc. There was a certain **re-Stalinization** of the U.S.S.R., but now dictatorship was collective rather than personal and coercion replaced terror. This compromise seemed to suit the leaders and a majority of the people.

A slowly rising standard of living for ordinary people contributed to the apparent stability in the Soviet Union, although long lines and innumerable shortages persisted. Ambitious individuals had tremendous incentive to do as the state wished in order to gain access to special, well-stocked stores, to attend special schools, and to travel abroad.

Another source of stability was the enduring nationalism of ordinary **Great Russians.** Party leaders successfully identified themselves with Russian patriotism, stressing their role in saving the country during the Second World War and protecting it now from foreign foes, including eastern European "counter-revolutionaries." Moreover, the politically dominant Great Russians, who were concentrated in the central Russian heartland and held through the Communist party the commanding leadership positions in the non-Russian republics, constituted less than half of the total Soviet population. The Great Russians generally feared that greater freedom might result in demands for autonomy and even independence not only by eastern European nationalities but also by the non-Russian nationalities within the Soviet Union itself. Thus liberalism and democracy generally appeared to Great Russians as alien political philosophies designed to undermine the U.S.S.R.'s power and greatness.

The strength of the government was expressed in the re-Stalinization of culture and art. Free expression disappeared and Brezhnev and company made certain that Soviet intellectuals did not engage in public protest. Acts of open nonconformity and protest were severely punished, but with sophisticated, cunning methods. Most frequently, dissidents were blacklisted and thus rendered unable to find decent jobs since the government was the only employer. This fate was enough to keep most in line. More determined protesters were quietly imprisoned, while celebrated nonconformists such as Aleksandr Solzhenitsyn were permanently expelled from the country. Eliminating the worst aspects of Stalin's dictatorship strengthened the regime, and almost all Western experts concluded that rule by a self-perpetuating Communist party elite in the Soviet Union appeared to be quite solid in the 1970s and early 1980s.

Yet beneath the dreary immobility of political life in the Brezhnev era, the Soviet Union was actually experiencing profound changes. As a perceptive British journalist put it in 1986, "The country went through a social revolution while Brezhnev slept."[1] Three aspects of this

1985 1990 1995 2000 2005

## POLITICAL/MILITARY

- August 1989 Solidarity gains power in Poland
- November 1989 Collapse of the Berlin Wall
- December 1989 Velvet Revolution ends communism in Czechoslovakia
- 1990–1991 First war with Iraq
- October 1990 Reunification of Germany
- 1991–2001 Civil war in Yugoslavia
- July 1991 Failed coup against Gorbachev in Russia
- December 1991 Dissolution of the Soviet Union
- 1993 Creation of the European Union
- September 2001 Terrorist attack on the United States
- 2001 War in Afghanistan
- 2003 Second war in Iraq begins
- 2004 Ten new states join European Union

## SOCIAL/ECONOMIC

- 1985– Decline in birthrate in industrialized nations continues
- 1986 Single European Act lays groundwork for single currency
- 1991 Maastricht treaty sets financial criteria for European monetary union
- 1992–1997 "Shock therapy" in Russia causes decline of the economy
- 1993– Growth of illegal immigration in Europe
- 1999 Russian economy booms
- January 2002 New euro currency goes into effect in the European Union

## INTELLECTUAL/RELIGIOUS

- 1985 Glasnost leads to greater freedom of speech and expression in the Soviet Union
- 1991–2000 Resurgence of nationalism and ethnic conflict in eastern Europe
- 1992 Fukuyama, *The End of History and the Last Man*
- 1996 Cronin, *The World the Cold War Made*
- 1998– Growing support for global human rights in Europe
- 2000 Controversy over Muslim headscarves in French schools begins

**"What's This? You Have Your Own Opinion?"** This cartoon, published in the Soviet Union's enormously popular satirical magazine *The Crocodile,* shows a Soviet manager getting into trouble for drawing a nonstandard doodle at a meeting. Jokes poking fun at communist bosses and human foibles permeated Soviet culture, especially the oral culture, in the Brezhnev era. *(© Vneshtorgizdat, Moscow)*

revolution, which was seldom appreciated by Western observers at the time, were particularly significant.

First, the growth of the urban population, which had raced forward at breakneck speed in the Stalin years, continued rapidly in the 1960s and 1970s. In 1985 two-thirds of all Soviet citizens lived in cities, and one-quarter lived in big cities. Of great significance, this expanding urban population lost its old peasant ways, exchanging them for more education, better job skills, and greater sophistication.

Second, the number of highly trained scientists, managers, and specialists expanded prodigiously, increasing fourfold between 1960 and 1985. Thus the class of well-educated, pragmatic, and self-confident experts, which played such an important role in restructuring industrial societies after World War II (see pages 1008–1009), developed rapidly in the Soviet Union. Moreover, leading Soviet scientists and technologists sought membership in the international "invisible college" of their disciplines. They sought the intellectual freedom necessary to do significant work, and they often obtained it because their research had practical (and military) value.

Third, education and freedom for experts in their special areas helped foster the growth of Soviet public opinion. Educated people read, discussed, and formed definite ideas about social questions. And if caution dictated conventional ideas (at least in public), many important issues could be approached and debated in "nonpolitical" terms. Developing definite ideas on such issues as environmental pollution and urban transportation, educated urban people increasingly saw themselves as worthy of having a voice in society's decisions, even its political decisions.

## Solidarity in Poland

Gorbachev's reforms interacted with a resurgence of popular protest in the Soviet Union's satellite empire. Developments in Poland were most striking and significant.

Poland had been an unruly satellite from the beginning. Stalin said that introducing communism to Poland was like putting a saddle on a cow. Efforts to saddle the cow—really a spirited stallion—led to widespread riots in 1956 (see page 1006). As a result, Polish Communists dropped their efforts to impose Soviet-style collectivization on the peasants and to break the Roman Catholic church. Most agricultural land remained in private hands, and the Catholic church thrived. Thus the Communists failed to monopolize society.

They also failed to manage the economy effectively. Even the booming 1960s saw little economic improve-

**Lech Walesa and Solidarity** An inspiration for fellow workers at the Lenin Shipyards in the dramatic and successful strike against the Communist bosses in August 1980, Walesa played a key role in Solidarity before and after it was outlawed. Speaking here to old comrades at the Lenin Shipyards after Solidarity was again legalized in 1988, Walesa personified an enduring opposition to Communist rule in eastern Europe. *(G. Merrillon/Gamma)*

ment. In 1970 Poland's working class rose again in angry protest. A new Communist leader came to power, and he wagered that massive inflows of Western capital and technology, especially from rich and now-friendly West Germany (see pages 1016–1017), could produce a Polish "economic miracle." Instead, bureaucratic incompetence and the first oil shock in 1973 put the economy into a nosedive. Workers, intellectuals, and the church became increasingly restive. Then the real Polish miracle occurred: Cardinal Karol Wojtyla, archbishop of Cracow, was elected pope in 1978. In June 1979, he returned from Rome, preaching love of Christ and country and the "inalienable rights of man." Pope John Paul II drew enormous crowds and electrified the Polish nation. The economic crisis became a moral and spiritual crisis as well.

In August 1980, the sixteen thousand workers at the gigantic Lenin Shipyards in Gdansk (formerly known as Danzig) laid down their tools and occupied the plant. As other workers joined "in solidarity," the strikers advanced revolutionary demands, including the right to form free trade unions, freedom of speech, release of political prisoners, and economic reforms. After eighteen days of shipyard occupation, the government gave in and accepted the workers' demands in the **Gdansk Agreement.** In a state where the Communist party claimed to rule on behalf of the proletariat, a working-class revolt had won an unprecedented victory.

Led by feisty Lenin Shipyards electrician and devout Catholic Lech Walesa (b. 1943), the workers proceeded to organize their free and democratic trade union. They called it **Solidarity.** Joined by intellectuals and supported by the Catholic church, Solidarity became the union of a nation. By March 1981, a full-time staff of 40,000 linked 9.5 million union members together as Solidarity published its own newspapers and cultural and intellectual freedom blossomed in Poland. Solidarity's leaders had tremendous support, and the ever-present threat of calling a nationwide strike gave them real power in ongoing negotiations with the Communist bosses.

But if Solidarity had power, it did not try to take the reins of government in 1981. History, the Brezhnev Doctrine, and virulent attacks from communist neighbors all seemed to guarantee the intervention of the Red Army and a terrible bloodbath if Polish Communists "lost control." Thus the Solidarity revolution remained a "self-limiting revolution" aimed at defending the cultural and trade-union freedoms won in the Gdansk Agreement, and it refused to use force to challenge directly the Communist monopoly of political power.

Solidarity's combination of strength and moderation postponed a showdown, as the Soviet Union played a waiting game of threats and pressure. After a confrontation in March 1981, Walesa settled for minor government concessions, and Solidarity dropped plans for a massive general strike. Criticism of Walesa's moderate leadership grew, and Solidarity lost its cohesiveness. The worsening economic crisis also encouraged grassroots radicalism, as the Polish Communist leadership shrewdly denounced Solidarity for promoting economic collapse and provoking Soviet invasion. In December 1981, Communist leader General Wojciech Jaruzelski suddenly struck, proclaiming martial law, arresting Solidarity's leaders, and "saving" the nation.

Outlawed and driven underground, Solidarity fought successfully to maintain its organization and to voice the aspirations of the Polish masses after 1981. Part of the reason for the union's survival was the government's unwillingness (and probably its inability) to impose full-scale terror. Moreover, millions of Poles decided to continue acting as if they were free, even though they were not. Cultural and intellectual life remained extremely vigorous as the faltering Polish economy continued to deteriorate. Thus popular support for outlawed Solidarity remained strong under martial law in the 1980s, preparing the way for the union's political rebirth toward the end of the decade.

The rise and survival of Solidarity showed the desire of millions of eastern Europeans for greater political liberty and the enduring appeal of cultural freedom, trade-union rights, patriotic nationalism, and religious feeling. Not least, Solidarity's challenge encouraged fresh thinking in the Soviet Union, ever the key to lasting change in the Eastern bloc.

## Gorbachev's Reforms in the Soviet Union

Fundamental change in Russian history has often come in short, intensive spurts, which contrast vividly with long periods of immobility. The era of reform launched by Mikhail Gorbachev in 1985 was one such decisive transformation. Gorbachev's initiatives brought political and cultural liberalization to the Soviet Union, and they then permitted democracy and national self-determination to triumph spectacularly in the old satellite empire and eventually in the Soviet Union itself, although this was certainly not Gorbachev's original intention.

As we have seen, the Soviet Union's Communist party elite seemed secure in the early 1980s as far as any challenge from below was concerned. The long-established system of administrative controls continued to stretch downward from the central ministries and state committees to provincial cities, and from there to factories, neighborhoods, and villages. At each level of this massive state bureaucracy, the overlapping hierarchy of the Communist party, with its 17.5 million members, continued to watch over all decisions and manipulate every aspect of national life. Organized opposition was impossible, and average people simply left politics to the bosses.

Yet the massive state and party bureaucracy was a mixed blessing. It safeguarded the elite, but it promoted apathy in the masses. Therefore, when the ailing Brezhnev finally died in 1982, his successor, the long-time chief of the secret police, Yuri Andropov (1914–1984), tried to invigorate the system. Relatively little came of these efforts, but they combined with a sharply worsening economic situation to set the stage for the emergence in 1985 of Mikhail Gorbachev (b. 1931), the most vigorous Soviet leader in a generation.

Trained as a lawyer and working his way up as a Communist party official in the northern Caucasus, Gorbachev was smart, charming, and tough. Gorbachev believed in communism, but he realized it was failing to keep up with Western capitalism and technology. This was eroding the Soviet Union's status as a superpower. Thus Gorbachev (and his intelligent, influential wife, Raisa, a dedicated professor of Marxist-Leninist thought) wanted to save the Soviet system by revitalizing it with fundamental reforms. Gorbachev was also an idealist. He wanted to improve conditions for ordinary citizens. Understanding that the endless waste and expense of the cold war arms race had had a disastrous impact on living conditions in the Soviet Union, he realized that improvement at home required better relations with the West.

In his first year in office, Gorbachev attacked corruption and incompetence in the bureaucracy, and he consolidated his power. He attacked alcoholism and drunkenness, which were deadly scourges of Soviet society, and elaborated his ambitious reform program.

The first set of reform policies was designed to transform and restructure the economy, in order to provide for the real needs of the Soviet population. To accomplish this economic "restructuring," or **perestroika,** Gorbachev and his supporters permitted an easing of government price controls on some goods, more independence for state enterprises, and the setting up of profit-seeking private cooperatives to provide personal services for consumers. These timid economic reforms initially produced a few improvements, but shortages then grew as the economy stalled at an intermediate point between central planning and free-market mechanisms. By late 1988, widespread consumer dissatisfaction posed a serious threat to Gorbachev's leadership and the entire reform program.

Gorbachev's bold and far-reaching campaign "to tell it like it is" was much more successful. Very popular in a country where censorship, dull uniformity, and outright lies had long characterized public discourse, the newfound "openness," or **glasnost,** of the government and the media marked an astonishing break with the past. Long-banned and vilified émigré writers sold millions of copies of their works in new editions, while denunciations of Stalin and his terror became standard fare in plays and movies. Thus initial openness in government pronouncements quickly went much further than Gorbachev intended and led to something approaching free speech and free expression, a veritable cultural revolution.

Democratization was the third element of reform. Beginning as an attack on corruption in the Communist party, it led to the first free elections in the Soviet Union since 1917. Gorbachev and the party remained in control, but a minority of critical independents was elected in April 1989 to a revitalized Congress of People's Deputies. Millions of Soviets then watched the new congress for hours on television as Gorbachev and his ministers saw their proposals debated and even rejected. Thus millions of Soviet citizens took practical lessons in open discussion, critical thinking, and representative government. The result was a new political culture at odds with the Communist party's monopoly of power and control.

Democratization ignited demands for greater autonomy and even for national independence by non-Russian minorities, especially in the Baltic region and in the Caucasus. In April 1989, troops with sharpened shovels charged into a rally of Georgian separatists in Tbilisi and left twenty dead. But whereas China's Communist leaders brutally massacred similar prodemocracy demonstrators in Beijing in June 1989 and reimposed rigid authoritarian rule, Gorbachev drew back from repression. Thus nationalist demands continued to grow in the non-Russian Soviet republics.

Finally, the Soviet leader brought "new political thinking" to the field of foreign affairs and acted on it. He withdrew Soviet troops from Afghanistan and sought to reduce East-West tensions. Of enormous importance, he sought to halt the arms race with the United States and convinced President Ronald Reagan of his sincerity. In December 1987, the two leaders agreed in a Washington

**Mikhail Gorbachev** In his acceptance speech before the Supreme Soviet (the U.S.S.R.'s parliament), newly elected president Mikhail Gorbachev vowed to assume "all responsibility" for the success or failure of perestroika. Previous parliaments were no more than tools of the Communist party, but this one actively debated and even opposed government programs. *(Vlastimir Shone/Gamma)*

**MAP 31.1 Democratic Movements in Eastern Europe, 1989** With Gorbachev's repudiation of the Brezhnev Doctrine, the revolutionary drive for freedom and democracy spread throughout eastern Europe. Countries that had been satellites in the orbit of the Soviet Union began to set themselves free to establish their own place in the universe of free nations.

summit to eliminate all land-based intermediate-range missiles in Europe, setting the stage for more arms reductions. Gorbachev also encouraged reform movements in Poland and Hungary and pledged to respect the political choices of the peoples of eastern Europe, repudiating the Brezhnev Doctrine. By early 1989, it seemed that if Gorbachev held to his word, the tragic Soviet occupation of eastern Europe might well wither away, taking the long cold war with it once and for all.

## The Revolutions of 1989

See DBQ 14

Instead, history accelerated. In 1989 Gorbachev's plan to reform communism in order to save it snowballed out of control. A series of largely peaceful revolutions swept across eastern Europe (see Map 31.1), overturning existing communist regimes and ending the communists' monopoly of power. Watched on television in the Soviet Union and around the world, these stirring events marked the triumph and the transformation of long-standing opposition to communist rule and foreign domination in eastern Europe.

The revolutions of 1989 had momentous consequences. First, the peoples of eastern Europe joyfully re-entered the mainstream of contemporary European life and culture, after having been conquered and brutalized by Nazis and communists for almost sixty years. Second, Gorbachev's reforms boomeranged, and a complicated anticommunist revolution swept through the Soviet Union, as the multinational empire broke into a large Russia and fourteen other independent states. Third, West Germany quickly absorbed its East German rival and emerged as the most influential country in Europe. Finally, the long cold war came to an abrupt end, and the United States suddenly stood as the world's only superpower.

## The Collapse of Communism in Eastern Europe

Solidarity and the Polish people led the way to revolution in eastern Europe. In 1988 widespread labor unrest, raging inflation, and the outlawed Solidarity's refusal to cooperate with the military government had brought Poland to the brink of economic collapse. Thus Solidarity skillfully pressured Poland's frustrated Communist leaders into another round of negotiations that might work out a sharing of power to resolve the political stalemate and the economic crisis. The subsequent agreement in early 1989 legalized Solidarity and declared that a large minority of representatives to the Polish parliament would be chosen by free elections in June 1989. Still guaranteed a parliamentary majority and expecting to win many of the contested seats, the Communists believed that their rule was guaranteed for four years and that Solidarity would keep the workers in line.

Lacking access to the state-run media, Solidarity succeeded nonetheless in mobilizing the country and winning most of the contested seats in an overwhelming victory. Moreover, many angry voters crossed off the names of unopposed party candidates, so that the Communist party

**Demonstrators During the Velvet Revolution** Hundreds of thousands of Czechoslovakian citizens flooded the streets of Prague in peaceful, daily protests after the police savagely beat student demonstrators in mid-November 1989. On the night of November 24, three hundred thousand people roared "Dubček-Havel" when Alexander Dubček, the aging reformer ousted in 1968 by the Soviets, stood on a balcony with Václav Havel, the leading opponent of communism. That night the communist government agreed to share power—the climax of the Velvet Revolution. *(Corbis)*

**The Fall of the Berlin Wall** The sudden opening of the Berlin Wall in November 1989 dramatized the spectacular collapse of communism throughout eastern Europe. Built by the Soviet leader Nikita Khrushchev in 1961, the hated barrier had stopped the flow of refugees from East Germany to West Germany. *(Patrick Piel/Gamma)*

failed to win the majority they had anticipated. Solidarity members jubilantly entered the Polish parliament, and a dangerous stalemate quickly developed. But Solidarity leader Lech Walesa, a gifted politician who always repudiated violence, adroitly obtained a majority by securing the allegiance of two minor procommunist parties that had been part of the coalition government after World War II. In August 1989, the editor of Solidarity's weekly newspaper was sworn in as Poland's new noncommunist leader.

In its first year and a half, the new Solidarity government cautiously introduced revolutionary political changes. It eliminated the hated secret police, the Communist ministers in the government, and finally Jaruzelski himself, but it did so step by step in order to avoid confrontation with the army or the Soviet Union. However, in economic affairs, the Solidarity-led government was radical from the beginning. It applied **shock therapy** designed to make a clean break with state planning and move quickly to market mechanisms and private property. Thus the Solidarity government abolished controls on many prices on January 1, 1990, and reformed the monetary system with a "big bang."

Hungary followed Poland. Hungary's Communist party boss, János Kádár, had permitted liberalization of the rigid planned economy after the 1956 uprising in exchange for political obedience and continued Communist control. In May 1988, in an effort to retain power by granting modest political concessions, the party replaced

Kádár with a reform communist. But opposition groups rejected piecemeal progress, and in the summer of 1989 the Hungarian Communist party agreed to hold free elections in early 1990. Welcoming Western investment and moving rapidly toward multiparty democracy, Hungary's Communists now enjoyed considerable popular support, and they believed, quite mistakenly it turned out, that they could defeat the opposition in the upcoming elections. In an effort to strengthen their support at home and also put pressure on East Germany's hard-line Communist regime, the Hungarians opened their border to East Germans and tore down the barbed-wire "iron curtain" with Austria. Thus tens of thousands of dissatisfied East German "vacationers" began pouring into Hungary, crossed into Austria as refugees, and continued on to immediate resettlement in thriving West Germany.

The flight of East Germans led to the rapid growth of a homegrown protest movement in East Germany. Intellectuals, environmentalists, and Protestant ministers took the lead, organizing huge candlelight demonstrations and arguing that a democratic but still socialist East Germany was both possible and desirable. These "stayers" failed to convince the "leavers," however, who continued to flee the country en masse. In a desperate attempt to stabilize the situation, the East German government opened the Berlin Wall in November 1989, and people danced for joy atop that grim symbol of the prison state. East Germany's aging Communist leaders were swept aside, and a reform government took power and scheduled free elections.

In Czechoslovakia, communism died in December 1989 in an almost good-humored ousting of Communist bosses in only ten days. This so-called **Velvet Revolution** grew out of popular demonstrations led by students, intellectuals, and a dissident playwright turned moral revolutionary named Václav Havel. The protesters practically took control of the streets and forced the Communists into a power-sharing arrangement, which quickly resulted in the resignation of the Communist government. As 1989 ended, the Czechoslovakian assembly elected Havel president.

Only in Romania was revolution violent and bloody. There ironfisted Communist dictator Nicolae Ceauşescu (1918–1989) had long combined Stalinist brutality with stubborn independence from Moscow. Faced with mass protests in December, Ceauşescu, alone among eastern European bosses, ordered his ruthless security forces to slaughter thousands, thereby sparking a classic armed uprising. After Ceauşescu's forces were defeated, the tyrant and his wife were captured and executed by a military court. A coalition government emerged from the fighting, although the legacy of Ceauşescu's oppression left a very troubled country.

## The Disintegration of the Soviet Union

As 1990 began, revolutionary changes had triumphed in all but two eastern European states—tiny Albania and the vast Soviet Union. The great question now became whether the Soviet Union would follow its former satellites and whether reform communism would give way to a popular anticommunist revolution.

In February 1990, as competing Russian politicians noisily presented their programs, and nationalists in the non-Russian republics demanded autonomy or independence from the Soviet Union, the Communist party suffered a stunning defeat in local elections throughout the country. As in the eastern European satellites, democrats and anticommunists won clear majorities in the leading cities of the Russian Federation. Moreover, in Lithuania the people elected an uncompromising nationalist as president, and the newly chosen parliament declared Lithuania an independent state. Gorbachev responded by placing an economic embargo on Lithuania, but he refused to use the army to crush the separatist government. The result was a tense political stalemate, which undermined popular support for Gorbachev. Separating himself further from Communist hard-liners, Gorbachev asked Soviet citizens to ratify a new constitution, which formally abolished the Communist party's monopoly of political power and expanded the power of the Congress of People's Deputies. Retaining his post as party secretary, Gorbachev convinced a majority of deputies to elect him president of the Soviet Union.

Gorbachev's eroding power and his unwillingness to risk a universal suffrage election for the presidency strengthened his great rival, Boris Yeltsin (b. 1931). A radical reform communist who had been purged by party conservatives in 1987, Yeltsin embraced the democratic movement, and in May 1990 he was elected leader of the Russian Federation's parliament. He boldly announced that Russia would put its interests first and declare its independence from the Soviet Union, thereby broadening the base of the anticommunist movement as he joined the patriotism of ordinary Russians with the democratic aspirations of big-city intellectuals. Gorbachev tried to save the Soviet Union with a new treaty that would link the member republics in a looser, freely accepted confederation, but six of the fifteen Soviet republics rejected Gorbachev's pleas.

Opposed by democrats and nationalists, Gorbachev was also challenged again by the Communist old guard. Defeated at the Communist party congress in July 1990,

**Celebrating Victory, August 1991** A Russian soldier flashes the victory sign in front of the Russian parliament, as the last-gasp coup attempt of Communist hard-liners is defeated by Boris Yeltsin and an enthusiastic public. The soldier has cut the hammer and sickle out of the Soviet flag, consigning those famous symbols of proletarian revolution to what Trotsky once called the "garbage can of history." *(Filip Horvat/Corbis Saba)*

a gang of hard-liners kidnapped a vacationing Gorbachev and his family in the Caucasus and tried to seize the Soviet government in August 1991. But the attempted coup collapsed in the face of massive popular resistance, which rallied around Yeltsin, recently elected president of the Russian Federation by universal suffrage. As the world watched spellbound on television, Yeltsin defiantly denounced the rebels from atop a stalled tank in central Moscow and declared the "rebirth of Russia." The army supported Yeltsin, and Gorbachev was rescued and returned to power as head of the Soviet Union.

The leaders of the coup wanted to preserve Communist power, state ownership, and the multinational Soviet Union, but they succeeded only in destroying all three. An anticommunist revolution swept the Russian Federation as Yeltsin and his supporters outlawed the Communist party and confiscated its property. Locked in a personal and political duel with Gorbachev, Yeltsin and his democratic allies declared Russia independent and withdrew from the Soviet Union. All the other Soviet republics also left. The Soviet Union—and Gorbachev's job—ceased to exist on December 25, 1991 (see Map 31.2). The independent republics of the old Soviet Union then established a loose confederation, the Commonwealth of Independent States, which played only a minor role in the 1990s.

## German Unification and the End of the Cold War

The sudden death of communism in East Germany in 1989 reopened the "German question," and raised the threat of renewed cold war conflict over Germany. Taking

**MAP 31.2 Russia and the Successor States** After the attempt in August 1991 to depose Gorbachev failed, an anticommunist revolution swept the Soviet Union. Led by Russia and Boris Yeltsin, the republics that formed the Soviet Union declared their sovereignty and independence. Eleven of the fifteen republics then formed a loose confederation called the Commonwealth of Independent States, but the integrated economy of the Soviet Union dissolved into separate national economies, each with its own goals and policies.

power in October 1989, East German reform communists, enthusiastically supported by leading East German intellectuals and former dissidents, wanted to preserve socialism by making it genuinely democratic and responsive to the needs of the people. They argued for a **third way,** which would go beyond the failed Stalinism they had experienced and the ruthless capitalism they saw in the West. These reformers supported closer ties with West Germany, but they feared unification and wanted to preserve a distinct East German identity.

These efforts failed, and within a few months East Germany was absorbed into an enlarged West Germany, much like a faltering company is merged into a stronger rival and ceases to exist. Three factors were particularly important in this sudden absorption. First, in the first week after the Berlin Wall was opened, almost 9 million East Germans—roughly one-half of the total population—poured across the border into West Germany. Almost all returned to their homes in the East, but the joy of warm welcomes from long-lost friends and loved ones and the exhilarating experience of shopping in the well-stocked stores of the much wealthier West aroused long-dormant hopes of unity among ordinary citizens.

Second, West German chancellor Helmut Kohl and his closest advisers skillfully exploited the historic opportunity on their doorstep. Sure of support from the United States, whose leadership he had steadfastly followed, in November 1989 Kohl presented a ten-point plan for a step-by-step unification in cooperation with both East Germany and the international community. Kohl then promised the struggling citizens of East Germany an immediate economic bonanza—a one-for-one exchange of all East German marks in savings accounts and pensions into much more valuable West German marks. This generous offer helped a well-financed conservative-liberal **Alliance for Germany,** which was set up in East Germany and was closely tied to Kohl's West German Christian Democrats, to overwhelm those who argued for the preservation of some kind of independent socialist society in East Germany. In March 1990, the Alliance outdistanced the Socialist party and won almost 50 percent of the votes in an East German parliamentary election. (The Communists ignominiously fell to fringe-party status.) The Alliance for Germany quickly negotiated an economic union on favorable terms with Chancellor Kohl.

Finally, in the summer of 1990, the crucial international aspect of German unification was successfully resolved. Unification would once again make Germany the strongest state in central Europe and would directly affect the security of the Soviet Union. But Gorbachev swallowed hard—Western cartoonists showed Stalin turning over in his grave—and negotiated the best deal he could. In a historic agreement signed by Gorbachev and Kohl in July 1990, a uniting Germany solemnly affirmed its peaceful intentions and pledged never to develop nuclear, biological, or chemical weapons. Germany also sweetened the deal by promising to make enormous loans to the hard-pressed Soviet Union. In October 1990, East Germany merged into West Germany, forming henceforth a single nation under the West German laws and constitution.

The peaceful reunification of Germany accelerated the pace of agreements to liquidate the cold war. In November 1990, delegates from twenty-two European countries joined those from the United States and the Soviet Union in Paris and agreed to a scaling down of all their armed forces. The delegates also solemnly affirmed that all existing borders in Europe—from unified Germany to the newly independent Baltic republics—were legal and valid. The **Paris Accord** was for all practical purposes a general peace treaty, bringing an end to World War II and the cold war that followed.

Peace in Europe encouraged the United States and the Soviet Union to scrap a significant portion of their nuclear weapons in a series of agreements. In September 1991, a confident President George H. W. Bush also canceled the around-the-clock alert status for American bombers outfitted with atomic bombs, and a floundering Gorbachev quickly followed suit. For the first time in four decades, Soviet and American nuclear weapons were no longer standing ready to destroy capitalism, communism, and life itself.

As anticommunist revolutions swept eastern Europe and East-West tensions rapidly disappeared, the Soviet Union lost both the will and the means to be a global superpower. Yet the United States retained the strength and the desire to influence political and economic developments on a global scale. Thus the United States, still flanked by many allies, emerged rather suddenly as the world's only surviving superpower.

In 1991 the United States used its military superiority on a grand scale in a quick war with Iraq in western Asia. Emerging in 1988 from an eight-year war with neighboring Iran with a big, tough army equipped by the Soviet bloc, western Europe, and the United States, Iraq's strongman Saddam Hussein (b. 1937) set out to make himself the leader of the entire Arab world. Eyeing the great oil wealth of his tiny southern neighbor, Saddam Hussein's forces suddenly invaded Kuwait in August 1990 and proclaimed the annexation of Kuwait.

Reacting vigorously to free Kuwait, the United States mobilized the U.N. Security Council, which in August 1990 imposed a strict naval blockade on Iraq. Receiving the support of some Arab states, as well as of Great Britain and France, the United States also landed 500,000 American soldiers in Saudi Arabia near the border of Kuwait. When a defiant Saddam Hussein refused to withdraw from Kuwait, the Security Council authorized the U.S.-led military coalition to attack Iraq. The American army and air force then smashed Iraqi forces in a lightning-quick desert campaign, although the United States stopped short of toppling Saddam because it feared a sudden disintegration of Iraq more than Saddam's hanging on to power.

The defeat of Iraqi armies in the Gulf War demonstrated the awesome power of the U.S. military, rebuilt and revitalized by the spending and patriotism of the 1980s. Little wonder that in the flush of yet another victory, the first President Bush spoke of a **"new world order,"** an order that would apparently feature the United States and a cooperative United Nations working together to impose stability throughout the world.

## Building a New Europe in the 1990s

The fall of communism, the end of the cold war, and the collapse of the Soviet Union opened a new era in European and world history. The dimensions and significance of this new era, opening suddenly and unexpectedly, are subject to debate. We are so close to what is going on that we lack vital perspective. Yet the historian must take a stand.

First, it seems clear that Europe took giant strides toward a loose unification of fundamental institutions and beliefs and that many broad economic, social, and political trends operated all across the continent in the 1990s. We shall focus on three of the most important trends: the pressure on national economies increasingly caught up in global capitalism; the defense of social achievements under attack; and a resurgence of nationalism and ethnic conflict. Second, with these common themes providing an organizational framework, we shall examine the course of development in the three overlapping but still distinct regions of contemporary Europe. These are Russia and the western states of the old Soviet Union, previously communist eastern Europe, and western Europe.

## Common Patterns and Problems

The end of the cold war and the disintegration of the Soviet Union ended the division of Europe into two opposing camps with two different political and economic systems. Thus, although Europe in the 1990s was a collage of diverse peoples with their own politics, cultures, and histories, the entire continent shared an underlying network of common developments and challenges.

Of great importance, in economic affairs European leaders embraced, or at least accepted, a large part of the neoliberal, free-market vision of capitalist development. This was most strikingly the case in eastern Europe, where states such as Poland and Hungary implemented market reforms and sought to create vibrant capitalist economies. Thus postcommunist governments in eastern Europe freed prices, turned state enterprises over to private owners, and sought to move toward strong currencies and balanced budgets. Milder doses of this same free-market medicine were administered by politicians and big business to the lackluster economies of western Europe. These initiatives and proposals for further changes marked a considerable modification in western Europe's still-dominant welfare capitalism, which featured government intervention, high taxes, and high levels of social benefits.

Two factors were particularly important in accounting for this ongoing shift from welfare state activism to tough-minded capitalism. First, Europeans were only following practices and ideologies revived and enshrined in the 1980s in the United States and Great Britain (see page 1020). Western Europeans especially took American prescriptions more seriously because U.S. prestige and power were so high after the United States "won the cold war" and because the U.S. economy continued to outperform its western European counterparts in the Clinton years. Second, the deregulation of markets and the privatization of state-controlled enterprises were an integral part of the powerful trend toward a wide-open, wheeler-dealer global economy. The rules of the global economy, which were laid down by Western governments, multinational corporations, and international financial organizations such as the International Monetary Fund (IMF), called for the free movement of capital and goods and services, as well as low inflation and limited government deficits. Accepting these rules and attempting to follow them was the price of full participation in the global economy.

The ongoing computer and electronics revolution strengthened the move toward a global economy. That revolution thrived on the diffusion of ever-cheaper computational and informational capacity to small research groups and private businesses, which were both cause and effect of the revolution itself. By the 1990s, an inexpensive personal computer had the power of a 1950s mainframe that filled a room and cost hundreds of thousands of dollars. The computer revolution reduced the costs of distance, speeding up communications and helping businesses tap cheaper labor overseas. Reducing the friction of distance made threats of moving factories abroad ring true and helped hold down wages at home.

**Globalization,** the emergence of a freer global economy, probably did speed up world economic growth as enthusiasts invariably claimed, but it also had powerful and quite negative social consequences. Millions of ordinary citizens in western Europe believed that global capitalism and freer markets were undermining hard-won social achievements. As in the United States and Great Britain in the 1980s, the public in other countries generally associated globalization with the increased unemployment that accompanied corporate downsizing, the efforts to reduce the power of labor unions, and, above all, government plans to reduce social benefits. The reaction was particularly intense in France and Germany, where unions remained strong and socialists championed a minimum of change in social policies.

Indeed, the broad movement toward neoliberal global development sparked a powerful counterattack as the 1990s ended. Financial crises, which devastated many of Asia's smaller economies and threatened to spread, triggered this reaction. Many critics and protesters argued increasingly that globalization damaged poor countries as much as wealthy ones. Above all, critics insisted that globalization hurt the world's poor, because multinational corporations destroyed local industries and paid pitiful wages, and because international financial organizations demanded harsh balanced budgets and deep cuts in government social programs. These attacks shook global neoliberalism, but it remained dominant.

Political developments across Europe also were loosely unified by common patterns and problems. The demise of European communism brought the apparent triumph of liberal democracy everywhere. All countries embraced

**Santiago Calatrava: Tenerife Concert Hall, 2003** One of the most celebrated of the "postmodern" architects, who go beyond the modernism that dominated from the 1920s to the 1970s, Calatrava is known for swooping shapes and unusual spaces that convey a sense of motion to his buildings. The enormous, free-standing "roof" of this concert hall rises on a waterfront property like a cresting, crashing wave, linking the ocean with the city and beckoning tourists to Tenerife and Portugal's Canary Islands. Postmodern architects rely heavily on three-dimensional computer modeling to fashion complex forms and translate them into construction blueprints. *(Barbara Burg and Oliver Schuh/Palladium Photodesign, Cologne, Germany)*

genuine electoral competition, with elected presidents and legislatures and the outward manifestations of representative liberal governments. With some notable exceptions, such as discrimination against Gypsies, countries also guaranteed basic civil liberties. Thus, for the first time since before the French Revolution, almost all of Europe followed the same general political model, although the variations were endless.

The triumph of the liberal democratic program led the American scholar Francis Fukuyama to discern in 1992 the "end of history" in his influential book by that title. According to Fukuyama, first fascism and Nazism and then communism had been definitively bested by liberal democratic politics and market economics. Conversely, as James Cronin perceptively noted in 1996 in *The World the Cold War Made,* the fall of communism also marked the return of nationalism and national history.[2] The cold war and the superpowers generally kept their allies and clients in line, either by force or by granting them conditional aid. As soon as the cold war was over, nationalism and ethnic conflict re-emerged, and history, as the story of different peoples, began again.

The resurgence of nationalism in the 1990s led to terrible tragedy and bloodshed in parts of eastern Europe, as it did in several hot spots in Africa and Asia. During the civil wars in Yugoslavia, many observers feared that national and ethnic hatreds would spread throughout eastern Europe and infect western Europe in the form of racial hostility toward minorities and immigrants. Yet if nationalist and racist incidents were a recurring European theme, they remained limited in the extent of their damage. Of critical importance in this regard was the fact that all European states wished to become or remain full-fledged members of the European society of nations and to join eventually an ever-expanding European Community, renamed the **European Union** in 1993. States that embraced national hatred and ethnic warfare, most notably Serbia, were branded as outlaws and boycotted and isolated by the European Union and the international community. The process of limiting resurgent nationalism in Europe was almost as significant as the resurgence itself.

## Recasting Russia

Politics and economics were closely intertwined in Russia after the attempted Communist coup in 1991 and the dissolution of the Soviet Union. President Boris Yeltsin, his democratic supporters, and his economic ministers wanted to create conditions that would prevent forever a return to communism and would also right the faltering economy. Following the example of some postcommunist governments in eastern Europe and agreeing with those Western advisers who argued that private economies were always best, the Russian reformers opted in January 1992 for breakneck liberalization. Their "shock therapy" freed prices on 90 percent of all Russian goods, with the exception of bread, vodka, oil, and public transportation. The government also launched a rapid privatization of industry and turned thousands of factories and mines over to new private companies. Each citizen received a voucher worth 10,000 rubles (about $22) to buy stock in private companies, but control of the privatized companies usually remained in the hands of the old bosses, the managers and government officials from the communist era.

President Yeltsin and his economic reformers believed that shock therapy would revive production and bring prosperity after a brief period of hardship. The results of the reforms were in fact quite different. Prices increased 250 percent on the very first day, and they kept on soaring, increasing twenty-six times in the course of 1992. At the same time, Russian production fell a staggering 20 percent. Nor did the situation stabilize quickly. Throughout 1995 rapid but gradually slowing inflation raged, and output continued to fall. According to most estimates, in 1996 the Russian economy produced at least one-third and possibly as much as one-half less than in 1991. Only in 1997 did the economy stop declining, before crashing yet again in 1998 in the wake of Asia's financial crisis.

Rapid economic liberalization worked poorly in Russia for several reasons. Soviet industry had been highly monopolized and strongly tilted toward military goods. Production of many items had been concentrated in one or two gigantic factories or in interconnected combines that supplied the entire economy. With privatization these powerful state monopolies became powerful private monopolies, which cut production and raised prices in order to maximize their financial returns. Moreover, powerful managers and bureaucrats forced Yeltsin's government to hand out enormous subsidies and credits to reinforce the positions of big firms and to avoid bankruptcies and the discipline of a free market. The managerial elite also combined with criminal elements to intimidate would-be rivals and prevent the formation of new businesses. Not that most ordinary Soviet citizens were eager to start businesses. In the end, enterprise directors and politicians succeeded in eliminating worker ownership and converted large portions of previously state-owned industry into their own private property.

Runaway inflation and poorly executed privatization brought a profound social revolution to Russia. A new capitalist elite acquired great wealth and power, while large numbers of people fell into abject poverty, and the majority struggled in the midst of decline to make ends meet.

Managers, former officials, and financiers who came out of the privatization process with large shares of the old state monopolies stood at the top of the reorganized elite. The richest plums were found in Russia's enormous oil and natural resources industries, where unscrupulous enterprise directors pocketed enormous dishonest gains. The new elite was more highly concentrated than ever before. By 1996 Moscow, with 5 percent of Russia's population, accounted for 35 percent of the country's national income and controlled 80 percent of its capital resources.

At the other extreme, the vast majority saw their savings become practically worthless. Pensions lost much of their value, and whole markets were devoted to people selling off their personal goods to survive. Perhaps the most telling statistic, summing up millions of hardships and tragedies, was the truly catastrophic decline in the life expectancy of the average Russian male from sixty-nine years in 1991 to only fifty-eight years in 1996.

Rapid economic decline in 1992 and 1993 and rising popular dissatisfaction encouraged a majority of communists, nationalists, and populists in the Russian parliament to oppose Yeltsin and his coalition of democratic reformers and big-business interests. The erratic, increasingly hard-drinking Yeltsin would accept no compromise and

**Russia's Leading Capitalist on Trial, 2004** Mikhail Khodorkovsky emerged from the privatization of Russian industry as the progressive chief and largest shareholder of Yukos, Russia's most successful oil company. But after he supported liberal opposition parties in 2002, an increasingly authoritarian President Putin jailed the billionaire, charged him with tax fraud, and confiscated his wealth before the trial even began. Putin's behavior was widely criticized in the West, but most ordinary Russians applauded because they believed the super rich had plundered the Russian state. *(Alexander Natruskin/Reuters/Corbis)*

insisted on a strong presidential system. Winning in April 1993 the support of 58 percent of the population in a referendum on his proposed constitution, Yeltsin then brought in tanks to crush a parliamentary mutiny in October 1993 and literally blew away the opposition. Subsequently, Yeltsin consolidated his power, and in 1996 he used his big-business cronies in the media to win an impressive come-from-behind victory. But effective representative government failed to develop, and many Russians came to equate "democracy" with the corruption, poverty, and national decline they experienced throughout the 1990s.

This widespread disillusionment set the stage for the "managed democracy" of Vladimir Putin, first elected president as Yeltsin's chosen successor in 2000 and re-elected in a landslide in March 2004. An officer in the secret police in the communist era, Putin maintained free markets in the economic sphere but re-established semi-authoritarian political rule. Aided by high oil prices for Russia's most valuable export, this combination worked remarkably well and seemed to suit most Russians. In 2004, the Russian economy had been booming for five years, the Russian middle class was expanding rapidly, and the elected parliament supported Putin overwhelmingly. Proponents of liberal democracy were in retreat, while conservative Russian intellectuals were on the offensive, arguing that free markets and capitalism required strong political rule to control corruption and prevent chaos. Historians saw a reassertion of Russia's long authoritarian tradition.

Putin's forceful, competent image in world affairs also soothed the country's injured pride and symbolized its national resurgence. Nor did the government permit any negative television reports on the civil war in Chechnya, the tiny republic of 1 million Muslims on Russia's southern border, which in 1991 had declared its independence from the Russian Federation (see Map 31.2). The savage conflict in Chechnya continued, largely unreported, with numerous atrocities on both sides.

## Progress and Tragedy in Eastern Europe

Developments in eastern Europe shared important similarities with those in Russia, as many of the problems were the same. Thus the postcommunist states of the former satellite empire worked to replace state planning and socialism with market mechanisms and private property. Western-style electoral politics also took hold, and as in Russia, these politics were marked by intense battles between presidents and parliaments and by weak political parties. The social consequences of these revolutionary changes were similar to those in Russia. Ordinary citizens and the elderly were once again the big losers, while the young and the ex-Communists were the big winners. Inequalities between richer and poorer regions also increased. Capital cities such as Warsaw, Prague, and Budapest concentrated wealth, power, and opportunity as never before, while provincial centers stagnated and old industrial areas declined. Crime and gangsterism increased in the streets and in the executive suites.

Yet the 1990s saw more than a difficult transition, with high social costs, to market economies and freely elected governments in eastern Europe. Many citizens had never fully accepted communism, which they equated with Russian imperialism and the loss of national independence. The joyous crowds that toppled communist regimes in 1989 believed that they were liberating the nation as well as the individual. Thus communism died and nationalism was reborn.

The surge of nationalism in eastern Europe recalled a similar surge of state creation after World War I. Then, too, authoritarian multinational empires had come crashing down in defeat and revolution. Then, too, nationalities with long histories and rich cultures had drawn upon ideologies of popular sovereignty and national self-determination to throw off foreign rule and found new democratic states.

The response to this opportunity in the former communist countries was quite varied in the 1990s, but most observers agreed that Poland, the Czech Republic, and Hungary were the most successful (see Map 31.3). Each of these three countries met the critical challenge of economic reconstruction more successfully than Russia, and each could claim to be the economic leader in eastern Europe, depending on the criteria selected. The reasons for these successes included considerable experience with limited market reforms before 1989, flexibility and lack of dogmatism in government policy, and an enthusiastic embrace of capitalism by a new entrepreneurial class. In the first five years of reform, Poland created twice as many new businesses as Russia, with a total population only one-fourth as large.

The three northern countries in the former Soviet bloc also did far better than Russia in creating new civic institutions, legal systems, and independent broadcasting networks that reinforced political freedom and national revival. Lech Walesa in Poland and Václav Havel in Czechoslovakia were elected presidents of their countries and proved as remarkable in power as in opposition. After Czechoslovakia's "Velvet Revolution" in 1989, Havel and the Czech parliament accepted a "velvet divorce" in 1993 when Slovakian nationalists wanted to break off and form their own state. All three northern countries managed to control national and ethnic tensions that might have destroyed their postcommunist reconstruction.

Above all, and in sharp contrast to Russia, the popular goal of "rejoining the West" reinforced political moderation and compromise. Seeing themselves as heirs to medieval Christendom and liberal democratic values in the 1920s, Poles, Hungarians, and Czechs hoped to find security in NATO membership and economic prosperity in western Europe's ever-tighter union. Membership required many proofs of character and stability, however. Providing these proofs and endorsed by the Clinton administration, Poland, Hungary, and the Czech Republic were accepted into the NATO alliance in 1997. Gaining admission to the European Union (EU) proved more difficult, because candidates also had to accept and be ready to apply all the rules and regulations that the EU had developed since 1956—an awesome task.

Romania and Bulgaria were the eastern European laggards in the postcommunist transition. Western traditions were much weaker there, and both countries were much poorer than neighbors to the north. In 1993 Bulgaria and Romania had per capita national incomes of $1,140, in contrast to Hungary ($3,830) and the Czech Republic ($2,710). Although Romania and Bulgaria eventually made progress in the late 1990s, full membership for both countries in either NATO or the EU still lay far in the future.

The great postcommunist tragedy was Yugoslavia, which under Josip Tito had been a federation of republics and regions under strict communist rule (see page 1003). After Tito's death in 1980, power passed increasingly to the sister republics, which encouraged a revival of regional and ethnic conflicts that were

**MAP 31.3 Contemporary Europe** No longer divided by ideological competition and the cold war, today's Europe features a large number of independent states. Several of these states were previously part of the Soviet Union and Yugoslavia, both of which broke into many different countries. Czechoslovakia also divided on ethnic lines, while a reunited Germany emerged, once again, as the dominant nation in central Europe.

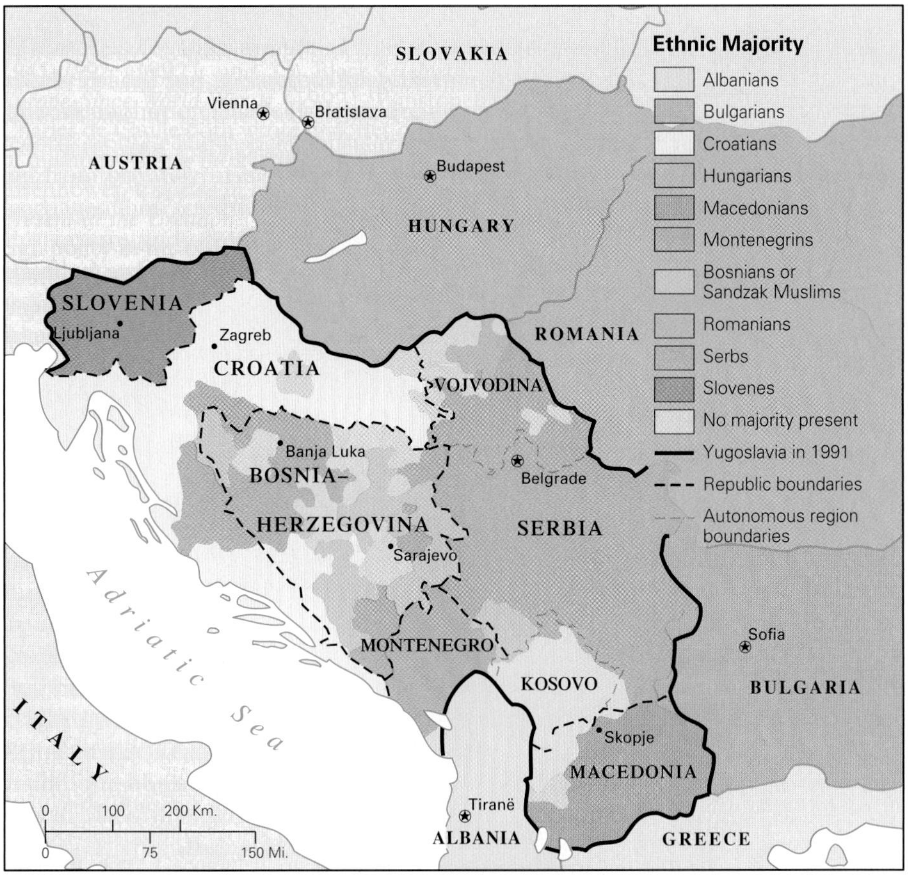


**MAP 31.4 The Ethnic Composition of Yugoslavia, 1991** Yugoslavia had the most ethnically diverse population in eastern Europe. The Republic of Croatia had substantial Serbian and Muslim minorities. Bosnia-Herzegovina had large Muslim, Serbian, and Croatian populations, none of which had a majority. In June 1991, Serbia's brutal effort to seize territory and unite all Serbs in a single state brought a tragic civil war.

exacerbated by charges of ethnically inspired massacres during World War II and a dramatic economic decline in the mid-1980s.

The revolutions of 1989 accelerated the breakup of Yugoslavia. Serbian president Slobodan Milosevic intended to grab land from other republics and unite all Serbs, regardless of where they lived, in a "greater Serbia." In 1989 Milosevic arbitrarily abolished self-rule in the Serbian province of Kosovo, where Albanian-speaking people constituted the overwhelming majority. Milosevic's moves strengthened the cause of separatism, and in June 1991 Slovenia and Croatia declared their independence. Slovenia repulsed a Serbian attack, but Milosevic's armies managed to take about 30 percent of Croatia. In 1992 the civil war spread to Bosnia-Herzegovina, which had declared its independence. Serbs—about 30 percent of that region's population—refused to live under the more numerous Bosnian Muslims (see Map 31.4). Yugoslavia had once been a tolerant and largely successful multiethnic state, with different groups living side by side and often intermarrying. The Bosnian civil war unleashed ruthless brutality, with murder, rape, destruction, and the herding of refugees into concentration camps.

While scenes of horror shocked the world, the Western nations had difficulty formulating an effective response. The turning point came in July 1995, when Bosnian Serbs overran Srebrenica—a Muslim city previously declared a United Nations "safe area"—and killed several thousand civilians. World outrage prompted NATO to bomb Bosnian Serb military targets intensively, and the Croatian army drove all the Serbs from Croatia. In November 1995, President Bill Clinton helped the warring sides hammer out a complicated accord that gave the Bosnian Serbs about 49 percent of Bosnia and the Muslim-Croatian peoples the rest. Troops from NATO countries patrolled Bosnia to try to keep the peace.

The Albanian Muslims of Kosovo had been hoping for a restoration of self-rule, but they gained nothing from the Bosnian agreement. In early 1998, frustrated Kosovar militants formed the **Kosovo Liberation Army (KLA)** and began to fight for independence. Serbian repression of the Kosovars increased, and in 1998 Serbian forces

**Escape from Srebrenica** A Bosnian Muslim refugee arrives at the United Nations base in Tuzla and with her anguished screams tells the world of the Serbian atrocities. Several thousand civilians were murdered at Srebrenica, and Western public opinion finally demanded decisive action. Efforts continue to arrest those Serbs believed responsible and to try them for crimes against humanity. *(J. Jones/Corbis Sygma)*

attacked both KLA guerrillas and unarmed villagers, displacing 250,000 people within Kosovo. By January 1999, the Western powers, led by the United States, were threatening Milosevic with heavy air raids if he did not withdraw Serbian armies from Kosovo and accept self-government (but not independence) for Kosovo. Milosevic refused, and in March 1999 NATO began bombing Yugoslavia. Serbian paramilitary forces responded by driving about 780,000 Kosovars into exile. NATO redoubled its highly destructive bombing campaign, which eventually forced Milosevic to withdraw and allowed the joyous Kosovars to regain their homeland. The impoverished Serbs eventually voted the still-defiant Milosevic out of office, and in July 2001 a new pro-Western Serbian government turned him over to the war crimes tribunal in the Netherlands, to stand trial for crimes against humanity. The civil wars in the former Yugoslavia were a monument to human cruelty and evil in the worst tradition of the twentieth century. But ongoing efforts to preserve peace, repatriate refugees, and try war criminals also testified to the regenerative power of liberal values and human rights as the twenty-first century unfolded.

## Unity and Identity in Western Europe

The movement toward western European unity, which since the late 1940s had inspired practical politicians seeking economic recovery and idealistic visionaries imagining a European identity that transcended destructive national rivalries, received a powerful second wind in the mid-1980s. The Single European Act of 1986 laid down a detailed legal framework for establishing a single market,

**A United Europe** As part of the festivities celebrating the entrance of ten new members into the European Union on May 1, 2004, the elected leaders of the Czech Republic, Germany, and Poland walked across the bridge separating the Czech Republic from Germany at the point where the three countries come together. For a region that had suffered terribly from world wars and iron-curtain division, the enlargement of the European Union marked the triumph of good sense and the human spirit. *(Sebastian Willnow/AFP/Getty Images)*

which would add the free movement of labor, capital, and services to the existing free trade in goods. With work proceeding vigorously toward the single market, which went into effect in 1993 as the European Community proudly rechristened itself the European Union (EU), French president François Mitterrand and German chancellor Helmut Kohl took the lead in pushing for a monetary union of EU members. After long negotiations and compromises, designed especially to overcome Britain's long-standing reluctance to cede aspects of sovereignty, in December 1991 the member states reached an agreement in the Dutch town of Maastricht. The **Maastricht treaty** set strict financial criteria for joining the proposed monetary union, with its single currency, and set 1999 as the target date for its establishment. The treaty also anticipated the development of common policies on defense and foreign affairs after achieving monetary union.

Western European elites and opinion makers generally supported the decisive step toward economic integration embodied in the Maastricht treaty. They saw monetary union as a means of coping with Europe's ongoing economic problems, imposing financial discipline, cutting costs, and reducing high unemployment. European elites also viewed monetary union as a historic, irreversible step toward a basic political unity. This unity would allow western Europe as a whole to regain its rightful place in world politics and to deal with the United States as an equal.

The Maastricht plan for monetary union encountered widespread skepticism and considerable opposition from ordinary people, leftist political parties, and patriotic nationalists. Ratification votes were close, especially when the public rather than the politicians could vote yes or no on the question.

There were several interrelated reasons for this widespread popular opposition. Many people resented the unending flow of rules handed down by the EU's ever-growing bureaucracy in Brussels, which sought to impose common standards on everything from cheese to day care and undermined national practices and local traditions. Moreover, increased unity meant yielding still more power to distant "Eureaucrats" and political insiders, thereby undermining popular sovereignty and democratic control through national politics and electoral competition. Above all, many ordinary citizens feared that the new Europe was being made at their expense. Joining the monetary union required national governments to meet stringent fiscal standards and impose budget cuts. The resulting reductions in health care and social benefits hit ordinary citizens and did nothing to reduce western Europe's high unemployment rate.

Events in France dramatically illustrated these developments. Mitterrand's Socialist government had been forced to adopt conservative financial policies in the 1980s (see page 1021), and more cuts followed the Maastricht treaty. In early 1993, frustrated French voters elected Jacques Chirac president and gave a coalition of conservatives and moderates an overwhelming victory over the Socialist party. Chirac had won by promising a vigorous attack on unemployment, but the Maastricht criteria demanded that he continue the unpopular retrenchment of the Socialists. After some hesitation, Chirac's government chose deficit-reducing cuts in health benefits and transportation services. France's powerful unions and railroad workers, seconded by the Socialist opposition, responded with massive protest marches and a crippling national strike that simply shut down rail traffic throughout France for almost a month. Paris freeways became creeping parking lots as exhausted workers struggled with nightmare commutes. Yet despite the enormous inconvenience and economic damage, the public supported the strike. Many people felt that the transport workers were also fighting for them. The government had to back down, although it continued its austerity program with less provocative measures until disgruntled French voters again gave the Socialists control of the National Assembly. The Socialists quickly passed a controversial new law to reduce the legal workweek to thirty-five hours, in an attempt to reduce France's stubborn 12 percent unemployment rate without budget-busting spending. More generally, much of the western European public increasingly saw laws to cut the workweek and share the work as a way to reconcile desires for social welfare and a humane market economy with financial discipline and global competition.

Battles over budgets and high unemployment throughout the European Union in the 1990s raised profound questions about the meaning of European unity and identity. Would the European Union expand as promised to include the postcommunist nations of eastern Europe, and if it did, how could Muslim Turkey's long-standing application be ignored? How could a European Union of twenty-five to thirty countries have any real cohesion and common identity? Conversely, would a large, cohesive Europe remain closely linked with the United States in the NATO alliance and with an evolving Western tradition?

The merging of East Germany into the German Federal Republic suggested the enormous difficulties of full East-West integration under the best conditions. After 1991 Helmut Kohl's Germany pumped massive investments into its new eastern provinces, but Germans in the east still saw factories closed and social dislocation. Unemployment in Germany reached a postwar high of 12.8 percent in late 1997, and it soared to 20 percent in the eastern region. Germany's generous social benefits cushioned the economic difficulties, but many ordinary citizens felt hurt and humiliated.

Eastern German women suffered in particular. Before unification, the overwhelming majority had worked outside the home, effectively supported by cheap child care, flexible hours, and the prevailing socialist ideology. Now they faced expensive child care and a variety of pressures to stay at home and let men take the hard-to-find jobs. Many of these women, who had found autonomy and self-esteem in paid work, felt a keen sense of loss. They helped vote Kohl out of office in 1998.

Instructed by the serious difficulties of unification in Germany, western Europeans proceeded cautiously in considering new requests for EU membership. Sweden, Finland, and Austria were admitted because they had strong capitalist economies and because they no longer needed to maintain the legal neutrality that the Soviet Union had required during the cold war.

At the same time the former communist states pressed toward meeting the EU's detailed criteria for membership. In December 2000, the EU's fifteen members agreed to begin final negotiations with the eight leading eastern candidates in the near future. The very smooth establishment of the euro on January 1, 2002, when brand-new euros entered the billfolds of all euro-zone citizens as their unified common currency, built confidence and brought an acceleration of arduous but triumphant negotiations. Thus on May 1, 2004, the European Union added 70 million people and expanded to include 455 million citizens in twenty-five different countries. The largest newcomer by far was Poland, followed in descending size by the Czech Republic, Hungary, Slovenia, Slovakia, Estonia, Lithuania, Latvia, Malta, and Cyprus.

In June 2004, more than two years after charging a special commission to write "a new constitution for European citizens," the leaders of the European Union reached agreement on the final document. Above all, the new constitution, with almost 350 articles, established a single rulebook to replace the complex network of treaties concluded by the member states since the 1957 creation of the European Economic Community. The EU constitution created a president, a foreign minister, and a voting system weighted to reflect the number of people in the different states. The result of intense debate and many compromises, the constitution moved toward a more centralized federal system in several fields, but each state retained veto power in the most sensitive areas, such as taxation, social policy, and foreign affairs. The constitution also omitted explicit reference to Europe's Christian heritage, a reference that Poland and Italy had most ardently championed and that France had most strongly opposed. In order for the constitution to take effect, each and every EU country needed to ratify it, and seven states planned to place the document before the voters. Although these referendum campaigns promised to be noisy and divisive, especially in Britain, where fears of surrendering sovereignty to a central European government were most acute, the new constitution was already a great achievement. The postwar dream of building a united, peaceful Europe, constantly evolving but never abandoned, had reached a new pinnacle.

## New Challenges in the Twenty-first Century

As the twenty-first century opened and the historic movement toward European unity moved forward, European society faced new uncertainties. Of great significance, Europe continued to experience a remarkable **baby bust,** as birthrates fell to levels that seemed to promise a shrinking and aging population in the future. At the same time, the peaceful, wealthy European Union attracted rapidly growing numbers of refugees and illegal immigrants. The unexpected arrival of so many newcomers raised many perplexing questions and prompted serious thinking about European identity and Europe's place in the world. These questions became particularly pressing after the terrorist attack on the United States in 2001, which brought at first a united Western response but eventually led to sharp divisions over war in Iraq and relations with the Middle East and Muslim countries.

### The Prospect of Population Decline

Population is still growing rapidly in many poor countries, but this is not the case in the world's industrialized nations. In 2000 women in developed countries had only 1.6 children on average; only in the United States did women have, almost exactly, the 2.1 children necessary to maintain a stable population. In European countries, where women have been steadily having fewer babies since the 1950s, national fertility rates ranged from 1.2 to 1.8 children per woman. Italy, once renowned for big Catholic families, had achieved the world's lowest birthrate—a mere 1.2 babies per woman. Spain, Germany, and Russia were only slightly higher, while France, Poland, and Britain were clustered around 1.6 children per woman.

If the current baby bust continues, the long-term consequences could be dramatic, though hardly predictable. At the least, Europe's population would decline and age. Projections for Germany are illustrative. Total German population, barring much greater immigration, would gradually decline from 82 million in 2001 to only 62 million around 2050. The number of people of working age would drop by a third, and almost half of the population would be over sixty. Social security taxes paid by the shrinking labor force would need to soar for the skyrocketing costs of pensions and health care for seniors to be met—a recipe for generational tension and conflict. As the premier of Bavaria, Germany's biggest state, warned, the prospect of demographic decline was a "ticking time bomb under our social welfare system and entire economy."[3]

Why, in time of peace, were Europeans failing to reproduce themselves? Certainly the uneven, uninspiring European economic conditions of the 1980s and much of the 1990s played some role. High unemployment fell heavily on young people and often frustrated their plans to settle down and have children. Some observers also argued that a partial rejection of motherhood and parenting was critical. They noted that many women chose to have no children or only one child. By 2000, 30 percent of German women born in 1965 were childless, whereas 90 percent would have had children in earlier generations. In the Catholic countries of southern Europe, where strong pressures to have children still exist, a quarter of the couples were fulfilling their "social duty" with a single child.

In our view, the ongoing impact of careers for married women and the related drive for gender equality remained the decisive factors in the long-term decline of postwar birthrates. After World War II, Western women married early, had their children early, and then turned increasingly to full-time employment, where they suffered from the discrimination that drove the women's movement (see pages 1017–1018). As the twenty-first century opened, women had attained many (but not all) of their objectives. They did as well as or better than men in school, and educated young women earned almost as much as their male counterparts.

Research showed that European women (and men) in their twenties, thirties, and early forties still wanted to have two or even three children—about the same number as their parents had wanted. But unlike their parents, young couples did not realize their ideal family size. Many women postponed the birth of their first child into their thirties in order to finish their education and establish themselves in their careers. Then, finding that raising even one child was more difficult and time-consuming than anticipated, new mothers tended to postpone and eventually forgo a second child. This was especially true of professional women. The better educated and the more economically successful a woman was, the more likely she was to stop with a single child or to have no children at all.

By 2002 some population experts believed that European women were no longer postponing having children. At the least, birthrates appeared to have stabilized. Moreover, the frightening implications of dramatic population decline emerged as a major public issue. Opinion leaders, politicians, and the media started to press the case for more babies and more support for families with children. Europeans may respond with enough vigor to limit the extent of their population decline and avoid societal disaster.

## The Growth of Immigration

As European demographic vitality waned in the 1990s, a surge of migrants from Africa, Asia, and eastern Europe headed for western Europe. Some migrants entered the European Union legally, but increasing numbers were smuggled in past beefed-up border patrols. Large-scale immigration emerged as a contentious and critical challenge.

Historically a source rather than a destination of immigrants, western Europe drew heavily on North Africa and Turkey for manual laborers until 1973, when unemployment started to rise and governments abruptly stopped the inflow. Many foreign workers stayed on, however, eventually bringing their families to western Europe and establishing permanent immigrant communities there.

A new and different surge of migration into western Europe began in the 1990s. The collapse of communism in the East and savage civil wars in Yugoslavia sent hundreds of thousands of refugees fleeing westward. Equally brutal conflicts in Afghanistan, Iraq, Somalia, and Rwanda—to name only four countries—brought thousands more from Asia and Africa. Illegal immigration into the European Union also exploded, rising from an estimated 50,000 people in 1993 to perhaps 500,000 a decade later. This movement exceeded the estimated 300,000 unauthorized foreigners entering the United States each year.

As the twenty-first century opened, many migrants still applied for political asylum and refugee status, but most were eventually rejected and classified as illegal job seekers. Certainly, greater economic opportunities exerted a powerful pull. Germans earned on average six times more than neighboring Poles, who in turn earned much more than people farther east and in North Africa.

Illegal immigration also soared because powerful criminal gangs turned to "people smuggling" for big, low-risk profits. Ruthless Russian-speaking gangs dominated much of the trade, passing their human cargo across Russia and through the war-torn Balkans to western Europe. A favorite final leg involved Albanian smugglers with speedy motorboats, who slipped across the narrow Adriatic Sea past Italian coastal patrols and landed their high-paying passengers on the beaches of southern Italy. From there new arrivals could head off unimpeded in almost any direction, because in 1998 the European Union abolished all border controls between member states. Substantial numbers tried similar entries across the Strait of Gibraltar into southern Spain.

A large portion of the illegal immigrants were young women from eastern Europe, especially Russia and Ukraine. Often lured by criminals promising jobs as maids or waitresses and sometimes simply kidnapped and sold like slaves from hand to hand for a few thousand dollars, these women were smuggled into the most prosperous parts of central Europe and into the European Community and forced into prostitution or worse.

Illegal immigration generated intense discussion and controversy in western Europe. A majority opposed the newcomers, who were accused of taking jobs from the unemployed and somehow undermining national unity. The idea that cultural and ethnic diversity could be a force for vitality and creativity ran counter to deep-seated beliefs. As busy mosques came to outnumber dying churches in parts of some European cities, rightist politicians especially tried to exploit widespread doubts that immigrants from Muslim countries would never assimilate to the different national cultures. In France, in a controversial and widely debated decision, the right-center government of Jacques Chirac in 2004 banned the wearing of headscarves by Muslim girls in public schools (as well as the wearing of large crosses by Christians and skullcaps by Jews). The government insisted that religious symbols in the classroom were incompatible with France's republican tradition of strictly secular, nonsectarian public education. Muslims in France protested vigorously, claiming

**Marching in Favor of Islamic Headscarves** Although the new French law banned the wearing of religious symbols in the classroom and the workplace, it affected primarily the headscarves of Muslim women. After protesting throughout France, almost all Muslim students accepted the law in 2004 in order to avoid expulsion and continue their education. *(Owen Franken/Corbis)*

that headscarves were part of their religion and that their religious freedom was being denied.

An articulate minority challenged the anti-immigrant campaign and its racist overtones. They argued that Europe badly needed newcomers—preferably talented newcomers—to limit the impending population decline and provide valuable technical skills. European leaders also focused on improved policing of EU borders and tougher common procedures to combat people smuggling and punish international crime. Above all, growing illegal immigration pushed Europeans to examine the whys of this dramatic human movement and to consider how it related to Europe's proper role in world affairs.

## Promoting Human Rights

The tide of refugees and illegal job seekers made thinking people in western Europe acutely aware of their current good fortune, the sweet fruit of more than fifty years of peace, security, and rising standards of living. The nearby agonies of barbarism and war in the former Yugoslavia vividly recalled the horrors of World War II, and they cast in bold relief the ever-present reality of collective violence in today's world. At the same time, western European countries were generally doing their best to limit or expel the foreigners arriving at their gates, as we have seen. This ongoing rejection gave some Europeans a guilty conscience and a feeling that they needed to do

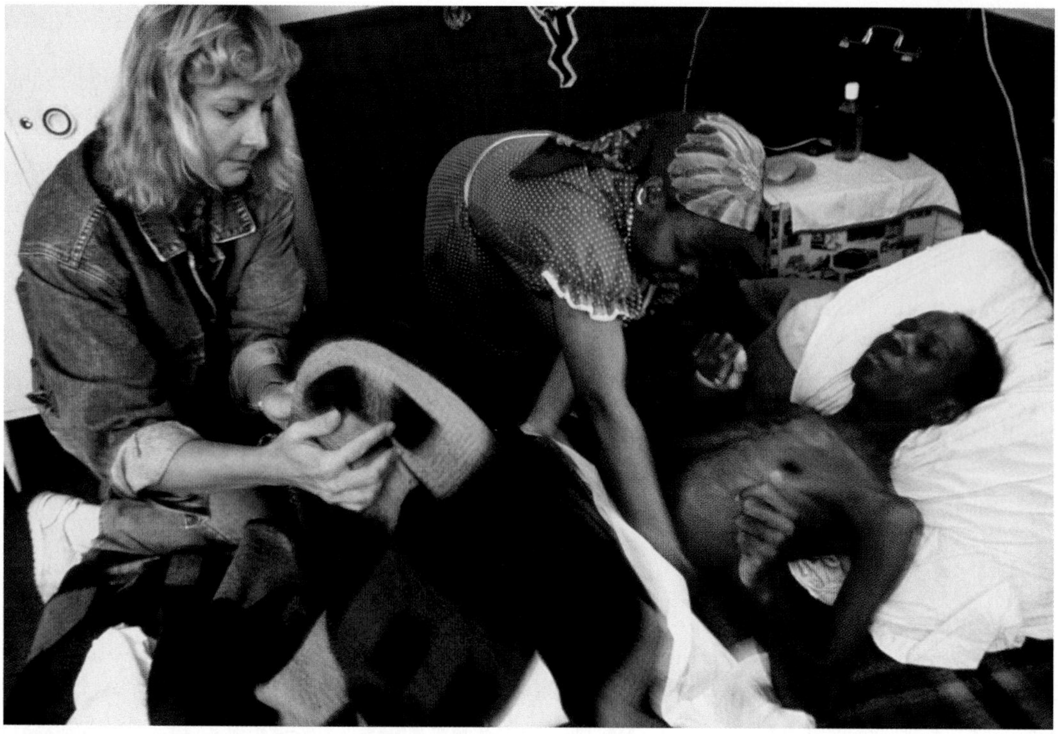

**Fighting the AIDS Epidemic** These women, financed in part by the European Union, are treating an AIDS patient at his home in Mozambique. In 2004 the United Nations estimated that about 42 million persons were infected with HIV, the virus that causes AIDS. AIDS is the fourth-leading cause of death in the world. *(Black Star/stockphoto.com)*

more when they had so much and so many others had so little. As a result, European intellectuals and opinion makers began to envision a new historic mission for Europe—the promotion of domestic peace and human rights in those lands plagued by instability, violence, and oppression.

European leaders and humanitarians believed that Europe's mission required more global agreements and new international institutions to set moral standards and to regulate countries, political leaders, armies, corporations, and individuals. In practice, this meant more curbs on the sovereign rights of the world's states, just as the states of the European Union had imposed increasingly strict standards of behavior on themselves in order to secure the rights and welfare of EU citizens. As Nicole Gnesotto, the director of the European Union's institute, concluded, the EU has a "historical responsibility" to make morality "a basis of policy," because "human rights are more important than states' rights."[4] In general, the United States reacted coolly to the idea of preferring human rights to states' rights. American leaders stressed the preservation of U.S. freedom of action in world affairs, particularly after George W. Bush was elected president in 2000.

In practical terms, western Europe's evolving human rights mission meant, first of all, humanitarian interventions to stop civil wars and to prevent tyrannical governments from slaughtering their own people. Thus the European Union joined with the United States to intervene militarily to stop the killing in Bosnia, Kosovo, and Macedonia and to protect the rights of embattled minorities (see pages 1045–1048). The states of the EU also vigorously supported U.N.-sponsored conferences and treaties that sought to verify the compliance of anti–germ warfare conventions, outlawed the use of hideously destructive land mines, and established a new international court to prosecute war criminals.

Europeans also pushed for broader definitions of individual rights. Abolishing the death penalty in the European Union, for example, they condemned its continued use in China, the United States, Saudi Arabia, and some other countries as inhumane and uncivilized. Rights for Europeans in their personal relations also continued to expand. In the pacesetting Netherlands, for example, a growing network of laws gave prostitutes (legally recognized since 1917) pensions and full workers' rights and legalized gay and lesbian marriages, the smoking of pot in licensed coffee shops, and assisted suicide (euthanasia) for the terminally ill.

As the twenty-first century opened, western Europeans also pushed as best they could to extend their broad-based concept of social and economic rights to the world's poor countries. These efforts were related to sharp criticism of globalization and unrestrained capitalism (see pages 1040–1041), criticism that in 2001 helped socialists regain power in twelve of the fifteen countries in the European Union. Quite typically, Europe's moderate social democrats combined with human rights campaigners in 2001 to help African governments secure drastic price cuts from the big international drug companies on the drug cocktails needed to combat Africa's AIDS crisis. Strong advocates of greater social equality and state-funded health care, European socialists embraced morality as a basis for action and the global expansion of human rights as a primary goal.

## The al-Qaeda Attack of September 11, 2001

On the morning of September 11, 2001, two hijacked passenger planes from Boston crashed into and destroyed the World Trade Center towers in New York City. Shortly thereafter a third plane crashed into the Pentagon, and a fourth, believed to be headed for the White House or the U.S. Capitol, crashed into a field in rural Pennsylvania. These terrorist attacks took the lives of more than three thousand people from many countries and put the personal safety of ordinary citizens at the top of the West's agenda. Stunned and horrified, the peoples and governments of the world joined the Americans in heartfelt solidarity.

The United States, led by President George W. Bush, launched a military campaign to destroy the perpetrators of the crime—Saudi-born millionaire Osama bin Laden's al-Qaeda network of terrorists and Afghanistan's reactionary Muslim government, the Taliban. Drawing on the world's sympathy and building a broad international coalition that included western Europe, Russia, and Pakistan, the United States joined its tremendous airpower with the faltering Northern Alliance in Afghanistan, which had been fighting the Taliban for years. By mid-October 2001 American special forces on the ground were directing precision air strikes that devastated Taliban and al-Qaeda troops, and a rejuvenated Northern Alliance took the offensive. In mid-November the Taliban collapsed, and jubilant crowds in the capital of Kabul welcomed Northern Alliance soldiers as liberators. Afghan opposition leaders and United Nations mediators worked out plans for a new broad-based government, while American planes, ground troops, and tribal fighters searched for bin Laden and his die-hard supporters in their mountain hideaways. In 2002 foreign governments, aid organizations, and the United Nations turned to the arduous task of helping the Afghans get themselves back on their feet after a generation of conflict and civil war following the 1979 Soviet invasion of their country.

In trying to make some sense out of the heinous attack of September 11, 2001, and the current wave of terrorist action in general, it is helpful to realize that civil war and terrorism often went hand in hand in the twentieth century. Beginning in the 1920s and peaking in the 1960s, many nationalist movements used terrorism in their battles to achieve political independence and decolonization. This was the case in several new states, including Algeria, Cyprus, Ireland, Israel, and Yemen.[5] Those fighting for independence and political power often targeted police forces for assassination campaigns, thereby breaking down confidence in the colonial government and provoking counter-atrocities that generated increased support for the independence movement.

In the Vietnam War era, a second wave of terrorism saw some far-left supporters of the communist Vietcong, such as the American Weathermen, the German Red Army Faction, and the Italian Red Brigade, practicing "revolutionary terror" in an effort to cripple the Western heartland. These groups engineered a series of deadly bombings, assassinations, and kidnappings. These terrorists also hijacked airplanes—more than one hundred each year in the 1970s—in order to take hostages and blackmail governments into meeting some demand, such as the release of convicted fellow terrorists. Some terrorists trained in the facilities of the PLO (the Palestine Liberation Organization) operated international networks and targeted Israel and U.S. installations abroad. This second wave receded in the 1980s as painstaking police work and international cooperation defeated these "revolutionaries" in country after country.

In recent years a third wave has been building, cresting in al-Qaeda's attack on the World Trade Center and the Pentagon on September 11, 2001. In analyzing this third wave, many commentators were quick to stress the role of extreme Islamic fundamentalism as a motivating factor. But the most perceptive scholars noted that recent deadly attacks had been committed by terrorists inspired by several religious faiths and religious sects and were by no means limited to Islamic extremists.[6] These scholars

**Terrorism in Spain** Flames from a powerful car bomb engulf the booby-trapped vehicle of a Spanish army officer and take another life in Madrid in January 2000. The bombing was attributed to the Basque separatist organization ETA, which assassinates officials and ordinary citizens in a violent campaign to obtain political independence for the Basque region in northern Spain. Similar terrorist attacks plague many countries divided by political and ethnic conflicts. *(AFP/Corbis)*

noted that the different terrorist movements in today's world need to be linked to underlying political conflicts and civil wars for meaningful understanding.

When this perspective is applied to Osama bin Laden and al-Qaeda members, two stages stand out. First, in the long bitter fighting against the Soviet Union and the local communists in Afghanistan, bin Laden and like-minded "holy warriors" developed terrorist skills and a narrow-minded, fanatical Islamic puritanism. They also developed a hatred of most existing Arab governments, which they viewed as corrupt, un-Islamic, and unresponsive to the needs of ordinary Muslims. The objects of their hostility included the absolute monarchy of oil-rich Saudi Arabia (bin Laden's own country), pro-Western but undemocratic Egypt, and the secular, one-party dictatorship of Saddam Hussein.

Second, when these Islamic extremists returned home from Afghanistan and began to organize, they usually met the fate of many earlier Islamic extremists and were jailed or forced into exile, often in tolerant Europe. There they blamed the United States for being the supporter and corrupter of existing Arab governments, and they organized murderous plots against the United States—a despised proxy for the Arab rulers they could not reach. This development set the stage for the 1998 bombing of the U.S. embassy in Nairobi, Kenya, which claimed nearly 200 lives, the World Trade Center atrocity, and the U.S.-led counterattack on al-Qaeda in Afghanistan.

## The West Divided and War in Iraq

Unfortunately, Western unity in Afghanistan soon turned into bitter quarreling and international crisis over the prospect of war with Iraq. As soon as he was elected in 2000, President Bush and his most influential advisers, led by Vice President Dick Cheney and Secretary of Defense Donald Rumsfeld, began to consider how to overthrow Iraq's Saddam Hussein and remake the Middle East. Paul O'Neill, Bush's secretary of the treasury, summed up discussions on Iraq by the president and his cabinet this way: "From the start, they were building the case against Hussein and looking at how we could take him out and change Iraq into a new country. And, if we did that, it would solve everything."[7] And indeed, many in the administration argued that a democratic, pro-American Iraq would transform the Middle East, make peace with Israel, provide easy access to the world's second-largest oil reserves, and show small states the folly of opposing the United States. The most effective prowar argument, however, played on American fears of renewed terrorism and charged that Saddam Hussein was still developing weapons of mass destruction in flagrant disregard of his promise to end all such programs following the first war with Iraq, in 1991 (see page 1040). Saddam had used chemical weapons in his war with Iran in the 1980s and against the Kurdish population of northern Iraq, and the Bush administration argued that sooner or later he would probably use these terrible weapons against the United States and its allies or would give them to anti-American fanatics like those who struck New York on September 11, 2001.

**Shi'ite Insurgents Leaving Najaf's Imam Ali Shrine** After three weeks of intense urban combat, U.S. forces and Shi'ite fighters loyal to a radical cleric agreed in August 2004 to a compromise cease-fire. The Americans withdrew and the insurgents left the sacred Shi'ite shrine with the golden dome (seen in the background) without surrendering or giving up their weapons. Other groups fighting against the Americans included Sunni Muslims from Saddam's regime and Islamic fundamentalists from home and abroad. (An ancient dispute split Muslims into Sunnis and Shi'ites.) *(Getty Images)*

In August 2002, Vice President Cheney promised Iraqi exiles that the United States would depose Saddam, although according to the United Nations charter, the Security Council has the sole authority to use armed force, except in self-defense, and Iraq, impoverished by a decade of tough United Nations sanctions, gave no indication of attacking any of its neighbors, much less the United States. Moreover, large numbers of Americans shared widespread doubts in Europe about the legality—and wisdom—of an American attack on Iraq and argued for a peaceful settlement of the Iraqi weapons crisis. (See the feature "Listening to the Past: The West in World Affairs" on pages 1062–1063.) So the Bush administration reluctantly agreed to new Security Council resolutions requiring Iraq to accept the return of United Nations weapons inspectors and destroy any remaining prohibited weapons. Iraq accepted the inspectors, declaring it had destroyed all prohibited weapons.

As 2002 ended and the inspections went forward, Kofi Annan, the United Nations secretary-general, coordinated efforts to achieve the Security Council's stated objectives and avoid war. (See the feature "Individuals in Society: Kofi Annan.") The inspectors operated freely in Iraq and found no weapons of mass destruction. However, the United States and Britain said Iraq was hiding prohibited weapons, moved armies to the Middle East, and lobbied for a new United Nations resolution authorizing immediate military action against Iraq. The world followed the debates in the Security Council with unprecedented interest and generally opposed an attack on Iraq. France, Russia, China, Germany, and a majority of the smaller states argued for continued weapons inspections. Western governments became bitterly divided, and the Security Council deadlocked and failed to act. Nevertheless, all parties in the crisis recognized the United Nations as a key source of international legality and the importance of the international organization was reaffirmed.

In March 2003 the United States and Britain invaded Iraq from bases in Kuwait and quickly overwhelmed the Iraqi army. Yet even as Saddam's dictatorship collapsed, the confident expectation of a long and peaceful occupation in a pro-American Iraq was impaired by serious errors of American judgment. As chaos spread and looters stripped government buildings and hospitals of everything from computers to faucets, American and British troops simply turned a blind eye and took no action. Disbanding the Iraqi army also alienated the population, worsened security, and created mass unemployment, while the failure to seize huge stocks of weapons left Iraqi insurgents with guns and explosives for subsequent counterattacks. The allies found no weapons of mass destruction, which raised many questions about a prewar manipulation of intelligence data. In November 2003, with security deteriorating and Islamic extremists slipping into Iraq to join the insurgents (as in the 1980s they had done in Afghanistan against the Soviets), the Bush administration abruptly decided to grant "full and complete sovereignty" to an interim Iraqi government by July 2004 and hold national elections the following year. In April 2004, as fighting reached a new intensity, pictures of American soldiers and contract workers sexually abusing and humiliating Iraqi prisoners shocked public opinion worldwide.

In late June 2004, after having turned to the United Nations for some limited support, a somewhat more pragmatic United States and Britain proclaimed a "fully sovereign" Iraqi government, headed by an Iraqi exile with close ties to the CIA and the Pentagon. American and British soldiers remained to support the new government, and fighting with Iraqi insurgents continued. The war in Iraq had split the West, the occupation of the country had gone poorly, and the legitimacy of the new government was in doubt. But it was impossible to predict the final outcome in Iraq or to know if the damage to the Western alliance would be repaired. Only time would tell.

## The Future in Perspective

For centuries astrologers and scientists, experts and ordinary people, have sought to peek into the future. And although it may seem that the study of the past has little to say about the future, the study of history over a long period is actually very useful in this regard. It helps put the future in perspective.

Certainly, history is full of erroneous predictions, a few of which we have mentioned in this book. Yet lack of success has not diminished the age-old desire to look into the future. Self-proclaimed experts even pretend that they have created a new science of futurology. With great pomposity, they often act as if their hunches and guesses about future human development are inescapable realities. Yet the study of history teaches healthy skepticism regarding such predictions, however scientific and learned they may appear. Past results suggest that most such predictions will simply not come true, or at least not in the anticipated ways. Thus history provides some psychological protection from the visions of modern prognosticators.

This protection is particularly valuable when we realize that views of the future tend to swing between pessimistic and optimistic extremes from one generation, or even from one decade, to the next. These swings back and forth between optimism and pessimism, which one

# Individuals in Society

## Kofi Annan

The key role of the Security Council in the Iraqi weapons crisis of 2002–2003 highlighted the renewed prominence of the United Nations in world affairs after a series of ambitious and sometimes unsuccessful peacekeeping missions in developing countries in the mid-1990s. This revival owed a great deal to Kofi Annan (b. 1938), the confident, compassionate African diplomat who headed the international organization beginning in 1997. Annan offered an inspiring moral vision of a global community committed to peace, democracy, and universal human rights.

Kofi Annan was born into the West African elite. His parents were hereditary nobles of the Fante people in Ghana, and his father was an elected provincial governor and business executive. As a boy, Annan attended excellent private schools, but he also grew up with deep roots in his African heritage. He later recalled, "My family moved in and out all the time from a traditional to a modern urban setting."* Active in student politics and winning a Ford Foundation scholarship for young foreign leaders, the winsome Annan attended Macalester College in St. Paul, Minnesota, where he developed an idealistic commitment to international peace and understanding.

Although he had intended to return to Ghana after graduation, the increasingly authoritarian rule of President Kwame Nkrumah caused him to reconsider. In 1962 Annan took a job as a budget officer with the World Health Organization (WHO), an important United Nations agency based in Geneva, Switzerland. In the following years he gradually worked his way up the ladder in the United Nations, experiencing the world's tragedies and emergencies firsthand and also learning to create budgets and plan programs as a skilled administrator.

In 1992 United Nations secretary-general Boutros Boutros-Ghali put Annan in charge of all United Nations peacekeeping operations. It proved to be a monumental challenge. As the cold war order disappeared, civil war enveloped a host of countries, including Bosnia, Croatia, Somalia, Haiti, Rwanda, Angola, Afghanistan, and Sudan. Annan had to manage an unprecedented explosion in the size, scope, and complexity of peacekeeping efforts. Civilian and military peacekeepers working for the United Nations skyrocketed from about ten thousand in 1992 to almost seventy thousand, from seventy-seven countries, in 1995. Widely praised from many sides for his sensitive and effective leadership, Annan was selected secretary-general for a five-year term beginning in 1997 and began serving a second term in 2002.

Annan's first act as secretary-general was to reform the United Nations. He reduced total spending, as the wealthy nations led by the United States adamantly demanded, but he did so by refocusing the organization's efforts on the welfare of the world's poorest citizens, many of whom were in Annan's native Africa. This focus in turn helped bolster the developing countries' support of United Nations efforts.

*Kofi Annan, secretary-general of the United Nations, discusses his Nobel Peace Prize in 2001.* (Reuters NewMedia Inc./Corbis)

Guided by an idealistic, moral view of the world, Annan believed that humanity should know no divisions. As he said when he and the United Nations were jointly awarded the Nobel Peace Prize in December 2001, the "poor and dispossessed are no less deserving of human dignity, fundamental freedoms, security and education than any of us." Moreover, he acted on his beliefs in countless ways, rallying humanitarian organizations, launching initiatives, and setting a moral agenda. His contribution to the global campaign for human rights, called the Annan Doctrine, argues that states must no longer use their rights of sovereignty as a shield for gross violations of human rights and that the global community has at times a "duty to intervene." Annan helped lead the international attack on the HIV/AIDS epidemic, which he called his "personal priority," and said that he tried "to place human beings at the center of everything we do" at the United Nations.

### Questions for Analysis

1. How was Annan able to rise out of the United Nations bureaucracy and reach the very top as secretary-general? What factors were most important? Why?
2. What is the Annan Doctrine? What, in your opinion, is the proper role of the United Nations in today's world?

*Quoted in J. Tessitore, *Kofi Annan: The Peacekeeper* (New York: Franklin Watts, 2000), p. 18.

*The* **history companion** *features additional information and activities related to this topic.*
**history.college.hmco.com/students**

historian has aptly called "the great seesaw" in the development of the Western world, reflect above all the current situation of the observers.[8] Thus in the economic stagnation and revived cold war of the 1970s and 1980s, many projections into the future were quite pessimistic, just as they were very optimistic in the 1950s and 1960s. Many people in the Western world feared that conditions were going to get worse rather than better. For example, there were fears that pollution would destroy the environment and that the traditional family would disappear. Some gloomy experts predicted that twenty to thirty states might well have nuclear weapons by the end of the twentieth century. Many forecasters and politicians predicted that the energy crisis—in the form of skyrocketing oil prices—meant disaster in the form of lower standards of living at best and the collapse of civilization at worst. In fact, oil prices collapsed in the early 1980s and generally stayed low until the second Iraq war in 2003. It was heartening in that time of pessimism to know that most dire predictions do not prove true, just as the same knowledge of likely error is sobering in times of optimistic expectations.

Optimistic visions of the future were certainly in the air after the end of the cold war. The pendulum had definitely swung, most notably in the United States. Untroubled in the late 1990s by the high unemployment and the early stages of corporate downsizing that soured the mood in western Europe, the United States celebrated its dynamic economy and its booming stock market. U.S. military power, leadership in world affairs, and excellence in advanced technologies also encouraged optimism and rosy projections.

In 2000 the American mood shifted. The dot-com bubble burst, and in 2001 the U.S. economy slid into a recession. The attack of September 11, 2001, accentuated economic problems, brought national grief and fear, and led to many pessimistic forecasts of a long uphill struggle against global extremism. Most frightening of all were grim warnings by some self-described experts who predicted that terrorist groups were likely to succeed in developing or buying biological and nuclear weapons of mass destruction, which they would then turn on millions of innocent people with unspeakable cruelty. Such nightmare scenarios are not impossible, but we should remember that modern governments possess tremendous resources that they can mobilize to control individuals and small opposition groups, especially when the leading states decide to work together, as they did immediately after September 11, 2001. Once again, just as it is sobering to know that the rosiest predictions in optimistic times usually do not prove true, so is it heartening to know that the direst projections in pessimistic times normally do not come to pass.

Whatever does or does not happen, the study of history puts the future in perspective in other ways. We have seen that every age has its problems and challenges. Others before us have trodden the paths of uncertainty and crisis. This knowledge helps save us from exaggerated self-pity in the face of our own predicaments.

Perhaps our Western heritage may rightly inspire us with pride and measured self-confidence. We stand, momentarily, at the head of the long procession of Western civilization. Sometimes the procession has wandered, or backtracked, or done terrible things. But it has also carried the efforts and sacrifices of generations of toiling, struggling ancestors. Through no effort of our own, we are the beneficiaries of those sacrifices and achievements. Now that it is our turn to carry the torch onward, we may remember these ties with our forebears.

To change the metaphor, we in the West are like a card player who has been dealt many good cards. Some of them are obvious, such as our technical and scientific heritage or our commitment to human rights, religious freedom, and the individual. Others are not so obvious, sometimes half-forgotten or even hidden up the sleeve. Think, for example, of the Christian Democrats, the moderate Catholic party that emerged after World War II to play such an important role in the western European renaissance. And in the almost miraculous victory of peaceful revolution in eastern Europe in 1989—in what Czech playwright turned president Václav Havel called "the power of the powerless"—we see again the regenerative strength of the Western ideals of individual rights, representative government, and nationhood in the European homeland. We hold a good hand.

Our study of history, of mighty struggles and fearsome challenges, of shining achievements and tragic failures, gives a sense of the essence of life itself: the process of change over time. Again and again we have seen how peoples and societies evolve, influenced by ideas, human passions, and material conditions. As surely as anything is sure, this process of change over time will continue as the future becomes the present and then the past. And students of history are better prepared to make sense of this unfolding process because they have already observed it. They know how change is rooted in existing historical forces, and their projections will probably be better than many of the trendy speculations of futurologists. Students of history are also prepared for the new and unexpected in human development, for they have already seen great breakthroughs and revolutions. They have an understanding of how things really happen.

## Key Terms

| | |
|---|---|
| re-Stalinization | Alliance for Germany |
| Great Russians | Paris Accord |
| Gdansk Agreement | "new world order" |
| Solidarity | globalization |
| perestroika | European Union |
| glasnost | Kosovo Liberation Army (KLA) |
| shock therapy | Maastricht treaty |
| Velvet Revolution | baby bust |
| third way | |

## Notes

1. M. Walker, *The Waking Giant: Gorbachev's Russia* (New York: Pantheon Books, 1987), p. 175.
2. F. Fukuyama, *The End of History and the Last Man* (New York: Free Press, 1992); and J. Cronin, *The World the Cold War Made: Order, Chaos, and Return of History* (New York: Routledge, 1996), pp. 267–281.
3. Quoted in *The Economist,* January 6, 2001, p. 6.
4. Quoted by Flora Lewis, *International Herald Tribune,* June 15, 2001, p. 6.
5. D. Rappaport, "The Fourth Wave: September 11 in the History of Terrorism," *Current History,* December 2001, pp. 419–424.
6. Ibid.
7. R. Suskind, *The Price of Loyalty: George W. Bush, the White House, and the Education of Paul O'Neill* (New York: Simon and Schuster, 2004), p. 86.
8. G. Blainey, *The Great Seesaw: A New View of the Western World* (London: Macmillan, 1988).

## Suggested Reading

Many of the studies cited in the Suggested Reading for Chapters 29 and 30 are of value for the years since 1985 as well. Among other general works, F. Gilbert, *The End of the European Era: 1890 to the Present* (1991), is particularly helpful with its evenhanded account and extensive bibliography. Journalistic accounts in major newspapers and magazines are also invaluable tools for an understanding of recent developments. *Current History,* which devotes each monthly issue to either a geographical region or a contemporary topic, is especially recommended. *The Economist* is an excellent newsmagazine with outstanding feature articles.

M. Dobbs, *Down with Big Brother: The Fall of the Soviet Empire* (1997), is a superb firsthand account by an inspired journalist who covered events in Russia and eastern Europe between 1977 and 1993. On the Soviet Union, in addition to works cited in Chapter 30, the book by Walker cited in the Notes is a fascinating eyewitness account of Soviet life in the mid-1980s. R. Suny, *The Soviet Experiment: Russia, the USSR, and the Successor States* (1998), is outstanding on Russia in the 1990s. M. Lewin, *The Gorbachev Phenomenon: A Historical Interpretation* (1988), is excellent on the origins of the reforms. Two valuable studies by leading authorities on Russia after communism are M. Goldman, *Lost Opportunity: What Has Made Economic Reform in Russia So Difficult?* (1996), and R. Brady, *Kapitalizm: Russia's Struggle to Free Its Economy* (1999). R. Sakwa, *Putin* (2004), puts the new Russian leader in social and historical context.

N. Naimark, *Fires of Hate: Ethnic Cleansing in Twentieth-Century Europe* (1999), argues that recent nationalism rather than "ancient hatreds" is decisive, while L. Johnson, *Central Europe: Enemies, Neighbors, Friends* (1996), ably interprets developments in eastern Europe before and after the revolutions of 1989. For developments in Poland, R. Leslie, *The History of Poland Since 1863* (1981), provides a long-term perspective. P. Kenney, *A Carnival of Revolution* (2003), is a well-written oral history blending personalities and broad movements, and T. Ash, *The Magic Lantern: The Revolution of '89 Witnessed in Warsaw, Budapest, Berlin, and Prague* (1990), is exciting instant history. G. Stokes, ed., *From Stalinism to Pluralism: A Documentary History of Eastern Europe Since 1945,* 2d ed. (1996), is another excellent collection. Two excellent, judicious studies on the tragedy in Yugoslavia are J. Lampe, *Yugoslavia as History: Twice There Was a Country,* 2d ed. (2000), and T. Judah, *The Serbs: History, Myth and the Destruction of Yugoslavia* (1997).

The work by Cronin cited in the Notes provides a stimulating view of the late cold war and the massive changes following it. P. Zelikow and C. Rice, *Germany Unified and Europe Transformed: A Study in Statecraft* (1995), is an award-winning study of relations between the Great Powers and the peaceful resolution of the German question. G. Rose, *Jacques Delors and European Integration* (1995), analyzes the controversies surrounding the European Union in the 1990s. E. Balibar, *We, the People of Europe? Reflections on Transnational Citizenship* (2004), considers problems of nationality in contemporary Europe. D. Calleo, *Rethinking Europe's Future* (2003), presents the ideas of a leading expert. J. Ardagh, *Germany and the Germans: The United Germany in the Mid-1990s,* is an insightful study.

The contemporary resurgence of nationalism is analyzed by R. Brubaker, *Nationalism Reframed: Nationhood and the National Question* (1996), and R. Caplan and John Feffer, *Europe's New Nationalism: States and Minorities in Conflict* (1996). N. Cantor, *The American Century: Varieties of Culture in Modern Times* (1997), is a lively consideration of many cultural developments that includes the 1990s. Important books on globalization include P. O'Meara et al., eds., *Globalization and the Challenges of the New Century* (2000); M. Hardt and A. Negri, *Empire* (2000); and S.

*(continued on page 1064)*

# Listening to the Past

## The West in World Affairs

*The foreign policies of the George W. Bush administration and the run-up to the American-led attack on Iraq created a firestorm of debate, revealing deep divisions in public opinion in Europe and the United States. One defender of American willingness to use military force to impose its will was Robert Kagan, a political analyst with close ties to the Bush administration, and the first reading presents a portion of a widely read Kagan essay. The second selection provides a critique of Kagan's argument by William Pfaff, an American political columnist and author noted for essays that often incorporate European views and resonate on both sides of the Atlantic.*

### Robert Kagan, May 26, 2002

President Bush is making a noble effort to pull together the fraying alliance, but the fact is Europeans and Americans no longer share a common view of the world. On the all-important question of power—the utility of power, the morality of power—they have parted ways. Europeans believe they are moving beyond power into a self-contained world of laws and rules and transnational negotiation and cooperation. . . . The United States, meanwhile, remains mired in history, exercising power in the anarchic Hobbesian world where international rules are unreliable and where security and the promotion of a liberal order still depend on the possession and use of military might. This is why, on major strategic and international questions today, Americans are from Mars and Europeans are from Venus: They agree on little and understand one another less and less. Why the divergent perspectives? . . .

Part of the reason is the enormous shift in the balance of power. The gap between the United States and Europe opened wide as a result of World War II and has grown wider in the past decade. America's unparalleled military strength has predictably given it a greater propensity to use force and a more confident belief in the moral legitimacy of power. . . .

For Americans, the Hobbesian world is not so frightening. Unilateralism is naturally more attractive to those with the capacity to act unilaterally. And international law constrains strong nations more than it does the weak. Because of the disparity of power, Americans and Europeans even view threats differently. A person armed only with a knife may decide that a bear prowling the forest is a tolerable danger—trying to kill the bear is riskier than lying low and hoping the bear never attacks. But a person with a rifle will likely make a different calculation: Why should he risk being mauled to death if he doesn't need to? Americans can imagine successfully invading Iraq and toppling Saddam, and therefore more than 70 percent of Americans favor such action, particularly after the experience of Sept. 11. Europeans, not surprisingly, find the prospect unimaginable and frightening. . . .

American realists may scoff, but within the confines of Europe the brutal laws of power politics really have been repealed. Since World War II European society has been shaped not by the traditional exercise of power but by the unfolding of a geopolitical miracle: The German lion has lain down with the French lamb. . . . The application of the European miracle to the rest of the world has become Europe's new [civilizing mission]. If Germany can be tamed through gentle rapprochement, why not Iraq? . . .

Most Europeans don't acknowledge the great paradox: that their passage into post-history has depended on the United States not making the same passage. Instead, they have come to view the United States simply as a rogue colossus, in many respects a bigger threat to the pacific ideals Europeans now cherish than Iraq or Iran. Americans, in turn, have come to view Europe as annoying, irrelevant, naive and ungrateful as it takes a free ride on American power. This is not just a family quarrel. If Americans and Europeans no longer agree on the utility and morality of power, then what remains to undergird their military alliance? . . .

### William Pfaff, August 1, 2002

A new metaphor has been introduced into the trans-Atlantic dialogue, portraying Europe as enjoying a "Kantian paradise" made possible by the United States' ordering of a Hobbesian world.

Europe, by virtue of its wartime and postwar experience, is said to have established "a post-historical paradise of peace and relative prosperity, the realization of Kant's 'perpetual peace.'" This benign achievement causes West Europeans to recoil from the use of force, and to see international problems generally as open to rational and negotiated solutions. My quotation, and the argument, are from Robert Kagan of the Carnegie Endowment in Washington. . . .

Kagan goes on to say that Europeans can enjoy this happy condition because a sober and illusion-free United States patrols the frontiers, beyond which lies a Hobbesian world where lions and tigers roam and good intentions unaccompanied by power can prove fatal. . . .

Kagan was an early promoter, in 1996, of the proposition that as circumstances have placed the United States in a position of world hegemony, this "hegemony must be actively maintained, just as it was actively obtained. . . . Any lessening of that influence will allow others to play a larger part in shaping the world to suit *their* needs."

He collaborated then with William Kristol, the [influential] neoconservative advocate of American foreign policy unilateralism. . . .

In 2000, the two observed that American hegemony is not only to American benefit but that of the world, since the United States "does not pursue a narrow, selfish definition of its national interest . . . and infuses its foreign policy with an unusually high degree of morality."

This is not an argument to which all will assent. . . . Currently, Washington is debating whether or not to attack or invade Iraq in order to overthrow and replace that country's unsavory government. This cannot possibly promote stability in the Middle East in the short term, or in the longer run, other than by resort to a forecast—which most specialists would classify as amateurish wishful thinking—that Saddam Hussein's overthrow would cause democratic governments to spring up in his country and throughout the region. Why? A second Washington debate is whether to make an unprovoked attack on Iran to destroy a nuclear power reactor being built there with Russian assistance, under inspection by the International Atomic Energy Agency, within the terms of the Nuclear Nonproliferation Treaty, of which Iran is a signatory. . . .

Protesters march in 2004 against an informal meeting of NATO in Munich; the lead banner reads "Stop the global war of NATO states." *(AFP/Getty Images)*

No other government in the world would support such an action, other than Israel's. Israel would do so not because it expected to be attacked by Iran but because it not unreasonably opposes any nuclear capacity in the hands of any Islamic government.

The Bush administration's policy of providing virtually unqualified support—out of essentially domestic political motives—to Israel's policies in the occupied territories and Gaza is a self-evident source of potential regional disorder, as every government in the Near and Middle East and the Maghreb, from Turkey to Morocco, has already advised Washington. The argument that the United States today protects international society from Hobbesian disorder is untrue. Washington acts as Kagan in 1996 urged it to act, to protect a hegemonic position that serves its political and economic interests, and its perceived security.

## Questions for Analysis

1. How does Kagan justify current U.S. policy?
2. What criticisms does Pfaff make? How does he evaluate American policies?

*Sources:* Robert Kagan, *Washington Post,* May 26, 2002. Reprinted by permission of the author; William Pfaff, *International Herald Tribune,* April 9, 2002. Reprinted by permission.

Strange, *The Retreat of the State: The Diffusion of Power in the World Economy* (1996).

Recent works on major developments include M. Klare, *Resource Wars: The New Landscape of Global Conflict* (2001), which stresses the importance of oil and other commodities, and R. Bernstein, *Out of the Blue: The Story of September 11, 2001, from Jihad to Ground Zero* (2002), a gripping account by a talented journalist. R. Suskind's excellent biography of Paul O'Neill, cited in the Notes, examines the Bush administration's early buildup for war in Iraq, as does the best-selling insider account by B. Woodward, *Plan of Attack* (2004). M. Viorst, *In the Shadow of the Prophet: The Struggle for the Soul of Islam* (2001), deftly charts the conflicting currents of contemporary Islam. P. Jenkins, *The Next Christianity: The Coming of Global Christianity* (2002), argues that new African and Asian converts are revitalizing Christianity. The work by Fukuyama cited in the Notes illustrates the widespread euphoria after the collapse of communism, arguing that democratic capitalism has defeated all its competitors. The pathbreaking study of Blainey cited in the Notes examines the cycle of pessimism and optimism in Western history in fascinating detail.

# Document-Based Questions (DBQs)

## Introduction

Think of a Document-Based Question (DBQ) as a mini-research paper, or a mini-investigation. It is a chance to show that you, like a professional historian or detective, can read the documents, question your sources, understand the backgrounds and motivations, and produce a good case/interpretation. In the words of the Advanced Placement European History course description book, a DBQ tests your ability "to formulate and support an answer from documentary evidence."* It *does not* test your historical recall; the multiple-choice questions and the free-response essays do that. The DBQ is a test of your document-reading and analytical skills.

That last point is worth repeating: the DBQ is a test of your skills. It is scored/graded with a list of skills: when the reader sees a skill demonstrated, the reader gives you a point. Your essay can receive a maximum of 9 points when it is scored by an AP reader. Your classroom teacher may use an easier system of grading (A–F and 100–0% come to mind) but s/he will be looking to see if you demonstrate the same skills.

This section is designed to be used in conjunction with your chapters in *A History of Western Society* and to give you practice on three of the most crucial and difficult skills: figuring out exactly what the question is asking you to do, writing an acceptable thesis statement, and analyzing a document for its content and point of view. For the most part, the DBQs in this section feature fewer documents than on the AP European Exam. The DBQs dealing with the earlier chapters of the text (DBQs 1 through 11) feature 3–6 documents; the last three DBQs (DBQs 12 through 14) are designed like those on the AP Exam and feature 10–12 documents. The mini-DBQs are to be completed in 40 minutes or less, while the full-length DBQs take an hour in "regulation" time.

*When working with documents, try the following three-step process:*

---

**1.** "Plot summary": What is this document's basic subject matter and content? What is its date? Does it relate to some other important events in the same time period?

---

**2.** "Point of View" (POV):

a. The first question about the document is "who produced it?": in terms of writer's gender, age, ethnicity, social status, religion, intellectual beliefs. (Almost all of the documents here are "primary sources," produced during the time in question. A few are "secondary sources," produced by historians after the fact. Take this difference into account.)

b. The second question is "who was the intended audience?": written privately, written to be read/heard by others (whom?), official document for a ruler to read, commissioned painting, and so on.

c. The third question, as any good detective knows, is "why?": what was the MOTIVATION of the writer/producer of the document, based on what you can surmise about him or her?

d. When you put these together, you get the POV: why THIS person produced THIS piece of information at THIS time. Then you can evaluate how much you "trust" the information in the document, or what you think was *really* going on. *Note:* It is useful to consider the tone/vocabulary of the document, just as you would in analyzing a piece of literature. Tone will sometimes convey the intent or the point of view of the author (anger, disdain, admiration, etc.).

---

**3.** "Analysis": Now that you know the basic information, and the POV of the author, how does this document help you to *answer the question that is being asked?*

---

*Quoted in 2004, 2005 Course Description for AP European History (College Entrance Examination Board, NY, 2003), p. 23. Available online at www.apcentral.collegeboard.com. AP and Advanced Placement Program are registered trademarks of the College Entrance Examination Board, which was not involved in the production of, and does not endorse, this product.

## DBQ 1: Attitudes About Religion in the Late Middle Ages and Early Renaissance (Chapters 12 and 13)

**Question: To what degree did criticism in the late Middle Ages influence attitudes toward religion during the early Renaissance?**

### Document 1

Source: Marsiglio of Padua (Rector of the University of Paris), *Defensor Pacis* [Defender of the Peace], 1324.

The Roman bishops wrongly wish to possess excessive temporal goods, and refuse to be subject to the laws and edicts of the rulers or the human legislator, thereby opposing the example and teaching of Christ and the apostles.

### Document 2

Source: The Council of Pisa, 1409.

This holy and general council, representing the universal church, decrees and declares that the united college of cardinals was empowered to call the council and that the power to call such a council belongs of right to the aforesaid holy college of cardinals, especially now when there is a detestable schism. The council further declared that this holy council, representing the universal church, caused both claimants of the papal throne to be cited in the gates and doors of the churches in Pisa to come and hear the final decision [in the matter of the schism] pronounced, or to give a good and sufficient reason why such sentence should not be rendered.

### Document 3

Source: Pico della Mirandola, *Oration on the Dignity of Man,* 1486.

On man when he came into life the Father conferred the seeds of all kinds and the germs of every way of life. Whatever seeds each man cultivates will grow to maturity and bear in him their own fruit. If they be vegetative, he will be like a plant. If sensitive, he will become brutish. If rational, he will grow into a heavenly being. If intellectual, he will be an angel and the son of God. And if, happy in the lot of no created thing, he withdraws into the center of his own unity, his spirit, made one with God, in the solitary darkness of God, who is set above all things, shall surpass them all.

### Document 4

Source: Erasmus, *The Praise of Folly,* 1509.

As for the theologians, perhaps it would be better to pass them over in silence, "*not stirring up the hornets' nest*" and "not laying a finger on the stinkweed," since this race of man is incredibly arrogant and touchy. For they might rise up en masse and march in ranks against me with six hundred conclusions and force me to recant. And if I should refuse, they would immediately shout "heretic." For this is the thunderbolt they always keep ready at a moment's notice to terrify anyone to whom they are not very favorably inclined.

**Document 5**

Source: Raphael, *Pope Leo X with Two Cardinals,* 1518.

Uffizi, Florence, Italy/Scala/Art Resource, NY.

## DBQ 2: Reform and Renewal in the Christian Church (Chapter 14)

**Question: Discuss to what extent the religious schism during the sixteenth century was symptomatic of political, social, and economic problems.**

### Document 1

Source: Martin Luther, *Address to the Christian Nobility of the German Nation Concerning the Reform of the Christian Estate,* 1520.

Therefore, when necessity demands it, and the pope is an offense to Christendom, the first man who is able should, as a true member of the whole body, do what he can to bring about a truly free council. No one can do this so well as the temporal authorities, especially since they are also fellow-Christians, fellow-priests, fellow-members of the spiritual estate, fellow lords over all things. Whenever it is necessary or profitable, they ought to exercise the office and work which they have received from God over everyone.

### Document 2

Source: Martin Luther, *Against the Murderous, Thieving Hordes of the Peasants*, ca 1525.

Let everyone who can smite, slay, and stab [the peasants], secretly and openly, remembering that nothing can be more poisonous, hurtful or devilish than a rebel.

### Document 3

Source: *The Twelve Articles,* manifesto of German peasants in Swabia, 1524.

It has been the custom hitherto for men to hold us as their own property, which is pitiable enough, considering that Christ has delivered and redeemed us all, without exception, by the shedding of his precious blood, the lowly as well as the great. Accordingly, it is consistent with Scripture that we should be free and should wish to be so. . . . We are aggrieved by the appropriation by individuals of meadows and fields which at one time belonged to the community. These we will take again into our own hands.

### Document 4

Source: The Act of Supremacy, English Parliament, 1534.

Albeit the king's Majesty justly and rightfully is and ought to be the supreme head of the Church of England, and so is recognized by the clergy of this realm in their convocations, yet nevertheless, for corroboration and confirmation thereof, and for increase of virtue in Christ's religion within this realm of England, and to repress and extirpate all errors, heresies, and other enormities and abuses heretofore used in the same, be it enacted, by authority of this present Parliament, that the king, our sovereign lord, his heirs and successors, kings of this realm, shall be taken, accepted, and reputed the only supreme head in earth of the Church of England, called *Anglicans Ecclesia;* and shall have and enjoy, annexed and united to the imperial crown of this realm, as well the title and style thereof, as all honors, dignities, preeminences, jurisdictions, privileges, authorities, immunities, profits, and commodities to the said dignity of the supreme head of the same Church belonging and appertaining.

## DBQ 3: Women in the Sixteenth and Seventeenth Centuries (Chapter 15)

**Question: In what ways were the lives of European women affected by the upheavals and changes of the sixteenth and seventeenth centuries?**

### Document 1

Source: Hans Jacob Christopher von Grimmelshausen (German writer), *Simplicissimus* (a novel), 1669.

The first thing these troopers did was, that they stabled their horses: thereafter each fell to his appointed task: which task was neither more nor less than ruin and destruction. . . . Our maid was so handled in the stable that she could not come out; which is a shame to tell of. . . . Of the women, girls, and maidservants whom they took, I have not much to say in particular, for the soldiers would not have me see how they dealt with them. Yet this I did know, that one heard some of them scream most piteously in divers corners of the house; and well I can judge it fared no better with my mother and our Ursel than with the rest.

### Document 2

Source: Confession of Bessie Wilson (Scotland?) (n.d.).

And then the Devil said, "Thee are a poor overworked body. Will thee be my servant and I will give thee abundance and thee shall never want."

### Document 3

Source: Natalie Zemon Davis, *Women on the Margins: Three Seventeenth-Century Lives* (1995), writing about Maria Sibylla Merian (1647–1717), Dutch artist, writer, naturalist.

In February 1699 she [Merian] asked a broker to sell a large collection of her paintings of fruit, plants, and insects, as well as many specimens acquired in Germany, Friesland, and Holland and sent to her from the Indies. She hoped to cover costs by the sale of rare specimens from Suriname upon her return. . . . It was an adventure for which her life changes had prepared her. Hadn't the men in her family traveled about Europe in pursuit of their art?

### Document 4

Source: Elizabeth I of England (r. 1558–1603), *On the Spanish Armada,* 1588.

And therefore I am come amongst you at this time, not as for my recreation or sport, but being resolved, in the midst and heat of the battle, to live or die amongst you all; to lay down, for my God, and for my kingdom, and for my people, my honor and my blood, even the dust. I know I have but the body of a weak and feeble woman; but I have the heart of a king, and of a king of England, too; and think foul scorn that Parma or Spain, or any prince of Europe, should dare to invade the borders of my realms: to which, rather than any dishonor should grow by me, I myself will take up arms; I myself will be your general, judge, and rewarder of every one of your virtues in the field. I know already, by your forwardness, that you have deserved rewards and crowns; and we do assure you, on the word of a prince, they shall be duly paid you.

## Document 5

Source: John Knox (Scottish), "The First Blast of the Trumpet Against the Monstrous Regiment of Women," 1558.

To promote a woman to bear rule, superiority, dominion, or empire above any realm, nation, or city, is repugnant to nature; contumely [*an insult*] to God, a thing most contrary to his revealed will and approved ordinance; and finally, it is the subversion of good order, of all equity and justice.

## DBQ 4: Absolutism (Chapters 16 and 17)

**Question: To what extent did rulers and their subjects view the proper role of an absolute monarch differently?**

### Document 1

Source: Frederick II of Prussia (r. 1740–1786), *Essay on the Forms of Government.*

The sovereign is representative of his state. He and his people form a single body. Ruler and ruled can be happy only if they are firmly united. The sovereign stands to his people in the same relation in which the head stands to the body.

### Document 2

Source: Holy Roman Emperor Joseph II (r. 1780–1790), excerpts from (1) a letter to Leopold of Tuscany, 1768; and (2) a confidential memorandum to his mother, Empress Maria Theresa, 1765.

Patriotism, the welfare of the monarchy, . . . are my only passion, and they would inspire me to do anything.

The aim of every measure is to have a total view, every action being related to the overall view, which only the monarch and his closest associates should share and pursue.

### Document 3

Source: *The Memoirs of the Duke of Saint-Simon on the Reign of Louis XIV [r. 1643–1715] and the Regency,* trans. Bayle St. John, 1857.

The frequent fêtes [parties], the private promenades at Versailles, the journey, were means on which the King seized in order to distinguish or mortify the courtiers, and thus render them more assiduous in pleasing him. . . . Louis XIV took great pains to be well-informed of all that passed everywhere; in the public places, in the private houses, in society and familiar intercourse. His spies and tell-tattlers were infinite . . . all these letters were seen by him alone, and always before everything else. . . . These unknown means ruined an infinite number of people of all classes, who never could discover the cause; often ruined them very unjustly; for the King, once prejudiced, never altered his opinion.

### Document 4

Source: Report of the Commission of Enquiry into the Conditions of the Peasants of Bohemia, presented to the Council of State in Vienna, 1769 (Holy Roman Empire).

Even those nobles who have the best intentions are unable to protect their peasants, because their [taxation] agents are rough, evil, violent and grasping. . . . The Kingdom of Bohemia is like a statue which is collapsing because its pedestal has been taken away, because all the charges of the Kingdom are born by the peasants, who are the sole taxpayers.

**Document 5**

Source: Arthur Young (English agronomist), *Travels [in France] During the Years 1787, 1788 and 1789.*

The abuses attending the levy of taxes were heavy and universal. . . . Such an enormous power, constantly acting and from which no man was free, must in the nature of things, degenerate in many cases into absolute tyranny. . . . What must have been the state of the poor people paying heavy taxes from which the nobility and clergy were exempted? A cruel aggravation of their misery to see those who could best afford to pay, exempted. . . . The *Capitaineries* [lords' exclusive hunting rights] were a dreadful scourge on all the occupiers of the land. . . . Such were the exertions of arbitrary power which the lower orders felt directly from the royal authority.

**Document 6**

Source: Adam Olearius (German diplomat to Moscow), *Travels in Moscovy,* ca 1630.

Although the Russians, especially the common populace living as slaves under a harsh yoke, can bear and endure a great deal out of love for their masters, yet if the pressure is beyond measure . . . a dangerous indignation results, turned not so much against their sovereign as against the lower authorities, especially if the people have been much oppressed by them . . . and have not been protected by the higher authorities.

## DBQ 5: Toward a New World-View (Chapter 18)

**Question: How did the new world-views of the seventeenth and eighteenth centuries affect the way Europeans thought about society and human relations?**

### Document 1

Source: René Descartes (French), *Discourse on Method,* 1637.

. . . [I]n my travels I had found that those who held opinions contrary to ours were neither barbarians nor savages, but that any of them were at least as reasonable as ourselves.

### Document 2

Source: John Locke (Scottish), *Some Thoughts Concerning Education,* 1693.

I think I may say that of all the men we meet with, nine parts of ten are what they are, good or evil, useful or not, by their education. 'Tis that which makes the great difference in Mankind.

### Document 3

Source: Catherine the Great of Russia, Decree on Serfs, 1767.

. . . [A]ccording to the laws that have been enacted from time immemorial by the autocratic forefathers of Her Imperial Majesty and which have not been repealed . . . all persons who dare to incite serfs and peasants to disobey their landlords shall be arrested and taken to the nearest government office, there to be punished forthwith as disturbers of the public tranquility, according to the laws and without leniency.

### Document 4

Source: Mary Wollstonecraft, *A Vindication of the Rights of Woman,* 1792.

. . . [W]omen, in particular, are rendered weak and wretched by a variety of concurring causes, originating from one hasty conclusion. The conduct and manners of women, in fact, evidently proof that their minds are not in a healthy state; for, like the flowers which are planted in too rich a soil, strength and usefulness are sacrificed to beauty; and the flaunting leaves, after having pleased a fastidious eye, fade, disregarded on the stalk, long before the season when they ought to have arrived at maturity. One cause of this barren blooming I attribute to a false system of education, gathered from the books written on this subject by men who, considering females rather as women than human creatures, have been more anxious to make them alluring mistresses than affectionate wives and rational mothers; and the understanding of the sex has been so bubbled by this specious homage, that the civilized women of the present century, with a few exceptions, are only anxious to inspire love, when they ought to cherish a nobler ambition, and by their abilities and virtues exact respect.

## DBQ 6: European Expansion and the Changing Life of the People (Chapter 19)

**Question: How did fundamental changes in the European economy in the eighteenth and early nineteenth centuries affect the standards of living of the urban and rural working classes?**

### Document 1

Source: Increase of Population in Europe, 1700–1800

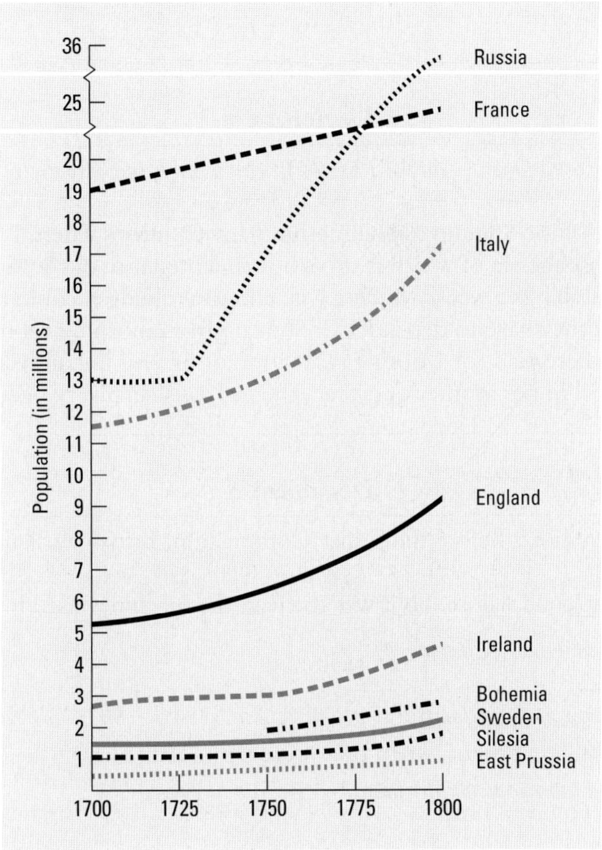


### Document 2

Source: Adam Smith, *An Inquiry into the Nature and Causes of the Wealth of Nations,* 1776.

[Every individual generally] neither intends to promote the public interest, nor knows how much he is promoting it. . . . He is in this case, as in many cases, led by an invisible hand to promote an end which was no part of his intention. Nor is it always worse for the society that it was not part of it. I have never known much good done by those who affected to trade for the public good.

## Document 3

Source: Inquiry of English Parliament, from English Parliamentary Papers, 1842.

West Riding of Yorkshire: Southern Part—In many of the collieries [coal mines] in this district, as far as relates to the underground employment, there is no distinction of sex, but the labour is distributed indifferently among both sexes, except that it is comparatively rare for the women to hew or get the coals, although there are numerous instances in which they regularly perform even this work. In great number of the coal-pits in this district the men work in a state of perfect nakedness and are in this state assisted in the labour by females of all ages, from girls of six years old to women of twenty-one, these females being themselves quite naked down to the waist.

## Document 4

Source: *Observations . . . on the Loss of Woollen Spinning* [anonymous], 1794.

But from the establishment of the Spinning Machines in many countries where I was last Summer, no Hand Work could be had, the consequence of which is the whole maintenance of the family devolves on the father, and instead of six or seven shillings a week, which a wife and four children could add by their [spinning] wheels, *his* weekly pay is *all* they have to depend. . . . Shut up from morning till night, except when they are sent home for their meals, these girls [of 14 or so] are ignorant of, and unhandy at every domestic employment, whereas if at her wheel in her mother's cottage, the girl assists in every occupation of the family.

## Document 5

Source: Testimony Before the Sadler Commission, British Parliament, 1832.

Elizabeth Bentley—a doffer (child whose job it was to clean the machines used in textile manufacturing)

**Q:** *What time did you begin to work at a factory?*
**A:** When I was six years old.

**Q:** *What were your hours of labor in that mill?*
**A:** From 5 in the morning till 9 at night, when they were thronged [busy].

**Q:** *Do you consider doffing a laborious employment?*
**A:** Yes.

**Q:** *Explain what you had to do.*
**A:** When the frames are full, they have to stop the frames, and take the flyers off, and take the full bobbins off, and carry them to the roller; and then put empty ones on, and set the frames on again.

**Q:** *Were they in the habit of strapping [beating with a strap] those who are last in doffing? Constantly? Girls as well as boys? Severely?*
**A:** Yes [to all].

**Q:** *Were you generally there on time?*
**A:** Yes, my mother has been up at 4 o'clock in the morning and at 2 o'clock in the morning. . . . I have sometimes been at Huslet Car at 2 o'clock in the morning, when it was streaming down with rain, and we had to stay till the mill was open.

## DBQ 7: The French Revolution (Chapter 21)

**Question: To what extent did the ideas and objectives of the men and women who participated in the French Revolution change over time?**

### Document 1

Source: M. Dufourny de Villiers, French revolutionary pamphlet: "Cahier of the Fourth Order [Estate] of the poor, the infirm, the indigent, etc., the Sacred Order of the Unfortunates: . . . To make up for the right to directly elect [representatives to] the Estates which appertains to all of France, but which this Order does not enjoy," April 1789 (Paris).

April 25, 1789

. . . Reason dictates that, contrary to the [current] configuration of the Orders [Estates] . . . the true Orders should be these: the poor; those who have only the necessities; the well-off; the rich; the opulent; the bloated. Now, according to this classification, the poor, far from paying, will have the right to receive assistance; those who have only necessities will neither pay nor receive, because only indigents will receive and because only those with excess will pay and those with real needs don't come close to having excess; if the well-off must pay a twentieth, the rich must pay two and half times [more than the twentieth], the opulent six [times that], the bloated ten [times that].

### Document 2

Source: Preamble to the Declaration of the Rights of Man, August 1789.

The representatives of the French people, organized as a National Assembly, believing that the ignorance, neglect, or contempt of the rights of man are the sole causes of public calamities and of the corruption of governments, have determined to set forth in a solemn declaration the natural, inalienable, and sacred rights of man, . . . in order that the grievances of the citizens, based hereafter upon simple and incontestable principles, shall tend to the maintenance of the constitution and redound to the happiness of all.

### Document 3

Source: Olympe de Gouges, "Declaration of the Rights of Woman and the Female Citizen," September 1791.

Mothers, daughters, sisters, [and] representatives of the nation demand to be constituted into a national assembly. Believing that ignorance, omission, or scorn for the rights of woman are the only causes of public misfortunes and of the corruption of governments, [the women] have resolved to set forth in a solemn declaration the natural, inalienable, and sacred rights of woman, . . . in order that citizens' demands, henceforth based on simple and incontestable principles, will always support the constitution, good morals, and the happiness of all.

**Document 4**

Source: Pierre Antoine Leseur, *The Planting of a Liberty Tree,* 1792.

Giraudon/Art Resource, NY.

**Document 5**

Source: Speech by Robespierre, February 1794.

The French are the first people in the world who have established true democracy by calling all men to equality and to full enjoyment of the rights of citizenship. . . . Since virtue [good citizenship] and equality are the soul of the republic . . . it follows that the first rule of your political conduct must be to relate all of your measures to the maintenance of equality and to the development of virtue. . . . That which is immoral is impolitic, and that which tends to corrupt is counterrevolutionary. Weakness, vices, and prejudices are the road to monarchy. . . . It is necessary to annihilate both the internal and external enemies of the republic or perish with its fall.

**Document 6**

Source: Excerpts from Napoleon's speech to his troops, April 1796.

Soldiers of liberty, only republican phalanxes [infantry troops] could have endured what you have endured. . . . The grateful Patrie [nation] will owe its prosperity to you. . . . All of you are consumed with a desire to extend the glory of the French people; all of you long to humiliate those arrogant kings who dare to contemplate placing us in fetters; all of you desire to dictate a glorious peace, one which will indemnify [compensate] the Patrie for the immense sacrifices it has made; all of you wish to be able to say with pride as you turn to your villages: "I was with the victorious army of Italy!"

## DBQ 8: Women in the Industrial Revolution (Chapter 22)

**Question: To what extent were women's experiences in the factories reflections of the profound social changes brought by the Industrial Revolution, and to what extent did women's experiences reflect continuities with traditional working-class ways of life?**

### Document 1

Source: Testimony to Parliament of an agricultural worker's wife and former factory worker, England.

I went to school till I was eight years old. . . . At ten years old I went to work at a factory, where I was till I was 26. . . . I have seven children, all boys. . . . I have worked in the fields, and when I went out I left the children in the care of the eldest boy, and frequently carried the baby with me as I could not go home to nurse it. I have worked at hay-making and at harvest, and at other times in weeding and keeping the ground clean. I generally work from half-past seven till five, or half past. When at work in the spring, I have received 10*d.* [pence] a day, that is higher than the wages of women in general; . . . I never felt that my health was hurt by the work. Hay-making is hard work, very fatiguing, but it never hurt me. Working in the fields is not such hard work as working in the factory. I am always better when I can get out to work in the fields.

### Document 2

Source: Journalist's report on the working conditions of female textile workers in Germany in the 1880s and 1890s.

[T]he dust is breathed in by the girls, since they are not allowed to open the windows. To this has to be added the terrible nerve-racking noise of the rattling machines so that no one can hear himself speak. . . . In consequence all the girls have screeching, irritating voices even when the shop has gone quiet. . . .

Many girls work happily, particularly those weaving small carpets or curtains woven as one piece who can observe the building up of the pattern. They love their machines like loving a faithful dog; they polish them, and tie colored ribbons. . . .

The girls work hard, very hard. . . . I could not have stood this for long. No one would dream of stopping work and taking a rest even when suffering from violent headache or toothache, not even a quarter of an hour of being late was tolerated without a substantial fine. . . .

The work of the carpet weavers should not be underrated, it is anything but monotonous or repetitive. . . . She [the weaver] has to think and coordinate, calculate and pay attention and concentrate all her thought.

## Document 3

Source: Annie Besant, "White Slavery in London," 1888, describing women working in a match factory.

The hour for commencing work is 6:30 in summer and 8 in winter, work concludes at 6 p.m. . . . the long day of work is performed by young girls, who have to stand the whole of the time. A typical case is that of a girl of 16, a piece-worker who earns 4*s.* [shillings] a week and lives with her sister, employed by the same firm, who "earns good money, as much as 8*s.* or 9*s.* per week."

Out of the earnings 2*s.* is paid for the rent of one room; the child lives on only bread-and-butter and tea, alike for breakfast and dinner. . . . The splendid salary of 4*s.* is subject to deductions in the shape of fines; if the feet are dirty, or the ground under the bench is left untidy, a fine of 3*d.* [pence] is inflicted; for putting "burnts"—matches that have caught fire during the work—on the bench 1*s.* has been forfeited. . . . Day work is a little better aid than piecework, and is done chiefly by married women, who earn as much sometimes as 10*s.* a week. . . . Such is a bald account of one form of white slavery as it exists in London. With chattel slaves, Mr. Bryant could not have made his huge fortune, for he could not have fed, clothed, and housed them for 4*s.* a week each.

## Document 4

Source: Testimony of Mr. Matthew Crabtree, a worker in a blanket mill. From Sadler Commission, British Parliament, *Report on Child Labor,* 1832.

**Q:** *Do you find that the children, the females especially, are very early demoralized in them [mills]?*
**A:** They are.
**Q:** *Is their language indecent?*
**A:** Very indecent, and both sexes take great familiarities with each other in the mills, without at all being ashamed of their conduct.
**Q:** *Do you connect their immorality of language and conduct with their excessive labor?*
**A:** It may be somewhat connected with it, for it is to be observed that most of that goes on towards night, when they begin to be drowsy, it is a kind of stimulus which they use to keep them awake; they say some pert thing or other to keep themselves from drowsiness, and it generally happens to be some obscene language.
**Q:** *Have not a considerable number of the females employed in mills illegitimate children very early in life?*
**A:** I believe there are; I have known some of them have illegitimate children when they were between 16 and 17 years of age.
**Q:** *How many of [the grown-up] females had illegitimate children?*
**A:** A great many of them. . . .
**Q:** *Did they generally marry the men by whom they had the children?*
**A:** No, it sometimes happens that young women have children by married men.

## DBQ 9: Ideologies and Nationalism (Chapters 23 and 25)

**Question: Discuss the concepts that become the foundations of aggressive nationalism during the period 1815–1914.**

### Document 1

Source: Delacroix, *Massacre at Chios,* 1824.

Réunion des Musées Nationaux/Art Resource, NY.

### Document 2

Source: Charles Darwin, *On the Origin of Species,* 1859.

Natural Selection acts solely through the preservation of variations in some way advantageous, which consequently endure. Owing to the high geometrical rate of increase of all organic beings, each area is already fully stocked with inhabitants; and it follows from this, that as the favoured forms increase in number, so, generally, will the less favoured decrease and become rare.

**Document 3**

Source: Friedrich Fabri, *Bedarf Deutschland der Kolonien?* [Does Germany Need Colonies?], 1879.

Even more important is the consideration that a people at the height of their political power can successfully maintain their historic position only as long as they recognize and prove themselves as the bearers of a cultural mission. That is the only way which guarantees the stability and growth of national prosperity, which is the necessary basis for an enduring source of power. . . . It would be good if we Germans would begin to learn from the colonial skill of our Anglo-Saxon cousins. . . . If the new German Reich wants to justify and maintain its power, then it will have to grasp it as a cultural mission and no longer hesitate to renew once again its colonial calling.

**Document 4**

Source: Theodor Herzl, *Der Judenstaat* [The Jewish State], 1896.

We are but one people—our enemies have made us one without our consent, as repeatedly happens in history. Distress binds us together, and thus united, we suddenly discover our strength. Yes, we are strong enough to form a State, and, indeed, a model State. We possess all human and material resources necessary for the purpose. . . . Let the sovereignty be granted us over a portion of the globe large enough to satisfy the rightful requirements of a nation; the rest we shall manage for ourselves.

## Document 5

Source: Maps of the unified Italian and German states, ca 1871.

0 50 100 Km.
0 50 100 Mi.
DENMARK
SWEDEN
Baltic Sea
North Sea
Neman
Königsberg
EAST PRUSSIA
Danzig
SCHLESWIG
Kiel
HOLSTEIN
Lübeck
Hamburg
MECKLENBURG
POMERANIA
WEST PRUSSIA
Bremen
OLDENBURG
HANOVER
Elbe
BRANDENBURG
Berlin
Warta
Vistula
Warsaw
Amsterdam
NETHERLANDS
Hanover
POSEN
RUSSIAN EMPIRE
WESTPHALIA
Essen
P R U S S I A
POLAND
Antwerp
Ruhr
Cologne
Leipzig
Mulde
Oder
BELGIUM
Bonn
RHINE PROVINCE
Weimar
Dresden
SAXONY
SILESIA
Sadowa 1866
Frankfurt
Moselle
Main
Prague
Cracow
Sedan 1870
Luxembourg
BOHEMIA
Nuremberg
Olmütz
Verdun
Rhine
Neckar
Vltava
MORAVIA
Morava
LORRAINE
Karlsruhe
Nancy
Stuttgart
BAVARIA
Strasbourg
WÜRTTEMBERG
Danube
ALSACE
Inn
Vienna
Munich
BADEN
AUSTRIAN EMPIRE
FRANCE
Buda Pest
Innsbruck
SWITZERLAND
ITALY
Prussia before 1866
Conquered by Prussia in Austro-Prussian War, 1866
Austrian territories excluded from North German Confederation, 1867
Joined with Prussia to form North German Confederation, 1867
South German states joining with Prussia to form German Empire, 1871
Won by Prussia in Franco-Prussian War, 1871
Major battles
German Confederation boundary, 1815–1866
Bismarck's German Empire, 1871

## DBQ 10: The West and the World (Chapter 26)

**Question: Discuss the variety of responses that the colonized peoples advocated toward the European colonizers in the late nineteenth and early twentieth centuries.**

### Document 1

Source: Mohandas K. Gandhi (1869–1948), *Hind Swaraj, or Indian Home Rule,* 1908.

Many examples can be given in which acts of majorities will be found to have been wrong and those of minorities to have been right. All reforms owe their origins to the initiation of minorities in opposition to majorities. . . . So long as the superstition that men should obey unjust laws exists, so long will their slavery exist. . . .

Passive resistance is a method of securing rights by personal suffering; it is the reverse of resistance by arms. When I refuse to do a thing that is repugnant to my conscience, I use soul-force [*satyagraha*]. For instance, the government of the day has passed a law which is applicable to me: I do not like it; if, by using violence, I force the government to repeal the law I am employing what may be termed body-force. If I do not obey the law and accept the penalty for its breach, I use soul-force. It involves sacrifice of self.

### Document 2

Source: Letter from Chinese imperial official Lin Zexu (1785–1850) to Queen Victoria, 1839.

They [British merchants] may not intend to harm others on purpose, but the fact remains that they are so obsessed with material gain that they have no concern whatever for the harm they can cause to others. Have they no conscience? I have heard you strictly prohibit opium in your own country, indication unmistakably that you know how harmful opium is. You do not wish opium to harm your own country, but you choose to bring that harm to other countries such as China. Why? . . . Since a foreigner who goes to England to trade has to obey the English law, how can an Englishman not obey the Chinese law when he is physically present within China? The present law calls for the imposition of the death sentence on any Chinese who had peddled or smoked opium.

### Document 3

Source: “Announcement to the Arabs” [anonymous], printed in Arabic in Cairo, 1914.

O sons of Quahtan [south Arabs]! Oh descendants of Adnan [north Arabs]! . . . When will you realize the truth? When will you know that your country has been sold to foreigners? See how your natural resources have been alienated from you and have come into the possession of England, France, and Germany. Have you no right to these resources? You have become humiliated slaves in the hands of the usurping tyrants; the foreigner unjustly dispossesses you of the fruit of your work and labor and leaves you to suffer the pangs of hunger. How long will it be before you understand that you have become the plaything in the hand of him who has no religion but to kill the Arabs and forcibly to seize their possessions?

**Document 4**

Source: Memorandum from the chiefs of Brass (a city-state on the Niger delta) to the (British) Royal Niger Company, June 1895.

The Niger Company are cleverer than we are. We humbly submit that we have a right, confirmed by our Treaty, to go and trade freely in the places we have traded at for all these generations. We are ready to pay to do so, but let us pay a fair duty, and conform to fair Regulations.

## DBQ 11: World War I and the Home Front (Chapter 27)

**Question: What effects did the Great War have on the European home fronts during the course of the fighting?**

### Document 1

Source: Employment of women in wartime British industry, 1914–1918. From report of the War Cabinet Committee on Women in British Industry, London, 1919.

| Trades | Est. Number Females Employed in July 1914 | Est. Number Females Employed in July 1918 | Difference Between Numbers of Females Employed in July 1914 and July 1918 | Percentage of Females to Total Number People Employed: July 1914 | Percentage of Females to Total Number People Employed: July 1918 | Est. Number Females Directly Replacing Males in Jan. 1918 |
|---|---|---|---|---|---|---|
| Metal | 170,000 | 594,000 | +424,000 | 9 | 25 | 195,000 |
| Chemical | 40,000 | 104,000 | +64,000 | 20 | 39 | 35,000 |
| Textile | 863,000 | 827,000 | −36,000 | 58 | 67 | 64,000 |
| Clothing | 612,000 | 568,000 | −44,000 | 68 | 76 | 43,000 |
| Food, drink, and tobacco | 196,000 | 235,000 | +39,000 | 35 | 49 | 60,000 |
| Paper and printing | 147,500 | 141,500 | −6,000 | 36 | 48 | 21,000 |
| Wood | 44,000 | 79,000 | +35,000 | 15 | 32 | 23,000 |
| China and earthenware | 32,000 | } 197,100 (China and earthenware, Leather, Other combined) | +93,000 | 4 | 10 | 62,000 |
| Leather | 23,100 | | | | | |
| Other | 49,000 | | | | | |
| Government establishments | 2,000 | 225,000 | +223,000 | 3 | 47 | 197,000 |
| Total | 2,178,600 | 2,970,600 | +792,000 | 26 | 37 | 704,000 |

### Document 2

Source: *Blockade: Diary of an Austrian Middle-Class Woman, 1914–24* (1932).

We housewives have during the last four years grown accustomed to standing in queues; we have also grown accustomed to being obliged to go home with empty hands and still emptier stomachs. Only very rarely do those who are sent away disappointed give cause for police intervention. On the other hand, it happens more and more frequently that one of the pale, tired women who have been waiting for hours collapses from exhaustion.

**Document 3**

Source: V. I. Lenin, "The Call to Power," October 24, 1917 [italics in the original].

It would be an infinite crime on the part of the revolutionaries were they to let the chance slip by, knowing that the *salvation of the revolution,* the offer of peace, the salvation of Petrograd, salvation from famine, the transfer of the land to the peasants depend on them.

The government is tottering. It must be *given the death-blow* at all costs.

To delay action is fatal.

**Document 4**

Source: Letter from the prefect (governor) of the department of Isère to France's minister of the interior, June 17, 1917.

I have the honour to reply herewithin to the questions contained in your confidential telegram circulated on 10 June: . . .

[The farmers] work, but they do not hide the fact that "it's been going on too long"; they are tired of their continuous over-exertion in the fields, of the lack of hands and of the very heavy burden of the requisitions. . . . In the towns . . . the workers, the ordinary people—are upset about the duration of the struggle, impatient with the increasing cost of living, irritated by the considerable profits being made out of the war by the big industrialists in their neighborhood, and increasingly taken in by the propagandists of the united Socialist Party and their internationalist ideas.

## DBQ 12: Age of Anxiety (Chapter 28)

**Question: In what ways did European culture after World War I challenge the assumptions of the prewar, nineteenth-century European culture?**

### Document 1

Source: Otto Dix (German), *War* (triptych), 1929–1932.

Staatliche Künstsammlungen Dresden, © 2002 Artists Rights Society [ARS], New York/VG Bild-Künst, Bonn).

## Document 2

Source: Pablo Picasso (Spanish), *Three Musicians*, 1921.

© MoMA/Scala/Art Resource, NY. © 2002 Artists Rights Society [ARS], New York/ADAGP, Paris.

## Document 3

Source: Sigmund Freud (Austrian), *Civilization and Its Discontents,* 1930.

The element of truth behind all this, which people are so ready to disavow, is that men are not gentle creatures who want to be loved, and who at most can defend themselves if they are attacked; they are, on the contrary, creatures among whose instinctual endowments is to be reckoned a powerful share of aggressiveness. . . . In consequence of this primary mutual hostility of human beings, civilized society is perpetually threatened with disintegration. The interest of work in common would not hold it together; instinctual passions are stronger than reasonable interests.

### Document 4

Source: Lines from W. B. Yeats (Irish), "The Second Coming," 1920–1921.

Turning and turning in the widening gyre [spiral]
The falcon cannot hear the falconer;
Things fall apart; the center cannot hold;
Mere anarchy is loosed upon the world,
The blood-dimmed tide is loosed, and everywhere
The ceremony of innocence is drowned;
The best lack all conviction, while the worst
Are full of passionate intensity.

Reprinted with the permission of Simon & Schuster from *The Poems of W. B. Yeats: A New Edition,* edited by Richard J. Finneran. Copyright © 1924 by Macmillan Publishing Company, renewed 1952 by Bertha Georgie Yeats.

### Document 5

Source: Erich Maria Remarque (German), *All Quiet on the Western Front*, 1929.

What would our fathers do if we suddenly stood up and came before them and proffered our accounts? . . . Through the years our business has been killing;—it was our first calling in life. Our knowledge of life is limited to death. What will happen afterwards? And what shall come out of us?

### Document 6

Source: Benito Mussolini (Italian), "The Political and Social Doctrine of Fascism," 1932.

For if the nineteenth century was a century of individualism (Liberalism always signifying individualism) it may be expected that this will be the century of collectivism, and hence the century of the State.

### Document 7

Source: Helena Swanwick (English), "The War in Its Effect upon Women," 1916.

The course and conduct of the war, throwing upon women greater and greater responsibilities, bringing home to them how intimately their own lives and all they hold dear and sacred are affected by the government of the country, will tend greatly to strengthen and enlarge their claim for a share in the government.

**Document 8**

Source: Salvador Dali (Spanish), *The Persistence of Memory,* 1931.

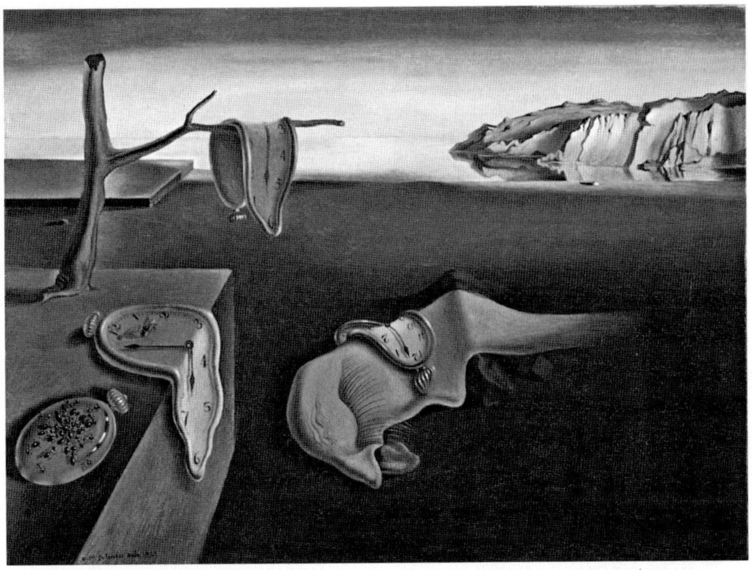

© The Museum of Modern Art/Scala/Art Resource, NY.

**Document 9**

Source: Sir Arthur S. Eddington, physicist and philosopher, referencing *The Nature of the Physical World,* Rutherford's work on the structure of the atom, 1928.

When we compare the universe as it is now supposed to be with the universe as we had ordinarily preconceived it, the most arresting change is not the rearrangement of space and time by Einstein but the dissolution of all that we regard as most solid into tiny specks floating in void.

**Document 10**

Source: Photograph of the Sylvester Jazz Band, 1927.

Ulstein Bilderdienst.

## DBQ 13: Dictatorships and the Second World War (Chapter 29)

**Question: What were the key concepts that motivated authoritarian governments and rulers in the interwar years (1919–1939), and why were those concepts so appealing?**

### Document 1

Source: Klara Zetkin, Rosa Luxemburg, Karl Liebknecht, and Franz Mehring (German revolutionaries), *Spartacist Manifesto*, November/December 1918, as it appeared in the *New York Times,* January 24, 1919.

Europe has been ruined through the infamous international murder. Twelve million bodies cover the grewsome [sic] scenes of the imperialistic crime. The flower of youth and the best man power [sic] of the peoples have been mowed down. Uncounted productive forces have been annihilated. . . . The great criminals of this fearful anarchy, of this chaos let loose—the ruling classes—are not able to control their own creation. The beast of capital that conjured up the hell of the world war is not capable of banishing it again, of restoring real order, of insuring bread and work, peace and civilization, justice and liberty, to tortured humanity.

### Document 2

Source: Paul Valéry (French philosopher), speech at the University of Zurich, November 1922.

One can say that all the fundamentals of the world have been affected by the war, or more exactly, by the circumstances of the war; something deeper has been worn away than the renewable parts of the machine. You know how greatly the general economic situation has been disturbed, and the polity of states, and the very life of the individual; you are familiar with the universal discomfort, hesitation, apprehension. *But among all these injured things is the Mind.* The Mind has indeed been cruelly wounded; its complaint is heard in the hearts of intellectual man; it passes a mournful judgment on itself. It doubts itself profoundly.

### Document 3

Source: German Nazi Party poster: "The String-Puller. White Collar and Manual Laborers: Vote for the Volkischen Block," 1924.

Anschläge, Ebenhausen, Laugewiesche/Bradt-Verlag.

### Document 4

Source: Jose Ortega y Gasset (Spanish), *Revolt of the Masses,* 1930.

Under . . . Fascism there appears for the first time in Europe a type of man who does not want to give reasons or to be right, but simply shows himself resolved to impose his opinions. This is the new thing: the right not to be reasonable, the "reason of unreason." Here I see the most palpable manifestation of the new mentality of the masses, due to their having decided to rule society without the capacity for doing so. . . . The average man . . . wishes to have opinions, but is unwilling to accept the conditions and presuppositions that underlie all opinion. Hence his ideas are in effect nothing more than appetites in words.

### Document 5

Source: Joseph Stalin, "Address to Industrial Managers," 1931.

Do you want our socialist fatherland to be beaten and to lose its independence? If you do not want this you must put an end to its backwardness in the shortest possible time and develop genuine Bolshevik tempo in building up its socialist system of economy. There is no other way. That is why Lenin said during the October Revolution: "Either perish, or overtake and outstrip the advanced capitalist countries." We are fifty or a hundred years behind the advanced countries. We must make good this distance in ten years. Either we do it or they crush us.

### Document 6

Source: Benito Mussolini, "Fascist Doctrines" (article in the *Italian Encyclopedia*), 1932.

Given that the nineteenth century was the century of Socialism, of Liberalism, and of Democracy, it does not necessarily follow that the twentieth century must also be the century of Socialism, Liberalism, and Democracy: political doctrines pass, but humanity remains; and it may rather be expected that this will be a century of authority, . . . a century of Fascism. For if the nineteenth century was a century of individualism (Liberalism always signifying individualism) it may be expected that this will be the century of collectivism and hence the century of the State.

### Document 7

Source: Map of the Great Depression in Europe: unemployment figures, 1932.

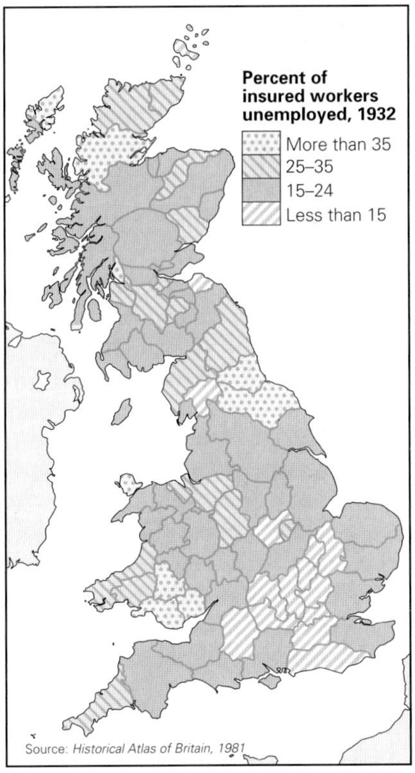


Source: *Historical Atlas of Britain, 1981*

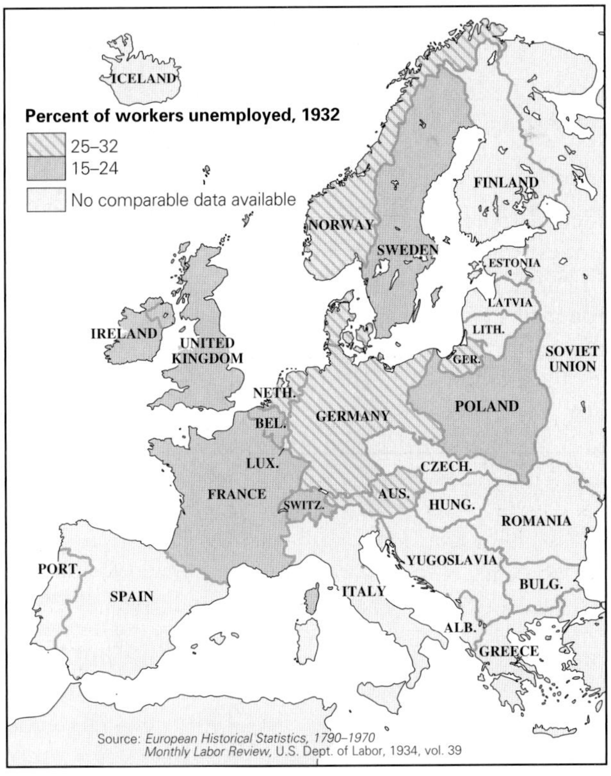


Source: *European Historical Statistics, 1790–1970*
*Monthly Labor Review*, U.S. Dept. of Labor, 1934, vol. 39

**Document 8**

Source: Excerpt from Jakob Graf, *Hereditary and Racial Biology for Students* (a German textbook), 1935.

HOW WE CAN LEARN TO RECOGNIZE A PERSON'S RACE

*Assignments*

1. Summarize the spiritual characteristics of the individual races. . . .
3. What are the expressions, gestures, and movements which allow us to make conclusions as to the attitude of the racial soul?
4. Determine also the physical features which go hand in hand with the specific racial soul characteristics of the individual figures. . . .
9. Observe people whose special racial features have drawn your attention, also with respect to their bearing when moving or speaking. Observe their expressions and gestures.
10. Observe the Jew: his way of walking, his bearing, gestures, and movements when walking.

**Document 9**

Source: Nicolas Berdyaev (an exiled Russian philosopher), *The Fate of Man in the Modern World,* 1935.

The new world which is taking form is moved by other values than the value of man or of human personality, or the value of truth: it is moved by such values as power, technics, race-purity, nationality, the state, the class, the collective. The will to justice is overcome by the will to power. . . . The results of the Christian-humanistic process of unifying humanity seem to be disappearing. We are witnessing the paganization of Christian society. Nationalism is polytheism: it is incompatible with monotheism.

**Document 10**

Source: Arthur Koestler (Hungarian-born British writer and journalist), "I Was Ripe to Be Converted," from *The God That Failed,* 1949.

A considerable portion of the middle classes in central Europe was, like ourselves, ruined by the inflation of the 'twenties. It was the beginning of Europe's decline. This disintegration of the middle strata of society started the fatal process of polarization which continues to this day. The pauperized bourgeois became rebels of the Right or Left; Schickelgruber [Hitler] and Djugashwili [Stalin] shared about equally the benefits of social migration. Those who . . . clung to the empty shell of gentility, joined the Nazis blaming their fate on Versailles and the Jews. . . . The other half turned Left, thus confirming the prophecy of the Communist Manifesto.

## DBQ 14: Communism and Eastern Europe (Chapters 30 and 31)

### Question: To what extent did the criticisms of communism from citizens of the Eastern European socialist states change over time?

### Document 1

Source: Andor Heller, "The Hungarian Revolution," 1956.

The walls of Budapest are plastered with leaflets put up by the students during the night. They list the fourteen demands adopted at the storm meetings held at the universities:

1. Withdrawal of all Soviet troops from Hungary
2. Complete economic and political equality with the Soviet Union, with no interference in Hungary's internal affairs . . .

8. A secret general multi-party election
9. The organization of Hungary's economy on the basis of her actual resources
10. Revision of the workers' output quotas and recognition of the right to strike
11. Revisions of the system of compulsory agricultural quotas
12. Equal rights for individual farms and cooperative members . . .

Someone grabs a Hungarian flag and cuts out the hated hammer and sickle that the Communists had placed at its center. One after another of the purified Hungarian flags appear. Suddenly someone remembers to put the old Kossuth [the leader of the Hungarian uprising of 1848–1849] coat-of-arms on the flag. . . . We have created a new flag of freedom!

### Document 2

Source: Milovan Djilas (Yugoslavia), *The New Class,* 1957.

In contrast to earlier revolutions, the Communist revolution, conducted in the name of doing away with classes, has resulted in the most complete authority of any single new class. Everything else is shame and an illusion. . . . This new class, the bureaucracy . . . may be said to be made up of those who have special privileges and economic preference because of the administrative monopoly they hold. . . . The Communist Party is the backbone of the entire political, economic and ideological activity. . . . The exclusive, if unwritten, law that only party members can become policemen, officers, diplomats, and only they can exercise actual authority, creates a special privileged group of bureaucrats. . . . The so-called "dictatorship of the proletariat" which is the beginning of and under the best circumstances becomes the authority of the party, inevitably evolves into the dictatorship of the leaders.

**Document 3**

Source: Ludvik Vaculik, "2,000 Words to Workers, Farmers, Scientists, Artists, and Everyone," Spring 1968 (published in the literary journal *Literarni listy* in Prague, Czechoslovakia).

The communist party betrayed the great trust the people put in it after the war [World War II]. It preferred the glories of office, until it had those and nothing more. The disappointment was great among communists as well as non-communists. . . . There was no criticism of the state and economic organizations. Parliament forgot how to deliberate, the government forgot how to rule and managers how to manage. Elections had no significance and the laws lost their value. . . . Personal and collective honor deteriorated. . . . No organization was run by its members, not even the communist party. . . . Honesty led nowhere, and it was useless to speak of rewards according to ability. As a result, most citizens lost interest in public affairs.

**Document 4**

Source: Cartoon, "Workers of All Countries Unite—Or I'll Shoot," August 28, 1968 (Czech journal).

**Document 5**

Source: Charter 77 (an informal and loosely structured organization of intellectuals, including Václav Havel, in Czechoslovakia), 1977.

Freedom of public expression is repressed by the centralized control of all the communications media and of publishing and cultural institutions. No philosophical, political, or scientific view or artistic expression that departs ever so slightly from the narrow bounds of official ideology or aesthetics is allowed to be published. Further civil rights are seriously vitiated by the various forms of interference in the private life of citizens exercised by the Ministry of the Interior, for example, by bugging telephones and houses, opening mail, following personal movements, searching homes, setting up networks of neighborhood informers.

## Document 6

Source: "Twenty-one Demands: A Call for Workers' Rights and Freedom in a Socialist State," issued by Solidarity in Poland, 1980.

1. Acceptance of Free Trade Unions independent of both the Party and employers, in accordance with the International Labor Organization's Convention number 87 on the freedom to form unions, which was ratified by the Polish government.
2. A guarantee of the right to strike and guarantees of security for strikers and their supporters.
3. Compliance with the freedoms of press and publishing guaranteed in the Polish constitution. A halt to repression of independent publications and access to the mass media for representatives of all faiths.
4. (a) Reinstatement to their former positions for: people fired for defending workers' rights, in particular those participating in the strikes of 1970 and 1976; students dismissed from school for their convictions. (b) The release of all political prisoners. . . . (c) A halt to repression for one's convictions. . . .
6. The undertaking of real measures to get the country out of its present crisis by: (a) providing comprehensive, public information about the socio-economic situation; (b) making it possible for people from every social class and stratum of society to participate in open discussions concerning the reform program. . . .
11. The rationing of meat and meat products through food coupons (until the market is stabilized).
12. Abolition of "commercial prices" and hard currency sales in so-called "internal export" shops.
13. A system of merit selection for management positions on the basis of qualifications rather than Party membership. . . .
19. Reduce the waiting time for apartments.

**Document 7**

Source: Undated cartoon published probably in the early 1980s, during the Brezhnev years, in the magazine *The Crocodile,* U.S.S.R.

***"What's this? You have your own opinion?"***

—А У ВАС ЧТО, СВОЕ МНЕНИЕ?

Vneshtorgizdat, Moscow.

**Document 8**

Source: Mikhail Gorbachev, *Perestroika.* Copyright 1987 by Mikhail Gorbachev.

The presentation of a "problem-free" reality backfired: a breach had formed between word and deed, which bred public passivity and disbelief in the slogans being proclaimed. . . . Decay began in public morals; . . . and the penetration of stereotypes of mass culture alien to us, which bred vulgarity and low tastes and brought about ideological barrenness, increased.

One specific feature of socialism . . . [is] the high degree of social protection in our society. On the one hand, it is, doubtless, a benefit and a major achievement of ours. On the other hand, it makes some people spongers. There is virtually no unemployment. . . . Health care is free, and so is education. People are protected from the vicissitudes of life, and we are proud of this. But we also see that dishonest people try to exploit these advantages of socialism: they know only their rights, but they do not want to know their duties: they work poorly, shirk, and drink hard.

**Document 9**

Source: Václav Havel (president of Czechoslovakia), "The Failure of Communism," New Year's Day address, 1990.

Our country is not flourishing. The great creative and spiritual potential of our nation is not being applied meaningfully. Entire branches of industry are producing things for which there is no demand while we are short of things we need.

The state, which calls itself a state of workers, is humiliating and exploiting them instead. Our outmoded economy wastes energy, which we have in short supply. The country, which could once be proud of the education of its people, is spending so little on education that today, in that respect, we rank 72nd in the world. We have spoiled our land, rivers, and forests, inherited from our ancestors, and have, today, the worst environment in the whole of Europe. Adults die here earlier than in the majority of European countries. . . .

The worst of it is that we live in a spoiled moral environment. . . . The previous regime, armed with a proud and intolerant ideology, reduced people into the means of production, and natures in its tools. So it attacked their very essence, and their mutual relations. . . . None of us are only its victims; we are all also responsible for it.

**Document 10**

Source: Olga Havlova (wife of Václav Havel), letter to the editor, *New York Review of Books,* June 14, 1990.

The handicapped in our country have been forced into isolation, removed from sight into homes and institutions. There are a million of them in Czechoslovakia, in a population of only fifteen million. This did not trouble us. The state said they were being looked after, so we chose to believe it.

This was our habit of inhumanity. It would have been inhuman even if the state had been looking after these people well. But it turns out that it has been looking after them badly. There is practically no equipment, no nursing, sometimes not even the most basic conditions for living in dignity.

We are now changing the state. But we also need to change our habits.

## Document 11

Source: Slavenka Drakulic (a Croatian columnist), "A Letter from the United States: The Critical Theory Approach." From *How We Survived Communism and Even Laughed,* 1991.

Every mother in Bulgaria can point to where communism failed, from the failure of the planned economy [and the consequent lack of food and milk], to the lack of apartments, child-care facilities, clothes, disposable diapers, or toilet paper. The banality of everyday life is where it has really failed, rather than on the level of ideology.

## Document 12

Source: Soviet soldier outside Russian parliament building, August 1991.

Filip Horvat/Saba.

# Index

# Timeline A History of Western Society: A Brief Overview

| | Government | Society and Economy |
|---|---|---|
| **3200 B.C.** | Dominance of Sumerian cities in Mesopotamia, ca 3200–2340<br>Unification of Egypt; Archaic Period, ca 3100–2660<br>Old Kingdom of Egypt, ca 2660–2180<br>Dominance of Akkadian empire in Mesopotamia, ca 2331–2200<br>Middle Kingdom in Egypt, ca 2080–1640 | Neolithic peoples rely on settled agriculture, while others pursue nomadic life, ca 7000–ca 3000<br>Development of wheeled transport in Mesopotamia, by ca 3200<br>Expansion of Mesopotamian trade and culture into modern Turkey, the Middle East, and Iran, ca 2600 |
| **2000 B.C.** | Babylonian empire, ca 2000–1595<br>Hyksos invade Egypt, ca 1640–1570<br>Hittite Empire, ca 1600–1200<br>New Kingdom in Egypt, ca 1570–1075 | First wave of Indo-European migrants, by 2000<br>Extended commerce in Egypt, by ca 2000<br>Horses introduced into western Asia, by ca 2000 |
| **1500 B.C.** | Third Intermediate Period in Egypt, ca 1100–700<br>Unified Hebrew Kingdom under Saul, David, and Solomon, ca 1025–925 | Use of iron increases in western Asia, by ca 1300–1100<br>Second wave of Indo-European migrants, by ca 1200 |
| **1000 B.C.** | Hebrew Kingdom divided into Israel and Judah, 925<br>Assyrian Empire, ca 900–612<br>Phoenicians found Carthage, 813<br>Kingdom of Kush conquers and reunifies Egypt, 8th c.<br>Medes conquers Persia, 710<br>Babylon wins independence from Assyria, 626<br>Dracon issues law code at Athens, 621<br>Cyrus the Great conquers Medes, founds Persian Empire, 550<br>Solon's reforms at Athens, ca 549<br>Persians complete conquest of ancient Near East, 521–464<br>Reforms of Cleisthenes in Athens, 508 | Concentration of landed wealth in Greece, ca 750–600<br>Greek overseas expansion, ca 750–550<br>Beginning of coinage in western Asia, ca 640 |
| **500 B.C.** | Battle of Marathon, 490<br>Xerxes' invasion of Greece, 480–479<br>Delian Confederacy, 478/7<br>Twelve Tables in Rome, 451/0<br>Valerio-Horatian laws in Rome, 449<br>Peloponnesian War, 431–404<br>Rome captures Veii, 396<br>Gauls sack Rome, 390<br>Roman expansion in Italy, 390–290<br>Conquests of Alexander the Great, 334–323<br>Punic Wars, 264–146<br>Reforms of the Gracchi, 133–121 | Building of the Via Appia begins, 312<br>Growth of Hellenistic trade and cities, ca 300–100<br>Beginning of Roman silver coinage, 269<br>Growth of slavery, decline of small farmers in Rome, ca 250–100<br>Agrarian reforms of the Gracchi, 133–121 |

| Religion and Philosophy | Science and Technology | Arts and Letters |
| --- | --- | --- |
| Growth of anthropomorphic religion in Mesopotamia, ca 3000–2000<br>Emergence of Egyptian polytheism and belief in personal immortality, ca 2660<br>Spread of Mesopotamian and Egyptian religious ideas as far north as modern Anatolia and as far south as central Africa, ca 2600 | Development of wheeled transport in Mesopotamia, by ca 3200<br>Use of widespread irrigation in Mesopotamia and Egypt, ca 3000<br>Construction of the first pyramid in Egypt, ca 2600 | Sumerian cuneiform writing, ca 3200<br>Egyptian hieroglyphic writing, ca 3100 |
| Emergence of Hebrew monotheism, ca 1700<br>Mixture of Hittite and Near Eastern religious beliefs, ca 1595 | Construction of the first ziggurats in Mesopotamia, ca 2000<br>Widespread use of bronze in the ancient Near East, ca 1900<br>Babylonian mathematical advances, ca 1800 | *Epic of Gilgamesh,* ca 1900<br>Code of Hammurabi, ca 1790 |
| Exodus of the Hebrews from Egypt into Palestine, 13th c.<br>Religious beliefs of Akhenaten, ca 1367 | Hittites introduce iron technology, ca 1400 | Phoenicians develop alphabet, ca 1400<br>Naturalistic art in Egypt under Akhenaten, ca 1367<br>Egyptian Book of the Dead, ca 1300 |
| Era of the prophets in Israel, ca 1100–500<br>Intermixture of Etruscan and Roman religious cults, ca 753–509<br>Growing popularity of local Greek religious cults, ca 700 B.C.–A.D. 337<br>Babylonian Captivity of the Hebrews, 586–539 | Babylonian astronomical advances, ca 750–400 | Beginning of the Hebrew Bible, ca 9th c.<br>First Olympic Games, 776<br>Babylonian astronomical advances, ca 750–400<br>Homer, traditional author of the *Iliad* and *Odyssey,* ca 700<br>Hesiod, author of the *Theogony* and *Works and Days,* ca 700<br>Archilochos, lyric poet, 648<br>Aeschylus, first significant Athenian tragedian, 525/4–456 |
| Pre-Socratic philosophers, 5th c.<br>Socrates, 469–399<br>Plato, 429–347<br>Diogenes, leading proponent of cynicism, ca 412–323<br>Aristotle, 384–322<br>Epicurus, 340–270<br>Zeno, founder of Stoic philosophy, 335–262<br>Emergence of Mithraism, ca 300<br>Spread of Hellenistic mystery religions, 2nd c.<br>Greek cults brought to Rome, ca 200 | Hippocrates, formal founder of medicine ca 430<br>Theophrastus, founder of botany, ca 372–288<br>Aristarchos of Samos, advances in astronomy, ca 310–230<br>Euclid codifies geometry, ca 300<br>Herophilus, discoveries in medicine, ca 300–250<br>Archimedes, works on physics and hydrologics, ca 287–212 | Sophocles, tragedian who used his plays to explore moral and political problems, ca 496–406<br>Euripides, the most personal of the Athenian tragedians, ca 480–406<br>Thucydides, historian of the Peloponnesian War, ca 460–400<br>Aristophanes, the greatest writer of Old Comedy, ca 457–ca 385<br>Herodotus, the father of history, ca 450 |

| | Government | Society and Economy |
|---|---|---|
| **100 B.C.** | Dictatorship of Sulla, 88–79<br>Civil war in Rome, 78–27<br>Dictatorship of Caesar, 45–44<br>Principate of Augustus, 31 B.C.–A.D. 14 | Reform of the Roman calendar, 46 |
| **A.D. 300** | Constantine removes capital of Roman Empire to Constantinople, ca 315<br>Visigoths defeat Roman army at Adrianople (378), signaling massive German invasions into the empire<br>Bishop Ambrose asserts church's independence from the state, 380<br>Death of emperor Romulus Augustus marks end of Roman Empire in the West, 476<br>Clovis issues Salic law of the Franks, ca 490 | Growth of serfdom in Roman Empire, ca 200–500<br>Economic contraction in Roman Empire, 3rd c. |
| **500** | Law Code of Justinian, 529<br>Dooms of Ethelbert, king of Kent, ca 604<br>Spread of Islam across Arabia, the Mediterranean region, Spain, North Africa, and Asia as far as India, ca 630–733 | Gallo-Roman aristocracy intermarries with Germanic chieftains<br>Decline of towns and trade, ca 500–700<br>Agrarian economy predominates in the West, ca 500–1800 |
| **700** | Charles Martel defeats Muslims at Tours, 732<br>Pippin III anointed king of the Franks, 754<br>Charlemagne secures Frankish crown, r. 768–814 | Height of Muslim commercial activity, ca 700–1300, with western Europe |
| **800** | Imperial coronation of Charlemagne, Christmas 800<br>Treaty of Verdun, 843<br>Viking, Magyar, and Muslim invasions, ca 845–900 | Byzantine commerce and industry, ca 800–1000<br>Invasions and unstable conditions lead to increase of serfdom |
| **1000** | Seljuk Turks conquer Muslim Baghdad, 1055<br>Norman conquest of England, 1066<br>Penance of Henry IV at Canossa, 1077 | Decline of Byzantine free peasantry, ca 1025–1100<br>Growth of towns and trade in the West, ca 1050–1300<br>Domesday Book, 1086 |
| **1100** | Henry I of England, r. 1100–1135<br>Louis VI of France, r. 1108–1137<br>Frederick I of Germany, r. 1152–1190<br>Henry II of England, r. 1154–1189<br>Thomas Becket murdered, 1170<br>Philip Augustus of France, r. 1180–1223 | Henry I of England establishes the Exchequer, 1130<br>Beginnings of the Hanseatic League, 1159 |

| Religion and Philosophy | Science and Technology | Arts and Letters |
| --- | --- | --- |
| Mithraism spreads to Rome, 27 B.C.–A.D. 270<br>Dedication of the Ara Pacis Augustae, 9<br>Traditional birth of Jesus, ca 3 | Pliny the Elder, student of natural history, 23 B.C.–A.D. 79<br>Frontinus, engineering advances in Rome, 30 B.C.–A.D. 104 | Virgil, 70–19 B.C.<br>Livy, ca 59 B.C.–A.D. 17<br>Ovid, 43 B.C.–A.D. 17 |
| Constantine legalizes Christianity, 312<br>Theodosius declares Christianity the official state religion, 380<br>Donatist heretical movement at its height, ca 400<br>St. Augustine, *The City of God,* ca 425<br>Clovis adopts Roman Christianity, 496 | | St. Jerome publishes the Latin *Vulgate,* late 4th c.<br>St. Augustine, *Confessions,* ca 390<br>Byzantines preserve Greco-Roman culture, ca 400–1000 |
| *Rule of St. Benedict,* 529<br>Monasteries established in Anglo-Saxon England, 7th c.<br>Muhammad preaches reform, ca 610<br>Publication of the Qu'ran, 651<br>Synod of Whitby, 664 | Using watermills, Benedictine monks exploit energy of fast-flowing rivers and streams<br>Heavy plow and improved harness facilitate use of multiple-ox teams; harrow widely used in northern Europe | Boethius, *The Consolation of Philosophy,* ca 520<br>Justinian constructs church of Santa Sophia, 532–537<br>Pope Gregory the Great publishes *Dialogues, Pastoral Care, Moralia,* 590–604 |
| Missionary work of St. Boniface in Germany, ca 710–750<br>Iconoclastic controversy in Byzantine Empire, 726–843<br>Pippin III donates Papal States to the papacy, 756 | Byzantines successfully use "Greek fire" in naval combat against Arab fleets attacking Constantinople, 673, 717 | Lindisfarne Gospel Book, ca 700<br>Bede, *Ecclesiastical History of the English Nation,* ca 700<br>*Beowulf,* ca 700<br>Carolingian Renaissance, ca 780–850 |
| Foundation of abbey of Cluny, 909<br>Byzantine conversion of Russia, late 10th c. | Stirrup and nailed horseshoes become widespread in shock combat<br>Paper, invented in China ca 2d c., enters Europe through Muslim Spain in 10th c. | Byzantines develop the Cyrillic script, late 10th c. |
| Beginning of reformed papacy, 1046<br>Schism between Roman and Greek Orthodox churches, 1054<br>Pope Gregory VII, 1073–1085<br>Peter Abelard, 1079–1142<br>St. Bernard of Clairvaux, 1090–1153<br>First Crusade, 1095–1099 | Arab conquests bring new irrigation methods, cotton cultivation, and manufacture to Spain, Sicily, southern Italy<br>Avicenna, Arab scientist, d. 1037 | Romanesque style in architecture and art, ca 1000–1200<br>*Song of Roland,* ca 1095<br>Muslim musicians introduce lute, rebec—stringed instruments and ancestors of violin |
| Universities begin, ca 1100–1300<br>Concordat of Worms ends investiture controversy, 1122<br>Height of Cistercian monasticism, 1125–1175<br>Aristotle's works translated into Latin, ca 1140–1260<br>Third Crusade, 1189–1192<br>Pope Innocent III, 1198–1216 | In castle construction Europeans, copying Muslim and Byzantine models, erect rounded towers and crenelated walls<br>Windmill invented, ca 1180<br>Some monasteries, such as Clairvaux and Canterbury Cathedral Priory, supplied by underground pipes with running water and indoor latrines, elsewhere rare until 19th c. | *Rubaiyat of Umar Khayyam,* ca 1120<br>Dedication of abbey church of Saint-Denis launches Gothic style, 1144<br>Hildegard of Bingen, 1098–1179<br>Court of troubador poetry, especially that of Chrétien de Troyes, circulates widely |

| | Government | Society and Economy |
|---|---|---|
| **1200** | Spanish victory over Muslims at Las Navas de Tolosa, 1212<br>Frederick II of Germany and Sicily, r. 1212–1250<br>Magna Carta, 1215<br>Louis IX of France, r. 1226–1270<br>Mongols end Abbasid caliphate, 1258<br>Edward I of England, r. 1272–1307<br>Philip IV (the Fair) of France, r. 1285–1314<br>England and France at war, 1296 | Economic revival, growth of towns, clearing of wasteland contribute to growth of personal freedom, 13th c.<br>Crusaders capture Constantinople (Fourth Crusade) and spur Venetian economy, 1204<br>Agricultural expansion leads to population growth, ca 1225–1300 |
| **1300** | Philip IV orders arrest of Pope Boniface at Anagni, 1303<br>Hundred Years' War, 1337–1453<br>Political disorder in Germany, ca 1350–1450<br>Merchant oligarchies or despots rule Italian city-states | European economic depression, ca 1300–1450<br>Black Death appears ca 1347; returns intermittently until 18th c.<br>Height of the Hanseatic League, 1350–1450<br>Peasant and working-class revolts: Flanders, 1302; France, 1358; Florence, 1378; England, 1381 |
| **1400** | Joan of Arc rallies French monarchy, 1429–1431<br>Medici domination of Florence begins, 1434<br>Princes in Germany consolidate power, ca 1450–1500<br>Ottoman Turks under Mahomet II capture Constantinople, May 1453<br>Wars of the Roses in England, 1453–1471<br>Ferdinand and Isabella complete reconquista in Spain, 1492<br>French invasion of Italy, 1494 | Population decline, peasants' revolts, high labor costs contribute to decline of serfdom in western Europe<br>Christopher Columbus reaches the Americas, October 1492<br>Portuguese gain control of East Indian spice trade, 1498–1511<br>Flow of Balkan slaves into eastern Mediterranean; of African slaves into Iberia and Italy, ca 1400–1500 |
| **1500** | Charles V, Holy Roman emperor, 1519–1556<br>Imperial sack of Rome, 1527<br>Philip II of Spain, r. 1556–1598<br>Revolt of the Netherlands, 1566–1609<br>St. Bartholomew's Day massacre, August 24, 1572<br>Defeat of the Spanish Armada, 1588<br>Henry IV of France issues Edict of Nantes, 1598 | Balboa discovers the Pacific, 1513<br>Magellan's crew circumnavigates the earth, 1519–1522<br>Spain and Portugal gain control of regions of Central and South America, ca 1520–1550<br>Peasants' Revolt in Germany, 1524–1525<br>"Time of Troubles" in Russia, 1598–1613 |
| **1600** | Thirty Years' War, 1618–1648<br>Richelieu dominates French government, 1624–1643<br>Frederick William, Elector of Brandenburg, r. 1640–1688<br>English Civil War, 1642–1649 | Chartering of British East India Company, 1600<br>Famine and taxation lead to widespread revolts, decline of serfdom in western Europe, ca 1600–1650<br>English Poor Law, 1601 |

| Religion and Philosophy | Science and Technology | Arts and Letters |
|---|---|---|
| Maimonides, d. 1204<br>Founding of Franciscan order, 1210<br>Fourth Lateran Council, 1215<br>Founding of Dominican order, 1216<br>Thomas Aquinas (1225–1274) marks height of Scholasticism<br>Pope Boniface VIII, 1294–1303 | *Notebooks* of Villard de Honnecourt, a master mason (architect), a major source for Gothic engineering, ca 1250<br>Development of double-entry bookkeeping in Florence and Genoa, ca 1250–1340<br>Venetians purchase secrets of glass manufacture from Syria, 1277<br>Mechanical clock invented, ca 1290 | *Parzifal, Roman de la Rose, King Arthur and the Round Table* celebrate virtues of knighthood<br>Height of Gothic style, ca 1225–1300 |
| Babylonian Captivity of the papacy, 1307–1377<br>John Wyclif, ca 1330–1384<br>Great Schism in the papacy, 1377–1418 | Edward III of England uses cannon in siege of Calais, 1346 | Petrarch, 1304–1374<br>Paintings of Giotto, ca 1305–1337<br>Dante, *Divine Comedy,* ca 1310<br>Boccaccio, *The Decameron,* ca 1350<br>Jan van Eyck, 1366–1441<br>Brunelleschi, 1377–1446<br>Chaucer, *Canterbury Tales,* ca 1385–1400 |
| Council of Constance, 1414–1418<br>Pragmatic Sanction of Bourges, 1438<br>Expulsion of Jews from Spain, 1492 | Water-powered blast furnaces operative in Sweden, Austria, the Rhine Valley, Liège, ca 1400<br>Leonardo Fibonacci's *Liber Abaci* (1202) popularizes use of Hindu-Arabic numerals, "a major factor in the rise of science in the Western world"<br>Paris and largest Italian cities pave streets, making street cleaning possible<br>Printing and movable type, ca 1450 | Masaccio, 1401–1428<br>Botticelli, 1444–1510<br>Leonardo da Vinci, 1452–1519<br>Albrecht Dürer, 1471–1528<br>Michelangelo, 1475–1564<br>Raphael, 1483–1520<br>Rabelais, ca 1490–1553 |
| Lateran Council attempts reforms of church abuses, 1512–1517<br>Machiavelli, *The Prince,* 1513<br>Concordat of Bologna, 1516<br>More, *Utopia,* 1516<br>Luther, *Ninety-five Theses,* 1517<br>Henry VIII of England breaks with Rome, 1532–1534<br>Loyola establishes Society of Jesus, 1540<br>Calvin establishes theocracy in Geneva, 1541<br>Merici establishes Ursuline order for education of women, 1544<br>Council of Trent, 1545–1563<br>Peace of Augsburg, 1555<br>Hobbes, 1588–1679<br>Descartes, 1596–1650 | Copernicus, *On the Revolutions of the Heavenly Bodies,* 1543<br>Galileo, 1564–1642<br>Kepler, 1571–1630<br>Harvey, 1578–1657 | Erasmus, *The Praise of Folly,* 1509<br>Castiglione, *The Courtier,* 1528<br>Cervantes, 1547–1616<br>Baroque movement in the arts, ca 1550–1725<br>Shakespeare, 1564–1616<br>Rubens, 1577–1640<br>Montaigne, *Essays,* 1598<br>Velazquez, 1599–1660 |
| Huguenot revolt in France, 1625 | Bacon, *The Advancement of Learning,* 1605<br>Boyle, 1627–1691<br>Leeuwenhoek, 1632–1723 | Rembrandt van Rijn, 1606–1669<br>Golden Age of Dutch culture, 1625–1675<br>Vermeer, 1632–1675<br>Racine, 1639–1699 |

| | Government | Society and Economy |
|---|---|---|
| **1600 (cont.)** | Louis XIV, r. 1643–1715<br>Peace of Westphalia, 1648<br>The Fronde in France, 1648–1660 | Chartering of Dutch East India Company, 1602<br>Height of Dutch commercial activity, ca 1630–1665 |
| **1650** | Protectorate in England, 1653–1658<br>Leopold I, Habsburg emperor, r. 1658–1705<br>Treaty of the Pyrenees, 1659<br>English monarchy restored, 1660<br>Ottoman Siege of Vienna, 1683<br>Glorious Revolution in England, 1688–1689<br>Peter the Great of Russia, r. 1689–1725 | Height of mercantilism in Europe, ca 1650–1750<br>Principle of peasants' "hereditary subjugation" to their lords affirmed in Prussia, 1653<br>Colbert's economic reforms in France, ca 1663–1683<br>Cossack revolt in Russia, 1670–1671 |
| **1700** | War of the Spanish Succession, 1701–1713<br>Peace of Utrecht, 1713<br>Frederick William I of Prussia, r. 1713–1740<br>Louis XV of France, r. 1715–1774<br>Maria Theresa of Austria, r. 1740–1780<br>Frederick the Great of Prussia, r. 1740–1786 | Foundation of St. Petersburg, 1701<br>Last appearance of bubonic plague in western Europe, ca 1720<br>Enclosure movement in England, ca 1730–1830<br>Jeremy Bentham, 1748–1823 |
| **1750** | Seven Years' War, 1756–1763<br>Catherine the Great of Russia, r. 1762–1796<br>Partition of Poland, 1772–1795<br>Louis XVI of France, r. 1774–1792<br>American Revolution, 1776–1783<br>Beginning of the French Revolution, 1789 | Start of general European population increase, ca 1750<br>Growth of illegitimate births, ca 1750–1850<br>Adam Smith, *The Wealth of Nations,* 1776<br>Thomas Malthus, *Essay of the Principle of Population,* 1798 |
| **1800** | Napoleonic era, 1799–1815<br>Congress of Vienna, 1814–1815<br>"Battle of Peterloo," Great Britain, 1819 | European economic imperialism, ca 1816–1880 |
| **1825** | Greece wins independence, 1830<br>French conquest of Algeria, 1830<br>Revolution in France, 1830<br>Great Britain: Reform Bill of 1832; Poor Law reform, 1834; Chartists, repeal of Corn Laws, 1838–1848<br>British complete occupation of India, 1848<br>Revolutions in Europe, 1848 | Height of French utopian socialism, 1830s–1840s<br>German Zollverein founded, 1834<br>European capitalists begin large-scale foreign investment, 1840s<br>Great Famine in Ireland, 1845–1851<br>Marx, *Communist Manifesto,* 1848 |
| **1850** | Second Empire in France, 1852–1870<br>Crimean War, 1853–1856<br>Unification of Italy, 1859–1870<br>Civil War, United States, 1861–1865<br>Bismarck leads Germany, 1862–1890<br>Unification of Germany, 1864–1871<br>Britain's Second Reform Bill, 1867<br>Third Republic in France, 1870–1940 | Crédit Mobilier founded in France, 1852<br>Japan opened to European influence, 1853<br>Mill, *On Liberty,* 1859<br>Russian serfs emancipated, 1861<br>First Socialist International, 1864–1871<br>Marx, *Das Capital,* 1867 |

| Religion and Philosophy | Science and Technology | Arts and Letters |
| --- | --- | --- |
| Patriarch Nikon's reforms split Russian Orthodox church, 1652<br>Test Act in England excludes Roman Catholics from public office, 1673<br>Revocation of Edict of Nantes, 1685<br>James II tries to restore Catholicism as state religion, 1685–1688<br>Montesquieu, 1689–1755<br>Locke, *Second Treatise on Civil Government,* 1690<br>Pierre Bayle, *Historical and Critical Dictionary,* 1697 | Tull (1674–1741) encourages innovation in English agriculture<br>Newton, *Principia Mathematica,* 1687<br>Newcomen develops steam engine, 1705 | Construction of baroque palaces and remodeling of capital cities throughout central and eastern Europe, ca 1650–1725<br>J. S. Bach, 1685–1750<br>Fontenelle, *Conversations on the Plurality of Worlds,* 1686<br>The Enlightenment, ca 1690–1790<br>Voltaire, 1694–1778 |
| Wesley, 1703–1791<br>Hume, 1711–1776<br>Diderot, 1713–1784<br>Condorcet, 1743–1794 | Charles Townsend introduces four-year crop rotation, 1730 | Montesquieu, *The Spirit of Laws,* 1748 |
| Ricardo, 1772–1823<br>Fourier, 1772–1837<br>Papacy dissolves the Jesuits, 1773<br>Church reforms of Joseph II in Austria, 1780s<br>Reorganization of the church in France, 1790s | Hargreaves's spinning jenny, ca 1765<br>Arkwright's water frame, ca 1765<br>Watt's steam engine promotes industrial breakthroughs, 1780s<br>War widens the gap in technology between Britain and the continent, 1792–1815<br>Jenner's smallpox vaccine, 1796 | *Encyclopedia,* edited by Diderot and d'Alembert, published, 1751–1765<br>Mozart, 1756–1791<br>Rousseau, *The Social Contract,* 1762<br>Beethoven, 1770–1827<br>Wordsworth, 1770–1850<br>Romanticism, ca 1790–1850<br>Wollstonecraft, *A Vindication of the Rights of Women,* 1792 |
| Napoleon signs Concordat with Pope Pius VII regulating Catholic church in France, 1801<br>Spencer, 1820–1903 | | Staël, *On Germany,* 1810<br>Liszt, 1811–1886 |
| Comte, *System of Positive Philosophy,* 1830–1842<br>List, *National System of Political Economy,* 1841<br>Nietzsche, 1844–1900<br>Sorel, 1847–1922 | First railroad, Great Britain, 1825<br>Faraday studies electromagnetism, 1830–1840s | Balzac, *The Human Comedy,* 1829–1841<br>Delacroix, *Liberty Leading the People,* 1830<br>Hugo, *Hunchback of Notre Dame,* 1831 |
| Decline in church attendance among working classes, ca 1850–1914<br>Pope Pius IX, *Syllabus of Errors,* denounces modern thoughts, 1864<br>Doctrine of papal infallibility, 1870 | Modernization of Paris, ca 1850–1870<br>Great Exhibition, London, 1851<br>Darwin, *Origin of Species,* 1859<br>Pasteur develops germ theory of disease, 1860s<br>Suez Canal opened, 1869<br>Mendeleev develops the periodic table, 1869 | Realism, ca 1850–1870<br>Freud, 1856–1939<br>Flaubert, *Madame Bovary,* 1857<br>Tolstoy, *War and Peace,* 1869<br>Impressionism in art, ca 1870–1900<br>Eliot (Mary Ann Evans), *Middlemarch,* 1872 |

| | Government | Society and Economy |
|---|---|---|
| **1875** | Congress of Berlin, 1878<br>European "scramble for Africa," 1880–1900<br>Britain's Third Reform Bill, 1884<br>Dreyfus affair in France, 1894–1899<br>Spanish-American War, 1898<br>Boer War, 1899–1902 | Full property rights for women, Great Britain, 1882<br>Social welfare legislation, Germany, 1883–1889<br>Second Socialist International, 1889–1914<br>Witte directs modernization of Russian economy, 1892–1899 |
| **1900** | Russo-Japanese War, 1904–1905<br>Revolution in Russia, 1905<br>Balkan wars, 1912–1913 | Women's suffrage movement, England, ca 1900–1914<br>Social welfare legislation, France, 1904, 1910; England, 1906–1914<br>Agrarian reforms in Russia, 1907–1912 |
| **1914** | World War I, 1914–1918<br>Armenian genocide, 1915<br>Easter Rebellion, 1916<br>U.S. declares war on Germany, 1917<br>Bolshevik Revolution, 1917–1918<br>Treaty of Versailles, 1919 | Planned economics in Europe, 1914<br>Auxiliary Service Law in Germany, 1916<br>Bread riots in Russia, March 1917 |
| **1920** | Mussolini seizes power, 1922<br>Stalin uses forced collectivization, police terror, ca 1929–1939<br>Hitler gains power, 1933<br>Rome-Berlin Axis, 1936<br>Nazi-Soviet Non-Aggression Pact, 1939<br>World War II, 1939–1945 | New Economic Policy in the Soviet Union, 1921<br>Dawes Plan for reparations and recovery, 1924<br>The Great Depression, 1929–1939<br>Rapid industrialization in Soviet Union, 1930s<br>Roosevelt's "New Deal," 1933 |
| **1940** | United Nations, 1945<br>Cold war begins, 1947<br>Fall of colonial empires, 1947–1962<br>Communist government in China, 1949<br>Korean War, 1950–1953<br>"De-Stalinization," 1955–1962 | The Holocaust, 1941–1945<br>Marshall Plan, 1947<br>European economic progress, ca 1950–1969<br>European Coal and Steel Community, 1952<br>European Economic Community, 1957 |
| **1960** | The Berlin Wall goes up, 1961<br>United States in Vietnam, ca 1961–1973<br>Student rebellion in France, 1968<br>Soviet tanks end Prague Spring, 1968<br>Détente, 1970s<br>Soviets in Afghanistan, 1979 | Civil rights movement in United States, 1960s<br>Collapse of postwar monetary system, 1971<br>OPEC oil price increases, 1973 and 1979<br>Stagflation, 1970s<br>Women's movement, 1970s |
| **1980** | U.S. military buildup, 1980s<br>Solidarity in Poland, 1980<br>Unification of Germany, 1989<br>Revolutions in eastern Europe, 1989–1990<br>End of Soviet Union, 1991<br>War in former Yugoslavia, 1991–1995<br>War in Chechnya, 1991–present | Growth of debt, 1980s<br>Economic crisis in Poland, 1988<br>Maastricht Treaty proposes monetary union, 1990<br>European Community becomes European Union, 1993<br>Migration to western Europe grows, 1990s |
| **2000** | Terrorist attack on U.S., Sept. 11, 2001<br>War in Afghanistan, 2001<br>War in Iraq, 2003–present | Euro note enters circulation, 2002<br>Israel begins construction of West Bank barrier, 2003<br>European Union approves constitution, 2004 |

| Religion and Philosophy | Science and Technology | Arts and Letters |
|---|---|---|
| Growth of public education in France, ca 1880–1900<br>Growth of mission schools in Africa, 1890–1914 | Emergence of modern immunology, ca 1875–1900<br>Trans-Siberian Railroad, 1890s<br>Marie Curie, discovery of radium, 1898<br>Electrical industry: lighting and streetcars, 1880–1900 | Zola, *Germinal,* 1885<br>Kipling, "The White Man's Burden," 1899 |
| Separation of church and state, France, 1901–1905<br>Jean-Paul Sartre, 1905–1980 | Planck develops quantum theory, ca 1900<br>First airplane flight, 1903<br>Einstein develops relativity theory, 1905–1910 | "Modernism," ca 1900–1929<br>Conrad, *Heart of Darkness,* 1902<br>Cubism in art, ca 1905–1930<br>Proust, *Remembrance of Things Past,* 1913–1927 |
| Schweitzer, *Quest of the Historical Jesus,* 1906 | Submarine warfare, 1915<br>Ernest Rutherford splits the atom, 1919 | Spengler, *The Decline of the West,* 1918 |
| Emergence of modern existentialism, 1920s<br>Wittgenstein, *Essay on Logical Philosophy,* 1922<br>Revival of Christianity, 1920s and 1930s | "Heroic age of physics," 1920s<br>First major public radio broadcasts in Great Britain and the United States, 1920<br>Heisenberg, "principle of uncertainty," 1927<br>Talking movies, 1930<br>Radar system in England, 1939 | Gropius, the Bauhaus, 1920s<br>Dadaism and surrealism, 1920s<br>Woolf, *Jacob's Room,* 1922<br>Joyce, *Ulysses,* 1922<br>Eliot, *The Waste Land,* 1922<br>Remarque, *All Quiet on the Western Front,* 1929<br>Picasso, *Guernica,* 1937 |
| De Beauvoir, *The Second Sex,* 1949<br>Communists fail to break Catholic church in Poland, 1950s | Oppenheimer, 1904–1967<br>"Big Science" in United States, ca 1940–1970<br>U.S. drops atomic bombs on Japan, 1945<br>Watson and Crick discover structure of DNA molecule, 1953<br>Russian satellite in orbit, 1957 | Cultural purge in Soviet Union, 1946–1952<br>Van der Rohe, Lake Shore Apartments, 1948–1951<br>Orwell, *1984,* 1949<br>Pasternak, *Doctor Zhivago,* 1956<br>The "beat" movement in the U.S., late 1950s |
| Catholic church opposes the legalization of divorce and abortion, 1970 to present<br>Pope John Paul II electrifies Poland, 1979 | European Council for Nuclear Research (CERN), 1960<br>Space race, 1960s<br>Russian cosmonaut first to orbit globe, 1961<br>American astronaut first person on the moon, 1969 | The Beatles, 1960s<br>Solzhenitsyn, *One Day in the Life of Ivan Denisovitch,* 1962<br>Friedan, *The Feminine Mystique,* 1963<br>Servan-Schreiber, *The American Challenge,* 1967 |
| Revival of religion in Soviet Union, 1985 to present<br>Fukuyama proclaims "end of history," 1991<br>Growth of Islam in Europe, 1990s | Reduced spending on Big Science, 1980s<br>Computer revolution continues, 1980s and 1990s<br>U.S. Genome Project begins, 1990<br>First WWW server/browser, 1991<br>Pentium processor invented, 1993<br>"Dolly," first genetically cloned sheep, 1996 | Solzhenitsyn returns to Russia, 1994<br>Author Salman Rushdie is exiled from Iran, 1989<br>Gehry, Guggenheim Museum, Bilbao, 1997 |
| France bans headscarves in public schools, 2004 | Segway human transporter, 2001<br>First hybrid car, 2003 | Calatrava, Tenerife Concert Hall, 2003 |

Elevation
Meters
Feet
4,000
13,120
2,000
6,560
500
1,640
200
656
Sea level
Sea level
Below sea level
Below sea level
National capital
Other city
0
250
500 Km.
0
250
500 Mi.
NORWAY
Oslo
SWEDE
SCOTLAND
North Sea
NORTHERN IRELAND
UNITED KINGDOM
IRELAND
Dublin
DENMARK
Copenhagen
ENGLAND
WALES
NETHERLANDS
Amsterdam
Thames
London
Berlin
Elbe
English Channel
Brussels
BELGIUM
GERMANY
LUXEMBOURG
Luxembourg
Seine
Paris
Prague
CZECH
REPUBI
Loire
Rhine
ATLANTIC OCEAN
Bay of Biscay
Vienna
Bern
FRANCE
SWITZERLAND
AUSTRIA
ALPS
SLOVENIA
Ljubljana
Po
Rhône
PYRENEES
Ebro
APENNINES
Adriatic Sea
PORTUGAL
SPAIN
Lisbon
Madrid
Corsica
Tiber
Rome
ITALY
Balearic Is.
Sardinia
Tyrrhenian Sea
Strait of Gibraltar
GIBRALTAR (U.K.)
Algiers
Rabat
Tunis
Sicily
MALTA
MOROCCO
TUNISIA
Tripoli
ALGERIA
LIBYA